CHILD DEVELOPMENT

A Topical Approach

CHILD DEVELOPMENT
A Topical Approach

Danuta Bukatko
COLLEGE OF THE HOLY CROSS

Marvin W. Daehler
UNIVERSITY OF MASSACHUSETTS, AMHERST

Houghton Mifflin Company   Boston   Toronto
Dallas   Geneva, Illinois   Palo Alto   Princeton, New Jersey

To Don and Nicholas
D. B.

To June, and to Curtis, Joshua, and Renée
M. W. D.

Sponsoring Editor: Michael DeRocco

Basic Book Editor: Jane Knetzger

Project Editor: Suzanne Morris

Design Coordinator: Sandra Gonzalez

Production Coordinator: Renée Le Verrier

Manufacturing Coordinator: Holly Schuster

Marketing Manager: Diane McOscar

Cover and interior design by Ron Kosciak

Cover photograph by James Scherer

Anatomical illustrations, charts, and graphs by Networkgraphics

Printed in the U.S.A.

Library of Congress Catalog Card Number: 91-72007

ISBN: 0-395-48144-9

ABCDEFGHIJ-D-9876543211

BRIEF CONTENTS

CONTENTS

8

COGNITION

10
EMOTION

12
SEX ROLES

16

**THE INFLUENCE OF SCHOOL
AND TELEVISION**

PREFACE

Those of us who teach courses on child development share the opportunity to consider an exciting and complex topic: the factors that influence and shape an individual in his or her most formative years. Yet, as instructors, we also share a dilemma: How do we capture the remarkable breadth and depth of the child's psychological development in the mere thirteen (or fewer) weeks that the course is scheduled? The task is made all the more challenging by the veritable explosion of research that our field has witnessed in the last two decades, research that is often necessarily quite specialized. How, then, do we help students to sift through the enormous number of developmental "facts" so that they carry away the central knowledge of our field? Furthermore, how do we give students a meaningful sense of the "whole" child, given the specialized study of so many different "parts" of the individual?

It is with these special challenges in mind that we wrote this text. Our goal has been to provide for the undergraduate student a comprehensive, topically organized, up-to-date picture of child development from conception through adolescence. We emphasize the classic and contemporary research and theory at the core of developmental psychology. Wherever possible, we draw on the growing body of cross-cultural research that helps to elucidate certain fundamental questions about development.

Most important, however, we explicitly draw the student's attention to the themes that replay themselves throughout the course of development, those fundamental, overarching issues that continually resurface and that provide coherence among seemingly disparate research findings. We highlight six basic themes in our discussion of child development:

- What roles do nature and nurture play in development?
- How does the sociocultural context influence development?
- How does the child play an active role in development?
- Is development continuous or stagelike?
- Are there sensitive periods in development?
- How do the various domains of development interact?

These themes have been part of the rich theoretical tradition of past decades and continue to play a prominent role in contemporary thinking about development.

By drawing out these themes, we hope to give the reader a means of discovering the "big picture," a way of making sense of the myriad facts that compose the child development literature and a way of understanding the child as a complex, yet integrated being. Moreover, we believe these themes will serve as a tool to stimulate critical thinking among students about the nature of development and how it is best conceptualized. They encourage the student to think about the *process* of development, or *why* development proceeds as it does. After all, many of the student's questions, and ultimately our goals as teachers and researchers, center on explaining rather than merely describing development. Furthermore, understanding why development proceeds as it does can have important ramifications for applied areas such as parenting practices, education, and social policy regarding children, which are ultimately concerns for us all.

ORGANIZATION AND COVERAGE

We begin the text with two chapters that set the stage for the balance of the book. Chapter 1 considers the historical roots of developmental psychology and the research methodologies the field typically employs. Along with many of our colleagues, we firmly believe that students must have a basic understanding of how researchers operate in order to understand and evaluate the findings they report. Consequently, we describe the most common research tactics, including newer approaches such as meta-analysis. Chapter 2 introduces six developmental themes followed by major theories of development. We include discussion of how various theorists have taken explicit or implicit positions on the six themes.

The next three chapters deal primarily with the biological underpinnings and physical changes that characterize child development. Chapter 3 explains the mechanisms of heredity that contribute to human development and evaluates the role of genetics in the expression of many human traits and behaviors. The chapter discusses the developmental implications of several gene disorders, such as the fragile X syndrome, that have been brought to light by advances in molecular biology. The chapter also addresses recent conceptualizations of gene–environment interactions espoused by behavior geneticists. Chapter 4 sketches the major features of prenatal development and focuses on how environmental factors such as teratogens can modify the genetic blueprint for physical and behavioral development. Chapter 5 outlines the major features of physical and motor skill development and includes a special section on brain growth and differentiation.

The next group of chapters focuses on the development of the child's various mental capacities. Chapter 6 reviews both the traditional literature on children's learning as well as more recent formulations that center on cognitive processes and the social aspects of the learning situation. The chapter also documents the development of perception, including the most recent findings on early intermodal perception as well as perceptual development in older children. Chapter 7 describes language development, highlighting the contemporary research on infant language and the social context of language acquisition and considers several different roles, in addition to communication, that language plays in development. Chapter 8 features contemporary explanations of children's thinking skills generated by information-processing theorists and, building on theoretical ideas introduced in Chapter 2, includes a treatment of Piaget's approach to cognitive development. Chapter 9 provides students with a picture of traditional models of intelligence along with more recent views, such as Sternberg's triarchic theory and Gardner's theory of multiple intelligences.

The child's growing social and emotional achievements constitute the focus of the next group of chapters. In light of the enormous growth of interest in children's emotions, we devote all of Chapter 10 to this topic. Within this context, we consider recent debates about the measurement and developmental significance of attachment. Chapter 11 covers another rapidly expanding area of interest: social cognition, the child's understanding and regulation of self and the development of perspective-taking and attribution skills in the understanding of others. Chapter 12 covers the most recent ideas about sex-role development, including substantial treatment of gender schema theory. Chapter 13, devoted to moral development, describes not only traditional ideas about moral judgment but also covers two specific aspects of moral behavior—altruism and aggression.

In the final portion of the text, we consider the most important external forces that shape the path of child development—the family, the peer group, and the schools and media. Chapter 14 adopts a family systems approach to emphasize how various family members continually influence one another. Specific topics include fatherhood, maternal employment and day care, and divorce. A separate chapter entirely dedicated to the influence of peers, Chapter 15, covers the burgeoning research on this topic. Chapter 16 considers the special influence of schools on child development, along with another powerful aspect of contemporary culture—television. The chapter makes special note of how computers can influence the child's growing skills and abilities.

SPECIAL FEATURES

We have incorporated several features in this text to achieve the goals we initially set for this project:

Key Themes in Development   Within each chapter, some or all of the six developmental themes listed above serve to organize and provide coherence for the material. As already noted, we see these themes as pedagogical tools designed to help students discern the importance and interrelatedness of various facts, and as vehicles for instructors to encourage critical analysis among students. The themes are highlighted for students in several ways. First, the themes most immediately relevant to a chapter are listed at its start. Throughout the body of the chapter, marginal indicators point to the discussion of a relevant theme. Finally, each chapter closes with a brief synopsis of how the key themes are illustrated in the chapter. Students may, of course, find other themes and additional instances of the six we explore; in fact, we encourage them to do so. Our point is to set in motion in the reader a search for integration and coherence in the vast material that constitutes the scientific study of child development.

Chronology Charts   From our own experience as teachers who have adopted a topical approach to child development, we know that students often get so immersed in the theories and research on a given topic that they lose a sense of the child's achievements over time. Consequently, within most chapters, we include one or more Chronology charts, which summarize the child's specific developmental attainments at various ages. One of the points we emphasize in this text, of course, is that there are individual differences in rates, and sometimes in paths, of development. We therefore caution students that these tables are meant only to give a picture of the overall trajectory of development, a loose outline of the sequence of attainments we expect to see in most children. Nonetheless, we believe that these rough guidelines will give students a sense of the patterns and typical timing of important events in the life of the child and that they will serve as another organizing device for the material related to each domain of development.

Controversies   Important questions about development often have no clear-cut answers. In fact, decisions must frequently be made about children and their families in the face of conflicting research findings or theoretical beliefs. Should children serve as eyewitnesses in courts of law? Should infants be taught how to read? Should children be academically tracked in school? A special feature found in each chapter considers questions like these to help students critically assess the opposing positions that experts take and to appreciate some of the applied implications of developmental research and theory. These controversies (and others in the research literature that are introduced in the text but not specifically highlighted) can serve as the foundation for debate and extended discussion in the classroom.

Study Aids   The chapter outlines, chapter summaries, marginal and end-of-text glossaries all serve to underscore important themes, terms, and concepts. We hope that students will actively utilize these aids to reinforce what they have read in the chapter body.

In addition, we employ several strategies to make the material in this text more accessible to students: opening vignettes to capture the reader's interest, the liberal use of examples throughout the text, and an extensive program of illustrations accompanied by instructive captions.

The result, we hope, is a text that captures for the reader all the excitement and wonder we ourselves feel when we watch a child growing up.

ANCILLARIES

The Test Bank, Instructor's Resource Manual, and Study Guide that accompany this text were prepared by Carolyn Greco-Vigorito of St. John's University, Staten Island, and Michael Vigorito of Seton Hall University, South Orange, NJ. A shared set of learning objectives unifies all three supplements.

Test Bank   The Test Bank contains 1600 multiple-choice items (100 per chapter). All items are keyed to the learning objectives presented in the Instructor's Resource Manual and Study Guide. Each question is accompanied by a key that provides the learning objective number, text page on which the answer can be found, type of question (Fact/Concept or Application), and correct answer.

Computerized Test Bank   All test items are available on disk in IBM or Macintosh formats. Instructors may integrate their own test items with those on disk.

Instructor's Resource Manual   The Instructor's Resource Manual contains a complete set of chapter lecture outlines and learning objectives. The manual also contains specific teaching aids such as lecture topics, classroom exercises, demonstrations, and handouts.

Study Guide   The Study Guide contains the same set of learning objectives that appear in the Instructor's Resource Manual and the Test Bank. In addition, each chapter of the Study Guide includes a detailed chapter outline, a key terms review section, and a self-quiz consisting of 30 multiple-choice questions. An answer key tells the student not only which response is correct but why each of the other choices is incorrect.

Transparencies   The set of forty transparencies, most in full color, features images from the text.

ACKNOWLEDGMENTS

No project of this magnitude could come to completion without the assistance of numerous colleagues, friends, and others who have provided their professional opinions, time, and inspiration. Our first thanks, though, go to our students at Holy Cross and the University of Massachusetts, who enroll in our classes in child development and show us so visibly how they appreciate what they learn. Because the material is important to them, it becomes even more important to us to try to tell this saga in the best way possible. It is the students who have served as the initial and primary inspiration to write this book.

The transformation from first draft to final printed book was a process that could be completed successfully only with the assistance of reviewers whose questions, comments, and helpful criticisms provided the impetus for a more accurate, complete, and readable discussion of children and their development. For their many generous contributions in reviewing these chapters, we thank the following individuals:

Linda Acredolo, *University of California, Davis*
Daniel Ashmead, *Vanderbilt University*
Janette B. Benson, *University of Denver*
Marvin W. Berkowitz, *Marquette University*
Dana W. Birnbaum, *University of Maine*
Theodore N. Bosack, *Providence College*
Duane Buhrmester, *University of Texas, Dallas*
Toni A. Campbell, *San Jose State University*
D. Bruce Carter, *Syracuse University*
Jane E. Clark, *University of Maryland*
John Colombo, *University of Kansas*
Anne P. Copeland, *Boston University*
Don Cousins, *Rhode Island College*
Susanne A. Denham, *George Mason University*
Claire Etaugh, *Bradley University*
Richard A. Fabes, *Arizona State University*
Tiffany Field, *University of Miami*
A. J. Finch, Jr., *Medical University of South Carolina*
Stanley K. Fitch, *El Camino College*

Harvey J. Ginsburg, *Southwest Texas State University*
John P. Gluck, *University of New Mexico*
Vernon C. Hall, *Syracuse University*
Carollee Howes, *University of California, Los Angeles*
Janice E. Jacobs, *University of Nebraska*
Kenneth D. Kallio, *State University of New York, Geneseo*
Daniel B. Kaye, *University of California, Los Angeles*
George P. Knight, *Arizona State University*
Claire B. Kopp, *University of California, Los Angeles*
Larry Kurdek, *Wright State University*
Mark R. Lepper, *Stanford University*
Elizabeth Pugzles Lorch, *University of Kentucky*
Adam P. Matheny, Jr., *University of Louisville*
Carol E. MacKinnon, *University of North Carolina, Greensboro*
Carolyn J. Mebert, *University of New Hampshire*
William E. Merriman, *Kent State University*
Leon Miller, *University of Illinois, Chicago*
Barbara E. Moely, *Tulane University*
Barbara A. Morrongiello, *University of Western Ontario*
Linda Smolak, *Kenyon College*
Leighton E. Stamps, *University of New Orleans*
Carolyn Ross Tomlin, *Union University*
Donald J. Tyrrell, *Franklin & Marshall College*

We also appreciate the contributions of D. Bruce Carter at Syracuse University and Clifford J. Drew at the University of Utah in the preparation of selected portions of this text. Their expertise has certainly added to the quality of the final product.

In addition, we are extremely grateful to colleagues at our respective institutions for reading and commenting on various chapters or just plain sharing ideas that helped us clarify what we were doing. At Holy Cross, John Axelson, Linda Carli, Andrew Futterman, Ogretta McNeil, Carleton Parkes, and Edward Thompson were invaluable sounding boards, critiquing chapters or suggesting directions to take as we hit an impasse. At the University of Massachusetts, Daniel Anderson, Rachel Clifton, Carolyn Mervis, Nancy Myers, Philippe Rochat, and Edward Tronick have provided a wealth of information and stimulating ideas in formal seminars and informal hallway conversations. Among those of special importance, too, are former teachers, particularly John Wright and John Flavell, whose inspiration and confidence served as the beginning link in the chain of events that eventually led to this work. A special thanks is due to Holy Cross for providing the first author with a Faculty Fellowship to work on this project. In addition, thanks go to Betsy Cracco, Deanna Canavan, Michael Villa, and the staff of Dinand Library for providing assistance with many last-minute tasks that may have seemed small but that absolutely needed to get done in a short period of time. They all assisted so graciously.

The editorial staff at Houghton Mifflin has been superb. We couldn't have asked for a more professional, talented, dedicated, and knowledgeable group of people to work with. Even though they undoubtedly wished we would have worked faster, they were patient and accommodating when we faced real obstacles to our work on this project and stimulated us to produce the book we said we had in mind.

Most of all, though, we would like to thank our families for their patience and unconditional support throughout the various phases of this project. To Don and Nicky, thanks for faithfully shuttling all those pieces of manuscript to the courier; but most of all thanks for understanding the importance of this project and tolerating sometimes frequent and long absences from home. Nicky, who was born almost right as we began writing, was an especially important source of inspiration, especially as the blank computer screen glared. Special thanks to June, who put up with the long evenings and weekends of separation and also to Curtis, Joshua, and Renée, who are now leaving the years that are central to the topic of this book. Their own development has been witness to so many of the points that we have tried to make and has reaffirmed the conviction that despite the many questions about development that remain, our children will become competent and resourceful young adults able to further improve the world and the lives of those who are a part of it.

Danuta Bukatko

Marvin W. Daehler

CHILD DEVELOPMENT
A Topical Approach

1

Studying Child Development

"When a few days over nine months," the noted evolutionary theorist Charles Darwin wrote of his infant son in 1840,

he associated his own name with his image in the looking-glass, and when called by name would turn toward the glass even when at some distance from it. When a few days over nine months, he learnt spontaneously that a hand or other object causing a shadow to fall on the wall in front of him was to be looked for behind. Whilst under a year old, it was sufficient to repeat two or three times at intervals any short sentence to fix firmly in his mind some associated idea. . . . The facility with which associated ideas due to instruction and others spontaneously arising were acquired, seemed to me by far the most strongly marked of all the distinctions between the mind of an infant and that of the cleverest full-grown dog that I have ever known. (Darwin, 1877, p. 290)

In just such informal records of their own offspring, Darwin and other nineteenth-century European scientists were taking the first steps toward the systematic observation of the child that would burgeon in the next century into a flourishing multidisciplinary field. The only surprise is that human development became a focus of serious study comparatively late in the history of Western science, for few fields offer a subject—the developing human being—that undergoes such dramatic transformations over time.

Development, as we will use the term, means all the physical and psychological changes a human being undergoes in a lifetime, from the moment of conception until death. The study of human development, above all, is the study of change. And at no other time of life does change take place at such a rapid pace as in childhood and adolescence. From the very moment of birth, changes in body and behaviors are swift and impressive. Even in a few short months, the newborn who looks so helpless— though we will see that the true state of affairs is otherwise—comes to control his own body, to locomote, and to master simple tasks such as feeding himself. In the years that follow, the child learns to understand and speak a language, displays more and more complex thinking abilities, shows a distinct personality, and develops a social network along with the skills necessary to interact with other people. The range and complexity of every child's achievements in the first decade and a half of life can only be called extraordinary.

One of our goals in this book is to give you an overview of the most significant changes in behavior and thinking processes that occur in this time span. Accordingly, much of the material you will encounter in the pages that follow will *describe* the growing child's accomplishments in many domains of development. We will begin by observing the formation of basic physical and mental capabilities in children; we will then examine the social and emotional skills children develop as they reach out to form relationships with their family members, peers, and others.

Development refers to the physical and psychological changes that occur over the span of life. Infancy is a period when children show numerous developmental achievements, such as learning to walk.

Our second important goal is to help you appreciate just why children develop in the specific ways that they do. That is, we will also try to *explain* development, at least as far as research up to now has led us to understand the causes of varying developmental outcomes in children. How do the genetic blueprints inherited from parents shape the growing child? What is the role of the environment—the people, objects, and events the child has experience with? How does the society or culture in which the child lives influence development? What role does the child play—is she passive or active in this entire process? Do the changes that take place occur gradually or suddenly? Are some particular experiences necessary for development to proceed normally? And how do the many facets of development influence one another? As you might imagine, the answers to these questions are neither simple nor always obvious. The story you are about to witness is more a complex, expanding web than it is a linear progression from point A—the newborn—to point B—the adult.

We will relay our account of the growing child as it has emerged in the past 150 years from the research of **developmental psychologists,** scientists who study changes in human behaviors and mental activities as they occur over a lifetime. Though popular accounts, some more mythical than true, abound, developmental psychologists rely on the general principles of scientific research to collect information about growth and change in children. This approach has its limitations—researchers have not necessarily studied every important aspect of child development, and sometimes research findings do not point to clear, unambiguous answers about the nature of development. Indeed, researchers often disagree on the conclusions they draw from a given set of data. Nonetheless, scientific fact finding has the advantage of being verifiable and is also more objective and systematic than personal interpretations of children's behavior. As you read the research accounts in the coming pages, the controversies as well as the unequivocal conclusions, we hope you will use them as opportunities to sharpen your own skills of critical analysis.

Research conducted around the world, especially in the last three decades, has yielded many important insights about the process of human development. Needless to say, a substantial number of these discoveries have implications for the practical side of interacting with children. For example, newborn nurseries for premature infants contain rocking chairs so that parents and nurses can rock and stimulate babies previously confined to isolettes. Bilingual education programs capitalize on the ease with which young children master the complexities of language. Many day-care centers stress the teaching of prosocial behaviors to young children. Throughout this book, we will emphasize both the importance of rigorous research and the practical implications of knowledge gathered by scientists.

development   Physical and psychological changes in the individual over a lifetime.

developmental psychology   Systematic and scientific study of changes in human behaviors and mental activities over time.

THE SCIENTIFIC STUDY OF THE CHILD IN WESTERN SOCIETY

Developmental psychology as a field has grown at an astonishing rate since Darwin recorded his observations of his baby boy. Each year hundreds of books and articles about children's growth are published for professionals interested in specific theoretical issues and for parents or teachers who wish to bring a more informed perspective to the challenging enterprises of child rearing and education. Neither scientists nor laypersons, however, always had such a focused and conscious desire to understand the process of child development. In fact, Western societal attitudes toward children have shifted considerably over the last several centuries, a phenomenon that has paved the way for the contemporary emphasis on children as the objects of scientific study.

Historical Perspectives on the Nature of Childhood

Contemporary American society views childhood as a separate, distinct, and unique period in the span of human life: during this special time children are to be protected, nurtured, loved, and for the most part kept free from the responsibilities and obligations that adults assume. Child labor laws try to ensure that children are not abused in the world of work, and the doctrine of public education signals our society's willingness to devote significant resources to their academic training. But childhood was not always viewed in this way. As we look back through time, we see that the prevailing general beliefs about human nature and the social order shape attitudes about the nature of childhood and hence the treatment and rearing of children (Borstelmann, 1983).

Children in Medieval and Renaissance Times
Europe during the Middle Ages and through premodern times fostered an attitude toward children strikingly different from our contemporary society's. Though their basic needs to be fed and clothed were attended to, children were not coddled or protected in the same way that infants in our society are. As soon as they were physically able, usually at age seven or so, children were incorporated into the adult world of work, in which they harvested grain, learned craft skills, and otherwise contributed to the local economy. In medieval times, Western European children did not have special clothes, toys, or games. Once they were old enough to shed swaddling clothes, they wore adult fashions, played archery and chess, and even gambled, all common adult pastimes (Ariès, 1962).

At the same time, premodern European society regarded children as vulnerable, fragile, and unable to assume the full responsibilities of adulthood. Medical writings alluded to the special illnesses of young children, and laws prohibited marriages of children under age twelve (Kroll, 1977). Religious movements of this era proclaimed the innocence of children and the need for educating them. Children's souls were also worth saving, said the clerics, and on this notion was founded the moral responsibility of parents to provide for their children's spiritual well-being. Parents also recognized that children needed to be financially provided for and helped them to set up their own households as they approached adulthood and marriage (Pollock, 1983; Shahar, 1990). Thus, even though medieval children were incorporated quickly into the adult world, they were also recognized both as different from adults and as possessing special needs.

A noticeable shift in attitudes toward children occurred in Europe during the sixteenth century. In 1545, the English physician and lawyer, Thomas Phayre, published the first book on pediatrics. The advent of the printing press during this century made possible the wide distribution of other manuals

In premodern Europe, children often dressed like adults and participated in many adult activities. At the same time, though, children were seen as fragile and in need of protection.

on the care of infants and children. The first grammar schools were established and became a vehicle for upper-class boys to gain knowledge about economics and politics. Girls of the upper classes attended convent schools or received private instruction intended to cultivate modesty and obedience, as well as other skills that would be useful in their future roles as wives and mothers (Shahar, 1990).

Probably one of the most significant social changes occurred as a result of the transition from agrarian to trade-based economies in the sixteenth and seventeenth centuries, along with the subsequent growth of industrialization in the eighteenth century. As people relocated from farms to towns and as the production of goods shifted to outside the home, the primary role of the family in Western society changed from economic survival to the nurturing of children (Hareven, 1985). Closeness and emotional attachment increasingly became the hallmarks of parent-child relations.

The Age of Enlightenment   By the eighteenth century, the impact of these sweeping social changes was consolidated by the writings of key thinkers who shaped the popular understanding of childhood. In the seventeenth and eighteenth centuries, two philosophers proposed important but distinctly different ideas about the nature and education of children. In his famous treatise *An Essay Concerning Human Understanding,* published in 1690, the British philosopher John Locke (1632–1704) described his beliefs about how human knowledge was acquired. Virtually no information is inborn, according to Locke. The newborn's mind is a **tabula rasa,** literally a "blank slate," upon which perceptual experiences are imprinted. Locke's philosophy of **empiricism,** the idea that environmental experiences shape the individual, foreshadowed the modern-day psychological school called behaviorism. Locke believed that rewards and punishments, imitation, and the associations that the child formed between stimuli are key elements in the formation of the mind.

In a second work, *Some Thoughts Concerning Education* (1693), Locke expounded further on his philosophy of training children:

> The great mistake I have observed in people's breeding their children . . . is that the mind has not been made obedient to discipline and pliant to reason when it was most tender, most easy to be bowed. . . . He that is not used to submit his will to the reason of others when he is young, will scarce hearken to submit to his own reason when he is of an age to make use of it.

> . . . If the mind be curbed and humbled too much in children, if their spirits be abased and broken by too strict a hand over them, they will lose all vigour and industry and are in a worse state than the former.

These statements convey Locke's belief that early experiences and proper training are important, but that child rearing and education should proceed through the use of reason rather than harsh discipline. Reason is the means by which self-control is exercised, and thus it is a behavior that should be modeled by parents. The goal for parents is to find a balance between being overly indulgent and overly restrictive as they manage their child's behavior. Physical punishment and nagging have no place in the training of children; instead, children should be encouraged to internalize adult standards of good behavior. As we will see, many of these same themes resound in contemporary research on the elements of good parenting and represent a contrast to the strict, restrictive discipline characteristic of Western society before the eighteenth century.

The second influential philosopher of the Enlightenment was Jean Jacques Rousseau (1712–1778), a French thinker who embraced the ideal of the child as a "noble savage." According to Rousseau, children are born with a propensity to act on impulses but not necessarily with the aim of wrongdoing. Children require the gentle guidance of adult authority to bring their natural instincts and tendencies in line with the social order. In his work *Émile,* Rousseau (1762) set forth these general beliefs about child rearing:

> Make a preparation in advance for the exercise of his liberty and the use of his strength by allowing his body to have its natural habits, by putting him in a condition to be always master of himself, and in everything to do his own will the moment he has one.

> . . . Never command him to do anything whatever, not the least thing in the world. Never allow him even to imagine that you assume to have any authority over him. Let him know merely that he is weak and that you are strong; that by virtue of his condition and your own he is necessarily at your mercy.

> . . . Do not give your scholar any sort of verbal lesson, for he is to be taught only by experience. Inflict on him no species of punishment, for he does not know what it is to be in fault.

Here Rousseau emphasizes the dynamic relationship between the curious and energetic child and the demands of his or her social environment, as represented by adults. A major aspect of the process of development, Rousseau

tabula rasa Literally, "blank slate"; the belief that infants are born with no innate knowledge or abilities.

empiricism Theory that environmental experiences shape the individual; more specifically, that all knowledge is derived from sensory experiences.

believed, is the resolution of conflicts between the individual tendencies of the child and the needs of the larger society; adults should not have to stifle the child's natural development and spirit through domination. Contemporary theories that acknowledge the active role of the child in the process of development have distinct roots in Rousseau's writings.

Rousseau also advanced some radical ideas about education. Children, he held, should not be forced to learn by rote the vast amounts of information that adults perceive as important. Instead, teachers should capitalize on the natural curiosity of children and allow them to discover on their own the myriad facts and phenomena that make up our world. Rousseau's ideas on the nature of education would be incorporated in the twentieth century in the writings of Jean Piaget, a prominent theorist who observed and described the cognitive development of children.

Both Locke and Rousseau emphasized the notion of the child as a *developing*, as opposed to a static, being. Both challenged the supposition that children are merely passive subjects of adult authority, and both advanced the idea that children should be treated with reason and respect. Having been elevated by the efforts of these worthy thinkers to an object of intellectual interest, the child was now ready to become the subject of scientific study.

The Origins of Developmental Psychology

By the mid- to late 1800s, scholars in the natural sciences, especially in biology, saw in the study of children an opportunity to support their emerging theories about the origins of human beings as a species and the dynamics of physiological processes. Charles Darwin, for example, hypothesized that the similarities between the behaviors of humans and those of other species were the result of common evolutionary ancestors. Darwin undertook his study of child development not so much to understand individual development for its own sake as to find further support for his theory of evolution. Similarly, Wilhelm Preyer, another biologist, was initially interested in the physiology of embryological development but soon extended his investigations to behavioral development after birth.

Although these early attempts to study childhood scientifically were fraught with methodological difficulties and were not explicitly conducted for the purpose of understanding child behavior, they paved the way for the systematic psychological study of the child that was to emerge by the end of that century. In the United States and in Europe, certain key researchers who participated in the birth of psychology as an academic discipline began to show an interest in studying children specifically and applied the general methods of scientific observation to this end. By the beginning of the twentieth century, developmental psychology was established as a legitimate area of psychological inquiry.

The Baby Biographers: Charles Darwin and Wilhelm Preyer   The excerpt from Charles Darwin's 1840 notes at the beginning of the chapter marks one of the first records of the close scrutiny of a child for the purpose of scientific understanding. With the goal of uncovering important clues about the origins of the human species in mind, Darwin undertook to record in great detail his infant son's behaviors during the first three years of life. Darwin

Charles Darwin, an early baby biographer, made extensive observations of his son during his first three years of life. Darwin's work helped set the stage for the scientific study of children that began in the late 19th and early 20th century.

documented the presence of early reflexes, such as sucking, as well as the emergence of voluntary motor movements, language, and emotions such as fear, anger, and affection. When he saw similarities, he linked the behaviors of the young child to other species, as when, for example, he concluded that the infant's comprehension of simple words was not unlike the ability of "lower animals" to understand words spoken by humans (Darwin, 1877).

In 1882, the German biologist Wilhelm Preyer published *The Mind of the Child,* a work that described in great detail the development of his son, Axel, during his first three years of life. Preyer wrote meticulously of his son's sensory development, motor accomplishments, language production, and memory, even noting indications of an emerging concept of self. Although Preyer followed in the footsteps of several previous "baby biographers," including Darwin, he was the first observer to insist that observations of children be conducted systematically and scientifically. Accordingly, Preyer advocated that observations be taken unobtrusively and recorded immediately, that observations be repeated several times each day, and that whenever possible the observations of more than one observer be compared.

Preyer also grappled with a long-standing controversy that has endured even in modern times, namely, the nature-nurture debate. Is the child the product of biological programs that dictate the course of development, or does experience shape the individual? Perhaps surprisingly, especially given his background as an embryologist, Preyer acknowledged that although biology predominates, both nature and nurture seem to exert a powerful influence on development.

The observations conducted by Darwin, Preyer, and other baby biographers were not without flaws. One major problem was the subjective nature of the interpretations they made about children's observable behaviors. How do we know, for example, that a given facial expression made by an infant actually signifies "sympathy," a notation Darwin made in his records about his son? The very fact that he was recording his own child's behavior introduces still another dimension of observer bias; parents typically are not the most objective observers of their own child's behavior. Moreover, the baby biographers did not always make their observations at regular intervals: sometimes entries were made in the "diary" on a daily basis; other times weeks would go by before an entry was made. Nonetheless, by advocating the application of scientific techniques to the study of children, the baby biographers, and Preyer in particular, set in motion the beginnings of the child development movement in the United States.

G. Stanley Hall: The Founder of Modern Child Psychology   The psychologist perhaps most responsible for beginning the new discipline of child study in the United States was G. Stanley Hall, the first American to obtain a Ph.D. in psychology (in 1878 under William James and Henry Bowditch at Harvard University). Hall is also known for founding in 1887 the first psychological journal in the United States and subsequently, in 1891, the first journal of developmental psychology, *Pedagogical Seminary* (now called the *Journal of Genetic Psychology*). In addition, he founded and served as the first president of the American Psychological Association.

As the first American to study in Europe with the pioneer psychologist Wilhelm Wundt, G. Stanley Hall returned to the United States in 1880 with an interest in studying the "content of children's minds." Adopting the questionnaire method he had learned about in Germany, he had teachers ask about two hundred kindergarten-aged children in the Boston area questions such as, "Have you ever seen a cow?" or "What are bricks made of?" The percent of children who gave particular answers was tabulated, and comparisons were made between the responses of boys and girls, city children and country children, and children of different ethnic backgrounds (Hall, 1891). For the first time, researchers were collecting group data and comparing groups of children, in contrast to previous approaches that had emphasized the detailed examination of individual children.

G. Stanley Hall later authored the first textbook on the psychology of adolescence, identifying this period as a special time in development. As a firm believer in evolutionary theory, Hall (along with many of his contemporaries) endorsed the notion that "ontogeny recapitulates phylogeny," the idea that the sequence of development observed in any individual parallels the evolutionary development of the species. The infant's eventual ability to walk, for example, resembles the transition to upright locomotion in the evolutionary ancestors of Homo sapiens. Early development, Hall maintained, was predominantly governed by biology, and the child's behaviors were largely based on instincts. Hall also believed, however, that adolescence was a time in development when the person could shape his or her individuality apart from the constraints imposed by evolution. He saw adolescence as a phase in which many developmental options were available and a wide range of human potentials could be achieved. Thus, Hall was also the first researcher to identify specific periods of special importance within the span of childhood.

Most historians of developmental psychology conclude that G. Stanley Hall's greatest contributions to the field lay not so much in the specific ideas he put forth about the nature of development, but rather in his role as "an importer and translator of ideas" (Cairns, 1983). By transplanting the questionnaire method from Europe to the United States, Hall introduced a new method by which researchers interested in children could approach their studies. As president of Clark University, he was further instrumental in bringing another preeminent psychologist to the United States in 1909 to deliver a series of lectures—Sigmund Freud. The ideas of psychoanalysis—specifically, that early childhood experiences could profoundly influence adult thinking and behavior and that development itself might be a stagelike process—were to find a new and receptive audience in America. The central tenets of Freud's theory will be discussed in Chapter 2.

Alfred Binet and the Study of Individual Differences   The French psychologist Alfred Binet is known primarily as the developer of the first formal assessment scale of intelligence. Binet's original interest lay in the general features of children's thinking, including memory and reasoning about numbers. His goal was to capture the complexity of children's cognition rather than to reduce it to its simplest elements, as many American researchers were apt to do. Binet's studies of children's thinking were to provide the basis for more formal tests of children's mental abilities. In response to a request from the Ministry of Public Instruction in Paris for a tool to screen for students with learning problems, Binet and another colleague, Théodore Simon, developed a series of tasks for the systematic measurement of motor skills, vocabulary, problem solving, and a wide range of other higher-order thought processes (Binet & Simon, 1905). The result was an instrument that would help to identify patterns in mental capabilities that were unique to each child.

For the first time, it was legitimate, even important, to consider variation in mental abilities from person to person. Binet was a pioneer in the study of **individual differences,** those unique characteristics that distinguish one person from others in the larger group. Although the trend in the United States at this time was to study the psychological characteristics or behaviors that groups of people shared in common, Binet's work underscored the importance of identifying varying patterns of abilities. The idea of mental testing caught on very quickly in the United States, especially among clinicians, school psychologists, and other professionals who were concerned with the practical side of dealing with children.

James Mark Baldwin: Developmental Theorist   Much of the emphasis in the early history of developmental psychology lay in constructing methodologies for studying children and collecting data about their behavior. Meanwhile James Mark Baldwin, one of the most historically important American developmental theorists of the early twentieth century, was making his own contributions on another front. Surprisingly, many of the ideas that Baldwin originally formulated went unacknowledged for another four decades. Now, however, many researchers and theorists appreciate the enormous contributions he made to our current explanations of the process of child development.

One of Baldwin's most important propositions was that development is a dynamic and hierarchical process involving more than just the accumulation of bits and pieces of knowledge or behavior. As he stated, "Every genetic change ushers in a real advance, a progression on the part of nature to a higher mode of reality" (Baldwin, 1930, p. 86). Moreover, two critical processes are part of development: habit, or simple repetition of behaviors, and accommodation, the

individual differences   Unique characteristics that distinguish a person from other members of a larger group.

adaptation of organisms to their new environments, a process that brings with it a new level of knowledge and awareness (Baldwin, 1895). Baldwin applied these ideas to the domain of cognitive development by suggesting that mental advances occur in a stagelike sequence. The earliest thought is prelogical but gives way to logical, and eventually hyperlogical (or formal), reasoning.

Baldwin is also recognized for his unique ideas about social development and the formation of personality. Instead of characterizing the child as a passive recipient of the behaviors and beliefs endorsed by the larger society, he described the child's emerging self as a product of continuing reciprocal interactions between the child and others. Children imitate those around them, but so, too, are others affected by the child's behaviors. The proposition that development results from a mutual dynamic between child and others took a long time to catch on among psychologists, but this idea, so popular today—and one of the themes of development we are emphasizing throughout this text—is actually almost a century old (Cairns & Ornstein, 1979).

By the start of the 1900s, the foundations of developmental psychology were well laid out. The handful of psychologists of that era who were specifically interested in development, however, were still obliged to invent their own methodologies and devise their own theories, sometimes apart from mainstream psychology (Cairns & Ornstein, 1979). During the early part of this century, several especially prominent theorists began to publish their ideas about the nature of development. Sigmund Freud detailed the stages in the emergence of personality in his psychoanalytic theory of development. John B. Watson elaborated on how the principles of learning theory could be applied to the development of emotions, such as fear, in children. Jean Piaget began to formulate what would become the most comprehensive theory of cognitive development to date in developmental psychology. The ideas of each of these theorists will be treated in more detail in the next chapter. Considering how few empirical data had been gathered about children up to that point, however, the theoretical writings of our predecessors were amazingly insightful. Table 1.1 summarizes the contributions of the major figures in the birth of developmental psychology.

Developmental Psychology in the Twentieth Century

From the beginning of the century to the mid-1940s, psychologists interested in development concentrated their efforts on gathering descriptive information about children. At what ages do most children achieve the milestones of motor development, such as sitting, crawling, and walking? When do children develop emotions such as fear and anger? What are children's beliefs about punishment, friendship, and morality? It was during this era of intensive fact gathering that many *norms* of development—that is, the ages at which most children are able to accomplish a given developmental task—were established. For example, Arnold Gesell established the norms of motor development for the first five years of life, guidelines that are still useful to psychologists, pediatricians, and other professionals who work with children in diagnosing developmental problems or delays (Gesell & Thompson, 1934; 1938).

The first half of the twentieth century also saw the founding of many major institutes or research centers devoted exclusively to the study of child devel-

TABLE 1.1

Major Figures in the Emergence of Developmental Psychology

John Locke (1632–1704)	Promoted the philosophy of tabula rasa, empiricism, and the use of reasoning in child rearing.
Jean Jacques Rousseau (1712–1778)	Defined the child as a "noble savage," endorsing the nurturance of natural tendencies and curiosity.
Charles Darwin (1809–1882) **Wilhelm Preyer** (1841–1897)	Systematically detailed the accomplishments of their own children in the form of baby biographies.
G. Stanley Hall (1844–1924)	Spearheaded the child-study movement in the United States, introduced the use of the questionnaire method, and wrote the first text on adolescence.
Alfred Binet (1857–1911)	Developed the first intelligence test and spurred the movement to study individual differences.
James Mark Baldwin (1861–1934)	Developed one of the first comprehensive theories of development.
Sigmund Freud (1856–1939)	Formulated a psychodynamic theory of personality development.
John B. Watson (1878–1958)	Demonstrated the usefulness of learning theory in understanding the development of emotions.
Jean Piaget (1896–1980)	Proposed an influential, broad theory of cognitive development.

opment. Child research laboratories were opened at the University of Iowa, the University of Minnesota, Yale, Columbia, and several other institutions of higher learning. In addition, the Fels Institute (in Yellow Springs, Ohio) was established to conduct extensive *longitudinal studies* in which the same children were tested repeatedly over time—often well into their adulthood—to determine how personality, thinking, and other human attributes might change with development. These centers attracted bright young scholars who dedicated their lives to the scientific study of children. A further sign of the professionalization of the discipline was the formation of the Society for Research in Child Development in 1933 for scientists who wished to share their growing knowledge of child behavior and development.

Scholars now approach child development from an assortment of disciplines, including anthropology, sociology, education, medicine, biology, and several subareas of psychology (for example, neuropsychology, comparative psychology, and clinical psychology), as well as the specialized area of developmental psychology. Each discipline has its own biases, as defined by the questions each asks about development and the methodological approaches it employs to answer those questions. Nonetheless, our pooled knowledge now gives us a better understanding of development than we might expect from a field that officially began only a century ago.

CONTROVERSY

Is Childhood Disappearing from Contemporary Society?

We have seen how our understanding of the nature of childhood has altered as a function of historical and social changes within our society. We have also seen how childhood slowly has come to be viewed as a unique and special time in life worthy of study and special attention. Childhood as an *idea* now occupies a privileged place in contemporary society. Our modern culture, some would even say, prolongs the actual experience of childhood into what bygone eras regarded as adult years. By midcentury, American society allowed many older teenagers and young adults to remain socially defined as children by virtue of remaining full-time students, relying on their parents for financial and emotional support, and delaying the start of their own families, households, and independent lives.

Other observers, however, warn that many signs in post-1950s contemporary culture point to the erosion of this relatively new distinction between childhood and adulthood and a return to the blurring of the boundaries between these two developmental periods characteristic of pre-Enlightenment times.

Some of the more visible evidence for this "adulteration" of a protected childhood comes from a merging of adults' and children's clothing styles, games, and tastes in food. Children frequently wear miniature versions of adult jeans, athletic shoes, designer clothing, make-up, and accessories. On the other hand, video games and fast-food restaurants, once thought of as appealing primarily to children, attract numerous adults. Thus, many of the activities and customs that distinguished adults from children in previous decades are now commonly shared by both age groups (Postman, 1982).

More alarming, however, is the suggestion that today's children now experience many of the problems once exclusively found among adults. Alcoholism, drug abuse, sexual promiscuity, and violent crime are increasingly found among adolescents and even younger children. In an era when many parents divorce, children are also forced to provide their parents with emotional support, a reversal of the usual parent-child roles (Winn, 1983). One of the factors that may contribute to the adultlike problems now increasingly experienced by children is the access children have to the media—the television programs, newspapers, and magazines that make available to children portrayals of violence and sexuality that were once taboo (Postman, 1982).

Contemporary society, this same argument holds, often pushes children to achieve more at earlier ages—as, for example, the young athlete in serious training or the child musician, practicing several hours before and after school to achieve new levels of proficiency. Children also experience pressures for academic achievement at earlier and earlier ages. Some parents enroll their two- and three-year-olds in highly structured preschool programs with the hopes that they will read at earlier ages, show increases in their IQ scores, and achieve more once they enter elementary and secondary school (Elkind, 1981b). Children, say the social critics, no longer have time to just be children, to engage in fantasy play and to live free from the responsibilities and pressures experienced by adults.

Is childhood disappearing? Most of us would probably say that we still hold children in a special place in society and that we do protect them from the harsher realities of life. Moreover, a noticeable proportion of society's resources are still allocated to children in the form of education, medical care, and social services (although some would argue that we do not do enough). Nevertheless, some children undoubtedly enter the world of adulthood too soon. The costs of their doing so—to the children themselves and to society at large—are worth our serious attention. ∎

RESEARCH METHODS IN DEVELOPMENTAL PSYCHOLOGY

Like their colleagues in all the sciences, researchers in child development seek to gather data that are objective, measurable, and capable of being replicated in controlled studies by other researchers. Their studies, in other words, are based on the **scientific method.** Frequently, they initiate research to evaluate the predictions of a specific theory (for example, is cognitive development stagelike as Piaget suggests?). Alternatively, they may formulate a research question to determine an application of theory to a real-world situation (for example, can IQ scores be boosted by early intervention programs for preschoolers?). Regardless of the motivation, the general principles of good science are as important to research in child development as they are to any other research arena. Moreover, even though many of the methods that child development researchers use are the very same techniques that psychologists routinely employ in other specialized areas, some methodological approaches are especially useful in studying changes in behavior or mental processes that occur over time.

The Role of Theories

An essential ingredient of the scientific process is the construction of theories. A **theory** is a set of ideas or propositions that helps to organize or explain observable phenomena. Children display a vast assortment of intellectual, linguistic, social, and physical behaviors, capabilities that also show changes with time. By describing children's accomplishments in a systematic, integrated way, theories serve to *organize* or make sense of the enormous amount of information researchers have gleaned.

Theories of development also help *explain* our observations. Is your neighbor's little boy shy because he inherited this trait, or did his social experiences encourage him to become this way? Did your niece's mathematical skills develop from her experience with her home computer, or does she just have a natural flair for numbers? Psychologists are interested in understanding the factors that contribute to the emergence of behavioral skills and capacities, and their theories are ways of articulating ideas about what causes various behaviors to develop in individual children.

A good theory goes beyond even description and explanation. It leads to *predictions* about behavior, predictions that are clear and easily tested. If shyness is the result of the child's social experiences, for example, then the withdrawn four-year-old should profit from a training program that teaches social

scientific method Use of objective, measurable, and repeatable techniques to gather information.

theory Set of ideas or propositions that helps organize or explain observable phenomena.

skills. If, on the other hand, shyness is a stable, unchangeable personality trait, then even extensive training in sociability might have very little impact.

Theories usually lead to *hypotheses* about the causes of or influences on behavior, hypotheses that the researcher then systematically tests. The scientific method dictates that theories must be revised or elaborated as new observations confirm or refute them. The process of scientific fact finding involves a constant cycle of theorizing, empirical testing of the resulting hypotheses, and revision (or even outright rejection) of theories as the new data come in. In Chapter 2 we will examine the major theories of child development and their impact on the field.

Measuring Attributes and Behaviors

All researchers are interested in identifying relationships among **variables,** those factors in a given situation having no fixed or constant value. In child development studies, the variables consist of individual attributes, experiences, or behaviors that differ from one time to the next or from one person to another. Ultimately, researchers are interested in determining the causal relationships among variables—that is, they wish to identify those variables directly responsible for the occurrence of other variables. Does watching television cause children to behave aggressively? Do withdrawn children have academic problems once they enroll in school? Does the way a parent interacts with a toddler raise or lower the child's later intelligence? To pose each of these questions, researchers are hypothesizing that some attribute or experience of the child is causally related to another attribute or behavior.

The first problem the researcher faces is that of **operationally defining,** or specifying in measurable terms, the variables under study. Take the case of aggression. This term can be defined as parental ratings of children's physical hostility, the child's own reports of his or her level of violent behavior, or the number of hits and kicks recorded by an observer of the child's behavior. The key point is that variables must be defined in terms of precise measurement procedures that other researchers can use if they wish to repeat the study.

The measurement of variables must also be **valid** and **reliable. Validity** refers to how well an assessment procedure actually measures the variable under study. Parental reports of physical violence, for example, or even the child's own self-reports may not be the best indicators of aggression. Parents may not want a researcher to know about their child's misbehavior, or they may not have complete knowledge of how their child behaves outside the home. Children's own reports may not be very accurate because they may wish to present themselves to adults in a certain way. If a trained observer records the number of hits or kicks the child displays during a school day, on the other hand, the resulting measurement of aggression is likely to be valid.

Reliability is the degree to which the same results will be obtained consistently if the measure is administered repeatedly or if several observers are viewing the same behavior episodes. In the first case, suppose a child takes an intelligence test one time, then two weeks later takes the test again. If the test is reliable, she should obtain similar scores on the two testing occasions. In the second case, two or more observers viewing a child's behavior should agree about what they are seeing (for example, did that child smile in the pres-

variable Factor having no fixed or constant value in a given situation.

operational definition Specification of variables in terms of measurable properties.

validity Degree to which an assessment procedure actually measures the variable under consideration.

reliability Degree to which a measure will yield the same results if administered repeatedly.

ence of a stranger?); if they do, the test has high **inter-rater reliability.** Both types of reliability are calculated mathematically and are usually reported by researchers in their published reports of experiments; both are very important factors in good scientific research. Measurements of behavior that fluctuate dramatically from one observation time to another or from one observer to another are virtually useless as data.

Collecting Data

Researchers in developmental psychology employ a range of strategies to gather information about children. Each approach offers both advantages and disadvantages, and the choice of research tactic will often depend on the nature of the investigator's questions. If we are interested in exploring children's spontaneous tendencies to behave aggressively as they play (for example, do boys play more aggressively than girls?), we would probably find a *naturalistic approach* most appropriate. If we want to examine how children understand aggression, its antecedents and consequences, then we might adopt another strategy, such as a *structured interview* or a *questionnaire*. Sometimes researchers combine data collection methods within a study or series of studies. Ultimately, there is no one right way to study children. Researchers must consider their overall goals and their available resources as they make decisions about how to construct a research study.

Naturalistic Observation　　Researchers have no better way to see how children really behave than to observe them in natural settings—in their homes, schools, playgrounds, and other places that are part of their everyday lives. After all, the ultimate goal of developmental psychology is to describe and explain changes in behavior that actually exist. **Naturalistic observations** do not involve the manipulation of variables; researchers simply observe and record behaviors of interest from the natural series of events that unfolds in a real-world setting. An important advantage of this approach is that researchers can see the events and behaviors that precede the target behaviors they are recording; they can also note the consequences of those same target behaviors. In this way they may be able to discern important relationships in sequences of events.

A study by Henry Wellman and Jacques Lempers (1977), for example, used naturalistic observations to assess the *referential communication skills* of two-year-old children, their ability to effectively describe, point out, or show an object to another child. Five boys and five girls were videotaped while they played with their age mates in a preschool class or play group over several sessions. To minimize the children's potential reactions to the presence of the experimenter, the videotapes were made unobtrusively from an observation booth. Later the researchers viewed the tapes and identified all instances in which children engaged in referential communication. Did these very young children understand some of the basic principles of effective communication?

Wellman and Lempers developed two scales to assess children's referential communication skills in this study. The first described the communicator's ability to appraise the communication situation. Did the communicator seek

inter-rater reliability　Degree to which two or more observers agree in their observations.

naturalistic observation　Study in which observations of naturally occurring behavior are made in real-life settings.

In naturalistic observations, researchers observe and record children's behaviors in real-life settings, such as playgrounds, schools, or homes.

close physical proximity to the listener? Did the communicator get the listener's attention before speaking? Did the communicator wait until the listener was ready to receive the message? The second scale described the communicator's behavior—the use of verbal attention getters (for example, "Hey"); nonverbal attention getters (for example, waving at the receiver); or any other behavior to make sure the message got across. A communication was considered to be effective if the listener looked at the object being talked about or verbally communicated that he or she understood the message. The investigators then computed the number of times communicators used any of the situations or behaviors that led to successful transmission of their message. They found that 80 percent of these young children's messages were met with a response from the listener and, furthermore, that two-year-olds were very much aware of the conditions and behaviors that lead to effective communication.

The methodology of this study had many positive features. First, Wellman and Lempers operationally defined the variables of interest by clearly identifying what a referential communication was and what constituted an effective communication. Second, they were aware that children might react to the presence of a stranger by behaving in untypical ways. To avoid such **subject reactivity** to the presence of the experimenter—in this case, the tendency of children to behave differently in the presence of a stranger (which could make their behavior "unnatural")—these researchers hid their camera. Finally, to minimize the effects of **observer bias**—the possibility that the researcher would interpret ongoing events to be consistent with his or her prior hypotheses—two independent observers (one of whom was unfamiliar with the purposes of the study) scored the videotapes to ensure reliability of the findings.

Naturalistic observations are especially useful in examining areas of child development that have not previously been the object of intensive research. Often the trends or phenomena identified in such preliminary studies become

subject reactivity   Tendency of subjects who know they are under observation to alter natural behavior.

observer bias   Tendency of researchers to interpret ongoing events as consistent with their research hypotheses.

the focus of more intensive, controlled laboratory experiments. And, as we mentioned earlier, naturalistic observations have the distinct advantage of examining real-life behaviors as opposed to behaviors that may emerge only in response to some contrived or artificial laboratory manipulation.

Some cautions, however, are in order about this method. First, a wide range of variables may be influencing the behaviors under observation, and it is not always clear which ones have the most impact. Do all preschoolers show sophisticated communication skills, or is it just those who have had extensive contact with peers? Do listeners receive the message more readily about some objects—say, an attractive toy—rather than less interesting objects? Cause-and-effect relationships, furthermore, are difficult to establish. Here, the circumstances that cause preschoolers to become aware of the strategies and techniques that foster effective communication cannot be specified. Answering questions like these often requires the systematic manipulation of variables, a tactic that is part of other research approaches.

Structured Observation   Researchers are not always fortunate enough to be able to count on a child to display behaviors of scientific interest to them. Researchers who observe a child in the home, school, or other natural setting may simply not be present when referential communication, sharing, aggression, or other behaviors they wish to study occur. Therefore, developmental psychologists may opt to observe behaviors in a more structured setting, usually the laboratory, where they devise situations to elicit those behaviors of interest to them. **Structured observations** are the record of specific behaviors displayed by the child in a situation constructed by the experimenter. Structured observations, like naturalistic observations, are a way of collecting data by *looking* at and recording the child's behaviors, but this form of looking takes place under highly controlled conditions.

A study on the effects of adult emotions on the emotions of two-year-olds illustrates how such structured observations are frequently conducted (Cummings, Iannotti, & Zahn-Waxler, 1985). Pairs of children were brought to a laboratory playroom along with their mothers. While the children played, two adults entered the room and engaged first in a friendly, pleasant interaction, then in an angry exchange, and finally in a friendly, conciliatory manner. The emotional reactions of children (particularly bodily or facial expressions of anxiety and vocalizations like crying) during the different phases of the experimental session were recorded by several trained observers. In addition, a control group of children witnessed the adults in a series of three neutral communications. The results (shown in Figure 1.1) indicated that exposure to the adults' angry exchanges generated significant distress among two-year-olds compared with their reactions in the presence of the friendly exchanges. Although these researchers could have attempted to conduct their study of reactions to adult emotions through naturalistic observation in children's homes or preschools, they might have had to wait a long time for the appropriate interactions to take place spontaneously. Furthermore, adults in natural settings display emotions with varying degrees of intensity, making it difficult for the experimenters to ensure that all of their subjects witnessed exactly the same emotional states. By doing a structured observation, the experimenters could control the precise nature of the adult emotional displays that children saw. The adult actors were carefully trained so that all children witnessed exactly the same emotional scenes in the same order.

structured observation   Study in which behaviors are recorded as they occur within a situation constructed by the experimenter, usually in the laboratory.

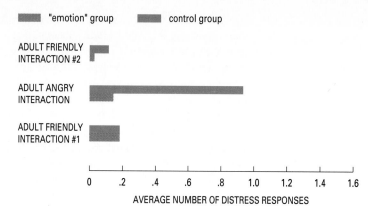

Source: Adapted from Cummings, Ianotti, & Zahn-Waxler, 1985.

FIGURE 1.1

A Structured Observation

What happens when two-year-old children observe two adults have a friendly interaction, followed by an angry exchange, then by another friendly interaction? The graph shows the average number of distress responses (expressions of anxiety, crying, and so forth) displayed by children who witnessed this sequence of events compared with those of a control group that saw a series of three neutral exchanges. This structured observation showed that exposure to adult anger heightened children's distress.

A liability of structured observations, especially if they are conducted in the laboratory, is that children may not react in the same ways in the research room as they do in "real life." Being in a strange environment with unfamiliar experimenters or other participants in the study may make children behave in ways that are not typical. For example, children may show heightened distress to adult anger when they are in an unfamiliar environment. One solution to this problem is to confirm the results of laboratory studies by conducting similar studies in children's natural environments.

Structured observations can focus on a variety of types of behaviors. Like many structured observations, the study by Cummings and colleagues focused on children's overt actions—in this case, their facial displays and physical activities. Researchers often record other behaviors, such as the number of errors children make in a problem-solving task, the kinds of memory strategies they display, or the amount of time it takes children to learn a specified task. When structured observations are conducted in the laboratory, it is also possible for researchers to obtain **physiological measures,** the shifts in heart rate, brain wave activity, or respiration rate that can indicate the child's reaction to changes in stimuli. This technique is especially useful in examining the behavior of infants, because the range of overt responses usually displayed by very young children is more limited than that of older children.

The Interview and the Questionnaire   Sometimes the best way to glean information about what children know or how they behave is not simply to observe them but to *ask* them directly. Researchers have found that talking with children about their conceptions of friendships, sex roles, problem-solving skills—in fact, almost anything in the child's world—has yielded a wealth of material for analysis.

Many investigators use the technique of **structured interviews,** studies in which each participating child is asked the same sequence of questions. When Deanna Kuhn and her associates (Kuhn, Nash, & Brucken, 1978) wanted to explore young children's understanding of sex roles, they showed the two- and three-year-old children in this study two paper dolls, one named Michael and one named Lisa. As the experimenter read a list of statements—for example,

physiological measure Measurement of heart rate, brain activity, respiration rate, or other bodily responses to stimulation.

structured interview Standardized set of questions administered orally to subjects.

"I like to play dolls,"—children were to identify which doll said it. The list included items that are frequently associated with male and female stereotypes, such as, "I like to clean house," "I like to cry sometimes," "I can hit you," and "I like to build things." These researchers found that even two-year-old children were well aware of sex-role stereotypes. Both boys and girls thought Lisa was the doll that played with dolls, helped mother, talked a lot, and liked to clean the house. Similarly, both boys and girls thought Michael liked to play with cars, build things, and talked about hitting. The knowledge these very young children possessed about traditional male and female roles was, in fact, quite extensive.

Another "asking" technique that researchers use with children is to obtain written responses to a standard set of items in a **questionnaire.** Because questionnaires can be administered to large numbers of children at the same time, researchers can use this method to obtain a large set of data very quickly. Questionnaires can also be scored quickly, particularly if the items ask subjects to pick from a set of multiple-choice items or to rate items on a numerical scale. Children, however, may have difficulty understanding the items and may not be able to answer accurately without guidance from an adult. Under those conditions, oral interviews with individual children may provide more reliable and valid information about how children think and feel.

Researchers who use interviews and questionnaires to collect data from children must be careful, though. Sometimes young respondents, like their adult counterparts, will try to present themselves in the most favorable light or answer questions as they think the researcher expects them to. In the study that used paper dolls, for example, children may have given stereotypical responses about the things that "Michael" and "Lisa" do simply because they thought the researcher wanted to hear these responses. To prompt subjects to answer as honestly as possible, researchers try not to react positively or negatively as the subject responds and also try to explain the importance of answering truthfully before the start of the interview or questionnaire.

Another way of collecting data by interview is the **clinical method,** a flexible, open-ended technique in which the investigator may modify the questions in reaction to the child's response. Jean Piaget was famous for using the clinical method to explore age-related changes in children's thinking capabilities. Consider the following segment, in which Piaget (1929) questions a six-year-old boy about the sun:

questionnaire Set of standardized questions administered to subjects in written form.

clinical method Flexible, open-ended interview method in which questions are modified in reaction to the child's responses.

PIAGET: How did the sun begin?
CHILD: It was when life began.

PIAGET: Has there always been a sun?
CHILD: No.

PIAGET: How did it begin?
CHILD: Because it knew that life had begun.

PIAGET: What is it made of?
CHILD: Of fire . . .

PIAGET: Where did the fire come from?
CHILD: From the sky.

PIAGET: How was the fire made in the sky?
CHILD: It was lighted with a match. (p. 258)

Notice how Piaget follows the child's line of thinking with each question he asks. The format of the interview changes with an older boy, age nine years:

PIAGET: How did the sun start?
CHILD: With heat.

PIAGET: What heat?
CHILD: From the fire.

PIAGET: Where is the fire?
CHILD: In heaven.

PIAGET: How did it start?
CHILD: God lit it with wood and coal.

PIAGET: Where did he get the wood and coal?
CHILD: He made it. (p. 265)

Piaget gained some enormous insights into the thinking processes of children by using the probing, interactive questions typical of the clinical method. Having the flexibility to follow the child's train of thought rather than sticking to a rigid protocol of predetermined questions allows the researcher to gather fresh insights. The weakness of this approach, though, lies in precisely this flexibility. Because the questions asked of different subjects are likely to vary, systematic comparisons of their answers are difficult to make. Moreover, the researcher may be tied to a theoretical orientation that biases the formulation of questions and the interpretation of answers. Nonetheless, the clinical method can be a valuable research tool, particularly in exploring the way children think and reason.

The Meta-analytic Study   Sometimes researchers do not actually collect empirical data themselves but instead make a statistical analysis of a body of previously published research on a specific topic that allows them to draw some general conclusions. Instead of looking or asking, they "crunch" data— that is, they combine the results of numerous studies to assess whether the central variable common to all has an important effect. This technique, called **meta-analysis,** is particularly useful when the results of studies in the same area are inconsistent or in conflict with one another.

A good example of meta-analysis is a study conducted by Janet Hyde and her colleagues to assess the existence of sex differences in children's mathematical skills (Hyde, Fennema, & Lamon, 1990). Many researchers have concluded that boys perform better than girls on tests of mathematical skill, particularly after the age of twelve or thirteen (Halpern, 1986; Maccoby & Jacklin, 1974). Such observations have spawned numerous debates about the origins of this sex difference. Is mathematical skill biologically given or is it learned through experiences in the environment? The answer to this question has important educational implications for male and female students. Hyde and her colleagues collected one hundred studies conducted from 1967 through 1987 that examined the question of sex differences in mathematics performance. (This body of studies represented the participation of over 3 million subjects!) For each study, a statistical measure representing *effect size* was computed, a mathematical way of expressing the size of the difference in male and female scores. Hyde and her colleagues (1990) found that the average difference between males and females across all studies was small, leading these

meta-analysis Statistical examination of a body of research studies to assess the effect of the common central variable.

researchers to conclude sex differences in mathematical ability are not large enough to be of great scientific significance.

Conducting a meta-analysis requires the careful transcription of hundreds of statistical figures, a powerful computer, and a good deal of computational skill. Because the researcher taking this approach did not design the original studies, she or he cannot always be sure that the central variables have been defined in identical ways across studies. Moreover, studies that do not present their data in the form necessary for analysis might have to be eliminated from the pool; potentially valuable information might thus be lost. Despite these difficulties, the meta-analytic approach allows us to draw conclusions based on a large corpus of research, not just individual studies, and thereby to profit from an accumulated body of knowledge. This technique has recently become increasingly popular in developmental research and has provoked the reevaluation of more than one traditional notion about children. Table 1.2 summarizes the advantages and disadvantages of these four broad types of data collection.

TABLE 1.2

Advantages and Disadvantages of Information-gathering Approaches

Approach	Description	Advantages	Disadvantages
Naturalistic Observations	Observations of behaviors as they occur in children's real-life environments.	Can note antecedents and consequences of behaviors; see real-life behaviors.	Possibility of subject reactivity and observer bias; less control over variables; cause-and-effect relationships difficult to establish.
Structured Observations	Observations of behaviors in situations constructed by the experimenter.	More control over conditions that elicit behaviors.	Children may not react as they would in real life.
Interviews and Questionnaires	Asking children (or parents) about what they know or how they behave.	Quick way to assess children's knowledge or reports of their behaviors.	Children may not always respond truthfully or accurately; systematic comparisons of responses may be difficult; theoretical orientation of researcher may bias questions and interpretations of answers.
Meta-analytic Studies	Statistical analysis of other researchers' findings to look for the size of a variable's effects.	Pools a large body of research findings to sort out conflicting findings; no subjects are observed.	Requires careful mathematical computation; variables may not have been defined identically across all studies.

Research Designs

Besides formulating their hypotheses, identifying the variables, and choosing a method of gathering information about children, investigators must select the research design they will use as part of their study. The *research design* is the overall conceptual approach that defines whether the variables will be manipulated, whether a large number of children will be studied or just a few, and what the precise sequence of events will be as the study proceeds. Research designs can get fairly complex, and an investigator might choose more than one design for each part of a large study. Generally, however, researchers select from one of three study types: the correlational, the experimental, and the single-case design.

The Correlational Design   Studies in which the researcher looks for systematic relationships between variables use the correlational design and are called **correlational studies.** Instead of manipulating the variables, in this design the investigator obtains measures of two or more characteristics of the subjects and sees if changes in one variable are accompanied by changes in the other. Some variables show a **positive correlation**—that is, as the values of one variable change, scores on the other variable change in the same direction. For example, if a positive correlation existed between children's television viewing and their aggression, as the number of hours of TV viewing increased, the number of aggressive acts committed would increase, as well. A **negative correlation** indicates that as scores on one variable change, scores on the other variable change in the opposite direction. Thus, using our example, a negative relationship would exist if aggression decreased as TV viewing increased.

The statistic used to describe the strength of a relationship between two variables is called the **correlation coefficient,** or **r.** Correlation coefficients may range from $+1.00$ (perfectly positively correlated) to -1.00 (perfectly negatively correlated). As the correlation coefficient approaches 0.00 (which signifies no relationship), the relationship between the two variables becomes weaker. A general rule of thumb is that correlations of .70 or higher usually signify strong relationships, whereas those below .20 represent weak relationships. In most cases, values falling in between indicate a moderate relationship between two variables.

We can use portions of a study conducted by M. Ann Easterbrooks and Wendy Goldberg (1984) to illustrate the key features of correlational research. The objective of these investigators was to see if the involvement of fathers in child rearing was related to the development of their preschool-aged children. The measure of father involvement was a composite number representing how much time fathers spent with their toddler children alone or playing with them each day. The investigators employed several measures of the children's development, including a score of "task orientation," in which a high score reflected self-direction and persistence in solving jigsaw puzzles. A second measure was a score of how emotionally attached children were to their mothers. Here, too, a high score indicated healthier development in the form of a secure, positive relationship with the mother. The results indicated that the correlation between father involvement and task orientation among female children was $r = .50$; fathers who spent more time with their daughters had

correlational study   Study assessing whether changes in one variable are accompanied by systematic changes in another variable.

positive correlation   Relationship in which changes in one variable are accompanied by systematic changes in another variable in the same direction.

negative correlation   Relationship in which changes in one variable are accompanied by systematic changes in another variable in the opposite direction.

correlation coefficient (r)   Statistical measure, ranging from $+1.00$ to -1.00, that summarizes the strength and direction of the relationship between two variables; does not provide information about causation.

girls who were better able to solve puzzles in an independent, thorough manner. In contrast, the value of the correlation between father involvement and task orientation in boys was $r = .11$, signifying no relationship. In addition, for boys, father involvement and attachment to mother were correlated $r = .29$. To some extent, the more time fathers spent with their sons, the healthier was the mother-son bond. This relationship was not significant for girls.

Because researchers do not actively manipulate the variables in correlational studies, it is not possible in these studies to make statements about cause and effect when strong relationships are found. In the Easterbrooks and Goldberg study, it is not clear whether father involvement caused greater task orientation in daughters or the other way around. It may be, for example, that toddler girls who are independent and persistent in solving problems attract more attention from their fathers. Still another possibility is that some third factor influences both father involvement and problem-solving behavior. Perhaps when fathers spend time with their daughters, mothers do too, making the maternal behavior the determining influence on their daughters. Despite these limitations on interpretation, correlational studies are often a useful first step in determining which variables might possibly have a causal relationship with each other. In addition, in many instances experimenters are unable to manipulate the variables that are the suspected causes of behavior. In the study of father involvement, for example, it would be difficult to ask some fathers to be involved with their children at home and some to avoid playing with them. In such cases, correlational studies represent the only approach available to understanding the influences on child development.

The Experimental Design   The **experimental design** involves the manipulation of one or more **independent variables** (the variables that are manipulated or controlled by the investigator, often because they are the suspected cause of a behavior) to observe the effects on the **dependent variable** (the suspected outcome). One of the major goals of this type of study is to control for as many of the factors that can influence the outcome aside from the independent variables. Experimental studies are frequently conducted in laboratory situations, where it is possible to make sure that all subjects are exposed to the same environmental conditions and the same task instructions. In addition, **random assignment** of subjects to different treatment groups (in which usually one group is a *control group* that receives no treatment) helps to avoid any systematic variation aside from that precipitated by the independent variables. As a consequence, one distinct advantage of the experimental study design is that cause-and-effect relationships among variables can be identified.

To illustrate the experimental design, consider the following question: Do infants change their emotional responses based on the facial expressions of their mothers? A team of investigators explored this question in an experimental study involving three- and six-month-old infants and their mothers in a laboratory setting (Gusella, Muir, & Tronick, 1988). Mothers were randomly assigned to one of two experimental conditions. In the first, the still-face condition, mothers were to interact normally with their infants for two minutes (Period 1); then to maintain a still, neutral face and refrain from touching their infants for the following two minutes (Period 2); and finally to resume normal interactions (Period 3). In the second condition, the control condition, mothers were instructed to interact normally with their babies for all three periods.

experimental design   Research method in which one or more independent variables are manipulated to determine the effect on other, dependent, variables.

independent variable   Variable manipulated by the experimenter; the suspected cause.

dependent variable   Behavior that is measured; suspected effect of an experimental manipulation.

random assignment   Use of principles of chance to assign subjects to treatment and control groups; avoids systematic bias.

During the sessions, the time the infant spent smiling was recorded. Thus the independent variable was the mother's facial expression and the dependent variable was the duration of the infant's smiling.

Figure 1.2 shows the average percent of time the younger and older infants spent smiling during the sessions. You can see that, especially for the six-month-olds, smiling decreased in the still-face condition compared with the control condition. In other words, the facial expressions of mothers directly influenced the facial expressions of their infants. Can any other hypotheses account for these findings? Because mothers and their babies were randomly assigned to the treatment conditions, it is not likely that happier babies appeared in the control group. And because all parent-infant pairs experienced the same experimental procedures except for the manipulation itself, it is difficult to argue for other explanations of these data.

The experimental approach has been the traditional design choice for many developmental psychologists because of the "clean" answers it provides about the causes of developmental phenomena. Yet it has also been criticized for providing a narrow portrait of child development. Development in the real world is likely to be caused by many variables; few changes are likely to be the result of a single or even a few independent variables. In that sense, experimental studies typically do not capture the complexities of age-related changes. Moreover, we have already mentioned that children may not react normally when they are brought into the laboratory setting, where most experiments are conducted. Children may "clam up" because they are shy about being in unfamiliar surroundings with strangers and mechanical equipment. Or they may rush through the experimental task just to get it over with.

In recognition of these problems, many researchers have tried to furnish their laboratories to achieve a more homelike feeling, with comfortable couches, chairs, tables, and rugs instead of sterile, bare-walled rooms filled

FIGURE 1.2

An Experimental Study

In this example of an experimental design, mothers of three- and six-month-old infants were randomly assigned to one of two groups. The first group interacted normally with their infants for two minutes (Period 1); then maintained a still, motionless face and refrained from touching their infants for two minutes (Period 2); and finally resumed normal interaction (Period 3). The control group simply interacted normally with their infants throughout the three periods. Most babies, but especially the six-month-olds, showed a drop in smiling during the mothers' still-face period. Babies in the control group showed little change in smiling.

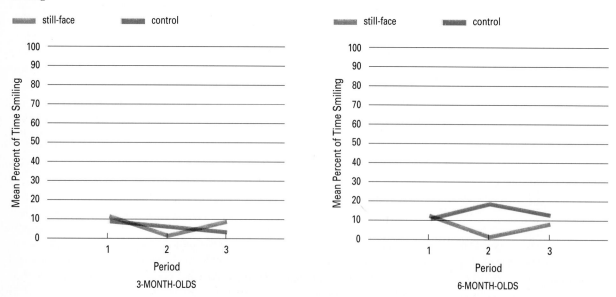

Source: Adapted from Gusella, Muir, & Tronick, 1988.

with wires and panels of equipment. Another tactic has been to conduct **field experiments,** in which the experimental manipulations are actually carried out in a natural setting, such as the child's home or school. In one classic field experiment, Lynette Friedrich and Aletha Stein (1973) randomly assigned preschoolers to one of three experimental conditions to see if the type of television program they watched over a period of time affected their behavior during free play. For four weeks, one-half hour each day, children viewed either: (1) aggressive cartoons ("Batman" and "Superman"), (2) prosocial shows ("Mr. Rogers' Neighborhood"), or (3) neutral films. The results showed that children exposed to aggressive shows declined in obedience to rules and their ability to tolerate delays. In addition, children who were above average in aggression at the start of the study showed more aggression during free play than children who viewed the neutral shows. Finally, children who watched prosocial programs were more likely to stick with tasks they had begun and were more likely to obey rules than children who viewed neutral films. As with laboratory experiments, this study identified a causal effect of television programs on children's social behaviors. Because the only known variation in children's experiences was systematically introduced by the researchers in their manipulation of the independent variable (the type of television show the children watched), changes in behavior could be attributed to type of show. The natural setting of this field experiment was an added feature that minimized the problems associated with bringing children into the artificial surroundings of a laboratory.

In some instances, it is not possible for the researcher to randomly assign subjects to treatment groups because of logistical or ethical difficulties. In these cases, the researcher may take advantage of the natural separation of subjects into different groups. **Quasi-experiments** are studies in which researchers investigate the effects of independent variables that they do not manipulate themselves but that occur as a result of children's natural experiences. Suppose, for example, that a researcher wanted to explore the effects of day-care centers of varying quality on children's social competence. It would be ethically problematic to assign children randomly to high- and low-quality centers. Yet in everyday life, children do attend centers that differ in the overall quality of experience they provide. Deborah Vandell and her colleagues (Vandell, Henderson, & Wilson, 1988) observed the free play of four-year-old children who attended good- and poor-quality day-care centers. Good-quality centers were defined as those with better-trained teachers, better adult-child ratios, smaller classes, and more materials than poor-quality centers. When children from the two types of centers were compared on a range of social behaviors, Vandell and her colleagues noted that children from the better centers were rated as more socially competent, happier, and capable of more friendly interactions with their peers than children from the poorer centers.

Because the researchers did not randomly assign subjects to each group, we must be careful in how we interpret the results of this and other quasi-experimental studies. The children who attended poor- and good-quality centers may have consistently differed in ways that better account for their differences in social behavior than simply the nature of the day-care center they attended. Families with children in poor-quality centers may have had more limited financial resources and may have been under more stress than those who sent

field experiment Experiment conducted in a "natural" real-world setting such as the child's home or school.

quasi-experiment Study in which the assignment of subjects to experimental groups is determined by their natural experiences.

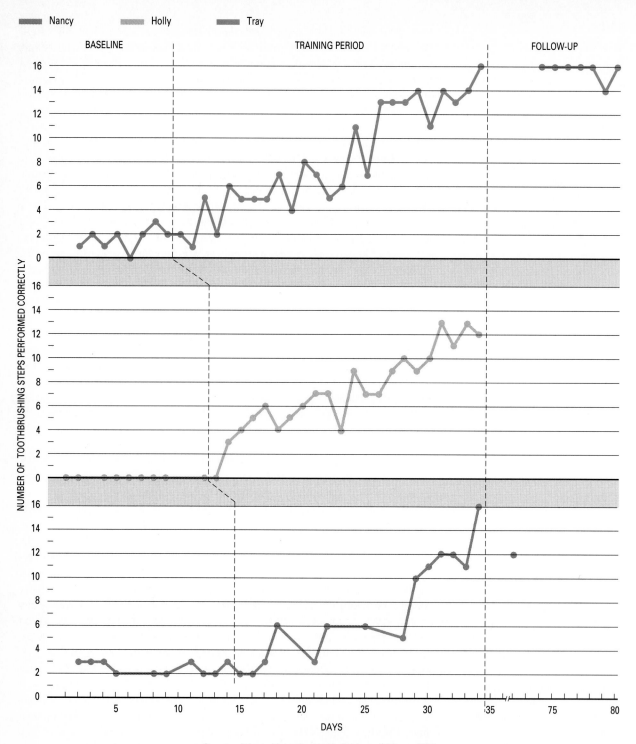

Source: Adapted from Poche, McCubbrey, & Munn, 1982.

FIGURE 1.3

A Single-Case Design

Can training increase correct toothbrushing in preschool children? In this example of a single-subject design, during the baseline period, little or no correct toothbrushing occurred; as training proceeded, however, the target behaviors increased dramatically and were maintained during the follow-up phase, as measured in two of the subjects. Because the three children showed similar patterns of change in these behaviors over time, and because the behaviors were maintained well after the program ended, the researchers concluded that their treatment had an effect.

their children to better centers. Aspects of the home climate, rather than qualities of the day-care experience, may in fact have caused differences in children's social behavior and general emotional disposition. At the same time, however, quasi-experimental studies do offer researchers a way of addressing important questions about the complex influences on child development, questions that often have powerful real-world implications.

The Single-Subject Design Some notable discoveries about developmental processes have come from the in-depth examination of a single child or just a few children. At times, psychologists make an intensive description of an individual child, much as the baby biographers did. Freud and Piaget both relied heavily on such **case studies** of individuals to formulate their broad theories of personality and cognitive development, respectively. In other instances, researchers introduce experimental treatments to one or a few children and note any changes in their behavior over time. In these **single-case designs,** the focus of the study is frequently to evaluate a clinical treatment for a problem behavior or an educational program designed to increase or decrease specific activities in the child.

Suppose, for example, we wish to evaluate a training program to increase the toothbrushing skills of preschool-aged children. One team of researchers devised such a program, which included instruction on the appropriate angle of the brush, the motion of the brush, and the duration of brushing (Poche, McCubbrey, & Munn, 1982). Would such a program increase the skills of children in this age group? The researchers selected three children and first noted the number of correct toothbrushing steps each showed before the start of the program. As Figure 1.3 shows, none of the children performed very many of these steps during the period of *baseline* observations. Next, the program was instituted and the children's behavior during the *training period* was recorded each day. As the graph shows, all children increased dramatically in their toothbrushing skills. Finally, a *follow-up* done on two of the children a month after the program ceased showed that they continued to display their toothbrushing skills at a high rate. Was the training program effective? The fact that three children showed similar increases in their toothbrushing skills once the program began and the fact that the two children evaluated in the follow-up maintained these behaviors well after the program ended suggests that it was.

Single-case designs do not require large groups of children or the random assignment of subjects to groups. Each subject essentially serves as his or her own control by experiencing all conditions in the experiment over a period of time. As with any study involving only one or a few individuals, however, researchers may be limited in their ability to generalize to a larger group of children. Perhaps the child or children they selected for the study were particularly responsive to the treatment, a treatment that might not work as well for other children. In addition, the researcher must be aware of any other circumstances concurrent with the treatment that might have actually produced the behavior changes. Did the children in the toothbrushing study have their first dental visits at the time of the training program, with the dental visits causing the increase in their skills? Did they watch a television show about brushing teeth? In this case, the fact that the training started at different times for each

case study In-depth description of psychological characteristics and behaviors of an individual.

single-case design Study that follows only one or a few children over a period of time.

Design	Description	Strengths	Weaknesses
Correlational Design	Researcher sees if changes in one variable are accompanied by systematic changes in another variable.	Useful when conditions do not permit the manipulation of variables.	Cannot determine cause-and-effect relationships.
Experimental Design	Researcher manipulates one or more independent variables to observe the effects on the dependent variable(s).	Can isolate cause-and-effect relationships.	May not yield information about real-life behaviors.
Field Experiment	Experiment conducted in real-life, naturalistic settings.	Can isolate cause-and-effect relationships; behaviors are observed in natural settings.	Less control over treatment conditions.
Quasi-Experiment	Assignment of subjects to groups is determined by their natural experiences.	Takes advantage of natural separation of children into groups.	Factors other than independent variables may be causing results.
Single-subject Design	In-depth observation of one or a few children over a period of time.	Does not require large pool of subjects.	Ability to generalize to the larger population may be limited.

TABLE 1.3

Strengths and Weaknesses of Research Designs

of the three children and was immediately followed by increases in toothbrushing skill suggests that the program and not some other factor caused the changes. Table 1.3 provides an overview of the strengths and weaknesses of single-subject and other research designs we have briefly examined here.

Strategies for Assessing Developmental Change

The developmental researcher faces a problem unique to this field: how to record the changes in behavior that occur over time. Basically, the investigator has two possible choices—to observe individual children repeatedly over time or to select children of different ages to participate in one study at a given time. Each approach has its strengths and limitations, and both have contributed substantially to our understanding of child development.

The Longitudinal Study   **Longitudinal studies** are studies in which the same sample of subjects is assessed repeatedly at various points in time, usually over a span of years. This approach has the longest historical tradition in developmental psychology. The early baby biographies were, in essence, longitudinal observations, and several major longitudinal projects initiated in the early part of the 1900s continued for decades beyond. One of the most famous is Lewis Terman's study of intellectually gifted children, begun in 1921 (Terman, 1925; Terman & Oden, 1959).

longitudinal study   Research in which the same subjects are repeatedly tested over a period of time, usually years.

Terman identified 952 children aged two to fourteen years who had scored 140 or above on a standardized test of intelligence. He was interested in answering several questions about these exceptionally bright children. Would they become extraordinarily successful later in life? Did they possess any specific cluster of common personality traits? Did they adapt well socially? The sample was followed until most subjects reached sixty years of age, and a wealth of information was collected over this long span of time. One finding was that many individuals in this sample had highly successful careers in science, academics, business, and other professions. In addition, contrary to many popular stereotypes, high intelligence was associated with greater physical and mental health and adaptive social functioning later in life.

Longitudinal research is costly and requires a substantial research effort. Subjects followed over a period of years often move or become unavailable for other reasons; just keeping track of them requires careful and constant record keeping. And questions can be raised about the characteristics of the people who remain in the study: perhaps they are less mobile or perhaps those who agree to participate in a thirty-year study have unique qualities that can affect the interpretation of the project's results (for example, they may be less energetic or they may be especially curious about themselves and introspective). Another difficulty lies in the fact that subjects who are tested repeatedly often get better at the tests, not because of any changes in their abilities, but

Longitudinal studies assess the same subjects over a span of years. This strategy for assessing developmental change allows researchers to identify the stability of many human characteristics.

because the tests become more familiar over time. Subjects who take a test of spatial skill again and again may improve because of practice with the test and not because of any developmental change in their abilities. If the researcher attempts to avert this outcome by designing a different version of the same test, the problem then becomes whether the two tests are similar enough!

One of the biggest methodological drawbacks of longitudinal research is the possibility of an **age-history confound.** Suppose a researcher began a twenty-year longitudinal study in 1950 and defined the variables that were influential in the process of child development. It is unlikely that a list of influences devised in 1950 would have included maternal employment, television, or day care because these factors were not major social forces at that time. Certainly a longitudinal study begun in 1990 would yield a very different picture of the variables that impinge on the child and adolescent. Therefore, the results obtained from a study begun four decades ago may have limited applicability to children growing up in the 1990s.

Despite all these difficulties, the longitudinal approach has distinct advantages not offered by any other research tactic; in fact, certain research questions in child development can only be answered longitudinally. If a researcher is interested in identifying the *stability* of human characteristics—that is, how likely early attributes are to be maintained later in development—the longitudinal approach is the only method of choice. Only by observing the same person over time can we answer such questions as, Do passive infants become shy adults? or, Do early experiences with peers affect the child's ability to form friendships in adolescence? For researchers interested in understanding the process of development and the factors that precede and follow particular developmental phenomena, the longitudinal strategy remains a powerful one.

The Cross-sectional Study   Possibly the most widely used strategy for studying developmental differences is the **cross-sectional study,** in which children of varying ages are examined at the same point in time. Cross-sectional studies take less time to complete and are usually more economical than longitudinal studies.

A good example of cross-sectional research is the investigation of children's memory development conducted by Peter Ornstein and his colleagues (Ornstein, Naus, & Liberty, 1975). The specific goal was to see if age-based changes occur in children's tendency to rehearse (or repeat) a series of words they are asked to remember. Furthermore, the researchers were interested in whether any tendencies to rehearse were accompanied by actual increases in the numbers of words that children remembered. Ornstein and his associates began by asking third-, sixth-, and eighth-graders to study a list of eighteen words and then recall them in any order they wished (a *free recall* procedure). Half of the subjects in each age group were also instructed to rehearse out loud as each word was presented during the study period. The number of times the children repeated the words as well as the number of different words in the rehearsal set (the block of items they actually verbalized each time they rehearsed) were noted. The three panels in Figure 1.4 show the results. First, third-graders had lower levels of recall than the two older age groups, especially for words that had appeared early in the list. Second, third-graders tended to rehearse individual items with less frequency than did older children, again primarily for items at the beginning of the list. Lastly, third-graders included fewer different items in their rehearsal sets; instead of saying

age-history confound In longitudinal studies, changes in originally defined variables due to changes in sociohistorical context; affects generalizability of findings.

cross-sectional study Study in which subjects of different ages are examined at the same point in time.

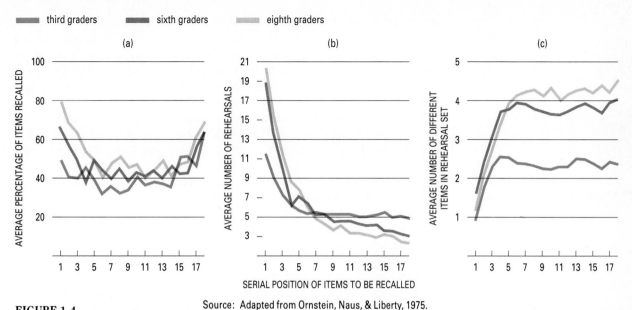

FIGURE 1.4

Source: Adapted from Ornstein, Naus, & Liberty, 1975.

A Cross-sectional Study

Age differences in behaviors can be assessed relatively quickly with the cross-sectional approach. In one such study, Ornstein, Naus, and Liberty found that older children remembered more words than younger children (a), older children rehearsed more frequently than younger children (b), and older children included more items in the set they rehearsed than younger children (c).

over and over several different words from the list to be remembered, they tended to repeat only one or two of the same words. Ornstein and his colleagues (1975) concluded that younger children's poorer levels of recall memory were linked to their use of less effective strategies for remembering.

Using the cross-sectional approach allowed the researchers to make a rapid assessment of changes in memory without waiting for children to grow three or five years older. They were, however, unable to draw conclusions about individual children and how characteristics observable at one age might be related to characteristics at another age. Did some of the third-graders spontaneously rehearse, even if most of their age mates did not? If so, would these children have the best memories three or five years later? The cross-sectional approach does not provide answers to these kinds of questions. Most cross-sectional studies involve pooling the scores of individual subjects in such a way that the average performance of an entire group of children of a specified age is reported; the average scores of two or more groups of children are then compared. The result is that information about individuals is not the focus of data analysis in this type of study.

Another difficulty with cross-sectional designs is that cohort effects may interfere with our ability to draw clear conclusions. **Cohort effects** are all the characteristics shared by children growing up in a specific social and historical context. For example, many of today's five-year-olds have had extensive peer experience through their enrollment in day-care and other preschool programs, whereas many fifteen-year-olds probably have not. A researcher comparing the two groups might mistakenly conclude that younger children are more sociable than older children, but the differential exposure to age mates early in life—that is, the cohort effect—may be responsible for the findings rather than changes in sociability with age. Cross-sectional studies are a quick means of providing descriptions of age changes in all sorts of behaviors. Where they sometimes fall short is in helping us to understand the processes underlying those age-related changes.

cohort effect   Characteristics shared by individuals growing up in a given sociohistorical context that can influence developmental outcomes.

The Sequential Study   One way to combine the advantages of both the longitudinal and cross-sectional approaches is the **sequential study,** in which
groups of children of different ages are followed repeatedly but for only a few
years. For example, a research group wanted to study age changes in patterns
of television viewing of the educational program "Sesame Street" (Pinon, Huston, & Wright, 1989). Two groups of children—a group of three- to five-year-
olds and a group of five- to seven-year-olds—were followed for a period of two
years. During specified weeks within this two-year period, families kept diaries of the children's television viewing. At the same time, the researchers
wanted to examine the relationship between a number of family characteristics, such as parental education and maternal employment, and children's tendency to watch "Sesame Street."

Figure 1.5 shows that children's viewing of "Sesame Street" peaked at about
age three and a half or four and then declined. These researchers also found
that age-related events in the children's lives were associated with the declines after age four. For example, as children entered preschools or kinder-
gartens, they tended to watch less television. Similarly, as mothers returned
to work and sent their children to child care, children's viewing decreased. The
benefit of the sequential design was that it allowed information about a four-
year age span to be obtained in two years. Information about the stability of
television viewing for individual children was available, just as it would have
been in a longitudinal study. At the same time, the researchers halved the
amount of time it took to find out about children's viewing tendencies from
ages three through seven. Although most developmental researchers still prefer to conduct cross-sectional studies because of their expediency, the sequen-

FIGURE 1.5

A Sequential Study

Age differences in behavior patterns over time can be assessed by
sequential studies. In one such
study, television viewing of "Sesame Street" by two age groups of
children, a group of three- to five-
year-olds and a group of five- to
seven-year-olds, was recorded
over a period of two years. (Some
of the subjects began the study in
the spring, others started in the
fall.) As the graphs show, children's interest in this show peaked
around age four, then declined
over the next several years. The
sequential approach combines the
advantages of the longitudinal and
cross-sectional approaches.

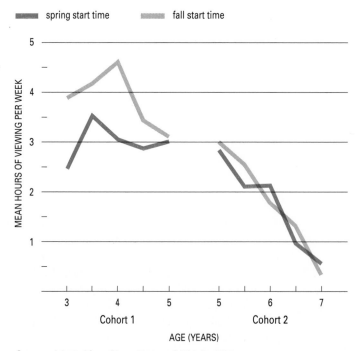

Source: Adapted from Pinon, Huston, & Wright, 1989.

Approach	Description	Advantages	Disadvantages
Longitudinal Study	Repeated testing of the same group of children over an extended period of time.	Can examine the stability of characteristics.	Requires a significant investment of time and resources; problems with subject attrition; can have age-history confound.
Cross-sectional Study	Comparison of children of different ages at the same point in time.	Requires less time, less costly than longitudinal study.	Cannot study individual patterns of development or the stability of traits; subject to cohort effects.
Sequential Study	Observation of children of two or more different ages over a shorter period of time than in longitudinal studies.	Combines the advantages of both longitudinal and cross-sectional approaches; can obtain information about stability of traits in a short period of time.	Has same problems as longitudinal studies but to a lesser degree.

TABLE 1.4

Strategies for Assessing Developmental Change

tial study provides a convenient way of reaping the advantages of both cross-sectional and longitudinal approaches to studying developmental change. Table 1.4 summarizes the relative benefits of each of the research strategies for assessing developmental change.

Cross-Cultural Studies of Development

Some of the most fundamental questions about the nature of development concern the universality of the various features of psychological growth. Do all children learn language the same way, regardless of the specific language they acquire? Does children's thinking develop in a universal sequence? Are certain emotions common to all children regardless of the attitudes about the appropriateness of crying, smiling, or feeling angry in the larger social group in which they live?

If psychological development does display universal features, this circumstance has far-reaching implications. It could imply, for a start, that a child's behavior is largely shaped by biological factors and, more specifically, by the genes that govern the unfolding of some human behaviors. Variations in aspects of psychological development across cultures, on the other hand, imply that the differences in the child's experiences weigh heavily in bringing about those behaviors. **Cross-cultural studies,** which compare children from different cultural groups on one or more behaviors or pattern of abilities, can be extremely useful in answering questions such as these.

Take, for example, a reported finding about infants' linguistic behaviors. Among young infants in the United States, it has been found that females vocalize more than males under age one year (Lewis, 1969; Lewis & Freedle,

sequential study Study that examines groups of children of different ages over a period of time; usually shorter than a longitudinal study.

cross-cultural study Study comparing subjects in different cultural contexts.

Cross-cultural studies compare children from different cultural groups on one or more behaviors or patterns of abilities. This type of research is especially useful in answering questions about universalities in development.

1973). Especially because this sex difference appears so early in life, it might be tempting to conclude that females are biologically predisposed toward strong verbal skills. Yet a recent study of Greek infants has demonstrated that male infants show greater vocal responsiveness to their mothers than females do (Roe, Drivas, Karagellis, & Roe, 1985). This one finding alone casts doubt on a strong biological explanation of sex differences in vocalization.

Cross-cultural studies can present unique challenges to the researcher. If children from two cultural backgrounds are being compared, the researcher must make sure that the tasks are well understood and have equivalent forms despite differences in language or the kinds of activities children are used to doing. For example, children in some cultures may never have seen a photograph or a two-dimensional drawing. Asking these children to categorize objects in pictorial form may place them at an unfair disadvantage if they are to be compared with children who have extensive experience with two-dimensional representations. Moreover, if the researcher is an outsider to the cultural group being observed, he or she may provoke atypical reactions from the individuals under study. Parent-child interactions, peer play, and many other behaviors may not occur as they would in the natural stream of events because of the presence of an outside observer. Cross-cultural researchers must thus pay special attention to the possibility of subject reactivity.

These problems aside, cross-cultural studies can provide important insights into almost all aspects of child development, especially the processes underlying that development. For this reason, we will draw on cross-cultural work whenever it is available as we discuss each aspect of the growth of children.

Ethical Issues in Developmental Research

All psychologists are bound by professional ethics to treat the subjects under study humanely and fairly. In general, researchers try to minimize the risk of any physical or emotional harm that might occur to subjects from participation in research and to maximize the benefits that will accrue from the findings of their work. The American Psychological Association has drawn up the following specific guidelines for the use of human subjects: First, subjects must give **informed consent** before participating in a research project; that is, they must be told the purposes of the study and informed of any potential risks to their well-being, and then they must formally agree to participate. Second, subjects have the right to decline to participate or to stop participation, even in the middle of the experiment. Third, if subjects cannot be told the true purpose of the experiment (sometimes knowing the experimenter's objective will influence how subjects behave), they must be **debriefed** at the conclusion of the study. When subjects are debriefed, they are told the true objective of the study and the reasons for any deception on the part of the experimenter. Finally, data collected from subjects must be kept confidential. To ensure that experimenters comply with these guidelines, most institutions in which research is conducted have institutional review boards that evaluate any potential risks to subjects and the researchers' compliance with ethical practice.

The same ethical guidelines apply to using children as subjects in research, but frequently the implementation of these guidelines becomes a difficult matter. Who provides informed consent in the case of an infant or young toddler, for example? (The parents do.) Is it proper to deceive children about the purposes of a study if they cannot understand the debriefing? (In general, it is a good idea to avoid any kind of deception with children, such as telling them you are interested in how quickly they learn a game when you are really interested in whether they will be altruistic with their play partner.) Are some subjects of study taboo, such as asking children about their concepts of death, suicide, or other frightening topics that might affect them emotionally? (Such studies, if conducted, must be planned very carefully and conducted only by trained professionals.) What about cases in which treatments are suspected to have beneficial outcomes for children? Can the control group properly have the treatment withheld? For example, if we suspect that children's participation in an early-intervention preschool program will have real benefits for them, should children in the control group be kept out of it? (One solution to this thorny problem is to offer the control group the beneficial treatment as soon as possible after the conclusion of the study, although this is not always a satisfactory compromise. The control group still has to wait for a beneficial treatment or intervention.)

Many researchers assume that the vulnerability of children to risk as they participate in psychological experiments decreases as they grow older. Because infants and young children have more limited cognitive skills and emotional coping strategies, they are viewed as less able to protect themselves and their rights during participation in research. This assumption certainly has some logical basis. Some types of research, however, may actually pose a greater threat to older children. As Ross Thompson (1990) has pointed out, older children are developing a self-concept and a more elaborate understanding of the ways in which others evaluate them. Older children may thus be more susceptible to psychological harm than younger children when the researcher compares their performance with that of others or when they think teachers or parents might learn about their performance. In addition, older children may be more sensitive to research results that reflect negatively on their family or sociocultural group. These are situations that require awareness in the researcher about the subtle ways in which children can be adversely affected by the research enterprise.

informed consent Subject's formal acknowledgement that he or she understands the purposes, procedures, and risks of a study and agrees to participate in it.

debriefing Providing research participants with a statement of the true goals of a study after initially deceiving them about its purposes.

• The investigator may not use any procedures that could impose physical or psychological harm on the child. In addition, the investigator should use the least stressful research operation whenever possible. If the investigator is in doubt about the possible harmful effects of the research, he or she should consult with others. If the child will be unavoidably exposed to stress in research that might provide some diagnostic or therapeutic benefits to the child, then the study should be reviewed by an institutional review board.

• The investigator should inform the child of all features of the research that might affect his or her willingness to participate and should answer all questions in a way that the child can comprehend. The child has the right to discontinue participation at any time.

• Informed consent should be obtained in writing from the child's parents or from other adults who have responsibility for the child. The adult has the right to know all features of the research that might affect the child's willingness to participate and can refuse consent.

• If the research necessitates concealment or deception about the nature of the study, the investigator should make sure that the child understands the reasons for the deception after the study is concluded.

• All information about participants in research must be kept confidential.

• If, during the research, the investigator learns of information that jeopardizes the child's well-being, the investigator must discuss the information with the parents or guardians and experts to arrange for assistance to the child.

• The investigator should clarify any misconceptions that may have arisen on the part of the child during the study.

Source: Adapted from the ethical standards set by the Society for Research in Child Development, 1990.

TABLE 1.5

**Ethical Guidelines in Conducting
Research with Children**

Table 1.5 sets forth the ethical guidelines on using children as subjects in research established by the Society for Research in Child Development. Probably the greatest guiding principle is that children should not be subjected to any physical or mental harm and should be treated with all the respect that can be afforded them. In fact, because children are frequently unable to voice their concerns and have less power than adults do, developmental researchers must be especially sensitive to their comfort and well-being.

SUMMARY

Developmental psychology has two main goals: to describe changes in behavior and mental processes that occur over time and to explain the reasons that development occurs in the way it does. Although development can be understood from many perspectives, the scientific method gives us information that is verifiable, objective, and capable of being repeated in other experiments.

Attitudes toward children have changed in Western society over the centuries. During medieval times, children were quickly incorporated into the adult world although their vulnerability was also recognized. Philosophers such as Locke and Rousseau contributed to the growing interest in the nature of childhood during the seventeenth and eighteenth centuries, preparing the way for the formal scientific study of children.

The systematic study of children began with the baby biographers of the nineteenth century, who made extensive observations of individual children.

At the beginning of the twentieth century, G. Stanley Hall introduced the questionnaire method for studying large groups of children and Alfred Binet led the movement to study individual differences in children's behavior and abilities. Theorists like James Mark Baldwin formulated hypotheses about the nature of the child, including ideas about the active role of the child that are still popular today. Much of the early empirical work in developmental psychology focused on establishing norms of behavior. Today, research in developmental psychology is guided by a rich array of theoretical, empirical, and applied questions.

Developmental psychologists rely on the *scientific method* to gather information about children. They formulate and test theories, then revise these theories based on the research findings they glean. Researchers are careful to define operationally the variables in their studies and select measures that are both valid and reliable. Researchers can choose from a number of specific techniques for gathering data about children. *Naturalistic observations* involve the systematic recording of behaviors as they occur in children's homes, schools, and other everyday environments. *Structured observations,* usually conducted in the laboratory, allow the experimenter more control over the situations that accompany children's behaviors. Researchers can employ *interviews* or *questionnaires* if they are interested in children's own reports of what they know or how they behave. Finally, *meta-analytic studies* permit investigators to analyze the results of a large body of published research in order to draw general conclusions about behavior.

Three basic research designs are employed in psychological research. In the *correlational design,* investigators see if changes in one variable are accompanied by systematic changes in another variable. However, correlations between variables do not prove cause-and-effect relationships. In the *experimental design,* the researcher manipulates one or more independent variables to see if they have an effect on the dependent variable. In the *single-subject design,* the researcher intensively studies one or a few individuals over a period of time. Each of these designs offers advantages and disadvantages, with the researcher's choice dictated by the specific questions to be answered as well as the types of resources available.

Developmental psychologists, who are specifically concerned with describing changes in individuals over time, must also choose among three strategies for assessing developmental change when they plan their research. *Longitudinal studies* test the same subjects repeatedly over an extended period of time. *Cross-sectional studies* examine subjects of different ages at the same time. *Sequential studies* examine children of two or more ages over a period of time, usually shorter than that used in longitudinal studies.

Cross-cultural studies have a special place in developmental psychology because they often address questions of the universality of human behaviors and have implications for biological versus environmental explanations of growth.

One last important consideration for the researcher is the ethical dimensions of conducting studies with children. Children, like all human subjects, must be treated with fairness and dignity. Because children are less powerful than adults and may be especially sensitive to the effects of participating in research studies, investigators must pay special attention to any potential harm they may suffer.

2
Themes and Theories

Right from the start Robert was a handful. A restless infant who slept poorly and cried frequently, he grew into an extremely active toddler who threw frequent temper tantrums. After his mother died in a car accident, leaving his father as a single parent to rear him, Robert's behavior became an even greater problem. By the time he entered kindergarten, he displayed serious difficulties in participating in group activities and minding teachers. Robert's father had always refused to use physical punishment to discipline his son but now found himself faced with a painful question: had he, in the words of an old saying, "spared the rod and spoiled the child"?

When we first think seriously about how children mature and the best ways to foster their development, common sense seems like the logical place to start. The caregivers responsible for your upbringing were most likely unacquainted with the theories of John Locke, Jean Jacques Rousseau, or other philosophers. Instead, they probably relied on their own experience and the advice of relatives and friends to make decisions about how to encourage your development. Even if you have not been actively involved in child rearing, you will also have preconceptions based on your childhood—perhaps further influenced by personal observations, study, or work with children—about "what's best" for them. These kinds of experiences form the common sense and parenting wisdom by which generations of caregivers have reared children, and they are frequently shared across cultures. In fact, Robert's father might have been even more likely to begin spanking his son if he had known that the Ovambo of southwest Africa say, "A cranky child has not been spanked," and that Japanese parents are traditionally advised, "Bring up your beloved child with a stick."

Yet at times common sense not only fails to provide answers but may promote unexpected and possibly even undesirable outcomes. The conventional wisdom just quoted, for example, suggests that physical punishment of children is a good thing. Caregivers in many societies often believe spanking, hitting, and even whipping the child for unacceptable behaviors such as aggression are the best ways to prevent those behaviors. But is this widely held tenet true, and is it the best solution to the child-rearing dilemma Robert's father faces? Perhaps not. Researchers, for example, have found that parents who typically resort to physical punishment often have children who initiate more aggressive acts toward others than children whose parents rely on alternative methods of disciplining in response to inappropriate conduct (Bandura & Walters, 1959; Olweus, 1980). Thus, under some circumstances, physical punishment may encourage, rather than discourage, aggressive actions. In Robert's case, an attentional deficit or some other disorder might underlie his hyperactive behavior, and spanking might be ineffective in helping him to control that behavior. As scientific knowledge of child development has evolved, we can step back from blind acceptance of the untested wisdom and insights of previous generations and validate the effectiveness of these "common sense" preconceptions using the systematic procedures and methods described in Chapter 1.

This is precisely the point at which *theory* enters the picture. As one researcher has flatly stated, "The basic aim of science is theory" (Kerlinger, 1964, p. 10). Reread this sentence, because it makes a claim you may find surprising. For many students, theories seem far less important and interesting than the many intriguing "facts" that cluster around children and their development. Why are theories so vital to science? The answer lies in what they are designed to do. Theories are formulated to move beyond describing and cataloging the behaviors of children. These are important goals, but theories additionally help to organize this information and to guide further research. But an even more important aim of theory is to *explain* those behaviors.

Theories are intended and designed to provide reliable explanations, a goal that is important in every scientific discipline, not just child development. Being able to explain behavior is not only gratifying, it is essential for translating ideas into applications—creating meaningful programs and ways to assist parents, teachers, and others who work to enhance and promote the development of children. Thus, for example, when a theory proposes that adults are an important source of imitative learning and that parents who display aggressive behavior provide a model for responding to a frustrating situation, we can begin to understand why common proverbs such as "spare the rod and spoil the child" sometimes need to be reevaluated.

In this chapter our discussion focuses on several broad theories and perspectives that have been influential in offering explanations of children's behavior and in promoting developmental research. We must always remember, however, that no one theory is sufficiently complete to provide a full explanation of all behavior. Some primarily strive to make sense of intellectual and cognitive development; others focus on social, emotional, and personality development. Theories also vary in the extent to which they present formalized, testable ideas. Thus, some are more useful than others in providing explanations for behavior that can be rigorously evaluated. And they often disagree in their answers to the fundamental questions and major recurring themes in development. In fact, before we examine specific theories, let us consider the cluster of basic themes that all theories of development must address.

SIX MAJOR THEMES IN DEVELOPMENTAL PSYCHOLOGY

As you read about each of the many dimensions in child development—language acquisition, peer relationships, motor skills, recognition of self-worth, or any number of others—you will find that certain key questions about the causes and nature of development surface again and again. Theories provide different answers to these questions—which we call here the *themes in development*. As you trace these major themes through each domain of development, that is, in our discussions of language, cognitive, emotional, social, and other aspects of development, notice the diversity in the ways theories attempt to address these questions. Ultimately, our understanding of these major themes and the best ways to think about them will emerge as good theories, grounded in careful research, and formulated to explain such matters.

What Roles Do Nature and Nurture Play in Development?

In an old joke, a child about to be chastised for misbehaving says to his parent, "Okay, so what made me do it—heredity or environment?" This is perhaps the most basic question of child development, one that has fueled a controversy among theorists since before the days of Locke and Rousseau and that continues to rage even today. Dubbed the **nature-nurture debate,** the dispute centers on whether the child's development is the result of genetic endowment or environmental influences.

Do children typically crawl at nine months and walk at twelve months of age because they have learned to do so or because of some inborn unfolding program? Do they acquire language easily and readily because their environment demands it or because they are genetically predisposed to do so? Are boys more aggressive than girls because of cultural conditioning or biological factors? Is the child's level of intellectual functioning an inherited trait or the result of environmental stimulation (or lack thereof)? In all these areas researchers want to do more than describe the course of the child's achievements; they also want to identify the factors influencing those achievements. And in some of these areas, such as the development of intelligence and the emergence of sex roles, the debate on nature versus nurture has become particularly heated.

Why all the sound and fury about such a question? One reason for the fervor of these discussions is the implications the answers carry for children's developmental outcomes. If, for example, tested theories suggest that intelligence is guided largely by heredity, then providing children with rich learning experiences may have minimal impact on their eventual levels of intellectual skill. If, on the other hand, research and theory more convincingly suggest that intellectual development is shaped by environmental experiences, it becomes of vital importance to provide children with the kinds of experience that will optimize their intellectual growth. Such theories can also have an impact on public policy in determining the allocation of funds to various social and educational programs.

Psychologists now recognize that both nature and nurture play a role in all aspects of behavior. Thus, the controversy has moved away from an either/or position concerned with *which* of these two factors is critical in any given situation to the question of *how,* specifically, each contributes to development. The problem for researchers is to determine the manner by which heredity and environment interact to produce the behaviors we see in children, and eventually in adults. More than any other factor, these two forces together play the major role in shaping what the child becomes, and theories have taken very different positions on the way nature and nurture contribute to development.

nature-nurture debate Ongoing theoretical controversy over whether development is the result of the child's genetic endowment or the kinds of experiences he or she has had.

How Does the Sociocultural Context Influence Development?

Development does not take place in a vacuum. Children grow up within a larger social group holding unique customs, values, and beliefs about the proper way

Children grow up in various cultures and social settings that stress unique customs, values, and beliefs. As a consequence, children differ in the kinds of experiences they receive throughout their childhood. Only some children in some societies spend part of their early years in nursery school activities like those shown here. Researchers must take into consideration these and many other kinds of sociocultural differences to fully understand development.

of rearing children and the ultimate goals of guiding their development. Think back to your family and the cultural standards and values that determined how you were treated. Were you allowed to be assertive and to speak your mind or expected to be compliant to adults and never challenge them? Were you encouraged to fend for yourself from a very early age, or were parents, other relatives, perhaps even cultural institutions such as the school, church, or a government agency expected to take care of most of your needs throughout childhood, adolescence, perhaps even into your early adult years? On an even broader scale, how was your development, both physical and social, affected by your family's economic status and educational attainments? By your gender and ethnic identity?

The values and resources of the society in which the child lives have important consequences for a broad spectrum of developmental areas, including physical, social, emotional, and cognitive growth. These values and resources affect everything from the kinds of child-rearing practices parents engage in to the level of health care and education children receive, from physical well-being, social standing, and sense of self-esteem to such aspects of "personality" as emotional expressiveness. As you explore the various domains of development, you will see how many developmental outcomes seemingly the result of inborn dispositions or the immediate environment are in fact heavily influenced by the sociocultural context. And, as with the nature-nurture debate, the precise nature of its influence in certain areas of development has attracted much heated discussion among theorists.

How Does the Child Play an Active Role in Development?

When children learn to speak, do they passively record the language they hear in their environment and reproduce it as if they were playing back a tape recording? Or are they more actively engaged in acquiring the sounds, grammar, and meanings of words and putting them together in new ways? Do children produce male and female sex roles simply by imitating the behaviors of men and women around them? Or do they somehow construct mental interpretations of male and female roles that in turn drive their own behavior? Do parents set the emotional tone for interactions with their young infants? Or do infants often take the initiative in determining whether playing or bathing will be stressful or happy events? In other words, do infants and children somehow regulate and determine their own development?

Most researchers today believe that children do take an active role in their own growth and development. That active role may be evident at two different levels. The first comprises the various qualities and attributes that children display or possess, including their curiosity and eagerness for engaging in the physical and social world surrounding them. For example, by virtue of being a boy or girl, being placid or temperamental, being helpful or refusing to cooperate, and of taking an interest in doorknobs, steps, and stairways, perhaps eventually dinosaurs, music, or sports, children elicit reactions from others that can affect their development in profound ways. In this sense children are not simply passive recipients of influences surrounding them, blank slates on which the environment writes; children's own characteristics and efforts to engage in, to get "mixed up" with, their physical and social world often modify the kinds of things that happen to them and that have an impact on their development.

A second, perhaps more fundamental way in which children may contribute to their own development is by actively forming and organizing internal mental, social, linguistic, and other psychological structures designed to assist them in making sense of the surrounding world. These conceptualizations are constructed by children to help organize and establish effective ways for responding to and understanding the physical and social events that make up their experience. As you will soon come to see, this view of how children may directly influence their own development is theoretically controversial.

Is Development Continuous or Stagelike?

Are children at some ages able to think only concretely—that is, only about things that they can see, feel, or touch—and not about abstract and hypothetical events? Does the way in which children think change radically after reaching some new level of maturity? Does the four-year-old child have unique personality traits that are different from those he or she will display as a twelve-year-old? What is the best way to explain the many changes that are so immediately apparent when we compare the behaviors and abilities of the one-year-old, four-year-old, nine-year-old, and sixteen-year-old?

Everyone agrees that children's behaviors and abilities change with development and sometimes in dramatic ways. But much less agreement exists on how best to explain these changes. Some theories describe development in terms of the child's progress through a series of **stages,** or periods when unique developmental accomplishments or qualities become evident, presumably because some fundamental reorganization in the thought or capacities underlying behavior has taken place. The concept of developmental stages suggests *qualitative* differences in how children perceive, think, feel or behave at certain periods in their lives. Additionally, development seems to undergo

stage Developmental period during which the organization of thought and behavior is qualitatively different from that of an earlier or later period.

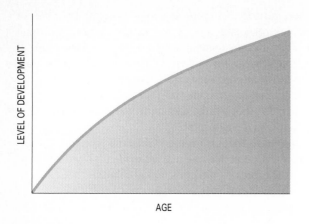

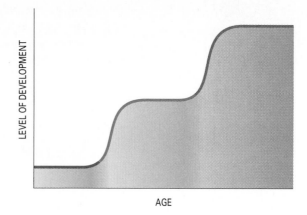

FIGURE 2.1

Development as a Continuous Versus a Discontinuous Process

Children display many changes in their abilities and behaviors throughout development. Theorists, however, disagree on how best to describe these changes. According to some, the best way to explain development is in terms of gradual changes in the structures and processes underlying growth. For others, however, development is believed to undergo a series of stagelike transformations during which underlying processes and structures exhibit rapid reorganization followed by a period of relative stability.

rapid transitions as one stage ends and a new one begins, followed by a relatively stable period during which the behavior and abilities of the child undergo minimum change (see Figure 2.1).

Alternatively, development can be viewed as a *continuous* process in which the child's attainments in thinking, language, social behavior, and so forth are characterized by steady, small advances. Another way of describing these gradual changes is to claim that development is *quantitative*. Changes in thinking might arise from increments in the child's ability to remember rather than as a result of a complete reorganization in the way he or she thinks. As neural coordination and muscle strength gradually increase, the infant begins to be able to walk as well as crawl, progress in behavior that is, by anyone's account, substantial. But the change has been brought about by continuously advancing physical processes rather than a total reorganization of some underlying motor program. The toddler's expanding displays of refusal to cooperate and shouts of "no!" might be viewed in terms of increasingly enterprising, if not always pleasing, efforts to exhibit independence rather than in terms of entry into some developmental stage labeled as the "terrible twos."

Evidence for and against the presence of stages in development is difficult to obtain. No aspects of human growth, for example, appear to mimic the dramatic stages found in the life cycle of an insect, which undergoes transformations from egg to larva, to pupa, and finally to adult, periods in which a stable physical organization is followed by rapid reorganization and emergence of a new period in the life cycle. In contrast, the changes in children's thinking and in other aspects of their development often seem gradual. Yet over a period of months and years children do indeed become quite different. The controversy over whether these changes are best understood in terms of qualitative or quantitative factors remains difficult to resolve.

Are There Sensitive Periods in Development?

If the infant does not develop a secure, positive emotional relationship with her caregiver in the first year of life, will her ability to establish positive relationships with others suffer throughout her development? If the child has not been exposed to a second language by the beginning of adolescence, will he ever be able to achieve native fluency and pronunciation in the new language? Questions like these imply the existence of certain **sensitive** or *critical periods* when the child is most responsive to, and influenced by, particular kinds of environmental events. In some cases, exposure to a specific experience may lead to problems in development. For example, during certain weeks of pregnancy, some drugs ingested by the mother appear to have an especially disruptive effect on the fetus's physical and intellectual development. In other cases, the *lack* of a specific experience during a sensitive time can lead to behavioral difficulties. For example, some experts believe that the failure to form a strong emotional bond with a caregiver in infancy predicts serious emotional problems later in childhood.

Not everyone agrees that the concept of a sensitive period is useful for all domains of development. Children may be vulnerable to or benefit from certain experiences at particular times, but they also display considerable resilience—that is, the ability to overcome many of the disruptive effects of inadequate or inappropriate experiences. Consider the child born into a poor, stressed family, whose parents divorce at some time in her childhood, who then undergoes separation from her biological mother and endures caregiving in an alternative strife-ridden home. That child may still grow up to become a bright and motivated, socially sensitive and productive adult (Werner & Smith, 1982). A major challenge for developmental psychology is to identify the most crucial experiences or deprivations and the circumstances that permit children to recover from any negative impacts of these factors.

How Do the Various Domains of Development Interact?

Many times the child's accomplishments in one domain will have a direct bearing on his or her accomplishments in other domains. Consider just one example: How the child interacts with friends (social development) is very likely to be influenced by his or her understanding of what friendship is (cognitive development). Young children define friendship in terms of shared activities. Friends are those you happen to play with, usually because of their proximity or availability. Older children define friendship in terms of peers with whom to share innermost thoughts; they attribute more internal, psychological dimensions to the definition. These advances in thinking influence the basis for establishing friendships. But just as importantly, social interactions involving friends also encourage cognitive development. Thus, in their interaction, social and cognitive development promote and enhance each other.

The interaction among domains of development constitutes an important theme that few theories so far have considered in much depth. Nevertheless, if we fail to attend to these relationships, we will have passed over a vital dimension of the complicated dynamics of development. Our ultimate aim is to understand the child as a whole individual, not just as someone who undergoes perceptual, emotional, cognitive, and social development. To do so, we must realize that no single component of development unfolds in isolation from the rest.

Where do you stand on each of these themes? Do you view development as a product of nature or of nurture? How extensively do you think a society's

sensitive period Brief period during which specific kinds of experiences have significant positive or negative consequences for development and behavior. Also called *critical period.*

Development takes place on many fronts. Abilities displayed in one domain often interact with abilities in other domains. For example, good physical skills and motor coordination can be a source of positive self esteem, which in turn may foster effective communication and social interactions with others.

trends, values, and resources affect an individual's development? To what extent do you believe children actively determine their own future? Would you describe changes throughout infancy and childhood in terms of stages or continuous processes? Can you identify sensitive periods during development, or do you believe any child, no matter how poor or limited his or her experience, can become a psychologically healthy and effective participant in society? How do you see advances or difficulties in one domain affecting the child's development in other domains?

These are not easy questions, to say the least. In fact, the theoretical models presented in this chapter often propose conflicting answers. It is time now for us to take a closer, more careful look at specific theoretical approaches and, along the way, begin to learn about the range of answers they offer to these difficult questions.

LEARNING THEORY APPROACHES

Learning theorists study how principles of learning cause the individual to change and develop. **Learning,** the relatively permanent change in behavior as a result of experience, is undoubtedly a contributing factor in the infant's smile to her approaching mother, the three-year-old's polite "thank you" in response to his grandmother's present, the five-year-old's newfound skill in tying her shoes, and the adolescent's impressionable choice about the most fashionable item of clothing to wear.

learning Relatively permanent change in behavior as a result of such experiences as exploration, observation, and practice.

In the extreme, some learning theorists believe, as John B. Watson did, that learning mechanisms can be exploited to create virtually any type of person:

> Give me a dozen healthy infants, well-formed, and my own specified world to bring them up in and I'll guarantee to take any one at random and train him to become any type of specialist I might select—doctor, lawyer, artist, merchant, chief, and yes, even beggarman and thief, regardless of his talents, penchants, tendencies, abilities, vocations, and race of his ancestors. (Watson, 1930, p. 104)

Although present-day supporters of learning theory may not take such a radical position on the modifiability of human potential, they are in agreement that basic principles of learning can have a powerful influence on development (Bijou, 1989).

Behavior Analysis

Behavior analysis is a theoretical account of development that relies on several basic principles of learning, particularly *classical* and *operant* conditioning, to explain developmental changes in behavior. Behavior analysis sprang from the radical learning position introduced by John B. Watson and was extended in more recent years by B. F. Skinner (1953, 1974) and others.

In his extensive work on digestion conducted nearly a century ago, the Russian physiologist Ivan Pavlov observed that dogs would often begin to salivate to the sound of a bell or some other arbitrary stimulus. Pavlov already knew that food innately triggered the release of saliva. But here was evidence that other, neutral stimuli could also come to have this effect. Pavlov soon realized the powerful implications of this observation; responses considered to be reflexive, such as salivation, could, in fact, occur in situations other than those that innately elicited them. This type of learning, in which a neutral stimulus, repeatedly paired with another that elicits a reflexive response, begins to elicit the reflexlike response by itself, is called **classical conditioning**. We acquire, or learn, certain behaviors and emotions as a result of classical conditioning. For example, both children and adults may become anxious upon entering a dental office because of its association with previous painful treatments performed by the dentist.

To understand the second basic principle of learning, consider two babies who smile as their caregivers approach. With one baby, the caregiver stops, says "Hi, baby!" and briefly rocks the cradle. With the other baby, the caregiver walks on past, preoccupied. Or consider two teenagers who are invited to gamble at their older friend's house. One comes away with twenty-five dollars more in her pocket, the other with ten dollars less than when he arrived. Which baby and which teenager are more likely to repeat their behavior? If you reasoned in both cases that the first is more likely than the second to carry out the behavior again because it results in a pleasing outcome, you know something about the principle of operant conditioning. **Operant conditioning** (also called *instrumental conditioning*) refers to the process in which patterns of behavior are learned; the frequency with which they are performed depends on whether the behaviors produce rewarding or desired outcomes. Nearly any response that an infant or child is able to emit can be operantly conditioned.

behavior analysis Learning theory perspective that explains the development of behavior by the principles of classical and operant conditioning.

classical conditioning Type of learning in which a neutral stimulus repeatedly paired with another stimulus that elicits a reflexive response eventually begins to elicit the reflexlike response by itself.

operant conditioning Type of learning in which patterns of behavior that are learned and the frequency with which they are performed depend on whether the behaviors produce rewarding or desired outcomes. Also called *instrumental conditioning*.

Behavior analysts have used this principle to account for such straightforward behaviors as the one-year-old's waving goodbye to his departing grandmother and far more complicated activities such as speech and problem solving.

Operant and classical conditioning have been shown to have enormous potential for changing behavior. *Behavior modification,* sometimes called *applied behavior analysis,* is concerned with the systematic application of principles of conditioning to affect human activity. In fact, operant and classical conditioning have become a powerful means by which teachers, therapists, and caregivers have brought about changes in behavior ranging from the elimination of temper tantrums or thumb sucking to encouraging healthy diets and safe driving habits.

Even some of its detractors have suggested that behavior analysis may have done more to benefit human welfare than any other psychological theory (Hebb, 1980). For this reason alone, classical and operant conditioning have appealed to many in their efforts to understand development. Yet extensive criticisms of behavior analysis exist. Critics, including some learning theorists, remain unconvinced that behavior can be understood without taking into account the presence of internal *psychological structures.* Experience is important in regulating behavior, but mental, emotional, and motivational conditions also play a role in determining how a child interprets and responds to the environment. Among various learning perspectives, social learning theory attempts to incorporate these factors into its explanation of complex behavior and development.

Social Learning Theory

Social learning theory emphasizes the importance of learning through observation and imitation of the behaviors displayed by others. This theoretical perspective first emerged in the 1930s, when anthropologists, psychologists, and sociologists at Yale University were endeavoring to explain the development of personality in terms of principles of learning. Social learning theorists start with the assumption that whether an adult will be friendly, outgoing, confident, and honest rather than shy and perhaps hostile and untrustworthy largely depends on the child-rearing practices parents and caregivers adopt to socialize her as a child. Although operant and classical conditioning play a substantial role in these child-rearing practices, social learning theorists emphasize **observational learning,** the acquisition of behaviors from simply listening to and watching other people, as a particularly important means of learning new behaviors. The two-year-old who stands before a mirror pretending to shave in imitation of his father is displaying observational learning. Similarly, you may have witnessed the embarrassed look of a parent whose three-year-old expressed a profanity, probably acquired by the same process.

social learning theory Theoretical approach emphasizing the importance of learning through observation and imitation of behaviors modeled by others.

observational learning Learning that takes place by simply observing another person's behavior.

According to Albert Bandura, psychology's most well known spokesperson for social learning, a society could never effectively convey complex language, social and moral customs, or other achievements to its younger members if each behavior had to be learned solely through operant and classical conditioning. Bandura (1965) notes that significant learning occurs, often completely without error, by the act of watching and imitating another person, a *model.*

Children often notice the behavior of others and frequently imitate their activities. Observational learning serves as an important mechanism for acquiring many socially desirable customs and behaviors.

For example, girls in one part of Guatemala learn to weave simply by watching an expert, an approach to learning new skills common to the fields, homes, and shops of communities all over the world. Social learning theorists propose that many kinds of complex social activities, including the acquisition of sex roles, aggression, prosocial responses (such as willingness to assist others), resistance to temptation, and other facets of moral development are learned primarily through observing others (Bandura & Walters, 1963).

In accounting for the acquisition of complex behaviors, Bandura (1977b) has increasingly made reference to cognitive processes within his theory, now known as *social cognitive theory.* Bandura (1989) has identified four sets of cognitive processes he believes to be especially important in observational learning. Attentional processes determine what information will be acquired from models, memory processes convert these observations into stored mental representations, production processes transform these mental representations into matching behaviors, and motivational processes define which behaviors are likely to be performed. Advances take place in each of these processes so that a child's observational learning becomes increasingly refined and proficient as development progresses.

Learning Theory and Themes in Development

As our discussions of behavior analysis and social cognitive theory suggest, learning theorists do not all share the same views about the prime determinants of development. What stance do behavior analysts and social cognitive theorists take on the six major developmental themes we introduced at the beginning of this chapter?

• *Roles of Nature and Nurture*   Behavior analysts believe that although biological and genetic factors may limit the kinds of responses that can be performed and help to define the events that are likely to be reinforcing or punishing, it is the environment that controls behavior. For behaviorists, each child's activity reflects an accumulated history of events associated with reinforcement or punishment, accidentally or intentionally delivered by the environment. In social cognitive theory, biological and other internal factors along with the environment are believed to play a mutual, interactive role in contributing to development (Bandura, 1989).

• *Sociocultural Influence*   Behaviorists believe that although societies differ in the behaviors viewed as desirable or unacceptable, the mechanisms of learning are universal for individuals in all cultures. Rewards and punishments provided by the immediate environment are the key to understanding development, although the circumstances under which reward and punishment occur may differ from one culture to the next. Social learning theorists have given the role of the sociocultural context more emphasis by pointing out, for example, that advances in communication technology such as television have expanded the opportunity for children and adults in many societies to acquire many novel skills and patterns of behavior through observational learning.

• *The Child's Active Role*   In keeping with their strong emphasis on environmental stimulation, behaviorists believe that the child plays a passive role in development. Skinner claimed that "a person does not act upon the world, the world acts upon him" (1971, p. 211). According to Skinner, psychologists should abolish references to unobservable mental or cognitive constructs such as motives, goals, needs, or thoughts in their explanations of behavior. Bandura's social cognitive theory moves far beyond behavior analysis by embracing mental and motivational constructs and processes for interpreting and understanding others as well as the self. Social cognitive theory therefore confers a much more active status on the child than does behavior analysis. Whereas behavior analysts see children adjusting and reacting to their environment, social cognitive theorists see them encoding and processing observations, selecting whether and when to perform modeled behaviors on the basis of cognitive skills and motivational factors. For example, the child who imitates aggressive behavior and gains a reputation as a bully experiences a changed environment when others attempt to avoid him. Thus, "people are both products and producers of their environment" (Bandura, 1989, p. 3).

• *Development as Continuous/Stagelike*   Both behavior analysts and social cognitive theorists consider development to be continuous rather than stagelike, undergoing relatively smooth transitions and without dramatic qualitative changes. Any departure from this pattern would stem from abrupt shifts in environmental circumstances such as might take place when the child enters school or the adolescent enters the work environment.

• *Sensitive Periods*   Neither behavior analysts nor social cognitive theorists emphasize sensitive periods in development, since experience is important throughout all of development.

• *Interaction Among Domains*   Finally, whereas behavior analysts explain development in all domains in terms of the basic principles of learning, social cognitive theorists stress that learning is linked to the child's physical, cognitive, and social development. Thus, this latter perspective gives attention to the reciprocal interaction among the different domains of development by recognizing that what the child learns from observing others is a consequence of what he or she feels, believes, and thinks.

COGNITIVE-DEVELOPMENTAL APPROACHES

For **cognitive-developmental** theorists, behavior reflects the emergence of various psychological *structures,* organized units or patterns of thinking, that influence how the child interprets experience. Cognitive-developmental theories tend to also share the fundamental assumptions that normal children (1) display similar mental, emotional, and social capabilities despite widely varying experiences and (2) undergo similar changes in capacities at roughly comparable ages (Horowitz, 1987a). Most three- and four-year-olds around the world, for example, believe that a gallon of water, poured from one container to another of a different shape, changes in amount or quantity, an error that is rarely made once children reach seven or eight years of age. Cognitive-developmental theorists explain this profound change in reasoning in terms of children acquiring new ways of understanding their world.

The most extensive and well-known cognitive-developmental theory has been put forward by Jean Piaget. His ideas about children have had a monumental impact on developmental psychology. In the more than sixty years he devoted to research, Piaget published dozens of books and hundreds of articles on infants and children. Many of his writings so challenged the beliefs of American psychologists that his theory was not taken seriously by many psychologists until the late 1960s and early 1970s. Today Piaget's vigorous defense of *action* as the basis for cognitive development and of mental structures that undergo *qualitative* reorganization at different stages of development is well known among educators and other professionals working with children. More than a decade after his death in 1980, Piagetian insights continue to be disseminated through the writings of his many students and collaborators (Beilin, 1989).

Piaget's initial research interests were in biology, not psychology, and this early biological training had a major impact on his ideas about the mind and how it develops. The few pages that we can devote here to Piaget's theory will permit us to touch upon only his core ideas and concepts. His keen observations and theoretical contributions, however, will be discussed in many chapters that follow.

Piaget's Theory

Piaget's vision of human intellectual development was based on two overriding assumptions about intelligence: (1) it is a kind of biological adaptation, and (2) it becomes organized in various ways as the individual interacts with the external world (Piaget, 1971). For Piaget, thought exhibits two kinds of inborn qualities. The first is **adaptation,** a tendency to adjust or become more attuned to the conditions imposed by the environment. The second is **organization,** a

cognitive-developmental theory Theoretical orientation, most frequently identified with Piaget, that explains development in terms of the active construction of psychological structures concerned with the interpretation of experience. These structures are assumed to be established at roughly similar ages by all children to form a series of qualitatively distinct stages in development.

adaptation In Piagetian theory, inborn tendency to adjust or become more attuned to conditions imposed by the environment; takes place through assimilation and accommodation.

organization In Piagetian theory, the inborn tendency for structures and processes to become more systematic and coherent.

Jean Piaget's keen observations and insights concerning the behavior of children laid the groundwork for his theory of cognitive development. Piaget's ideas about how children's thinking develops have influenced psychologists, educators, and many others in their attempts to understand children.

scheme   In Piagetian theory, the mental structure underlying a co-ordinated and systematic pattern of behaviors or thinking applied across similar objects or situations.

assimilation   In Piagetian theory, a component of adaptation; process of interpreting an experience in terms of current ways (schemes) of understanding things.

accommodation   In Piagetian theory, a component of adaptation; process of modification in thinking (schemes) that takes place when old ways of understanding something no longer fit.

tendency for intellectual structures and processes to become more systematic and coherent. Just as arms, eyes, lungs, heart, and other physical structures organize and take shape to carry out biological functions, so too, mental structures become organized in ever more powerful ways to carry out more complex thought. These changes, however, do not simply proceed in a vacuum; they depend upon the opportunity to look and touch, to manipulate and play with objects, to sort and order materials, to encounter unexpected and puzzling outcomes, and to reflect upon complex and challenging tasks and events—in other words, the physical and social events that comprise everyday experience.

Schemes   The basic mental structure in Piaget's theory is a **scheme,** a coordinated and systematic pattern of actions, behaviors, and ways of reasoning, a kind of template for acting or thinking applied across similar classes of objects or situations. The infant who sucks at her mother's breast, at her favorite pacifier, and at her thumb is exercising a scheme. The toddler who stacks blocks, pots and pans, and then shoe boxes is exercising a scheme. The six-year-old who realizes that his eight matchbox cars can be stored in an equal number of boxes regardless of how they are scattered about the floor is also exercising a scheme. Each of these is a kind of intelligence, a way of knowing and structuring reality.

The infant's schemes are patterns of action applied to objects—sucking, grasping, shaking, and so forth. The older child's schemes will likely involve mental processes and be far more complex as she reasons about number, spatial relations, and by adolescence, the universe. But at all levels of development, individuals have a tendency to apply schemes, to exercise them as a means of interacting with the environment. For Piaget, this tendency sets the stage for constructing new and more complex schemes—in other words, for development. From simple reflexes like grasping and sucking emerge schemes for holding or hugging or hitting. From these actions emerge ideas about classifying objects, for relating to family and friends, and so forth.

Assimilation and Accommodation   Piaget believed that schemes change through two complementary processes. The first, **assimilation,** refers to the process of interpreting an experience in terms of current ways of understanding things. The second, **accommodation,** refers to the modifications in thinking that take place when the old ways of understanding something, the old schemes, no longer fit.

To illustrate these two processes, Piaget used the biological analogy of ingesting and digesting food. For the child to take in nutrients for physical growth, she must first ingest food. The way she chews it, how enzymes react to it, and the speed and manner in which the muscles of the stomach contract to move food along the digestive tract are examples of accommodating to the particular form or type of food that has been eaten. Once food has been broken down into easily digestible components, the body can assimilate the nutrients using the physical structures available.

Consider another example, this time one that might challenge the toddler who has begun to walk. He freely moves about the main floor of his home but when approaching the steps leading to either the bedroom upstairs or to the basement below, he stops and says, "Stairs." He does the same when coming across sets of stairs while visiting his grandmother's or neighbor's house. He recognizes, in other words, after repeatedly hearing his mother and father say, "Stop! You'll fall down! Stay away from the stairs!" that steps are forbidden and *assimilates* instances of staircases in other situations within this scheme or knowledge of forbidden things.

But one day at the beginning of winter when the temperature has fallen below freezing, he and his father go for a walk outdoors. Following some distance behind, his father suddenly shouts, "Stop! You'll fall down!" The toddler appears puzzled, looking around as if searching for something and at the same time utters, "Stairs." His father, sensing his son's confusion, points to the ice that has formed on the sidewalk on which he is standing and adds, "There aren't any stairs here, but you can fall down on ice, too." In this new experience, the child must *accommodate* his understanding of "fall down" to include other factors that can cause him to take a tumble, not just stairs, but also ice and, eventually, a slippery rug and perhaps toys left lying about on the floor. So too, when the baby first begins to drink from a cup instead of feeding from his mother's breast, he must accommodate to this new experience, shape his lips and mouth in new ways to take in the milk. In a similar manner, the child's intellectual capacities become reshaped and reorganized as she attempts to adjust—that is, accommodate—to new experiences.

For Piaget, assimilation and accommodation are complementary aspects of all psychological activity, processes engaged in a constant tug of war with experience. We attempt to assimilate experience within our current schemes or level of intellectual knowledge. At the same time, however, we are continually pressured to change our understanding, to accommodate, since we are regularly confronted with new experiences that fail to fit our schemes. Just as the toddler needs to recognize the many circumstances that may contribute to her falling down, so too, she and other children throughout their development need to establish increasingly mature schemes for thinking about their world.

Fortunately, adaptation in the form of newer and more complex schemes is the result of this never-ending dynamic. The outcome of increased adaptation is a greater *equilibrium* or balance, a more effective fitting together of the many pieces of knowledge that make up the child's understanding. The process by which assimilation and accommodation bring about more organized and powerful schemes for thinking is called **equilibration**. Each new experience can cause imbalance, which can only be corrected by modification in the child's schemes. In trying to make sense of his or her world, the child develops more adaptive ways of thinking. At some periods in development, schemes may undergo substantial reorganization. These more effective levels of knowledge are the basis for distinguishing one stage of development from another.

equilibration In Piagetian theory, an innate self-regulatory process that begins with the discovery of a discrepancy between the child's cognitive structures or schemes and results, through accommodation and assimilation, in more organized and powerful schemes for effectively thinking about and adapting to the environment.

The Piagetian Stages   Piaget is probably most widely known for his description of stages of cognitive development. Piaget proposed that development proceeds through four stages: sensorimotor, preoperational, concrete, and formal. These stages, which are briefly identified in Table 2.1, will be described more fully in Chapter 8 when we discuss cognitive development. In Piaget's theory, each higher stage is defined by the appearance of a qualitatively different level of thinking, an increasingly sophisticated form of knowledge that achieves greater intellectual balance for responding to the environment. However, each new stage does not suddenly appear full blown; rather, it arises from the integration and incorporation of earlier ways of thinking.

Stage	Emerging Cognitive Structure (Schemes)	Typical Achievements and Behaviors
Sensorimotor (birth until 1½–2 years)	Sensory and motor actions, initially as reflexes, quickly differentiate by means of accommodation and coordinate to form adaptive ways of acting upon the environment.	Infants suck, grasp, look, reach, and so forth, responses that become organized into complex activities such as hand-eye coordination and are applied to the environment to solve problems such as reaching for and manipulating objects. Practical knowledge of space and the consequences of physical actions is acquired. Object permanence and rudimentary symbols, although still closely tied to sensorimotor events, emerge.
Preoperational (1½–7 years)	Symbols stand for or represent objects and events, but communication and thought remain relatively inflexible, heavily influenced by physical appearance and the child's own perspective.	Children begin to acquire language and mental imagery, to understand drawings, and to display pretend play. They may have difficulty understanding that another person sees, feels, or thinks differently from themselves. Thinking appears unidimensional, focused on a single perceptual aspect. Reasoning about classes, relations, space, time, and causality is inconsistent.
Concrete Operational (7–11 years)	Cognitive operations permit logical reasoning about objects, events, and relationships. Thought, however, remains limited to concrete objects and events.	Children are no longer fooled by appearance. They recognize that some things do not affect quantity and other characteristics of objects and can reason effectively about classes of objects and their relationships.
Formal Operational (11 years and above)	Operations can be performed upon operations. Thought becomes abstract, and all possible outcomes can be considered.	Adolescents are able not only to imagine, but to reason about hypothetical outcomes. Abstract issues (for example, religion, morality, alternative lifestyles) can be considered and systematically evaluated. Adolescents are able to think about their own thinking.

TABLE 2.1

Piaget's Stages of Cognitive Development

Piaget's Theory and Themes in Development

How does Piaget's theory address the six major themes of development?

• *Roles of Nature and Nurture* Piaget theorized that a number of biologically based factors contribute to cognitive development. Among them is **maturation,** the gradual unfolding over time of genetic programs for development. Another factor is the child's inherent tendency to act, physically or mentally, upon the environment. As a result of those actions, schemes become modified and changed. Still another factor is equilibration, the self-regulatory process of achieving a more adaptive balance in physically responding to and mentally understanding objects, events, and the relationships among them. Nevertheless, for Piaget development is clearly the product of these factors interacting with experience. Piaget emphasized the interaction between nature and nurture in his cognitive-developmental theory.

maturation Gradual unfolding over time of genetic programs for development that are independent of experience.

• *Sociocultural Influence* For Piaget, children develop in much the same way in all cultures around the world, partly as a result of the common physical world to which all humans must adapt, partly as a result of the common threads that exist within their social environments as well. Social experience in the form of cultural or educational opportunities could affect the speed and ultimate level of progress in cognitive development, but generally all children are expected to advance through the stages of development at roughly similar ages.

• *The Child's Active Role* In Piaget's theory, knowledge is far more than simply a mirror or copy of the physical or social world. Instead, knowledge is *constructed*—that is, created and formed by the continuous revision and reorganization of intellectual structures in conjunction with experience. Piaget's constructivist model depicts a mind actively engaged in knowing and understanding its environment. Thinking is active. That activity leads to increasingly more effective ways of thinking. Children, then, are highly active participants in determining what they learn and how they understand reality.

• *Development as Continuous/Stagelike* Although recognizing continuous changes, Piaget's theory focuses on describing and understanding the ways schemes undergo reorganization and change to form distinctive stages in development. In his later writings and conversations, Piaget began to downplay the importance of stages (Piaget, 1971; Vuyk, 1981). He felt that an overemphasis on stages led to too much concern with describing periods of intellectual stability or equilibrium when, in fact, cognition is always undergoing development. Cognitive development, he eventually concluded, is more like a spiral in which change constantly occurs, although sometimes at faster rates than at others (Beilin, 1989).

• *Sensitive Periods* Piaget did not emphasize sensitive periods in development. However, the way in which experiences are interpreted will depend on the child's level of development. Thus, the child still in the sensorimotor stage of development will be unable to assimilate a complex verbal description of adding and subtracting numbers. There is, then, a notion of "readiness" for various kinds of experiences evident in Piaget's theory. Moreover, Piaget theorized that progress through the various stages followed the same pattern for all children; no stage could be skipped. Thus, cognitive development will depend on the child's successful completion of earlier stages.

• *Interaction Among Domains* Piaget's cognitive-developmental theory has implications for many other domains of development. For example, his ideas about cognitive development have been used to explain developmental changes in communication, moral thinking, and aspects of *social cognition*, how children understand the thoughts, intentions, feelings, and views of others. Nevertheless, Piaget has been criticized for paying relatively little attention to emotional factors and how social and emotional domains influence cognitive development.

Neo-Piagetian Views

Piaget's wide range of observations, his frequently surprising findings about what infants and children can and cannot do, and his challenging theoretical explanations and assumptions have sparked a wealth of research on cognitive development and in other domains as well, including social and moral development. Many researchers agree with his findings but disagree with his interpretations of them. For example, although Piaget's notion of children as active participants in their development has been widely embraced, the central concept of qualitative differences in thinking between children and adults—and particularly of stagelike transformations—has been criticized extensively.

Many researchers also suggest that Piaget underestimated how quickly children can display certain kinds of thinking (for example, Flavell, 1985; Gelman & Gallistel, 1978; Meltzoff, 1988a). There is evidence to suggest that children can use symbols or can reason logically, indicators of significant intellectual advances, far earlier than Piaget proposed. Others question whether the child of a particular age will exhibit a consistent level of cognitive development. The six-year-old expert on dinosaurs or chess may display far more sophisticated thinking about these topics than about things she is less familiar with—for example, plants or kickball. Several researchers have modified and expanded Piaget's theory to address some of these criticisms.

Fischer's Theory   Kurt Fischer proposes that transitions in levels of thinking should be considered only within specific domains or skills, such as understanding numbers or classification of objects familiar to the child (Fischer, 1980; Fischer & Pipp, 1984). In the same individual, development may proceed far more rapidly in some domains than in others, depending upon the child's opportunity to engage in experiences relevant to each. The child who is given ample access to art materials but not to math training may show greater skill in the first area. Similarly, development may differ from child to child for the same reason: the child who has the chance to explore her community by taking different paths as she walks to various shops and homes, for example, will come to represent and think about large-scale space such as her neighborhood more effectively than the child who cannot go out on the streets alone.

Skills in Fischer's theory are similar to Piaget's schemes. They are mental structures that stem from action. In contrast to schemes, however, which are highly generalized structures, skills are more specific to particular objects and tasks. If the environment supports a variety of skills, development in all the skills will proceed relatively evenly. Fischer suggests, however, that such uniform access to skill development is unlikely. Levels of skill displayed by the child at a specific age involving number, classification, space, perspective taking, and so forth are likely to be quite different. By making variation in the rate of progress through each skill a central part of his theory—that is, by emphasizing the emergence of separate skills that are not joined in lock-step fashion but are heavily dependent on the specific experiences available to a child—Fischer offers a picture of development that is more continuous and gradual than that proposed by Piaget.

Case's Theory   Robbie Case (1985) has also built on and revised many Piagetian ideas. Case proposes four stages of development similar to those outlined by Piaget. Case's theory differs most noticeably from Piaget's, however, in terms of its explanation of transitions from one stage to the next. Case proposes that infants begin life with certain innate capacities and attentional resources. These resources, however, are limited. As a consequence, an infant can only carry out actions involving objects or entities that are immediately available. Through both maturation and sensorimotor practice, these actions gradually become more efficient and automatic, eventually permitting a child to think about as well as to act upon these objects and entities, and eventually to integrate information about their dimensions, features, and qualities to solve problems. According to Case, then, developmental change comes about through increasingly efficient abilities to remember and operate on information rather than through equilibration, the elimination of inconsistencies, and the restructuring of concepts and ideas so that they become more logically organized.

INFORMATION-PROCESSING APPROACHES

Information processing as a metaphor for human thinking has generated so many theories that it is difficult to single out any one approach as a prototype. In fact, many research programs, including the work of Albert Bandura and Robbie Case, are based on assumptions often associated with this perspective. Researchers adopting an **information-processing** point of view have proposed many kinds of models, but one common thread is the notion that humans, like computers, have a *limited capacity* for processing information. With development, changes in the capacities of intellectual structures and more efficient skills, including the implementation of sophisticated strategies, help older children to process information more fully and effectively.

Why have information-processing ideas become so popular in psychology? One reason is the disenchantment with learning, Piagetian, and other perspectives for explaining behavior. Although learning theories attempt to identify which kinds of human behaviors are acquired and performed, they have offered fewer insights into what kind of mind we possess to be able to do those things. Piaget's cognitive-developmental theory addresses this latter issue, but his explanations have been difficult to translate into ideas about how the mind actually functions. Contributing to the surge in interest in information processing has been the popularity of the computer as an alternative, albeit limited, model of symbol manipulation.

Humans operate with symbols (information). So do computers. To carry out these manipulations, computers have physical structures (hardware) that follow nonphysical, conceptual programs (software) to function. What entities analogous to the computer's physical structures and programs might exist in the human mind? The human mind can be said to possess cognitive structures (a sensory store, short- and long-term memory, executive systems, response systems) and processes (strategies, hypotheses, rules, and plans that influence attention, categorization and decision making, storage and retrieval, and so forth), respectively. Thus, information-processing theories attempt to explain how the child comes to identify the letters of the alphabet, remember the tables of multiplication, recall the main ideas of a story, give a classmate directions to her home, decide whether it is safe to cross the street, or recognize that a friend has become angry—abilities that are influenced by sensing, perceiving, representing, storing, retrieving, and manipulating a set of information.

A highly simplified information-processing model is shown in Figure 2.2.

information processing Theoretical approach that views humans, much like computers, as having a limited ability to process information.

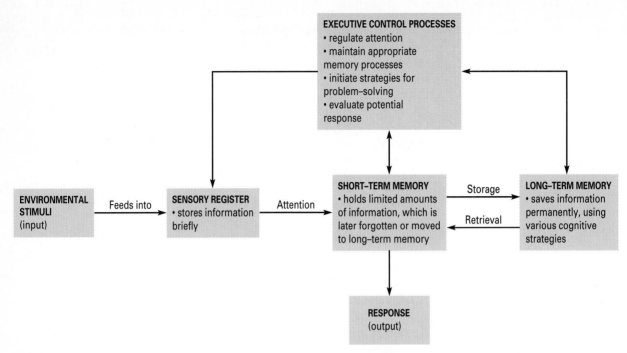

FIGURE 2.2

A Schematic Model of Human Information Processing

This highly simplified model includes several cognitive structures and processes many information-processing theorists believe to be important in cognitive development. As the arrows indicate, information often flows in several directions between various structures. The goal of information-processing models is to identify those structures and processes at work when the child responds to his or her environment.

Source: Adapted from Atkinson & Shiffrin, 1968.

This model identifies several mental structures through which information may flow as it is registered, manipulated, and stored. In addition, the model suggests ways in which cognitive processes operate on this information to produce behavior. Executive control processes, for instance, may regulate attention; implement strategies for maintaining information within working memory and for storing and retrieving information in long-term memory; initiate strategies, hypotheses, and plans for solving problems; and evaluate potential response output.

Information-processing models often rely on measures such as time to complete a task, kinds of responses, or errors in performing a task to evaluate what cognitive structures and processes may be involved in reasoning, problem solving, or some other activity. Consider the six-year-old who successfully completes a few simple addition problems. The question, from an information-processing perspective, might be, How did she do this task? She may have had lots of practice with this activity, having learned the answer to each particular problem by rote over many weeks and months of exposure. Or she might carry out some kind of strategy that permits her to consistently arrive at the correct answer. For example, she could start with the first number of the addition problem, and then add one unit the number of times indicated by the second number. Thus, for the problem 3 + 5, she may begin at 3 and add 1 to it the necessary five times indicated by the second number to arrive at the correct answer.

How could we tell whether she was engaging in the first procedure, primarily retrieving information from long-term memory, or the second, utilizing a rule for arriving at the answer? One clue could come from the length of time it takes to solve a set of different addition problems. If she is using the first technique, she can be expected to solve each problem given to her in about the same length of time. If she uses the second technique, however, she will likely take much longer to answer those problems where the second number is very large and requires more addition.

As the preceding example illustrates, information-processing theorists often attempt to describe the rules and procedures that the child follows in completing a task as a convenient way for summarizing children's knowledge and how it changes with development. Marshall Haith (1980), for example, believes that looking behavior in newborns follows these rules:

- *Rule 1:* If awake and alert and the light is not too bright, then open your eyes.
- *Rule 2:* If it is dark, then look by broadly scanning the environment.
- *Rule 3:* If it is light, but not too bright, then broadly scan the environment.
- *Rule 4:* If an edge is detected, then stop scanning broadly and look in the vicinity of the edge, border, or boundary, scanning back and forth across it.
- *Rule 5:* If other edges or visual contours are nearby, then limit scanning to the first edge detected.

This set of rules summarizes the finding that, given an environment with moderate illumination, newborns tend to focus on an edge or corner of a triangle, square, or other available figure and fail to look at all the edges that form the figure. By the time they are two months of age, these rules will have changed because infants now scan the entire figure. Jean Berko (1958) and many other linguists and psychologists studying children's language acquisition also conclude that children follow rules in producing grammatical utterances and that these rules change as children hear more language. Developmental advances in memory, concept formation, and problem-solving tasks are often theorized to result from changes in the rules, strategies, or procedures children employ.

Information-processing Approaches and Themes in Development

Because of the wide variety of information-processing models theorized to account for changes in cognitive development, we can draw only broad conclusions concerning their positions on the various themes in development.

- *Roles of Nature and Nurture* In contrast to most other theories, information-processing models have often had little to say about the nature versus nurture debate. Some basic capacities to perceive and process information are assumed to be present at or before birth, and the system may be attuned to respond in certain ways—for example, to language and other kinds of information. The environment has an obvious impact on development since it provides input for processing by the mind. The implicit assumption in most models is that basic cognitive structures and processes interact with experience to produce changes in the system.

- *Sociocultural Influence* As in the case of learning theory, the sociocultural context of development has largely been ignored by information-processing theorists. This is probably because researchers have typically focused on identifying how the mind operates on specific problems rather than on how the mind is affected by the kinds of problems a culture presents to it.

• *The Child's Active Role*   The limitations of the computer as a metaphor for human information processing are most evident when we consider the child's active contributions to development. Whereas computers are generally perceived as passive machines that must be programmed, few information-processing theorists accept this view of the mind. While we do, of course, react to the environment, we also initiate and construct strategies and procedures that assist in processing information more effectively. From this perspective, children take an increasingly active role in controlling their own learning and development.

• *Development as Continuous/Stagelike*   In most information-processing models, cognitive development is typically theorized to undergo quantitative rather than qualitative changes. For example, children remember increasingly greater numbers of items both in short-term and long-term memory and interpret information and apply various strategies more efficiently and effectively with development. Similarly, the acquisition of new strategies for storing and retrieving information, new rules for problem solving, and new ways of thinking about and processing information are usually interpreted as shifts in ability that come about because of relatively small, continuous improvements in the capacity to process information.

• *Sensitive Periods*   Little emphasis is placed on sensitive periods by information-processing perspectives.

• *Interaction Among Domains*   A notable limitation of many information-processing models is their failure to consider emotional, motivational, and other domains of behavior. How social factors such as instructions, modeling, and the cultural context of learning lead to developmental changes in processing information are also rarely spelled out (Klahr, 1989). Increasingly, however, information-processing approaches have been adopted to examine other domains of development. For example, the development of peer relationships has been frequently interpreted in terms of changes in information-processing capacities. Thus, this type of model has begun to provide surprisingly fruitful ways of documenting and explaining age-related differences in language, social, and personality development as well as in cognitive development.

PSYCHOANALYTIC APPROACHES

psychoanalytic models Set of theories, most frequently associated with Freud and his followers, that emphasizes the importance of unconscious motivations in determining personality development and behavior.

The theoretical models we have examined so far have been concerned for the most part with learning and cognitive development. With **psychoanalytic models,** which emphasize the unconscious motivations that contribute to behavior, we shift to a substantially greater focus on socioemotional and personality development. If Piaget has been the dominating figure in the field of cognitive development, then Freud has been his counterpart in personality development. Freud's influence on psychology, however, came several decades earlier than Piaget's. As a consequence, more than one generation of researchers has had the opportunity to reinterpret and expand on Freud's ideas. Among these is Erik Erikson, whose work represents another major contri-

Sigmund Freud, shown here with his granddaughter, emphasized the importance of early experience for development. A child who successfully negotiated each successive psychosexual stage of development could be expected to display a healthy personality in adulthood.

bution to developmental psychology. Both Freud and Erikson theorize that personality development progresses through stages. During each stage the child must resolve conflicts between biologically based needs or feelings and external obstacles, particularly those that are socially induced. The satisfactory resolution of these conflicts leads to a healthy personality and a productive lifestyle. We begin with a brief summary of Freud's theory.

Freud's Psychosexual Theory

Trained as a medical doctor and interested in neurology, Freud devoted much of his clinical practice to the investigation of mental disorders. Following the lead of other pioneers, Freud first used hypnosis to study the distinctive behaviors that often accompany mental illness. Eventually he realized, however, that having patients simply describe their early emotional experiences often led to a reduction in the symptoms associated with mental illness. As a consequence, Freud advocated the method of *free association*—that is, letting a patient candidly report whatever came into his or her mind to understand and eventually help relieve these symptoms of illness. From these observations, Freud established his **psychosexual theory of development,** the notion that many aspects of the individual's personality originate in an early and broad form of childhood sexuality.

Psychoanalytic Concepts The fuel that powers human behavior in Freud's theory is a set of biological instincts that makes demands on the mind by initiating a form of psychological tension called *libido* or *libidinal energy.* Libidinal energy surrounds sexual and other biological needs such as eating and elimination. Tension arises as libidinal energy gradually builds, demanding eventual discharge. Under many circumstances this tension is reduced as rapidly as possible, the basis for a premise Freud termed the *pleasure principle,* the desire to obtain immediate gratification regardless of whether the action taken to discharge the tension is effective or socially acceptable.

Sometimes tensions, such as those associated with hunger or pain in infants, cannot be discharged immediately. The consequence for the baby is likely to be more and more intense crying until the need is satisfied. From these experiences, however, mental structures and behavioral responses are eventually organized to achieve more satisfactory means of tension reduction. These behaviors might include calling out to the caregiver as a signal to be fed or eventually learning to feed oneself, responses that fit with Freud's conceptualization of the *reality principle,* that is, the act of reducing libidinal urges by effective, rational, and socially acceptable means. That humans develop mental structures that allow for satisfying and socially acceptable methods of gratifying libidinal energy is a central tenet of Freud's psychoanalytic theory. But Freud also emphasized that the mind can establish indirect means of reducing these energies, as when sexual desire is transformed into athletic exertion or intense hatred of another person into self-destructive tendencies.

The Structures of the Mind: Id, Ego, and Superego Freud identified three major agents of personality that influence how libidinal energy is expressed: id, ego, and superego. He conceptualized the **id** as a primitive, un-

psychosexual theory of development Freud's theory that many aspects of an individual's personality originate in an early and broad form of childhood sexuality. The focus of gratification of this sexuality, however, changes from one region of the body to another throughout various stages of development.

id In Freudian theory, a mental structure that is the seat of libidinal energy and that operates according to the pleasure principle.

conscious segment of the mind, the source of the biologically based libidinal energy much like a "cauldron full of seething excitations" (1933/1965, p. 73). Because it is ruled by the pleasure principle, the id does not function according to logic or any other constraints of reality in its efforts to maximize pleasure and minimize pain. It may generate wish-fulfilling hallucinations or primitive images that provide only partial and incomplete satisfaction, murky and chaotic exercises that come nearest to consciousness during dreams. During infancy the human personality structure is mostly id; the baby's goal is to reduce tensions as rapidly as possible. Even in an optimal caregiving environment, however, no infant consistently achieves immediate hunger reduction or body comfort. The infant must experience many frustrations, diminished somewhat initially by wish-fulfilling images or inadequate responses such as thumb sucking that are usually feeble substitutes for stemming the rising tide of hunger pains or some other need.

The **ego,** the structure designed to satisfy libidinal energy more realistically than the id, gains increasing control over behavior throughout infancy and childhood. The ego contains the representational and cognitive mechanisms required to carry out adaptive reductions in tension that accord with the reality principle. Relying on perception, rational thought, memory, and problem solving, the ego utilizes present, past, and expected outcomes, attempting to delay impulsive action or behavior to plan and initiate more satisfactory means of tension reduction. At first, these actions are performed largely through motor responses: turning toward, reaching for, or crawling after an object that will satisfy the need. As the ego becomes stronger, however, it operates with a variety of cognitive structures and strategies for reaching a goal. The ego attempts to harness the energies of the id, threading these energies through a narrow course in conformity with the pressures of the external world, yet still remaining within the constraints imposed by yet another mental structure, the superego.

The **superego,** which monitors both id and ego and fosters socially acceptable tension resolution, is the final structure to develop, according to Freud's theory. The superego emerges from the resolution of a major crisis during the preschool years called the *Oedipal complex* in boys and the *Electra complex* in girls. Between the ages of three and six, Freud postulated, sexual impulses and fantasies are particularly active and dangerous. At this time a child not only becomes aware of the physical differences between males and females but unconsciously wants to take the place of his father, if a boy, or her mother, if a girl, to establish an intimate social and sexual relationship with the parent of the opposite sex. But this desire promotes anxiety and fear about what the same-sex parent can and might do in retaliation, including physical harm. The child reduces this anxiety through the process of *identification,* the strong desire to look, act, and feel like the parent of the same sex.

Through identification, then, the child arrives at his or her gender identity and a sense of moral values, internalizing parental and cultural standards for acceptable and desirable behavior. The superego consists of two parts, the conscience and the ego ideal. The **conscience** attempts to influence behavior by defining the things that the individual should *not* do, the "thou shalt nots" communicated by caregivers. Transgressions of the dictates of conscience lead to feelings of guilt. The **ego ideal** comprises the positive standards toward

ego In Freudian theory, a mental structure that fosters the formation of representational and cognitive mechanisms and operates according to the reality principle.

superego In Freudian theory, a mental structure that monitors socially acceptable and unacceptable behavior.

conscience In Freudian theory, the part of the superego that defines unacceptable behaviors and actions, usually as also defined by the parents.

ego ideal In Freudian theory, the part of the superego that defines the positive standards for which an individual strives. This component is acquired via parental rewarding of desired behaviors.

Stage	Focus	Consequences for Personality
Oral (birth to 12 months)	Libidinal energy centered on the mouth. Gratification through sucking, chewing, eating, and biting.	Inadequate opportunity to suck may lead to fixations in the form of thumb sucking or other oral activity such as preoccupation with food, eating, or other forms of taking things in (for example, wealth or power). Also possibility of "biting" (sarcastic) personality.
Anal (1–3 years)	Libidinal energy centered on the anal region. Gratification through controlling and expelling fecal waste through the anal sphincters.	If toilet-training demands are too lax, fixations may occur in the form of being messy, disorderly, wasteful, or excessively demonstrative. Strict toilet training may result in possessive, retentive (frugal and stingy) personality and excessive concern with cleanliness and orderliness.
Phallic (3–5 years)	Libidinal energy centered on genitals. Gratification possible through masturbation but more likely through expressions of desire for opposite-sex parent. Period of Oedipal and Electra complex.	Beginning rivalry with members of the same sex. Fixations appear as inordinate ties to opposite-sex parent or difficulty in achieving appropriate relationships with members of same and opposite sex. Possible failure of superego development.
Latency (5 years to adolescence)	Libidinal energy is submerged (latent) and not exhibited through any specific body region.	Because libidinal energy is submerged, there are relatively few important long-term consequences. Much of the energy is channeled into emotionally safe areas, such as intellectual, athletic, and social achievements.
Genital (adolescence and beyond)	Libidinal energy centered on mature forms of genital stimulation. Gratification directed toward reproductive functions.	Complete independence from parents becomes possible. Strong ego and superego structure permit balance between love and work.

TABLE 2.2

Freud's Five Psychosexual Stages of Development

oral stage In Freudian theory, the first psychosexual stage, between birth and about one year of age, during which libidinal energy is focused on the mouth.

anal stage In Freudian theory, the second psychosexual stage, between about one and three years of age, during which libidinal energy is focused on control of defecation.

which the individual strives, the kinds of behaviors desired by and rewarded by parents rather than punished. The achievement of these ideals leads to a sense of pride and positive self-esteem.

The Psychosexual Stages of Development One of Freud's greatest contributions to psychology was his emphasis on the importance of early experience in human development. He theorized that the way in which caregivers respond to the child's basic needs serves as the foundation for either normal or abnormal personality. The locus of tension and the optimal way to reduce needs, furthermore, change with age. Freud identified five stages of psychosexual development, periods during which libidinal energy is usually associated with a specific area of the body. These stages were called the **oral stage,** the **anal stage,** the **phallic stage,** and, after a period of **latency** during middle childhood, the **genital stage.** Table 2.2 summarizes the characteristics of these stages.

Freud believed that the individual's advances through these stages were greatly influenced by maturation. From this perspective, normal personality development proceeded through periods in which libidinal energy could be satisfactorily reduced by activities associated with the dominant region of the body. However, the environment also played a critical role in this normal progression. Lack of opportunity to have needs sufficiently met or to express them adequately during a critical period was predicted to have negative consequences for the ways in which the child related to others and for feelings of self-worth. The infant whose sucking needs were not gratified, for example, became *fixated,* that is, preoccupied with actions associated with the mouth for the rest of his life.

Freud's theory of psychosexual development has been criticized extensively by later schools of psychology, and by anthropologists and others who argue that Freud's theory is culture bound. In particular, it was early noted that the sources of conflict that affect social and personality development differ among societies, especially where family composition and locus of authority depart from the pattern of strong parental influence found in traditional Western societies (Malinowski, 1927). One major theory to expand upon Freud's perspective and address these criticisms has been offered by Erik Erikson.

Erikson's Psychosocial Theory

Despite the fact that he never received a formal degree after high school, his contributions to psychoanalytic theory have earned Erik Erikson prestigious clinical and academic positions as well as the admiration of many psychologists. In his classic work *Childhood and Society* (1950), Erikson built upon Freudian theory to chart eight stages of development, as summarized in Table 2.3. The first five stages match Freud's psychosexual model in their time of appearance. The last three describe additional stages of personality development during adulthood.

In his description of these eight stages, Erikson modified Freudian theory in two significant ways. His first modification was to emphasize the critical role of the ego or reality-oriented processes for the successful negotiation of each stage. During the first stage (comparable to Freud's oral stage), for example, he theorized that *incorporation* or taking in was the primary mode for acting adaptively toward the world. In Erikson's view, this mode of activity extended beyond the mouth and included other senses such as looking and hearing, and motor systems such as reaching and grasping, systems designed to begin to expand the infant's ways for responding to reality. Each subsequent stage identified another important mode for adapting to the environment.

Erikson's second major modification to Freudian theory was to assign society a fundamental role in shaping and forming reality for the child. Societies create their own demands and set their own criteria for socializing the child. In one society an infant may be permitted to breast-feed whenever hungry over a period of several years, whereas infants in another society may be nursed or bottle-fed on a meticulously arranged schedule and weaned within the first year of life. As another example, the timing and severity of toilet training as well as the means by which it is initiated by caregivers may differ vastly from one society to another. Cultures disagree in the requirements they impose on the child, yet the child must adapt to his own culture's regulations. Thus, for Erikson, development is **psychosocial,** a term that highlights the child's com-

phallic stage   In Freudian theory, the third psychosexual stage, between about three and five years of age, when libidinal energy is focused on the genitals and resolution of unconscious conflict with the parent of the same sex leads to establishment of the superego.

latency   In Freudian theory, a period from about six to eleven years of age, when libidinal energy is suppressed and energies are focused on intellectual, athletic, and social achievements appropriate to the adult years.

genital stage   In Freudian theory, the final psychosexual stage, beginning with adolescence, in which sexual energy is directed to peers of the opposite sex.

psychosocial theory of development   Erikson's theory that personality development proceeds through eight stages during which adaptive modes of functioning are established to meet the variety of demands framed by society.

Stage	Adaptive Mode	Significant Events and Outcomes
Basic Trust Versus Mistrust (birth to 1 year)	Incorporation— to take in (and give in return)	Babies must find consistency, predictability, and reliability in their caregivers' behaviors. Out of these experiences babies learn to trust the world and themselves or to gain a sense of hope.
Autonomy Versus Shame and Doubt (1–3 years)	Control—to hold on and to let go	The child begins to explore, to make messes, to say "no!", to make choices. From these opportunities the child comes to understand what is socially acceptable or unacceptable without losing the feeling of being able to manage or the sense of will.
Initiative Versus Guilt (3–6 years)	Intrusion—to go after	The child begins to make plans, set goals, and persist in both physical and social exchanges. Even though frustration is inevitable, the child's goal is to remain enthusiastic and bold and to gain a sense of purpose.
Industry Versus Inferiority (6 years to puberty)	Construction— to build things and relationships	The child acquires and extends skills to the wider culture, to perform "work," in the sense of education or support of the family. Failure and feelings of inadequacy occur, but the child must be able to feel competent and achieve a sense of skill.
Identity Versus Identity Confusion (puberty to adulthood)	Integration—to be oneself (or not to be oneself)	The adolescent attempts to bring together experiences to discover his or her identity and place in society. This trying out of many roles should lead to an answer for the question, Who am I? or a sense of fidelity to self.
Intimacy Versus Isolation (young adulthood)	Solidarity—to lose and find oneself in another	The young adult who has achieved a sense of identity is no longer self-absorbed and can now share himself or herself with another. Inability to do so contributes to feelings of isolation and self-absorption and the absence of a sense of love.
Generativity Versus Stagnation (middle adulthood)	Productivity—to make and to take care of	The adult not only produces things and ideas through work, but also creates and cares for the next generation. Lack of productive endeavors leads to boredom, stagnation, and the absence of a sense of caring.
Integrity Versus Despair (old age)	Acceptance—to be (by having been) and to face not being	The older adult reviews his or her life and reevaluates its worth. Acceptance of that life, even though all goals have not been achieved, and of death, contributes to a sense of wisdom.

TABLE 2.3

Erikson's Eight Stages of Psychosocial Development

posite need to initiate adaptive modes of functioning while meeting the variety of demands framed by the society in which she lives.

As in Freudian stages, maturation plays an important role in the movement from one to another of the eight Eriksonian stages. Similarly, Erikson theorized that the individual confronts a specific crisis as new demands are imposed by society in each stage. The resolution of each crisis may or may not be successful, but success at earlier stages lays the groundwork for the negotiation of later stages. The individual unable to work through a crisis at one time in her life, however, may still successfully resolve it at a later stage. From this perspective, Erikson's theory places less emphasis on critical periods than

Erik Erikson outlined eight stages of personality development. His psychosocial theory emphasized that at each stage, individuals must successfully adapt to new forms of demands placed upon them by society. He also stressed that cultures frequently differ in how they help individuals to negotiate these demands.

does Freud's. Moreover, each society has evolved ways of helping individuals meet their needs. Caregiving practices, educational programs, social organizations, occupational training, and moral and ethical support are examples of cultural systems established to foster healthy, productive psychosocial development.

Perhaps the common theme underlying the various features of Erikson's theory is the search for **identity,** or the acceptance of both self and one's society. At each stage this search is manifested in a specific way. The need to develop a feeling of trust for a caregiver, to acquire a sense of autonomy, to initiate exchanges with the world, and to learn and become competent in school and other settings are examples of how the infant and child discovers who and what she is and will become. During adolescence the individual confronts the issue of identity directly. But the answer to "Who am I?" is elaborated and made clearer as the individual progresses through each psychosocial stage.

In summary, Erikson has rechanneled Freud's somewhat pessimistic views of personality development away from the need to restrain and control biological desires toward a consideration of the practices society uses to encourage and promote healthy social and personality development. Erikson, however, paints development with a broad brush, and consequently his theory is frequently criticized for its vagueness. Such a flaw, of course, is not unique to his theory. Still, just as Piaget's insights seem to have highlighted meaningful issues in cognitive development, so too, Erikson—regardless of the correctness of his specific formulations—had a flair for targeting crucial issues in social and personality development.

Psychoanalytic Theories and Themes in Development

Our discussion of Freud's and Erikson's theories has already focused on a number of themes in development, but let's consider them once more.

• *Roles of Nature and Nurture*   A biological contribution to behavior is conspicuous in both Freud's and Erikson's theories, yet both theories must be considered interactionist given the momentous role that the presence and absence of appropriate experiences play in development.

• *Sociocultural Influence*   Freud and Erikson differ with respect to the role of sociocultural influences on development. For Freud, events within the immediate environment, particularly the way caregivers respond to feeding, toilet training, and other needs of the child, especially during the first five or so years of life, play the most central role. For Erikson, the broader sociocultural context in which these and other caregiving activities take place has the more powerful influence. Thus, the sociocultural context of development is relatively unimportant in Freud's theory, but a critical factor in Erikson's theory of development.

• *The Child's Active Role*   In Freud's theory, the infant seems almost enslaved by his or her libidinal urges, but the ego is an active structure in its efforts to cope with and organize more effective and socially acceptable ways of responding to these urges. Nevertheless, its actions certainly have a more reactive

identity In Eriksonian psychosocial theory, the acceptance of both self and society, a concept that must be achieved at every stage but is especially important during adolescence.

flavor than, say, Piaget's view of a child as constructing his or her own knowledge. In Erikson's theory, the emphasis on establishing an identity for self and within society also suggests an active role for the child in development.

• *Development as Continuous/Stagelike*   Both theories propose stages in personality development. The successful negotiation of earlier stages lays the groundwork for continued psychological growth.

• *Sensitive Periods*   For Freud, in contrast to Erikson, advances from one stage to the next are critically dependent on adequate experiences at the right times. Thus, Freud's theory emphasizes sensitive periods for personality development whereas Erikson's theory places less emphasis on sensitive periods.

• *Interaction Among Domains*   Although not spelled out in detail, Freud's emphasis on motivation and emotion as contributors to intellectual growth reveals an appreciation for the interaction among various domains of development. His theory challenges researchers to consider the close relationships between emotion and thought and vice versa. Rarely is thought cold and completely rational, and Freud would likely applaud efforts to demonstrate how children think about love, violence, and the broad spectrum of human emotions. Similarly, Erikson links social, emotional, and cognitive development together in the individual's efforts to achieve identity.

CONTEXTUAL APPROACHES

Psychologists have long recognized not only that children live in vastly different environments, but that each child experiences a number of overlapping environments. First is the environment of the immediate family, which is subject to enormous variation: some children grow up in households with only a single parent, others with two parents, and still others with grandparents and other relatives; children in foster care may be frequently shuffled from one family to another. Number of siblings, economic resources, space and privacy, independence, and emotional atmosphere are among the vast number of factors that vary in the immediate surroundings of children.

Differences in the contexts of development extend far beyond a child's immediate family, however. Physical surroundings, access to schools, job opportunities, technological innovations, natural disasters, political systems, war, and the cultural dictates of the community in which children are reared permeate the way they are viewed and treated. Some of these environments are likely to be more supportive of social and cognitive development than others. Beyond the physical and sociocultural contexts in which each child lives is still another—the innate and species-specific predispositions humans come equipped with that make some types of learning easier than others.

In other words, the context of development extends far beyond family or even society. Developmental theories usually take into account immediate experience along with inner psychological structures and processes to explain development. Most, however, define experience fairly narrowly and in terms of specific events and circumstances currently affecting the child. Yet culture, the historical legacy of earlier generations of a given social group as well as the evolutionary pressures that have shaped humans to exist in their natural environment, are also major determinants of development. **Contextual models** are concerned with the broad range of biological, physical, and sociocultural settings that influence development. Let us examine first theories that attempt to address the sociocultural contributions to a child's development.

Ecological Systems Theory

The most extensive model of a contextual approach to development is the ecological systems theory proposed by Urie Bronfenbrenner (1979, 1989). Ecological theories stress the need to understand development in terms of the everyday environment in which children are reared, a need fervently advocated by Bronfenbrenner, who argues that "much of contemporary developmental psychology is the science of the strange behavior of children in strange situations with strange adults for the briefest possible periods of time" (Bronfenbrenner, 1977, p. 513). Development, he believes, must be studied not only in the home, but also in the schools, neighborhoods, and communities where it takes place. His **ecological systems theory** emphasizes the broad range of situations and contexts individual children encounter and the consequences for the roles children play and the relationships they establish in the physical and social environment.

One of Bronfenbrenner's major theoretical contributions is his broadened and comprehensive portrait of the environment—the ecological forces and systems that exist at several different, but interrelated, levels. These levels can be conceptualized as a series of concentric rings, as shown in Figure 2.3. At the center is the child's biological and psychological makeup, not only inherited and biologically based factors, but also cognitive capacities and socioemotional and motivational propensities (for example, temperament and personality) for responding to and acting upon the environment. These characteristics and traits have evolved to make humans unique from other organisms, and they are also potential sources of individual differences among children.

Systems with the most immediate and direct impact upon an individual are part of the next ring, the **microsystem,** and include the home and members of the household; social and educational settings (including classmates, teachers, and classroom resources); neighborhoods (including physical layout, friends, and acquaintances); and the workplace. The microsystem includes the personal qualities of others, the physical and material properties of everyday settings, and the "activities, roles, and interpersonal relations experienced by the developing person" (Bronfenbrenner, 1989, p. 227).

The **mesosystem,** the next ring, is concerned with the interrelationships among the various settings within the microsystem. For example, expectations and events within the family, such as access to books and learning to read, or an emphasis on acquiring basic academic and socialization skills, may have a critical impact on the child's opportunities and experiences in school. When the households of divorced parents are in different neighborhoods, regular and frequent moves back and forth between the two homes have an effect not only on family relationships but also on the range and kinds of friendships that the child can establish with peers.

contextual model   Theoretical orientation in developmental psychology that recognizes that, for each individual, the environment consists of a wide range of biological, physical, and sociocultural settings.

ecological systems theory   Bronfenbrenner's theory that development is the joint outcome of individual and experiential events. Experience consists not only of immediate surroundings but also of the larger social and cultural systems that affect an individual's life.

microsystem   In Bronfenbrenner's ecological systems theory, the immediate environment provided in such settings as the home, school, workplace, and neighborhood.

mesosystem   In Bronfenbrenner's ecological systems theory, the environment provided by the interrelationships among the various settings of the microsystem.

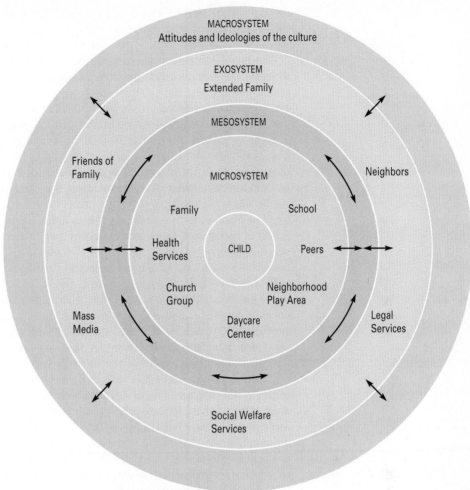

MACROSYSTEM
Attitudes and Ideologies of the culture

EXOSYSTEM
Extended Family

MESOSYSTEM

Friends of Family

Neighbors

MICROSYSTEM

Family

School

Health Services

CHILD

Peers

Church Group

Neighborhood Play Area

Mass Media

Daycare Center

Legal Services

Social Welfare Services

FIGURE 2.3

Bronfenbrenner's Ecological Model

Source: Adapted from Garabino, 1982.

At the core of Bronfenbrenner's ecological model is the child's biological and psychological makeup, based on individual genetic and developmental history. This makeup continues to be affected and modified by the child's immediate physical and social environment (*microsystem*) as well as by interactions among the systems within this environment (*mesosystem*). Other broader social, political, and economic conditions (*exosystem*) influence the structure and availability of microsystems and the manner in which they affect the child. Finally, social, political, and economic conditions are themselves influenced by the general beliefs and attitudes (*macrosystem*) shared by members of a society.

Social, economic, political, religious, and other settings in which the child takes no immediate part but that directly bear upon those who interact with the child can also influence development. These wider contexts make up the **exosystem.** In technological societies, for example, the child is seldom a member of either parent's work environment. Nevertheless, the parent who encounters a difficult problem at work may bring frustrations home and express them through angry exchanges with members of the family. A neighborhood playground taken over by drug pushers could very well end afternoon softball

exosystem In Bronfenbrenner's ecological systems theory, environmental settings that indirectly affect the child by influencing the various microsystems forming the child's immediate environment.

games with friends. Skirmishes between rival villages or countries may bring poverty if the family breadwinner is killed in fighting. Thus, contexts removed from the child's environment can still have a powerful impact on development.

The broadest context, the one that embraces all the others, is the **macro-system.** The macrosystem includes the major historical events (for example, famines, wars) and the spiritual and religious values, legal and political practices, ceremonies and customs shared by a cultural group. Natural disasters and wars can have a devastating impact on conventional microsystems such as schools and neighborhoods as well as on individual families. Cultural beliefs about child rearing, the role of schools and family in education, the importance of specific kinship affiliations, tolerance for different lifestyles, and the ethical and moral conventions of a society affect the child both directly and through the broad strokes the macrosystem paints for acceptable and desirable behavior. The macrosystem represents the accumulated insights of previous generations of caregivers, an evolving wisdom that continues to be transformed by succeeding generations. This historical context, too, has far-reaching consequences for each individual's psychological development.

Bronfenbrenner's ecological systems theory underscores that many levels of the environment directly and indirectly interact with the individual to influence development. Specific settings within the microsystem have direct consequences for behavior but are often affected in turn by larger settings and contexts. Bronfenbrenner points out that researchers frequently use labels that stand for some aspect of the environment (for example, socioeconomic class, ethnic group, or region such as rural and urban) to incorporate broader contexts into explanations of development. But such labels, Bronfenbrenner argues, fail to give adequate credit to the belief systems, resources, lifestyles, and cultural values that are the critical determining factors in these contexts. To simply state that ethnic differences exist within a culture, for example, does not identify the elements of the broader cultural belief systems that lead to specific developmental consequences, nor does it acknowledge the interactive, multidimensional nature of the different levels of these systems.

Vygotsky's Sociohistorical Theory

What is culture? It is, of course, the part of the environment that has and continues to be made and produced by humans—physical artifacts such as tools and buildings—but also language and the practices, values, and beliefs accumulated over many generations. A culture, in other words is a *historical,* human-generated aspect of the environment that has enormous influences on the ways that children are reared and the experiences they receive. Children grow up in an environment different from any other creature's because of the extensive cultural influences that affect them. Lev Vygotsky's **sociohistorical theory** emphasizes the unique contextual blend of the cultural (historical) and social processes that are the legacy for every child's development.

The range and variety of cultural practices is immense. Some communities emphasize skill in weaving; others, fishing and hunting; still others, athletic prowess. Some encourage allegiance and respect for kin and various groups such as grandparents and elders; others do not. Some view peacemaking efforts superior to war; others do not. A central tenet of Vygotsky's sociohistorical theory is that as children become exposed to and participate in their cul-

macrosystem In Bronfenbrenner's ecological systems theory, major historical events and the broad values, practices, and customs promoted by a culture.

sociohistorical theory Vygotsky's theory of development emphasizing the historical (cultural) and social processes that are part of the context of development for every child.

ture, they begin to internalize, to take in and adopt, often with the guidance of a skilled partner such as a caregiver or teacher, more mature and effective ways of thinking about and solving problems with respect to their environment.

Children, of course, are not born with the cultural tools and ways of thinking that are part of a community's history, but these can be channeled to children by those who are more skilled or knowledgeable in their use. Thus, social interactions involving observations of and communications with others familiar with a culture's artifacts, including its language and approaches to problem solving, are an indispensable part of every child's experience and, therefore, of his or her development (Wertsch, 1989). For example, in sitting down with and reading to the child, the caregiver is communicating the importance of this activity so that the child eventually comes to value it in her own behavior and as part of her own culture. Vygotsky believed that language is an especially important cultural tool in this dialogue because it too is internalized by the child to affect thinking and how problems are solved. We will have more opportunity to discuss Vygotsky's ideas on the relationship between language and cognition in Chapter 7, but as you will see, his views have become especially important in considering the larger context, the cultural (or sociohistorical) context, in which development takes place.

Transactional Theory

Transactional theory begins with and builds upon ecological and sociohistorical theories to emphasize the seamless alloy that comprises development as a consequence of the child's being affected by and, in turn, actively influencing, the environment (Sameroff, 1987). Development is viewed as a dynamic, never-ending process involving a continuing, reciprocal exchange: the surrounding people and contextual settings transform the child, who in turn produces changes in the surrounding people and environment, which then transform the child again, and so on. In **transactional theory,** development consists of progressive movement and mutual construction of both the environment and the individual—an ongoing process with no final goal, measure, or outcome by which to conclude that either development or the context in which it takes place is complete.

A major innovative element in transactional theory is the child's active influence on the environment so that experience is never independent of the child. Consider the baby born with low birth weight. Such an infant often has a sharp, shrill cry and has difficulty nursing. Because of these factors and his fragile appearance, a mother who might otherwise feel confident may become anxious and uncertain about her caregiving abilities. Her apprehensions may be translated into inconsistent behaviors to which the baby responds with irregular patterns of feeding and sleeping. These difficulties further reduce the mother's confidence in her abilities and enjoyment of her baby, resulting in fewer social interactions and less positive stimulation for her baby. As a consequence, achievements in other areas of development, such as language acquisition, may be delayed. What factors, precisely, caused the delay? To answer this question, we might point to the mother's avoidance of her child, but this explanation falls far short of portraying the many complex factors that led up to the mother's avoidance (Sameroff, 1987).

transactional theory Theoretical perspective in psychology that highlights the reciprocal relationship between child and environment, emphasizing that development is a seamless alloy formed by the child's being affected by and, in turn, actively influencing the environment.

The teenage years offer many good examples of transactional events. The adolescent caught shoplifting at the urging of a friend may set into motion a change in his parents' perceptions of him that further elevates conflict between them. The girl unable to resist her boyfriend's urges to engage in sexual activity may become part of a course of events that dramatically alters her role from that of student with many friends and freedoms to that of mother with many responsibilities and little time to herself. The contexts of her own development have changed dramatically. Can we realistically single out one critical factor to explain her current situation? Many factors, both historical and immediate, have contributed and formed an intricate and complex web of interacting events that have led to these outcomes.

The importance of transactional models becomes even more apparent when psychologists apply theories to interventions that attempt to alter the course of development. The mother who has avoided her premature infant because of a widening gulf of anxious reactions brought about by disappointments and unhappy exchanges will need more than simply to be told to start talking to her child to encourage his language development. She may need to develop a greater understanding of the typical problems faced by prematures, receive personal support and reinforcement from others for her efforts to initiate confident caregiving skills, and acquire richer insights into how the context of development affects multifaceted levels of experience.

Ethological Theory

Development is influenced by yet one more broad context. That context is the biological history and constraints that have been a part of human evolution. In the nineteenth century, Charles Darwin and other biologists concluded that adaptive traits—those that improved the likelihood of survival and thus a greater number of offspring for further reproduction—were more likely to be found in succeeding generations of a species. He hypothesized that through *evolution,* the descent of living species from earlier species of animals, humans possessed a biological heritage that also included traits that would improve the likelihood of their survival. While other theorists have discussed biology's influence on development in terms of genetic and maturational processes, **ethology** is the discipline especially concerned with understanding how adaptive behaviors evolved and the functions they continue to serve for the survival of the species.

Ethological theory had its start in the 1930s, when European zoologists such as Konrad Lorenz (1963/1966) and Niko Tinbergen (1951) carried out extensive investigations of aggressive actions and the courtship and mating rituals of such animals as the mallard duck and stickleback fish. Their observations led to explanations that took into account the *mutual* interchange between the inherited, biological bases of behavior and the environment in which that behavior was exhibited (Hinde, 1989). Consider, for example, the kinds of questions that Robert Hinde (1965), another well-known ethologist, wanted to answer. How is hormone production in female canaries influenced by temperature and length of daylight and how does this hormone production contribute to, and in turn become affected by, responsivity to male courtship displays and the initiation of nest building? Questions such as these, concerned with behaviors that arise from the interaction between biological and environmental fac-

ethology Theoretical orientation and discipline concerned with the evolutionary origins of behavior and its adaptive and survival value in animals, including humans.

Konrad Lorenz, an ethologist, is being followed by young geese who have imprinted to him. Imprinting in young animals typically occurs to other members of the same species who, under normal circumstances, are present shortly after hatching or the birth of an animal. One question posed by ethologists is whether human infants also show some form of imprinting.

tors, are typical in research on animals in their natural habitats and are also relevant to the complex behaviors of human beings.

Topics ethologists have frequently studied include caregiver-offspring behaviors designed to provide support and protection, behavioral exchanges between adversaries competing for territory or potential mates, and courtship and other rituals leading to the production of offspring. These social interactions are among the most powerful and important for the survival of any species, including humans. Ethological studies propose answers to questions such as the following: Why do babies cry or smile? Why might the ten-year-old fight or be friendly? Ethologists point out the need to consider the adaptive value that such activities have for the individual in the specific environment in which he or she is growing up. In providing answers to these questions, both the evolutionary as well as the cultural heritage are considered.

Ethological theory proposes that human infants, as well as the offspring of other species of animals, begin life with a set of innate, *species-specific* behaviors common to all members. In human babies, these include reflexes such as sucking and grasping and may also include more complex activities such as babbling, smiling, and orienting to interesting sensory events, behaviors exhibited by normal infants around the world. These species-specific behaviors help infants meet their survival needs either directly, as in the case of sucking as a means of ingesting food, or indirectly, as in the case of smiling, a behavior that attracts caregivers and encourages them to provide support.

Besides displaying innate behaviors, the young of many species have predispositions for certain kinds of learning that are not easily reversed and promote their continued survival. These kinds of learning may occur only during sensitive periods. One of the best-known examples has been observed in various species of birds, including geese. Usually within a very short time after hatching, the gosling begins to follow and to prefer being near a particular stimulus. Under normal circumstances that stimulus will be another goose, its mother. In acquiring this behavior, the gosling not only learns about its mother and its species more generally, but also increases the likelihood of being fed and protected. This form of learning that takes place during a brief interval early in life and that is difficult to modify once established is known as **imprinting.**

An imprinted stimulus must meet certain requirements. A gosling, for example, will become imprinted to things that make only certain kinds of sounds or movements. As Lorenz has shown, however, goslings can become imprinted on objects ranging from electric trains to quacking humans. If such a stimulus is present instead of the mother goose, the stimulus continues to be treated as the gosling's "mother" and will even be sought out for mating purposes when the goose becomes mature.

Do other animals show imprinting? Mammals such as horses and sheep do. What about human infants? John Bowlby's (1969) theory of attachment suggests that they do, at least to some degree. Bowlby noted that the crying, babbling, and smiling behaviors of young infants signal needs and elicit supportive and protective responses from adults. These behaviors, along with following and talking in older infants, become organized and integrated with the social and emotional reactions of caregivers to form the basis for *attachment,* a mutual system of physical, social, and emotional stimulation and support between caregiver and young. We will discuss attachment more fully in Chapter 10, but ethological principles are evident in a related controversial issue that we introduce here, the issue of bonding of a mother to her infant.

imprinting Form of learning, difficult to reverse, during a sensitive period in development in which an organism tends to stay near a particular stimulus.

CONTROVERSY

How Important Is Bonding?

Does it matter whether infants and their caregivers are together during the first few hours and days after birth? It may make a difference for some species of animals, but what about for humans? In 1976 Marshall Klaus and John Kennell reported the results of an intriguing experiment that suggested that the events occurring within the first few hours following human birth are extremely important for the development of a positive relationship between a mother and her infant. One group of mothers received the typical sequence of events followed in most hospitals in the United States at that time, a brief glance or two at the baby immediately after delivery and then regularly scheduled twenty- to thirty-minute visits for feeding every three to four hours during the day. A second group of mothers was permitted to cuddle and engage in skin-to-skin contact with their babies for an hour immediately after birth and to interact with them several additional hours each day during the hospital stay. Observations of these two groups of mothers during the first few days in the hospital, a month later, and even after one and two years, revealed that those permitted the extra interactions cuddled, looked at, soothed, and nurtured their babies more than mothers given the usual hospital routine. Furthermore, infants who were cuddled immediately after birth tended to perform better on various tests of physical and mental development (Klaus & Kennell, 1976, 1982).

Klaus and Kennell concluded that during the first few hours after giving birth, human mothers enter a sensitive period during which they can establish a strong emotional bond to their infants. This bond may come about because hormones present during the birth process lead the mother to be especially receptive to forming an early attachment. Alternatively, the intense emotional and anxiety-ridden experiences accompanying the delivery process are suddenly replaced and reinterpreted as intensely positive feelings as the mother has the opportunity to focus on her cuddly, responsive baby. Whatever the reason for this finding, it had an immense impact upon hospital practices throughout the nation, leading many doctors and nurses to encourage early and frequent interactions between mothers, and even fathers, and their newborns.

Others, however, have challenged the findings reported by Klaus and Kennell and have argued that bonding is not a necessary route by which early positive relationships are established between infants and their caregivers. Some researchers have been unable to replicate differences in interactions of the kind reported by Klaus and Kennell for mothers who do and do not have the opportunity to establish an early bond (Chess & Thomas, 1986; Goldberg, 1983; Svejda, Campos, & Emde, 1980). Some have also pointed out that mothers of adopted infants often feel as closely bonded to their offspring as biological mothers do to theirs (Singer et al., 1985). Furthermore, when cultures that encourage mothers to have early contact with their babies or fathers to be involved with the birth process are compared with cultures that do not promote these activities, few differences emerge in the extent to which nurturance or affection for infants is expressed (Lozoff, 1983).

The importance of early bonding continues to be a popular, but controversial issue. For some caregivers it may indeed be an important means of establishing a positive relationship with their infants. Yet it appears that for humans, other routes exist for establishing positive and supportive relationships with their young. Mothers or fathers need not feel that their newborns will be permanently harmed by the lack of opportunity to establish early contact. On the other hand, because parents seem to enjoy and appreciate immediate involvement with their infants, they can be encouraged to participate in the birth and caregiving process to whatever extent it is possible and comfortable for them. ■

Contextual Approaches and Themes in Development

Contextual models are generally in agreement on many of the themes in development, and where differences exist, they are most often found in ethological theories.

• *The Roles of Nature and Nurture*   For most contextual theories, nurture is emphasized. Except for ethological theories, the biological contributions to development receive little attention in contextual models. For ethologists, however, behaviors are closely linked to nature because they have helped, or continue to help, humans survive. Thus, the biological context is every bit as important as other contexts for development. Yet even in ethological theories, the interaction between nature and nurture is considered paramount.

• *Sociocultural Influence*   Most contextual theories are concerned with the ways that broad sociocultural patterns affect development. Contextual theories attempt to find evidence for how the larger social systems and cultural settings in which children are reared affect their behavior and shape their minds. Often the focus is less on universal experiences and more on the particular circumstances that foster cognitive, linguistic, social, and personality development. Ethological principles of development, however, are assumed to be applicable in all cultural contexts.

• *The Child's Active Role*   Contextual models, even those having an ethological focus, tend to view the child as actively engaged with the environment. In calling for their caregivers, exploring, playing, solving problems, and seeking out playmates, infants and children elicit reactions from the adults and peers around them. Contextual models emphasize that characteristics of the child trigger and alter environmental events and these changes further impact development. Both individual and environment change in highly interdependent ways, and their relationship is *bidirectional,* each influencing the other (Bell, 1968).

• *Development as Continuous/Stagelike*   Contextual models place little emphasis on major qualitative changes in development. Instead, contextual models describe the continuous ebb and flow of interactions that transpire throughout development to produce incremental change. Most contextual theorists emphasize how the child's unique circumstances promote gradual advances in thought and behavior rather than claim a universal sequence of developmental stages.

• *Sensitive Periods*   Sensitive periods are an important part of aspects of development according to ethological theories. For example, infancy is considered a crucial time for forming emotional ties with caregivers according to this perspective. However, other contextual models place little emphasis on this theme in development.

• *Interaction Among Domains*   Not surprisingly, most contextual models are typically concerned with the entire fabric of human growth and claim substantial interactions among cognitive, linguistic, social, and other domains. Ethological theorists especially focus on the interrelationship between biological and other aspects of development.

WHICH THEME AND WHICH THEORY?

All theories of development, of course, are ultimately concerned with the simple question, What develops? As you have seen amply demonstrated in this chapter, the answers differ. For learning theorists, what develops is a set of responses. For Jean Piaget, it is a set of cognitive structures. For information-processing enthusiasts, it is mental structures and strategies for responding. For psychoanalytic theorists, it is personality structures. For ecological, sociohistorical, and transactional theorists, it is a pattern of mutually supportive individual and cultural relationships. For ethologists, it is adaptive behaviors.

Theories give us models for observing and interpreting behavior. They have had an enormous influence on the way we view children and their development, as the chapters to follow will demonstrate. Why so many different theories? The reason is that each brings an important perspective to understanding development. Some remind us of the importance of emotions, others of cognitive structures. Some keep us honest about the role of our biological nature; others perform the same service for the culture in which we are born and reared. Various theories enrich and broaden our understanding of development. We will frequently draw on their contributions to promoting research and interpreting the many behaviors of children. We hope you will, too.

At the beginning of this chapter, we asked you to note your position on each of six major themes of development. As we have introduced developmental theories, we have also discussed their positions on these themes. Table 2.4 summarizes these positions for the major theories introduced in this chapter. As you read further in this book, you may find yourself revising your own stand on the six themes. We trace their presence throughout the remainder of this book with marginal cues placed beside important research and discussion that bear on each theme. We also open each chapter with a list of the most relevant themes to consider as you read, and we conclude each chapter by summarizing how the themes have applied to the developmental domain under discussion.

SUMMARY

Theories provide models for understanding the complex phenomenon of human development. At the beginning of this chapter we formulated six recurring investigative questions that developmental theories must answer:

- What roles do nature and nurture play in development?
- How does the sociocultural context influence development?
- How does the child play an active role in development?
- Is development continuous or stagelike?
- Are there sensitive periods in development?
- How do the various domains of development interact?

Not surprisingly, the various theories examined in this chapter differ in their emphases on one theme or another, or on one aspect of a theme over another aspect.

TABLE 2.4

The Main Developmental Theories and Where They Stand on Six Themes in Development
(Continued on next page.)

Theme	Learning Theories	Piagetian Theory	Information-processing Models	Psychoanalytic Theories	Contextual Sociocultural	Theories Ethological
What roles do nature and nurture play in development?	Environment is more important than heredity.	Maturation sets limits on how rapidly development proceeds, but experience is necessary for the formation of cognitive structures. Interaction between nature and nurture.	Of relatively minor concern. Structures and processes presumably have an inherent basis, but experience is likely to be important for effective operation of structures and processes.	Freud: Biologically determined motivational urges are the fuel for development of more reality-oriented structures. Erikson: A more interactional position that emphasizes the socialization demands of the society in which a child is reared.	A major emphasis on the environmental factors that interact with biological structures.	Behavior is biologically based, but the environment elicits and influences these biologically based patterns.
How does the sociocultural context influence development?	Sociocultural factors are likely to determine which behaviors are reinforced, punished, or available from models, but this level of context is not stressed since the principles of learning are considered to be universal.	Piaget believed the cognitive structures underlying thought are universal. Sociocultural context might affect the rapidity or final level of thinking, but sociocultural differences are not stressed.	Of relatively minor concern. However, the rules, strategies, and procedures acquired to perform tasks may differ from one culture to another.	Freud has been widely criticized for failure to consider the sociocultural context of psychosexual development. Erikson incorporated sociocultural context as a major component of his theory.	A critically important determinant of behavior. Culture contains the historical knowledge that has permitted former and current members of the group to interact successfully with the environment.	Not emphasized. Ethological principles of development are presumed to apply in all cultures.
How does the child play an active role in development?	The child is not active in behavior analysis, but more actively engages the environment to determine what is learned in social cognitive theory.	Knowledge is based on underlying cognitive structures constructed by the child.	The child determines what information is processed and the rules, strategies, and procedures initiated to perform tasks.	Freud: Initially, the child is at the whim of libidinal and unconscious urges early in development, but emerging ego structures lead to more active role in development. Erikson: Child is actively in search of an identity.	The child plays a central role in determining what kind of environment is established, and may influence changes in the environment that further affect behavior. The influences of the child and the environment are bidirectional.	The child is biologically equipped to interact with the environment and actively contributes to developmental outcomes.

Theme	Learning Theories	Piagetian Theory	Information-processing Models	Psychoanalytic Theories	Contextual Theories Sociocultural	Contextual Theories Ethological
Is development continuous or stagelike?	Continuous. Development is cumulative, consisting of the acquisition of a greater and greater number of learned responses.	Stagelike. Four qualitatively different stages emerge, each involving a reorganization of cognitive structures that permits more effective adaptation to the demands of the world. Neo-Piagetian theories see stagelike changes as more domain specific.	Usually continuous. Development consists of the acquisition of more effective structures and processes for performing tasks.	Stagelike. Freud: Qualitatively different psychosexual stages. Erikson: Psychosocial stages.	Continuous. Development involves transactions between the individual and the environment.	Continuous.
Are there sensitive periods in development?	No. Learning is equally important during all periods of development.	No. The active role of the child and the universal experiences of responding to the physical environment are usually sufficient to spawn normal intellectual development.	No.	Yes. Freud: Sensitive periods are definitely present. Failure to negotiate the psychosexual stages successfully results in major disruption in personality development. Erikson: Sensitive periods are present, but individual has an opportunity to work through necessary conflicts even at later periods.	No.	Yes. Critical periods are strongly emphasized, especially during early development.
How do the various domains of development interact?	Learning proceeds on many different fronts and is highly situational.	In Piaget's theory, stagelike advances in cognition not only have implications for thinking and problem solving, but also for moral and social development since many achievements in these domains depend on cognitive skills.	Development is usually considered to be domain specific. However, recent efforts have been made to understand social and emotional relationships in terms of information-processing models.	Failure to progress through psychosexual stages may disrupt progress, not only for personality development, but also for social, emotional, and perhaps even cognitive development.	Because of the strong mutual interdependence between individual and environment, all aspects of development are closely interrelated.	Social and psychological aspects of development are intimately linked to biological aspects, and all domains of development are linked together by their common contribution to adaptation.

TABLE 2.4 (Continued)

The Main Developmental Theories and Where They Stand on Six Themes in Development

Learning theories, originating with the ideas of Watson, emphasize the critical role of the environment and *operant* and *classical conditioning* for bringing about behavioral change. Even complex behaviors are the outcome of simple learning principles involving reinforcement and punishment. *Social learning theories,* particularly *social cognitive theory* as outlined by Bandura, adds *obser-*

vational learning as an important mechanism by which behavior is continuously modified and changed. *Behavior analysis* views the child as passively shaped by the environment, but Bandura's social cognitive theory views the child as a more active participant in determining what is learned.

Jean Piaget's *cognitive-developmental theory* focuses on the child's construction of schemes or patterns of thought as development progresses through a series of qualitatively different stages. By *assimilation* and *accommodation* a child's *schemes,* or mental structures, actively adapt to the demands of the environment and become more organized, rational, and logical, thereby establishing equilibrium with the environment. Cognitive structures not only determine the way the child interprets and understands the world but also influence social and moral development.

Information-processing models use the computer as a metaphor to describe the cognitive structures and processes available to children in their efforts to comprehend, reason about, and respond to information in the environment. Various perceptual, memory, and other structures as well as attentional, storage, retrieval, and other processes involving rules, plans, and strategies are posited to explain behavior. Improvements in performance in cognitive and other activities are viewed as gradual over time.

Psychoanalytic theories focus on personality development. Sigmund Freud's *psychosexual theory* proposed that the mind consists of three parts, the *id,* the *ego,* and the *superego.* Behavior is motivated by the need to discharge a buildup of *libidinal energy.* Reduction of libidinal energy in infancy takes place only through the *pleasure principle,* associated with the id. With the development of the ego and superego, the child becomes equipped with mechanisms and criteria for reducing libidinal energy through more socially acceptable and adaptive means. Behavior accordingly becomes governed by the *reality principle.* Development proceeds maturationally through several stages in which specific body organs become especially effective in reducing libidinal energy. Failure to negotiate these stages successfully results in personality disturbances. Erik Erikson's *psychosocial theory* emphasizes the sociocultural context in which behavioral needs are met. Development proceeds through a series of crises involving an individual's identity. Individuals who manage to resolve these crises become people who can successfully contribute to society.

Contextual models attempt to step back and view human development from a broader framework. *Ecological systems theory* looks beyond the immediate context of an individual interacting with family, peers, and friends to the broader sociocultural contexts of his or her society. Vygotsky's *sociohistorical theory* views culture as the historical legacy of a community and emphasizes that development results from social interactions in which this legacy is transferred to and becomes part of an individual's way of thinking. His and other *transactional theories* view the child as actively modifying and affecting the environment so that development is a process that is unending for both the child and the culture in which he or she grows. *Ethological theory* pays special attention to the biological heritage each individual brings into the world. This heritage includes a history of species-specific behaviors that have been found to be adaptive throughout evolution. The emergence of many adaptive behaviors takes place during sensitive periods when specific kinds of experiences are necessary for normal development.

3

Genetics and Heredity

▶ **What roles do nature and nurture play in development?**

▶ **How does the child play an active role in the effects of heredity on development?**

"He was shy," Jeremy's mother said. "He's always been shy, ever since he was a baby. I remember those first weeks at the day-care center, how Jeremy clung to me, clutched my hand, even grabbed my leg whenever I started to walk toward a group of children. The teacher said he would get over this timid behavior. But when I came to observe, Jeremy would be off to the side watching what everyone else was doing; he was hardly ever in the center of a group. Every time I saw him like that, it reminded me of myself in grade school. The other kids talked with each other and shared things so easily and always seemed so popular. I guess Jeremy just takes after me. No matter how I tried to encourage him, he hung back from the rest of the group just like I did."

She paused. "Cindy was so different. She was usually the center of attention and never bashful about walking up to a stranger. Her school teachers often commented about Cindy's enthusiasm in class. She'd usually be one of the first to raise her hand, answer a question, or volunteer to lead the group in some kind of activity. She has all her father's outgoing personality and charm. It comes so naturally to both of them!"

Parents often describe their children in ways like this, but what precisely are the mechanisms by which we "take after" our parents, grandparents, and other genetic forebears? Can a personality trait like introversion or extroversion be inherited? Though we may readily acknowledge the contribution of nature to eye color, gender, height, and many other physical traits, heredity's role in whether we are shy or outgoing, quick tempered or complacent, prone to alcoholism, likely to suffer depression, and other social, emotional, and intellectual traits continues to be questioned. However, as Sandra Scarr, a leading researcher in behavioral genetics, a field we will examine later in the chapter, has stated, "Parents of two or more children know perfectly well that their children are different for reasons that have nothing to do with their training regimens" (1987, p. 227).

Scarr's comment was made to counter several decades of theorizing in which the importance of biology for understanding development was minimized. In Chapter 2, we pointed out how researchers have debated the contributions of nature and nurture for many domains of development. That debate continues today. In fact, in recent years some researchers have become so sympathetic to biologically based explanations of development that Robert Plomin, another leading behavioral geneticist, cautions, "As the pendulum swings from environmentalism, it is important that the pendulum be caught midswing before its momentum carries it to biological determinism" (1989, p. 110).

This chapter considers the role of heredity in development. Major advances in our understanding of the basic biological units of inheritance and their effects on behavior have swung the pendulum away from extreme environmentalism to a greater appreciation of the reciprocal, interactive relationship between nature and nurture. We no longer think of the rich variety of physical and social experiences encountered daily as elements that can replace biological determinants of development or vice versa. Instead, we attempt to understand how experiences mold, modify, and enhance biological predispositions, and conversely, how our genetic endowment regulates development and actively promotes selection and preference for certain kinds of environments.

The chapter begins with a brief overview of the laws of heredity and the biological structures determining these laws. The blueprint for human development is replicated in nearly every cell of our body. This blueprint includes genetic instructions that help distinguish humans from all other species of plants and animals. Regardless of the language we speak, the work we do, the color of our skin, or how friendly we are, we share a genetic underpinning that makes us unambiguously human. But this biological inheritance also contributes to our uniqueness as individuals. All of us, with the exception of identical twins, began our lives with a set of genetic instructions that, when combined with a variety of experiences, ensures that each of us is and continues to be unique, different from everyone else, though we belong to the same species. Imagine the monotony of a world populated by a single kind of man and a single kind of woman. Biologists emphasize that genetic diversity is important for another reason: it helps ensure the survival of our species.

The chapter also examines several examples of genetic anomalies and diseases that pose problems for development, focusing on specific disorders to illustrate how each person's genetic makeup and life experiences interact. As researchers have come to learn more about the ways in which genetic abnormalities arise, they have begun to design environments that sometimes help minimize the negative impact of these disorders. The chapter also looks at how genetic counseling assists parents in deciding whether to have children.

Most psychological development, of course, cannot be linked to simple genetic instructions. Intelligence, temperament, and personality along with mental disorders such as schizophrenia and manic depression are the product of complex interactions between genetic and environmental events. The final section of this chapter considers research involving identical and fraternal twins, siblings, adopted children, and other family relationships for the purpose of unraveling the complex tapestry that genetic and environmental factors weave for cognitive, social-emotional, and personality development. Arguments about the extent to which specific behaviors are inherited or acquired have been voiced repeatedly throughout the history of psychology. Research bearing on these topics has often attempted to identify *how much* nature and nurture, respectively, contribute to development. But efforts to understand how these factors *interact* to account for behavior will ultimately yield more insights concerning the process of human development (Wachs, 1983).

The biological heritage passed on from mother to daughter is one source of similarities in the four generations of women shown here. Psychologists are interested in determining how this biological heritage interacts with experience to affect physical appearance, intellectual development, personality, and other traits and behaviors.

PRINCIPLES OF HEREDITARY TRANSMISSION

Historical records of agricultural practices in most civilizations reveal a simple knowledge of principles of inheritance. The concept of "like begets like," routinely applied to the propagation of plants and the breeding of animals, often served to explain similarities among human family members as well. The first known genetic theory, attributed to Hippocrates in ancient Greece, proposed that each component of the body produced an element somehow collected and physically transferred to offspring through the seminal fluid of males. Aristotle, however, suggested that only the *potential* for specific characteristics is inherited (Sturtevant, 1965). Thus, whether we have freckles, blonde hair, or display a certain type of personality may be influenced by genetic factors but is not given to us at conception any more directly than our height, which is finally realized only at our maturity. In making this distinction, Aristotle set the stage for differentiating between **genotype,** a person's constant, inherited genetic endowment, and **phenotype,** the developing person's observable, measurable features, characteristics, and behaviors. Today we know that a given phenotype is the product of complex interactions involving the genotype and the many events the individual *experiences* in his or her environment.

The beginning of modern theories of the genotype can be traced to a series of experiments on peas reported in 1866 by Gregor Mendel, an Austrian monk. From his observations, Mendel outlined several basic principles of inheritance still accepted today. For example, Mendel theorized hereditary characteristics are determined by *pairs* of particles called factors (later termed **genes,** the

▶ **Roles of nature and nurture**

genotype Total genetic endowment inherited by an individual.

phenotype Observable and measurable characteristics and traits of an individual; a product of the interaction of the genotype with the environment.

gene Large segment of nucleotides within a chromosome that codes for the production of proteins and enzymes. These proteins and enzymes underlie traits and characteristics inherited from one generation to the next.

specialized sequences of molecules that form the genotype). He proposed that the information carried by the individual members of a pair of genes is not always identical. If differences between the two genes in a pair exist, each member does not necessarily contribute equally to the expression of a specific characteristic. The information carried by one gene might dominate or mask the information carried by another gene. In other cases, the information might interact so that the phenotype would reflect the combined influence of both genes.

Mendel also outlined the basic principle by which genes are transferred from one generation to another. He concluded that offspring randomly receive one member of every gene pair from the mother and one from the father. The parents' **gametes,** or sex cells (egg and sperm), carry individual genes, rather than pairs of genes. Thus, when egg and sperm combine during fertilization, a pair of genes, one from each parent, is established in the newly created offspring, who in turn may pass on either member of this pair to subsequent offspring. In this way, a given genotype can be inherited from one generation to the next.

About the same time that Mendel's research was published, biologists discovered **chromosomes,** long threadlike structures in the nucleus of cells. By the early 1900s, several researchers independently hypothesized that genes are located on chromosomes. Other biological research during the first half of this century revealed that genes are not immutable; they can be altered by environmental events such as radiation (Muller, 1927). Yet another major breakthrough occurred in 1953 when James Watson and Francis Crick deciphered the structure of chromosomes, and in so doing, proposed a powerfully elegant way by which genes are duplicated during cell division. By 1956, researchers documented the existence of forty-six chromosomes in normal human body cells. Research in the 1990s may result in the mapping of the entire **human genome,** the identification of the set of genes and sequence of complex molecules that makes up the genetic information contained in all forty-six chromosomes.

▶ **Roles of nature and nurture**

gametes   Sperm cells in males, egg cells in females, normally containing only twenty-three chromosomes.

chromosomes   Threadlike structures of DNA, located in the nucleus of cells, that form a collection of genes. A human body cell normally contains forty-six chromosomes.

human genome   Entire inventory of nucleotide base pairs comprising the genes and chromosomes of humans.

nucleotide   Repeating basic building block of DNA consisting of nitrogen-based molecules of adenine, thymine, cytosine, and guanine.

The Building Blocks of Heredity

The way in which the genotype contributes to traits and behaviors in the individual is of major interest to psychologists. We are eager to learn how biological factors might play a part in Jeremy's shyness and Cindy's friendliness, in another child's remarkable mathematical ability or mental retardation. To achieve their effects on appearance, behavior, personality, or intellectual ability, genetic mechanisms operate at cellular and even more fine grained levels.

Every living organism is composed of cells—and in the case of mature humans, trillions of cells. As Figure 3.1 indicates, within the nucleus of nearly all of these cells are the chromosomes that carry genetic information critical to the functioning of that cell. Genes, regions within the strands of chromosomes, determine the production of specific proteins and enzymes in the cell. The genes are, in turn, made up of various arrangements of four different chemical building blocks, nitrogen-based molecules called **nucleotides**

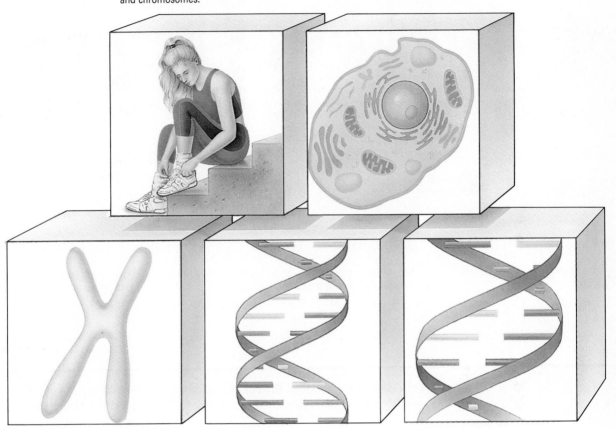

1. The **human body** has about 10 trillion cells. Proteins determine the structure and function of each cell. A project is now under way to map and sequence the 3 billion pairs of nucleotides that make up the total complement of genes and chromosomes.

2. A **cell** contains the chromosomes in its nucleus and uses the information in the chromosomes to manufacture proteins.

3. A **chromosome** is a long DNA double helix coiled and packed with proteins. A full set of 46 chromosomes contains about 100,000 genes.

4. A **gene** contains thousands of nucleotide pairs and has enough information in it to specify a particular protein.

5. **Nucleotides**, four different kinds represented by the letters A, C, G, and T, are the smallest genetic unit and are paired in specific combinations within the double helix of DNA.

FIGURE 3.1

The Building Blocks of Heredity

Source: Adapted from Isensee, 1986.

Hereditary contributions to development occur at many different levels. In this figure you can see how each level, numbered 1 through 5, is important in human development. Nearly every cell in the human body carries the genetic blueprint for development in the chromosomes. Specific regions on each chromosome, the genes, regulate protein and enzyme production and can be further examined at the level of nucleotides, chemical molecules that are the building blocks for the genes. Each of these different levels of the individual's biological makeup can offer insights into the mechanisms by which the genotype affects the phenotype, the observable expression of traits and behaviors.

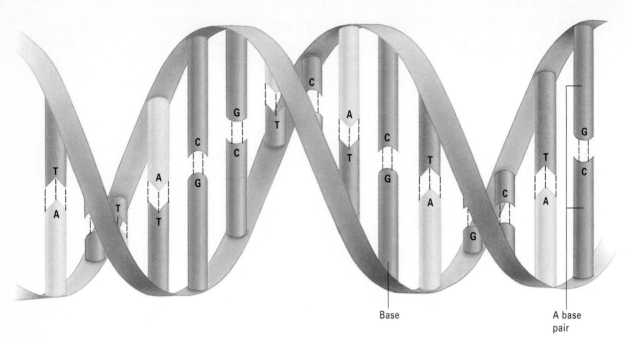

Base

A base
pair

FIGURE 3.2

Base Pairs: Steps on the DNA Ladder

Source: Adapted from Alberts et al., 1983.

The four basic building blocks of the human genome are nitrogen-based molecules called nucleotides. Each of the four nucleotides—adenine (A), thymine (T), cytosine (C), and guanine (G)—binds with only one other, and these links are known as base pairs.

deoxyribonucleic acid (DNA) Long, spiral staircase-like sequence of molecules created by nucleotides identified with the blueprint for genetic inheritance.

karyotype Pictorial representation of an individual's chromosomes.

autosomes Twenty-two pairs of homologous chromosomes. The two members of each pair are similar in size, shape, and genetic function. The two sex chromosomes are excluded from this class.

X chromosome Larger of the two sex chromosomes associated with genetic determination of sex. Normally females have two X chromosomes; males, only one.

(*adenine, thymine, cytosine, and guanine*) that form a remarkably long, spiral, ladderlike staircase called **DNA** or **deoxyribonucleic acid.** Each rung or step of the DNA ladder is constructed of two different nucleotides linked together, called a *base pair* (see Figure 3.2). An average of about a thousand nucleotide pairs make up each gene, although some have substantially more pairings (National Research Council, 1988). Genes differ from each other in the sequencing as well as the number of their base pairs and in the location of these pairs on the chemical staircase. Each human body cell normally contains forty-six of the chemical spiral staircases, or chains of DNA, the chromosomes.

Just as Mendel had theorized, hereditary attributes are determined by *pairs* of genes, one member of each pair inherited from the mother and one from the father. Since genes are segments of chromosomes, chromosomes, too, come in pairs. The two chromosomes in a pair are called *homologous* (similar) because they code for the same kinds of genetic events. Of the forty-six chromosomes in humans, twenty-three different pairs can be identified. Figure 3.3 shows a **karyotype** or photomicrograph of these paired chromosomes. They are numbered from 1 to 22 in the case of the **autosomes,** those pairs of homologous chromosomes that are distinguished from the remaining set of two chromosomes, which genetically determine sex. The two members of the twenty-third pair in females, called **X chromosomes,** are relatively large and similar in size and shape. But the two members of the twenty-third pair for males are quite different. The normal male has one X chromosome and one much smaller

FIGURE 3.3

Chromosomes for the Normal Human Male

This karyotype depicts the twenty-two homologous pairs of autosomes and the two sex chromosomes for the normal human male. In females the twenty-third pair of chromosomes consists of an XX instead of an XY pair.

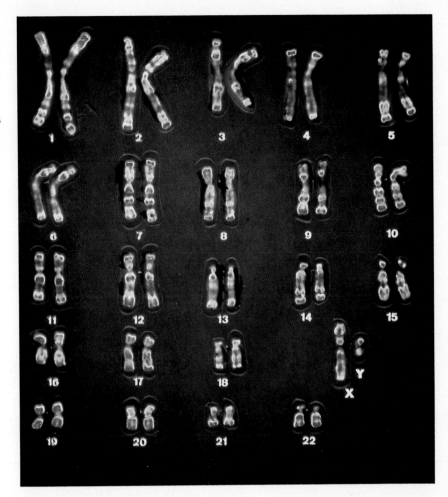

Y chromosome, a chain of DNA that is believed to carry far less genetic information. Nevertheless, the Y chromosome has a major function in promoting the development of the male *gonads* (testes) and, consequently, whether an individual will be identified as male or female.

Cell Division and Chromosome Duplication

Each child begins life as a single cell created when a sperm cell from the father unites with an ovum (egg) from the mother to form a **zygote,** or fertilized egg cell. The developmental processes started by this union and that lead to the newborn with arms and legs, eyes and ears, neurons and muscle tissue are more fully described in Chapter 4. Remarkably, however, nearly every one of the millions of different cells in the newborn, whether specialized for bone or skin, heart or brain, or in some other way, contains the same genetic blueprint established in the initial zygote. The rare exceptions include the red blood cells, which have no nucleus, and the gametes, which contain only twenty-three chromosomes.

Y chromosome Smaller of the two sex chromosomes associated with genetic determination of sex. Normally males have one Y chromosome; females, none.

zygote Fertilized egg cell.

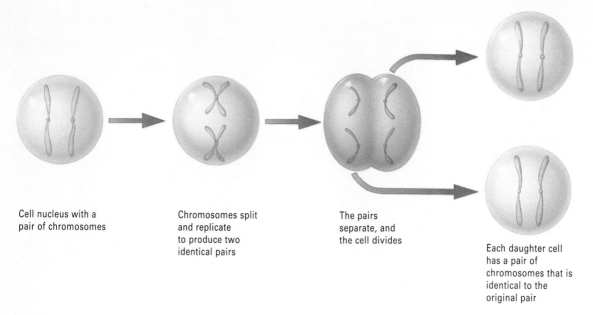

Cell nucleus with a
pair of chromosomes

Chromosomes split
and replicate
to produce two
identical pairs

The pairs
separate, and
the cell divides

Each daughter cell
has a pair of
chromosomes that is
identical to the
original pair

FIGURE 3.4

The Process of Mitosis

The process of mitotic cell division generates virtually all the cells of the body except the gametes. During mitosis, each chromosome replicates to form two chromosomes with identical genetic blueprints. As the cell divides, one member of each identical pair becomes a member of each of the daughter cells. In this manner complete genetic endowment is replicated in nearly every cell of the body.

mitosis   Process of cell division taking place in most cells of the human body that results in a full complement of forty-six chromosomes in each cell; reproduces identical genetic material in succeeding generations of cells.

meiosis   Process of cell division that takes place to form the gametes; normally results in twenty-three chromosomes in each human egg and sperm cell rather than the full complement of forty-six chromosomes.

How does this extraordinary ability for DNA to duplicate itself from one cell to the next or from one generation to the next take place? The division process for most cells is called **mitosis.** During mitosis, genetic material in the nucleus is duplicated so that a full complement of DNA becomes available to each new cell. The process of cell division associated with the gametes is called **meiosis.** As a result of this process, each egg and sperm cell receives only twenty-three of the normal array of forty-six chromosomes.

In *mitosis,* before cell division occurs, the chemical bonds linking the nucleotides to form the rungs of the DNA ladder begin to weaken. Each base pair separates as if each nucleotide is being unzipped from its complementary nucleotide on the opposite side. While this process is taking place, additional nucleotides are being manufactured in the cell. Because each type of nucleotide can connect with only one other type, these newly formed molecules can only rebuild the missing components of the ladder in their original sequence. The resulting two replicas of the original DNA ladder are known as *sister chromatids,* both with the same sequence of base pairs. At this phase of cell division the chromosome appears x-shaped because the sister chromatids remain attached at the *centromere,* a genetically inactive region where the chromosome looks as if it has been pinched. As cell division proceeds, the centromere finally splits. Now the two separate and complete chromosomes migrate away from each other to become members of two separate new daughter cells, as depicted in Figure 3.4.

Meiosis, the process of cell division resulting in twenty-three chromosomes in the egg and sperm cells, actually involves *two* successive generations of cell divisions. In the first stage, each of the forty-six chromosomes replicates to form a pair of identical sister chromatids joined at the centromere. However, before the chromatids split apart, the cell divides. Each of the resulting two cells receives only twenty-three chromosomes, one from each of the twenty-

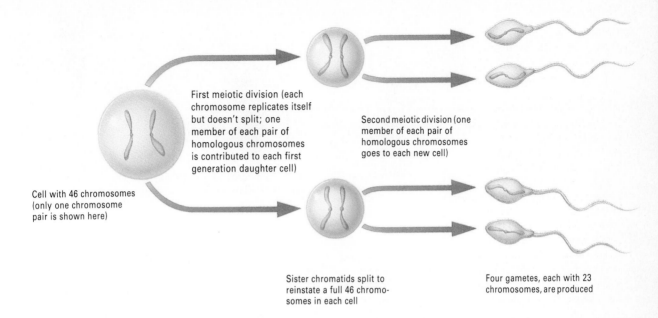

First meiotic division (each chromosome replicates itself but doesn't split; one member of each pair of homologous chromosomes is contributed to each first generation daughter cell)

Cell with 46 chromosomes (only one chromosome pair is shown here)

Second meiotic division (one member of each pair of homologous chromosomes goes to each new cell)

Sister chromatids split to reinstate a full 46 chromosomes in each cell

Four gametes, each with 23 chromosomes, are produced

FIGURE 3.5

The Process of Meiosis

As meiosis begins, sister chromatids are formed as in mitotic cell division. One member of each pair of homologous chromosomes is then contributed to each first-generation daughter cell. Sister chromatids then split apart to reinstate a full complement of forty-six chromosomes to these cells. In the second meiotic division, one member of each pair of chromosomes is again contributed to each second-generation daughter cell. From these two successive divisions, four cells, each with twenty-three chromosomes, are produced.

three pairs of chromosomes, as pictured in Figure 3.3. But the gamete has not finished forming. In the second stage, the sister chromatids split apart and the two cells divide once more, each again receiving one member of each pair of chromosomes. Thus, from these two successive generations, four cells have been produced, each with twenty-three chromosomes. Figure 3.5 illustrates the process of meiosis.

Random segregation of the twenty-three homologous chromosome pairs in the first stage of meiosis yields over 8 million possible combinations of gametes with one or more different sets of chromosomes. This number, along with an equivalent number of possible unique arrangements from a mate, means that a mother and father have the potential for producing 64 trillion offspring differing by one or more chromosomes. But the potential for genetic variability is actually far greater because of the phenomenon known as **crossing over,** a key part of the first stage of meiosis. Before homologous chromosome pairs are separated by the first cell division, they mysteriously align, and segments of DNA transfer, or cross over, from chromatids on one member of a homologous pair to chromatids on the other member of the pair, as shown in Figure 3.6. As a result of the genetic variability ensured by crossing over, it is virtually impossible for you to have the same genetic makeup as anyone else, even another sibling, unless you are an identical twin, in which case your genetic endowment is based on the same fertilized ovum.

▶ **Roles of nature and nurture**

crossing over Process during the first stage of meiosis when genetic material is exchanged between autosomes.

Gene Expression

We have briefly described key structures of inheritance: nucleotide bases, genes, and chromosomes, and how those structures are replicated in cells of the body, including gametes. But how is this genetic information expressed or

FIGURE 3.6

Crossing Over: The Exchange of Genetic Material Between Chromosomes

In the process known as crossing over, genetic material is exchanged between autosomes during the first stage of meiotic cell division. (a) Initially, autosomes that have begun DNA replication and formed sister chromatids align with each other. (b) Genetic material between nonsister chromatids is exchanged. (c) One member of each homologous pair of chromosomes randomly segregates or relocates to two different regions of the parent cell, and the first generation of cell division in meiosis takes place.

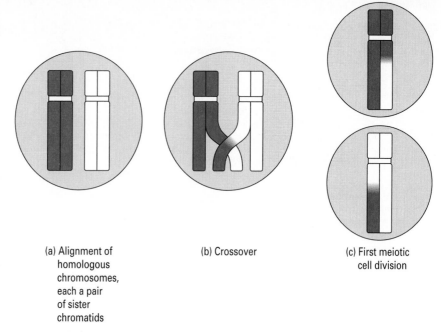

(a) Alignment of
      homologous
      chromosomes,
      each a pair
      of sister
      chromatids

(b) Crossover

(c) First meiotic
      cell division

Source: Adapted from Knowles, 1985.

allele   Alternate form of a specific gene; provides a genetic basis for many individual differences.

homozygous   Genotype in which two alleles of a gene are identical, thus having the same effects on a trait.

heterozygous   Genotype in which two alleles of a gene are different. The effects on a trait will depend on how the two alleles interact.

reflected in the traits or behaviors of the individual human? In raising this question, we confront the phenomenon of how the genotype affects the phenotype—how the underlying genetic blueprint promotes the appearance of blue eyes, baldness, and dark skin, or such complex behaviors as shyness, schizophrenia, and intelligent problem solving. The answer begins with the fact that individual genes often exhibit alternate forms called **alleles.** For example, in the case of a specific gene that affects eye color, the different alleles of that gene are the hereditary factors that contribute to determining whether your eyes are blue or brown or hazel.

Autosomes contain two genes that code for an event, one inherited from the mother and the other from the father, each located at the same place on the two homologous chromosomes. These genes may be identical—that is, have the same allelic form—or they may differ. When both have the same allelic form, a person's genotype is said to be **homozygous** for whatever trait that gene affects. For example, three alleles exist for the gene that governs blood type: A, B, and O. When both inherited versions have the same allelic form— that is, both are A, both B, or both O—a person has a homozygous genotype for this means of classifying blood. But if an individual has inherited two different alleles, that person's genotype is **heterozygous** for the trait the gene affects. Thus, for example, the person with Type AB blood has inherited two different alleles for blood type and is heterozygous for that trait.

The consequences of a homozygous genotype are usually straightforward: the child's phenotype will be influenced by whatever characteristics are specified by that allele. But the outcome of a heterozygous genotype depends on

FIGURE 3.7

The Pattern of Inheritance for Cystic Fibrosis

The inheritance of cystic fibrosis is one of many traits and diseases that is influenced by a single pair of genes. In this figure, F symbolizes a normal allele and f symbolizes the allele for cystic fibrosis. When parents with a heterozygous genotype for this disease have children, their offspring may inherit a homozygous genotype with normal alleles (FF), a heterozygous genotype with one normal and one abnormal allele (Ff), or a homozygous genotype with two abnormal alleles (ff). Because the normal allele dominates, children with a heterozygous genotype will not exhibit cystic fibrosis. When both alleles carry genetic information for the disease, however, cystic fibrosis will occur.

FATHER'S GENOTYPE (Ff)

Meiosis

	F sperm	f sperm
F ovum	FF Zygote (Homozygous) Phenotype–Normal	Ff Zygote (Heterozygous) Phenotype–Normal
f ovum	fF Zygote (Heterozygous) Phenotype–Normal	ff Zygote (Homozygous) Phenotype–Cystic Fibrosis

MOTHER'S GENOTYPE (Ff)

Meiosis

dominant allele Allele whose characteristics are reflected in the phenotype even when part of a heterozygous genotype. Its genetic characteristics tend to mask the characteristics of other alleles.

recessive allele Allele whose characteristics do not tend to be expressed when part of a heterozygous genotype. Its genetic characteristics tend to be masked by other alleles.

how the alleles influence each other. For some genes, the child's phenotype will show the effects of only one of the two alleles. When this happens, the allele whose characteristics are observed in the phenotype is considered **dominant;** the allele whose influence is not evident in the phenotype is considered **recessive.** For example, a person who inherits both an A and O allele for blood type will still be classified as having Type A; the allele for Type A is dominant; the allele for Type O, recessive.

Cystic fibrosis, a leading cause of childhood death among children of European ancestry in the United States, provides another example of a dominant-recessive relationship between alleles of a gene. The vast majority of Americans inherit a gene pair that does not include the allele for cystic fibrosis and thus have a homozygous genotype that contributes to a normal phenotype. About one in twenty people, however, has a heterozygous genotype in which one allele is normal, but the other carries the genetic information that leads to cystic fibrosis. The normal allele is *dominant.* Thus, someone who is heterozygous for this condition can lead an ordinary, productive life. But should two individuals, each with a heterozygous genotype, have children, some of the children can be expected to inherit two normal alleles, some both a normal and an abnormal allele, and some two abnormal alleles for cystic fibrosis (see Figure 3.7). In the latter homozygous condition, the two recessive abnormal alleles are no longer masked by a normal allele; children with these two abnormal alleles (about one in every two thousand newborns in the United States) will suffer from cystic fibrosis, a disease that some day may be treated by *gene therapy,* the replacement of the allele that codes for cystic fibrosis by a normal allele.

For other genes, the child's phenotype will reflect the influence of both alleles, either in some blended form intermediate to the pattern expressed when the alleles are homozygous or in some unblended form in which elements or characteristics of both alleles are evident. An individual's mature height, for example, is probably affected by several genes. Nevertheless, some of the specific genes that have a bearing on height are likely expressed as a blend of the two alleles inherited from the parents (Mange & Mange, 1990). When the characteristics of both alleles are observed in some unblended form, the alleles exhibit **codominance.** For example, a child with Type AB blood has inherited an allele for Type A blood from one parent and another allele for Type B blood from the other parent.

A number of traits and characteristics of individuals are affected by single genes exhibiting dominant-recessive patterns between alleles (see Table 3.1). But we must be cautious in drawing inferences about these dominant-recessive relationships, even for the characteristics listed in Table 3.1. Many traits are **polygenic**—that is, determined by more than one and possibly many genes. Eye color, for example, although recognized to be largely governed by the dominant-recessive relationship between alleles of a single gene, is influenced by other genes as well. A further complication is that determining whether two alleles exhibit a dominant-recessive pattern, some intermediate blend, or a codominant relationship depends on the yardstick of measurement we use (Mange & Mange, 1990). We will see this chameleon-like quality of allele relationships later when we discuss sickle-cell anemia, a condition that affects a high proportion of individuals in some African and African American populations. Depending on whether sickle cell anemia is measured in terms of its implications for medical care, certain behavioral limitations, or biochemical analysis of the blood, it can be considered to have a recessive, a blended, or a codominant expression.

▶ **Roles of nature and nurture**

Gene Functioning and Regulation of Development

How do genes influence the development of a phenotype? Although exceptions are known to exist, one fundamental principle is that genetic information is conveyed from the DNA in the cell's nucleus to the *cytoplasm,* the complex of organic and inorganic substances in the cell outside the nucleus. This process is carried out by *ribonucleic acid,* or *RNA,* a molecule somewhat similar to DNA. RNA copies segments of the nucleotide sequences making up genes and then moves from the nucleus to the cytoplasm. The message carried by the RNA undergoes a series of biochemical steps that eventually accomplishes the production of complex enzymes or proteins that give the cell its unique ability to function. Enzymes act as catalysts, promoting additional biochemical reactions whose presence and timing are fundamental to the development and operation of all organs and systems of the human body. Thus, our appearance and our behavior are, in part, the end result of an extensive chain of biochemical processes started by the instructions carried in the genotype.

codominance   Condition in which individual, unblended characteristics of two alleles are reflected in the phenotype.

polygenic   Phenotypic characteristic influenced by two or more genes.

phenylketonuria (PKU)   Autosomal recessive disorder involving protein metabolism; can lead to severe mental retardation. Dietary intervention can dramatically reduce negative impact.

The varying initial information in alleles of a gene may cause one or more biochemical events in the chain to be modified, sometimes in substantial ways. Such a modification occurs, for example, in **phenylketonuria,** or **PKU,** a genetic condition in which *phenylalanine,* an amino acid in milk and other foods, is unable to be metabolized as it is by most individuals. One outcome for those with PKU can be severe mental retardation. Remember, however, that a phenotype is the product of the interaction between genotype and environment. Thus, extrinsic factors can promote or disrupt developmental processes initiated by the genotype. In the case of PKU, environmental intervention in the

TABLE 3.1

Alleles of Genes That Display a Dominant and Recessive Pattern of Phenotypic Expression

Dominant Traits	Recessive Traits
Brown eyes	Gray, green, blue, hazel eyes
Curly hair	Straight hair
Normal hair	Baldness
Dark hair	Light or blond hair
Nonred hair (blond, brunette)	Red hair
Normal skin coloring	Albinism (lack of pigment)
Immunity to poison ivy	Susceptibility to poison ivy
Normal skin	Xeroderma pigmentosum (heavy freckling and skin cancers)
Thick lips	Thin lips
Roman nose	Straight nose
Cheek dimples	No dimples
Extra, fused, or short digits	Normal digits
Double-jointedness	Normal joints
Normal color vision	Red-green color blindness
Farsightedness	Normal vision
Normal vision	Congenital eye cataracts
Retinoblastoma (cancer of the eye)	Normal eye development
Normal hearing	Congenital deafness
Type A blood	Type O blood
Type B blood	Type O blood
Rh-positive blood	Rh-negative blood
Normal blood clotting	Hemophilia
Normal metabolism	Phenylketonuria
Normal blood cells	Sickle cell anemia
Familial hypercholesterolemia (error of fat metabolism)	Normal cholesteral level at birth
Wilms tumor (cancer of the kidney)	Normal kidney
Huntington's chorea	Normal brain and body maturation
Normal respiratory and gastrointestinal functioning	Cystic fibrosis
Normal neural and physical development	Tay-Sachs disease

form of reducing phenylalanine in the diet can help prevent severe mental retardation. Here, then, is an excellent example illustrating that genes do not have all the information built into them to cause particular developmental outcomes; external factors interact with the genotype to yield a specific phenotype.

Consider another example of genotype-environment interaction, one of less significance for individual differences and of more importance for development in all humans. Most mammals are able to manufacture their own vitamin C. At some time in the early evolution of the human genome, however, a **mutation,** or sudden change in the genetic material underlying this capacity, took place. The mutation may have occurred spontaneously or in response to some environmental condition, but it became a permanent part of the human genome. That change left humans unable to biochemically produce their own vitamin C. As a result, we, but not most other mammals, must eat fresh fruits and vegetables or other vitamin-fortified foods to obtain it. Otherwise we suffer from *scurvy,* a potentially fatal disease that gained public notice in the seventeenth and eighteenth centuries when sailors fell ill during long voyages. All humans inherit this genetic limitation involving synthesis of vitamin C. Fortunately, an environment that permits humans to receive a normal diet serves to prevent scurvy.

Many mysteries remain concerning how genes influence development. For example, humans are estimated to have about 100,000 **structural genes,** genes that code for the production of different kinds of enzymes and other proteins governing the physiological functions of a cell. Yet structural genes account for only about 3 percent of the 100 million nucleotide pairs estimated to be in the human genome (National Research Council, 1988). Large segments of DNA interspersed both within the boundaries of a gene and between genes do not code for the production of proteins. One recent finding is the discovery of other types of genes, called **regulator genes,** that start and stop the functioning of structural genes. Many structural genes do not always function immediately after conception and continuously throughout development. They turn on and off (Plomin, 1987). Regulator genes appear to be responsive to environmental signals, factors within and from outside the cell itself, to determine when structural genes become activated. Such genes would help explain how cells become differentiated—for example, how a nerve cell, liver cell, or muscle cell is formed despite their identical genetic makeup.

Vast networks of structural, regulator, and probably other kinds of genes interact, not just with themselves, but with the environment in which they operate, to affect development. Some may speed or slow the timing and organization of developmental events (Ambros & Horvitz, 1984). For example, one short sequence of 180 nucleotide pairs found among numerous genes in organisms as different as insects and humans may be especially important in *pattern formation,* helping to organize embryonic development so that the various organs of the body are positioned alike in every member of the species (Brownlee, 1987; Gould, 1985).

No single gene, of course, codes for development in the broad sense of determining childhood, adolescence, or adulthood. Complex human activities are affected by many genes, but how they influence the many behaviors of interest to psychologists remains largely unknown. Nonetheless, the consequences of several specific gene mutations and chromosomal disturbances are easily rec-

mutation   Sudden change in molecular structure of a gene; may occur spontaneously or be caused by an environmental event such as radiation. Some mutations are lethal, but others are not and may be passed on from one generation to the next in the form of alleles of a gene.

structural gene   Gene responsible for the production of enzymes and other protein molecules. Humans are estimated to have about 100,000 structural genes, some of which have been located on particular chromosomes.

regulator gene   Gene that switches other genes on and off.

ognized and have serious repercussions for development. We examine some of these gene and chromosomal abnormalities now to further illustrate the contribution of the genotype to human development.

GENE AND CHROMOSOMAL ABNORMALITIES

Changes in genes, or *mutations,* introduce genetic diversity among individuals. Mutations occur relatively often. Nearly half of all human conceptions have been estimated to have some kind of genetic or chromosomal error (Plomin, DeFries, & McClearn, 1990). Most of these conceptions are lost through spontaneous abortion. A few mutations have little impact, but others can have enduring, usually negative, consequences, especially when the mutation occurs very early after conception to affect much of an individual's development. If the mutation in a single gene is not immediately devastating, it may be inherited from one generation to the next, a major way different alleles of a gene are established in populations of individuals. Still other disorders can be linked to disturbances involving the larger structural units of inheritance, the chromosomes.

Between three and four thousand different disorders associated with specific genes, some inherited from parents and grandparents and some occurring as mutations early in development, have been identified in humans (National Research Council, 1988; DeLisi, 1988). Many additional inherited gene disorders may be discovered in the near future as the human genome is mapped more completely.

Gene Disorders

An estimated 100,000 infants are born each year with some kind of disorder caused by a single dominant or recessive gene. For about 20,000 of these babies the problem is serious (Knowles, 1985). Table 3.2 lists a few of the more important gene disorders that are currently known. Only about 3 percent are completely understood in terms of their genetic locus and biochemical consequences (National Research Council, 1988). The effects of inherited disorders are often evident at birth (*congenital*), but the consequences of some are not observed until childhood or even late adulthood. We will discuss several dominant and recessive disorders to illustrate their effects on development and the medical interventions and treatments they engender.

Huntington's Disease: A Dilemma for Genetic Counseling About twenty-five thousand Americans have **Huntington's disease.** Many more are at risk for developing it as they enter their adult years. Because Huntington's disease is caused by a dominant gene, each child with an affected parent has a 50 percent chance of acquiring it. The disease continues to be transmitted from one generation to the next since its onset is usually delayed until an individual is thirty-five to forty years of age. By this time, of course, before its symptoms begin to appear, a carrier may have children. The symptoms, which often appear slowly but relentlessly increase in severity over a period of about

Huntington's disease Dominant genetic disorder characterized by involuntary movements of the limbs, mental deterioration, and premature death. Symptoms appear between thirty and fifty years of age and death within twenty years of onset of these symptoms.

Disorder	Estimated Frequency (live births in U.S.)	Phenotype, Prognosis, and Prenatal Detection
Autosomal Dominant Disorders		
Familial Alzheimer's Disease	Unknown.	Premature onset of loss of cognitive and social functioning often characteristic of senility. Gene located on chromosome 21. Prenatal detection possible.
Huntington's Disease	1 in 18,000.	See text. Gene located on chromosome 4.
Marfan Syndrome	1 in 5,000–25,000.	Phenotype tall, lean, long limbed, with gaunt face (some believe Abraham Lincoln had syndrome). Frequent eye problems. Cardiac failure in young adulthood common. Suicide second most common cause of death. Associated with increased paternal age.
Neurofi- bromatosis (von Reckling- hausen's disease)	1 in 2,500–3,300.	Symptoms range from a few pale brown spots on skin to severe tumors affecting peripheral nervous system and visibly distorting appearance. Minimal intellectual deficits in about 40% of cases. Gene for major form located on chromosome 17. Gene for other form located on chromosome 22. Prenatal detection possible.
Autosomal Recessive Disorders		
Albinism	1 in 10,000–20,000. Several forms; frequency differs among various populations. Most common form occurs in about 1 in 15,000 African Americans; 1 in 40,000 Caucasians; but much more frequently among some Native American tribes (1 in 200 among Hopi and Navajo, 1 in 132 among San Blas Indians of Panama).	Affected individuals lack pigment *melanin*. Extreme sensitivity to sunlight and visual problems. Prenatal detection possible.
Congenital Hypothy- roidism	1 in 3,000 of European origin.	Dwarfism, severe mental deficiency. Treatment with thyroid hormones successful but must be continued throughout life. All states currently screen newborns for disease.
Cystic Fibrosis	Most common genetic disease in Caucasian populations in U.S., affecting about 1 in 1,600–2,000. One in 20–25 Americans is carrier. Very rare among African American and Asian American populations.	Respiratory tract becomes clogged with mucous; lungs likely to become infected. Gene located on chromosome 7. Death usually before age 20, but individuals may have children. Prognosis for females poorer than for males. Therapy helps delay effects. Prenatal detection possible. Some states regularly screen newborns for disease.
Galacto- semia	1 in 40,000.	Mental retardation, cataracts, cirrhosis of the liver caused by accumulation of galactose in body tissues because of absence of enzyme to convert this sugar into glucose. Those heterozygous for this condition have half the normal enzyme activity, but this is enough for normal development. Galactose-free diet only treatment. Prenatal detection possible. 34 states currently screen newborns for defect.

Disorder	Estimated Frequency (live births in U.S.)	Phenotype, Prognosis, and Prenatal Detection
Phenylketonuria	1 in 14,000. Somewhat higher rate of incidence in Caucasian and Asian than in African American populations.	See text. Prenatal detection possible.
Sickle Cell Anemia	1 in 600 African Americans. Also frequently found in malaria-prone regions of world.	See text. Prenatal detection possible.
Tay-Sachs Disease	1 in 3,600 Ashkenazic Jews. Very rare in other populations. 1 in 30 Ashkenazic Jews are carriers; in other populations 1 in 300 are carriers.	Signs of mental retardation, blindness, deafness, and paralysis begin 1 to 6 months after birth. Death normally occurs by 3 or 4 years of age. Prenatal detection possible.
Thalassemia (Cooley's anemia)	1 in 800–2,500 in populations of Greek and Italian descent. Much less frequent in other populations.	Severe anemia beginning within 2 to 3 months of birth, stunted growth, increased susceptibility to infections. Death usually occurs in 20s or 30s. Prenatal detection possible.

Sex-linked Disorders

Disorder	Estimated Frequency (live births in U.S.)	Phenotype, Prognosis, and Prenatal Detection
Color Blindness (red-green)	About 1 in 100 males of Caucasian descent see no red or green. About 1 in 15 males of Caucasian descent experience some decrease in sensitivity to red or green colors.	Those who are completely red-green color blind lack either green-sensitive or red-sensitive pigment for distinguishing these colors and see them as yellow. Those who show lesser sensitivity to red or green perceive reds as reddish browns, bright greens as tan, and olive greens as brown.
Duchenne Muscular Dystrophy	1 in 3,500 males. Most common of many different forms of muscular dystrophy. Most forms, including Duchenne, are X linked.	Progressive muscle weakness and muscle fiber loss. Mental retardation in about ⅓ of cases. Few ever live long enough to reproduce. Responsible gene located on short arm of X chromosome; appears to be massive in number of nucleotide pairs. Prenatal detection possible.
Hemophilia	1 in 10,000 Caucasian male births for the most common form.	Failure of blood to clot. Several different forms; not all are sex linked. Queen Victoria of England carrier for the most common form. Potential for bleeding to death, but administration of clot-inducing drugs and blood transfusions reduces hazard. At risk for exposure to blood-transmitted diseases such as AIDS. Prenatal detection possible.
Lesch-Nylan Disease	1 in 15,000. In more than ⅓ of affected males, cause is new mutations.	Recurrent vomiting, cerebral palsy, and mental retardation; self-mutilation, including gnawing of fingers, lips, or mouth. Death at relatively early age. Prenatal detection possible.

Sources: Based on Dorozynski, 1986; Fishler et al., 1987; Grady, 1987; Headings, 1988; Knowles, 1985; Lowitzer, 1987; Martin, 1987; National Genetics Foundation, 1987; Ostrer & Hejtmancik, 1988; Plomin, DeFries, & McClearn, 1990; Scriver & Clow, 1988; Smith et al., 1988.

TABLE 3.2

Some Inherited Gene Disorders

fifteen to twenty years, usually include personality changes, depression, a gradual loss of motor control and memory, and other mental impairments.

Recent progress in molecular genetics now permits testing to determine whether an individual is likely to have inherited Huntington's disease. Unfortunately, however, it cannot be cured or treated at the present time. Thus, the decision to carry out such screening presents an enormous conflict for those who have a family history of the disease; the test results can provide a potentially devastating glimpse into their future. *Genetic counselors,* professionals who advise parents about whether their children may or may not inherit a genetic defect, are also confronted with the ethical dilemma of whether to encourage prospective parents to have the test since its results are important for determining if offspring are at risk for the disease (Grady, 1987). Tests can also be conducted prenatally to determine whether the fetus has a 50 percent risk of eventually manifesting the disease or a far lower risk.

Sickle Cell Anemia: A Problem for Genetic Classification   **Sickle cell anemia** is a genetic disorder whose incidence is extremely high in many regions of West Africa and around the Mediterranean basin. It is also found in about one of every six hundred African Americans and in high numbers among Greek Americans and others in the United States whose ancestors came from areas where malaria commonly occurs. Sickle cell anemia is generally considered to be a recessive autosomal disorder associated with an allele located on chromosome 11. The genetic defect introduces a change in a single amino acid in hemoglobin, the molecule permitting the red blood cells to carry oxygen. As a result, red blood cells of individuals with sickle cell anemia become crescent shaped rather than round. These sickle-shaped cells are ineffective in transporting oxygen; they also survive for a much shorter duration than normal red blood cells, and the bone marrow has difficulty replacing them. The consequence is often anemia, jaundice, low resistance to infection, and severe pain and damage to various organs when the distorted cells block small blood vessels.

More than 2 million, or about one in every ten, African Americans are carriers of the sickle cell allele. These individuals, who possess a heterozygous genotype, have the **sickle cell trait.** Individuals with sickle cell trait manufacture a relatively small proportion of cells with abnormal hemoglobin. Few of these individuals show symptoms of sickle cell anemia, and most live normal lives. But insufficient oxygen can trigger sickling of red blood cells in those who have the trait. Oxygen depletion can occur in high altitude regions, when flying in unpressurized airplane cabins, or after strenuous exercise. However, carriers of the sickle cell allele are more resistant to malaria than are individuals who have normal hemoglobin. This adaptive feature of the allele probably accounts for the high incidence and persistence of the trait in populations where malaria is present.

Sickle cell trait provides a good illustration of the arbitrary nature of classifying alleles as dominant, recessive, or as bearing some other phenotypic relationship to each other (Mange & Mange, 1990). From a medical or clinical perspective, the sickle cell allele is considered recessive; an individual is likely to suffer anemia and need hospitalization only when the genotype is homozygous and both alleles code for the production of the abnormal red blood cells. From a broader social perspective, however, the sickle cell allele reflects an

sickle cell anemia   Genetic blood disorder common in regions of Africa and other areas of the world where malaria is found and among descendants of these regions. Abnormal blood cells are unable to carry adequate amounts of oxygen.

sickle cell trait   Symptoms shown by those possessing a heterozygous genotype for sickle cell anemia.

Individuals who suffer from sickle cell anemia, a genetically inherited disorder, have a large proportion of crescent-shaped red blood cells like the ones shown here. Normal red blood cells are round. Sickle-shaped cells are ineffective in transporting oxygen and may cause damage to various organs and pain by blocking small blood vessels.

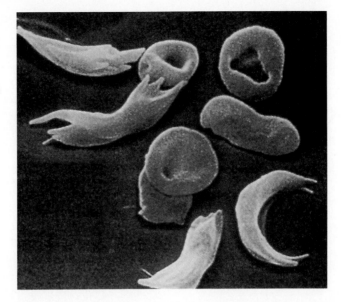

intermediate phenotypic pattern; individuals with a heterozygous genotype have *some* sickled cells, although far fewer than those homozygous for the condition and suffering sickle cell anemia. Nevertheless, individuals with the sickle cell trait *may* endure symptoms of sickle cell anemia under conditions of oxygen deprivation. From the perspective of biochemists, however, who analyze chains of amino acids, normal and abnormal alleles are really codominant; both kinds of chains are present in heterozygotes. In other words, as we pointed out earlier in our discussion of phenotypic expression, the label we use to describe the relationship between two alleles really depends on the level of the phenotype we are observing.

▶ **Roles of nature and nurture**

Phenylketonuria: An Environmentally Modifiable Genetic Disorder
Phenylketonuria (PKU), a recessive metabolic disorder affecting about one in every fourteen thousand children born in the United States, is caused by the mutation of a gene on chromosome 12. It was one of the first gene disorders to be fully understood at the biochemical level and provides a good illustration of how genes interact with the environment to foster a particular phenotype or capacity. Treatment in the form of changing the child's environment—in this case, diet—can be initiated to reduce the effects of this debilitating genetic disorder. As indicated earlier, when PKU is inherited, the child's liver is unable to produce an enzyme responsible for metabolizing *phenylalanine,* an amino acid commonly found in milk and high-protein foods such as meat. As a result, phenylalanine and other metabolic products accumulate in the blood, and the nervous system becomes deprived of needed nutrients. The eventual consequences are often convulsions, severe mental retardation, hyperactivity, and other behavioral problems. At one time, PKU contributed to the institutionalization of large numbers of mentally retarded children.

An infant with PKU is normal at birth. Within six months, however, if the condition is untreated, developmental retardation will begin; if the condition remains untreated, mental retardation becomes severe by four years of age.

Fortunately, screening performed shortly after birth can detect elevated levels of phenylalanine. Today, nearly all states in the United States require such screening. An infant identified as having PKU can then be placed on a diet low in phenylalanine to prevent its more serious effects. Debate continues, however, on how to monitor the diet effectively and how long it should be maintained. Experts agree the diet must be started relatively early, within the first few months after birth, to be most effective. At one time, researchers believed the diet could be discontinued when a child reached six to eight years of age. Today, researchers recommend early and continued adherence to phenylalanine-restricted diets at least through adolescence to ensure nearly normal mental development (Fishler et al., 1987).

The dietary treatment of children with PKU can prevent the more serious consequences of this genetic disorder, but a completely normal prognosis for these children remains outside the realm of current treatment programs (Scriver & Clow, 1988). The diet is difficult to maintain; it requires a careful balance between excessive phenylalanine to prevent neural damage and sufficient nutrients to permit reasonably normal growth. Blood tests may be needed as often as twice a month to keep metabolite concentrations within an acceptable range, a regimen for which child, parents, and testing centers may be ill prepared. Even under optimal dietary and testing conditions, children with PKU show some growth and intellectual deficiencies in comparison to other children. They are also somewhat more likely to display deviant behaviors such as mannerisms, hyperactivity, and reduced social responsivity (Smith, Beasley, Wolff, & Ades, 1988). The bland and unappetizing diet can be a source of conflict between child and caregiver as well, creating management problems within households attempting to lead relatively normal lives (Scriver & Clow, 1988).

Even those who successfully reach adulthood may not escape further consequences of their inherited disorder. Children born to mothers with PKU often suffer congenital heart defects and mental retardation (Lowitzer, 1987). Elevated levels of phenylalanine in the mother's blood appear to cause serious damage to fetal development. If a mother returns to a low phenylalanine diet before and during pregnancy, the risks can be reduced, but continue to be higher than normal (Lenke & Levy, 1982). Apparently an abnormal intrauterine environment exists in mothers with PKU. While dietary modifications are helpful, this environmental intervention has been unable to eradicate the negative consequences of PKU completely.

Sex-linked Disorders   Relatively few genes are known to exist on the Y chromosome, but the X chromosome carries many. This imbalance has substantial implications for a number of disorders that are said to be **sex linked** because the gene associated with them is carried on the X chromosome. Disorders such as hemophilia, red-green color blindness, and Duchenne muscular dystrophy (see Table 3.2) have nothing to do with differentiation of sex but are sex linked because they are fostered by genes on the X chromosome and, as a consequence, are found much more frequently in males than in females.

As with alleles for autosomes, those that are sex linked often have a dominant-recessive relationship. Thus, females, who inherit two genes for sex-linked traits, one on each of the X chromosomes, are much less likely to dis-

sex linked   Attribute, trait, or disorder inherited from genes located on the X chromosome.

play the deleterious effects associated with an abnormal recessive allele than are males, who, if they inherit the damaging allele, have no second, normal allele to mask its effects. Hemophilia, a condition in which blood does not clot normally, is a good example since it is nearly always associated with a defective gene on the X chromosome. Because the allele for hemophilia is recessive, females who inherit it typically do not exhibit hemophilia; the condition is averted by an ordinary gene on the second X chromosome that promotes normal blood clotting. Unless her father has hemophilia, the X chromosome the female inherits from her father will provide genetic information for normal blood clotting. A female can, however, serve as a carrier. If she possesses a heterozygous genotype for hemophilia, the X chromosome with the abnormal allele has a fifty-fifty chance of being transmitted to either her son or daughter. If the abnormal allele is inherited by a son, he will exhibit hemophilia because the Y chromosome does not contain genetic information to counter the allele's effects. If the abnormal allele is inherited by a daughter, she will be a carrier who may then transmit the allele to her sons and daughters, as has occurred in several interrelated royal families of Europe.

Autosomal Anomalies

Mutations in specific genes are only one of several sources of variation in the human genome. Occasionally whole sections of a chromosome are deleted or duplicated, or an extra chromosome is transmitted to daughter cells during cell division. When this happens, either during meiosis or during early embryonic development, the consequences for normal development are often devastating.

Human embryonic growth virtually never proceeds either when a complete set of autosomes is missing or when an extra set of autosomes is inherited. But **trisomy,** the inheritance of an extra chromosome, may be tolerated. Trisomy has been observed for virtually every set of autosomes. However, the typical outcome for this condition is loss of the zygote or miscarriage in early pregnancy (Boué, Boué, & Gropp, 1985). Nevertheless, human newborns with several different trisomic patterns are known to survive. One of these, **trisomy 21,** or **Down syndrome,** occurs relatively frequently and has a substantial impact on the child's development and the caregiving responsibilities of the child's family and community.

Trisomy 21 (Down Syndrome) Trisomy 21, the most common genetic cause of mental retardation in the United States and many other countries, occurs in one of about seven hundred live births (Patterson, 1987). Physically observable features associated with trisomy 21 include an epicanthal fold of the eye; flattened facial features; poor muscle tone; short stature; and short, broad hands, including an unusual crease in the palms of the hands. Infants with Down syndrome are likely to have congenital heart defects, cataracts or other visual impairments, and deficiencies in the immune system so that susceptibility to infection and leukemia is increased.

Approximately 95 percent of babies born with Down syndrome have an extra twenty-first chromosome because of failure of that autosome to segregate

trisomy Condition in which an extra chromosome is present.

trisomy 21 Inheritance of an extra copy of chromosome 21; associated with a distinct set of physical features and moderate to severe mental retardation. Commonly known as *Down syndrome.*

This child has trisomy 21, or Down syndrome. Although trisomy 21 is the leading cause of mental retardation in the United States, when given the opportunity to learn, many children with this chromosomal anomaly can acquire some skills in reading and writing.

appropriately during meiosis. The majority of these errors originate in egg cells, but a small percentage stem from errors of meiosis during the production of sperm cells (Stewart, Hassold, & Kunit, 1988). Karyotypes of another 4 percent of infants with Down syndrome reveal that a part of chromosome 21, perhaps as little as its bottom third, has been shifted to another chromosome (National Genetics Foundation, 1987; Patterson, 1987). Another 1 percent of infants born with Down syndrome display a *mosaic* genotype, that is, have chromosomal deviations in only a portion of their body cells as a result of an error in normal mitotic cell division during early embryonic development. The severity of Down syndrome in these individuals seems to be related to the proportion of cells exhibiting trisomy.

The probability of giving birth to an infant with Down syndrome increases with the age of the mother (see Table 3.3). Although mothers over age thirty-five give birth to only about 16 percent of all babies, they bear over half the infants with Down syndrome. The age of the father shows little relationship to the occurrence of Down syndrome. To explain this finding, experts have often proposed an "older egg" hypothesis. According to this view, the mother's egg cells, which have begun the first steps in meiosis even before her own birth, undergo some change as a result of aging, either because of the simple passage of time or because of increased exposure to potentially hazardous biological and environmental conditions. As a consequence, the older egg cells, those released from the ovaries later in the childbearing years, become more susceptible to chromosomal errors while undergoing the final steps of meiosis that take place when ovulation occurs.

Recent research, however, has not confirmed that errors occur more often in the ova of older than of younger mothers (Stewart et al., 1988). Thus, other researchers have proposed a "relaxed selection" hypothesis to account for the increased frequency of Down syndrome in older mothers. According to this view, older mothers are less likely than younger mothers to spontaneously abort a zygote with trisomy 21. Though this is a plausible explanation, other research findings fail to support it. For example, Down syndrome caused by the relocation of a part of the twenty-first chromosome to another chromosome is not associated with maternal age. Why is a pregnancy in younger women more likely to end when there is an extra chromosome, but not when other kinds of chromosomal errors occur (Stewart et al., 1988)?

Sixty years ago, an infant born with Down syndrome typically died before ten years of age. Today more than half live over thirty years and a quarter beyond fifty years because of better medical and physical care (Patterson, 1987). Furthermore, a few decades ago, children born with Down syndrome in the United States were never expected to learn to read or write, and many were warehoused in institutions where they seldom received educational training that would foster such abilities. Yet today, many of these children are provided the opportunity to acquire such skills, and some have shown considerable proficiency in reading and writing.

We still have much to learn about Down syndrome. Individuals with trisomy 21 who do survive beyond age thirty-five, for example, frequently develop the same kinds of abnormal brain cells and show the same behavioral symptoms as people who acquire Alzheimer's disease. Alzheimer's disease is characterized by memory and speech disturbances, personality changes, and increasing loss of intellectual functioning, typically in individuals between fifty and seventy-five years of age, although the symptoms may begin much earlier. At least one form of Alzheimer's disease is known to be inherited, and perhaps not surprisingly, the responsible gene appears to be located on chromosome 21.

Structural Aberrations of Autosomes Other changes in the structure of chromosomes, including deletions, duplications, and relocations of *parts* of DNA also occur for all twenty-two pairs of autosomes. As with trisomy, the consequences in most cases are so severe that the pregnancy ends soon after conception. But individuals are occasionally born with aberrations in the composition of chromosomes. For example, deletion of a small segment of the fifth chromosome is responsible for *cri du chat* or *cat-cry syndrome*. Infants with this syndrome exhibit a cry similar to a cat's (and thus its name), severe mental retardation, short stature, and microcephaly (very small head size), as well as

TABLE 3.3

Relationship Between Maternal Age and the Incidence of Down Syndrome

According to the "older egg" hypothesis, an older mother's gametes are more susceptible to chromosomal errors during the final steps of meiosis. This table shows the incidence of Down syndrome among mothers of various ages. One in every 1,500 babies born to mothers aged twenty-one has Down syndrome. For forty-nine-year-old mothers, the incidence is much higher: 1 in every 10 babies has Down syndrome.

Maternal Age	Estimated Frequency of Down Syndrome (live births in U.S.)
21	1/1,500
27	1/1,000
33	1/600
34	1/450
35	1/400
36	1/300
37	1/220
38	1/175
39	1/140
40	1/100
41	1/80
42	1/60
43	1/50
44	1/40
45	1/30
46	1/25
47	1/20
48	1/15
49	1/10

Source: Adapted from Hook, 1982.

other congenital anomalies. Many survive to adulthood. Mental retardation and severe physical deformations often accompany structural aberrations observed in other chromosomes as well.

Sex Chromosome Abnormalities

As we have frequently noted, the twenty-third pair of chromosomes differs for males and females. Males normally have an X and a Y, and females have a pair of X chromosomes. But other variations in the number of sex chromosomes have been reported in humans. For example, an individual may inherit only a single X (XO), an extra chromosome (XXX, XXY, XYY), or even pairs of extra chromosomes (for example, XXXX, XXYY, XXXY). Several of these variations are described in more detail in Table 3.4.

Abnormalities and Phenotypic Variations   Children with sex chromosome anomalies display a wide range of phenotypic expressions. In fact, substantial proportions of individuals with an extra sex chromosome lead normal lives. But when anomalies in the number of sex chromosomes were first identified, a few researchers contended that an extra chromosome was closely linked to an assortment of abnormal and socially unacceptable behaviors. For example, in the 1960s several published reports claimed the XYY pattern existed surprisingly often in the karyotypes of hard-to-manage retarded men and highly aggressive inmates in penal institutions and was the basis for their antisocial behaviors. Despite a number of methodological problems with this research, the belief that XYY males are more aggressive than other males was widely disseminated by the media. The extra Y chromosome was even used in courts of law to argue for leniency for criminals who inherited this chromosomal pattern. Today we know that the extra Y chromosome is linked to above-average height and sometimes lowered intelligence. This physical and intellectual combination may account for the slightly elevated percentage of XYY men in prison compared with normal XY males. The crimes these men commit, however, are no more violent than those committed by other men (Witkin et al., 1976).

Researchers have discovered wide variation in the phenotypic expression associated with sex chromosome anomalies, even when bearing the same karyotype. These variations may be due to environmental factors. Bruce Bender and his colleagues at the University of Colorado School of Medicine have been studying forty-six children with sex chromosome abnormalities such as those described in Table 3.4 (Bender, Linden, & Robinson, 1987). These children, born between 1964 and 1974, were identified by screening forty thousand consecutive births in the Denver area. Children with chromosome abnormalities were more likely to have neuromotor, psychosocial, school, and language impairments compared with control subjects, siblings who had normal sex chromosome complements (see Figure 3.8). But this was true for school and psychosocial problems in dysfunctional families only—that is, those families frequently exposed to severe stress such as drug abuse or death, lacking effective parenting skills, or living in poverty. In families in which such problems were absent, children with sex chromosome abnormalities showed no greater evidence of school or psychosocial problems than con-

▶ **Roles of nature and nurture**

trol children, although they did show more neuromotor and language impairment. Thus, children with sex chromosome abnormalities may be vulnerable to environmental events; a normal complement of sex chromosomes may help to buffer the potentially adverse consequences of environmental stressors.

Fragile X Syndrome Genetic researchers have recently identified a structural anomaly that consists of a pinched or constricted site near the end of the

TABLE 3.4

Examples of Observed Sex Chromosome Abnormalities

Disorder	Estimated Frequency (live births in U.S.)	Phenotype and Prognosis
XO (Turner syndrome)	1 in 1,200–2,500 females (90% are spontaneously aborted)	*Characteristics.* Short stature, usually normal psychomotor development, but limited development of secondary sexual characteristics. Failure to menstruate and sterility due to underdeveloped ovaries. Webbed, short neck. Near-average range of intelligence but serious deficiencies in spatial ability and directional sense. *Prognosis.* Increased stature and sexual development, including menstruation, but not fertility, can be induced through administration of estrogen and other hormones. In vitro fertilization permits carrying of child when adult.
XXX (Triple-X syndrome or "superfemale")	1 in 500–1,200 females	*Characteristics.* Not generally distinguishable. Some evidence of delay in speech and language development, lack of coordination, poor academic performance and immature behavior. Sexual development usually normal. *Prognosis.* Many are essentially normal, but greater proportion have language, cognitive, and social-emotional problems.
XXY (Klinefelter syndrome)	1 in 500–1,000 males (increased risk among older mothers)	*Characteristics.* Tend to be tall, beardless, with feminine body contour, high-pitched voice. Some evidence for poor auditory short-term memory and difficulty with reading. Testes underdeveloped, individuals sterile. *Prognosis.* Many with normal IQ, but about 20% may have occasional mild to moderate retardation.
XYY ("supermale")	1 in 700–1000 males	*Characteristics.* Above-average height, near-average range of intelligence. *Prognosis.* Most lead normal lives and have normal offspring. Higher proportion than normal incarcerated, but crimes no more violent than those of XY men.

Sources: Based on Bender, Linden, & Robinson, 1987; Brook, 1986; Gorlin, 1977; Knowles, 1985; Linden et al., 1988; Plomin, DeFries, & McClearn, 1990; National Genetics Foundation, 1987.

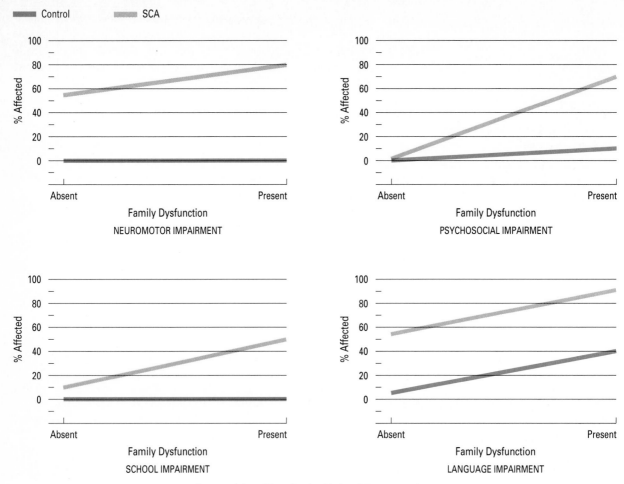

FIGURE 3.8

The Influence of Family Dysfunction on Children with Sex Chromosome Anomalies

Source: Adapted from Bender, Linden, & Robinson, 1987.

Sex chromosome anomalies (SCA) are associated with a substantial range of phenotypic expressions, possibly because of environmental factors. A longitudinal study of SCA children showed that they are more likely to exhibit neuromotor, psychosocial, school, and language impairments than control children (normal siblings). However, compared with siblings, SCA children exhibit more psychosocial and school impairments only when they are members of dysfunctional families. Children with sex chromosome anomalies may be at greater developmental risk than those with a normal set of sex chromosomes, but for some kinds of problems only when stressful family conditions exist.

fragile X syndrome   Disorder associated with a pinched region of the X chromosome; a leading genetic cause of mental retardation in males.

long arm of the X chromosome. This anomaly, termed **fragile X syndrome,** affects about one in every thousand infants and can be inherited from one generation to the next. Fragile X syndrome has attracted widespread attention primarily because of its link to mental retardation. In fact, it runs a close second to Down syndrome as the most frequent known genetic cause of mental retardation in the United States (Hagerman, 1987).

Males with fragile X syndrome commonly have a long narrow face, large or prominent ears, and large testes. Cardiac defects and relaxed ligaments (permitting, for example, hyperextension of finger joints) are also frequent components of the disorder. Behavioral attributes include poor eye contact and other attentional problems as well as hand flapping, hand biting, and other unusual mannerisms such as mimicry that are frequently associated with *autism,* a disorder in which the child shows little responsiveness to most forms of external stimulation. Females who possess a heterozygous genotype often show some reduction in intelligence and, to a much lesser extent, some of the physical characteristics of the disorder. Most of these women are normal, although they are carriers for the syndrome just as for other sex-linked gene disorders. Fragile X syndrome is probably caused by a single gene on the X chromosome (Nussbaum & Ledbetter, 1986). We include it in our discussion of chromosomal errors, however, because its diagnosis is made on the basis of a change in the chromosomal structure.

GENETIC COUNSELING

Advances in detecting gene and chromosomal defects as well as in understanding the biochemical and metabolic consequences of various inherited disorders have led to a rapidly expanding medical and guidance specialty called **genetic counseling.** Using family histories showing the occurrence of various diseases among ancestors and relatives and the results of diagnostic tests, genetic counselors are able to provide prospective parents with estimates of the likelihood of bearing a child with a specific disorder. For many conditions, genetic counselors today are able to go beyond providing estimates. Through a variety of prenatal tests, they can determine if a particular fetus has a chromosomal abnormality or one of many other kinds of genetic defects.

Prospective parents may wish to consult genetic counselors for a variety of reasons. The National Genetics Foundation indicates that genetic counseling is particularly warranted when a history of disorders is found in a family and in certain other circumstances. Conditions existing among prospective parents and their families that warrant genetic counseling include birth defects, mental retardation, unusual physical features, and medical conditions with a genetic component, such as cancer and heart disease (National Genetics Foundation, 1987). Obtaining family medical histories is usually the first step. If warranted, parental **genetic screening** may be carried out. Tests can now be performed on adults for many genetic disorders to determine if the individual may have a heterozygous genotype for specific conditions. For example, screening can be completed for Tay-Sachs disease in Ashkenazic Jews, sickle cell trait among African Americans, thalassemia for individuals of Mediterranean ancestry, and for other disorders in which a family history raises the possibility that one or both parents are carriers. Assuring couples about the absence of a particular genetic concern is always the preferred message from a genetic counselor, but if hereditary disorders are found to be a possibility, counselors can help couples understand the likelihood of and reasons for various outcomes and the options available in deciding whether to have children.

genetic counseling Medical and counseling specialty concerned with determining and communicating the likelihood that prospective parents will give birth to a baby with a genetic disorder.

genetic screening Systematic search for certain genotypes using a variety of tests to detect individuals at risk for developing genetic anomalies, bearing offspring with potential chromosome or gene defects, or having genetic susceptibility to environmental agents.

Prenatal Screening

If couples at risk for children with a genetic disease elect to conceive, prenatal tests may be carried out for many genetic disorders. These tests, including *amniocentesis, chorionic villus sampling,* and other procedures, are discussed in detail in Chapter 4. They can often replace probabilistic estimates with precise answers about whether a condition is present or absent in the fetus. The number of disorders for which prenatal diagnosis is possible is increasing at a remarkable rate and today stands at over two hundred different defects.

Technical advances in genetic screening have provided many benefits to couples. Parents can often be reassured that their child will be normal with respect to some potential condition. These advances have also led to a number of questions. For example, should screening be mandatory under some conditions, such as when inexpensive procedures are available and treatments exist to help alleviate or minimize the impact of a condition? The discovery that one is a carrier for a genetic disease can have devastating psychological effects. Adequate counseling resources must be planned and provided if screening procedures are to become more widespread. Who should have access to the results of such tests? Should insurance companies be allowed to obtain such information? Should such tests be carried out solely to determine the sex of the baby? These are just a few of the many legal and ethical issues to emerge in this rapidly advancing field.

CONTROVERSY

When Is a Mother a Mother and a Father a Father?

Recent sweeping advances in the field of genetics and reproductive technology have revolutionized human conception and childbearing along with our traditional notions about definitions of motherhood and fatherhood. Parents at risk for children with a genetic disease or couples among the one in six estimated to be unable to have children now have many options in addition to adoption in their efforts to become parents. Each new alternative has brought with it hope for many couples but a tangle of ethical and legal issues as well.

If a male carries a genetic disorder or is infertile, couples may elect *artificial insemination by donor.* In this procedure, a donor, usually anonymous and often selected because of his similarity in physical and other characteristics to a prospective father, contributes sperm that are then artificially provided to the mother when ovulation occurs. Some six thousand to ten thousand children are thought to be conceived by this means every year in the United States (Curie-Cohen, Luttrell, & Shapiro, 1979). Little information exists about how donors are chosen and screened or about how they subsequently feel about being the possible biological father to an unknown number of children. Donors in rural areas have voiced concerns about whether their known children might inadvertently marry and bear offspring with unknown half-siblings (Baran & Pannor, 1989). A greater problem, however, may exist for children conceived in this way. Whereas children are often informed that they have been adopted, children born via artificial insemination are seldom aware that their legal and

Baby M, shown here with her surrogate mother, has been in the center of legal battles over who should be allowed to rear her. New advances in reproductive technology, including in vitro fertilization and surrogate motherhood, have raised medical and social issues that are yet to be fully resolved in our society.

biological fathers are not the same person. Even if told, such children would typically be unable to obtain further information since the approximately thirty sperm banks currently operating in the United States rarely make their records public (Baran & Pannor, 1989).

If a female is the carrier of a genetic disease or is infertile, options include *surrogate motherhood* and *in vitro fertilization*. Surrogate motherhood has sometimes been termed the "renting" of another woman's womb, but this concept is a bit misleading in most cases since the surrogate mother often donates an egg, as well as her womb, for prenatal development. She is thus the biological mother as well as bearer of the child who has been conceived by artificial insemination using the prospective father's sperm (Holbrook, 1990). More recent advances involving in vitro fertilization, in which eggs are removed from a woman's ovaries and fertilized in a laboratory dish before their transfer to a woman's uterus, make it possible for biological and social mother to be one and the same except during the gestational period when a surrogate mother's womb might be used. This technique also permits a woman who cannot conceive normally to sometimes bear her own child.

Legal, medical, and social controversy swirl around both surrogate motherhood and in vitro fertilization (American Fertility Society, 1988; Congregation for the Doctrine of Faith, 1987; Elias & Annas, 1987; Lauritzen, 1990). Legal debates center on who is the rightful father or mother. For example, in one highly publicized case involving Baby M, a woman was impregnated by artificial insemination by a man whose wife was afflicted by multiple sclerosis. According to the contract between the couple and the surrogate mother, the surrogate mother was to receive $10,000 for carrying the child. At birth, she would then surrender the child to the couple for adoption. After delivering the baby, however, she refused to relinquish custody of the child. Who should be the legal parent of such a child? In the Baby M case, the court ruled against the surrogate mother. In another recent case in California, the courts also ruled that a baby conceived from a woman's egg and her husband's sperm via in vitro fertilization and then carried to term by another woman should be reared by the genetic couple rather than the surrogate mother. Yet the debate surrounding these and similar cases continues as the judicial system tries to resolve who is the legal parent when motherhood can be splintered into at least three levels: genetic, gestational, and caregiving or social mother.

Other controversies surround the costly medical procedures and complicated ethical and social issues associated with in vitro fertilization and surrogate motherhood. For example, perhaps as many as two hundred clinics in the United States, many as commercial businesses, provide in vitro fertilization services. But their success has been limited, and perhaps less than 20 percent of their attempts result in live births. Should medical insurance pay the approximately $5,000 it costs per attempt (Holbrook, 1990)? What about meeting the immeasurable psychological costs to parents who repeatedly try and fail to have children using these new technologies? What social and ethical dangers exist in paying for surrogacy arrangements? Will there be increased pressures toward genetic engineering to ensure only healthy offspring? The desire to have their own children is a powerful motive for most couples. New advances in reproductive technology will help many to reach that goal. Yet these new opportunities include risks and uncertainties for defining motherhood and fatherhood that our society has not fully resolved. ■

BEHAVIORAL AND DEVELOPMENTAL GENETICS

Chromosomal errors and alleles of particular genes can have drastic, often devastating, effects on physical, intellectual, and social development, as our previous discussion has indicated. Yet the frequent similarities observed among relatives—the sudden outburst of anger brother shares with brother; the wry sense of humor in a mother and daughter; the musical talent of a grandfather and his grandchildren; and for Jeremy's mother, her son's shy, reserved personality, so reminiscent of her own childhood—are not likely to have been influenced by a single, isolated gene. These phenotypic resemblances may, of course, be inspired by common experiences shared by kin. Still, researchers have often wondered whether these attributes and behaviors, if not regulated by a *single* gene, might reflect a hereditary contribution involving *many* genes. In fact, most attributes and behaviors that signal differences between individuals are undoubtedly influenced by polygenic relationships.

▶ **Roles of nature and nurture**

Behavior geneticists are researchers concerned with learning to what extent the diversity of traits, abilities, and behaviors exhibited by individuals is influenced by combinations of genes versus experience. This focus on the hereditary and experiential basis of individual differences distinguishes behavior geneticists from ethologists, who are interested in understanding the adaptive value of activities such as attachment and aggression that have biologically evolved and are universally shared by members of the same species.

The Methods of Behavioral Geneticists

Working with animals such as the fruit fly or mouse, behavior geneticists often use *selective breeding* experiments to learn whether certain phenotypic expressions can be increased or decreased in offspring. In this procedure, members of a species that display a specific attribute are bred to each other, usually over many generations. If the attribute is inherited, subsequent generations of offspring can be expected to display it more and more frequently or strongly. For example, in a study to determine whether activity level has a genetic basis, mice displaying a high level of activity were bred only to each other, as were mice showing only a low level of activity (DeFries, Gervais, & Thomas, 1978). After thirty generations of selective breeding, the mice in the two groups showed no overlap in terms of the amount of activity displayed; in fact, those bred for high activity were thirty times more active than those bred for low activity. Whereas the high-activity mice would run the equivalent of a football field during two 3-minute test periods, the low-activity mice would not even run the equivalent of a first down (Plomin, 1986).

behavior genetics Study of how characteristics and behaviors of individuals such as intelligence and personality are influenced by the interaction between genotype and experience.

Can we conclude that activity level is completely inherited? Certainly not, since the environment, as in most selective-breeding studies, was held constant. In other words, any potential environmental contribution to activity level was minimized. Nevertheless, research involving selective breeding in animals has revealed genetic contributions to many different attributes, including aggressiveness, emotionality, maze learning, and sex drive in mice, rats, chickens, and other species of animals (Plomin, DeFries, & McClearn, 1990; Tryon, 1940).

Because their genetic makeup is the same, identical or monozygotic twins often look very much alike and display very similar traits and behaviors. The study of such twins provides important information about the contributions of heredity and environment to development.

identical twins Two individuals who originate from a single zygote (one egg fertilized by one sperm), which early in cell division separates to form two separate cell masses. Such twins have an identical genetic makeup. Also called *monozygotic twins.*

fraternal twins Siblings sharing the same womb at the same time but who originate from two different eggs fertilized by two different sperm cells. Also called *dizygotic twins.*

concordance rate Percentage of pairs of twins in which both members have a specific trait identified in one of the twins.

Selective breeding, of course, cannot be used to study human behavior. Instead, behavior geneticists gain information about hereditary and environmental influences on humans by studying resemblances among family members. These studies investigate similarities among *identical* and *fraternal* twins, siblings, and other members of families who are genetically different from one another to varying degrees. **Identical,** or **monozygotic, twins** come from the same zygote: a single egg fertilized by a single sperm. A cell division takes place early in development that creates two separate embryos from this zygote, but the twins are genetically identical. **Fraternal,** or **dizygotic, twins** come from two different zygotes, each created from a separate egg and separate sperm. Although sharing the womb at the same time, fraternal twins are no more genetically similar than siblings born at different times, each averaging about half their genes in common.

If identical twins resemble each other more than fraternal twins in some behavioral attribute such as intelligence or shyness, one *potential* explanation for this similarity is their common genotype. The degree of resemblance is usually estimated from one of two statistical measures: concordance rate or correlation coefficient. The concordance rate is used when measuring attributes that are either present or absent, such as schizophrenia or depression. The **concordance rate** is the percentage of pairs of twins in which both members have a specific attribute when one of the twins is identified as having that attribute. Thus, if both members of every twin pair have a particular trait, the concordance rate would be 100 percent. If only one member of every pair of twins has some particular trait, the concordance rate would be 0 percent.

When attributes vary on a continuous scale so that they can be measured in terms of amount or degree, resemblances are estimated from a *correlation coefficient.* This statistic helps to determine whether variables such as intelligence or shyness, which are measured in some quantifiable way from lower to higher, are more similar among identical twins than among fraternal twins or more similar among siblings than among unrelated children. The attributes may be positively correlated, negatively correlated, or uncorrelated. For example, a positive correlation exists when both members of a pair of twins typically score at similar levels on an intelligence test. A negative correlation is found when one member of the pair of twins tends to score high, but the other low. Uncorrelated attributes show no relationship to one another. One member of a pair of twins may score high, but this information does not help us to anticipate how high the other member of the pair is likely to score.

Remember that a negative or positive correlation between two variables, no matter how strong, does *not* imply causation. This should be fairly evident in our discussion of twin relationships. For example, scores on intelligence tests by identical twins are often found to be positively correlated. But when both members of a pair of twins score well on an intelligence test, the high score of one twin does not *cause* the score for the other twin to be high. Similarity in genotype, experience, or both may be responsible for this correlation.

One reason that identical twins might resemble one another more than fraternal twins is the fact that identical twins share the same genotype. However, an alternative explanation for this greater resemblance may be that identical twins share more similar experiences. Some behavior geneticists do not feel the similarity of their experiences represents a major problem in twin research (Plomin, DeFries, & McClearn, 1990). However, one way to reduce its effects is to study biologically related family members who have been adopted or reared apart from one another in very different environments. If an attribute is greatly influenced by genetic factors, children should still resemble their biological siblings, parents, or other family members more than their adoptive relatives. On the other hand, if the environment is the primary determinant of an attribute, separated children might be expected to resemble their adoptive parents or other adopted siblings more closely than their biological parents or siblings.

Adoption studies pose substantial challenges for evaluating hereditary and environmental influences because children are often placed in homes similar to those of their biological parents. As a consequence, the separate contributions of family environment and heredity to an attribute become extremely difficult to identify. In addition, information on the biological family may not be readily available in the case of adoption. Because of these kinds of difficulties, major family resemblance projects investigating genotype-environment interactions in Colorado, Kentucky, Texas, and other locations throughout the United States and the world often combine family, twin, and adoption methods. The Colorado Adoption Project, for example, has been conducting longitudinal research on resemblances between (1) parents and their natural children, (2) adoptive parents and their adopted children, and (3) parents and their biological children who have been adopted into other homes (Horn, 1983). This and other such longitudinal studies have provided us with valuable new information on the genetic and experiential contributions to family resemblance.

▶ **Roles of nature and nurture**   Conceptualizing the Interaction Between Genotype and Environment

Before examining some of the conclusions emerging from family resemblance projects, we must further clarify the roles that genotype and environment play in fostering behavior and its development. Historically, theories have typically claimed one of two extremes: behavior is completely determined by the genes, or behavior is completely determined by the environment. Neither position, of course, at least in its extreme form, is advocated today; both genotypic and environmental factors are essential for any phenotypic expression. Thus, researchers often propose an interaction between the two. But what is the nature of this interaction and how does it help to clarify our understanding of behavior and its development?

Genotype-Environment Interaction and the Range of Reaction The way in which a genotype influences development may depend to a great extent on the environment. Similarly, the effects of different environments upon behavior often depend on the genotype. These conditional relationships signify an *interaction* between genotype and environment; the influence of one upon the other is not always constant across different kinds of environments or different kinds of genotypes. We can illustrate this principle by considering the repercussions of inheriting the single-gene condition phenylketonuria (PKU), discussed earlier in the chapter. Consuming a protein-laden diet will lead to severe mental retardation for someone with PKU. By not eating foods containing high amounts of phenylalanine, the debilitating consequences of this genetic defect can be greatly minimized; mental development may be nearly normal. Thus, for persons bearing this genotype, intellectual development depends on a diet in which phenylalanine is minimized. In contrast, intellectual development for someone without PKU will be largely unaffected by either kind of diet or may possibly even be improved by the presence of substantial protein in the diet.

The same principle of interaction accounting for the relationship between a single-gene condition and the environment can be extended to polygenic factors and experience. The nature of the individual child plays a role here. Some children seem to be highly vulnerable to certain rearing conditions, whereas other children seem to succeed despite those conditions. For example, many children are members of families who encounter severe forms of stress; a parent may commit crimes, be mentally ill, or the family may live in poverty or be dysfunctional for other reasons. Norman Garmezy (1985) at the University of Minnesota has identified some children in these families who seem to be enormously resilient and able to function despite such stresses, who are capable of personal and intellectual achievement, and who are socially far above the norm for children reared in such contexts. A distinctive array of family, community, and other experiential factors, as yet not fully understood, may promote these competencies. But it is also possible that these successful children have a biological makeup less affected by the environmental conditions that seem so devastating to many other children.

Any generalizations we might want to make about the *degree* to which genotype and environment, respectively, contribute to behavior are limited by the interactive relationship of these factors. The genotype may be far more influential in accounting for individual differences in some environmental settings than in others. For an extreme hypothetical example, assume that psychologists somehow discovered, and parents around the world were able to implement, optimal rearing conditions for every child for some attribute such as intelligence. Any remaining differences in children's intelligence must necessarily be entirely due to the genotype. It is, of course, impossible to know how well families are able to provide optimal rearing conditions. Thus, we can only

FIGURE 3.9

The Concept of Range of Reaction for Intellectual Performance

As the product of the interaction between genotype and environment, the phenotype for any attribute shows a typical range of reaction. For example, the intelligence score of the child, even though mentally retarded (Child C), will be higher when the environment is optimal for intellectual development. The same is true of the child whose genotype suggests normal or higher intelligence; the effects of the environment, in fact, may even be more substantial for such a child.

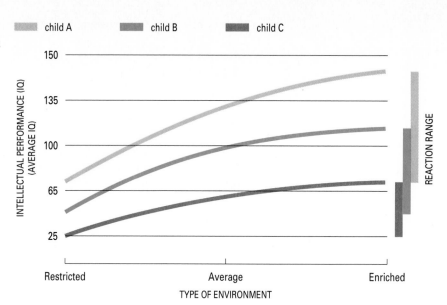

Source: Adapted from Gottesman, 1963.

identify the relative contribution of genotype and environment to some attribute on the basis of actual practices and procedures initiated in a specific sample of children.

The interactive quality of genotype and environment can be made clearer using a concept offered by Irving Gottesman (1963). Gottesman has proposed that genotypes establish limits on the kinds of phenotypes displayed in different environments. This concept of a **range of reaction** (or **norm of reaction**) associated with different genotypes is illustrated in Figure 3.9. For example, how well the child performs on an intelligence test may be dramatically influenced by the type of environment in which he or she is reared. Removing children with Down syndrome from unstimulating institutional settings has helped many of them to achieve much higher ranges of intellectual functioning than would have been achieved had they remained in institutions. The intellectual level they reach is affected by the kinds of experiences they have. Nevertheless, at the present time we do not know of any environment that will promote in the child born with Down syndrome a level of intelligence routinely exhibited by most children with a normal complement of chromosomes. It is important to remember that environmental conditions also have an impact on children with normal intelligence. As Figure 3.9 suggests, the range of intellectual ability created by a restricted versus enriched environment for someone of average intelligence may be even greater than for someone who is retarded.

range of reaction   Range of phenotypic differences possible as a result of different environments interacting with a specific genotype. Also called *norm of reaction.*

canalization   Concept that the development of some attributes is governed primarily by the genotype and that only extreme environmental conditions will alter the phenotypic pattern for these attributes.

Canalization   Conrad Waddington, a biologist, has proposed the principle of **canalization,** or a kind of "channeling" of development, to suggest another way of thinking about genotype-environment relationships. This principle helps to shed light on how genotype and experience contribute to the emergence of behaviors common to all members of a species as well as to the development of individual differences. According to this principle, a highly canalized attribute is one that is primarily influenced by the genotype; experiential factors modify the impact of the genotype only under extreme conditions. Think about the developing phenotype as something like a stream or river seeking its course over terrain in which channels of varying depth have previously been cut. The terrain organized by the genotype includes many choices of direction. However, channels are so deeply cut for some phenotypes that only extreme environmental pressures can change their course.

Many aspects of early motor behavior emerge on a fairly regular basis during infancy. Presumably the genotype has carved a relatively deep channel for these aspects of development; the emergence of various early motor skills is protected well, but not completely, from experience (see Chapter 5). This may be true for many other aspects of early development, including the onset of babbling and such important aspects of social responsivity as smiling to interesting events. Channels for other phenotypes are shallower, and the direction the phenotype takes can be diverted to another course with relative ease by experience.

The further possibility exists that some attributes and behaviors are highly canalized early in development but become less so with increasing age. Robert McCall (1981) suggests this is true for intellectual development. The development of early mental abilities, he suggests, is primarily organized by the genotype, and only relatively extreme conditions are likely to change their initial course. With development, however, intellectual abilities become less heavily influenced by the genotype. Their channels flow into an increasingly shallow terrain, and the potential for environmental conditions to affect their direction and progression rises. It is as if the canyons through which these phenotype "rivers" first flowed gradually give way to a flatter plain of developmental choices. In accounting for a particular attribute or behavior, the interactive relationship between genotype and environment does not remain constant but, in fact, changes throughout development.

Passive, Evocative, and Niche-picking Links We can determine quantitatively that water is made up of two parts hydrogen and one part oxygen. But even though researchers have theorized that some portion of various traits such as activity level, sociability, or intelligence derives from the genes and the remainder from the environment, we cannot precisely determine what portion each contributes. Because genotype and experience interact, numerical estimates of their respective contributions to the development of a particular behavior must be interpreted extremely cautiously.

Identifying discrete contributions of genotype and environment to behavior is difficult for other reasons as well. Not only do genotype and environment interact directly, they are linked or correlated with each other in more complex ways (Plomin, DeFries, & Loehlin, 1977; Scarr & McCartney, 1983). One correlation between genotype and experience arises from the tendency for parents to establish a child-rearing environment in harmony with their own interests and preferences. Assume, for example, that sociability has some genetic basis. Sociable parents may transmit this orientation to their children either through the genes, through the social environment created in their home, or through an intertwining of both mechanisms.

This kind of correlation between genotype and environment is considered to be *passive* since it has been created for the child by the parents. Jeremy and

Cindy might have been influenced by this passive correlation. Jeremy's mother stayed home with him during his first three years of life. But soon after Cindy was born, her mother returned to work. Cindy spent much more of her infancy and toddler years with a day-care provider. Thus, while Jeremy was young, his mother, who was shy, had the opportunity to structure her household and interactions in ways that met her needs, and Jeremy had considerable opportunity to experience the kind of environment his mother preferred. Jeremy's wariness could stem from the genotype and the environment he experienced. In contrast, Cindy's toddler days were spent with a day-care provider who was much more outgoing and sociable. Because for these two siblings both genotype and environment may have been different, we cannot distinguish their separate contributions to later social development.

In most families the correlation between the genetic and environmental components of child rearing is likely to be positive—that is, the environment will contain features that support and complement the child's genetic potential. But a negative correlation between genotype and environment is also possible, as when a highly active child is adopted into a sedentary family or when parents elect to provide a rearing environment that departs from their own experience and genetic propensities. A parent who feels that he or she was too shy during childhood and, as a consequence, missed out on many social activities may actively initiate parties and other activities designed to promote sociability in a child.

▶ **The child's active role**

Another type of correlation between the genotype and the environment, termed *reactive* or *evocative,* occurs when elements in the environment, particularly other people, support or encourage individual differences that may have a genetic component (Scarr & McCartney, 1983). An active preschooler is likely to prompt teachers to make sure enough large-muscle toys are available to dissipate some of that energy. A sociable child is more likely to attract the attention of peers than a shy or passive child. Jeremy's preference for standing on the sidelines resulted in a tendency for other children in the preschool to ignore him; Cindy's gregariousness helped to ensure that she was often called on by others in her group. Thus, attributes that may have a biological basis are likely to evoke certain patterns of social interaction involving others, providing an environment complementary to the child's genetic proclivity.

▶ **The child's active role**

In a final type of correlation between genotype and environment, termed *active,* the child may eagerly seek out and be attracted to experiences more compatible with his or her genotype. Bright children may prefer to engage in exercises that challenge their intellect and to play with peers who are also bright. The athletic child may find little pleasure in practicing the piano but spend countless hours skateboarding and playing on the basketball court. Jeremy preferred to play by himself, Cindy to play with others. Traits and activities such as these, which we assume can have a genetic basis, may, in turn, influence the kind of environment a child attempts to create and experience. Sandra Scarr and Kathleen McCartney (1983) describe this kind of linkage as **niche picking** to emphasize that children and adults selectively construct and engage environments responsive to their genetic orientations.

niche picking Tendency to actively select an environment compatible with a genotype.

Scarr and McCartney (1983) believe that the impact of these three types of correlations between genotype and environment change with development. Although infants may actively attend to some parts of their environment more than others, their experiences are often determined for them by their care-

Niche picking, the tendency of a child to seek out and become attracted to activities that are compatible with her genotype, may be an important aspect of the interaction between nature and nurture. A child with musical abilities may work hard to display her talents and gain much satisfaction from her efforts.

givers. Thus, initial correlations between genotype and environment are likely to be established by passive factors. As children gain greater independence and control of their environment, however, others around them may begin to notice and support their individual differences and niche picking becomes an increasingly greater potential source of correlation between genotype and environment. Here again we observe the interplay between the child's active and passive roles in his or her own development.

This analysis allows us to make one important developmental prediction: under some circumstances, children within the same family will become less similar to each other as they grow older and move away from the common environment provided by their parents. In other words, siblings will select environmental niches more fitting to their individual genotypes than the one they were first presented with. When Sandra Scarr and Richard Weinberg (1977) studied adopted children, they obtained support for this prediction. During early and middle childhood, adopted but biologically unrelated children did show similarities in intelligence, personality, and other traits. These resemblances may have come from two sources: (1) adoption procedures that tend to encourage the placement of children in homes that are somewhat like the child's biological home and (2) the common family environment children share when adopted into the same home. As adopted siblings neared the end of adolescence, however, they no longer exhibited similarities in intelligence, personality, or other traits. Scarr and Weinberg concluded the passive influence of the common environment established by the adoptive parents had been supplanted by active niche picking. Older siblings more and more effectively exposed themselves to environments agreeing with and supportive of their own individual genotypes.

The notion of niche picking may provide us with an even more startling prediction. When identical twins are reared apart, they might, in some ways and with increasing age, actually come to resemble each other as much as, possibly even more so than, identical twins reared together! This similarity could come about as people have more and more occasions to react to the similar behaviors influenced by the twins' identical genotypes and as opportunities arise for the twins to make more choices in their environment. While evidence for this prediction remains limited, Thomas Bouchard, Jr., and colleagues (Bouchard, 1984; Bouchard et al., 1990) have studied identical twins reared apart from early in life. The twins were given a variety of personality, cognitive, and interest tests. Bouchard (1984) found that they repeatedly displayed similarities in gait, posture, gesture, and habits such as straightening glasses, as well as similar levels of intellectual ability. Moreover, identical twins reared apart showed as high a correlation on many personality variables as those reared together. These results suggest that niche picking could be a powerful means by which behaviors initiated by the genotype are maintained.

▶ **Roles of nature and nurture**

Hereditary and Environmental Influences on Behavior

If, as we have already learned, single-gene mutations can affect human development in dramatic ways, we have little reason to doubt that multiple genes, perhaps often with subtle effects, can touch on and influence intellectual and personality development, mental illness, and many other aspects of human behavior. As always, however, sifting through the genetic and environmental contributions for complex human traits and behaviors is an extremely difficult task. Research involving studies of family resemblances, identical and fraternal twins reared together and apart, and adopted children has not always been interpreted with purely scientific goals in mind. The results and their implications have often been misunderstood and used to promote social and political ends. Nevertheless, *real* genetic as well as *real* environmental contributions to human traits and behaviors exist, and the more we learn about their relationships, the more we will understand children and their development.

Intelligence   In Chapter 9 we discuss the limitations of using the intelligence quotient (IQ) as the primary symbol of intellectual ability. Unfortunately, most studies have relied on IQ to determine the contributions of genotype and environment to intelligence, and many of these studies suffer from other methodological problems as well. Nevertheless, the combined findings of 111 studies involving a variety of tests designed to measure intelligence (summarized in Figure 3.10) reveal that *both* environmental and genetic factors make important contributions to intelligence (Bouchard & McGue, 1981).

The data in Figure 3.10 are presented as correlation coefficients between pairs of individuals who share different genetic relationships with one another. The contribution of environmental factors is revealed in several ways. For example, the twenty-three studies investigating the correlation in intelligence between unrelated persons living together (such as two adopted children, an adopted and natural child, or a parent and an adopted child) reveal a median correlation of about .20. But no correlation should be expected if environmental influences are absent. Another indicator of the environment's influence is reflected in the finding that identical twins reared together are more alike in performance on intelligence tests than identical twins reared apart. Nevertheless, a substantial role for the genotype in intelligence is also evident. There is a pattern of increases in the correlation for IQs as similarity in genotype increases. In fact, the median correlation for studies examining intelligence in identical twins reared apart is fairly high (.67).

Scarr and McCartney's (1983) analysis of developmental changes in patterns of genetic and environmental influences helps make sense of several additional findings from research on family relatedness and intelligence. For example, some researchers have observed that intelligence for *both* identical and fraternal twins during infancy and early childhood is highly correlated. With increasing age, the correlations become even greater for identical twins, but tend to decline to the level reported in Figure 3.10 for fraternal twins (Fischbein, 1981; Wilson, 1978; 1983; 1986). These results suggest a greater influence of passive factors (the similar rearing environment created by the parents) on intelligence early in development and more opportunity for niche picking later in development. It would be misleading, however, to conclude that identical twins always become more similar when they grow older. In fact, a recent meta-analysis of twin studies reveals that as twins become older, not only fraternal twins, but also to some extent identical twins, become more dissimilar on many aspects of intelligence tests. In other words, twins, including identical twins, often do grow apart as they grow older (McCartney, Harris, & Bernieri, 1990). This may come about because identical twins actively

▶ **The child's active role**

FIGURE 3.10

The Contributions of Genetic and Environmental Factors to Intelligence

Correlation coefficients between pairs of individuals given various kinds of intelligence tests suggest that both genetic and environmental factors make important contributions to intelligence. Bars indicate the range of correlation coefficients obtained from different studies (the number of studies appears in parentheses). Dots above bars indicate the median correlation obtained; arrows mark the correlation that would be expected assuming that intelligence is entirely influenced by hereditary factors. Evidence for a contribution from genetic factors comes from the finding that correlations in intelligence increase as genetic relationships increase. The discrepancy between the dots and arrows, however, indicates that environmental factors are also influencing performance.

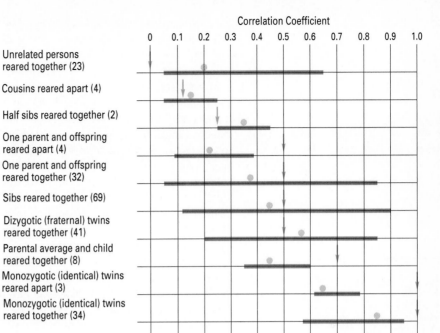

Source: Adapted from Bouchard & McGue, 1981.

heritability Proportion of variability in the phenotype that is estimated to be accounted for by genetic influences.

attempt to establish a *unique* niche in the family and community, efforts that may also be encouraged by parents of the twins (Schachter, 1982).

How significant is heredity for intellectual development? Assessments of **heritability,** the proportion of variability in the phenotype that can be accounted for by genetic influences, are typically estimated to be about 50 percent for intelligence (Plomin, 1990). In other words, about half of the variability in intelligence appears to be attributable to genetic factors and the remainder to environmental factors, at least among white American and European middle-class populations, the groups studied most thoroughly (Plomin & DeFries, 1980; Scarr & Carter-Saltzman, 1983). But because of the limitations of IQ scores (see Chapter 9) and the interactive nature of genotype-environment relationships, generalizations about the heritability of intelligence are hazardous at best.

Even if an attribute like intelligence is highly influenced by hereditary factors, environmental influences can still have an enormous impact on the level displayed by the individual. A classic investigation carried out by Marie Skodak and Harold Skeels (1949) illustrates this point. One hundred children born to retarded mothers, most of whom were from low socioeconomic backgrounds, were adopted before six months of age into homes that were economically and educationally well above average. The IQs of these children were found to be above average throughout the childhood and adolescent years and substantially higher than their biological parents, an outcome reflecting the contribution of environmental factors on this measure of intelligence. But despite their high levels, the children's IQs still were substantially correlated with those of their biological mothers, indicating a hereditary contribution to these scores as well. Furthermore, children whose biological mothers had higher IQs benefited more from adoption than children whose biological mothers had lower IQs, a further illustration of the interactive nature of environment and heredity.

More recent adoption studies have reached similar conclusions concerning the importance of both environment and heredity (Dumaret, 1985; Horn, Loehlin, & Willerman, 1979; Scarr & Weinberg, 1983). In the Texas Adoption Project, children who had been adopted into similar homes but who were born to two extreme groups of biological mothers—those who scored below average on an intelligence test (less than 95) and those who scored well above average (greater than 120)—were tested during middle childhood (Horn, 1983). Children of the low-IQ mothers scored above average on the test, suggesting an impact of environmental factors, but they still did not score as well as those of high-IQ mothers. In addition, the correlation of children's IQ scores with biological mothers' scores was higher than with adoptive mothers' scores. Even though IQ can undergo impressive boosts in some kinds of environments, measures of intelligence for adopted children continue to be more highly correlated with their biological parents than with their adopted parents (Loehlin, Willerman, & Horn, 1988). The environment does affect the various abilities assessed on standard intelligence tests, but the genotype grants a broad range of reaction for expressing those abilities.

Personality and Temperament   Many personality traits also reflect genetic influences, although their heritability may be less than for intelligence (Loehlin, Willerman, & Horn, 1988). Perhaps the most extensive research on this topic has been concerned with **temperament,** an early appearing constellation of personality traits theorized to have some genetic basis (Buss & Plomin, 1975; 1984; Rothbart & Derryberry, 1981; Thomas & Chess, 1977). Arnold Buss and Robert Plomin have identified three broad traits frequently describing the temperaments of infants and very young children. One of these is *sociability,* the tendency to be shy or outgoing in infancy or early childhood, the likely precursor to introversion and extroversion in older children and adults. Another trait is *emotionality,* how easily an individual becomes distressed, upset, angry, or fearful and how intensely these emotions are expressed. The third trait is *activity,* as evidenced by the tempo and vigor with which behaviors are performed.

Selective breeding studies with various species of animals indicate that sociability, emotionality, and activity level have a hereditary component; family resemblance and adoption studies in humans lead to the same conclusion. For example, a review of seven studies of infants revealed that identical twins consistently show higher correlations for sociability (typically between .40 and .60 on various measures) than fraternal twins (typically between .10 and .30) (Plomin, 1987). Inherited differences in physiological reactivity may underlie these variations in social responsiveness (Kagan, Reznick, & Snidman, 1988). Young children like Jeremy who remain aloof from strangers, including peers, and who are reluctant to begin to play with novel toys, display increased heart rate and muscle tension in unfamiliar situations compared with children like Cindy, who are more outgoing and spontaneous. Although other studies provide further evidence for a genetic basis for this aspect of temperament (Matheny, 1989), adoption studies also suggest that the personality of adoptive

temperament Stable, early appearing constellation of individual personality attributes believed to have a hereditary basis; includes sociability, emotionality, and activity level.

parents can play some role in influencing sociability; for example, the shyness of adopted infants has been found to be somewhat related to the shyness of their adoptive parents (Plomin & DeFries, 1985).

Studies comparing infant twins on the other two aspects of temperament, emotionality and activity, also consistently reveal higher correlations for identical than for fraternal twins (Plomin, 1987). These studies have used different kinds of procedures to evaluate emotionality and activity: parent interviews, parent questionnaire ratings, experimenter ratings of infants being tested, and observations carried out in a playroom setting. Furthermore, consistent racial and ethnic differences have also been reported and have been attributed to genetic differences in temperament. When Daniel Freedman (1979) compared the temperaments of Caucasian and Chinese American newborns, he found Caucasian babies were more irritable and harder to comfort than Chinese American infants. As older infants, Chinese American babies also tended to be more wary when confronted with novel or uncertain situations (Kagan, Kearsley, & Zelazo, 1978).

Does the environment play a significant role in personality development? Just like Jeremy and Cindy's mother, parents of siblings sometimes think not and often comment on how different their children are. While parents rarely believe that their baby might have been switched for someone else's at the hospital, they are amazed at how compliant, responsive, and cheerful one child might be but how stubborn, independent, and active another is. Furthermore, most studies comparing the personalities of unrelated children in the same household report that the correlations are fairly low and often approach zero especially in later childhood and adolescence (Plomin & Daniels, 1987). Does this mean that such traits are really not influenced by the environment and only by heredity? Probably not, since the environment may be contributing to personality development by promoting *differences* among individual children as well as similarities.

Evidence that many parents do encourage differences in personality is perhaps most evident in the dissimilar ways they often interact with boys and girls (see Chapter 12). But variations in personality also seem to be related to whether a child is first-born or later-born, tall or short, and as a result of other factors that are part of their position in the family, and their physical and psychological makeup. Parents and other family members, even the broader community, may react to encourage a unique status and role in the family for individual children. Of course, individuals within a family may also actively seek ways to be different, to "stand out" from their siblings and others, as we have already suggested with respect to intellectual development (Schachter et al., 1976). As both identical and fraternal twins grow older, they also grow apart in terms of their personalities (McCartney, Harris, & Bernieri, 1990). These reactions and active niche-picking efforts could counter child-rearing and other parenting patterns that are likely to foster consistency and similarities among members of families. In other words, environmental factors exist within families that both promote and deter similarities in personality. The relative strengths of these oppositional factors for personality development are not easily teased apart by behavioral geneticists.

▶ **The child's active role**

Mental Illness Investigators are currently conducting intensive research on whether some forms of *manic depression,* a disorder characterized by rapid and large mood swings between feverish activity and withdrawn, depressed behaviors, is influenced by a single gene (Barinaga, 1989). However, manic depression may be influenced by many factors, and some subtypes may have a polygenic component. Family studies reveal children of a manic-depressive parent are at substantially greater risk for displaying the illness than children without such a parent. For example, the rate of occurrence of manic depression in the general population is about 0.7 percent. But when one parent has manic depression, the rate of occurrence for the same illness among the children increases to more than 11 percent (Rosenthal, 1970). This risk triples for children born to two manic-depressive parents.

Studies of twins and adoptees provide further evidence to indicate that genotype, not just the environment, plays a role in the transmission of manic depression. Based on a number of studies, the overall concordance rate for identical twins for manic depression is about 70 percent. For fraternal twins, the concordance rate is only about 15 percent, not much higher than the rate observed for nontwin siblings (Rosenthal, 1970). The data on adopted children reveal manic depression is about three times greater for adopted children whose biological parents have the illness than for adopted children whose biological parents do not have the illness (Knowles, 1985).

A form of psychopathology that has received even greater attention from researchers is *schizophrenia*, a disorder that may include disturbances in thoughts and emotions, including delusions and hallucinations. As the biological relationship to someone diagnosed as having schizophrenia increases, an individual's risk for the same diagnosis rises. In general, when one twin has schizophrenia, the other twin is about three times more likely to display schizophrenia if identical than if fraternal. Adoption studies provide further confirmation for a role of the genotype (Gottesman & Shields, 1982). Schizophrenia is far more prevalent among adopted children who are the biological offspring of schizophrenic parents than of nonschizophrenic parents. The risk is similar whether the parent is the mother or the father. The exact nature of the genetic basis for schizophrenia remains unknown. Although the search continues for contributions of a single gene, many researchers feel a polygenic model, which claims schizophrenia is influenced by many genes, provides a better explanation for these findings.

An important point to remember about various forms of mental illness—and about all the other traits we are studying—is that none are 100 percent concordant even in identical twins, despite the similarity of their genetic makeup. Environmental factors most likely play a significant role in the emergence of mental illness as well as in other forms of behavior. Whether children come to display mental illness is greatly influenced by the number and intensity of environmental stresses such as parental disharmony, poverty, and other dysfunctional living arrangements (Rutter, 1979). Once again, the interaction between genotype and environment must be taken into account to understand how heredity and experience are interwoven.

Other Characteristics   A variety of other characteristics, including alcoholism, reading disabilities, inclinations to committing crimes, and susceptibility to various illnesses such as heart disease and cancer, have also been linked to family histories (Mange & Mange, 1990; Vandenberg, Singer, & Pauls, 1986). For example, alcoholism in a parent or sibling is a better predictor of alcoholism in an individual than any other measure researchers have attempted to identify (Mednick, Moffitt, & Stack, 1987). This relationship, of course, may exist because of either genetic or environmental factors. Nevertheless, research on adopted children strongly implicates a hereditary contribution (Cadoret, Cain, & Grove, 1980). One study examined sons who were separated from their biological fathers early in infancy. Some of the biological fathers were alcoholics; others were not. Those fathered by an alcoholic parent were almost four times more likely to become alcoholic as adults than those fathered by a nonalcoholic parent (Goodwin et al., 1973). Sons separated from their alcoholic fathers early in infancy are often just as likely to become alcoholic as sons who remain with their alcoholic fathers throughout their childhood years.

Concordance rates for identical and fraternal twins for a variety of diseases are indicated in Table 3.5. Although the number of twins from whom data have been collected is small (shown in parentheses in Table 3.5) and it is not possible to determine to what extent heredity and environment are responsible for the typically higher concordance rates in identical twins, researchers are becoming increasingly convinced that both single-gene and polygenic factors contribute to some forms of cancer, diabetes mellitus, hypertension, and many other diseases. But again, should hereditary factors be found to be associated with such diseases, we cannot overlook the major contribution that the environment often has in their expression.

TABLE 3.5

The Genetic Basis of Selected Diseases: Twin Data

Evidence for the genetic basis of diseases and other traits is often supported from comparisons involving the concordance rates observed in identical and fraternal twins. The numbers in parentheses indicate the number of pairs of twins studied.

Trait	Concordance in Identical Twins	Concordance in Fraternal Twins
Schizophrenia	34% (203)	12% (222)
Tuberculosis	37% (135)	15% (513)
Manic-depressive psychosis	67% (15)	5% (40)
Hypertension	25% (80)	7% (212)
Mental deficiency	67% (18)	0% (49)
Rheumatic fever	20% (148)	6% (428)
Rheumatoid arthritis	34% (47)	7% (141)
Bronchial asthma	47% (64)	24% (192)
Epilepsy	37% (27)	10% (100)
Diabetes mellitus	47% (76)	10% (238)
Smoking habits (females only)	83% (53)	50% (18)
Cancer (at same site)	7% (207)	3% (767)
Cancer (at any site)	16% (207)	13% (212)
Death from acute infection	8% (127)	9% (454)

Source: Adapted from Hartl, 1977.

THEMES IN DEVELOPMENT

GENETICS AND HEREDITY

▶ **What roles do nature and nurture play in development?**

Because of our emphasis on exploring heredity, basic endogenous structures such as nucleotide pairs, genes and chromosomes, and the principles by which they are inherited and expressed have been a primary interest in this chapter. These form the genetic building blocks contributing to a series of biochemical events that transform enzymes and proteins into functioning cells throughout the human body. Nevertheless, the phenotype, the observable behaviors and characteristics of an individual, is the product of a complex interaction between the genotype and the environment. Environment includes the foods that are eaten, as our discussion of the effects of protein on the intellectual development of children with phenylketonuria has indicated. More frequently, however, we examine the role of nature and nurture within the framework of trying to understand how various kinds of stimulation provided by caregivers and others promote or have little consequence for intellectual development, temperament, mental illness, and other behaviors. The relationship between genotype and phenotype is complicated because passive, reactive, and niche picking factors may enter into the equation to various degrees throughout development. As a consequence, experiential factors become tightly interwoven with the genotype to produce the range and variety of behaviors and characteristics displayed by an individual.

▶ **How does the child play an active role in the effects of heredity on development?**

Researchers have begun to recognize the child's active efforts to seek out environments that support and maintain behavioral orientations and preferences that are influenced by hereditary factors. As the child achieves greater control over the environment, he or she has increasing opportunities to find a niche. In other words, behaviors, activities, and skills displayed by the child are not only a consequence of imposed social and physical experiences, but also reflect the selective efforts of the child to find environments that are interesting, challenging, and supportive. Inherited and environmentally imposed influences may be met with eager support or active resistance to determine each child's unique life history.

SUMMARY

In this chapter we have focused on several distinct levels at which the structures and principles of heredity must be understood. These levels include the (1) individual; (2) the cells making up the body of that individual; (3) the chromosomes located within the nucleus of those cells; (4) the genes comprising segments of each chromosome; and (5) the nucleotide pairs that form the biochemical building blocks for the genes. The arrangement of hundreds of couplings of two sets of two different nitrogen-based molecules (*nucleotide pairs*) constitutes the central unit of hereditary information, the *gene*. Pairs of genes affect particular traits or characteristics. The sequence of nucleotide bases is not always identical for each member of the pair. These variants, or *alleles,* interact with each other in *dominant-recessive* and other ways to establish different patterns of inheritance in the genotype and expression in the phenotype. The alleles are the hereditary source of differences between individuals.

Genes are made up of *deoxyribonucleic acid,* or *DNA,* the spiral staircase–like molecular structure that comprises the twenty-three pairs of *chromosomes* present in most body cells. *Mitosis* is the process of cell division by which these forty-six chromosomes are duplicated. The *gametes,* or sex cells, are formed by *meiosis,* a process of cell division by which one member of each pair of chromosomes is randomly selected for each cell. This random process, combined with *crossing over,* ensures that every individual, with the exception of identical twins, has a unique hereditary blueprint.

Hereditary contributions to development begin at conception, when the twenty-three chromosomes in a sperm cell are added to the twenty-three chromosomes in the egg. Males and females differ in the composition of the twenty-third pair of chromosomes. For females, both members of the pair are X chromosomes. For males, one is an X and the other a Y chromosome. Gene disorders associated with this twenty-third pair of chromosomes are said to be *sex linked.*

Sometimes abnormal chromosomes and alleles are inherited. Such inherited abnormalities as Down syndrome, fragile X syndrome, Huntington's disease, and sickle cell anemia lead to severe disruptions in physical and behavioral development. Environmental input in the form of treatment and remediation programs exists to counter the consequences of some of these genetic defects. *Genetic counseling* can provide prospective parents with information on the likelihood of having children who will be affected by birth defects.

A *genotype* constitutes the hereditary information that contributes to the *phenotype,* a measurable characteristic, trait, or behavior. Every phenotype is the product of the interaction between genotype and environment. The genotype may establish a range of possible outcomes for development. Thus, the relative contribution of genotype to a phenotype cannot be readily determined and may differ from one individual to the next as a function of both hereditary and environmental conditions. Understanding the genotype-environment interaction is made even more difficult by correlated passive events, such as the creation of particular environments by caregivers with similar genotypes; reactive events such as siblings, peers, and others responding to genetic inclinations in specified ways; and by active *niche picking* by children to locate and create environments supportive of their individual genetic propensities.

Most human attributes, whether simple physical traits or complex capacities such as intelligence and personality, are *polygenic;* they are influenced by several genes. Behavior geneticists conduct studies of family members, including identical and fraternal twins, siblings, and adopted children, to demonstrate that both the genotype and the environment make important contributions to intelligence, temperament, personality characteristics, mental illness, and other patterns of human behavior. Identifying to what degree genotype and environment each separately contribute to development may not be possible, but determining how they influence each other remains a major goal of *behavior genetics.*

4

The Prenatal Period and Birth

Don Talayesva, Hopi Indian, begins his autobiography Sun Chief *(1942) with the story of his life in his mother's womb and the precautions his mother took while carrying him:*

She had nothing to do with the tanning of skins or the dyeing of anything lest she spoil the goods and also injure me. When she grew big, she was careful to sit in such a way that other people would not walk in front of her and thus make my birth difficult. She would not look at the serpent images displayed in the ceremonies, lest I turn myself into a water snake while still in her womb and raise up my head at the time of birth, instead of lying with head down seeking a way out. (p. 25)

Recognition of the potentially powerful role the environment plays in prenatal development has been shared across human cultures since the dawn of history. Although societies differ enormously in their specific beliefs, anthropologists report expectant mothers around the world are urged to avoid certain activities and to carry out various rituals for the sake of their unborn children. Western societies have their quotas of admonitions about pregnancy as well. Whereas Don Talayesva's mother was careful not to allow other people to walk in front of her, American obstetricians may advise a pregnant woman to stop smoking, avoid alcohol, and let someone else clean the cat litter.

Environmental factors do in fact disrupt prenatal development, though these disruptions may not directly affect the fetus through the mother's sensory perceptions, as much traditional folklore suggests. Unless we understand precisely how drugs, diseases, and other external factors influence prenatal development, however, an obstetrician's advice may seem every bit as arbitrary and equivocal as the practices Talayesva's mother adopted from her Hopi forebears. A major goal of this chapter, then, is to examine carefully the circumstances under which environmental factors can affect prenatal development.

We begin our discussion of prenatal development with a brief description of the remarkable sequence of events occurring from conception to birth. At no other time during human life does growth proceed so rapidly or do so many physical changes take place in a matter of weeks, days, and even hours. Some cultures, such as the Chinese, give tacit recognition to these dramatic events by crediting an infant with about a year of life at birth. As we will soon discover, in the nine months the newborn typically has been confined to the mother's womb, he has indeed undergone an epic adventure that we are only now beginning to understand.

THE STAGES OF PRENATAL DEVELOPMENT

▶ **Development as continuous/ stagelike**

prenatal development Period in development from conception to the onset of labor.

perinatal environment Medical, physical, and social environment established immediately before, during, and after birth of an infant.

postnatal development Period in development following birth.

germinal period Period lasting about ten to fourteen days following conception before the fertilized egg becomes implanted into the uterine wall. Also called *period of the zygote.*

embryonic period Period of prenatal development during which major biological organs and systems are formed. Begins at about the tenth to fourteenth day after conception when implantation occurs, and ends at about the eighth week after conception, with the onset of bone formation.

fetal period Period of prenatal development marked by relatively rapid growth of organs and preparation of body systems for functioning in postnatal environment. Begins about the eighth week after conception and ends at birth.

The importance of the environment for early development is indicated first of all in the fact that the three major periods in an infant's life—before, during, and after birth—are defined in terms of the dramatic changes in her surroundings. **Prenatal development** takes place from the moment of conception to the beginning of labor; all but the first few days of this time are spent within the confines of the mother's womb. The events surrounding the beginning of birth and the social and physical setting into which the newborn enters is called the **perinatal environment.** These events include the medical and obstetrical practices associated with delivery and also the preparations and care provided by parents and others to assist in the transition from the womb to life outside. **Postnatal development** begins after this transitional period. The environment now includes the broader physical and social world afforded by caregivers and others responsible for the infant's continued development.

Prenatal development itself is subdivided into three stages following fertilization of the egg. These are the **germinal period,** also known as the **period of the zygote** (from fertilization to about the first ten to fourteen days after conception), the **embryonic period** (from about two to eight weeks after conception), and the **fetal period** (from about eight weeks after conception to birth). The germinal period is characterized by movement, cell division, and implantation of the fertilized egg into the uterine wall. The embryonic period is marked by the formation of structures such as the nervous, circulatory, and respiratory systems and organs. In the fetal period, the body grows rapidly, and the organs and systems are refined in preparation for functioning in the postnatal environment outside the womb. This series of events in all its complexity is initiated by the act of fertilization.

Fertilization

Even before birth, the human female has already formed hundreds of thousands of primitive egg cells in her ovaries. Their numbers, however, decline with development; by puberty perhaps only 30,000 remain available. Of this abundant supply, about 400 will mature and be released for potential fertilization during the childbearing years (Samuels & Samuels, 1986). In contrast, male sperm production begins only at puberty, when an incredible 300 million sperm may be formed daily.

The opportunity for human conception begins around the fourteenth day after the start of the menstrual period. At this time a follicle housing a primitive egg cell in one of the ovaries begins to mature. In the course of its maturing, the follicle moves, eventually ruptures, and discharges its valuable contents from the ovary. The expelled egg cell, or *ovum,* is carried into and begins its journey through the Fallopian tube. This organ not only serves as a conduit for

Human development begins with the penetration of the egg by a single sperm, as shown here (egg and sperm are magnified greatly). Although the egg is the body's largest cell and the sperm its smallest, each contributes 23 chromosomes to form the hereditary basis for the development of a new living entity.

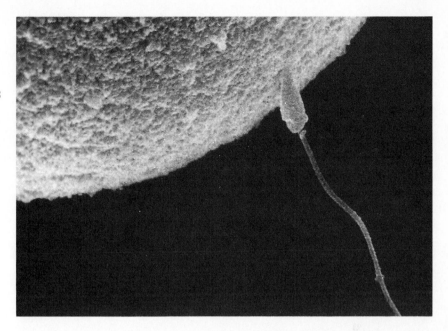

the egg as it moves on its way to the uterus at the leisurely rate of about one-sixteenth inch an hour, but also provides a receptive environment for fertilization if sperm are present (Abel, 1989). The unfertilized ovum, however, can survive for only about twenty-four hours.

Sperm reach the Fallopian tube by moving from the vagina through the cervix and the uterus. Sperm may migrate several inches an hour with the assistance of their tail-like appendages. Fewer than a hundred may negotiate the six- or more hour trip into the Fallopian tube, but these can survive about forty-eight hours.

If an ovum is present, sperm become attracted to it. The egg cell also prepares for fertilization in the presence of sperm. Cells initially surrounding the ovum loosen their protective grip, permitting the egg to be penetrated by a sperm cell (Nilsson, 1977). As soon as a sperm cell passes through the egg's protective linings, enzymes rapidly transform the ovum's outer membrane to prevent other sperm from penetrating its surface. The tail of the successful sperm disintegrates, and its head enlarges as it migrates toward the center of the egg. Genetic material from both cells mixes to reestablish a normal complement of forty-six chromosomes as described in Chapter 3. The egg, the body's largest cell, barely visible to the naked eye, weighs about 100,000 times more than the sperm, the body's smallest cell. Despite the enormous difference in their size, both contribute an equal number of chromosomes to form the new living entity.

The Germinal Period

The fertilized egg cell, called a *zygote,* continues to migrate down the Fallopian tube (see Figure 4.1). Within twenty-four to thirty hours after conception, the zygote divides into two cells, the first of a series of mitotic divisions called **cleavages.** At roughly twelve-hour intervals, these cells divide again to form

cleavage Mitotic cell division of the zygote.

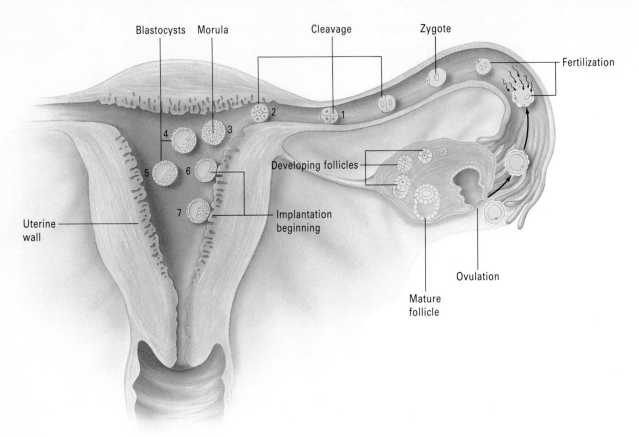

FIGURE 4.1

Source: Adapted from Moore, 1988.

Fertilization and the Germinal Period

During the early development of the human embryo, an egg cell is released from a maturing follicle within the ovary and fertilization takes place in the Fallopian tube, transforming the egg cell or ovum into a zygote. Cleavage and multiplication of cells proceed as the zygote migrates toward the uterus. Differentiation of the zygote begins within the uterus, becoming a solid 16-cell sphere known as the morula, then a differentiated set of cells known as the blastocyst, which prepares for implantation in the uterine wall. Once implanted, it taps a vital source of nutriments to sustain further development. (The numbers indicate days following fertilization.)

four, then eight, then sixteen cells. During these cleavages, the zygote remains about the same size; thus, individual cells become smaller and smaller.

After three days, about the time the migrating zygote is ready to enter the uterus, it has become a solid sphere of sixteen cells called a **morula.** The cells of the morula are alike in their capacity to generate a separate, identical organism; all contain and have access to the master genetic blueprint. By the fourth day after conception, however, these cells begin to segregate to carry out specific functions. One group forms a spherical outer cellular layer that will eventually form various membranes serving to provide nutritive support for the embryo (Moore, 1973). A second, inner group of cells begins to organize to one side to form a cell mass that will develop into the embryo. This differentiated group of cells is now called a **blastocyst.**

About the sixth day after conception, the blastocyst begins the process of attaching to the uterine wall, generating fingerlike projections that actively invade the blood-rich lining of the uterus to tap a critical new supply of nutriments. The blastocyst appears only as a slight prominence on the uterine lining once implantation is completed, about the tenth to fourteenth day after conception. In preparing for this event, the blastocyst began secreting hormones and other substances to inhibit menstruation, or the shedding of the uterine lining, and to keep the mother's immune system from rejecting this foreign entity. One of these hormones will eventually become detectable in the mother's urine as a marker in a common pregnancy test.

The Embryonic Period

The embryonic period begins after implantation of the blastocyst in the uterine wall. This stage of development, lasting until about the eighth week after conception, is marked by the rapid differentiation of embryonic cells to form most of the organs and systems within the body. Differentiation is achieved by the migration and formation of specialized cells having distinctive shapes and functions.

Formation of Body Organs and Systems   The first step in the formation of various body organs and systems involves the migration of unspecialized embryonic cells to form a three-layered embryo (Abel, 1989). These three layers—the endoderm, the ectoderm, and the mesoderm—serve as the foundation for all tissues and organs in the body. The *endoderm,* or lower layer, will give rise to many of the linings of such inner organs as lungs, the gastrointestinal tract, liver, pancreas, bladder, and some glands. The *ectoderm,* or upper layer, will eventually form skin, hair, and nails, but its earliest derivatives will be the central nervous system and nerves. The *mesoderm,* or middle layer, will eventually develop into skeleton and muscles, urogenital system, lymph and cardiovascular systems, and other connective tissues.

> ▶ **Roles of nature and nurture**

How, by simply migrating to a layered configuration, do undifferentiated cells come to establish highly distinctive sets of organs and systems? Here is a striking instance in which immediate environment plays a major role. Although cells at first may be unspecialized, their potentiality or fate becomes narrowed by their association with neighboring tissues. They are, in other words, induced to take on certain forms and functions by their surrounding environment. For example, if cells from the ectodermal layer are removed and placed in a culture where they grow isolated from other cell layers, they form epidermal or skinlike tissues. If placed with a layer of mesodermal cells, however, a nervous system will emerge from the ectoderm instead; their developmental course has been modified by the presence of mesodermal cells. The inducing mechanisms remain unknown, but biochemical substances are likely to be involved in this excellent example of the immediate environment's influence on cellular growth (Abel, 1989).

Because the embryonic period is the major time during which development of organs and systems takes place, many possibilities exist for disruption. We will examine some examples later as we discuss the influence of environmental factors on the embryo. Under normal conditions, however, embryological development proceeds in a fairly regular pattern. The sequence of major changes in prenatal development during the embryonic and fetal periods is summarized in the Chronology on page 134. We will emphasize major aspects of cell differentiation for only the brain and nervous system here because these are especially significant for psychological and behavioral development.

morula   Solid ball of cells formed by cleavage of the zygote as it passes through the Fallopian tube.

blastocyst   Hollow, spherical cell mass formed about the fourth day after conception by differentiation of the morula; embeds in uterine lining.

neural tube   Tube in which central nervous system develops. Failure of tube to close can cause spina bifida or no brain growth.

Early Brain and Nervous System Development   On about the fifteenth day after conception, a small group of cells at one end of the embryonic ectoderm begins growing rapidly. This growth creates a reference point for the cephalo (head) and the caudal (tail) end of the embryo and helps to distinguish its left from its right side. These cells induce the development of the **neural tube,** which initiates the formation of the spinal cord, nerves, and eventually the brain.

CHRONOLOGY   **Prenatal Development**

3 WEEKS*

Precursors to vertebrae begin to organize.
Blood vessels form and connect to precursor of umbilical cord.
Blood vessels and tubes establish primitive, one-chambered heart that starts to beat by 21st day.
Major segments of brain begin to differentiate.
Embryo grows to about 2 millimeters in length (about ⅛ inch).

4 WEEKS

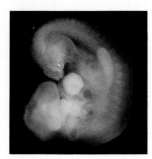

Disc-shaped embryo forms more cylindrical appearance as it folds on cephalo and caudal ends and on right and left side.
Thickening stripe of tissue develops on either side of trunk to begin chest and stomach muscle production. Swelling occurs near upper end of stripe to form arm buds by about day 26. Two days later similar swellings begin at caudal end of stripe to form early buds for lower limbs.
Rudimentary liver, gall bladder, stomach, intestines, pancreas, thyroid, and lungs created.
Nerves begin to form.
Embryo appears to have tail-like cartilage curving under rump.

5 WEEKS

Basic mouth and esophagus develop.
Elbow, wrist regions, and paddle-shaped plate with ridges for future fingers take shape.
Heart differentiates into upper and lower regions.
Embryo grows rapidly, about 1 millimeter a day (.04 inches), but is still less than ½ inch in length.

6–7 WEEKS

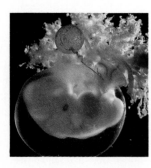

Upper lip, jaws, teeth, eyelids, nostrils, tip of nose, and tongue are formed as head size becomes dominant.
Embryo possesses short, webbed fingers, and foot plate has also begun to differentiate.
Heart divides into four chambers.
Many muscles differentiate and take final shape.
Neurons form rapidly.
Tail-like cartilage regresses.

8–12 WEEKS

Fetus appears to have widely separated eyes and ears set lower in head than they eventually will be.
Eyelids fuse shut about 9th week.
Fingernails, toenails, and hair follicles form.

Fetus begins to show differentiation of reproductive organs (if male about 9th week, if female, several weeks later).
Bones start to grow.
Fetus shows reflexive responses to touch, first around the facial region, then in other regions of body.

13–16 WEEKS

Fingerprints and footprints established.
Spinal cord begins to form.
If female, large numbers of primitive egg cells created.
Other reflexes, including swallowing and sucking, emerge.

17–20 WEEKS

Fetus becomes covered by cheeselike, fatty material secreted by oil glands that probably protects the skin constantly bathed in amniotic fluid.
Fetus sprouts soft downlike hair at end of this period.
Eyebrows and hair visible.
Fetal heartbeat can be heard through mother's abdomen.
Fetus displays stable pattern of sleep and wakefulness and often assumes a favorite position.

21–25 WEEKS

Skin appears wrinkled and has a pink to reddish cast caused by blood in capillaries, which are highly visible through translucent skin.
Eyes fully formed and may be opened and closed.
Fetus can see and hear and produce crying sounds.

26–29 WEEKS

Fat deposits accumulate beneath surface of skin to give fetus a much less wrinkled appearance.
Downy hair may disappear or may remain and be present at birth.
Hair may begin to grow on head.
Lungs are sufficiently developed to permit breathing of air should birth occur.
Nerve cell formation completed, and brain begins to take on wrinkled and fissured appearance.

30–38 WEEKS

Fat continues to accumulate, giving full-term newborn chubby appearance and helping to insulate baby from varying temperatures once born.
Fetus adds about half its total weight.
Skin color turns from red to pink to white or bluish pink for all babies, regardless of racial make-up.

*From conception.
This chart describes the sequence of prenatal development based on the findings of research. There are individual differences in the exact ages at which embryos and fetuses display the various developmental achievements outlined here.

Rapid growth takes place in the region of the neural tube starting about the fourth week. At first, the neural tube is open at both ends. The tube, however, first begins closing in the brain region and a few days later in the caudal region. This sequence exhibits a general principle associated with many aspects of development, the *cephalocaudal principle,* in which organs and systems near the head develop somewhat more rapidly than organs and systems in lower regions of the body.

Failure of the neural tube to knit shut or close at either end can have drastic consequences for development. In *anencephaly,* a condition that results when the cephalic region of the neural tube does not close, the cerebral hemispheres do not develop and most of the cortex is missing at birth. Anencephaly occurs in about one of every thousand live births; newborns with such a condition survive only a short time. *Spina bifida* is a condition that arises when the caudal region of the neural tube fails to close. The resulting cleft in the vertebral column permits spinal nerves to grow outside the protective vertebrae. In more serious cases, the infant may be paralysed and lack sensation in the legs. Surgery after birth often must be performed to keep the condition from getting worse, but lost capacities cannot be restored. Malformations in brain development and impaired intellectual development often accompany spina bifida (Abel, 1989).

The second month after conception is marked by continued rapid development of the head and brain. Nerve cells show an explosive increase in number and undergo extensive migration once the neural tube closes. Because of rapid brain growth, the head becomes extremely large in relation to the rest of the body, making up about half of total body length by the end of the embryonic period. By any standard the embryo is still tiny: it is less than an inch long and weighs only about one-thirteenth of an ounce. Nevertheless, it is recognizably human.

Perhaps one of the most striking milestones occurs about the fifth week after conception, when the nervous system begins to function. Now irregular and faint brain wave activity can be recorded. Touch elicits reflex body movements. Soon, if the head or upper body is touched, the embryo efficiently turns away. Muscles may also flex, but it will still be some time before the mother is able to feel any of these movements.

The Fetal Period

The transition signaling the change from embryo to fetus is the emergence of bone tissue about the eighth week after conception. While organ development continues, particularly in the reproductive system and the brain, many organs and structures within the human body are already formed by this time. The fetal period is dedicated primarily to growth in size and the addition of finishing touches to assist the functioning of various organs and systems. As a consequence, the fetus becomes much less susceptible to potentially damaging environmental influences.

During the third month following conception, the fetus increases to about 3½ inches in length and about 1½ ounces in weight. Its movements become more pronounced. At nine weeks, the fetus opens and closes its lips, wrinkles its forehead, raises and lowers its eyebrows, and turns its head. By the end of twelve weeks, these behaviors have become more coordinated; the fetus can now, for example, display sucking and the basic motions of breathing and swallowing. Its fingers will bend if the arm is touched, and the thumb can be opposed to fingers, an indication that peripheral muscles and nerves are functioning in increasingly sophisticated ways (Samuels & Samuels, 1986).

The Second Trimester By the end of the third month, the fetus has completed the first of three *trimesters* of prenatal development. In the second trimester, the human body grows more rapidly than it will at any other time. By the end of the fourth month, the fetus is about 8 to 10 inches long, although it still weighs only about 6 ounces. During the sixth month, the fetus rapidly starts to gain weight, growing to about 1 and ½ pounds while reaching a length of about 14 inches.

By the middle of the second trimester, fetal kicks, commonly identified as *quickening,* are unmistakable to the mother. Other movements, such as stretching, squirming, and hiccuping, are exhibited as well. Near the end of this trimester, brain wave patterns begin to look like those observed in the newborn. At this time the baby has a small chance to survive if birth should occur, although only when specialized medical facilities are available. A baby born at this age can breathe regularly for a number of hours because the air sacs in the lungs are sufficiently developed to allow transfer of oxygen and carbon dioxide. The surfaces of these air sacs, however, tend to stick together unless production of a substance that prevents this problem has begun. The probability of survival for a baby born during the second trimester therefore still remains quite low.

The Third Trimester The final months of prenatal development add finishing touches to an amazing progression. The cerebral hemispheres, the parts of the brain most responsible for complex mental processes, grow rapidly, folding and developing fissures to give them a wrinkled appearance. *Myelin,* which helps insulate and speed the transmission of neuronal impulses, begins to form and surround some nerve fibers. Brain wave patterns indicating different stages of sleep and wakefulness can also be observed. The sense organs are sufficiently developed so that the fetus is capable of responding to smell and taste as well as auditory, visual, and tactual stimulation; learning also appears to be possible. The fetus continues to gain weight rapidly, although growth slows in the weeks just preceding birth. Control of body temperature and rhythmic respiratory activity remain problematic if birth should occur at the beginning of the third trimester. Nevertheless, **viability,** or the ability of the baby to survive outside the mother's womb, shows dramatic improvement over the course of these three months.

A Caucasian baby can be expected to be born about 269 to 274 days after conception; there is evidence that this gestation time may be a few days shorter for Japanese and Black babies (Mittendorf et al., 1990). Within the medical profession, the common reference for prenatal development is **gestational age** which is based on the date of onset of the mother's last menstrual period prior to conception. This method of calculating prenatal age makes the embryo or fetus fourteen days older than when it was actually conceived.

viability Ability of the baby to survive outside the mother's womb.

gestational age Age of fetus derived from onset of mother's last menstrual period.

Despite the differences used to assess the age of a developing baby and our emphasis on the stages in prenatal development, one other important principle stands out. Underlying the dramatic changes during this time are a continuous set of processes that operate to foster the division of cells, their differentiation, and their organization and functioning. As a consequence, the events that begin at conception and continue to take place throughout prenatal development provide the basis for a baby's ability to adapt to the perinatal and postnatal events soon to be experienced.

Prenatal Diagnosis

We saw in Chapter 3 how the new field of genetic counseling assists couples at risk for children with a genetic disease. Prenatal diagnostic procedures are now available that can detect over two hundred types of hereditary and environmentally-induced defects. We will briefly examine a few of these procedures here.

Amniocentesis   In **amniocentesis** a small amount of amniotic fluid is withdrawn by means of a syringe inserted through the abdominal wall (see Figure 4.2). Cells from the fetus collected by this process are tested for biochemical composition and chromosomal makeup. Amniocentesis is usually performed during the sixteenth to eighteenth week after the last menstrual period; tests carried out on the cells often require several additional weeks for completion. The effectiveness of the procedure at earlier times (when the fetus is eleven to fourteen weeks old) is still being explored (Evans et al., 1989).

Amniocentesis as well as other fetal tests are typically performed only when there is an increased risk of having a genetically defective child. Mothers who are over thirty-five years of age, who have had frequent miscarriages, or who have previous children or other relatives with genetic defects are good candidates for the test. The risks from the procedure are small, but infection and a possible increased likelihood of spontaneous abortion exist.

Chorionic Villus Sampling   In **chorionic villus sampling,** a biopsy or small sample of hairlike projections (*villi*) is taken from the *chorion,* the outer wall of the membrane in which the embryo develops. The villi are obtained by means of a thin tube inserted into the uterus through the vagina. Villi divide rapidly and can be cultured for chromosomal and biochemical analysis. This relatively new test can be performed earlier than amniocentesis—as early as the fifth week of prenatal development—although it is usually performed between the eighth and twelfth week after conception. Its primary advantage is that information can be gained much earlier in pregnancy, thus reducing uncertainty and anxiety about possible genetic or developmental defects. The procedure is somewhat more difficult to perform than amniocentesis and is associated with a slightly greater risk of miscarriage than amniocentesis unless it is performed by highly qualified experts (Green et al., 1988).

Ultrasonography   Other less intrusive tests are now often performed to

amniocentesis Method of sampling the fluid surrounding the developing fetus by insertion of a needle; usually performed in sixteenth week of pregnancy. Used to diagnose fetal genetic and developmental disorders.

chorionic villus sampling Method of sampling fetal chorionic cells; usually performed in eighth or ninth week of pregnancy. Used to diagnose embryonic genetic and developmental disorders.

ultrasonography Method of using sound wave reflections to provide a representation of the developing fetus. Used to estimate gestational age and to detect fetal physical abnormalities.

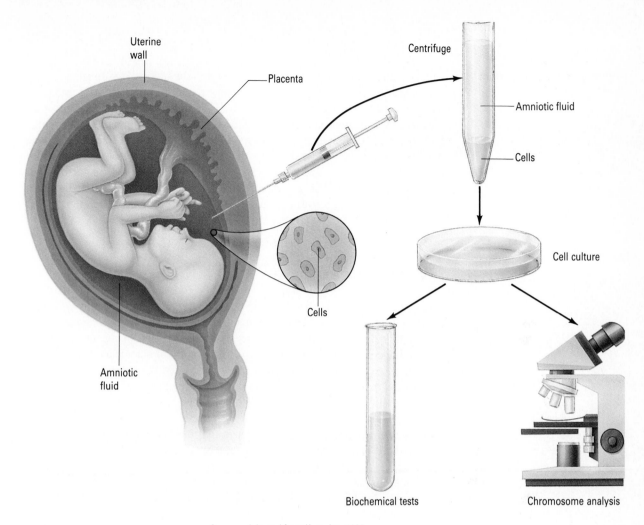

Uterine wall

Placenta

Centrifuge

Amniotic fluid

Cells

Cells

Cell culture

Amniotic fluid

Cells

Biochemical tests

Chromosome analysis

FIGURE 4.2

The Process of Amniocentesis

Source: Adapted from Knowles, 1985.

In this prenatal screening procedure, a needle is inserted into the amniotic fluid surrounding the fetus. A small amount of fluid is withdrawn, and cells shed by the fetus are separated from the fluid by centrifuge. The cells are cultured and submitted to various biochemical and other tests to determine whether chromosomal, genetic, or other developmental defects exist.

provide information on fetal development. **Ultrasonography,** once used primarily to assist in amniocentesis and chorionic villus sampling, is now carried out as a procedure in its own right to help determine if fetal growth is proceeding normally. Sound waves reflecting at different rates from tissues of varying density can be represented on monitors and even printed to form a picture of the baby. This picture can reveal such problems as microcephaly, cardiac malformations, cleft lip and palate, and neural tube and other physical defects. Studies reveal that the procedure is safe, and it is becoming widely used to verify the age of the fetus.

ENVIRONMENTAL FACTORS INFLUENCING PRENATAL DEVELOPMENT

▶ **Roles of nature and nurture**

The amazing events taking place before birth—the union of ovum with sperm, the migration of the zygote to the uterus, the differentiation of organs and systems within the embryo, the growth of the fetus—are among the most intricate and complex phenomena that take place in the universe. As greater knowledge of these events has emerged, both professionals and parents have become increasingly interested in determining how environmental factors influence this process. We have already noted that individual cells form an environmental context that can have dramatic consequences for tissue development. We now consider other aspects of the environment of the embryo and fetus that affect prenatal development within the womb.

Support Within the Womb

The embryo and fetus are supported by a number of major structures, including the placenta, the umbilical cord, and the amniotic sac. The **placenta,** jointly formed by cells from both the blastocyst and the uterine lining, produces important hormones for the fetus. Just as importantly, it serves as the exchange site where oxygen and nutrients are absorbed from the mother's circulatory system and carbon dioxide and waste products are excreted from the embryo's circulatory system. This transfer takes place via a network of intermingling blood-rich capillaries originating from both the mother's and the fetus's circulatory systems. Blood cells are too large to cross the membranes separating the two systems, but smaller molecules of oxygen, carbon dioxide, nutrients, and hormones are able to traverse this barrier. So, too, are chemicals, drugs, and diseases that can interfere with fetal development.

The **umbilical cord** acts as the conduit transporting blood from the placenta to the fetus via two arteries and a vein embedded in a gelatin-like substance about the consistency of a firm rubber hose. The pressure from the circulating blood helps prevent the cord from kinking or knotting.

The fetus lives in the womb surrounded by the fluid-filled **amniotic sac.** Amniotic fluid helps to stabilize temperature, insulates the fetus from bumps and shocks, and contains substances necessary for lung and other aspects of development. The amniotic fluid is constantly being recirculated and renewed as the fetus ingests nutrients and urinates. The fluid consequently contains cells from the fetus and fetal membranes that can be examined by amniocentesis, the prenatal screening procedure described earlier.

placenta   Support organ formed by cells from both blastocyst and uterine lining; serves as exchange site for oxygen, nutrients, and waste products.

umbilical cord   Conduit of blood vessels through which oxygen, nutrients, and waste products are transported between placenta and embryo.

amniotic sac   Fluid-filled, transparent protective membrane surrounding the fetus.

Teratogens

Most babies who negotiate the average thirty-eight-week period from conception to birth emerge healthy, vigorous newborns. Between 95 and 97 percent of infants born within the United States show no evidence of disruptions in their development. Yet, as we saw in Chapter 3, genetic factors can modify normal progress. So, too, can environmental factors. The consequences may range from death to physical malformations to disturbances in behavioral functioning. The study of birth defects and behavioral problems that arise from environmental influences during the prenatal period is called teratology. Environmental agents causing such disruptions are known as **teratogens.**

The Historical and Cultural Context of Teratogens Measured against the span of human interest in such phenomena, the scientific study of birth anomalies has had an extremely brief history. A representation found in Turkey depicting conjoined twins dates to about 6500 B.C. Writings on clay tablets by Babylonian priests from about 4000 B.C. describe *congenital* malformations—birth defects, either genetically or environmentally caused—that are present before or shortly after birth (Warkany, 1983). Then, as in some cultures today, such atypical births were used to divine and predict the future, and because births of abnormal babies were often associated with impending disaster, deformed infants, and even members of the infants' families, might be put to death (Warkany, 1983). Today we know that interference in normal prenatal development arises from two kinds of factors: (1) errors caused by faulty genetic instructions (see Chapter 3), and (2) environmental agents that upset the course of development following conception (Beckman & Brent, 1987). Determining which of these factors is the cause of a given fetal anomaly, however, is not always easy.

Research begun in the late 1800s on animal embryos revealed that several kinds of foreign agents could influence fetal development. However, superstition dominated explanations of congenital malformations in Western civilization until the middle of this century. In 1941, an ophthalmologist named McAllister Gregg theorized that rubella, a form of measles, caused visual anomalies in the fetus. During this same decade many infants born to mothers exposed to the atomic bomb were reported to have birth defects—a finding that, along with studies involving animals, implicated radiation as a teratogen (Warkany & Schraffenberger, 1947). Yet the full import of these isolated observations did not become apparent until researchers documented that mothers who had taken a presumably harmless drug called thalidomide frequently bore infants with arm and leg malformations (McBride, 1961). The thalidomide tragedy made absolutely clear, as no previous finding had, that human embryos could be seriously harmed by an environmental agent without adverse effects on the mother or others already born (Wilson, 1977).

To be convinced that environmental agents can disrupt prenatal development, researchers had to give up a fundamental misconception about the relationship between the fetus and its mother. Many experts claimed that a placental barrier filtered out virtually all harmful agents so that the fetus lived in a highly insulated, protective world. But researchers now realize that the fetus may be susceptible to exposure to virtually any substance if sufficiently concentrated (Samuels & Samuels, 1986).

Principles of Teratology A number of broad generalizations have emerged from extensive research on teratogens within the past thirty years (Abel, 1989; Vorhees, 1986; Wilson, 1977). These principles help establish order among the sometimes bewildering array of adverse consequences that specific drugs, diseases, and other agents have been found to have on development.

teratogen Any environmental agent that can cause deviations in prenatal development. Consequences may range from death to behavioral problems.

• *The Principle of Susceptibility: Individuals within species as well as species themselves show major differences in susceptibility to different teratogens* The thalidomide tragedy resulted, in part, from the failure to realize that the effects of this drug differed among species. Extremely large doses of thalidomide were known to cause abnormal fetal development in rats (Cohen, 1966), but the level given to pregnant mothers in Europe and Canada, where thalidomide was administered to reduce morning sickness and anxiety, was considerably lower. For reasons unknown, human and other primate embryos are far more sensitive than embryos of other species to small doses of thalidomide. More than seven thousand babies were born with limb defects and intellectual retardation before this species difference was recognized. The genotype of an individual mother and her fetus may also affect susceptibility to a teratogen: some babies were exposed to thalidomide between the third and eighth week after conception, the interval during which it usually causes anomalies, yet showed no ill effects from the drug (Kajii, Kida, & Takahaski, 1973).

▶ **Sensitive periods**

• *The Principle of Critical or Sensitive Periods: The extent to which a teratogen will affect the fetus depends on the stage of development during which exposure occurs* The majority of human organs and systems are most sensitive to toxic agents during the period from the third to eighth week after conception, when they are still being formed. Thus, numerous teratogenic agents produce their most severe congenital malformations at this time. Figure 4.3 illustrates periods when specific organs of the body show the greatest susceptibility to teratogens. It also confirms that many body systems show vulnerability to teratogens throughout much of prenatal development. In fact, the brain continues to undergo substantial neural differentiation, migration, and growth during the second and third trimesters of pregnancy and even the weeks and months following birth. As a consequence, exposure to teratogens throughout much of prenatal development may have significant behavioral consequences for the infant.

The impact of teratogens on the zygote are not well known. Some researchers believe that many agents typically have no effect in this earliest stage, but others suggest that a common outcome is loss of the zygote. A large proportion of pregnancies terminate very early, well before the mother is aware that she is pregnant. Whether these spontaneous abortions are a consequence of genetic or teratogenic factors, however, is unknown.

▶ **Sociocultural influence**

• *The Principle of Access: The accessibility of a given teratogen to a fetus or embryo influences the extent of its damage* Many factors determine when and to what extent an embryo or fetus is exposed to a teratogen. Cultural and social practices may prevent or encourage whether a pregnant mother has access to drugs, is inoculated for certain diseases, or works in locations exposing her to chemicals and other toxins. Even when the mother is exposed to the teratogen, it must still gain entry into the uterine environment. The way the mother has been exposed to the agent, how she metabolizes it, and how the agent is transported to the womb all influence whether a teratogen reaches a sufficient threshold to affect the baby.

• *The Principle of Dose-Response Relationships: The extent of exposure or dosage level of a given teratogen influences the extent of its damage* Once an agent gains access to the fetus and reaches a critical threshold, the severity of its effects is often related to level of dosage. The more a mother smokes, for example, the greater the likelihood that her baby will weigh less at birth and be born prematurely. The concentration of a toxic agent reaching the fetus, however,

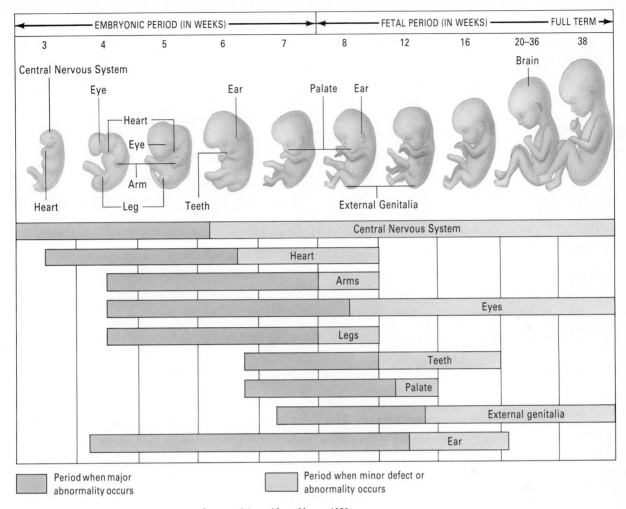

FIGURE 4.3

Source: Adapted from Moore, 1989.

Sensitive Periods in Prenatal Development

During prenatal development, organs and systems undergo periods in which they are more or less sensitive to teratogenic influences—environmental agents that can cause deviations in development. The potential for major structural defects (dark-colored sections) is usually greatest during the embryonic period, when many organs are being formed. However, many regions of the body, including the central nervous system, continue to have some susceptibility to teratogens (light-colored sections) during the fetal period.

cannot always be determined based on the mother's exposure to it. The severity of illness a mother experiences, for example, does not always predict the impact of a disease on the fetus. The mother's physical condition also determines how much of a teratogen reaches the fetus.

• *The Principle of Teratogenic Response: Teratogens do not uniformly show the same effects on prenatal development* Teratogens may cause death or disrupt development of specific organs and systems. They may also have behavioral consequences, impairing sensorimotor, cognitive, social, and emotional development. As earlier principles suggest, species and individual differences, as well as time, duration, and intensity of exposure play a role in determining the impact of a specific teratogen on prenatal development. Rubella, for example, may cause visual, auditory, cardiac, or nervous system anomalies depending on which week of pregnancy the mother acquires the disease. Alcohol can cause congenital defects during the embryonic period but may interfere with prenatal weight gain and contribute to postnatal behavioral problems during the second and third trimesters of pregnancy (Abel, 1989).

TABLE 4.1

Causes of Congenital Malformations

Suspected Cause	Percent of Total
Unknown	65%
Genetic	
Autosomal genetic disease	15%–20%
Chromosomal abnormalities	5%
Environmental	
Teratogens	3%–5%
Maternal conditions and uterine problems	4%–6%

Source: Adapted from Beckman and Brent, 1987.

One other important implication of this principle is that very different teratogenic agents can produce a similar pattern of defects. Thus, efforts to pinpoint the reason that a baby was born with a given anomaly are frequently unsuccessful. As Table 4.1 indicates, the cause of the majority of congenital malformations in human babies born in the United States cannot be traced to any single teratogenic event.

• *The Principle of Interference with Specific Mechanisms: Teratogens affect prenatal development by interfering with biochemical processes contributing to the differentiation, migration, or other basic functions of cells* This principle helps winnow out folk beliefs from scientific explanations of fetal anomalies. Looking at a frightening visual stimulus, for example, has no direct consequence for the fetus. On the other hand, a teratogen such as alcohol may affect development because it can interfere with normal fetal metabolism, including neural cell growth and migration. These changes may, in turn, have physical, behavioral and other consequences for the developing fetus.

• *The Principle of Developmental Delay and "Sleeper Effects": Some teratogens may cause temporary delays in development with no long-term negative consequences, but others will cause developmental problems only late in development* Although many teratogenic effects may be observed at birth and are permanent and irreversible, the impact of teratogens on development is probably substantially underestimated because many produce "sleeper effects" that go unnoticed for some time after birth but sow the seed for problems that become apparent in childhood and even later. One of the most highly publicized examples of a "sleeper effect" involves mothers who were treated with diethylstilbestrol (DES), a hormone administered from the 1940s through the 1960s to prevent miscarriages. When the children of these mothers became adults, women showed a high rate of genital tract cancers and men displayed a high incidence of abnormalities of the testes.

Drugs as Teratogens

Now that we have considered general principles involving teratogens, we can examine the effects that specific kinds of environmental agents have on the unborn baby. Among them are a number of substances expectant mothers may use either as medicine or as mood-altering devices. Some are frequently a part of the unborn baby's world.

▶ **Sociocultural influence**

Alcohol   Because alcohol readily crosses the placenta, its concentration in the fetus is likely to be similar to that in the mother (Abel, 1981). Simply stated, this means that every time a pregnant mother takes a drink, she may be giving her baby a drink of proportionate size. Nevertheless, alcohol consumption by pregnant women continues to be acceptable in many cultures. From 9 to 11 percent of pregnant American women are considered heavy or problem drinkers (Abel, 1982). The proportion may be substantially greater in Portugal, France, Italy, Switzerland, West Germany, and some other countries (U.S. Department of HEW, 1978). The definition of heavy drinking varies but usually refers to consumption of two or more drinks a day (two 12-ounce glasses of beer, two 2½-ounce glasses of wine, or two ⅝-ounce glasses of distilled spirits) or ten to fourteen drinks over a week's duration. About 300,000 infants born each year in the United States are estimated to be exposed to this amount of alcohol on a regular basis.

Widespread recognition of the potential dangers of alcohol emerged in the early 1970s when Kenneth Jones and David Smith (1973) reported a constellation of deficits frequently observed in babies born of alcoholic mothers. Babies displaying this **fetal alcohol syndrome (FAS)** showed prenatal and postnatal growth retardation, microcephaly (small head size), and abnormal eye and other facial features. Nearly two in every thousand mothers (about one in forty alcoholic mothers) are estimated to deliver a baby displaying FAS (Abel & Sokol, 1987). Approximately 85 percent of these children will be mildly to moderately retarded, with intelligence quotients typically ranging between 65 and 80 (Eskenazi, 1984). Many will show physical withdrawal symptoms shortly after birth.

The effects of alcohol are dose related. Mothers who drink heavily are far more likely to have children diagnosed with FAS than mothers who drink moderately or infrequently (Weiner & Morse, 1988). Heavy drinkers are also more likely than moderate or light drinkers to give birth to infants with *fetal alcohol effects (FAE)*. These less severe effects include mental and growth retardation, hyperactivity, behavior problems, learning and language disabilities, shortened attention span, and sleep disturbances that extend into early childhood and perhaps beyond (Landesman-Dwyer, Ragozin, & Little, 1981; Rosett & Weiner, 1984). Ann Streissguth and colleagues found the children of mothers who consumed more than three drinks of alcohol per day showed an average five-point decrement in IQ at age four compared with children whose mothers drank less or no alcohol (Streissguth et al., 1989). These effects appear to be caused by alcohol consumption alone rather than poorer nutrition, use of other drugs (including cigarettes), or other frequently accompanying social and cultural factors. Moreover, unlike infants with growth delays produced by malnutrition and some other drugs, infants with FAE fail to show catch-up or compensatory growth once nutritional circumstances are improved (Rodgers & Lee, 1988; Weiner & Morse, 1988).

How does alcohol produce these effects? One way is by directly modifying cell functioning, including cell differentiation, migration, and growth. Infants with fetal alcohol syndrome who have died shortly after birth and whose brains

This baby, born to an alcoholic mother, displays the characteristics of fetal alcohol syndrome. These characteristics include microcephaly (small head size), eyes widely set apart, thin, flat upper lip, delayed physical growth, and mental retardation.

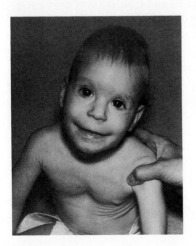

have been examined evidence structural changes caused by delays and errors in the ways neurons migrate to form the cortex, or outer layers, of the brain (Clarren et al., 1978). The metabolism of alcohol also requires substantial amounts of oxygen. If the oxygen available to the fetus is consumed to metabolize the alcohol, then less may be available for the growth and functioning of neural and other cells, and those cells may be impaired or lost (Abel, 1982). Alcohol is also associated with a reduction in respiration rate, disturbances of placental functioning, and changes in maternal physiology that further diminish availability of oxygen to the fetus (Abel, 1982).

Binge drinking, even on an infrequent basis, may be especially hazardous because it exposes the fetus to highly concentrated alcohol levels (Chasnoff, 1986). But what about the effects of moderate amounts of alcohol? Even a single drink a day throughout pregnancy poses risks, according to some researchers. A drink a day has been linked to a substantial increase in number of spontaneous abortions and to reduced alertness, less vigorous body activity, more tremors, and less rapid learning in newborns as compared with babies of mothers who do not drink (Kline et al., 1980; Streissguth, Barr, & Martin, 1983). The effects of small amounts of alcohol on prenatal development remain controversial, but most physicians advise that total abstinence is the most effective way to minimize risk to the baby (Rodgers & Lee, 1988; Samuels & Samuels, 1986).

Cigarette Smoking   A decade ago nearly one-third of expectant mothers smoked (Merritt, 1981). Since then, the popularity of cigarette smoking has continued to increase, especially among younger women, and so, too, have concerns about its impact on prenatal development. Researchers agree that smoking does not cause major congenital defects, but nicotine, or some other of the more than two thousand pharmacological agents found in cigarette smoke (U.S. Public Health Service, 1979), does have serious consequences for fetal and infant mortality, birth weight, and possibly postnatal development (Weinberger & Weiss, 1988; Zuckerman, 1988). The most consistent finding from studies of babies born to smokers, compared with those born to non-smokers, is their smaller size. The more a mother smokes during pregnancy, the lower the baby's average weight at birth; babies of mothers who smoke typically weigh about two hundred grams (about seven ounces) less than other babies. Babies of mothers who smoke are likely to be born a few days early, but even those carried to full term will be smaller and lighter, on average, than infants who have not experienced cigarette smoke.

A second consistent finding is an increase in spontaneous abortions, still-births, and neonatal deaths in pregnant women who smoke (Abel, 1980). The Ontario Perinatal Mortality Study examined the effects of no smoking, light smoking (less than one pack a day), and heavy smoking (more than one pack a day) on death rate in more than fifty-one thousand births (Meyer & Tonascia, 1977). Various factors such as race, socioeconomic status, mother's age, number of previous children, and occurrence of anemia were found to be linked to a number of deaths, but even when these variables were controlled, light smoking was found to increase the risk of fetal death by 20 percent, and heavy smoking by 35 percent.

As with alcohol consumption, a reduction in oxygen may account for these effects. Smoking increases carbon monoxide in the blood of both the mother

fetal alcohol syndrome (FAS)
Cluster of fetal abnormalities stemming from mother's consumption of alcohol; includes growth retardation, defects in facial features, and intellectual retardation.

and fetus. Because carbon monoxide displaces oxygen in red blood cells, smoking may cause as much as 12 percent less oxygen to be circulated by the fetal blood (Abel, 1980). Nicotine is also associated with reduced blood flow to the placenta. These events can help explain why a fetus's heart rate goes up when its mother smokes, a reaction possibly designed to maintain adequate oxygen (Samuels & Samuels, 1986). Perhaps for the same reason, babies of mothers who smoke tend to have larger placentas and more frequent placental abnormalities compared with babies of the same weight born to nonsmoking mothers (Meyer & Tonascia, 1977; Weinberger & Weiss, 1988).

The behavioral and long-term consequences of smoking for the newborn are less well understood. Studies have reported that newborns display poorer learning (Martin et al., 1977) and reduced visual alertness (Landesman-Dwyer, Keller, & Streissguth, 1978), but infant tests of development have failed to uncover any consistent pattern of deficits for infants born to smokers (Abel, 1980; Eskenazi, 1984). At older ages, children of mothers who smoked during pregnancy have been found to perform lower than children of nonsmokers on a variety of academic measures, but this finding is confounded by possible postnatal differences in exposure to smoke. In one study of twelve thousand children in Great Britain in which socioeconomic class and mother's age were controlled, seven-year-old children of mothers who smoked were four months behind in reading level compared with children of mothers who did not smoke. By eleven years of age, children of smokers lagged several months behind other children on general ability, reading, and mathematics tests (Butler & Goldstein, 1973). In another, more recent study of nine- to eleven-year-olds, however, children of smokers did not differ on a variety of academic, social, and other measures compared with children of nonsmokers (Lefkowitz, 1981). Thus, the long-term behavioral consequences of maternal smoking remain controversial.

Prescription and Over-the-Counter Drugs   Other legal drugs besides alcohol and cigarette smoke can be hazardous for fetal development. Some are known teratogens (see Table 4.2), but our knowledge of the effects of many others remains perilously limited. Aspirin, for example, has been demonstrated to impair behavioral competence in the offspring of lower animals. One recent well-controlled study found that aspirin may also be associated with lower IQ in early childhood (Streissguth et al., 1984). Because of inconsistencies in the findings, however, many drugs, including aspirin, must be categorized as suspected or possibly toxic rather than as either established teratogens or completely safe under normal conditions of usage.

Somewhere between 60 and 80 percent of pregnant women in the United States take prescription and over-the-counter drugs at some time while they are pregnant (Lewis, P., 1983; Schnoll, 1986). Perhaps of greater concern is the number of medications women consume during pregnancy, an average of 3.7 prescription drugs alone (Samuels & Samuels, 1986). Little is known about the effects of many of these drugs and even less about possible interactive effects when multiple drugs are used. Thus, expectant mothers are often advised to take *no* drugs during pregnancy, including many over-the-counter remedies, or to take them only under the close supervision of their physician. Cautions printed on the labels of cough syrups, pain relievers, antacids, vitamins, and other readily available health aids are placed there for good reasons.

Drug	Description and Known or Suspected Effects
Alcohol	Growth retardation, congenital malformations, mental retardation, and behavioral problems (fetal alcohol syndrome).
Amniopterin	Anticancer agent. Facial defects and a number of other congenital malformations as well as mental retardation.
Amphetamines	Stimulants for the central nervous system, some types frequently used for weight control. Readily cross placental barrier. Fetal intrauterine growth retardation often reported but may be a result of accompanying malnutrition or multiple-drug use (Little, Snell, & Gilstrapp, 1988; Rodgers & Lee, 1988).
Antibiotics (streptomycin) (tetracycline)	Streptomycin associated with hearing loss. Tetracycline associated with staining of baby's teeth if exposure occurs during second or third trimester.
Aspirin	Possibility of increased bleeding in both mother and infant. Possible association with lower IQ.
Barbiturates (pentobarbital) (phenobarbital) (secobarbital)	Sedatives and anxiety reducers. Considerable evidence of neurobiological and behavioral complications in rats. Readily cross human placenta; concentrations in fetus may be greater than in mother. Newborns may show withdrawal symptoms (Brown & Fishman, 1984). No consistent evidence of long-term effects in humans.
Benzodiazepines (chlordiazepoxide) (diazepam)	Tranquilizers. Not shown to have teratogenic effects (Rogers & Lee, 1988). Newborns may display withdrawal symptoms (Eskenazi, 1984).
Caffeine	High levels of consumption reported associated with prematurity and lower birth weights. Birth defects suspected.
Hydantoins	Treatment for epilepsy. Produce *fetal hydantoin syndrome,* including heart defects, cleft lip or palate, decreased head size, and mental retardation. Controversy continues over whether effects are entirely caused by drug or by conditions associated with the mother, including her epilepsy (Eskenazi, 1984).
Lithium	Treatment for manic depression. Crosses placenta freely. Known to be teratogenic in pre-mammalian animals. Strong suggestive evidence of increased cardiovascular defects in human infants. Behavioral effects unknown. Administration at time of delivery markedly reduces infant responsivity (Kerns & Davis, 1986).
Sex Hormones (androgens) (estrogens) (progestins)	Contained in birth control pills, fertility drugs, and other drugs to prevent miscarriages. Continued use of birth control pills during pregnancy associated with heart and circulatory disorders. Behavioral and personality implications suspected.
Thalidomide	Reduce morning sickness and anxiety. Deformities of the limbs, depending on time of exposure, often accompanied by mental retardation (Gouin-Decarie, 1969).
Tobacco	Lower birth weight and increased risk of spontaneous abortion, stillbirth, and neonatal deaths.
Tricyclics (imipramine) (desimipramine)	Antidepressants. Some tricyclics cross the placenta. Studies with rats reveal developmental and behavioral disturbances. Studies with humans reveal no consistent findings (Kerns & Davis, 1986).
Vitamins	Large amounts of vitamin A known to cause major birth defects. Excess amounts of other vitamins may also cause prenatal malformations.

Note: This listing is not meant to be exhaustive and other drugs may have teratogenic effects. No drug should be taken during pregnancy without consultation with a qualified physician.

TABLE 4.2

Some Prescription and Other Frequently Used Drugs and Their Known or Suspected Effects on Prenatal Development

Illegal Drugs The effects of illegal drugs such as marijuana, heroin, and cocaine on prenatal development are even more difficult to untangle than the effects of prescription and over-the-counter medications. Drug users are rarely certain of the concentrations or the contents of the drugs they consume. Wide variability in frequency of use, possible interactions from exposure to multiple drugs, poor nutritional status, inadequate or no prenatal care, and possible psychological and physiological differences created by taking such drugs before or even after pregnancy, compared to those who do not take such drugs, compound the problem of isolating the teratogenic effects of illegal drugs. Yet the need to understand their impact on development has never been greater. About 11 percent of expectant mothers in the United States are estimated to be drug abusers; some 375,000 infants are born to them each year (National Association for Perinatal Addiction Research and Education, 1988).

As many as 10 to 14 percent of expectant mothers are estimated to use marijuana at some time during pregnancy (Abel, Rockwood, & Riley, 1986), although for many that use is infrequent. Nevertheless, researchers have long known from animal experiments that the psychoactive ingredients associated with marijuana cross the placenta and are stored in the amniotic fluid (Harbison & Mantilla-Plata, 1972). These ingredients may even be transferred postnatally through the mother's milk (Dalterio & Bartke, 1979).

One large study conducted in Ottawa, Canada, enlisted the cooperation of approximately seven hundred pregnant women to investigate whether marijuana affects development (Fried, 1986). About 3 percent of the sample reported heavy use during pregnancy, defined as smoking marijuana more than five times per week or exposure to equivalent amounts of its active ingredients in other ways. When heavy users were matched with nonusers for alcohol and cigarette consumption as well as income level, several differences emerged. Length of gestation was shorter for heavy marijuana users, a finding that was anticipated because at one time in Europe marijuana was given to speed labor. Even so, the frequency of miscarriages, birth complications, or major congenital anomalies was similar for both groups. Infants born to heavy marijuana users, however, exhibited wider eye separation and more skin covering the nasal regions of the eyes than other infants (Fried, 1986).

As newborns, infants of both heavy users and nonusers were similar in irritability, ability to be soothed, activity level, alertness, and measures of physical adjustment to their new environment. But infant tests given three to four days after birth revealed less responsivity and slower habituation to light in infants exposed to heavy marijuana use. Visual problems throughout early childhood continued among these children (Fried, 1986). Participation in the Ottawa project was voluntary, limiting generalization of the findings, but visual and attentional disturbances associated with marijuana have also been reported in animal research and other studies with humans (Brown & Fishman, 1984; Golub, Sassenrath, & Chapman, 1981).

The effects of heroin and morphine on the infant came to the attention of the public as early as the late 1800s when doctors reported withdrawal symptoms in newborns whose mothers used these drugs (Zagon & McLaughlin, 1984). By the early 1900s heroin and morphine were known to be transmitted through the placenta as well as through the mother's milk. Today, approximately one in every thousand infants born in the United States has been exposed to heroin or another opium-based product called methadone (Zagon & McLaughlin, 1984). Often given under regulated conditions as a heroin substitute, methadone may have effects on fetal development that are just as serious as heroin's.

Between 60 and 90 percent of infants born to heroin- and methadone-addicted mothers undergo withdrawal symptoms such as tremors, diarrhea, high-pitched cries, and sweating. These signs of fetal distress peak in severity at about six weeks following birth but persist for four to six months (Chasnoff, Hatcher, & Burns, 1980). Although congenital malformations have not been positively linked to either drug, stillbirths and infant deaths are more frequent and lower birth weight is common. Sleep disturbances, retarded sensorimotor development, and visual and auditory problems are often found in these infants as well (Hans et al., 1984). Such problems continue to be reported in older infants and children, although these difficulties may, of course, arise from the disruptive postnatal environment in which many of them grow up. Methadone programs that provide high-quality prenatal care, emphasize adequate nutrition, and furnish other kinds of support to the addict can reduce the frequency of low birth weight, mortality, and behavioral teratogenic effects associated with these drugs (Rodgers & Lee, 1988).

Cocaine has become the most widely used illegal substance among many drug-dependent pregnant women today. Whereas the frequency of use of other drugs stayed level or declined from the mid-1970s to the mid-1980s, cocaine use in the United States tripled and quadrupled among several age groups, including young adults (Atkins, 1988). Perhaps as many as 200,000 infants a year in the United States are now born to mothers who use cocaine during pregnancy. In some major metropolitan areas, one in four mothers bearing a baby has abused cocaine during her pregnancy. Mothers of many of these infants use crack, an especially potent and addictive form of cocaine.

Infants exposed to cocaine while in the womb are at substantial risk. Cocaine readily crosses into the placenta, and once it reaches the fetus, it stays longer than in adults because of the difficulty the fetus has in breaking the substance down. It can continue to influence the baby after birth through the mother's milk. Babies exposed to cocaine during prenatal development are likely to be born prematurely, have lower birth weight and small head size, suffer seizures and strokes, experience respiratory problems, and have kidney and genital malformations (Taylor, 1989). Behaviorally, cocaine-exposed newborns have difficulty moving from sleep to being awake and alert, seem irritable and tense, and display sensorimotor retardation (Chasnoff, 1988). Cocaine babies often show extremes in behavior—jitteriness and excitability or depression and lethargy—and some babies act both ways at different times. Many of these infants continue to have significant behavioral problems at least into the preschool years (*Crack Children,* 1990). The extent to which these problems can be attributed to cocaine, to the lower birth weight associated with cocaine exposure, or to other factors remains difficult to sort out, but well-controlled experiments with animals provide additional evidence that prenatal exposure to cocaine significantly impairs development and behavior.

Diseases as Teratogens

From 2 to 8 percent of babies born to American women are exposed to one or more infectious or parasitic diseases or other forms of illness during pregnancy (Andiman & Horstmann, 1984; Saltzman & Jordan, 1988). Fortunately, most babies are unaffected by these exposures. But some diseases have physical and behavioral consequences for some babies (see Table 4.3). These effects may occur even when the mother may be completely unaware of illness.

▶ **Sociocultural influence**

Rubella   Rubella (German measles) continues to be a major cause of congenital malformations and death in many regions of the world. Fewer than twenty cases of congenital defects associated with the disease were reported in the United States in the early 1980s (Orenstein et al., 1984). Before widespread vaccination, however, the last major outbreak of rubella in this country in 1964 caused congenital defects in an estimated twenty thousand infants (Andiman & Horstmann, 1984). Unfortunately, no vaccination programs exist in many Third World countries, making rubella of more than merely historical concern for many populations.

▶ **Sensitive periods**

The most common problems associated with rubella include growth retardation, cataracts, hearing impairment, heart defects, and mental retardation. Virtually every organ, however, may be affected, depending on when the disease is contracted during prenatal development (Andiman & Horstmann, 1984). Up to 50 percent of infants born to mothers with rubella during the first month of pregnancy will have congenital abnormalities, but this percent declines to 22 percent, 6 percent, and less than 1 percent during the second, third, and fourth months, respectively (Saltzman & Jordan, 1988).

▶ **Sensitive periods**

Toxoplasmosis   Toxoplasmosis is caused by a parasite found in many mammals and birds. From 20 to 40 percent of adults in various regions of the United States have been exposed to it (Feldman, 1982). Its prevalence around the world varies widely, but as a rule toxoplasmosis is found more frequently in tropical climates than in colder regions of the earth.

Perhaps the most unique aspect of the parasite causing toxoplasmosis is that its life cycle can only be completed in cats. Humans obtain the disease by touching cat feces containing the parasite or by eating raw or partially cooked meat, especially pork and lamb, that has also been infected by exposure to cat feces. Children and adults are frequently unaware of their exposure because the infection may have no symptoms or cause only a minor fever or rash. Fortunately, only about 3 percent of mothers contracting the disease during pregnancy will have an infected baby (MacLeod & Lee, 1988). The risk of infection is much greater during the last trimester of pregnancy, but the developmental consequences are minimal by then. An earlier fetal infection, although less likely, can have far more devastating consequences. Growth retardation, jaundice, accumulation of fluid in the brain, and visual and central nervous system defects are the most typical effects. In many cases, however, mental retardation, neuromuscular abnormalities, impaired vision, and other eye problems become apparent only later in development (MacLeod & Lee, 1988; Pass, 1987). Thus, the prognosis for infants exposed to the disease who lack any symptoms at or shortly after birth is difficult to predict.

Because some drugs can reduce the risk of the disease, widespread screening of pregnant mothers for exposure to toxoplasmosis has sometimes been proposed. Simply avoiding maternal infection during pregnancy, however, is currently the most cost-effective method of preventing congenital toxoplasmosis.

Sexually Transmitted Diseases

Acquired Immune Deficiency Syndrome (AIDS)	See text.
Gonorrhea	If acquired prenatally, may cause premature birth. Most frequently contracted during delivery through infected birth canal and may then attack eyes. In the United States, silver nitrate eye drops are administered to all newborns to prevent blindness.
Hepatitis B	Associated with premature birth, low birth weight, increased neonatal death, and liver disorders (Pass, 1987). Most frequently contracted during delivery through birth canal or postnatally.
Herpes Simplex	Of its two forms, only one is transmitted primarily through sexual activity. Both forms, however, can be transmitted to the fetus, causing severe damage to the central nervous system (Pass, 1987). Most infections occur during delivery through birth canal containing active herpes lesions. Even when treated, the majority of infants will die or suffer central nervous system damage (Nahmias, Keyserling, & Kernick, 1983). Mothers may be unaware of symptoms even when disease is active, so may be frequently tested if known to have virus. If the disease is active, caesarian delivery is used to avoid infecting the baby.
Syphilis	Damage to fetus does not begin until about 18 weeks after conception. May then cause death, mental retardation, and other congenital defects. Infected newborns may not show signs of disease until early childhood.

Other Diseases and Maternal Conditions

Cholera	Increased risk of stillbirth.
Cytomegalovirus	See text.
Diabetes	Risk of congenital malformations and death to fetus two to three times higher than for babies born to nondiabetic mothers (Coustan & Felig, 1988). Excessive size at birth also common. Effects are likely to be a consequence of metabolic disturbances rather than of insulin. Rapid advances in care have helped reduce risks substantially for diabetic mothers.
Hypertension (chronic)	Probability of miscarriage or infant death increased.
Influenza	Some forms linked to increased heart and central nervous system abnormalities as well as spontaneous abortions.
Mumps	Increased risk of spontaneous abortion and stillbirth.
Pregnancy-induced Hypertension	5%–10% of expectant mothers experience significant increase in blood pressure, often accompanied by *edema* (swelling of face and extremities as a result of water retention), rapid weight gain, and protein in urine during later months of pregnancy. Condition is also known as *pre-eclampsia* (or *eclampsia,* if severe) and *toxemia.* Under severe conditions, mother may suffer seizures and coma. The fetus is at increased risk for death, brain damage, and lower birth weight. Adequate protein consumption helps minimize problems. Drugs used to treat high blood pressure may be just as hazardous to fetus as the condition itself.

TABLE 4.3

Maternal Diseases and Other Maternal Conditions That May Affect Prenatal Development

Rh Incompatibility	Blood containing a certain protein is Rh-positive, Rh-negative if it lacks that protein. Hereditary factors determine which type the individual possesses. If fetus's blood is Rh-positive, it can cause formation of antibodies in blood of mother who is Rh-negative. These antibodies can cross placental barrier to destroy red blood cells of fetus. May result in miscarriage or stillbirth, jaundice, anemia, heart defects, and mental retardation. Likelihood of birth defects increases with succeeding pregnancies because antibodies are usually not present until after birth of first Rh-positive child. A vaccine (Rhogam) can be administered to the mother within 3 days after childbirth, miscarriage, or abortion to prevent antibody formation.
Rubella	See text.
Smallpox	Increased risk of spontaneous abortion and stillbirth.
Toxoplasmosis	See text.
Varicellazoster (chicken pox)	Skin and muscle defects, intrauterine growth retardation, limb reduction.

TABLE 4.3 (continued)

Maternal Diseases and Other Maternal Conditions That May Affect Prenatal Development

▶ **Sociocultural influence**

Meat should be fully cooked and hands frequently washed following meat preparation. Cat litter must be disposed of carefully. Because the parasite can survive in cat feces for as long as a year under some conditions (Pass, 1987), even work in gardens frequented by cats can be hazardous.

Cytomegalovirus Cytomegalovirus (CMV), which causes swelling of the salivary glands and mononucleosis-like symptoms in adults, is probably the single most frequent cause of infection in newborns today. It affects one to two of every hundred babies (Saltzman & Jordan, 1988), and as many as 20 percent of these infected infants can be expected to sustain some congenital damage. CMV, along with other members of the herpesvirus family, shares the property of latency; after contacting the disease, an individual may show no signs of it for many years. It may, however, reappear at any time, and neither the initial occurrence or its reappearance, often without symptoms, can be treated. CMV is most frequently reported in Japan and Africa and among lower socioeconomic groups, yet 60 percent of middle- and high-income groups in the United States have been exposed to it (Wentworth & Alexander, 1971). Transmission occurs sexually, through blood transfusions, and by other body fluids. CMV is particularly common in day-care centers, where it can easily be passed from child to child or between child and adult through physical contact.

Babies are most frequently exposed to CMV during birth or early thereafter if the disease is active in the mother at these times. But infection can occur within the womb. For infants who acquire the disease prenatally, growth retardation, jaundice, skin disorders, and small head size are common consequences. About one-third of infants showing these characteristics at birth will die in early infancy (Pass et al., 1980); a large percentage of those who survive will be mentally retarded. About half of infants sustaining congenital damage from CMV will have no symptoms at birth. Many of these infants show progressive loss of hearing caused by damage to the auditory nerve (Andiman & Horstmann, 1984), or other more subtle defects emerge, including minimal brain dysfunction, visual or dental abnormalities, or motor and neural problems (Pass, 1987; Saltzman & Jordan, 1988).

Sexually Transmitted and Other Diseases   Several diseases identified as teratogenic are primarily transmitted sexually, or the infection and its symptoms are usually centered around the genitourinary tract (see Table 4.3). Most sexually transmitted diseases (STDs), however, have limited means of transmission. Acquired immune deficiency syndrome (AIDS) and hepatitis B, for example, can be acquired only through exposure to blood or infected sexual partners; syphilis and certain strains of herpes simplex are virtually always contracted from infected sexual partners. STDs can interfere with reproduction in a number of ways. They may compromise the mother's health (AIDS, gonorrhea, hepatitis B, herpes simplex, syphilis); scar or disturb reproductive organs so conception and normal pregnancy cannot proceed (chlamydia, gonorrhea); directly infect the fetus (AIDS, herpes simplex); and interfere with healthy postnatal development (AIDS, hepatitis B, herpes simplex, syphilis) (Lee, 1988).

In recent years the frequency of most of these diseases has risen rapidly in populations around the world. None, however, has had so dramatic an impact as acquired immune deficiency syndrome (AIDS). AIDS already is, or will soon be, one of the top five leading causes of death among children and adolescents today (Novello et al., 1989). Of the estimated ten thousand to twenty-thousand HIV-infected children alive in the United States, most were infected prenatally or during birth. Approximately one-third of expectant mothers with human immunodeficiency virus type 1 (HIV) infection, the precursor to AIDS, will give birth to infected infants (Valleroy, Harris, & Way, 1990). Many of these infants will show poor growth and mental and motor retardation, and those whose infections have progressed to AIDS will die, often within a matter of months after their birth (Minkoff et al., 1987).

Environmental Hazards as Teratogens

Radiation was one of the earliest confirmed teratogens, and it is known to cause genetic mutation as well. Radiation's teratogenic effects include spontaneous abortion, small head size, and other defects associated with the skeleton, genitals, and sensory organs. Even low doses of radiation have been linked to increased risks of cancer and neural damage so that mothers are urged to avoid unnecessary x-rays and other circumstances where radiation exposure may be increased.

Chemicals and other elements in the environment pose another significant source of potential risks. Known teratogens include lead, mercury, and cadmium, as well as many elements found in paints, dyes and coloring agents, solvents, oven cleaners, pesticides, insecticides, food additives, artificial sweeteners, and cosmetic products. Careless handling and disposal of such elements and their excessive production and use, so that they enter the foods we eat and the air we breathe, is one problem. But additionally, many women of childbearing age are exposed to these hazardous substances in the workplace (see Table 4.4).

TABLE 4.4

Occupational Hazards for Women of Childbearing Age

Occupation	Hazardous Substances
Cleaning Personnel	Soaps, detergents, solvents
Electronic Assemblers	Lead, tin, antimony, trichloroethylene, methyl chloride, resins
Hair Dressers and Cosmetologists	Hair-spray resins, aerosol propellants, solvents, dyes
Health Personnel	Anesthetic gases, x-rays, laboratory chemicals
Painters	Lead, titanium, toluene
Photographic Processors	Caustics, bromides, iodides, silver nitrate
Plastic Workers	Formaldehyde, vinyl chloride
Printing Personnel	Ink mists, methanol, carbon tetrachloride, lead, solvents, trichloroethylene
Textile and Garment Workers	Formaldehyde, dyes, asbestos, solvents, flame retardants
Transportation Personnel	Carbon monoxide, lead

Source: Adapted from Samuels & Bennett, 1983.

CONTROVERSY

Should Companies Bar Women from Jobs with Environmental Hazards?

With increasing awareness of the negative impact of certain chemicals and other environmental elements on prenatal development have come new and complex social and legal issues pertaining to women in the workplace. Some companies have barred women from jobs involving hazardous substances as a way of reducing risks to potential offspring, generating enormous controversy.

One manufacturer of automobile batteries, where lead is an essential ingredient, has demanded that any woman, regardless of her age and childbearing plans, must prove that she is sterile before she may be considered for any job in which the lead content in the air is high enough to risk fetal health. The company instituted this extreme requirement because exposure to lead has been shown to cause severe birth defects, and because they feared future lawsuits from women or their offspring. Company administrators had also found that some pregnant women continued to work in high-risk jobs even though they had been warned about dangers to the fetus and given opportunities to transfer to other jobs.

▶ **Sensitive periods**

Proponents of such policies believe that companies are legally responsible for the hazards that exist in their workplaces. If fetal protection rules are eliminated, companies might be liable for damages to unborn children. Sensitive periods occur early in prenatal development, often before a mother knows that she is pregnant. Even if a pregnant woman relinquished her job voluntarily, damage to the fetus may have been done before she knew she was pregnant.

Opponents of fetal protection policies argue that the slightest risks could be used as a pretext for keeping women from certain jobs, whether they are pregnant or not. In fact, millions of jobs could be restricted to men should the possibility of pregnancy be used to determine eligibility for those jobs. Some even argue that lead poses equal danger to men and to their offspring, but the policies are restricted to women.

Title VII of the Civil Rights Act forbids job discrimination based on gender and other factors. Laws are currently in place to protect pregnant women from losing jobs that they are capable of performing. Just as debatable is the question of whether women should be barred from certain jobs simply because they might *someday* become pregnant. Employers could monitor whether a woman is pregnant and change her job accordingly, but monitoring is an invasion of privacy. And a woman who knows she is pregnant may want to have the choice to keep her job regardless of the potential risks.

Responsibility for children, born or unborn, has traditionally fallen on parents; other parties are now taking an unprecedented fundamental role in fetal protection. Educating women about potential dangers and improving the workplace to eliminate those dangers might help to resolve this controversy. For now, both employers and employees are caught in the middle: should women have equal access to jobs or should employers be responsible for ensuring that unborn offspring are adequately protected? In 1991, the U.S. Supreme Court overturned a lower court's decision and ruled that women could not be excluded from jobs on the basis of possible harm to a developing fetus. The Court was divided, however, on whether circumstances might sometimes permit employers to exclude women from jobs to protect the welfare of the fetus. The issue continues to be controversial for both prospective mothers and employers, as well as those who must make decisions when conflicts arise between the rights of employees and the companies that hire them. ■

Maternal Conditions and Prenatal Development

In addition to teratogens, a number of maternal conditions are associated with increased risk during pregnancy. Several of these (diabetes, pregnancy-induced and chronic hypertension, Rh incompatibility) and their consequences for the fetus are summarized in Table 4.3. Additional maternal factors influencing the prenatal environment include the age of the mother, her nutritional status, and her emotional state.

▶ **Sociocultural influence**

Age   The number of older mothers is on the rise in the United States as women postpone pregnancy until careers are established or for other reasons. Is pregnancy in older women more risky? As we saw in Chapter 3, the likelihood of having a child with Down syndrome increases markedly during the later childbearing years. Some studies also report increased prematurity and

Teenage mothers give birth to approximately 500,000 babies in the United States each year. Many of them will be unmarried teens who have received little or even no prenatal care, factors that increase the risk for delivering less healthy babies.

mortality as well as greater difficulty during labor, especially for older mothers having their first child. Other evidence, however, suggests that these findings stem from an increase in health-related problems that generally accompany aging. Healthy mothers over thirty-five have no more complications during pregnancy than mothers younger than thirty-five (Grimes & Gross, 1981; Stein, 1983).

Teenage mothers, on the other hand, are at considerable risk for delivering less healthy babies (McAnarney, 1987). Lack of adequate prenatal care may be one primary reason. Pregnant teenagers in the United States, particularly those who are very young and unmarried, are much less likely than other women to seek out medical services. Although pregnancy among young adults has declined over the last decade, in any given year one in twenty teenagers is likely to bear a child. Nearly 60 percent of these approximately 500,000 births each year will be to unmarried teens (Children's Defense Fund, 1988).

Nutrition What foods eaten during pregnancy are best for the health of mother and infant? Theories and fads on this topic abound in virtually every

▶ **Sociocultural influence**

society. Clellan Ford (1964), in fact, found that only four of sixty-four cultures he examined from around the world failed to have some kind of dietary proscriptions for expectant mothers. In many societies dietary taboos limit the variety of foods eaten, a practice that may not be beneficial for prenatal development. Furthermore, as early as the eighteenth century, mothers in Western societies were encouraged to limit their weight gain during pregnancy. Perhaps this advice became popular because women whose pelvic cavities were small and misshapened by rickets or other forms of malnutrition often had difficulty delivering large babies (Samuels & Samuels, 1986).

Today, however, we know that adequate nutrition is extremely important for fetal development. Physical and neural growth can be impaired when a mother fails to maintain a balanced diet or to gain sufficient weight, typically about twenty-five pounds, during pregnancy. Extreme malnutrition is especially detrimental to fetal development. During World War II, famines occurred in parts of Holland and in Leningrad in the Soviet Union. The incidence of spontaneous abortions, stillbirths, abnormalities of the nervous system, and deaths at or shortly after birth increased markedly in these locations.

▶ **Sensitive periods**

When extreme malnutrition occurred during the first few months of pregnancy, death, premature birth, and nervous system defects were especially frequent. When famine occurred later in prenatal development, retardation in fetal growth and low birth weights were more likely (Antonov, 1947). Unfortunately, provision of an adequate diet with sufficient proteins, vitamins, and other nutrients continues to be one of the major problems for fetal development in many parts of the world today.

▶ **Sociocultural influence**

Stress   Cultural beliefs about potentially harmful consequences of frightening or stressful events on fetal development are pervasive, and many societies encourage a calm atmosphere for the mother (Samuels & Samuels, 1986). Though the impact of stressful events is not nearly as specific as most folklore suggests, physiological reactions accompanying chronic or high levels of stress may directly influence prenatal development. Research with animals indicates that when the mother is under stress, blood flow is diverted from the womb and hormones that can interfere with normal growth are released. Alternatively, the existence of stress may indirectly affect prenatal development by leading a mother to increase smoking, consume more alcohol, or engage in other activities that are known to have teratogenic effects on the fetus (McAnarney & Stevens-Simon, 1990).

A consistent picture of the relationship between stress and complications associated with pregnancy, however, has not emerged (Norbeck & Tilden, 1983). Many early studies with humans were methodologically unsound and simply asked mothers whether they felt anxious during pregnancy. In more recent experiments, researchers have tried to make more careful measurements of the existence of family conflict, the frequency of positive and negative life events, and the availability of physical and social support for the mother. These studies have revealed that stressful conditions before and during pregnancy result in a pattern of greater complications during pregnancy and birth, such as preeclampsia or premature labor for the mother and, for the infant, lower birth weight, poorer respiration, and other reasons for admission to intensive care.

The mother's prior medical condition, age, personality, and the social support she receives from family and friends, however, are important factors that mediate the consequences of stress during pregnancy. Among women who experience a variety of life changes two years prior to and during pregnancy, those with strong social and personal support, for example, have far fewer complications than women without these resources (Nuckolls, Cassel, & Kaplan, 1972). Similarly, Jane Norbeck and Virgina Tilden (1983) found that life stress during the previous year was correlated with complications such as high blood pressure during pregnancy or early delivery. Complications for the infant (low birth weight, respiratory difficulties, and so forth) were more frequently observed only when a mother had few tangible sources of support (to borrow money, to get a ride somewhere, or to get help if sick) along with high life stress. Gabriel Smilkstein and colleagues reported that stress and previous obstetrical history were less important predictors of complications during and after pregnancy than how well the family functioned together during these times (Smilkstein et al., 1984).

Mothers, like anyone else, cannot completely eliminate stress in their lives; they must often juggle work, family, and other obligations. To the extent that mothers and the people around them help to manage their stress by supplying opportunities for relaxation and by providing emotional and social support, however, they can minimize many potentially negative consequences. Efforts

A prospective mother who receives support from family and friends seems to experience less stress during her pregnancy. This support appears to be especially important for mothers who undergo a variety of other stressful changes in the two years prior to and during pregnancy.

parents initiate to reduce stress or respond to it in adaptive ways can serve as effective preventive medicine during pregnancy (Samuels & Samuels, 1986). These are sound practices not only during pregnancy but throughout the child-rearing years as well.

A Final Note on Environment and Prenatal Development

After examining the range of teratogens and other factors affecting prenatal development, we may be surprised to learn that babies manage to be born healthy at all. But they are—every day. We should wonder rather at the rich complexity of prenatal development and appreciate more deeply the fact that it proceeds normally so much of the time. Between 90 and 95 percent of babies born in the United States are healthy infants well prepared to respond and adapt to their new environment. Knowledge of teratogenic influences allows for mothers and fathers as well as others in the community to maximize the chances that every infant is equipped to act upon its world with as many resources as possible.

BIRTH AND THE PERINATAL ENVIRONMENT

When a mother goes into labor, the wet, warm, and supportive world surrounding the fetus undergoes a rapid transformation and the fetus must adjust to an earthshaking series of events. During a normal birth the baby is subjected first to pressure—pressure that becomes increasingly stronger as labor continues. Uterine contractions, occurring first at about ten- to fifteen-minute intervals and for relatively brief durations, begin to take place at shorter intervals and become increasingly stronger, forcing the baby to enter the birth canal. In the journey through the narrow canal, pressure up to thirty pounds of force will probably cause the baby's head to become somewhat elongated and misshapen (Trevarthen, 1987). At times the baby may experience difficulty in receiving a sufficient supply of oxygen when the flow of blood in the umbilical cord or head is temporarily disrupted by these intense pressures. And then the infant emerges head first into an utterly different world—drier, possibly colder, and often much brighter and noisier than his or her only previous home. The newborn must cope with other shocking surprises as well. Within minutes of birth, the infant must begin to take in oxygen unassisted, except perhaps by the sharp slap of a physician or midwife. The baby must also quickly learn to manage and coordinate sucking, swallowing, and breathing to obtain sufficient nutrients.

▶ **Roles of nature and nurture**

Passage from the womb to the outside world is a momentous physical change for a newborn, but there are other kinds of changes, too. This new world contains separate living beings, entities that actively relate to the baby. If the baby is wanted, she will be cuddled and talked to, fussed over, and rocked by one, maybe two, perhaps many people. If she is unwanted, she may rarely receive such experiences. The newborn, in other words, enters a social environment that can be supportive and responsive, barren and uninviting, or any number of degrees in between. Physical needs that were formerly automatically met by the placenta and other physical structures in the womb now depend on social interaction for their gratification. Mothers, fathers, grandparents, siblings, and others become the major environmental resource for physical and psychological growth alike.

▶ **Sociocultural influence**

Childbirth Techniques

The events and agents surrounding the baby's transition from the womb to its new physical and social surroundings make up the perinatal environment. Societies vary enormously in the rituals and techniques they have developed to smooth this transition for newborns. One basic difference among cultures involves the contrasting views of pregnancy and birth as natural and healthy or as an illness requiring medical care and attention (Newton, 1955). The !Kung, a hunting and gathering people living in the Kalahari Desert of Africa, build no huts or facilities for the delivery of their babies because they regard birth as part of the natural order of events requiring no special intervention (Shostak, 1981). Pregnancy and childbirth in the United States during this century, in contrast, have been placed within the illness model and managed by professionally trained medical personnel (Dye, 1986).

In 1900, only 5 percent of babies were born in hospitals in the United States. At that time, survival rates for both mother and baby may have been no higher in the hospital than at home because doctors inadvertently spread infection between patients. The subsequent discovery of antiseptic practices, anesthesia and other painkilling drugs, new delivery techniques, and greater knowledge of the anatomy and physiology of gestation, however, definitively moved childbirth from a natural process to a medical and surgical event. By 1960, nearly 100 percent of all babies in the United States were born in hospital maternity wards (Devitt, 1977). Nearly all of these deliveries were accompanied by some form of medication (Brackbill, 1979).

Societies differ enormously in their approach to the birth of a baby. Here a midwife from Mauritania, with her own baby swaddled on her back, assists in tying the newborn's umbilical cord.

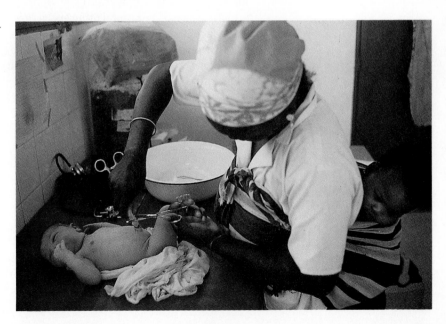

CONTROVERSY

The first use of medication in Western societies to reduce pain associated with childbirth was criticized for both religious and medical reasons (Cianfrani, 1960). On one hand, Old Testament scripture was interpreted to mean childbirth *should* be painful (Genesis 3:16). On the other hand, medical concerns centered on the safety of drugs for the baby. Religious objections were quickly muted, but controversy over pain-lessening drugs has persisted because of the possibility of teratogenic effects. Anesthesia to block the transmission of pain, analgesics to lessen feelings of pain, and sedatives to relax the mother all pass readily through the placenta and enter the baby's circulatory system.

Critics of the use of childbirth medication point out that babies whose mothers receive high doses of drugs during labor are reported to be less responsive and more irritable, to gain weight more slowly, and to show other behavioral consequences that decrease interactions with caregivers compared with babies exposed to small amounts of drugs or none at all (Brackbill, 1979; Brazelton, Nugent, & Lester, 1987; Hollenbeck, Gewirtz, & Sebris, 1984). Moreover, some behavioral differences may persist well beyond infancy. Heavy use of drugs during labor has been associated, for example, with an increased incidence of learning disorders in school-aged children (Brackbill, McManus, & Woodward, 1985).

Many of these studies, however, have been extensively criticized. Some researchers have failed to find that babies born to medicated and nonmedicated mothers show significant differences on such measures as strength, activity, irritability, sensitivity, or sleep patterns and believe the negative effects of drugs at birth have been markedly overstated (Kraemer et al., 1985). In addition, research on the effects of medication at birth has been methodologically inadequate. Indeed, it may be argued that increased medication is only a symptom of poor maternal health, labor difficulties, or other factors that are the primary cause of behavioral differences reported in babies born to heavily versus lightly medicated or unmedicated mothers. As a consequence of pressures to avoid medication, mothers who might have been made more comfortable have stoically experienced unnecessary pain or have felt considerable guilt when drugs are administered.

As you can see, considerably more research is necessary to resolve this controversy. For the present time obstetricians are advised by the Committee on Drugs of the American Academy of Pediatrics to administer drugs during labor only in minimal amounts necessary to relieve pain. ∎

▶ **Sociocultural influence**

Prepared Childbirth   Concerns about the effects of drugs used during labor along with reports of unmedicated but seemingly pain-free delivery by mothers in other cultures have led professionals and expectant parents to consider more natural ways of preparing for the birth of a baby. After observing one woman who reported a pain-free delivery, Grantley Dick-Read, a medical practitioner in Great Britain, concluded that difficult childbirth was fostered largely by the tension and anxiety in which Western civilization cloaked this event. Dick-Read (1959) proposed that mothers be (1) taught methods of physical relaxation, (2) given knowledge of the process of childbirth, and (3) encouraged to cultivate a cooperative relationship with their doctors to foster a more natural childbirth experience. Others, including Fernand Lamaze (1970), adopted similar ideas, adding procedures to divert thoughts away from pain and encouraging breathing activities to support the labor process.

Lamaze and other childbirth relaxation programs have become popular in the United States in recent years. Mothers who attend such classes and adhere to their recommendations generally require reduced amounts of drugs during delivery compared with mothers who have not participated in prepared childbirth. Mothers who attend childbirth classes may experience no less pain, but along with relaxation techniques, an additional element often required in these programs—the assistance of a coach or trainer, usually the father—seems to help counter the pain. Human birth differs from birth in other species of mammals in typically requiring some form of assistance. In many cultures this help is provided by friends and relatives or by midwives who specialize in such activity. Even in the United States childbirth until the middle of the eighteenth century was a "social" event attended by friends and neighbors in the community (Wertz & Wertz, 1977). With the relocation of childbirth to hospitals, however, mothers were often isolated from family and friends during labor, and a more private and impersonal procedure emerged.

A supportive companion during delivery is helpful to mothers. In a study carried out in Guatemala, first-time mothers were randomly assigned to receive routine nursing care or were provided with a lay woman, previously unknown to them, who talked to them and stayed with them during the entire labor period (Klaus & Kennell, 1982). Mothers with personal attendants spent far shorter time in labor (nine versus nineteen hours), required drugs or forceps less frequently, and delivered babies who showed less fetal distress and difficulty in breathing than mothers who received routine nursing care. The attended mothers also spent more time than the unattended mothers touching, smiling at, and talking to their newborns. The presence of fathers in the delivery room may have similar effects and seems to provide a greater sense of inclusion of the father within the family although there is little convincing evidence that such involvement influences the quality and amount of subsequent caregiving provided by fathers to their babies (Palkovitz, 1985).

▶ **Sociocultural influence**

Birth Settings

The perception of hospital settings as impersonal and regimented, coupled with a desire to make delivery more relaxing and natural, has led to revolutionary changes in childbirth practices in the United States in recent years. Hospitals began to allow fathers into the delivery room in the early 1970s. Birthing centers within hospitals have become less institutional and more homelike. Home delivery and freestanding birthing centers (FSBCs) are further new options. Although relatively few births in the United States take place outside hospitals, nearly 5 percent of babies born in Oregon in the early 1980s were delivered at home or in FSBCs. These alternatives have become popular for three reasons: (1) mothers feel more relaxed surrounded by family or friends in a familiar setting, (2) they wish to distance the experience of pregnancy from the concept of illness, and (3) they feel greater control over what happens to both themselves and their babies (Eakins, 1984).

Alternative birthing environments do raise the issue of safety, however. Virtually all of the nearly 150 freestanding birthing centers currently operating in the United States encourage mothers at risk for complications to use traditional medical facilities and have arrangements with nearby hospitals if emergencies should arise. But back-up services for home deliveries are often less available, especially since the rise in home births may be partly for economic reasons. For those without health insurance, financial considerations play a significant role in the home birth choice. The safety of planned home births with licensed midwives in attendance matches that for hospital births, but the mortality rate increases nearly twentyfold when home deliveries are unplanned. Prenatal planning and screening along with adequate training of birth attendants are among the most important factors helping to make home births relatively safe (Burnett et al., 1980; Clarke & Bennets, 1982).

Labor and Delivery

Labor is a complicated interactive process involving three elements: the baby, the mother, and the placenta. What actually causes labor to begin remains unknown, although the pituitary gland of the fetus itself seems to play a significant role (Trevarthen, 1987). Irregular contractions or "false" labor often occurs late in pregnancy, but true labor is marked by regular, increasingly frequent contractions.

Stages of Labor   Labor is traditionally divided into three stages. The first stage begins with mild but increasingly severe and frequent contractions that alter the shape of the cervix, preparing it for the baby's descent. Near the end of this first stage, which lasts an average of eleven hours for first-borns and about seven hours in later-borns, dilation of the cervix proceeds rapidly to allow the baby's passage through the birth canal (Friedman, 1978). The second stage consists of the continued descent and birth of the baby. This stage usually requires a little less than an hour in first-borns and about twenty minutes in later-borns. In the third stage, lasting about fifteen minutes, the placenta is expelled.

▶ **Sociocultural influence**

Caesarean Birth   A caesarean birth is the delivery of a baby through a surgical incision of the mother's abdomen and uterus. Traditionally, caesarean births were recommended when labor failed to progress normally, when the baby's head was very large, or when birth was *breech* (foot or rump first) rather than head first. Today, however, concerns about stress on the baby during birth—often measured by sophisticated fetal monitors and including increased risk of brain damage, vaginal infections associated with sexually transmitted diseases, and expensive malpractice suits (should things go awry during vaginal delivery)—have led to a substantial increase in the frequency of caesarean sections. In fact, the rate of caesarean births has more than tripled in the last decade (Summey, 1986). Today about one in five deliveries in the United States is caesarean rather than vaginal (Notzon, Placek, & Taffel, 1987), a rate that is substantially higher than that in some other Western European countries.

Mothers who undergo caesarean birth face an increased risk of infection and a longer hospital stay compared with mothers who give birth vaginally (Consensus Development Conference, 1981). Moreover, caesarean babies are likely to be exposed to greater maternal medication. Other concerns center on the different experience both mother and infant receive under such circumstances. When caesarean babies are delivered before labor begins, they do not have a misshapen head and appear perfectly healthy, but they have substantially lower levels of two stress hormones, adrenaline and noradrenaline. These hormones facilitate respiration by helping keep the lungs open and clear. They also enhance cell metabolism, circulation of the blood to the brain, and activity level, factors that help the infant make the transition to the new environment and respond to caregivers. Thus, caesarean babies generally tend to have more trouble breathing, are less active, sleep more, and cry less than other babies (Trevarthen, 1987). Because of these behavioral differences as well as indications that caesarean births often fail to yield clear benefits to many infants (DeRegt et al., 1986), medical experts have called for a reduction in the frequency of such births.

Birth Trauma   The increase in the frequency of caesarean sections in the United States has come about partly because of concerns about birth trauma, or injuries sustained at birth. A potentially serious consequence is *anoxia,* or deprivation of oxygen. Anoxia can result from damage to or lengthy compression of the umbilical cord or head during birth. It may also result from failure of the baby to begin regular breathing after birth. If oxygen deprivation lasts more than a few minutes, the baby can suffer severe damage to the central nervous system.

Fortunately, the brain of the fetus and newborn requires relatively low rates of oxygen consumption. Thus, brief periods of anoxia appear to have few long-lasting effects on development. Furthermore, an adequate postnatal caregiving environment can be extremely important in helping counter potentially negative long-range outcomes for infants experiencing periods of anoxia (Sameroff & Chandler, 1975). Concerns about anoxia and other birth traumas, however, have led to the rapidly expanded use of **fetal monitoring devices** during labor. Most of these devices record fetal heartbeat to determine whether the infant is undergoing stress during delivery. Unfortunately, some mothers find them uncomfortable and disruptive. Moreover, experts question whether these devices are more beneficial than the ordinary stethoscope for making medical decisions in all but high-risk pregnancies (Shy et al., 1990).

Low Birth Weight

fetal monitoring device Medical device used to monitor fetal heartbeat during delivery.

As infant and childhood diseases have come under greater control in recent decades, prevention and treatment of low–birth weight infants has gained increased attention in the United States. Study after study has confirmed that as birth weight increases to a reasonable level, mortality rate rapidly declines (see Figure 4.4). Within the first four weeks of life, low–birth weight infants (less than 2,500 grams or 5½ pounds) are about forty times more likely to die than infants of normal birth weight. Very low–birth weight infants (less than 1,500 grams or about 3¼ pounds) are nearly two hundred times more likely to die (Shapiro et al., 1980). The United States has a higher proportion of infants

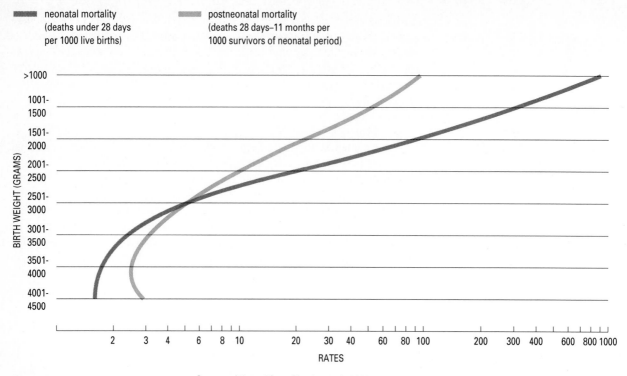

FIGURE 4.4   Source: Adapted from Shapiro et al., 1980.

Birth Weight and Infant Mortality   Mortality rate is much greater in infants of very low (<1500 grams) and low birth
weight (<2500 grams) compared with infants of normal birth weight. Advances in the
treatment of these infants can help lower the mortality rate, but an even more effective means of reducing infant mortality may be to provide medical, educational, and
social resources geared to preventing the causes of low birth weight in infants in the
first place.

▶ **Sociocultural influence**   born with very low or low birth weight than a number of other developed countries, one major reason for this country's correspondingly higher infant mortal-
ity rate (see Figure 4.5). A relatively large number of births to teenaged mothers and the lack of resources for obtaining prenatal care by some members of
the population are cited among the reasons why the United States does not
fare well in comparison to many other countries.

Infants born with low birth weight face many obstacles. Cerebral palsy, sei-
zure disorders, and other neurological problems are more likely in low–birth
weight babies than in babies of normal birth weight (McCormick et al., 1981).
The risk is even greater for infants of very or extremely low birth weight (less
than 1,000 grams or about 2¼ pounds). Respiratory difficulties, hyperactivity,
greater frequency of illness, and disruption of parental caregiving and family
functioning are frequent problems for these infants (Kitchen et al., 1987;
McCormick, Shapiro, & Starfield, 1982).

Despite the immediate problems, long-term followup of low–birth weight
children who manage to survive reveals that they often do surprisingly well.
They are more likely to have speech and hearing deficits and exhibit hyperactivity, learning disabilities, and behavior problems, but many low–birth weight

infants fall within the range of normal intellectual development (Field, 1986; Korner, 1987; McCormick, Gortmaker, & Sobol, 1990). A recent analysis of data from more than eighty different studies conducted in North America, Europe, Australia, and New Zealand concluded that only small differences in intellectual and developmental capabilities exist between low–birth weight and normal children (Aylward et al., 1989). Although greater percentages of very and extremely low–birth weight infants suffer handicapping conditions, supportive caregiving appears to play an extremely important role in minimizing the extent to which deficits are exhibited by these children (Ehrenhaft, Wagner, & Herdman, 1989; Kitchen et al., 1987; Resnick et al., 1990).

Infants with low birth weight fall into two major groups: those born *preterm* (less than thirty-five weeks conceptual age) and those born near their expected arrival date who are *small for gestational age* (SGA). This distinction gives recognition to the fact that low–birth weight infants comprise a heterogeneous group, perhaps needing separate types of medical treatment and intervention with differing developmental outcomes. Congenital anomalies are somewhat more frequent in SGA infants, for example, whereas respiratory

FIGURE 4.5

Infant Mortality and Low Birth Weight in Selected Developed Countries

The percentage of the infant mortality rate (deaths before one year per thousand live births) and low–birth weight live births are measures that provide an indication of the overall health of a nation. The United States ranks below a substantial number of other countries on each of these measures.

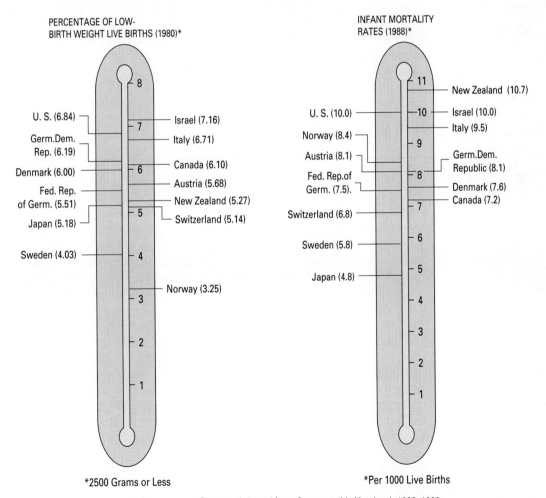

Source: Adapted from *Demographic Yearbook,* 1983, 1990.

distress is more likely among infants who are born preterm (Starfield et al., 1982).

▶ **Sociocultural influence**

Reducing Problems Associated with Low Birth Weight   Attempts to manage problems associated with low birth weight have proceeded on two fronts. Medical intervention has advanced to permit more low–birth weight, especially extremely low–birth weight, infants to survive and develop normally. Improved regulation of temperature, careful and effective use of drugs, sensitive monitoring of biochemical functions, and other advances in intensive care have all proven beneficial in reducing mortality rate (Ehrenhaft, Wagner, & Herdman, 1989). Some forms of treatment, however, can be harmful. Too much oxygen to alleviate respiratory distress can lead to blindness, excess levels of antibiotics to fight infection can contribute to deafness, and prolonged use of ventilators to assist breathing can cause respiratory problems (Korner, 1987).

▶ **Sociocultural influence**

A second major assault on the problem of low birth weight has been directed at preventing or at least minimizing its occurrence. Researchers have cataloged a long list of risks, including demographic, medical, and behavioral factors associated with low birth weight. Providing adequate prenatal care, meeting nutritional needs, and initiating early and frequent education about the effects of smoking, drugs, and other risk factors both before and during pregnancy can help reduce the enormous medical, social, and psychological costs associated with low birth weight. In the years to come, more significant progress in dealing with the problems associated with low birth weight will likely come through prevention rather than through improved treatment of the condition.

▶ **Roles of nature and nurture**

Caring for Low–Birth Weight Babies   Once an infant with low birth weight can maintain physiological stability, the next developmental task appears to be achieving regular cycles or patterns of activity involving sleep and wakefulness—patterns that full-term infants routinely display within a few weeks of birth but that infants of low birth weight often take many more weeks to achieve (Barnard, 1987; Horowitz, 1987b; Gunzenhauser, 1987). The ability to move smoothly from one state to another is part of this task. Infants of low birth weight have trouble falling asleep, awakening, maintaining alertness, and establishing regular and efficient feeding schedules (Barnard, 1987).

Such difficult transitions and irregular states complicate the task of caring for low–birth weight babies. At one time, these infants were thought to be too fragile to receive any stimulation beyond that necessarily imposed by medical treatment. Parents were either excluded completely from intensive care units, where their babies were sustained on life-support equipment, or were cautioned to handle them as little as possible. Gradually, however, various views of child development—Freud's theory of psychosexual development, ethological observations of the importance of imprinting and early attachment,

▶ **Sensitive periods**

and new experimental evidence for sensitive periods in the development of both social and intellectual development—gained wide enough acceptance among professionals to challenge and modify these practices (Ramey, Bryant, & Suarez, 1987). Giving these babies certain kinds of stimulation, professionals agreed, was highly desirable.

What kind of stimulation is appropriate for newborn babies? Should caregivers introduce *compensatory* kinds of experience, attempting to duplicate what the baby would have gained while still in its womb? Or, by the reasoning that preterm babies must perform such tasks as responding to gravity, organizing respiratory and digestive functions, and process stimulation much like full-term infants, should caregiving be *enriching*, more closely matching the experiences confronting healthy newborns? A number of studies have examined the effects of both compensatory and enriching stimulation on the development of low–birth weight babies (Korner, 1987). Compensatory stimulation has consisted of supplementary handling or the use of oscillating devices such as waterbeds to provide the experience of motion similar to that the fetus receives in its mother's womb (Korner, Schneider, & Forrest, 1983). Sometimes muffled auditory recordings of a human voice, a heartbeat, or other intrauterine sounds as well as the opportunity for nonnutritive sucking, an activity that the fetus occasionally engages in while in the womb, have been added. Enriching stimulation, on the other hand, has included extra visual and auditory stimulation, handling, and social contact more closely approximating what a typical newborn might receive (Scarr-Salapatek & Williams, 1973; Solkoff et al., 1969; White & Labarba, 1976).

Although they vary enormously in their procedures, studies have reported some at least temporary benefits from both types of extra stimulation. Perhaps the most consistent outcome of compensatory and enrichment experiments alike has been increased weight gain. Tiffany Field and her colleagues (Field, Ignatoff, et al., 1982), for example, gave one group of premature infants having respiratory problems and weighing less than 1,800 grams the opportunity to suck on a pacifier whenever they were fed through tubes. The group receiving this extra nonnutritive sucking gained weight more rapidly, stayed in the hospital fewer days, and had fewer medical and eating problems later than infants not given this opportunity. Weight differences between the two groups of infants in this study were found even a year after birth. Benefits reported in other studies have included more regular patterns of breathing and heart rate, improvements in sensorimotor development, more regular and longer periods in quiet states, and more appropriate and effective transitions from one state to another (Barnard & Bee, 1983; Burns et al., 1983; Edelman, Kraemer, & Korner, 1982).

A major question remains unanswered. Are the positive benefits of added stimulation enduring? Few studies have been able to show long-term gains from either compensatory stimulation or enrichment (Field, 1986; Korner, 1987). Perhaps this is not surprising; treatment conditions are usually of limited breadth or duration. Moreover, both treatment and control groups may be exposed to social and rearing conditions upon leaving the hospital that can have a far more powerful influence on later development (Korner, 1987). In fact, an essential component of successful intervention both during hospitalization and after the baby goes home may be to provide parents support and encouragement in their caregiving efforts with low–birth weight infants.

▶ **Sociocultural influence**

Encouraging opportunities for parent-child bonding in the atypical hospital situation, instructing parents about what behaviors to expect, teaching them to recognize and care for the specific needs of their infant, and emotional support from the hospital staff, other parents, and service agencies are all special forms of assistance that can be offered to parents of low–birth weight children and others with special needs (Korner, 1987). Such intervention can have a powerful effect. Even very simple parent training, such as having the mother observe the administration of a standard infant test or report on the infant's capacities on a weekly basis, has been found to increase the mother's sensitivity to and involvement with the infant and to promote the development of infants with low birth weight (Szajnberg et al., 1987; Widmayer & Field, 1981; Worobey & Belsky, 1982). It seems important, then, to include the primary caregivers, the parents, in any efforts to foster the development of low–birth weight infants.

THE NEWBORN

Even parents of a healthy infant may be in for a surprise when they see their baby for the first time. Unless it was delivered by caesarean section, the baby is likely to have a flattened nose and a large distorted head, produced when the bones of the skull override one another during passage through the narrow birth canal. The skin of all babies, regardless of racial background, is a pale, pinkish color, covered by an oily, cheeselike substance (the vernix caseosa) that protects against infection. Sex organs are swollen by high levels of sex hormones.

If the parents are startled, though, just imagine what kind of adjustment the baby is having to make! An infant's most immediate need after emerging from the birth canal is to breathe. Pressure on the chest during delivery probably helps to clear the baby's fluid-filled lungs, but the shock of cool air, perhaps accompanied by jiggling, a slap, or some other less-than-gentle activity by a birth attendant, makes the first breath of air more like a gasp, quickly followed by a reflexive cry. A baby's first respirations are typically shallow and erratic, becoming deeper and more regular within fifteen to thirty minutes in unmedi-

Giving birth can be an intensely emotional experience for all those who have awaited the baby's arrival. Even the newborn may have played some role in determining when this experience takes place. What begins the process of labor remains unknown, but the pituitary gland of the fetus may be involved in some way.

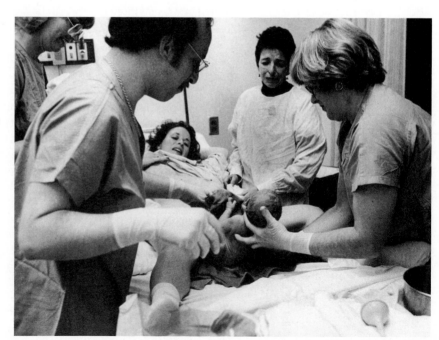

cated deliveries and in about ninety minutes in medicated deliveries (Desmond et al., 1963). The umbilical cord can continue to pulse for several minutes after birth, and in most societies the cord is not cut until after it ceases to function in this way (Trevarthen, 1987). In the United States, however, the cord is usually cut immediately, a practice under criticism since the placenta continues to provide an oxygen-rich source of blood for a short time after delivery (Desmond, Rudolph, & Phitaksphraiwan, 1963).

The second major task the baby must accomplish upon entering the world is to regulate body temperature. Sudden exposure to cool air may help to stimulate breathing, but babies lose body heat about four times more rapidly than adults because of their lower fat reserves and relatively large body surface (Bruck, 1962). Newborns are often quickly separated from their mothers and placed under radiant heaters to prevent heat loss. They can, however, effectively maintain their temperature when they are held by their mothers (Hill & Shronk, 1979).

Assessing Newborns

Babies come in a more or less standard size. The average newborn in the United States weighs about seven and a half pounds and is about twenty inches in length. Nearly 95 percent will weigh between five and a half and ten pounds and measure between eighteen and twenty-two inches in length. Heavier or lighter infants may receive further medical attention, especially if they score low on the *Apgar Scale* (Apgar, 1953), a measure that diagnoses the physical state of newborns. Widely administered to infants throughout the United States at one minute and five minutes after birth, the Apgar scale assesses five vital signs: heart rate, respiratory effort, muscle tone, reflex responsivity, and color. Each vital sign is assessed and assigned a score of 0, 1, or 2, based on the criteria described in Table 4.5. These scores are added for a total ranging from 0 to 10 points. Ninety percent of infants score 7 or better. An infant who scores less than 4 is considered to be at risk and will receive immediate medical attention to ensure its survival.

TABLE 4.5

The Apgar Scoring System

The Apgar Scale is given at and shortly after birth to diagnose the physical condition of a newborn. The ratings for each vital sign are added for a total score ranging from 0 to 10. An infant who scores less than 4 is considered to be at risk.

Vital Sign	Ratings		
	0	1	2
Heart rate	Absent	Slow (below 100)	Over 100
Respiratory effort	Absent	Slow, irregular	Good, crying
Muscle tone	Flaccid	Some flexion of extremities	Active motion
Reflex responsivity	No response	Grimace	Vigorous cry
Color	Blue, pale	Body pink, extremities blue	Completely pink

Source: From Apgar, 1953.

The *Neonatal Behavioral Assessment Scale (NBAS),* a more recent measure developed by T. Berry Brazelton (1973), evaluates the baby's behavior on a variety of dimensions such as ability to interact with the tester, responsiveness to objects in the environment, reflex motor capacities, and ability to control behavioral state. Typical questions include: Does the baby watch while the examiner moves her head back and forth and side to side and calls out the baby's name in a high-pitched voice? Does the baby cuddle or resist being held? Does the baby remove a cloth placed over the face, grasp a forefinger placed in the hand, attempt to hold head upright while in a sitting position, and fall quiet within a reasonable time after being fussy?

Performance on the NBAS has been used to assess a newborn's neurological condition and can indicate whether certain prenatal or perinatal conditions, as well as intervention programs, have had an impact (Korner, 1987; Tronick, 1987). An NBAS score can also predict later developmental outcomes. Babies who score poorly on the scale continue to be somewhat less responsive to caregivers in the first few months after birth (Vaughn et al., 1980). In general, however, the ability of the NBAS (along with other infant tests) to predict long-term development is only modest at best (Brazelton, Nugent, & Lester, 1987). Nevertheless, as we saw in examining caregiving techniques for low–birth weight infants, the mere administration of a test like the NBAS can have an educational function. Parents of normal as well as at-risk babies who observe examiners give the NBAS or who are trained to give it themselves seem to become more responsive to and effective in interactions with their infants (Worobey, 1985).

Newborn Sleep States

We all know that babies sleep. They sleep a great deal, in fact. The sleep of infants, however, is not a totally constant condition but rather one of a shifting range of interrelated states. In fact, newborns and young infants display an amazing variety of states: regular and irregular sleep, drowsiness, alert inactivity, alert activity, and crying. Crying or distress usually begins with whimpering but swiftly shifts to full-scale cries, often accompanied by thrashing of arms and legs. During alert activity, the infant also engages in vigorous but diffuse motor activity, although such exertions are not accompanied by signs of distress. During alert inactivity, the baby is relatively quiet, at least in terms of motor activity, but is still quite actively engaged in scanning the environment. It is in this stage, therefore, that the baby appears most responsive to sensory stimulation and may be engaged in considerable learning activity.

Despite their different states, infants still spend most of their time asleep. Although individual differences are great, full-term babies average between sixteen and seventeen hours of sleep a day. Their sleep patterns, however, change dramatically, especially within the first year (see Figure 4.6). In newborns the duration of sleep and wake cycles is extremely short, and states are easily disrupted by external stimulation. As the weeks pass, babies gradually sleep less, but for longer periods. At first these longer periods of sleep may take place at any time, but by about three to five weeks of age a pattern begins to emerge in which the longest sleep periods take place at night (Thompson, 1982). But naps during the day continue to be a regular occurrence for chil-

FIGURE 4.6

Sleep-Wake Cycles for Newborns, Children, and Adults

Most newborns already follow a fairly regular sleep-wake cycle (blue areas represent sleep). That cycle, however, is markedly different from a parent's typical sleep pattern. Within three or four months of birth, the infant may be sleeping through a good proportion of the night. But naps during the day continue to be a regular part of the sleep-wake cycle for children through the preschool years.

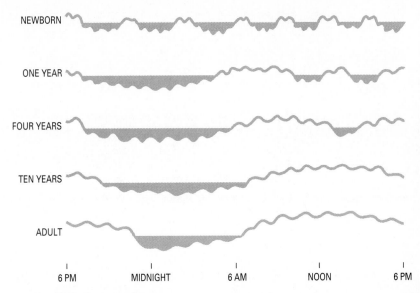

Source: Adapted from Kleitman, 1963.

▶ **Sociocultural influence**

dren through the preschool years. In fact, in some cultures such naps are never eliminated.

The development of sleep patterns shows extensive cultural differences. In the United States, parents are often eager to have their infants adopt a routine that matches their own. A significant milestone is reached when the baby of three or four months finally sleeps through the night; younger infants are unable to exhibit such a long sleep duration. In some cultures, however, such as the Kipsigi of rural Kenya, infants are permitted more flexible sleep patterns and they will not sleep through the night until they are much older (Super & Harkness, 1982).

Even infants display two distinct sleep states. During active or *REM* (rapid eye movement) sleep, eye movements and muscle jerks are frequent and breathing and heart rate are irregular. During quiet sleep (NREM), eye and muscle movements are few, and physiological activity is more regular. The proportion of time spent in these two states, however, shifts dramatically during the first year of life (see Figure 4.7). In fact, the large amount of sleep required by infants compared with adults is largely a result of their greater need for REM sleep.

Active or REM sleep has been linked to dreaming, but it is not clear that young infants dream. Even if they do, why is so much time spent in REM sleep? *Autostimulation theory* proposes that REM sleep provides powerful stimulation to the central nervous system. In adults, that stimulation is interpreted as sensory and motor activity—that is, as a dream. Though it seems unlikely that babies can interpret stimulation as dreams, it may still be important for normal brain activity (Roffwarg, Muzio, & Dement, 1966). According to this theory, stimulation during REM sleep compensates for the relatively brief number of hours each day the infant is awake. Infants kept awake for relatively lengthy periods of time show reduced amounts of REM sleep, and premature infants, whose wakeful periods are even more limited, show more

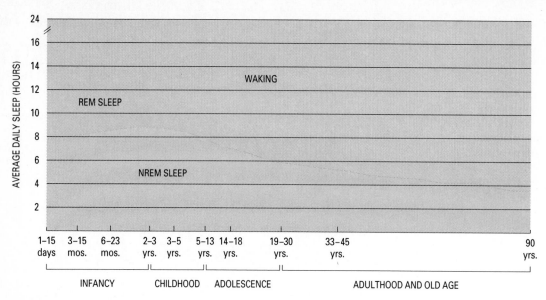

FIGURE 4.7   Source: Adapted from Roffwarg, Muzio, & Dement, 1966.

Developmental Changes in Sleep   The young infant not only sleeps more than children or adults but also spends a sub-
Requirements   stantially greater proportion of that time in rapid-eye-movement (REM) sleep. New-
                                       borns fall asleep and wake up in the REM state. By about age two or three, however,
                                       children begin sleep in the non-REM (NREM) state, the pattern also observed for
                                       older individuals. Moreover, very young infants may alternate between REM and
                                       NREM sleep every fifteen to twenty minutes, changes that occur much less frequently
                                       in older individuals.

▶ **Roles of nature and nurture**   REM sleep than full-term babies (Boismer, 1977; Roffwarg, Muzio, & De-
                                       ment, 1966). If this explanation is correct, we have once again, another pow-
                                       erful demonstration of how important stimulation is for development even at
                                       those times when considerable sleep is essential as well. It is the effects of
                                       stimulation during the waking hours in postnatal development, however, that
                                       has become a major focus of psychological research, and this is an issue we
                                       consider in more detail in the chapters ahead.

THEMES IN DEVELOPMENT

THE PRENATAL PERIOD AND BIRTH

▶ **What roles do nature and nurture play in prenatal development and birth?**

Prenatal development is the product of complex interactions involving genetic
instructions and programs inherited from parents (see Chapter 3) and the expectant mother's physical and emotional conditions; her exposure to drugs,
diseases, hazardous chemicals, stressful living conditions, an inadequate diet,
and other environmental influences; and her use of medication during preg-

nancy and at birth. We have seen, for example, that the differentiation of organs and systems in the embryo typically obeys a sequence of principles established by biochemical and physiological processes and directed by inherited genetic programs. Yet these processes do not operate in a vacuum. Exposure to teratogens and various maternal conditions can radically alter this normal path. In this way the actions of the mother may change the immediate environment within the womb, with drastic consequences for the fetus within. The reactions, attitudes, and availability of the newborn's caregivers and the stimulation they provide are other major sources of potential influence on the baby's development.

▶ How does the sociocultural context influence prenatal development and birth?

The immediate internal environment of the fetus and the interactions of caregivers for the newborn can be dramatically influenced by the larger social, economic, and cultural settings in which pregnancy and birth takes place. The mother's actions during pregnancy are often governed by a larger network of expectations, advice, and resources provided by the community in which she lives. An expectant mother in one community, for example, may have access to medical and other kinds of care that provide a more healthy environment for the fetus than a mother in another community. Industry or governing units may legislate controls on chemical pollution in one country, ignore them in another. Scientific and technological advances in prenatal testing, birthing practices, and newborn care may be available in many regions of the world; even when they are, however, not all parents may have the economic resources or desire to access them. Low–birth weight infants may require social, psychological, and economic supports that stretch the capacities of many families. Support provided by societies to deal with these problems can be a major factor contributing to the low–birth weight infant's successful development.

▶ Is development before and after birth continuous or stagelike?

When the zygote attaches to the uterine wall and taps a new source of nourishment, its course of development has changed dramatically. Once the various organs and systems have completed their formation to become much less susceptible to various teratogens, the fetus has achieved a vastly different status. The process of birth, itself, is a major transition. These kinds of dramatic changes fit with stagelike descriptions of development. Underlying these changes, however, are a set of biochemical and physiological processes governing cell proliferation, differentiation, and the emergence and functioning of biological organs and systems that are effectively conceptualized as continuous. This is why a preterm baby differs from a full-term baby. Even though both are no longer developing prenatally, they are at different points in the continuing process begun at conception.

▶ Are there sensitive periods in prenatal development and shortly after birth?

The answer here must be a resounding yes. Our discussion of teratogens should make it abundantly clear that there are periods in prenatal development when the embryo is far more susceptible to specific kinds of insults than at other times. Indeed, at few other times in development can environmental factors have such a dramatic impact on physical, cognitive, and social development. Early experience, too, may be important for low–birth weight infants. Consistent and appropriate stimulation during this highly vulnerable period seems to assist normal development in such babies.

SUMMARY

Prenatal development is the period that extends from conception to birth. During this time, a newly fertilized ovum is transformed from a single-celled zygote into the complex, active organism we know as the newborn. Prenatal development is subdivided into three periods. During the *germinal period*, about the first ten to fourteen days following conception, the zygote migrates from the Fallopian tube to the uterus, becomes a *morula*, and then a multi-celled *blastula*, and implants into the uterine wall to gain access to a new source of nutrients directly from the mother.

The *embryonic period* begins after implantation and continues until about the eighth week after conception. This period is marked by development of the placenta and other supportive structures within the uterine environment and by the differentiation of cells into tissues that form the major organs and systems of the body. Because many vital organs, including the brain, begin forming at this time, the embryo is susceptible to a variety of teratogens, environmental agents that can disrupt development and interfere with later behavior.

The *fetal period*, beginning about the eighth week after conception and lasting until birth, is marked by continued growth and refinement of organs and systems. Neurons continue to form and migrate during this period. Brain activity, sensory reactions, and movement become more easily detected, and by the beginning of the third trimester of pregnancy, the infant may be able to survive should birth occur prematurely.

At one time the *placenta* was believed to form an effective barrier that protected the embryo and fetus from potentially damaging environmental influences. Today researchers realize that many drugs, diseases, chemicals, and other agents can cross the placental barrier and induce fetal death, produce congenital malformations, and contribute to other negative outcomes in development. The effects of exposure to a specific *teratogen* depend on many factors such as the genetic susceptibility of mother and fetus, stage of fetal development, and means of access and level of exposure of the teratogen to the fetus. A specific teratogen can have different consequences ranging from transient delays to irreversible defects to outcomes apparent only much later in development. In addition, characteristics of the mother can influence fetal development. These characteristics include the extent of stress she experiences and the availability of others for social and emotional support as well as her nutritional and health status. These factors are, in part, determined by the larger social, political, and economic context in which the unborn baby and mother live.

The practices and procedures surrounding the birth and initial care of a baby constitute its *perinatal environment.* Cultures differ enormously in their methods of managing childbirth. Among some of the biggest differences are where the baby is born, who is present at birth, and how much and what kinds of medication are made available to the mother during labor. Concerns about isolated and restrictive regimens as well as an overreliance on medication in traditional Western hospital settings have led to the advent of a variety of more "natural" methods of preparing for and delivering children in the United States. These changes seem to foster more satisfying experiences surrounding childbirth for many parents without increasing and perhaps even diminishing risks for newborns.

As infant and childhood diseases have come under increasing control, researchers have redirected their attention to the prevention and treatment of low–birth weight infants. Despite the immediate obstacles facing both preterm and small-for-gestational-age babies, many become normal children and adults. Compensatory and enrichment programs increase early weight gains and other aspects of early development in low–birth weight babies.

The brief but climactic beginnings taking place prenatally and perinatally have set the stage for the long course of *postnatal development.* Newborns have the immediate task of responding to their new environment. Infant scales such as the Apgar and Neonatal Behavioral Assessment scales provide some indication of the baby's physiological state and ability to interact with caregivers and respond to stimulation. Newborns and young infants display a number of different sleeping and waking states, and a relatively large proportion of their sleep time is engaged in REM sleep, a state that may provide them with stimulation even when asleep.

5

Physical Growth and Motor Skills

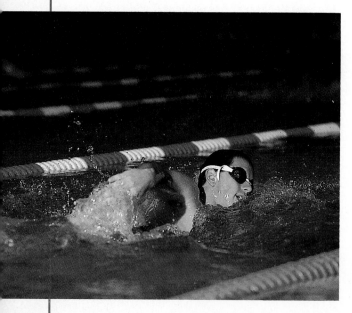

KEY THEMES

▶ **What roles do nature and nurture play in physical growth and motor skill development?**

▶ **How does the sociocultural context influence physical growth and motor skill development?**

▶ **How does the child play an active role in the process of physical growth and motor skill development?**

▶ **Are physical growth and motor skill development continuous or stagelike?**

▶ **Are there sensitive periods in physical growth and motor skill development?**

▶ **How do physical growth and motor skill development interact with other domains of development?**

She had not been able to sleep very well last night. Maybe that's why she felt so tired now. Or maybe it was the grueling tennis match in which she was now engaged. She was only fourteen, but this match was for the high school state championship. Erin had faced situations like it before. Just three months ago her teammates had looked to her to score the final five points to win the league basketball title. She had not let them down. Now she was on the spot again, in a completely different sport.

"Competitive from the day she was born," her mother always said of Erin, but there was much in Erin's family life to encourage her to develop her athletic abilities. Her father had been a university basketball player, and her brothers were constantly playing basketball in her front yard; she joined them whenever they'd let her. From the age of eight she attended sports camp faithfully, spending two months each summer swimming and playing field hockey, soccer, tennis, any game she could. The specialized training markedly increased her naturally good motor coordination in each of these sports. By the age of ten, Erin was good—very good—at most sports even though she was one of the shortest girls in her class. After she turned twelve, however, Erin began to grow rapidly, and now had become taller than many of her classmates, including some of the boys.

Erin played a tough match, but she lost the state championship. She was disappointed, but not devastated. She knew she played well. And she could also take pride in her academic work and her social life outside school. Over the years of childhood, Erin's athletic achievements contributed to a core of self-esteem that extended to other areas of her life and was solid enough to survive temporary setbacks. The burgeoning adult in Erin would need to draw on this reserve of confidence many times in the course of the complicated blend of physical, social/emotional, and cognitive transformations that comprise adolescence.

Physical and brain growth and the development of motor skills vary enormously in degree from one individual to another, and they do not take place at an even rate over childhood. These are among the many principles exhibited by bodily changes that are evident in social, emotional, and cognitive development as well. What's more, physical growth and the development of motor skills significantly influence, and in turn are influenced by, these other dimensions of development. Consider how newfound motor skills, for example, can dramatically affect cognition. The infant who begins to reach for and grasp objects acquires a fresh and powerful means of gaining information and controlling the world. Equally, the child just beginning to crawl learns a tremendous amount about the world simply by being forced to pay attention to the surfaces that will support her weight or the location of interesting objects to investigate. In return, and for her own safety, she may confront new barriers—the side of a playpen, a gate, a locked door.

The reactions of others to the child's new accomplishments, in fact, can elicit and encourage further efforts or stifle and interfere with them. The toddler who insists on dressing himself but still lacks the fine motor skills for buttoning and unbuttoning may become easily frustrated, overtaxing his mother's patience as she tries to get her son to day care and herself to work on time. His need for increasing autonomy and his efforts to master new motor skills are two facets of the same developmental impulse, but his parent in turn has other agendas to balance in fostering them. The child's increasingly sophisticated techniques for engaging the environment at all levels are constantly being influenced by the responses of caregivers.

Along with its attributes and accomplishments, the human body itself provokes emotional reactions, positive and negative, in others. The responses of

TABLE 5.1

A Premodern Measurement System of Human Metamorphosis

Chronological Age (in years)	Time of Year	Time of Day
Birth–2	Frozen	Before daybreak
2–7	Thawing	Dawn
7–14	Budding	Daybreak
14–21	Leafing Out	Sunrise
21–28	Blossoming	Breakfast
28–35	Increasing in size	Before noon
35–42	Maturing	Noon
42–49	Reaping	Afternoon
49–56	Spreading about	Dinner
56–63	Falling of leaves	Sunset
63–70	Freezing	Twilight
70–death	Wintertime	Night

Source: Adapted from Wadstroem, 1769.

peers and adults strongly influence the child's feelings about self and other competencies. A young adolescent like Erin, satisfied with her body and the changes it has undergone, is likely to feel confident not only about learning new physical activities such as dancing, but about establishing new social relationships as well. Conversely, the child who fails to display physical attributes or motor skills valued in a society—the child who is shorter, less coordinated, or otherwise physically distinctive—may receive strikingly different treatment than the child who is tall, strong, or athletic.

Yet another factor besides interdependence of influences must be considered in the complex process of physical development: To what extent are age-related changes in body, brain, and motor skills genetically programmed? To what extent are they determined by parenting, cultural, or other environmental events? As in every other aspect of child development, once again we face the nature-nurture issue. Did Erin's athletic prowess come about "naturally," or had years of practice shaped her exceptional skills? Conversely, the same question could be asked about her determination to succeed: was it a "family" trait genetically passed on, or did she absorb it in her competitive, sports-oriented home environment?

To answer these questions as well as to gauge the effect of broad principles of physical growth and development on other domains of development, we must examine the distinctive ways in which the child's body, brain, and motor skills conjointly develop.

HOW THE BODY GROWS AND DEVELOPS

The mysterious ability of a living organism to *grow* is a phenomenon that never loses its wonder. For parent and child alike, the ever-higher pencil marks on the bathroom wall are eloquent testimony to the passage of time. A long-absent aunt who cries, "My, how you've grown!" may summon a grin from the wary seven-year-old or a blush from the self-conscious thirteen-year-old, but she is confirming for them the social importance of this mark of increasing physical maturity.

We tend to use the words *grow* and *develop* interchangeably in describing the physical transformations of childhood, but they do not refer to the same processes. Strictly speaking, *growth* is the increase in physical size of the body or its parts. *Development* refers not only to changes in size, but also to the accompanying orderly patterns, such as growth spurts, and the increasingly more complicated levels of functioning associated with physical and other changes.

Norms of Growth

For as far back as we possess written records, we find evidence that testifies to the power of the phenomenon of physical growth to excite the human imagination as well as a fascination with measuring and evaluating growth by drawing parallels to other natural events. As recently as the eighteenth century, Western European scientists used seasonal and day-night metaphors as yardsticks for human growth and aging. Table 5.1 lists a few of these analogical measurement systems.

The height of children of the same age varies enormously. These individual differences are most pronounced as children approach the teenage years.

Today we have more precise ways of determining **norms,** quantitative measures that provide typical values and variations in height, weight, and size of body parts as a function of chronological age. These norms have become an essential yardstick for attempting to answer questions about how biological and experiential factors influence growth.

Length and Height   In Chapter 4 we saw that the most rapid change in body length occurs during the fourth month of prenatal development, when the size of the fetus increases about 1.5 millimeters a day (Sinclair, 1985). Babies also typically undergo distinct periods of rapid growth, no matter what their differences in size at birth. The rate is especially rapid during the first six months of life; if this growth rate were sustained unchecked, in fact, the average ten-year-old would be about a hundred feet tall (McCall, 1979). In the first twelve months of life, the baby's length increases by nearly half. By age two, the toddler will be approximately half his or her adult height.

Throughout infancy and childhood, boys and girls grow at very similar rates. Around ten or eleven years of age, however, many girls begin an adolescent growth spurt, a period when the rate of growth nearly doubles the rate maintained during childhood. Because this growth spurt does not usually start in boys until about two years later, girls may tower over their male peers for a brief period in early adolescence. Figure 5.1 depicts this pattern of growth for children during their first eighteen years. Derived from measurements obtained in a cross-sectional sample of boys and girls in England in 1965, it is typical of populations of children around the world.

norms Measure of average values and variations in some aspect of development such as physical size and motor skill development in relation to age.

Weight   In contrast to height, the maximum rate of increase in weight occurs shortly *after* birth, as shown in Figure 5.1. In the first few days after delivery, newborns typically lose excess body fluids and shed 5 to 10 percent of their birth weight. But then infants usually make rapid weight gains, normally doubling their birth weight in about five months and tripling it by the end of the first year. If the gains for the first six months were sustained, the average ten-year-old would weigh in at about 240,000 tons (McCall, 1979)! The lowest weight gain during childhood takes place between the ages of two and three. After that, gains gradually increase until just before adolescence. During the adolescent growth spurt, however, weight and height gains combine: a girl can be expected to put on another thirty-five pounds; a boy, another forty-five pounds.

Patterns in Physical Growth

So far we have examined typical changes in the rate of overall body size during childhood. The physical development of individual systems within the body, however, often proceeds at different rates than that of the body as a whole. The most dramatic example of this phenomenon is probably head size. Think

FIGURE 5.1

Growth Curves for Height and Weight in Boys and Girls

Babies shoot up faster than teenagers and gain weight just as rapidly, as this chart of average individual growth in height and weight for British boys and girls in 1965 shows. Note how boys and girls are very similar in height and weight until adolescence, when girls typically show an adolescent growth spurt about two years before boys. The later growth spurt found in boys, however, is usually more intense, and they often overtake girls in height and weight.

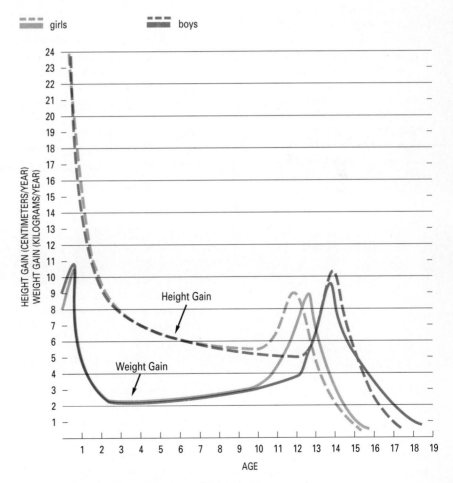

Source: Adapted from Tanner, Whitehouse, & Takaishi, 1966.

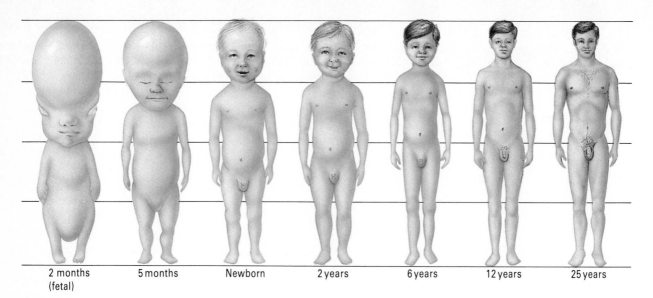

| 2 months (fetal) | 5 months | Newborn | 2 years | 6 years | 12 years | 25 years |

FIGURE 5.2

Source: Adapted from Robbins et al., 1928.

Changes in Body Proportions During Prenatal and Postnatal Growth

The size of the human head in proportion to the rest of the body shows striking changes over the course of prenatal to adult development. Two months after conception, the head comprises about half of the entire length of the body. By adulthood, the head makes up only about 12 to 13 percent of total body length. The fact that the head tends to grow more rapidly than regions of the body near the "tail" demonstrates the pattern of cephalocaudal development.

cephalocaudal development
Pattern that organs, systems, and motor movements near the head tend to develop earlier than those near the feet.

proximodistal development Pattern that organs and systems of the body near the middle tend to develop earlier than those near the periphery.

of paintings you may have seen from the Renaissance in which children are rendered simply as "little grownups" with proportionately small, adult-sized heads. Perhaps because their societies also tended to regard children as miniature adults, European artists of those times failed to draw head size in infants and young children as relatively large compared to the rest of the body.

Directionality of Growth   The varying growth trends we observe in many parts of the body follow the cephalocaudal and proximodistal patterns of development. **Cephalocaudal development**—cephalocaudal combines the Greek words for "head" and "tail"—describes the tendency for systems and parts of the body near the head to grow more rapidly than those more distant from the head. In Chapter 4 we noted that prenatal development of the upper limbs typically precedes development of the lower limbs, an order predicted by cephalocaudal development. This pattern is also evident in the head's rate of development compared with that of the rest of the body. Two months after conception, the head constitutes nearly 50 percent of total body length. By birth, however, head size represents only about 25 percent, and by adulthood, 12 to 13 percent of total body length, as Figure 5.2 shows. **Proximodistal development** refers to the finding, discussed in Chapter 4, that regions near the middle of the body tend to differentiate more rapidly than regions near the periphery. An infant is able to control body parts nearer the trunk much sooner than many areas more distant, such as fingers and toes.

Not all physical changes, however, conform to the cephalocaudal or proximodistal principles of development. During the adolescent growth spurt, for example, parts of the body undergo rapid growth in a pattern almost the reverse of the proximodistal principle. We are all familiar with the spectacle of the gawky teenager who seems to be all hands and feet. Hands and feet are in fact usually the first body parts to show a dramatic change during this period; they are followed by arms and legs and, last of all, the trunk (Tanner, 1978).

An adolescent, in other words, is likely to outgrow his shoes first, then his trousers, and finally his jacket.

Independent Growth of Body Parts As we have just seen, various organs and systems of the body grow to adult levels at different rates. Many organs, including the muscles and the respiratory and digestive systems, follow the pattern of overall weight change shown by the gold line in Figure 5.3: substantial gains during the first two years; a slower, more stable increase throughout childhood; and a rapid increase during adolescence.

As the other lines in Figure 5.3 demonstrate, however, not all systems of the body exhibit this pattern of growth. The central nervous system and the head, as already pointed out, show an early and extremely rapid increase in weight. By five or six years of age, 90 percent of the adult level for brain and head size has been reached. The reproductive system, not surprisingly, follows a strikingly different pattern; only during adolescence do organs associated with reproduction begin to mature and rapidly approach their adult size. Finally, the lymphoid system, which includes the tonsils, thymus, and lymph nodes, undergoes a steep rise in weight throughout early childhood and achieves maximum size near the onset of adolescence. This system, however, subsequently shows a precipitous decrease in weight during the remaining years before early adulthood.

FIGURE 5.3

Growth Curves of Different Parts and Systems of the Body

Body parts and systems grow at unequal rates. The weight of various body systems during development is shown here as a percentage of adult weight; the general curve indicates body growth as a whole (excluding head) and also growth of respiratory, digestive, and muscle systems. The weight of the brain and head approaches adult weight much more rapidly than the weights of other body systems do. The weight of the reproductive organs remains low until the onset of puberty. Some organs, such as those that make up the lymphoid system (tonsil, thymus, and lymph nodes), actually weigh more during middle childhood than at maturity.

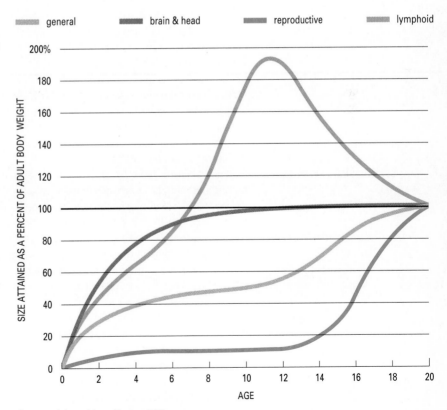

Source: Adapted from Tanner, 1978.

Each of these patterns reflects the critical functional importance of various systems of the body at specific points in development. The brain's relatively early maturity makes neural involvement possible in many aspects of early behavior acquisition and development. Similarly, the increase in the weight of the reproductive organs during adolescence is an important component in the emergence of adult sexual maturity.

Individual and Group Differences in Physical Growth

▶ **Roles of nature and nurture**

Children can show substantial deviations from the norm in their rate of physical growth and development. Variations in size are already noticeable at birth. In the United States, infants weighing between five and a half and nine pounds and measuring between nineteen and twenty-one inches in length are considered within the normal range (National Center for Health Statistics, 1976). As we have seen in Chapter 4, however, environmental factors such as exposure to teratogens, maternal health conditions, genetic factors, and other circumstances may cause weight and length at birth to be substantially below or above these figures.

▶ **Development as continuous/ stagelike**

After birth, individual differences in growth continue through infancy and childhood, often becoming most visible during the adolescent years, when children are likely to show enormous variation in the timing, speed, and duration of the adolescent growth spurt. In the United States, the onset of rapid adolescent growth normally occurs between the ages of ten and fourteen for girls and twelve and sixteen for boys (Sinclair, 1985). A girl who once towered over her childhood girlfriends may suddenly find, at age thirteen, that she is looking up to them—temporarily, at least. A boy whose athletic skills were nothing remarkable may find himself the starting center for the junior high basketball team if he undergoes an early adolescent growth spurt. These swift transformations in size produce correspondingly dramatic emotional reactions as well. As we will see in our discussion of the psychological effects of early and late maturity, individual responses run the gamut from pride and excitement to embarrassment and anxiety.

▶ **Sociocultural influence**

▶ **Roles of nature and nurture**

Variability in growth occurs among ethnic and cultural groups as well as among individuals, a fact confirmed by anthropologists, pediatricians, and developmental psychologists. The average height of eight-year-old girls from thirty-seven cultures shown in Figure 5.4 demonstrates this ethnic and cultural variability. These group variations help scientists explore the role of heredity and environment in physical development. Both factors contribute to these differences, and we will shortly have much more to say about the complex ways in which they interact.

Measuring and Defining Physical Maturity

Together with enormous variations in adult stature, the large variability in rate of growth we have been examining here—not only among individuals and groups but for different parts of the body—obliges us to use criteria other than size to determine physical maturity.

FIGURE 5.4

Ethnic and Cultural Differences in Growth

Ethnic and cultural differences in growth are strikingly apparent in this graph of the average height of eight-year-old girls from selected regions of the world. Girls in northern and eastern Europe are nearly a half a foot taller, on average, than girls in India at this age; similar results are found for boys. These variations may reflect both hereditary and environmental conditions.

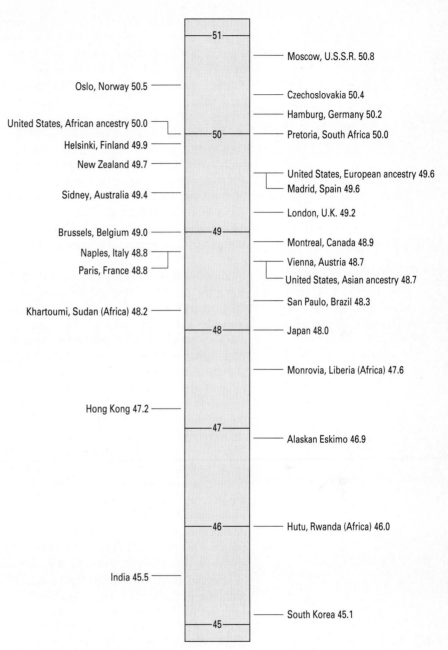

Source: Adapted from Meredith, 1978.

Skeletal Maturity   One reliable measure of growth changes is provided by *ossification,* the chemical transformation of cartilage into bony tissue. As noted in Chapter 4, ossification begins prenatally about the eighth week after conception when cartilage in the ribs and in the center of the long bones of the arms and legs is transformed into bone. The ossifying process continues after birth through late adolescence or early adulthood, when bones in the wrist and ankle are finally completely formed.

The extent to which cartilage has ossified thus provides an excellent index of **skeletal age** or **maturity.** Degree of ossification is measured by x-rays of the size, shape, and position of bones, particularly those in the hand and forearm. This measure is sometimes used by archaeologists and practitioners of forensic medicine to determine the age of death of a young individual when other information is unavailable. It has even been used to make decisions about training and education, as a true story demonstrates. A very short ten-year-old aspiring dancer was denied admission to England's Royal Ballet School because school officials feared she would never reach the minimum height of five feet two inches required for a position in a ballet company. Because of the girl's unusual talents, however, the school's director was persuaded to obtain x-rays of her hand to determine whether she was simply showing a slower-than-normal rate of maturation. When the x-rays revealed that this was indeed the case, the girl was admitted. She eventually grew to the height of five feet four inches and became a professional dancer (Tanner & Taylor, 1965).

Sexual Maturity   Although skeletal age rather than individual size has become the scientific standard for determining physical maturity, other highly visible markers of maturity appear just before and during the adolescent years. Typically important indicators to young teenagers and their parents, these markers include both the adolescent growth spurt and a series of transformations associated with **puberty,** that developmental milestone when a young person gains the ability to reproduce. Indeed, rapid and dramatic changes in many aspects of physical development during the teenage years often provoke questions about whether adolescence represents a unique stage in development.

During puberty the *primary sexual organs*—testes and penis in males; vagina, uterus, and ovaries in females—enlarge and begin to function. *Secondary sexual characteristics* that distinguish males from females, such as facial hair or breasts, also mature. Puberty is accompanied by other changes that catapult adolescents from "childish"-looking to adult-looking persons. Boys take on a more muscular and angular appearance as shoulders widen and the fat tissue of childhood is replaced with muscle. Girls' hips broaden, a change especially adaptive in bearing children. Girls also tend to retain a higher proportion of fat to muscle tissue and assume a more rounded appearance overall than boys.

Like the growth spurt, the timing of each of the range of events associated with puberty varies enormously from one young person to another. Within each individual, moreover, the various signs of puberty emerge at different times. As a rule, however, this cluster of characteristics tends to appear somewhat earlier in girls than in boys. Figure 5.5 identifies several events associated with sexual maturity and the average age at which those events take place for boys and girls.

Typically, enlargement of the testes in boys begins at about eleven and a half years of age, pubic hair starts to appear about six months afterwards, and growth of the penis, spurt in height, and deepening of the voice begin another six months later. The first spontaneous ejaculation of semen normally occurs about a year after the penis begins to enlarge. Further markers, such as the growth of facial and body hair, appear in boys even later. In some boys, however, these indicators of increased sexual maturity make their appearance at much younger or older chronological ages. The growth of the testes, for example, may begin as early as nine and a half years of age and be nearly com-

▶ **Development as continuous/ stagelike**

skeletal maturity   Extent to which cartilage has ossified to form bone; provides the most accurate estimate of how much additional growth will take place in the individual.

puberty   Developmental period during which a sequence of physical changes takes place that transforms the individual from immaturity to one capable of reproduction.

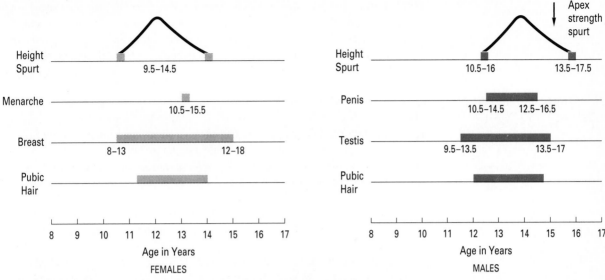

FIGURE 5.5

Normal Range of Ages in the Development of Sexual Characteristics in Males and Females

Source: Adapted from Marshall & Tanner, 1970.

The various changes accompanying puberty for males and females have a typical age of onset and cessation, but the specific times vary within individuals as well as between individuals. The peaking lines connecting onset and cessation of the timeline for height spurt reflect changes in the rate of increase in height over the duration of the growth spurt. The numbers under the time lines mark the earlier and later ages when these transitions take place for many children. Note especially the age differences for girls and boys.

plete by age thirteen and a half for some boys, the time in which this growth is just beginning for other boys.

The various signs of approaching sexual maturity typically begin somewhat earlier for girls. The age of onset, however, is every bit as variable as that for boys. Breast development and the growth spurt typically begin in the tenth year, the appearance of pubic hair in the eleventh year, and underarm hair about the thirteenth year. **Menarche,** the first menstrual period, tends to occur relatively late in this sequence—at about the thirteenth birthday—but, as with all other indicators of puberty, its age of onset varies considerably from one girl to the next. Menarche is usually considered the indicator of sexual maturity in females even though it is not synonymous with actual reproductive ability. *Ovulation,* the release of an egg cell during menstruation, may not occur for another twelve to eighteen months after menarche.

WHAT DETERMINES PHYSICAL GROWTH AND DEVELOPMENT?

▶ **Roles of nature and nurture**

menarche First occurrence of menstruation.

Developmental psychologists try to understand the role of nature and nurture in human physical growth just as in other domains of development. On the one hand, the contributions of nature or heredity are often suggested by correlations in the onset and pattern of physical changes among biologically related family members and cultural groups and by studies revealing significant consequences of brain and hormonal functioning for physical development. On the other hand, nurture or environment—factors including diet, disease, and even seasonal and climatic conditions—have a bearing on physical growth as well.

▶ **Roles of nature and nurture**

Biological Determinants

The influence of biological factors on physical development is readily apparent—tall parents usually have tall children, for example, an indication that hereditary factors may be at work in influencing growth. But just how does biology affect physical development?

Genetic Factors   Your height is likely to be closely related to that of your mother and father. A late-maturing adolescent often shares late maturity with other family members (Rallison, 1986). What is true for the family in miniature is also true for larger human populations that are genetically related. The Mbuti of Zaire, for example, are much taller as a group than their close neighbors the Efe, the pygmies of the Ituri rain forest. Even body proportions differ among ethnic groups; leg and arm lengths are relatively greater in individuals of African descent than in other racial groups when length of the torso is the same (Sinclair, 1985). Similarities and differences like these implicate genetic factors in physical development.

Researchers are fairly certain that human growth and final stature are normally influenced by many genes (Gillis, 1982). Chromosomal errors or specific gene defects, however, can also play a role by causing growth retardation and interfering with various aspects of physical development, as we saw in Chapter 3 when we examined the impact of hereditary anomalies. It is important to remember, though, that genes do not control growth *directly*. Genes regulate physical development by means of biochemical instructions that affect the neural and hormonal functioning of different organs and body systems. Thus, neural and hormonal factors make up the biological systems that carry out genetic instructions.

catch-up growth Increase in growth rate after some factor such as illness or poor nutrition has disrupted the expected, normal growth rate.

lagging-down growth Condition in which, after periods of rapid acceleration because of congenital or hormonal disorders, growth is slowed so that subsequent increases in height conform to those normally expected for the individual.

Neural Control   Many researchers believe the brain includes a "growth center," a genetically established program or template against which it can monitor and compare the actual rate and level of growth taking place in the individual (Sinclair, 1985). This claim has been supported with observations of **catch-up growth,** the phenomenon that occurs after some environmental factor interferes with normal increases in height during infancy or childhood. Illness or malnutrition, for example, may disrupt a child's expected increase in height; if the duration and severity of these problems are limited and do not occur at a critical time, however, the rate of growth is likely to accelerate once these conditions are removed. The accelerated rate of growth continues until height "catches up" to the level expected if no disruption had occurred.

The presence of a growth center is suggested equally by the converse of catch-up growth—that is—**lagging-down growth** (Prader, 1978). Some rare congenital and hormonal disorders produce accelerated increases in height; if the disorder is corrected, growth halts or slows until actual height matches projected height based on the pattern of growth before the disruption.

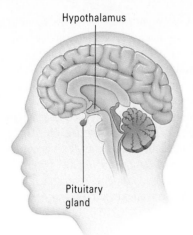

Hypothalamus

Pituitary gland

FIGURE 5.6

Two Important Organs of the Brain That Affect Growth and Physical Development

The hypothalamus and the pituitary gland, located near each other at the base of the brain, are two organs believed to play a central role in the regulation of growth. The hypothalamus may possibly be the locus for a growth center that compares actual height with a genetically determined template for height. Hormones released by the hypothalamus stimulate the release of other hormones by the pituitary gland that promote growth.

pituitary gland Major gland located near the hypothalamus that releases a number of hormones affecting physical growth and development.

testosterone Hormone produced by the testes of males that contributes to fetal sex differentiation and also triggers the emergence of pubertal changes.

estrogen Hormone produced by the ovaries that contributes to pubertal changes in primary and secondary sexual characteristics and that helps prepare the uterus for implantation by a zygote.

If catch-up and lagging-down growth provide evidence that the brain has the means of monitoring the phenotype and determining whether it conforms to the genotype for height, where is this growth center located? Researchers have theorized that the orchestrator of genetic instructions on growth may be the *hypothalamus,* a small region near the base of the brain (see Figure 5.6). Special cells in the hypothalamus may maintain the records for comparing actual to genetically programmed growth and may regulate other cells in the hypothalamus to produce hormones that directly affect growth.

Hormonal Influences One of the key mechanisms for converting genetic instructions into physical development is provided by hormones, the secretions of substances from various glands of the body. Hormones travel in the bloodstream to influence cells in other regions of the body. A dozen or more hormones affect growth, often by regulating the manufacture of other hormones that directly stimulate cell division (Tanner, 1978).

Besides being the possible site of the growth center, the hypothalamus may also play an important role in coordinating the formation and release of many growth-related hormones. Chemical instructions from cells in the hypothalamus trigger or inhibit production of several hormones in the nearby **pituitary gland** (see Figure 5.6), including one known as *human growth hormone,* or *HGH.* An infant whose pituitary gland fails to manufacture enough HGH may be nearly normal in size at birth, but growth will slow dramatically over the ensuing months and years; such a person typically reaches an adult height of only about four or four and a half feet. When HGH deficiencies were first discovered, endocrinologists assumed that this hormone directly promoted growth in bone and other cells. Later research, however, revealed that *somatomedin,* a hormone produced in response to HGH by specialized cells in the liver, is the immediate regulator of cell division for growth (Rallison, 1986). Somatomedin in the bloodstream also closes an important link in the feedback loop to the brain; cells in the hypothalamus sensitive to somatomedin transmit further chemical instructions to the pituitary to produce more or less HGH.

The hypothalamus and pituitary gland interact to stimulate the production of other hormones important for physical changes, including those that take place during puberty. A single pituitary secretion stimulates the *adrenal glands,* located just above the kidneys, to increase the manufacture of a hormone that plays an important role in the growth spurt and the emergence of underarm and pubic hair in girls. Still other *gonadotropic* (gonad-seeking) hormones released by the pituitary gland contribute to the production of sperm and elevate the production of **testosterone** by the testes in boys; they also regulate the menstrual cycle and stimulate the production of **estrogen** and **progesterone** by the ovaries in girls. For boys, testosterone promotes growth in height, an increase in size of the penis and testes, and the appearance of secondary sexual characteristics such as pubic and facial hair. In girls, estrogen promotes the development of the breasts, uterus, and vagina as well as the broadening of the pelvis (Malina, 1975). Estrogen and progesterone together prepare the uterine environment to receive a fertilized ovum.

How these various biological processes interact to determine individual differences in physical growth and development remains a difficult puzzle to solve. We do not know, for example, what kinds of events trigger the hypothalamus to send instructions to the pituitary to release hormones that initiate puberty. The hypothalamus may monitor metabolic cues associated with body size or the ratio of fat to muscle, because extremely high levels of exercise and poor nutrition seem to delay menarche in girls (Frisch, 1983).

Moreover, variations in amounts of a hormone, as long as they fall within a reasonable range, fail to provide a consistent explanation for individual differences. Tall and short persons may both manufacture ample supplies of HGH and somatomedin, but differences in height seem to depend on the sensitivity of cartilage cells to these hormones (Tanner, 1978). The absence of either HGH or somatomedin, as we have seen, can have a dramatic impact on growth but so, too can other poorly understood biological substances. The "pygmy" Efe of Zaire produce normal quantities of HGH but seem unable to utilize it for normal growth because they lack a body substance identified as *insulinlike growth factor (IGI-I)* (Merimee, Zapf, & Froesch, 1981).

▶ **Roles of nature and nurture**

Environmental Determinants

Physical growth may seem to be a phenomenon so closely determined by its biological regulators that it is impervious to experiential influences. Once again, however, we find this dimension of development to be a flexible, interactive process affected by a range of environmental factors. Nutrition, health, and exercise are all potential experiential variables affecting human physical growth and development. Other environmental factors, including social and emotional circumstances, even climate and geographic conditions, should be added to this list. Let's examine some of these influences more closely.

Nutrition and Health   We identified some consequences of malnutrition for fetal development in Chapter 4, and as the phenomenon of catch-up growth indicates, illness and poor nutrition can affect postnatal growth as well. In one study of the growth of children based on data collected over much of the first half of the twentieth century from a city in Germany, the average height of children at various ages was found to increase gradually over the years, a trend reported in most Western societies. However, during World Wars I and II, when food was far more limited in this city, the pattern of gradual increments in average height leveled off and in some years for some age groups even showed a decline (Howe & Schiller, 1952).

Dietary supplements can raise poor nutrition to an adequate level, thereby exerting a positive influence on children's physical growth and development, suggests a recent study conducted by the Harvard School of Public Health in Bogota, Colombia. All family members in a group in which infants were at risk for malnutrition were given additional food to raise their dietary intake. These supplements were begun when the mother was in her third trimester of pregnancy and were continued for all family members until the target child reached three years of age. At the end of this period, children receiving the supplement averaged over an inch taller and nearly one and a half pounds heavier than children in families who did not receive the supplement. Though these were not enormous differences, size differences in the targeted children continued to be found at age six as well, three years after the supplements were discontinued (Super, Herrara, & Mora, 1990).

progesterone   Hormone produced by the ovaries that helps prepare uterus for implantation by a zygote.

Extreme malnutrition can, of course, have a devastating impact on growth. Infants with *marasmus* fail to grow because they lack sufficient calories. Consequences include eventual loss in weight; wrinkly, aged skin; an abdomen that is either shrunken or swollen and distended; and a "hollow" appearance to the body. An even more prevalent form of malnutrition around the world is *kwashiorkor,* or failure to develop because of a diet inadequate in protein. Kwashiorkor typically appears in a child between one and three years of age who has been deposed from his or her mother's breast, usually by a newborn, when no other adequate source of protein replaces the mother's milk. The symptoms of kwashiorkor—lethargic behavior and apathetic look, the wrinkled skin, distended stomach, and thin, wispy, reddish orange cast of hair—have been depicted over and over again in all their horror by the world media. Yet despite international efforts to respond to this preventable condition, kwashiorkor continues to be an ominous, life-threatening reality for a large proportion of the 100 million or 18 percent of the world's younger citizens who are estimated to be malnourished (De Maeyer, 1976). Deficiencies linked to specific nutritional elements—for example, vitamins A, D, B complexes, and K, as well as iron and calcium—are also linked to growth disorders affecting hundreds of thousands of children in various regions of the world (Hansen, 1990).

Influences of the Physical Environment   It may seem hard to believe, but even the earth's broader physical conditions may affect rate of growth. Physical growth actually shows seasonal variations: height increases more in the spring, and weight increases more in the fall, at least for populations of children in the Northern Hemisphere (Sinclair, 1985). Light, known to accelerate growth in other species of animals, may influence human growth as well. High altitude may also affect age of menarche and the adolescent growth spurt. Some populations living in the Andes and Himalayan mountains as well as the Ethiopian highlands reveal a late age of onset for menarche among girls and a fairly prolonged, stable growth period during adolescence, especially for boys. As always, of course, more than one factor may be involved; these developmental differences may stem from poor nutritional or other environmental conditions. The pattern of findings from several regions of the world, however, suggests that less oxygen at higher altitudes plays a contributing role as well (Malik & Hauspic, 1986).

▶ **Interaction among domains**

Social-Emotional Factors   We have noted that physical development and the acquisition of motor skills can strongly impact a child's social-emotional development. Surprisingly enough, studies have proven that the reverse is also true. Early studies of institutionalized children (Ribble, 1943; Spitz, 1946b) painted vivid images of massive disruption in physical growth if a warm, consistent caregiver was unavailable to the young infant. Pediatricians and psychologists continue to be concerned about how social and emotional factors affect growth—in particular, whether lack of social-emotional support contributes to **failure to thrive,** a label applied to any child below the third percentile on weight or height compared with other children of the same age.

failure to thrive   Label applied to any child whose growth in height or weight is below the third percentile for children of the same age; may arise from inadequate social-emotional relationships with caregivers.

Failure to thrive occurs for many different reasons. In one survey of a half-dozen studies conducted in the United States, about 20 percent of the children

Even the earth's geography may have an influence on physical development. The girls shown here are growing up in the Andes Mountains and can be expected to display a more prolonged, stable pattern of increase in height and weight, rather than a rapid growth spurt during adolescence, and a later age for menarche compared to children living in lower altitudes.

showing failure to thrive were found to be merely constitutionally small and happened to fall at the low end of the range of normal development because of their genetic makeup. Organic factors such as gastrointestinal, neurological, and endocrinological disorders accounted for lack of growth in another 53 percent of children. For the remaining 27 percent, however, researchers theorized that environmental (for example, undernutrition) or other nonorganic factors were responsible for the lack of gain in height and weight (Berwick, 1980).

When no specific organic or other cause (such as poor nutrition) can be identified, such growth retardation is labeled *nonorganic failure to thrive syndrome.* Infants with this syndrome show more than just the physical signs of failure to thrive; they also tend to be passive and apathetic as well as unresponsive to stimulation, although they may intently observe the events going on around them (Oates, 1984). Emotional deprivations, psychological traumas, or some other aspect of abusive, neglectful, or inadequate caregiving appear to underlie many cases of nonorganic failure to thrive (English, 1978; Rallison, 1986).

▶ **The child's active role**

Although the syndrome may stem partly from characteristics of the infant or child—for example, difficulty in nursing or unresponsiveness to the caregiver—nonorganic failure to thrive is probably initiated or further aggravated by the caregiver's misperceptions, indifference, and less positive interactions (Skuse, 1985). For example, mothers of infants who fail to thrive tend to display less pleasure and positive support for their babies compared with other mothers. Communications are also more inappropriate, and these mothers interfere or act more arbitrarily while engaging in activities with their infants (Drotar et al., 1990; Skuse, 1985).

A growth disorder occasionally found in older children for which no genetic, organic, or nutritional basis can be identified is called **deprivational dwarfism.** Children with this disorder, usually between the ages of two and fifteen, differ from failure-to-thrive children in that height and weight are often at parallel levels and that the child does not appear malnourished. Nevertheless, these children are surprisingly small for their age. This growth deficit is believed to result solely from emotional deprivation, a powerful negative factor in the caregiving environment that appears to inhibit the release of sufficient levels of human growth hormone. If placed in a more emotionally supportive environment before adolescence, the child suffering from deprivational dwarfism often shows an increase in the production of human growth hormone, followed by catch-up growth (Oates, Peacock, & Forrest, 1985).

▶ **Sensitive periods**

The importance of the environment for physical development seems to go beyond simply making available adequate nutrition and minimum emotional support. Undernutrition-related growth retardation may be reduced by social and educational programs concerned with promoting development. In the study carried out on infants at risk in Colombia, researchers included a condition in which home visits were made twice weekly to stimulate learning and development of the target child. These visits were carried out until the child was three years of age and were designed to improve caregiver-child interactions even after the intervention ended. They were based on a curriculum for lower-income parents in the United States. The home visitor provided advice and support to the parents, but *no* specific instructions on nutrition or other health-related topics. This intervention by itself eventually resulted in positive benefits in height and weight by the time the children were six years of age. Even greater growth benefits occurred when food supplements were combined with the home visits. Fewer than 20 percent of the children who received both types of intervention were considered growth retarded, as compared with more than half the children in the control condition (Super, Herrara, & Mora, 1990). These findings demonstrate that programs designed to improve interactions within the family as well as those designed to provide adequate nutrition can have a substantial impact on physical growth.

▶ **Sociocultural influence**

▶ **Sociocultural influence**

Secular Trends The environment is not always the same from one generation to the next. Knowledge of nutrition and medical treatment of disease in some societies, for example, have changed dramatically in recent generations. These changes can exert long-term influences on populations as well as specific effects on individuals. When a pattern of change in the environment occurs over generations, it is called a **secular trend.** As any young woman who has ever tried on her grandmother's wedding dress knows, for example, children today not only grow faster, they are also taller than previous generations of children in most regions of the world. In many European countries, slight increases in average height took place from 1825 to 1875. Substantially greater increases occurred from the late 1800s to the middle of this century, and a slower increase or even stability in size has been found since the 1960s. Between 1880 and 1950, the average height of Western European and American children increased by nearly four inches. Similar findings have been reported for other cultures, although for different generations. For example, the most

deprivational dwarfism Condition in which child's low levels of human growth hormone and failure to grow at normal rates are believed to be due solely to emotional deprivation. If placed in a supportive environment before adolescence, these children return to normal growth rate.

secular trend Consistent pattern of change over generations.

substantial changes in height in Japan have taken place between 1950 and 1970 (Tanner, 1978).

Even more dramatic changes over generations have been reported for the age at which physical and sexual maturity is reached. Today growth in height among adolescents in most industrialized societies typically halts by about age seventeen; a century ago final height was often not achieved until about age twenty-three (Rallison, 1986). Changes in the age of menarche reveal a similar trend to increasingly earlier and earlier occurrences over recent generations (see Figure 5.7).

What accounts for these dramatic progressive increases in human size and the age of menarche? Generational differences in growth probably stem from improved nutrition, medical care, the abolition of child labor, and, as the recent data from Colombia suggest, a better understanding of the ways to support and encourage child development and family relationships. These same kinds of factors may account for the greater height and more rapid maturation, within a single generation, of children from professional, highly educated, and urban families compared with children from poorer families and those in rural populations (Tanner, 1978).

Medical and economic changes have brought significant improvements to the physical growth and development of children around the world, but greater knowledge of the social, emotional, and psychological needs of children may provide yet another range of enhancements in this vital domain. In the next section we examine yet another facet of the complex interaction among these spheres of development.

THE SOCIAL-EMOTIONAL CONSEQUENCES OF BODY CHANGE

We have seen in the previous section a few of the ways in which social and emotional contexts can affect growth. As Erin's story at the beginning of the chapter showed, however, the converse is also true. Our height, our weight, and the relative speed of our physical maturation can influence the way others respond to us and, in turn, our own sense of worth. Let us explore some of the areas in which the physical affects other domains of development.

▶ **Interaction among domains**

Height

Many societies share a mystique of tallness, the notion that height is directly correlated with such traits as competence and leadership. John Gillis (1982) and others have argued that our height has a dramatic bearing upon the work we do, our success in that work, the social lives we lead, our attractiveness to others, our political choices and willingness to accept authority, and our self-esteem and sense of worth. Studies have shown that the height of a child does affect impressions of his or her ability. Mothers of young children, for example, perceive taller boys as more competent (able to get along better with others, less likely to cry when frustrated, and so forth) and treat smaller boys of the same age as younger and in a more overprotective manner (Eisenberg

FIGURE 5.7

Secular Trends in the Age of Menarche

A secular trend is a pattern of change occurring over generations. There is evidence for a secular trend in the decrease in age for the onset of menarche from 1845 through 1960. Though most of the data were obtained by questioning adolescents and young adults, some, especially from earlier generations, depended on the memory of older individuals.

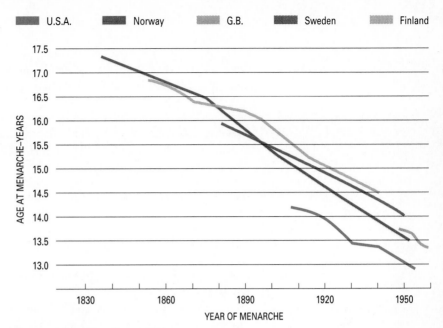

Source: Adapted from Tanner, 1962.

et al., 1984; Rotnem, 1986). Moreover, boys believe it is important to be tall and muscular (Cobb, 1954); those substantially below the average height for their age report extensive teasing from their peers, greater dissatisfaction with their skills, especially in athletic endeavors, and increasing unhappiness as they approach adolescence (Finch, 1978).

Contemporary preferences for being tall, thin, athletic, and "grown up" seem to have promoted considerable apprehension about physical appearance, especially among older children and adolescents in our society, but to some extent among parents as well. Recent advances in science have added an option for addressing this concern, one that, in turn, raises many other new issues.

CONTROVERSY

▶ **Interaction among domains**

When Should Human Growth Hormone Be Made Available to Foster Growth?

Until recently, very little could be done to alter the course of the child's rate of growth or eventual height. Once human growth hormone could be synthetically produced, however, new possibilities emerged. Although costly to manufacture, HGH is now available for the first time in fairly large quantities. For those children whose lack of growth stems from insufficient HGH, this breakthrough represents an enormously positive step. However, perhaps because stereotypical attitudes about height are difficult to modify, increasing numbers of parents are asking pediatricians to administer HGH to offspring who are genetically short or whose delay in growth is a normal part of their pattern of maturation (Law, 1987).

Should such treatments, motivated by self-perceptions and expectations about the benefits of being tall rather than by a medical condition, be encouraged? Relatively large doses of HGH are needed to have any effect on growth in normal children. Moreover, large doses have been administered for only short periods of time; little is known about possible long-term consequences, including their effectiveness and potential negative side effects (Wilson & Rosenfeld, 1987). The cost of HGH is also high; thus, widespread treatment could foster another kind of class difference—rich and tall or short and poor. As a consequence, the American Academy of Pediatrics has concluded that only children with confirmed deficiencies in HGH warrant treatment at this time (Law, 1987). But do possible advantages of HGH outweigh these medical concerns? Some argue that if short stature in otherwise healthy children contributes to poor self-esteem and social disadvantages and growth can be modified without significant risk, HGH should be made more readily available.

Altering normal physical development to conform to a cultural stereotype is a drastic action that raises many ethical issues. The argument that such treatment forestalls negative consequences in the social and emotional domains of development is often countered with the charge that the stereotype itself, and not the child, needs modification. ∎

Obesity and Other Eating Disorders

▶ **Interaction among domains**

Obesity is a physical condition with strong social-emotional consequences in all cultures. Our society tends to view obesity negatively, even though in previous eras it carried, and in many developing countries today it still carries, positive connotations of "substance" and prosperity (Sobal & Stunkard, 1989). In some cultures, for example, adolescent females are encouraged to increase body fat in preparation for marriage (Brown & Konner, 1987). In industrialized societies, however, excess body fat is rarely viewed positively by people of any age (Feldman, Feldman, & Goodman, 1988). When children as young as six years of age are asked to describe drawings or photographs of people who are chubby or thin in appearance, obese figures are more likely to be labeled "lazy," "cheater," or "liar," even though such terms are seldom applied to the children's overweight friends (Kirkpatrick & Sanders, 1978; Lawson, 1980). Moreover, overweight ten- and eleven-year-olds are more likely to experience negative interactions involving peers than are children of normal weight (Baum & Foreham, 1984).

Definitions of obesity vary enormously. A common criterion in our society, however, is 20 percent over the weight considered ideal for a person's height, age, and sex (Epstein & Wing, 1987) or when other indicators of fatness (such as skin fold thickness) measure above the eightieth percentile for the child's reference group (Dietz, 1983). Despite these ambiguous parameters, national health surveys conducted in the United States reveal a substantial increase in obesity in African American and Caucasian girls and boys over recent decades (Gortmaker et al., 1987).

▶ **Sociocultural influence**

What are the reasons for this secular trend? Researchers have advanced various hypotheses. Compared with a generation ago, children spend larger amounts of time in more sedentary activities such as watching television

(Gortmaker et al., 1987). Limited physical activity as well as dietary shifts away from fresh fruits and vegetables toward calorie-laden snack and convenience foods are often advanced as contributing factors. Thus we see an instance in which the social context, while attaching a negative label to a physical condition on one hand, can actively promote it on the other.

▶ **Roles of nature and nurture**

Disease or medical conditions rarely cause obesity (Dietz, 1983). Genetic factors, however, may predispose some children to overnutrition. The weights of adopted children show a closer relationship to weights of biological parents than to weights of adoptive parents (Stunkard et al., 1986). Having overweight parents also greatly increases the probability of being obese as a child (Epstein, Wing, & Valoski, 1985). This relationship, however, may arise through either hereditary or environmental influences since the parents serve as models for their children's eating and exercise habits.

Does a fat baby stay fat? At one time people routinely assumed that overweight infants became overweight adults, but recent studies indicate this relationship is lower than originally believed (Woolston, 1987). Nevertheless, about 20 percent of overweight babies continue to be obese as children. In fact, a heavy infant is about twice as likely as an infant of normal weight to be obese later in life, and the longer a child continues to be overweight, the more likely he or she will remain obese as an adult (Epstein, Wing, & Valoski, 1985; Spence, 1986). Heavier infants and young children appear to form greater numbers of fat cells than their counterparts of average weight (Hirsch, 1975). As a consequence, overweight children may have difficulty escaping a pattern of obesity laid down by these cells early in development. Regardless of whether this pattern stems from hereditary or environmental factors, the problem of weight control is made more complicated by the tendency for obese children to be more sensitive to external food-related cues and less responsive to internal hunger cues than their normal-weight peers (Ballard et al., 1980; Costanzo & Woody, 1979).

The finding that many factors can contribute to obesity may help explain why weight reduction programs have had limited success in children and suggests that effective treatment procedures will need to approach the problem from many different fronts (Spence, 1986). The generally unimpressive results of therapeutic efforts to control weight stand in stark contrast with recent evidence that a substantial number of teenagers, especially girls, many who are not obese, go to great, and sometimes life-threatening, lengths to reduce their weight. *Anorexia nervosa* and *bulimia nervosa* are two self-initiated forms of such weight control (Blinder & Goodman, 1986).

▶ **The child's active role**

Anorexia nervosa is a self-imposed kind of starvation (Halmi, 1985). Anorexics appear to be obsessed with the avoidance of appearing too heavy and, as a consequence, become dangerously thin. As weight loss becomes extreme, muscle tissue degenerates and bone marrow changes, menstrual periods are disrupted, and cardiac stress and arrhythmia can occur. Bulimia nervosa is an eating disorder in which the individual engages in recurrent bouts of binge eating, consuming enormous quantities of food, alternating with self-induced vomiting of what has been eaten. Although sharing an extreme concern about their body weight with anorexics, bulimics typically fall within a normal range of weight for their age and height.

These eating disorders often stem from complex interactions between perceived cultural ideals of physical attractiveness, insecurities about family and friends, possible hormonal or physiological factors, and concerns about changes taking place throughout puberty (Blinder & Goodman, 1986). These extreme behaviors may sometimes emerge as part of the larger spectrum of anxieties many adolescents and young adults are assumed to experience about the events taking place during puberty. One potential source of that anxiety is the relative speed or slowness of physical change at crucial points during the teenage years.

▶ **Interaction among domains**

Early Versus Late Maturity

In describing the striking variability individuals show in their rate of physical development, Tanner (1978) suggests that "some children play out their growth andante, others allegro, a few lentissimo" (p. 78). How do these individual, often transitory, differences during adolescence impact socioemotional development? Let's first consider how young people feel generally about the changes accompanying puberty.

Most teenagers express concerns about their appearance. Their worries may stem from increasingly sophisticated cognitive skills as well as from the physical changes taking place during the adolescent years. But because most indicators of maturity at this age show gradual transformations, research investigating how young people view puberty has focused on girls and their reactions to menarche—the sudden, sometimes unexpected first menstrual period (Greif & Ulman, 1982). This limited focus, as well as the absence of information about social class and ethnic differences, means that generalizations about the psychological impact of puberty must be interpreted cautiously. However, girls who are relatively unprepared for menarche, either because of lack of information or because of its early onset, perceive the event more negatively than other girls, whose reactions are often a mixture of positive and negative feelings (Koff, Rierdan, & Sheingold, 1982; Ruble & Brooks-Gunn, 1982).

▶ **Sociocultural influence**

Because both earlier and more complete education takes place today within many families, in the school, and in other health-related contexts, girls' reactions to menarche appear to be less negative than in previous generations, at least in developed countries (Brooks-Gunn, 1984). Whereas greater communication within the family is correlated with a more positive attitude about menstruation (Brooks-Gunn & Ruble, 1980), girls are still reluctant to talk about their experience with friends, at least at first (Brooks-Gunn et al., 1986).

Limited research conducted with boys suggests that they are often uninformed, other than through reading, about their first spontaneous, nocturnal emission of sperm. Perhaps for this reason, their feelings about this event are mixed and they seldom talk about it with others (Gaddis & Brooks-Gunn, 1985). Nevertheless, in our culture, and probably in most, early maturity seems to be beneficial for boys. Compared with early maturers, late maturers report more negative feelings about themselves, feel more rejected, express stronger dependency and affiliative needs, and are more rebellious toward their parents (Mussen & Jones, 1957). Although late maturers want to be well liked and accepted, they are more likely to belittle or ridicule, even attack others, compared with early maturers (Jones, 1957; Mussen & Jones, 1958).

In other words, their efforts to obtain social approval often translate into attention-getting and compensatory, childish behaviors disruptive to successful relationships with peers and adults. These differences continue to be observed even into adulthood (Jones, 1965).

Given an emphasis on strength and size in many societies, it is not surprising that early maturity seems to benefit boys. But what about the impact of pubertal differences for girls? The outcome here remains much more clouded (Greif & Ulman, 1982; Simmons, Blyth, & McKinney, 1983). Early maturity may enhance status and prestige in girls, as seems to be the case with boys. But it may also be embarrassing, decrease popularity, at least among age mates, and lead to greater social pressure from older friends and greater expectations from parents and other adults to conform to more mature interaction patterns (Brooks-Gunn, 1989).

The findings of one recent project that studied the behaviors of Swedish girls beginning when they were ten years of age reveal some of the social consequences of early maturity (Magnusson, Stattin, & Allen, 1986). Girls reaching menarche earlier were more likely than late-maturing girls to engage in a variety of norm-breaking activities—staying out late, cheating on exams, pilfering, or using alcohol. This was especially true for the earliest-maturing girls. These girls also preferred older and more mature friends, friendships that may have inspired tendencies to express greater independence from socially approved conventions of behavior. Indeed, among those who matured early but reported no older friends, norm-breaking activities were no greater than for girls who matured later (see Figure 5.8). With increasing age, those with and without older friends no longer differed in the frequency of many norm-breaking activities, and later maturers began to engage in some norm-breaking activities such as use of alcohol as frequently as early maturers. Still,

FIGURE 5.8

Norm-breaking and Menarcheal Age for Girls With and Without Older Friends

Among adolescent girls, a correlation has been found between norm-breaking activities, age of menarche, and availability of older friends. Although early maturers tended to engage in more norm-breaking activities than late maturers, their behavior was markedly influenced by the availability of older friends. The presence of older friends, in contrast, had little influence on norm-breaking activities for those girls who matured at later ages.

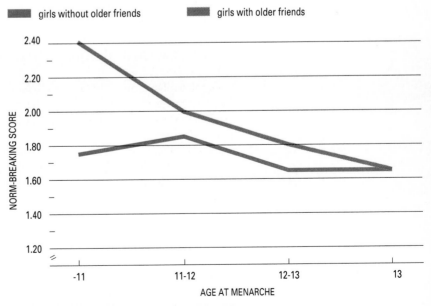

Source: Adapted from Magnusson, Stattin, & Allen, 1986.

a few unacceptable behaviors, such as use of drugs, remained higher among early-maturing girls than among late-maturing girls throughout adolescence.

▶ **Sociocultural influence**

How individual adolescents feel about pubertal changes and how they evaluate their own status in relation to their peers help to explain many of these findings on early and late maturity. Consider the cultural ideals of beauty and maturity for men and women that exist in most Western societies. Slenderness and long legs are considered desirable traits in women. Early-maturing girls, although initially taller than their peers during the growth spurt, have less opportunity to grow tall and often end up being shorter, and at the same time heavier and more robust, than their later-maturing peers (Faust, 1983). These physical outcomes deviate from the ideal portrayed in the media; not surprisingly, therefore, early-maturing girls are less satisfied with their weight and appearance than late-maturing girls. Early-maturing boys, on the other hand, more quickly assume the rugged, muscular physique stereotypically portrayed as ideal for men in our society. As you might expect, then, early maturing boys are more pleased by their weight and appearance than late-maturing boys (Peterson, 1987).

Girls who mature early and boys who mature late are also out of step with most of their classmates. Young people usually prefer friends who share the same interests, and those interests change with increasing maturity. Late-maturing boys find that their friends are likely to move on to other pursuits, making it more difficult to maintain positive relationships with their peers. Early-maturing girls may redirect friendships to older peers. But the desire to be with older friends can be a double-edged sword: it may contribute to increased behavior and school problems, and it may also lead to greater personal unhappiness as a result of pressures to conform with older peers (Magnusson, Stattin, & Allen, 1986; Simmons et al., 1987). Thus, we must consider the interconnecting links among biological, immediate social, and broader cultural events to fully understand the consequences of early and late maturity for children.

HOW THE BRAIN AND NERVOUS SYSTEM DEVELOP

Researchers have long sought to attribute every human activity—from the knee-jerk reflex to the formulation of quantum physics—to the workings of the developing structures and functions of the central nervous system. But progress in delineating specific connections between behavior and mental processes on one hand and brain and neuronal development on the other has been slow (Parmelee & Sigman, 1983), and psychologists believe that an understanding of these connections demands more than knowledge of the physiology of brain development. Human functioning, however, is the product of complex interactions and events involving the biological "hardware" of the brain and other organs, the operations of the nervous system, and the rich variety of external events that engage the human mind and body. Therefore, learning about the central nervous system and some of the basic issues of neuroscientific research can be helpful in unraveling the intertwined complexities of motor, cognitive, and social development (Crnic & Pennington, 1987).

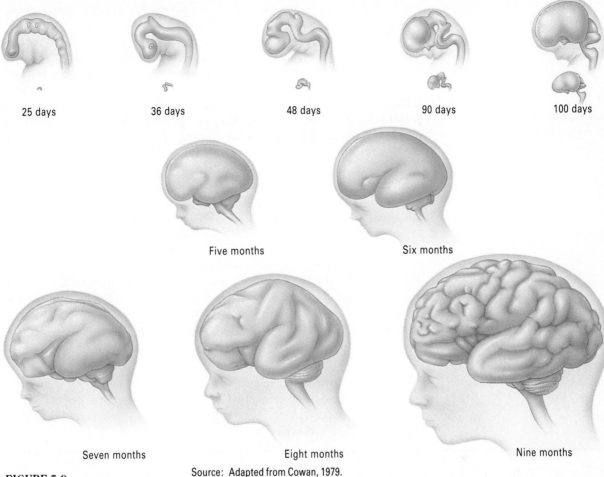

25 days   36 days   48 days   90 days   100 days

Five months   Six months

Seven months   Eight months   Nine months

FIGURE 5.9

The Developing Human Brain

Source: Adapted from Cowan, 1979.

During prenatal development, the human brain shows dramatic increases in size, and the cerebral cortex takes on a convoluted pattern to increase surface area. During the last trimester of prenatal development, the shape of the brain takes on an adultlike appearance, and by birth most of the neurons have been formed. The brain's weight increases most dramatically from about the fifth prenatal month until the infant is about two and a half years of age. The drawings have been made to a common scale; however, the first five have been enlarged to a common size to show details.

cerebral cortex Uppermost, outer, and largest portion of the brain; undergoes rapid differentiation during last few months of prenatal development and first few years of life. Various regions are specialized to carry out sensory, motor, associative, and other neural processing.

The Developing Brain

The growth of the brain before birth is rapid, as is shown in Figure 5.9. The weight of the brain swiftly increases, from about 51 grams (4 percent of adult weight) at five months after conception to about 350 grams (25 percent of adult weight) at birth, to about 1,100 grams (80 percent of adult weight) by four years of age (Spreen et al., 1984). Much of that growth takes place in the **cerebral cortex,** the region of the brain most closely identified with mental processing and complex human behavior.

Compared with other regions of the brain, the cerebral cortex is relatively late in its development. The *brain stem* and *midbrain,* involved in basic reflexes and sensory processing as well as essential biological functions such as digestion, elimination, and respiration, are fairly well established at birth. Within the cerebral cortex, regions associated with motor and sensory functions tend to be among the first to mature. Even within these areas, cell maturity and accompanying changes reflect a cephalocaudal and proximodistal pattern of growth: neural development involved in the control of the head and upper body progresses more quickly than neural development associated with the lower trunk or legs.

The adult cerebral cortex is estimated to contain 10 to 20 billion **neurons,** cells designed to carry electrochemical messages as neural impulses (Nowakowski, 1987). With development, neurons *proliferate*—that is, increase in number; *migrate*—move to various regions of the brain; and *differentiate*—increase in size, complexity, function, and in terms of the number and kinds of contacts with other neurons. Parts of many neurons also become surrounded by **myelin,** a sheath of fatty material that serves to insulate and speed neural impulses by about tenfold. An estimated ten times more **glial cells** (from the Greek word for "glue") than neurons also form within the brain (Blinkov & Glezer, 1968). Glial cells provide the material from which myelin develops, facilitate the transfer of nutrients to neurons, and establish a scaffolding for neuron migration (Tanner, 1978).

▶ **Development as continuous/ stagelike**

Neuron Proliferation   The production of new nerve cells is known as neuron proliferation. Neuron production in humans begins near the end of the first month of fetal development, shortly after the *neural tube* closes, and ends about a month or two before birth (Parmelee & Sigman, 1983). Thus, during this important period only a finite number of young neurons are formed. Rapid postnatal brain growth results from increases in the size and complexity of the neurons rather than from an increase in their numbers (Nowakowski, 1987). Growth of glial cells and other supportive tissues, including myelin, also contributes to the growth of the brain postnatally.

Neuron Migration   Shortly after their formation, neurons move from the neural tube, where they were produced, to other locations within the brain. In fact, it is this migration that shapes the complex cerebral cortex. For some parts of the brain, neurons move only a short distance as they are passively pushed away from the neural tube by the production of new neurons. But a noticeably different kind of movement occurs among neurons in the cerebral cortex and many other regions of the brain. Young neurons in these regions often migrate a great distance, passing through levels of older neurons that have previously reached their final destination. The consequence is an *inside-out pattern* of development; areas nearer the outer surface of the cortex are actually younger than areas deeper in the cortex (Rakic, 1981).

neuron   Nerve cell within central nervous system electrochemically designed to transmit messages between cells.

myelin   Sheath of fatty cells that insulates and speeds neural impulses by about tenfold.

glial cells   Brain cells that provide the material from which myelin is created, nourish neurons, and provide a scaffolding for neuron migration.

How do neurons know where to migrate and when to stop this process? Both neurochemical and mechanical information probably contributes to these activities. For example, young neurons attach to fibers of glial cells radiating to the region of the neuron's destination. The neuron is somehow programmed to move along the surface of the fiber and detach at its final location. Moreover, the production and migration of neurons in the cortex proceeds in waves beginning about the seventh and eleventh weeks of gestational age to form several different layers of neurons in the brain (Berry, 1982; Spreen et al., 1984). Some teratogens, including mercury and alcohol, are known to interfere with the onset and path of neuron migration (Abel, 1989). In fact, developmental defects ranging from mental retardation to behavioral disorders, including some forms of schizophrenia and dyslexia, have been linked to interference in the migratory patterns of nerve cells (Nowakowski, 1987).

▶ **Sensitive periods**

Neuron Differentiation Whereas neurons proliferate and migrate prenatally, neuron differentiation—the process of enlarging, forming connections with other neurons, and beginning to function—continues postnatally, perhaps even into adulthood. Some aspects of this process proceed without external stimulation. Experience, however, often plays a major role in the selection, maintenance, and strengthening of specific connections among neurons. Work on brain development associated with the processing of visual information by cats illustrates this complex relationship (Hubel & Wiesel, 1979). By the time a young kitten's eyes open, neurons in the cerebral cortex receiving input from the visual receptors have already established some connections so that, for example, they may respond to sensory input from either eye and to visual patterns having a broad range of orientations and characteristics. But these neurons will show much further differentiation, becoming far more selective and tuned to specific kinds of sensory input as the kitten experiences various kinds of visual stimulation. Some may, for example, begin to respond to information arising from one or the other eye only and to transitions in dark-light patterns in the visual field that are vertical or horizontal or at some other spatial orientation.

▶ **Roles of nature and nurture**

One of the most startling recent discoveries about brain development is that differentiation never advances for many neurons, and that massive neuron death typically follows migration. In birds, for example, from 40 to 75 percent of all neurons are estimated to die within a few days of completing cell migration (Spreen et al., 1984), and the same is hypothesized to occur in mammalian brains. Neuron death appears to be intimately tied to the process of differentiation. As neurons grow and begin to form contacts with neighboring nerve cells they compete for space (Berry, 1982). Those that are unsuccessful in this process die out, often because of lack of stimulation. Even then, stimulation appears to be critical for the continued survival of the remaining neurons. Unstimulated cells fail to establish new connections and to acquire myelin sheaths (Kalil, 1989).

▶ **Roles of nature and nurture**

These kinds of findings indicate that the process of neuron differentiation is heavily influenced by experience. In fact, the formation and functioning of neurons within the brain provides a superb example of the complex interaction between hereditary and environmental determinants of development (Suomi, 1982). The infant comes biologically equipped with genetic information that helps to generate and position far more neurons in the cortex than will ever be used (Kalil, 1989). That surplus provides the opportunity for a rich variety of experiences to influence development and, should damage or destruction occur to some neurons early in life, for other nerve cells to replace them. In fact, experience is probably essential for many aspects of neural development (Kalil, 1989).

▶ **Sensitive periods**

Plasticity and Sensitive Periods in Brain Development

A substantial amount of brain development takes place during the final weeks of prenatal life. A condition like prematurity, therefore, poses the hazard of considerable trauma, since a premature baby confronts a markedly different environment than an unborn baby during these critical weeks. Fortunately, several factors help to buffer the effects of trauma, although, of course, the brain is limited in ability to recover from severe injury. One such buffer, as we suggested earlier, is the large number of excess neurons. If some are lost by other than natural attrition, enough others may exist to permit normal functioning.

Another buffer derives from the unspecialized nature of young neurons. The brain possesses **plasticity,** or the ability of alternate regions to take on the specialized sensory, linguistic, and other information-processing requirements handled by various parts of the cerebral cortex. This plasticity is most evident in the nervous system of infants and younger children. Thus, for example, infants or children who suffer damage to regions of the cerebral cortex that process speech are often able to recover as neurons in other parts of the cortex take on this function. But the prognosis for recovery of language in adults after an accident or stroke is often much poorer because the remaining neurons in various regions of the brain have already become dedicated to processing certain kinds of experiences (Lenneberg, 1967).

The plasticity of brain development provides a further indication of how important experience can be for neuron differentiation, a process that advances at a remarkable rate. In the much simpler brain of the rat, an estimated quarter of a million connections between neurons are established *each second* during the first month of its postnatal life (Schuz, 1978). Some kinds of experience, however, are important at sensitive or critical periods in development. These *sensitive periods* are like brief openings of a window, limited times during which specific types of stimulation can have positive or, as in the case of teratogens, negative consequences for development (Bateson, 1979).

William Greenough and his colleagues have proposed that neurons in human and other mammalian brains exhibit two different kinds of plasticity (Greenough, Black, & Wallace, 1987). Some neurons are sensitive to *experience-expectant information.* As a result of a long evolutionary process, these neurons begin to grow and differentiate rapidly about the time they can be *expected* to receive the kinds of stimulation important to their functioning. In many mammals, for example, parts of the visual cortex involved in depth or pattern perception develop quite rapidly shortly before and after the eyes open or, in the case of human infants, shortly before and after birth. Research with lower animals indicates that visual deprivation during these periods—rearing in the dark or without patterned light, for example—results in the permanent loss of some kinds of depth and pattern vision, losses that do not occur when equivalent lengths of deprivation occur at other times in development (Movshon & Van Sluyters, 1981).

Other neurons are sensitive to *experience-dependent information.* Many kinds of events cannot be expected to occur at predicted times during development. Each of us learns different and unique things even into old age. The distinctive perceptual features forming an image of one's neighbor or the attributes defining our concept of democracy are unique representations recorded

plasticity   Capacity of immature systems, including regions of the brain and the individual neurons within those regions, to take on different functions as a result of experience.

▶ **Roles of nature and nurture**

within our neural system. This type of learning, also assumed to be linked in some way to neuron differentiation, can take place at any time in development. Analyses of the cerebral cortex of lower animals reared in enriched environments, filled with objects to explore and play with, compared with analyses of the cortex of animals reared in nonstimulating settings, individual cages with few objects to interact with, reveal neurons with larger cell bodies and greater numbers of synaptic connections and more glial cells. Furthermore, brain differences resulting from individual learning experiences continue to be exhibited in parts of the cerebral cortex of lower animals even in adulthood (Greenough, Black, & Wallace, 1987). Here, then, is a form of plasticity that extends beyond sensitive periods of development and implicates neural differentiation as a critical aspect of brain functioning throughout one's lifetime.

Brain Lateralization

One of the brain's most obvious physical characteristics is that it can be divided into two mirrorlike structures, a *left* and *right hemisphere.* By and large, in humans sensory input and motor responses on the left side of the body are processed by the right hemisphere; sensory input and motor responses on the right side of the body are processed by the left hemisphere. In addition, in most adults the left hemisphere is especially involved in language functioning, whereas the right hemisphere is usually involved in processing spatial, emotional, or other nonverbal information (Michel, 1988; Saxby & Bryden, 1985). But these differences are by no means absolute. Speech is primarily controlled by the left hemisphere in about 95 percent of right-handed adults but only in about 70 percent of left-handed adults (Kinsbourne & Hiscock, 1983), another indication of the brain's plasticity. Furthermore, in all individuals the right hemisphere can comprehend and initiate speech, although it may be more limited in capacity to do so.

A major developmental question is whether hemispheric specialization exists already at birth or whether the brain shows progressive **lateralization,** the process of one hemisphere dominating the other in terms of a particular function. Based on research on left-hemisphere damage in children, Lenneberg (1967) proposed that at least until two years of age, both hemispheres were capable of carrying out language functions equally well and that lateralization only gradually increased until adolescence. In other words, even throughout childhood either hemisphere could process language nearly as well as the other. Other researchers suggest lateralization begins much earlier (for example, Kinsbourne & Hiscock, 1983). Most infants lie with the head oriented to the right rather than to the left (Michel, 1988), an orientation that later predicts hand preference (Michel & Harkins, 1986), and turn more frequently to stimulation coming from the right rather than the left side (Siqueland & Lipsitt, 1966). Furthermore, most one- to three-month-olds more actively use and hold objects longer in the right hand rather than the left (Hawn & Harris, 1983; Michel & Harkins, 1986). By this age, infants are also better able to identify changes in speech sounds delivered to the right ear than those delivered to the left ear and to detect changes in the timbre of musical notes better in the left than in the right ear (Best, Hoffman, & Glanville, 1982).

lateralization Process by which one hemisphere of the brain dominates the other. In most individuals the left hemisphere, is more involved in language processing, whereas the right is more involved in processing spatial and emotional information.

We cannot be entirely certain that lateralization exists either at birth or as a progressive phenomenon because most lateral preferences become stronger and more consistently displayed with development in complex motor, linguistic, and other behaviors—behaviors that younger children are less likely to display. Conceivably, the hemispheric specialization underlying those behaviors may have existed all along (Witelson, 1985). Moreover, evidence of early hemispheric differences does not preclude the possibility that the other hemisphere is still capable of taking over the same functions if necessary.

HOW MOTOR SKILLS DEVELOP

As the human body develops, cartilage is transformed to bone, and bones elongate and increase in number to become scaffolding to support the body in new physical orientations. Muscles thicken and enlarge, producing more powerful and refined movements among the bones and joints. As the central nervous system matures, neural commands begin to coordinate the complex muscles that effortlessly and routinely initiate skilled motor actions in mature humans. Cephalocaudal and proximodistal patterns of development underlie the emergence of many of these abilities. To these are added two other complementary patterns in the development of movement: *differentiation,* the progression from global, relatively unorganized actions to more refined and skilled ones, and *integration,* the coordinated alliance among actions involving various muscles and sensory systems.

The earliest movements, many occurring prenatally, are **reflexes,** involuntary reactions to touch, light, sound, pressure, or other kinds of stimulation. Reflexes are the building blocks that soon make way for voluntary movements and the acquisition of developmental milestones or significant achievements in motor skills during the first years of life. Throughout early and later childhood, motor skills become increasingly efficient, organized, and coordinated. At the end of this period, many skills have become highly specialized talents: youngsters like Erin, with training, are already athletes; others her age, concert musicians.

Motor skills were the preeminent focus of study in the early days of developmental psychology. Many of these studies yielded descriptive and normative information still valuable today (Bayley, 1935; Gesell, 1929; Gesell & Thompson, 1934; Halverson, 1931; McGraw, 1935, 1943; Shirley, 1931). But one key question for these pioneer researchers—the role of maturation and experience in the acquisition of motor skills—has proven difficult to answer. Research on motor behavior waned during the 1950s and 1960s (Benson, 1988), but interest in this topic has reemerged in recent decades because of the importance that Jean Piaget and others have assigned to action in cognitive development. If, as Piaget suggested, sensorimotor activity serves as the prototype and first stage in the construction of knowledge, the acquisition of basic motor skills, and particularly their coordination and integration, provides an important means by which to understand cognitive development. The mastery of innovative motor skills offers further opportunities for gaining information about the world (Benson, 1988; Bullinger, 1987).

▶ **Interaction among domains**

reflex Involuntary movement in response to touch, light, sound, and other forms of stimulation; controlled by subcortical neural mechanisms.

A touch on an infant's cheeks close to the lips is often enough to elicit the rooting response, an opening of the mouth in anticipation of something to suck on.

The First Actions: Reflexes

At first glance, newborns seem helpless and incompetent. Babies eat, sleep, and cry; their diapers always seem to need changing. If we take a more careful look, however, we see that infants are equipped to do much more than we might first think. They enter their new world with reflexes and surprisingly competent sensory capacities that, combined with the support of a loving caregiver, provide the basis for the remarkable physical and behavioral transitions that are about to take place.

The earliest movements of newborns are **primitive** and **postural reflexes,** relatively fixed and rigid reactions to specific kinds of stimulation. Along with breathing and swallowing, reflexes assist in the survival of the infant. Rooting and sucking, as Table 5.2 shows, provide nourishment, and others such as the Moro and palmar reflexes, at least among our evolutionary ancestors, helped protect newborns from danger. Postural reflexes such as stepping, swimming, and body righting, surprisingly similar to later voluntary movements, seem designed to maintain a specific, usually upright, orientation to the environment.

Both primitive and postural reflexes have the important consequence of providing stimulation to, and information about, the brain. If some of these reflexes are absent, are too strong or too weak, are of unequal strength when

primitive reflexes Reflexes identified with survival and protection of the individual that usually disappear during the first year of life.

postural reflexes Reflexes associated with maintaining a particular, usually upright, orientation and that disappear or become incorporated within voluntary behavior.

Name of Reflex	Testing Procedure	Response	Developmental Course	Significance
Primitive Reflexes				
Palmar or Hand Grasp	Finger placed in hand.	Hand grasps object	Birth to about 4 months	Absence may signal neurological defects; persistence could interfere with voluntary grasping.
Rooting	Stroke corner of mouth lightly.	Head and tongue move toward stimulus.	Birth to about 5 months	Mouth is brought to stimulus to permit sucking.
Sucking	Finger placed in mouth or on lips.	Sucking begins.	Birth to about 6 months	Ensures intake of potential nutrients.
Moro	(1) Sitting, head allowed to drop about 20 degrees backward, or (2) loud noise, or (3) baby rapidly lowered.	Arms are extended outward, hands open; then hands brought to midline, hands clenched, spine straightened.	Birth to about 5–7 months	Absence may signal neurological defects; persistence could interfere with acquisition of sitting.
Plantar or Foot Grasp	Pressure on ball of foot.	Toes curl as if grasping.	Birth to about 9 months	Absence may signal spinal cord defect.
Babinski	Stroke bottom of foot.	Toes fan and then curl.	Birth to about 1 year	Absence may signal neurological defects.
Asymmetric Tonic Neck Reflex	Arms and legs extended, baby on back, rotate head 90 degrees.	Arm on face side extends, arm on back side of head flexes.	About 1 month to 4 months	Absence may signal neurological defects; persistence could prevent rolling over, coordination.
Postural Reflexes				
Stepping	Baby held under arms, upright, leaning forward.	Walklike stepping movements.	Birth to about 3 months	Absence may signal neurological defects.
Labyrinthine	(1) Baby on back. (2) Baby on stomach.	Arms and legs are extended. Arms and legs are flexed.	Birth to about 4 months	Absence may signal neurological defects.
Swimming	Baby placed in water	Breath is involuntarily held; arms and legs move as if trying to swim.	Birth to about 4 to 6 months	Absence may signal neurological defects.

TABLE 5.2

Typical Reflexes Observed in Newborns and Infants

Name of Reflex	Testing Procedure	Response	Developmental Course	Significance
Placing	Baby held under arms, upright, top of foot touches bottom edge of table.	Foot lifted and placed on top of table.	Birth through 12 months	Absence may signal neurological defects.
Landau Reaction	Baby on stomach, held under chest.	Head, eventually other parts of body lifted above chest.	Head at 2 months, other parts of body later.	Absence may signal neurological defects; inadequate muscle tone for motor development.
Body Righting	Rotate hips or shoulder.	Remainder of body is rotated.	4 months to more than 12 months	Absence may signal neurological defects; difficulty in gaining postural control and walking.

Many of the reflexes displayed by the newborn can also be elicited during the later weeks of fetal development (Gundy, 1987). Considerable variability exists among infants in the way in which many of these reflexes are displayed and ages during which they can be elicited (Touwen, 1974). The presence or absence of any single reflex provides only one among many indicators of healthy or atypical development.

TABLE 5.2 (continued)

Typical Reflexes Observed in Newborns and Infants

▶ **Roles of nature and nurture**

normally elicited from either side of the body, or continue to be exhibited beyond certain ages, a pediatrician may begin to suspect neurological impairment and possible developmental difficulties for the baby.

Because of its biological importance and interesting qualities, we will consider *sucking* in more detail. This reflex can be separated into two major components exhibiting both reflexive and learned characteristics right from birth. One component, *expression,* is a lapping action the infant performs with the tongue, squeezing the nipple against the roof of his or her mouth. The other component, *suction,* creates negative pressure within the mouth. An infant normally produces both components when nursing from breast or bottle. Arnold Sameroff (1968), however, devised a special nipple that yielded milk only when the baby exhibited *either* expression or suction, but not both. He found that both components increased in frequency when either was necessary to obtain milk. Only suction, however, gradually disappeared if it was no longer required to obtain milk. Thus, although sucking is initially a reflex, a baby can learn to modify this behavior in certain ways very early in development.

Sucking activity often generalizes to a wide range of objects at an early age, including fingers and toes. As we saw in Chapter 4, such nonnutritive sucking even occurs prenatally. But to survive in the postnatal environment, the infant must synchronize reflexes such as rooting and sucking with swallowing and breathing. In fact, the inability to coordinate these reflexes, rather than their absence, often makes premature infants unable to nurse. They must be fed instead by a tube inserted into the stomach through the esophagus (Rosenblith & Sims-Knight, 1985). Certain neurological or other medical conditions such as jaundice can also disrupt coordination of these reflexes in full-term newborns (Kazmeier, Keenan, & Sutherland, 1977).

Sudden Infant Death Syndrome

As you might imagine, the modification of reflexes such as sucking so that they become more organized and more effectively controlled is a significant part of development. This appears to be true even for such a basic response as breathing. The sudden, unexplained death during sleep of any infant or toddler is known as **sudden infant death syndrome (SIDS).** These deaths are particularly alarming since no identifiable clues signal their occurrence. Although concern about SIDS, sometimes known as crib death, has received public attention only within the last three decades, notes from a physician in 1834 suggest it has existed for some time (Peterson, 1984). In fact, SIDS is reported in countries around the world and is estimated to occur in about two of every thousand live births, leading to nearly eight thousand deaths every year (Peterson, 1984). Although no specific cause has been identified, SIDS is associated with a bewildering number of factors: the colder months of the year, infant colds, bottle feeding, economically depressed neighborhoods, males, infant members of a multiple birth, younger siblings of children who have already died of SIDS, later-born infants, low birth weight, maternal cigarette smoking, and maternal drug dependency (Goyco & Beckerman, 1990).

The frequency of SIDS peaks during the second and third months after birth and rarely occurs in infants younger than three weeks or over a year of age. Thus, the highest incidence of SIDS exists during a developmental period when basic, automatic reflexes governed by the brainstem become supplemented by voluntary, learned behaviors controlled by the cortex. Among these transitions is a reorganization in breathing as neural networks developing between the cortex and brainstem begin to integrate involuntary, automatic breathing with voluntary, regulated breathing and vocal movements essential for the emergence of speech. During this developmental period the voluntary and involuntary breathing patterns may not be sufficiently orchestrated to provide a fail-safe system (Rovee-Collier & Lipsitt, 1987); in deep sleep there is a disruption in breathing that, if prolonged, leads to death.

Unfortunately, attempts to monitor breathing to determine whether SIDS victims show more irregular breathing patterns or temporary cessation in breathing (*apnea*) have not been very successful (Hunt & Brouillette, 1987). SIDS victims often display apnea, but so do many other infants, including prematures. Home monitors designed to signal alarms in response to apnea have yet to demonstrate that they are sufficiently sensitive or specific to predict incidences of SIDS or significantly help to reduce its occurrence (Hunt & Brouillette, 1987).

Many hypotheses exist concerning the causes of SIDS, and more research is needed on this puzzling syndrome. No single factor may be responsible (Goyco & Beckerman, 1990). But perhaps an important lesson we can learn is that even simple-appearing reflex behaviors are often complex systems worth understanding more fully if we are to fathom the entire fabric of development.

▶ **Sensitive periods**

sudden infant death syndrome (SIDS) Sudden, unexplained death of infant or toddler as a result of failure to continue breathing during sleep.

rhythmical stereotypies Repeated sequences of movements such as leg kicking and hand waving or banging that seem to have no apparent goal.

Motor Milestones

Reflexes are not the only motor activities displayed by young infants. Babies also exhibit **rhythmical stereotypies,** repeated sequences of motions performed for relatively long periods of time with no apparent external goal (Thelen, 1979). Rubbing one foot against the other, rocking back and forth, bouncing up and down, swaying side to side, striking or banging objects, mouthing and tonguing activities, and shaking and nodding the head are just a few of these activities that seem to be produced as part of exercising movements among bones, joints, and muscles. In children and adults, the continuation of such behaviors is generally considered evidence of abnormal development, but in infants these actions are entirely normal. Although probably not entirely governed by deliberate, directed efforts, stereotypies, along with some early reflexes, may eventually become recruited and progressively integrated into organized, voluntary motor skills and activities (Thelen, Kelso, & Fogel, 1987).

▶ **The child's active role**

During the first year of life, infants also begin to display a wide variety of directed, voluntary actions as they gradually gain neuromotor control of head, arms, and legs. Some of these—grasping, crawling, and walking, for example—are motor milestones: once they have been mastered, new worlds are opened to the infant. Moreover, they cause caregivers to respond to the infant in different ways—child-proofing the home to prevent accidents, encouraging greater independence, expecting more mature behavior. Most achievements in infant movement illustrate progress in (1) *postural control,* the ability to maintain an upright orientation to the environment; (2) *locomotion,* the ability to maneuver oneself through space; and (3) *manual control,* the ability to manipulate objects (Keogh & Sugden, 1985).

Postural Control The capacity to keep head upright and stable at about two to three months of age represents one of the first milestones in infant motor development. As shown in the Chronology on page 214, this achievement is followed by mastery of other significant postural skills such as maintaining an upright sitting position, moving to a standing position, and standing alone without assistance. These milestones, built on various postural reflexes, among other things, often reflect a cephalocaudal progression in development. Head control, for example, is achieved before control of the trunk, and control of the legs is the last to develop. The integration of postural skills is also evident in this progression. For example, being able to keep head upright while lying, sitting, or standing on a stable surface is one important accomplishment, but being able to do these things when motion is added from being carried about or during self-movement is an even more complex task requiring integration of additional information (Keogh & Sugden, 1985).

Locomotion Achievements in prewalking and walking are also summarized in the Chronology on page 214. One early milestone in this domain is the ability to roll over. Then comes success at initiating forward motion, a skill marked by variability in timing and method. For example, some infants use their arms to pull and their legs to push, others use only arms or legs, and still others scoot forward while sitting. *Crawling,* locomotion with stomach touching the floor, may soon give way to *creeping,* locomotion on hands and knees. Then again, it may not, and the varieties of forward motion invented by babies often generate lively and entertaining discussions among caregivers.

Once babies are able to pull themselves upright, they often *cruise*—that is, move by holding onto furniture or other objects while stepping side to side.

Once a baby can stand, he will often cruise or move about by stepping side to side while holding onto objects or other people. It is one of the many milestones infants achieve in their diligent attempts to gain independent locomotion.

CHRONOLOGY	Motor Skill Development
2 MONTHS*	Holds head steady when held upright. Lifts head up.
3 MONTHS	Holds head steady while being carried. Rolls over.
4 MONTHS	Grasps cube.
6 MONTHS	Sits without support. Pulls self to stand. Stands holding on to something.
7 MONTHS	Rolls: back to stomach. Begins to attempt to crawl and/or creep. True thumb opposition in holding cube.
8 MONTHS	Achieves sitting position without help. Pulls to standing.
9 MONTHS	Walks holding furniture (cruises). Fine prehension (neat pincer grasp). Bangs two objects held in hands.
10 MONTHS	Walks with help. Plays pat-a-cake.
11 MONTHS	Stands alone.
12 MONTHS	Walks alone. Turns pages of book. Drinks from cup.
14 MONTHS	Builds tower using two cubes.
15 MONTHS	Walks sideways and backwards.
17 MONTHS	Walks up steps.
20 MONTHS	Kicks ball forward.

*Age at which approximately half of the infants tested in the United States have achieved the skill.

Source: Bayley, 1969; Frankenburg & Dodds, 1967.

This chart describes the sequence of motor skill development based on the findings of research. Children often shown individual differences in the exact ages at which they display the various developmental achievements outlined here.

Forward walking while holding on to someone's hand often follows. By about twelve months of age, half of American babies are able to walk alone, a skill that continues to be refined throughout infancy and early childhood. Mary Shirley (1931), for example, placed olive oil or powder on the soles of babies' feet to record how they attempted to walk across a length of paper. When walking first began, toddlers' feet were widely separated, and their toes were pointed outward to yield a waddling gait. Beginning walkers also took more rapid, shorter steps than mature walkers. Pace, however, slowed, and length of stride gradually increased as walking became more automatic and natural.

▶ **Roles of nature and nurture**

Prewalking and walking skills probably depend on the maturation of higher brain centers that build upon stereotypies and inhibit some reflexes, such as the asymmetric tonic neck reflex, which interferes with voluntary locomotion (see Table 5.2). Even before walking, however, motion in one leg is not independent of motion in the other. While lying on their backs, babies as young as six weeks of age produce surprisingly coordinated leg movements; if weights, for example, are placed on one leg, the unweighted leg compensates by speeding up its rate of kicking, an association that may set the stage for later coordinated movements involved in walking (Thelen, Skala, & Kelso, 1987).

Manual Control Infants display a progression of skills in grasping and manipulating objects. At birth and in the first few weeks that follow, babies typically keep their hands closed in fistlike fashion. By about four months of age, infants awkwardly pick up an object by grasping it with the palm of the hand. Extensive films taken more than fifty years ago (Halverson, 1931) and analyzed in greater detail more recently (Connolly & Elliott, 1972) reveal the shift in grasping from inner palm to thumb and finger tips, a progression that culminates in a *neat pincer grasp* at about nine months of age (see Figure 5.10). This development, in turn, sets the stage for the elegant manual control required to hold, inspect, and manipulate a wide variety of objects. The outcome,

FIGURE 5.10

Changes in Grasping Techniques

Changes in grasping progress along several dimensions. With development, the infant becomes increasingly capable of rotating the thumb so that it closes opposite the index finger rather than to the side. Additionally, at first objects are clutched near the inner palm. As finger and thumb dexterity increase, grasping takes place nearer the thumb region and the tips of the fingers, culminating in the neat pincer grasp.

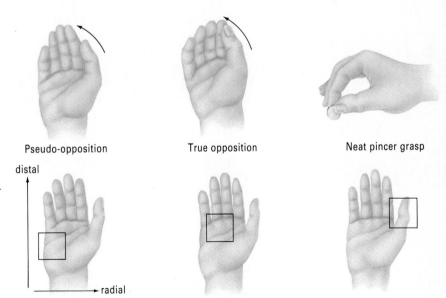

Pseudo-opposition   True opposition   Neat pincer grasp

distal

radial

Source: Adapted from Connolly & Elliott, 1972.

Sophisticated eye-hand coordination and the ability to simultaneously perform different functions with each hand are two important accomplishments that assist the curious toddler in gaining increasingly effective manual control of her environment.

of course, is not only a chance to learn about the objects in the environment, but also an opportunity for the infant to discover his or her own abilities to control those objects (Karniol, 1989).

Before deliberate grasping can take place, the infant must also make progress in *eye-hand coordination*. Newborns display evidence of *prereaching*, attempting to initiate contact with objects that catch their attention, but these reaches are neither accurate nor coordinated with grasping (Bushnell, 1985; Hofsten, 1984). In fact, prereaching appears more like a reflex. More deliberate reaching guided by vision begins about two or three months of age, after maturation of visual and motor areas of the cerebral cortex. Even then, it is more like swiping and continues to be inaccurate and limited, for example, to objects on the same side of the body as the reaching hand. Over the next few months, infants evidence more visual control of reaching. For example, they may gradually move a hand to the object while glancing back and forth between the two. By about five to six months, infants display mature, *ballistic* reaches, rapidly and accurately retrieving an object in the visual field (White, 1971).

Another important step in manual control is gaining coordination between the two hands. Although the child may use both hands to hold an object such as a toy, manual control often involves complementary hand orientations—for example, holding a toy dump truck in one hand while using the other hand to fill it with sand. This *functional asymmetry* emerges at about five to six months of age and becomes even more important as the child enters the second year and begins to display self-help and advanced motor tasks requiring sophisticated coordination of arms and hands.

Motor Skills in Preschool and Later-Childhood Years

The fundamental motor skills the infant acquires in the first two years of life continue to be modified and refined into childhood. The norms for preschoolers and older children on basic abilities such as jumping, hopping, running, balancing, and catching or throwing a ball document increasing speed, strength, and efficiency as children mature and have the opportunity to engage in a wide variety of physical activities. These changes contribute to greater competence in self-help skills (such as dressing and grooming), assembling items (such as stacking and puzzle construction), and writing and drawing. In general, activities that permit the exercise of large muscles are of more interest to toddlers and young preschoolers. These activities include pulling and pushing things, stacking and nesting large objects, and, eventually, riding toys such as kiddie cars and tricycles. Older preschoolers begin to supplement these exercises with coloring and drawing, cutting and sculpting, and many other activities that require small-muscle coordination, a longer attention span, and more sophisticated planning and organization.

▶ **The child's active role**

Changes in motor skills during the middle childhood years usually consist of doing things faster, coordinating more muscles, and producing more complex movements in a wider variety of circumstances and contexts (Keogh & Sugden, 1985). Movements become more efficient and effective as well as better controlled in relation to the force needed to complete them. Any parent who has tried to avoid a three-year-old's fastball fired at point blank range will have a healthy appreciation for developmental changes in performing such actions with reasonable force! The acquisition of expertise or specialized motor skills in sports, dance, crafts, hobbies, playing musical instruments, and, in some cultures, trade or work-related endeavors permit older children to engage their environment with increasing competence, become more effective members of their society, and gain greater social status among peers and adults.

WHAT DETERMINES MOTOR DEVELOPMENT?

▶ **Roles of nature and nurture**

Once again we must ask the question: To what extent do the emergence, refinement, and integration of motor skills depend on genetic factors? To what extent are they determined by maturational events? Are the dramatic changes we see unfolding a consequence of practice, cultural, or other experiential factors?

Many pioneers in developmental psychology advocated a strong maturational theory to account for individual differences in the acquisition of motor skills and relied on demonstrations of limited benefits from training and practice to support their position. But the empirical findings often raised enough questions to suggest that changes in motor skills, as in other domains of development, are better understood as a consequence of the interaction of biological and experiential factors.

▶ **Roles of nature and nurture**   ## Biological Determinants

The tendency for motor skills to develop in predictable ways in accordance with a cephalocaudal and proximodistal pattern and to show progressively more differentiation and integration has provided one of the strongest logical arguments to suggest that motor skill development has a biological or maturational basis. Although individual differences exist, children in many cultures achieve milestones at similar ages and in a consistent order. This finding has led to the notion that infants are *genetically preadapted,* possessing righting and balancing reflexes, bone and muscle growth, and a maturing central nervous system designed to interact with their physical and social environment (Kopp, 1979).

Even handicapped and retarded babies routinely achieve major milestones in the same order as normal children. For example, blind children acquire many motor skills at ages remarkably similar to those of sighted infants; only actions involving visual-motor coordination and independent locomotion are delayed (Adelson & Fraiberg, 1974). Children with Down syndrome evidence a similar order of motor achievements although they need more time, particularly when health complications such as heart disease are present (Zausmer & Shea, 1984). Furthermore, studies have revealed greater concordance in sitting up and walking for monozygotic than for dizygotic twins and increasing similarity in gross motor activities, including running, jumping, and throwing, as children are more closely related biologically (Malina, 1980). As we saw in Chapter 3, however, genetic or maturational interpretations for these kinds of findings can often be challenged.

▶ **Roles of nature and nurture**   ## Environmental Determinants

Cultures differ immensely in the freedom infants and children are given to manipulate, explore, and engage their environment. Because the infant is so physically immature at birth, the potential exists for a variety of environmental factors such as these to influence motor development. Do these and other experiential variables play a role in motor development?

Training and Practice   In the 1930s, several researchers conducted studies with sets of twins to confirm the view, prevalent at the time, that motor development is maturationally determined. Typically, one twin received extensive training on a specific motor skill, such as handling blocks, climbing stairs, or roller skating, and the other twin did not (Gesell & Thompson, 1934; Hilgard, 1932; McGraw, 1935). Given the opportunity to perform these activities without special training or practice, the untrained twin often rapidly achieved the skill level of the trained twin, leading researchers to conclude that maturation was the primary determinant of motor development.

Wayne Dennis carried out other research frequently cited to support the

In the Navajo culture babies are often swaddled for most of the day. Wayne Dennis' research with Hopi infants who received the same kind of experience suggests that this baby, despite the lack of opportunity to practice sitting up, crawling, and standing alone, will begin to walk about the same time as an infant who has not been swaddled.

maturation position (Dennis & Dennis, 1940). Dennis found that some Hopi Indian mothers continued to practice the tribal tradition of rearing their babies tightly swaddled in a cradle board. The board was strapped to the mother's back for all but about an hour a day during the mother's waking hours for the first six to twelve months of life so that these babies had little opportunity to practice sitting up, crawling, and walking. Other Hopi mothers adopted the practice of rearing infants without swaddling. Dennis found swaddling had little bearing on when infants began to walk, an observation reconfirmed in a more recent examination of the effects of Hopi rearing customs (Harriman & Lukosius, 1982).

Limitations and alternative interpretations exist for many of these findings. In the twin-training studies, the twins were not always identical (Scientific American, 1987). Moreover, the kinds of experiences they received outside the experimental setting were seldom regulated; the untrained twin may have gained substantial practice on important components of the target motor skill. Similarly, babies reared on cradle boards receive far more upright experience than other babies, and this postural orientation could promote locomotor development (Rosenblith & Sims-Knight, 1985). Thus, these early studies failed to provide conclusive evidence in support of either nature or nurture.

The controversy over the effects of practice and training on the acquisition of motor skills has resurfaced in recent years. Philip Zelazo and his colleagues asked whether infants, given a few minutes of daily practice on the placing and stepping reflex from one week of age to seven weeks of age, retained these reflexes and began walking earlier than infants who received no special experience or whose legs were passively moved back and forth (Zelazo, 1983; Zelazo, Zelazo, & Kolb, 1972). The answer to both questions was yes. Zelazo (1983) concluded that the loss of these infant reflexes stems from a failure to exercise them. Maintaining them provides a later foundation for early walking. Thus, his research suggests experience can influence the development of motor skills. On the other hand, Thelen (1983) has argued that the onset of walking is the product of complex events including maturation of the nervous system's control of posture and balance, increases in bone and muscle strength, and changes in body proportions, as well as the motivation to move forward. According to Thelen, the stepping reflex is a minor part of many maturational components, some already functioning at birth, that gradually coalesce to produce walking.

▶ **Sociocultural influence**

Cross-Cultural Differences   Robert Malina (1980), reviewing the findings of a number of studies involving babies from Europe and the United States, found that the median age for the onset of walking was between 11.4 and 14.5 months. This range is remarkably narrow given the complexity of walking activity—one reason, as suggested earlier, why maturational factors are considered important. Charles Super (1976), however, observed several cultures in East Africa in which infants began walking about a month earlier than those in most Western societies. Caregivers in these cultures believed it was important to teach babies to walk, and infants continued to exhibit the stepping reflex until walking began, a finding that confirms Zelazo's hypothesis about its importance for walking.

In still other cultures, walking begins surprisingly late. Among the Ache of Eastern Paraguay, children are significantly delayed in acquiring a host of motor skills, but the disparity is best illustrated by walking, reported not to begin until twenty-one to twenty-three months of age (Kaplan & Dove, 1987). This small band of people, engaged in hunting and gathering, do not encourage the acquisition of motor skills in infants. When families migrate to the forests, the women closely supervise their children under three years of age, preventing them from venturing more than a yard or so into the uncleared vegetation and spending 80 to 100 percent of their time in physical contact with the children (Kaplan & Dove, 1987). For the Ache, keeping infants in close contact may be crucial for their continued survival. One consequence is less opportunity for infants to practice motor skills. Because the Ache have been relatively isolated and the total population at times quite small, however, genetic factors cannot be completely ruled out as the possible basis for the delay.

Cultural and ethnic differences are sometimes reported in the ages at which skills other than walking are acquired (Werner, 1972). These differences may again reflect genetic and maturational factors that have evolved among different groups of people to enhance survival in specific kinds of environments. But this explanation has been challenged in recent years as child-rearing practices have been more closely examined. Consider again the work of Super (1976), conducted in a fairly prosperous rural community in Africa.

Super spent three years testing all sixty-four children born from 1972 to 1975 in a high-altitude region of Kenya. His monthly tests revealed that these babies were able to sit, stand, and walk an average of a month earlier than babies in the United States. Parents carried out extensive efforts to teach these skills to their children. For example, they provided special props to encourage the infant to sit or held the baby's hands in a sequence of structured activities involving walking. In fact, their language contained distinctive words to denote this specialized training, practices also observed in a dozen other regions of East Africa. The more likely caregivers were to teach specific motor skills, the earlier their children tended to display them. For example, 93 percent of one group of caregivers said they taught their babies to crawl, and babies in this group began crawling at about five and a half months of age. In contrast, only 13 percent of the caregivers in a nearby cultural group expressed support for teaching their infants to crawl, and these babies did not crawl until they were about eight months of age.

Although genetic and biological factors could be responsible for these cultural differences, one finding strongly implicates child-rearing efforts. Super found that advanced motor development in this part of Kenya was limited to sitting, standing, and walking, skills considered important to these cultures. Skills that were not taught or valued, such as head control or the ability to roll over, were acquired later than by American infants. A similar finding has been reported in Jamaica, where some mothers perform special stretching and massaging exercises to encourage their infants to sit and walk alone (Hopkins & Westra, 1990). Those mothers who performed these activities and expected their children to sit and walk early did have children who achieved these milestones sooner compared with other children.

Still, we cannot be certain whether training focused on specific skills or more general experiences are responsible for cultural differences. Children in East Africa, for example, spend more time in an upright position, seated on a caregiver's lap or riding on her back, than children in the United States (Super,

Different cultures may implement a variety of practices to foster the development of motor skills and physical coordination. Here Mexican girls are encouraged to acquire the graceful movements of a folkdance by practicing with bottles on their heads.

1976). These activities may strengthen trunk and leg muscles to aid the earlier appearance of sitting, standing, and walking. We can conclude, however, that cultural concerns and efforts to promote the acquisition of motor skills do have a significant impact on their development.

▶ **Roles of nature and nurture**

Experience Deprivation   Despite its importance, researchers have often overestimated nature's contribution to the emergence of motor skills (Parmalee & Sigman, 1983). The lack of opportunity to engage in motor activities *can* seriously interfere with their acquisition, as research conducted in the 1940s and 1950s on children reared in institutions has revealed. Children in these institutions were delayed in virtually every aspect of development, including motor behavior. For example, in an orphanage in Teheran, Iran, Wayne Dennis (1960) found that infants who spent most of their first year lying in cribs and receiving few other experiences typically did not walk before three or four years of age. Other evidence that motor skills do not simply follow a maturational course comes from observations of blind children. Even though blind infants achieve many milestones at ages similar to the sighted, reaching for objects and crawling and walking are substantially delayed. These findings have led researchers to design special programs to encourage blind infants to acquire self-initiated movement at an earlier age (Fraiberg, 1977). Thus, a complete theory of motor skill development needs to give recognition to the contribution of both nature *and* nurture.

THEMES IN DEVELOPMENT

PHYSICAL GROWTH AND MOTOR SKILLS

▶ **What roles do nature and nurture play in physical growth and motor skill development?**

Physical growth and the development of motor skills are the product of complex events involving genetic and biological factors. Genetic programs, both for growth and for the proliferation and migration of neurons, combine with hormonal factors and various maturational principles of skill acquisition to establish the broad "nature" parameters of development. At the same time, the physical transformation from relatively helpless infant into increasingly competent child and adolescent is further affected by the environment, specifically the many different resources and forms of stimulation provided by caregivers. These responses include their emotional and social support, their knowledge of nutrition and how to respond to illness, and their beliefs about the importance of providing practice, training, and encouragement for the acquisition of motor skills and talents.

▶ **How does the sociocultural context influence physical growth and motor skill development?**

Caregivers' beliefs about physical growth and motor skill development are embedded within and often determined by the resources, standards, and settings available to and promoted by the society in which they live. In some cultures, for example, babies are encouraged to acquire motor skills as quickly as possible; in others, far less attention is given to such matters, and these different views affect when such skills are acquired. Furthermore, new advances in knowledge of nutrition, views about appearance, and leisure time and educational practices have affected secular trends for many aspects of development, including growth in height, onset of menarche, and the prevalence of obesity. In addition, the extent to which a culture promotes specific skills, such as athletic ability, or a particular physical appearance, such as being slender, affects the efforts children initiate to acquire these qualities.

▶ How does the child actively contribute to the process of physical growth and the development of motor skills?

Babies seem to be intrinsically motivated to exercise rudimentary motor skills, as displays of rhythmic stereotypies suggest, and these efforts may contribute to the eventual organization of more voluntary motor behaviors. Furthermore, once a child attains locomotion skills, she provokes new reactions from caregivers that may include instituting ways of preventing the one-year-old from getting into cupboards and light sockets, falling down stairs, and pouncing on the usually patient family dog. The child's world is filled with activity, and the physical exercises the child undertakes undoubtedly contribute to further improvements in the speed, accuracy, and efficiency with which motor skills are performed. Out of these efforts can emerge expertise and the acquisition of competencies that fuel further progress in athletic, artistic, and other endeavors. In addition, rapid growth or early maturity may affect not only the child's interests, but also the expectations and reactions of others. Other conditions—for example, difficulty in nursing or obesity—are likely to further influence the kinds of interactions that take place in the home and the infant's or child's opportunities for additional experiences that affect physical development.

▶ Are physical growth and motor skill development continuous or stagelike?

Physical growth, brain development, and the acquisition of motor skills show spurts at certain times in development. These patterns often give rise to conceptions of stagelike development in these domains. But even dramatic changes such as those taking place in the acquisition of motor milestones in infancy or during the pubertal changes of adolescence are grounded in prior continuous changes. Little evidence exists for major kinds of reorganization, and even small, incremental changes in the production of hormones during puberty, for example, can serve to explain how development changes at this time. Perhaps physical and skill changes observed in children bring about dramatic reactions from others and these are the primary basis for stagelike conceptions of growth and motor skill development.

▶ Are there sensitive periods in physical growth and motor skill development?

Brain development, particularly of the neural structures, exhibits sensitive periods for the processing of certain kinds of information. Moreover, the plasticity of the brain is considerably reduced as individuals reach maturity. This process, in turn, may limit changes in physical growth and motor skill development beyond adolescence, although support for sensitive periods in these domains is limited.

▶ How do physical growth and motor skills interact with other domains of development?

A child's physical size and weight, as well as improvements in the execution and coordination of motor skills, have dramatic influences on the responses and expectations of caregivers, peers, and others, and in turn, on how the child feels about his or her body and abilities. For example, once capable of moving autonomously, the child's greater ability to initiate independence may also lead parents to grant more freedoms and, at the same time, demand more responsibilities. Similarly, the young adolescent's status with peers is often influenced by signs of a physically maturing body and other aspects of physical stature, coordination, and skill. These qualities are not only evaluated by others, but influence the child's evaluation of self.

SUMMARY

Norms obtained on the physical growth of the newborn as measured in height and weight reveal a common pattern of (1) rapid changes in the months before and after birth, (2) much slower but regular increases in size beginning about two years of age, and (3) a final growth spurt before or during early adolescence. Growth is also marked by considerable variability among individuals and among cultural groups and by different growth patterns for specific systems of the body. *Cephalocaudal* and *proximodistal* principles summarize many patterns of development. Maturity, however, is most effectively defined not by size but by ossification of bone material.

Genetic factors help regulate growth, and cells in the hypothalamus may determine whether growth is proceeding according to genetic instructions. Many *hormones,* some sensitive to instructions from the hypothalamus (such as HGH) and some sensitive to hormones released by the pituitary and other glands (such as somatomedin), interact in complex ways to influence growth. Nutrition, disease, the physical environment, and even social-emotional experiences also influence physical development. Improved nutrition and prevention of disease have yielded increases in average height over the last several centuries in many regions of the world. Yet marasmus and kwashiorkor, two extreme forms of malnutrition, and nonorganic *failure to thrive* syndrome, stemming from inadequate, neglectful, or abusive caregiving, can result in severe stunting of growth.

Physical size, weight, and early versus late onset of maturity have significant consequences for the child's social interactions with others. From these interactions the child may develop feelings of self-confidence or dissatisfaction. The adolescent growth spurt begins earlier for girls than for boys, as does the appearance of most signs of puberty. Boys in Western societies seem to benefit from early maturity, but the effects for girls are less clear. These different consequences may stem from the reactions and pressures of peers and perceived cultural values about body size and shape. Technical advances in fostering growth present the potential for new ethical dilemmas. Obesity among children appears to be increasing in the United States; various environmental factors such as increased sedentary behaviors have been advanced as reasons.

Brain growth proceeds rapidly during fetal and early postnatal development. Neurons proliferate and migrate to various locations in the brain before birth; however, differentiation of neurons continues throughout development. Differentiation may proceed at critical or sensitive times for experience-expectant information but occurs throughout development for experience-dependent information. *Glial cell* formation, *myelination,* and the operation and organization of nervous system networks also begin prenatally and continue to develop after birth. Infants display behaviors suggestive of hemispheric specialization, or *lateralization,* at birth, but both hemispheres may have equal potential for higher-order processing of information.

Infants display *primitive* and *postural reflexes* and spend considerable time in producing stereotypies that may serve as building blocks and neuromotor programs for complex voluntary behavior. Postural, locomotor, and manual control undergo regular patterns of development. Throughout infancy and childhood, motor skills become increasingly differentiated and integrated and are performed more efficiently and speedily. Failure to integrate higher-order voluntary and lower-order reflex brain mechanisms controlling breathing may be one cause of *sudden infant death syndrome (SIDS).*

Genetic preadaptation probably assists in initiating the emergence of motor milestones, but research indicates that experience is equally important for their acquisition. Both genetic and environmental factors contribute to individual and cross-cultural differences in the appearance of early skill acquisition, but practice greatly affects skill development in later childhood.

6

Learning and Perception

> ▶ **What roles do nature and nurture play in learning and perceptual development?**

> ▶ **How does the sociocultural context influence learning and perceptual development?**

> ▶ **How does the child play an active role in learning and perceptual development?**

> ▶ **Are there sensitive periods in learning and perceptual development?**

> ▶ **How do learning and perceptual development interact with development in other domains?**

Imagine you are a parent approached by a psychologist. The psychologist politely asks for permission to study whether your young son or daughter will imitate a stranger who sticks out her tongue! Andrew Meltzoff and M. Keith Moore (1983) explained the reasons for their interest in this unorthodox behavior and were able to convince many parents to let their young offspring take part in the study. In their research Meltzoff and Moore discovered that boys and girls at ages three, two, and even younger than one would indeed imitate tongue protrusions.

By now you may be thinking, "I always knew psychologists did strange things." More to the point, however, you may also be wondering, "So what? I'd like a quarter for every preschooler and toddler I've seen sticking out their tongues—and usually at each other!" The children Meltzoff and Moore observed, however, were not one or two or three years of age, as you may have first assumed; these imitators were very young. "All right," you say, "maybe babies a month old can learn to imitate new responses." But these subjects were not even that age. They were three, two, and in some cases, less than one day *old!*

If newborns can imitate tongue protrusion, then they cannot be functionally blind, a belief sometimes taught to pediatricians and obstetricians as recently as twenty years ago (Haith, 1990). But what do babies actually see? The experimenter's face? And if so, what might they learn about it? How can young babies already "know" that their own tongue protrusion, an activity that they cannot see themselves produce, matches the model? Do day-old infants possess an innate capacity to link the actions of another person to their own mouth movements? And if newborns can see their surroundings, can they also hear sounds—for example, a mother's lullaby? Can they identify the subtle smells of their own mother's body, feel the prick of a nurse's pin or the pain of circumcision? If perceptual abilities improve with age, do these changes depend on exposure to certain sights, noises, odors, or other events at sensitive periods? Might a child reared in the angular world of city skyscrapers see and learn about things far differently than a child reared in a tropical rain forest?

These are precisely the kinds of questions psychologists have often asked about infants and children. Why? Because the answers not only tell us about what infants and children can sense and distinguish, but also provide clues about the many things children can learn about the people, objects, and events around them. Learning, a means of acquiring new skills and behaviors from experience, is an extremely important form of adaptation to the environment. Through learning children avoid dangers, achieve satisfactions, and eventually become contributing members of the family, community, and culture in which they are born. Let's begin with the amazing story of how infants and children learn.

LEARNING IN INFANCY AND CHILDHOOD

Learning, as we will see, includes mechanisms that permit adaptation to the environment. Along with the reflexes described in Chapter 5 and various sensory capacities, the wide variety of learning infants and children display helps them to increase their likelihood of survival, respond to the demands of their physical and social environments, and achieve goals and solve problems. Children learn, for example, that a stove can be hot, that hitting a sibling makes their parents angry, and by watching another child climb a chair to reach the cupboard, that they too can reach the cookie jar in their own home. Because learning is mostly concerned with how experience affects development, our exploration of this topic stresses the "nurture" side of the nature-nurture theme. But, even here, you will see that biology sets limits on what children can or cannot learn, especially during early infancy.

▶ **Roles of nature and nurture**

Basic Learning Processes in Infancy

Developmental psychologists are fascinated by indications of learning in newborns and infants, and they have demonstrated that basic forms of learning appear very early in infancy. Let's examine the evidence supporting this conclusion more closely.

unconditioned stimulus (UCS) A stimulus that, without prior training, elicits a reflexlike response (unconditioned response).

unconditioned response (UCR) The response that is automatically elicited by the unconditioned stimulus (UCS).

conditioned stimulus (CS) A neutral stimulus that begins to elicit a response similar to the unconditioned stimulus (UCS) with which it has been paired.

Classical Conditioning   Because both *classical* and *operant* conditioning involve the acquisition and performance of behaviors in new situations, they are powerful forms of learning. As we saw in Chapter 2, in classical conditioning a neutral stimulus associated with an event that elicits an inborn reaction eventually produces a similar kind of reaction. A nipple placed in a newborn's mouth, for example, tends to elicit sucking behavior. The nipple is called an **unconditioned stimulus (UCS),** and the sucking response it elicits is called an **unconditioned response (UCR)** (see Step 1 in Table 6.1). After a series of trials in which a neutral stimulus—let's say a distinctive odor—is presented with the nipple (the UCS) (Step 2), the odor may also begin to elicit sucking even when the UCS is not present (Step 3). The odor has become a **conditioned stimulus (CS),** and the sucking response it elicits, a **conditioned re-**

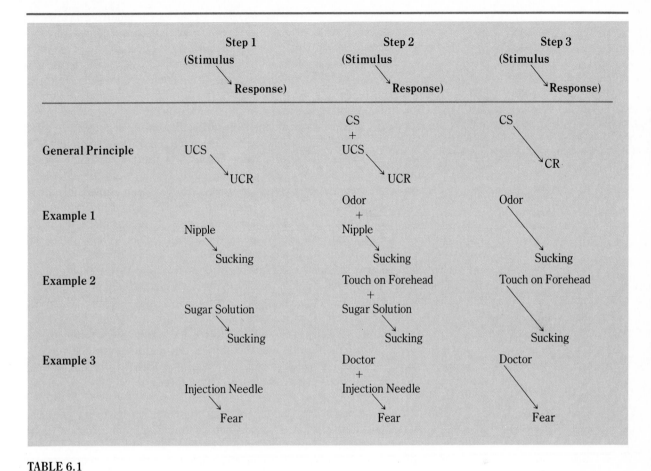

TABLE 6.1

Examples of Classical Conditioning

Classical conditioning is learning in which a neutral cue (conditioned stimulus), through its association with a cue (unconditioned stimulus) that naturally elicits a reflex-like response (unconditioned response), comes to elicit the same response (conditioned response).

conditioned response (CR) A learned response that is exhibited to a previously neutral stimulus (CS) as a result of pairing the CS with an unconditioned stimulus (UCS).

sponse (CR). Table 6.1 summarizes several examples of classical conditioning.

Instances of classical conditioning in infants can be demonstrated within two hours after birth. Elliot Blass and his colleagues paired a tactile stimulus, stroking of the newborn's forehead (CS), with the delivery of a sugar solution to the mouth (UCS) that elicited sucking (UCR) (Blass, Ganchrow, & Steiner, 1984). Newborns learned to orient their heads and to produce sucking responses (CR) to stroking of the forehead (CS) alone. Other types of classical conditioning are difficult to demonstrate in very young babies (Sameroff & Cavanagh, 1979). For example, responses to aversive stimuli such as loud noises and pain have not been successfully conditioned before three or four weeks of age. Carolyn Rovee-Collier (1987) does not find this failure surprising because very young infants do not have the motor skills to escape noxious events; they must depend upon their caregivers for protection. Thus, learning involving aversive stimuli emerges during or only just before the onset of simple locomotor abilities. Nevertheless, other biologically meaningful associations, particularly those surrounding feeding activity, may be acquired through classical conditioning shortly after birth.

Operant Conditioning In *operant* (or *instrumental*) *conditioning*, the frequency of spontaneous, sometimes novel, behaviors is changed as a result of their relationship to positive and negative consequences. Put more simply, behaviors tend to increase when followed by a reward (**positive reinforcement**) or the removal of an aversive event (**negative reinforcement**) and to decrease when followed by the loss of rewards or the occurrence of an aversive outcome (**punishments**). Table 6.2 summarizes these relationships and provides examples of positive and negative reinforcement as well as different forms of punishment.

Operant conditioning is evident in the first few hours and days after birth. As we saw in Chapter 5, for example, newborns increase or decrease pressure during sucking in response to the availability of milk, a positive reinforcement (Sameroff, 1972). And like classical conditioning, operant conditioning seems to work best with behaviors significant to infants, such as searching for (head turning, mouthing) and obtaining food (sucking). Moreover, babies only a few weeks of age can acquire complex chains of behavior through operant conditioning. Hanus Papousek (1967) was able to teach infants to make two head turns in one direction and two in the other through this procedure, although younger infants usually took longer than older infants to learn these relatively complex behaviors. Sensory stimuli seem to provide powerful reinforcements for infants. Babies will work hard, modifying the frequency or rate of vocalizing, smiling, and other behaviors under their control to see and hear things or

▶ **Interaction among domains**

to be touched and continue receiving stimulation (Lipsitt, 1982). This sensory input, of course, typically occurs in a social context as parents, grandparents, neighbors, and siblings encourage the baby to become outgoing and responsive to them. Thus, simple forms of learning are probably a major source of developmental changes in behavior very early in life.

Imitation   We began this chapter by suggesting that newborns may be able to imitate tongue protrusions. Controversy surrounds this observation, however. Piaget (1962), for example, claimed infants less than eight to twelve months of age could imitate, but only when able to *see* their own imitative responses. Since babies cannot view their own face, imitative facial gestures were assumed to be impossible until about a year of age when, according to

TABLE 6.2

Positive Reinforcement, Negative Reinforcement, and Punishment

Action of Stimulus	Type of Stimulus	
	Positive (pleasant)	Negative (unpleasant)

Delivered	*Positive reinforcement* (increases behavior through administration of a desired stimulus)
	Example: Infant says "cookie" →
	      Mother gives praise →
	      Infant says "cookie" again
		Punishment (decreases behavior through administration of an aversive stimulus)
		Example: Toddler throws toys →
		      Father yells, "Stop it" →
		      Toddler stops throwing toys

Withdrawn	*Punishment* (decreases behavior through the removal of a desired stimulus)
	Example: Teenager out past curfew →
	      Parent grounds teenager →
	      Teenager meets curfew next week
		Negative reinforcement (increases behavior by removing an aversive stimulus)
		Example: Child cleans messy room →
		      Parent stops "nagging" →
		      Child keeps room clean

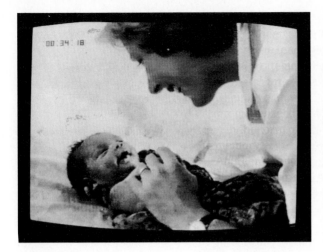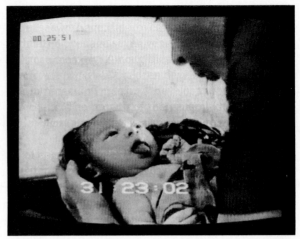

FIGURE 6.1

Facial Imitation in Newborns

Within an hour after their birth, babies in Nepal showed different responses when an experimenter modeled pursed versus widened lip movements. On the left, the baby broadens his lips in response to widened lips by the model. On the right, the baby exposes his tongue in response to pursed lips by the model. These findings support the highly controversial position that even newborns are capable of imitating facial gestures.

Piaget, new symbolic capacities emerged. Although some researchers have been unable to replicate the findings reported by Meltzoff and Moore, other experimenters, including one study involving infants from Nepal (see Figure 6.1), report success in observing imitation by very young infants (Reissland, 1988).

Tiffany Field and her colleagues indicate that newborns are even able to imitate facial expressions portraying emotions such as happiness, sadness, and surprise (Field, Woodson, et al., 1982). Some researchers have challenged this claim and have offered other explanations for such behaviors (Anisfeld, 1991; Kaitz et al., 1988; Over, 1987). One proposal is that facial gestures are rigid and stereotyped reflexive responses triggered and "tethered," so to speak, to limited forms of stimulation. In other words, infants are innately responsive to just a few kinds of stimuli and this behavior is not a result of imitation (Jacobson, 1979). Meltzoff and Moore (1989), however, counter that the variety of responses imitated, the variability in their expression, and the tendency for imitations to follow several seconds after the model's behavior work against the view that such behaviors are innately released. Whatever the explanation, these imitations are fragile and easily disrupted; the lighting, for example, must be arranged to ensure the model's face is highlighted and the baby is attending to it. Moreover, the model must display active movement; when a protruding static tongue is displayed, for example, newborns do not respond (Vinter, 1986). Furthermore, imitations seem more difficult to obtain in babies a few weeks of age, suggesting a change in the mechanisms underlying imitation as infants become older.

In the second six months after birth, imitations by infants become more frequent and precise, matching a wide range of modeled behaviors (Kaye & Marcus, 1981). Around eighteen to twenty-four months of age, according to Piaget

▶ **Roles of nature and nurture**

positive reinforcement Occurrence of a stimulus that strengthens a response when it follows that response. Also known as a reward.

negative reinforcement Withdrawal of an aversive stimulus that, upon its removal, serves to strengthen a preceding response.

punishment Aversive stimulus, or the removal of a pleasant stimulus, that decreases the frequency of a response when it is the outcome of that response.

▶ **Interaction among domains**

and others (McCall, Parke, & Kavanaugh, 1977), young children exhibit **deferred imitation,** the ability to imitate hours, days, and eventually weeks *after* some activity has been modeled. For Piaget, this was a particularly important achievement. Along with pretend play and the emergence of language, he believed, deferred imitation marked the transition from one stage of thinking to the next and provided one of the first major sources of evidence for symbolic capacities.

Other researchers have reported that deferred imitation occurs much earlier than eighteen to twenty-four months of age (Meltzoff, 1988b). For example, nine-month-olds are able to imitate simple actions with novel objects, such as knocking a particular block over or pushing a button, equally well both immediately and twenty-four hours after seeing the actions. These results suggest that the capacity for representing information in memory exists much sooner than previously assumed (Mandler, 1988). In fact, the results accord well with research on memory indicating that infants under a year of age can recognize stimuli hours and days later. These findings are also important from a social learning perspective. Imitation, a specific form of observational learning in which responses are produced to match behaviors displayed by a model, provides clear and convincing evidence that infants, as well as older children, can acquire many new behaviors by watching others.

Habituation   The gradual decline in the intensity, frequency, or duration of a response to the repetitive occurrence of the same stimulus is known as **habituation.** Even newborns display habituation. For example, they may evidence less arousal as they are repeatedly patted on the arm or hear the same noise again and again. Habituation is thus a simple form of learning—learning to ignore things that have become uninformative or "boring." It is also adaptive in the sense that the baby has come to "ignore" a stimulus that provides little new information. Unlike classical and operant conditioning, however, habituation does not usually lead to new behaviors.

When babies have habituated to an event, they will often exhibit a renewed response to a change in the stimulus. For example, they may become aroused once again as a result of being touched on the leg instead of the arm or by the presentation of a sound that is different from the noise repeatedly offered before. This return of a response is an example of **recovery from habituation** (sometimes called **dishabituation**). Recovery from habituation indicates that the baby perceives the new stimulus as different from the old one. As we shall soon discover, recovery from habituation has proven to be an important way in which babies provide information to researchers about their sensory capacities.

▶ **Interaction among domains**

Although premature as well as normal newborns habituate to repetitive events, premature, brain-damaged, and younger babies tend to habituate less rapidly than older, more mature infants (Krafchuk, Tronick, & Clifton, 1983; Rovee-Collier, 1987). In fact, growing evidence suggests that both rapid habituation and rapid recovery from habituation to novel stimuli by infants is associated with greater intelligence and cognitive capacities in childhood (Bornstein & Sigman, 1986; Fagan, Shepherd, & Montie, 1987; Rose et al., 1989). Thus, habituation, although a simple form of learning, may nevertheless be an extremely important indicator of intellectual development.

Learning Throughout Childhood

Of course, classical and operant conditioning as well as imitation and habituation continue after infancy and provide a rich contribution to the many new behaviors children begin to exhibit. For example, around two years of age, children begin more readily to imitate actions performed on objects by another person. When that happens between children, it seems to promote continued play with the objects by both model and observer and the awakening of more advanced social and imitative games between them (Eckerman & Stein, 1990). Around this age, moreover, mothers report that children increasingly imitate responsible behaviors such as those involved with chores and self-care (pretending to cook, brushing teeth) rather than affective or attention-getting actions such as laughing and sighing or shouting and pounding (Kuczynski, Zahn-Waxler, & Radke-Yarrow, 1987). These findings suggest that imitation and observational learning, along with the parents' direct manipulation of reinforcers and punishments, play a powerful role in the socialization of young children.

▶ **Interaction among domains**

▶ **Sociocultural influence**

The Cultural Context of Learning Learning is essential for completing many vital tasks of childhood. The sophisticated conventions required for interacting with others; the physical and intellectual skills, techniques, and procedures demanded in complex play and work; and the rapidly escalating knowledge of the world that evolves throughout childhood all depend on learning (Paris & Cross, 1983). Knowing the way to address a revered elder, care for a flock of sheep, read and solve complex mathematics problems, and the cues to use in moving or navigating from one location to another within the city, mountainous countryside, or between widely dispersed islands are skills not innately present in children; all are acquired through learning. Furthermore, much of what children learn is culturally prescribed: the games to be played, the chores to be performed, the relationships to be respected, and the activities to be valued.

As we saw in Chapter 2, social learning theorists have focused on observational learning as the means by which children acquire many complex social and cognitive skills (Bandura, 1977b). One outcome of this focus has been increasing recognition that learning is carried out in the presence and under the tutelage of others. Both children and adults often learn by watching others engaged in the tasks and interactions important to the culture. Lev Vygotsky also made *social activity* the cornerstone of his theory of development. A child's knowledge is cultivated by formal and informal interactions with caregivers, peers, and tutors who convey the knowledge a culture has accumulated (Vygotsky, 1978). Consider, for example, how a sensitive caregiver arranges tasks and activities to help a child solve a problem. The caregiver controls the difficulty of the task by providing useful background information, modeling appropriate actions, guiding and directing behavior, and allowing the child to take control whenever possible. For effective learning to take place, the teacher or caregiver may sometimes lead and oversee an activity; at other times, stand back and let the student demonstrate his or her skill.

deferred imitation Ability to imitate a model's behavior hours, days, and even weeks after observation.

habituation Gradual decline in intensity, frequency, or duration of a response over repeated or lengthy occurrence of the same stimulus.

recovery from habituation Reinstatement of the intensity, frequency, or duration of a response to a stimulus that has changed. Also called *dishabituation*.

scaffolding Temporary aid provided by one person to encourage, support, and assist a lesser-skilled person in carrying out a task or completing a problem. The model provides knowledge and skills that are learned and gradually transferred to the learner.

Scaffolding The concept of **scaffolding** is a way of thinking about the social relationship involved in learning from another (Wood, Bruner, & Ross, 1976).

A scaffold, as its name implies, is a temporary structure and gives support to accomplish a task that could not be completed otherwise. An effective caregiver or teacher provides a scaffold in learning situations, perhaps by defining the activity to be accomplished and by providing supporting skills and techniques in which the child is still deficient. These collaborative interactions advance the knowledge and abilities of the learner, as the following study of a toddler learning to label objects illustrates. Anat Ninio and Jerome Bruner (1978) visited the young child in his home every two weeks from his eighth month until he was two years old. During these visits they videotaped the boy's activities as he played with his mother. One commonly shared activity was "reading" from a picture book, with the mother providing the scaffold for the child to learn some things about his language.

> The mother's (often quite unconscious) approach is exquisitely tuned. When the child responds to her "Look!" by looking, she follows immediately with a query. When the child responds to the query with a gesture or a smile, she supplies a label. But as soon as the child shows the ability to vocalize in a way that might indicate a label, she raises the ante. She withholds the label and repeats the query until the child vocalizes, and then she gives the label if the child does not have it fully or correctly.
>
> Later, when the child has learned to respond with shorter vocalizations that correspond to words, she no longer accepts an indifferent vocalization. When the child begins producing a recognizable, constant label for an object, she holds out for it. Finally, the child produces appropriate words at the appropriate place in the dialogue. Even then the mother remains tuned to the developing pattern, helping her child recognize labels and make them increasingly accurate. For example, she develops two ways of asking, "What's that?" One, with a falling intonation, inquires about those words for which she believes her child already knows the label; the other, with a rising intonation, marks words that are new. (Bruner, 1981, pp. 49–50)

In this example, at first the mother takes responsibility for labeling the pictures. As the child becomes accomplished in labeling, however, she withdraws one kind of scaffold and replaces it with a new one involving different demands for learning.

▶ **Sociocultural influence**

Scaffolding involves a teaching/learning relationship that utilizes the expert or tutor who intervenes as required and gradually withdraws as assistance becomes unnecessary. Patricia Greenfield (1984) observed this phenomenon among girls learning to weave in Zinacantan, Mexico. Unless the girls had already achieved expert status as weavers, at least one expert weaver or teacher (usually the mother) was present. Beginning weavers started with smaller items to weave, but they also performed only the simpler parts of the task and the teacher intervened to complete the more technically difficult steps. The more experienced the weaver, the less likely the teacher was to assist. Novices were also more likely to receive direct commands from the teachers, whereas experienced weavers were more likely to receive statements or comments. In fact, both verbal and nonverbal assistance declined as the girls became increasingly expert weavers. Remarkably, the scaffolding provided by the tutor yielded a woven product from beginners indistinguishable from those completed by expert weavers! Nevertheless, the scaffolding of the teacher also provided a model from which the student could learn both specific techniques and more general principles of weaving.

With the assistance of an expert, children can often contribute to the completion of tasks that they would otherwise be unable to perform. By providing support, encouragement, and direction, this grandmother provides the scaffolding necessary for making cookies, a task the granddaughter would be unable to complete by herself.

These examples, consisting of carefully monitored support designed to help children complete activities that they will eventually do on their own, illustrate what Lev Vygotsky (1978) called the **zone of proximal development,** an extremely important aspect of child-adult interactions. In adopting the concept of *zone*, Vygotsky highlighted the disparity between what children are able to do without the assistance of others and what they are able to accomplish by having someone more expert assist them at key points. Typically a gap or discrepancy, a zone, exists between the two. In using the term *proximal* (near the center or core), Vygotsky emphasized that the most effective assistance from the expert will be that just slightly beyond or ahead of the child's current capacities. For Vygotsky, beginning with the child's level and building on it served as a key concept in his theory of development.

Modeling by Caregivers and Teachers   As the phenomenon of scaffolding and the zone of proximal development suggest, a model who is sensitive to the learner's level of knowledge contributes greatly to the effective transmission of skills. James Wertsch and his colleagues report an example of how teachers sometimes differ from parents in their approach to modeling activities (Wertsch, Minick, & Arns, 1984). Five- and six-year-olds from rural Brazil were asked to construct a replica of a toy barnyard. Either a mother or a teacher assisted in completing the task. Mothers were far more directive with their children than were teachers, pointing to specific pieces in the model or identifying pieces by explicit verbal references to them. This kind of social interaction provides very different opportunities for the problem solver than do situations in which the child is expected to take more initiative. A child who is given direct instruction by a parent may not be learning to plan and organize

zone of proximal development Range of various kinds of support and assistance provided by an expert (usually an adult) who helps children to carry out activities they currently cannot complete but will later be able to accomplish independently.

her approach to the problem, an essential part of many social and cognitive tasks.

Despite these differences, parents, who are usually the first models for their children, can be remarkably effective in their role as models and teachers. They have the opportunity to engage in frequent one-on-one interactions with their children, to monitor closely and assess progress in all domains of development, and to gain substantial knowledge of their children's abilities. They also have a greater personal and emotional investment in the development of their offspring than do most teachers. Still, teachers provide important social models for children as well. Although formal schooling is often viewed as nonsocial, there are many reasons to believe that effective teachers capitalize on interpersonal interactions with students to enhance learning even in large classroom settings (Brown & Reeve, 1987). Social interactions can provide tools and ways of thinking at many choice points along the path to what and how children learn.

▶ **Interaction among domains**

CONTROVERSY

When Should Children Learn to Read?

▶ **Sociocultural influence**

Among many cultures today, *literacy*, the ability to read and write, has become an extremely important skill for children to acquire and display. The illiterate or barely literate individual has few opportunities to advance in most jobs and can be severely hindered in effectively performing many of the essential tasks within a community that demand sophisticated reading ability. Not surprisingly, then, many parents express concerns about their children learning to read. Indeed, if such a skill is so valuable, attentive and loving parents might be eager to encourage their children to begin reading as soon as possible. But just how early should children learn to read?

Glenn Doman (1983), a physical therapist and founder of the Better Baby Institute, argues that beginning to read at five or six years, the age when many children acquire this skill, is far too late; that it can and should be accomplished, instead, by the time a child is two years of age. He believes that learning to read can proceed just as easily in infants and toddlers as learning to talk. To do so, parents should print words in large red letters on flash cards and repeatedly show the cards to their child while saying each word. For example, one card might say *mommy,* another *daddy,* still others spell out parts of the body as well as toys and objects the toddler plays with. Whenever the child correctly recognizes a word on the flash card, she is given lavish praise. Through this procedure, according to Doman, the child will learn to read, perhaps even before she is out of diapers. As a result she will be brighter and less frustrated than children who must still achieve this skill in school. In fact, for Doman, this is just one activity that can be adopted for fostering precocious development or *superbabies,* infants who through special kinds of stimulation become smarter and more competent in later childhood.

Some psychologists and reading specialists are highly critical of such efforts. Among their concerns are fears that parents may establish inappropriate expectations for children who do not yet have the requisite attentional and cog-

▶ **Interaction among domains**

nitive skills to read at such an early age. Failure to show anticipated progress in reading could then impair social interactions between parent and child, decrease a child's self-esteem, and increase the likelihood of reading problems later (Elkind, 1978; Moore & Moore, 1975). The intense, formalized routine surrounding efforts to instill early reading might create situations begetting tension and conflict rather than pleasure and enthusiasm for the child and parent.

Well-designed studies of the long-term consequences of structured early reading programs have not been carried out. However, at the present time there is no good evidence to indicate that these efforts lead to greater success in school, gains in intelligence, and greater happiness or other emotional benefits (Henig, 1988; Jackson, 1988). Formal programs to promote early reading remain unproven both in their benefits and in their potential for harmful effects. There is, however, much evidence that very young children often take an interest in text and reading materials. If parents nourish this interest by making available opportunities for children to become familiar with books, by reading to their young children, and by responding to their questions about letters, words, and text in a positive and supportive way, many children will learn to read well before they enter a formal school setting. Even if children have not yet acquired this skill, their readiness to learn to read in school is clearly increased (Durkin, 1966). Reading, then, may be promoted just as effectively in contexts in which the parent follows the child's own interests in books as in highly structured interactions in which the parent "drills" the young child on letters and words. Exactly how much structure parents should provide in encouraging very young children to acquire reading remains uncertain. ∎

SENSORY AND PERCEPTUAL CAPACITIES IN INFANTS

Can she see me? Can she hear me talking to her? This is what many people wonder when they hold a very young baby, even as they seem to be answering their own question with a resounding "Yes!" by vocalizing, making exaggerated facial expressions, and touching, caressing, and rocking the baby. Still the uncertainty remains: do infants register this information and if so, how do they interpret it?

The process of learning in infants and children is closely intertwined with the development of sensation and perception. After all, if babies cannot see or hear or feel the things that are part of their environment, then they would be unlikely to learn much from it. But what do very young infants perceive?

More than a century ago, William James (1890) theorized that for the newborn the world must consist of a "big blooming buzzing confusion." Is this a valid hypothesis today? To help decide the answer, psychologists often distinguish between **sensation**, the registration of a basic unit of information such as a visual feature or aspect of sound by a sensory receptor and the brain, and **perception,** the process of organizing and interpreting sensations. Perception occurs when a mother's face is visually recognized or a sequence of sound is interpreted as a familiar lullaby. Sensations are the building blocks; perception, the order and meaning imposed on those basic elements.

Today, most developmental psychologists think that the sensory world of

sensation Basic information in the external world processed by the sensory receptors.

perception Process of organizing and interpreting sensory information.

the very young infant is less chaotic and more organized than William James suggested. As we consider evidence supporting this view, we can make two broad observations about research on sensory and perceptual development. First, vision has been studied far more thoroughly than any other sensory domain. To some extent, this bias reflects the widespread belief that sight provides the major source of information for humans. Visual development, however, has also been easier to study than hearing, smell, and other sensory capacities. Second, in recent years our knowledge of sensory and perceptual development in newborns and young infants has expanded far more rapidly than our knowledge about these matters in older infants and children (Aslin & Smith, 1988). This disparity stems from the desire of researchers to uncover the earliest appearance of various sensory and perceptual capacities and the discovery that many major changes in sensation and perception take place during the first few months after birth.

Studying Infant Sensory and Perceptual Capacities

How can we possibly know what babies perceive when they are unable to tell us in words what they see or hear or taste? Researchers have devised ingenious techniques, some quite simple, to answer this question. Most of these techniques are based on measures of **attention**—that is, alertness or arousal focused on a selected aspect of the environment and revealed, for example, by extensive gazing toward a particular stimulus. Infants respond to various stimuli in dissimilar ways, attending to some more than others. When they display these attentional differences, they are demonstrating that they can perceive differences among the stimuli. Let's take a closer look at several types of studies that have given us much of our knowledge about what infants perceive.

Preferential Behaviors   In 1958, Robert Fantz placed babies on their backs in an enclosed, criblike chamber. Through a peephole, he and his colleagues observed how long the babies gazed at different visual stimuli inserted in the top of the brightly illuminated chamber. The observers had no difficulty determining what the infant was looking at because the reflection of the stimulus could be seen on the *cornea,* the outer surface of the baby's eyes, while he or she looked at it. Using this method, Fantz (1961) found that infants attended to some kinds of visual arrays longer than others. Babies as young as one to six months of age, for example, looked at patterned discs such as bull's eyes, stripes, newsprint, or facelike figures far longer than at solid-colored circles (see Figure 6.2).

   This methodologically simple demonstration encouraged many researchers to study the visual capacities of infants by observing their *preferential looking,* their tendency to look at some things more than others. The procedure has some limitations, however. What can we conclude, for example, when both members of a pair of stimuli are attended to the same length of time? Is the infant unable to discriminate the two, or does he prefer to look at one about as much as the other? Nor can we be certain that, when the baby gazes at a stimulus, she is processing its features.

   Despite these limitations in our ability to interpret the baby's response, preferential looking is often displayed by babies, and it has proven to be enor-

attention   State of alertness or arousal that allows the individual to focus on a selected aspect of the environment.

FIGURE 6.2

Preferential Looking

When Robert Fantz showed infants two to three months of age the different visual stimuli shown here, he found that babies preferred to look at those that illustrated some pattern (for example, a facelike figure, newsprint, or a bull's eye) more than those that consisted of a single solid color. This finding, using the preferential looking procedure, was an important early demonstration that young infants have the capacity to discriminate different visual stimuli. Note that the greatest preference was exhibited toward the facelike stimulus.

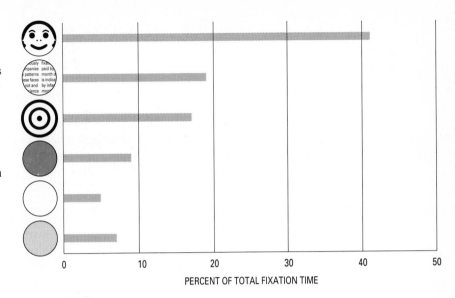

Source: Adapted from Fantz, 1961.

mously useful as a means of assessing infant visual capacities. In fact, highly sophisticated techniques now permit researchers to pinpoint the specific regions and aspects of a figure at which the baby gazes. Using specialized photographic techniques involving infrared lights and appropriate film, researchers can determine with great accuracy not only where the infant looks, but also how he or she scans a stimulus. Such procedures have revealed, for example, which aspects of a human face infants are most likely to attend to, as shown in Figure 6.3.

FIGURE 6.3

Visual Scanning

Using specialized techniques, researchers can often pinpoint the specific features in a visual stimulus at which infants are looking. Here the typical patterns of scanning these facelike stimuli by a one- and two-month-old have been recorded. Note how the younger infant's gaze tends to be directed toward the outer or external regions of the facial stimulus—that is, hair and chin. The older infant's gaze is more frequently directed toward inner features such as the eyes and mouth.

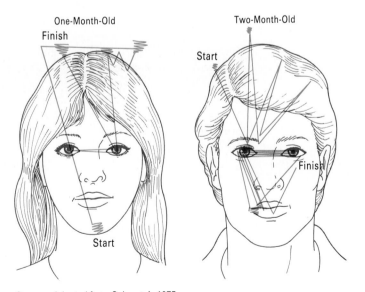

Source: Adapted from Salapatek, 1975.

Habituation   In another technique that takes advantage of the infant's tendency to prefer looking at some things more than others, babies are presented with the *same* stimulus for relatively lengthy periods, often over a series of trials. *Habituation,* a simple form of learning described earlier in the chapter, is often the outcome of repetitious stimulation. At first babies may attend to an interesting visual figure or object for a considerable amount of time. Just like adults, however, babies often tire of seeing the same stimulus over and over again, whether it be a simple line or a smiling face. This decline in attending to the repeated occurrence of the stimulus signals habituation. A change in the stimulus, however, may elicit *recovery from habituation,* a powerful indication that the infant has noticed something different, that a novel stimulus has been introduced.

By measuring habituation and recovery from habituation to angles, Marcelle Schwartz and R. H. Day (1979) demonstrated that two- to four-month-old infants could distinguish both the size of a visual angle and its orientation. Infants were shown stimulus A illustrated in Figure 6.4 over eight 20-second trials. The amount of time infants attended to the figure declined as trials continued, thereby demonstrating the presence of habituation. On the ninth, or test, trial, some infants were shown the same stimulus, some the stimulus rotated ninety degrees (B), and still others a stimulus in which the size of the angle had been reduced (C). Infants shown stimuli B and C exhibited recovery of habituation, attending more to the novel test stimulus than to the familiar stimulus on the immediately preceding trial. Infants who continued to be shown figure A, however, did not exhibit recovery from habituation on the test trial. Thus, infants this young were clearly able to discriminate the size and the orientation of this simple stimulus.

Habituation and recovery from habituation are processes that reveal abilities in other sensory domains. Infants, for example, often turn their heads away from unpleasant odors. Yet just as adults frequently report that they no longer notice an ongoing unpleasant smell, head turning to repeated presentations of the same odor typically habituates in infants. An infant, however, who starts turning his head away again when a slightly different odor is presented demonstrates that he can distinguish between the old and new smells.

Operant Conditioning   More complex forms of learning such as operant conditioning also can be used within days and weeks after birth to test the infant's ability to discriminate visual, auditory, and other sensory cues. In order to receive milk and other tangible rewards, including interesting visual and auditory patterns, for example, infants will learn to suck faster or slower, to turn their heads, to look, and to perform other behaviors that indicate discrimination of sensory stimuli.

Operant conditioning procedures have figured prominently in research on infants' auditory perception because there is no easily measured attentional response for the domain of hearing comparable to looking in the visual domain. One procedure popularized by Peter Eimas and his colleagues, called *high-amplitude sucking,* has proven especially informative (Eimas et al., 1971). Babies are given a special nipple designed to record their rate of sucking. A baby who sucks energetically or at a very rapid rate may be rewarded by hearing some pleasant sound—for example, the consonant-vowel pairing *pa,* a

FIGURE 6.4

Discriminating Orientation and Angle

Using a procedure involving habituation and recovery from habituation, Schwartz and Day demonstrated that two- to four-month-old infants could discriminate both the size of an angle and its orientation. The amount of time infants looked at figure A declined over the series of trials it was shown to them. But when figure B or C was then shown to the infants, they looked longer at it than at figure A, indicating that infants could discriminate the orientation and size of the angle of this simple stimulus. Researchers have found that habituation and recovery from habituation can provide considerable information about many of the sensory and perceptual capacities of young infants.

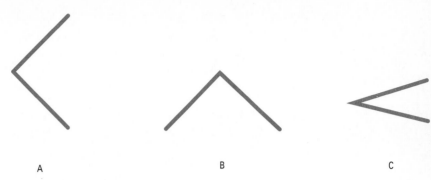

A   B   C

Source: Adapted from Schwartz & Day, 1979.

sound that babies seem to like to hear. After the infant hears *pa* over and over, however, the rate of sucking typically declines as she habituates to the stimulus.

What do you think the baby will do when a different pleasant sound, such as *ba*, is introduced? If the baby cannot detect the change in the sound, then of course we would not expect to see any change in the rate of sucking. But babies as young as one month of age begin to suck at a high rate again in order to keep hearing *ba*, thereby confirming that they can discriminate this novel consonant-vowel pair from *pa*. In other words, very young infants are already able to distinguish some important sounds that occur in language. By recording the energy level of sucking that infants display when given a choice of sounds to listen to, developmental psychologists can further determine whether infants prefer some sounds over others as well as whether they are able to discriminate among them.

Besides these behavioral methods involving preferential looking, habituation, and operant conditioning, other procedures utilizing physiological responses such as heart rate or the neurological activity of the brain and even of individual neurons have helped to clarify the sensory and perceptual abilities of infants. Fortunately, the results of these various methods have often complemented each other in providing information about the sensory and perceptual capacities of infants.

How Vision Develops

▶ **The child's active role**

The fact that newborns have such limited motor skills tempts us to assume that their sensory systems—their eyes, ears, nose, mouth, and skin—are passive receptors waiting to be stimulated by light, sound, aroma, taste, touch, and perhaps even painful sensations. But Eleanor and James J. Gibson convincingly argue that perceiving is an active "process of *obtaining* information about the world" (J. J. Gibson, 1966). "We don't simply see, we look" (E. J. Gibson, 1988, p. 5). The Gibsons' emphasis upon the active nature of the visual system applies to all sensory domains at every developmental level. Even the senses of newborns are adjusting and adapting to explore the happenings in the world surrounding them.

Until recently the active nature of infants' looking and the vibrant quality of stimulation that they often receive were largely ignored. Researchers routinely showed babies static, two-dimensional pictures to test their visual capacities. But the experiences of infants, as well as our own, are dynamic; the optical flow of information from the fluctuating spatial and temporal cues of a bustling environment is constantly modified by eye, head, and body movements as well. Young infants are attuned to this engaging world, utilizing active visuomotor systems that contribute to the development of what they see.

Visuomotor Skills: Looking   Each of our eyes includes a lens designed to refract, or bend, light passing through it. When the lens works effectively, visual images are projected onto the *retina,* that part of the back of the eye housing the sensory receptors for light. The lens of the human eye is variable; small involuntary muscles change its shape so that images of objects viewed at different distances are brought into focus, a process called **accommodation.**

Newborns display limited accommodation, but the process undergoes rapid improvement and reaches nearly adultlike levels by about three months of age (Aslin, 1987a). The newborn's poorer accommodative ability, along with the relatively small size of the eye, contribute to a tendency for images to be projected behind rather than on the retina (Banks, 1980). In addition, the reflex controlling the amount of light entering the eye, which further affects ability to focus, tends to be sluggish during the first few months (Aslin, 1987a). As a result, very young infants often receive somewhat unfocused visual input and are unable to detect fine details of stimuli. Their clearest visual discriminations are likely to be for patterns and objects about eight to twenty inches away, a convenient distance since a caregiver's face will often be about this far away when holding and feeding the baby.

Eye movements are another essential part of looking. **Saccades,** rapid movements of the eye to inspect an object or to view a stimulus in the periphery, occur within hours of birth (Lewis, Maurer, & Kay, 1978). At first, saccades are performed sluggishly and cover only small distances; young infants must initiate a sequence of them before "catching up" to a peripheral target (Aslin, 1987a). Under other conditions, such as when inspecting complex arrays, one-month-olds produce saccades similar to those of adults. Saccades, however, typically become more accurate over the first three to four months, although the precise age when they become fully adultlike remains uncertain (Bronson, 1990; Hainline et al., 1984; Shupert & Fuchs, 1988).

Humans exhibit another pattern of eye movements, **smooth visual pursuit,** which consists of maintaining fixation on a slowly moving target almost as if the eyes were locked onto it. Even under optimal conditions such as viewing a large object, newborns display only brief periods of smooth pursuit and show saccadic responses instead (Kremenitzer et al., 1979). Smooth visual pursuit remains fragile up to eight weeks of age and continues to improve through eight months of age (Shupert & Fuchs, 1988). Despite the relatively late appearance of smooth pursuit, very young babies readily turn eyes and head to continue viewing a moving object and, in fact, prefer looking at a moving rather than a static visual array (Nelson & Horowitz, 1987).

In pursuing a visual object, both eyes normally move together in the same direction. Sometimes, however, our eyes must rotate in opposite directions, as when we try to see a fly that has landed on our nose. This response, called

accommodation (visual)   Visuomotor process by which small involuntary muscles change the shape of the lens of the eye so that images of objects seen at different distances are brought into focus on the retina.

saccade   Rapid eye movement to inspect an object or to view a stimulus in the periphery of the visual field.

smooth visual pursuit   Consistent, unbroken tracking by the eyes that serves to maintain focus on a moving visual target.

The newborn must perform a variety of visuomotor responses including focusing his eyes on the features of his mother's face if he is to make sense of this new source of information. Visuomotor skills undergo rapid improvement during the first few months of life, one factor that permits a baby to soon recognize his caregiver's face.

▶ **Sensitive periods**

vergence Ability of the eyes to rotate in opposite directions to fixate objects at different distances; improves rapidly during first few months after birth.

visual acuity Ability to make fine discriminations among elements in a visual array by detecting contours, transitions in light patterns that signal borders and edges.

vergence, occurs when eye fixations shift between far and near objects; if it fails, we may see double images. Vergence occurs irregularly in infants less than two months of age (Aslin, 1987b). Thus, young babies' eyes often fail to turn sufficiently toward each other to converge on a visual target. By three months of age, however, vergence, an important visuomotor skill, is more regularly exhibited. The development of some mechanisms for perceiving depth depend on the coordination of the two eyes, and if vergence is not attained during a sensitive period in the first few years of life, individuals may suffer a permanent loss in some aspects of depth perception (Banks, Aslin, & Letson, 1975).

Sensation: Seeing How well are young infants able to see despite their somewhat immature visuomotor skills? One approach to providing an answer attempts to measure **visual acuity,** the ability to make discriminations between *contours*—that is, transitions in dark-light shading that signal borders and edges of elements in a visual array. One common test of visual acuity in children and adults, the *Snellen test,* requires identifying letters or other symbols on a chart located twenty feet away. If you need glasses, those letters look fuzzy and like ill-formed gray masses rather than sharply focused images distinguishing letter from background.

Babies, of course, cannot name letters, so other procedures are necessary to test their visual acuity. Although several methods have been devised, one that provides a reasonably good estimate of acuity relies on preferential looking. As a pattern of, say, black and white stripes become more frequent (the stripes become narrower), the pattern becomes more difficult to detect, and the stimulus begins to appear gray. If infants are unable to detect the stripes, they are unlikely to attend to the stimulus very long, preferring instead one in which the pattern can still be detected. By pairing stimuli with different frequencies of stripes and observing preferential looking, researchers can then gauge the visual acuity of infants.

Two key findings emerge from the many investigations of visual acuity in infants. First, even newborns detect contours, although their acuity is much poorer than that of children or adults. In fact, acuity under some conditions is estimated to improve more than forty-five-fold from birth to adulthood (Banks & Dannemiller, 1987). Other studies suggest far better acuity in very young infants, but babies are certainly not able to detect detailed features of stimuli. Second, acuity improves rapidly, especially during the first six months after birth. This improvement comes about through increasing accommodation and convergence skills, growth and maturation of the neural pathways for vision, and changes in the shape and physical characteristics of the eye, including a dramatic increase in the number of visual receptors in the retina.

▶ **Interaction among domains**

Acuity alone provides a limited measure of the ability to see. Visual discrimination is also affected by *brightness contrast,* or the degree of discrepancy in the brightness of light and dark contours. Research indicates that, to detect contours, brightness contrast must be substantially greater for very young infants than for adults. Nevertheless, by six months of age, infants' sensitivity to brightness contrast is nearly adultlike (Banks & Dannemiller, 1987).

Can babies also see colors? Once again, the answer is yes, and at very young ages. The retina contains two major types of receptor cells: *rods,* sensitive only to the intensity of light (functioning already at birth) and *cones,* sensitive to the different wavelengths of light that underlie color perception. Although very young infants may not perceive the full range of colors available to adults, the cones are functioning by two or three months after birth, possibly even earlier (Adams, 1989; Adams, Maurer & Davis, 1986). In fact, by four months of age, babies prefer to look at red and blue rather than green or yellow, a preference also evident in adults (Teller & Bornstein, 1987). Thus, color preferences may not be simply learned but may instead reflect certain biological contributions.

▶ **Roles of nature and nurture**

In summary, basic visuomotor and sensory capacities are available to the very young infant. These permit babies to look at and see a richly patterned and probably colorful array of elements and features. Their vision is not as keen as it soon will become, but newborns and young infants are certainly not blind. In the first few months their vision is limited to the more glaring and distinctive elements, but these seem more than adequate for perception—that is, for interpreting and giving meaning to the visual environment that is part of their sensory world.

Perception: Interpreting Depth   Visual images are received on our retina in two dimensions, yet we see our world in three dimensions. Not only do we see objects to the left and right and above and below, we also note their depth or distance. When and how do we acquire the ability to perceive depth? One source of information comes from our *binocular* vision; we receive input to two eyes, and that input is slightly different for each. The process of fusing these two distinct images to form a single percept is called **stereopsis,** a capacity that improves markedly during the first four months after birth. Despite this fusion, stereopsis provides clues to the depth or distance of a stimulus as effectively for six-month-old infants as for adults (Fox et al., 1980; Held, Birch, & Gwiazda, 1980).

stereopsis   Ability to perceive a single image of an object even though perceptual input is binocular and differs slightly for each eye; significant source of cues for depth perception.

FIGURE 6.5

The Visual Cliff

In the visual cliff, used to test depth perception, a baby is placed on the plank at the center and a caregiver attempts to coax the child to cross to either side. Infants are much less likely to crawl on the glass support when the textured surface appears far below than when it is immediately beneath the glass.

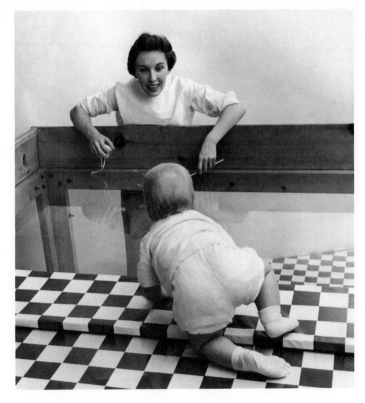

kinetic cue Perceptual information provided by movement of eyes, head, body, or of objects in the environment; important source of information for depth perception, even for infants.

visual cliff Experimental apparatus used to test depth perception in which the surface on one side of a glass-covered table is made to appear far below the surface on the other side.

Still other cues to depth and distance, known collectively as **kinetic cues,** are provided by the movement of our eyes, head, or body and by the actions of objects in the environment. When we or aspects of the environment move, our visual input undergoes a variety of informative transformations. If you rotate your head while staring at an object some distance away, for example, nearer objects appear to move more rapidly than objects more distant. This difference in the rate of movement of near and far objects is an important source of information about depth, especially if you cover one eye to eliminate depth cues associated with stereopsis.

A classic series of studies of depth perception involving the visual cliff suggests that kinetic cues are important to depth perception for infants who are able to crawl. The **visual cliff** consists of a large sheet of glass bisected by a relatively narrow plank. A patterned surface is located immediately under the glass on one side, but much farther below the glass on the other side (see Figure 6.5). Richard Walk (1968) found that an infant placed on the plank and old enough to crawl can usually be coaxed to cross the shallow side to reach a caregiver, but is much less likely to crawl over the deep side. In one study Walk put a patch on one eye of each young subject to eliminate binocular cues to depth. Infants were still far more reluctant to crawl over the deep side, perhaps because they were sensitive to the kinetic cues signaling depth provided by their own head and body movements. In fact, these cues may be influencing attention already at birth since newborns prefer to look at three-dimensional objects more than at two-dimensional figures (Slater, Rose, & Morison, 1984).

The shallow and deep sides of the visual cliff can even be identified by babies too young to crawl. Placed face down on the glass surface, two- to three-month-old infants give different responses to the two sides of the cliff; they become quieter, less fussy, and show a greater decrease in heart rate on the deep side than on the shallow side (Campos, Langer, & Krowitz, 1970). Such reactions suggest that infants have not yet associated anxiety or fear with the cues that can signal depth in the visual cliff, but find the visual cues on the deep side more interesting than on the shallow side.

Sudden expansion or contraction of an image provides another kind of kinetic cue to an object's possible location. When an image enlarges rapidly, an object may appear to be approaching, possibly on a collision course with the viewer; when an image recedes, an object may appear to be moving away. Infants from three to six weeks of age produce avoidance-like behaviors such as blinking and backward head movements to rapidly expanding shadows that suggest an impending collision but do not show these behaviors to rapidly shrinking shadows (Náñez, 1988). Infants do not display these responses if the expansion suggests that the object will "miss" or appears as an opening, such as a doorway (Ball & Tronick, 1971; Carroll & Gibson, 1981; Nanez, 1988). Moreover, infants under three weeks of age do not exhibit these defensive reactions, an indication that the behavior to this particular kind of motion must be rapidly learned or that the visual system quickly matures to respond to these cues (Yonas, 1981). The role of maturation may indeed be important since premature infants do not demonstrate the behavior until several weeks after full-term infants (Pettersen, Yonas, & Fisch, 1980).

▶ **Roles of nature and nurture**

Another kinetic cue to depth is change in texture. As we walk past a tree, cues behind it disappear and reappear. The same thing happens when someone walks in front of us and temporarily blocks our view of a distant object. This information is used by seven-month-olds to reach for "nearer" objects even when stimuli are computer-generated visual arrays (Granrud et al., 1984). In fact, around five to seven months of age, infants begin to interpret many *pictorial* depth cues, those in photos and two-dimensional displays, such as relative size (near objects appear larger), shadows, interposition of surfaces (one surface "hides" another), and linear perspective (lines converging towards a horizon) to indicate depth (Yonas & Owsley, 1987).

▶ **Roles of nature and nurture**

As with other cues to depth, we cannot assume that infants' responsivity to pictorial cues is innate. The ability to interpret them is probably acquired rapidly around six months of age as a result of neurological maturation, experience, or both. However, we can conclude that infants respond to an abundant array of depth cues very early in development. These cues provide the necessary information for perceiving space and the objects in it as three-dimensional. While some of these cues may be detected in the first months of life, they may, of course, not be recognized as cues to depth until the middle of the first year, when rapid advances in manipulatory and locomotor skills assist to give consistent meaning to them.

▶ **Interaction among domains**

Perception: Interpreting Patterns and Form   Few questions have fascinated psychologists more than when and how infants recognize patterns and other configurations of visual features. Some researchers have proposed that babies are born with the ability to perceive larger wholes and units; others have argued that this capacity is acquired only through extensive visual expe-

▶ **Roles of nature and nurture**

▶ **The child's active role**

▶ **The child's active role**

externality effect   Tendency for infants younger than two months of age to focus on the external features of a complex stimulus and to explore the internal features less systematically.

rience. Neither extreme position, of course, is likely to be correct, but psychologists traditionally have tended to place greater emphasis on experience. According to this perspective, infants construct perceptions of integrated, holistic, and meaningful visual figures through repeated opportunities to process contours, angles, shading, and other basic sensory features. Nevertheless, this nurture-oriented explanation continues to be challenged (Dodwell, Humphrey, & Muir, 1987).

The visual world of infants younger than two months of age does appear to be governed primarily by basic and relatively simple features of stimuli (Haith, 1980; Karmel & Maisel, 1975). The receptors and neural pathways of the visual system respond to elements such as contour, angles, and motion at or shortly after birth (Bronson, 1974; Maurer & Lewis, 1979). By two months of age, however, things change. Now infants inspect and analyze visual arrays more systematically and are more likely to scan a greater variety of features in a complex stimulus. A good example of this developmental change is the **externality effect**—infants less than about two months of age tend to look at only a few features, typically the outer contours of a complex stimulus. Older infants, however, tend to scan the internal features of a complex stimulus as well (Maurer, 1983; Salapatek, 1975).

We saw an illustration of the externality effect in our discussion of preferential looking. Babies less than two months of age tend to fixate—that is, look at—external contours of the face such as hair or chin line; older infants fixate internal features such as eyes or mouth much more frequently. This developmental difference is found when babies view other stimuli, such as two geometric figures, one inside the other. Very young infants *can* attend to the smaller figure when it is not encircled by the larger, when it shows movement, or when its brightness is increased, but their attention is usually affected by the presence of an outer contour (Bushnell, Gerry, & Burt, 1983; Ganon & Swartz, 1980). Older infants seem to be able to carry out a more deliberate, organized visual search, looking geared toward exploring and more fully perceiving the entire pattern or array.

Other experiments provide evidence for perception of entire forms and patterns within a few months of birth. For example, when two-month-olds are habituated to a rectangle, they show recovery of habituation if the shape changes to a square, but not if the rectangle is rotated (Schwartz & Day, 1979). In other words, they recognize that the figure has changed, not just its orientation. From two to six months of age, infants also display increasingly greater preference for looking at more complex and varied patterns (Fantz & Yeh, 1979). By four or five months of age, babies distinguish symmetrical from asymmetrical patterns (Bornstein & Krinsky, 1985). These findings confirm that attention to the configuration of a pattern begins very early after birth and continues to improve throughout infancy (Dodwell, Humphrey, & Muir, 1987).

Perhaps one of the most intriguing examples of form perception involves "subjective" or "gradient-free" contours. Look at the Kanizsa figure in Figure 6.6. You probably see a highly visible white triangle standing above three black disklike figures located at each of its corners. But you are subjectively assuming the triangular form; no contour is present to mark its sides. Habituation experiments reveal that infants, perhaps as young as one or two months of age, and certainly by three to four months of age, perceive these subjective

FIGURE 6.6

Infants' Subjective Perception of Form

Infants as well as adults perceive the subjective triangular figure appearing in the Kanizsa figure (a) even though no contour is present to define it. After becoming habituated to the Kanizsa figure, babies are shown other figures, including a standard triangle formed by visible contours (B), the indented circular figures rotated to abolish the subjective triangle (C), or a completely different array of stimuli (D). Infants show the least recovery from habituation to the normal triangle (B), suggesting that they perceived the triangular shape produced by the Kanizsa figure.

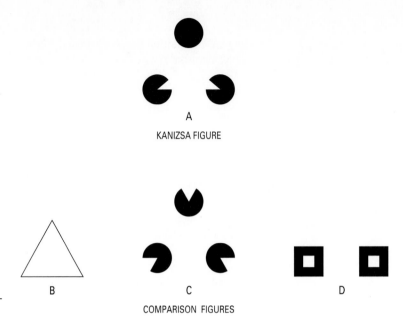

KANIZSA FIGURE

COMPARISON FIGURES

Source: Adapted from Treiber & Wilcox, 1980.

▶ **Interaction among domains**

▶ **Roles of nature and nurture**

figures, too, another powerful demonstration of the perception of patterns, not isolated features (Ghim, 1990; Treiber & Wilcox, 1980).

Some perceptual patterns are especially significant in the social life of the infant. Remember the results shown in Figure 6.2, where it appears that babies prefer to look at facelike stimuli over some other kinds of visual patterns? One question often posed by students and parents alike is, Do very young infants, perhaps even newborns, recognize faces, especially the faces of their caregivers? An early, perhaps innate, ability to do so makes evolutionary sense because faces are a vital source of information for social and emotional relationships. Based on our discussion so far, you should not be surprised to learn that by two months of age infants do begin to assign great importance to faces. Before this age, infants attend to a stimulus whose features and contours are organized either in the form of a face or in a scrambled arrangement for about the same length of time (Maurer, 1985). Thus, specific features visible in a face may be interesting to newborns, but whether they are arranged in a facial configuration does not seem to matter. About two months of age, however, a change takes place; infants now show more attention to a pattern whose features are organized to look like a face.

Between two and four months of age, babies display additional progress in perceiving faces. Three-month-olds recognize photographs of their mothers and prefer to look at pictures of her rather than of strangers (Barrera & Maurer, 1981b). They also discriminate facial expressions such as sad and angry and prefer faces displaying a broad smile over ones with a more neutral expression (Barrera & Maurer, 1981a; Kuchuk, Vibbert, & Bornstein, 1986). But can we be certain that a baby recognizes her mother (Walker-Andrews, 1986)? Or only some specific feature in her face? Even babies a few days old appear to distinguish a mother from a stranger on this latter basis (Bushnell, Sai, & Mullin, 1989). We can conclude, however, that newborns and young

FIGURE 6.7

Inference of Unity and Coherence

Under some conditions, four-month-olds respond as if they perceive an occluded rod as a single, complete figure. Infants are habituated to one of the seven familiarization displays shown here and then are presented with the test displays. After viewing conditions A, B, and C, infants respond to the complete rod in the test display as novel, indicating they perceived the rod in A, B, and C to be broken. When shown conditions D, E, F, or G, however, infants appear to perceive the rod as a connected whole, showing less attention to the complete rod than to the broken rod in the test display. These results indicate the ability of young infants to infer unity and coherence for objects. Recent research suggests newborns do not make these perceptual inferences.

infants are attracted to and identify important aspects of the human face and that in the first few months they make rapid strides in perceiving and recognizing this important social stimulus.

Perception: Interpreting Objects   Our visual environment is not made up of flat, fixed pictures, but of objects that must be distinguished from each other and from various background surfaces and contours. How does a baby perceive a rattle as separate from the table on which it lies? The family dog as distinct from the floor on which he sits? James J. Gibson (1979) argued that the dynamic flow of visual information created by movement of both objects and self—that is, *kinetic cues,* helpful to perceiving depth—also provides infants with abundant cues for identifying objects. A series of experiments carried out by Philip Kellman and Elizabeth Spelke reveals evidence in support of Gibson's position (Kellman & Spelke, 1983; Kellman, Spelke, & Short, 1986). Four-month-olds viewed a rod whose midsection was occluded by a rectangular block; only the ends of the rod were visible (see Figure 6.7). What do infants see in these circumstances? A single, complete rod partially hidden by the block? Or two short rods with a space between them covered by the block? To find out, the babies were habituated to the rod and block. As Figure 6.7 shows, in some conditions the rod and block underwent different kinds of motion during the process of habituation.

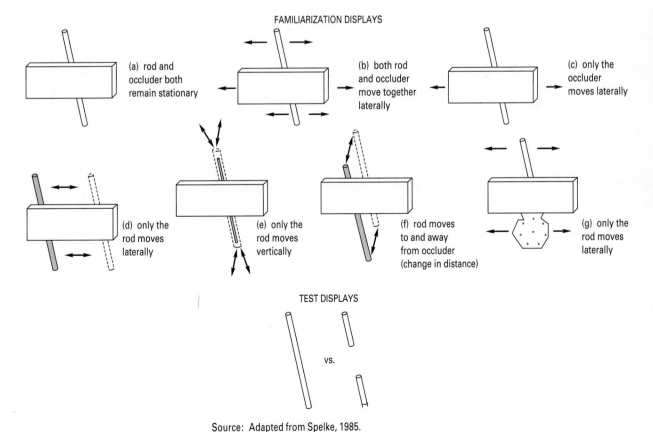

FAMILIARIZATION DISPLAYS

(a) rod and occluder both remain stationary

(b) both rod and occluder move together laterally

(c) only the occluder moves laterally

(d) only the rod moves laterally

(e) only the rod moves vertically

(f) rod moves to and away from occluder (change in distance)

(g) only the rod moves laterally

TEST DISPLAYS

vs.

Source: Adapted from Spelke, 1985.

The results revealed that infants interpret the occluded rod as complete rather than broken as long as its two ends are seen moving together and independently of the block during habituation trials, even when the two visible rod ends are quite different. But if, during habituation trials, neither the rod nor block move, both rod and block shift together in the same direction, or only the occluding block moves, four-month-olds and also three-month-olds do not "fill in" the unseen portion of the rod; they do not respond to the separate segments as if they are novel (Spelke, von Hofsten, & Kestenbaum, 1989).

▶ **Roles of nature and nurture**

Is this perception of coherence associated with certain kinds of movement innate? Would even newborns see complete objects in such a situation? One recent study with newborns suggests that the answer is no (Slater et al., 1990). Under movement conditions in which older four-month-olds treat the separated segments as novel, newborns treat the complete rod as novel. Newborns do not seem to "fill in" or make perceptual inferences about the occluded segment of the stimulus.

The importance of kinetic cues, motion in general, for early infant perceptual development is demonstrated in yet another phenomenon known as *biological motion*. Bennett Bertenthal and his colleagues programmed lights to move as if attached to the head and major joints of a person walking. In other conditions the pattern of lights was inverted or an equivalent amount of motion occurred in the lights, but the lights were scrambled and the motion did not simulate the appearance of a person walking. After habituating to one of these displays, three-month-olds could perceive the change when either of the other displays was shown. By five months of age, however, infants exhibited greater reactions after habituating to the display organized to correspond with humanlike movement, suggesting that the "walker" had taken on special meaning for infants this young (Proffitt & Bertenthal, 1990).

As with the basic abilities to look and see, the main question about perception is, *When* does the infant begin to perceive patterns, form, and objects? These and other studies suggest that the answer is, At least within the first two to four months (Ghim & Eimas, 1988). Newborns detect features of their visual environment, but their capacity to process larger, more organized and meaningful patterns and arrays remains uncertain. Of course, as visuomotor and sensory processes mature and are modified by experience, the ability to organize and interpret visual arrays rapidly improves. Visual development in the infant is summarized in the Chronology on page 251. Researchers are just beginning to ask what role specific kinds of experiences play in these continuing advances. It should be evident, however, that the young infant's visual world is far less of a "blooming buzzing confusion" than William James suspected.

How Hearing Develops

Just as medical opinion once held that newborns are blind, so too it asserted that newborns are deaf (Spears & Hohle, 1967). Convincing evidence exists, however, to indicate that young infants hear, and perhaps surprisingly well. In fact, babies respond to sound several weeks before birth; noises affect brain wave patterns and the heart rate of babies during their last few weeks in utero (Aslin, 1987b). But perhaps the most persuasive evidence that babies hear

CHRONOLOGY	Visual Development
NEWBORN	Shows minimal accommodation; limited, sluggish saccades; incomplete vergence. Detects contours, but acuity and contrast sensitivity remain relatively poor. Prefers attending to highly visible contours, angles, features in motion, and three-dimensional over two-dimensional stimuli. Exhibits externality effect.
1–3 MONTHS	Shows accommodation; near normal adultlike vergence. Smooth visual pursuit emerges, as does color vision. Discriminates cues to depth. Responsive to rapidly expanding visual images. Explores internal as well as external features of stimuli. Recognizes shape of simple figures and more detailed patterns and objects. Prefers attending to increasingly complex patterns, including those with facelike organization.
4–8 MONTHS	Exhibits stereopsis. Saccadic eye movements become larger, more rapid and accurate. Shows adultlike smooth visual pursuit. Acuity and contrast sensitivity approach normal. Displays fear of depth on visual cliff. Discriminates many pictorial (two-dimensional) cues to depth. Distinguishes symmetrical from asymmetrical patterns. Processes "subjective" contours. Perceives occluded objects as wholes. Becomes responsive to "biological motion."

This chart describes the sequence of visual development in infancy based on the findings of research. Children often show individual differences in the exact ages at which they display the various developmental achievements outlined here.

prenatally comes from several recent studies indicating that newborns prefer to listen to the sounds they heard before birth!

Anthony DeCasper and Melanie Spence (1986) asked expectant mothers to read aloud a passage from Dr. Seuss's *The Cat in the Hat*. Mothers read this passage twice a day during the last six weeks of pregnancy so that their babies were exposed to the story for a total of about three and a half hours before they were born. Two or three days after birth, the babies could hear either the same passage or a new story while outfitted with a special pacifier that recorded rate of sucking. Depending on rate of sucking, the recording of the story would turn on or off. When newborns could hear *The Cat in the Hat*, they modified their rate of sucking to listen to it, but they did not do this for the new story. The results suggest that some kind of learning took place prenatally. The fluid-filled prenatal environment maintains a relatively constant level of background noise; many sounds, particularly of higher frequencies,

▶ **Roles of nature and nurture**

must be muffled and even completely masked (Kuhl, 1987). Thus, the precise nature of what the unborn heard and how newborns recognize that the auditory noises conducted by air are somehow related to their previous experience remain a mystery. Nevertheless, prenatal familiarity with a mother's voice may help to explain why newborns prefer to listen to their mother rather than to a stranger speaking (DeCasper & Fifer, 1980).

Sensation: Hearing   Though we know that the unborn can hear during the last few weeks before birth, we know little of the range and variety of sounds reaching them and how well these are detected. The same can be said for the newborn and very young infant; very little research exists to reveal exactly how well babies hear the first few months after birth. Six-month-olds, however, detect high-frequency sounds nearly as well as preschoolers, who, in turn, are able to hear such sounds better than adults (Schneider et al., 1986). Furthermore, by six months of age babies are able to distinguish between two different high-frequency sounds much as adults do (Olsho, 1984). On the other hand, the ability to hear low-frequency sounds improves substantially over the first two years and probably improves until about ten years of age (Trehub et al., 1988; Yoneshige & Elliott, 1981). Thus, in contrast to visual sensitivity, which becomes nearly adultlike by six to eight months, some aspects of auditory sensitivity take a lengthy period to develop.

Can infants determine where a sound is coming from? Shortly after birth, babies display **sound localization,** the ability to locate a sound, by turning their head or eyes to the left or right side. This early ability, which may be reflexive, declines during the first two months and then reemerges about four months of age in the form of more deliberate search for sound (Field et al., 1980). Yet babies are much less precise than children or adults in locating the position of a noise. For example, adults can tell when sounds are displaced only one or two degrees from a center position; eighteen-month-olds can only make this distinction when the sounds are about four degrees apart (Morrongiello, 1988). Six-month-olds, however, require sounds to be displaced somewhere between twelve and nineteen degrees before they detect the difference in position, and younger infants require even larger shifts from midline (Ashmead, Clifton, & Perris, 1987; Morrongiello, Fenwick, & Chance, 1990). Thus, the infant's capacity to localize sound improves rapidly over the first two years of life.

Perception: Interpreting Patterns   Are babies able to perceive sound patterns? Perhaps they can distinguish music from noise, even have a preference for some kinds of music over others? Although younger infants have not been extensively tested, two- and three-month-olds do recognize changes in the duration of intervals between four brief bursts of sound (Demany, McKenzie, & Vurpillot, 1977). Six-month-olds can distinguish more complex rhythms; they can, for example, detect a change from three groups of three bursts of noise (a three-three-three pattern) to either two groups (a five-four pattern) or one group (a nine-element pattern). By one year of age, infants also distinguish among different numbers of elements in a group (for example, a four-one-four versus three-three-three pattern) (Morrongiello, 1984).

At eight months of age, babies recognize changes in short six-note melodies, including a transposition in key and a change to an either higher or lower

sound localization   Ability to determine a sound's point of origin.

frequency of a single note in the sequence (Trehub, Bull, & Thorpe, 1984; Trehub, Thorpe, & Morrongiello, 1985). Babies are, indeed, sensitive to rhythmic and melodic contour (Trehub, 1987). In fact, four-and-a-half- to six-month-olds can boast some budding capacities as music critics. Carol Krumhansl and Peter Jusczyk (1990) chose short passages of Mozart minuets and introduced brief pauses at locations judged by adults to be either "natural" or "awkward" places for a musical phrase to end. Babies preferred looking at a loudspeaker that played only "natural" versions rather than "unnatural" versions of the Mozart selections. This ability to detect satisfying musical phrasings may be important not only for appreciating music, but also for recognizing the phrasing and sound rhythms that commonly underlie speech.

▶ **Interaction among domains**

Perception: Speech Research on infants' basic hearing abilities has often been conducted to answer one question: how soon do babies perceive human speech? The ability to interpret speech sounds as meaningful elements of language probably begins during the second six months of life. That developmental story is discussed in Chapter 7. Nevertheless, we can ask whether even younger infants discriminate speech sounds and, if so, how they are able to do this.

The basic, distinctive sounds of speech, called *phonemes,* consist of bursts of acoustic energy produced at several different frequencies. Phonemes are surprisingly complicated stimuli, and a difference, for example, of less than 20/1000 second in the onset or transition of a frequency of sound is enough for adults to discriminate distinctive phonemes such as /p/, /b/, and /t/ as in the sounds *pa, ba,* and *ta.* (Linguists identify the phonemes of a language by slashes.)

Are very young infants able to hear these differences? Indeed they are. In fact, by six months of age babies probably distinguish every sound of importance in any of the hundreds of languages spoken around the world, and many of these sounds can be discriminated much earlier (Werker, 1989).

▶ **Roles of nature and nurture**

How are infants able to detect these subtle differences? Two answers with very different implications for language development have been proposed. One possibility is that babies are born with special mechanisms for the perception of speech. Newborns have a "speech module," an innate capacity to detect and process the subtle and complicated sounds that make up human language (Fodor, 1983). This explanation supports a belief, widespread among linguists, that the complexity of language acquisition requires specialized abilities for infants and young children since other cognitive skills remain limited at this age. Another viewpoint is that phoneme discrimination is possible through more general auditory capacities, capacities not limited to processing speech sounds nor even necessarily unique to humans. Infants, however, are quickly able to utilize these capacities along with basic cognitive skills to develop representations for the various sounds that are meaningful in the language they hear.

Do infants have a perceptual system innately programmed and uniquely sensitive to language or a more general auditory capacity, more likely influenced by experience, to assist in discriminating all sounds, including phonemes? What evidence exists to support either explanation? Two research findings lend support to the view that speech perception involves special language-oriented mechanisms. The first comes from the extremely complex relationship between the acoustic properties of phonemes and their perception. For example, the /b/ phonemes that we hear in the two words *beak* and *book* are quite different acoustically even though we treat the sounds as equivalent. Researchers argue that the absence of a simple set of rules for perceiving the phoneme /b/ in these two contexts makes the presence of a "special mechanism" for speech perception highly likely (Kuhl, 1987).

A second important finding supporting the view that infants possess a special innate capacity for speech perception focuses on categorical perception. **Categorical perception** is the act of classifying sounds that vary on some continuous physical dimension as the same *except* when they fall on opposite sides of a critical juncture point on that dimension. For example, the English consonants /b/ and /p/ in the sounds *ba* and *pa* are quite similar and differ only in *voice onset time* or *VOT,* the time when the vocal chords begin vibrating in relation to the release of air by the vocal apparatus. English speakers perceive *ba* and *pa* categorically. Small changes in VOT are not heard as "more or less" like *ba* or *pa.* Instead, we hear the *ba* as long as the VOT continues to fall on one side of the categorical boundary and *pa* when it continues to fall on the other. But if the small difference in VOT crosses a critical point, the phoneme boundary, the two sounds are readily distinguishable. Infants as young as one month of age already demonstrate categorical perception for many different speech sounds (Aslin, 1987b; Kuhl, 1987).

However, researchers remain uncertain about whether babies are born with a special sensory mode for speech perception. Monkeys, even chinchillas, for example, distinguish speech sounds categorically (Kuhl & Miller, 1978; Kuhl & Padden, 1983). Moreover, categorical perception occurs with other sounds than speech. Both of these findings argue against a specialized, innate ability to process phonemes.

▶ **Sensitive periods**

Younger infants actually appear more sensitive than older infants to phonemes that are found in different languages. In one study, six- to eight-month-olds who were being reared in an English-speaking environment could readily discriminate among phonemes used in Hindi, whereas eleven- to thirteen-month-olds had more difficulty with this task (Werker & Lalonde, 1988). Adults could regain these "lost" discriminations only with considerable practice (Werker, 1989). Thus, the linguistic environment that surrounds a child has a substantial impact on the sounds to which she continues to be responsive. Regardless of the answer to what accounts for speech perception, developmental psychologists fully concur that young infants have or quickly gain many discriminative auditory abilities, including those important for acquiring language, as is summarized in the Chronology on page 255.

How Smell, Taste, and the Cutaneous Senses Develop

▶ **Interaction among domains**

Developmental researchers have given far less attention to smell, taste, and the *cutaneous senses*—the receptor systems of the skin responsible for perceiving touch, pressure, pain, and temperature—than to either vision or hearing. These senses, however, do function shortly after birth and furnish crucial adaptive and survival cues for the very young baby. Smell, for example, may be critical for determining what is acceptable for eating and may also be involved in early attachment between infant and caregiver.

CHRONOLOGY	Auditory Development
NEWBORN	Recognizes auditory events that were repeatedly produced by the mother when baby was still in utero. Discriminates mother's and stranger's voice. Localizes sound reflexively.
1–3 MONTHS	Recognizes simple auditory patterns. Discriminates many, if not all, basic sounds used in language. Makes deliberate efforts to locate sound, an ability that continues to improve throughout early childhood.
4–8 MONTHS	Detects and discriminates high-frequency tones nearly as well as, sometimes better than, children or adults; ability to detect low-frequency tones continues to improve throughout childhood. Recognizes melodic rhythms, transposition in key, note changes, phrasing in music. Begins to lose some phoneme discriminations if not heard in native language.

This chart describes the sequence of auditory development in infancy based on the findings of research. Children often show individual differences in the exact ages at which they display the various developmental achievements outlined here.

categorical perception Inability to distinguish between sounds that vary on some basic physical dimension except when those sounds lie at opposite sides of a critical juncture point on that dimension.

Smell   Facial expressions, changes in rate of respiration, and avoidance-approach activities involving head turning are just a few of the responses indicating that newborns detect odors. But studying infants' olfactory capacities is difficult because no simple system exists for classifying odors and because the intensity of these odors at the receptor level is extremely difficult to control. The typical procedure consists of a series of trials in which a researcher holds a stimulus-saturated cotton swab just beneath the baby's nose for a few seconds. Do babies "turn up their noses" at the unpleasant smell of rotten eggs? Turn away from the harsh odor of ammonia? Detect the food-related smells of fish, butter, banana, or vanilla? They most certainly do (Engen, Lipsitt, & Kaye, 1963; Rieser, Yonas, & Wikner, 1976; Steiner, 1979). Moreover, newborns become increasingly sensitive to these and other odors over the first few days of life (Lipsitt, Engen, & Kaye, 1963; Self, Horowitz, & Paden, 1972).

Parent-infant recognition occurs by smell among many species of animals (Porter, Balogh, & Makin, 1988). Can human infants identify their caregivers this way as well? Aidan Macfarlane (1975) offered two breast pads to newborns, one worn by the infant's mother and the other unused. Two- to four-day-olds oriented toward both pads about the same amount of time, but by five days of age infants turned their heads longer in the direction of the pad the mother had used. By six days of age, infants also preferred a pad obtained from their own mother over one from an unfamiliar mother.

What cues are babies detecting, a mother's milk or odors from her body?

Perhaps both. Two-week-old female babies, whether breast or bottle fed, orient more toward breast pads worn by unfamiliar nursing mothers than toward the underarm pads worn by these mothers or the breast pads of non-nursing women (Makin & Porter, 1989). Thus, either milk, body odors associated with nursing, or both are identified and preferred by very young infants. But the sensitivity of babies to these cues also depends on whether they are breast or bottle fed. At two weeks of age, breast-fed, but not bottle-fed, babies orient longer to the underarm pads worn by their mothers than to those of unfamiliar women. Neither group recognized their fathers' underarm pads from those of other males (Cernoch & Porter, 1985). Taken together, these findings suggest that after close and frequent contact such as that involved with nursing, very young infants become able to discriminate their caregivers from others on the basis of odor.

To test this familiarity hypothesis, Rene Balogh and Richard Porter (1986) taped one of two substances releasing either a cherry or ginger fragrance inside the bassinets of twenty-four newborn infants. The substance remained for about twenty-three hours, and babies were tested with the familiar and the unfamiliar odor within forty-eight hours of birth. Girls, but not boys, demonstrated a clear preference for the familiar stimulus, results consistent with the hypothesis that early exposure to an odor can lead to its preference. Sex differences in this and other studies with infants have indicated that females are more sensitive to odors than males, a finding also reported in tests of olfactory capacities of children and adults (Doty et al., 1984; Makin & Porter, 1989).

One additional finding of interest is that within the first few days of birth and after brief contact, mothers can identify their own infants on the basis of odor alone. So too, can fathers, grandmothers, and aunts recognize newborn kin by their smell alone. In other words, each of us may have inherited some family olfactory signature to which we are sensitive or are able to learn very quickly (Porter, Balogh, & Makin, 1988).

Taste   Receptors for the basic tastes of sweet, sour, salty, and bitter are located mostly on the tongue and nearby regions of the mouth. Because these receptors develop well before birth, it is possible that the fetus "tastes" as it swallows amniotic fluid. Facial expressions and rate of sucking provide strong evidence that newborns can certainly discriminate among tastes (see Figure 6.8). Sweet stimuli, for example, elicit a relaxed facial expression often resembling a smile of enjoyment; sour stimuli, lip pursing or a puckered expression; bitter stimuli, mouth openings often described as an expression of disgust (Steiner, 1979).

▶ **Roles of nature and nurture**

Innate preferences for some tastes may help infants to meet nutritional needs and protect them from harmful or dangerous substances (Crook, 1987). These preferences, however, can be modified by experience. For example, babies fed sweeter fluids in the first few months after birth ingest more sweet water at six months of age than babies not given this experience (Beauchamp & Moran, 1982). Other researchers suggest that the desire for salt in a specific food can also be established in infancy and becomes strongest during early childhood (Beauchamp & Cowart, 1990; Harris & Booth, 1985; Sullivan & Birch, 1990). Regardless of how important learning is for the emergence of odor and taste preferences, we should also note that until they reach about two years of age, children will put just about anything they can into their

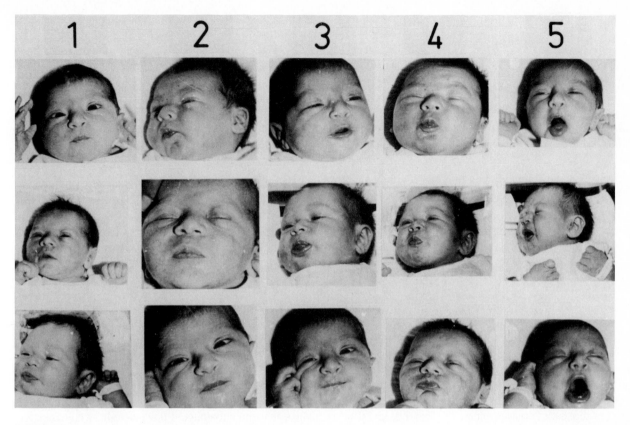

FIGURE 6.8

Discriminating Tastes

Babies produce different facial expressions depending on what they taste. The first column shows the resting face of three different newborns. Column 2 shows the same babies after they received distilled water—their expressions show very little change. The babies' facial expressions after sweet stimulation are more likely to be positive and relaxed, resembling a smile or licking of the upper lip as shown in column 3. However, their mouths become more pursed after sour stimulation (column 4) and more arch-shaped after bitter stimulation (column 5).

mouths. Thus, among the most important things they must learn is what *not* to eat (Rozin, 1990).

Touch, Pressure, Pain, and Temperature Our skin contains over a hundred types of receptors sensitive to touch, pressure, pain, and temperature (Reisman, 1987). As we saw in Chapter 4, even the fetus responds to touch. In the newborn, stimulation of the skin and muscles elicits a variety of reflexes (see Chapter 5), and pin pricks and other painful events initiate crying. The skin's receptors undergo further development after birth, and during the first month, babies become increasingly sensitive to painful events (Humphrey, 1964; McGraw, 1941). Although work on pain sensitivity is obviously limited because of ethical concerns, circumcision and other medical procedures involving newborns have come under increasing scrutiny because these operations are performed without anaesthesia. Babies recover from such surgery rapidly, however, feeding and responding to their mothers normally after only a few minutes (Marshall et al., 1982). They also typically fall asleep following surgery, which may assist in their recovery from stress within a few hours (Gunnar et al., 1985).

A difficult problem for newborns, particularly premature infants, is regulation of body temperature (Moffat & Hackel, 1985). Cooling results in awakening, greater restless movements, and increased oxygen consumption, responses that may facilitate heat production. Because newborns are unable to sweat or pant, exposure to high temperatures produces skin reddening, less

This toddler very likely feels the soft, cold texture of snow while at the same time sees its white, fluffy qualities. Both visual and tactual cues will change if she holds onto it long enough and she may soon add another sensory input, taste, if she hasn't done so already. Stimulation often takes place through several sensory modalities.

▶ **Roles of nature and nurture**

intermodal perception Coordination of information from more than one sensory modality to perceive an object or to make inferences about its characteristics.

perceptual differentiation Process postulated by Eleanor and James Gibson in which experience contributes to the ability to make increasingly finer perceptual discriminations and to distinguish stimulation arising from each sensory modality.

activity, and more sleep, events that decrease heat production and assist heat loss (Harpin, Chellapah, & Rutter, 1983). When they are warm, babies also assume a "sunbathing" position, extending their extremities, perhaps a good clue for caregivers trying to decide whether a baby is too warm or cold (Reisman, 1987).

As with their abilities to see and hear, we cannot help but be impressed with the sensitivity infants show to the smells, tastes, and cutaneous information that is part of their surroundings. But do they perceive the many sensory inputs available from the environment as discrete and separate, only gradually integrating sight, sound, smell, and all the other senses? That question, too, has often been asked, and the answer is the focus of enormous debate.

How Intermodal Perception Develops

We can see, smell, even hear a steak sizzling on a platter before us. Sometimes we can obtain identical information from two or more different senses. For example, we can distinguish the texture and shape of a box or a pillow often by looking at or feeling them. Besides hearing rhythm, we can see it as when we watch the performance of a drummer on television with the volume turned off. When we coordinate information arriving from several sense organs to perceive an entity or to make inferences about its various qualities, we are demonstrating **intermodal perception.** The toddler who hears his mother's voice calling from another room also expects to see her as he enters it. When we see a cup, its appearance tells us how to shape our mouth to drink from it, and if we recognize that the substance it holds is milk, we also expect it to taste a certain way and that we cannot pick it up with our fingers like pieces of popcorn. Sometimes, of course, we can be fooled. A luscious-looking dessert may have the flavor of cardboard. A good ventriloquist really does make you think the dummy is doing the talking.

How can we explain intermodal perception? How does it develop? These two questions have been debated for decades. In fact, the study of infant tongue protrusion we described at the beginning of this chapter suggests intermodal perception in newborns. If newborns really imitate such an action, they must be able to recognize that the sight of another person's actions can somehow be coordinated with their own mouth movements. Some researchers argue that intermodal perception would have to be innate for infants to produce such behaviors.

A kind of intermodal perception may indeed exist at birth, according to James and Eleanor Gibson (E. J. Gibson, 1982; J. J. Gibson, 1979). They argue that perception is initially amodal—that is, undifferentiated—so that a newborn is unable to distinguish which sensory system is being stimulated. For example, if an object is both seen and heard, the infant is able to perceive only "something stimulating" and orients, to whatever extent possible, all receptors to it. Thus, intermodal perception does not depend on learning to coordinate information from the various senses (Spelke, 1987). Instead, as infants and children gain experience, they become aware of their various senses and begin to distinguish information arising from each of them, part of a process the Gibsons have labeled **perceptual differentiation.**

The Gibsons' position is a controversial one. Another explanation of inter-

▶ **Roles of nature and nurture**

▶ **The child's active role**

▶ **Interaction among domains**

modal perception emphasizes the initial separateness of the senses; only after repeated experiences, this argument runs, are babies able to coordinate different sensory information. Thus, intermodal perception involves learning, for example, that when objects are shaken, some rattle and make noise, others do not; an object that feels soft can also look soft; a square peg does not fit into a hole that appears round. According to this viewpoint, intermodal perception is the outcome of *enrichment,* the association of sensations from two or more modalities, or, from a more Piagetian perspective, the consequence of *constructing* schemes involving multisensory experiences (Spelke, 1987).

Note that learning is important in each of these views. The point of contention is over whether learning occurs as a form of unpacking unique sensory qualities from complex, undifferentiated stimulation or as a form of recognizing links and associations and better understanding the relationships between distinctive sensory cues. Each position may contain some truth (Spelke, 1987).

Auditory-Visual Coordination We indicated earlier that newborns display sound localization, a tendency to turn the eyes in the direction from which a sound comes. Such behaviors, however, are probably reflexive because they also occur to sounds produced in the dark and with eyes either closed or open (Mendelson & Haith, 1976). Very young infants do not seem to be "looking for" a noisy object in the same way that three- or four-month-old infants purposefully look at things they hear, as work by Elizabeth Spelke and her colleagues has demonstrated.

Spelke (1976) developed a simple procedure to demonstrate the integration of auditory and visual information in infants. In her initial study, four-month-olds were able to view two films shown side by side. At the same time, infants could hear a sound track coming from a speaker located between the two viewing screens. This sound track matched events in one of the two films, either an unfamiliar woman engaged in a game of "peekaboo" or someone playing on percussion instruments. Would infants pay more attention to the film synchronized with the sound track? Spelke found this to be the case, at least when the percussion sounds could be heard.

Other research has confirmed that four-month-olds can not only match auditory and visual tempo and rhythm, but other auditory-visual cues as well. In one study babies were shown two films, one depicting wet sponges being squeezed, the other, two blocks being clapped together (Bahrick, 1983). When babies heard a "squishing" sound, they attended more to the film showing the sponges; when they heard a banging sound, they attended more to the film of the rigid blocks. In other words, four-month-olds integrate visual events involving rigid and nonrigid objects with certain kinds of sounds. Five-month-olds even link sounds and visual progressions of approaching and retreating movement—as, for example, an auto coming and going (Walker-Andrews & Lennon, 1985). If babies are learning these relationships, they are doing so very quickly!

Infants also display intermodal perception involving social relationships. They quickly learn to match up the face that goes with a parent's voice. When the mother is positioned on one side and the father on the other, three-and-a-half-month-olds are more likely to look at the parent whose voice comes from a speaker centered in front of them (Spelke & Owsley, 1979). By six months, babies who hear a strange male or female voice also look longer at a face of the same sex, although three-month-olds do not show this ability (Francis & McCroy, 1983). Five-month-olds can even link vocal expressions of happiness or sadness to facial expressions of emotion, an ability that continues to improve for several more months (Walker-Andrews, 1986). But what if visual and auditory cues send mixed messages? Does one cue dominate the other?

Research with young children and adults has consistently revealed that visual cues tend to dominate auditory cues when the two are in conflict (O'Connor & Hermelin, 1965). But this may not be the case for babies less than six months of age. For example, six-month-olds were habituated to a flashing checkerboard occurring along with a pulsing sound. Then a change was introduced in the duration or rate of either the flashing checkerboard or the pulsing sound. Babies this age were far more likely to detect an auditory change than a visual change. On the other hand, by ten months of age babies were likely to respond to changes in either the sound or visual pattern (Lewkowicz, 1988a, 1988b). Thus, during the second six months of life visual information appears to attain greater importance for infants as they become able to respond to more complex information arising from multiple senses.

The dominance, or at least the influence, of visual cues on perception in children and adults can be found in some unexpected situations. Speech perception, for example, which most of us assume to be an entirely auditory event, may be greatly affected by what we see. Harry McGurk and John MacDonald (1976) played videotapes of an adult uttering simple syllables such as *ba ba*. Sometimes, however, the video picture was synchronized with another sound, such as *ga ga*. Three-year-olds as well as older children and adults often reported hearing something quite different—for example, *da da* or another utterance—in these conflict situations. If viewers turned away so they no longer saw the incompatible visual input, they identified the sounds correctly. McGurk and MacDonald concluded that visual cues such as lip movements can provide substantial information for speech perception in face-to-face situations, a finding that accords with other research involving children and adults suggesting that visual cues tend to dominate auditory cues. Maybe then, we shouldn't be too surprised when we are fooled by a ventriloquist!

Coordination of Vision and Touch   Infants at six months of age who explore an object with their hands alone can then recognize it by sight alone (Rose, Gottfried, & Bridger, 1981; Ruff & Kohler, 1978). But several experiments suggest that coordination between vision and touch exists much earlier as long as the mouth, rather than hands, is able to explore objects. In one study, one-month-olds were allowed to mouth either a smooth sphere or a sphere with nubs, neither of which they could see. When they were then shown the objects, they preferred to look at the one they had not mouthed (Meltzoff & Borton, 1979). In another experiment, one-month-olds also recognized objects they mouthed, but—perhaps because of a difference in the procedure—these infants preferred to look at the familiar rather than the novel object (Gibson & Walker, 1984). Nevertheless, in both experiments the infants could discriminate between the novel and the familiar. By nine months of age, babies are even surprised by a discrepancy between vision and touch. Emily Bushnell (1981) showed infants a solid object within a box. But the location of the object was displaced by mirrors so that when babies reached for it, they touched another object differing in size, shape, and texture. Infants younger than nine months of age failed to investigate the novel object actively or search for the one they could see, but older infants did both.

▶ **Roles of nature and nurture**

Research has not yet yielded a simple verdict on whether intermodal perception is present at birth or is only gradually acquired. Both positions may contain some kernel of truth. Coordination among looking, listening, and touching can be found a few weeks after birth, if not earlier, a serious challenge to the view that these abilities are learned or constructed only after much experience involving each separate sensory modality. Yet there is substantial evidence that intermodal perception also changes with experience. Infants surely lack some, if not much of the knowledge and skill that contributes to intermodal perception. That can only be gained through opportunities to look, listen, smell, taste, touch, and act upon the world surrounding them.

Drawing Conclusions About Infant Perceptual Development

Very young infants can boast of surprisingly sophisticated sensory and perceptual capacities, capacities that will further undergo extraordinarily rapid improvement and refinement. Babies come equipped to gain access to the rich variety of stimulation that surrounds them. They are able to detect and discriminate sensory inputs and make sense of them quickly. Their perceptual development reveals an order and purpose beautifully adapted to the process of responding to and learning from experience. We must conclude that babies are highly competent information processors, able to explore and learn from their environment through vision, audition, touch, smell, and taste. Furthermore, they interpret and organize the inputs in many ways that appear to be similar to the older child and adult. This does not mean, of course, that infants perceive and interpret their surroundings in exactly the same way that children and adults do. It does mean that they are equipped with sensory and perceptual tools that allow them to become responsive to their family, community, and culture in an astonishingly short amount of time.

PERCEPTION IN CHILDHOOD

▶ **Interaction among domains**

Richard Aslin and Linda Smith (1988) recently noted a predicament facing anyone interested in learning about perceptual development after infancy. As research has increasingly uncovered sophisticated abilities in newborns and infants, the importance of studying perceptual development at older ages has seemingly faded. Perception also becomes more difficult to investigate without considering at the same time the child's developing linguistic and cognitive skills. Nevertheless, studies of attention and part-whole perception have brought out several important features of perceptual development in children. Were you intrigued as a child by those pages in children's magazines challenging you to find which of two pictures were exactly alike among the six on the page? Or by segments of "Sesame Street" asking you, "Which of these things is not like the others?" As you became older, you solved these problems better and faster. Children's attention becomes more focused, organized, and confined to the more meaningful and important features of the environment—in other words, it becomes increasingly efficient and less easily distracted with age. Eleanor Gibson (1969, 1982, 1988) has outlined one major view of perceptual learning to account for these kinds of findings.

How Perceptual Learning Develops

Gibson's theory of perceptual learning emphasizes three changes with age: increasing specificity in perception, improved attention, and more economical and efficient acquisition of perceptual information. As we have already learned, infants perceive important aspects of their environment. Much of their first year is spent in discovering the sensory properties of objects, the spatial layout of their world, and the perceptual repercussions of their actions. But perceptual learning continues. For example, children acquire new kinds of visual discriminations when they learn to read. They must begin to pay attention to consistencies and variations in letters and text, aspects of their visual environment that they may have largely ignored before.

▶ **The child's active role**

One good example of this increased sensitivity to perceptual differences comes from a study by Gibson and her colleagues (Gibson et al., 1962). They created different sets of letterlike figures like those shown in Figure 6.9. One member of each set was designated a standard, but each set also included variations of that standard. A straight line, for example, might be changed to a curved line, the standard rotated or reversed, a variation introduced by cre-

When they begin to learn to read, children must pay attention to consistencies and variations in letters and text, aspects of their visual environment that they may have largely ignored before.

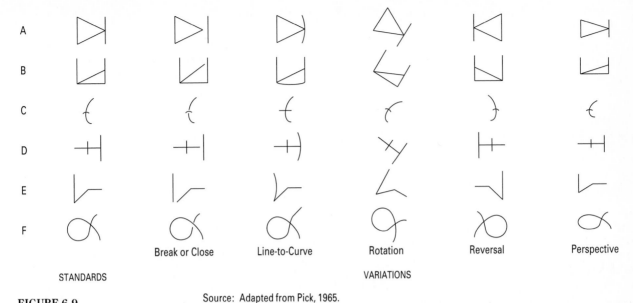

	Break or Close	Line-to-Curve	Rotation	Reversal	Perspective

STANDARDS   VARIATIONS

FIGURE 6.9   Source: Adapted from Pick, 1965.

Sensitivity to Perceptual Differences

Column 1 of this figure gives different letterlike forms used as standards in a sorting task. Columns 2 through 6 display various transformations of each standard. Four- to eight-year-olds, shown a stack of these figures and asked to select only those identical to the standard, commit relatively few errors on variations that involve a break in the figure, presumably because this distinction is important for identifying many objects as well as alphabetic symbols. With increasing age, errors involving rotation, reversal, and line/curve variations decrease substantially because, according to Gibson, children who are beginning to learn to read must pay attention to these features of the stimuli. Errors involving perspective remain high at all ages, perhaps because this transformation is not important for identifying either objects or letters of the alphabet.

ating a break in a continuous line, or its perspective changed by tipping, elongating, or changing other aspects of the specific components of the figure. Children four through eight years of age were shown a stack of each set of figures and asked to pick out only those identical to the standard.

Children made many more errors in this sorting task for some kinds of variations in the stimuli than for others. For example, children of all ages seldom confused the standard with variations that contained breaks, probably because these visual features are important for identifying common objects in the environment as well as letters of the alphabet. On the other hand, older children did substantially better than younger children in discriminating rotations and reversals as well as line/curve transformations, presumably because children learning to read must begin to pay attention to these kinds of variations. Finally, children of all ages found it difficult to discriminate changes in perspective from the standard, a variation that can and should normally be ignored for identifying both physical objects as well as letters of the alphabet.

Gibson believes age-related improvements in performance on this sorting activity do not come about from reinforcing children for making these discriminations. In fact, given the opportunity to classify these letterlike forms over a series of trials, children showed steady improvement in their sorting even though they were never given any feedback about how accurate they were. Gibson argues that in their repeated exposure to and inspection of letters of the alphabet, children are afforded the opportunity to recognize that certain critical features distinguish such figures. It is opportunities to experience the regularities and differences among similar stimuli, not the systematic reinforcements of parents or teachers, that enable children to distinguish perceptual events. While infants can make basic discriminations, perceptual learning is an indispensable part of learning to read and accomplishing many other technical skills that demand subtle and sophisticated perceptual distinctions.

How Part-Whole Perception Develops

A major research question about infant perception has been whether babies can see patterns, forms, and objects—the wholes, so to speak, rather than just their isolated features. As we have already learned, they can do so within a matter of weeks after birth, and we cannot rule out the possibility that they do so even earlier. The perception of preschoolers appears to be frequently influenced by wholes; they occasionally have difficulty making analytic—that is, precise and systematic—judgments about the similarity of objects based on specific features and attributes (Smith, 1989). Whereas older children are more likely to classify or discriminate among stimuli on one or a few dimensions (for example, size, shape, color, or some other specific dimension), preschoolers seem to approach such tasks from a more global perspective, grouping and discriminating things on the basis of their overall similarity. Whether they see the parts or features rather than the whole, however, is probably greatly influenced by how complex and distinctive both are. But a related question is whether they are able to see *both* the wholes and parts.

Consider the stimuli shown in Figure 6.10, a set of figures with identifiable pieces arranged to form meaningful wholes. David Elkind and his colleagues asked children from ages four to nine years to describe what they saw (Elkind, Koegler, & Go, 1964). Younger children generally reported only the parts. Only eight- and nine-year-olds were likely to mention both wholes and parts, leading these researchers to conclude that younger children have difficulty perceiving both features. But a more recent study has demonstrated that when the parts and the whole are relatively simple stimuli, children as young as three years of age will report seeing both (Prather & Bacon, 1986).

In summary, any developmental trends in childhood concerning the perception of parts and wholes must be interpreted cautiously. On simpler perceptual tasks preschoolers can perform like older children, and if older children, even

FIGURE 6.10

Part-Whole Perception

Stimuli were created by Elkind and his colleagues to test whether young children can perceive both the parts and the whole. Younger children reported only seeing the parts. When the wholes are made simpler than those shown here, however, even three-year-olds can see both the parts and the whole. Difficulty in reporting both may stem from conceptual and verbal constraints rather than from perceptual limitations.

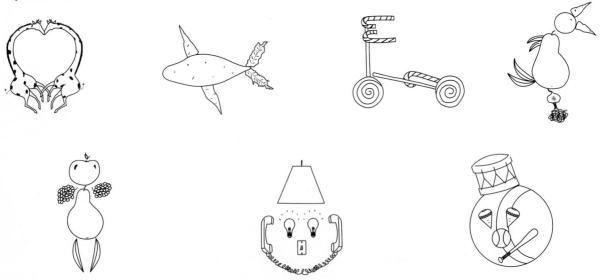

Source: Adapted from Elkind, Koegler, & Go, 1964.

▶ **Interaction among domains**

adults, are given limited time or a difficult task, their perception is likely to take on a less complicated quality, such as reporting only the whole (Smith & Kemler-Nelson, 1984). These findings suggest that cognitive rather than perceptual factors may be primarily affecting performance on many perceptual tasks (Smith & Evans, 1989).

How Attention Develops

Many of the findings we examined under perceptual learning and part-whole perception may reflect developmental differences in *attention*. With increasing age, children's attention to aspects of the environment becomes more organized, systematic, and selective. How can we tell? Simply by watching children explore things with their hands and their eyes. Asked to examine an unfamiliar object for the purpose of recognizing it later, three-year-olds are likely to hold it or play with it, four-year-olds to feel it with one hand, five-year-olds to explore a few features with their finger tips, and older children to investigate it thoroughly with their finger tips. Not surprisingly, as they gain familiarity with the object by exploring it more thoroughly, children also become better at recognizing it later (Abravanel, 1968; Zaporozhets, 1965).

These developmental changes can be observed from eye movements alone. In one study children three to seven years of age were instructed to look at outlines of irregular forms that were projected onto a screen in order to identify them later (Zaporozhets, 1965). Their eye movements were filmed through a hole in the center of the screen. Children younger than four appeared to be distracted by the camera; they looked toward the lens rather than toward the task-relevant outline of the figure. Children four to five years of age were more likely to attend to sections of the outline of the figure. Seven-year-olds scanned the figures far more systematically and, of course, performed more accurately on the recognition task than younger children.

Other demonstrations of developmental changes in the ways children attend to their environment come from the work of Eliane Vurpillot (1968; Vurpillot & Ball, 1979). Children were shown a picture of two houses, each having six windows, and were asked to judge whether the houses were identical (see Figure 6.11). As they inspected the houses, their eye movements were filmed by a camera located between the two pictures. Preschoolers scanned the windows less thoroughly, efficiently, and systematically than older children. For example, when the houses were identical, four- and five-year-olds looked at only about half of the windows before making a decision, but older children looked at nearly all of them. When the windows differed, older children were more likely than younger children to stop scanning as soon as they detected a discrepancy. Finally, older children were more likely to look back and forth at windows in the same locations of the two houses; younger children displayed more haphazard fixations, looking at a window in one house, then a different window in the other house. Here again we see evidence of developmental changes in attention, although it is not possible to determine whether the changes are solely perceptual or also benefit from more sophisticated cognitive strategies or processes that direct attention.

▶ **Interaction among domains**

FIGURE 6.11

Comparing Houses

Children were asked to explore houses to make judgments about whether they were the same or different while a camera photographed their eye movements. Preschoolers explored the windows less thoroughly, efficiently, and systematically than older children.

Source: Adapted from Vurpillot, 1968.

▶ **Roles of nature and nurture**

The Interaction of Experience and Perceptual Development

How do experience and inborn sensory capacities interact to determine perception? This question has been important throughout the history of psychology, and it continues to be of enormous interest as medical and technical advances provide opportunities to compensate for some kinds of sensory deficits. For example, blind children are able to perceive the existence of objects at a distance, presumably because of changes in auditory cues they receive while navigating in an environment that includes obstacles (Ashmead, Hill, & Talor, 1989). Blind infants are now being fitted with sonic devices to help them hear echoes to signal the direction, distance, and other qualities of objects. The effects of these efforts are not well known, but we can be sure of one thing based on research on perceptual deprivation in laboratory animals: experience is extremely important for *maintaining* many perceptual capacities.

Evidence for the importance of experience in maintaining perceptual capacities comes from many sources. When infant monkeys are reared with light, but no contours or patterns are visible, the ability to discriminate objects visually is gradually and permanently lost over a period of time (Riesen, 1965). The same appears true in humans as studies of infants born with cataracts has demonstrated (Walk, 1981). Research with kittens indicates that responsivity

▶ **Sensitive periods**

▶ **Sociocultural influence**

to contours of different orientations requires exposure to a variety of horizontal, vertical, and oblique patterns of stimulation (Blakemore & Mitchell, 1973). Moreover, if both of their (and our) eyes do not function together over the first months and years of life, binocular vision may be permanently affected (Aslin & Dumais, 1980). Thus, sensitive periods exist early in perceptual development during which perceptual capacities may be lost if the range of visual stimulation is limited.

Experiential factors may also help to explain cross-cultural differences in perception. Environments around the world differ in their degree of "carpenteredness" (Segall, Campbell, & Herskovits, 1966). In most urban, technically advanced societies, houses are constructed on rectilinear principles involving perpendicular and right-angle dimensions. Even the layout of roads and other artifacts of the environment often follow these principles. In other environments, such as in Oceanic and many African cultures, walls and roofs may be curved and there may be few straight lines and angular intersections.

In one study, field workers administered several optical illusions to samples of children and adults in twelve locations in Africa, the Philippines, and the United States (Segall, Campbell, & Herskovits, 1966). The two horizontal lines in the Müller-Lyer illusion (see Figure 6.12) are actually the same length, as are the horizontal and vertical segments of the horizontal-vertical illusion. The researchers theorized that individuals living in a carpentered environment, who often see rectangular intersecting contours, would have greater difficulty seeing the lines as equal in the Müller-Lyer illusion than people living in noncarpentered environments. They made this prediction based on the fact that inward-pointing finlike perspectives often accompany lines that are seen nearer, and outward-pointing finlike perspectives are frequently associated with lines seen farther away. Thus, in the case of the Müller-Lyer illusion, an individual gains the expression of greater depth and the line is judged to be longer when the fins point outward rather than inward. They also predicted

Does the environment influence perceptual development? Some have argued that a child who grows up in a culture where linear perspective is uncommon, as is the case in many parts of Africa and island regions in the Pacific Ocean, will perceive things differently than a child who grows up in a "carpentered" environment—one filled with straight lines, right angles, and many opportunities to see distances based on orderly linear cues.

FIGURE 6.12

Cross-Cultural Differences in Perception

Is one of the two horizontal lines in the Müller-Lyer illusion longer than the other? What about the vertical and horizontal lines in the horizontal-vertical illusion? Children and adults who live in "carpentered" environments are more susceptible to these illusions than people who live in forested regions where cues to distance are less prevalent.

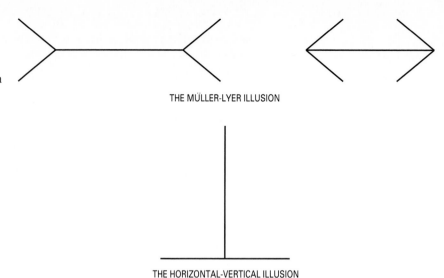

THE MÜLLER-LYER ILLUSION

THE HORIZONTAL-VERTICAL ILLUSION

that because the vertical line in the horizontal-vertical illusion might signal depth, that is, a line receding in space, the illusion of the vertical line as longer should be greater among people living in open plains or deserts who regularly experience such cues to distance than among people residing in heavily wooded tropical forests. In fact, their results conformed to these predictions.

Other research has challenged the "carpentered-world" hypothesis. Nevertheless, children and adults in cultures who receive minimal formal education, have little experience with pictures, or whose artworks incorporate few depth cues are unlikely to perceive pictures or photos in three dimensions (Pick, 1987). Thus, the ways in which children and adults interpret their sensory environment can be greatly affected by cultural opportunities, a finding that fits well with the conclusion that perception is influenced by experience.

THEMES IN DEVELOPMENT

LEARNING AND PERCEPTION

▶ **What roles do nature and nurture play in learning and perceptual development?**

When we review the enormous advances in learning and perceptual development made by infants and children, we can only be impressed by the remarkably adaptive resources immediately available to them for gaining knowledge of their environment. The basic mechanisms of learning—habituation, classical and operant conditioning, perhaps even imitation—are found ready to influence development at or shortly after birth. Although newborns' sense organs and brain still undergo many changes, they are sufficiently developed to provide rudimentary capacities to see, hear, feel, taste, and smell. Thus, babies are biologically ready to begin to perceive the world, and their behavior is readily influenced by the familiar and the novel that enter into their experience. We have also seen, though, that sensory and perceptual capacities improve substantially as a result of further maturation and the fine-tuning of receptors to the rich variety of experiences available to them. Through such mechanisms, the environment begins to have an early and powerful role in determining what behaviors are acquired and maintained.

▶ How does the sociocultural context influence learning and perceptual development?

Occasions provided by the culture—the behaviors that are reinforced and punished and the opportunity to observe others engaged in work, play, and social interactions—have substantial effects on what is learned. Although formal instruction and education may be provided to assist learning in some societies, in all cultures the actions of caregivers and models provide plentiful opportunities for children to gain knowledge of what is socially accepted and expected within a community. Specific cultural demands, such as discriminating the printed word, and culturally related physical layouts, such as "carpentered environments," may also have considerable bearing on perceptual development.

▶ How does the child play an active role in learning and perceptual development?

While mechanisms of learning do not emphasize an active role for the child, what the child has learned certainly contributes to the kinds of interactions he or she will be exposed to and the kinds of opportunities for further learning that he or she will have. In this sense, the knowledge and skills that the child possesses actively contribute to further social interactions, learning, and development. With respect to perceptual development, Gibson's theory highlights the important role that the activity of the child, including visuomotor and other sensorimotor mechanisms, plays in perception and its development. Children construct perceptions of whole, multisensory arrays at an early age and their attention increasingly reflects deliberate and organized exploration of the environment.

▶ Are there sensitive periods in learning and perceptual development?

Sensitive periods with respect to learning are not known to exist. However, the perception of patterns and forms, of depth, perhaps even of the sounds of language, which begin in the first months of life, appear to be heavily dependent on experience. In the absence of some kinds of sights and sounds and perhaps other sorts of sensory stimulation, infants do not acquire or may lose certain perceptual capacities. Thus, there appear to be sensitive periods for some aspects of perceptual development.

▶ How do learning and perceptual development interact with development in other domains?

Learning plays a substantial role in almost every aspect of development as much of the rest of this book details. The child learns social skills, labels and acceptable ways to express thoughts and feelings, and numerous other behaviors, at least in part through the basic principles of learning. The child who has had the opportunity to learn about the alphabet, about having to sit quietly in the classroom, about when and when not to speak to an elder, or about behaviors effective in hunting, shepherding, domestic, or other activities can be expected, depending on her culture, to achieve social status, prestige, and other resources that will benefit other aspects of development. Moreover, through perceptual development, the child effectively recognizes the stimuli and events that are important for his world, an essential, adaptive aspect of virtually all other domains of an individual's development. The gains in perception observed throughout infancy and childhood are substantially influenced by physiological and neural advances. Rapidly improving intellectual and motor skills introduce demands for making new perceptual discriminations that, once mastered, as in the case of reading, lead to further cognitive, social, and other advances.

SUMMARY

Learning includes mechanisms that permit adaptation to the environment. Very young infants are capable of *classical* and *operant conditioning, habituation* and *recovery from habituation,* and possibly *imitation* as well. Thus, babies are equipped to adapt to their environment and to learn from it. Observational learning plays a major role in the socialization of infants and children as well as in their acquisition of knowledge. Caregivers and tutors often provide a *scaffold* to assist learning, permitting children to make progress in the acquisition of a wide range of skills in a social context. For Vygotsky, social interactions taking place in the *zone of proximal development* provide maximal opportunities for children to acquire the knowledge and skills important to society.

Although at one time it was assumed that newborns' sensory receptors did not yet function, today we know that every sense is operative at birth, and in some cases even before birth. This conclusion has emerged from studies of the numerous discriminative responses displayed by young infants. Specific responses observed include preferential behaviors to certain kinds of stimuli, habituation of responses to familiar stimuli and recovery to novel ones, and learning to respond to various kinds of stimuli.

Newborns have the capacity both to look for and see visual events. Whereas the lens of the newborn's eye is initially relatively inflexible, within a few months it readily *accommodates* to the varying distances of objects to permit seeing them in focus. Newborns also display *saccadic* eye movements, which in a matter of weeks become more rapid and accurate in the exploration and search for stimuli in the visual field. Infants' ability to perform *smooth visual pursuit,* the consistent, unbroken tracking that serves to maintain focus on a moving visual target, is limited but improves over the first eight months as well. *Vergence,* the capacity to focus both eyes on an object, reaches a mature level even sooner.

Visual acuity, the ability to make fine discriminations, is limited, but newborns can detect contour, and their ability to see edges and transitions in surfaces under varying intensities of light is nearly adultlike by six months of age. Color vision and *stereopsis,* the capacity to perceive depth through the fusion of the separate images to the two eyes, emerge within the first few months of life and, in fact, may be present even earlier. Other cues to depth, such as *kinetic cues* based on self-induced movement or movement in the environment are available to young infants as well. Sensitivity to many two-dimensional cues in pictures begins to be evident around five to seven months of age, at least among children in the United States.

Newborns do not examine patterns of stimuli systematically and are often attracted to larger external features or patterns showing high contrast or movement. By two to three months of age, however, infants perceive more detailed patterns and begin to prefer looking at such things as the human face. Kinetic cues are important for the detection of the unity and coherence of objects and signal movement arising from another person.

Newborns have the basic ability to detect sounds and their location, although this ability shows substantial improvement over the first few months. In fact, auditory sensitivities continue to improve throughout childhood. Auditory pattern perception is present beginning about three months of age, and infants this young prefer patterns that conform to acceptable phrasing in musical passages. Moreover, infants are able to discriminate most, if not all, the phonemes used in different languages around the world, a capacity that will become limited by the end of the first year as a result of exposure to only a subset of the sounds used in the language(s) the baby hears. This phenomenon, along with *categorical perception* of speech sounds, has given rise to theoretical debates about whether speech perception is performed by special acoustic mechanisms or by more general auditory capacities.

Newborns can distinguish among basic tastes and can distinguish pleasant and unpleasant smells. They agree with adults' judgments of the pleasantness of odors and very quickly recognize the smell of their caregiver. Babies also respond to a variety of tactual stimuli and readily demonstrate intermodal perception. This latter capacity has raised numerous questions about whether the senses are differentiated at birth and whether knowledge that objects provide multiple sensory cues is learned or constructed as a result of experience. Although visual cues seem to dominate perception in young children and adults, auditory cues seem to be most important for infants.

Research on perceptual development in children, as opposed to infants, has been infrequent and most concerned with changes in *attention*. Children's attention becomes more focused, organized, and confined to the meaningful and important features of the environment—in other words, increasingly efficient and less easily distracted—as they have opportunities to learn about the invariant and critical features of the environment. Children perceive both the parts and whole of stimuli. Opportunity to perceive patterns, depth, and the auditory sounds important in language early in development helps maintain those perceptual distinctions that have a biological base. Perceptual learning may lead to differences among children from various cultures in their attention to their environment.

7
Language

It is hard to believe just how quickly and easily infants and children master the range of complex verbal and nonverbal skills that make up human communication. Just consider the sophisticated efforts of an infant named Carlotta, after less than a year of life, to gain an adult's attention:

At [10 months, 18 days], we observed the first instance in which Carlotta extends her arm forward to show an object to the adult. She is playing with a toy already in her hand; suddenly, she looks toward the observer and extends her arm forward holding the toy. In the next 2–3 weeks, this behavior increases and stabilizes until we observe Carlotta looking around for objects not already in her grasp, and immediately presenting them while awaiting adult response. (Bates, Camaioni, & Volterra, 1975, p. 216)

Carlotta's gesture, as documented by Elizabeth Bates and her coresearchers, seems to be sending the nonverbal message "Here, look at this!"

A few months later, as Carlotta sits outside the kitchen, she looks at her mother, says, "Ha," and looks toward the kitchen. After her mother carries her in, Carlotta points to the sink. Her mother gives her a drink of water. On two separate occasions this infant has been able to make her communications perfectly clear to observers.

Consider next the following statement, made by a five-year-old boy: "Daddy, look how your pants are sulking!" (Chukovsky, 1963). By about four years later, most children have moved from Carlotta's effective but rudimentary mix of verbal and nonverbal messages to the complex achievements reflected in this sentence. They have mastered the bewildering variety of sounds in their native language to produce recognizable words, and they understand the meanings of words reasonably well. Even though in this case the boy may not yet possess the vocabulary to describe sagging pants accurately, he can still state the words in correct order so that his meaning is clear. And if he spares his father embarrassment by whispering his message so that other people cannot hear, this child has shown himself to be aware of the interactive and sociocultural rules of human communication.

By the age of five, in fact, most children have become highly proficient listeners and speakers, a marvel indeed when we consider the plethora of sounds, vocabulary words, grammatical rules, and social conventions that go into producing mature, adult-sounding speech. Even though you may not have a vivid memory of the way in which you learned to speak—most of us, in fact, have little specific recall of this extremely complex yet somehow entirely "natural" process—you probably have some sense of how remarkable children's mastery of communication is if you have ever tried to learn a foreign language. How do infants and children manage such a seemingly overwhelming task?

In this chapter we will first examine the major milestones in the acquisition of communication and language skills from infancy through childhood: what is the sequence of events that occurs as the child comes to comprehend and produce language, the core of communication? Next, we will look at the most important theories of language development. What factors account for the observable regularities in how children acquire language? Here we may note that, of all the themes of development, none has been more central to theories of language development than the nature versus nurture debate—the extent to which either biological predispositions or environmental influences dictate the child's developing linguistic competence. Finally, we will briefly examine the functions of language, particularly as they interact with children's growing cognitive skills and ability to regulate their own behavior.

THE COURSE OF LANGUAGE ACQUISITION

A baby's contact with language is—initially, at least—noticeably one sided. Although she may gurgle or coo, most of her experience takes place as a listener. Among her first tasks in this role will be learning to identify the myriad sounds that make up her native language. That is, she must distinguish specific sounds in the stream of spoken language, note the regularities in how they are combined, and eventually—when she makes the transition from listener to speaker—form the consonant-vowel combinations that are the building blocks of words and sentences. The fundamental sound units and the rules for combining them in a given language make up that language's **phonology.** If you have studied a foreign language, you will recognize that some sounds appear only in certain languages, such as the prolonged nasal *n* sound in Spanish or the French vowel that is spoken as if *e* and *u* are combined. Each language, furthermore, has its own rules for combining sounds. In English, for example, the *sr* combination does not occur, whereas *sl* and *st* appear frequently. Even at this basic level of phonology, the child has an enormous amount of information to absorb about those sounds and combinations of sounds that are acceptable to make in her native language.

Another basic language skill the child must master is that of linking the combinations of sounds she hears to the objects, people, events, or relationships they label. The *meaning* of words or combinations of words is called **semantics.** *Cookie* is an arbitrary grouping of sounds, but it is used by speakers of English to refer to a specific class of objects. The child thus attaches words to conceptual groups, learning when it is appropriate to use them and when it is

phonology Fundamental sound units and combinations of units in a given language.

semantics Meanings of words or combinations of words.

not (for example, *cookie* does not refer to all objects or edible goods found in the bakery shop). Not only does the child learn the labels for objects, he also learns that some words describe actions (*eat*), whereas others describe relations (*under* or *over*) or modify objects (*tasty* cookie). Mapping combinations of sounds to their referents (that is, the things words refer to) is a major task in the acquisition of language.

As the child begins combining words, she learns the principles of **syntax,** or the grammatical rules that dictate how words can be combined. The order in which words are spoken conveys meaning—"Eat kitty" and "Kitty eat" do not mean the same thing, even in the simplified language of the young child. A word's position in a sentence can signify whether it is an agent or the object of an action, for example. The rules of syntax vary widely from one language to another, but within a given language they operate with consistency and regularity. One of the most remarkable features of language acquisition is the child's ability to detect that regularity of syntax and use it to create meaningful utterances of her own.

▶ **Interaction among domains**

The process of acquiring language also includes learning **pragmatics,** the rules for employing language effectively and appropriately according to social conventions. The effective use of language includes a host of nonverbal behaviors, rules of etiquette, and even a change in the content of speech depending on the identity of the listener and the context of the communication. How do you ask someone for a favor? Not, the child soon learns, by saying, "Hey, you—get me that ball"! The pragmatic element missing in this situation is courtesy. If someone doesn't hear what you've said, the child also learns that adding a gesture can sometimes complete the communication. And the way you speak to an adult with some authority will probably include more polite forms and fewer terms of familiarity than the way you speak to a peer. At the same time as they are acquiring language itself, then, children are also engaged in absorbing the equally important sociocultural dimension of pragmatics.

We can see that language is a multifaceted skill with many overlapping dimensions, from understanding and uttering sounds to appreciating the sometimes subtle rules of social communication. Despite the complexities involved in this learning process, however, most children speak much like adults by the time they are four or five years old. Their progress in mastering vocabulary, syntax, and pragmatics continues during the school years and thereafter, but one of the most impressive aspects of language development in children is that the essential elements of learning the language system occur in a relatively brief period of time.

From Sound to Meaning: Phonological and Other Prelinguistic Skills

syntax Grammatical rules that dictate how words can be combined.

pragmatics Rules for using language effectively within a social context.

What does it take to learn a language? The very first step the infant makes consists both of attending to the sounds of speech as a special type of auditory stimulation and also of deciphering phonology, the units of sound that occur in a given language. Thus, during much of the infant's first year the emphasis is on phonological development, both in receiving messages from others and in being able to produce them on his own.

Early Responses to Human Speech   Right from birth, the human infant has a special sensitivity to the sounds made by other human beings. Newborns show a distinct preference for human voices over other sounds and like to hear their own mothers' voices more than a stranger's (DeCasper & Fifer, 1980; Gibson & Spelke, 1983). Of most significance, though, is the fact that infants respond in specific ways to certain qualities of human speech.

Speech signals vary in several ways. First, the actual sounds heard by the listener vary acoustically. As you learned in Chapter 6, the basic building blocks of spoken language are called **phonemes**—the smallest units of sound that change the meanings of words or parts of words. In the words *pat* and *bat,* for example, the phonemes /p/ and /b/ make a big difference in the meaning of the word. You have already seen that infants as young as one month of age can discriminate among different phonemes and that they do so *categorically,* ignoring small acoustic variations in a sound unless the sound pattern crosses a phonemic "boundary" (Aslin, Pisoni, & Jusczyk, 1983; Kuhl, 1987). The ability of infants to detect phonemes is relevant to their eventual ability to distinguish among words. As we also pointed out in Chapter 6, younger infants are actually more sensitive than older infants to differences in phonemes that occur across languages.

Spoken language also varies in its **prosodic features**—the patterns of intonation, stress, and rhythm that communicate meaning. One example of a prosodic feature is the patterns of intonation that distinguish questions from declarative statements. When you raise your voice at the end of a question, you are signaling a different communicative intent than when you let your voice fall at the end of a declarative sentence. Researchers have discovered that infants prefer the prosodic features associated with the high-pitched, exaggerated, musical speech, often called "baby talk," that mothers typically speak to their young children. Figure 7.1 illustrates some of the acoustical properties of mothers' speech to infants. In one study, Anne Fernald (1985) trained four-month-old infants to turn their heads to activate a loudspeaker positioned on either side of them. Infants were more likely to make this response if their "reward" was a female stranger's voice speaking as she would to a baby than if it was normal adult speech. In a subsequent study, researchers found that it was the high pitch of the "baby talk" that was preferred as opposed to the loudness or rhythm of that speech (Fernald & Kuhl, 1987).

Besides possessing the ability to discriminate extremely subtle differences in speech sounds, infants are also able to detect larger differences, such as variations in the language being spoken. For example, researchers reported that four-day-old French infants could distinguish their native language from another language, Russian. After they displayed habituation of their sucking response in the presence of one language, the infants showed dishabituation in the presence of the new language. They also preferred their native language. These infants, however, could not detect the difference between two unfamiliar languages (Mehler et al., 1988).

In summary, then, infants show an amazing ability to respond to some important elements of human speech. Their ability to discriminate among phonemes, their sensitivity to the prosodic features of speech, and their ability to detect differences in languages are fundamental skills that prepare the path for even more sophisticated language achievements to come. Many of these early abilities, such as the initial capacity to distinguish phonemes in many

phoneme   Smallest unit of sound that changes the meanings of words.

prosody   Patterns of intonation, stress, and rhythm that communicate meaning in speech.

FIGURE 7.1

The Acoustical Properties of Maternal Speech to Infants

These two samples of maternal speech show the special acoustical qualities that make speech to infants (bottom) distinct from speech to adults (top). The Y-axis represents fundamental frequency, a measure of auditory pitch. Note the frequent use of modulation of pitch and the predominant presence of high pitch in maternal speech to infants. Babies seem to be especially responsive to the qualities of this type of speech.

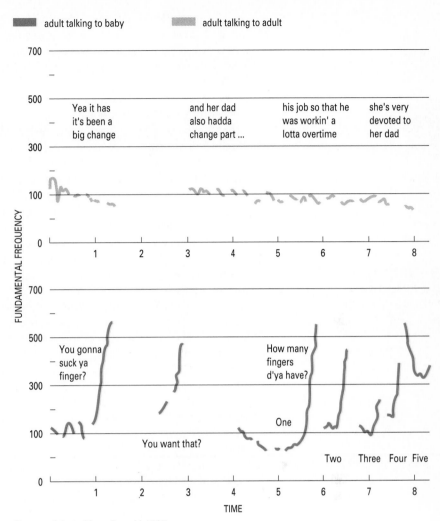

Source: Adapted from Fernald, 1985.

▶ **Roles of nature and nurture**

cooing Vowel-like utterances that characterize the infant's first attempts to vocalize.

languages and the preference for high-pitched speech, suggest that human language ability has biological underpinnings. At the same time, however, we can see the role of the environment in language acquisition. The young baby's ability to distinguish her own native language from others and her increasing difficulty in making phoneme discriminations from nonnative languages demonstrate that the specific language the child hears exerts a steady influence on her linguistic skills even in the first year of life.

Cooing and Babbling: Prelinguistic Speech Well before the child utters her first word, she produces sounds that, over the months, increasingly resemble the language spoken in her environment. At birth, the infant's vocal capabilities are limited to *crying* and a few other brief sounds such as grunts, sighs, or clicks. Between six and eight weeks, though, a new type of vocalization—**cooing**—emerges. These brief vowel-like utterances are sometimes accompanied by consonants, usually those produced in the back of the mouth, such as /g/ or /k/. Infants coo when they are in a comfortable state or when a parent has made some attempt to communicate, either with speech or "coos" of his own. In the weeks that follow, the infant's vocalizations become longer and begin to include consonants formed at the front of the mouth, as in /m/ or /b/.

The next significant accomplishment is the emergence of **babbling,** the production of consonant-vowel combinations such as *da* or *ba* through the purposeful maneuvering of the tongue. Most children begin to babble at about three to six months of age and refine their skills in the succeeding months. To many listeners, the infant's babbling appears to be an active experimentation with the production of different sounds. In the succeeding weeks, the infant will repeat syllables, such as *bababa* or *dadada*. This repetition of the same consonant-vowel pair is called **reduplicated babbling.** At age nine or ten months, the child's babbling includes more numerous and complex consonant-vowel combinations, as well as variations in intonation. In fact, a casual listener might think that the child is actually speaking, even though no real words are being produced yet.

▶ **Interaction among domains**

These changes in the child's productive capabilities are linked to physiological changes in the vocal apparatus and the central nervous system that occur during the first year. In the months following birth, the infant's larynx descends further into the neck, the oral cavity grows, and the tongue can be placed in different positions in the mouth (not just forward and back as at birth). In addition, the infant develops a greater sensitivity to sensations of touch, pressure, and movement in the mouth. At the same time, the cortex of the brain replaces the brain stem in controlling many of the child's behaviors. In general, early reflexlike vocalizations, such as cries, fade as more controlled, voluntary utterances, such as coos and babbles, enter the child's repertoire (Stark, 1986).

▶ **Roles of nature and nurture**

An important question raised by some language researchers is the extent to which infants' prelinguistic utterances are influenced by the language they hear spoken in their environment. Until the 1980s, the *independence hypothesis* was popular. Proponents of this position believed that infant babbling is predominantly under the control of biological maturation and is influenced very little by the native language (Lenneberg, 1967). According to this view, infants from different cultures should evidence the same patterns and sounds of babbling, with only random variations among individuals. Another implication of this hypothesis is that a discontinuity exists between the babbling stage and first words. In other words, there is not necessarily a close relationship between the varied sounds made in babbling and the child's eventual production of real words.

▶ **Development as continuous/ stagelike**

The proponents of an alternative viewpoint, the *interactional hypothesis,* assume that the language the infant hears in his surroundings influences the nature of his vocalizations, even those that precede intelligible words. Furthermore, the transition from babbling to first words is seen as a continuous process, with the child's language environment exerting a steady influence on the nature of his emerging language capabilities.

babbling   Consonant-vowel utterances that characterize the infant's first attempts to vocalize.

reduplicated babbling   Repetition of simple consonant-vowel combinations in the early stages of language development.

Are there universals or variations in children's babbling across different language environments? Several studies have demonstrated that adult listeners are unable to distinguish the vocalizations made by infants exposed to different language environments, such as American English, Chinese, or Spanish

(Oller & Eilers, 1982; Olney & Scholnick, 1976). Yet other more recent studies have detected distinct differences in babbling among infants from varying cultures. For example, a group of researchers asked French-speaking adults if they could discern the babbling of a French infant from that of an Arabic and a Chinese child without knowing which speech sample came from which child. Listeners were able to identify the French infant from its vocalizations, provided that the speech segments were long and contained extended intonation patterns (Boysson-Bardies, Sagart, & Durand, 1984). In a more recent study, this same group of researchers conducted a *spectral analysis* of the vowel sounds made by ten-month-old babies in Paris, London, Algiers, and Hong Kong. The procedure involved translating the acoustic properties of speech into a visual representation depicting the intensity, onset, and pattern of vocalization. Infants from different cultural backgrounds varied in the average frequencies of the sounds they produced, with the differences paralleling those of adult speakers from the same cultures (Boysson-Bardies, Halle, Sagart, & Durand, 1989). This research group concluded that the child's linguistic environment has a distinct impact on his own speech before true words are spoken.

A second way to assess the role of experience in the development of babbling is to compare the preverbal utterances and other language-related behaviors of deaf children with those of hearing children. If exposure to spoken language is a critical element in the development of babbling, deaf children should show different patterns of linguistic production than hearing children. For many years, psychologists thought that there were strong resemblances between the vocal babbling of deaf and hearing infants (Appleton, Clifton, & Goldberg, 1975; Fry, 1966). Moreover, a recent study of two deaf infants exposed to sign language showed that they made repetitive, rhythmic hand gestures akin to babbling at ten months of age (Petitto & Marentette, 1991). Such findings support a maturational explanation of babbling. Another study of nine deaf infants, however, showed that none of these children had reached the stage of vocal reduplicated babbling by ten months of age, whereas all twenty-one of the hearing subjects produced well-formed syllables by this time (Oller & Eilers, 1988). Evidently, exposure to spoken language plays a significant role, at least in the production of speech sounds.

The fact that most infants, regardless of their culture, begin to coo and babble at similar ages suggests that biological factors direct the onset of these behaviors. In addition, the child's brain and vocal apparatus must mature physiologically so that she can voluntarily produce the sounds that are the precursors of speech. "Nature" thus plays a distinct role in the emergence of the child's utterances. But even at this early stage of language development, the form of the child's vocalizations is influenced by her language environment. And, as the case of spoken speech among deaf infants suggests, the biological blueprint of language emergence can be altered when children are not able to process spoken language.

Gesture as a Communication Tool   Late in the first year, before or at the same time that they speak their first words, many children begin to use gestures such as pointing, showing, or giving as a means of communicating with other persons. As we saw at the beginning of the chapter, Carlotta, the infant that Bates and her colleagues observed, was able to display several kinds of

Beginning at about one year of age, many young children begin to use gestures to communicate with others, a sign that they are making progress in putting into practice the various facets of language.

nonverbal communication (Bates, Camaioni, & Volterra, 1975). When Carlotta held up her toy, this kind of "showing" was a **protodeclarative** communication that, much like a declarative sentence, functioned to make a statement that would call the adult's attention to the object. When she pointed to the kitchen sink, Carlotta used a **protoimperative** communication intended to get the adult to perform an action (Bates, 1979).

Often (as was the case when Carlotta wanted her drink of water), children's gestures are accompanied by direct eye contact with the communication's recipient. They may also repeat their communications if the message is not understood. This constellation of behaviors and the context in which they occur suggest that children use gestures as a purposeful means to an end (Scoville, 1983).

Young children also use gestures symbolically—to represent objects, events, and needs. Linda Acredolo and Susan Goodwyn (1988) found that when a child is between eleven and twenty-four months of age, a nonverbal symbolic system commonly develops alongside the child's verbal skills. The child may designate a flower, for example, by making a "sniffing" gesture or the desire to go outside by a knob-turning motion. A significant number of children's gestures recreate the function of objects, rather than their form or shape. For example, subjects would put their fist to the ear to signify a "telephone" or wave their hands to signify a "butterfly." Acredolo and Goodwyn (1988) believe in a strong relationship between the development of gestures and verbal abilities since both appear at approximately the same time in development and are often used together in communication. Gestures eventually drop out by the middle of the second year, however, because they are less useful when the "listener" is out of view and they are usually correctly understood by a limited number of adults in the child's environment. Parents also probably tend to encourage the child's verbalizations more than they do the use of gestures (Acredolo & Goodwyn, 1990a).

protodeclarative communication
Use of a gesture to call attention to an object or event.

protoimperative communication
Use of a gesture to issue a command or request.

▶ **Interaction among domains**

Gesturing to communicate is a significant accomplishment for the young child. When he signals for the door to open or indicates a flower, he understands that an action or object can be symbolized by turning his wrist or sniffing with his nose. Realizing first of all that one thing can symbolize or stand for another represents a major cognitive advance and is essential to the use of spoken language. Moreover, when the child makes a protodeclarative or protoimperative gesture, he understands that symbols can be used to communicate with other people, another major ingredient in the process of language acquisition. The child's gestures are not merely cute or amusing behaviors but indicators that he is making progress in understanding and putting into practice the various facets of the communication tool we call language.

Content: The Acquisition of Semantics

Few moments in life rival the excitement parents feel when they hear their daughter or son say her or his first words, typically at about one year of age. "Cookie," "Mama," and "Dada" are joyfully entered into the baby book alongside other momentous events, such as the infant's first steps. Certainly, the uttering of first words is a major accomplishment, marking the visible entry of the child into the world of spoken, shared communication with her social partners. The child's comprehension and production of words also signals a new focus in her mastery of language—semantic development. Although she continues to refine her understanding of phonology, the major task confronting her now is unraveling the meanings of words.

The One-Word Stage From about twelve to twenty months of age, most children speak only one word at a time. Children's first words are most frequently **nominals,** labels for objects, people, or events, although action words (*give*), modifiers (*dirty*), and personal-social words (*please*) also occur (Nelson, 1973). Children's early words usually refer to people or objects important in their lives, such as parents and other relatives, pets, or familiar objects. Children are also more likely to have labels for dynamic objects (*clock, car, ball*) or those they can use (*cup, cookie*) than for items that are stationary (*wall, window*). Figure 7.2 shows how the proportion of word types changes in the vocabularies of children in the one-word stage.

Many of the child's first words are bound to a specific context: that is, he or she uses the word to label objects in very limited situations. Lois Bloom (1973) observed that one nine-month-old infant used the word *car* only when she was looking out the living room window at cars moving on the street. She did not say *car* to parked cars, pictures of cars, or cars she was sitting in. Similarly, Martyn Barrett (1986) noted that one of his subjects began to use the word *duck* only when he was knocking a toy duck off the edge of the bathtub. Over time, the child begins to use single words more flexibly in a wider variety of contexts. He will say *duck,* for example, when the toy duck is lying on the floor or when he is playing with it in a room other than the bathroom; later he will use the same word to label real ducks and not just toys (Barrett, 1986).

Children acquire their first ten words slowly; the typical child adds about one to three words to her repertoire each month (Barrett, 1989). From about age eighteen months onward, however, many children show a period of rapid

nominal Word that labels objects, people, or events; the first type of word most children produce.

FIGURE 7.2

Changes in the Proportion of Word Types in Children's Vocabularies

As children's vocabularies grow from only a few words to fifty words (the horizontal axis on this graph), the proportion of general nominals (*cat, dog*) increases dramatically. The proportion of other types of words children learn— such as specific nominals (*Mommy*), action words (*go*), modifiers (*pretty*), and personal-social words (*please*)—remains fairly stable or even declines slightly as their vocabulary increases.

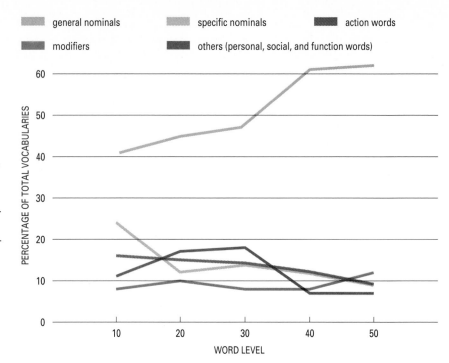

Source: Adapted from Nelson, 1973.

▶ **Sensitive periods**

vocabulary spurt Period of rapid word acquisition that typically occurs early in language development.

receptive language Ability to comprehend spoken speech.

productive language Meaningful language spoken or otherwise produced by the individual.

acquisition of new words. This critical period in language development is called the **vocabulary spurt** (Barrett, 1985; Bloom, 1973). In one recent longitudinal study of vocabulary growth in one- to two-year-old children, some children learned as many as twenty new words every week during the vocabulary spurt. Almost three quarters of the words they learned were nouns (Goldfield & Reznick, 1990). Figure 7.3 shows that rapid rate of vocabulary growth for three children in the middle of their "spurt." Besides learning new labels for objects and actions, children also begin to use words to express internal states (*yay!*) and to direct the actions of others (*go*) (Nelson, 1973).

Comprehension Versus Production   If you have ever tried learning a new language, you undoubtedly found that it was easier to understand what another speaker was saying than to produce a sentence in the new language yourself. An important point to remember about early child language is that the child's **receptive language,** what she comprehends, far exceeds her **productive language,** her ability to say and use the words herself. In one study, children were found capable of comprehending their first 50 words by the time they were thirteen months of age but incapable of producing 50 words until the age of nineteen months (Benedict, 1979). In another study, parents reported an average of 5.7 words produced by their ten-month-olds but a comprehension average about three times greater, 17.9 words (Bates, Bretherton, & Snyder, 1988).

The fact that young children understand so much of what is said to them means they have acquired some important knowledge about language before they actually speak. They know that people, objects, and events have names.

They know that specific patterns of sounds represent objects and events in their environment. Most important, they are beginning to appreciate the usefulness of language as a means of expressing ideas, needs, and feelings.

Individual Differences in Language Development Although children show many common general trends in the way they acquire language, they also show significant individual differences in rates and types of language production. You may have heard a family member or friend report that their child said virtually nothing for two or three years and then began speaking in complete sentences. Although such dramatic variations in language milestones are not frequent, children sometimes show unique patterns in their linguistic accomplishments, patterns that still lead to the attainment of normal language by later childhood.

One example of wide individual variation is the age at which children say their first word. Some children produce their first distinguishable word as early as nine months of age, whereas others may not do so until sixteen months of age (Barrett, 1989). Similarly, some children show good pronunciation, whereas others have difficulty making certain sounds, consistently substituting *t* for *k*, or *b* for *v*, for example (Smith, 1988). In addition, not all children display the vocabulary spurt, or they may start their spurts at different ages (Acredolo & Goodwyn, 1990b).

Children may also differ in the content of their one-word speech. Most of the one-year-olds in Katherine Nelson's (1973) study of early words tended to use predominantly nominals in their speech, displaying what this researcher

FIGURE 7.3

The Vocabulary Spurt in Three Young Children

Many children show a vocabulary spurt, a sharp rise in the number of new words they learn, as they approach two years of age. However, children may begin their spurts at different ages, as the graph clearly shows. Child A showed an early spurt, beginning at fifteen months. Child B's spurt began at the more typical age of eighteen months. Child C showed a late spurt at twenty-one months.

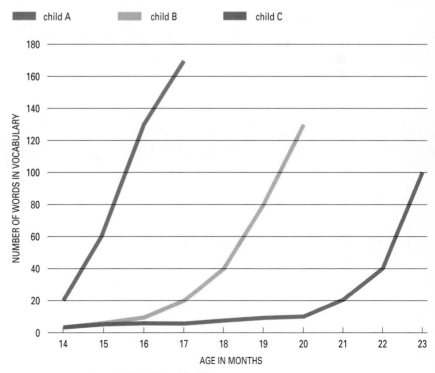

Source: Adapted from Goldfield & Reznick, 1990.

termed a **referential style.** Referential children tend to have mostly object labels in their vocabulary. Another group of children, however, showed a different pattern in their speech. Rather than naming objects, these children frequently used words that had social functions, such as *hello* or *please,* thus displaying an **expressive style.** Expressive children use words to direct the behavior of other people or to comment on them. Referential children, in contrast, tend to have larger vocabularies and show more rapid advances in language development, at least in the early stages (Bates, Bretherton, & Snyder, 1988; Nelson, 1973).

How can we explain these individual differences in the rates and styles in which children acquire language? There are several possible hypotheses. One is that individual differences might result either from differences in the neurological structures that control language or from inborn differences in temperament (for example, expressive children may be more sociable in temperament). Another possibility is that parents may influence the rate and form of children's vocabulary development. Some parents, for example, may spend a great deal of time encouraging their infants to speak, and they may focus especially on labeling objects. Others may be more relaxed about letting the infant proceed at her own pace. A recent study in which several infants and their parents were observed in the period from fourteen to twenty-six months of age confirmed that the overall amount of parental speech at sixteen months was related to the acceleration of vocabulary growth in infants (Huttenlocher et al., 1991).

Deriving the Meanings of Words   The number of new words the child learns grows rapidly from the age of eighteen months through the preschool years. According to one estimate, children learn more than fourteen thousand new words by the time they enter school (Carey, 1978). How can we explain this remarkable feat? There are several hypotheses about how children learn the meanings of words.

Some researchers believe that the child acquires word meanings by a process called **fast-mapping,** in which the context in which the child hears words spoken provides the key to their meaning. Often the child's initial comprehension of a word is an incomplete "guess," but a fuller understanding of its meaning follows from successive encounters with it in other contexts (Carey, 1978). Suppose the child hears his mother say, "This room looks *messy!*" in the midst of the youngster's toy-strewn bedroom. He might surmise that the word *messy* refers to some characteristic of the room that has to do with the toys being out of the toybox. At another time, he might hear his father say, "You look *messy,*" as the child climbs out of the sandbox. Noticing his dirty T-shirt and sneakers and drawing on his previous interpretation of the word, he concludes that *messy* refers to a state of disarray. Children are often able to derive the meanings of words very quickly, even when the exposure is brief, if the context in which new words are heard is meaningful (Rice & Woodsmall, 1988).

Certain elements in early parent-child interactions also provide children with clues to the meanings of words. For example, parents of infants tend to label many objects, often in the context of joint book reading or the child's manifest interest in a particular object or person in her surroundings (Ninio & Bruner, 1978). A typical scenario goes like this: The infant turns her head, points, and maybe even coos as the family dog enters the room. The mother

▶ **Roles of nature and nurture**

referential style   Type of early language production in which the child uses mostly nominals.

expressive style   Type of early language production in which children use many social words.

fast-mapping   Deriving meanings of words from the context in which they are spoken.

turns and looks, too, saying, "Doggy." Such interactions, in which the parent follows the child's attention and labels the target of her interest, are common between nine and eighteen months of age.

One researcher found that parental labeling of objects that children *point to* has special significance. Parents tend to label many objects for children, including those he reaches for or shows to the parent. But the child's vocabulary development is related most strongly to the tendency of parents to label objects the child actually points to (Masur, 1982). Besides providing information on how children learn the names of objects, this study illustrates one of the basic themes of development—the child's active role in language acquisition. In this case, the child's own actions, pointing, lead to the parental labels that foster his own linguistic development.

As the child begins speaking herself, parents continue to supply her with information about word meaning, often in the form of corrections when she makes a mistake. "That's not a glass; that's a cup," or "Your soup is not hot; it's cool" are examples of parental verbalizations that not only point out the child's error but provide the correct words. Children profit from these forms of **linguistic contrast** to learn new terms and labels (Au & Laframboise, 1990).

A number of developmental psychologists also believe that semantic development is intimately tied to the child's emerging conceptual skills. Eve Clark (1973) has proposed the **semantic feature hypothesis,** which suggests that the child's early concepts and the labels used to identify them are based on the child's perception of the shared features of objects. For example, the child's initial concept of *dog,* and hence the meaning of that word, might include all four-legged creatures with tails. Children frequently base their concepts on fewer features than adults do and consequently make mistakes in labeling objects, as in calling both a horse and a cow "dog," for example. This kind of error, the tendency to apply a label to a broader category than the term signifies, is known as **overextension.** Only when children have abstracted other features that distinguish horses and cows from dogs do their concepts become more adultlike, as do their names for objects.

An alternative position on semantic development called **functional theory,** described by Katherine Nelson (1973), holds that children's early concepts are based on the uses of objects. The concept *ball,* for example, is derived from all of the actions that can be performed on or with a ball, by the child himself and by others he has observed. Actions such as rolling, throwing, and bouncing might all be elements of his early understanding of *ball.* This hypothesis helps to explain the occurrence of **underextensions,** the error in which a label is applied to a narrower class of objects than the term signifies. A child, for example, might refer to her mother's automobile, and only her mother's, as *car,* since she has only had the opportunity to ride in this one vehicle. According to Nelson (1973), children's concepts often include personal and irrelevant components, but, with development, they come to include broader, more general features typical of adult categories.

A more recent hypothesis about semantic development is that young children tend to assume that new words label unfamiliar objects. Suppose the child sees an eggbeater and a fork on the kitchen table. Her father says, "Bring me the eggbeater." Even if the child did not previously know what an eggbeater is, she correctly picks that object because she assumes the new word does not

▶ **The child's active role**

▶ **Interaction among domains**

linguistic contrast   Correction of the child's incorrect utterance by pointing out both the error and the correct term.

semantic feature hypothesis Hypothesis that early concepts are based on the child's perception of the shared features of objects.

overextension   Tendency to apply a label to a broader category than the term actually signifies.

functional theory   Hypothesis that early concepts are based on the child's perception of the uses of objects.

underextension   Application of a label to a narrower class of objects than the term signifies.

The child's early concepts and the labels used to identify them may be based on her perception of the shared features of objects. The child's initial concept of *dog,* for example, might include all four-legged creatures with tails.

refer to the fork, an item she already knows the name of. This tendency of children to assume that unfamiliar words label new objects is called the **mutual exclusivity bias** (Markman, 1987, 1990). Researchers have been able to demonstrate experimentally that children tend to treat new words as labels for new objects rather than as synonyms for words they already know. Ellen Markman and Gwyn Wachtel (1988) showed three-year-old children pairs of objects with one familiar item and one unfamiliar item in each set (for example, banana and tongs). When children were asked to "Show me the *x*," where *x* was a nonsense syllable, they tended to select the unfamiliar objects. The mutual exclusivity bias emerges at around age three years and continues to play a role in the way in which older children and adults attach meaning to new words (Merriman & Bowman, 1989).

Which explanation of semantic development is most satisfactory? There is no reason to believe that just one process accounts for children's acquisition of the meanings of words. Parents undoubtedly help when they label objects for the child or correct his verbal errors. The child also plays an active role by using context and the mutual exclusivity assumption to "figure out" the meanings of words. At the same time, the child's growing understanding of concepts—because of shared perceptual features or functions—also contributes to his increased ability to attach meanings to new words.

▶ **The child's active role**

▶ **Interaction among domains**

Form: The Acquisition of Syntax

At just about the time of the child's second birthday, another significant achievement in language production appears—the child becomes able to produce more than one word at a time to express ideas, needs, and desires. At first, two-word utterances, such as "Doggie go" and "More juice," prevail; but it does not take long for the child to combine greater numbers of words in forms that loosely resemble the grammatical structure of the native language.

mutual exclusivity bias Tendency for children to assume that unfamiliar words label new objects.

What is the significance of the child's production of more than one word at a time? For one thing, in combining words, the child is displaying an awareness of the different syntactic categories words fall into. "Doggie go" illustrates the child's understanding of nouns and verbs as distinct classes of words. Moreover, when children combine words, they are stating more than just labels for familiar items; they are expressing relations among objects and events in the world. All this represents no small feat for a two-year-old child.

An important tool used to assess the complexity of the child's early speech is the **mean length utterance,** or MLU. This technique, developed by Roger Brown (1973), involves taking a fairly lengthy sample of a child's speech (usually a hundred verbalizations) and computing the average number of morphemes per utterance. A **morpheme** is the smallest unit of meaning in speech (in contrast to the phoneme, which is the basic unit of sound in speech). The verbalization "Doggie walk" contains two morphemes; "Doggie walked," in contrast, contains three, since the addition of *-ed* changes the meaning of the statement. Because children of a given age may differ dramatically in the MLUs they produce, language researchers often prefer to use the MLU as an index of linguistic skill. Even though there may be individual differences in the rate of growth of MLUs, the child's utterances generally expand in length very rapidly between one and a half and four years of age.

Early Grammars: The Two-Word Stage   At first, children's two-word utterances consist of combinations of nouns, verbs, and adjectives, without the conjunctions, prepositions, and other modifiers that give speech its familiar flow. Because speech at this stage often contains only the elements essential to getting the message across, it is often described as **telegraphic.**

Martin Braine (1976), in his systematic observations of the language of three children, noted that speech at this stage contained a unique syntactic structure, which he dubbed **pivot grammar.** The speech of the children he observed contained noticeable regularities: one word often functioned in a fixed position while other words filled in the empty "slot." For example, one child in this study said, "More car, more cookie, more juice, more read." In this string of utterances, *more* functions as a **pivot word,** an anchor for a variety of **open words.** The child's "grammar" could consist of [pivot word + open word] as in the example above, or [open word + pivot word], as in "Boots off, pants off, water off." Table 7.1 contains several other examples of one two-year-old's early word combinations.

Other linguists have described alternative child grammars, grammars that reflect the incorporation of semantic knowledge with the use of syntax. Roger Brown (1973) believes that the categories appearing in Table 7.2 capture the regularities of child speech in the two-word stage in ten different cultures. In children's verbalizations, agents consistently precede actions, as in "Mommy come" or "Daddy sit." At the same time, inanimate objects are usually not named as agents. The child rarely says, "Wall go." She must know the meaning of wall and the fact that walls do not move to avoid making this utterance. The child's semantic knowledge is thus related to the production of highly ordered two-word utterances.

Many experts currently believe that no one syntactic system defines the structure of early language for all children (Maratsos, 1983; Tager-Flusberg, 1985). Some children may speak using nouns, verbs, adjectives, and sometimes adverbs in the pivot grammar described by Braine, whereas others pep-

mean length utterance Average number of morphemes per utterance.

morpheme Smallest unit of meaning in speech.

telegraphic speech Early two-word speech that contains few modifiers, prepositions, or other connective words.

pivot grammar Early two-word grammar in which one word is repeated and a series of other words fills the second slot.

pivot word Repeated, or anchor, word in a pivot grammar.

open word Variable word that accompanies the pivot word in a pivot grammar.

TABLE 7.1

One Child's Pivot Grammar

This table shows several examples of one two-year-old's two-word speech. Frequently, one word—the pivot word—is repeated while several other words—open words—fill the other slot. The pivot word can occupy either the first or second position in the child's utterances.

no bed	boot off	more car	airplane all gone
no down	light off	more cereal	Calico all gone
no fix	pants off	more cookie	Calico all done
no home	shirt off	more fish	all done milk
no mama	shoe off	more high	all done now
no more	water off	more hot	all gone juice
no pee	off bib	more juice	all gone outside
no plug		more read	all gone pacifier
no water		more sing	salt all shut
no wet		more toast	
		more walk	
		outside more	

Source: Adapted from Braine, 1976.

per their speech with pronouns and other words such as *I, it,* and *here* (Bloom, Lightbown, & Hood, 1975). Most researchers agree, however, that individual children frequently use consistent word orders and that their understanding of at least a small set of semantic relationships is related to that word order.

Later Syntactic Development   At age two and a half years, children's speech often exceeds two words in length and includes many more of the modifiers and connective words that enrich the quality of speech. Adjectives, pronouns, and prepositions are added to the child's repertoire (Valian, 1986). Between the ages of three and five, the child's speech also includes more and more sophisticated grammatical structures. **Inflections**—endings to words (such as *-s, -ed,* and *-ing*) that signal plurals or verb tense—become incorporated in routine utterances, as do more articles and conjunctions. Gradually negatives, questions, and passives also come to be used correctly.

Ursula Bellugi (1967) found a predictable sequence in the child's use of negatives. Initially, children mark the negative at the beginning of an utterance, as in "No sit down" or "No Mommy do it." In the second stage, the negative occupies an internal place in the utterance, usually next to the main verb, as in "I no like it." Finally, children correctly place the negative as an adult would, as in "You can't have this." Peter and Jill de Villiers (1979) have provided additional details on the acquisition of negatives through a case study of their own son, Nicholas. Nicholas's first attempts to create a negative were not limited to markers at the beginning of a statement. On occasion, particularly when he was expressing denial, he would place the negative in an internal position ("My sweetie's no gone"). At the same time, expressions of rejection ("No you tuts dat") followed the ["no" + sentence] format described by Bellugi. Thus, even the earliest expressions of the negative suggest the child's sensitivity to different meanings he or she intends to communicate.

Questions, too, are formed in a fairly consistent developmental sequence,

inflection Alteration to a word, such as tense or plural form, that indicates its syntactical function.

although not all children necessarily display the pattern we are about to describe (Maratsos, 1983). Children's earliest questions do not contain inverted word order but consist instead of an affirmative sentence, or a declarative preceded by a *wh-* word (*who, what, why, when, where*), with a rising intonation at the end of the statement ("Mommy is tired?" "Where Mommy go?"). Subsequently, questions are formed by inverting word order for affirmative questions such as "Where will you go?" but not negative ones ("Why you can't do it?"). Finally, by age four, children form questions for both positive and negative instances as adults do (Klima & Bellugi, 1966).

One of the more difficult linguistic constructions for children to understand is the passive voice, as in "The car was hit by the truck." Though children typically begin to comprehend the meaning of a passive construction by the later preschool years, they may not use this grammatical form spontaneously and correctly until several years later. Generally, passive constructions that convey some action, such as "The boy was kissed by the girl," are understood before those without action, such as "John was liked by Mary" (Maratsos et al., 1979). In addition, it is easier to train children to use passive constructions when the object or person being acted upon in the sentence is animate ("The baby is being touched by the frog") as opposed to inanimate ("The drum is being touched by the frog") (Lempert, 1989). These findings suggest that action is a salient feature, not only as children learn their first words, but also as they acquire the rules of syntax.

What are the common patterns in children's acquisition of the complexities of syntax? In the case of negatives, questions, and passives, we have seen that children comprehend the adult's constructions well before they can correctly produce them on their own. In addition, children's own utterances of these sophisticated grammatical forms begin as imperfect versions that gradually approach the more adult forms. Thus, the child's progression to mature speech shows a distinct orderliness. Accounting for these consistencies in children's acquisition of syntax remains a major challenge for psychologists concerned with language development.

TABLE 7.2

Examples of Semantic Relations in Child Syntax

Children's word orders often reflect knowledge of semantic relationships, such as the idea that agents precede actions or that actions are followed by locations. Brown believes that the semantic relations shown in this table are incorporated in the syntactic constructions of children in many different cultures.

Semantic Relation	Examples
agent + action	Mommy come; Adam write
action + object	eat cookie; wash hand
agent + object	Mommy sock; Eve lunch
action + location	sit chair; go park
entity + location	lady home; baby highchair
possessor + possession	my teddy; Daddy chair
entity + attribute	block yellow; box shiny
demonstrative + entity	dat book; dis doggie

Source: Adapted from Brown, 1973

Context: The Acquisition of Pragmatics

▶ **Sociocultural influence**

Just as important as the semantic and syntactic rules and conventions governing the production of meaningful, correctly ordered speech are cultural requirements or customs pertaining to the proper use of speech in a social context. Is the child speaking with an elder or a peer? Is the context formal or informal? How does the speaker express politeness? Each of these situations suggests some unique characteristics of speech, a tone of voice, a formal or more casual syntactic structure, and the choice of specific words. In the context of play with one's closest friend, a "Gimme that" might be perfectly appropriate; when speaking with the first-grade teacher, saying "Could I please have that toy?" will probably produce a more favorable reaction. All these examples demonstrate the child's grasp of pragmatics.

Acquiring Social Conventions in Speech   When do children first realize that different situations call for different forms of speech? When Jean Gleason and Rivka Perlmann (1985) asked two- to five-year-old children and their parents to play "store," they observed that at age three some of the children modified their speech depending on the role they were playing. For example, one three-and-a-half-year-old boy who was the "customer" pointed to a pretend milk bottle and said, "I want . . . I would like milk." In his revision, he indicated an understanding that an element of politeness is required of a customer. Preschoolers also have some limited understanding that different listeners are appropriately spoken to in different ways. In a study in which four- and five-year-olds were asked to speak to dolls portraying adults, peers, or younger children, they were observed to use more imperatives with dolls representing children and fewer with dolls that were adults and peers (James, 1978).

The child's facility with social forms of politeness increases with age. Researchers in one study instructed two- to six-year-old children to *ask* or *tell* another person to give them a puzzle piece. Adults rated the politeness of children's verbal requests. Older children were rated as being more polite than the younger children, particularly when they were *asking* for the puzzle piece. Usually older children included words like *please* in their requests of another person (Bock & Hornsby, 1981).

Parents undoubtedly play a significant role in at least some aspects of the acquisition of pragmatics, especially because they deliberately train their children to speak politely. In another of Jean Gleason's studies (Greif & Gleason, 1980), she observed the reactions of parents and children after children had received a gift from a laboratory assistant. If the child did not say "Thank you" spontaneously (and most of the preschoolers in the sample did not), the parent typically prompted the child with "What do you say?" or "Say thank you." Parents also serve as models for politeness routines; most of the parents in this study greeted the laboratory assistant upon entry and said "Goodbye" when the assistant departed.

Incorporating social conventions into language use often involves learning subtle nuances in behaviors, the correct words, vocal intonations, gestures, or facial expressions that accompany speech in different contexts. Though children may get direct instruction on the use of forms of politeness, it is as yet unclear exactly how they acquire the other behaviors that accompany socially skilled communication.

FIGURE 7.4

An Experiment in Referential Communication

In Krauss and Glucksberg's (1969) study of referential communication, four- and five-year-old children had to describe a series of unfamiliar geometric forms (represented here as blocks) to other children who could not see them. In this illustration, for example, the speaker on the left must explain to the listener on the right which forms to place on the stacking peg. The results showed that children this age are generally ineffective in transmitting this type of information. Research in more naturalistic settings, however, demonstrates that preschoolers can engage in effective referential communication.

Source: Adapted from Krauss & Glucksberg, 1969.

▶ **Interaction among domains**

referential communication
Communication in situations that require the speaker to describe an object to a listener or to evaluate the effectiveness of a message.

Referential Communication A group of experiments that has been especially useful in providing information on children's awareness of themselves and others as effective communicators centers on **referential communication** tasks, situations that require the child either to talk about a topic specified by the experimenter or to evaluate the effectiveness of a message describing some sequence of events. Researchers note if the child's own message is sufficient to communicate its intent or, alternatively, if the child is able to detect ambiguous or uninformative components in the messages he hears.

A classic experiment in referential communication was conducted by Robert Krauss and Sam Glucksberg (1969), who asked four- and five-year-olds to describe a series of unfamiliar geometric forms to another child who could not see them (see Figure 7.4). The speaker had to provide enough information so that the listener could duplicate an array the speaker was constructing. The results showed that children at this age often rely on personal, self-based descriptions of the stimuli ("It looks like Daddy's shirt"), messages that are not particularly helpful to the listener. Thus, young children's ability to understand the requirements of the listener and to adjust their speech to meet those needs is limited when they are describing novel items.

Initially, children's poor performance in referential communication tasks conducted under highly controlled laboratory conditions was attributed to their cognitive *egocentrism*—that is, their inability to understand the perspectives of other individuals. Observations of children's natural interactions with one another, however, suggest that well before they enter school, children appreciate the requirements of the listener and can modify their speech in accordance with those requirements.

In a study of the communication skills of preschool-aged children, Marilyn Shatz and Rochel Gelman (1973) asked four-year-olds to describe a toy to

Observations of children's interactions with each other suggest that even at an early age children appreciate the requirements of the listener and can modify their speech in accordance with those requirements.

either an adult or a two-year-old listener. When children spoke to a younger child, they shortened their utterances, used simple constructions, repeated utterances, and employed more attention-getting devices than when they spoke to an adult. As we saw in Chapter 1, Wellman and Lempers (1977) also observed that even two-year-olds use techniques to make sure their message gets across during the normal interactions that occur in a nursery school. Children point, seek eye contact with listeners, and use verbal attention getters such as "Hey" to ensure that listeners hear what they have to say.

Older children—for example, those in the first or second grade—show the ability to detect problems in the messages of others and can even provide suggestions for revision. Carole Beal (1987) asked children to trace a route on a road map in accordance with a set of oral instructions that was read to them. Most children were able to identify uninformative instructions as such and to suggest revisions that would make the message clearer. The child's ability to evaluate the adequacy of a communication, called **comprehension monitoring**, appears to be stronger for written materials than for oral communications, however (Bonitatibus & Flavell, 1985). We will have more to say about children's ability to keep tabs on their own cognitive processes in the next chapter.

The mature use of language thus involves the ability to understand the demands of the communicative situation, to be sensitive to the needs of the listener, and to employ subtle nuances in speech compatible with the situation. The child's failure to acquire the social skills that are a part of effective communication can have broad consequences in the qualities of relationships he or she establishes with parents, teachers, and peers, among others. The child's mastery of pragmatics is an excellent example of how development in one

▶ **Interaction among domains**

domain—language—is related to development in another domain—social development.

Abstraction: The Acquisition of Metalinguistic Awareness

During the time of most rapid language learning—from about eighteen months through age five years—children may not have a full realization of what it means for a sentence to be "grammatical" or how to gauge their own linguistic competencies even when their speech is syntactically correct and effective in delivering a communication. The ability to reflect abstractly on the properties of language and to conceptualize the self as a more or less proficient user of this communication tool is called **metalinguistic awareness.** By most accounts, the child does not begin to think about language in this way until at least the early school years, although some early indicators of this emerging ability are evident before that time.

Reflecting on Properties of Language   One of the first studies to explore children's ideas of the function of grammar was conducted by Lila Gleitman and her colleagues (Gleitman, Gleitman, & Shipley, 1972). These investigators had mothers read grammatically correct and incorrect passages to their two-, five-, and eight-year-old children. After each sentence, an experimenter said either "good" following an acceptable passage, such as "Bring me the ball," or "silly" after an unacceptable one, such as "Box the open." When the children were given the opportunity to judge sentences themselves, even the youngest children were generally able to discriminate between correct and incorrect versions. They were not able, however, to correct improper constructions or to explain the nature of the syntactic problem until age five.

Not until the age of six or seven do most children appreciate that words are different from the concepts to which they are linked. Four-year-olds frequently believe that *train* is a long word, for example, because its referent is long (Berthoud-Papandropoulou, 1978). Similarly, preschoolers believe that the labels for objects can be changed—that is, a *dog* can arbitrarily be called a *cat,* but at the same time the animal will shift from barking to meowing (Osherson & Markman, 1975). Some of these changes in metalinguisitic understanding are undoubtedly linked to advances in cognition, particularly the development of more flexible and abstract thought.

▶ **Interaction among domains**

Humor and Metaphor   One visible way in which children demonstrate their metalinguistic awareness is through language play—creating funny words, telling jokes or riddles, or using words in a figurative sense. The way in which children comprehend and produce humorous verbalizations undergoes clear developmental changes from the preschool to later school years. Children who are three to five years of age frequently experiment with the sounds of words, altering phonemes to create humorous facsimiles (for example, *watermelon* becomes *fatermelon*) (McGhee, 1979). By the early school years, the basis for children's humor expands to include riddles or jokes based on semantic ambiguities, as in the following:

comprehension monitoring Ability to evaluate the adequacy of a communication.

metalinguistic awareness Ability to reflect on language as a communication tool and on the self as a user of language.

QUESTION: How can hunters in the woods find their lost dogs?
ANSWER: By putting their ears to a tree and listening to the bark.

Still later—as every parent who has ever had to listen to a seemingly endless string of riddles and jokes from a school-aged child can testify—children begin to understand and be fascinated by jokes and riddles that require them to discern syntactic ambiguities:

QUESTION: Where would you go to see a man-eating shark?
ANSWER: A seafood restaurant.
(Hirsch-Pasek, Gleitman, & Gleitman, 1978)

Thus, children's appreciation of humor mirrors their increasingly sophisticated knowledge about the various features of language, beginning with its fundamental sounds and culminating with the complexities of syntactic and semantic rules. It appears that each change in the orientation of children's humor comes after they have conquered a particular facet of language.

Similarly, children's understanding of **metaphor,** figurative language in which a term that typically describes one object or event is directly applied to another context (for example, calling a *shadow* a "piece of the night," or *skywriting* a "scar in the sky"), undergoes developmental change. Even preschoolers show a rudimentary comprehension of figurative language, especially when it refers to perceptual similarities between two objects. A four-year-old understands expressions such as "A string is like a snake," for example (Winner, 1979). In later childhood and adolescence, children understand and even prefer metaphors grounded in conceptual relationships, such as "The volcano is a very angry man" (Silberstein et al., 1982). An interesting phenomenon is the fact that even though metaphorical comprehension increases during the middle childhood years, the likelihood that the child will actually use figurative language decreases during this time (Pollio & Pickens, 1980). One hypothesis is that children believe that figurative language will not be accepted or approved of by adults.

The development of metalinguistic skills necessarily follows the acquisition of phonological, semantic, and syntactic knowledge. After all, to be able to reflect on and even "play" with the properties of language demands that one first possess a basic understanding of those properties. In addition, metalinguistic skill is probably tied to advances in thinking skills in general. Just how children move from concrete to abstract thinking and come to reflect on their thought processes are topics we will return to in the next chapter when we discuss the development of cognition.

▶ **Interaction among domains**

The Sequence of Language Acquisition: An Overview

The Chronology on page 295 provides a summary of the child's progression in attaining language. Two points about this sequence are especially noteworthy. First, language development proceeds in an orderly fashion, starting with the infant's ability to perceive and produce sounds and proceeding to the older child's metalinguistic awareness. Although there may be individual differences in the ages at which language milestones are acquired or in the precise form of the child's achievements, children do not acquire language in a haphazard fashion. Second, the child learns language very rapidly and with seemingly little effort. With the exception of those with some serious physical or psychological problem, all children learn to speak within only a few years in spite of the

metaphor Figurative language in which a term is transferred from the object it customarily designates to describe a comparable object or event.

CHRONOLOGY	Language Development
NEWBORN	Prefers human voices. Discriminates among phonemes. Discriminates own language from others. Cries.
1–4 MONTHS	Is sensitive to prosodic features of speech. Coos.
6 MONTHS	Babbles.
9–12 MONTHS	Engages in reduplicated babbling. Produces gestures to communicate and symbolize objects.
12–18 MONTHS	Produces single-word utterances. Comprehends 50 + words.
18–24 MONTHS	Displays a vocabulary spurt.
2 YEARS	Produces two-word utterances.
2½–5 YEARS	Produces three-word utterances. Uses inflections, negatives, questions, and passive voice. Shows growth in vocabulary and use of syntax. Appreciates humor and metaphor. Shows growth in referential communication skills and other aspects of pragmatics.
6 + YEARS	Displays metalinguistic awareness.

This chart describes the sequence of language development based on the findings of research. Children often show individual differences in the exact ages at which they display the various developmental achievements outlined here.

diverse range of skills this activity requires. How can we account for these outstanding achievements? This is the puzzle we will examine next.

HOW DO WE EXPLAIN LANGUAGE ACQUISITION?

generative language Unique and novel combinations of words and sentences that speakers produce without having heard them before.

Any comprehensive explanation of language acquisition must capture not only the extraordinary complexity and rapidity of children's accomplishments but also their ability to use language in a **generative** way. Most of what children say, in other words, consists not merely of duplication of what they have already heard but rather of novel, creative combinations of words to express unique thoughts.

Psychologists have proposed a number of hypotheses to account for specific aspects of language development, ranging from biological accounts to theories that emphasize the children's experiences in the environment. In this section we will examine five major theoretical perspectives on the development of language. Although each captures the essence of some dimensions of the child's changing linguistic attainments, no one position manages to provide a complete explanation for the emergence and refinement of language skills. Most contemporary theorists believe that children have strong biological predispositions to acquire language but that the nature of their experiences with language, along with their growing cognitive abilities, also plays a role in shaping children's developing linguistic competence.

The Behaviorist Perspective

▶ **Roles of nature and nurture**

One of the earliest attempts to explain language acquisition came from the behaviorists. Skinner (1957) and other behaviorists regarded language as a behavior like any other, whose appearance and development could be accounted for by the basic principles of learning. Reinforcement and imitation were the mechanisms that explained the child's acquisition of phonology, semantics, syntax, and pragmatic rules. According to this view, the child's role in this process is minimal; she is merely a passive recipient of what the environment supplies.

Behaviorists believed that productive language is initially shaped through the selective reinforcement of the child's earliest vocalizations. At first, utterances that even remotely resemble the child's native language are rewarded by caregivers with smiles, hugs, or an enthusiastic "Good!" whereas other random sounds are ignored or discouraged. Gradually, parents and others expect the child's verbalizations to conform more closely to the phonological and syntactic structure of their language before they will reward her. Later in infancy, the verbalization "Baba" may not receive the reinforcements it once did when the child signals for her bottle; only a more accurate pronunciation will.

Imitation also plays a significant role, according to the behaviorist perspective. As parents and other more experienced users of language label objects for the child and speak in syntactically correct sentences, they provide models of competent and mature language use for young language learners. Children do, after all, learn the phonology, syntax, and conversational rules of the culture they are born into; they must be influenced by the linguistic models in their environment.

Although reinforcement and imitation undoubtedly play a role in language development, it is difficult to account for many aspects of children's language use with behavior theory exclusively. For one thing, there is little evidence that parents systematically tutor their children in producing grammatically correct speech or that they differentially reinforce grammatically correct and incorrect sentences with any consistency. Instead, parents respond on the basis of the truth value of children's utterances, so that a grammatically flawed statement like "I no like spinach" might be followed by "Yes, I know" from the parent, whereas a perfectly constructed "I'm sleeping" would probably be met with "No, you're not" (Brown & Hanlon, 1970).

Imitation plays an important role in language acquisition; children learn the sounds, words, grammatical constructions, and gestures that accompany spoken language by observing those around them.

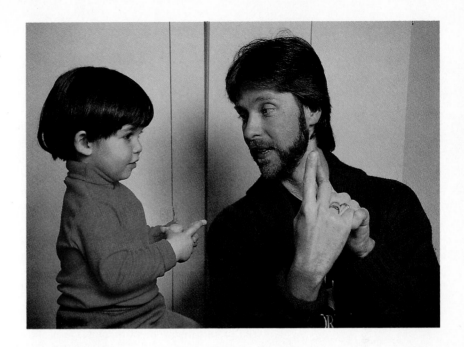

Parents, however, do sometimes provide *indirect* feedback about the correctness of child speech. Mothers (the parent whose speech to the child has been studied most) often follow the child's grammatically incorrect utterances with **expansions,** repetitions of the child's verbalization with some elaboration: when the child says, "Ball fall," his mother might reply, "Yes, the ball fell." Expansions provide the child with cues that his verbalization needs improvement along with a model for how to do this. On the other hand, parents frequently follow the child's grammatically correct utterances with extensions of the topic rather than expansion of the child's syntactic form. Extensions of the topic suggest to the child that her message was understood and, therefore, correctly expressed (Penner, 1987). Other researchers have noted that parents are more likely to repeat the child's well-formed sentence than a poorly formed sentence and more frequently ask for clarification after a poorly formed sentence than a well-formed one (Bohannon & Stanowicz, 1988; Demetras, Post, & Snow, 1986). Thus, although parents do not always directly reinforce the grammatical correctness of child speech, they occasionally do provide subtle messages regarding the child's use of syntactic rules.

▶ **The child's active role**

Another limitation of behavior theory in explaining language development is its inability to account for the occurrence of **overregularizations,** the application of grammatical rules to words that require exceptions to those rules. Preschoolers often say words such as "goed" or "runned" to express past tense, for example. The child is not likely to encounter models for these grammatical mistakes in her language environment. It is also unlikely that parents encourage children to generate these erroneous constructions. The phenomenon of overregularization suggests that children abstract the general rules for forming tenses, plurals, and other grammatical forms from the language they hear spoken around them and then overuse the rules. This tendency

expansion Adult's repetition and elaboration of the child's utterance.

overregularization Inappropriate application of syntactic rules to words and grammatical forms that show exceptions.

seems to represent an active application of rules rather than mere modeling of behavior.

Finally, one of the greatest limitations of the behaviorist perspective is the assumption that the child plays a passive role in acquiring language. We have already seen that even in the earliest stages of learning language, children actively experiment with the production of sounds regardless of the reactions of caregivers. They point to objects that their parents subsequently label for them and create two- or three-word utterances that others have never spoken to them. Indeed, the fact that so much of language acquisition is "child driven" lies behind the emergence of subsequent theories of language development.

The Biological Perspective

The human brain contains several areas associated with the understanding and production of language. As we saw in Chapter 5, the right and left hemispheres of the brain have specialized functions, a phenomenon called *lateralization.* The primary regions that control language processing in most persons are found in the left hemisphere. A major question arising from our knowledge of the brain's involvement in language is the extent to which the milestones of language acquisition are controlled by physiological maturation of brain structures and, more specifically, by lateralization.

The Brain and Language   Studies of adults who have suffered brain damage because of stroke, traumatic injury, or illness have pinpointed two specific regions in the left hemisphere that play a vital role in the ability to use language. The first is **Broca's area,** located in the left frontal region near the motor cortex (see Figure 7.5). Patients who have damage in this region evidence **expressive aphasia,** or the inability to speak fluently even though their comprehension abilities remain intact. The second region, **Wernicke's area,** is situated in the temporal region of the left hemisphere, close to the areas of the brain responsible for auditory processing. Damage to Wernicke's area results in **receptive aphasia,** in which speech seems fluent, at least on the surface, but contains nonsense or incomprehensible words; the ability to understand the spoken speech of others is also impaired.

An important finding is that children with lesions, or injuries, to the left side of the brain show language impairments more frequently than those whose lesions occur in the right side of the brain (Witelson, 1987). This is precisely the same pattern that adults with similar lesions show. Children, however, are more likely to recover language functions than are adults. Eric Lenneberg (1967) hypothesized that children are less vulnerable to aphasias only if brain damage occurs before puberty. Before the age of two years, he contended, children's brains are not lateralized, and each side thus has equal potential for controlling language; damage to one area may be overcome by another part of the brain "taking over" those functions. Lenneberg believed that lateralization proceeded slowly through childhood until adultlike characteristics emerged at puberty. Chief among these mature characteristics is a loss of *plasticity,* the ability of the brain to recover from damage.

Many clinical studies of children who suffered left hemisphere brain damage before the onset of speech show that the effects are less severe than when the

▶ **The child's active role**

▶ **Interaction among domains**

▶ **Sensitive periods**

Broca's area   Portion of the cerebral cortex that controls expressive language.

expressive aphasia   Loss of the ability to speak fluently.

FIGURE 7.5

The Two Portions of the Left Cortex of the Brain Responsible for Language Processing

Broca's area governs the production of speech, and Wernicke's area is responsible for the comprehension of speech. Damage to the former produces expressive aphasia, whereas damage to the latter leads to receptive aphasia.

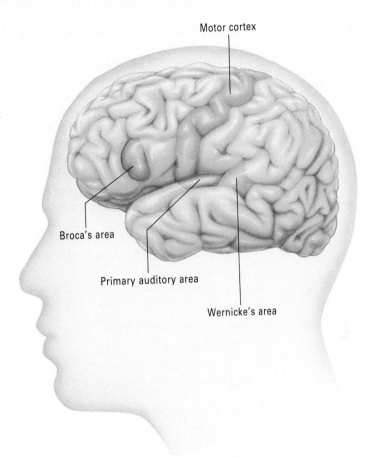

Motor cortex

Broca's area

Primary auditory area

Wernicke's area

▶ **Roles of nature and nurture**

Wernicke's area Portion of the cerebral cortex that controls language comprehension.

receptive aphasia Loss of the ability to comprehend the speech of others.

damage occurs after speech has already begun, although in most cases children still suffer less permanent effects than do adults (Annett, 1973; Basser, 1962). New evidence suggests, though, that children already show lateralization of the hemispheres by the first few months of life and do not become more "lateralized" with age (Best, Hoffman, & Glanville, 1982; Molfese & Molfese, 1979, 1980, 1985). For example, Dennis and Victoria Molfese (1980) found greater brain wave activity to speech stimuli in the left hemisphere compared with the right hemisphere in infants aged one week to ten months. Thus, greater plasticity of the human brain during childhood may be independent of the phenomenon of lateralization (Witelson, 1987).

Lenneberg (1967) also argued that several other features of language acquisition suggest a strong biological component. Language milestones, like motor milestones, emerge in a predictable time sequence regardless of the environment in which the child grows up (except for a few rare cases of extreme environmental deprivation). In addition, all languages share common features such as phonology, semantics, and syntax, elements that Lenneberg and others believed were derived from the biologically determined capabilities of human beings. Indeed, children do seem to be driven to learn language, even in the absence of linguistic input. One group of researchers found a group of congenitally deaf children who were not taught sign language and failed to learn oral communication (Feldman, Goldin-Meadow, & Gleitman, 1978). Even so, these children developed their own unique gestural system of communication that followed the same sequence as that of hearing children (that is, a one-symbol stage followed by a two-symbol stage, and so forth).

The fact that children generally show a common sequence in the emergence of language abilities is the strongest evidence for a biological explanation of language development. An explanation based solely on biology, however, cannot account for all aspects of language development. Languages vary enormously in the way they express relations and concepts. Let us take one example: how "definiteness" versus "indefiniteness" is expressed. In English, we say "I want *the* car" or "I want *a* car" to represent these two ideas. In some African languages, though, different intonation patterns rather than different words convey this distinction (Maratsos, 1989). Clearly, biology alone cannot explain the vast differences in the way languages express ideas, nor the fact that children do, in fact, end up speaking different languages, depending on their culture. It is obvious that a place must be found for the role of "nurture" or experience.

▶ **Sociocultural influence**

CONTROVERSY

▶ **Sensitive periods**

Is There a Critical Period for Second-Language Learning?

Lenneberg (1967) suggested that the span from age one year to puberty is a critical period for the acquisition of language. To speak and comprehend normally, children must have acquired all language basics by adolescence, when physiological changes in the brain make language learning more difficult. One implication of Lenneberg's hypothesis is that children will also find it difficult to learn a second language if they begin during or after adolescence. In fact, Lenneberg claims that few of those who learn a second language after adolescence will sound like native speakers. Is there evidence that childhood is a critical period for learning language, including a second language?

On one side, some language researchers believe that at least some version of a critical-period hypothesis is correct. One line of support comes from clinical studies of children with aphasias; as we just saw, children who suffer brain lesions to language areas before puberty have a higher likelihood of recovering language than those who experience brain damage later in life. A few rare case studies of children who have been isolated from social contact for protracted periods of time also bear on this issue. One girl, Genie, had minimal human contact from the age of twenty months until thirteen years because of isolation imposed by her parents. She did not speak at all. After her discovery and with extensive therapy, Genie made some progress in learning words but never learned to speak normally, showing special difficulty in completely mastering the rules of syntax (Curtiss, 1977). Other evidence comes from studies of deaf persons who learned American Sign Language (ASL) at different times in life. Elissa Newport (1990) found that subjects who learned ASL after the age of twelve showed consistent errors in the use of grammar, whereas subjects who learned ASL from birth (from parents who signed) displayed a normal course in the development of this language.

The same principles may also apply to second-language learning. Jacqueline Johnson and Elissa Newport (1989) assessed the ability of Chinese and Korean subjects who learned English as a second language to judge the grammatical correctness of over two hundred English sentences. Some of the subjects started to learn English as early as age three, whereas others began to learn at age seventeen or later. Performance was related to the age at which subjects began learning English. The older they were when they arrived in the United States, the poorer their scores on the grammar test. Other analyses showed that factors such as length of experience with English, amount of formal instruction in English, or identification with American culture could not account for these findings. Newport (1990) concludes that "in language . . . the child, and not the adult, appears to be especially privileged as a learner" (p. 12).

On the other side of the argument, critics point to problems in interpreting some of the research cited in support of the critical-period hypothesis. Genie, for example, may have suffered serious cognitive, physiological, and emotional deficits because of her prolonged isolation from other humans, deficits that could very well account for her lack of mature language. Deaf persons who learn ASL later in life still learn a good deal about the syntactic system and are able to communicate. And many individuals who learn a second language in adulthood acquire the phonology, vocabulary, and syntax of that language with native like proficiency (Snow, 1987b). In fact, in the early stages of acquisition, adults typically learn a second language more rapidly than children (McLaughlin, 1984). In other words, it is difficult to find unequivocal support for a strong version of the critical-period hypothesis for either first- or second-language learning.

Children may have a slight advantage over adults in language learning, making early childhood an ideal time to acquire a second language. However, the end of childhood by no means signals a sudden drop in the ability to learn new

Studies of second language learners indicate that younger children may have an advantage over older children and adults in attaining proficiency. At the same time, however, data do not support a strong version of the critical period hypothesis for language learning.

languages with facility and proficiency. Because older children and adults have already learned one language, they may actually be more sensitive to the phonological, semantic, and syntactic features of a second language, facilitating more rapid learning. Another factor to consider is that older children and adults rarely learn a second language as children do, by immersion in the sounds, meanings, and grammar of the nonnative tongue. We might very well find that teaching second languages by the "immersion method" as opposed to drill-and-practice of vocabulary and syntax produces more proficiency among older learners. In other words, language learning may not be exclusively for the very young but a lifelong possibility. ■

The Linguistic Perspective

One of the first challenges to behaviorist accounts of language acquisition was made by the linguist Noam Chomsky, who proposed in a revolutionary book called *Syntactic Structures* (1957) that language is generative—in other words that specific utterances are created by a rule-governed structure that can produce all sorts of novel verbalizations, provided they conform to grammatical conventions. Chomsky called this innate grammatical "processor" the language acquisition device, or LAD. According to Chomsky, the language spoken in the child's environment is filtered through the LAD, where the grammatical regularities are recognized and abstracted into rules. The LAD then uses these generalized rules to create new combinations of words, combinations the child may not have heard others speak. Such a capability could account for the vast number of original verbalizations that children make and explains furthermore how children manage to acquire language with very little formal instruction or feedback on the correctness of their verbalizations.

▶ **The child's active role**

Chomsky and other linguists have emphasized the structures that all languages share, those syntactic regularities that are quickly identified by the young language learner in the course of everyday exposure to speech—as when the child learning English notices that nouns representing agents precede verbs and nouns representing the objects of actions follow verbs. Linguists thus lean heavily toward a "nature" perspective in accounting for language attainments. According to them, the human organism is biologically predisposed to be sensitive to the organized features of language.

▶ **Roles of nature and nurture**

Research evidence supports many of the tenets held by linguists about how language is acquired. Children learn syntactic rules for forming plurals, past tense, and other grammatical forms very rapidly in their first five years and can even apply them to words they have never heard before, indicating that they detect and correctly employ regularities in language from a very early age. In a famous experiment, Jean Berko (1958) presented children with several nonsense words accompanied by pictures like the example in Figure 7.6. Children were able to state correctly that there were two "wugs" even though they had never heard made-up words such as these. Moreover, linguistic theories fare better than behaviorist accounts in explaining the occurrence of overregularizations; these can be seen as the product of an LAD that has done too good a job, one that has not yet stored the exceptions to the rules.

Despite the excitement and new thinking that followed the linguistic revolution, Chomsky and his fellow linguists leave many questions unanswered about how language is learned. The idea that children abstract a generative grammar system helps us to understand the rapid development of syntax, but by its very nature as an approach that emphasizes the grammatical structure of language, Chomsky's theory gives us little information on the development of semantics. Similarly, the LAD is a useful hypothetical construct, but the characteristics of this device and exactly how it functions remain to be filled in. Whatever its shortcomings, though, the linguistic approach has helped to capture some of the complexities of language development overlooked by behaviorists.

▶ **Interaction among domains**

The Cognitive Perspective

Language follows from advances in the child's thinking processes, according to the cognitive perspective on language. Theorists vary, however, in the way they hypothesize exactly how cognitive development paves the way for linguistic accomplishments.

In Piaget's framework, children must have certain knowledge about the concept a given label stands for before they can use labels for objects, events, or people. In particular, infants must have grasped fully the notion of *object permanence,* the fact that an object continues to exist even when it is no longer in view, before they can use symbolic names for parents, pets, or toys. In addition, Piaget believes that during most of their first two years, children do not yet use symbolic schemes; hence, their language abilities are very limited before this age. Once the **semiotic function,** or the cognitive ability to symbolize, emerges, however, language becomes possible. According to Piaget, both the fact that children's first words usually name objects rather than other semantic categories and the rapid expansion of vocabulary at the age of eighteen months are explained by changes in underlying cognitive structures that precede language.

As we saw earlier in this chapter, other theorists such as Eve Clark (1973) and Katherine Nelson (1973) also argue that children's early words reflect developments and refinements in cognition, but these researchers' emphasis is on other aspects of the child's underlying conceptual knowledge. Children first establish conceptual groupings of objects, based on either shared perceptual or functional features (for example, four-legged things or things that roll). Only then can they begin speaking the labels that apply to these groupings. In other words, achievements in conceptual understanding lay the groundwork for the ability to apply linguistic labels to those very same concepts.

Do cognitive achievements precede linguistic milestones, as Piaget, Clark, and Nelson suggest? If anything, it now seems more likely that the two domains tend to develop at the same time, and there may be some overlap, especially at the early stages of language learning (Rice, 1989). In studies in which researchers have explored the relationship between attainment of object permanence and language, for example, the correlations have been only moderate or weak (Corrigan, 1979). In fact, Elizabeth Bates and her colleagues found that other skills such as imitation, tool use, and the complex manipulation of objects predict language attainments better than measures of object

FIGURE 7.6

A Sample Item from the WUG Test

In the WUG test, children are presented with nonsense words such as "wug" and must supply a grammatical variation. Children are able to form plurals and past tenses for words they have never heard before, suggesting that they abstract general rules of syntax from the language in their environment.

THIS IS A WUG.

NOW THERE IS ANOTHER ONE.
THERE ARE TWO OF THEM.
THERE ARE TWO _____.

Source: From Berko, 1958.

permanence (Bates et al., 1979). Nonetheless, abilities such as tool use do reflect cognitive sophistication and, as such, suggest that specific cognitive skills may have some bearing on the emergence of language.

Alison Gopnik and Andrew Meltzoff (1986) have been able to identify some specific language attainments that closely follow the acquisition of certain cognitive skills. For example, children who can find a hidden object after it has been moved from one location to another begin to use words to signify disappearance, such as "gone," within a few weeks. Similarly, they begin to employ words representing success and failure (for example, "there" and "uh-oh") after learning to solve a complex means-ends task, such as using a stick to obtain an object. Gopnik and Meltzoff (1987) also noted that the "naming explosion" that children typically demonstrate at about one and a half years of age is related to the ability to sort groups of toys into two distinct categories, such as dolls versus cars or boxes versus balls. According to these researchers' **specificity hypothesis,** children display strong relationships between particular cognitive achievements and specific semantic developments. Gopnik and Meltzoff maintain that children develop linguistic labels consistent with cognitive problems that interest them at a given stage of development.

In another attempt to relate specific cognitive skills to language development, Keith Nelson (1989) has recently proposed a model in which language learning is seen as the result of the application of a cognitive mechanism called the **rare event learning mechanism** (or **RELM**). According to this model, children make advances in linguistic understanding when they notice discrepancies between linguistic structures they already know ("the boy ran") and those they newly encounter ("the boy will run"). To make this distinction, children must employ cognitive processes such as attention, comparison, categorization, and memory.

Look at the following exchange between child and caregiver to illustrate this phenomenon:

CHILD: "Ball roll."
CAREGIVER: "Yes, the ball is rolling."

▶ **The child's active role**

When adults repeat the child's utterance but embed it in a more complex syntactic structure, they are using a **recast.** By doing so, they are highlighting discrepancies between the child's simple utterance and a more advanced one. It is up to the child to attend to those discrepancies, compare her own utterance with that of the caregiver, and remember the adult's more sophisticated grammatical form. According to Nelson (1989), the strategies for learning language resemble strategies for learning any complex, rule-based skill. In other words, the child's cognitive capabilities must be sufficiently developed before she can master all the intricacies of language. At the same time, his model points out the important role of interactions with the caregiver, leading us to another major perspective on the acquisition of language.

▶ **Interaction among domains**

A Social Interaction Perspective

▶ **Roles of nature and nurture**

Many observers of child language hold as a central tenet that language is a social activity, one that arises from the desire to communicate with others and that is nurtured in social interactive contexts. Proponents of this position represent a compromise between the nature and nurture advocates. While ac-

When caregivers talk to infants and young children, they employ simple sentences, exaggerate their intonation, and speak with a high pitch. Infants are especially responsive to these qualities of "motherese."

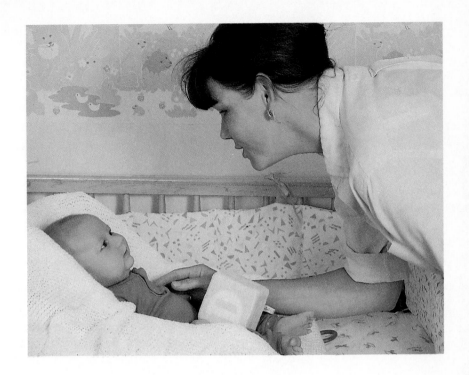

semiotic function   Ability to symbolize objects.

specificity hypothesis   Hypothesis that specific cognitive achievements precede specific language achievements.

rare event learning mechanism   Learning model that postulates the development of attention, memory, and other cognitive processes as a prerequisite to language achievements.

recast   Repetition of a child's utterance along with some new elements.

motherese   Simple, repetitive, high-pitched speech of caregivers to young children; includes many questions.

turn taking   Alternating vocalization by parent and child.

turnabout   Element of conversation that requests a response from the child.

knowledging the biological and innate predispositions of the young human organism to learn language, they emphasize at the same time the role that experiences with more mature, expert speakers play in fostering linguistic skill. Children need support and feedback as they make their first attempts at communication. They also need models of appropriate speech, models that do not exceed their processing abilities. Many of the qualities of parental speech directed at children are well suited to the child's emerging receptive and productive skills. That is, parental speech often operates within the child's *zone of proximal development* to provide the *scaffolding* for language development, concepts outlined in Chapter 6 in relation to the child's general learning process.

Parents have a unique way of talking to their young children. Most parents present a "scaled-down" version of spoken language as they interact with their young offspring, a version that contains simple, well-formed sentences and is punctuated by exaggerated intonation, high pitch, and clear pauses between segments of speech (Newport, 1977). Caregivers describe concrete events taking place in the present and often refer to objects with diminutive names, such as "kitty" or "doggie." **Motherese,** as this form of communication is called, also includes repetitions of what the child has said as well as a large number of questions. The latter, in particular, serve to facilitate the occurrence of **turn taking,** the alternating vocalization by parent and child. Some questions are also used as **turnabouts,** elements of conversation that explicitly request a response from the child, as in "You like that, don't you?" or "What did you say?" And as we saw above, *recasts,* the repetition of the child's utterance with the addition of a new element of sentence structure, are an especially important component of motherese.

Some good examples of motherese in its varying forms are provided in Catherine Snow's (1977) detailed study of the speech of two mothers to their infants. Consider the following segment observed when one child, Ann, was seven months of age:*

MOTHER	ANN
Ghhhhh ghhhhh ghhhhh ghhhhh	
Grrrrr grrrrr grrrrr grrrrr	
	(protest cry)
Oh, you don't feel like it, do you?	
	aaaaa aaaaa aaaaa
No, I wasn't making that noise.	
I wasn't going *aaaaa aaaaa.*	
	aaaaa aaaaa
Yes, that's right.	

(p. 16)

Notable in this exchange is the mother's pattern of waiting for her child's vocalization to end before she began her response, an example of turn taking. If the child had spoken actual words, a real conversation would have taken place. The mother also repeated the child's vowel-like sound but embedded it in more elaborate speech. By the time the infant reaches eighteen months, the mother's tendency to expand or explain her utterances becomes even more pronounced, as in the following brief episode:

MOTHER	ANN
	(blowing noises)
That's a bit rude.	
	Mouth.
Mouth, that's right.	
	Face.
Face, yes, mouth is in your face.	
What else have you got in your face?	
	Face. (closing eyes)
You're making a face, aren't you?	

(Snow, 1977, p. 18)

Snow's (1977) research demonstrated how mothers adjust their speech according to the growing capabilities of their infants, promoting a conversational partnership. According to Snow (1984), two general principles operate during these caregiver-child interactions. First, parents generally interpret their infants' behaviors as attempts to communicate, even when that interpretation may not seem warranted to an objective observer. Second, children actively seek relationships between objects, events, and people in their world and the vocal behaviors of their caregiver. Because of the correspondence between adult verbalizations and the objects of infants' attention, they are able to learn

▶ **The child's active role**

---

* Excerpts reprinted from Snow, C.E. (1977). "The Development of Conversation Between Babies and Mothers," *Journal of Child Language,* 4, 1–22. Reprinted by permission of Cambridge University Press.

the basic elements of language. The result of these two tendencies is that parents are motivated to converse with their children and children have a mechanism for learning language.

Motherese may serve a number of functions in the child's growing competence with language. First, this form of speech may assist the child's acquisition of word meaning. Mothers tend to say the names for objects more loudly than other words in their speech to infants, and often they place the object label in the last position in their sentence, as in "Do you see the *rattle?*" (Messer, 1981). Mothers also tend to highlight new words by raising their pitch as they say them (Fernald & Mazzie, 1983). Second, the intonations of motherese may facilitate the child's acquisition of syntax. A recent study demonstrated that seven- to ten-month-old infants oriented more frequently to motherese that contained pauses at clausal boundaries, as opposed to motherese that was interrupted within clauses. They did not show these differential preferences in response to regular adult speech. The prosodic features of motherese may thus assist the infant in identifying syntactically salient elements of language (Nelson et al., 1989). Finally, exposure to motherese may provide lessons in conversational turn taking, one of the aspects of pragmatics that governs speech in interactions with others.

Are there any other effects of interactions with caregivers on child language development? Researchers have observed that the more time mothers spend in joint encounters with their year-old children, the larger the children's vocabularies are six months later (Tomasello & Todd, 1983). And the more mothers talk, the more words their children acquire (Olson, Bayles, & Bates, 1986; Huttenlocher et al., 1991). It is not just *how much* mothers talk to their children that makes a difference, however; *how* they talk also matters. When mothers use a large number of directives to control their children's behaviors and are generally intrusive, language development is slowed. When mothers use questions and conversational turn taking to elicit language from their children and follow their children's lead with a response, language development proceeds more rapidly (Hoff-Ginsberg, 1986; McDonald & Pien, 1982; Nelson, 1973). By engaging their young children in conversations, mothers are increasing children's attention to the properties of language and are at the same time providing them with a rich set of information about those characteristics (Hoff-Ginsberg, 1990).

▶ **Sociocultural influence**

As important as motherese may seem, it is not a universal phenomenon. Although features of motherese have been observed in fourteen different languages (Gleason & Weintraub, 1978), mothers in some cultures adopt a distinctly different style in talking with their infants. For example, Japanese mothers use fewer questions but more nonsense sounds compared with American mothers (Toda, Fogel, & Kawai, 1990). In the Kaluli society of Papua New Guinea, talking with others is a highly valued social skill, yet few adult verbalizations are directed toward infants. Infants may be called by their names, but until they pass their first year, little else is said to them. When mothers do begin to talk to their babies, their speech contains few of the elements of motherese. Turn taking, repetitions, and elaborations are absent; usually mothers simply make a directive statement that requires no response from the child. Despite the absence of a rich interchange between mother and child, Kaluli children eventually become proficient users of their language (Schieffelin & Ochs, 1983). Joint linguistic interactions between caregiver and child may thus not be absolutely essential to the emergence of language, but such interactions probably spur the rate at which children achieve various language milestones.

The social interaction perspective, if it is to give an accurate picture of language acquisition, will have to be extended beyond mothers to include the child's other interaction partners. Linguistic exchanges with fathers, siblings, peers, and others may uniquely influence the child's eventual level of linguistic skill. For example, when fifteen-month-olds "converse" with their fathers, they experience more communication breakdowns than when they talk with their mothers. Fathers more often request clarification, change the topic, or do not acknowledge the child's utterance after they fail to understand what she says (Tomasello, Conti-Ramsden, & Ewert, 1990). Thus, in communicating with fathers, children are challenged to make adjustments in order to maintain the interaction. Recent evidence also suggests that by three years of age, children monitor the conversations of mothers with older siblings and are effective both in entering into those conversations and eliciting responses (Dunn & Shatz, 1989). Children are normally exposed to a rich and varied range of linguistic input; many theorists believe that this fact ensures that children will learn the details of linguistic structures that may not be present in the verbalizations of a single conversation partner, such as the mother (Gleitman, Newport, & Gleitman, 1984; Wexler, 1982). A broader version of the social interaction perspective is thus likely to provide additional insights into the process of language acquisition.

In summary, each of these five theoretical positions makes a contribution to our understanding of language development. Specialized biological structures are responsible for human language processing, and biology evidently also sets the child's early predispositions to be responsive to the unique features of language. The child's cognitive growth, especially her tendency to form concepts and the development of attention, memory, and comparison skills, assists in the acquisition process. Part of the child's task, one which she does very well, is to filter out the regularities that occur in spoken language so that she can use these general rules to create her own utterances. At the same time, caregivers provide models of correct speech, deliver indirect feedback as to the correctness of the child's utterances, and in the use of motherese, provide linguistic data compatible with the child's level of language skill. Given the complexities involved in language development, it is no wonder that our explanations of this phenomenon are multifaceted.

THE FUNCTIONS OF LANGUAGE

Aside from its obvious usefulness as a social communication tool, what functions does language serve? How does the human propensity to learn and employ language affect other aspects of functioning—specifically, mental processes, the regulation of behavior, and socialization? At the very least we would have to say that language enriches the human experience by providing a useful vehicle to enhance cognition and behavior; it also exerts powerful influences on other areas of human activity. Here we will examine briefly some of the broad effects of language on the domains of cognition, behavior, and socialization.

▶ **Interaction among domains**   **How Language Influences Cognition**

The relationship between language and cognition has been a controversial subject for many years, especially with respect to the issue of which activity precedes the other. Some psychologists and anthropologists have argued for the primacy of language over cognition (that is, that language shapes thinking), whereas others contend that cognition paves the way for language. Most contemporary researchers and theorists now acknowledge that the link between language and cognition is bidirectional and that each domain exerts influence on the other. For the purposes of our present discussion, though, it is reasonable to state that language can have a powerful influence on the child's cognitive attainments.

If you ask the child to perform a cognitive task, such as remembering a list of words or grouping a set of similar objects, you will notice that he will often spontaneously use language to aid his performance. The best examples of this behavior come from research findings on developmental changes in children's memory. Many observers of children's memory performance have noted distinct differences in the way preschool- and school-aged children approach the task of remembering. Older children are far more likely to employ deliberate strategies for remembering than are younger children, strategies that typically involve the use of verbal skills. In one early study, John Flavell and his colleagues (Flavell, Beach, & Chinsky, 1966) asked kindergarten, second-, and fifth-graders to watch as the experimenter pointed to three pictures in an array of seven. The children's job was to point to the same three pictures either immediately or after a delay of fifteen seconds. During the delay, the experimenters noticed that most of the children in the oldest group made spontaneous lip movements, suggesting that they were verbally repeating the items to be recalled. Moreover, the superior performance of the oldest group on the memory test was attributed to their spontaneous repetition of the names of the items. The use of verbal labels seemed to bridge the gap between the time the items were first seen and the time they were to be recalled. Since this landmark study, numerous other researchers have observed that children who employ verbal rehearsal strategies display superior memory performance compared with children who do not (Daehler & Bukatko, 1985).

Language can also influence how children categorize related groups of objects. Stan Kuczaj and his colleagues showed children twelve novel objects that could be grouped into three sets (Kuczaj, Borys, & Jones, 1989). Children who were taught the names of one category member from each group were more successful in sorting these objects than children who were not given labels. Language provides children with cues that classes of stimuli differ from each other and can thus influence how children form conceptual groups. If some four-legged animals are called "dogs" and others are called "cats," the fact that different linguistic labels are applied will highlight for the child the relevant differences in the features of these two groups.

One of the more interesting ways in which the influence of language on thought has been studied has been to compare, on a variety of tasks, the performance of bilingual children equally fluent in two languages with monolinguals fluent in only one. Bilingual children have been characterized as more analytic and flexible in their approach to different types of thought problems. Sandra Ben-Zeev (1977) compared monolingual children with children who

FIGURE 7.7

Cognitive Achievements of Bilingual and Monolingual Children

Bilingual children outperform monolinguals on nonverbal tests like the Raven Progressive Matrices, which requires children to select the segment that correctly fits into the larger pattern. Bilingual children generally seem to be more analytical than monolinguals in their approach to various problem-solving tasks.

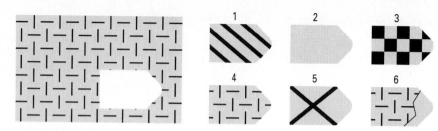

Source: From Raven, 1948.

spoke both Hebrew and English and found that bilinguals performed better on a symbol substitution task. The task required that subjects substitute certain words in a series of sentences for others, such as "spaghetti" for "I" in the sentence "I am cold." Bilingual children also perform better than monolinguals on nonverbal problems, such as the Raven Progressive Matrices (see Figure 7.7) (Hakuta & Diaz, 1985). One hypothesis to explain their superior performance is that bilingual children are forced to think more abstractly and analytically because they are sensitized to the structure and detail of not just one language but two. Alternatively, they may have a greater tendency to produce verbalizations that enhance their performance even in nonverbal tasks. Whatever the mechanism, these studies demonstrate that speaking a second language has an impact on cognitive processes.

▶ **Interaction among domains**

How Language Influences Self-Regulation

Language takes on special significance in its increasing role in regulating behavior during the course of child development, according to two prominent Soviet psychologists, Lev Vygotsky and Alexander Luria. Vygotsky (1962) be-

TABLE 7.3

Luria's Stages of the Verbal Regulation of Behavior

Age	Characteristics	Example
18 Months–3 Years	Verbalizations of others initiate child's motor behavior but do not inhibit it.	Child squeezes ball when adult says, "Go," but does not stop squeezing when adult says, "Don't press."
3–5 Years	Adult's or child's own speech initiates and inhibits behavior but only if physical qualities of speech match task requirements.	If child says, "Go, go," child squeezes ball twice; if child says, "I shall press twice," child will only squeeze once.
5+ Years	Content of child's internalized speech controls thoughts and actions.	Child says, "I shall press twice" and squeezes rubber ball two times.

Young children often use private speech when they are engaged in new or challenging tasks. This overt, audible speech guides children's behaviors and eventually becomes interiorized.

▶ **Development as continuous/stagelike**

private speech Child's vocalized speech to himself that directs behavior.

inner speech Interiorized form of private speech.

lieved that the child's initial utterances serve an interpersonal function, signaling others about his or her affective state. In the preschool years, though, speech takes on a different function. Specifically, the child's **private speech,** or overt, audible "speech-for-self," comes to guide his or her observable activities. If you have ever observed a toddler coloring and simultaneously saying something like, "Now, I'll use the blue crayon. I'll make the sky blue," you have seen an example of private speech. Eventually, "speech-for-self" becomes interiorized in such a way that **inner speech** dictates the direction of the child's thoughts. Inner speech resembles the "little voice" many of us listen to if we have a series of important tasks to do.

Luria (1961) expanded these ideas by proposing three stages in the verbal regulation of behavior (see Table 7.3). In the first stage, encompassing the ages of about eighteen months to three years, the verbalizations of others can prompt motor activity but they rarely inhibit behavior. In an experiment in which children were to squeeze a rubber ball following the commands of an adult, they would start pressing following the command "Go!" but did not stop this behavior following negative commands such as "Don't squeeze." In the second stage, lasting from about three to five years of age, children's external speech (either from others or overtly vocalized by the self) can increasingly initiate and inhibit behavior, but only if the physical qualities of the speech match the requirements of the task. If children said, "Go, go," they squeezed the rubber ball twice; if they said, "I shall press twice," however, they still squeezed the ball only once. Finally, at about age five, children's speech becomes internalized to control thoughts and actions. In addition, the content of speech, and not just its superficial qualities, becomes effective in regulating behavior.

Attempts by American researchers to find empirical support for the ideas of Vygotsky and Luria have met with mixed success. One problem has been the failure to observe much overt "speech-for-self" among preschoolers, although that may be a function of the particular settings and tasks American psychologists have used (Fuson, 1979). A few studies, however, do provide general support for the Soviet view of language and thought. For example, in one investigation, when children under age four and a half were given negative commands—such as "Don't touch your toes!"—in a loud voice, they were more likely to perform the prohibited act than when the instruction was issued softly. That is, the loudness of the command was more powerful in initiating a behavior than the content was in stopping it. In contrast, older children attended more to the content of the message than its physical qualities (Saltz, Campbell, & Skotko, 1983). More recently, Laura Berk (1986) noted that when first-graders were engaged in solving math problems in school, they engaged in high levels of externalized private speech to guide their problem solving. Third-graders also showed evidence of private speech, but a more internalized form, through mutterings and lip movements as they attempted to solve math problems. Thus, children do use private speech, and they progress from overt private speech to a more interiorized form.

How important is private speech in directing behavior? You may have noticed that you tend to "talk to yourself" when you are under stress or when you have a lot of things to do. Research has confirmed that children, like adults, use private speech when they find tasks difficult or when they make errors (Berk, 1984). In addition, a recent longitudinal study has demonstrated that as children progress from overt to more internal private speech, they also show fewer distracting body movements and greater sustained attention in school (Bivens & Berk, 1990). Studies such as these suggest that language becomes an increasingly powerful regulator of children's behavior with development.

▶ **Sociocultural influence**

How Language Influences Cultural Socialization

Still another way in which language can have a broad influence on development is by helping children to discern the social roles, relationships, and values of their culture. Many languages have specific grammatical forms that are used to convey gender, age, or social power. In acquiring language, children are sensitized to the specific ways their own culture creates social order. For example, in Japanese, the word particle *zo* signifies affective intensity and a male speaker; the particle *wa*, hesitancy and a female speaker. Children learning Japanese are therefore likely to associate hesitancy with females and forcefulness with males (Ochs, 1990). In many other languages, specific words have formal and informal versions, with the former used when speaking with individuals who have more authority or power and the latter with individuals of equal status or who are related. Again, such linguistic distinctions highlight important social relationships within the cultural group.

A good example of how language can influence socialization comes from traditional Samoan culture, in which community and group accomplishments are emphasized over the attainments of individuals. In Samoan speech, very few verbalizations include praise or blame for individuals. Most statements concern the success or failure of the group and emphasize the life of the community. When Samoan children are exposed to verbalizations of this type, they are being socialized into the collective orientation of their culture (Ochs, 1990).

Researchers are just beginning to explore the ways in which the words and social conventions within a specific language are related to cultural values and beliefs. However, it is apparent that, through language, children are learning far more than simply how to communicate; they are also learning about the broader belief systems of their society.

THEMES IN DEVELOPMENT

LANGUAGE

▶ **What roles do nature and nurture play in language development?**

There are several indicators that nature sets early human dispositions to develop language: the infant's sensitivity to phonemes and the prosodic features of speech, the child's tendency to progress through language milestones in a predictable sequence, and the fact that certain portions of the brain are devoted to language functions are just some examples. Nurture, in the form of the child's experiences with more mature language users, interfaces with these biological tendencies to lead her to acquire the phonology, semantics, and syntax of a particular language and to learn the social conventions that accompany spoken language in her culture.

▶ **How does the sociocultural context influence language development?**

Cultures vary in the extent to which caregivers employ motherese with their growing children, a factor that may influence rate of language acquisition. The specific elements of phonology, semantics, syntax, and pragmatics also vary widely across languages. Often, the content and structure of a specific language provide cues as to the culture's social order and values. Language thereby plays a role in the child's socialization.

▶ **How does the child play an active role in the process of language development?**

Even in the earliest stages of language acquisition, the child often influences which objects or people caregivers will label when she looks at or points to specific items. Although the child does benefit by merely listening to models of language use in the environment, she also actively employs context and the mutual exclusivity bias to derive the meanings of words. In addition, her rapid acquisition of the rules of syntax and her production of overregularizations suggest that the child abstracts out the regularities in language to generate her own verbalizations.

▶ **Is language development continuous or stagelike?**

Descriptions of early language production, in particular, often seem stagelike; children appear to spend distinct periods of time in a babbling stage, one-word stage, and so on. However, recent studies suggest that there are more continuities than previously thought between different "stages" in language acquisition. For example, the sounds in infant babbling are related to the language the child will eventually speak, as the interactional hypothesis suggests. Finally, Luria posits stages in the verbal regulation of behavior. However, rather than disappearing at a particular age, private speech often resurfaces, even among older children, when tasks become difficult or stressful.

▶ Are there sensitive periods in language development?

A prominent hypothesis has been that the entire period from infancy to adolescence is a sensitive period for the acquisition of language. Studies of brain-injured children suggest that children recover language functions to a greater extent than adults with similar damage, for example. Children learning a second language also seem to achieve somewhat greater proficiency than adults who learn a second language. However, there is no firm evidence that the ability to learn language drops off dramatically at adolescence. Adults, for example, sometimes acquire a second language with native-like proficiency.

▶ How does language development interact with development in other domains?

In early childhood, the ability to produce spoken language parallels the physiological maturation of the vocal apparatus and the central nervous system. The emergence of language also coincides with the onset of certain cognitive skills, such as conceptual understanding, memory, and attention. Later, the ability to monitor one's own thinking processes is tied to the child's metalinguistic awareness. Language itself is nurtured largely within the context of social interactions with caregivers. Thus, physical, cognitive, and social factors all impinge on the process of language acquisition.

By the same token, language has a clear impact on other domains. The child's use of language enhances her ability to remember, form concepts, and as studies of bilinguals suggest, may even promote analytic thinking and mental flexibility. In addition, children's ability to be successful communicators can have important repercussions for social relationships with parents, peers, and others.

SUMMARY

Acquiring language is a developmental task with four main components: phonology, semantics, syntax, and pragmatics. Children master these components of language in a distinct sequence. In the early stages of acquisition, children focus on *phonology;* they learn to segment and produce the basic sounds of language and show a predisposition to respond to language as a unique auditory stimulus. During the first year, they vocalize by *cooing* and *babbling* but also communicate and symbolize objects by producing gestures.

By one year, most children are speaking in one-word utterances, usually *nominals,* or nouns. A general characteristic of *semantic* development, the learning of word meanings, is that children comprehend far more language than they are able to produce. Children learn the meanings of words through *fast-mapping,* parental labeling of objects that children point to, *linguistic contrast,* and their tendency to have a *mutual exclusivity bias.* Their growing conceptual knowledge is also thought to be part of learning word meanings. Although there are specific ages at which most children acquire language milestones, children also show individual differences in patterns of acquisition.

Once children begin combining two or more words, they show evidence of *syntactic* awareness, the grammatical rules that state how words are combined. Although it is difficult to describe a single child's grammar, many children employ *pivot grammars* or other systematic relationships between words to convey meaning. Later in childhood, children learn to form negatives, questions, and use the passive voice. Two other later developments are the acquisition of *pragmatics*, the social conventions regarding effective communication, and *metalinguistic awareness,* the ability to reflect abstractly on language as a communication tool and the self as a language user.

Theories of language development have centered primarily on the nature-nurture debate. Behaviorists have emphasized the role of shaping, reinforcement, and imitation in language acquisition. Those leaning toward a biological explanation have pointed to the regularities in language attainments across cultures and the brain structures specifically devoted to language processing. A major question stemming from the biological position has been whether a critical period exists for the acquisition of language. Other approaches that have contributed to our understanding of language are the linguistic, cognitive, and social interaction perspectives. Linguistic theorists emphasize the child's abstraction of general grammatical principles from the stream of speech. Cognitive theorists point out that certain advances in thinking precede language attainments, such as concept formation and attention skills. Finally, social interaction theorists highlight the characteristics of caregiver-child speech that facilitate development, such as the use of *recasts, turn taking,* and simple, clear verbalizations. Each of these theoretical perspectives helps us to grasp the complexities of the child's attainment of language as well as the apparent ease with which this task is accomplished.

Language serves numerous functions in the child's life besides simply communication. It can influence specific cognitive processes, such as memory or classification. It can serve to direct the child's behavior in the form of *private speech* and, later, *inner speech,* particularly when tasks are new or difficult. Lastly, it can play a role in the socialization of the child by introducing him or her directly to specific values and expectations of the child's native culture.

8

Cognition

▶ **What roles do nature and nurture play in cognitive development?**

▶ **How does the sociocultural context influence cognitive development?**

▶ **How does the child play an active role in the process of cognitive development?**

▶ **Is cognitive development continuous or stagelike?**

▶ **How does cognitive development interact with development in other domains?**

Observing his sixteen-month-old daughter Lucienne, the developmental psychologist Jean Piaget recounts what happened when he placed an intriguing watch chain inside an empty matchbox:

I put the chain back into the box and reduce the opening to 3 mm. It is understood that Lucienne is not aware of the functioning of the opening and closing of the match box and has not seen me prepare for this experiment. She only possesses two preceding schemas: turning the box over in order to empty it of its contents, and sliding her fingers into the slit to make the chain come out. It is of course this last procedure that she tries first: she puts her finger inside and gropes to reach the chain, but fails completely. A pause follows during which Lucienne manifests a very curious reaction. . . . She looks at the slit with great attention; then, several times in succession, she opens and shuts her mouth, at first lightly, then wider and wider! [Then] . . . Lucienne unhesitatingly puts her finger in the slit, and instead of trying as before to reach the chain, she pulls so as to enlarge the opening. She succeeds and grabs the chain. (Piaget, 1952b, pp. 337–338).

What Piaget witnessed in this episode is a very clear demonstration of a young child in the process of *thinking*. Lucienne solved a simple problem by paying attention to the dilemma before her, relying on her memory for information about what could be done with matchboxes, and testing out potential solutions "in her head." The opening and closing of her mouth signaled her ability to symbolize internally what needed to be done with the matchbox. Although Lucienne's problem-solving behavior is a far cry from the more sophisticated thought of, say, an adolescent, who can solve complex logical problems or remember vast amounts of new information, she is displaying some impressive cognitive skills for a child not far past her first birthday.

One of the most active research areas of child development focuses on ***cognition***—those thought processes and mental activities including attention, memory, and problem solving that are evident and grow from early infancy onward. Do young children remember as well as older children? Do children change in the way they form concepts? Do older children solve problems the same way that younger children do? These are the types of questions that psychologists interested in cognitive development ask.

Virtually every aspect of a child's development, in fact, has some connection with emerging cognitive capabilities. We have already seen in Chapter 7 that a child's use of language is linked to her growing conceptual development. Once she understands concepts such as "animal" or "flower," she can apply the labels to members of these classes. Similarly, the child's growing knowledge of effective social interaction can influence the quality of her relations with peers. In the domain of emotional development, the infant's fear of separation from the caregiver follows from the realization that people continue to exist even when they are no longer within sight, another cognitive advance. These are just a few of the numerous examples of how changes in thinking influence and interact with other areas of the child's development.

We begin our discussion of cognitive development by considering two important theoretical positions that have jointly framed the research on children's thought, those of Piaget and the information-processing theorists. Next we will discuss the development of four fundamental areas of cognition—attention, memory, concept formation, and problem solving. We will see, in each of these areas, how children become increasingly organized and *planful,* employing deliberate strategies to accomplish the tasks that confront them. Children, we will also see, profit from their expanding general knowledge base as they perform more advanced cognitive skills. Finally, we will examine the ways in which the child's social and cultural environment shapes cognitive skills. How do parents and other adults influence the child's thinking processes, and how do cultural norms and expectations come into play?

PIAGET'S THEORY OF COGNITIVE DEVELOPMENT

▶ **The child's active role**

In Chapter 2, we discussed the major ideas of Jean Piaget, the most important theorist to provide a comprehensive theory of cognitive development. As we saw there, Piaget believed that children are actively involved in the construction of knowledge, incorporating new information into already existing knowledge structures, or *schemes,* through *assimilation.* As a result, schemes are modified or expanded through the process of *accommodation.* The outcome is greater *equilibrium* or balance among the pieces of knowledge that make up the child's understanding.

▶ **Development as continuous/ stagelike**

As a stage theorist, Piaget maintained that thought becomes qualitatively reorganized at several points in development. Even though early schemes lay the foundation for later knowledge structures, schemes in one stage bear little resemblance to those in other stages. The child's progression through the *sensorimotor, preoperational, concrete operational,* and *formal operational* stages reflects major transitions in thought in which early action-based schemes evolve into symbolic, then logical, and finally abstract mental structures.

cognition   Processes involved in thinking and mental activity, such as attention, memory, and problem solving.

Stages of Development

Piaget maintained that all children progress through the stages of cognitive development in an invariable sequence—that is, in the same order. No stage can be skipped. In addition, each stage contains a period of formation and a period of attainment. When the child begins a new stage, his schemes are somewhat unstable and loosely organized. By the end of the stage, his schemes are well formed and well organized. Even though Piaget provided age norms for the acquisition of each stage, he believed that because cognitive development is the result of maturational factors working in concert with environmental experiences, some children might reach each stage more quickly or more slowly, depending on the opportunities for learning that they are exposed to.

▶ **Roles of nature and nurture**

The Sensorimotor Stage (Birth to Two Years)   The most striking characteristic of human thinking during the **sensorimotor stage**—the first two years of life—is its solid basis in action. Each time the child reaches for an object, sucks on a nipple, or crawls along the floor, she is obtaining varied feedback about her body and its relationship to the environment that becomes part of her internal schemes. At first, the infant's movements are reflexive, not deliberate or planned. As the child passes through each of the six substages of the sensorimotor stage, her actions become progressively more goal directed and aimed at solving problems. Moreover, she is able to distinguish self from environment and learns about the properties of objects and how they are related to one another. Table 8.1 summarizes the major features of each substage of the sensorimotor period.

▶ **The child's active role**

A significant accomplishment of the sensorimotor stage is the infant's progression toward **means-ends behavior,** the deliberate use of an action to accomplish some goal. During the early substages of sensorimotor development, the infant often initiates actions accidentally rather than purposefully. When Piaget's daughter Lucienne was three months old, she was observed to shake her bassinet

> by moving her legs violently (bending and unbending them, etc.), which makes the cloth dolls swing from the hood. Lucienne looks at them, smiling, and recommences at once. (Piaget, 1952b, pp. 157–158.)

Lucienne repeated her kicking to make the dolls shake in what Piaget calls a **circular reaction,** the repetition of a motor act because of the pleasure it brings. Her first kick, however, was totally accidental and not intentional. Several months afterward, when Lucienne was eight months old, Piaget placed a new doll over the hood of her bassinet. This time her behavior reveals an even greater degree of intentionality:

> She looks at it for a long time, touches it, then feels it by touching its feet, clothes, head, etc. She then ventures to grasp it, which makes the hood sway. She then pulls the doll while watching the effects of this movement. (Piaget, 1952b, p. 256).

Throughout the first two years, then, the child increasingly uses actions as a means of obtaining some end or goal. She experiments with new means toward reaching the same goal and uses familiar behaviors to attain new goals.

A second aspect of sensorimotor development is the child's gradual separation of self from the external environment. Initially, the child derives pleasure from actions that center on her own body. At three months of age, Lucienne "strikes her quilt with her right hand; she scratches it while carefully watching what she is doing, then lets it go, grasps it again, etc." (Piaget, 1952b, p. 92). The circular reaction, in this case, was repeated because of the satisfying sensations it brought to Lucienne's hands. A few months later, in the episode of

sensorimotor stage   In Piagetian theory, the first stage of cognitive development—from birth to approximately two years of age—in which thought is based primarily on action.

means-ends behavior   Deliberate behavior employed to attain a goal.

circular reaction   In Piagetian theory, repetition of some action or behavior because of the pleasure it brings.

Substage	Major Features	Object Concept
Reflexive Activity (0–1 month)	Formation and modification of early schemes based on reflexes such as sucking, looking, and grasping	No attempt to locate objects that have disappeared
Primary Circular Reactions (1–4 months)	Repetition of behaviors that produce interesting results centered on own body	No attempt to locate objects that have disappeared
Secondary Circular Reactions (4–8 months)	Repetition of behaviors that produce interesting results in the external world	Search for objects that have dropped from view or are partially hidden
Coordination of Secondary Schemes (8–12 months)	Combination of actions in order to achieve a goal	Search for completely hidden objects
Tertiary Circular Reactions (12–18 months)	Experimentation with different actions to achieve the same goal or observe the outcomes	Ability to follow visible displacements of an object
Invention of New Means Through Mental Combinations (18–24 months)	Thinking through of potential solutions to problems and imitation of absent models	Ability to follow invisible displacements of an object

TABLE 8.1

The Six Substages of Piaget's Sensorimotor Stage

the swinging dolls, Lucienne's kicking in the bassinet produced a gratifying result in the external environment. In general, the child becomes less centered on the self during this stage and more oriented to the external world.

A third important accomplishment of this stage is the attainment of the **object concept,** or **object permanence.** Infants who possess the object concept realize that objects continue to exist even though they are not within immediate sight or within reach to be acted upon. Up to three months of age, the saying "out of sight, out of mind" characterizes the child's understanding of objects. At about four months of age, she will lift a cloth from a partially covered object or show some reaction, such as surprise or puzzlement, when an object disappears. At about eight months of age, she will search for an object that has completely disappeared—for example, when it has been covered entirely by a cloth. In the last two phases of the attainment of the object concept, she will be able to follow visible and then invisible displacements of the object. In the first instance, the twelve-month-old will be able to follow and find a toy that has been moved from under one cloth to another, as long as the movement is done while she is watching. In the second instance, the eighteen-month-old can find an object moved from location A to location B, even if the displacement from A to B is done while the infant is not looking.

The completion of the sensorimotor stage and the beginning of the next stage is signaled by the child's display of *deferred imitation,* the ability to imitate a model who is no longer present. At age sixteen months, Piaget's daughter Jacqueline was playing with a boy who suddenly had a dramatic temper

object concept Realization that objects exist even when they are not within view. Also called *object permanence.*

A significant attainment in infancy is the child's understanding of object permanence. Children under about 3 to 4 months of age act as if a hidden or obstructed object no longer exists.

tantrum. The next day, the normally well-behaved Jacqueline mimicked the little boy's behaviors with remarkable accuracy. To do so, she must have had the ability to represent the boy's overt behaviors in internal form and to draw on that representation hours later. It is this ability to represent events and objects internally that marks the beginning of a major transition in thought.

The Preoperational Stage (About Two to Seven Years) The key feature of the young child's thought in the **preoperational stage** is the *semiotic function,* the child's ability to use a symbol, object, or word to stand for something. He can play with a cardboard tube as if it were a car or draw a picture of the balloons he had at his third birthday party. The semiotic function is a powerful cognitive ability because it permits the child to think about past and future events and to employ language. In fact, Piaget asserted that language would not be possible without this significant characteristic of thought; the child must possess the general cognitive ability to let one thing stand for another before words can be used to represent objects, events, and relationships. The semiotic function is also a prerequisite for imagery, fantasy play, and drawing, all of which the preschool child begins to manifest.

preoperational stage In Piagetian theory, the second stage of development—approximately from two to seven years of age—in which thought is now symbolic in form.

Despite this tremendous advance in thinking, preoperational thought has distinct limitations. One is that children in this stage are said to be **egocentric,** a term that describes the child's inability to separate his own perspective from that of others. Put into words, his guiding principle might be, "You see what I see, you think what I think." An example is the three-year-old who thinks he is hiding from an older sibling or parent by crouching behind a chair. Even though his legs and feet might be sticking out for all present to see, the youngster

egocentrism Preoperational child's inability to separate his or her own perspective from that of others.

▶ **Interaction among domains**

believes he is well concealed because he himself is unable to see anyone. According to Piaget, the preschooler's egocentrism has ramifications for both his social communicative behavior and his perceptual skills. As we saw in Chapter 7, Piagetian theory predicts poor referential communication skills in children under age seven and, as we will see in Chapter 11, the inability to appreciate the perspectives of others in perceptual tasks.

The second limitation of preoperational thought lies in the child's inability to solve problems flexibly and logically. The tasks that Piaget used to assess the status of the child's cognitive development are called **conservation tasks.** These problems generally require the child to observe some transformation in physical quantities that are initially equivalent and to reason about the impact of the transformation. Figure 8.1 shows several conservation tasks.

Suppose we use the conservation of liquid quantity task to illustrate how the preoperational child thinks. The four- or five-year-old will usually quickly agree that two beakers (A and B) of water have the same amount of liquid. If the liquid from A is poured into the tall cylinder C, however, the child will state that C now has more than B. According to Piaget, this error is the result of several cognitive traits of preoperational children. One is **centration**—that is, focusing on one aspect of the problem, in this case the height of the cylinder—to the exclusion of all other information, such as its narrower width, that could help produce a correct solution. A second cognitive trait at work here is lack of **reversibility.** The preoperational child cannot mentally reverse the action of pouring from C to A; if he could, he would realize that the two containers still contain the same amount of liquid as they did at the start of the problem. Third, the preoperational child tends to **focus on states** rather than on the events that occur between states. It is as if he has stored two static photographs of containers A and B, and then B and C, rather than a video of the sequence of events. He fails to realize the connection between the two components of the conservation problem and, as a result, fails the conservation task.

conservation tasks Problems that require the child to make judgments about the equivalence of two displays; used to assess stage of cognitive development.

centration In Piagetian theory, tendency of the child to focus on only one aspect of a problem.

reversibility In Piagetian theory, the ability to mentally reverse or negate an action or transformation.

focus on states Preoperational child's tendency to treat two or more connected events as unrelated.

concrete operational stage In Piagetian theory, the third stage of development—approximately from seven to eleven years of age—in which thought is logical when stimuli are physically present.

operation In Piagetian theory, mental action such as reversibility;

The Concrete Operational Stage (About Seven to Eleven Years)   Children enter the **concrete operational stage** when they begin to be able to solve the conservation tasks correctly. At first, the six- or seven-year-old may solve only a few of the simpler problems, such as conservation of length, number, or liquid quantity. Later, he will be able to conserve on tasks that involve area or volume. The use of the same cognitive structures to solve increasingly difficult problems within a given stage Piaget called *horizontal décalage.*

The reason for this shift is that the child is now capable of performing **operations,** mental actions such as reversibility that allow him to reason about the events that have transpired. He can pour the liquid back from C to A "in his head" or think about the narrow width of the tall cylinder as compensating for its height. In other words, the child now thinks logically, although the physical components of the problem must still be present (if not externally in the world, then as images in the head). The child's thought is also less egocentric, allowing him to understand that other individuals' perceptions, beliefs, and feelings might be different from his own. The concrete operational child is becoming a true "thinker," as long as there are specific objects or events that his logic can be applied to.

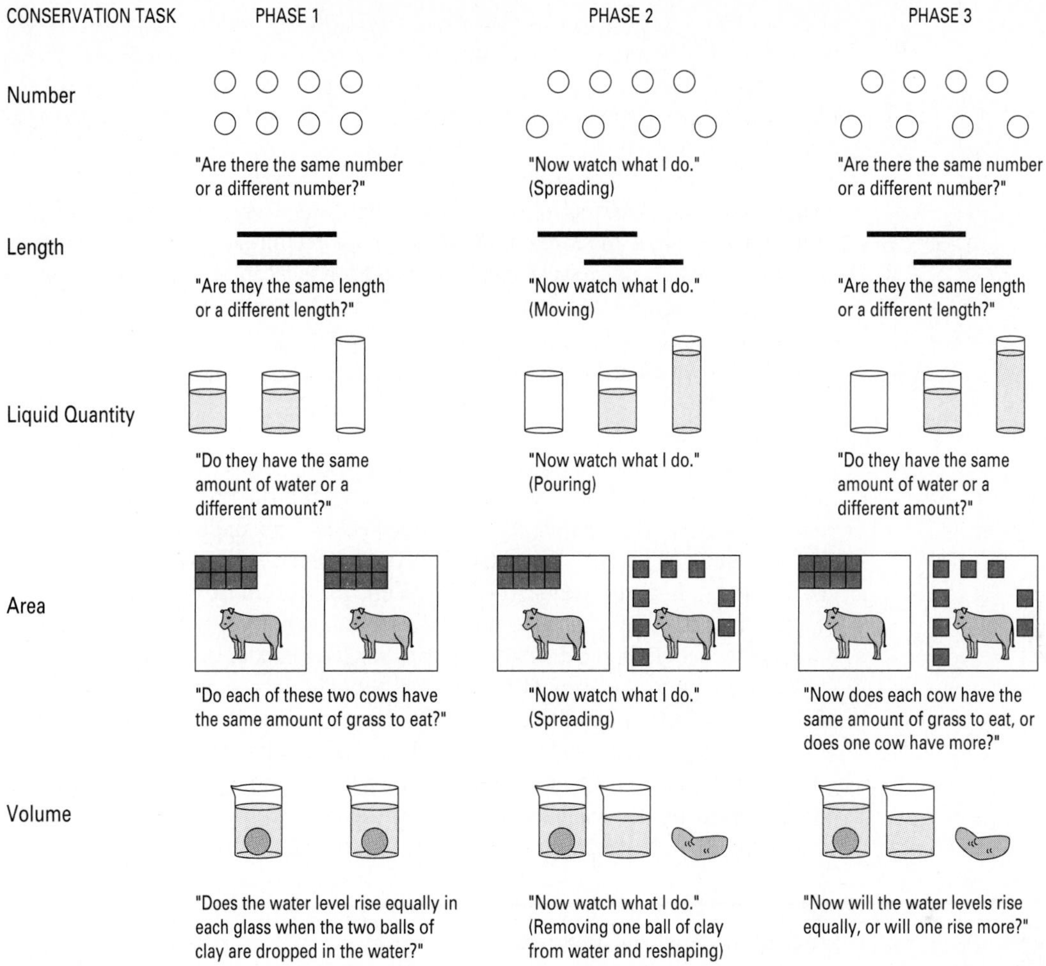

CONSERVATION TASK	PHASE 1	PHASE 2	PHASE 3

Number

"Are there the same number or a different number?"

"Now watch what I do." (Spreading)

"Are there the same number or a different number?"

Length

"Are they the same length or a different length?"

"Now watch what I do." (Moving)

"Are they the same length or a different length?"

Liquid Quantity

"Do they have the same amount of water or a different amount?"

"Now watch what I do." (Pouring)

"Do they have the same amount of water or a different amount?"

Area

"Do each of these two cows have the same amount of grass to eat?"

"Now watch what I do." (Spreading)

"Now does each cow have the same amount of grass to eat, or does one cow have more?"

Volume

"Does the water level rise equally in each glass when the two balls of clay are dropped in the water?"

"Now watch what I do." (Removing one ball of clay from water and reshaping)

"Now will the water levels rise equally, or will one rise more?"

FIGURE 8.1

Examples of Conservation Tasks   In the first phase of all conservation tasks, the child agrees that two stimulus arrays are equivalent. In the second phase, one of the stimuli is physically altered but remains equivalent to the other. In the third phase, the child is questioned about the equivalence of the arrays. The child who conserves will respond that the arrays remain the same.

formal operational stage   In Piagetian theory, the last stage of development—approximately from eleven to fifteen years of age—in which thought is abstract and hypothetical.

hypothetical reasoning   Ability to systematically generate and evaluate potential solutions to a problem.

The Formal Operational Stage (About Eleven to Fifteen Years)   By the time the child reaches adolescence, she will most likely have moved to the final stage in Piaget's theory, the **formal operational stage.** Thinking in this stage is both logical and abstract. Problems like "Bill is shorter than Sam, but taller than Jim. Who is taller?" can now be solved without seeing the individuals or conjuring up concrete images of them. The adolescent can also reason **hypothetically;** that is, she can generate potential solutions to problems in a thoroughly systematic fashion, much as a scientist approaches an experiment.

Piaget's pendulum problem allows us to examine the thinking of the formal operational adolescent. In this task, the subject is shown an object hanging from a string and is asked to determine the factor that influences the frequency of oscillation, the rate at which the pendulum swings. The length of the string, the weight of the object, the force of the push on the object, and the height from which the object is released can all be varied. How do children in earlier Piagetian stages approach this problem? Children in the preoperational and concrete operational stages typically try various manipulations in a haphazard fashion. They might compare the effect of a long string attached to a heavy weight and a short string tied to a light weight. Or they experiment with the weight of the object and force of the push, but leave out length of the string. In contrast, formal operational children are both systematic and complete in varying the potential influences on oscillation. For example, they might keep the weight constant; examine the effects of varying length, push, and height; and write down their conclusions. Most adolescents, Piaget observed, could correctly discover that length of the string was the critical factor in how fast the pendulum swings (Inhelder & Piaget, 1958).

In the social realm, achieving abstract thought means that the adolescent can think about the nature of society and her own future role in it. Idealism is not uncommon at this developmental stage because she understands more fully concepts such as justice, love, and liberty and thinks about possibilities, not just realities. In some ways, the adolescent may be more of a "dreamer" or utopian than the adult because the adolescent has not yet had to confront the practical facts of living and working in the world (Inhelder & Piaget, 1958).

The development of formal operational thought represents the culmination of the reorganizations in thought that have taken place throughout each stage in childhood. Even though older children and adults continue to manifest growth in thinking, they experience no further qualitative alterations in cognitive structures. By adolescence thought has become logical, flexible, and abstract, and its internal guiding structures are now highly organized.

Implications for Education

Although Piaget was not explicitly concerned with the process of education, his theory carries some clear implications for the teaching of children. The first implication is that the individual child's current stage of development must be carefully taken into account as teachers plan lessons. For example, if a particular seven-year-old is in the stage of concrete operations, she should be given problems involving actual physical objects to observe or manipulate rather than abstract word problems or diagrams (Flavell, 1963). An addition or subtraction problem could be presented by adding or taking away wooden blocks from an array in front of the child rather than by writing numerical symbols on the chalkboard. Similarly, a four-year-old preoperational child might have difficulty with tasks requiring the use of logic; a more fruitful strategy might be to foster the imagination and creativity that result from the recently acquired semiotic function. By encouraging drawing, pretend play, and vocal expression, teachers can capitalize on the preschooler's cognitive strengths and encourage development within that stage.

A second, related implication is that what the child knows already will determine what new information he is able to absorb. Because his current cognitive structures limit what he will be able to assimilate, it is important for the teacher to be aware of the child's current state of knowledge. In addition, cognitive advances are most optimally made when new material is very slightly different or novel from what the child already knows (Ginsberg & Opper, 1988). The teacher's task, then, is to plan lessons that are tailored to the needs of the individual child rather than of the class as a whole and to be flexible in devising instructional materials that stretch the child one step beyond what he already knows.

▶ **The child's active role**

One of Piaget's most important statements about cognitive development is that it is the result of the *active engagement of the child.* Early sensorimotor schemes and later mental operations are all founded first on the child's physical activity and later on mental actions. Thus education, too, must be structured in such a way that it will promote the child's active participation. Instead of imparting a list of theories or scientific facts to learn by rote, teachers following a Piagetian model provide children with experiments that allow them to discover scientific principles on their own. Children do not memorize numerical relationships, such as the multiplication tables, but discover them by manipulating sets of objects under the close guidance of the teacher. According to Piagetian thinking, active learning of this sort promotes deeper and more enduring understanding.

Educational programs based on a Piagetian model have varied in their instructional goals—some have emphasized the teaching of specific skills such as conservation, and others have focused on more general principles, such as fostering children's active participation in the educational process (Crain, 1985). Many of these programs have been specifically targeted for preschool-aged children, probably for good reasons. One difficulty in implementing Piagetian-based education in higher grades is that individualized instruction is not always possible when there are twenty or more students in a classroom; in preschool classrooms, which tend to have fewer students, individualized instruction is more normative. Nevertheless, many teachers have found inspiration in the rich theoretical framework Jean Piaget devised for thinking about how and what to teach children.

According to Piaget, the ideal way to educate children is to actively involve them in the discovery of scientific or mathematical principles.

Evaluating Piaget's Theory

Given its wide-ranging scope, we should not be surprised that Piaget's theory has stimulated so much research in developmental psychology. Without Piaget's dominating presence, one wonders whether the object concept, logical reasoning, and other aspects of children's thought would have been researched as extensively as they have been. In sheer numbers of empirical studies generated by the writings of one person, Jean Piaget probably has few rivals in developmental psychology. Like all good theories, Piaget's ideas have also spawned a host of debates about the fundamental nature of cognitive change. These debates do not reflect any failure on Piaget's part to provide a "correct" account of cognitive development. Rather, they are a tribute to the power of his ideas and his contribution to the scientific process.

Contemporary evaluations of Piaget's theory have raised several key points. First, did Piaget provide an accurate portrayal of the ages at which different cognitive skills are acquired? Second, does cognitive development proceed in a stage-like fashion? Third, could there be alternative explanations for the behaviors Piaget observed in children of different ages?

What Are the Ages of Acquisition?   One major criticism of Piaget's theory is that he underestimated the abilities of young children. Many researchers have found that when cognitive tasks are simplified or restructured or when children are observed in more naturalistic settings, they display cognitive skills at much earlier ages than Piaget believed them capable of.

Take the object concept, for example. Piaget maintained that the first real notions about the permanence of objects do not occur until about ten months of age, when infants will search for objects that are completely covered. Renée Baillargeon (1987), however, was able to demonstrate that infants as young as four months old have a rudimentary understanding of the continuing existence of objects. Figure 8.2 shows the phases of this experiment. At first, the infants observed a screen that rotated 180 degrees over repeated trials. As you might expect, they showed habituation of visual fixation to this display. Next, a box was placed behind the screen so that as the screen rotated, it occluded the box. In the *possible-event* condition, the screen stopped moving at the point where it hit the box. In the *impossible-event* condition, the box was surreptitiously removed and the screen passed through the space the box would have occupied. In two control conditions, the screen either moved or stopped, as in the two experimental conditions, but no box was present. Infants looked significantly longer at the impossible event than the possible event, apparently noticing that the screen was moving through the space that should have been occupied by the box. Looking did not differ in the two control conditions, indicating that the type of movement did not determine the infants' looking. Thus, infants seemed to be aware that the box in the impossible-event condition should have had an effect on the movement of the screen, even though they could not see it. This awareness, argues Baillargeon, is an indicator of the object concept.

Similarly, Rochel Gelman (1969) noted that conservation of number could be demonstrated in five-year-old children, who in Piaget's view are still in the preoperational stage of development and lack the logical thought structures to perform this task correctly. Gelman first determined that all the subjects in her sample were unable to conserve number. Then she provided training on

FIGURE 8.2

Do Infants Have an Object Concept?

In Baillargeon's experiment, infants were habituated to a screen rotating 180 degrees (A). Next, infants in the *impossible event* condition saw the screen seeming to pass through the location of a box (B, on left), while infants in the *possible event* condition saw the screen stopping at the location of the box (C, on left). Infants in the *impossible event* condition looked significantly longer at this event, suggesting that they were puzzled by what they saw and therefore had an object concept. The control conditions (shown at right) were included to make sure that infants were not responding to the arc of the screen's movement.

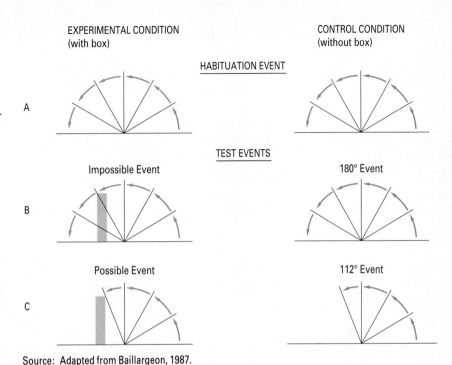

EXPERIMENTAL CONDITION (with box)

CONTROL CONDITION (without box)

HABITUATION EVENT

A

TEST EVENTS

Impossible Event

180° Event

B

Possible Event

112° Event

C

Source: Adapted from Baillargeon, 1987.

the "oddity problem." On each trial, children saw three stimuli and were directed to indicate which one was different from the other two. On some trials, the "odd" stimulus differed in number from the other two; on others, the "odd" stimulus was different in length. After the training period, the children were tested on the conservation of length and number. The majority performed correctly even when they were tested several weeks after the training period. In fact, in later work, Gelman has shown that under some circumstances, even three- and four-year-olds are able to conserve number (Gelman, 1972).

Naturalistic studies of children's communications with each other also demonstrate that egocentrism is not as prevalent among preschoolers as Piaget thought. Recall the studies of referential communication described in Chapter 7, in which we saw that two-year-olds employ behaviors such as pointing and repetition to ensure that peer listeners understand them (Wellman & Lempers, 1977) and that four-year-olds adjust their speech depending on whether the listener is a child or adult (Shatz & Gelman, 1973). Being responsive to the needs of the listener requires sensitivity to the perspective of another, a distinctly nonegocentric characteristic.

Piaget himself was not so concerned with the specific ages at which children acquired cognitive skills as he was with the sequence of development. Thus, the fact that many cognitive attainments occur earlier than he suggested is, by itself, not problematic. As researchers sought explanations for the presence of cognitive skills at earlier ages, however, they were drawn to deeper questions about the nature of cognitive development.

▶ **Development as continuous/ stagelike**

Is Cognitive Development Stagelike? If cognitive development proceeds in stages, there should be common features in how children think within a stage and distinctive differences in how they think across stages. One problem with Piagetian theory is that it posits more consistency in performance within a given stage than is actually found in the behavior of children. In one study, Ina Uzgiris (1968) tested children who should have been in the stage of concrete operations on conservation of quantity, weight, and volume. The same tasks were tested with different materials, such as plasticine balls, metal cubes, and plastic wires. Many children were able to conserve when one material was used (say, plasticine balls) but not when another was employed (say, metal cubes). If, indeed, conservation is tied to the presence of logical thought structures, it should not matter which materials are used to conduct the conservation tests.

Other researchers have noted that the correlations among various abilities predicted to co-occur within the stage of concrete operations are much lower than would be expected if development were truly stagelike (Gelman & Baillargeon, 1983). Piaget maintained, for example, that before children could conserve number they had to understand the principle of *class inclusion,* the idea that some groups of objects are subsets within a larger set. "Tulips" are a subset of "flowers," just as "five" is a set contained within "six." Yet children can conserve number by the age of six or seven and still not fully understand the concept of class inclusion (Brainerd, 1978).

Because of these findings many contemporary researchers now favor the position that development shows more continuity than Piaget allowed for. The fact that children display signs of logical thinking and a lack of egocentrism well before the age of seven years suggests that the thinking of younger and older children shows more common features than differences. What seems to vary among children of different ages is not their cognitive skills but the degree to which the same basic skills are displayed.

Are There Alternative Explanations for Development?   Many studies have confirmed Piaget's general claims about the patterns of behavior children display at different ages. Without special training, for example, most children under age six or seven fail conservation tasks, whereas older children perform them successfully. Adolescents are indeed capable of solving problems more systematically and abstractly than their younger counterparts. Yet many psychologists disagree with Piaget about the precise mechanisms that account for such patterns in the development of thinking processes.

The basic challenge to Piaget's theory centers on whether cognitive development is best understood in terms of emerging symbolic, logical, and hypothetical thought structures or whether some other explanation is more tenable. A case in point is the successful training of conservation provided by Rochel Gelman (1969) just described. Gelman suggests that young children normally fail conservation tasks because they fail to attend to the correct portions of the problem, not because they lack mental operations like reversibility. If children's attention is directed to the salient cues, Gelman and others argue, they will be successful in conserving. Younger children may also be less skilled at remembering than older children, forgetting elements of problems that are essential to reaching the correct solution. Thus, cognitive development results from a change in how information is gathered, manipulated, and stored rather than from the alteration of cognitive structures themselves.

▶ **Roles of nature and nurture**

Another central Piagetian tenet is that maturation, in conjunction with experience, is responsible for the unfolding of more sophisticated thought structures. The heavy emphasis Piaget places on maturation implies that the sequence of development is universal. Yet not all children reach the stage of formal operations, and some do not even attain the highest levels of concrete operations. Many American adults, in fact, fail to display formal operational thought (Neimark, 1979). Moreover, members of many non-Western cultures do not display formal operational thinking, especially when they have little experience with formal schooling (Dasen, 1972; Rogoff, 1981). At the same time, specific kinds of cultural experiences may accelerate the emergence of conservation and formal operational thought. Douglass Price-Williams and his colleagues (Price-Williams, Gordon, & Ramirez, 1969) examined two groups of rural Mexican children six to nine years old on standard conservation problems. Half of the children came from pottery-making families, the other half from families who practiced other trades. Children who had experience in manipulating clay for pottery making were far more likely to conserve than the other children. Studies such as these imply that the child's experiences in the surrounding sociocultural context may shape the nature of thought to a greater degree than Piaget acknowledged. They also challenge the notion that Western scientific thinking represents the highest form of thought and the end point of development (Greenfield, 1976). The ability to solve problems like a miniature scientist may be highly valued in our own culture, but less so in cultures in which other skills such as hunting, farming, or even social facility are more essential to successful living.

Despite these criticisms, several important threads from Piaget's work continue to run through contemporary ideas about cognitive development. First and foremost, the idea that children are active participants in their own growth is well accepted. Few researchers believe that children merely absorb information like sponges swelling with liquid. Moreover, many modern accounts of cognition assume that what the individual knows at a given time determines the knowledge he or she can acquire, a distinctly Piagetian idea. Contemporary theorists owe an enormous debt to Piaget for his tremendous insights into the workings of the developing mind.

▶ **Sociocultural influence**

▶ **The child's active role**

THE INFORMATION-PROCESSING APPROACH

Another theoretical framework we can apply to cognitive development is the information-processing model. As we saw in Chapter 2, information-processing theorists believe that human cognition is best understood as the management of information through a system with limited space or resources. Many traditional information-processing models are called **multistore models** because they posit several mental structures through which information flows sequentially, much as data passes through a computer. Other theorists in this field have advanced a **limited-resource model** of the cognitive system that emphasizes a finite amount of available cognitive energy that can be deployed in numerous ways, but only with certain tradeoffs.

Most multistore models distinguish between psychological structures and control processes. Psychological *structures,* as we saw in Chapter 2, are analogous to the "hardware" of a computer and typically include (1) a *sensory store,*

multistore model Information-processing model that describes a sequence of mental structures through which information flows.

limited-resource model Information-processing model that emphasizes the allocation of finite energy within the cognitive system.

which holds new information in essentially raw form, like an echo or an enduring visual image, for very brief periods of time; (2) *memory stores* (often separated into *working memory* and *long-term memory*), which retain information
for seconds, minutes, or even years; (3) a *central processor* that oversees and
coordinates the components in the system; and (4) a *response system* that allows the individual to produce an answer to a problem or question. The *control
processes* are mental activities that move information from one structure to
another, much like "software" functions for the computer.

Suppose someone asks you to repeat a list of words: shoe, car, truck, hat,
coat, bus. If you have paid attention to all of the words and have "input" them
like a good computer into your cognitive system, the first stage of processing
would take place in the **sensory store.** Information is held here for a fraction of
a second in a form very close to the audible sounds in which you experienced
it. Next, the words may move to the memory stores. The first is **working
memory** (often also called **short-term store**), which holds information for no
more than a couple of minutes. If you were to repeat the words over and over
to yourself in an attempt to rehearse them, you would be employing a control
process to retain information in working memory. You might also make contact
with **long-term memory,** the repository of more enduring information you
have stored, and notice that the items belong to two categories, clothing and
vehicles. The central processor, which functions like an "executive decision
maker," oversees this communication among the structures of the information-processing system. Finally, when you are asked to say the words aloud,
your response system functions to help you reproduce the sounds you heard
moments earlier. Figure 8.3 illustrates this process.

Unlike multistore models, limited-resource models of cognition put their
emphasis on the allocation of energy for various cognitive activities rather than
on the mental structures themselves. The basic assumption is that the pool of
resources available for processing, retaining, and reporting information is finite (Bjorkland & Harnishfeger, 1990). In one such model, first introduced in
Chapter 2, Robbie Case proposes an inverse relationship between the amount
of space available for operating on information and that available for storage
(Case, 1985; Case, Kurland, & Goldberg, 1982). *Operations* include processes
such as identifying the stimuli and recognizing relationships among them; *storage* refers to the retention of information for use at a later time. If a substantial
amount of mental effort is expended on operations, less space is available for
storage or retention.

In the simple memory experiment we just examined, the effort we use to
identify the words and notice the categorical relationships among them will
determine the space we have left over for storing those words. If we are proficient at recognizing words and their relationships, storage space will be available. If these tasks cost us substantial effort, however, our resources will be
taxed and few of them will be left for the task of remembering.

How do these two general information-processing frameworks, the multistore model and the limited-resource model, account for cognitive development? Multistore models allow for two possibilities. Changes in cognition can
stem from either an increase in the size of the structures—the "hardware"—
or from increasing proficiency in employing control processes. For example,
the capacity of working memory may increase with age, or as they grow older,
children may increase in the tendency to rehearse items and thereby remember them. Limited-resource models like Case's suggest that what changes dur-

sensory store   Memory store that
holds information for very brief periods of time in a form that closely
resembles the initial input.

working memory   Short-term
memory store in which mental
operations such as rehearsal and
categorization take place.

long-term memory   Memory that
holds information for extended periods of time.

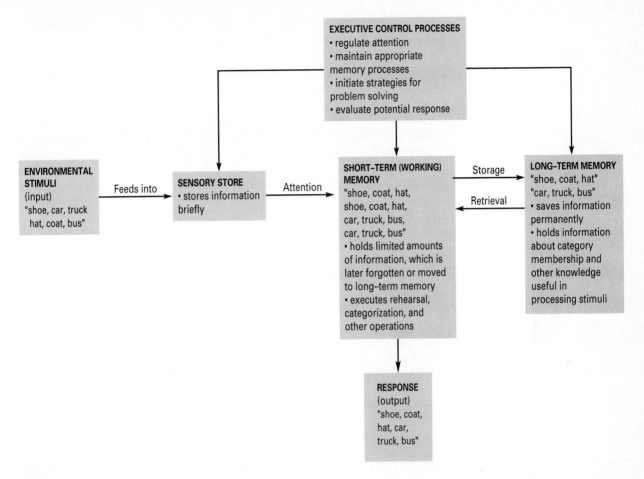

FIGURE 8.3

Memory: The Multistore Model

According to multistore models, information to be remembered passes through a series of structures, such as the sensory store, working memory, and long-term memory. The various components of the information-processing system often communicate with one another and are overseen by a central (or executive) processor.

ing development is operational efficiency. As children become more proficient in manipulating information, more internal space is freed up for storage. Thus, limited-resource models posit that developmental changes in operations influence the capacity of memory.

The Development of Attention

Have you ever noticed that sometimes a seven- or eight-year-old can spend hours absorbed in a single activity, like doing a jigsaw puzzle or playing Nintendo, whereas a toddler seems to bound back and forth from activity to activity? Even if your experience with children is not extensive, most of us have a sense that older children are better able to "pay attention" to a given task than younger children. Parents read brief stories to their two-year-olds but expect their adolescent offspring to read novels. Preschool teachers present their charges with only occasional brief structured tasks, like painting or coloring; high school teachers expect their students to follow their lessons for an hour or more at a time. Clearly, children's attentional processes undergo recognizable changes with development.

As we saw in Chapter 6, *attention* has been conceptualized as a state of alertness or arousal that allows the individual to focus on a selected aspect of the environment, often in preparation for learning or problem solving (Kahneman, 1973). Attention represents the first step in the flow of information through the cognitive processing system and, as such, is a critical phase. Unless information enters the system in the first place, there will be few opportunities to develop memory, concepts, or other cognitive skills. Children with a poor capacity to attend will have difficulties in learning, the ramifications of which can be enormous, especially as they enter school. Recent evidence corroborates that children who have greater attention spans and persistence in tasks at ages four to five years have higher intelligence scores and school achievement by the time they get to second grade (Palisin, 1986).

Focusing Attention   One of the most obvious developmental trends that takes place approximately from ages one through six is the dramatic increase in the child's ability to *focus* attention on some activity or set of stimuli. Holly Ruff and Katharine Lawson (1990) observed one-, two-, and three-and-a-half-year-old children while they played with an array of six toys. There was a steady linear increase with age in the amount of sustained attention directed to individual toys. On average, one-year-olds showed focused attention for 3.33 seconds, two-year-olds for 5.36 seconds, and three-and-a-half-year-olds for 8.17 seconds. The attention span continues to increase throughout the early school years and adolescence (Yendovitskaya, 1971).

▶ **Interaction among domains**

Why does focused attention increase with age? It may be that maturation of the central nervous system is partly responsible. The reticular activating system, the portion of the lower brain stem that regulates levels of arousal in the organism, is not fully mature until adolescence. Another factor may be the increasing complexity of the child's interests. Young children seem to be intrigued by the physical properties of objects, but since these are often not too complex, simply looking at or touching objects leads quickly to habituation. On the other hand, older children are more concerned with creative and varied ways of playing with objects (Ruff & Lawson, 1990). As the child actively generates more possible uses for stimuli, her attention becomes more captivated by them. Thus, the child's overall cognitive development and her active engagement with stimuli feed back to influence attention.

▶ **The child's active role**

One other aspect of sustained attention has been revealed in studies examining how children watch television. Daniel Anderson and his colleagues have noted that when children watch programs like "Sesame Street," the longer they look at the screen, the longer they keep looking (Anderson, Choi, & Lorch, 1987). If preschool children attended to the TV program for fifteen seconds, it was highly unlikely that they would be distracted by other environmental events. This greater likelihood of continued looking after longer initial looks is called **attentional inertia**. Research has yet to reveal how attentional inertia might change with age. However, it may serve a valuable function in cognitive growth by maintaining the flow of information passing through the system. The end result is that the child is exposed to new stimuli that she might not have noticed if she had looked away.

attentional inertia   Continued sustained attention after an initial period of focused attention.

Deploying Attention   A second developmental change that takes place in attentional processes is that older children become more able to control their attention in a systematic manner—that is, they *deploy* their attention effectively—as, for example, when they are comparing two complex stimuli. The

As children grow older, they become increasingly skilled at attending to some stimuli and ignoring distracting information.

Vurpillot (1968) study described in Chapter 6 illustrates how children over the age of six make *exhaustive* comparisons of two pictures as they attempt to determine if they are identical or different.

In a more recent experiment, Patricia Miller and Yvette Harris (1988) found that children also use more *efficient* attentional strategies as they grow older. Preschoolers were asked to determine whether two rows of six drawings of toys were the same or different. To accomplish this task, they had to open doors that covered the pictures. Three-year-olds tended to be systematic, but not very efficient; they opened one entire row first, then opened the next row. In contrast, the four-year-olds adopted a systematic *and* more efficient strategy for comparing; they opened each vertically aligned pair from one end of the array to the next. As a consequence, the older subjects were more accurate in their judgments about whether the rows were identical or not.

Selective Attention   Still another aspect of attention that changes with development is the ability to be *selective*. Older children are much more likely to ignore information that is irrelevant or that distracts from some central activity or problem than younger children are (Lane & Pearson, 1982). An experiment conducted by George Strutt and his colleagues (Strutt, Anderson, & Well, 1975) illustrates this effect.

Children of ages six, nine, and twelve years, as well as adults, participated in a *speeded classification task*. They were given decks of cards that varied on one or more stimulus dimensions: form (circle or square), orientation of a line (horizontal or vertical), and location of a star (above or below the center). The objective was to sort the cards on the basis of one predetermined dimension as quickly as they could. But what happened when an irrelevant dimension was added to the cards in the deck? This manipulation interfered with the ability of six-year-olds to sort the cards but had little effect on the performance of older children. What about the effect of adding a second irrelevant dimension? Again, the six-year-olds were the most dramatically affected by the addition of distracting information.

The ability to attend to some parts of an event or activity to the exclusion of others signals the child's increasing skill at controlling his or her own cognitive processing. Contributing to this change may be a growing understanding that there are limits to the child's attentional capacity and that cognitive tasks are best accomplished with focused attention. In other words, the child shows gains in **metacognition,** the knowledge and awareness of one's own cognitive processes. Some evidence of that knowledge appears during the preschool years. In a recent study, three- and four-year-olds were asked if they would rather listen to pairs of stories simultaneously or one at a time. The three-year-olds were willing to listen to two tape recorders at once, but the four-year-olds preferred to listen to one at a time (Pillow, 1988). Thus, the development of attention involves an awareness of attention as a limited resource, coupled with more focused, systematic, and selective allocation of that resource.

The Development of Memory

metacognition Awareness and knowledge of cognitive processes.

Few cognitive skills are as basic as the ability to store information encountered at a given time for potential retrieval seconds, minutes, days, or even years later. It is hard to imagine how any other cognitive activity, such as problem solving or concept formation, could take place without the ability to draw on previously experienced information. How could we classify dogs, horses, and giraffes into the category "animals" unless we remember the common shared features of each? How could we solve a problem like Piaget's pendulum task without remembering the results of each of our miniexperiments with length of the string, weight of the object, and so on? In one way or another, memory is a crucial element in most of our thinking.

Memory, however, is far from a simple or unitary construct. One distinction, for example, is drawn between episodic and semantic memory. **Episodic memory** is defined as memory for events that have occurred at a specific time and place in the past ("What did you do on your first day of school?"). **Semantic memory,** on the other hand, consists of general concepts or facts that are stored without reference to a specific previous event ("How many inches are there in a foot?"). We can make another distinction, between recognition and recall memory. Tasks that measure **recognition memory** require subjects to indicate if a picture, word, or other stimulus has been encountered before ("Have you seen this picture on previous trials of this experiment?"). All that is usually required of the subject is a simple "yes" or "no" answer or some other simple response that signals an item has been encountered before. In **recall memory** tasks, subjects must reproduce previously presented stimuli ("Tell me the twelve words you heard me say a few minutes ago").

The fact that memory can be conceptualized in such different ways has complicated the task of describing developmental processes. Nevertheless, two decades of research on this multifaceted area of cognition have begun to suggest some clear and predictable trends in the development of memory.

Early Recognition Memory   How early can we demonstrate the presence of memory? Essentially, almost from birth, if we are talking about recognition. A characteristic useful for documenting young infants' perceptual abilities and discussed in Chapter 6, *habituation,* has also been fruitful in yielding information about infants' abilities to recognize previously viewed stimuli.

Much of the research on infant recognition memory has been conducted by Joseph Fagan, who has used the following general procedure. First, a visual stimulus such as a photograph of a human face or geometric figure (some examples are shown in Figure 8.4) is presented to the infant for a predetermined period of time. On a subsequent trial, the same stimulus is paired with a completely new item, and the time the infant spends looking at each is recorded. In this *paired-comparison procedure,* infants typically look longer at the novel stimulus than at the familiar one, suggesting that they remember the familiar item.

Using this basic approach, Fagan (1974) has demonstrated that five- to six-month-olds familiarized with black-and-white photos of human faces for only a few minutes retain information about them for surprisingly long periods of time. When the recognition test occurred three hours or up to fourteen days after the initial familiarization, infants showed consistently longer visual fixations to the novel stimulus. This is an impressive level of performance for infants only a few months old.

Researchers have reported similarly high levels of recognition memory among preschool-aged children. Marvin Daehler and Danuta Bukatko (1977) showed one-and-a-half- to three-and-a-half-year-old children forty pictures of

episodic memory   Memory for events that took place at a specific time and place.

semantic memory   Memory for general concepts or facts.

recognition memory   Ability to identify whether a stimulus has been previously encountered.

recall memory   Ability to reproduce stimuli that have previously been encountered.

FIGURE 8.4

Infant Recognition Memory

Fagan tested infant recognition memory by using visual stimuli in a paired-comparison procedure. For each row, one of the stimuli was presented repeatedly until habituation occurred. Then one of the other stimuli in the row was paired with the familiar stimulus to see if infants preferred the novel item. Infants only a few months old looked longer at novel items up to fourteen days after the initial familiarization.

Source: Adapted from Fagan, 1974.

▶ **Roles of nature and nurture**

memory span Number of stimulus items that can be recalled after a brief interval of time.

memory strategy Mental activity, such as rehearsal, that enhances memory performance.

common objects. The stimuli reappeared paired with novel pictures after up to fifty intervening stimuli. Nevertheless, children of all ages showed consistently greater visual attention to the new pictures, indicating good memory for pictures they had previously seen. With somewhat older children who are able to verbalize what they have seen, researchers have found that three- to five-year-olds recognize more than three-fourths of the hundred pictures they had viewed as many as twenty-eight days earlier (Brown & Scott, 1971).

The ability to recognize previously viewed stimuli thus appears to be rudimentary, present almost right from birth. The ability to distinguish the familiar from the novel probably has a biological basis because it appears so early in human infants and is evident in other species as well. Considering how important memory is to other cognitive activities, it is not surprising that this early form of retention should appear so early in the developmental process.

Developmental Changes in Recall Suppose someone asks you to repeat a string of digits, such as a phone number. Provided the number is not too long, like most adults, you should be able to repeat between seven and nine digits with relatively little difficulty as long as no more than approximately thirty seconds elapse after you first hear the digits. Tasks like these measure **memory span,** the number of stimulus items that can be *recalled* after a brief interval of time. Children under the age of ten remember fewer items than do adults. As Figure 8.5 shows, two-year-olds typically remember only about two items, four-year-olds about three or four, and seven-year-olds about five items (Dempster, 1981).

Do these changes in memory span occur because the storage capacity of memory increases? That is, does the "hardware" of the information-processing system hold increasingly greater amounts of information as the child grows? The findings of numerous memory experiments suggest that this is not necessarily the case. Instead, children's ability to employ **memory strategies,** activities to enhance the encoding and retrieval of information, increases with

FIGURE 8.5

Developmental Changes in Memory Span

In the memory span task, subjects are asked to repeat a string of digits after an interval of a few seconds. The points on the curve represent the average number of digits subjects are able to recall. The bars represent the ranges of typical performance at each age. Memory span increases throughout childhood and approaches the adult level between ages ten and twelve years.

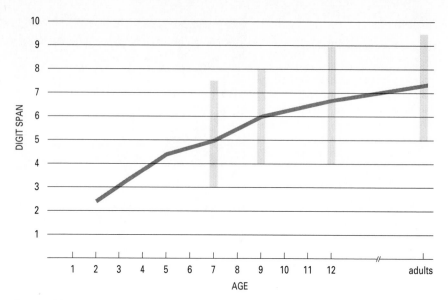

Source: Adapted from Dempster, 1981.

age. Children seven years and older are more likely than younger children to rehearse items or reorganize them into more meaningful, and hence more memorable, units. For instance, noting that the numbers 1, 3, 5, and 7 form the sequence of odd numbers makes the list easier to recall. So does simply repeating them over and over.

Robbie Case and his colleagues have proposed that increases in memory span can also be understood as a result of the increasing operational efficiency children display as they mature (Case, Kurland, & Goldberg, 1982). These researchers asked three- to six-year-olds to perform two tasks—repeat a list of words one at a time as fast as possible and then recall those same lists of words. Children who were quick to repeat the words had higher levels of memory compared with children who were slower at repetition. Thus, as operational efficiency increased, more cognitive resources were available for storage.

▶ **Interaction among domains**

Case (1985) has suggested that increases in the ability of children to process information quickly are tied to maturational changes in the nervous system as well as to practice with various cognitive activities. One important physiological change that occurs through adolescence is the *myelinization* of areas of the cortex that control alertness and higher-order thinking processes (Yakovlev & Lecours, 1967). Because myelinization is responsible for speeding neural transmissions, it is plausible that this process is related to increasing speed of cognitive processing. Practice also helps. The more times the child identifies numbers, words, or other stimuli, the more facile she will become in this activity. Thus, developmental increases in memory span are probably due to biological maturation as well as the child's increasingly active engagement with the material she must remember.

▶ **The child's active role**

The memory span task is usually believed to tap working memory, or short-term memory, because the interval between presentation of the stimuli and the memory test is relatively brief. Other recall studies have examined the

FIGURE 8.6

Developmental Differences in Free Recall

This graph shows the probability that a word will be recalled by third-, sixth-, and eighth-graders in a free-recall task. Few developmental differences appear in memory for the last few items in the list, but older children show elevated levels of recall for the first few items. This pattern suggests that older children are more likely to produce memory strategies such as rehearsal to remember the early items.

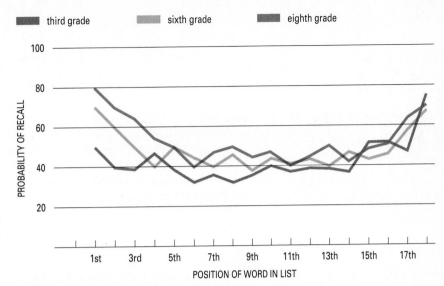

Source: Adapted from Ornstein, Naus, & Liberty, 1975.

ability of children to remember lists of words, sentences, or other items for longer than a few seconds. One of the most consistent findings in nearly all of these experiments is that older children remember more information than younger children do.

In *free-recall* tasks, children are given a list of words or objects that they are to repeat after a specified delay period in any order they wish. As Figure 8.6 shows, few developmental differences in recall are usually noted for items later in the list. Children of all ages recall these well, at least by the time they are of elementary school age. Older children, however, show a clear advantage for recalling items that had appeared in the early or middle positions (Ornstein & Naus, 1978; Ornstein, Naus, & Liberty, 1975). The fact that older children show good memory for early items is called the **primacy effect,** whereas elevated memory for later items is called the **recency effect.**

How can we account for age-related differences in patterns of recall? The recency effect is viewed as the extraction of information from more immediate memory, a task that is usually not too demanding for children aged four years and older. However, as we saw with memory span, as children grow older they tend to display more memory strategies. Developmental differences in the primacy effect can be explained as the result of the tendency of older children, those aged seven years or greater, to engage in deliberate strategies to improve recall. They repeat items aloud, make up sentences connecting the items, or think of mental images that connect the items. In fact, much of the research on memory development has centered on detailing the types of strategies that children of different ages display. We now turn to these investigations.

Memory Strategies   How do you make sure that you remember your grocery list or where you hung your coat in a restaurant coatroom? To do so, you must ordinarily perform some activity to make sure that the stimuli are correctly and enduringly encoded in the first place. As a mature rememberer, you

primacy effect   Tendency for subjects to display good recall for early items in a list.

recency effect   Tendency for subjects to show good recall for the last few items in a list.

often capitalize on cues that may later "trigger" retrieval. Thus, you might say the words in your grocery list over and over to yourself ("milk, eggs, cat food; milk, eggs, cat food") or note the characteristics of the location of an object ("I hung my coat next to the bright red one"). In general, as children grow older, they become more likely to employ self-generated strategies for both encoding and retrieval and to take advantage of external information that can potentially aid recall.

▶ **The child's active role**

We have already identified one useful memory tactic—**rehearsal**—simply repeating, either aloud or silently, items to be remembered. The fact that young children are unlikely to engage spontaneously in rehearsal is well documented. In a study mentioned in Chapter 7, investigators asked kindergarten, second-, and fifth-graders to observe as an experimenter pointed to three specific pictures in an array of seven (Flavell, Beach, & Chinsky, 1966). When children were asked to point to the same sequence after a fifteen-second delay, fifth-graders showed significantly greater accuracy than the other two age groups. More important, during the delay period the researchers recorded any signs that children might have been rehearsing the items to be remembered, such as moving their lips or vocalizing to themselves. They found that 85 percent of the fifth-graders engaged in this form of spontaneous rehearsal, whereas only 10 percent of the kindergarteners did. Moreover, children who rehearsed showed the best recall. In other words, there was a direct link between the child's production of this mnemonic strategy and memory performance.

Not only does the tendency to rehearse increase with age, the nature of the **rehearsal set** (the items actually repeated by the subject during the delay period) changes, too. Peter Ornstein and his coresearchers (Ornstein, Naus, & Liberty, 1975) asked third-, sixth-, and eighth-graders to remember a list of eighteen unrelated words. In one condition of the experiment, subjects were instructed to rehearse out loud whatever list items went through their minds as each stimulus word was presented. Table 8.2 shows the rehearsal sets for a third- and an eighth-grade subject. In general, third-graders tended to repeat only the current item and perhaps one immediately preceding word, whereas eighth-graders constructed a more cumulative rehearsal set. Studies such as these emphasize the tendency for older children to engage in active, purposive behaviors designed to ensure that they remember as many stimulus items as possible.

Older children also engage in another important memory strategy called **organization,** the tendency to reorder items to fit some category or higher-order scheme. If the items to be recalled can be grouped conceptually, older children do so, and the amount they recall increases accordingly. For example, if the stimulus list contains *animals, furniture, vehicles,* and *clothing,* ten- and eleven-year-olds spontaneously cluster conceptually related items together as they recall, whereas five- and six-year-olds do not (Moely et al., 1969). Furthermore, giving children explicit instructions to group the words or objects they are to remember into categories significantly enhances recall (Bjorkland, Ornstein, & Haig, 1977; Black & Rollins, 1982). Even if young children do not cluster stimulus lists categorically on their own and are not shown how to do so, they are often still able to profit from organizational structure. For example, Marion Perlmutter and Nancy Myers (1979) presented two- to four-year-old children with objects from related categories (animals, transportation,

rehearsal Memory strategy that involves repetition of items to be remembered.

rehearsal set Items actually repeated by subjects as they engage in rehearsal.

organization Memory strategy in which subjects reorder items to be remembered on the basis of category or some other higher-order relationships.

	Rehearsal Sets	
Word Presented	**Eighth-Grade Subject**	**Third-Grade Subject**
Yard	Yard, yard, yard	Yard, yard, yard, yard, yard
Cat	Cat, yard, yard, cat	Cat, cat, cat, cat, yard
Man	Man, cat, yard, man, yard, cat	Man, man, man, man, man
Desk	Desk, man, yard, cat, man, desk, cat, yard	Desk, desk, desk, desk

Source: Adapted from Ornstein, Naus, & Liberty, 1975.

TABLE 8.2

Rehearsal Sets of a Third- and an Eighth-Grader

As children grow older, they are more likely to employ a rehearsal set that includes more items from the list to be remembered. In this example, with one exception, the third-grader repeats only the word that has just been presented by the experimenter. In contrast, the eighth-grader incorporates previous items from the stimulus list into the rehearsal set.

▶ **The child's active role**

utensils) or unrelated categories (bell, clock, drum, flag, horse, leaf, pen, star, truck). Children from both age groups remembered significantly more objects from the related list. The fact that older, school-aged children tend to order items spontaneously within some meaningful framework means that they have a powerful tool in the service of memory.

Still another helpful memory technique is the use of **elaboration,** thinking of a sentence or image that links together items to be remembered. If you have to remember the list "cat, shoe, piano," you might construct the sentence "The cat wearing shoes played the piano" or think of a visual image portraying this scene. Elaboration is one of the latest memory strategies to appear; usually children do not spontaneously use images or elaborative verbalizations until adolescence or later (Pressley & Levin, 1977).

One last facet of the strategic behavior of older children is their tendency to use **retrieval cues,** aids that help them to extract information already stored in memory. One of the best illustrations of this phenomenon comes from a study conducted by Akira Kobasigawa (1974). Children ranging in age from six through eleven years were shown twenty-four pictures of objects that belonged to eight categories. For each stimulus item, a cue card was provided that served to categorize it. For example, pictures of a monkey, camel, and bear were accompanied by a picture of a zoo with three cages; a seesaw, slide, and swing were presented with a picture of a park. There were three experimental conditions: (1) a control condition, in which children were given standard free recall instructions; (2) a cue condition, in which at the time of recall, children were told they could consult the cue cards if they wanted to; and (3) a directive-cue condition, in which children were specifically asked to name the items that went with each cue card. Figure 8.7 shows the results. In the directive-cue condition, few developmental differences in recall emerged—children of all ages performed at high levels compared with the control condition. When left to their own devices in the cue condition, however, only the older children chose to use the cue cards as retrieval aids. As a result, their memory was clearly superior to that of the younger subjects in the same condition.

Throughout this discussion, the recurring theme has been the tendency of children over seven years of age to initiate some activity that will improve their recall. It is important to note that when younger, nonstrategic children are instructed to employ strategies such as rehearsal, organization, or the use

FIGURE 8.7

Developmental Differences in the Use of Retrieval Cues

These data from Kobasigawa's experiment show that children directed to use retrieval cues performed extremely well on a memory test regardless of age. When they were given the option of using retrieval cues, however, only the oldest children chose to use the cues and therefore recalled the greatest number of items. The free-recall condition shows the typical levels of performance when no cues were available to assist memory.

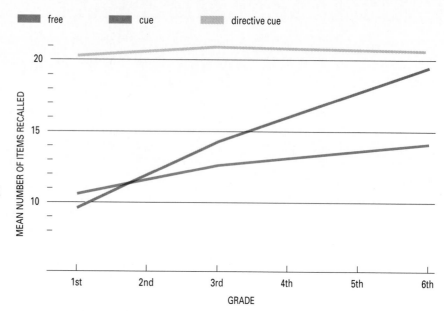

Source: Adapted from Kobasigawa, 1974.

of retrieval cues, their recall markedly improves (Bjorkland, Ornstein, & Haig, 1977; Keeney, Cannizzo, & Flavell, 1967; Moely et al., 1969; Ornstein & Naus, 1978). That is, the point is not that younger children's strategies fail to facilitate memory but that younger children simply do not generate the strategies on their own. This failure to generate memory strategies on their own has been termed a **production deficiency** (Flavell, 1970). At the same time, preschool-aged children are not completely deficient in the use of strategies. For example, when preschoolers are instructed to "remember" a set of objects, they are more likely to name and look at them than children who are instructed to "play with" the objects (Baker-Ward, Ornstein, & Holden, 1984). Thus, strategy use does not suddenly appear among seven-year-olds. There is a developmental progression that leads to a greater degree and more varied forms of strategy use.

How can we explain children's tendency to become more strategic and planful with age? There are several possibilities. One is that children are taught memory strategies directly or indirectly by parents and teachers. Barbara Moely and her colleagues (Moely et al., 1989) noted that 83 percent of the elementary school teachers they interviewed said that they encouraged their pupils to employ repetition to learn vocabulary words, science concepts, and other material. Many teachers also reported teaching organization and elaboration strategies. In another study, Hilary Ratner (1984) found a positive relationship between three-year-olds' memory performance and the frequency with which their mothers asked them questions about past events. Such memory demands may help children to learn about encoding and retrieval processes that aid memory.

Another possibility is that children become more conscious of their own thinking capabilities with age and realize the need to produce strategies. **Metamemory,** an aspect of metacognition, refers to the understanding and ability

elaboration Memory strategy in which subjects link items to be remembered in the form of an image or sentence.

retrieval cue Aid or cue to extract information that has already been stored in memory.

production deficiency Failure of children under age seven years to spontaneously generate memory strategies.

metamemory Understanding of memory as a cognitive process.

to reflect on memory as a process. It includes the ability to assess one's own memory characteristics and limitations, the demands made by different memory tasks, and the strategies likely to benefit memory (Flavell & Wellman, 1977; Guttentag, 1987). It also includes the ability to monitor the contents of one's own memory and to make decisions about how to allocate cognitive resources ("Have I memorized everything thoroughly? Do I still need to study some items?") (Kail, 1990). Advances in each of these aspects of metamemory may be responsible for improvements in memory as children get older. For example, unlike older children, younger children often manifest unrealistic ideas about the extent of their memories. When John Flavell and his colleagues (Flavell, Friedrichs, & Hoyt, 1970) asked nursery school through fourth-grade children to predict the number of pictures they could recall in a set of ten, many of the youngest subjects stated that they could remember them all. In fact, they could actually recall only three or four. In contrast, older children were much more accurate in estimating their memory span. Similarly, older children have a better understanding that shorter lists are easier to remember than longer ones and that events from the distant past are more difficult to remember than more recent events (Kreutzer, Leonard, & Flavell, 1975; Wellman, 1977). Thus, children's general knowledge about the characteristics of memory increases with age.

Finally, it may be that the child's general knowledge about the world must develop. For example, for a child to use the strategy of organization, she must appreciate the conceptual categories that objects can belong to. Before she can categorically cluster *couch, chair,* and *table* in a list of words to be recalled, she must understand that they all belong to the category *furniture*. In other words, the child's production of memory strategies arises, in part, from her expanding general knowledge base.

Memory and the Growth of General Knowledge Do younger children ever remember more than older children or adults? In a unique experiment, Michelene Chi (1978) found that in certain situations they do. Part of the experiment resembled the standard laboratory recall task: adults along with children averaging ten years of age were asked to remember lists of ten digits presented by the experimenter. Typically, the adults' performance surpassed the children's. In another portion of the experiment, however, the memory task consisted of reproducing chess positions previously seen for only ten seconds on a chessboard. Here the children significantly outperformed their adult counterparts. How did they accomplish this remarkable feat? Chi (1978) explains that the children who participated were experts in the game of chess, whereas the adults (who were college educated) had only casual knowledge of the game. These children's greater knowledge probably enabled them to see familiar patterns of chess pieces that they could efficiently encode, whereas adults were probably seeing random arrangements of rooks, knights, and pawns. Thus, **domain-specific knowledge,** information about a specific content area, can be influential in the individual's ability to remember.

Memory researchers now recognize that the knowledge the child has already acquired can influence subsequent memory. Thus, many psychologists have begun to explore the nature and development of *semantic memory,* knowledge about the meanings of words, concepts, and other general knowledge. An important question here is, How is knowledge stored internally? One popular

domain-specific knowledge
Knowledge about a specific content area.

By the time they reach three or four years of age, many children have general knowledge, or *scripts,* for familiar events, such as Halloween.

hypothesis is that information about the world is stored in the form of **networks,** groups of associations in which closely related items are represented in close proximity. Thus, for example, the concepts "sunset," "sunrise," and "clouds" are stored in close proximity to one another, while "apples" or "ambulance" are more distant.

If a network representation of semantic memory is accurate, then David Bjorkland (1987) suggests that what changes with development is the number of items stored in semantic memory, the number of features or links associated with each item, and the strength of the relationships among items. As children become more familiar with new and different objects and concepts, more and stronger links are established with other concepts and relations among items are more easily activated. Thus, Bjorkland maintains that as children mature, they become more able to retrieve information automatically. Memory development, according to Bjorkland, is more than just the emergence of effortful strategy use—it is the greater use of *effortless* processing. This, in turn, leaves more space available for storage. These ideas are consistent with the limited-resources concept of cognition.

The effect of a growing knowledge base on memory has been described in one other way—in terms of scripts. **Scripts** are the organized schemes of knowledge individuals possess about commonly encountered events. For example, by the time they are three or four years old, most children have a general schematic representation for the events that occur at dinner time—cooking the food, setting the table, sitting down to eat—as well as for other routine events such as going to school or attending a birthday party (Fivush, 1984; Nelson & Gruendel, 1981). When they are asked to remember stories based on such familiar scripts, children typically recall script-based activities like "eating dinner" better than other details less related to scripts (McCartney & Nelson, 1981). Thus, scripts serve as general frameworks within which specific memories can be stored.

One of the great challenges facing those interested in cognitive development is finding the most useful way of describing semantic memory and accounting for developmental changes in the representations and relationships among the items it contains. Moreover, research will undoubtedly continue to illuminate how general knowledge plays an important role in the child's ability to recall information for specific objects and events.

CONTROVERSY

Should Children Provide Eyewitness Testimony?

The research on children's memory, particularly recognition memory, suggests that their ability to remember events from the past is very impressive. But as children are increasingly called upon to testify in courts after they have witnessed or been victims of abuse, neglect, or other crimes, their capability of rendering an accurate account of past events has been questioned by some.

At the heart of the matter is whether children's memories of past events are susceptible to suggestive or leading questions by attorneys, clinicians, or other interrogators. Stephen Ceci and his colleagues (Ceci, Ross, & Toglia,

network   Model of semantic memory that consists of associations among closely related items.

script   Organized scheme or framework for commonly experienced events.

1987) tested children ages three through twelve years on their ability to remember the details of a story. A day later, children in one of the experimental conditions were asked leading questions that distorted the original information, such as "Do you remember the story about Loren, who had a headache because she ate her cereal too fast?" In the original story, Loren had a stomachache from eating her eggs too fast. Compared with children who did not hear misleading questions, children who heard biased questions made more errors on a subsequent test in which they were required to select pictures that depicted the original story—they chose the pictures showing a girl eating cereal and having a headache. This tendency to err was especially pronounced in children ages four and under.

On the other hand, other researchers who had children witness a live staged event of an argument between two adults found no age differences in susceptibility to misinformation (Marin et al., 1979). Although college students in this study were able to recall more of the details of the event two weeks later, children aged five, eight, and twelve years were no more likely to "fall for" misleading information than young adults. The tendency for children to resist leading questions is most evident when they are asked about the central, most important details of an event (Goodman & Reed, 1986).

One of the most influential factors in children's suggestibility is the perceived power of the person doing the questioning. For example, in Ceci's study described above, misinformation provided by an adult had more of an impact on distorting memory than misinformation provided by another child. Moreover, children may be particularly vulnerable in the emotionally charged atmosphere of the courtroom, especially when they are the victims of abuse or assault and are in the presence of the person they are accusing (Goodman et al., 1991). Most experts agree that the best way to encourage children to give reliable eyewitness accounts is to relieve the social pressures surrounding their questioning, even allowing them to testify outside of the courtroom or on videotape. ■

Memory Development: An Overview

What is it, then, that develops during memory development? First, effective and deliberate strategies, such as rehearsal and organization, that serve to strengthen or impose meaning on stimuli to be recalled. Second, knowledge in the broader sense—knowledge about one's own cognitive processes, general information about objects and their relations, and knowledge about common sequences of events. In the multistore model of information processing, memory development means the development of control processes that move information to long-term storage and facilitate the communication among stores. In the limited-resource model, strategy use and greater access to semantic memory promote operational efficiency, leaving more room for storage.

Concept Development: Class, Number, and Space

When and how does the child begin to understand that horses, dogs, and cats all belong to a common category called "animals"? When does she realize that numbers like "2" or "4" represent specific quantities, no matter what objects are being counted, and that the latter number is greater than the former? And how does she mentally organize her spatial environment, such as the layout of her house or the path from home to school? In each case, we are concerned with the ways in which the child organizes a set of information about the world, using some general or abstract principle as the basis for that organization. In other words, we are describing the child's use of **concepts.**

As one psychologist recently put it, "Concepts and categories serve as the building blocks for human thought and behavior" (Medin, 1989). Concepts allow us to group isolated pieces of information on the basis of common themes or properties. The result is greater efficiency in cognitive processing. Suppose someone tells you, "A quarf is an animal." Without even seeing one, you already know many of the quarf's properties—it breathes, eats, locomotes, and so on. As we have already seen, concepts also underlie language and many other information-processing activities, such as strategies for improving memory. Understanding how concepts develop is an important concern of developmental psychologists.

Classification   Objects can be classified on the basis of a number of relations. They can be grouped together because they look alike (triangles go with other triangles, circles with circles), a *perceptually based grouping.* Objects can also be grouped together because they often function together or complement one another (spoon goes with cereal), a *thematic relation.* Finally, objects can be grouped together because they belong to a common higher-order group, as in pear-apple, both fruits, or horse-dog, examples of animals. *Taxonomic groupings,* as these classes are called, require children to cluster objects that may not always look alike or function similarly into a grouping based on some abstract principle.

One of the earliest signs of classification skills in young children occurs toward the end of the first year, when they begin to group perceptually similar objects together. Susan Sugarman (1982, 1983) carefully watched the behaviors of one- to three-year-old children as they played with successive sets of stimuli that could be grouped into two classes, such as plates and square blocks, or dolls and boats. Even the youngest subjects displayed a spontaneous tendency to group similar objects together by pointing consecutively to items that were alike. At age two, children went one step further and began to move objects resembling each other into two distinct groups—that is, plates with plates and blocks with blocks. Thus, the tendency to group objects together on the basis of shared perceptual characteristics emerges early in development.

Between ages one and three years, children experience a rapid growth in classification skills. Infants as young as fourteen months successively touch objects that appear in common contexts, such as "kitchen things" and "bathroom things" (Mandler, Fivush, & Reznick, 1987). Two-year-olds will match items on the basis of both thematic and taxonomic relations, putting a baby bottle with a baby or a shoe with a boot. Younger children, though, are more likely to group items taxonomically when items show perceptual similarities. For example, linking a shoe with a boot is easier for the two-year-old than linking a shoe with a shirt. By age three years, children put even perceptually dissimilar items together if they belong to the same taxonomic category (Fenson, Vella, & Kennedy, 1989). Thus, as they grow older, preschoolers become

concept   Organization of a set of information on the basis of some general or abstract principle.

Preschoolers display rapid growth of *classification skills,* the ability to group objects according to some rule or principle.

capable of using a wider range of relations to classify objects, and their exclusive reliance on shared perceptual features lessens.

Eleanor Rosch and her colleagues (Rosch et al., 1976) have proposed another way of framing our understanding of the way concepts develop in children. These researchers believe that some groupings of objects are *basic level;* that is, objects go together when they look alike, can be used in similar ways, and "average" members of the class can be thought of. "Chair" is an example of a basic-level concept because all chairs have seats, legs, and backs; all are used for sitting; and we can think of such a thing as an "average" chair. In contrast, other concepts are *superordinate level.* Members of superordinate-level concepts, such as "furniture," do not necessarily share many perceptual attributes, and they are broader and more general than basic-level concepts. Rosch and her colleagues believe that because basic-level groups carry more information, especially perceptual information, than superordinate-level groups, they are the easiest for children to process.

Rosch and her colleagues (Rosch et al., 1976) found that children under the age of five readily put together four pictures of different shoes or four pictures of different cars; that is, they could sort according to basic-level groupings. Children could not, however, proficiently sort on the basis of superordinate category by putting a shoe, shirt, sock, and pants together until they reached the age of eight or nine years.

In summary, children's earliest concepts appear to be based largely on perceptual similarities. The child's conceptual understanding quickly expands to include thematic and taxonomic relations, especially if shared perceptual features are present to provide cues about category membership. Finally, toward the middle school years, children understand hierarchical relations among stimuli that bear few perceptual resemblances to one another.

Just why classification skills develop precisely as they do is still unclear. One variable, however—the experience of formal schooling—may play a role in the development of taxonomic classification, at least among older children. One group of researchers found that residents of rural Mexico without much formal schooling tended to group objects on the basis of their functional relations. "Chicken" and "egg" were frequently classified together because "the chicken lays eggs." On the other hand, subjects with more education relied on taxonomic classification, grouping "chicken" with "horse" because "they are animals" (Sharp, Cole, & Lave, 1979). It may be that taxonomic classification strategies are taught directly in schools or that education fosters the development of more abstract thought, a basic requirement for taxonomic grouping. Either way, any full explanation of the development of classification skills will have to take into account the experiences of children within their specific sociocultural context.

▶ **Sociocultural influence**

Numerical Concepts   Children as young as two years of age frequently use number terms, either to count toys, snacks, or other items or in playful ways, such as shouting, "One, two, three, jump!" as they dive off their bed (Saxe, Guberman, & Gerhart, 1987). But do young children really understand the full significance of numbers as a tool for establishing quantitative relationships? Or are they merely repeating a series of words they have heard someone else say without fully appreciating the conceptual underpinnings of those words?

Piaget's (1952a) position was that children under the age of seven years or so, before they enter the concrete operational stage, do not have a full grasp of the meaning of numbers. One indication is the failure of preoperational children to succeed in the conservation-of-number task. In this problem, you will recall, children see two equal rows of objects—say, red and white poker chips—as shown in Figure 8.1 earlier. Initially, the rows are aligned identically, and most children will agree that they have equal numbers of chips. But when the chips in one row are spread out, the majority of children state that this row now has more chips even though no chips have been added or subtracted.

Preoperational children, Piaget maintained, fail to comprehend the **one-to-one correspondence** that still exists among items in the two rows; that is, each element in a row can be mapped onto an element in the second row with none left over. Moreover, he believed that young children have not yet attained an understanding of two important aspects of number. The first is **cardinality,** or the total number of elements in a class—as in *six* red poker chips. The second is **ordinality,** the order in which an item appears in the set, as in the *second* poker chip. According to Piaget, the child must grasp both these concepts in order to judge two sets of items equivalent.

Many contemporary researchers believe that Piaget underestimated preschool children's understanding of number concepts. For example, we know

one-to-one correspondence Understanding that two sets are equivalent in number if each element in one set can be mapped onto a unique element in the second set with none left over.

cardinality Principle that the last number in a set of counted numbers refers to the number of items in that set.

ordinality Principle that a number refers to an item's order within a set, as in the third finisher in a race.

that many children aged four years and under say number words in sequence and, in so doing, appreciate at least some basic principles of numerical relationships. Rochel Gelman and her associates have argued that even young children have knowledge of certain important fundamental principles of counting (Gelman & Gallistel, 1978; Gelman & Meck, 1983). Among these principles are (1) using the same sequence of counting words when counting different sets; (2) employing only one counting word per object; (3) using the last counting word in the set to represent the total number; (4) understanding that any set of objects can be counted; and (5) appreciating that objects can be counted in any order.

Recent studies suggest that when young children count, their words are not empty of numerical meaning. In one experiment, three- and four-year-olds saw six dolls and five rings and were asked, "There are six dolls. Is there a ring for every doll?" Most of the four-year-olds used number words to answer questions about one-to-one correspondence. For example, many said, "No, because there are six dolls and five rings" (Becker, 1989). In addition, children aged four years are able to compare quantities, answering correctly such questions as "Which is bigger, five or two?" (Siegler & Robinson, 1982). Thus, their understanding of number terms includes quantitative relations such as "larger" and "smaller." One interesting pattern, though, is that young children have more difficulty in making such comparisons when the numbers themselves are large (ten versus fourteen) or when the difference between two numbers is small (eight versus nine).

Once children enter school, of course, they are expected to master the formal properties of numbers through mathematics. Lauren Resnick (1986) believes that before children learn the systematic rules for addition, subtraction, algebra, and the like, they develop intuitive concepts about how numbers can be manipulated. How would Pitt, one of her seven-year-old subjects, add 152 and 149?

> I would have the two 100's, which equals 200. Then I would have 50 and the 40, which equals 90. So I have 290. Then plus the 9 from 49, and the 2 from the 52 equals 11. And then I add the 90 plus the 11 . . . equals 102. 102? 101. So I put the 200 and the 101, which equals 301. (p. 164)

All this came from a young boy who had mastered only first-grade arithmetic! Resnick suggests that the additive properties of numbers are relatively easy for children to understand, whereas relations, such as ratios, and transformations, such as algebraic expressions, are more difficult. Therefore it is not surprising that many children experience difficulties with mathematics beyond the early elementary school years. One way to ameliorate the difficulty might be to frame more complex mathematical operations in terms of simple additive properties, at least when they are first being learned.

Thus, young children understand a good deal about numbers and their usefulness in describing relations among objects. In the course of their cognitive development, children become more adept at dealing with larger quantities and manipulate numbers in more sophisticated ways, such as addition, subtraction, and other mathematical operations. Many of their intuitive understandings about the properties of numbers can help them as they learn the more formal aspects of quantitative relations.

Spatial Relationships   From early infancy onward, children organize the objects in their world in still another way—according to relationships in space. Where does the toddler find his shoes or an enticing snack? Usually, the infant and young child have developed a mental picture of their homes and other familiar physical spaces to guide their search for missing objects or to reach a desired location. For the older child, spatial understanding extends to finding her way to school, grandparents' homes, or other more remote locations. As he did for many other areas of cognitive development, Piaget set forth some of the first hypotheses about the child's concepts of space, ideas that have been modified or enriched by later researchers.

During infancy, Piaget (1954) stated, the child's knowledge of space is based on her sensorimotor activities within that space. The child, for example, searches for objects by using *egocentric* frames of reference. That is, if a ball disappears under a couch or chair, the infant represents its location in relation to her own body ("to the left of my arm") rather than in relation to some other external object ("to the left of the door"). Only with the advent of symbolic ability at the end of the sensorimotor stage are children able to use frames of reference external to the self.

Many researchers have confirmed that children, in the absence of environmental cues, indeed rely on the positions of their own bodies in space to locate objects. For example, experimenters in one study hid an object under one of two covers situated to the left and right of their nine-month-old subjects. The infants readily learned to locate the item in one of the two positions, either to the right or to the left, depending on which training condition they were in. After the training trials, the children were shifted to the opposite side of the table, a 180-degree change in position. Now infants were unable to locate the hidden objects, a finding that suggests they were relying on the position of the object relative to their own bodies in order to find it (Bremner & Bryant, 1977). In an interesting modification, however, the investigator made the covers of the two hiding locations of distinctively different colors. Under these conditions, infants were able to locate the hidden toy even when they were moved to a different position around the table (Bremner, 1978). Thus, infants are *not* egocentric when other information is available to assist in finding objects.

The ability to use cues or **landmarks** denoting the physical locations of objects helps preschool-aged children find objects in larger spatial environments. Linda Acredolo and her colleagues (Acredolo, Pick, & Olsen, 1975) demonstrated this skill in an experiment in which three- through eight-year-olds were taken on a walk through an unfamiliar building in one of two conditions. In the first condition, the hallway through which the experimenter led each subject contained two chairs. In the second, there were no chairs. The subjects saw the experimenter drop a set of keys during the walk with each child, and in the "landmark" condition this event occurred near one of the chairs. Later, when children were asked to retrieve the keys, performance was best in the "landmark" condition for the preschoolers; older children did well regardless of the experimental condition. Thus, prominent landmarks help younger children to encode specific locations within their spatial environment.

Alexander Siegel and his associates (Siegel, Kirasic, & Kail, 1978) believe that knowledge about large-scale spaces proceeds from landmark knowledge

landmark   Distinctive location or cue that the child uses to negotiate or represent a spatial environment.

to route mapping. **Route mapping** consists of knowledge about sequential directional changes that must take place as one negotiates a path through space, such as, "Take a left at the store, then a right at the traffic light." Children rely on this form of spatial representation during their early school years. At age ten years or so, children display even more sophisticated spatial understanding, called **configurational knowledge,** which is the ability to represent landmarks and routes as integrated, holistic entities. They can draw reasonably accurate maps of their neighborhood or the spatial layout of their school (Anooshian & Young, 1981; Curtis, Siegel, & Furlong, 1981). Developmental improvements in spatial knowledge are associated with the child's increasing familiarity with a given physical space. In the study conducted by Siegel and his associates, when kindergartners were walked through a model town several times, they were able to produce maps of the town as accurate as those of fifth-graders. Their ability to produce a mature spatial layout, one that required configurational representation, was enhanced simply by having experience with that physical space (Siegel, Kirasic, & Kail, 1978).

In summary, young children initially locate objects in space by using simple cues, such as the position of objects relative to their own bodies or distinctive landmarks. Gradually, their spatial representations include more discrete elements and become better integrated. Why does spatial knowledge develop in this way? A likely explanation is that the child's growing attentional and memory skills contribute to his ability to process, retain, and integrate more numerous physical cues.

The Development of Problem-solving Skills

One of the most powerful human cognitive skills is the ability to solve problems. Whether you are completing an analogy, computing an arithmetic solution, or testing a scientific hypothesis, problem solving typically involves several steps or phases. Usually you must draw on a body of information from memory and examine relationships among several pieces of information in order to solve a problem. Once you have the solution, you will often apply this new knowledge in other similar contexts.

What are the earliest instances of problem-solving activity in humans? In the beginning of this chapter, we saw a good example of problem solving in the young toddler when Lucienne Piaget opened the matchbox. Recent evidence suggests that even younger infants are capable of solving problems, combining several subgoals in order to reach an interesting toy. In an experiment conducted by Peter Willatts and Karen Rosie (1989), twelve-month-old infants saw a barrier in front of a cloth, on which was placed a string attached to a toy (Figure 8.8). To get the toy, infants had to remove the barrier, pull the cloth, and then pull the string. In a control condition, the toy was not attached to the string. Infants in the first group tended to remove the barrier without playing with it, quickly pulled the cloth, and grasped the string in order to reach the toy. Their behavior suggested that reaching the attractive toy was of utmost interest. In contrast, infants in the control group played with the barrier, were slower to reach for the cloth, and frequently did not grasp the string, probably

▶ **Roles of nature and nurture**

route mapping   Child's use of sequential directional changes to negotiate or represent a spatial environment.

configurational knowledge   Child's use of landmarks and routes in integrated, holistic ways to represent physical space.

FIGURE 8.8

**Simple Problem Solving
by Infants**

This one-year-old knocks down the barrier and pulls the cloth to obtain the string to which an attractive toy is attached. Such behavior suggests that young infants can deliberately put together several subgoals in order to reach a goal.

because they recognized that the barrier, cloth, and string could not help in bringing the toy closer. Willatts and Rosie (1989) concluded that infants are capable of putting together several subgoals in an intentional way to reach a goal.

▶ **Development as continuous/
stagelike**

Problem-solving skills become more elaborate as children get older. A major question has been whether the child's increasing proficiency in solving complex and abstract problems results from an abrupt, qualitative shift in the ability to think logically or whether improvements in problem solving occur because of gradual gains in memory, attention, and other component cognitive skills. Piaget believed in abrupt, qualitative shifts; he felt that the cognitive structures that permit completely logical and abstract thought do not evolve until adolescence. In contrast, many information-processing theorists have emphasized the growth and refinement of component skills; according to them, children of all ages possess the fundamental ability to combine pieces of information in a logical fashion but may forget some of those elements or not attend to them sufficiently in the first place.

The Development of Formal Reasoning

If A is greater than B, and B is greater than C, then what is the relationship between A and C? To solve this problem, the child must perform a *transitive inference;* that is, she must decide on the relationship between two objects based on their relationships to other objects. Because all the information necessary to solve the problem is available and the child must simply put it together correctly, this is a problem requiring formal reasoning (Galotti, 1989).

Children as young as four years of age show at least some ability to engage in formal reasoning. Peter Bryant and Tom Trabasso (1971) asked preschoolers to learn the relationships among a series of sticks of different sizes, although the children could not see the actual length of the sticks. Thus, they learned that A is greater than B, B is greater than C, C is greater than D, and D is greater than E. Bryant and Trabasso made sure that their subjects thoroughly learned this initial premise information. In the next portion of the experiment, children were asked to compare the lengths of B and D, even though they had not directly learned about the relationship between these two specific sticks. Approximately 78 percent of the four-year-olds correctly stated that B is greater than D, showing that they were able to make a transitive inference when their memory for each component was ensured.

Another area of formal reasoning that undergoes development involves the concept of *logical necessity,* which does not emerge until adolescence. In one study, researchers presented fourth- and seventh-graders, as well as college students, with premises and conclusions, some of which did not describe truthful relations (Moshman & Franks, 1986). For example, one set was "If dogs are bigger than elephants and elephants are bigger than mice, then dogs are bigger than mice." This task required the use of *deductive reasoning,* putting the two premises together to draw a logical conclusion. Could subjects agree that the conclusion was logically necessary even though the premise information was not necessarily true? Not until about age ten to twelve years, according to the findings. Young children cannot separate the concept of an inference's validity from the content of the premise information; they use the truth value of the statements to justify their conclusions. Older children and adults, in contrast, can think more abstractly about the logical necessity of relations apart from their content. In other words, they can manipulate the elements of a problem using logic, regardless of the problem's content. In general, the ability to engage in formal deductive reasoning does not appear until adolescence (Byrnes & Overton, 1988).

In summary, young children show some rudimentary skill in solving formal reasoning problems, as they do in many other aspects of cognitive development. In some specific domains of cognition, however, the most notable advances occur during adolescence, when children employ formal systems of logic to solve deductive reasoning problems. Whether these advances result from qualitative shifts in the nature of thought or from the honing of component cognitive skills remains a matter of debate.

Transferring Skills   How well do children apply their existing problem-solving skills to new situations? This has been a longstanding question in psychology, particularly among researchers who have studied the role of *generalization* in learning. It has also been a question of paramount importance to educators, who assume that children will find some application in their everyday lives from what they learn in the classroom.

The ability to transfer knowledge across problems requires children to have learned the original problem well, to note the resemblance between the old and new problems, and to apply the appropriate activities to the new problem. This process is called **analogical transfer** in that the child must notice the one-to-one correspondence that exists between the elements of one problem and another, and then must apply the familiar skills to the novel context.

An experiment by Ann Brown and her coresearchers (Brown, Kane, & Echols, 1986) illustrates just how this process can occur. In this study, three- to five-year-old children were read a story in which a magical genie had to move his jewels from one bottle across a high wall to another bottle. Several items were available to help the genie: glue, paper clips, sheets of paper, and so on. The experimenter and each child enacted the solution, rolling up the paper into a tube and using it to transport the jewels from one bottle to the other. The children were then presented with a different problem having the same general solution (a rabbit who needs to get his Easter eggs across a river can roll paper into a tube to transport them). Whether the children were able to transfer the solution to the new problem depended on whether they recalled the goal structure of the previous problem. If they remembered the major actor, his goal, and the solution to his problem, even three-year-olds could solve the new problem.

Brown hypothesizes that for transfer of problem solving to take place, the child must represent the problem in general mental terms, that is, to abstract out the goal, problem, and solution dissociated from the specific fact that it was a genie who had to transfer jewels. Children can be encouraged to discern such common goal structures in consecutive problems. Zhe Chen and Marvin Daehler (1989) found that when six-year-olds were explicitly prompted to formulate an answer to the question of how problems were alike, they then performed significantly better on a transfer problem than control subjects who did not receive this training. Thus, parents and teachers may play a crucial role in facilitating the transfer of learning by pointing out commonalities across the solutions to several problems.

The Process of Cognitive Development: An Overview

To summarize, the process of cognitive development includes notable achievements in attention, memory, concept formation, and problem solving, achievements that are highlighted in the Chronology on page 354. From the information-processing perspective, changes occur in the child's ability to input, store, and manipulate information—in other words, in every phase of the processing system. Moreover, changes in one component of processing, such

analogical transfer   Ability to employ the solution to one problem in other similar problems.

as memory, often have an impact on other components, such as attention or problem solving. Manifesting the distinct influence of Piaget, modern-day accounts of cognitive development universally recognize the richness and complexity of the child's developing mind.

THE CONTEXT OF COGNITIVE DEVELOPMENT

▶ **Sociocultural influence**

As we saw in Chapters 2 and 6, Lev Vygotsky (1978), the prominent Soviet psychologist, wrote that the child's cognitive growth must be understood in the context of the culture in which the child lives. Vygotsky believed that adults cultivate in children the particular skills and abilities valued by their cultural group and that the regulation and guidance of the child's behavior by others is gradually replaced by internalized self-regulation. As adults engage in interactions with children, they provide the *scaffolding,* or framework, for the child's subsequent attainments, especially when those experiences are just one step ahead of what the child already knows within the *zone of proximal development.* In this section we explore the ways in which children's cognitive skills vary across different cultures and look at the microcosm of adult-child interactions as a way of understanding the development of cognition.

Cross-Cultural Differences in Cognition

Many of us probably assume that cognitive processes function in similar ways across cultures, that there are universal qualities to the nature of thinking. But researchers who have studied memory, classification, and other cognitive skills among children from diverse cultures have shown that although children's thinking from culture to culture may show common features, there are notable differences as well.

Take, for example, the typical free-recall task described earlier in this chapter. Michael Cole and his colleagues (Cole et al., 1971) examined how children and adults from the Kpelle tribe of Liberia remembered two kinds of lists— words that were potentially categorizable and unrelated words. We already know that American children remember more words as they grow older and tend to categorize them into conceptual groups with age. The Kpelle, however, exhibited few developmental differences in recall—all age groups performed rather poorly. Moreover, Kpelle subjects showed almost no evidence of clustering similar items together in their recall. The only exception was that subjects who had some experience in school tended to perform better (and cluster more) than their nonliterate counterparts.

Similar findings come from studies of other cognitive skills. Earlier in this chapter, we saw that children and adults living in the rural Yucatán region of Mexico tended to classify objects together on the basis of functional similarities rather than taxonomically. For example, they would group a food item with a utensil rather than putting food items and utensils into two separate groups. Once again, formally educated children and adults behaved differently from their less educated peers—they were more likely to group items taxonomically, just as older American children are (Sharp, Cole, & Lave, 1979).

CHRONOLOGY	**Cognitive Development**
NEWBORN	Shows recognition memory for simple stimuli.
4–8 MONTHS	Develops object concept.
1 YEAR	Attends to physical properties of objects. Performs simple problem solving by combining subgoals. Classifies objects according to physical similarities.
2 YEARS	Has memory span of two items. Attends to potential uses of objects. Uses naming and looking as early memory strategies.
3 YEARS	Shows recognition memory for fifty-plus items. Knows scripts for familiar routines. Classifies according to taxonomic relations. Understands basic principles of counting. Uses landmarks to negotiate spatial environments. Shows analogical transfer following training.
4 YEARS	Uses systematic and efficient attention strategies. Shows memory span of three to four items.
7 YEARS	Displays intuitive concepts about numbers. Produces rehearsal as a memory strategy. Has memory span of about five items. Displays selective attention.
8 YEARS	Uses route mapping to represent spatial environments.
9 YEARS	Classifies according to superordinate relations. Produces accurate estimates of memory span.
10 YEARS	Produces organizational strategies for memory. Appreciates the concept of logical necessity. Shows configurational knowledge in spatial relations.
11 YEARS	Uses retrieval strategies for memory. Produces elaboration strategies for memory.
13 YEARS	Uses cumulative rehearsal sets.

This chart describes the sequence of cognitive development based on the findings of research. Children often show individual differences in the exact ages at which they display the various developmental achievements outlined here.

An important variable that influences performance in these diverse contexts, then, is children's experience with formal instruction in school. Barbara Rogoff (1981) suggests that schooling may influence the development of cognitive skills in four ways: (1) by emphasizing the importance of searching for general rules; (2) by teachers' use of verbal instruction, which invites abstract thought; (3) by teaching specific skills such as memorizing and classifying; and

(4) by leading to literacy, the ability to read and write, which, in turn, enhances specific cognitive skills.

But children from other cultures, even when they have little or no schooling, do not always do more poorly than educated American children on cognitive tasks. Barbara Rogoff and Kathryn Waddell (1982) compared Mayan children living in rural Guatemala with American children on a memory test that required the reconstruction of an organized spatial scene. Both groups of children were shown a scene containing mountains, buildings, a road, lake, and trees. Children watched as the experimenter placed twenty objects in the scene and removed them. They were then asked to place the objects in the same locations. The children from these two cultural groups showed no differences in performance on this task. When memory for meaningful, spatially organized information was being tapped, children of both cultures performed well. On the other hand, Mayan children performed poorly on memory tasks they had little experience with, such as learning lists of unrelated words.

Studies such as this suggest that it is important to consider the activities that are valued and common within a culture in trying to explain the emergence of cognitive skills. Some cultures may provide children with more experience in grouping objects together on the basis of function, for example. In other cultures, in which many children attend school, other modes of classification may be directly taught. Some cultures value literacy, whereas others value trade skills such as weaving or making pottery. Thus, children ultimately show different cognitive attainments depending on the skills and abilities that are promoted in the context in which they grow up.

Although the cognitive end products may differ, however, the process through which children learn to think in culturally specific ways may be universal. Many developmental psychologists now agree with Vygotsky that at least one critical process is the way adults convey particular cognitive skills as they engage in cognitive activities and problem-solving tasks with children (Rogoff, 1989).

The cognitive activities emphasized within various cultures can influence the modes of thinking that children develop. For example, researchers have observed that cross-cultural differences in children's memory and classification skills parallel their cultural experiences.

▶ **Roles of nature and nurture**

The Role of Parents and Teachers

Just how are the cognitive skills and activities valued in a given sociocultural context transmitted to children? One mechanism could well be imitation—children learn by watching how parents, older siblings, and other skilled thinkers approach various cognitive tasks (Azmitia & Perlmutter, 1989). Another is the instruction provided by parents and teachers within the zone of proximal development. Two recent studies illustrate how this process takes place with two rather different skills: planning the solution to a problem and reading.

In the first study, Barbara Radziszewska and Barbara Rogoff (1988) examined how nine- and ten-year-old children learned to plan errands. One group of children first worked with their parents to organize a shopping trip through an imaginary town, and a second group of subjects worked with a peer to plan their expedition. Children who worked with adults were exposed to more sophisticated planning strategies; they explored a map of the town more frequently, planned longer sequences of activities, and verbalized more of their plans. Instead of using a step-by-step strategy ("Let's go from this store to the next closest store") as the peer pairs did, children working with adults formulated an integrated sequence of actions ("Let's mark all the stores we have to go to in blue and see what is the best way between them.") In the second part of the experiment, all the children were observed as they planned a new errand in the same town, this time by themselves. Children who had initially worked with their parents employed more efficient planning strategies than children who had worked with peers.

The second study was an exploration of how teachers might foster the emergence of reading comprehension strategies in junior high school students (Palinscar & Brown, 1984). The students received instruction in four reading skills: summarizing, clarifying, self-directed questioning, and predicting. Using an instructional method called *reciprocal teaching*, students and teachers took turns in generating these activities. For one paragraph, the teacher summarized the theme, isolated material that needed to be clarified, anticipated questions, and predicted what would happen next. For the next paragraph, the students engaged in these four activities. The results of training were impressive. Whereas during the pretest students averaged 20 percent correct in answering ten questions from reading a paragraph of material, after twenty sessions of reciprocal teaching, they averaged 80 percent correct on similar tests. Six months later, students trained in this method moved up from the twentieth percentile in reading ability in their school to the fifty-sixth percentile. The key to the success of reciprocal teaching was the interaction between teacher and students. Teachers modeled the appropriate use of each of the four comprehension skills and adjusted their instructions according to the needs of the individual students.

Both studies described here show that parents and teachers can and do provide children with direct instruction about how to succeed in different cognitive tasks. But several ingredients are necessary for the child to fully grasp that skill and be able to use it on his or her own in other contexts. First, both adult and child must be motivated—the adult to find occasions to push the child forward and the child to engage in the activity in the first place. Second, the adult must be facile at modifying the skill in question so that it suits the needs of the child. Last, the adult must be adept at assessing the child's current level of competence and judging the level of difficulty the child is able to master.

That is, the adult must be able to locate and work within the zone of proximal development (Belmont, 1989). The result is a constantly modulated interaction leading to the child's cognitive advancement.

THEMES IN DEVELOPMENT

COGNITION

▶ What roles do nature and nurture play in cognitive development?

A central tenet of Piaget's theory is that maturation, in conjunction with experience, is responsible for the child's cognitive growth. Information-processing researchers have found that some cognitive processes, like recognition memory and attention, are present early in childhood, implying that certain fundamental skills are "wired in" and are part of the child's physiological makeup. At the same time, we have seen how the experiences of the child with parents and others in the environment can shape or refine emergent cognitive skills. Whereas nature may be important in providing the underpinnings for cognitive development, nurture has an extremely important role in determining what specific cognitive skills are acquired.

▶ How does the sociocultural context influence cognitive development?

Adults transmit to children those cognitive skills that are highly valued within their society. For children growing up in our Western technological society, this means that cognitive processes become more abstract, planned, and oriented toward problem solving. In addition, when cultures emphasize formal schooling, children acquire literacy, mathematical, and scientific reasoning skills that further affect the ways they think and organize their behaviors. One of the clearest illustrations comes from research showing that schooled children employ taxonomic classification more frequently than unschooled children.

▶ How does the child play an active role in the process of cognitive development?

A central assumption in Piaget's theory of cognitive development is that the child actively organizes cognitive schemes and knowledge to more effectively adapt to the demands of the environment. A major element of information-processing approaches to cognitive development is the child's increasing control of her own thought processes. Attention, memory, and reasoning are used deliberately and flexibly, depending on the demands of the task at hand. The active nature of the child's cognitive processing is thus accepted by Piagetians and information-processing theorists alike.

▶ Is cognitive development continuous or stagelike?

The extent to which cognitive advances are stage determined is an issue that remains to be resolved. We have seen how many changes in thinking processes seem to be more gradual than stage theorists like Piaget hypothesized. Yet we have also seen that young children are not as capable of some forms of thought, such as abstract formal reasoning, as adolescents are. For those who favor a nonstage approach, a major task is to explain why some cognitive tasks remain markedly difficult for children until they reach a specific point in development.

▶ **How does cognitive development interact with development in other domains?**

The child's emergent cognitive skills interface with almost every other aspect of development, from language to socioemotional development. For example, a child's decreasing cognitive egocentrism will affect his ability to communicate effectively, as in referential communication tasks. By the same token, development in other domains can influence cognitive growth. For example, cognition may be affected by maturation of the central nervous system, which is hypothesized to contribute to the development of focused attention and speed of information-processing. The child's thinking is thus both the product of as well as a contributor to development in many other domains.

SUMMARY

One of the most comprehensive theories of cognitive development was proposed by Jean Piaget, who described the active role of the child in the construction of knowledge as well as the transformation of cognitive schemes as a result of maturation combined with experience. Piaget believed that cognitive development proceeded in the following stages: *sensorimotor, preoperational, concrete operational,* and *formal operational.* The child's thought in each stage has unique characteristics, beginning with the action-based schemes of the sensorimotor stage and progressing to the symbolic, then logical, and finally abstract thought of succeeding stages.

Challenges to Piaget's theory have focused on whether his description of the ages of acquisition of cognitive skills is accurate, whether development is indeed stagelike, and whether there are alternative explanations for the behaviors he observed among children.

Information-processing theories have emphasized the flow of information through the cognitive system, using the model of processors with either multiple stores or limited resources. *Multistore models* include such structures as the *sensory store, working memory,* and *long-term memory,* along with *control processes* such as *rehearsal. Limited-resource models* describe tradeoffs made between the energy used to operate on stimuli and the room left over for storage.

Information-processing theorists view the development of attention in terms of the child's increasing ability to focus attention for longer durations, to control attention efficiently and systematically, and to select certain aspects of the environment to attend to while ignoring others. These changes seem to be tied to maturation of the central nervous system during the early and middle childhood years as well as to advances in other aspects of cognition, such as the ability to think about the potential uses of objects and knowledge about the limits of the child's own attentional capabilities.

Although even infants display good *recognition memory*, the ability to *recall* previously seen stimuli increases with age. Improvements in memory result in part from the tendency of children over age seven years or so to spontaneously produce strategies that enhance memory. Among these are *rehearsal, organization, elaboration,* and *retrieval strategies.* Children develop these strategies as their *metamemory,* or awareness of memory, develops; they also learn strategies directly from teachers. The growth of the general knowledge system in the form of *semantic memory* and *scripts* is also related to improvements in memory.

Another important area of cognitive development is the emergence of concepts. One-year-olds group items together on the basis of perceptual similarities, but even very young children can rely on thematic and taxonomic relations. Later, children are able to employ more complex hierarchical relations as they sort objects. Similarly, children show an awareness of the concept of numbers before starting school and later develop an intuitive understanding of mathematical operations such as addition. The development of spatial concepts begins with the child's use of *landmarks* and proceeds to *route mapping* and *configurational knowledge.* Spatial knowledge is related to the child's ability to select useful landmarks and familiarity with a given physical space.

Even though infants show the ability to solve simple problems, significant advances in problem solving continue during adolescence. It is not until then that children can reason deductively and understand the principle of *logical necessity.* Another important problem-solving skill is the ability to transfer learning from one problem to another, called *analogical transfer.* Training can help even preschool-aged children show transfer of skills.

The culture in which the child lives is an important influence on cognitive development. According to Vygotsky, adults play a critical role in the transmission of skills, particularly as they teach children within the zone of proximal development. The availability of formal schooling is another key variable. In describing and explaining cognitive development, we must take into consideration the valued and frequently used skills within a given cultural context.

9

Intelligence

▶ **What roles do nature and nurture play in the development of intelligence?**

▶ **How does the sociocultural context influence the development of intelligence?**

▶ **How does the child play an active role in the development of intelligence?**

▶ **Is the development of intelligence continuous or stagelike?**

▶ **Are there sensitive periods in the development of intelligence?**

▶ **How does the development of intelligence interact with development in other domains?**

Son Van Nguyen stared intently at the questions he couldn't answer while the other students in the test room kept on busily marking their score sheets. Son was embarrassed to be stuck, and especially embarrassed about the nature of the questions he was having trouble with. After only nine months in America, this ten-year-old was proud of the English he had learned, and he was tops in math. Now he was in serious trouble on portions of a test some of his slower American classmates seemed to be sailing through.

At lunchtime he compared notes with Manuela Gomez, who sat across from him in class and was his counselor on all things American because her family had lived in the States a good four years longer than his family had. "What does inscription *mean?"*

"Oh, that's easy. It's words you write or carve on something, like a tombstone."

Son was impressed but suspicious. He knew the only thing Manuela really liked reading in English was comic books. "How did you know that?"

"It's the same in Spanish, inscripción.*"*

She was acting so superior he almost didn't want to confess his ignorance. Just as he feared, when he asked her another question about the test, she hooted with laughter. "Are you ever dumb! Don't you know anything? Everybody knows Christopher Columbus discovered America. We all knew that back in Chihuahua before we even moved here."

Son's worst fears about himself had just been confirmed. Although the teachers never mentioned the word, he knew, like all the other children did, that he had just taken an intelligence test. And at that moment the truth seemed only too plain to Son: compared with his classmates, he was not intelligent.

Psychologists who have tested large numbers of children and adults on intelligence tests have found noticeable differences in individual performance, like those that presumably occurred between Son and many of his classmates. What do these differences mean? In contrast to cognitive psychologists, who are interested in identifying *common processes* in the thinking of children and adults, some researchers focus on identifying and explaining *individual differences* in mental capabilities. Researchers look for these differences in subjects' responses on tests of word meanings, general knowledge, and visual-spatial performance and describe the results as a measure of intelligence.

What is intelligence? To the layperson, that term usually includes the ability to reason logically, speak fluently, solve problems, learn efficiently, and display an interest in the world at large (Siegler & Richards, 1982; Sternberg et al., 1981). Most of us probably have a sense that the ability to profit from experience and adapt to the environment are also part of intelligent human functioning. We might even postulate that intelligent behavior is defined by different kinds of skills at different ages, as did the college-aged subjects in one study of popular notions of intelligence (see Table 9.1). Yet despite the average person's ability to give what sounds like a reasonable description of intelligent behavior, in the field of psychology the formal definition of intelligence has proven surprisingly elusive. Even though the concept has been the object of intensive research and theorizing for over a century, no one definition has been commonly agreed upon, and no one measurement tool assesses intelligence to everyone's satisfaction.

Despite the lack of consensus on how to define and measure it, we now have many tests designed to measure intelligence in children as well as adults. These tests are routinely used in schools as well as in medical, mental health, and employment settings to make decisions about educational strategies, therapeutic interventions, or job placements. Moreover, numerous research studies have examined the origins of intelligence and the relationship between intelligence test scores and other human characteristics and abilities. Considering this widespread use of intelligence tests in research and in applied settings, it is especially vital that we closely examine the concept of intelligence and how it is measured. As we can see in Son Van Nguyen's case, whether

TABLE 9.1

Popular Notions of Age-Specific Intelligence

This table shows the five most important traits that characterize intelligence at different ages according to one survey of college students. The students identified perceptual and motor abilities as most important for infants. They saw problem solving and reasoning, on the other hand, as abilities that become increasingly important later in development.

6-Month-Olds	2-Year-Olds	10-Year-Olds	Adults
Recognition of people and objects	Verbal ability	Verbal ability	Reasoning
Motor coordination	Learning ability	Learning ability; problem solving; reasoning (all three tied)	Verbal ability
Alertness	Awareness of people and environment		Problem solving
Awareness of environment	Motor coordination		Learning ability
Verbalization	Curiosity	Creativity	Creativity

Source: Adapted from Siegler & Richards, 1982.

intelligence can even be measured as an absolute quantity free of cultural bias is a compelling issue in the field of intelligence testing.

Intelligence has been a particularly important topic for developmental psychologists because the nature-nurture controversy, a central concern among developmentalists over the decades, has had an especially long and stormy history in this area. On one side, some researchers believe that intelligence in large part is an inherited human characteristic displayed in the phenotype as long as the person's experiences in the environment fall within the broad range of normality. Other psychologists argue that intelligence is primarily molded by the individual's cumulative experiences within a given sociocultural context and that answers to intelligence test questions reflect that experience.

Furthermore, intelligence has been a pivotal concept for developmental researchers, educators, and all those professionals concerned with the role of early experience in child development. Two important goals of research in this area have been to identify the eventual developmental outcomes for children who score both high and low on intelligence tests and to identify the factors in early development that determine whether children obtain above-average, normal, or below-average test scores later in life.

Our goal in this chapter is to present both historical and contemporary ideas about intelligence—what it is, how we measure it, and the factors that influence it—while keeping in mind the fact that many of the long-standing controversies about this topic are still unresolved. For the most part, the type of intelligence we will be describing is academic intelligence, which includes the kinds of perceptual, verbal, spatial, and reasoning skills traditionally associated with successful performance in school. We will see, though, that because psychologists have taken a renewed interest in intelligence in recent years, newer definitions of this concept incorporate broader skills such as social adaptability or artistic talent in their frameworks.

WHAT IS INTELLIGENCE?

Among the many attempts to define intelligence, the most pressing issue has been and continues to be whether intelligence is a unitary phenomenon or whether it consists of various separate skills and abilities. In the first view, an intelligent person has a global ability to reason and acquire knowledge that manifests itself in all sorts of ways, such as memorizing a long poem, solving a maze problem, or writing a complicated computer program. Intelligence by this definition is a general characteristic that shows up in multiple and varied observable behaviors and activities within any one person. In the second view, an intelligent person may possess specific talents in some areas but not others and so may be able to compose a sonata but not solve a simple mathematics problem. The various component skills of intelligence are seen as essentially independent, and each individual may have areas of strength and weakness.

The second major issue has been the best way to conceptualize intelligence. Should it be defined in terms of the *products* individuals generate, such as test scores on vocabulary items or problems of visual-spatial thinking? Or should it be defined in terms of the *processes* people use to solve problems? The earliest theories about intelligence came from the *psychometric tradition,* which emphasized the quantification of individual differences in test scores to establish a rank order of capabilities among the subjects tested. More recently, psychologists from the learning and information-processing traditions have put forth alternative ideas about the nature of intelligence based on theoretical propositions about the way in which people learn or acquire knowledge. Regardless of theoretical approach, the fundamental debate about the nature of intelligence—whether it is a global attribute or a composite of discrete skills—continues to be a lively one.

Psychometric Approaches

The notion that human beings might differ from each other in certain skills originated in the late nineteenth century with the work of Sir Francis Galton, a cousin of Charles Darwin. Galton (1883) believed that people differ in their ability to discriminate among varying physical stimuli, such as auditory tones of different pitch or heavier and lighter objects, and in their speed of reaction to sensory stimuli. Such differences, according to Galton, are largely innate. Expanding on these ideas, James McKean Cattell (1890) devised a series of fifty psychophysical tests that assessed a person's ability to sense physical stimuli or perform different motor actions, such as the length of time needed to move one's arm fifty centimeters or identify the name of a color. It was Cattell who coined the term *mental test.* Few relationships emerged between the scores that students in Cattell's studies obtained on these "mental tests" and their levels of achievement in college, presumably another measure of intellectual ability (Wissler, 1901). But even though the idea that intelligence is functionally equivalent to psychophysical skill was temporarily shelved, the idea of testing individuals to compare their levels of performance was not.

The first formal intelligence test was created in 1905 by Alfred Binet and Théodore Simon. Commissioned by the minister of public instruction in Paris to devise a test that would identify children who could not profit from the regular curriculum in the public schools because of lower mental ability, Binet and Simon (1905) designed a test that assessed children's ability to reason verbally, solve simple problems, and think logically. With the Binet-Simon test, the mental testing movement was born, and psychometrics was firmly entrenched as a model for understanding intelligence.

Psychometric models of intelligence are based on the testing of large groups of individuals to quantify differences in abilities. The basic assumption is that some people will perform better than others and that those who perform below some average or normative level are less intelligent, whereas those who perform above that level are more intelligent. Thus, if a large group of ten-year-olds scores an average of 20 out of 40 points on a test, and one ten-year-old youngster scores 35, she is considered more intelligent than other children her age. Within the general psychometric framework, though, theorists have taken contrasting positions on the exact nature of intelligence.

psychometric model Theoretical perspective that quantifies individual differences in test scores to establish a rank order of abilities.

Spearman's Two-Factor Theory Charles Spearman (1904) believed that intelligence consisted of two parts: *g,* a general intelligence factor that he equated with "mental energy," and *s*'s, or specific knowledge and abilities such as verbal reasoning or spatial problem solving that were evident only in specific tasks. According to Spearman, *g* is involved in any task requiring cognitive activity and accounts for commonalities in levels of performance that people typically demonstrate in various kinds of intellectual tasks. Thus, the influence of *g* might enable a person to obtain a high score on a verbal test as well as on a test of visual-spatial skill.

Spearman (1923, 1927) developed a statistical technique called **factor analysis** that led to his theory of an underlying general intellectual skill. Factor analysis, simply put, allows researchers to examine the relationships among a large number of correlations to find a smaller number of "factors," or sources of variability that explain those relationships. These factors are groupings that presumably represent a particular skill or characteristic. Spearman claimed that the high correlations among tests of various mental abilities are caused by the presence of the single factor *g*. Not all statisticians agreed with Spearman that the data on relatedness of test scores fit his conceptual model. The idea that intelligence was a unitary phenomenon, however, took hold at least in some theoretical camps.

Thurstone's Primary Mental Abilities In contrast to Spearman, Louis Thurstone (1938) believed that intelligence is comprised of several distinct fundamental capabilities that are completely independent of one another. After factor analyzing the intelligence test scores of many college students, Thurstone concluded that there was little evidence for *g*. Instead, he proposed that the following seven mental abilities are components of the concept called intelligence: *visual comprehension,* as measured by vocabulary and reading comprehension tests; *word fluency,* or the ability to generate a number of words (for example, those beginning with "b") in a short period of time; *number facility,* or the ability to solve arithmetic problems; *spatial visualization,* the mental manipulation of geometric forms or symbols; *memory,* the ability to recall lists of words, sentences, or pictures; *reasoning,* the ability to solve analogies or other problems involving formal relations; and *perceptual speed,* the ability to recognize symbols rapidly.

Although he did find some overlap among the specific skills constituting the "primary mental abilities," Thurstone concluded that no single underlying factor influences all of them. Subsequent studies found that the correlations among Thurstone's seven skill areas were higher than he initially thought (Thurstone, 1947), but Thurstone continued to maintain that any underlying general skill is secondary in importance to the separate skill areas themselves. In this new conception of intelligence, individuals possess areas of strength and weakness rather than the global entity of intelligence.

Guilford's Structure-of-Intellect Approach J. P. Guilford (1967, 1985) extended Thurstone's ideas about discrete mental abilities in a model that proposes 150 factors in intelligence. These factors are the product of three elements: *operations, contents,* and *products.* According to Guilford, there are five types of operations—cognition, memory, divergent production, convergent production, and evaluation (see Table 9.2). At the same time, there are five types of contents—visual, auditory, symbolic, semantic, and behavioral. Finally, there are six products—units, classes, relations, systems, transformations, and implications. Operations, contents, and products can all be combined with each other in a multiplicative fashion to create a $5 \times 5 \times 6$ matrix,

factor analysis Statistical technique that examines relationships among a large number of correlations to find a smaller set of explanatory "factors."

OPERATIONS

Cognition	Comprehension or knowledge, as in knowing the meaning of a word
Memory	Committing information to storage in the brain, as in memorizing a license plate number
Divergent Production	Producing several responses to a question, as in suggesting alternative titles for a short story
Convergent Production	Retrieving a specific item from memory, as in selecting the word to fit a specific space in a crossword puzzle
Evaluation	Deciding whether a piece of information satisfies certain logical requirements, as in determining which of four stimuli is both round and hard

CONTENTS

Visual	Information derived from stimulation of the retina
Auditory	Information derived from stimulation of the inner ear
Symbolic	Information that represents other items, such as digits or letters
Semantic	Meanings, usually of words
Behavioral	Information about the mental states or behaviors of others

PRODUCTS

Units	Single objects, such as a word or musical chord
Classes	Sets of similar units, such as a set of rectangles
Relations	Connections between two items, such as two names in alphabetical order
Systems	Three or more related items that constitute a whole, such as a melody
Transformations	Changes in a piece of information, such as variation in a melody
Implications	Stimuli suggested by other stimuli, such as expecting thunder to follow lightning

TABLE 9.2

Source: Adapted from Guilford, 1985.

Guilford's Structure-of-Intellect Model

Guilford proposes three basic elements that produce 150 factors of intelligence: operations, contents, and products. This table provides examples of each.

▶ **Interaction among domains**

resulting in 150 different aspects of intelligence. Furthermore, each combination can be assessed by a unique test. Whereas one person, for example, might obtain an exceptionally high score on memory for visual units, such as pictures of distinct items, another might do well on a test of evaluating symbolic units, such as noting small differences in pairs of numbers.

Guilford's model is represented in the form of 150 small cubes that make up the larger cube of intelligence (see Figure 9.1). Each small cube represents a unique combination of operations, products, and contents and signifies an independent skill. A unique feature of the model is its acknowledgment of the role of social knowledge, which is represented as behavioral content, as in the ability to read "body language" or facial expressions of another person. Until

FIGURE 9.1

The Intelligence Cube

Guilford's model of intelligence consists of 150 factors, the products of 5 types of content × 6 products × 5 operations. Each factor (the small cubes) represents a unique feature of intelligence as a whole, represented by the larger cube.

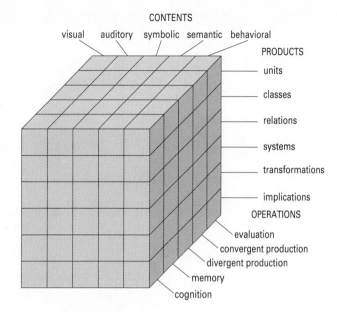

Source: Adapted from Guilford, 1985.

Guilford proposed his model, few tests of intelligence included items from the social realm. Guilford (1985) has claimed to find empirical evidence for a substantial number of these factors by giving individuals tests designed to assess specific combinations of contents, operations, and products. Not all researchers agree, however, that human intellectual abilities fall into 150 separate categories.

Fluid and Crystallized Intelligence   According to Raymond Cattell and John Horn, a distinction can be made between two types of intelligence, each with a distinct developmental course (Cattell, 1971; Horn, 1968; Horn & Cattell, 1967). **Fluid intelligence** consists of biologically based mental abilities that are relatively free from cultural influence, such as the ability to remember a list of words or to group abstract figures together. **Crystallized intelligence** consists of skills that are acquired as a result of living in a specific culture, such as knowledge of vocabulary, reading comprehension, or general information about the world. Because it is thought to be tied to physiological maturation, fluid intelligence is believed to increase until adolescence, when it levels off and then declines in later adulthood. On the other hand, crystallized intelligence is hypothesized to increase over much of the life span because individuals are continually acquiring knowledge as they live in their cultural group.

Horn and Cattell's (1967) early studies substantiated the idea that fluid intelligence increases until subjects are in their twenties and then declines. They also found that older adults obtained higher scores on tests of crystallized intelligence than younger adults did. Other researchers have failed to replicate these findings, however, and have pointed out the problems of cross-sectional studies, in which cohort effects could account for apparent declines in intelligence (Schaie, 1974).

Suppose, for example, we examine a group of ten- and forty-year-old subjects on a test of visual-spatial skill and find that the ten-year-olds outperform

▶ **Roles of nature and nurture**

▶ **Sociocultural influence**

fluid intelligence Biologically based mental abilities that are relatively uninfluenced by cultural experiences.

crystallized intelligence Mental skills derived from cultural experience.

According to Raymond Cattell and
John Horn, crystallized intelligence is
comprised of skills that are acquired as
the result of living in a specific culture.
For example, here a Navajo woman
shows her daughter how to weave, an
ability that is valued in that sociocultural context.

▶ **Sociocultural influence**

the forty-year-olds. Can we definitively conclude that fluid intelligence
declines? The answer is no. In contrast to the forty-year-olds, the group of
ten-year-olds has grown up in an age of technological advances, in which many
children have substantial experience with video games and other forms of electronic media. Perhaps these experiences have influenced their ability to
perform on the test of visual-spatial skill. Longitudinal studies are also problematic because a group of forty-year-olds that has been followed for the past
thirty years may not share many educational, cultural, or historical experiences with a group of ten-year-olds who are moving into adulthood today. In
other words, generalizability of the findings from one cohort to another may
be limited. When researchers have combined the longitudinal and cross-
sectional designs to address some of these methodological problems, they find
that decreases in intelligence test scores, if they occur, happen after the age
of sixty years or so (Schaie, 1983; Schaie & Hertzog, 1986).

Psychometric models of intelligence have been valuable in demonstrating
individual differences in performance on questions about general information,
vocabulary, nonverbal reasoning, and on a variety of other mental tasks.
Moreover, although psychometric models have not definitively resolved the
debate about whether intelligence is a unitary trait or a cluster of separate
abilities, the patterns of correlations among tests for different skills suggest
the presence of some underlying general factor as well as several specific
skills (Kail & Pellegrino, 1985). Some researchers, however, have challenged
the idea that asking people questions about knowledge they have *already* acquired is a good indicator of intelligence. Many have chosen an alternative
path to understanding intelligence—studying the processes by which people
learn and acquire information.

Learning Approaches

To many of us, intelligence is closely linked to the ability to learn. The intelligent person, we believe, is someone who learns quickly, who can absorb large amounts of information with relative ease, who can "learn how to learn," or who can make connections between a problem already mastered and a brand new one. Yet surprisingly few psychologists who have studied learning processes have made explicit links between learning and intelligence. There are some notable exceptions, however.

▶ **Roles of nature and nurture**

▶ **Development as continuous/stagelike**

Gagné's Hierarchy of Learning Like traditional learning theorists, Robert Gagné believes that children acquire knowledge through their experiences in the world, particularly those experiences that have been reinforced (Gagné, 1968; Gagné, Briggs, & Wager, 1988). The unique twist he adds to this familiar equation is that learning proceeds in increasingly complex and cumulative ways as the child grows older, with intelligence as the end product. Early learning, says Gagné, consists of simple associations between stimuli and responses as well as discriminations among stimuli. These early skills eventually become the building blocks of more complex learning processes, such as concept learning and problem solving. Thus, learning proceeds in a continuous, hierarchical fashion, and intelligence is the product of its cumulative effects.

Figure 9.2 shows how Gagné's hierarchy of learning can be applied to a specific task such as learning to read. Implicit in this model is the assumption that

FIGURE 9.2

Example of a Learning Hierarchy

Gagné's learning hierarchy explains the process of reading in the following way: At the lowest level of the hierarchy (bottom of figure), children learn to associate printed letters and words with the sounds of language. At a somewhat higher level, they comprehend the concepts associated with nouns, verbs, and other words. At the highest level, children discern the organization of text according to paragraphs.

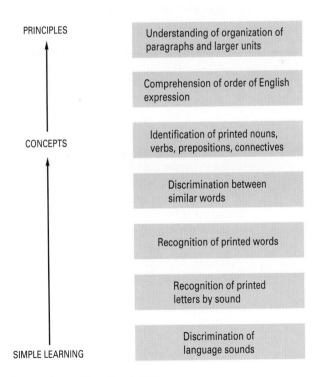

PRINCIPLES

Understanding of organization of paragraphs and larger units

Comprehension of order of English expression

CONCEPTS

Identification of printed nouns, verbs, prepositions, connectives

Discrimination between similar words

Recognition of printed words

Recognition of printed letters by sound

SIMPLE LEARNING

Discrimination of language sounds

Source: Adapted from Gagné, 1968.

children must learn and master lower-order skills before higher-order thinking processes can take place. Thus, they must learn the configurations of lines and curves that distinguish one letter from another and the sounds associated with each letter, as well as the concepts signified by words, before they can distinguish phrases and paragraphs. This model has direct implications for educators. Gagné has proposed that teachers carefully analyze the requirements of the intellectual tasks they present to students, with special attention to the hierarchy of skills needed to perform these tasks (Gagné, Briggs, & Wager, 1988). In Gagné's model, individual lessons and entire curricula should be analyzed and structured so that students thoroughly master lower-level skills before they are expected to perform higher-order skills.

A hierarchical model like Gagné's is more useful in understanding developmental processes in intelligence than the psychometric models we discussed in the previous section for the following reason: Theories such as Spearman's, Thurstone's, and Guilford's are essentially static models of the *structure* of intelligence. They describe what children know at a given point in time but say very little about the developmental *processes* that move children from lower to higher levels of intellectual functioning. In contrast, Gagné's approach helps us to understand how children might move from more rudimentary to sophisticated forms of intellectual functioning. Moreover, Gagné's model carries the implicit idea that children can be helped by those in their environment to master complex intellectual tasks. What educators need to have is an appreciation for the learning hierarchy accompanied by a diligent effort to ensure that children are successful at every level of the learning process.

Campione and Brown's Transfer Theory   Joseph Campione and Ann Brown believe that two learning processes are critical to intelligent functioning: the speed or efficiency of learning and the ability of individuals to transfer what they have learned in one context to another (Campione & Brown, 1978; Campione, Brown, & Ferrara, 1982). As a corollary, intelligent persons can actively employ executive control skills to monitor, evaluate, and compare their performance as they are learning. Thus, the Campione-Brown hypotheses about intelligence incorporate some of the basic assumptions of information-processing theory with traditional tenets of learning theory.

▶ **The child's active role**

Many of Campione and Brown's conclusions are drawn from their review of studies comparing the performance of children of normal and below-normal intelligence as they attempt to execute learning tasks. For example, children of below-average intelligence need a good deal of instruction, such as in the use of verbal rehearsal in memory tasks, before they can employ the learning strategies routinely and readily employed by children of normal intelligence. Moreover, even when they are trained so that they are able to use a learning technique, children with below-average intelligence rarely apply that skill to other new situations in which it might also be useful (Brown & Barclay, 1976; Brown, Campione, & Barclay, 1979).

Campione and Brown believe that a fundamental hallmark of intelligence is the ability to generalize information and skills already acquired to new situations in a flexible and efficient fashion without guidance or instruction from someone else. An essential ingredient in this process is the ability of the individual to monitor his or her own cognitive processes, the *metacognitive* or executive control skills we described in Chapter 8. An intelligent person is able to monitor her own mental processes, seek relations between past and current events, and check the effectiveness of what she is doing.

One of the implications of this model is that intelligence results from many of the normal developmental achievements we discussed in Chapter 8. That is, as children mature, they are increasingly able to determine and employ the cognitive activities necessary to perform a given mental task. If the problem is to remember a list of words, most older children realize that they need to engage in an activity such as rehearsal or categorical clustering to enhance their recall. Similarly, most children, by the time they reach the middle school years, are able to gauge if they have allocated enough study time to material they are supposed to remember. If intelligence is equivalent to reaching some final product or level of functioning, then normal development does lead to higher intelligence.

On the other hand, some children always seem to be one step ahead of their peers in their ability to learn quickly and efficiently. If individual differences in the speed of learning exist—and studies of lower-functioning children suggest they do—then there is more to intelligence than normal developmental advances in cognition account for (Campione, Brown, & Ferrara, 1982). The idea that individual differences in intelligence are related to speed of processing has surfaced in several information-processing accounts of intelligence.

Information-processing Approaches

The newest theoretical ideas about intelligence are directly derived from the information-processing model of cognition discussed in Chapter 8. The analysis of each step involved in the chain of cognitive processes from encoding to retrieval has led to definitions of intelligence that refer to concepts such as speed of processing, growing knowledge base, or metacognitive skill. Rather than identifying the structures of mental ability, as the psychometricians did, information-processing theorists have focused on describing the mental processes necessary to accomplish different types of tasks. In this section, we will briefly consider three formulations of intelligence that are based on the general principles of information-processing theory.

Intelligence as Speed of Processing Individuals vary in the speed with which they conduct certain cognitive activities. For example, studies with infants show that some babies habituate more quickly than others to visual stimuli and show a more pronounced reaction when a novel stimulus appears. Michael Lewis and Jeanne Brooks-Gunn (1981) showed a group of three-month-old infants a picture of twenty straight colored lines repeated over six trials. On the seventh trial, twenty curved colored lines appeared. Some infants in this study were more likely than others to habituate quickly to the repeated straight lines and to show rapid recovery of attention to the novel stimulus. Data from this and other studies suggest that individual differences in visual attention or recognition memory may exist from early childhood (Bornstein & Benasich, 1986; Colombo et al., 1987).

People also vary in the time it takes them to react in simple psychophysical tasks, an idea that goes back to the work of Galton and Cattell we examined earlier in this chapter. Consider, for example, a typical *choice reaction-time* task. Subjects sit in front of an apparatus that contains eight lights, their finger resting on a "home" button. As soon as one of the eight lights comes on, the subject is required to move her finger to a button below that light to turn it off. People show notable differences in the speed with which they carry out this task. Several researchers have proposed that such individual differences in speed of processing information might be related to intelligence, particularly *g*, the general intelligence originally described by Spearman (Jensen, 1982; Jensen & Munroe, 1979; Vernon, 1983).

Is there evidence that speed of information processing is a component of intelligence? Lewis and Brooks-Gunn (1981) noted that infants who were rapid habituators at age three months also had high intelligence test scores at twenty-four months on the *Bayley Scales of Infant Development,* a test that we will describe more fully later in this chapter. Similarly, other researchers have observed at least moderate relationships between reaction-time measures and scores on standardized tests of intelligence among adults (Jensen, 1982; Vernon, 1983). At the same time, though, individuals may differ in the speed of their processing because of variations in motivation and attention to the task rather than because of differences in intellectual ability (Marr & Sternberg, 1987). Some subjects in the choice reaction-time task may become distracted by the equipment in the experimental room or may become anxious (hence slower) in their attempts to do their best. Because reaction times are measured in fractions of a second, they are particularly vulnerable to these types of disruptions.

▶ **Sociocultural influence**

In addition, different cultures and ethnic groups place varying emphases on the value of speed in mental processes. In our own Western culture, we place high priority on getting things done quickly, but the same may not be true for cultures in which time is not a major part of daily routines. If a person does not have a heightened consciousness of time and speed, he might not choose to perform mental tasks rapidly, even when he has the capability to do so (Marr & Sternberg, 1987). Thus, we must be cautious about interpreting the results of tasks like choice reaction-time tasks that assess speed of processing as an element of intelligence.

Sternberg's Triarchic Theory of Intelligence   A major new theory of intelligence based on the principles of information processing has recently been proposed by Robert Sternberg (1985). The **triarchic theory of intelligence** (see Figure 9.3) took its name from three major subtheories that describe mental functioning in broader terms than theories we have described thus far, incorporating what cognitive psychologists have learned in the past two decades about how people think.

▶ **Sociocultural influence**

In the first of these subtheories, called the *contextual subtheory,* the essential idea is that intelligence must be considered as an adaptation to the unique environment in which the individual lives. This means, for example, that we would not administer an intelligence test designed for children in the United States to children from a completely different culture, such as that of the Australian aborigines. In Sternberg's words, intelligence consists of "purposive adaptation to, and selection and shaping of, real-world environments relevant to one's life" (1985, p. 45). Intelligent persons are thus able to meet the specific demands placed on them by their environment, by learning to hunt if that skill is required by their culture, or by perfecting reading or mathematical

FIGURE 9.3

The Triarchic Theory of Intelligence

According to Sternberg, intelligence has three major facets, or "subtheories," all based on the individual's ability to process information.

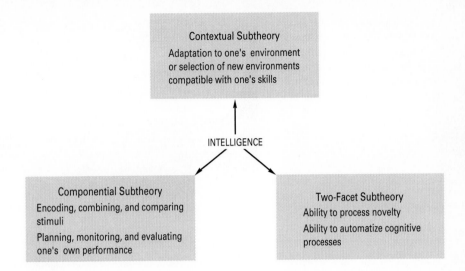

Contextual Subtheory
Adaptation to one's environment or selection of new environments compatible with one's skills

INTELLIGENCE

Componential Subtheory
Encoding, combining, and comparing stimuli
Planning, monitoring, and evaluating one's own performance

Two-Facet Subtheory
Ability to process novelty
Ability to automatize cognitive processes

▶ **The child's active role**

triarchic theory Theory developed by Robert Sternberg that intelligence consists of three major components: (1) the ability to adapt to the environment; (2) the ability to employ fundamental information-processing skills; and (3) the ability to deal with novelty and automatize processing.

skills in societies in which formal education is stressed. By the same token, intelligent persons will change their environment to utilize their skills and abilities most effectively. Changing jobs or moving to a different locale may actually be more adaptive in some circumstances than sticking with the status quo, according to Sternberg.

The *componential subtheory* focuses on the internal mental processes involved in intelligent functioning, including the ability to encode, combine, and compare stimuli—those basic aspects of information processing described in Chapter 8. Other components of intelligence are the higher-order processes, such as relating new information to what is already known. Finally, the ability to plan, monitor, and evaluate one's performance—the metacognitive activities we described in Chapter 8—are also part of intelligent functioning. Thus, Sternberg stresses *how* individuals acquire knowledge rather than *what* they know as indicators of intelligence.

The *two-facet subtheory* describes the intelligent person in terms of his ability to deal with novelty and his tendency to automatize cognitive processes. Devising a creative solution to an unfamiliar problem or figuring out how to get around in a foreign country are examples of coping successfully with novelty. Automatization takes place when the individual has learned initially unfamiliar routines so well that executing them requires little conscious effort. Learning to read is a good example of this process. The beginning reader concentrates on the sounds symbolized by groups of letters and is very aware of the process of decoding a string of letters. The advanced reader scans groups of words effortlessly and may not even be aware of her mental activities while in the act of reading.

Sternberg has drawn many of the mental activities described in his triarchic theory from more traditional theories that view verbal reasoning, spatial manipulation, and numerical thinking as components of intelligence. One of Sternberg's major contributions is the fact that he identified more precisely than previous researchers the cognitive processes needed to engage in these kinds of tasks, processes such as selecting information or monitoring one's own performance. Even more important, the triarchic theory captures the

An important aspect of Robert Sternberg's triarchic theory of intelligence
is the individual's ability to adapt to
his or her own unique environment.
For example, an urban environment
may make different demands on children than a rural environment would.

enormous breadth and complexity of what it means to be intelligent. Sternberg
believes that it is futile to try to encapsulate this human quality with one measure or number because such a number would mask the extremely different
patterns of abilities that individuals show. One child might have exceptional
componential skills but behave maladaptively in her environment. Another
might be highly creative in encountering novel problems but show poor componential skills. Devising a test of intelligence that could be applied to groups
of individuals thus becomes a tricky matter.

Gardner's Theory of Multiple Intelligences   Howard Gardner defines intelligence as "an ability (or skill) to solve problems or to fashion products which
are valued within one or more cultural settings" (1986, p. 74). Gardner (1983)
also noted, though, that people often show marked individual differences in
their ability to process specific kinds of information. Accordingly he identified
seven distinct intelligences:

- *Linguistic:*   A sensitivity to the meaning and order of words, as well as the
  functions of language
- *Musical:*   A sensitivity to pitch, tone, and timbre, as well as musical
  patterns
- *Logico-mathematical:*   The ability to handle chains of reasoning, numerical
  relations, and hierarchical relations
- *Spatial:*   The capacity to perceive the world accurately and to transform and
  recreate perceptions
- *Bodily-kinesthetic:*   The ability to use one's body or to work with objects in
  highly differentiated and skillful ways
- *Intrapersonal:*   The capacity to understand one's own feelings and use them
  to guide behavior

▶ **Interaction among domains**

▶ **Roles of nature and nurture**

▶ **Sociocultural influence**

• *Interpersonal:*   The ability to notice and make distinctions among the moods, temperaments, motivations, and intentions of others

Gardner finds support for the existence of these discrete areas of intelligence from several fronts. For each skill, he says, it is possible to find people who excel or show genius, as in the examples of Mozart, T. S. Eliot, or Einstein. It is also possible, in many instances, to show a loss of or deficit in a specific ability through damage to particular areas of the brain. Lesions to the parts of the left cortex specifically dedicated to language function, for example, produce a loss of linguistic intelligence. Yet the other intelligences usually remain intact. Finally, it is possible to identify a core of information-processing operations uniquely relevant to each of the areas. For musical intelligence, one core process is sensitivity to pitch. For bodily-kinesthetic intelligence, it is the ability to imitate the movement made by another person. Not all the core operations have yet been identified, but Gardner's presumption is that they can be.

How do each of the intelligences develop? Gardner believes that propensities or talents in certain areas may be inborn but that the child's experiences are of paramount importance. Some children, for example, may show a unique ability to remember melodies, but all children can profit from exposure to musical sequences. Moreover, Gardner reminds us that it is important to remember the cultural values the child is exposed to. In our culture, linguistic and logico-mathematical skills are highly valued and are emphasized as measures of school success. Among the Puluwat islanders of the South Pacific, the navigational skills required for successful sailing are of paramount importance, hence spatial intelligence receives great recognition in that culture.

Although no formal test is available to assess individuals on the various intelligences, Gardner's theory has refueled the debate over intelligence as a unitary construct or a set of distinct skills. The theory of multiple intelligences clearly falls into the latter category.

One of the distinct abilities identified by Howard Gardner in his theory of multiple intelligences is musical intelligence, a sensitivity to pitch, tone, timbre, and musical patterns.

TABLE 9.3

Major Theoretical Approaches to Intelligence

Some researchers maintain that all these models, taken together, contribute to our understanding of intelligence. However, few of these models address the issue of how intelligence develops.

Model	Emphasis on Mental Products vs. Process	Skills Viewed as Global vs. Specific
Psychometric		
Spearman	Mental products	Global skill
Thurstone	Mental products	Specific skills
Guilford	Mental products	Specific skills
Horn & Cattell	Mental products	Both
Learning		
Gagné	Mental processes	Not applicable
Campione & Brown	Mental processes	Not applicable
Information-processing		
Speed of processing	Mental processes	Global skill
Sternberg	Mental processes	Both
Gardner	Mental processes	Specific skills

Approaches to Intelligence: An Overview

Table 9.3 summarizes the major models of intelligence put forth by psychometric, learning, and information-processing theorists. Even though each viewpoint emphasizes reasoning and problem-solving skills, newer approaches have broadened our understanding of intelligence to include adaptability to the individual's environment, social skill, and even control of one's body and self-understanding. Many contemporary theorists believe that all these theoretical models must be drawn on to provide a full description of the nature of intelligence. Although psychometric models help to identify patterns of individual differences in performance, learning and information-processing models have made a start toward identifying and describing the precise mental activities involved in intelligent behavior. At the same time, however, few theories so far (with the exception of Piaget's, which will be discussed below) explicitly describe the *development* of intelligence. Most models of intelligence are derived from data gathered from young adults and provide few suggestions about the way intelligence changes from early childhood throughout adulthood. This represents an obvious gap that future research and theory needs to fill.

MEASURING INTELLIGENCE

Over the years, we have come to use the term *IQ* as a synonym for *intelligence*. In fact, the abbreviation *IQ* means "intelligence quotient" and refers only to the score a person obtains on the standardized intelligence tests now widely used in Western societies. The results of these tests have become so closely associated with intelligence as an attribute of human functioning that we have virtually ceased to make a distinction between them. Yet as we saw in our opening scene about Son, the IQ score may or may not be a good indicator of intelligent functioning.

Standardized tests of intelligence share many assumptions about how this characteristic is distributed among individuals. IQ scores are assumed to be normally distributed in the population, as shown in Figure 9.4, with the majority falling in the middle of the distribution and fewer at the upper and lower extremes. The average or *mean* IQ score on most tests is 100. Usually a statistical measure of the average variability of scores around the mean, or *standard deviation,* is also calculated. The standard deviation gives a picture of how clustered or spread out the scores are around the mean. On many tests, the standard deviation has a value of 15, which means that most individuals differ from the mean score of 100 by 15 points or less. The normal distribution of scores can also be partitioned into "standard deviation units."

As Figure 9.4 shows, the majority of IQ scores (about 68 percent) fall within one standard deviation on either side of the mean, and almost all scores in the population (about 99 percent) fall within three standard deviations above or below the mean. In actuality, the percent of scores below the mean is slightly greater than the theoretical normal distribution would predict. This fact is probably the result of genetic, prenatal, or early postnatal factors that can put young infants at risk for lower intellectual development (Vandenberg & Vogler, 1985; Zigler, 1967). Generally, a child who obtains an IQ score greater than 130 is regarded as gifted (although psychologists typically add other criteria to determine giftedness), whereas a child who obtains a score below 70 is regarded as mentally retarded. Less than 3 percent of the population falls into either of these two categories of exceptionality.

FIGURE 9.4

How Intelligence Is Distributed in the General Population

Intelligence scores are assumed to be normally distributed in the population, with a mean score of 100. Most people's scores fall within 15 points (or one standard deviation) above or below the mean, and almost the entire population falls within three standard deviation units of the mean. In actuality, a slightly greater number of individuals than we would theoretically expect fall at the lower end of the distribution, probably because of genetic, prenatal, or early postnatal risks that can affect intelligence.

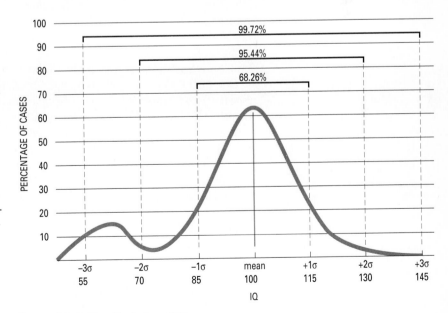

Source: Adapted from Vandenberg, 1971.

Standardized Tests of Intelligence

Educators, clinicians, and others who must assess and diagnose children have a number of standardized tests to choose from. **Psychometricians,** psychologists who specialize in the construction and interpretation of tests, typically administer a new test to a large sample of subjects during the test construction phase, both to assess the test's reliability and validity (see Chapter 1) and to establish the norms of performance against which other individuals will be compared. Some intelligence tests are designed to be administered to individual children; others can be given to large groups.

Infant Intelligence Tests   Most tests of infant intelligence are based on norms for behaviors that are expected to occur in the first year or two of life. Because most of the infant's accomplishments are in the domains of motor, language, and socioemotional development, these areas appear most frequently on the various tests. Almost without exception, the tests are administered individually to infants, require careful and astute observation, and frequently take several hours to complete.

▶ **Interaction among domains**

Perhaps the most widely used infant test is the *Bayley Scales of Infant Mental and Motor Development.* Originally developed in the 1930s by Nancy Bayley (1936, 1969), this test was explicitly designed to predict later childhood competence. The test consists of two scales: The Mental Scale assesses the young child's sensory and perceptual skills, memory, learning, acquisition of the object concept, and linguistic skill. The Motor Scale measures the child's ability to control and coordinate the body, from large motor skills to finer manipulation of the hands and fingers. Table 9.4 shows some sample items from each scale. Designed for infants from one through thirty months of age, the test yields a *developmental index* for both the mental and the motor scale. That is, the infant's scores are compared to the scores for the standardization sample (the large sample of normal infants whose performance was assessed at the time the test was developed) and are expressed in terms of how much they deviate from the average scores of that sample. The Bayley scales also contain an Infant Behavior Record to assess the infant's interests, emotions, and general level of activity as compared with the standardization sample.

One of the most recently developed measures of infant intelligence is the *Fagan Test of Infant Intelligence,* designed for infants between six and twelve months old and based on infants' recognition memory capabilities. During the test, the child sits on the parent's lap and views a picture for a predetermined period of time. The familiar picture is then presented alongside a novel one and the infant's looking time to the novel stimulus is recorded. As you saw in Chapter 8, infants show their "memory" for the familiar stimulus by looking longer at the new item. Several of these "novelty problems" are presented in succession, although the entire test session usually takes no more than fifteen minutes. The test is designed to screen for children at risk for intellectual deficits, based on the premise that their response to novelty is depressed. In one study, scores that infants obtained on the Fagan Test of Infant Intelligence correlated $+.49$ with their scores on several standard tests of intelligence at age three years. Furthermore, it was found over a series of studies that if infants

psychometrician Psychologist who specializes in the construction and interpretation of standardized tests.

TABLE 9.4

Sample Items from the Bayley Scales of Infant Development

Age	Mental Scale	Motor Scale
2 Months	Searches with eyes for sound Vocalizes 2 different sounds Visually recognizes mother	Elevates self by arms in prone position Holds head steady Sits with support
6 Months	Looks for fallen spoon Manipulates bell Playful response to mirror	Sits alone for 30 seconds or more Rolls from back to stomach
10 Months	Looks at pictures in book Attempts to imitate scribble	Brings hands together at midline while playing pat-a-cake
14 Months	Says 2 words Closes round box	Walks sideways or backwards
24 Months	Names 3 objects (ball, watch, scissors, pencil, cup) Imitates vertical and horizontal stroke	Jumps from bottom step
30 Months	Builds tower of 8 blocks Understands 3 prepositions (in, on, under)	Jumps over string 2 inches high Hops on one foot 2 or more times

Source: From the Bayley Scales of Infant Development. Copyright © 1969 by The Psychological Corporation. Reproduced by permission. All rights reserved.

directed less than 53 percent of their visual fixations to the novel stimuli, they were especially likely to fall into the category of "intellectually delayed" (Fagan & Montie, 1988).

Individual IQ Tests for Older Children   The two most widely used individually administered intelligence tests for school-aged children are the Stanford-Binet Intelligence Scale and the Wechsler Intelligence Scale for Children–Revised (or WISC-R). Both are based on the psychometric model and measure similar mental skills.

The *Stanford-Binet Intelligence Scale,* adapted from the original Binet scales by Lewis Terman of Stanford University, was most recently revised in 1986 (Terman, 1916; Terman & Merrill, 1937; Terman & Merrill, 1973; Thorndike, Hagen, & Sattler, 1986). When Binet originally designed the test, he chose mental tasks the average child at each age could perform. He also assumed that if children of a specific age—say, eight years—performed like their older counterparts—say, ten years—they had a higher **mental age.** By the same token, if an eight-year-old passed only the items the average

mental age   Expression of the child's mental abilities by comparing performance with that of children of the same, younger, or older ages.

six-year-old could answer, he had a lower mental age. Thus, intelligence was the extent to which children resembled their age mates in performance.

Terman translated, modified, and standardized the Binet scales for use in the United States. He also borrowed from William Stern, a German psychologist, an equation for expressing the results of the test. The child's **intelligence quotient,** or **IQ,** was computed as follows:

$$\frac{\text{mental age}}{\text{chronological age}} \times 100$$

Thus, a ten-year-old who obtained a mental age score of 12 would have an IQ of 120. The Stanford-Binet Intelligence Scale came rapidly into use among educators and clinicians eager to find a useful diagnostic tool for children.

The Stanford-Binet test assesses four broad areas of mental functioning: verbal reasoning, abstract/visual reasoning, quantitative reasoning, and short-term memory. The test is scaled for use with individuals from two years of age through adulthood. During the administration of the test, children are given tasks according to year level. Once they fail all or most of the tasks for two consecutive year levels, the test session is terminated. In the newest edition of the Stanford-Binet, the concept of mental age has been replaced by a **deviation IQ.** The child's score in each of the four test areas is compared with the performance of similar-aged children in the standardization sample, and an IQ score is obtained for each. An overall IQ score can also be computed. Thus, this test permits psychologists not only to assess the child's overall abilities but also to isolate specific areas of strength and weakness.

The *Wechsler Intelligence Scale for Children,* the major alternative to the Stanford-Binet, is scaled for use with children aged six through sixteen years. The original version was constructed in 1949 by David Wechsler. The revised version, called the WISC-R, contains three scales: (1) the Verbal Scale, which includes items assessing vocabulary, arithmetic skills, digit span performance, and knowledge of general information; (2) the Performance Scale, which includes tests of visual spatial skill, puzzle assembly, and arranging pictures to form a story; and (3) a Full Scale IQ, which represents a composite of the two (Wechsler, 1974). Figure 9.5 shows some items resembling those from each scale of the WISC-R. Thus, like the Stanford-Binet, this test allows the examiner to assess patterns of strength and weakness in the child's mental abilities. In addition, like the Stanford-Binet, the child's score on the WISC-R is computed on the basis of the deviation IQ.

A relatively new intelligence test for two- through twelve-year-olds is the *Kaufman Assessment Battery for Children* or *K-ABC* (Kaufman & Kaufman, 1983). This test is based on the assumption that intelligence is related to the quality of mental processing; the focus is on how children produce correct solutions to problems rather than on the content of their knowledge. One important mental skill tapped by the K-ABC is the ability to arrange stimuli in serial order, as in reproducing an ordered series of hand movements displayed by the test administrator. Another is the ability to process information holistically by integrating and synthesizing, as in identifying an object in a partially completed drawing. The test includes three scales: (1) the Sequential Processing Scale, which assesses the ability to solve problems in a step-by-step fashion; (2) the Simultaneous Processing Scale, which tests the ability to solve problems through integration and organization of many pieces of information; and (3) the

intelligence quotient (IQ) Numerical score received on an intelligence test.

deviation IQ IQ score computed by comparing the child's performance with that of a standardization sample.

FIGURE 9.5

Sample Items from the Wechsler Intelligence Scale for Children–Revised

The WISC-R contains two scales: the Verbal Scale and the Performance Scale. Shown here are examples that resemble items from the several subtests that contribute to each scale.

VERBAL SCALE

General Information
1. How many nickels make a dime?
2. Who wrote *Tom Sawyer?*

General Comprehension
1. What is the advantage of keeping money in a bank?
2. Why is copper often used in electrical wires?

Arithmetic
1. Sam had three pieces of candy and Joe gave him four more. How many pieces of candy did Sam have all together?
2. If two buttons cost fifteen cents, what will be the cost of a dozen buttons?

Similarities
1. In what way are a saw and a hammer alike?
2. In what way are an hour and a week alike?

Vocabulary
This test consists simply of asking, "What is a _____?" or "What does _____ mean?" The words cover a wide range of difficulty.

PERFORMANCE SCALE

Picture Arrangement

I want you to arrange these pictures in the right order so they tell a story that makes sense. Work as quickly as you can. Tell me when you have finished.

Object Assembly

Put this one together as quickly as you can.

SEQUENTIAL PROCESSING

HAND
MOVEMENTS: Watch my hand. Now, you try it.

NUMBER
RECALL: Say these numbers just as I do.   5 – 4 – 8 – 1 – 10

WORD
ORDER: Cat–hand–shoe–ball. Now touch
                  the pictures that I named.

SIMULTANEOUS PROCESSING

GESTALT
CLOSURE: What is this?

TRIANGLES: (Child is given three triangles). Now
                  try to make one like this.

SPATIAL
MEMORY: See these pictures?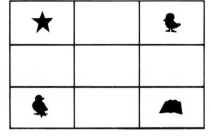

                  Point to where you saw the pictures.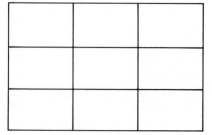

Source: Kaufman & Kaufman, 1983.

FIGURE 9.6

Sample Items from the Kaufman Assessment Battery for Children

The K-ABC contains a Sequential and a Simultaneous Processing Scale. One of the goals of this test is to assess intelligence apart from the specific content children may already have learned.

Mental Processing Composite, a combination of the first two scales. The K-ABC also includes an Achievement Scale to assess knowledge the child has acquired in the home and school. Figure 9.6 illustrates some of the items found on the K-ABC.

Most of the items on the K-ABC were specifically designed to be neutral in content so that processing differences among children could be validly assessed. That is, the intent was to minimize the influence of the child's previous learning history on performance. In addition, the emphasis in test administration is on obtaining the best performance the child is capable of. Whereas administration of the Stanford-Binet and the WISC-R requires strict adherence to test protocol, examiners giving the K-ABC are encouraged to use alternate wording, gestures, or even languages other than English to make sure the child understands what is expected. Thus, in terms of its content and its mode of administration, the K-ABC represents a departure from many traditional tests of intelligence.

Group Tests of Intelligence   Not all intelligence tests are administered to individual children. Many of us probably remember the experience of having our normal school routine altered to take a special test, one that we were told would assess our special talents and abilities. Group intelligence tests were first used on a large scale during World War I, when the U.S. Army administered its Alpha and Beta tests to over 1 million soldiers. Educators, seeing the possibilities, quickly jumped on the bandwagon. Arthur Otis, who helped to design the army tests, published the first version of a test for schools in 1918, and within a year's time it was necessary to print 1 million copies (Lennon, 1985). The idea that children's intelligence should be tested had caught on in the public consciousness.

Group tests are obviously less time consuming and more efficient to administer and score than are individual tests. Because the child must work relatively independently on the group test, however, she may be at a disadvantage if she has poor reading skills or language difficulties. Moreover, individual tests often provide the examiner with clinical insights apart from the responses to the test items themselves; a school psychologist, for example, might note during the test session that a child is overly anxious or has a poor attention span. Such insights are lost in group testing situations. Despite their drawbacks, though, group tests have been shown to be as reliable and valid as individual tests (Lennon, 1985). Some examples of group tests include the *Otis-Lennon School Ability Test,* the *Differential Aptitude Tests,* and the *Test of Cognitive Skills.*

Piagetian Tests of Intelligence   Piaget's theory, which we described in Chapter 2 and again in Chapter 8, is an elegant exposition on how children acquire knowledge, and in a broad sense it also represents an approach to understanding intelligence. Piaget's description of cognitive development as an adaptive process and his delineation of the child's progression from simple, sensorimotor-based mental activities to rational, abstract thought clearly portrays the growth of the child's intellectual functioning. In that sense, it is one of the few conceptualizations of intelligence that is distinctly developmental. Piaget emphasized process and structure—that is, how children come to know what they do and how internal representations of their knowledge change—

rather than the specific contents of children's minds. Given that theoretical backdrop, some researchers have attempted to devise a standardized test that taps Piagetian notions of intelligence.

Although few Piagetian tests are available, one called the *Concept Assessment Kit* has received some attention (Goldschmid & Bentler, 1968). In this test, the child must solve a number of conservation problems that assess her ability to think in a concrete operational way. Among the tasks tested are conservation of number, mass, and liquid. The child's responses to each conservation problem are noted, as well as any rationale or justification she provides for the answer, and her scores are compared with those of a normative sample. Using Piaget's theory as a guideline, this test is appropriate for children aged four through seven years, when the transition from preoperational to concrete operational thought is typically made. Scores on the Concept Assessment Kit are moderately correlated with scores on more traditional measures of IQ (Goldschmid, 1967).

Intelligence Tests: An Overview

In summary, the most widely used intelligence tests are based on the idea that levels of performance on academic types of tasks reveal something about an individual's general mental abilities. They assume that intelligent persons will have acquired a specific body of knowledge that many other members of our Western industrialized culture have also learned. Newer tests like the *Fagan Test of Infant Intelligence,* the *Kaufman Assessment Battery,* and the Piagetian *Concept Assessment Kit* assess intelligence from alternative perspectives that emphasize differences in mental processing activities such as recognition memory capacity or the ability to think logically. So far, though, no test captures the breadth of human intelligent functioning as it displays itself in adaptive behavior overall and in specific dimensions such as social competence, artistic talent, or other nonacademic skills.

Stability and Prediction: Key Factors in Testing

Intelligence tests were first developed with the goal of predicting children's future functioning. Binet, you recall, was asked to design a tool to predict children's achievement in school. Those who followed with other theories and assessment tools for measuring intelligence likewise assumed, either explicitly or implicitly, that scores on the tests would forecast the individual's successes or failures in some areas of life. Moreover, many (although not all) psychologists assumed that "intelligence" was a quality people carried with them over the whole span of their lives. They believed, in other words, that IQ scores would show continuity and stability. A person was expected to obtain reasonably similar scores no matter when she took the test, though some points of development or decline might be apparent at the extremes of the life span. The belief that intelligence was a stable characteristic further fueled attempts to examine its predictive power.

The Stability of IQ   If intelligence is a reasonably invariant characteristic, then a child tested repeatedly at various ages should obtain approximately the same IQ scores. In one major longitudinal research project, the Berkeley Growth Study, a group of children was given intelligence tests every year from infancy through adulthood. The correlations between the scores obtained during the early school years and scores at ages seventeen and eighteen years were generally high; the correlation between IQ scores at ages seven and eighteen years, for example, was .80 (Jones & Bayley, 1941; Pinneau, 1961). Even though the results point to a great deal of stability, however, about half of the sample showed differences of 10 points or more when IQ in the early school years was compared with IQ in adolescence.

In another extensive project, the Fels Longitudinal Study, the stability of intelligence was assessed from the preschool years to early adulthood. Although correlations for scores were high when the ages were adjacent, they were much lower as the years between testing increased; the correlation between IQ score at ages three and four years was .83, but dropped to .46 between ages three and twelve years. Furthermore, as in the Berkeley data, individual children frequently showed dramatic changes in scores—sometimes as much as 40 points—between the ages of two and seventeen years (McCall, Appelbaum, & Hogarty, 1973; Sontag, Baker, & Nelson, 1958). Taken together, the results of these two major longitudinal studies suggest that, for many children, IQ scores are often remarkably stable, especially if the two test times are close together, but that large fluctuations in individual scores are also possible.

Why do the scores of some children shift so dramatically? The presence or absence of family stress can be one factor. Children in the Berkeley study who showed significant declines in IQ often also experienced a dramatic alteration in life experience, such as loss of a parent or a serious illness (Honzik, Macfarlane, & Allen, 1948). The child's personality attributes or parental interaction styles can also play a role. In the Fels study, children who showed gains in IQ were described as independent, competitive in academics, and self-initiating. In addition, the parents of these children encouraged intellectual achievement

Longitudinal studies have demonstrated that parents who encourage intellectual achievement have children who show noticeable gains in IQ.

and used a discipline style that emphasized moderation and explanation. In contrast, children whose IQ scores decreased with age had parents who were overly restrictive or permissive in discipline style (McCall, Appelbaum, & Hogarty, 1973). These studies suggest that IQ scores are vulnerable to environmental influences that can affect the child's performance on a test at a given point in time or, more broadly, his motivation to achieve in the intellectual domain.

The Stability of Infant Intelligence   The correlations between scores on infant intelligence tests and IQ scores in later childhood have been particularly low (Kopp & McCall, 1980; McCall, Hogarty, & Hurlburt, 1972). In one review of studies measuring IQ at age one year and again at ages three through six years, it was found that the average correlation was only .14 (Fagan & Singer, 1983). In another, Nancy Bayley (1949) reported essentially no relationships between scores obtained in the first four years of life and young adulthood. Only when children reached age five years were correlations of .60 seen with adult scores (see Figure 9.7).

Several hypotheses have been advanced to explain why infant IQ scores do not correlate well with scores later in childhood. One possibility, of course, is that there is no such thing as a general intelligence factor (or *g*) or that if it exists, it is not a stable trait. Another possibility is that intelligence in infancy differs qualitatively from intelligence in later years, implying that intellectual development is discontinuous. One problem in drawing any conclusions is that the types of skills measured by infant intelligence tests are very different from those measured by tests such as the Stanford-Binet and WISC-R. Recall, for example, some of the items from the *Bayley Scales of Infant Development*, many of which center on the infant's sensory and motor accomplishments: the

▶ **Development as continuous/ stagelike**

FIGURE 9.7

Is Intelligence Stable over Time?

The graph shows the correlations between IQ scores obtained in infancy and childhood and IQ score at age eighteen years. Note that IQ scores obtained before age four years are poor predictors of subsequent IQ.

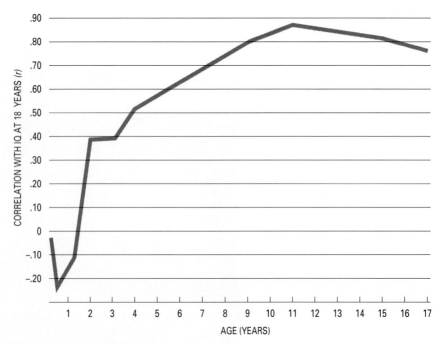

Source: Adapted from Bayley, 1949.

ability to roll over, reach, or jump on one foot. We have little reason to believe that the infant's skill in these areas should be related to the verbal, memory, and problem-solving skills measured by traditional IQ tests for older children.

On the other hand, tests that assess the infant's response to familiar and novel stimulus items hold more promise in identifying those features of mental functioning that might remain constant over a span of years. Recall that the *Fagan Test of Infant Intelligence,* based on the infant's tendency to respond to novelty, correlates well with IQ scores three years later. Several other researchers have reported strong relationships between habituation and response to novelty during infancy and cognitive and language proficiency at ages three through five years (Bornstein & Sigman, 1986). The strong possibility exists that mental development is more continuous than developmental psychologists had previously thought if the characteristics of visual attention are used as measures. Moreover, these data suggest that the ability to discern familiar from novel may represent a fundamental cognitive skill that plays a role in other higher-order mental processes.

▶ **Interaction among domains**

Qualities of infant temperament, specifically attention span and task persistence, may also be related to later mental functioning (Berg & Sternberg, 1985). Like the infant's response to novelty, these dimensions of temperament are related to the ways in which the infant encodes and processes information. In a longitudinal study of temperament in twins called the Collaborative Perinatal Project, researchers tested children at eight months, four years, and seven years of age (Goldsmith & Gottesman, 1981). They obtained behavioral observations of children's tendency to manipulate objects actively and to attend to stimuli for long periods of time along with other standard measures of mental development. The results indicated moderate relationships between children's vigorous, persistent activity on the behavioral dimension at eight months and later mental level, with the correlation coefficient, or *r*, ranging between .50 and .60. Persistence also showed a notable relationship to intelligence at four years of age, at least for boys ($r = .31$ for males and $r = .12$ for females).

Infant recognition memory, attention span, and task persistence all involve the child's ability to discern similarities and differences across stimuli and to extract information from the environment (Fagan, 1984; Lerner & Lerner, 1983). Children who are easily distracted or who do not "stick with" the task at hand will not acquire information to the same extent as children who remain more focused. Each of these dimensions of infant behavior may be tapping fundamental capabilities in mental processing that are related to intellectual functioning later in life. Thus, there may be more continuity (and stability) in some elements of intelligence than was previously thought.

The Predictive Utility of IQ Tests What do IQ tests predict? Not surprisingly, they do a good job of telling us which children will be successful in school and which will have difficulties. Most studies have found that the correlations between intelligence tests and measures of educational achievement average about .50, with the correlations slightly higher for elementary school children than for high school or college students (Brody & Brody, 1976; Jensen, 1980). In addition, the correlations are strongest with academic subjects emphasizing verbal skills. In one study, the correlation between IQ and reading comprehension was .73, but only .48 in geometry (Bond, 1940). One reason that IQ scores are so successful at predicting school achievement is that many of the skills required in intelligence tests overlap with the skills essential to educational success. Verbal fluency, the ability to solve arithmetic problems, and rote memory, some of the abilities measured by IQ tests, are part of most children's school routines. Thus, IQ tests predict best exactly what they were designed to foretell.

Do IQ tests predict any other developmental outcomes besides school success? One extensive review found a notable relationship between IQ and job performance during adulthood. There was a moderate correlation of .42 between IQ and job trainability, and a lower correlation of .23 between IQ and job proficiency (Ghiselli, 1966). IQ scores are also related to job status. In his longitudinal study of children with IQs of 140 or higher, Lewis Terman (Terman, 1925; Terman & Oden, 1959) found that many of these exceptionally bright individuals eventually became scientists, executives, and college faculty members. As usual, however, we must be cautious about how we interpret correlational data. If, as we saw earlier, IQ scores are strongly related to educational achievement, it may be that occupational success is the result of education and not a direct result of IQ. In fact, researchers who have applied advanced statistical techniques to unravel the directions of influence among IQ, education, and occupation have demonstrated that IQ influences educational attainment and has little additional direct influence on occupation (Fulker & Eysenck, 1979; Jencks, 1972).

Aside from these relationships, though, IQ scores have typically not been found to be related to other measures of success in life. IQ scores do not predict the amount of money an individual earns, physical or mental health, or general life satisfaction (Lewis, M., 1983; McClelland, 1973). A likely explanation is that IQ tests measure only a restricted set of skills that do not provide a full picture of intelligence as the ability to adapt to the environment.

Because IQ tests predict a limited number of developmental outcomes, many psychologists advocate their use only for educational purposes—to identify gifted children or to provide students who have lower intellectual capabilities with special educational services. Even here, though, some experts caution that making major educational decisions based solely on IQ test scores can be dangerous. For example, the child may obtain a low score on a given test because of poor motivation, unfamiliarity with the English language, or vastly different cultural experiences. Moreover, when the child is labeled an "underachiever" or a "slow learner" on the basis of an IQ score, teachers and parents may have lower expectations of that child, a phenomenon that can further lower her achievement. Finally, IQ test scores usually do not have direct implications for specific remedial education practices or instructional techniques (Boehm, 1985). Thus, many recommend that psychologists who employ IQ tests also rely on other measures of the child's abilities, such as classroom observations or teacher reports, and that examiners be familiar with the cultural backgrounds of the children they assess (Weinberg, 1989).

▶ **Sociocultural influence**

FACTORS THAT INFLUENCE INTELLIGENCE

In Chapter 3 we saw that genetics can influence intelligence. Chromosomal abnormalities and single-gene effects such as the fragile X syndrome, Down

▶ **Roles of nature and nurture**

syndrome, and PKU can have profound effects on the child's intellectual growth. The higher correlations among IQ scores of identical twins reared apart compared with fraternal twins or nontwin siblings reared in the same environment and the strong correlations between IQs of adopted children and their biological parents also suggest a role for heredity.

Yet even if we agree that genetic differences contribute, perhaps even substantially, to the child's intellectual competence, it would be a mistake to conclude that IQ scores are not influenced by environmental experiences (Angoff, 1988; Scarr, 1981). Take, for example, two traits very strongly influenced by heredity—physical height and the presence of the trait for PKU. In each instance, the presence of the genotype bears a great resemblance to the phenotype. Yet it is also true, as you learned in Chapters 3 and 5, that environmental factors can influence the eventual outcome for the child. Recall the secular trends in physical height discussed in Chapter 5, and remember also from Chapter 3 that dietary modifications for infants born with PKU can result in essentially normal mental development. In each case a highly canalized human characteristic is modified by the environment. The ever present role of the environment is an important idea to keep in mind as we discuss the roots of intelligence.

What factors are especially important in shaping the child's intellectual attainments? We begin by examining group differences in IQ scores, findings that have provided much of the backdrop for the nature-nurture debate. Next we examine those elements of the child's home experience that might be especially crucial to mental growth as well as the role of the sociocultural environment in shaping specific mental skills. Finally, we consider the impact of early-intervention programs on the intellectual attainment of children from culturally different backgrounds. In each case we will see that there are conditions, even given the contributions of heredity, under which IQ scores are not necessarily fixed but malleable by the timing, extent, and range of environmental experiences. In addition, a recurring question throughout this discussion continues to be whether IQ scores ultimately provide a valid measure of intelligence.

Group Differences in IQ Scores

▶ **Sociocultural influence**

Children from different socioeconomic and ethnic backgrounds do not perform equally well on traditional IQ tests. One well-established finding is that African American children in the United States typically score 15 points lower than Caucasian children on tests such as the Stanford-Binet and the WISC-R (Jensen, 1980; Loehlin, Lindzey, & Spuhler, 1975). Another finding is that children from lower socioeconomic classes obtain lower IQ scores than those from middle and upper classes (Deutsch, Katz, & Jensen, 1968; Lesser, Fifer, & Clark, 1965). Of the many hypotheses put forward about the sources of these differences, some have rekindled the nature-nurture debate and others focus on the validity of IQ tests for minority and lower-class children.

Racial Differences in IQ and Nature vs. Nurture In 1969, Arthur Jensen published a paper suggesting that racial differences in IQ scores could, in large

▶ **Roles of nature and nurture**

part, be accounted for by heredity. According to Jensen (1969), there is a high degree of *heritability* in IQ; that is, about 80 percent of the variation in IQ scores in the population could be explained by genetic variation. Because racial and ethnic subgroups within the population tend not to marry outside their groups, he argued that African American–Caucasian differences in IQ scores had a strong genetic component.

Jensen's propositions created a storm of controversy. One of the most immediate criticisms was that *within-group* estimates of heritability could not be used to explain *between-group* differences in performance. Even if the heritability of IQ were .80 for both Caucasian and African American populations (actually the heritability estimates for IQ had been derived solely from samples of Caucasian children and their families), other factors, such as differences in the environmental experiences of each group, could still not be ruled out in explaining racial differences in IQ scores (Loehlin, Lindzey, & Spuhler, 1975). For example, although the heritability estimates of IQ for Caucasians and African Americans may be .80, a 15-point difference in IQ could still arise if most Caucasian children grew up in enriched environments and most African American children experienced environments that did not promote optimal intellectual development.

Sandra Scarr and Richard Weinberg's (1976, 1978, 1983) **cross-fostering study,** in which children were raised in environments markedly different from that of their biological families, demonstrated just how this effect might take place. In their transracial adoption study, Scarr and Weinberg selected 101 Caucasian middle-class families who had adopted African American children, most frequently when the children were under one year of age. Many of these families also had biological children of their own. The adoptive families were highly educated, were above average in occupational status and income, and had high to superior IQ scores. The biological families of the adopted children had lower educational levels and lower-status occupations.

Scarr and Weinberg found that the average IQ of the African American adopted children during childhood was 106, higher than the average score of both African Americans and the general population. The researchers argued that because the adopted children were raised in environments in which they were exposed to Caucasian culture and the verbal and cognitive skills customarily assessed in IQ tests, they performed better than African American children with similar genetic backgrounds who did not have that experience. At the same time, though, the IQs of the adopted children were more strongly correlated with the educational levels of their biological parents ($r = 0.36$) than with the IQs of their adoptive parents ($r = 0.19$). Thus, the role of heredity cannot be ruled out. However, these latter findings do not necessarily mean that racial *differences* in IQ are the result of heredity; they suggest rather that heredity plays a role *regardless* of race.

Many researchers reject a genetic explanation of racial differences in IQ as too simplistic. We have seen in Chapter 3 that heredity and environment interact in complex ways to produce varied developmental outcomes and that neither by itself is sufficient to explain most human behaviors. Furthermore, in the United States race is a variable confounded by the other variables of social class, educational achievement, educational opportunities, and income. All these factors can contribute to the types of learning experiences young chil-

cross-fostering study   Research study in which children are reared in environments that differ from those of their biological parents.

dren are exposed to. Parents with greater financial resources can provide the books, toys, and other materials that stimulate intellectual growth. Moreover, families with economic stability are likely to experience less stress than economically unstable families, a factor that can be related to intellectual performance, as we saw earlier in this chapter. Rather than settling the nature-nurture question, racial differences in IQ have served to highlight just how interwoven many variables are in explaining intelligence.

Test Bias   Another hypothesis to account for group differences in IQ scores is based on the notion of **test bias.** According to this view, the content of traditional tests is not familiar to children from some social or cultural backgrounds. Another way of expressing this concept is to state that traditional psychometric tests are not *culturally fair;* they do not necessarily test the knowledge and skills that are adaptive or important in the child's own culture. Recall the dilemma faced by Son Van Nguyen at the beginning of this chapter and the erroneous conclusion he drew about his own intelligence based on his failure to answer the question "Who discovered America?" Unfortunately his test score may reflect the same conclusion. Children who have not encountered such specialized information in their own cultural experience will fail those items and score lower on many intelligence tests.

▶ **Sociocultural influence**

What happens when tests that are more culturally fair are administered to children from varied sociocultural backgrounds? The research findings are mixed. In Chapter 7, you were introduced to the *Raven Progressive Matrices,* a nonverbal test of reasoning ability that is assumed to contain minimal cultural bias. Caucasian children still score significantly higher on this test than African American children do (Jensen, 1980). Yet when another culturally fair test, the *Kaufman Assessment Battery,* was administered to children of different cultural backgrounds, the difference in test scores between Caucasian and African American children was smaller than when tests such as the WISC-R are given (Kaufman, Kamphaus, & Kaufman, 1985).

Finally, there are questions about whether minority children have the same experiences with, and attitudes toward, taking tests as majority children do. Some of the skills required to perform well on standardized tests include understanding directions, considering all response alternatives before selecting one, and attending to one item at a time (Oakland, 1982). Minority children may not have this basic "savvy" about how to take tests. Since most tests do not permit examiners to be flexible in how the test is administered, they may underestimate minority children's skills (Miller-Jones, 1989). Nor do minority children always have the same attitudes as majority children about trying to do their best on intelligence tests. Minority children may score lower simply because they do not see the point of performing well or have not acquired the same drive to achieve in academic settings that is part of the majority culture (Gruen, Ottinger, & Zigler, 1970; Zigler & Butterfield, 1968).

test bias Idea that the content of traditional standardized tests does not adequately measure the competencies of children from diverse cultural backgrounds.

Not all researchers are convinced that test bias and motivational factors play a large part in explaining the lower IQ scores of certain groups of children (Jensen, 1980). Even for the skeptics, however, these ideas have highlighted the importance of trying to structure test situations so that *all* children are given the opportunity to display their best performance.

▶ **Roles of nature and nurture**

Experiences in the Child's Home

The generally lower performance of children from minority groups and lower socioeconomic classes on IQ tests has prompted many researchers to take a closer look at how environmental circumstances, such as interactions in the home or the values of the larger culture, might affect intellectual development. Not surprisingly, some elements in caregiver-child and teacher-child interactions are related to higher scores on IQ tests.

The HOME Inventory   In 1970, an ambitious project got under way in Little Rock, Arkansas. Initiated by Bettye Caldwell and her associates, the goal of the project was to identify characteristics of the young child's environment that might be related to later competence, including intellectual achievement. A measure of the quality of the home environment, called the *Home Observation for Measurement of the Environment (HOME),* was developed (Caldwell & Bradley, 1978), and a sample of infants and their parents was recruited for a longitudinal study that would last eleven years.

The HOME inventory was designed to measure a number of characteristics of the child's home surroundings, including the quality of caregiver-child interactions, the availability of objects and activities that might stimulate the child, and the types of experiences family members provide to nurture and provoke the child's development (see Table 9.5 for the subscales and some sample items). Researchers collected data for the inventory through interviews and direct observations in the children's homes and gave children in the original sample standard intelligence and school achievement tests throughout the study. The results of this study showed a number of significant relationships and identified several key features of the home environment as related to subsequent IQ (Bradley, 1989).

TABLE 9.5

Subscales of the Home Observation for Measurement of the Environment (HOME)

The HOME Inventory assesses several features of the home environment. Subscales (1), (4), and (5) were found to be significantly correlated with the child's later IQ and language competence.

(1) Emotional and Verbal Responsivity of Mother
Sample item: Mother caresses or kisses child at least once during visit.

(2) Avoidance of Restriction and Punishment
Sample item: Mother does not interfere with child's actions or restrict child's movements more than three times during visit.

(3) Organization of Physical and Temporal Environment
Sample item: Child's play environment appears safe and free of hazards.

(4) Provision of Appropriate Play Materials
Sample item: Mother provides toys or interesting activities for child during interview.

(5) Maternal Involvement with Child
Sample item: Mother tends to keep child within visual range and to look at the child often.

(6) Opportunities for Variety in Daily Stimulation
Sample item: Child eats at least one meal per day with mother and father.

Source: Adapted from Elardo & Bradley, 1981.

First, although there was a weak relationship between the home environment and children's IQ scores during the first year of life, significant correlations were found among several measures of the home environment taken at twelve months and children's IQ scores at ages three and four and a half years. Particularly important were scales on the HOME that measured parental emotional and verbal responsivity to the child, the availability of appropriate play materials, and parental involvement with their children (Bradley & Caldwell, 1976; Elardo, Bradley, & Caldwell, 1975). The correlations among these factors and the child's later IQ ranged from .39 to .56. Second, HOME scores at age two years were significantly related to language competencies at age three years (Elardo, Bradley, & Caldwell, 1977). Again, the same three scales on the HOME inventory were especially related to the child's linguistic competence. The most recent follow-up of these children showed that parental involvement and provision of toys at age two years was significantly related to school achievement at age eleven years (Bradley, 1989).

▶ **Interaction among domains**

This series of studies shows that important processes occur between children and their parents early in life that can have long-lasting implications for future intellectual achievement. For one thing, children who have responsive parents may develop a sense of control over their environments, and their resulting general socioemotional health may facilitate intellectual growth. In addition, the opportunity to play with toys may provide contexts for children to learn problem-solving skills from their parents as well as the chance to develop knowledge from direct manipulation of the play materials. Language development is also enhanced because verbal interactions with parents during play and at other times provide children with the chance to learn the properties of spoken speech (Bradley & Caldwell, 1984).

Parenting Practices Several other variables are related to children's subsequent IQ scores. Kevin Marjoribanks (1972) interviewed almost two hundred parents about their intellectual expectations for their eleven-year-old boys, their emphasis on the use of language, and their desire to promote independence and activity in their children. The boys were also given several mental tests. The results showed that parents who "pressed" for achievement, independence, and linguistic skill and, in general, valued intellectual accomplishment had sons with higher scores, particularly on verbal tests. One caution is in order in interpreting these data, however, as well as the results of the HOME studies. As with any correlational research that uncovers relationships, we do not necessarily know the direction of influence. In the case of the Marjoribanks (1972) study, for example, it could be that bright, intelligent boys elicited higher expectations from their parents rather than the other way around. Similarly, in the HOME studies intelligent infants may have engendered more parental responsiveness and involvement simply because of their greater exploration of the environment or advanced verbal skills.

Some of these difficulties are addressed in a study by Luis Laosa (1982), who used sophisticated statistical techniques to extract information about the directions of influence in correlational relationships. Wishing to see if a number of parental characteristics and behaviors might directly influence children's intellectual development at age three years, Laosa studied fifty families through interviews, observations of mother-child interactions, and standardized tests of children's intellectual levels. Some of the variables measured

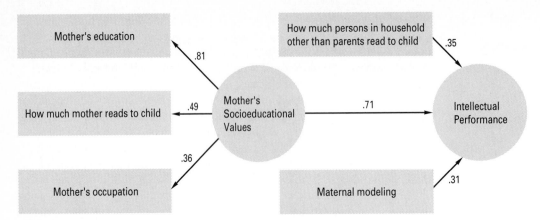

FIGURE 9.8

Source: Adapted from Laosa, 1982.

How Do Family Characteristics Influence Intelligence?

Laosa explored the causal relationships among family characteristics and behaviors and the child's intellectual development. As the figure shows, the highest correlation is between the mother's socioeducational values and the child's IQ. The mother's values, in turn, are highly related to how much she reads to the child and her own educational background. Other important factors are specific maternal teaching practices, or modeling, and how much others in the family read to the child.

included parental expectations concerning education, how much time was spent reading to children, styles of maternal teaching, the variety of toys available to children, and the amount of television viewing among children. From this rich set of data, a number of strong causal relationships emerged.

As Figure 9.8 shows, several aspects of parenting practices predicted children's IQ scores. Among them were how much time family members, including siblings, spent reading to the child, as well as the extent to which mothers used physical demonstration, or modeling, as a teaching strategy with their children. Another extremely important factor was the mothers' socioeducational values. This variable was expressed through the mothers' educational and occupational status, as well as the amount of reading they did with their children.

The results of this study suggest that several specific behaviors, especially on the part of mothers (probably because they remain the primary caregivers), play a causal role in intellectual development. It is significant that reading to children and modeling problem-solving tasks proved to be substantial influences. Reading and the verbal exchanges that accompany it provide an excellent context for the development of verbal skills, skills that are a primary ingredient in intelligence tests. Furthermore, three-year-old children are cognitively capable of profiting from modeling as a teaching style, whereas more complex forms of teaching such as the inquiry method (asking questions such as "What can you do with that part?") may be beyond the preschooler's cognitive reach.

Of course, many questions remain about the specific ways in which the child's home environment influences intellectual attainment. For example, are there teaching strategies aside from modeling that may be even more effective in promoting intellectual advances in older children? Are there other important parental behaviors besides teaching that have not yet been identified? And—in keeping with the position that parent-child effects are often reciprocal—what is the child's role in the parent-child interactions that foster intellectual development? One of the principle aims of current research is to identify more of the specific family characteristics that lead to intellectual advances across the span of childhood.

CONTROVERSY

Do Birth Order and Sibling Spacing Explain Intelligence?

Robert Zajonc and his colleagues have proposed that IQ scores are influenced by the configuration of the child's family (Zajonc & Markus, 1975; Zajonc, Markus, & Markus, 1979). In their **confluence model,** the child's intellectual environment is an average of the intellectual maturity of all members of the family, the child included. The family intellectual environment is "diluted" by the birth of a new child but is enriched as each young child grows older. This effect occurs because young infants do not contribute much to the overall intellectual environment in the home but begin to approach, as they mature, the intellectual contributions made by the adults in the family.

The confluence model predicts that first-born children should have an intellectual edge because they are reared in an environment influenced primarily by adults. Second-born children, however, experience an overall intellectual environment weakened by the presence of two children. The exception occurs when the spacing between two children is large, in which case the average intellectual level has been strengthened by the more mature older sibling. Have the predictions of this complex model been substantiated?

Several studies have found that as family size increases, IQ scores for all the children in the family decrease and that first-borns generally score higher than later-born children (Belmont & Marolla, 1973; Berbaum & Moreland, 1985). In addition, Robert McCall (1984) has confirmed that when children experience the birth of a sibling, their IQs drop an average of 10 points in the following two years, as compared with children who remain only children. Other specific predictions of the confluence model, however, have not been upheld. When children grow up in families with more than two adults, for example, their IQs are not higher than children from two-adult households (Brackbill & Nichols, 1982). Furthermore, other critics point to the small differences in IQ that usually arise as family size increases. Specifically, as the number of children in the family increases from one to nine, the drop in IQ scores seldom exceeds 3 points (Belmont & Marolla, 1973). Thus, large differences in family size produce only minimal changes in IQ.

Perhaps the confluence model's greatest contribution to developmental theory is its suggestion that interactions within the family, among siblings as well as between parents and children, are important to investigate. Although researchers have started to glean important information about how parents influence their children's intellectual accomplishments, we still know surprisingly little about how siblings affect each other in the intellectual domain. ∎

▶ **Sociocultural influence**

confluence model Hypothesis that intellectual attainment is influenced by birth order and spacing among children in the family.

The Child's Sociocultural Environment

Children from different cultural backgrounds often display unique patterns of intellectual abilities. For example, the Inuit people of the Arctic region show exceptional visual-spatial skills compared with those of United States residents (Berry, 1966; Vernon, 1966). How does the larger culture within which the child lives influence his or her level or pattern of mental abilities?

The child's sociocultural background can influence specific patterns of intellectual skills. For example, among the Inuits, superior visual-spatial skills may be tied to that culture's emphasis on hunting and gathering in large, expansive terrains.

One way to understand the role of culture in intellectual development is in terms of activities and behaviors essential for adaptation and survival. The Inuits depend on hunting and gathering in their native terrain, activities that require the ability to perceive small changes in large, expansive fields of vision; the prominence of their visual-spatial skills is understandable in this context. Similarly, as we saw in Chapter 8, Mexican children with extensive experience in making clay pottery were more advanced in a Piagetian measure of intelligence—the conservation-of-quantity task—compared with children without experience in pottery making (Price-Williams, Gordon, & Ramirez, 1969). Intensive practice in specialized skills because they are an integral part of one's cultural experience can lead to heightened "intelligence" in those domains.

Another way to understand the role of culture is in terms of parental beliefs about children that affect their interaction styles. When Shirley Brice Heath (1983) examined the communication patterns of middle- and lower-class parents as they interacted with their children, she found some striking differences. Middle-class parents tended to ask their children frequent questions and expected children to be able to provide explanations. They tended to give their children lots of reasons for events and behaviors even when their children were only one month of age. Lower-class parents, in contrast, delivered frequent commands without providing a rationale and expected children to show what they knew rather than to tell what they knew. Moreover, children in these families were discouraged rather than encouraged to ask questions, which were viewed as a sign of disrespect. Although this study focused on social class differences more than cultural differences, we can see how a culture's views about the proper place of children and the behaviors appropriate for parents and their offspring may translate into specific interaction styles that influence intellectual styles.

One further way in which the culture into which the child is born can influence patterns of intellectual activity is the degree to which that culture emphasizes formal schooling. Cross-cultural studies have shown that children with formal education are more likely to use mnemonic strategies to learn lists of words and to classify objects according to a consistent rule (Sharp, Cole, & Lave, 1979; Wagner, 1978). Although memory and classification performance, the dependent measures in these studies, are not explicitly indices of intelligence, they are cognitive skills frequently embedded in psychometric tests. Moreover, if intelligence is assumed to be reflected in IQ scores, children may learn specific skills in school that enable them to do well on intelligence tests. Performing on a time-limited test, understanding and following directions, and being able to consider a number of response alternatives are all general test-taking skills that children are likely to absorb in school. Furthermore, the answers to specific questions found on intelligence tests, such as "Who discovered America?" or "What is the distance from New York to Los Angeles?" are usually learned in school.

Early Intervention Programs and IQ

▶ **Roles of nature and nurture**

Besides looking at the child's experiences in the home and the role of culture, there is one other approach to understanding the role of the environment in the development of intelligence. During the 1960s, the idea of *compensatory education* became popular in the United States. Researchers wanted to see if the poorer performance of children from lower socioeconomic classes on IQ and achievement tests could be ameliorated if they received the doses of cognitive stimulation presumably present in the lives of middle-class children. If compensatory education programs worked, the idea that IQ is malleable or modifiable by experience would receive strong support, and a genetic explanation of class and race differences in IQ would be less tenable.

Project Head Start The first federally funded program for compensatory education was Project Head Start, begun in the 1960s as a preschool enrichment program for "underprivileged children." The program's aims have been to break the cycle of poverty by improving the educational and social outcomes for children; the assumption is that enriching the "deprived" environments of poor children will allow them to raise their levels of intellectual competence and school achievement. Project Head Start includes nutritional and medical assistance as well as a structured educational program designed to provide cognitive stimulation.

The first evaluations of Head Start were disappointing. In 1969, the Westinghouse Learning Corporation/Ohio University report compared the intellectual development of about four thousand children, half of whom had participated in the first Head Start programs around the country and half of whom came from the same backgrounds but did not participate in Head Start. There were essentially no differences in the intellectual performance of the two groups; both remained below the norms for their age groups. This evaluation, however, has been criticized on a number of grounds. One problem was that many of the children in the program had participated for only one summer, or at most one year. The program had just begun in the previous year and was not well organized in its early stages. The evaluation was thus done prematurely, just barely after the program got off the ground.

More recent evaluations of Head Start have yielded increasingly optimistic results. The Head Start Evaluation, Synthesis, and Utilization Project was an attempt to summarize all research on the impact of Head Start (McKey et al., 1985). This review concluded that Head Start produced significant effects on the intellectual performance of program participants, at least for the short term. Head Start children performed well in the first year or two after they started elementary school, showing average gains of 10 points in IQ score, but the effects of the program faded in subsequent years.

One of the methodological problems in many evaluations of Head Start is that initial differences between Head Start and control children have not been taken into consideration. In an assessment of the early Head Start data, researchers have recently found that Head Start children scored significantly lower than the comparison groups on cognitive measures (Lee, Brooks-Gunn, & Schnur, 1988). They also found differences on several demographic variables. Mothers of the Head Start children had less education, the children belonged to larger families, and they were less likely to have their fathers living in the household. Thus, they may have represented the most disadvantaged of the lower-class children who participated in the study. When these initial differences were statistically controlled, the Head Start children made the greatest gains after one year, although they still lagged behind children from lower-

Project Head Start is a federally funded program designed to provide nutritional and medical assistance, as well as to strengthen the school readiness skills of children growing up in poverty. Children who attend Head Start show gains in some measures of educational achievement and social competence, and at least short-term increases in IQ scores.

class backgrounds who attended some other sort of preschool program or who did not attend preschool at all.

Is Head Start a social experiment that failed? Perhaps not. One reason the initial gains Head Start children showed may have "washed out" is that their subsequent school experience was of poor quality. It may be too much to expect that a year or so of educational intervention will sustain the child's intellectual growth without continuing educational support. Minority and poor children are likely to attend schools with few resources and are often treated less favorably within schools than majority children and children from economically advantaged backgrounds. The schooling experience may thus actually "undo" the effects of Head Start (Lee, Brooks-Gunn, Schnur, & Liaw, 1990).

Another issue involves whether tests of intellectual performance are, in fact, the best indicators of the impact of Head Start. A collaborative study of the effects of eleven early-intervention programs showed that children who had participated were less likely to be assigned to special education classes, less likely to be "held back" in grade, and were more likely to cite their school achievements as a source of pride than nonparticipants (Lazar & Darlington, 1982). Edward Zigler, a consultant in the formulation of Project Head Start, and his colleagues have also suggested that Head Start children show gains in social competence, gains that are at least as important as those on IQ scores (Zigler & Berman, 1983; Zigler & Trickett, 1978).

The Carolina Abecedarian Project   Another important project, aimed at preventing the lower intellectual functioning of children at risk, was begun in 1972 at the University of North Carolina by Craig Ramey and his associates (Ramey & Campbell, 1981; Ramey, Lee, & Burchinal, 1989). One of the ideas behind this project was the notion that to be effective, interventions with children at risk must begin early in life, well before the ages of three or four that characterize most Head Start participants. A sample of 121 pregnant women whose children were at risk for lower intellectual achievement was selected. For the most part, the mothers were young, African American, single, poor, and had not completed high school. Once the infants were born, roughly half were assigned to the experimental group and half to the control group. The average IQ of the mothers in each condition was 84.

The experimental treatment for the infants consisted of medical care, nutritional supplements, and a structured program of day care. Infants attended the day-care center all day, five days a week, until they entered school. The curriculum emphasized the development of cognitive, language, social, and motor skills. In addition, the researchers provided a toy-lending library and a home visiting program as well as parent support groups. This was a comprehensive, multifaceted program intended to alter as much as possible the developmental outcomes for this high-risk sample.

During the first year, there were few differences between infants in the experimental and control groups on their Bayley scores. From age eighteen months onward, however, the IQs of the experimental group consistently exceeded those of the control group. Yet some researchers remain pessimistic about the significance of these findings. Herman Spitz (1986) points out that by age five years, the differences between the experimental and control groups revert back to the magnitude of difference seen at age 2 years. Therefore, the effects of the intervention were only transitory. Ramey and his colleagues counter that there were important patterns in the results that are not

▶ **Sensitive periods**

apparent when group means are compared (Ramey, Lee, & Burchinal, 1989). Some children's scores were always above the mean over the repeated testings, whereas others showed a pattern of consistently falling below the mean. Children who were in the intervention group tended to fall into the first category more frequently than children in the control group. The researchers concluded that even though the differences between groups might have looked small, the program actually had significant effects on a large group of children.

Do early-intervention programs work? If the definition of success is a permanent rise in IQ score for all or most participants in these programs, then the answer is somewhat pessimistic. If success, however, is gauged in terms of school success, motivation to achieve, or social competence, all part of a broader concept of intelligence, then there is room for optimism. Craig and Sharon Ramey point out that early-intervention programs can significantly improve the intellectual development of economically disadvantaged children if they (1) are of high intensity in terms of amount of time children spend in the program each month and how long they are enrolled; (2) are coordinated with health, housing, and other social services; and (3) are followed by educational supports once children have entered school (Ramey & Ramey, 1990).

The primary goal of developmental psychologists, parents, and teachers should be to determine how they can ensure that all children have the fullest opportunities to realize their native talents. Moreover, new formulations of the concept of intelligence suggest alternative possibilities for how we might measure intelligence. New assessment tools might be especially valuable as researchers strive to identify the factors that promote optimal intellectual growth.

THEMES IN DEVELOPMENT

INTELLIGENCE

▶ **What roles do nature and nurture play in the development of intelligence?**

The nature-nurture debate becomes an especially charged and thorny issue in the matter of intelligence. Few psychologists would dispute that heredity plays a role in the child's intellectual development. For example, early individual differences in the speed of infant habituation and recognition memory may signal differences in some aspects of later intellectual functioning. In addition, genetic effects such as Down Syndrome and the high correlations between IQ scores of identical twins reared apart suggest a role for "nature." Yet research also shows that the child's early experiences within the home or in educational intervention programs, together with the intellectual skills that are touted by the larger culture, modulate how her genetic blueprint comes to actual fruition.

▶ **How does the sociocultural context influence the development of intelligence?**

Culture broadly influences the kinds of skills that its members value and nurture and that will be considered "intelligent." Is speed of executing tasks important? Are good visual-spatial or verbal skills essential in successful adaptation to the environment? A culture's demands and expectations frame the way in which intelligent behavior will be defined in the first place. From the narrower perspective of performance on standardized IQ tests, children who have experiences consistent with the knowledge tapped by test items will perform well, while those whose backgrounds are different will be at a disadvantage. Other sociocultural factors often associated with social class, such as parental emphasis on intellectual achievement or the amount of emotional stress within the family system, can also impinge on IQ test performance.

▶ How does the child play an active role in the development of intelligence?

Traditional psychometric theories have rarely assumed that the child plays an active role in affecting his or her own intelligence. However, learning and information-processing perspectives have focused on executive control skills, the child's ability to monitor his or her own cognitive processes and other cognitive activities, as significant contributors to intellectual development. Moreover, Piaget's theory, which can be viewed as a theory of intelligence, emphasizes the child's active construction of knowledge.

▶ Is the development of intelligence continuous or stagelike?

There are those who would argue that intelligence does not really develop at all—that it is a stable, relatively unchanging human characteristic that each child is born with. Learning and information-processing theorists, in contrast, see intelligence as largely the by-product of normal developmental processes wherein the child learns more complex relations about stimuli in the world or becomes capable of more sophisticated cognitive processing with age. Piaget, of course, views intellectual development as stagelike, and formal tests based on his theory assess which stage of thinking best characterizes the child.

▶ Are there sensitive periods in the development of intelligence?

Intervention programs aimed at boosting children's IQ scores through intensive cognitive enrichment usually target young children in the preschool years or even earlier. Since the results show that children benefit from participation, early childhood may be the prime time to lay the foundations for intellectual development. On the other hand, such findings do not preclude the possibility that children can show significant intellectual gains later in development. In fact, some empirical evidence shows that crystallized intelligence increases well into adulthood.

▶ How does the development of intelligence interact with development in other domains?

Children who obtain high scores on intelligence tests are more likely to be successful in school and, as adults, to hold high-status jobs and be successful in them. Thus, to some extent, intelligence (as measured by IQ tests) can predict some aspects of success in life. From another perspective, the child's experiences in various domains can influence intelligence, as defined by newer theoretical perspectives. For example, in Gardner's theory of multiple intelligences, bodily-kinesthetic intelligence can be fostered through athletic experiences and interpersonal intelligence can grow through extensive social experiences.

SUMMARY

Definitions of intelligence vary in two major ways: (1) whether intelligence is seen as a global characteristic or a set of separate abilities, and (2) whether the emphasis is on the products or processes of intelligent behavior. The *psychometric model* emphasizes individual differences in test scores, whereas learning and information-processing models underscore the mental activities that individuals engage in as they solve problems. Both approaches have explanatory value, but few theories of intelligence describe precisely how development takes place in this domain.

Within the psychometric tradition, Spearman used *factor analysis,* a statistical technique that determines correlations, to identify an underlying general intellectual skill he called the *g* factor. Thurstone believed that intelligence was composed of a small set of distinct components, or "primary memory abilities," and Guilford extended the categories to 150 such components. Cattell and Horn hypothesized two specific types of intelligence, *fluid* and *crystallized,* to identify, respectively, biologically and culturally based skills.

From the learning perspective, Gagné proposes a hierarchy of learning that becomes qualitatively more complex as the child matures. Campione and Brown suggest that intelligence consists of two learning processes: the speed of learning and the ability to transfer learning from one context to another.

Within the information-processing framework, intelligence has been linked with speed of processing. There are individual differences among infants in the rapidity of habituation and differences among adults in speed of reaction in psychophysical tasks. Sternberg has proposed a *triarchic theory of intelligence* that includes the contextual, componential, and two-facet subtheories. Gardner has postulated a theory of multiple intelligences in which there are seven discrete areas of intellectual skill.

Intelligence is usually expressed in terms of the *intelligence quotient (IQ),* the individual's score derived from an intelligence test. Most intelligence tests, administered both individually and to groups, are based on the psychometric model and assess a range of verbal, visual-spatial, and problem-solving skills. Common intelligence tests for infants are the *Bayley Scales of Infant Mental and Motor Development* and the *Fagan Test of Infant Intelligence.* School-aged children are most frequently tested with either the *Stanford-Binet Intelligence Scale* or the *Wechsler Intelligence Scale for Children–Revised (WISC-R).* More recently, tests based on alternative conceptions of intelligence, such as the *Kaufman Assessment Battery for Children (K-ABC)* and the Piagetian *Concept Assessment Kit,* have also grown in popularity.

For many children the scores obtained on IQ tests are stable over time, especially after the age of five years, although individual children can show dramatic fluctuations. Studies of infant attention and memory suggest that some continuities in mental abilities may exist. IQ scores generally predict academic and job success but are not necessarily related to other measures of life satisfaction.

Intelligence is the result of the complex interaction between heredity and environment. Racial and social class differences in IQ scores illustrate the difficulty of drawing simple conclusions about the sources of intelligence. One problem is that estimates of the heritability of IQ do not necessarily explain between-group differences in scores. In addition, *cross-fostering studies* demonstrate that although adopted children's IQ scores are correlated with their biological parents' educational levels, they are at the same time higher than their predicted IQ scores. *Test bias* can be a factor in the performance of children from some social or cultural backgrounds on tests designed for the cultural mainstream. The presence or absence of motivation and mothers' socio-educational values also play a role. Researchers have demonstrated that the child's experiences in the home and the skills valued by the larger culture can have an impact on the child's level and pattern of intellectual performance.

Early-intervention programs that provide rich cognitive experiences for children at risk for lower intellectual achievement also show that there may be some long-term gains. This is especially true if alternative measures of intelligent behavior are employed and if the intervention is intensive.

10
Emotion

▶ What roles do nature and nurture play in emotional development?

▶ How does the sociocultural context influence emotional development?

▶ How does the child play an active role in the process of emotional development?

▶ Are there sensitive periods in emotional development?

▶ How does emotional development interact with development in other domains?

Among the Gusii tribe of Kenya, a typical interaction between mother and child takes place: The Gusii mother maintains a bland, neutral expression, constantly avoiding her infant's gaze, especially when the child becomes excited or agitated. When the infant begins to show strong signs of emotion by crying, laughing, or thrashing her arms and legs, the mother physically restrains her. The mother also nods her head and makes repetitive noises to maintain a calm emotional state in her infant. Although mother and child rarely engage in face-to-face play, when they do the mother makes a deliberate attempt to minimize strong emotional content (Dixon et al., 1981).

Contrast this scene with a representative exchange in our own culture: The mother raises her eyebrows and opens her mouth, making an "Oohh" sound suggesting surprise. Her baby eyes her with fascination, chortles, then smiles. Mother reacts with an expressive "Yeesss!" and claps her hands. American mothers generally engage in a great deal of animated face-to-face interaction with their infants, often with the explicit goal of eliciting an emotional reaction such as joy or surprise. The game of peek-a-boo, we suspect, enjoys a great deal of popularity among American parents and children because of the squeals of delight it usually prompts from the child, encouraging the parent to keep playing for long periods of time. In fact, parents in our culture often develop some unusual and elaborate behaviors—sounds and actions alike—just to get their infants to smile and laugh.

The very different nature of these two interactions raises some fundamental questions about the nature of human emotions and the forces that guide emotional development. Are our emotions innately determined, the result of a biological "prewiring"? Or are all our displays and conceptions of emotions derived from learning the rules and conventions of our sociocultural environment? On the surface, the two mother-and-child scenes might suggest that nurture, not nature, is the determining factor in emotional development. The Gusii culture places great importance on suppressing intense emotions, probably to maintain harmony in the small tribal living units characteristic of that group. In the United States, in contrast, intensity of emotional expression is consistent with the dynamic, energetic approach to life that Americans value (Dixon et al., 1981). These differing cultural norms are reflected in the parenting styles of each culture and the behaviors eventually displayed by children. At the same time, however, as we will see in this chapter, recent research with young infants suggests that emotions may possess biological underpinnings as well.

The exchange between the American mother and her infant suggests another related question about emotional development: to what extent do children play an active role in the emergence of the full range of their emotions? Do children passively record and mimic the emotional expressions of others at the same time as they are learning the contexts in which to display them? Do emotions appear when some internal biological clock marks the appropriate developmental moment for them to appear, again suggesting a passive role for the child? Or is there something special about the context of social interactions in which the interaction of *both* partners, caregiver and child, produces the emotional capabilities and dispositions we eventually observe in the adolescent and young adult?

In this chapter we will also see how children's expression and understanding of emotions change with age. Many of their accomplishments are tied to advances in cognition that permit them to think about complex feeling states in themselves as well as in others. And even though emotions are the personal expression of the individual's moods or feeling states, they also function as a mode of communicating with others. Given the social dimension of emotions, we can investigate the role they play in the child's relationships with others, specifically in the special "attachments" that emerge between child and caregivers. What is the psychological significance of these emotional bonds and how do they influence the child's later development?

WHAT ARE EMOTIONS?

Although many of us have an intuitive understanding of what an emotion is, the formal psychological definition of this term proves to be surprisingly elusive. Many theorists agree, however, that **emotions** are a complex set of behaviors produced in response to some external or internal event, or *elicitor,* and that they include several components. First, emotions have a *physiological* component, involving changes in autonomic nervous system activities such as respiration and heart rate. Fear or anxiety, for example, may be accompanied by more rapid breathing, increased heart rate and blood pressure, and perspiration. Second, emotions include an *expressive* component, usually a facial display that signals the emotion. Smiles, grimaces, cries, and laughter overtly express a person's emotional state. Third, emotions have an *experiential* component, the subjective feeling or cognitive judgment of having an emotion (Izard, Kagan, & Zajonc, 1984). Just how a person interprets and evaluates an emotional state depends on his level of cognitive development and the experiences he has had. For a child to state, "I feel happy," he must recognize the internal cues and external contexts associated with "happiness," which are derived from experience. In addition, he must have a relatively mature concept of the self as a feeling, responding being, a sign of cognitive maturity.

▶ **Interaction among domains**

emotions Complex behaviors involving physiological, expressive, and experiential components produced in response to some external or internal event.

Measuring Emotions

Given the complex nature of emotions, how to measure them becomes an important issue for researchers because all three dimensions—physiological, expressive, and cognitive—must be taken into consideration. One approach is to record changes in physiological functions such as heart rate (acceleration or deceleration), heart rate variability (the individual's basic heart rate pattern), or EEG patterns showing brain activity as affective stimuli are presented (Fox & Davidson, 1986). Another strategy is to conduct fine-grained analyses of the child's facial expressions or vocalizations. Tiny movements of the muscles in the brow, eye, and mouth regions produce the facial configurations associated with joy, sadness, anger, and other emotions (Izard & Dougherty, 1982). Similarly, the frequency, loudness, duration, and sound patterns of the child's vocalizations (see Figure 10.1) indicate emotion (Papoušek, Papoušek, & Koester, 1986). Finally, the child's interpretations of her own and others' emotions can be assessed through the use of self-report measures (for example, "Tell me how often you felt cheerful in the last week") and tasks requiring the child to label, match, or produce emotional expressions ("Tell me how the person in this picture feels" or "Show me the person who feels sad").

Although each methodological approach has helped to illuminate aspects of the child's emotional life, researchers must be cautious when they interpret

One way to assess emotions is to observe the facial expressions of infants. Researchers code tiny muscle movements in the brows, eyes, mouth, and other portions of the face to determine the particular emotion. The infants here are showing anger (top left), sadness (top right), joy (bottom left), and fear (bottom right).

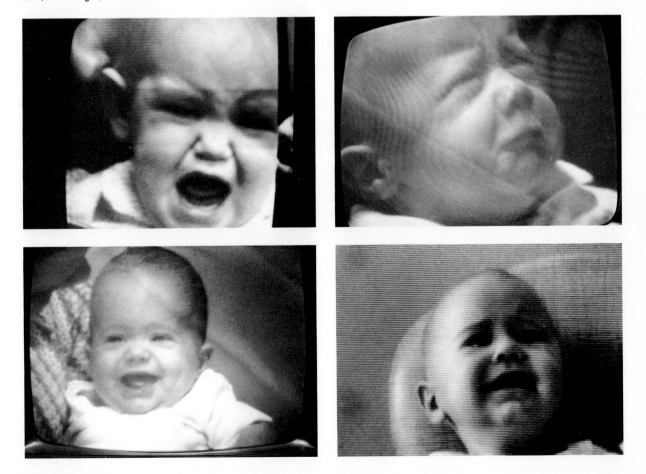

FIGURE 10.1

Sonograms of Infant Vocalizations of Emotion

Like facial expressions, sonograms (sound patterns) can be used to measure emotion. In the top panel, a two-month-old is expressing pleasure with a loud, rising pitch that culminates in a high-frequency squeal. In the bottom panel, the infant is crying with a rising and falling pitch and harsh voicing.

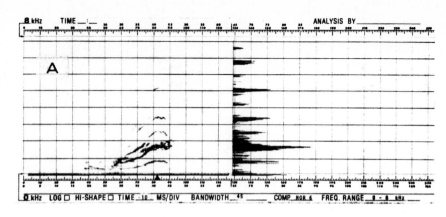

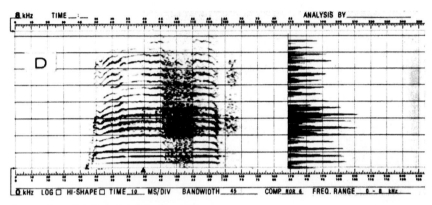

Source: Papoušek, Papoušek, & Koester, 1986.

their findings. When physiological changes such as decelerated heart rate occur as the infant watches a lively segment of "Sesame Street," is he experiencing happiness, interest, or fear? The emotion that corresponds to a specific reaction of the nervous system is not always clear. Likewise, an overt emotional expression such as crying might represent a number of possible internal emotional states, such as sadness, joy, or anger. Self-reports of the child's emotional states present their own difficulties. As we saw in Chapter 1, children may answer researchers' questions in the way they think they *should* rather than on the basis of how they really feel. Others may be reluctant to discuss their inner feelings at all. Despite these methodological difficulties, researchers have learned a good deal about emotional development in the last two decades.

▶ **Interaction among domains**

The Functions of Emotions

What role do emotions play in the psychological development of the child? On one level, they serve to organize and regulate the child's own behavior. If a child is learning to ride a two-wheel bicycle and succeeds in tottering down the sidewalk without keeling over, she will undoubtedly feel elated and probably more motivated to practice this new skill for a few more minutes or even hours. If, on the other hand, she falls repeatedly or even injures herself, she may feel angry and discouraged and quit riding for a few days. Thus, the child's emotional states regulate other internal psychological processes—what she will think and desire to do (Campos et al., 1983).

The link between emotions and cognition has been especially useful to researchers attempting to document children's knowledge and skills. Children often smile, show surprise, or even display fear as they engage in cognitive activities. For example, the infant who perceives depth as she is perched over the rail of her crib will express wariness. A ten-month-old who observes an object disappear behind a screen acts surprised; he has the concept of object permanence and understands the object still exists but is perplexed over its whereabouts. The school-aged child often beams at the mastery of an intellectual challenge such as completing a difficult puzzle or school assignment. In each case, the child's cognitive activity leads to the display of an emotion. Researchers often use these emotional responses to assess children's mental skills.

Not only do many cognitive processes produce emotional expressions, the child's emotional state can also influence cognitive processes, such as level of attention or ability to learn, as well. In one experiment, children were instructed to think of an event that made them feel either happy or sad. Children who were induced in this way to feel a positive affective state learned a shape discrimination problem significantly faster than those induced to feel a negative emotion (Masters, Barden, & Ford, 1979).

Of special importance, though, is the fact that emotions serve to initiate, maintain, or terminate interactions with others. The baby's cry or smile almost invariably prompts contact with the caregiver. A toddler's frustration and anger over an unshared toy may lead her to abandon a playmate temporarily. In fact, a social dialogue completely devoid of emotional content is unusual. "Moods," more enduring emotional states, may help us to understand the child's personality attributes, such as the tendency to be shy, dependent, or aggressive. Personality traits, too, can influence the frequency and form of the child's social contacts. Thus, understanding emotional development can increase our appreciation of a broad range of children's accomplishments in other domains.

THEORIES OF EMOTIONAL DEVELOPMENT: NATURE VERSUS NURTURE

Are human emotions biologically based, preprogrammed responses to specific environmental stimuli, or are they the products of the myriad learning experiences that accumulate over the course of infant and childhood development? The familiar nature-nurture debate has a historically rich tradition when we turn to the varying ways in which the emergence of human emotions has been explained.

▶ **Roles of nature and nurture**   ### The Foundations of Modern Theory: Darwin and Watson

The biological underpinnings of emotion were emphasized by Charles Darwin, the nineteenth-century scientist most known for his theory of evolution.

According to Darwin (1872, 1877), emotions and their expression in humans and animals are derived through evolution and serve a survival function by preparing the organism for action and signaling to others the action to be taken. On encountering a predator, for example, some apes will express fear with a bared-teeth grimace before fleeing. Other members of the troop read this expression and take similar action. In this way emotions play a role in the survival of both organisms and species.

In his investigation of human emotions, Darwin, as we saw in Chapter 1, made extensive observations of his own children, keeping a diary of their emotional expressions and states. He identified seven basic emotions, each with its own accompanying facial expression: anger, fear, affection, pleasure, amusement, discomfort, and jealousy. The facial expressions exhibited by children, he claimed, were virtually identical to those shown by adults. Furthermore, he argued for the universality across cultures of expressions for the basic emotions and maintained that human expressions were similar to those of other primates. Darwin concluded that emotions and their expression are innate and biologically determined.

With the emergence of behaviorism in the first part of the twentieth century, the prevailing view shifted. Emotions, like most other responses in the child's repertoire, were now seen as products of the child's learning experiences. John Watson, in his book *Behaviorism* (1930), stated that three emotional reactions—fear, rage, and love—are originally unlearned and are emitted to only a limited range of stimuli. Loud noises, for example, automatically result in the display of fear in very young infants. Through learning, these primitive emotions culminate in the more complex affective responses that children and adults produce to a wide array of stimuli.

To illustrate his theory, Watson demonstrated in his famous case study of little Albert that fear of a specific object could be learned through the process of classical conditioning. Albert, an eleven-month-old infant, initially showed no fear responses to a white rat, although loud sounds did elicit a marked reaction from him. Watson systematically paired the sound of a steel bar being struck by a hammer, producing a startle or fear reaction, with every attempt Albert made to touch the white rat. Eventually the sight of the rat alone made Albert begin to whimper and cry, a reaction Watson called a **conditioned emotional response**. Moreover, Albert showed a generalization of the fear response to other objects that were similar in appearance, such as a rabbit and a piece of fluffy cotton. Today researchers would raise ethical questions about conducting an experiment of this type because of the potential psychological harm to the child. Nevertheless, this early study points out how basic learning processes can account for the display of emotions to initially neutral stimuli.

▶ **Roles of nature and nurture**

conditioned emotional response
Emergence of an emotional reaction to an originally neutral stimulus through classical conditioning.

Contemporary Perspectives on Emotional Development

Modern-day theorists are more likely than either Darwin or Watson to acknowledge the interaction of biological and environmental factors in explaining the complexity and range of the child's emotional behaviors and experiences. Nevertheless, some investigators continue to stress the biological foundations of emotions, whereas others believe that the child's socialization history and the cognitions underlying emotions play a more significant role.

Biologically Based Explanations The main champions today of a strong biological view of emotions are Paul Ekman and Carroll Izard. Ekman (1972, 1973) has conducted numerous studies of how people in various cultures understand emotions and has concluded that there are universal facial expressions for certain basic emotions and that they are interpreted in common ways across cultures. Ekman showed photographs of six faces depicting happiness, sadness, anger, fear, surprise, and disgust to subjects in the United States, Japan, Chile, Brazil, and Argentina. As they looked at each photograph, subjects were asked to identify the emotion displayed. Ekman (1972) found a high degree of agreement across cultures as to which emotions were being depicted, leading him to conclude:

> We have isolated and demonstrated the basic set of universal facial expressions of emotion. They are not a language which varies from one place to another; one need not be taught a totally new set of muscular movements and a totally new set of rules for interpreting facial behavior if one travels from one culture to another. (p. 277)

Similarly, Izard believes that because certain emotional expressions are displayed by very young infants, they are necessarily innate and have distinct adaptive value (Izard, 1978; Izard & Malatesta, 1987). When the newborn infant tastes a bitter substance such as quinine, for example, she will pull up her

There are many cross-cultural commonalities in the expression of certain emotions. Such commonalities suggest biological underpinnings to emotional displays.

upper lip, wrinkle her nose, and squint her eyes, indicating that she has detected the unpleasant stimulus. No learning is necessary to produce this reaction of disgust. The caregiver observing this signal might respond by removing a potentially harmful substance from the baby's mouth, thereby protecting her well-being. The experience of emotion, Izard states, is the automatic product of the internal sensory feedback the individual gets from making the facial expression; wrinkling the face produces the feeling of disgust. Izard also maintains that once an emotion is activated, it motivates the individual in turn to act. The experience of disgust, in other words, may lead the baby to spit out the distasteful substance.

Biological models of emotions emphasize the direct relationship between the environmental stimulus and the emotional response. In our previous example, the presence of quinine automatically elicits the disgust expression, which in turn results in the experience of that emotion. Each of the basic emotions is associated with an innate neural mechanism that detects the sensory stimulation and produces a characteristic facial configuration. Both Ekman and Izard acknowledge that learning may play a role in emotional development, especially as children learn to control and regulate their emotions. They maintain, however, that the role of biological factors is paramount and that emotions originate in the genetic blueprints the child begins life with.

A Cognitive-Socialization Explanation   Michael Lewis and Linda Michalson (1983) have provided an alternative account of the emotional life of the child, one that emphasizes both the cognitive activities involved in emotional experiences and the role of socialization. According to these theorists, an environmental event does not directly produce an emotional expression. Instead, cognitive processes assess the nature of the event, how it compares with past events, and the social rules surrounding the event. Suppose, for example, the child encounters a barking dog. Whether he cries with fear or smiles at the noisy animal depends on the child's past experiences with dogs (has he ever been bitten?) and on what parents and others have instructed him to believe about animals ("Barking dogs will bite—stay away!" or "Some dogs get excited when they want to play—it's okay"). Cognitive processes thus act as **mediators,** or mental events that bridge the gap between environmental stimuli and the response the individual ultimately expresses. According to Lewis and Michalson, this conceptualization has the unique advantage of allowing us to explain individual differences in emotional reactions when the same event produces different responses from two persons. In other words, the relationship between environmental events and emotional expressions is not always automatic and fixed.

According to Lewis and Michalson, socialization plays a specific role in shaping both the time and the manner in which emotions are displayed. Children in our culture learn that it is appropriate to feel happy at birthday parties and sad when a friend's grandmother dies and that a smiling and sad face should be made at these events, respectively. Socialization also guides the way in which emotions are managed. Young children in our culture, for example, learn to inhibit expressions of fear and anger. Finally, socialization directs the way in which children label and interpret emotions. When the young child cries because of a physical injury and the parent says, "That hurts, doesn't it?" the interpretation provides pain as the reason for the tears. When crying is the

▶ **Interaction among domains**

mediator   Cognitive process that bridges the gap between an environmental event and the individual's eventual response to it.

response to a tower of toy blocks falling over, the parent may provide a different interpretation for the child, such as "That's frustrating." These kinds of communications serve as an important vehicle for children to learn how to interpret their own emotional states.

The two contemporary points of view presented here mirror the tension between an emphasis on nature or on nurture that continues to permeate explanations of emotional development. As we examine empirical studies of how children express emotions and learn to detect them in others, we will see that *both* perspectives help explain the development of emotions in children.

EXPRESSING, RECOGNIZING, AND UNDERSTANDING EMOTIONS

Researchers focus on emotional development from various angles. First, they examine whether children change in the way they *express* their own emotions. Do infants exhibit the full range of emotions that we see in adults or does a developmental progression occur in the types of emotions that children display? Second, do children change in their skill in *recognizing* emotions in others, in reading the facial expressions, vocalizations, and other body movements that carry messages about positive or negative affect? Last, are children likely to change in how they *understand* emotions, such as the events that precipitate and follow an emotional display or the complexities of masking emotions?

Early Emotional Development

Much of the groundwork for emotional development occurs during the first year or so of life. Parents and young infants rely less on language to communicate with each other than on nonverbal signals that are frequently laden with emotional overtones. Just what behaviors are infants capable of showing and "reading"? The answer to this question has direct implications for the nature-nurture debate in explaining how emotions develop.

Emotional Expressions in Infancy Even newborn infants are capable of producing the facial expressions associated with several emotions, including interest, distress, disgust, joy, sadness, and surprise (Field, Woodson et al., 1982; Izard, 1978). In studies of infants' affective displays, observers who are asked to label emotions depicted in slides and videotapes of infant faces have reliably identified each of these discrete emotions. By four months of age, the infant has added anger to her repertoire; by seven months, expressions of fear appear (Izard et al., 1980). The fact that these discrete facial expressions appear so early in infancy, before much learning could have taken place, provides strong support for the idea that emotional expressions are to some extent biologically determined. Moreover, because these emotions appear to be genetically determined, they are often called **basic** (or primary) **emotions.**

Besides displaying a wide range of expressive signals, infants show a high rate of change in their facial displays, sometimes spontaneously and sometimes in response to the expressions of others. Carol Malatesta and Jeannette

▶ **Roles of nature and nurture**

basic emotion Emotion such as joy, sadness, or surprise that appears early in infancy and seems to have a biological foundation. Also called *primary emotion.*

Haviland (1982), for example, found that as three-month-olds engaged in face-to-face play with their mothers, they changed their expression once every seven seconds. Six-month-olds changed once every nine seconds. As you might expect, the facial displays of infants often produce a reaction from the caregiver—delight at the infant's smile and concern at an expression of distress. In fact, Malatesta and Haviland (1982) noted that mothers responded to infant expressions 25 percent of the time, often by matching expressions. Thus, caregivers have ample opportunities to respond to infants' signals, leading to interactions that play a crucial role in their developing relationship.

Although even the earliest displays of basic emotions are usually readily recognized by adults, their form and the conditions that elicit them may change over the first few months. The development of two important emotional expressions in infancy—smiling and crying—demonstrates these changes.

Smiling   One of the most captivating and irresistible infant behaviors is the smile. In the newborn this phenomenon occurs primarily during the state of REM sleep, when dreaming is thought to occur, in bursts of several smiles in succession (Emde & Koenig, 1969). The mouth stretches sideways and up, producing a simple version of the eagerly anticipated expression. Although many hypotheses attempt to explain why very young infants produce this facial gesture (including the popular but mistaken notion that "gas" is responsible), the most consistent finding is that neonates smile when they experience a shift in physiological state, as when they fall asleep or become drowsy (Wolff, 1987).

When the newborn is approximately two weeks of age, the form of the smile changes. The corners of the lips retract even further, the cheek muscles contract, and the skin around the eyes wrinkles. Now the infant smiles during states of wakefulness, sometimes in response to familiar voices and sounds, sweet tastes, and pleasant food odors (Fogel, 1982; Steiner, 1979). By three months of age, smiles increase in frequency and occur in the presence of visual stimuli, most notably the sight of the baby's primary caregiver, usually the

▶ **The child's active role**

mother (Adamson & Bakeman, 1985; Fogel, 1982). Because this "social smile" plays a substantial role in initiating and maintaining interactions between the infant and significant adults in his life, it is considered an important milestone in infant development. Researchers have noted individual differences in the tendency to smile (Field & Walden, 1982). Such variations in responding may help explain the varying strengths of attachments between caregivers and infants, a topic that will be discussed in detail later in this chapter.

At about four months of age, infants begin to laugh as well as smile, initially at the presence of tactile or auditory stimuli such as tickling or interesting verbalizations, and later to amusing visual events such as the game of peek-a-boo (Sroufe & Waters, 1976). Thus, what began as a spontaneous, reflexlike behavior that occurs during certain physiological states becomes a voluntary, controlled response that serves an important social-communicative function.

▶ **Interaction among domains**

Several aspects of smiling and laughter are especially important to note. First, the developmental course of these positive emotional expressions is related to the child's increasing cognitive maturity. With age, the child smiles and laughs to increasingly complex stimuli, stimuli that are incongruent with her past experiences, or events that she remembers from the past. One-year-olds laugh at stimuli such as their mother walking like a penguin or sucking on a baby bottle; they also laugh in anticipation of being kissed on the stomach (Sroufe & Wunsch, 1972). In each situation, children rely on their memory of familiar events to perceive novelty or incongruity. Second, children become increasingly active in producing on their own the stimuli that generate smiling and laughter. After age two years, for example, children will laugh more when they cover an observer's face with a cloth than when the observer covers his or her own face (Sroufe & Wunsch, 1972). Finally, the shift from smiling as a reflexlike behavior to a controlled, voluntary response parallels the increasing maturation of the cerebral cortex, which is responsible for higher-order mental processes and deliberate, goal-directed behaviors.

Crying   Crying is another common way in which infants express emotion. Newborn babies cry for a variety of reasons, but primarily because they are hungry, cold, wet, in pain, or disturbed from their sleep. The nature of the baby's distress is often reflected in the type of cry he emits. In an extensive study of eighteen infants observed in their homes, Peter Wolff (1969) identified three patterns of crying. The first is the *basic* (or hungry) *cry,* a rhythmical sequence consisting of a vocalization, pause, intake of air, and pause. The second is the *angry cry,* in which extra air is forced through the vocal cords during the vocalization segment of the basic cry. Finally, in the *pain* cry, the infant produces a long vocalization followed by an even longer silence as he holds his breath and then gasps.

By the time the infant is one or two months of age, the causes of crying are no longer purely physiological. Infants will cry when the caregiver leaves the room or when a favorite toy is taken away. At about this time, a new type of cry emerges—the *fussy* or *irregular cry,* which varies in intensity, is less rhythmical, and seems to function as a demand for particular objects or actions. At eight months of age, the infant will pause in crying to see if the mother or other adults are receiving the message (Bruner, 1983).

Like smiling, crying is a response that promotes contact between the infant and caregiver. Mothers usually react to their young infant's cries promptly, especially an angry or pain cry (Wolff, 1969). The first order of business is usually to make sure that the infant's physical needs are met. Other effective techniques for soothing the crying infant include providing a pacifier, swaddling with a blanket, and tapping some part of the body—that is, providing some form of rhythmic or continuous stimulation (Brackbill, 1975). Picking up the baby and holding her on the caregiver's shoulder is also soothing, probably because this act provides the infant with a broad range of stimulation that distracts her from crying (Korner, 1972).

Like smiles, the earliest cries have a distinct pattern and are linked to physiological states, in this case some type of physical discomfort. As the infant gains more voluntary control over his vocalizations, however, cry patterns become more varied and controlled and are displayed in a wider range of situations to signal an assortment of different messages. Individual differences in the crying patterns of some infants might also be useful in diagnosing developmental abnormalities. Malnourished infants, for example, display more variability in the pitch of their cries, whereas children who have suffered oxygen deprivation have shorter cries of high pitch (Michelsson, Sirvio, & Wasz-Hockert, 1977; Zeskind, 1981). As with the smile, variations in individual patterns of crying may affect caregiver-infant relationships. In particular, the infant's

According to some research, three-day-old infants are capable of imitating expressions for happiness (top), sadness (middle), and surprise (bottom) when they are modeled by an adult.

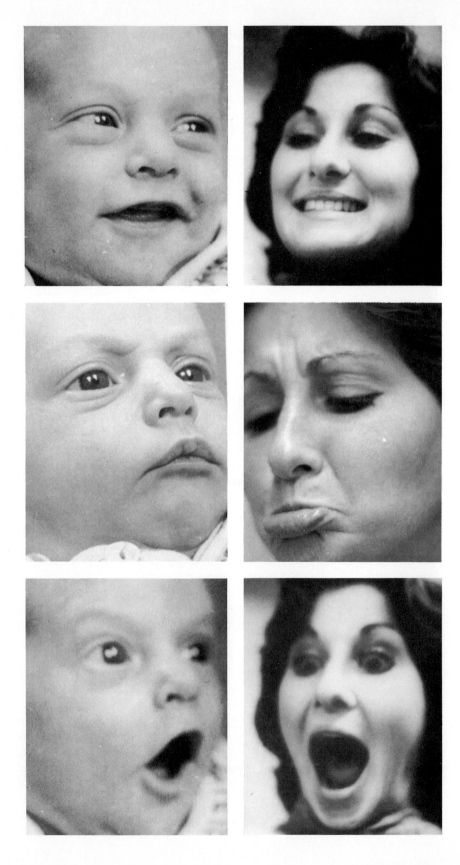

shrill or *aversive cry,* typical of the preterm baby, may interfere with the normal interactions that pave the way for healthy parent-child relationships (Zeskind & Lester, 1981).

Recognizing and Imitating Others' Emotions Besides producing expressions themselves, infants are capable of discriminating and responding to emotional displays in others. Several remarkable studies conducted by Tiffany Field and her colleagues suggest that three-day-old infants are capable of imitating the facial expressions for happiness, surprise, and sadness when they are modeled by an adult (Field, Woodson et al., 1982, 1983). In these experiments, the neonate was held in an upright position, with the face approximately ten inches from the female model. The model made one of the three expressions until the infant looked away. At the same time observers, who could see only the infant, recorded changes in the baby's eyes, brows, and mouth and also guessed which expression was being modeled for the infant. Infants widened their eyes and mouths on the "surprise" trials, widened their lips on the "happiness" trials, and tightened their mouths and furrowed their brows on the "sadness" trials. Moreover, based on the faces the babies made, observers correctly guessed which expressions the babies had seen at levels significantly above chance. Although some researchers offer alternative explanations for these findings (see Chapter 6), many believe that infants have an early sensitivity to emotional expressions.

Other researchers use the *habituation paradigm* to examine the infant's ability to recognize facial expressions in photographs. Typically, a stimulus representing one emotional expression is presented repeatedly while the amount of the infant's visual fixation is monitored. After looking time decreases to a certain predetermined level, a stimulus containing a new expression is presented. If the infant's looking time increases, there is good reason to believe that she has detected the change in expression. Researchers have also examined whether infants show preferences for looking at some expressions over others.

The use of these experimental procedures has shown that three- and four-month-olds are able to distinguish among several expressions, particularly happiness versus anger, surprise, and sadness and that they prefer to see joy over anger (Barrera & Maurer, 1981a; LaBarbera et al., 1976; Young-Browne, Rosenfeld, & Horowitz, 1977). They can even identify variations in a single expression. When three-month-olds saw pairs of photographs of a woman exhibiting a neutral expression versus varying degrees of a smile (see Figure 10.2), they consistently preferred looking at the smiling faces and looked longer at increasingly intense versions of the smile (Kuchuk, Vibbert, &

FIGURE 10.2

Showing Preferences for Adult Facial Expressions

When three-month-olds were shown a neutral face (far left) paired with one of the other photos of a smile, they consistently preferred to look at the smile and looked longer at the more intense smiles.

Bornstein, 1986). It is interesting to note that in many of these studies infants appear to recognize positive expressions more readily than negative expressions. In addition, infants find it easier to recognize the facial expressions of their mothers as opposed to strangers (Barrera & Maurer, 1981a), a fact that may not be surprising in light of the extensive experience they have with this person's face.

Social Referencing   Do infants derive meaning from the facial expressions they observe in others, or are they simply responding to changes in isolated facial features that contribute to these expressions (for example, the upward curve of the mouth in the smile)? Because some researchers report, as noted in Chapter 6, that infants under the age of two or three months do not systematically scan the entire human face, it seems unlikely that they are responding to any expression as a totality, and therefore they probably do not comprehend its meaning. In fact, it is not until the latter half of the first year that infants show evidence they understand the meaning of facial expressions.

At this age, a phenomenon called **social referencing** indicates an infant's ability to interpret facial expressions. If infants are placed in an unfamiliar situation or encounter a strange object and are uncertain how to respond, they will often look to their caregiver for cues. The facial expression displayed by the caregiver will typically influence the infant's own emotional response and subsequent actions. For example, in one study, twelve-month-olds were placed on the shallow side of the visual cliff apparatus, which as we saw in Chapter 6, can be used to assess the perception of depth. They were coaxed to move toward the place on the cliff where the surface apparently drops away. At this point, half of the subjects' mothers posed a happy expression and the other half exhibited fear. Seventy-four percent of the infants whose mothers smiled crossed the deep side of the cliff. In contrast, *none* of the infants whose mothers showed fear crossed the deep side. Moreover, these babies tended to produce fearful expressions on their own faces (Sorce et al., 1985). Thus, not only did infants "read" the expression they saw on their mother's face, they also correctly interpreted its message.

▶ **The child's active role**

Social referencing provides a good example of the child's active involvement in the process of emotional development. When he encounters a puzzling or ambiguous event, he actively seeks information from the environment about how to react. He then uses the emotional expression of others to derive meaning from that event and decide on a course of action (Tronick, 1989).

▶ **The child's active role**

Emotions as Regulators of Social Interactions   Observations of infants' ability to express and identify emotions in the context of interactions with others has led developmental psychologists to realize that emotions serve an important function in regulating and modulating early social exchanges. This dynamic begins at about two or three months of age, when, as in the scene that opened this chapter, the infant looks into the adult's eyes and shows a "social smile" or a cry, to which the adult responds. The adult vocalization or facial expression, in turn, often precipitates another emotional response from the infant. Such episodes of reciprocal, mutually engaging cycles of caregiver-child behaviors are called **interactive synchrony**. During the first year, interactive synchrony characterizes about 30 percent of face-to-face interactions between infants and caregivers (Tronick & Cohn, 1989).

social referencing   Looking to another individual for emotional cues in interpreting a strange or ambiguous event.

interactive synchrony   Reciprocal, mutually engaging cycles of caregiver-child behaviors.

Beginning at about two to three months of age, infants and their caregivers begin to show *interactive synchrony,* cycles of reciprocal, coordinated face-to-face interactions.

At about three months, primary caregivers typically assume the major responsibility for guiding interactions, producing repetitions of exaggerated faces and vocalizations to which the infant pays rapt attention (Stern, 1974). Infants, without doubt, notice and react to their mothers' displays. When mothers do not return a smile but show a still face or a neutral pose, infants respond with a quizzical look and withdraw from the social interaction (Tronick et al., 1978). When mothers show a positive expression, the infant follows suit. If mothers look depressed, infants react by averting their gaze and sometimes crying (Cohn & Tronick, 1983). By about six to nine months of age, infants more clearly take the initiative; the infant's displays of positive affect now more often precede the mother's (Cohn & Tronick, 1987). Thus, throughout early infancy, the child becomes an increasingly active partner in an emotionally toned interactive "duet" with the caregiver.

But what about the other 70 percent of the time, when infant-caregiver interactions are *asynchronous* or uncoordinated with each other? Edward Tronick and his colleagues believe that these episodes, which constitute the majority of infant-caregiver relations, also play an important part in normal emotional development. A common occurrence after a sequence in which infant and caregiver are not coordinated is the infant's attempt to repair the "interactive error." When the mother looks sad, for example, the infant's subsequent gaze aversion or crying encourages the mother to modify her own behavior, and frequently she does (Cohn & Tronick, 1983). Thus, episodes of asynchrony provide infants with the opportunity to learn about the rules of interaction, and in cases in which they are able to repair an interaction, give them a sense of mastery or control over their environment (Tronick & Cohn, 1989).

Affective exchanges between infant and caregiver lay the groundwork for social behavior and emotional dispositions at later ages. For example, researchers find that infants of clinically depressed mothers express a good deal of negative affect in face-to-face interactions, probably in response to the disengagement of the mothers (Cohn et al., 1986). The negative affect of these infants extends to other adults who are not depressed (Field et al., 1988). Moreover, the dominance of specific emotions during early mother-child interactions culminates in a general mood or background emotional state that pervades the child's own behaviors (Tronick, Ricks, & Cohn, 1982). The child then brings this general affective tone to new situations—for example, an anxious child is likely to interpret a new event as fearful, whereas a happy child might react with curiosity. Finally, the nature of the affective exchanges between mother and child influences the strength of the emotional bond—or *attachment*—between them. Infants who engage in attempts to elicit responses from mothers by smiling, vocalizing, or crying at six months of age are more likely to have high-quality attachments at the age of one year than children who withdraw from such interactions (Tronick, Ricks, & Cohn, 1982). As we will see later in this chapter, high-quality attachments, in turn, have been found to be related to many other positive developmental outcomes in social and cognitive functioning. Hence, the tone of these early interactions is a crucial facet of child development.

Later Emotional Development

Beyond infancy, the child's emerging linguistic capabilities and cognitive growth result in still more changes in emotions. He expresses new and more complex emotions, such as guilt, shame, and pride, or more varied forms of earlier emotions, such as joy and fear. With the advent of language, he can communicate feelings by verbalizing instead of just furrowing his brow and crying or making some other facial display. He also gains a more comprehensive understanding of emotions, their antecedents and their consequences, both in himself and in others.

▶ **Interaction among domains**

Expressing Complex Emotions   By their second year, many children begin to show emotions that reflect a more complex understanding of social relationships. Shame, guilt, and envy, for example, each require the child to understand the perspective of another person—that they might be disappointed in the child, might be hurt, or might feel affection for a third party. Such emotions also require a consciousness about the self and one's relations to others, a facet of cognitive development (Campos et al., 1983; Lewis, 1989). Emotions like envy and guilt are accordingly known as **complex emotions.**

complex emotion   Emotion such as guilt and envy that appears later in childhood and requires more complex cognitive and social skills.

Mothers report seeing the first signs of guilt and shame at about eighteen months of age (Emde, 1980; Izard & Malatesta, 1987). This is the same age at which children begin to make reparations for damage they have caused to others, such as hugging a peer hit a few moments earlier or showing remorse for coloring on the couch (Zahn-Waxler & Radke-Yarrow, 1982). At age two years, children also show visible signs of jealousy. The child might wedge herself between mother and father as they are hugging, or hit a sibling that a parent just kissed (Cummings, Zahn-Waxler, & Radke-Yarrow, 1981). You might recall from Chapter 7 that this is the same age at which children begin to evidence early referential communication skills, which also require an awareness of the perspectives of others. As the child understands more about the social world and the relationships and feelings of others, her own feeling states become increasingly sophisticated as well.

At the same time that more complex emotions emerge, the child also begins expressing the basic emotions in more varied and controlled ways. During the preschool years, for example, children show an increase in the tendency to smile by raising their upper lip and exposing the upper teeth, a form of smile that is considered the most sociable. By age four years, children begin to reserve this smile almost exclusively for same-sex peers (Cheyne, 1976).

Another emotion, fear, also undergoes developmental changes, particularly in the types of stimuli that elicit it. Whereas early expressions of fear are made in response to loud noises or strange people, later in childhood fear occurs as a response to more complex events, such as the possibility of failing in school or being rejected by peers (Morris & Kratochwill, 1983; Rutter & Garmezy, 1983). Thus, as the child's cognitive skills and social awareness become more elaborate, he expresses more complex emotions or more elaborate and controlled forms of the basic emotions.

▶ **Interaction among domains**

Understanding Emotions Children begin to use language to describe feeling states between eighteen and thirty-six months of age, shortly after they begin to talk. Inge Bretherton and Marjorie Beeghly (1982) asked mothers of twenty-eight-month-olds to keep a diary of their children's verbalizations that referred to psychological states. Table 10.1 shows the percentage of children who used words for various emotions to describe either themselves or others. Besides being able to apply a wide range of terms to express both positive and negative feelings, these children were also able to discuss the conditions that led to a specific emotion and the actions that followed as a consequence. Several children, for example, made statements similar to "Grandma mad. I wrote on wall," suggesting an understanding of the reasons for another's emotion. Another type of utterance made by several children—"I cry. Lady pick me up and hold me"—signifies an understanding that emotions may be related to subsequent actions.

From the age of three to four years and onward, children become more proficient in verbally describing the causes and consequences of emotions (Barden et al., 1980). Children tend to agree that certain events, such as receiving a compliment, lead to happy emotions, whereas others, such as being shoved, lead to negative feelings. Furthermore, they are able to suggest ways of ameliorating another's negative emotions, such as hugging a crying sibling or sharing toys to placate an angered playmate (Fabes et al., 1988). One recent study demonstrated that children who have substantial knowledge about the emotions that usually accompany given situations, such as fear during a nightmare, were better liked by their peers (Denham et al., 1990). The reason may be that children who have greater knowledge about emotions are more likely to respond appropriately to the emotional expressions of their peers. Thus, knowledge about emotions can have ramifications for the child's social development.

▶ **Interaction among domains**

By the time they enter school, children possess an even more sophisticated understanding of emotions. They appreciate the phenomenon that emotions fade with time (Harris, 1983). They also begin to understand that changes in thoughts may lead to changes in feelings—that thinking happier thoughts, for

TABLE 10.1

The Emotion Vocabulary of 28-month-olds

Mothers of thirty 28-month-old children collected data on their children's verbalizations that referred to psychological states. This table shows the percentage of children who used emotion terms to describe themselves and others. The majority of children used at least some emotion terms, and the ability to apply emotion labels to the self *and* others did not lag far behind the ability to use them for either the self *or* others.

Emotion Terms	Percentage of Children Using Word	
	For Self or Others	For Self and Others
Positive		
Good (moral)	93	67
Love	87	60
Like	80	60
Funny	77	40
Have fun	67	53
Happy	60	40
(Feel) good	47	27
To be all right	37	30
Have a good time	30	20
Proud	27	13
(Feel) better	27	10
Surprised	13	3
Negative		
Bad (moral)	87	60
Scared	73	43
Mad	73	33
Sad	57	50
Scary	40	13
Yucky	33	13
Messy	30	13
Angry	17	7
(Feel) bad	10	3

Source: Adapted from Bretherton & Beeghly, 1982.

example, might make a sad mood go away (Weiner & Handel, 1985). As children approach adolescence, they comprehend the possibility of experiencing two contrasting emotions at the same time, like feeling happy to get a bike as a gift but disappointed that it is not a ten-speed (Harter & Buddin, 1987).

One of the skills that appears later in childhood is the ability to mask or "fake" an emotional state. By this time, children understand behaviors prescribed by cultural rules (for example, you are supposed to look happy when you are given a gift even if you don't like it) or behaviors necessary to obtain certain goals (you should smile even if you don't feel well if you want your mother to allow you to go to a friend's party). Paul Harris and his associates (Harris et al., 1986) examined this skill in using emotional **display rules,** the cultural guidelines about when and how to express emotions, by asking six- and ten-year-old children to listen to stories in which the central character felt either a positive or negative emotion but had to hide it. Here is one such story:

display rules   Cultural guidelines about when, how, and to what degree to display emotions.

Diana has just had a haircut. The hairdresser cut off too much hair and she looks really silly. At school Diana's friends laugh at her and tell her that she looks like a hedgehog. Diana tries to pretend that she doesn't mind.

After hearing the story, children were to describe verbally the facial expression of the protagonist along with how this person *really* felt. Even six-year-olds could state that the emotion displayed would not match the emotion felt, although ten-year-olds provided a fuller explanation. These results suggest that by the middle school years children have developed a broad understanding of the social norms and expectations that surround the display of feelings.

As they approach adolescence, children's concepts of emotions center increasingly on internal psychological states. That is, whereas younger children identify their own emotional states based on the situations they are in ("I'm happy when it's my birthday"), preadolescents and adolescents refer more frequently to their mental states ("I'm happy when I feel good inside") (Harris, Olthof, & Meerum Terwogt, 1981). In explaining why emotions fade with time, younger children refer to the fact that situations change—sadness over a lost dog gives way to happiness when the family adopts another dog. At age ten years, their explanations center around notions of forgetting or not thinking about one's previous emotional state (Harris et al., 1985). Preadolescents also have better insights into the feelings and motives of others than do younger children. Fifth-graders in one study, for example, accurately identified the emotions felt by an adult based on the content of a conversation the adult was having with a third party. They were also able to elaborate on the reasons that person felt the way he did (Rothenberg, 1970).

In summary, emotional development in older children is closely affiliated with advances in cognition that allow them to think in more abstract and complex terms. In addition, it is apparent that the way in which children express and understand emotions can be a major ingredient in their success with social relationships. We will see in Chapter 15 that children who are popular with their peers know how to deliver positively toned messages to their playmates. Similarly, the emergence of guilt and shame is related to moral development and altruism, two other facets of social development.

Variations in Emotional Development

▶ **Roles of nature and nurture**

A strong biological account of emotional development emphasizes commonalities across children in the expression and interpretation of emotions. Yet despite the generalities we have observed, especially in the emotional behaviors of infants, noteworthy variations among individuals and cultural groups suggest an influential role for environmental factors, particularly socialization, in explaining emotional development.

Sex Differences in Emotions According to the familiar stereotype, females are more emotionally expressive and more sensitive to the emotional states of others than are males. Do boys and girls actually differ in any facet of emotional development? Before the adolescent years, there are few reported differences in the frequency or ways of expressing emotions, or in the child's understanding of emotions. Compared with boys, however, girls in late adolescence smile more either on their own initiative or in response to the smile of another (Hall & Halberstadt, 1986). Girls also begin to show more anxieties than boys during the school years—fears about tests, family issues, health, and other concerns (Orton, 1982; Scarr et al., 1981). Finally, some researchers report that girls are better than boys at decoding the emotional expressions of others (Hall, 1978; 1984).

Observations of parents' behaviors suggest that many of these sex differences are directly taught or modeled. For example, mothers and fathers spend more time trying to get their infant daughters to smile than they do their infant sons (Moss, 1974). Mothers of preschoolers also mention feeling states more often when they talk with their daughters than with their sons (Dunn, Bretherton, & Munn, 1987). When a group of researchers recorded the facial expressions of mothers as they played with their two-year-old children, they found that mothers were significantly more expressive with girls than with boys. Girls were exposed to a greater range of emotions and received more social smiles (Malatesta et al., 1989). In general, parents encourage girls to maintain close emotional relationships and to show affection, whereas they instruct boys to control their emotions (Block, 1973). Thus, for better or worse, many of the stereotyped emotional behaviors we see in males and females result from their learning histories.

▶ **Sociocultural influence**

Cross-Cultural Differences in Emotions   The tendency of children to express and detect emotions varies as a function of the culture in which they grow up. American children, for example, tend to smile more in response to the smile of a stranger than do Israeli children (Alexander & Babad, 1981). On the other side of the emotional spectrum, Chinese children are better able to identify fearful and sad situations than are American children (Borke, 1973). Although the relationship of these differences to specific parenting practices is unclear, it is significant that the Chinese culture tends to value protection of children and emphasizes the embarrassment of "losing face." These cultural mores are rapidly and effectively incorporated into the emotional life of the child.

A study of crying among the Kipsigis of Kenya provides a clear example of how parenting practices reflect cultural values and how those practices in turn shape the child's emotional responses. In the Kipsigis culture, crying is regarded as a positive behavior among infants, but as a negative behavior among older children, particularly as they approach their passage to adulthood. To discourage crying in her growing children, the Kipsigi mother does not hurry to pick up or hug her crying child. Instead, she waits for the child to approach her. And rather than focusing on the child's behavior and the reasons for it, she encourages the child to talk about other things and to return to the activities in which she had been engaged (Harkness & Super, 1985). We saw at the beginning of this chapter how, in a similar fashion, Gusii mothers prepare their children for a style of emotionally neutral interactions with others.

▶ **Roles of nature and nurture**

▶ **Interaction among domains**

In weighing the role of biology versus a cognitive-socialization explanation of emotional development, we have seen that biological factors predominate in the expressions of young infants. The early presence of basic emotions suggests a role for genetics, and the increasing control over emotional responses is probably tied to the physiological maturation of the cerebral cortex. But as children's conceptualizations of emotions become more complex and their behaviors take on the patterns characteristic of their cultural or sex group, we must draw on the concepts of cognitive development and socialization to provide a fuller explanation. As Michael Lewis and Carol Saarni (1985) have stated:

> Although the biology of human beings disposes us to emotional, as well as cognitive and social, behavior, the nature of that behavior, the situations that elicit it, the ways of thinking and speaking about it, the things we feel, and whether we feel or not are all dependent on an elaborate set of socialization rules. (p. 15)

Thus expanding intellectual capabilities, socialization experiences, and the cultural norms governing emotions all serve to elaborate and refine the child's earliest emotional tendencies.

ATTACHMENT: EMOTIONAL RELATIONSHIPS WITH OTHERS

One of the most widely discussed and actively researched aspects of emotional and social development is **attachment,** the strong and special emotional bond that emerges between infant and caregivers. Even a casual perusal of any popular book on child care will show an enormous emphasis on the importance of an affective relationship between infant and caregiver. Attachment is not the same as dependency, which refers to the child's reliance on others to meet his physical needs. The child may become more independent with age while still remaining attached to certain people in his life. A distinction is also sometimes made between attachment and *bonding,* which we saw in Chapter 2 refers, in particular, to the caregiver's emotional tie to the infant. The concept of attachment occupies a prominent place in developmental psychology because its presence is linked with successful cognitive, social, and emotional development throughout childhood.

How does attachment emerge between infant and caregiver? In what ways is this emotional bond expressed? What roles do the caregiver and infant each play in its formation? What is the significance of attachment in the later development of the child? And do we observe the same patterns of attachment among children across cultures? In this portion of the chapter we will describe the course of attachment in infancy and early childhood and explore the answers to these questions.

The Origins of Attachment: Theoretical Perspectives

What forces govern the emergence of attachment? Psychological explanations have varied over the last several decades depending on the dominant theoretical orientation at any given time. Psychodynamic and learning theorists emphasize the importance of the feeding situation, ethologists identify biological predispositions, and cognitive theorists focus on the child's advances in thinking. Let us examine each of these perspectives in turn.

The Psychodynamic View   As we saw in Chapter 2, Freud believed that infants derive gratification almost exclusively from oral activities such as feeding and sucking. Because the mother is closely associated with the child's pleasure during feeding, she too becomes a source of gratification and the object

attachment   Strong emotional bond that emerges between infant and caregiver.

Harlow's experiments showed that infant monkeys reared with surrogate mothers preferred the cloth mother even when the wire mother provided nourishment. Here, the infant monkey is actually nursing from the wire mother but still maintains contact with the cloth mother.

of the infant's attachment. The infant's role in the process is essentially a passive one, but the result is a bond that has profound implications for her later psychological development. The security provided by the attachment relationship with the mother enables the child to have healthy emotional relationships with others later in life and to develop a sense of mastery and curiosity.

Learning Theory   Learning theorists believe that certain basic drives of organisms, such as hunger, are satisfied by **primary reinforcers,** rewards that gratify biological needs. In the case of the young infant, an important primary reinforcer is food. Other rewards, called **secondary reinforcers,** acquire their reinforcing qualities because of their association with primary reinforcers. Because they are repeatedly connected with the reduction of the hunger drive, mothers acquire secondary reinforcing properties. Thus, the mother's presence in contexts outside feeding is eventually rewarding to the infant. Some theorists add that mothers behave in other ways that gratify the infant; they touch, vocalize, and provide visual stimulation. Again, because mothers are associated with these rewarding activities, infants become attached to them. In general, then, learning theorists stress the role of environmental experiences rather than the infant's own behaviors in promoting attachments. Like the psychodynamic theorists, they regard the infant as a passive participant in the formation of attachment.

Is the activity of feeding related to the emergence of infant-mother attachments, as both psychodynamic and learning theorists predict? Evidently not, according to a series of classic experiments conducted by Harry Harlow and his associates (Harlow & Zimmerman, 1959). These investigators separated infant monkeys from their mothers and provided them instead with extended contact with two surrogate mothers, one a figure made of wire mesh and the

primary reinforcer   Reward that gratifies biological needs or drives.

secondary reinforcer   Object or person that attains rewarding value because of its association with a primary reinforcer.

FIGURE 10.3

Forming Attachments: The "Cloth Mother" and "Wire Mother" Experiment

Harlow's research showed that infant monkeys spent more time with a cloth surrogate mother than a wire surrogate mother, regardless of which one fed them. This graph shows how much time infant monkeys spent with each surrogate as a function of feeding condition.

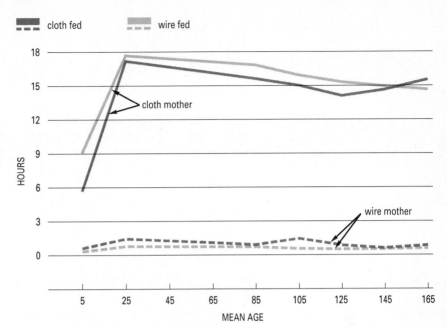

Source: Adapted from Harlow & Zimmerman, 1959.

other a figure covered with terry cloth. The wire surrogate was equipped for feeding half the monkeys; the terry-cloth surrogate fed the other half. The infant monkeys lived with both their surrogates for at least 165 days, during which time several observations were made of the monkeys' behaviors. One measure was the number of hours per day spent with each surrogate. As Figure 10.3 shows, infant monkeys preferred the cloth "mother" regardless of which surrogate was providing nourishment. In a subsequent test of attachment, when a frightening stimulus such as a mechanical spider was introduced into the monkeys' cage, the monkeys chose the cloth mother to run and cling to, even if they had been fed by the wire mother.

Harlow's findings challenged the view that attachments are based on the mother's acquisition of secondary-drive characteristics. The fact that the infant monkeys did not seek out the surrogate that fed them under either normal or stressful conditions led Harlow to conclude that "contact comfort," the security provided by a physically soothing object, played a greater role in attachments than the simple act of feeding. Interestingly enough, the results of Harlow's experiments also contested the idea that infants are merely passive players in the process of attachment formation. In this case, it was the inanimate mothers who were passive and the infant monkeys who actively sought them out.

▶ **The child's active role**

The Ethological View   Proponents of the ethological position state that attachments occur as the result of the infant's innate tendency to signal the caregiver and the caregiver's corresponding predisposition to react to these signals. As a result, the infant and caregiver are brought together, a bond is forged between them, and the survival of the infant is ensured. In other words, attachment is an adaptive, biologically programmed response system that is activated early in the infant's development and that follows many of the principles of *imprinting* described in Chapter 2.

▶ **Roles of nature and nurture**

▶ **Sensitive periods**

The principal spokesperson for this perspective, John Bowlby (1958, 1969), was initially concerned with accounting for the detrimental effects of institutionalization on infants and young children. Scientists in the late 1940s had reported that many children who spent extended periods of time in hospitals and orphanages during their early years often showed serious developmental problems, including profound withdrawal from social interactions, intellectual impairments, and in some cases, physical delays (Skodak & Skeels, 1949; Spitz, 1946a). Bowlby proposed that the cause lay in the lack of a close emotional bond between child and primary caregiver.

Bowlby maintained that attachments develop in a fixed sequence, beginning with the infant's emission of **signaling behaviors,** such as crying and smiling. In the first two months, most infants emit these signals indiscriminately, but by six months of age, smiles and cries become increasingly restricted to the presence of the caregiver, usually the mother. From six to twelve months of age, clearer signs of the infant's strong attachment to the caregiver develop. Most infants will now become visibly upset at the mother's departure, a phenomenon called **separation anxiety,** and will also show signs of greeting her upon her return. Once they are able to move about, infants will ensure their nearness to their mother by approaching and clinging to her. About the same time, they also display **stranger anxiety,** a wariness and fear at the approach of someone unfamiliar. The final phase of attachment occurs at about three years of age, when the relationship between mother and child becomes more of a partnership and the child comes to appreciate the mother's feelings, motives, and goals. The regularity with which infants show this sequence of behaviors, says Bowlby, suggests its biological basis.

According to Bowlby, the biological programs that control attachment prepare the infant to be especially attuned to behaviors of the caregiver. For example, the promptness of the adult's response to the infant's crying and smiling signals is essential to their emerging relationship. Infants become attached to those persons who respond consistently and appropriately to their signalling behaviors. Thus, Bowlby saw the maladaptive development of institutionalized infants as a consequence of the absence of the dynamic, contingent interaction between child and caregiver. Although the basic physical needs of children were met in institutional settings, it was often at the convenience of the caregiver's schedule rather than in response to the child's behaviors. Today, some researchers have moved away from the idea that infants' signals and caregivers' responses to them are innately wired in. Nonetheless, Bowlby's general scheme about the origins and course of attachment have framed numerous investigations of the development of attachment.

▶ **Interaction among domains**

Cognitive-Developmental Theory   Followers of Piaget assert that the development of attachment depends on the child's prior acquisition of certain cognitive capabilities, specifically the concept of *object permanence*. Before he can show stranger or separation anxiety, the infant must have an understanding of the continuing existence of objects and people. To be able to show stranger anxiety, for example, the child must have some internalized representation of the caregiver against which to compare the stranger's face. Similarly, separation protest depends on the infant's realization that the caregiver continues to exist, in a location apart from him.

signaling behavior   In ethological theory, a behavior such as crying or smiling that brings the caregiver physically close to the infant.

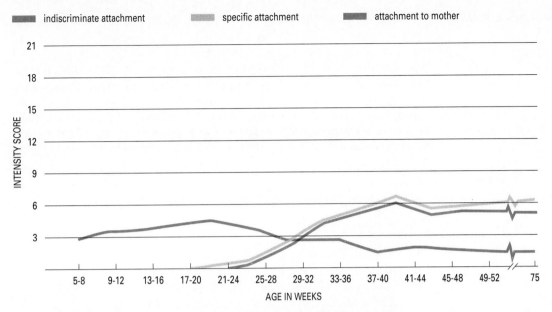

FIGURE 10.4

Source: Adapted from Schaffer & Emerson, 1964.

The Changing Pattern of Infant Attachments

During the first year, indiscriminate attachments decline and attachment to the mother increases beginning at about seven or eight months of age. The line labeled *specific attachment* refers to infant attachment behaviors directed to specific individuals, such as fathers, grandparents, and other caregivers, but also includes the mother. Specific attachments also increase toward the latter half of the first year.

Is there evidence to suggest that recognition of object permanence either precedes or accompanies stranger and separation anxiety? Research has shown that object permanence and strong indications of attachment are present in eight-month-olds almost simultaneously (Schaffer & Emerson, 1964). Moreover, infants who are in the more advanced stages of the development of object concept display stronger, more forceful protests when their mother departs (Lester et al., 1974). Evidently, advances in thinking do play a role in the development of attachments.

The Developmental Course of Attachment

For the most part, research has confirmed the sequence of behaviors outlined by Bowlby in the emergence of attachment. Infants can discriminate their mother's face from that of a stranger at two days of age and their mother's voice and smell a few days after that (DeCasper & Fifer, 1980; Field et al., 1984; Macfarlane, 1975). But they emit their social signals to anyone who is available—they simply like human company. By about seven months of age, these indiscriminate attachments give way to attachments to specific people, most notably the mother or primary caregiver. Stranger anxiety becomes full blown, and separation anxiety is usually manifested as well. In the months that follow, children show evidence of multiple attachments to persons such as fathers, substitute caregivers, and grandparents (Schaffer & Emerson, 1964). Figure 10.4 displays these developmental trends.

At age two years most children continue to show strong attachments, but by age three years some of the manifestations of this bond begin to change.

separation anxiety Distress shown by the infant when the caregiver leaves the immediate environment.

stranger anxiety Fear or distress shown by an infant at the approach of an unfamiliar person.

▶ **Interaction among domains**

Separation distress diminishes for most children, probably because of advances in cognition. For example, children begin to appreciate the fact that even though the caregiver may depart for several hours, she always returns (Marvin, 1977). Four-year-olds have even less of a need to maintain close physical proximity to the caregiver. As they develop insights into the perspectives of others and as their communication skills improve, they can understand better the reasons for temporary separations and can express their emotions in ways other than crying or clinging. The sequence of changes in emotional development and attachment is summarized in the Chronology below.

CHRONOLOGY	Emotional Development
NEWBORN	Discriminates mother's face, voice, and smell from others. Expresses interest, distress, disgust, joy, and sadness. Imitates facial expressions for happiness, surprise, and sadness. Smiles during REM sleep. Cries when has physical needs.
1 MONTH	Displays "fussy cry."
3 MONTHS	Smiles at caregiver. Distinguishes among anger, surprise, and sadness. Participates in interactive synchrony.
4 MONTHS	Expresses anger. Laughs in response to tactile and auditory stimuli.
7 MONTHS	Expresses fear. Begins to display social referencing. Shows specific attachments, stranger anxiety, and separation anxiety.
18–24 MONTHS	Displays guilt, shame, and envy. Uses words to describe feeling states.
3–4 YEARS	Smiles more to same-sex peers. Describes the causes and consequences of emotions. Shows decline in separation distress and other attachment behaviors typical of infancy.
6–7 YEARS	Understands that emotions fade with time and that thoughts can control emotions.
10–12 YEARS	Understands the possibility of feeling two emotions at once. Can mask or "fake" emotions. Has concepts of emotions based on internal feeling states.

This chart describes the sequence of emotional development based on the findings of research. Children often show individual differences in the exact ages at which they display the various developmental achievements outlined here.

Number of Episode	Persons Present	Duration	Brief Description of Action
1	Mother, baby, and observer	30 seconds	Observer introduces mother and baby to experimental room, then leaves.
2	Mother and baby	3 minutes	Mother is nonparticipant while baby explores; if necessary, play is stimulated after 2 minutes
3	Stranger, mother, and baby	3 minutes	Stranger enters. Minute 1: stranger silent. Minute 2: stranger converses with mother. Minute 3: stranger approaches baby. After 3 minutes mother leaves unobtrusively.
4	Stranger and baby	3 minutes or less[a]	First separation episode. Stranger's behavior is geared to that of baby.
5	Mother and baby	3 minutes or more[b]	First reunion episode. Mother greets and comforts baby, then tries to settle him again in play. Mother then leaves, saying bye-bye.
6	Baby alone	3 minutes or less[a]	Second separation episode.
7	Stranger and baby	3 minutes or less[a]	Continuation of second separation. Stranger enters and gears her behavior to that of baby.
8	Mother and baby	3 minutes	Second reunion episode. Mother enters, greets baby, then picks him up. Meanwhile stranger leaves unobtrusively.

TABLE 10.2

The Episodes of the Strange Situation

[a]Episode is curtailed if the baby is unduly distressed.
[b]Episode is prolonged if more time is required for the baby to become reinvolved in play.
Source: Haith & Campos, 1983.

Because attachments are thought to play a special role in the child's subsequent development, researchers have devised a uniform test to assess the quality of children's relationships with their caregivers. Researchers have used this measure to examine other important questions: What are the antecedents of strong, healthy attachments (and on the flip side of the question, what are the causes of poor attachment relations)? How modifiable are the child's early attachment relations? And what are the consequences of healthy and unhealthy attachments?

Measuring Attachment The **Strange Situation,** developed by Mary Ainsworth and her associates, is a standardized task that is now frequently employed to measure the quality of the child's emotional ties to her or his mother (Ainsworth et al., 1978). Table 10.2 shows the eight episodes that comprise this measure, which is administered in a laboratory setting. According to the

Strange Situation Standardized test that assesses the quality of infant-caregiver attachment.

criteria used by Ainsworth and her associates, infants who are attached use the mother as a **secure base for exploration,** exploring their new surroundings but looking or moving back to their mother as if to "check in" with her. They also show stranger anxiety, separation anxiety, and greet the mother enthusiastically upon her return.

On the basis of her extensive observations of infants and mothers, Ainsworth (Ainsworth et al., 1978) identified three patterns of attachment:

• *Secure attachment*   Children in this group showed clear signs of attachment by all or most of the indices mentioned. They obviously felt comfortable in the presence of their mother and distressed and apprehensive in her absence.

• *Avoidant attachment*   Infants in this category were not as enthusiastic in greeting the mother when she returned to the laboratory room. In fact, they tended to avoid or ignore her, playing in isolation even when she was present in the room.

• *Ambivalent attachment*   Tension characterized the behaviors these children showed toward their mothers. Although they displayed noticeable proximity-seeking behaviors when the mother was in the room, sometimes clinging excessively to her, they also showed angry, rejecting behavior, even hitting or pushing her away. Some children in this category were extremely passive, showing limited exploratory play, except for bouts of crying that were used as signals to be picked up and held.

In Ainsworth's original study, 63 percent of the infants were categorized as securely attached, 29 percent were avoidantly attached, and 8 percent were ambivalently attached. In our society, the behaviors of the securely attached group are generally seen as being the healthiest, most desirable pattern against which other patterns are compared.

The Antecedents of Secure Attachment   How do secure, high-quality attachments develop? Research by Mary Ainsworth and her colleagues suggests that the mother's style of interacting with her infant and her responsivity to the baby's signals are key factors. In addition, the ability of the caregiver and infant to achieve moments of interactive synchrony are also important.

Ainsworth and her associates visited the homes of twenty-six infants and their mothers for about four hours every three weeks during the entire first year of the infants' lives (Ainsworth, Bell, & Stayton, 1971, 1972, 1974). When they were about a year old, infants were brought to the laboratory to be tested in the Strange Situation and were classified according to the quality of attachment to their mother. An attempt was then made to find relationships between the attachment classification and specific maternal behaviors observed earlier. The results of this study indicated that mothers of securely attached infants were *sensitive* to the child's signals, noticing her cues and interpreting them correctly. These mothers were *accepting* of their role as caregiver. They displayed *cooperation;* mothers of securely attached infants would wait until the child finished his activity or was in a good mood before imposing a request. Gentle persuasion was used rather than assertive control. Mothers in this group were also *accessible,* providing quick responses to the child's signals, particularly crying. They were not distracted by their own thoughts and activities. In contrast, mothers of the insecurely attached group were often

secure base for exploration   Infant's use of the mother as a reference point during active exploration of a new environment.

secure attachment   Child's display of close affectional ties to the mother.

avoidant attachment   Infant-caregiver relations characterized by neutral emotion in the infant and few affectional behaviors directed to the caregiver.

ambivalent attachment   Infant-caregiver relations characterized by tension in the infant and a combination of clinging and avoidance behaviors.

rigid, unresponsive, and demanding in their parenting style and did not feel positively about their role as caregiver.

Some researchers have criticized the methodology of Ainsworth's study, raising the possibility of *observer bias*. Because assessments of mothers' behaviors and classifications of infant attachment were made by the same observers, they might have been predisposed to find relationships between these variables, especially if they were familiar with the hypotheses that guided the research. Ainsworth's general conclusions, however, have been supported by other studies. Edward Tronick and his associates found that mothers of securely attached infants had higher self-esteem, felt more competent, and saw themselves as more accepted by their own parents and peers than did mothers of insecurely attached infants (Tronick, Ricks, & Cohn, 1982). Mothers of securely attached children have also been found to be more affectionate and more positive in their vocalizations compared with mothers of insecurely attached infants (Bates, Maslin, & Frankel, 1985; Roggman, Langlois, & Hubbs-Tait, 1987). These findings suggest that when the mother creates a warm emotional climate in her interactions with her child and when she has a healthy regard for herself and her role as caregiver, a strong emotional bond of child to mother is likely to develop.

Other researchers have demonstrated that interactive synchrony is also important to consider in the emergence of attachments. One group of researchers observed the interactions of mothers and their infants at one, three, and nine months of age, recording each instance in which the infants' and mothers' behaviors co-occurred and produced a mutually satisfying outcome. For example, if the infant gazed at the mother, the mother verbalized, or if the infant fussed and cried, the mother soothed her. The infants' attachments were then assessed at one year of age. According to the results, securely attached infants had experienced a greater number of synchronous interactions in the prior months (Isabella, Belsky, & von Eye, 1989). Therefore, maternal behavior *as it is related to the child's behavior* is important to consider.

Attachments to Fathers   Because mothers have traditionally fulfilled the role of primary caregiver, most of the emphasis in this chapter, and in the field of child psychology, has been on the emotional bond that develops between child and mother. With large numbers of women participating in the labor force, however, and with the questioning of assumptions that females have the exclusive role in child care, many of the responsibilities of caregiving have been assumed by others either within or outside the family. Moreover, researchers in developmental psychology have begun to recognize the glaring absence of information on how another important family member—the father—interacts with his children. The result has been a growing literature on father-child interaction; we now have a far greater understanding of the paternal role than we did just a few years ago.

Undoubtedly exceptions exist, but in general fathers spend far less time interacting with and caring for their children than mothers do. Estimates on just how much time vary, ranging from an average of fifteen to twenty minutes per day to about three hours a day, compared with an average of eight or nine hours each day for the mother (Kotelchuk, 1975; Lewis & Weinraub, 1974). Nevertheless, many infants clearly do form attachments to their fathers. In the Strange Situation, these infants show signs of separation anxiety when

Infants show clear signs of attachment to fathers, especially when fathers spend time in rewarding, mutually engaging interactions with them.

their father leaves the room and greet him upon his return. They also use him as a secure base for exploration (Kotelchuck, 1976). Mothers may still be preferred in certain circumstances, as in the presence of a stranger or when children seek to be comforted (Cohen & Campos, 1974). When fathers spend time in face-to-face interactions with their infants and display sensitivity and playfulness, though, their infants show clear signs of attachment to them (Chibucos & Kail, 1981). Thus, the amount of time fathers spend with their infants seems to be less important than the nature of their interactions when they are together.

The fact that fathers can serve as objects of attachment is not inconsistent with the ideas of Bowlby and Ainsworth, who have repeatedly emphasized the caregiver's specific behaviors rather than the caregiver's gender. Given the opportunity to respond sensitively to the behaviors of their infants, fathers become partners in strong, secure attachments.

▶ **The child's active role**

Temperament and Attachment   Caregivers are not solely responsible for the emergence of attachment. Because the formation of attachments takes place in the context of interactions between caregiver and infant, it seems reasonable to postulate that the infant's own style as a communication partner might be influential in the growth of an affectional bond. Many parents report that one of their children was an "easier" baby than another, that the general disposition of that child was more positive, that the child was predictable in terms of times for feeding, sleeping, and playing, and that the responsibilities of caregiving were not nearly so challenging as for another child. It is plausible to think that two babies that contrast markedly in their general patterns of behaviors might elicit very different reactions from the same set of parents, perhaps producing different attachment profiles.

This was precisely the idea put forth by Stella Chess and Alexander Thomas (1982), who believe that infants vary in *temperament,* a biologically based style of behavioral functioning that encompasses the intensity of expression of moods, distractibility, adaptability, and persistence (see Chapter 3). Individual differences among infants in these qualities often remain relatively stable over time and affect the responses of others to the child. Chess and Thomas identified three basic patterns that infants might display:

- *The "easy" baby* generally has positive moods, regular body functions, a low to moderate energy level in responses, and a positive approach to new situations. This child establishes regular feeding and sleeping schedules right from early infancy and adapts quickly to new routines, people, and places.
- *The "difficult" baby* is often in a negative mood, has irregular body functions, shows high-intensity reactions, withdraws from new stimuli, and is slow to adapt to new situations. The difficult child sleeps and eats on an unpredictable schedule, cries a good deal (and loudly), and has trouble with new routines.
- *The "slow-to-warm-up" baby* is somewhat negative in mood, has a low level of activity and intensity of reaction, and withdraws from new stimuli.

Chess and Thomas suggest that "easy" children evoke the most positive parental reactions, whereas children in the other two categories cause parents to react more negatively. Because the quality of caregiver-child interactions influences attachment patterns, we would predict that "easy" children would be most likely to exhibit secure attachments.

Unfortunately, the relationship between temperament and attachment is not as clear and unequivocal as we might think (Sroufe, 1985). Although a few researchers have reported a link between infant characteristics (for example, irritability) and subsequent behaviors in the Strange Situation (Bates, Maslin, & Frankel, 1985; Miyake, Chen, & Campos, 1985), it is not clear whether temperament produced these outcomes or whether parental behaviors influenced both temperament and attachment in the infant. Even if children have biologically based temperaments, these might be modified by specific parenting practices very early in development. A young infant who is hard to arouse, for example, might elicit vigorous stimulation from the caregivers. In response, that child may become much more active, even irritable. Thus, her original temperament has been modified and parents may develop an entirely new mode of interaction in conjunction with the infant's altered style (Sroufe, 1985). On the other hand, a recent meta-analysis of thirty-three attachment studies suggests that one element of temperament, the infant's proneness to distress, predicted insecure attachments (Goldsmith & Alansky, 1987).

> ▶ **Roles of nature and nurture**

What can we conclude about the causes of attachment? The characteristics of both caregiver and infant play a role, as does the synchrony between the behaviors they emit toward each other. It is also important to realize, however, that healthy emotional relationships do not consist of fixed amounts of ingredients, as in cooking from a recipe. Because relationships are dynamic, constantly evolving forms of human interaction, much more about the complex story of attachment remains to be revealed.

The Modifiability of Attachments How stable are attachments, once they are formed? The attachment classification given to an infant at age twelve months typically remains the same when measured at eighteen months

(Waters, 1978). Using a measure of attachment specifically developed for testing older children and based on behavior during a reunion with the mother, Mary Main and Jude Cassidy (1988) found that classifications made at six years of age could be predicted from classifications that had been made at twelve months for 84 percent of the sample. Thus, attachment patterns established during the course of the first year are maintained for relatively long periods of time. Given Ainsworth's emphasis on aspects of maternal responding that account for different qualities of attachment, it seems likely that the enduring nature of maternal styles contributes to such stabilities, although researchers must still verify this possibility.

Attachment patterns do not always remain stable, however. Research has shown that stresses or changes in the family's circumstances can affect the quality of attachment. In a large-scale study conducted in Minneapolis, Brian Vaughn and his colleagues examined attachment classifications of infants at twelve months and again at eighteen months of age (Vaughn et al., 1979). The majority of these infants' families were living at or below the poverty level. Most of the mothers were single parents, and many of the families experienced a significant change such as a shift in residence or the addition or loss of an adult in the living group during the six months between observations. In this study, 20 percent of the infants who had been securely attached at twelve months were insecurely attached at eighteen months. Furthermore, shifts from secure to anxious attachments were associated with maternal reports of a greater number of stressful events in their lives, such as loss of employment, financial problems, or illness.

Similar findings have been reported for a middle-class sample in which many participants reported some alteration in family circumstances, such as the mother's return to work or a change in child care arrangements (Thompson, Lamb, & Estes, 1982). Shifts in attachment classification often accompanied the new events experienced in the family. Just as we accounted for the stability of attachments by referring to the dynamics of mother-infant interaction, so, too, can these same factors explain instabilities. Changes in important life situations and the stresses they create undoubtedly influence the mother's ability to be a sensitive, accessible, and cooperative partner in interactions and may have an impact on the interactive synchrony that characterizes healthy caregiver-child relationships.

▶ **Interaction among domains**

Attachment and Later Development   The importance of attachment has been underscored by research findings showing that secure attachments are related to positive developmental outcomes in both social and cognitive spheres when children become older. Leah Matas and her associates assessed the quality of attachments of forty-eight infants when they were eighteen months of age (Matas, Arend, & Sroufe, 1978). Six months later, these same children were observed for the quality of their play and their problem-solving style. Children who had earlier been categorized as securely attached were more enthusiastic and compliant with their mothers' suggestions in the problem-solving tasks and showed more positive affect and persistence than their insecurely attached counterparts. They also engaged in more symbolic play and displayed less crying and whining. According to the researchers, "the well-functioning or competent twelve- to eighteen-month-old is one who has formed an attachment relationship which effectively supports active exploration and mastery of the inanimate and social environments" (p. 547).

These same securely attached children were found to be more socially competent with their peers at age three and a half years, showing more leadership, greater sympathy, and less withdrawal from social interactions (Waters, Wippman, & Sroufe, 1979). They also evidenced stronger signs of "ego-resiliency" at age five years, meaning they responded to problems in a flexible, persistent, and resourceful manner (Arend, Gove, & Sroufe, 1979). In contrast, anxiously attached infants do not fare so well in the preschool years, according to another study (Erickson, Sroufe, & Egeland, 1985). Children with this attachment classification were found to display many maladaptive and undesirable behaviors, such as high dependency, noncompliance, and poor social skills in peer interactions. They were also described by teachers as hostile, impulsive, and withdrawn. It seems, then, that many of the characteristics parents in our culture value and hope to nurture are found in children who have had secure attachments.

The effects of early attachments may carry over well into adolescence and the adult years. Adolescents who are attached to their parents, in the sense of expressing affection for and trust in their parents, generally have high self-esteem, a strong sense of personal identity, and display social competence (Rice, 1990). The quality of an individual's attachment during childhood may also influence her parenting style as an adult. Margaret Ricks (1985) studied the intergenerational effects of attachment by assessing the self-esteem and childhood recollections of twenty-eight middle-class mothers. Mothers of securely attached infants had higher self-esteem scores and more positive recollections of their own childhood relationships with parents and peers.

Whether attachment per se is responsible for the outcomes described here is not clear. It may be that the same parenting styles that foster strong and secure attachments contribute directly to the desirable behaviors observed in children several years later. We will see in Chapter 14, for example, that parents who are nurturant, make liberal use of rewards for desirable behaviors, and explain the reasons for their requests have children who are successful in the cognitive and social domains. Evidently, there are strong links between the quality of parent-child interactions and developmental outcomes throughout childhood.

Three Special Cases: Prematurity, Adoption, and Abuse

In some contexts, the ideal pattern of caregiver-child interaction may be disrupted—as, for example, when mother and infant are physically separated during the early days of their partnership because of the infant's premature birth or when the child is placed for adoption and nonbiological parents assume the caregiving role. Other children are the unfortunate victims of physical abuse or neglect. Is there any evidence that attachments suffer in such cases? A consideration of these issues will illuminate further the ways in which early caregiver-child relationships are related to subsequent child development.

Prematurity The preterm infant looks and behaves differently from the infant with the benefit of a full thirty-eight weeks in utero. The premature in all likelihood will be very small and fragile looking, less alert and responsive to stimulation, and more difficult to comfort. Cries, but not smiles, are very frequent (Goldberg, 1979). In addition, mothers and their premature infants are

FIGURE 10.5

Maternal Interactions with Premature Babies

After an initial period of inactivity following the birth of their child, mothers of premature infants become more active in their exchanges with their infants compared with mothers of full- and post-term infants. At the same time, premature babies display more gaze aversion, as if they are seeking to terminate their mothers' overstimulation.

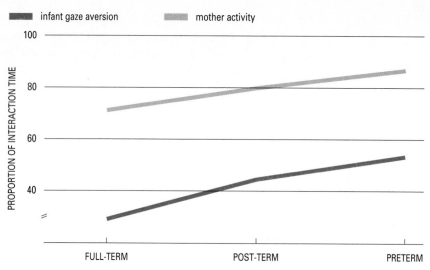

Source: Adapted from Field, 1982.

usually physically separated, sometimes for several weeks, while the baby receives the medical care necessary to insure her well-being and even survival. If attachments were based solely on mutually rewarding infant-caregiver interactions, we might expect premature infants to develop poor-quality emotional bonds with their mothers.

When they get the opportunity, mothers of premature infants do indeed behave in a markedly different manner than mothers of full-term infants in the hospital nursery. Mothers of prematures touch, hold, and smile at their babies less often than do mothers of full-term infants (DiVitto & Goldberg, 1979). As their babies get older, however, mothers of prematures actually become more active than mothers of full-term babies in stimulating them; they initiate and maintain more interactions, even to the point of being excessive. These behaviors may stem from the mother's desire to alter the premature's unresponsive pattern or to stimulate the child in an effort to spur slowed development. As Figure 10.5 shows, infants often react to these maternal behaviors by averting their gaze, as if to shut out the added stimulation (Field, 1977, 1982).

If maternal styles are so different with prematures, is there a corresponding impact on the attachments of these infants? In a comparison of twenty full-term and twenty premature infants at eleven months of age, Ann Frodi and Ross Thompson (1985) observed no significant differences in the patterns of attachments. Most of the children in both groups were observed to be securely attached. By one year of age, many premature infants "rebound" from the negative effects of early birth, especially if they encounter a responsive, supportive environment. Mothers may also adapt their styles in later months to conform more closely with the rhythms and needs of the child. Regardless of which explanation is correct, it is reassuring that the early developmental risk posed by prematurity does not automatically lead to enduring problems in mother-child relations or other developmental patterns.

Adoption   By the time they reach middle childhood and adolescence, adopted children show a noticeably higher incidence of psychological and academic problems compared with children who are not adopted (Brodzinsky et al., 1984). Obviously, a multitude of possible reasons might explain this outcome. Adopted children might feel rejected by their biological parents or believe that being adopted carries a social stigma. Because most adoptions involve the separation of the infant from the biological mother at an early age, the disruption of the attachment process might also play a role.

▶ **Sensitive periods**

One of the few investigations of this issue showed that separation of the infant from the biological parents at six to seven months of age produces socioemotional difficulties even ten years later, particularly in the child's ability to form relationships with others (Yarrow et al., 1973). Separation at an earlier age, however, may have less of an impact. When Leslie Singer and her colleagues assessed the attachments of adoptive and nonadoptive infants between thirteen and eighteen months of age, they found no difference in the classifications of attachments between these two groups (Singer et al., 1985). Most of the infants fell into the securely attached category. In this group, most of the adoptive placements had occurred at fairly early ages, the majority by three months of age. At this age children have not yet developed the concepts of object permanence, and the early manifestations of attachment, such as stranger anxiety and separation anxiety, have not occurred. As in the case of prematures, events that interfere with the establishment of stable relationships in the first part of infancy do not necessarily forecast poor attachment. These studies of adoption, however, also suggest that disrupting stable relationships with caregivers later in infancy can be more harmful and that the first few months of life may represent a sensitive period for emotional development.

Abuse Physically or psychologically abused children are at risk for an assortment of cognitive and socioemotional difficulties. Because the trauma that accompanies within-family violence can be enduring, especially with repeated episodes of abuse, it should not be surprising that attachments between abused children and their parents take on an aberrant character.

Infants and toddlers who have been maltreated by their caregivers are significantly more likely to have insecure attachments than are normal children (Egeland & Sroufe, 1981b). According to one estimate, 70 to 100 percent of abused children can be classified as insecurely attached (Cicchetti, 1987). Given the relationship between insecure attachments and subsequent maladaptive development discussed earlier in this chapter, this figure is a cause for serious concern. Moreover, recent research has identified a fourth classification of attachment called **disorganized/disoriented attachment,** in which children show fear of their caregiver, confused facial expressions, and an assortment of avoidant and ambivalent attachment behaviors (Main & Solomon, 1986). Approximately 80 percent of maltreated infants fit this attachment profile (Carlson et al., 1989).

disorganized/disoriented attachment Infant-caregiver relations characterized by the infant's fear of the caregiver, confused facial expressions, and a combination of anxious and resistant attachment behaviors.

Abusive parents tend to react negatively to many of their child's social signals, even positive ones. When Ann Frodi and Michael Lamb (1980) observed the reactions of abusive and nonabusive mothers to videotapes of smiling and crying infants, abusive mothers were more physiologically aroused by both cries and smiles than were nonabusive mothers and were less willing to interact with an infant, even a smiling one, than nonabusive mothers. Oftentimes, stimuli that are perceived as aversive can elicit aggression. These findings suggest, at the very least, that the abused infant has an unwilling and psychologically distant partner in any interactions that do take place.

In addition, abused children experience fear, an emotion that leads them to seek comfort from the caregiver but also makes them wary of further abuse. Thus, the tendency to seek proximity to the caregiver is counterbalanced by the tendency to avoid that same person. The resulting behaviors, such as freezing and appearing dazed, are characteristic of children in the disorganized/disoriented attachment category. To date, we know little about the consequences of this type of attachment, although one study found that when these children were six years old, they tended to be depressed, disorganized in behavior, and even self-destructive in response to questions about their parents or family life (Main, Kaplan, & Cassidy, 1985).

Taken together, studies of prematures, adoptees, and abused children reveal that secure attachment relationships can develop in a variety of circumstances that are less than optimal. At the same time, though, when interactions between caregivers and infants deviate too much from the ideal, either in terms of their partnership's time of onset or in the emotional tone of interactions, the consequences for the child can be serious and enduring.

▶ **Sociocultural influence**   **Cross-Cultural Variations in Patterns of Attachment**

In their original research, Ainsworth and her associates observed that 60 to 70 percent of the infants tested in the Strange Situation were securely attached (Ainsworth et al., 1978). In recent years, the Strange Situation has been used to assess the nature of attachments of infants in other cultures, primarily in Western Europe, Japan, and Israel. If, as Bowlby claimed, there are strong biological roots to the emergence of attachments, patterns and antecedents of attachments among infants of different cultures should show similarities.

In one of the first uses of the Strange Situation outside the United States, Karin and Klaus Grossmann and their associates observed infants and mothers in the German town of Bielefeld during the infants' first year of life (Grossmann et al., 1985). As in the Ainsworth studies, these researchers noted a relationship between maternal sensitivity and infant attachment; securely attached infants had mothers who responded to them in the sensitive manner initially described in the American studies. They noted some interesting variations as well, however. First, most infants (49 percent) were not classified as securely attached but instead fell into the category of avoidantly attached. Second, although mothers varied in the sensitivity of responding when infants were two months of age, they did not vary by the time the infants were ten months old—most mothers had *low* sensitivity ratings by this time.

Grossmann and her colleagues interpret their findings in the context of the different attitudes toward child rearing held by parents in Germany and the United States. The emphasis in German culture is on fostering independence in one's offspring, encouraging the development of an obedient child who does not make demands on the parents. Responding to the infant's every cry is considered inappropriate because it is seen as "spoiling" the child. Thus, German mothers' tendency to pick up their children less frequently and for shorter periods of time and to display less affection reflects the goals of socialization in that culture.

Many Israeli children are raised in the group setting of the kibbutz. Children visit with their parents in the evening and at other times during the day, but most of their time is spent with the nonparental caregiver and peers.

Studies of children in Israel portray a similar theme. Many Israeli infants are raised in the group setting of the kibbutz. While parents go to work, children are attended to by the *metapelet,* or caregiver, beginning some time between six and twelve weeks of age and continuing after the first year. Children visit with their parents in the early evening and often during other parts of the day, but most of their time is spent with the nonparental caregiver and peers. Do such arrangements interfere with the formation of attachments? Early studies suggested that such was not the case; infants raised on the kibbutz displayed clear signs of protest at separation from their mothers. At the same time they also displayed signs of attachment to the metapelet (Fox, 1977). A more recent study, however, showed that the experience of being raised on the kibbutz was related to the more frequent display of insecure, and in particular, ambivalent, attachments compared with American children and Israeli children raised in cities (Sagi et al., 1985). How are we to interpret these latter findings?

One possibility, of course, is that being raised in a group setting results in greater insecurity. In the child care setting of the kibbutz, it may not always be possible for the metapelet to respond to each infant's signals promptly and predictably. It would be consistent with attachment theory, then, to predict the insecure patterns that have been found. There is, however, another feasible explanation. Children in the kibbutz have relatively few experiences with strangers compared with American children, who often visit shopping malls, playgrounds, and other locations filled with unfamiliar people. It may be, then, that kibbutz infants are no less attached to their parents than any other children but are simply fearful in the unfamiliar context of the Strange Situation.

Michael Lamb and his associates suggest that the Strange Situation is not the optimal measure of the child's emotional feelings toward the caregiver

(Lamb et al., 1985). Instead of assessing the impact of maternal caregiving practices on children's affective bonds, it may instead be gauging the influence of other social and cultural experiences. This idea is supported by studies that show specific experiences in infancy may dampen the child's protests to the mother's departure. A child who has had frequent experiences with the mother leaving and subsequently returning may show little or no separation protest even though he is securely attached (Kagan, 1976).

The cross-cultural studies reviewed in this section underscore the point that variations in cultural expectations for children's behavior and what experiences they are exposed to may influence responses to all elements of the Strange Situation without reflecting on the actual intensity of emotional bonds between caregiver and child. As we begin to evaluate the impact of nonmaternal child care on children in our own society, we should be cautious about the measures we use to draw our conclusions.

Attachment, then, is an important developmental phenomenon that is shaped by the behaviors of caregivers, the dispositional traits of the child, and the amount of interactive synchrony between caregiver and child. The child's cognitive attainments are also related to attachment formation. Healthy attachments in infancy predict many favorable cognitive, emotional, and social outcomes later in childhood, whereas disruptions in attachment may lead to problems with peer relationships, achievement, and other vital aspects of development. Even though some developmental psychologists now dispute the way in which attachment is measured, and even whether the concept itself has broad explanatory value, this line of inquiry has highlighted the importance of understanding the dynamics of caregiver-child interactions as they lay the foundations for later development.

CONTROVERSY

Does Day Care Affect Attachment?

One of the most troublesome and difficult decisions many parents have to face is what to do about alternative child care arrangements when both mother and father work. As Table 10.3 shows, over 60 percent of mothers with preschool-aged children work, and 50 percent of women with infants under one year of age are employed (U.S. Bureau of the Census, 1990a). In fact, this latter group represents the fastest-growing category of women in the labor force. A substantial number of children are therefore receiving nonparental care, many beginning very early in their lives. The effects of maternal employment on child development will be discussed in greater detail in Chapter 14. For the moment, we will focus on the effects of alternative caregiving on emotional development. More specifically, because working mothers (and fathers) are necessarily less available to their children, does this form of early experience influence the formation of attachments?

Unfortunately, there is no simple answer to what seems to be a straightforward and obvious question. Beginning in the late 1970s and continuing through the present, numerous studies have attempted to provide information on this

TABLE 10.3

Labor Force Participation Rates of Women with Children Under Age 18

This table shows the percentage of women with children under age eighteen who are employed outside the home (the table shows only the data for women whose husbands are present in the home). The participation rates for this group of women have grown rapidly since 1975, especially for those with children age one year and under.

Age of Child	Percent of Women in the Labor Force			
	1975	1980	1985	1988
With children under 18	44.9	54.3	61.0	65.2
Under 6, total	36.8	45.3	53.7	57.4
Under 3	32.6	41.5	50.7	54.8
1 year or under	30.8	39.0	49.4	51.9
2 years	37.1	48.1	54.0	61.7
3 to 5 years	42.2	51.7	58.6	61.4
6 to 13 years	51.8	62.6	68.1	72.3
14 to 17 years	53.8	60.5	67.0	72.9

Source: Adapted from U.S. Bureau of the Census, 1990a.

issue. But the data paint a picture that is gray, not crisply black and white. Part of the problem is that many variables are operating when the child receives nonparental care. Is it the mother's absence or the quality of substitute care that produces any observable effects on child behavior? These two factors are difficult to unravel from each other. Does the age at which alternative care began make a difference? It may, but researchers have not always considered this variable when conducting their studies. Does it matter whether the child receives full-time or part-time care? Perhaps—but again, it has been difficult to control this factor in research studies because of the tremendous variation in caregiving schedules. In addition, the kinds of alternative care children receive vary tremendously, ranging from a single caregiver coming to the home, to out-of-home family day care in which another parent may provide care for several children, to center-based care. Given these complexities, it is easy enough to see why simple and direct answers to parents' questions have not been forthcoming.

Despite the many factors that vary in research concerned with day care and attachment, some researchers believe that the effects of alternative care on children's responses to mothers are minimal or nonexistent and that the few differences that have been observed can be explained in ways that do not rely on the concept of attachment. Others assert that constant experiences of separation from the mother take their toll and produce insecure attachments. The impaired relationships between mothers and children may be harbingers of poor developmental outcomes.

When Alison Clarke-Stewart and Greta Fein (1983) reviewed a large number of studies on day care and attachment, they concluded that children in day care may behave differently from home-reared children but only in some components of the Strange Situation. Day-care children do not react differently from home-reared children to the mother's departure; they both protest or ignore her to the same degree. Day-care children, however, tend to spend less time in close proximity to their mothers, both in the presence and in the absence of a stranger. In addition, although the majority of studies show no difference, a sizable minority find more avoidant responses in day-care children than home-reared children when they are reunited with their mothers.

Jay Belsky and Michael Rovine (1988), for example, reported that infants who received more than twenty hours per week of nonmaternal care when they were under one year of age were more likely to be classified as insecurely attached and showed more avoidance of the mother at reunion compared with infants who received less nonmaternal care. Boys seemed to be the most vulnerable. Belsky and Rovine point out that 50 percent of the infants receiving nonmaternal care did form secure attachments. Positive relationships were related to several child and mother characteristics: the child was more likely to be an "easy" baby, the mother was more sensitive and empathetic, and the mother expressed more satisfaction with her marriage. Also, secure attachments with mothers were more prevalent when the nonmaternal caregiver was the father. Overall, though, Belsky and Rovine conclude that "extensive nonmaternal (and nonpaternal) care in the first year is a risk factor in the development of insecure infant-parent attachment relationships" (p. 165).

Does this mean that day care predisposes children toward impaired attachments? The answer is no, according to Clarke-Stewart and Fein (1983). The behaviors observed in day-care children are subject to a number of other interpretations. It is possible that day-care children are showing a precocious move toward independence, an adaptive response since most parents see this as a desirable goal of socialization. They may also be used to interacting with unfamiliar people and to the comings and goings of their mother, and their behavior may simply reflect these socialization experiences, not insecure attachment.

As you can see, this controversy is far from resolved. Yet in the meantime parents must make practical decisions, not about whether to provide alternative care for their children, but how best to do so. For various economic and personal reasons, nonparental care is a necessity in most families. At issue is how to find the best affordable care so that the child will flourish. Whatever form that care takes—family day care, an individual caregiver, or a day-care center—the material covered in this chapter suggests that it should provide the child with all of the qualities of good "mothering" and "fathering"—namely, sensitivity, responsivity, and warmth. Translating these requirements into practical terms means searching for a day-care setting with favorable teacher-student ratios so that caregivers are available to respond to the behaviors of their charges. In addition, evaluating the overall affective tone of caregiver-child interactions is an essential task for parents to perform. ∎

THEMES IN DEVELOPMENT

EMOTION

▶ **What roles do nature and nurture play in emotional development?**

As we have stressed throughout this chapter, both nature and nurture contribute to the child's emotional development. Biology assumes a larger role in the child's early emotional capacities, as in the infant's ability to express and detect basic emotions such as joy and sadness. However, socialization and cognitive development become more prominent as explanations of later emotional expression and understanding, particularly for complex emotions such as guilt and envy.

▶ How does the sociocultural context influence emotional development?

Different cultures place varying emphases on emotionality itself and on those specific emotions considered appropriate to display. For example, among the Kipsigis, crying is actively discouraged almost as soon as children complete their infancy. A culture's beliefs and values can also influence the child's responses in the Strange Situation. For example, German children are often classified as avoidantly attached, but their behavior may simply reflect parental stress on independence.

▶ How does the child play an active role in the process of emotional development?

Whether it is through the thoughts she generates that lead to laughter or the behaviors she emits during the formation of attachments, the child is hardly docile in the construction of her emotional repertoire. There are numerous examples of how the child plays an active role in emotional development, including the phenomenon of social referencing, the infant's role in producing interactive synchrony with the caregiver, and the role of the child's temperament in the formation of attachments.

▶ Are there sensitive periods in emotional development?

The development of healthy attachments during infancy does forecast many desirable developmental outcomes later in childhood. Institutionalized children, who typically do not have opportunities to form attachments, show aberrant development. Studies of adopted infants, in particular, suggest that better socioemotional outcomes result when infants are placed with their adoptive parents prior to the age of six months. Early infancy may thus indeed be a sensitive period for emotional development.

▶ How does emotional development interact with development in other domains?

Emotions are closely intertwined with both cognition and social behavior. On the one hand, cognitive achievements, such as the attainment of object permanence or the ability to interpret social and personal experiences, lay the groundwork for advances in attachment and emotional expression. Similarly, children often learn about emotions through social experiences, such as interactions with their caregivers. On the other side of the equation, successful emotional development in the form of attachment is associated with positive social and cognitive achievements later in childhood. Children who are skilled at understanding and expressing emotions also have better relations with their peers.

SUMMARY

Emotions are complex responses to internal or external events that include physiological, expressive, and experiential components. They are measured in a variety of ways, ranging from physiological measures and observer judgments of facial expressions to self-reports about moods and feelings. Emotions serve to organize and motivate the child's behavior, influence cognitive processes, and regulate social interactions. Thus they play a comprehensive role in the child's development.

Most theories of emotional development pit nature against nurture. Biological theorists, like Izard, propose that certain *basic emotions* such as joy and disgust are innate and their expression has adaptive value. Environmental stimuli directly produce emotional responses that result in the experience of emotion. Cognitive-socialization theorists, like Lewis, emphasize the role of experience in transmitting to the child the appropriate times and ways of expressing emotions. Thus individuals may express different emotions in response to the same stimulus.

Research with infants reveals that many emotional expressions are made beginning from birth. Among these are joy, sadness, surprise, and disgust. But the form of such emotional expressions as smiling and crying changes over the first year, as do the circumstances in which these emotions are displayed. Advances in cognition are, in part, responsible, as is the maturation of portions of the brain that direct voluntary behaviors. Young infants also identify the emotional expressions of others and in many instances will imitate them. By the latter half of the first year, infants will use the emotional expressions of others to guide their behaviors, a phenomenon called *social referencing*. Infants' emotional expressions, in conjunction with those of caregivers, often co-occur in a synchronous manner, called *interactive synchrony*, laying the foundations for the formation of attachments.

Older children display more *complex emotions* such as guilt and envy, as well as more controlled use of basic emotions. Preschoolers understand many of the situations that give rise to specific emotions and the consequences of displaying them. School-aged children appreciate that they can control emotions with their own thoughts and that sometimes two emotions can be experienced simultaneously. The ability to disguise emotions appears later in childhood, as does an understanding of the nature of emotions based on internal feeling states. Many of these changes are related to cognitive development. Sex differences and cultural variations in the display of emotions also suggest a role for socialization.

One of the most intensively studied aspects of emotion is the strong affectional bond between child and caregiver known as *attachment*. Psychodynamic and learning theorists explain attachment as the product of the mother's association with feeding and other activities the infant finds pleasurable. Ethologists say that attachment is an innate, adaptive phenomenon that promotes proximity between infant and caregiver and thus the infant's survival. Cognitive-developmental theorists link attachment to the infant's cognitive advances, specifically the emergence of object permanence.

Stranger anxiety and *separation anxiety*, two of the most pronounced indicators of attachment, typically emerge at about seven or eight months of age. Three basic patterns of attachment—*secure, avoidant,* and *ambivalent*—have been identified on the basis of the *Strange Situation* task. Secure attachments, in particular, are related to the most favorable developmental outcomes for the child. Several variables predict the formation of secure attachments, including the sensitivity and responsiveness of the caregiver, the temperament of the child, and the synchrony in their interactional behaviors. Studies of prematures, adoptees, and abused children indicate that attachments can be formed under less than optimal circumstances, but that extreme deviations in caregiver-child interactional patterns can have serious negative consequences for the child. For example, many abused children show *disorganized/disoriented attachments*. Cultural variations in attachment patterns, as well as the attachment behaviors of day-care children, suggest that what seem to be insecure attachments may be caused by factors other than inadequate caregiver-child interactions.

11
Social Cognition

▶ **What roles do nature and nurture play in the development of social cognition?**

▶ **How does the sociocultural context influence the development of social cognition?**

▶ **How does the child play an active role in the development of social cognition?**

▶ **Is the development of social cognition continuous or stagelike?**

▶ **How does the development of social cognition interact with development in other domains?**

Who am I?

Depending on their age, children answer this most basic of questions in very different ways. Here's how Jason, a preschooler, describes himself:

I'm a boy, my name is Jason. I live with my mother and father in a big house, I have a kitty that's orange and a sister named Lisa and a television that's in my own room. I'm four years old and I know all my A, B, C's. Listen to me say them: A, B, C, D, E, F, G, H, J, L, K, O, M, P, R, Q, X, Z. I can run faster than anyone. I like pizza and I have a nice teacher. I can count up to 100, want to hear me? I love my dog, Skipper. I can climb to the top of the jungle gym. I have brown hair and I go to preschool. I'm really strong, I can lift this chair, watch me! (Harter, 1988, p. 47)

Now consider what one of Jason's older sisters, Lisa, a fifth-grader, might say:

I'm pretty popular. That's because I'm nice and helpful, the other girls in my class say I am. I have two girlfriends who are really close friends, and I'm good at keeping their secrets. Most of the boys are pretty yukky . . . I've always been smart at school, ever since the first grade and I'm proud of myself for that . . . But some of them (other kids) do better than me in math, like on tests where sometimes I goof up. When that happens, I feel really dumb, but usually not for long. I don't worry about it that much, and most of the time I feel like I'm smart. I'm not very good at sports . . . I don't really see why they even have sports in school since they just aren't that important. I'd like to be an actress when I grow up but nobody thinks I am pretty enough. Jennifer, my older sister is really pretty, but I'm smarter than she is. (Harter, 1988, p. 49)

Now let's hear from Jennifer, her older sister, who is fifteen:

I'm pretty complicated, actually. Most people don't understand me, especially my parents! I'm sensitive, moody, affectionate, and sometimes self-conscious. It depends on who I am with. When I'm with my friends, mostly my best friends that is, I'm sensitive and understanding. But sometimes I can also be extremely uncaring and selfish. At home, with my parents I'm affectionate, but I can also get very moody; sometimes I get really depressed . . . I also don't really understand why I treat my friends the way I do. I'm a naturally sensitive person and I care a lot about their feelings, but sometimes I say really nasty things to them. I'm not a horrible person, I know that, but then how can I *say* horrible things that I don't really mean? Sometimes I feel pretty confused and mixed up about it. Talking to my best girlfriends, Tammy and Sharon, helps. We talk on the phone for hours. They understand me better than anyone else. You probably don't understand what I'm trying to say. (Harter, 1988, p. 54)

How do these dramatically different self-descriptions supplant each other as the child grows to maturity? How can they be understood as a function of development? Are they a product of unfolding biological and intellectual capacities inherent in all children of all cultures? Do the early socialization practices of caregivers play a major role in their emergence and development? What impact do the child's own active social and cognitive efforts have on her understanding of self? These are not easy questions to answer. Yet they are important because what we think of ourselves can have important implications for the way we approach and establish relationships with the people around us and, in turn, how they respond to us.

These are the kinds of issues that make up **social cognition,** the broad knowledge that individuals acquire about motives, feelings, capacities, needs, interests, and thoughts, not only in themselves, but in others as well. When and how do children learn that the beliefs and intentions of friends or neighbors can be strikingly different from their own? What brings about the discovery that we share with others the ability to think and feel and initiate change in the world? How is this awareness linked to other emerging cognitive and social skills? To begin our exploration of these questions, we focus on how the very young child gains control over and begins to regulate his or her own behavior, one of the most significant goals in early socialization. This capacity, as we will soon discover, plays a key role in defining the way parents, peers, and teachers perceive us and, in turn, how we think about ourselves and others.

HOW SELF-REGULATION DEVELOPS

Imagine being in a state of such helplessness that you could neither walk or talk and were moved from place to place entirely at the whim of another person. As adults we forget the total dependence on others we experienced as infants, but that was indeed a time when we had little, if any, control over the things that happened to us. Eventually, through cries and whimpers, coy smiles and bursts of laughter, ever more sophisticated motor and verbal coordinations, we gained increasingly powerful ways of making things happen, perhaps first with the help of others and then by ourselves. The transition from being relatively helpless and dependent to becoming responsible and self-reliant, however, was not always a smooth one. Our caregiver may not have shared our enthusiasm for experimenting with the principles of gravity as we dispatched a bowl of cereal from highchair to floor. And why was our mother so unhappy when we eagerly shoved our friend off the tricycle so we could display our trike-riding prowess?

Impulsive and easily upset, infants and very young children have difficulty behaving in a patient, planful, or deliberate manner. As babies mature, how-

social cognition Individual's knowledge of humans and the activities in which they engage, including knowledge of self, the traits and qualities of others, and the roles and rules for interacting in social settings and structures.

ever, parents and others begin to place greater demands on them to regulate their behavior. Parents teach the baby to control motor, linguistic, and bodily functions and to manage or channel emotions appropriately. They expect the toddler to use the toilet, to give hugs and kisses and withhold tantrums, to avoid knocking over grandmother's knickknacks, to say thank you, to wait until candy is purchased before eating it, to share and put away toys, not to let the cat out or hit playmates, and to work toward long-term goals and delay of gratification. This increasing pressure to assume responsibility and accountability for one's own actions continues. Older children and teenagers are expected to adopt socially acceptable behaviors and conform to certain rules and standards.

▶ **Interaction among domains**

Self-regulation is often defined in terms of standards of conduct involving ethical or moral behavior, questions of right and wrong and of putting others before self. Self-regulation of ethical behavior is addressed in Chapter 13, which examines moral development. In its broadest sense, however, **self-regulation** means controlling one's behavior to conform to the expectations of caregivers or other adults, especially in their absence, and covers an enormous number of day-to-day activities (Harter, 1983; Kopp, 1982). We will explore the development of these aspects of self-regulation in this chapter.

▶ **The child's active role**

Self-Regulation in Late Infancy and Early Childhood

Self-regulation, especially in younger children, might be more appropriately labeled *co-regulation* (Kopp, 1987). Throughout development, but especially during the earlier years, caregivers play an important role in this activity (Maccoby, 1984a). Attempts to regulate infant behaviors start in many families when babies are about eight to nine months of age, when their developing motor skills begin to allow babies to throw things, pinch and kick, and perform other annoying, even potentially injurious activities (Kopp, 1987). Verbal imperatives such as "No, no!" and "Stop that!" may begin to ring out, and in some households restraining devices such as playpens and gates appear. These efforts to "childproof" the home help caregivers to reduce dangers without putting a total damper on the naturally inquisitive desires of toddlers to explore and learn.

▶ **Interaction among domains**

When infants approach eighteen months of age, caregivers often initiate a new set of efforts to control their children's behaviors. Designed to help organize the young child's activities, these efforts include touching and other non-verbal attempts to get the toddler's attention as well as pointing out things to be done and how to do them. The parent may ask the child to clean up the playroom and assist in putting away toys. As children's understanding of language increases, parents increase their use of verbal instructions for carrying out activities. By the time children are twenty-four to thirty months of age, these parental organizing activities often decline in frequency as children become familiar with the requests and respond to them more routinely (Kopp, 1987).

self-regulation Process by which children are expected to control their own behaviors in accordance with the standards and desires of their caregivers and community, especially in the absence of other adults.

Children's *self-initiated* attempts to obey standards appear during the second year. A thirteen-month-old, for example, may look at, perhaps even approach and touch, an electrical outlet while saying "No, no!" at the same time. During the second and third year self-restraint undergoes rapid improvement, as Brian Vaughn, Claire Kopp, and Joanne Krakow (1984) discovered when they tested eighteen-, twenty-four- and thirty-month-old children in a series of

Toddlers are often asked to begin to regulate behaviors and activities so that they are displayed in socially acceptable ways. One such activity that most toddlers are expected to master is control of body functions.

delay-of-gratification tasks, in which the child is asked to wait some period of time before performing a tempting activity or attaining some highly desired outcome. In this study the experimenter brought an unusually shaped telephone into the room, pointed out some of its features, then left the room to get more toys. Before leaving, the experimenter told the child to "sit right there and *don't touch* the phone while I am gone." In another task the child was instructed not to uncover or eat a raisin hidden under a cup until the experimenter gave permission to do so. In a third task the child was asked not to touch a brightly wrapped present until the experimenter finished some work.

Eighteen-month-olds had considerable difficulty complying with these instructions. By two years of age, children more effectively inhibited their behaviors, although thirty-month-olds showed even greater improvement in this ability. Thus, the development of self-regulatory behavior first begins with efforts by others to govern and control the very young child's actions. These efforts are gradually relinquished and transferred; the warnings and guidance of others become less direct, perhaps even less necessary, and the child takes on more responsibility for regulating her own behavior. How does this shift come about?

Factors Influencing Self-Regulation

Freud (1922) theorized that the ability to delay gratification and regulate one's own behavior emerged from the *ego,* that mental structure involving perceptual and cognitive processes designed to respond realistically to needs and desires. Skinner (1948) proposed that this ability could be established by *learning* appropriate responses to compete with impulsive, inappropriate, or unacceptable behavior. Although neither Freud nor Skinner systematically tested their ideas themselves, two programs of research on the development of self-regulatory behavior—one examining the role of language, the other the role of attention—have been carried out to explore what factors influence self-regulation. Let's examine each to understand what unfolds in this critical area of development.

▶ **Interaction among domains**

Language: Vygotsky's Theory   As we saw in Chapter 7, Lev Vygotsky (1962) and his students, particularly Alexander Luria (1961, 1969), theorized that language plays a pivotal role in the regulation of behavior. Consider what David, a preschooler, says while playing alone with Tinkertoys, as recorded by an observer at a desk on the other side of the room:

> The wheels go here, the wheels go here. Oh we need to start it all over again. We need to close it up. See, it closes up. We're starting all over again. Do you know why we wanted to do that? Because I needed it to go a different way. Isn't it going to be pretty clever, don't you think? But we have to cover up the motor just like a real car (Kohlberg, Yaeger, & Hjertholm, 1968, p. 695).

delay of gratification Capacity to wait for some period of time before performing a tempting activity or attaining some highly desired outcome; a measure of individuals' ability to regulate their own behavior.

According to Vygotsky, this *private speech* of David's serves as a form of self-regulation (Wertsch, 1985). Intended for no one else, this conversation with himself appears to keep David on track by organizing and praising his own efforts to construct a toy car. Before about three years of age, Vygotsky maintained, only the speech of others exerts any kind of control. By four or five years of age, however, the child's own speech becomes effective in initiating, maintaining, or inhibiting behavior. During the early phases of this new self-regulatory power, private speech must be spoken out loud, as in David's case. Over the next several years, however, self-regulatory verbalization is more likely to be expressed silently, in one's mind, rather than aloud.

As we pointed out in Chapter 7, observations of preschoolers' speech habits as they carry out motor and problem-solving activities do not always support Vygotsky's theory that verbalization contributes to more competent performance (Kopp, 1987). One reason may be that expressions intended for self-regulation are most likely to occur in circumstances especially challenging to the child (Frauenglass & Diaz, 1985). Thus, children who talk to themselves should not always be expected to do better on a task than others who do not verbalize; after all, the latter may no longer need verbalizations to assist them in solving the problem.

With development children come to believe that their own verbalizations can regulate their behavior, although it may eventually be seen as unnecessary, as research by Walter and Harriet Mischel (1977) has shown. The Mischels asked children what they might do to control their behavior. Children of nine or ten years of age report that verbalizations can be important, as the following example given by one girl indicates:

> To control myself not to get so angry and mad and not hit so much I can just say (before I get into a fight), "Now, Joannie, do you want to get hurt? No! Do you want to get hit? No! Do you want to get into trouble? No!" So then, I don't hit as much 'cause I don't want to get hurt and everyone else is stronger than me. (p. 52)

An older child, an eleven-year-old, realized that he could regulate his own behavior by more short-circuited, silent means:

> If I had to teach a plan to someone who grew up in the jungle—like a plan to work on a project at 10:00 A.M. tomorrow—I'd tell him what to say to himself to make it easier at the start for him. Like if I do this *plan* [emphasized word] on time I'll get a reward and the teacher will be proud. But for myself, I know all that already so I don't have to say to myself—besides it would take too long to say and my mind doesn't have the time for all that, so I just remember that stuff about why I should do it real quick without saying—it's like a method I know already in math; once you have the method you don't have to say every little step. (p. 53).

Donald Meichenbaum and Joseph Goodman (1971) have carried the relationship between verbalization and self-regulation one step further by training children to use language to control their behavior. In one study, they asked impulsive seven- to nine-year-olds to observe an adult engaged in a pencil-and-paper motor task. The adult verbalized task requirements, ways of directing and guiding responses, and positive feelings about performance by uttering comments such as "I have to go slowly . . . Draw the line down, good. Good, I'm doing fine so far."

Meichenbaum and Goodman found that simply having children observe this activity was not enough to help their performance. Successful training required a series of steps. Children had to carry out the task first while being instructed by an adult, then while instructing themselves out loud, and finally by instructing themselves silently. The procedures and findings of this training program mirror Vygotsky's developmental model of self-regulation. In other words, there was substantial evidence that the verbal communications provided by the caregiver and eventually adopted by children played an important part in helping them meet the demands for self-reliant, systematic, and planful behavior.

▶ **Interaction among domains**

Attention and Other Cognitive Mechanisms   Meichenbaum (1977) suggests that verbalizations help regulate behavior effectively because they direct attention to key dimensions and features of a task, assist in establishing and organizing ways to engage in activities, and preserve important task-related information in memory. The importance of attentional factors becomes apparent when we examine the kinds of verbal expressions most effective in delay-of-gratification tasks. For example, in a situation in which a child is directed not to eat a marshmallow until a certain time, the child who verbalizes "The marshmallow is yummy"—words that direct attention *to* the forbidden treat—or talks about things that are sad, such as falling down and hurting himself, an activity that provides little diversion, will show *less* delay than the child who sings a pleasant but distracting nursery rhyme such as "Three Blind Mice" (see Figure 11.1) (Mischel, Ebbesen, & Zeiss, 1972).

Once again, a developmental shift can be found for who assumes the responsibility for regulating attention. At first, caregivers are more likely to initiate attempts to focus or distract children's attention. To illustrate this point, George Holden (1983) observed twenty-four mothers accompanied by their two-and-a-half-year-olds as they completed their family grocery shopping, an activity that can rapidly test the limits of most caregivers since items are enticingly displayed in grocery stores. Moreover, the public nature of a grocery store often puts caregivers on the spot as they attempt to manage their children's behaviors.

Holden found mothers were frequently forced to respond to their children's numerous requests in this setting and used a variety of tactics to do so: reasoning, physically or verbally intervening, not responding, acknowledging children's desires, and attempting to distract children. Mothers who tried to *anticipate* potential conflicts, however, either by diverting children's attention in advance or by engaging them in an interesting conversation, were most effective in preventing conflict in these circumstances. In fact, mothers intentionally used such techniques with this goal in mind. Thus, sensitive and consistent mothers who have learned to employ strategies to direct, maintain, and redirect attention are most effective in the regulation of their young children's behavior (Holden & West, 1989; Kopp, 1987).

▶ **The child's active role**

During the late preschool and early school years, children adopt their own attentional strategies as a means of preserving goals and supporting long-term ambitions. They acquire this ability only gradually, however. For example, preschoolers who are waiting in a delay-of-gratification task often prefer to have a tempting reward in front of them rather than a picture of it or some other irrelevant item. In doing so, they unnecessarily expose themselves to the forbidden object, look at it more, and as a consequence have greater difficulty delaying their response to it. By age five, children are less likely to create these kinds of self-defeating circumstances; they prefer to wait with the tempting reward covered rather than uncovered (Mischel & Mischel, 1983).

FIGURE 11.1

Delay of Gratification and Attention to the Desired Goal Object

Preschoolers find it far easier to delay gratification if they are asked to think and talk about things that are fun than if asked to think and talk about either sad things or about the reward that they can eventually receive. Encouraging young children to consider fun things effectively distracts their attention from other highly desired goal objects.

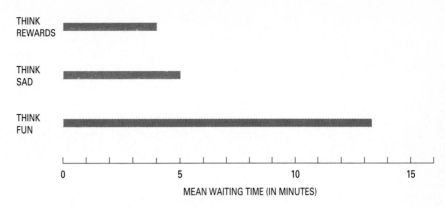

Source: Adapted from Mischel, Ebbesen, & Zeiss, 1972.

Some preschoolers begin to redirect their attention away from a forbidden object. Those who do so, by covering their eyes with their hands or by bowing their heads on their arms, are able to delay longer. They are also more successful if they sing distracting songs, play games with their hands and feet, even try to go to sleep (Mischel, Shoda, & Rodriguez, 1989). As they become older, they also are better able to recognize that self-instructions such as "I am waiting for the two marshmallows" are more helpful for delaying gratification than statements focused on consuming the reward ("The marshmallows taste yummy and chewy") (Mischel & Mischel, 1983). Based on these findings, Walter Mischel and others have concluded that attentional, verbal, and other strategies that encourage thinking about things more abstractly rather than in terms of their more immediately arousing or rewarding aspects are effective ways in which young children succeed in delay of gratification and come to regulate their own behavior (Kopp, 1987; Mischel, Shoda, & Rodriguez, 1989).

Older children show greater metacognitive understanding of helpful attentional and other tactics for regulating their own activities (Mischel & Mischel, 1983). As we saw in Chapter 8, *metacognition* is the knowledge of one's own thought processes and how they affect behavior. An eleven-year-old, for example, offered the following recommendation about distracting oneself: "You can take your mind off of it, and think of Christmas or something like that. But the point is—think about something else." By this age, then, children are beginning to reflect on the ways they can most effectively influence and control their own behavior, ideas that they will very likely also use to regulate their own children's activities once they become parents.

Individual Differences in Self-Regulation   Even ten years later, children who were better able to initiate their own delay-of-gratification strategies as preschoolers stand apart from children who were less able to delay gratification as preschoolers. Adolescents who had greater self-regulatory capacities as preschoolers are described by their parents as more academically and socially competent and better able to handle frustration and temptation. They are also reported to be more attentive, planful, and intelligent, and they score higher on the Scholastic Aptitude Test. In addition, they seem better able to tolerate stress and cope with social and personal problems even when they show the same level of intellectual performance as those less able to delay gratification (Mischel, Shoda, & Rodriguez, 1989; Shoda, Mischel, & Peake, 1990).

Jeanne and Jack Block (1980) have identified yet another component of self-regulation—flexible and adaptive behavior in appropriate settings—that shows evidence of stable individual differences. Shouting, running, and responding impulsively, for example, may be unacceptable within the classroom but highly appropriate behaviors during recess. The Blocks used a variety of methodologies, including observations, self-reports, and standardized tests, to garner evidence in support of stable individual differences in the manner in which children three to eleven years of age organize impulses and desires appropriate to the context in which they are exhibited. They found that individual differences in these capacities remain fairly consistent. Some children display elasticity and are easily able to modify their behavior as the situation demands throughout their childhood years, whereas others consistently show far less of this flexibility.

▶ **Roles of nature and nurture**

What brings about individual differences in the ability to regulate behavior? It is possible, of course, that genetic and constitutional factors underlie these patterns. Researchers are generally agreed, however, that socialization practices play a significant role as well. Caregivers who encourage and model self-regulation provide opportunities for children to acquire skills, habits, and attitudes that increase persistence and effort and reduce frustration. These experiences may yield both social and academic benefits to young children (Mischel, Shoda, & Rodriguez, 1989). It may also be important for the caregiver to strike a proper balance between providing adequate control and encouraging self-regulation. Overcontrolling adults tend to have grown up in families emphasizing considerable structure, order, and traditional values (Block, 1971). Adults with relatively little control, on the other hand, tend to have grown up in families in which less emphasis has been placed on achievement and responsible behavior and in which each parent has differing caregiving values. In other words, a good balance between control by parents and the opportunity to acquire self-regulatory abilities during childhood can be important for self-regulatory style in adulthood.

Self-regulation, in summary, is one of the first major demands placed on young children by their caregivers and the community in which they are reared. Some of the major transitions in that ability are summarized in the Chronology on page 457. This ability begins as a joint venture between child and caregiver, but as children mature, most parents gradually relinquish and transfer a supervisory role to their offspring. By verbally directing children's activities and attention, caregivers provide models and specific techniques that children can adopt as they begin to understand instructions and initiate more sophisticated social interactions and perform more complicated behaviors. Individual differences in these abilities emerge by the preschool years and are consistently maintained throughout adolescence. Gradual mastery of self-regulation in turn helps organize and solidify children's broader sense of self, the topic to which we now turn.

CHRONOLOGY	Self-Regulation
8–9 MONTHS	Parent intensifies attempts to regulate infant's behavior; infant begins to comply.
12–15 MONTHS	Child shows signs of self-regulation.
15–18 MONTHS	Increases efforts at co-regulation.
24–30 MONTHS	Begins to be capable of delaying gratification.
3–5 YEARS	Exercises overt self-regulation using own language.
5–6 YEARS	Recognizes increasingly effective ways to delay gratification.
5–8 YEARS	Exercises self-regulation through own internalized language.
8⁺ YEARS	Shows metacognitive understanding of self-regulation.

This chart describes the sequence in the development of self-regulation based on the findings of research. Children often show individual differences in the exact ages at which they display the various developmental achievements outlined here.

HOW THE CONCEPT OF SELF DEVELOPS

"I know how."

"Look! See what I did!"

"I'm smart."

"I'm stronger than you!"

"I'm really good at this!"

These familiar expressions tell us in no uncertain terms what a child believes he can do, what she thinks she is like, how he feels about his abilities. They are statements that seem to reveal something about the child's awareness of herself as an individual. How does this understanding of **self**—as someone who is an independent, unique, and stable entity able to reflect on his or her own set of beliefs, knowledge, feelings, and characteristics—emerge and develop throughout childhood?

To answer these questions, researchers have sometimes found it useful to adopt a distinction first offered by William James (1892) more than a century ago. For James, there were two components of self, the "me" or *objective self* and the "I" or *subjective self*. The "I" or subjective component consists of several essential realizations about the self that bear upon how one initiates, organizes, and interprets experience. These realizations are: (1) I can be an agent of change and can control life events; (2) my own experiences are unique and accessible to no one else in exactly the same way; (3) my past, present, and future are continuous; and (4) I can reflect upon—that is, think about—my own self. These four realizations are the basis of a sense of *autonomy*, a

self Realization of being an independent, unique, stable, and self-reflective entity; the beliefs, knowledge, feelings, and characteristics that the individual ascribes to his or her own personhood.

sense of *individuality,* a sense of *stability,* and a sense of *reflection* or *self-consciousness,* respectively. All contribute to the sense of the subjective *"I."*

James's objective or "me" aspect of self, on the other hand, is often called a *self-concept.* This "me" or objective component consists of all the ideas the individual forms to label or define self—that is, the multiple perceptions, conceptions, and values held to be applicable to oneself. An individual's self-concept includes an understanding of his or her own physical qualities, possessions and status in the community, skills, talents, interests, and other psychological characteristics, including personality, beliefs, and value systems. Let's examine the development of this "me," or self as object, first.

Self as Object

Self as object, one's **self-concept,** consists of that unique set of traits and characteristics that exemplify *me,* as one who is observed. In this case, however, that observation is not by another person, but rather by oneself. As we focus on how children see themselves and how that view changes with development, we begin with a seemingly simple question, a question that involves self-recognition: when does a young child identify her own face and body? When can she say to herself, "That's me!"?

Self-Recognition   When do babies recognize themselves? When do they know what they look like? To answer these questions researchers have found the household mirror to be a useful tool. Studies reveal that babies less than fifteen to eighteen months of age show little evidence of recognizing themselves in a mirror. About this age, however, many infants begin to notice, while looking in the mirror, when something peculiar has been done to them. If a spot of rouge has been placed surreptitiously on her nose, a toddler at this age now looking in the mirror is likely to touch or rub her own nose, an indication that she has formed a concept of what her face ordinarily looks like (Amsterdam, 1972; Bertenthal & Fischer, 1978; Lewis & Brooks-Gunn, 1979). In just a few more months, she will also be able to say, "That's me," when asked, "Who's that?" as she stares at a picture or mirror-image of herself.

Self-recognition may be aided by sensitivity to very basic information such as one's own movements. Michael Lewis and Jeanne Brooks-Gunn (1979) used television to illustrate this point. Consider, for example, the difference between a photograph, which provides a fixed image, and a mirror, which reflects *contingent* movement; activity by the viewer produces accompanying changes in what is viewed. Television reveals contingent movement if an image is transmitted "live" but not if it is videotaped and shown later. Lewis and Brooks-Gunn found that nine-month-olds imitated, played, and responded more positively when live images of themselves were available than when prerecordings of either themselves or another child of the same age were presented. The contingent movement seemed to attract their attention, and was probably the basis for the greater attraction to their own live image. By fifteen months of age, children distinguished a pretaped recording of themselves, smiling at, imitating, and playing more during its presentation than during a recording of another infant. Infants this age also point to themselves in a photograph when their name is called. In other words, over a short period of a few months they

self-concept Perceptions, conceptions, and values one holds about oneself.

This nine-month-old boy seems to be enormously attracted to his mirror image, perhaps because of the contingent movement that is part of such an environment. His response is to try to assimilate the event into the common scheme of eating as well as looking. It will be several months more before he recognizes whose image appears in the mirror.

make substantial progress from being attracted by correlated movements to a growing awareness of their own perceptual features.

The consequences of becoming aware of oneself can be enormous for a toddler. For one thing, it may be linked to the appearance of self-conscious emotions such as embarrassment, shame, and pride that emerge about this age, as we saw in the discussion of emotional development in Chapter 10 (Lewis, 1990; Lewis et al., 1989). Perhaps that is why, by the end of the second year, a toddler not only recognizes, but enthusiastically communicates by proudly proclaiming, "That's me!" in response to his picture. By this age, young children have begun to unwrap a major piece of the total package making up their self-concept, the first of many steps in the development of their own identity.

Self-Definition   A self-concept is made up of much more than the details of one's appearance. Remember Jason's description of himself at the beginning of this chapter. As a preschooler, he said he was a boy, strong, knows things like the alphabet, likes pizza, lives with his mother and father, and attends preschool. During these years, knowledge of self includes physical features, the activities one likes and is good at, one's possessions, and relationships to others. In defining themselves, a common theme for children this age is to establish a **categorical self**—that is, to classify themselves in terms of membership in certain groups based on their sex, age, skills, what they own, where they live, and who their friends are.

Are preschoolers, however, aware of having social and psychological attributes? Claims such as "I have a friend" or "I'm a happy person" are offered in their self-descriptions, but researchers have often theorized that young children have difficulty distinguishing their **inner self,** their mind and private

▶ **Interaction among domains**

categorical self   Conceptual process starting in the early preschool years in which the child begins to classify him- or herself according to easily observable categories (sex, age, physical capacities, skills, and so forth) that can be used to distinguish people.

inner self   Aspects of the self, such as thoughts and feelings, that are associated with the mind which are private and unobservable by others.

thoughts and feelings, from external characteristics such as their body and the observable actions that can be performed (Damon & Hart, 1988). Piaget (1929), for example, reported that preschoolers describe thinking as talking and dreams as pictures visible to everyone.

Evidence is rapidly accumulating to suggest, however, that preschoolers know quite a bit about their own mental activity and feelings and that these are different from things physically present in their environment. For example, three-year-olds are aware that real things can be seen and touched but not those that they imagine (Estes, Wellman, & Woolley, 1989). Furthermore, by four or five years of age, children begin to understand that the mind is an invisible entity within the body separate from the head or physical actions (Johnson & Wellman, 1982). These recent findings, then, disclose that preschoolers possess knowledge of themselves that extends beyond their appearance and actions. Furthermore, self as object, as me, even for a young child, includes a sense of a psychological and social being (Damon & Hart, 1988; Eder, 1990). For example, preschoolers can consistently select statements that reflect achievement, aggression, and other psychological and social orientations to apply to themselves. Young children may find it easier to comment on appearance and actions rather than mental states, but their knowledge is not limited to the purely observable aspects of their lives (Lillard & Flavell, 1990).

When children reach about seven years of age, a new element enters into their self-descriptions. Whereas younger children describe themselves in terms of *typical* categorical activities ("I run fast"), older children begin to make *relational* statements ("I can run *faster* than anyone else in my class"). Thus, the emphasis shifts from a kind of itemization of skills, actions, or social and psychological qualities to a comparison of these qualities with others (Livesley & Bromley, 1973; Ruble, 1983; Secord & Peevers, 1974). This shift was evident in the self-description at the beginning of the chapter given by Lisa, the fifth-grader, who thinks she is not as pretty as her older sister and that other children in the class are better than she at math. During the early elementary school years, various aspects of self are framed as comparisons that weigh real or imagined differences between self and others in appearance, skills, reactions, and social and psychological traits. Social evaluation becomes an important factor in defining self during these years.

Social roles take on ever-increasing importance in the assessment of self during early adolescence (Maccoby, 1980), and these roles are seen in terms of more abstract qualities instead of comparisons involving specific traits and characteristics (Secord & Peevers, 1974). The emphasis further shifts to how one's attributes spur interactions with others and help in getting along in the social environment. This change is evident in the physical realm in such expressions as "I'm very strong and I'm in terrific shape . . . *everybody I meet respects me for it*" or "I'm a four-eyed person . . . I wear glasses. *That's what all the kids call me . . . they make fun of me.*" Activities and skills are seen in a similar light ("I play sports . . . *because all the kids like athletes*"), and so is the social and psychological self ("I'm an honest person, and I was raised that way, *and people trust me because of it*") (Damon & Hart, 1988, p. 66).

Self can also be viewed from multiple and conflicting perspectives. For example, Susan Harter (1986) asked whether someone can have both positive and negative values. Can one be both "smart" and "dumb"? She found a substantial increase in the belief in this possibility between seventh and ninth grades. Remember fifteen-year-old Jennifer's concerns, described at the beginning of this chapter, about being both sensitive and selfish, nice as well as nasty.

Older adolescents establish an integrated and coherent picture of themselves, more effectively organizing potentially contradictory self-descriptions into a framework of principled ideas and comprehensive plans that include the future and the larger world. For example, whether a girl is pretty or not, she should just be herself as far as physical appearance goes. Good grades or athletic abilities are a matter of pride in oneself. Perceiving oneself as helpful is an important social quality because it makes the world a better place in which to live. Being someone who treats others fairly is valued because it conforms to an important ethical principle. By this age, self-definitions are evaluated within the context of a more abstract and encompassing personal identity and moral belief system.

▶ **Sociocultural influence**

How universal is this developmental picture? Can cultural, religious, and social class differences influence the development of children's self-concepts? William Damon and Daniel Hart (1988) believe that a sequence other than the one outlined here for middle-class children in the United States is possible, even likely, in other communities in view of the different levels of autonomy and independence granted to individuals in various cultures. In some societies, for example, possessions or category membership (e.g., family or social group) may be far more important in determining perceptions of self than individual qualities, abilities, and achievements (Levine & White, 1986).

To illustrate their point, Damon and Hart (1988) studied children living in a fishing village in Puerto Rico. The residents of the village were relatively poor, and few social and educational services were available to them. For example, children typically attended school no more than three or four years, and jobs often depended on a network of family and social relationships. Compared with American middle-class youngsters, these children voiced far more apprehension about whether their *behavior* was good or bad rather than whether they were competent or talented. A twelve-year-old might say it is important to be nice and respect people because if bad *"everybody will hit and hate me or not help me."* (p. 164) These children consistently expressed greater concern about how others approved of their actions than about whether they were better or poorer with respect to some skill or capacity.

In cultures in which individual superiority is rewarded less than contributions to the collective community—for example, the Samoan culture—researchers may find that evaluations of self in terms of individual competencies are not seen as desirable. Many cultural factors could be responsible, of course, for variations that are observed. The lives of children differ across cultures and communities in terms of styles of parenting, formal education, social structure, and the expectations of parents, peers, and community leaders. Any of these factors may contribute to the kinds of self-concepts children develop.

social comparison Process in which individuals define themselves in relation to the skills, attributes, and qualities of others; believed to become especially important in contributing to self-concept during the middle childhood years.

Social Comparison We indicated that during the early and middle school years children begin referencing others in describing themselves. Whether Jim feels he can run fast or is nice or Ellen believes she throws a ball well or is smart depends on how he or she stacks up against age mates and friends. How important is this process called **social comparison**—the tendency to use others as "mirrors" to evaluate one's own actions, abilities, interests, and values—in acquiring self-understanding?

Diane Ruble and her colleagues asked five-, seven-, and nine-year-olds to participate in an achievement task to help answer this question (Ruble et al., 1980). The task was to throw a ball into a hoop. Each child tried a few shots when the hoop was visible. Then a curtain was drawn in front of the child to conceal the hoop. Participants were told to remember the location of the hoop and to try to throw the ball through the hidden target four more times. After doing so, each child was informed that he or she had made the basket on the second and fourth try.

To determine how social comparisons influenced self-concept, one group of children was told that they made more shots than other children, another group was told that they made fewer shots, and a third group was provided no information about how well they did. Participants were then asked how they expected to do compared with others when the game was played again. The nine-year-olds utilized the information they received: those told that they were successful predicted they would continue to do better; those told that they were less successful expected to continue to do more poorly than children who received no feedback. Five- and seven-year-olds, however, were unaffected by this information: they predicted that they would do equally well regardless of how they compared with others. Thus, younger children did not exploit information about others, an indication that they were not using social comparisons to judge their abilities.

Children, of course, observe things happening to others even in the preschool years. Two pieces of candy of unequal size given to two four-year-olds can initiate conflict, and so can unequal amounts of attention from a caregiver or teacher. In many situations, however, the desire to identify appropriate norms and ways for responding and the desire to gain skills for mastering a task seem to be the primary reasons why younger children observe the activities of other children (Butler, 1989; Ruble, 1983). The motivation of younger children for attending to others often seems to be "How can I do this and can I do it better?" (Veroff, 1969).

In a recent observational study, Diane Ruble (1987) recorded how frequently children in kindergarten, first, second, and fourth grades spontaneously looked at or made comparative comments to others as they independently worked on projects in the classroom. These comparisons were identified as showing an interest in achievement ("What page are you on?") or nonachievement (looking at another child but not her work). The latter kind of activity provides more information on how to behave than on how well one is doing. Comparisons involving achievement increased substantially between kindergarten and first grades and continued at high levels among older children. On the other hand, nonachievement comparisons declined from kindergarten through fourth grades; older children seemed to be making social comparisons as a way of determining how well they were doing, whereas younger children seemed to be checking on what they should be doing.

In fact, young children are frequently unrealistic about their skills; they claim that they will do far better than they actually can on various tasks (Butler, 1990). By actively attending to the attributes and qualities of others, children may gain a more realistic means of predicting how well they can do. For example, Ruble (1987) found that children in kindergarten and first grade who frequently made social comparisons involving achievement tended to have greater knowledge of their relative standing in the classroom.

Compared with children who do better on a task, those who perform poorly

▶ **The child's active role**

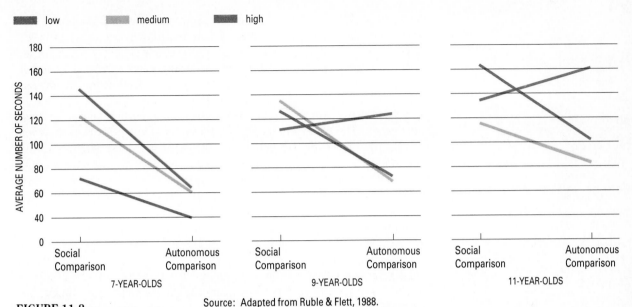

FIGURE 11.2

Source: Adapted from Ruble & Flett, 1988.

The Development of Social and Autonomous Comparison

Children from 7 to 11 years of age with high, medium, and low math abilities were asked to take part in a new kind of arithmetic-related activity but were not provided clear information on how well they performed. When given the opportunity to gain more information, children at these ages generally spend more time obtaining information about the performance of others (social comparison) than about their own previous performance (autonomous comparison), as can be seen in this figure. Both social and autonomous comparison increase with age, although social comparison seems to become less important than autonomous comparison for those with high mathematics ability. In fact, among older children with high ability, more time is spent making autonomous comparisons than social comparisons, an indication that these children are beginning to display a more principled standard for evaluating themselves on this particular activity.

and whose self-descriptions of that ability are low also show less interest in social comparisons involving the performance of others. In one study seven- to eleven-year-olds with different levels of ability in mathematics were asked to take part in a new kind of arithmetic-related test (Ruble & Flett, 1988). Children were not given clear information about how well they did on the task. This was done to determine how much, when given the chance to compare their performance during rest intervals, they would examine the scores of others (social comparisons) or their own scores on prior versions of the test (autonomous comparisons).

As Figure 11.2 shows, older children generally spent more time obtaining information about the performance of both others and themselves than younger children did. In other words, interest in obtaining information about performance, regardless of its source, increased with age. Those with low or medium math ability, however, sought out *less* information than those who did well. This finding may indicate that those who felt they were not very good at mathematics had some concern about receiving negative feedback.

Still another important finding in this study was that, in general, children spent more time making social comparisons than autonomous comparisons. Those with high math ability in the two older age groups, however, began to show a different pattern than the seven-year-olds and older children with lower math ability. These older, highly capable children displayed relatively more interest in looking at their *own* previous tests than in seeing whether they did better than others. This finding may be showing the dawning of a shift from social comparison toward a more self-reliant and principled standard for evaluating self. This basis for a self-concept, rooted in an internalized norm of mastery and competence, fits the mature criteria for evaluating one's own identity often observed in later adolescence and early adulthood.

In summary, the development of self as object reveals a fascinating progression that begins with the toddler's recognition of his or her own separateness from others in terms of physical appearance and features. Among preschoolers, self is usually organized around category membership, but children this young are capable of understanding that they possess psychological capacities. Older children's self-concepts increasingly reflect a consideration of others and involve active comparison. For many children this process eventually gives way during the adolescent years to formalized, autonomous standards for judging self, especially in areas in which the child feels competent. Of course, social and cultural conditions may have an important impact on these progressions. The traits and qualities children ascribe to themselves—their self-concepts—however, are only a part of that larger, increasingly sophisticated awareness of self that also includes subjective self or "I," the topic to which we now turn.

Self as Subject

The subjective "I" cannot be observed directly. George Herbert Mead (1934), however, proposed that we can study an individual's *knowledge* of her subjective self. In other words, just as we can ask what a child knows about her physical features or personal characteristics, we can also inquire whether a child realizes that she can influence and control her surroundings, and although unique and continuously changing, remains the same person over time. We can, in other words, investigate a child's understanding of her sense of agency or autonomy, individuality, stability, and capacity to reflect on her abilities. What do children know about these matters, the kinds of issues that preoccupy the thoughts of some of our wisest philosophers?

▶ **The child's active role**

▶ **Roles of nature and nurture**

The Sense of Agency   The belief that one can determine and influence things that happen probably begins in infancy, when a baby receives various kinds of feedback while acting upon the environment (Lewis & Brooks-Gunn, 1979). The motivation promoting this sense may be inborn. Robert White (1959) suggested that babies have within them an intrinsic desire to "master" their environment, an ambition he termed **effectance motivation.** The active infant repeatedly stacks blocks, bangs pots, smiles to caregivers, and plays peek-a-boo, activities that often lead to consistent and expected consequences. If he cries, he is typically picked up, rocked, and nursed. The one-year-old who says "Mama" or other new words may repeatedly become the center of attention. The preschooler who learns to ride a tricycle acquires a new means of exploring and learning. From the feedback connected with actions such as these in various domains, children learn to have expectations about what will happen and how to make it happen again. As a result, they eventually begin to see themselves in control: capable of achieving desired goals and having the knowledge and means to do so.

▶ **Interaction among domains**

effectance motivation Inborn desire theorized by Robert White to be the basis for the infant's and child's efforts to master and gain control of the environment.

As children mature, they believe that the world becomes more responsive to their own actions. Preschoolers first think that their own efforts are responsible for physical and cognitive achievements but that success in social relationships is still beyond their control (Harter, 1980). When children reach the early school years, they view even social success as a product of their own efforts, perhaps because they acquire more ways of relating to others and of thinking about these social interactions.

A developmental change in understanding their own agency is evident in how children answer such questions as, "How did you get to be the way you are?"

This infant may have already gained a rudimentary sense of agency. His outstretched arms seem to say, "Pick me up!" His behavior illustrates one of the many ways that even babies actively influence the things that happen to them.

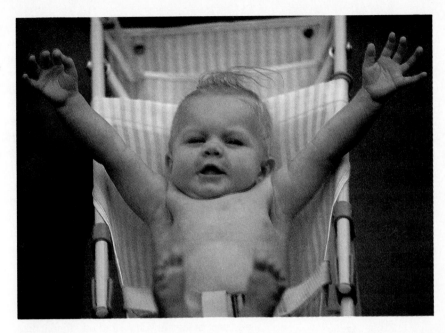

A preschooler is likely to refer to uncontrollable factors ("I just grew . . . My body just got bigger"), whereas a ten-year-old mentions her own efforts ("From getting good grades in school from studying"). By age thirteen years, children acknowledge the contributions of others to their sense of agency ("I learned from my parents, I even learned from friends, just listening to 'em and talking to 'em"), and older adolescents provide an assessment that incorporates principled personal and moral decisions about behaving in particular ways ("Well, I decided to be kind to people because I've seen lots of kids hurt other kids' feelings for no reason, and it's not right or fair . . ."). (Damon & Hart, 1988, p. 71) Thus children progress from little awareness of their own impact to having far greater knowledge of their own efforts, the assistance of others, and the status of their own reasoning in determining their actions and behaviors.

Do individual children differ in their sense of control and self-determination? Indeed they do! Some children are convinced that what happens to them depends on their own efforts and actions. They feel their choices, decisions, and abilities govern whether outcomes are good or bad, successful or unsuccessful. Asked how to find a friend, such a child might say, "Go up to someone you like and ask them to play with you," or how she became so tall, "I eat and sleep and drink, and it helps me grow," or how to do well on a test, "Study for it and you'll get smart!" These children are said to have an **internal locus of control** (Rotter, 1966). A similar distinction has been made by Carol Dweck and her colleagues (Dweck & Elliott, 1983). Dweck finds that some children have a strong **mastery orientation,** a belief that success is a consequence of trying hard; failures, these children believe, are usually conditions that can be overcome by working harder or putting in more effort. A positive outcome of this orientation is a sense that one has an important personal quality, the *ability* to do well in a variety of situations.

Other children exhibit an **external locus of control;** they feel that luck, fate,

internal locus of control Individual's sense that his or her own efforts and activities influence success and failure and the events that happen to him or her. Contrast with *external locus of control.*

mastery orientation Belief that achievements are based on one's own efforts rather than luck or other factors beyond one's control.

external locus of control Individual's sense that outside factors such as luck, fate, and other people primarily influence success and failure and the events that happen to him or her. Contrast with *internal locus of control.*

or others have an inordinate influence on what happens to them (Rotter, 1966). Asked why she cannot catch a ball, such a child might say, "The others throw it too fast," or why he got a poor grade, "The teacher doesn't like me," or why someone else sold more tickets, "He was lucky!" Such children often feel powerless and have little confidence in their ability to influence the future. Effort and hard work go unrecognized as ways to respond to a challenge because these children perceive themselves as not having the *ability* to achieve, perhaps because their efforts have been unsuccessful in the past. In place of a sense of mastery, a sense of **learned helplessness,** the feeling of having little ability and therefore no reason to initiate efforts at doing well, has emerged (Dweck & Elliott, 1983).

▶ **Interaction among domains**

The sense of agency reflected in these contrasting beliefs can have a bearing on academic achievement, participation in athletics and physical activities, popularity, and self-esteem (Nowicki & Strickland, 1973). The child who thinks passing to the next grade depends on whether a teacher likes her rather than on how hard she works or who believes performance on a test hinges on the level of its difficulty rather than on the amount of time she studies for it may have little reason to strive for success. Internalizers, particularly those who recognize that they have a choice of means available for pursuing a goal, perform better in school and on standardized tests of achievement than externalizers or those who do not seem to be aware of different ways of doing well (Chapman, Skinner, & Baltes, 1990; Findley & Cooper, 1983).

Children who exhibit learned helplessness *believe* that they are less capable and often do more poorly than other children in achievement tasks even though in prior situations they often demonstrated that they were just as competent (Dweck & Elliott, 1983). They are easily convinced that they are failures both in and out of the classroom. Because they anticipate lack of success, rationalize that they have little control over what happens, and often display academic difficulty, they are caught in a vicious cycle of self-fulfilling events. Learned helplessness, however, affects many children, not just those having academic difficulty. Deborah Phillips (1984) reports that nearly 20 percent of fifth-graders with high ability do not realize their level of competence and as a result, limit their goals and persistence in school activities. In the academic realm this pattern is found more frequently among girls than boys, perhaps because girls are more likely than boys to view their failures in terms of such uncontrollable factors as lack of ability (Crandall, 1969; Dweck, Goetz, & Strauss, 1980; Dweck & Repucci, 1973; Stipek & Hoffman, 1980).

How does an orientation toward mastery or a sense of learned helplessness come about? Is a physically and socially responsive environment important? Do parental reassurances encouraging active exploration within a safe environment promote a greater sense of self-determination than a family setting in which few freedoms or standards are established? How important are teachers and peers in acquiring either sense? The answers to these questions are complex. A responsive environment can be important in averting learned helplessness. For example, in one study researchers placed mobiles above the heads of infants for ten minutes a day over a period of fourteen weeks (see Figure 11.3). Some babies could make the mobile rotate by moving their heads on a pressure-sensitive pillow. For other babies the mobile either rotated independently of their activity or simply remained stationary. Babies who could make the mobile rotate rapidly learned to do so. The others, of course, could not learn this response, but later, when given the opportunity to control the

▶ **Roles of nature and nurture**

learned helplessness Belief that one has little control over situations, perhaps because of lack of ability or inconsistent outcomes.

FIGURE 11.3

Learning Not to Learn

Babies who are given the ability to control the motion of a mobile by moving their head on a special pillow normally learn to master the mobile's movement quite rapidly. However, infants who are initially not enabled to control the mobile but then are given the opportunity to do so have great difficulty learning to make the mobile move. Lack of opportunity to have an impact on one's environment may sow the seeds for learned helplessness.

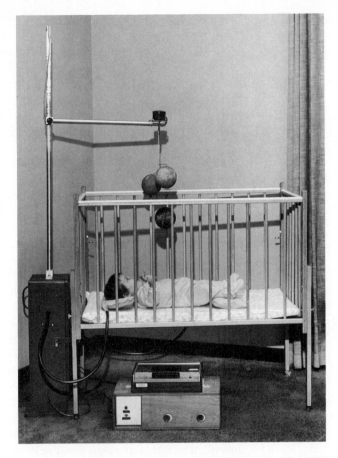

▶ **Roles of nature and nurture**

mobile using the pillow, they did not do so even after extensive training (Watson, 1971; Watson & Ramey, 1972). These infants had learned to be helpless in this situation and failed to make the connection between their head movements and the motion of the mobile.

Children who gain little mastery over their environment or who are offered conflicting and inconsistent reactions—as, for example, by abusive parents—seem most likely to display learned helplessness. Competent adults grow up in families in which they are encouraged to take on appropriate responsibilities as children, invited to participate in family discussion and encouraged to be independent, and in which their parents are available to provide clear and consistent discipline (Block, 1971).

Dweck believes teachers also play a major role in fostering a sense of mastery or helplessness, at least in academic achievement (Dweck et al., 1978). When children already do well, teachers can further promote a mastery orientation and build a greater sense of security about student competencies by rewarding stable, inner qualities such as ability as they encourage children's efforts. When children do poorly, however, teacher criticisms should focus on nonintellectual and temporary factors that may have reduced performance rather than on intrinsic ability, thereby encouraging effort and improvement in performance when the next opportunity arises.

To demonstrate how children are affected by the feedback they receive,

Dweck and her colleagues asked fifth-graders to complete a series of word puzzles (anagrams), some of which were easy, others difficult (Dweck et al., 1978). When children failed, they either heard criticisms of their ability ("You didn't do very well that time—you didn't get the word right") or of some non-intellectual aspect of performance ("You didn't do very well that time—it wasn't neat enough"). After the anagrams and another task, children were asked to say why someone might think they had not done very well. Choices included "I did not try hard enough," "The person was too fussy," or "I am not very good at it." When children heard criticisms of their ability, they were far more likely to conclude that they lacked ability than when they heard criticism directed at nonintellectual aspects of the task.

This brief demonstration suggests that over a period of weeks and months, even years, teachers can dramatically affect whether children see themselves as effective agents in a school setting. Dweck (1975) proposes that for those who perceive themselves as helpless, a sense of agency will only be established when *beliefs* about the causes of their failures are changed. These children must be convinced that their failures are not caused by their lack of ability but rather by insufficient effort or some other factor that can be easily modified. To illustrate her point, Dweck identified twelve children who displayed learned helplessness on math tasks and asked them to complete a series of difficult math problems that they did not solve. The children then received twenty-five training sessions. Six children were given problems on which they could be consistently successful and received tokens to emphasize their success, a procedure that has often been proposed to build self-confidence. The other six children were assigned to *attribution retraining,* a procedure designed to change beliefs about the factors causing their failures. During each session these children received a small number of "failures" in which they were explicitly told that they needed to work harder on such problems. Thus, for these children lack of success was directly tied to effort rather than inability.

When the two groups of children attempted the initial set of problems once again, those in the attribution retraining condition showed a clear improvement in performance; the other children did not. The children whose training emphasized "success" continued to view themselves as unable to do well on mathematics problems, but children receiving attribution retraining persisted longer and were more likely to credit their remaining failures to lack of effort. In other words, the attribution retraining led them to recognize that they had the means to change the outcomes they experienced, an important element in encouraging them to be agents in charge of their own behavior. Attribution retraining has now become an important way by which parents and teachers are able to replace self-limiting styles and attitudes with positive and fulfilling approaches to success, a means of converting learned helplessness into a greater sense of mastery and agency (Dweck, 1986).

The Sense of Individuality   When does the child realize he can't really be Batman? How does Kim know that she cannot become a different child in her day-care center? What do children understand, in other words, about their own individuality and uniqueness? In one recent study, young people were asked, "What makes you different from everybody else in the world?" Preschoolers usually reported that their uniqueness derived from their name, their possessions, or specific features of their bodies ("Cause there is only one person with my name," "My fingerprints . . . My voice . . . Cause nobody has the same voice"). Eight- to ten-year-olds added comparative statements involving abilities, activities, and personality ("Well, I think I'm friendlier than most kids I know," "I got more home runs than anybody else"). Young adolescents were more likely to identify unique sets of psychological and other kinds of traits that made them different ("The way I act . . . One thing else, I worry a lot . . . Yeah, I worry too much and a lot of things that a lot of kids don't care about"). Older adolescents adopted even stronger views involving unique personal feelings and orientations ("Nobody else sees things or feels the same way about things as I do") (Damon & Hart, 1988, pp. 74–76).

The picture emerging from this research is that the child gains her sense of individuality very early and first links it with observable physical characteristics and features. As children grow, they begin to compare themselves with others, especially their private feelings and thoughts, and these qualities become the central criteria for the child's claim to uniqueness.

The Sense of Stability Most of us would agree that although we do change over time, we are essentially the same person now as we were a year ago or will be a year from now. What goes into the child's judgments about such weighty matters? Just like his sense of individuality, the child's understanding of his own continuity begins quite early, but the explanation for this stability changes with development.

Asked the question, "If you change from year to year, how do you know it's still always you?" preschoolers cite personal name, physical features, possessions, or other categorical qualities as proof ("My name, and then I would know if it was me if someone called me," "I still have my toys . . . 'cause they are mine and will always be mine"). An eight- to ten-year-old is likely to refer to stable personal or internal qualities ("I know it's me because I still know the things I knew five years ago," "Like if you still had a good personality, if you still liked to talk to people, you'd know that it was you"). Young adolescents link the sense of continuity to others ("I'll still have my family . . . They always know I'm me and not someone else," "I know who I am . . . Every year I know who I am . . . By the way my friends tell me, I hope"). An older adolescent is likely to state her certainty more abstractly ("Well, nothing about me always stays the same, but I am always kind of like I was a while ago, and there is always some connection") (Damon & Hart, 1988, pp. 72–74).

Here, just as for a sense of individuality, children's sense of a stable self gradually expands and consolidates from physical, highly observable attributes to include both inner psychological and broader contextual elements. Moreover, as children mature, they not only name inner psychological qualities more frequently but judge them to be increasingly important in decisions about stability of self (Aboud & Skerry, 1983).

The Sense of Reflection When does the ability to reflect upon or contemplate the self emerge? Robert Selman (1980) suggests that this cognitive act begins relatively late, perhaps not until early adolescence. The emergence of reflection along with new ways of thinking abstractly helps to explain the preoccupations of young teenagers with appearance and worth—that is, their growing *self-consciousness* about who they are. In fact, David Elkind (1981a) has proposed that young adolescents exhibit a kind of egocentrism, an

▶ **Interaction among domains**

The ability to reflect upon or contemplate one's own looks, feelings, and ideas may not emerge until the adolescent years. Although surrounded by homework and listening to music, this teenager could also be preoccupied with thoughts about herself.

excessive preoccupation with themselves as the object of their thought. They go overboard in assuming that others are just as concerned as they about their looks, feelings, and thoughts. For them there is an *imaginary audience,* a sense of continually being on stage and being observed by others.

Another consequence of this emerging capacity to reflect upon the self is a greater appreciation of the mind's role as a processor and manipulator of one's own experience. A fourteen-year-old's comments about the loss of a pet illustrates this point: "I can fool myself into not wanting another puppy if I keep saying to myself, I don't want a puppy; I don't ever want to see another puppy." Of course, an older adolescent might show even further progress in her contemplations about how the mind works. She may be able to take her reflections one step further to realize that she cannot always completely control her feelings; just as thoughts can influence feelings, so, too, feelings can influence thoughts. Moreover, the mind continues to affect behavior even though we are unaware of those feelings. In other words, the sense of reflection forms the basis for eventually realizing that a distinction can be made between conscious and unconscious psychological processes (Damon & Hart, 1988).

identity (personal)   Coherent view of who one is and wants to be along with values and beliefs that emerge during adolescence.

Personal Identity   The burgeoning sense of self as subject, as a capable, unique, and stable individual, along with the capacity to reflect on these qualities, serves as the nucleus for the construction of a **personal identity,** a coherent, internalized view of who and what one is, wants to be, believes, and values. A strong sense of identity helps the person answer such fundamental questions as, Who am I? Why do I exist? and What am I to become? It is the conception of a solid, unique, and continuous entity woven out of the many roles the person plays in society. This conception, as Erik Erikson pointed out (see Chapter 2), makes its appearance during late adolescence and early adulthood.

Achieving a healthy personal identity, according to Erikson, springs from earlier progress in accepting and trusting others, in being encouraged to explore and pursue interests and desires, and in acquiring and building feelings of competence and skill. The teenager must also be free to evaluate and test various attempts to answer questions about who she is and how she compares with others, both in reality and in her imagination. With the formation of a fully integrated identity, the adolescent forms a healthy personality and makes the transition into the world of mature adulthood (see the Chronology below). We will have more to say about this important transition after we have examined the development of self-esteem, another aspect of self.

CHRONOLOGY	Understanding Self and Others
9–12 MONTHS	Prefers contingent movement by self.
15–18 MONTHS	Recognizes self in mirror and photos.
18–30 MONTHS	Realizes others can have different visual perspectives.
2½–6 YEARS	Defines self by categorical judgments. Recognizes agency for physical and cognitive achievements. Distinguishes inner and outer self. Is aware of specific limitations in visual perspectives of others. Begins to consider privileged information. Overgeneralizes intent as cause of behavior in others.
6–9 YEARS	Recognizes agency for social achievements. Defines self by social comparisons. Displays global self-esteem. Realizes others can reflect on the child's own thoughts and feelings. Attributes stable personality and dispositional qualities to others.
10–13 YEARS	Defines self in terms of social roles. Begins to use autonomous criteria for evaluating self. Can consider own and the perspective of others simultaneously.
13–17 YEARS	Defines self in terms of principled values. Shows personal identity. Recognizes views of the broader society.

This chart describes the sequence in the development of understanding self and others based on the findings of research. Children often show individual differences in the exact ages at which they display the various developmental achievements outlined here.

Self-Esteem: Evaluating Self

So far, we have addressed the child's definition and understanding of self as object ("me") and self as subject ("I"). Now we turn to another component of self, beliefs and feelings of worth and merit. **Self-esteem,** or self-worth, consists of the positive feelings arising from evaluations of self, the extent to which the child believes his or her attributes and actions are good, desired, and valuable. These judgments are important for establishing social relationships, for success in school and elsewhere, and for a child's overall mental health. Indeed, later life satisfaction and happiness have been linked to high self-esteem (Bachman, 1970; Crandall, 1973); depression, anxiety, and poor adjustment in school and social relations have been linked to low self-esteem (Damon, 1983).

Describing Self-Esteem   Lisa, the fifth-grader introduced earlier in this chapter, described herself as proud of how smart she was, not very good at sports (but sports are unimportant), and somewhat ambivalent about not being pretty enough to become an actress. How should we describe Lisa's self-esteem? Work by Susan Harter (1987) has consistently revealed that the child often gives different evaluations of self when asked about academic competence, athletic skill, social acceptance, or physical appearance. By about eight years of age, however, children can make global assessments and answer such broad questions as, "Do you like yourself?" "Do you like the way you are leading your life?" and "Are you happy the way you are?" Still, the positive or negative judgments children give to these broader questions are not a simple averaging of their answers to questions about individual areas of their lives. In other words, global self-esteem is not a composite of all the different evaluations children make of their specific attributes and abilities.

▶ **Interaction among domains**

Factors Influencing Self-Esteem   How does the child arrive at a sense of worth? William James (1892) theorized self-esteem depends on the success one feels in areas in which one wants to be successful. Others have emphasized social and cognitive elements; self-esteem originates in how we *think* others see us (Cooley, 1902; Mead, 1934). These latter factors could indeed be important. Children's self-ratings of competence in various domains correspond to others' evaluations of them. For example, the child rated high in physical ability by a teacher and preferred by peers as a teammate for games usually considers herself good at physical activities (Harter, 1982). Thus, the *generalized other*—the combined evaluations of parents, peers, and other people influential in one's life—may contribute to determining sense of worth (Mead, 1934). But remember that correlations between the generalized other and self-esteem may stem from other factors. For example, perhaps the child uses the same criteria and is just as effective as others in evaluating how skillful she is in various domains. Thus, her own independent self-evaluations may underlie feelings of self-worth.

To determine whether both the importance of being successful in a highly regarded domain and the perceived evaluations of others affect self-esteem, Susan Harter (1987) obtained ratings of how children viewed themselves in five areas (scholastic competence, athletic competence, social acceptance, physical appearance, and behavioral conduct) and in terms of global success. In

self-esteem   One's feelings of worth; extent to which one senses one's attributes and actions are good, desired, and valued.

addition, Harter asked children to rate how critical it was for them to do well in each of these domains in order to feel good about themselves. This rating provided a measure of the importance of, or desire for success in, each area. Harter reasoned that greater discrepancies between perceived competence and the importance of a domain, especially those areas highly valued by the child, would be linked to lower self-esteem.

Harter's prediction appears to be true. For children ranging from third to eighth grades, the competence/importance discrepancy score correlates highly with self-esteem; the more a rating of importance outstrips perceived competence, the lower the child's sense of overall worth. In fact, children with low self-esteem seem to have trouble disregarding the significance of areas in which they are not skilled (Harter, 1985). In contrast, children with high self-esteem minimize the importance of those domains in which they are not especially competent and build up and gain satisfaction from those areas in which they are relatively successful. Lisa, not very good at athletics, did not think sports were very important anyway. Academic activities (in which she was more likely to excel), however, she did value. For Lisa, then, the competence/importance discrepancy for the two domains was small, and her overall sense of worth should be reasonably high.

Harter also asked children to rate how other people in their lives (parents, peers) viewed them, felt they were important, liked them, and so on. This measure of perceived social support and positive regard was designed to provide an indication of the role that others' evaluations had in determining self-esteem. Harter found here that the perceived social support of others also correlates with the child's sense of self-worth.

Are both low competence/importance discrepancy score and strong social support essential for developing high self-esteem? Harter's research suggests they are. To illustrate the relationship, the children in her study were divided into three groups based on their discrepancy and social support scores. As Figure 11.4 shows, elementary school children with low discrepancy *and* high social support scores showed superior levels of self-worth. Children with high discrepancy *and* low social support, however, displayed the lowest levels of self-esteem. Furthermore, both factors contributed to overall sense of worth. Similar results were found for children in a middle school. These results suggest that efforts to improve self-esteem in children require both a supportive social milieu and the formation and acceptance of personal goals that are realistically based. Although Lisa may want to be an actress, she has already begun to realize that she has other important and desirable competencies and, as a consequence, has taken another step in maintaining high self-esteem regardless of how pretty she is.

Are some domains more important than others for a child's overall sense of worth? The answer may be yes. Harter (1987) has found that physical appearance seems most influential for both elementary and middle school children. Boys and girls who were dissatisfied with their physical appearance and were keenly concerned about it tended to have especially low self-esteem. Although discrepancies were also important in other domains, they were less highly correlated with judgments of overall self-worth. Harter (1987) speculates that in American culture this relationship stems from the enormous emphasis placed on appearance in movies, television, rock videos, and teen magazines that constantly bombard children and teenagers with the message that appearance is

▶ **Sociocultural influence**

FIGURE 11.4

How Self-Esteem Develops

Self-esteem reflects the combined influence of social support and the discrepancy between the child's perceived and desired competence in some ability or attribute. Harter divided elementary school children into three groups based on these two measures. Those with highest self-esteem reported high social support and a low discrepancy between perceived and desired competence. Those with lowest self-esteem reported low social support and a high discrepancy between perceived and desired competence. These findings suggest that parents, teachers, and others concerned with increasing self-esteem need to consider both the kind of social encouragement and positive regard they provide and the child's own feelings about what he or she believes is important.

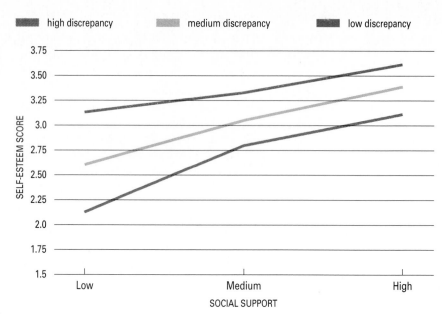

Source: Adapted from Harter, 1987.

the key to success and acceptance. Harter also found that for older children, discrepancy scores on social acceptance took on increasingly greater significance, whereas discrepancy scores on athletic competence showed some decline in importance.

What about the other factor—the role of other persons—in building self-esteem? Are some people more influential than others? To answer this question, Harter (1987) examined the relationship between the regard of various "others" and self-worth. Parents and classmates appeared to be somewhat more influential than friends or teachers for both elementary and middle school children. Furthermore, she found that the strength of the parent's influence did not decline during the early teenage years, although it may do so in later adolescence.

CONTROVERSY

▶ **Development as continuous/ stagelike**

Is There Such a Thing as an Adolescent Identity Crisis?

Anna Freud, a highly respected psychoanalyst as well as daughter of Sigmund Freud, wrote that "to be normal during the adolescent period is by itself abnormal" (1958, p. 275). With these words, Anna Freud summarized the popular view that the period of adolescence is filled with stress, including rapid and frequent mood shifts, ranging from feelings of discouragement to euphoria along with enormous uncertainty about self. We sense that quality in fifteen-year-old Jennifer's comments summarized at the beginning of this chapter. She described herself as sometimes self-conscious, moody, and depressed, but at other times sensitive and caring about, as well as close to, others. Jennifer's self-disclosed confusions are the kinds of ingredients leading to the notion that adolescents undergo a period of intense uncertainty about themselves and their place in society, an event dubbed the **identity crisis.** Such a crisis is often considered an inevitable and necessary part of separation from the family and the formation of a normal adult personality. From this perspective, adolescence is often viewed as a unique stage in development, a time in which an individual must sort out a number of personal issues in order to construct a more mature and integrated sense of self.

Does such a crisis really take place during adolescence? Erikson (1963) pointed out that in establishing a personal identity, adolescents enter a period of intense reflection on and dissatisfaction with who they are and what they are like. Some researchers have found that overall self-esteem declines as children approach and enter these years, especially for girls (American Association of University Women, 1991). These changes may be rooted in the myriad biological, cognitive, and social transitions taking place at this time. Adolescents certainly do engage in new ways of behaving and thinking involving greater autonomy, independence, and expressions of intimacy with others. For example, teenagers increasingly view their actions and conduct as personal, their own business, so to speak (Smetana, 1988), and come to strongly believe that such things as family chores, eating habits, curfews, and personal appearance are up to them, not their parents. Needless to say, this view can introduce conflict within the family, especially for parents who may attempt to continue to maintain control.

Other research suggests, however, that conflict for many adolescents is far less frequent and traumatic than the idea of a "crisis" would suggest (Powers, Hauser, & Kilner, 1989). Using a variety of research methods ranging from surveys to interviews to the use of electronic beepers that signal adolescents to record their moods and circumstances at a specific point in time, researchers claim that conflict, unhappiness, and turmoil are not the typical pattern (Hill, 1987). In fact, some researchers argue that the vast majority of adolescents are sociable, adjusted individuals who are well on their way to adopting the mores and values of their culture and effectively coping with the pressures and demands placed on them by their society (Offer, 1987).

This more positive image of the teenage years, however, should not overshadow the many important conflicts that do occur for normal adolescents, especially with their parents. A key element in the successful resolution of these conflicts appears to be negotiation. Out of disagreements that emerge over choice of friends and activities or use of the telephone or the family car, adolescents not only explore new roles and relationships but also ways of communicating with and relating to parents and others in authority (Powers, Hauser, & Kilner, 1989). Conflict, then, may be born less out of "crisis" than from a healthy form of adaptation that eventually culminates in shared respect, a new way of maintaining a close and caring relationship among members of the family and others with whom the young adult will come to work and play. Parents have an important role in this process; those who provide reassurance and support while permitting teenagers to establish their own point of view seem most effective at promoting the strongest sense of personal identity (Grotevant & Cooper, 1986; Hauser et al., 1987).

Is there an identity crisis during adolescence? Perhaps not for the vast majority of teenagers. Yet from 10 to 20 percent of adolescents do experience

▶ **Interaction among domains**

identity crisis Period, usually during adolescence, characterized by considerable uncertainty about the self and the role the individual is to fulfill in society.

serious mental health problems during this time in their lives. Although that percentage is about the same as for populations of adults (Offer, 1987), many troubled teenagers receive little attention from health professionals.

One especially significant problem area concerns suicide. The number of individuals between 15 and 24 years of age who committed suicide in the United States increased by 140 percent between 1960 and 1984. Unfortunately, the 5000 suicides reported for this age group in 1984, constitute only a small part of the problem. The number of attempted suicides is estimated to be 100 times the number of suicides that are actually completed (Berman, 1987). Deciding that these problems are or are not part of an "identity crisis" must never hinder efforts to ensure that the many serious mental health issues affecting adolescents receive adequate treatment. ■

HOW UNDERSTANDING OTHERS DEVELOPS

In examining how an understanding of self develops, we emphasized that what children know is intimately tied to their perceptions of other people. During the early school years children begin to compare themselves to their peers and actively seek out information about the performance of classmates to evaluate their own success. Now we will examine how children understand and judge the motives, feelings, needs, interests, capacities, and thoughts of others as summarized in the Chronology on page 471.

▶ **Interaction among domains**

For theorists like Jean Piaget, children's thinking about self and others develops in ways that mirror their reasoning about physical objects and events. Just as preschoolers, for example, focus on surface appearance to judge quantity in a conservation task, they tend to zero in on highly visible features and activities in assessing others and pay little heed to underlying intentions, feelings, and other psychological attributes. Preschoolers unable to coordinate height and width to conserve amount of liquid could also be expected to have trouble integrating information about various traits to form an overall opinion about another person's personality.

Social cognition, however, may demand other intellectual processes and capacities (Damon & Hart, 1988; Hoffman, 1981b). Not only do people act unpredictably, their feelings and moods, even to some extent, their appearance may shift, sometimes in seemingly random ways. From this perspective, other people pose an enormous cognitive challenge for young children. Fortunately, this challenge may be made easier by feedback and communication, mutual interchanges that furnish valuable opportunities for forming the child's thoughts about, and evaluations of, others.

▶ **Interaction among domains**

Progress in understanding the social world begins in the first year or two of life. In examining emotional development in Chapter 10, we learned that infants engage in *social referencing,* using others to interpret a strange or ambiguous event. *Attachment* reveals another form of social knowledge, this time about whom to run to when afraid or hurt or to seek out proudly when a new task has been mastered. The content of toddlers' speech also suggests rudimentary knowledge of mental, emotional, motivational, and perceptual states in others (Miller & Aloise, 1989). Two-year-olds, for example, frequently make such comments as "Baby sad" or "Sally angry" during exchanges with others or in pretend games (Dunn, Bretherton, & Munn, 1987). Several lines of research, however, including tasks requiring the child to take the role of another person, help to explain how the child advances from these rudimentary levels of social cognition.

Perspective Taking: Taking the Role of Others

Perspective taking is the ability to put oneself in another person's place, to consider that person's thoughts, feelings, or knowledge in order to interact with him more effectively. We have already seen one aspect of perspective taking in Chapter 7, which examined developmental differences in communicating with another person. To effectively explain or tell another person something, the child often must have knowledge of the other's background and abilities. By "putting oneself in another's shoes," a child can also more effectively assist and support that person, if in need. Or consider the popular children's game "rocks, scissors, and paper." You try to guess whether your opponent will show a fist (rock), two fingers (scissors), or flat hand (paper). Since a rock smashes scissors, scissors cuts paper, and paper covers a rock, your own choice must be one that prevails over your opponents in order to win. To anticipate your opponent's choice requires perspective taking. When and how does this ability develop in young children?

What Do Others See? Visual Perspective Taking One basic feature of perspective taking is understanding what others see. For example, does the child realize that his sister, standing across the room, cannot see the brightly colored pictures in the book he is attentively examining? In 1956, Jean Piaget and Barbel Inhelder published a classic experiment illustrating children's limited knowledge of the visual perspective of others. Children seated in front of three different papier-mâché mountains (see Figure 11.5) were asked to indicate what a doll would see in viewing the array from various locations. Four- to six-year-olds showed considerable *egocentrism* in their responses; they typically indicated that the doll's view would be identical to their own. By six to nine years of age, children began to realize the doll's perspective would be different, although they still had difficulty figuring out what the doll would actually see. Nine- and ten-year-olds were able to determine the doll's perspective accurately. More recent research has shown that the difficulty of the doll-and-mountain task may have led Piaget and Inhelder to underestimate children's role-taking competence. When simpler visual arrays or familiar everyday scenes are used, three- and four-year-olds can answer some of these kinds of questions reasonably well (Borke, 1975).

perspective taking Ability to take the role of another person and understand what that person is thinking, feeling, or knows, often with the purpose of solving some problem in communicating or interacting with that individual. Also called *role taking*.

John Flavell and his colleagues have identified two levels of visual perspective-taking skill in children (Flavell, 1978; Lempers, Flavell, & Flavell, 1977). At the first level, from late infancy until about three years, children realize that their own and another's view are not identical. Thirty-month-olds, for example, acknowledge that an object they can see, but screened from another person, will be visible to only themselves. Toddlers may even adjust pictures or objects to help others see them more easily (Flavell, Shipstead, & Croft,

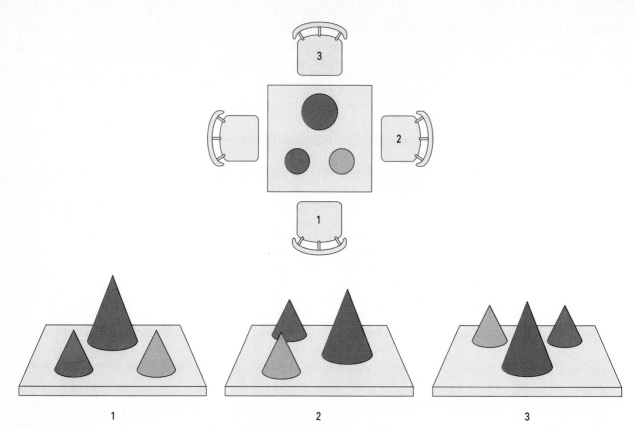

FIGURE 11.5

Visual Perspective Taking

Source: Adapted from Phillips, 1975.

How well can children adopt another person's visual perspective? Piaget asked this question by seating a child at a table (in location 1) containing three "mountains" of different size and color, then asking the child how the scene would look to a doll (or another person) seated at other locations (locations 2 and 3) around the table. Piaget found that preschoolers often chose a view similar to their own. More recent research indicates that preschoolers can be more successful with this task when familiar and easily distinguishable scenes are used.

1978). Thus, very young children recognize a different visual perspective for others.

A second, more advanced level of visual perspective taking appears in three- and four-year-olds and continues to be refined for several years thereafter. Now children begin to be successful in determining the *specific* limitations of another's view. Four-year-olds, for example, can say whether an object seen by another will look right side up (Masangkay et al., 1974). They also realize that a view of one portion of an animal may not provide enough cues to allow someone else to determine what the animal is *doing* but, until age six, believe others will have little difficulty *identifying* the animal even if only a few ambiguous details are visible (Taylor, 1988). Throughout the early school years children become increasingly proficient at determining how the relationships among specific features of a complex array will change when viewed from sev-

▶ **Interaction among domains**

eral perspectives (Rosser, 1983). These advances reflect cognitive gains both in differentiating oneself from another and in knowledge of space and spatial relationships (Shantz, 1983).

What Do Others Think? Conceptual Perspective Taking   To interact effectively with others, children must learn that friends, family members, and classmates not only see things in other ways than their own, but also have different kinds of knowledge about things. In Chapter 7, we discussed how younger children sometimes have trouble effectively communicating with others because they fail to consider what information another person possesses. What further evidence exists for developmental differences in children's conceptualizations of the thoughts and cognitions of others? A simple illustration comes from research on privileged information.

The typical procedure in experiments involving privileged information is to provide facts to the child that are unavailable to another and then to observe whether the child is aware of the discrepancy. In one study, two- to six-year-olds watched a film of a boy seated at a table (Mossler, Marvin, & Greenberg, 1976). The accompanying sound track described how much the boy wanted to have a cookie. Children then viewed the film again, this time with their mothers. For the second showing, however, the sound track was turned off. Asked if their mothers knew the boy wanted a cookie, children two to four years of age had difficulty realizing that their mothers would be unaware of this desire. But children between four and six years of age recognized that their mothers did not have this information. By this age, then, children begin making a distinction between what they and others know.

In his extensive research on children's conceptualization of others, John Flavell studied their emerging ability to understand the *recursive* nature of thought (Flavell, 1985; Flavell et al., 1968; Miller, Kessel, & Flavell, 1970). Recursive events refer to those that can take place repeatedly, perhaps indefinitely, over a series of steps. Thought is considered to be recursive because we can reflect on the possibility that others are thinking about what we are thinking, and so on, through many levels of "you're thinking that I'm thinking. . . ." Figure 11.6 illustrates an example of a one-loop recursion ("The boy is thinking that the girl is thinking of the father") and a two-loop recursion ("The boy is thinking that the girl is thinking of the father thinking of the mother").

Throughout the elementary school years, children's responses hint at an increasing understanding of the recursive nature of thought. Flavell found, however, that many children have difficulty understanding the sophisticated level of reasoning required in this process. For example, only about half the children at eleven years of age grasped a one-loop recursion, and about a third of eleven-year-olds understood two-loop recursions. This knowledge improves well into adolescence and may depend upon the more abstract and hypothetical reasoning associated with formal operational thought (Shantz, 1983).

▶ **Interaction among domains**

Perspective-taking Approaches

How should we describe and explain developmental changes in visual and conceptual perspective taking? Should we emphasize the specific mechanisms and

FIGURE 11.6

How Recursive Thinking Develops

Children often have difficulty with complex levels of recursive thinking. In this one-loop example, they must understand that "the boy is thinking that the girl is thinking of father" and in the two-loop example, that "the boy is thinking that the girl is thinking of the father thinking of the mother." Recursive thought continues to improve into adolescence, an indication that advanced levels of perspective taking probably require abstract and hypothetical reasoning available only to individuals capable of formal operational thought.

ONE-LOOP RECURSION   TWO-LOOP RECURSION

Source: Adapted from Miller, Kessel, & Flavell, 1970.

processes that are acquired to give the child the capacity to engage in social cognitive activities such as role taking? Or should we stress the broad, qualitative changes that may characterize children's conceptualizations of their relationship to others? Fortunately, two analyses of the development of perspective taking, one offered by John Flavell and his colleagues and the other by Robert Selman, permit us to consider both of these orientations.

Flavell's Analysis   Flavell argues that to be able to take the role of another person the child must draw upon four cognitive skills (Flavell, 1985; Flavell et al., 1968). Over development, these skills emerge and are executed in a more orderly sequence during occasions of perspective taking. The first skill is recognizing that a different point of view *exists* in others. At this level, the child realizes others have perceptions, thoughts, and motives different from her own but may be unable to specify their nature or comprehend their importance for social interactions. The second skill is an appreciation of the *need* to consider the other's perspective in order to carry out effective social interchanges. The third is *inferring* those attributes of another that are relevant to the social activity at hand. The child must not only know that another perspective exists and realize its importance but must also have the information-processing skills to determine what someone else sees, thinks, feels, or knows. Finally, the child must be able to *apply* these inferences and monitor their successful application while engaging in interactions with that person.

Flavell has not attempted to identify when each of these skills emerges. Their implementation may actually depend more upon the complexity of the social cognitive task at hand. By identifying this set of skills, however, we begin to appreciate the multitude of information-processing demands that confront children when they carry out tasks involving social cognition.

▶ **Development as continuous/ stagelike**

Selman's Stages Analysis Robert Selman has proposed a second model of perspective taking, one that also emphasizes an orderly sequence in children's understanding of the perspective of others (Selman, 1976, 1980; Selman & Byrne, 1974). According to Selman, however, and in contrast to Flavell's analysis, role taking undergoes qualitative differences from one age to the next. Selman used children's responses to social dilemmas to formulate this model. Children are presented stories like the following in which two individuals are in conflict:

> Holly is an eight-year-old girl who likes to climb trees. She is the best tree climber in the neighborhood. One day while climbing down from a tall tree she falls off the bottom branch but does not hurt herself. Her father sees her fall. He is upset and asks her to promise not to climb trees any more. Holly promises.
>
> Later that day, Holly and her friends meet Sean. Sean's kitten is caught up in a tree and cannot get down. Something has to be done right away or the kitten may fall. Holly is the only one who climbs trees well enough to reach the kitten and get it down, but she remembers her promise to her father. (Selman & Byrne, 1974, p. 805).

After listening to this story, children were asked the following kinds of questions: Does Holly know how Sean feels about the kitten? How will Holly's father feel if he finds out she climbed the tree? What does Holly think her father will do if he finds out that she climbed the tree? Children were expected to identify with Holly in order to answer these questions, but they were also asked what they would do in this situation.

Based on children's responses to these dilemmas, Selman distinguished five levels or stages of role-taking ability (see Table 11.1). Children approximately three to six years of age are either unable to recognize that others have a different perspective or, if able to do so, have little desire to maintain the distinction between their own and the other's perspective. On the other hand, children from about six to eight years of age begin to recognize that people with different information or other responsibilities may have dissimilar thoughts and feelings about a situation. Children this age, however, continue to have difficulty anticipating viewpoints that conflict with their own. Furthermore, even though the child realizes other perspectives can exist, he makes little effort to resolve disagreements between them.

Around eight to ten years of age, children realize that others are able to think about the child's perspective. Thus, at this age children become aware of one-loop recursions in thought, anticipating how others will think about their actions. Still, the perspectives of self and others are not considered simultaneously or from a neutral, third-party position. This capacity emerges at the next stage, sometime between ten and twelve years of age. Now children can, in a sense, step outside the situation to consider several points of view at

Level	Features	Typical Responses to the Story of Holly
0 *Egocentric Role Taking* (about 3–6 years)	The child has little understanding of another's point of view; the child's perspective extends to everyone else.	If child concludes Holly will rescue the kitten, other characters in the story, including the father, are assumed to approve of the action. "She will save the kitten because she doesn't want the kitten to die"; if her father finds out he will be "Happy, he likes kittens" (p. 305). If the punitive consequences of breaking a promise to the father are brought to the child's attention, he may decide Holly would not save the kitten after all; the child fails to grasp the discrepancy in his conflicting responses.
1 *Subjective or Differentiated Perspective* (about 6–8 years)	The child realizes that others may have another perspective but thinks all will agree if everyone has the same information and has difficulty anticipating disagreements and resolving any conflicts that remain.	The child who says Holly should climb the tree realizes her father might get angry, but only if she fails to tell him about the good reason for climbing the tree. She thinks that as long as both Holly and her father have the same information, they will arrive at similar evaluations of the situation. "If he didn't know why she climbed the tree, he would be angry. But if Holly tells him why she did it, he would realize she has a good reason" (p. 304).
2 *Self-reflective Role Taking* (about 8–10 years)	In addition to realizing that others may have different perspectives, the child also becomes aware that they can appreciate his perspective. Thus, the child understands that two perspectives may differ even though the same information is available to both of them. One consequence is that the child can begin to anticipate the reactions of others to his behaviors. He still, however, cannot consider his own and others' perspectives simultaneously.	The child might respond to Holly's dilemma by saying her father will understand Holly's feelings and will not punish her. By making such a claim, the child recognizes that Holly and her father can have different perspectives. "The father may think breaking a promise is worse, but he'd understand that Holly thinks saving the kitten's life is more important" (p. 305). Although the child realizes Holly's father will be unhappy, he is still unable to consider how that conflicting perspective might need to be resolved in a way that is fair for both Holly and her father.
3 *Mutual Role Taking* (about 10–12 years)	The child begins to appreciate the recursive and embedded nature of thinking about others. Both self and others can be viewed mutually and simultaneously.	Now the child is able to consider the views of both Holly and her father at the same time. He describes Holly's and her father's positions from the vantage point of a neutral person.
4 *Societal and In-depth Role Taking* (about 12–15 years)	Social conventions are seen as a means of attempting to resolve the dilemma. Different values are respected, but if the dispute remains unresolved, the values of the larger social or cultural group or "generalized other" become the arbiter.	Holly's rationale for retrieving the kitten might make reference to society's beliefs concerning humaneness to animals or assisting neighbors in times of difficulty. Alternatively, if she elected not to climb the tree, she might refer to the importance of honoring and respecting adult authority and demands.

Source: Based on Selman, 1976.

TABLE 11.1

Selman's Stages of Social Perspective Taking

Holly has promised her father that she will not climb trees any more. But she is the only person able to climb a tree to get a kitten that is caught in it. This table summarizes the perspectives that children at different ages take in attempting to resolve this kind of conflict.

▶ **Interaction among domains**

the same time. Finally, young adolescents consider the views of the larger society and bring them to bear upon the dilemma. The teenager can take the group perspective and recognizes that conflicts and problems need to be resolved in ways that satisfy the society at large.

Research provides some support for Selman's developmental model. For example, when researchers tested forty-one first- to sixth-grade boys two and five years later, all children showed increases in their level of responding over the period (see Figure 11.7) (Gurucharri & Selman, 1982). Only eight boys failed to advance at least one full level in five years, and only one child showed a decline in responding at any time during testing. The finding that children do not regress to lower levels and other research, indicating that they progressively advance to higher levels without skipping previous ones (Selman, 1980; Selman & Byrne, 1974), furnishes important evidence for the claim that perspective taking undergoes invariant stagelike advances during childhood.

Explaining the Development of Perspective-taking Ability How can we account for the important developmental changes found in perspective-taking ability? Certainly cognitive factors play a significant role. Flavell's analysis highlights several necessary cognitive skills that children must display. Children must realize that individuals can have different views and be able to process the ways in which those views converge or diverge. These skills, however, are not simply a reflection of intelligence as measured on standardized

FIGURE 11.7

Improvements in Perspective Taking

Children in first grade who were evaluated on their social perspective-taking ability showed substantially higher levels of performance over a five-year period between testing at time 1 and time 3, as the results shown here indicate. Each line in the graph shows the performance of an individual child. Similar changes were observed for children in the second through sixth grades. In fact, only one child showed a measurable decline in performance over testing intervals. Failure to find many regressions and other evidence to indicate that children do not skip levels provide support for Selman's claim that perspective taking progresses through qualitatively different stages of development.

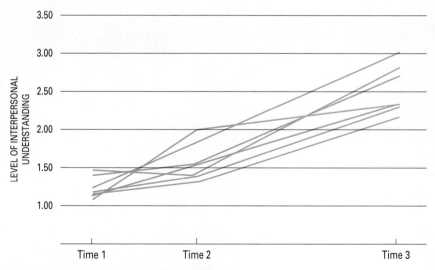

Source: Adapted from Gurucharri & Selman, 1982.

intelligence tests. Performance on intelligence tests and perspective-taking tasks typically show relatively low correlations (from about .20 to .40). Furthermore, intelligence tests provide few insights into the processes that lead to more effective communication, problem solving, and social interactions involving others (Shantz, 1983).

As Selman's analysis might lead us to suspect, performance on Piagetian conservation tasks is also associated with the development of perspective-taking skill. Children unable to think at a concrete operational level typically fall at the lowest level in Selman's model (Keating & Clark, 1980; Krebs & Gilmore, 1982). We are uncertain, however, about whether reversibility or other aspects of concrete and formal operational thought account for advances in perspective-taking skills (Shantz, 1983).

Even if cognitive and intellectual factors are found to be important in the emergence of perspective taking, we can not rule out possible contributions from other factors (Higgins & Parsons, 1983). Why not? Because numerous changes take place in children's environments that can affect their role-taking activities as well. For example, in Western cultures children typically enter school around five or six years of age. This transition often brings about a dramatic increase in the range and variety of experiences with others.

▶ **Sociocultural influence**

When a child enters a formal school, her roles expand to include pupil as well as daughter, athlete or musician as well as playmate, leader or follower among her peers as well as dutiful member of her family. While engaged in these various roles, the child must begin to juggle assorted perspectives and put into practice many different strategies to achieve effective social goals. These expanding opportunities to participate in social interactions with peers and others are likely to foster developmental changes in role-taking ability.

In summary, although cognitive development is undoubtedly a necessary component in perspective taking, we cannot overlook the potential importance of social contributions. Although little research has been carried out on the effects of parental socialization practices or cultural factors (Rubin & Everett,

In Western cultures children typically enter school around five or six years of age. This transition often brings about a dramatic increase in the range and variety of the child's experiences with others.

1982), visual and conceptual perspective taking fall within the broad domain of *social* cognition. Thus the universe of social experiences, including those provided within the family and those promoted by the larger culture, may be fertile ground for further insights about the development of perspective-taking skills.

How Attribution Skills Develop

Knowledge of others involves more than recognizing that someone else sees and understands things differently. Children also attribute intentions, motives, desires, feelings, and relatively stable characteristics such as personality traits and dispositions to others. These **attributions,** conjectures about the qualities underlying and causing behavior, must frequently be inferred from the actions of others. If someone steps on my toe, how I respond is very likely to depend on whether I believe the other's deed was intentional or not. If a friend loans me money but I fail to return it, my friend's reaction is very likely to depend on whether he accepts my proposal to eventually pay him back or concludes, perhaps based on previous incidents, that I am untrustworthy and a risky bet for future loans. When do children become aware of desires, intentions, and other internal causes of behavior in others? How do they put all this information together to reach a conclusion about someone's personality and character?

Attributions Involving Motivations and Intentions   Behavior may be selfish or selfless, morally indefensible or blameless, antisocial or ill fated, irresponsible or justified, aggressive or accidental depending on what motives are judged to underlie it. Given how important intentions are for interpreting another's actions, we should not be surprised to find researchers are interested in determining when children understand their role in causing behavior. In Chapter 13 we examine comprehension of moral dilemmas to explore this issue, but here we focus on children's basic knowledge of intentionality in the behavior of others.

Preschoolers do make inferences about intentions in others. For example, when asked to provide commentary while watching a silent film showing someone getting up, eating breakfast, carrying out routine household activities, and going to work, four- and five-year-olds often referred to the model's inner qualities, including his needs and intentions ("He wants to know," "He's trying to . . . ," "He needs . . .") (Livesley & Bromley, 1973). Studies of early language also suggest that young children understand motives as long as they are closely linked to behavior (Damon & Hart, 1988; Miller & Aloise, 1989). In many situations, in fact, three- and four-year-olds infer about as well as adults that beliefs and desires are responsible for the actions of others (Bartsch & Wellman, 1989).

▶ **The child's active role**

attribution   Inference about a person's characteristics that cause that person's behavior.

Preschoolers are actually overzealous in their attribution of intentions. When Michael Smith (1978) showed brief films depicting human movements involving voluntary acts (sitting down, chewing), involuntary acts (sneezing, yawning), and acts caused by objects (being pushed by a file cabinet, stumbling over a box), four-year-olds judged nearly all as *intentional.* By five years of age children were more likely to claim intention for actions with positive rather

These two boys are making numerous inferences about one another as they interact. While one boy may have decided that his companion's words are not worth listening to, his companion tries to get around the problem by yelling. But as long as they can recognize these behaviors as having a playful intent, the boys can continue to be good friends.

than negative consequences, but by six years of age their judgments of intentionality matched those of adults.

The bias of preschoolers to infer intentionality for accidental and involuntary events has been reported by others, including Piaget (1926), who noted that children at this age sometimes believe physical objects are capable of independent action and intention. Piaget proposed that this confusion arises from preschoolers' egocentrism—that is, the inability to differentiate their own thinking from events occurring in the physical world. Thomas Shultz (1982) suggests, however, that the overgeneralization stems from the desire to have a clear and simple explanation for cause-effect relationships.

Other research by Shultz and his colleagues reveals that overattributing intentionality is not simply a consequence of preschoolers trying to explain an outcome. Consider the "matching rule," which initially governs children's inferences about intent. According to this rule, an action whose outcome matches a plan or motive will be accepted as intentional. But if a plan is stated and the outcome does not match, a preschooler will not assume the unexpected event was *intended*. For example, if told that an actor is planning to shoot target A but instead hits target B, preschoolers do not infer the actor *intended* to hit B (Shultz & Wells, 1985). They also do not attribute intention to outcomes caused by unforeseen circumstances or mistakes (Nelson-LeGall, 1985; Shultz, Wells, & Sarda, 1980). For example, three-year-olds realize a child who commits an error while saying a tongue twister or while wearing distorting glasses is making a mistake and does not intend to do these things. Clearly, errors in attributing intention depend upon the information available and the child's familiarity with the situation.

We can conclude from these data that very young children have little difficulty attributing intention to the behavior of others. Imputing intent when none exists or the wrong intent is most frequent when a preschooler has little or no knowledge of a person's motives or the circumstances surrounding the behavior. Of course, in many situations information about desires and plans is not available and must be inferred. These circumstances are likely to be difficult to understand and lead young children to claim intentions when they do not exist (Shultz, 1982). In other words, an important developmental task is learning to infer the causes of behavior correctly and when *not* to use intention as an explanation for the actions of another.

Internal Versus External Attributions Virtually all theories of attribution distinguish between two types of causes of behavior: *internal* factors, those within a person, such as attitudes, interests, efforts, desires, and intentions, and *external* factors, such as parental pressure, financial rewards, and other aspects of a situation. Developmental psychologists have often argued that preschoolers believe the actions of others are rooted in external, situational, and context-dependent factors, whereas older, school-aged children are more likely to believe that actions are the outcome of internal, psychological dispositions or traits (Shantz, 1983).

We have already seen that preschoolers often overgeneralize intentions in others. Why, then, is it commonly thought that young children fail to consider internal factors in accounting for another's actions? Pat Miller and Patricia Aloise (1989) believe that the structured interviews and the clinical method typically employed to obtain information about the causes of behavior are largely responsible. These procedures bias young children toward simpler, more readily accessible explanations; preschoolers have neither the will nor the skill to describe effectively the internal psychological qualities underlying the actions of others. But if other procedures are used, children this young are able and sometimes prefer internal psychological explanations for the behavior of others.

Support for Miller and Aloise's view comes from a study in which Miller (1985) created a series of brief stories involving two dolls playing with blocks, doing puzzles, learning the names of birds, or learning about numbers. For one of the dolls, the reason for the activity was given in terms of some intrinsic attribute such as interest ("likes to learn about birds") or psychological effort ("thinking hard about birds"). For the other doll, the reason was given in terms of some external cause such as parental pressure ("mother makes her learn about birds") or external reward ("gets a dime for every bird she learns"). Children were then asked which doll would learn more, for example, the one thinking hard about the birds or the one whose mother made her learn their names. Three-year-olds showed little preference for either external or internal causes in deciding which doll would do most of an activity, although they did favor one intrinsic attribute (intellectual ability) over external causes. Four- and five-year-olds, however, preferred internal causes as the basis for most of their judgments, just as did eight-year-olds. Thus, we see that although some methods of testing reveal that older children are more capable of describing and elaborating psychological causes, alternative methods reveal that even very young children can and frequently prefer to use such explanations for the behavior of others.

Attributions About Personality and Dispositional Traits As we have just pointed out, children can make inferences about the thoughts, feelings, motivations, and intentions of others at a very early age. When such inferences are primarily formed to describe or conceptualize another's personality or some other quality, they are known as **person perception.** When do young

person perception Process of describing and conceptualizing someone's personality.

children realize that their friends and acquaintances have stable personalities and **dispositions**—that is, enduring tendencies and competencies—and are there developmental changes in these conceptualizations?

The procedure usually followed in research on person perception again consists of asking children to describe someone they know. Just as Jason, Lisa, and Jennifer described themselves somewhat differently, so, too, this research has shown developmental changes in how children describe others. The descriptions of children Jason's age, preschoolers, typically highlight physical characteristics such as where others live, members of their family, or things they own along with overt appearance and behaviors (Barenboim, 1981; Livesley & Bromley, 1973; Peevers & Secord, 1973). Shantz (1983) summarizes person perception at these younger ages as "A person 'is' what he owns and where he lives" (p. 505). Furthermore, even when young children do apply personality or dispositional terms to others, the labels are seldom used to describe stable, enduring qualities that will predict future behavior. For example, a friend might be labeled as generous because he shared a toy with another person, yet five-year-olds do not consistently predict that this same person will share in another situation (Rholes & Ruble, 1984). Still, this awareness of internal psychological qualities may form the basis by which children begin to conceptualize stable personality and dispositional traits in others (Eder, 1989).

Throughout the elementary school years, children increasingly frame their descriptions in the form of loosely connected personality and dispositional traits, making inferences about the values and beliefs of others in global terms such as "mean," "nice," and "smart" (Shantz, 1983). By adolescence, these descriptions begin to take into account contradictions and qualifications. Future research, however, that does not rely on the verbal competencies demanded by structured and other interview methods may reveal that children understand personality and dispositional traits much better than outlined here. For example, Jackie Gnepp and Chinni Chilamkurti (1988) gave children and adults stories describing a child's past behavior. These stories described consistent behaviors that would permit the listeners to predict how the child would behave in a future situation. Under these circumstances even kindergarten children could recognize and make inferences about a stable and generalizable trait in another. Of course, in everyday situations the information the child receives from others may not be so clear and consistent. Thus, the development of person perception during the school-age years is probably one of identifying stability and enduring qualities in the face of exceptions and variability in the behavior of others.

In summary, the ability to understand others, to take their perspective as well as to comprehend their personal qualities, reveals a complicated developmental progression that parallels changes observed for understanding self. It likely begins with a basic distinction, that others are different from self, and advances through increasingly sophisticated awareness of the ways in which the visual and conceptual perspectives and the traits and qualities of parents, peers, and others differ from one's own. These distinctions are important for effective communication and social interactions. Young children have often been perceived as egocentric and focused on external qualities when engaged in social relationships. Yet recent research challenges these ideas and claims that children begin to understand psychological and other inner qualities very early, although their ability to do so becomes increasingly effective throughout childhood.

disposition Enduring tendencies and competencies characterizing the individual.

THEMES IN DEVELOPMENT

SOCIAL COGNITION

▶ **What roles do nature and nurture play in the development of social cognition?**

Children borrow strategies from caregivers, teachers, and others for instructing themselves, controlling their attention, and planning as effective means of taking on responsibility for their own behavior. The feedback children receive from their environment also seems to be especially important for promoting a mastery orientation and preventing learned helplessness. And children clearly rely on the people in their environment for learning about themselves and others. For these reasons, nurture is often assumed to be paramount for the development of social cognition. Nevertheless, some competencies—for example, the desire to master the environment or effectance motivation, as well as various self-regulatory capacities—may build upon children's innate nature.

▶ **How does the sociocultural context influence the development of social cognition?**

Because children acquire so much of their knowledge of self through their interactions with others, the evaluations they place on themselves will be the consequence of whether the culture stresses autonomy, loyalty, perseverance, cooperation or some other qualities and how closely they measure up to them. Self-esteem is likely to be greatly influenced by how well children adhere to societies' expectations in terms of beauty, athletic skill, hunting prowess, academic ability, and so forth. Moreover, the stress a society places on proper social etiquette, effective communication, mutual cooperation, and other interpersonal skills may have a significant impact on how effectively children master and exhibit proficiency in activities involving social cognition.

▶ **How does the child play an active role in the development of social cognition?**

We have seen that caregivers take on the initial responsibility for instituting limits and standards in the behavior of young children, often in response to developing motor and other skills that may lead to danger for the child or annoyance to the caregiver. In time, as children gain cognitive and social skills, they initiate their own efforts to control their activities. Children can also begin to realize that they are competent individuals capable of influencing and controlling their environment in realistic ways and may even perceive intentions in the actions of others where none exists. They actively search out information from others, perhaps at first in order to "fit in" and learn how they are expected to behave in a specific situation. Comparison becomes an increasingly central part of social cognition in middle childhood. With the onset of adolescence, however, a more satisfying and fully integrated concept of self, a personal identity, becomes an important goal.

▶ **Is the development of social cognition continuous or stagelike?**

Selman's analysis of the development of perspective taking provides an example of how the development of social cognition can be viewed as stagelike, subject to the acquisition of qualitatively distinct conceptual capacities. Others such as Flavell consider information-processing skills central to this capacity and see perspective taking as continuously improving and expanding to various domains. While many developmental changes have been described for social cognition, some appearing to portray qualitative differences, evidence that these represent stagelike changes remains limited. Even the emergence and resolution of the identity crisis, often considered a hallmark of adolescence, may not be experienced by all youth, although new concerns about social relationships and other competencies during this time can have significant personal consequences for many young people.

▶ **How does the development of social cognition interact with development in other domains?**

The transformation from impulsive infant to a socially confident, self-assured adult is a remarkable one involving increasingly effective regulation of one's own behavior and greater awareness of the qualities of self and of others. With development, cognitive resources and socialization practices intersect to permit children to take charge of their own lives. Cognitive, linguistic, emotional, and physical aspects of development, along with the social environment, have been emphasized as contributing to the development of social cognition throughout this chapter. Perhaps it is not necessary to add that growth in social cognition may further promote development in these other domains as children learn to effectively interact with others.

SUMMARY

Social cognition is the broad knowledge that individuals acquire about humans and the activities in which they engage. It includes the motives, feelings, capacities, needs, interests, and thoughts that we come to grant to self and to others as well.

Among the earliest endeavors associated with self is *self-regulation,* learning to govern and control one's own behavior. Efforts to control behavior in most societies begin in the second half of the first year of life and continue throughout childhood. At first, these efforts are initiated primarily by caregivers, then take the form of co-regulation. Self-initiated attempts to control behavior become more evident as children demonstrate increasing capacities for *delay of gratification* and other forms of compliance, planning, and orderly behavior.

Vygotsky theorized that language is pivotal for regulation of behavior. At first, only the language of others influences a child's actions, but eventually the child's private speech takes on the same function. Others propose that attentional and cognitive mechanisms are the means by which behavior comes under control. Again, caregivers take initial responsibility for regulating these mechanisms. Attentional and cognitive tools, too, are eventually adopted by children to facilitate self-regulation. Individual differences in self-regulation may be related to genetic or constitutional factors, but socialization practices that encourage and model self-control, and that provide opportunities for children to acquire means of increasing persistence and taking on responsibility, are also important.

Researchers concerned with the development of *self*—the beliefs, knowledge, and feelings that an individual uses to describe and explain his or her own characteristics—distinguish between self as object and self as subject. Self as object consists of one's *self-concept,* the perceptions, ideas, and beliefs one holds to be true of oneself. Self as subject consists of how one initiates, organizes, and interprets experience.

Children's sense of themselves as objects is first evident in their self-recognition around fifteen to eighteen months of age. During the preschool years they begin defining themselves in terms of a *categorical self*—that is, by referring to various categories that provide membership in one group or another. By the early school years, *social comparisons* involving others become important, and by the adolescent years their own impact on others and their relationship to broader sociocultural ideals become a central part of defining themselves. At all ages, however, self-concept includes an appreciation of physical, behavioral, social, and psychological traits and characteristics.

Among the elements of self as subject are a sense of agency, individuality, stability, and reflection. Infants seem to be born with an intrinsic desire to gain control of their world, but to the extent an environment provides consistent feedback, children acquire an increasing sense of agency. Individual differences in the sense of agency have significant consequences for behavior. Children with an *internal locus of control* or a *mastery orientation* believe that they have considerable influence over the things that happen to them. Children with an *external locus of control* or who experience *learned helplessness* feel that they have little influence over the things that happen to them. This difference has major consequences in the ways children approach and respond to academic and other challenges. Socialization practices by caregivers, teachers, and others appear to have an important bearing on the emergence and continuation of this individual difference.

Self-esteem consists of the positive or negative feelings one grants to oneself. Preschoolers are able to make this evaluation for specific domains; by the early school years self-esteem takes the form of an overall sense of worth. Self-esteem is affected by feedback from others as well as how successful the child feels he is in areas that are believed to be important. Although self-esteem in adolescents is often assumed to undergo a precipitous decline, many teenagers successfully establish a *personal identity* with relatively minimal disruption to their lives and those around them.

Children begin to acquire *perspective taking*, the ability to assume the visual and conceptual perspective of others, during the preschool years, and this ability improves for many years thereafter. The developmental changes include a greater ability to balance the perspectives of both self and other as well as to consider the broader needs of society in resolving differences of opinion. Increasingly effective ability to process information permits perspective taking in more complex situations.

Children are capable of recognizing intention and other psychological causes of behavior very early in development, although young children may prefer or find it easier to identify external explanations as the cause of behavior in others. In fact, preschoolers often overgeneralize intentions where they do not exist. Children's perceptions of others, however, often include an understanding not only of their observable physical and behavioral attributes but also of their social and psychological qualities and dispositions.

12
Sex Roles

KEY THEMES

▶ **What roles do nature and nurture play in sex-role development?**

▶ **How does the sociocultural context influence sex-role development?**

▶ **How does the child play an active role in the process of sex-role development?**

▶ **Is sex-role development continuous or stagelike?**

▶ **Are there sensitive periods in sex-role development?**

▶ **How does sex-role development interact with development in other domains?**

Let the first words in this discussion go to Jason, a seven-year-old. "You see," Jason explains patiently, "there are boys' toys and girls' toys. I mean, G.I. Joe looks like a doll, but 'cause he's a boy's toy, he can't be a doll. Only girls play with dolls. G.I. Joe's an action figure!"

This brief but telling comment shows that Jason already has some clear-cut ideas about the activities that boys and girls properly engage in, even to the point of making fine discriminations between toys that are virtually alike. At a very young age Jason is displaying his knowledge of **sex-role stereotypes,** the expectations or beliefs that individuals within a given culture hold about the behaviors characteristic of females and males. His views are not atypical for children growing up in our culture. One popular stereotype is that only girls play with dolls, with which they can display the kind of maternal nurturance and affection usually regarded as "feminine." Because the stereotype for male behaviors includes activity and aggression, a boy's doll in this perspective is *not* a doll, but an "action figure" with which boys can mimic combat. Where do children learn such powerful and clearly articulated beliefs about maleness and femaleness? Are these stereotypes based on actual empirically confirmed *sex differences* in behavior between males and females? And if so, are these differences due to innate factors or to socialization? These are three of the central questions we will address in this chapter.

Each of us is classified at birth as either a boy or a girl. As it turns out, this simple classification—the result of differences in sex chromosomes and the prenatal differentiation of the genitalia—has enormous implications for our social development. The process by which children acquire the characteristics and behaviors that are prescribed for males and females in their culture is called *sex-role development,* or **sex typing.** To some extent, sex roles may have biological foundations; the sex chromosomes, hormones, and physical characteristics of boys and girls can potentially influence how they behave. By the same token, how children think about sex roles (including sex-role stereotypes) as well as their socialization experiences are also powerful factors in this domain. One of the major issues facing developmental psychologists is to identify how biology, cognition, and socialization experiences interact in the process of sex-role development.

Before the mid-1960s, most psychologists regarded the socialization of children into traditional masculine and feminine roles as both a natural and a desirable outcome of development. Behavioral sex differences were viewed as inevitable and were linked to comparable sex differences among nonhumans (Kohlberg, 1966; Mischel, 1966; Shaw & Darling, 1985). But changes in social values in the mid-1960s, especially those accompanying the rise of the modern women's movement, produced a shift in the ways in which psychologists approached sex differences and sex-role socialization. Many of the questions that interest developmental psychologists today represent both a challenge to traditional assumptions about the nature and origins of sex roles and sex differences and a concerted effort to determine the developmental processes that underlie children's acquisition and enactment of sex roles.

SEX DIFFERENCES: REAL OR IMAGINED?

Throughout the recorded history of Western civilization, considerable attention has been paid to the perceived characteristics of males and females. The Greek philosopher Plato (d. 347 B.C.) described sex differences in the temperaments of women and men, as did Judeo-Christian scriptural tradition and the religious philosophers of the Middle Ages. Females and males were assumed to differ in temperament, interests, educability, and susceptibility to mental illness, among other characteristics. Many of these beliefs persist unchanged in contemporary sex stereotypes.

The Stereotypes: What Are They?

Suppose a large group of college students is asked to rate the typical man or woman on a number of psychological attributes. Will they rate certain traits as more typical of males than of females, and vice versa? A study in which 128 college students were asked to do precisely this task revealed that characteristics such as independence, aggression, and self-confidence were associated with masculinity, and emotional expressiveness, kindness, and gentleness were associated with femininity (Ruble, 1983). Table 12.1 lists many additional traits the students ascribed to each sex.

sex-role stereotype Expectation or belief that individuals within a given culture hold about behavior characteristic of males and females.

sex typing Process by which individuals acquire the characteristics and behaviors prescribed by their culture for their sex. Also called *sex-role development.*

These sex-role stereotypes are not limited to our own society. Researchers asked children and adults from thirty nations in North and South America, Europe, Africa, and Asia to indicate whether certain traits are associated with men or women more frequently in their culture. The results showed that children from all the countries begin to acquire information about sex stereotypes before the age of five years (the youngest age studied), that this information is consolidated in the early school-age years (six to nine years of age), and that the process of learning sex stereotypes is completed by early adolescence.

TABLE 12.1

Stereotypic Characteristics Attributed to Males and Females

When college students were asked to rate a typical man or woman on a number of personality traits, strong patterns emerged among traits that were seen as associated with each sex. Male traits generally fall into a cluster called *instrumentality,* female traits into a cluster called *expressiveness.*

Male Characteristics	Female Characteristics
Independent	Emotional
Aggressive	Grateful
Acts as leader	Kind
Self-confident	Creative
Dominant	Gentle
Active	Understanding
Ambitious	Aware of others' feelings
Outspoken	Enjoys art and music
Adventurous	Tactful
Competitive	Considerate
Likes math and science	Home oriented
Takes a stand	Cries easily
Makes decisions easily	Devotes self to others
Skilled in business	Strong conscience

Source: Adapted from Ruble, 1983.

Interestingly, children consistently acquired stereotypes about male roles earlier than they acquired stereotypes about female roles (Williams & Best, 1982).

This same research also showed many cross-cultural similarities in the stereotypes adults attributed to males and females. Perceived masculine personality characteristics generally fell in a category psychologists describe as **instrumental** characteristics, or attributes associated with acting upon the world, such as being assertive, achievement oriented, and independent. Perceived feminine characteristics may be classified as **expressive,** or associated with emotions and interactions with other people. The results showed substantial agreement between sex-role stereotypes in the United States and in other cultures.

Despite the many similarities in sex-role stereotypes across cultures, some differences occurred between nations in the specific characteristics attributed to males and females. For example, Italian adults stereotypically associated "endurance" with women, although most adults in other countries felt that this was a masculine trait. Nigerian adults felt that "affiliation" was sex neutral, whereas adults in other countries said it was a feminine characteristic. Thus, we cannot say that specific characteristics are always attributed to males or to females. We can say, however, that the tendency to stereotype on the basis of sex is found in a variety of cultural settings.

Why do sex-role stereotypes exist? Probably because, like all stereotypes, they provide guidance for our own behavior—for instance, in situations in

▶ **Sociocultural influence**

instrumental personality characteristics Characteristics associated with acting on the world; usually considered masculine.

expressive personality characteristics Characteristics associated with emotions or relationships with people; usually considered feminine.

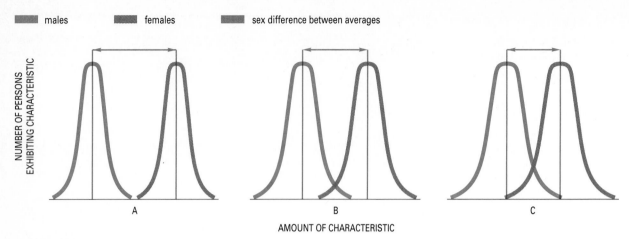

FIGURE 12.1

Possible Patterns of Sex Differences

Differences of any sort, including sex differences, may be of several varieties. The horizontal axis in this series of graphs represents scores on some psychological test that assesses a skill or attribute. In this particular example, females show higher average scores than males. Graph A illustrates a difference in which no overlap exists between the sexes. Graph B illustrates a sex difference in which males and females, on average, differ dramatically, although some males have scores that are higher than the lowest scores of females. Graph C illustrates a sex difference in which considerable overlap exists in the scores of males and females, although the averages of the two groups are still different. Most of the psychological differences between the sexes are of the sort illustrated in graph C.

▶ **Interaction among domains**

which we know little else about a person. Although stereotypes may not accurately predict any one person's behavior, and in fact can lead to woefully wrong assumptions about an individual's interests or abilities, they are retained because of their general usefulness in understanding our complex social worlds. Stereotyping appears to be a common way in which humans of all ages process information about their world (Martin & Halverson, 1981).

What Sex Differences Actually Exist?

In light of such durable and pervasive stereotypes about "femaleness" and "maleness," it is logical to ask whether researchers have documented actual differences in the characteristics or behaviors of females and males. Before we address this question, however, let us first consider a number of possible patterns for how such differences can occur.

Figure 12.1 illustrates three possible kinds of sex differences for any hypothetical set of scores, be they verbal skills, visual-spatial ability, or any other measure of an attribute or behavior. In graph A, males and females show no overlap and a wide average difference. In graphs B and C, the two sexes overlap (minimally in graph B and considerably in graph C), but males and females both display a greater range than in graph A, illustrated by the wider bell-shaped curves. Notice, in fact, that in graph C, some females are more different from other females (and some males from other males) than the two sexes are on average different from one another. The pattern of sex differences illustrated in graph C is far more common than those in graphs A and B. In general, average differences between the sexes are less than the variability in performance within each sex. This is an important point to keep in mind as we examine the empirical evidence.

Physical Attributes   Females and males physically differ in a number of ways, including the makeup of their chromosomes, their genitalia, and levels of certain hormones. By later childhood and adolescence, males have greater muscle mass than females, but females are physically more mature at birth and walk, talk, and reach puberty earlier than boys (Maccoby & Jacklin, 1974). Males show a special physical vunerability during infancy. Compared with females, males are more likely to be miscarried, die in infancy, or develop hereditary diseases. They are also more likely than females to experience longer and more difficult births (Jacklin, 1989).

▶ **Interaction among domains**

Cognition   In 1974, Eleanor Maccoby and Carol Jacklin performed an extensive review of the psychological literature on sex differences. They surveyed sixteen hundred studies that examined sex differences in behaviors and tabulated the number of studies that found sex differences favoring girls, the number favoring boys, and the number showing no sex differences. In the area of cognitive skills, Maccoby and Jacklin concluded that girls are more skilled in verbal areas such as reading and vocabulary, whereas boys excel in tasks requiring visual-spatial skills.

Visual-spatial skills involve a number of abilities, all of which require the ability to visualize and transform figures or objects in the mind. Figure 12.2 illustrates three tests of visual-spatial skills—spatial perception, mental rotation, and spatial visualization. As you can see, spatial perception tasks require subjects to ignore distracting information to locate horizontal and vertical. Mental rotation tasks demand that subjects transform two- and three-dimensional figures "in their heads." Spatial visualization tasks require

FIGURE 12.2

Sex Differences in Visual-Spatial Skills

Tests of visual-spatial skills typically assess spatial perception (top), mental rotation ability (middle), or spatial visualization (bottom). In the top panel, subjects are asked to indicate which bottle has a horizontal water line. In the middle panel, subjects must identify the two responses that depict rotated versions of the standard. In the bottom panel, subjects are asked to identify the simple geometric figure on the top within the more complex figure underneath. Generally, males perform better than females on spatial perception and mental rotation tasks.

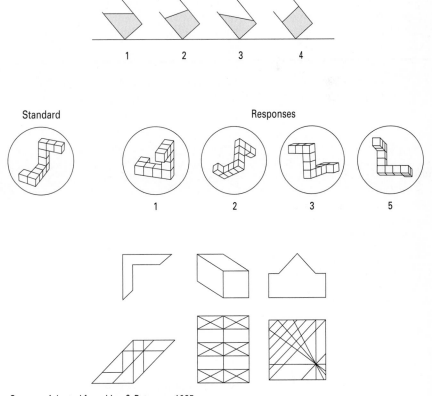

Source: Adapted from Linn & Petersen, 1985.

subjects to analyze relationships among different spatial representations. Up to and during the 1970s, boys' greater visual-spatial skills were also thought to be positively related to their greater mathematical skills, which some studies showed to emerge in adolescence.

More recent meta-analyses of cognitive sex differences, however, indicate no substantial sex differences in verbal skills (Feingold, 1988; Hyde & Linn, 1988). Interestingly, Maccoby and Jacklin's conclusion about verbal skills may have been accurate at the time it was made. Alan Feingold's (1988) meta-analysis of Preliminary Scholastic Aptitude Test (PSAT) scores from over seventy thousand high school juniors who took the test in the years 1960, 1966, 1974, and 1983 indicates that before 1974, girls outperformed boys on the verbal section of this test. Beginning in 1974 (the date of publication of Maccoby and Jacklin's review), however, sex differences in verbal skills disappeared.

In another meta-analysis of over a hundred studies of sex differences in mathematics skills, the investigators concluded that boys and girls showed no overall sex differences in mathematics skills either (Hyde, Fennema, & Lamon, 1990). When the scores of participants of different ages and from specific groups were examined separately, however, sex differences in certain aspects of mathematics performance did emerge. During elementary school, for example, girls showed a slight superiority over boys in the area of computation; in the high school and college years, on the other hand, males did moderately better than females on tests of mathematical problem solving. Among groups selected for either poor performance (such as children from Head Start programs) or exceptional performance (such as students in gifted and talented programs), males performed better than females in tests of mathematical problem solving. Interestingly, sex differences in mathematics skills seem to be diminishing just as they did in verbal skills: studies published before 1973 are more likely to show a sex difference in this area than studies published after 1973. When differences across all the studies are averaged, males show only a very slight advantage. Figure 12.3 illustrates the overall size of this sex difference.

FIGURE 12.3

**Sex Differences in
Mathematics Skills**

Although sex differences in mathematics skills do exist, these differences are quite small. This graph illustrates the size of the average sex difference. The horizontal axis represents scores converted to a standardized form.

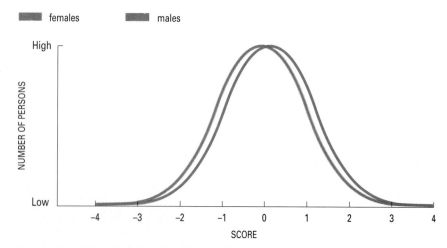

Source: Adapted from Hyde, Fennema, & Lamon, 1990.

In fact, the only notable sex difference in cognitive skills currently supported by empirical evidence is visual-spatial skills. Marcia Linn and Anne Petersen (1985, 1986) conducted a meta-analysis of thirty-eight studies of visual-spatial skills in boys and girls that had been published between 1974 and 1982. The results indicated that males show superior performance on two types of visual-spatial tasks, mental rotation, and, to a lesser extent, spatial perception (the tasks depicted in the middle and top portions of Figure 12.2, respectively). Sex differences in mental rotation ability emerge at about age ten years, usually the youngest age at which such tests can be used. Sex differences in spatial perception are noticeably larger after age eighteen years.

Social Behaviors Maccoby and Jacklin (1974) concluded that few actual sex differences exist in the area of social behaviors. Overall, the sex differences observed in social behaviors are most often the type illustrated in graph C of Figure 12.1. Although average scores of boys and girls are consistently different in some areas, there is considerable variability in the performance of children within each sex. The single most notable exception to this pattern is aggression.

One of the most consistent findings in the research on sex differences is that males are more aggressive than females starting from the preschool years. As we shall see in the next two chapters, they engage in more rough-and-tumble play, display more physical aggression, try to dominate peers, and subsequently display more antisocial behaviors than girls (Block, 1983; Huston, 1985). Meta-analyses substantiate that sex differences in aggression are

One of the consistent sex differences in social behavior is the tendency for boys to display more aggression than girls, especially during the preschool years.

the greatest among preschoolers, decreasing in size up through the college years (Eagley & Steffan, 1986; Hyde, 1984, 1986). Even though males generally are more aggressive than females, however, the size of the sex difference varies as a function of where the aggression occurs and the type of aggression being measured. Males are more likely to aggress in naturalistic settings and to engage in physical rather than verbal aggression than females are.

Meta-analyses also confirm that sex differences in other social behaviors, when they occur at all, tend to be fairly small. For example, studies show few consistent differences between the sexes in empathic behavior (Eisenberg & Lennon, 1983). Women report that they are more empathetic and cry more than men do, but no sex differences emerge when physiological or unobtrusive measures are used to assess empathy. Some researchers report that girls display more social smiles and gazing than boys do, especially in late adolescence (Eisenberg & Lennon, 1983; Hall & Halberstadt, 1986). Other evidence also suggests that females may be more vulnerable to anxiety and less confident in problem-solving situations than males (Block, 1983). These findings, however, may simply reflect the fact that females are more likely than males to report their feelings and emotional states.

One last area in which moderate sex differences have been noted is in the ability to decode the nonverbal expressions of others. Judith Hall's (1984) review of research on this issue shows that female children and adults from widely varying cultures are better than males at identifying the positive versus negative emotions signified by nonverbal cues, particularly as they are transmitted through facial expressions. Moreover, after infancy, females are better than males at recognizing faces.

In general research shows that there are fewer actual sex differences in behavior than sex role stereotypes lead us to believe. Stereotypes may persist, though, because we attribute behaviors inconsistent with the stereotypes to individual differences among children.

Sex Differences: An Overview

In summary, the research literature on actual sex differences in behavior indicates that even though the behavior of people in general shows great variability, males and females are more alike than they are different. Psychologically, male and female children reliably differ on very few dimensions, most notably visual-spatial skills, aggression, and to some extent the ability to decode social messages from nonverbal cues. In fact, many sex differences that we think are "real" actually exist only in the form of sex-role stereotypes. For example, girls are not more talkative, more emotional, or more dependent than boys. Boys are not less suggestible or more logical, nor do they show consistently higher levels of achievement motivation, than girls.

If the research indicates greater similarity than differences between males and females, why do stereotypical beliefs persist? One explanation may be that we notice when boys and girls display behaviors consistent with stereotypes and thus justify the stereotype. In contrast, when a girl or boy behaves in a manner inconsistent with a stereotype, we ascribe this pattern to an individual difference. Thus, when Billy fights (a stereotypically masculine activity), we say that "boys will be boys." But when he cooks and helps around the house in stereotypically feminine tasks, we comment on "how helpful" (not "how feminine") he is compared with other boys his age. Thus, our expectations for sex differences in behavior may cause us to see sex differences where none exist or to exaggerate the importance or magnitude of the sex differences we actually observe.

THEORIES OF SEX-ROLE DEVELOPMENT

What are the origins of sex differences in behavior? This question was on the minds of many researchers in the 1960s and 1970s, when it was assumed that actual sex differences were more numerous among children than contemporary research indicates. Biological, psychoanalytic, social learning, and cognitive theorists all had ideas to contribute about the origins of male and female characteristics. Naturally, biological theories emphasize the role of nature and regard sex-typed behaviors as less malleable than theories that emphasize the child's cognitions or experiences in the environment.

Even though contemporary research shows that actual sex differences in behavior are relatively few, they are still differences that must be explained. Most researchers today, however, are less interested in choosing one particular theoretical position over another than in identifying the complex interplay that occurs among nature, nurture, and the child's understanding in accounting for sex-role development.

Biological Theories

▶ **Roles of nature and nurture**

Biologically based explanations for sex differences focus largely on the influence of chromosomes, hormones, and the interaction of biological systems on behavior. Certain physical and behavioral characteristics can be influenced either directly by the sex chromosomes, indirectly through the interaction of chromosomes and hormones, or by hormones.

As we saw in Chapter 3, the presence of an X or Y sex chromosome begins a complex process that leads to sexual differentiation. Between six and twelve weeks after conception, the XY chromosomal configuration leads to the development of testes and the secretion of a class of male hormones called **androgens,** a process that leads to further sexual differentiation. The penis and scrotum develop in response to the metabolism of *testosterone,* an androgen that is actually present in both sexes, but in greater amounts in males (Whalen, 1984). In the absence of an XY configuration and greater amounts of androgens, at approximately twelve to fourteen weeks after conception the genitalia begin to develop into the female structures (Hood et al., 1987). These differences in biological structures form the bases for children to be labeled "boy" or "girl," the categorization of *biological sex,* which can set in motion a host of stereotyped expectations about the child's attributes and behaviors, as we shall soon see.

▶ **Roles of nature and nurture**

Hormones and Behavior   Prenatal exposure to hormones, particularly androgens, influences the developing fetus in ways that may have an impact on both biology and postnatal behavior. Most important for our discussion, androgens influence the developing organization of the central nervous system and the brain (Gorski, 1980; MacLusky & Naftolin, 1981). Sex differences have been found in the structure of certain neurons, including the size of their nuclei and the number of their *dendrites,* the branchlike structures of neurons that receive messages from other neurons (Moore, 1985). Hormone-related sex differences in structure and organization may, in turn, have important influences on behavior and abilities.

Take the example of aggression. Explanations of sex differences in aggression from a biological perspective have relied on two major sources: experiments in which levels of hormones have been systematically manipulated in animals and human studies that have found correlations between levels of androgens and aggressive behavior. The animal studies show that prenatally administered androgens do, in fact, increase the aggressive behaviors, such as threats and rough-and-tumble play, displayed by female rats, monkeys, and a number of other species (Goy, 1970; Parsons, 1980). Among humans, females may be prenatally exposed to large amounts of androgens either because their adrenocortical glands malfunction and allow excess androgens to circulate (a condition called *adrenogenital syndrome* or *AGS*) or because their mothers received drugs to prevent miscarriage that elevated androgen levels. These females are often born with masculinized genitals and behaviorally are more likely to engage in rough and active physical play than are females unexposed to prenatal androgens (Money & Ehrhardt, 1972). During puberty, moreover, when levels of testosterone in males begin to rise, aggressive behavior increases (Hood et al., 1987; Olweus et al., 1980; Susman et al., 1987).

Although this type of evidence supports a link between male hormones and aggression, some controversy about the relationship exists (Tieger, 1980). First, levels of hormones, including testosterone, change in response to changes in the environment (Hood et al., 1987). In stressful situations, for example, testosterone levels in males decrease (Parsons, 1980). Similarly,

androgen   Class of male or masculinizing hormones.

among nonhuman males, increases in androgen levels frequently follow, rather than precede, an aggressive encounter (Hood et al., 1987). Thus, the link between aggression and levels of androgens does not appear to be a direct one in which the presence of the hormone always precedes aggression. Moreover, studies of androgenized girls are difficult to interpret because parents were aware of their daughters' masculinized appearance and may have tolerated or even encouraged more "boylike" behaviors. Finally, as we will see later in this chapter, there is ample evidence to show how powerful a factor socialization can be in promoting aggression in boys. Even if biology sets some early predispositions toward aggression in males, the role of social experiences cannot be ruled out.

Prenatal exposure to female hormones, such as *estrogen*, appears to have minimal effects on children's development (Ehrhardt & Meyer-Bahlburg, 1981; Ehrhardt et al., 1984; Kester, 1984). In general, although parental ratings of children prenatally exposed to high doses of female hormones indicate greater levels of femininity, no differences are found when the behavior of these children is compared with that of unexposed children. The absence of a difference between these groups of children probably reflects the fact that all children are exposed to the female hormones produced by their mothers' bodies during the prenatal period.

If hormones do, indeed, affect sex-typed behaviors, their effects are both subtle and complex. In a longitudinal study of the relationship between sex hormones in the blood at birth and later behaviors, Jacklin, Maccoby, and their colleagues found that these substances affect males and females differently (Jacklin, Maccoby, & Doering, 1983; Jacklin et al., 1984; Jacklin, Wilcox, & Maccoby, 1988). One set of outcomes concerned *progesterone,* a hormone found in both males and females, but in greater amounts in females. In males, higher levels of progesterone in infancy are associated with greater physical strength and less timidity at age three years; in girls, however, higher levels of progesterone are linked to lower strength and are unrelated to timidity. Similarly, elevated levels of testosterone in infancy are unrelated to visual-spatial skills at age six years among boys; among girls, greater amounts of testosterone are associated with worse performance on tests of visual-spatial skills at age six years.

The sex-differentiating effects of sex hormones on male and female development are puzzling. It may be that males and females differ in the levels of hormones needed to produce an effect, such as poor visual-spatial skill. Sex hormones also may be metabolized by males and females in different fashions, resulting in paradoxical, or at least different, effects.

▶ **Roles of nature and nurture**

Brain Lateralization   A second way in which biology can influence sex differences in behavior is through the organization and functions of the brain. A prominent biological explanation for sex differences in verbal and visual-spatial skills involves the process known as *lateralization of the brain.* During the course of development, as we saw in Chapter 5, the two halves of the brain become increasingly specialized to handle different types of information, such as speech perception and speech production. According to one version of the lateralization hypothesis, girls have brains that mature more quickly and lateralize earlier than those of boys. Since verbal skills are thought to develop sooner than visual-spatial skills, and since rapid maturation of the brain is assumed to produce less lateralization, the verbal skills of girls are presumed to be more evenly distributed across hemispheres. Verbal processing in the right *and* left hemispheres, in turn, interferes with the visual-spatial processing that usually takes place predominantly in the right hemisphere. Because lateralization takes longer in boys, their cerebral hemispheres are hypothesized to become more specialized than in girls. The net result is that their visual-spatial skills are stronger. Some research evidence confirms that children (regardless of sex) who mature early score better on verbal tasks than on spatial tasks, whereas the reverse pattern holds true for late maturers (Waber, 1976).

On the other hand, nonbiological explanations of sex differences in visual-spatial skills also exist. One such explanation relies on the contrasting play experiences of boys and girls. According to this formulation, masculine play activities, such as using building blocks, facilitate the development of visual-spatial skills in boys (Block, 1983). Evidence for this explanation was found in a study in which preschool children were given practice in discerning a diamond within a patterned background. The data indicated that even though boys were initially superior on visual-spatial problems, their superiority disappeared after the practice sessions (Connor, Schackman, & Serbin, 1978). Thus, sex-typed play activities provide one alternative account for sex differences in visual-spatial skills.

▶ **Sociocultural influence**

Cross-Cultural Patterns of Sex Differences   The contexts in which sex-role development occurs are many and varied. Children who grow up in urban, suburban, and rural areas in industrialized nations and children who grow up in nonindustrialized societies all acquire the sex roles exhibited in their culture. If sex typing is a process that results solely from biological influences, then we would expect to see great unanimity in sex roles across periods of

Cultures sometimes vary in their beliefs about sex roles. For example, some cultures promote nurturance among boys, a characteristic that is considered feminine in our society.

history and in different cultures. If, on the other hand, sex roles reflect values that are peculiar to a given era or culture, then we would expect to see variability in the characteristics defined as masculine and feminine by different cultures or at different points in time. The meta-analyses showing that verbal superiority of girls has disappeared in the last two decades suggests that sociocultural forces play a role, for example.

Margaret Mead's (1967/1949) classic research on sex differences in Melanesian societies illustrates the differences that can emerge in cultures. In the 1930s, before the onset of modernizing influences, Mead studied three nonindustrial tribes living in New Guinea: the Arapesh, the Tchambuli, and the Mundugumor. These three tribes exhibited sex roles that differed both from each other and from those seen in our society. Among the Arapesh and Mundugumor tribes, roles were not strongly differentiated by sex although the two tribes exhibited very different personality characteristics and behavior. Arapesh men and women both adopted what we would identify as a "feminine" role. Both parents cared for children, were emotional, cooperative, and nonassertive. The Mundugumor men and women, in contrast, adopted "masculine" roles regardless of their biological sex. Men and women alike were extremely aggressive, and the women detested childbearing and child rearing. Mead (1967/1949) describes this tribe as devoting "all of their time to quarreling and headhunting" (p. 54). Finally, the roles Tchambuli men and women played in their society, though sex differentiated, were the reverse of what we consider masculine and feminine. Tchambuli men, adopting sex roles our society would deem feminine, were artistic, socially sensitive, and concerned with the feelings of other people. Tchambuli women were assertive and industrious, roles our society would deem as masculine. Indeed, in this society women handled business affairs while the men stayed at home, painting and practicing their dance steps.

The patterns of sex typing Mead observed in these three tribes provide evidence that the sex roles seen in our society are neither natural nor universal. Sex roles are prescribed by cultures to fill specific social needs and goals. But, as we can see from the Arapesh and the Mundugumor, sex differentiation in roles does not always occur. Thus, although biological factors in sex-role development cannot be ignored, neither can they account for the diversity of roles that occurs across cultures.

Psychodynamic Theories

▶ **Sensitive periods**
▶ **Development as continuous/stagelike**

Sigmund Freud and his heirs the neo-Freudians believe that sex-role development is largely an unconscious process that results from the interaction of biological sex differences and the differential identification processes experienced by boys and girls. The most important period in Freud's theory of sex-role socialization is the phallic stage, which begins around four years of age and lasts until the child is about age seven years. As we saw in Chapter 2, Freud believed that during this stage both boys and girls begin to develop erotic feelings toward the parent of the opposite sex (boys toward their mothers and girls toward their fathers) and rivalrous feelings toward the same-sex parent. Boys resolve their *Oedipal complex* and girls their *Electra complex* by *identifying* with the same-sex parent and adopting that parent's masculine or feminine behaviors. During the subsequent latency stage, personality characteristics become consolidated. Although this process occurs unconsciously, Freud believed that children's adoption of differing masculine and feminine roles in their play as well as behavioral sex differences facilitates the consolidation of masculine and feminine roles that begins in the Oedipal and Electra complexes.

Thus, according to the Freudians, sex-role development is a process that emerges as a result of children's identification with the same-sex parent. This process occurs largely at an unconscious level and is not under the direct control of either the child or of other socialization agents (parents, schools, the media, peers, and so forth). From the psychodynamic perspective, children's sex-role development and personality development are intimately connected. The process of identification that determines our sex typing is one of the most important aspects of personality development.

Freud's psychoanalytic theory of sex-role development, we must note, appears unsuccessful in explaining the process of sex-role development. The major theoretical mechanism, identification, should result in minimal differences between the sex typing of children and that observed in their parents, yet differences between father and son or mother and daughter are frequently found. For example, "feminized" boys can have very masculine fathers. Moreover, Freud's theory fails to predict a variety of important phenomena such as the development of sex stereotyping, the modification of sex-typed behavior by peers, and other trends to be discussed later in this chapter. Although some sex typing begins to appear during the period Freud suggested, several aspects of the theory have been proven false.

Social Learning Theories

▶ **Roles of nature and nurture**

One of the primary mechanisms accounting for sex differences in behavior, social learning theorists maintain, is sex-differentiated treatment of boys and girls. According to this position, boys and girls are differently reinforced and punished for specific behaviors, which leads them to behave in sex-typed ways. Girls, for example, may be rewarded for playing with dolls and punished for climbing trees, whereas boys may receive just the opposite treatment. Thus, because children are motivated to seek reinforcement and avoid punishment, they will behave in a sex-typed fashion.

Children attend both to the consequences of their own behavior and to the consequences others face for their behavior. Therefore, imitation, or modeling, is perhaps an even more powerful means by which children learn sex roles. By observing the experiences of other people, children develop expectancies for reinforcement and punishment of their own behavior. Expectancies may influence an individual's behavior as strongly as do the actual experiences of reward or punishment (Bandura, 1969, 1977a). Children have numerous opportunities to observe models behaving in sex-stereotypic ways in the home, in the outside world, and in the media. Each time a child sees that Dad fixes things around the house and Mom does most of the cooking and cleaning, or that most little boys play baseball while little girls play house and with dolls, she is adding to her storehouse of sex-typed behaviors.

Several factors influence whether children will imitate the sex-typed behaviors of others. Albert Bandura (1977a) has proposed that children's *attention*

According to social learning theory, a powerful vehicle for the transmission of sex roles is imitation. Parents can be especially potent models for sex-typed behaviors.

to models in the first place is influenced by both the sex of the model and the **sex typicality** of the model's behavior—how characteristic it is of the model's own sex. According to this hypothesis, boys would, in general, be more likely than girls to attend to the behavior of male models, although they would be less likely to attend to a male model who was exhibiting "feminine" behavior (Masters, Ford et al., 1979; Perry & Bussey, 1979). The prediction that individuals will pay greater attention to same-sex models is based on the notion that observation of same-sex models should provide us with greater information about potential consequences for our own behavior. As a corollary, children *recognize* that certain behaviors are sex typed, especially as they observe whether the behavior of models is sex typical or not. Finally, Bandura (1977) proposes that *motivational* factors, such as reward seeking and attempts to retain a sense of mastery, will influence behavior in a variety of realms. The incorporation of these factors—attention, recognition, and motivation—into traditional social learning theories has led to a greater emphasis on the ways that nonobservable cognitive processes influence observable behavior (Bandura, 1977a).

Several studies have supported the idea that children are more likely to imitate same-sex than other-sex models (Bussey & Bandura, 1984; Bussey & Perry, 1982). Thus, same-sex parents, peers, and characters in the media are powerful influences on the child. In addition, the sex typicality of the model's behavior also helps determine whether imitation will occur; children are more likely to imitate models who behave in sex-typical ways.

David Perry and Kay Bussey (1979) elaborated the ways that information about the sex typicality of a model influences imitation. Eight-year-old boys and girls were randomly assigned to one of two experimental conditions: prior film or no film. In the first phase of the experiment, children in the prior-film condition watched a movie of eight adult panelists (four men and four women) who indicated their preferences for a series of pairs of novel, sex-neutral objects such as banana-apple and horse-cow. In indicating which object in each pair they preferred, three females and one male consistently made the same choices, whereas three males and one female consistently chose the other

▶ **Interaction among domains**

sex-typical behavior Behavior usually associated with one sex.

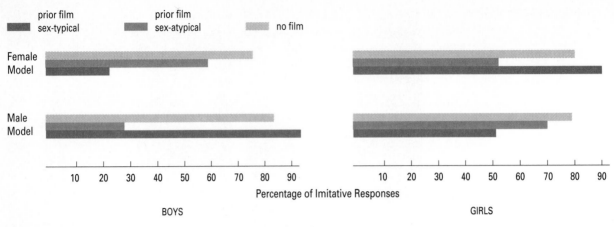

Source: Adapted from Perry & Bussey, 1979.

FIGURE 12.4

The Influence of a Model's Sex and Sex Typicality on Imitation

In a study by Perry and Bussey, half of the children first saw a videotape depicting a group of adults whose behavior was either typical or atypical of their sex (the prior-film condition). The remaining children were in the no-film condition—they did not view the initial videotape. The results indicated that both boys and girls were likely to imitate a same-sex model whose behavior was sex typical or about whom they had no prior information. Children also imitated other-sex models whose behavior was sex atypical. Children use complex information to decide whether they will imitate a model.

object in the pair. Thus, one male and one female made choices that were inconsistent with those made by their same-sex peers; their behavior was consistently **sex atypical,** or inconsistent with the norm for a particular sex.

During phase 2 of the experiment, children in both conditions watched either a male or a female panel member making choices between a second set of sex-neutral pairs of objects. For children in the no-film condition, this phase was the first time they had seen a model. Thus, the only information they had was the model's sex and his or her choices. In contrast, children in the prior-film condition had additional information from phase 1 on the sex typicality of the model's behavior. At this point in the experiment, children were asked to choose between pairs of objects identical to those they had just seen the model choose between. Did children use information about the prior sex typicality of a model's behavior in imitating the model?

As Figure 12.4 shows, children in the prior-film condition were more likely to imitate the choices of same-sex sex-typical models and other-sex sex-atypical models than they were to imitate same-sex models whose prior behavior had been sex atypical. Children in the no-film condition, who had no prior information about the models or their sex typing, were as likely to imitate male models as female models. These results indicate that children use fairly complex sources of information in determining whether to imitate a model.

Social learning theories offer the best explanation for the roles that parents, peers, and others play in sex-role development. They provide as well a credible set of explanations for children's imitation of sex-typical behavior. Traditional social learning explanations, however, appear to be limited by the theoretical emphasis on observable behavior rather than on cognitive processes. The recent inclusion of cognitive and emotional phenomena such as attention, recognition, and motivation may facilitate the ability of this theory to explain nonbehavioral aspects of sex-role development.

Cognitive-Developmental Theories

sex-atypical behavior Behavior inconsistent with the norm for a particular sex.

Cognitive-developmental theories are based on Jean Piaget's pioneer work in this area and employ concepts drawn from his approach. Their primary focus is the ways in which children understand sex roles in general and themselves as males and females in particular. In cognitive-developmental theories, *gender* is emphasized as a conceptual category, a way of classifying people on the basis of their overt appearance or behaviors, as opposed to *biological sex,* the actual physical characteristics of males and females, or *sex role,* the social roles, behaviors, and characteristics associated with maleness and femaleness.

▶ **Development as continuous/ stagelike**

▶ **Interaction among domains**

Kohlberg's Cognitive-Developmental Theory Lawrence Kohlberg (1966) proposed that sex-roles emerge as a consequence of stagelike developments in cognition. The most basic of these cognitive milestones is acquisition of **gender identity,** the knowledge that one is a female or male. This concept, which is acquired around the age of thirty months, is crucial to later sex-role development because it provides a basic categorizing principle along which children begin to divide the world.

After acquiring gender identity, around their fourth birthday children develop **gender stability,** a sense that gender does not change over time. Children who have acquired gender stability recognize that they were born one sex and will grow up to be a member of that sex. Despite this knowledge, however, they may not yet be aware of the fact that genitalia determine biological sex. Rather, children assume that external factors (such as clothing or hair length) are the determinants of sex. Thus, a young boy may believe that he was a baby boy and will grow up to be a "daddy" (gender stability), but only if his behavior and physical characteristics (such as hair length) remain masculine.

Children's lack of awareness of the genital basis of gender indicates their lack of **gender constancy.** This term refers to the child's awareness that changes in external characteristics, behaviors, or desires are not accompanied by a change in biological sex. Thus, a boy may wear a dress and a girl may play with toy soldiers without altering their respective biological sexes. Kohlberg proposes that gender constancy, like other forms of Piagetian cognitive skills (such as conservation skills), is acquired at about age seven years.

For Kohlberg, the acquisition of gender constancy marks the child's mature awareness of the concept of sex differentiation. Moreover, because children value both their own sex and themselves, they are motivated to behave in a sex-typed fashion. From Kohlberg's perspective, cognitive development facilitates *self-socialization* among children. Kohlberg believes that children are internally motivated by their positive self- and same-sex evaluations to behave in a manner consonant with their conceptions of what is sex appropriate. External motivators (such as reinforcements and punishments) are of minimal importance in the process of self-socialization.

▶ **The child's active role**

gender identity Knowledge, usually gained by age three years, that one is male or female.

gender stability Knowledge, usually gained by age four years, that one's gender does not change over time.

gender constancy Knowledge, usually gained around age six or seven years, that one's gender does not change as a result of alterations in appearance, behaviors, or desires.

Research has confirmed that children progress from attaining gender identity to gender stability and, finally, gender constancy from about two to six years of age (Fagot, 1985; Slaby & Frey, 1975). In recent years, the notion that children actively organize social information on the basis of gender has been even further elaborated.

Gender Schema Theory Another cognitive developmental theory is *gender schema theory* (Bem, 1981; Martin & Halverson, 1981, 1987). Like Kohlberg's theory, gender schema theory adopts Piagetian concepts and stresses the importance of the acquisition of gender identity and children's intrinsic motivations to behave in a sex-typical manner. Unlike Kohlberg, however, gender

▶ **The child's active role**

schema theory does not stress the attainment of gender constancy but rather focuses on the influence of children's active construction of gender knowledge on sex-typing in their behavior (Bem, 1981; Martin & Halverson, 1987; Signorella, 1987).

Carol Martin and Charles Halverson (1981) have proposed that children first acquire gender identity and then, in their attempts to create order in their social worlds, begin to construct two **gender schemas,** or cognitive organizing structures for information relevant to sex typing. The first one, the *same-sex/opposite-sex schema,* refers to the child's knowledge of one sex or the other. This is a fairly primitive cognitive structure comprised largely of sex stereotypes, such as "boys fix cars" and "girls sew." Children also develop a second, more elaborate, gender schema about behaviors relevant to their own sex. This *own-sex schema* provides a basis for guiding children's behavior. Thus, even though both boys and girls know that girls sew, girls are more likely to be motivated to learn to sew, whereas they may not want to learn how to fix a car. Researchers have confirmed that children explore non-sex-typed novel objects labeled as intended for their sex more than they explore such objects labeled for the other sex. Moreover, up to one week later, children remember more details about the "same-sex" objects than they do about the "other-sex" objects, even when they are offered a reward for remembering details (Bradbard et al., 1986).

According to Martin and Halverson (1981), children's gender schemas serve as a potent means of organizing information about their social worlds. Gender schemas may also have the effect of distorting information inconsistent with the schema. Thus, when children see a female doctor, for example, they may distort the information to make it consistent with their gender schema, turning the doctor, in their minds, into a nurse (Cordua, McGraw, & Drabman, 1979). Many studies have documented these kinds of distortions in children's memories for stereotype-inconsistent information (Carter & Levy, 1988; Martin & Halverson, 1987).

Cognitive-developmental theories are an effective way of explaining how children's own knowledge contributes to their sex-role development. Concepts such as gender identity and self-socialization have proven to be useful ways to explain sex typing. In addition, we have seen how children employ their prior conceptions of the sex typicality of models in deciding whether to imitate modeled behavior. This phenomenon is predicted directly by cognitive-developmental theories. Cognitive-developmental theories also appear to offer the best explanation for phenomena such as children's distortion of information that is inconsistent with sex stereotypes. Cognitive-developmental theories fall short, however, in explaining certain behavioral patterns, such as sex differences in children's play. As we shall soon see, the social learning perspective, with its emphasis on the direct reinforcements provided by parents and peers, provides a more satisfactory account of such phenomena.

▶ **Interaction among domains**

Theories of Sex-Role Development: An Overview

gender schema   Cognitive organizing structure for information relevant to sex typing.

Each of the preceding theories has some value for explaining the source of sex differences. The biological theories provide a basis for understanding the physiological factors that might influence masculinity and femininity. Social learning theory provides a mechanism for explaining how children learn discrete aspects of sex-typed behavior, and the cognitive-developmental approaches explain how children's concepts of gender become integrated in their minds. Although each of the theories explains a specific feature of sex typing better than the other theories do, none of them taken alone is adequate to explain the multifaceted nature of sex-role development.

HOW CHILDREN'S KNOWLEDGE OF SEX ROLES DEVELOPS

Contemporary explanations of sex-role development emphasize the importance of children's understanding of gender concepts on sex typing in their behavior. Kohlberg's theory, for example, stressed how the notions of gender identity, stability, and constancy set the stage for the emergence of sex-typed behaviors, and gender schema theory underlines the importance of the child's active constructions of gender. Exactly what do children know about sex roles at various ages and, further, how does this knowledge influence their actual behavior?

Gender Identity

Theories of sex-role development, especially cognitive theories, are virtually unanimous in contending that children's gender identity plays a vital role in sex typing. Gender identity is such a basic psychological categorization that, except in rare circumstances, individuals are unlikely to desire a change, nor is a change likely to be easy. John Money and Anke Ehrhardt (1972) maintain that once a child has attained gender identity, any attempt to change it would have negative outcomes such as depression or severe psychopathology. In clinical studies of children who were born one sex but subsequently relabeled as another (for example, because of ambiguous genitalia or surgical accidents), Money and Ehrhardt conclude that gender reassignment is only successful if it occurs before three or four years of age.

▶ **Sensitive periods**

Most children learn to label themselves correctly as female or male and begin to show a preference for toys consistent with their own gender between the ages of two and three years (Huston, 1985; O'Brien, Huston, & Risley, 1983). Precisely when children develop a gender identity can forecast subsequent patterns of sex typing. Beverly Fagot and Mary Leinbach (1989) found that children who developed gender identity early (before the age of twenty-eight months) differed from those who developed gender identity later on a variety of dimensions. Boys and girls who were early identifiers engaged in significantly more sex-typical play, such as play with building toys for boys and doll play for girls, than did late identifiers. At four years of age, early identifiers expressed greater knowledge of sex-role stereotypes than late identifiers did.

How does gender identity develop? Perhaps parents and others provide this information directly by saying things to their young children like, "There's another little boy just like you" or "Be a good girl now, won't you?" Many

Although gender constancy is an important developmental achievement, children display sex-typed behaviors and preferences for same-sex peers even before this concept emerges.

researchers contend, though, that the messages about sex roles are so clear and pervasive in our society that children simply spontaneously categorize the world—and themselves—in this way.

Gender Constancy

Unlike gender identity, gender constancy plays a less clearly defined part in early sex-role development. Some researchers find that children's knowledge of gender as a fixed, unchangeable characteristic is related to the models they select to imitate. In one study, researchers measured gender constancy by asking children to identify their sex and to respond to a series of questions about whether a doll changed sex when alterations were made in the doll's hair length and clothing. Boys who had acquired gender constancy spent more time watching a film of a boy model than a film of a girl model. On the other hand, girls and boys who were not gender constant paid approximately equal amounts of attention to both models (Slaby & Frey, 1975). Other investigators, however, report that children are more likely to imitate same-sex than opposite-sex models, regardless of their stage of gender constancy (Bussey & Bandura, 1984).

Gender constancy also is unrelated to sex-stereotype knowledge or sex-typed preferences for toys or activities (Carter & Levy, 1988; Marcus & Overton, 1978). In fact, Carol Martin and Jane Little (1990) note that children show a tendency to select sex-typed toys or play with same-sex peers well before the complex knowledge that constitutes gender constancy emerges. In their study, preschoolers who could simply discriminate and label the sexes already showed sex-typed behaviors. Thus, even though the acquisition of gender constancy is a significant cognitive accomplishment in its own right, it may not prompt or direct other aspects of sex-typed behavior.

Gender Schemas

Most children can select pictures labeled as "boy" or "girl" at about two to two and a half years of age (Etaugh, Grinnell, & Etaugh, 1989; Leinbach & Fagot, 1986; Thompson, 1975). And as we saw earlier, they also apply gender labels to themselves and choose toys appropriate for their sex at about the same age. Thus, children show the ability to categorize social information on the basis of gender at an early age. Some children, however, seem to be more likely to use gender as a classification scheme than others, and this tendency is related to their sex-typed behaviors.

As we saw earlier in this chapter, gender schemas are cognitive constructions that influence children's behavior and their interpretation of gender-relevant information. Some children tend to be *gender schematic*—that is, they possess a strong gender schema, exhibit more consistent sex typing in their behavior, and process information along gender lines. In contrast, children who are *gender aschematic* possess a weaker gender schema, are less sex typed behaviorally, and focus their attention on aspects of information that are not related to gender.

How do researchers determine whether children are gender schematic or aschematic? A popular technique is to measure the amount of time children take to choose between pairs of toys that are differently (masculine-feminine pairs) or similarly (feminine-feminine pairs) sex typed. Researchers assume that gender-schematic children should choose relatively quickly between masculine-feminine pairs of toys and take relatively longer to choose from masculine-masculine and feminine-feminine toy pairs. Gender-aschematic children, on the other hand, should take comparable amounts of time to choose between all pairs of toys (Carter & Levy, 1988).

▶ **Interaction among domains**   Results from a number of studies indicate that gender schemas influence the way in which children process sex-typed information. For example, gender-schematic children find it difficult to remember information about pictures of people engaged in sex-atypical activities, such as a boy playing with a doll, whereas they can easily remember information about people engaged in sex-typical activities, such as a girl playing with a tea set (Signorella, 1987). Similarly, children distort stereotype-inconsistent information by actually changing the sex of the person engaged in the sex-atypical behavior. Gender-schematic children who see a picture of a boy playing with a doll are more likely to remember seeing a picture of a girl playing with a doll than a picture of a boy playing with a sex-typical toy (Carter & Levy, 1988).

The development of gender schemas in young children has important implications for sex typing in children's behavior. Because gender-schematic children often distort information according to their beliefs about gender, they are unlikely to remember events that are inconsistent with those beliefs. Thus, they are less likely to believe that violations of sex-role norms are acceptable because they remember so few instances (if any) of people who behaved in a sex-atypical fashion. Gender-aschematic children, in contrast, are more likely to believe that stereotypes are flexible and that they are permitted to engage in a wider variety of behaviors regardless of the sex typing of those activities.

Why do many children become gender schematic? According to Bem (1983), children become gender schematic to the extent that they experience gender as a relevant social category. Thus, for example, when differences between males and females are frequently pointed out to them by parents, teachers, or peers, children themselves will use gender as a way of classifying social information. Furthermore, both peers and adults stress conformity to sex-typical roles, a fact that makes it difficult for most children in our society to become truly gender aschematic (Bem, 1983).

Sex-Role Stereotypes

Children begin to acquire *sex-role stereotypes* and employ them as guides for their behavior from very early ages on. For example, Spencer Thompson (1975) examined the levels of sex-stereotype knowledge and sex-typed preferences exhibited among a group of twenty-four-, thirty-, and thirty-six-month-old children. Children's sex-typed preferences were assessed by asking them to choose between pairs of photographs of identical objects, one of which was stated to be "for girls" and the other "for boys." Stereotype knowledge was assessed by asking children to sort photos of common sex-typed objects into boxes called things "for boys and men" and "for girls and women."

Children's performance on these tasks indicated significant developmental differences in children's sex-typed preferences and knowledge of stereotypes. Although twenty-four-month-olds did not show consistent sex-typed preferences, thirty-month-old children consistently preferred "same-sex" over "opposite-sex" objects. This tendency was even stronger among the thirty-six-month-old children tested.

Similarly, older children were more accurate in identifying sex-role stereotypes than the younger children were, although the youngest children were surprisingly accurate. Twenty-four-month-olds were able to identify 61 percent of the stereotypes accurately; thirty-month-olds identified 78 percent correctly; and thirty-six-month-olds identified 86 percent of the stereotypes accurately. These scores were consistently above the score (50 percent) we might expect children to receive if they were responding randomly to the questions. Thus, these data indicate that children have already begun to develop a knowledge of sex-role stereotypes by the age of two years and that they develop preferences for behaviors and objects associated with their own sex by thirty months of age.

As we saw in Chapter 1, Deanna Kuhn and her colleagues also have shown that children as young as two to three years of age begin to associate specific behaviors and future roles with each sex with startling levels of accuracy (Kuhn, Nash, & Brucken, 1978). Kuhn's data indicate that young preschoolers believe that girls are nonaggressive, talk a lot, play with dolls, and will grow up to be a nurse or a teacher. They say, in contrast, that boys are aggressive, play with trucks and cars, and will grow up to be the boss. It would be interesting for researchers to examine whether such dramatic findings occur now fifteen years later, in light of the increasing participation of mothers in the work force and their movement into professional roles in which they are indeed the "boss."

As children grow older, their knowledge of stereotypes also becomes more flexible. When D. Bruce Carter and Charlotte Patterson (1982) studied a group of kindergarten through eighth-graders, their data indicated that both stereotype knowledge and stereotype flexibility increase with age. Older children were more likely to indicate that sex stereotypes could be broken (for example, a man could be a nurse) than were younger children. Even when children believe that stereotypes can be violated, however, they do not want to associate with people who engage in counterstereotypical behavior (Carter & McCloskey, 1984). Thus, recognition of flexibility of sex stereotypes does not indicate that children find sex-atypical behavior acceptable, but merely that they recognize that exceptions can occur.

The Chronology below summarizes the attainment of sex-role stereotypes and other aspects of sex-role development described in this chapter. How do children acquire sex-role stereotypes and other knowledge about gender so thoroughly and so early in life? Children may be taught this information by

---

CHRONOLOGY	Sex-Role Development
PRENATAL PERIOD	Sex chromosomes and genitalia develop. Sex hormones influence brain and physical development.
BIRTH	Infant receives label as boy or girl.
2–3 YEARS	Child labels own gender. Identifies pictures labeled as "boy" or "girl." Shows knowledge of sex-role stereotypes. Prefers same-sex playmates and toys. If boy, shows more aggression. If girl, shows better ability to recognize faces.
4–5 YEARS	Attains gender stability. Shows even stronger preferences for same-sex playmates and toys. Displays decline in cross-sex behavior. Enforces sex-role norms in peers.
6–10 YEARS	Attains gender constancy. Responds increasingly negatively to cross-gender play in peers. If girl, shows greater ability to decode nonverbal social cues. If boy, shows better performance in mental rotation tasks. Shows more flexibility in sex-role stereotypes.
16–18 YEARS	Shows less interest in sex-segregated interactions. If girl, shows more social smiles and gazing. If boy, shows better performance in spatial-perception tasks. Shows greater tolerance for sex-atypical behaviors. Sex differences in aggression diminish.

This chart describes the sequence of sex-role development based on the findings of research. Children often show individual differences in the exact ages at which they display the various developmental achievements outlined here.

their parents, peers, teachers, or the media, or they may infer that a stereo-type or actual sex difference exists by observing systematic patterns of behaviors in the males and females around them (Martin & Halverson, 1987). In fact, the messages sent from the social world are so profound that many psychologists look to the child's socialization experiences as a primary way of explaining sex-role development.

THE SOCIALIZATION OF SEX ROLES

▶ **Roles of nature and nurture**

The earliest messages about the social world, of course, come from the child's parents, and in this regard communication about sex roles is no different from any other aspect of social development. From the moment of birth, when parents in our culture ask, "Is it a boy or a girl?" the sex of their child is a very prominent characteristic—one that elicits specific behaviors and reactions from mothers and fathers. As children branch out to social relationships with their peers, sex-role socialization continues in very powerful ways—in the games children play, the relationships they form, and how they react to each other's behaviors. Finally, another significant influence on sex-role development is the child's experiences in schools, in which teachers and the instructional materials they use can confirm (or disconfirm) early sex-role beliefs and behaviors.

The Influence of Parents

Traditionally, developmental psychologists have believed that one of the most important sources of sex-typing information for children is the behavior of their parents and the sex-typing environment they create (Katz, 1987). Sometimes the messages are subtle. Parents commonly provide their children with sex-differentiated toys and room furnishings (Rheingold & Cook, 1975). They buy sports equipment, tools, and vehicles for their sons and dolls and doll furniture for their daughters. Boys' rooms are typically decorated in blue, girls' in yellow (Pomerleau et al., 1990). When parents provide boys and girls with differing physical environments, they send messages that boys are indeed different from girls and set sex-related limits on the types of behavior that are acceptable and appropriate.

Other times the messages are more direct. Research has shown that parents, especially fathers, treat children differently on the basis of sex in early infancy, beginning at ages younger than those at which actual behavioral sex differences emerge (Fagot & Leinbach, 1987). Adults play more roughly with a male infant, tossing him in the air and tickling him vigorously, than they do with female infants (Huston, 1983). During infancy and childhood, girls are more likely than boys to be protected and sheltered by adults, whereas boy babies are given greater opportunities to explore their environments than girl babies are given (Block, 1983; Burns, Mitchell, & Obradovich, 1989). Adult females respond more quickly to crying babies whom they think are little girls, and parents encourage more nurturance in the play of their daughters than in the play of their sons (Condry, Condry, & Pogatshynik, 1978; Huston, 1983).

A revealing series of studies has been conducted to determine whether sex-differentiated treatment of infants results from infant behaviors or from sex stereotypes adults hold. In these "Baby X" studies, adults, who are often parents, are asked to interact with or observe a baby who is labeled as either male or female regardless of the child's actual sex. Information about a baby's sex has proved to be an important determinant of adults' behavior. Adults interpret the motivations of babies differently depending on the sex they believe the child to be. When subjects were asked to interpret why a baby was crying, people who thought the baby was a boy said "he" was angry, whereas those who thought the baby was a girl said "she" was frightened (Condry & Condry, 1976). Similarly, adults interacting with "boy" babies rarely offer them dolls even when these infants expressed an interest in dolls by reaching or grabbing at them (Seavey, Katz, & Zalk, 1975). Clearly the perceived, not the actual, sex of a child influences adults' responses in at least some instances.

Direct Reinforcement Parents take an active role in teaching and encouraging sex-typical behavior in their children, at least according to some research findings. For example, parents reinforce sex typing in the behavior of their sons and daughters beginning in toddlerhood (Fagot & Leinbach, 1987). Children, but especially boys, are likely to be encouraged to engage in sex-typical behavior. Parents respond positively to boys who play with blocks and manipulate objects and reinforce girls' play with dolls and requests for help. Fathers appear to be especially concerned about what they perceive as masculinity in their sons and less concerned about femininity in their daughters, at least during the preschool years (Jacklin, DiPietro, & Maccoby, 1984). Such concern is often expressed in parental interviews as well as in the consistently negative manner in which fathers respond to sex-atypical behavior in their sons.

A study of preschool children and their parents vividly illustrates these patterns of parental responses (Langlois & Downs, 1980). In this study, children served as the confederates of the experimenter, and parents were the actual subjects. Children played with a variety of toys while their mothers and fathers watched. Unbeknownst to the parents, however, the children had been instructed to play with both male-typed and female-typed toys because the researchers were interested in the responses of parents to both sex-typical and sex-atypical behavior.

Mothers consistently reinforced their daughters' play with sex-typical toys and punished play with sex-atypical toys. Their responses to their sons' behavior were more mixed: they alternately punished and reinforced sex-atypical play and responded with indifference to sex-typical play. In contrast, fathers appeared to be the consistent enforcers of sex-role norms. Both sons and daughters were punished for playing with sex-atypical toys and rewarded when they played with sex-typical toys.

A recent meta-analysis of 172 studies of parents' differential socialization of girls and boys suggests, however, that we must be cautious about how much weight we give to the role of direct parental reinforcement in accounting for the various facets of sex-role development. In general, the overall impact of parental socialization was judged to be small in most areas of socialization, including achievement expectations, dependency, and aggression. The only socialization area that showed a significant effect was in parental encouragement of sex-typed activities, such as doll play for girls and playing with tools for boys (Lytton & Romney, 1991). It is in these contexts in particular, then, that children may acquire well-defined ideas about maleness and femaleness. Sex-typed activities may also promote the actual sex differences in behavior that we identified earlier in this chapter—namely, aggression, visual-spatial skill, and the ability to interpret social cues.

Parental Attitudes   Another way in which parents influence sex typing in their children is more indirect—through their own general beliefs about masculine and feminine roles. Many parents believe that children as young as two years old differ along sex-stereotypic lines (McGuire, 1988). They report, for example, that their own sons like sports, enjoy using tools, and are energetic. On the other hand, parents of girls say their daughters like to be admired, play with dolls, and like clothes. Such beliefs are often translated into sex-differentiated treatment in the types of chores boys and girls are assigned to do around the house—boys take out the garbage and mow the lawn; girls do more chores within the house, such as cleaning and cooking (Lackey, 1989).

The father's role in the sex-role development of his children is apparently very important (Jacklin et al., 1984). Parents, but especially fathers, are likely to stress academic and nonacademic achievement more for their sons than for their daughters (Eccles, 1983). In elementary school, parents have higher academic achievement expectations for their daughters than for their sons (Maccoby & Jacklin, 1974). Beginning in adolescence, however, parents expect their sons to perform better in academics than their daughters, especially in areas such as mathematics (Eccles, 1983). Parents may convey such expectations directly (for example, through statements such as, "Girls are never very good at math") or indirectly (for example, through encouraging boys and girls to pursue differing occupational goals). Parents' encouragement of children's play with traditionally sex-typed toys may also have an impact on their academic endeavors. For example, parents may discourage daughters from male-typed play, such as with blocks or construction toys, a pattern that may have the unintended consequence of inhibiting the development of visual-spatial skills in girls.

▶ **Sociocultural influence**

Sex Typing in Nontraditional Families   A series of profound changes that have taken place in the traditional American family over the last several decades may have an impact on the sex-typing process. First, an increasing number of children spend a large part of their lives in families headed by a single parent, usually the mother (Huston, 1983). Theoretically, the absence of significant male models from the home should have an effect on the process of identification (for Freudians) or imitation (for social learning researchers), especially among boys. Second, as we described in Chapter 10, mothers increasingly are employed outside the home while their children are still young. Thus, these women may be providing their children with alternative models for feminine behavior. Contemporary researchers are interested in examining whether children from nontraditional families exhibit greater flexibility in sex typing and a less traditional adherence to sex-role norms.

A large number of studies have been conducted on the development of sex typing in children from families in which mothers are employed outside the home. In general, maternal employment facilitates the development of flexibil-

Children whose mothers work possess more flexible sex-role concepts compared with children whose mothers do not work outside the home. Girls also show higher levels of achievement motivation when their mothers are employed outside the home.

ity in children's conceptions of sex roles. Children with employed mothers are more likely to believe that both males and females can exhibit a wider variety of behaviors and personality characteristics than children whose mothers are not employed outside the home. The effects on the sex typing of daughters of employed mothers are particularly dramatic. Mothers who work outside the home have daughters who show higher levels of achievement motivation and are more likely to have personality styles that blend male-typed and female-typed traits than are the daughters of mothers who do not work outside the home (Hoffman, 1979; Huston, 1983). The effects of maternal employment on sons are mixed. Boys whose mothers work outside the home are more likely to have flexible views of women's roles than are the sons of nonworking mothers, but sons of both types of mothers have equally masculine personalities and display equally masculine types of behavior (Hoffman, 1979).

Psychologists are also interested in the effects of nontraditional fathers—that is, those who take primary responsibility for child care—on children's sex-role development. Despite the high level of interest in the topic, however, little work to date has been conducted on this group of men because very few fathers adopt even a moderate amount of child-care responsibility. Indeed, studies of labor distribution in households in which both parents work indicate that husbands' child-rearing behavior increases very little when their wives go to work (Nielsen, 1990).

Raising Children in a Nonsexist Fashion We are currently witnessing a shift in thinking about sex-role socialization in our society. Increasingly, some experts are questioning the desirability of socializing children into differing roles on the basis of sex alone—that is, they advocate raising children in a *nonsexist* fashion (Bem, 1983; Pogrebin, 1980). Advocates of nonsexist child rearing point out that traditional sex typing encourages children to learn specific skills and roles that may be inconsistent with their interests or abilities.

Sex typing, they argue, narrows the field of choices that children can make, forcing them to choose among alternatives that limit the myriad possible behaviors available to human beings.

Sandra Bem (1983) has made several suggestions for ways in which parents can minimize sex typing in their children. First, she suggests that parents provide their children with information about the biological bases of gender at about the time children form their gender identities. Children should be appraised of the fact that genitals—not clothing, appearance, or behavior—determine gender. Second, parents should screen reading materials, television, and movies so that children have opportunities to view both sexes engaged in sex-typical and sex-atypical activities. Finally, Bem suggests that parents provide their children with a "sexism schema." According to Bem, just as we may teach our children to recognize that other families have social values that are different from those held in our family, we can teach children that other people may hold beliefs about the sexes that are different from our own. The fact that other people hold such beliefs does not mean that we must follow their lead any more than we must follow their religion or political views. By preparing children for the fact that they will encounter sexism in the world outside the family, Bem maintains that parents will foster the retention of nonsexist ideals in these children.

Because gender is strongly emphasized in contemporary culture, raising children to be nonsexist may be an arduous, if not impossible, task for most parents (Bem, 1983). Children are exposed to sex-typing messages in their interactions with their peers and teachers as well as from the media—for, as we will now see, parents are only one of the many factors that influence sex typing during childhood.

The Influence of Peers

Another major influence on children's sex-role development is the peer group. Peer groups not only provide children with opportunities for particular kinds of play, but also offer a valuable forum in which children can learn about social behavior and social interactions by watching models and obtaining feedback about their own behaviors. From the moment children begin to interact with their peers, they enter a situation in which adult input is indirect and the opinions and behaviors of age mates become increasingly important. And though peers influence children in a variety of social dimensions, nowhere is their influence more marked than in the area of sex-role socialization (Carter, 1987).

Early Play Patterns   The influence of peers on sex typing in children's behavior can be observed even among very young children. Carol Jacklin and Eleanor Maccoby (1978) observed pairs of unacquainted same-sex and mixed-sex pairs of two-year-olds to determine the influence of peers on toddlers' behavior. Children were dressed in a sex-neutral fashion (in yellow jumpsuits) and allowed to play in a room with their mothers present but nondirective. As Figure 12.5 shows, the behavior of toddlers varied as a function of the sex of their play partner even though the toddlers were unaware of the true sex of the other child. In other words, the *behaviors* of the neutrally dressed children seemed to precipitate different reactions in their play partners. In general,

FIGURE 12.5

Social Behavior as a Function of the Child's Play Partner

In a study by Jacklin and Maccoby, unacquainted two-year-olds were observed as they interacted with either a same-sex or opposite-sex partner. The amount of social behavior (both positive overtures and negative acts such as aggression) was greater when children played with a peer of the same sex.

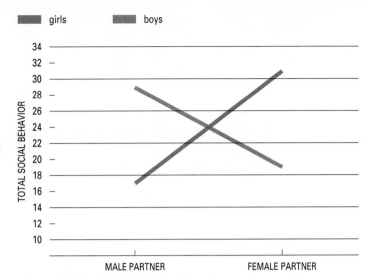

Source: Adapted from Jacklin & Maccoby, 1978.

children displayed more social behaviors—both positive overtures and negative acts—when they played with a peer of the same sex. Girls were more likely to be passive when they played with a boy peer than when they played with a girl peer. In addition, girls in girl-girl pairs exhibited greater sharing of toys and were less likely to become upset and cry than when they were in mixed-sex pairs. Finally, boys were less likely to obey a verbal prohibition from a girl than from a boy. Already at this young age, the dynamics of peer interactions were markedly influenced by the sex of the partners.

Peer Enforcement of Sex Roles Peers continue to exert a strong influence on children's adoption of sex-typed behaviors as they begin preschool. A number of studies have shown, for example, that children respond differentially to sex-typical and sex-atypical behavior in their peers. Children may reward behavior they like by complimenting a child or by engaging in mutual play, and they may punish a behavior they do not approve of by name calling. Preschoolers and kindergartners reliably punish boys who engage in sex-atypical behavior, such as playing with dolls, while rewarding them for engaging in sex-typical behavior, such as playing with trucks (Fagot, 1977; Lamb, Easterbrooks, & Holden, 1980; Lamb & Roopnarine, 1979). In contrast, girls are rewarded for engaging in sex-typical behavior, such as playing house, but apparently there are no consequences for them when they engage in sex-atypical behavior (Fagot, 1977). The differential responses of peers toward boys and girls who engage in sex-atypical behavior persist through at least the sixth grade (Carter & McCloskey, 1984).

The pressures exerted by the peer group apparently work. Children are responsive to the positive and negative feedback they receive from their peers. They are more likely to continue to engage in a sex-typical behavior in response to reinforcement and to terminate behaviors that are punished by their peers (Lamb, Easterbrooks, & Holden, 1980). Furthermore, feedback from same-sex peers may be especially important. Beverly Fagot (1978a) found that both two-year-old girls and boys were more likely to continue a behavior if a same-sex peer responded positively and to discontinue a behavior if a same-sex peer responded negatively. If the peer was of the other sex, however, the peer's feedback was largely ineffective. Interestingly, data indicate at the same time that among these young children, sex-atypical play is likely to be inhibited even in the presence of a peer of the other sex (Serbin et al., 1979).

Cross-Gender Children   Children who fail to respond to their peers' disapproval of sex-atypical behavior are a fascinating group. These children exhibit **cross-gender behavior;** that is, they adopt, in whole or in part, a variety of characteristics typical of the other sex (Fagot, 1977). Cross-gender boys, for example, exhibit a strong interest in feminine games and activities and play "dress-up" in girls' clothes. Cross-gender boys are likely to become social isolates over time because their male peers refuse to interact with them even when they play in a masculine fashion, and their female peers seem merely to tolerate their presence. Cross-gender girls, in contrast, appear to suffer very little for their sex-atypical behavior. At least in the preschool years, cross-gender girls cross play groups easily, playing with boys at boy games and girls at girl games (Fagot, 1977). Thus, the consequences of cross-gender behavior are much more severe and long lasting for boys than for girls.

The tendency for children to disapprove of cross-gender behavior increases with age. When researchers interviewed kindergartners through sixth-graders to determine how these children would respond to hypothetical cases of cross-gender behavior in their peers, older children reported that they would respond more negatively to cross-gender behavior than did younger children (Carter & McCloskey, 1984). Moreover, children stated that they would respond more negatively to cross-gender behavior in their male than in their female peers. The degree of negativity exhibited by children was particularly

Both boys and girls may engage in cross-gender activities. However, peers react more negatively to cross-gender behavior in boys than in girls.

surprising. Only one child reported that she would respond positively toward a cross-gender child, and children were virtually unanimous in their opinion that they would not want to play with a cross-gender child. Children's reports of how they would respond ranged from the fairly innocuous "I'd stay away" to reports that they would physically abuse cross-gender children. Children's negative attitudes towards cross-gender behavior may be reflective of their expectancies for punishment for cross-gender behavior.

Sex Segregation   The influence of peers on sex typing in children's behavior is undoubtedly enhanced as a result of the fact that boys and girls tend to interact in separate groups: starting at age three or four, boys play with boys and girls play with girls (Maccoby, 1988, 1990). This phenomenon is called **sex segregation.** In one observation of a hundred children on their preschool playgrounds, four-year-olds spent three times as much time with same-sex partners as with opposite-sex partners. By age six, they spent eleven times more time with peers of the same sex (Maccoby & Jacklin, 1987). This tendency to prefer same-sex peers is maintained at least until early adolescence (Maccoby, 1990). As a result, the range of behaviors open to children and acceptable to their peers is limited by their choice of playmates of the same sex.

Maccoby (1990) believes that children's experiences in same-sex groups foster different styles of social interaction in boys and girls. As boys play in their characteristic rough-and-tumble fashion or in team sports and games, they develop assertive, dominance-seeking styles of interaction. In contrast, girls' groups, which are oriented toward relationships and shared intimacy, promote cooperation and mutual support as well as a tendency to preserve the cohesiveness of the group. According to Maccoby, the same-sex peer group is an extremely powerful socialization environment throughout childhood.

Sex segregation begins to break down as children enter the period of adolescence and begin to think about dating. The pressures of heterosexual interactions, however, appear to enhance rather than diminish the push toward conformity with sex-role norms (Eccles, 1987; Petersen, 1980). This pattern is particularly obvious among teenage girls, many of whom abandon "tomboyish" behaviors that were acceptable during an earlier period of development (Huston & Alvarez, 1990).

Adolescent Peer Influences   Peer acceptance and rejection become increasingly important during adolescence. Though sex-typing pressures remain high, popularity among adolescents in both sexes relies more on positive personality characteristics, such as leadership abilities and politeness, rather than merely the presence of sex-typed behavior (Sigelman, Carr, & Begley, 1986). Thus, the presence of cross-gender personality characteristics may not lead to isolation from peers among adolescents (Huston & Alvarez, 1990). Adolescents' greater tolerance for sex-atypical personality characteristics may reflect their increasing cognitive abilities—specifically, their ability to consider multiple dimensions as they make judgments about individuals, including abstract qualities such as their trustworthiness or loyalty. It is also during adolescence that males and females show more attributes characteristic of both sexes as they begin to think about how gender roles affect their life decisions, such as career choice (Eccles, 1987).

▶ **Interaction among domains**

cross-gender behavior   Behavior usually seen in a member of the opposite sex. Term generally is reserved for behavior that is persistently sex atypical.

sex segregation   Clustering of individuals into same-sex groups.

Adolescents show greater tolerance than younger children for cross-gender behavior in their peers, probably because they consider multiple qualities as they make judgments about individuals.

The Influence of Teachers and Schools

Teachers, like peers and parents, treat children differentially according to sex, reinforce and punish sex-typed behaviors, and model sex-typical behavior for the children who study with them. Moreover, schools may foster sex typing through the teaching materials and curriculum that children are exposed to. For example, a recent survey of children's readers found that although boys and girls were portrayed with almost equal frequency, girls were more often the characters in stories in need of rescue and boys were rarely shown doing housework or displaying emotions (Purcell & Stewart, 1990).

Teacher Attitudes and Behaviors   Teachers, like other adults, often express stereotypical, gender-based views about the capacities of their students. They believe that female students are feminine and male students are masculine, although more experienced teachers are less likely to hold stereotyped beliefs and are more likely to treat students in an egalitarian fashion than less experienced teachers are (Fagot, 1978a; Huston, 1983). When teachers are asked to nominate their best students or those with the most potential, they are more likely to nominate boys than girls. They are especially likely to name boys as most skilled in mathematics. When teachers are asked to think of students who excel in language or social skill, they are more likely to name girls

(BenTsvi-Mayer, Hertz-Lazarowitz, & Safir, 1989). These patterns in teacher responses occur despite the fact that actual sex differences in many of these domains are minimal.

In addition, teachers respond differently to students on the basis of student sex as opposed to student behavior. Boys, for example, receive more disapproval from teachers than girls do during preschool and elementary school, even when boys and girls are engaged in similar amounts of disruptive behavior (Huston, 1983; Serbin et al., 1973). Teachers' behavior may reflect a belief that boys are more likely than girls to cause trouble in the classroom unless rules are strictly enforced (Huston, 1983). On the other hand, teachers pay more attention to girls when they sit quietly in the front of the classroom, whereas the amount of attention paid to boys is high regardless of where they sit (Serbin et al., 1973). Despite differences in the ways teachers respond to boys and girls, however, teachers tend to reinforce academic behaviors and punish disruptive behaviors regardless of their sex typing and to ignore behavior that is sex atypical but nondisruptive (Huston, 1983).

Just as teacher behavior can perpetuate stereotypes, though, it may also be used to change sex-typing patterns among children in classroom settings. Lisa Serbin and her colleagues (Serbin, Connor, & Iler, 1979; Serbin, Tonick, & Sternglanz, 1977) have found that teachers can reduce sex segregation by using reinforcement to facilitate cooperative cross-sex play among preschoolers and kindergartners. For example, when teachers praise children who play in mixed-sex groups by pointing out their cooperative play to the class and complimenting the children, cross-sex play increases.

Student Attitudes Toward Coursework Research indicates that students, teachers, and parents alike view some academic subjects as masculine and others as feminine (Huston, 1983). As we have noted earlier, mathematics is generally seen as a masculine activity and reading is seen as feminine (Eccles, 1983; Huston, 1983; Yee & Eccles, 1988). This sex typing is not limited to American schoolchildren. In a study of first- through fifth-grade Taiwanese Chinese, Japanese, and American boys and girls, the investigators found that most children felt that boys were better in mathematics and girls were better at reading (Lummis & Stevenson, 1990). Moreover, boys in these three societies predicted that they would do better in mathematics in high school than girls predicted they would do although no sex differences were found in children's predictions of their future reading skills.

Students' attitudes toward academic subjects can influence whether they will, in fact, be exposed to these subjects and acquire their specific skills. Jacquelynne Eccles (1983; Yee & Eccles, 1988) asked fifth- through twelfth-graders to complete questionnaires about their perceptions of their mathematics skills, their attributions for success and failure in mathematics, the value of mathematics for them, and their plans to take mathematics courses in the future. In addition, she gathered scores on both classroom and standardized mathematics tests. Eccles and her colleagues collected data over a two-year period, allowing them to examine how mathematics attitudes at one point were related to later attitudes and experiences.

Though there were no sex differences in children's classroom or standardized mathematics test scores, girls perceived themselves as less competent at mathematics, were less willing to take mathematics courses in the future, and saw mathematics as less valuable than did boys. Moreover, girls and boys differed in their explanations for success and failure in mathematics. Girls explained success in terms of *external attributions,* such as luck or teacher liking, and failure in terms of *internal attributions,* such as a lack of intelligence or skill. Boys, in contrast, explained failure by external attributions ("the teacher hates me") and success by internal attributions ("I'm smart"). Children's attitudes were predictive of later enrollment in mathematics classes. Girls were more likely to drop out of mathematics courses or to take lower-level mathematics courses than were boys of the same ability levels. Moreover, girls developed higher levels of anxiety about mathematics than boys did. Clearly, children's sex-stereotyped views of courses can have an enormous impact on the direction their studies take.

Sex Differences in Achievement Expectancies   A variety of factors may contribute to sex differences in children's interest in academic subjects and their expectancies for academic success. One of these factors may be sex typing in the content of the curriculum. In one study a group of investigators used two computer-based mathematics tutorials differing in sex typing to assess children's skills (Cooper, Hall, & Huff, 1990). The "masculine" tutorial was a typical arcade-type game designed to teach division in a war game format in which guns fired at tanks in response to children's answers to the problems. Tanks exploded when children answered correctly; incorrect responses produced misses. The "feminine" tutorial taught division of fractions using a word-oriented, nonaggressive format. Besides measuring children's liking for the two programs, the investigators collected children's perceptions of stress and their competence on the war game program (no scores were available for the feminine tutorial). Overall, children preferred the tutorial program designed for their own sex and reported feeling less stress when working on the same-sex than the other-sex tutorial. In addition, boys' performance was superior to the performance of girls on the masculine tutorial. (No comparisons of performance were made on the feminine task.) Thus, sex typing of curricular content may affect children's preferences and performance in academic areas.

Another factor that appears to influence children's academic expectancies is the nature of evaluative feedback they receive for their academic work and nonacademic behavior. Carol Dweck and her colleagues have proposed that evaluative criticism is more likely to result in both feelings of incompetence and lowered expectations of success if it is *discriminate*—in this case, directed primarily at academic work—than if it is *indiscriminate*—that is, directed at both academic and social behavior (Dweck et al., 1978). Dweck and her colleagues found that boys received greater indiscriminate criticism from teachers (over two-thirds was for nonacademic behavior), whereas over two-thirds of the criticism girls received concerned their academic efforts. Thus, girls' lower academic expectations may reflect the fact that their academic work is more likely to be criticized. In contrast, since teachers are generally more critical of them, boys may attribute negative feedback to the attitude of teachers rather than to the intellectual quality of their performance.

Girls do, in fact, show greater self-criticism of their academic work than boys do. Karin Frey and Diane Ruble (1987) have studied instances of self- and peer criticism for academic work in classroom settings. Children between the

FIGURE 12.6

Self-Evaluation in Boys and Girls

In a study of kindergartners through fourth-graders, Frey and Ruble found that both boys and girls make more self-congratulatory comments than self-critical ones, but girls show a greater proportion of self-critical comments relative to self-congratulatory comments about their classroom performance. The data here are shown as the proportion of self-congratulatory comments minus self-critical comments.

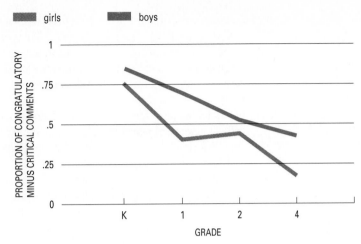

Source: Adapted from Frey & Ruble, 1987.

ages of five and ten years were observed at work in academic tasks in their classrooms, and their spontaneous critical and complimentary comments about themselves and their peers were tallied. Several sex differences emerged in the nature of comments children made. Overall, both girls and boys made more self-compliments than self-criticisms, but boys showed a greater number of self-congratulatory statements relative to self-criticisms than girls did (see Figure 12.6). Boys complimented themselves and criticized their peers more than girls did, whereas girls criticized themselves and complimented their peers more than boys did. Girls also were more likely to attribute their failures to a lack of ability ("I'm so stupid") than boys were. Thus, the patterns of girls' self-criticism match the discriminate criticism they hear from their teachers.

CONTROVERSY

Why Are Boys Better at Certain Mathematics Skills Than Girls?

In 1980, Camille Benbow and Julian Stanley (1980) presented data from an eight-year longitudinal study of intellectually gifted adolescents indicating that males and females differed significantly in their mathematics skills. The adolescents participating in this study were ten thousand seventh- through ninth-graders who scored in at least the top 5 percent on standardized mathematics achievement tests designed for students their ages. Boys and girls comprised 57 percent and 43 percent, respectively, of the resulting sample. These students then took the mathematics and verbal subtests of the Scholastic Aptitude Test (SAT), an instrument designed to assess the skills of college-bound high school juniors and seniors. In both their original and a subsequent study, these researchers found that boys outscored girls by about 30 points (Benbow & Stanley, 1983). When the numbers of boys and girls achieving particular scores were compared, it was found that as scores increased, the proportion of boys to girls who achieved a particular score became greater. For example, among students scoring at the fiftieth percentile (493 points), the ratio of boys to girls was two to one; at the seventy-ninth percentile (a score of 600), the ratio was four to one; for scores above 700, the ratio of boys to girls was thirteen to one. No differences were found for SAT verbal subtest scores. Benbow and Stanley (1980, 1983) conclude that because boys and girls were enrolled in identical mathematics classes before the seventh grade, the observed sex differences must be caused by a biological difference in mathematics abilities.

This conclusion raised a controversy that was discussed in both professional journals and the popular media (Hyde, Fennema, & Lamon, 1990). Critics point out that alternative factors can account for the sex difference. For example, although girls and boys are enrolled in comparable mathematics classes before the seventh grade, achievement expectations in mathematics differ for boys and girls beginning in late elementary school, when girls already rate their math ability lower than boys do (Eccles, 1983; Lummis & Stevenson, 1990). These expectancies most probably have their origins still earlier in development and may influence even talented girls' willingness (or confidence) in learning the higher forms of mathematics tested by the SAT. In addition, parents express the belief that their sons are more competent than their daughters in mathematics. Parental attitudes, in turn, are more strongly related to children's beliefs about their math competence than the children's actual past performance in math. This effect is especially pronounced when children are in junior or senior high school (Eccles & Jacobs, 1986; Eccles-Parsons, Adler, & Kaczala, 1982). Finally, when boys and girls of all ability levels, not just the gifted, are compared, sex differences in mathematics skills are small to nonexistent (Hyde, Fennema, & Lamon, 1990). Taken together, this evidence suggests that even when there are sex differences in mathematics, the causes of those differences are unlikely to be a single factor like genetics. ■

ANDROGYNY: A PSYCHOLOGICAL CONCEPT

▶ **Sociocultural influence**

Changes in society's conceptions of the desirability of traditional sex typing have been reflected in changes in psychological theories. Although earlier theorists and researchers (Kohlberg, 1966; Mischel, 1966) assumed that sex-atypical behavior was undesirable and perhaps indicative of psychopathology, recent conceptions of sex-role development have taken a different direction. Rather than assuming that traditional masculine and feminine roles are the most desirable, psychologists have increasingly recognized that conventional roles may restrict our abilities to respond adaptively to the demands of our environments.

Traditionally, psychologists treated masculinity and femininity as opposite ends of a bipolar dimension: the more masculine one was, the less feminine, by definition, one could be. Sandra Bem (1974, 1975) challenged this view by proposing that masculinity and femininity were not mutually exclusive, as the

TABLE 12.2

Classification of Sex Typing

In Sandra Bem's (1974, 1975) classification scheme, persons who score high on traits associated with both masculinity and femininity are "androgynous"; those low on both dimensions are classified as "undifferentiated." "Feminine" and "masculine" individuals are those who score high on one sex-typing dimension and low on the other.

		Masculinity Score	
		High	Low
Femininity Score	High	Androgynous	Feminine
	Low	Masculine	Undifferentiated

bipolar formulation would suggest, but rather were separate dimensions of personality measurable along two different poles. Thus, a person of either sex could be assertive in situations in which that behavior was necessary and nurturant when nurturance was required. From Bem's perspective, the coexistence of masculine and feminine characteristics allows the individual to be maximally adaptive. Bem called persons exhibiting high levels of both masculine and feminine characteristics **androgynous.**

Psychological androgyny should not be confused with the ways in which androgyny is presented in the popular media. From a psychological perspective, people whose physical appearance is ambiguous, neither distinctively male nor distinctively female, are not necessarily androgynous. In Bem's formulation, androgynous people are those who exhibit high levels of both masculine and feminine personality characteristics. Persons who are highly masculine but possess fewer feminine characteristics are designated as *masculine,* whereas those who are highly feminine but possess fewer masculine characteristics are designated as *feminine.* Persons who have few masculine and feminine characteristics are classified as *undifferentiated.* Table 12.2 presents this classification scheme.

Bem (1975) proposed that androgynous people should behave more adaptively and be psychologically healthier than nonandrogynous persons. She tested her predictions in two separate settings with college students. In the first setting, students were asked to rate a series of cartoons for funniness. Students were told that they were rating these cartoons with a group of peers, when in actuality only tape recordings of other students' voices were heard. Before rating each cartoon, students heard their "peers" make judgments that indicated, in some instances, that funny cartoons were not funny or that unfunny cartoons were funny. Of interest was whether sex-typing characteristics were related to independence (a masculine characteristic) in students' judgments. In the second setting, Bem rated the quality of subjects' play with a kitten. Of interest in this study was whether sex-typing characteristics would be related to students' nurturance (a feminine characteristic). Androgynous and masculine subjects exhibited the greatest independence in the first study, and androgynous and feminine subjects exhibited the greatest nurturance in the second study. In both cases, undifferentiated persons performed the least well. Thus, behavioral adaptability is associated with psychological androgyny.

androgyny Sex-role orientation in which a person possesses high levels of personality characteristics associated with both sexes.

▶ **Interaction among domains**

Psychological health and popularity with peers have also been found to be associated with psychological androgyny. For example, androgynous adolescents are better adjusted psychologically than are sex-typed or undifferentiated persons (Ziegler, Dusek, & Carter, 1984). Similarly, androgynous adolescents are liked better by their peers and report feeling less lonely than do other groups of adolescents (Avery, 1982; Massad, 1981). Androgynous adolescents also are more likely to have resolved identity crises than are nonandrogynous adolescents (Dusek, 1987). Finally, androgynous girls are more likely to attribute success to internal factors than to external factors (Huston, 1983).

How does an individual become androgynous? A variety of theories have been proposed to account for the development of androgyny. It has been proposed, for example, that parental characteristics such as nurturance or maternal employment are likely to lead to the development of androgyny. The data on relationships between parental characteristics and androgyny in children are sparse, however.

▶ **Interaction among domains**

Another possibility involves the child's growing ability to conceptualize the self and social roles in complex, abstract terms. Eccles (1987) has proposed that children cannot become androgynous before adolescence. She maintains that children are unlikely to exhibit androgynous behavior while they are still in the process of acquiring a sex role. During adolescence, however, children's abilities to conceptualize sex roles in a more abstract manner lead them to view sex-role stereotypes as descriptive statements about regularities in behavior rather than as prescriptions for acceptable behavior. Simultaneously, as adolescents strive to define their identities, they may consider factors other than gender as a means of characterizing themselves. Though androgynous role models are likely to foster gender-role transcendence, according to Eccles (1987), it is the convergence of cognitive developmental changes and the emergence of self-definition, rather than external factors such as models, that allow children to transcend traditional roles and emerge as androgynous.

THEMES IN DEVELOPMENT

SEX ROLES

▶ **What roles do nature and nurture play in sex-role development?**

According to some theorists, biological influences such as hormones and brain lateralization underlie sex differences in aggression and visual-spatial skill, and some experimental evidence is indeed consistent with such hypotheses. However, just as hormones, for example, can influence behavior, so too can behavior influence levels of hormones. According to social learning theorists, the child's socialization experiences with parents and peers, and in schools contribute substantially to observed sex differences as well as the child's knowledge of sex-role stereotypes. Children indeed learn about sex roles very early in life, well before actual sex differences in most behaviors are observed. Research also shows that parents, peers, and teachers treat boys and girls differently, providing support for the nurture position.

▶ How does the sociocultural context influence sex-role development?

Most cultures hold stereotypical beliefs about sex roles, although the specific characteristics associated with each sex can vary. The particular behaviors exhibited by males and females can also vary according to culture. Such findings demonstrate that although the tendency to stereotype is widespread, the characteristics associated with each sex are not necessarily fixed. Changes within American society, as in the proportion of women who are employed outside the home, underscore the idea that children's sex-role development can be affected by shifting sociocultural trends.

▶ How does the child play an active role in sex-role development?

The child's active role in the construction of gender-based knowledge is emphasized in cognitive-developmental theories of sex-role development. For example, many children construct gender schemas based on their socialization experiences, schemas that in turn influence how they process gender-related information and how they themselves behave.

▶ Is sex-role development continuous or stagelike?

Theorists like Freud and Kohlberg describe sex-role development as a stagelike process. Freud believed that the phallic stage in particular was a crucial time for sex-role development. Kohlberg hypothesized that children progress through a sequence of attaining gender identity, gender stability, and gender constancy. In contrast, social learning theorists describe the cumulative and incremental effects of reinforcement and modeling on sex-role development. Research evaluating stage theories has confirmed that children pass through the sequence of gender awareness outlined by Kohlberg but has failed to validate the relationship of the entire sequence to sex-role behaviors.

▶ Are there sensitive periods in sex-role development?

In Freud's theory, the resolution of the Oedipal and Electra complexes during the phallic stage was a critical time in personality formation. However, little empirical research confirms his claims. Some research also suggests that the first three or four years may be a sensitive period for gender identity. Children may have psychological difficulties if they are classified as a different sex after this time.

▶ How does sex-role development interact with development in other domains?

Attainments in cognition are thought to be related to many aspects of sex-role development. Bandura describes cognitive processes such as attention that influence which models, male or female, children will imitate. Kohlberg suggests that general cognitive advances pave the way for gender knowledge, such as gender constancy.

By the same token, the child's state of sex-role development can influence cognitive processing. Gender-schematic children, for example, may show memory distortions consistent with their sex-role beliefs. Moreover, a particular classification of sex role, androgyny, is associated with psychological health and popularity with peers.

SUMMARY

Sex-role development refers to the process by which children acquire the characteristics that are prescribed for males and females in their culture. *Sex-role stereotypes,* beliefs about the typical behaviors and characteristics of females and males, exist in numerous cultures. Often, identified male characteristics are *instrumental,* including traits like independence and assertiveness, whereas identified female characteristics are *expressive,* emphasizing emotionality and sociability. In actual fact, though, male and female characteristics show more similarities than differences.

In terms of real and quantifiable differences between the sexes, males are physically stronger but more vulnerable in infancy compared with females. Though past research showed that females had superior verbal skills and males excelled in mathematics and visual-spatial skills, recent studies suggest that verbal and mathematical skill differences, for the most part, have disappeared. In social behavior, the most consistent finding is that males are more aggressive than females, particularly during early childhood. In addition, some evidence suggests that females are more skilled than males at decoding nonverbal social-emotional messages, such as the meanings of facial expressions.

Different theories of sex-role development make unique contributions to our understanding of this phenomenon. Biological theories suggest that hormones, such as *androgens,* and brain lateralization help to explain sex differences in aggression and visual-spatial skill. Psychodynamic theories emphasize the process of identification with the same-sex parent. Social learning theories claim that reinforcement and imitation of same-sex models who behave in sex-typical ways explain many sex differences. Cognitive developmental theories stress how the child's growing awareness of and identification with her own sex—in the successive notions of *gender identity, gender stability,* and *gender constancy*—influence sex typing. Alternatively, *gender schemas,* or cognitive constructs, are thought to influence sex-role development.

Children's knowledge about sex roles grows rapidly during early childhood. Gender identity is usually formed by age three, an accomplishment that appears to be linked to sex-typed preferences in play activities and knowledge of stereotypes. Some children also tend to rely on gender schemas more than others as they process social information, a tendency that often makes them distort perceptions about sex-atypical behavior. Children become aware of sex-role stereotypes for many activities and traits during the preschool years, but their ideas become more flexible as they approach adolescence.

From birth onward, parents treat children differently on the basis of biological sex. Boys and girls are provided with sex-differentiated toys, and their parents tend to stress adherence to traditional sex-role norms. Fathers, in particular, appear concerned about their children's sex typing and exert an important influence on the development of sex-typed behavior in children.

Both parents are particularly upset when sons engage in sex-atypical behavior.

Children are perhaps the most ardent enforcers of sex-role norms. They develop a firm grasp on behaviors that are expected of their sex and enforce compliance with sex-role norms in their peers. Same-sex play and preferences for sex-typical toys and activities become the norm during the preschool and early elementary school years. These patterns of preferences persist at least through adolescence. Children who consistently behave in a cross-gender fashion are likely to become socially isolated from the rest of their peer group.

Schools also exert an important influence on the development of sex typing in children. Teachers treat children differently in some areas, but generally not in the academic realm. Boys and girls acquire differing expectations about their academic skills. These separate expectations can influence the child's choice of academic courses and, ultimately, of occupation.

13
Moral Judgment and Behavior

One day Ross, a four-year-old, tells his father, "I have some bad ideas." When his father wants to know what some of these bad ideas are, Ross says, "I want to be a he-man."

"That's not a bad idea," his father says.

"Uh-huh," answers Ross. "Marky and I are going to slap each other, and that's why he-man is bad."

This exchange, recorded by Catherine Snow (1987a, p. 119), demonstrates just how early in life youngsters begin to develop insights into what constitutes "good" and "bad." One of the primary goals of socialization is to instill in children a sense of morality, the standards of conduct considered ethical within his or her culture. We expect them to learn to judge right from wrong, to inhibit behaviors that harm others and display behaviors that are helpful and sensitive to others' needs. Children display this awareness very early on, but the basis for their moral judgments undergoes noticeable changes over development. One goal of this chapter is to describe age-related changes in moral reasoning and to explain why these changes occur.

Broadly speaking, the survival of social groups depends on their ability to control aggression and to foster behaviors that benefit their members, behaviors such as helping, cooperation, and sharing. Philosophers, theologians, and scientists have argued for years over the basic "goodness" or "evil" of human nature and the role of the child's experiences in channeling whatever inborn tendencies they may have in either direction. Modern-day psychologists tend to steer clear of framing the issue in terms of moral absolutes, but they are interested in identifying the sources of aggressive and prosocial behaviors in children. In that sense, the nature-nurture debate remains a part of contemporary discussions of the roots of moral behavior. A second goal of this chapter, then, is to examine the research on aggression and prosocial behavior, two opposite sides of morality, with an eye to understanding how to limit aggression and nurture prosocial actions.

PSYCHOLOGICAL THEORIES OF MORAL DEVELOPMENT

Psychologists became interested in the topic of moral development during the early years of the twentieth century. Debates about the fledgling theory of evolution sparked by Darwin led to scientific inquiries into the sources of morality. What aspect of human nature is more related to the survival of the species than moral thought and action, especially as it is expressed in terms of aggression or altruism toward others? On a more practical level, with the emergence of handbooks for parents on the "how-to's" of raising a child, experts attempted to identify those disciplinary techniques that would produce a child of good moral character. Educators, too, were interested in finding ways in which the school curriculum could foster high moral standards and conduct in students.

Psychological theories differ in the areas of moral development they emphasize. Psychodynamic theories focus on the *affective* dimensions of moral development. According to this perspective, the emotional relationships children have with their parents influence the degree to which they incorporate parental standards of conduct. Social learning theories emphasize the child's acquisition of moral *behaviors,* such as the tendency to behave aggressively or to resist temptation. Cognitive-developmental theories center on moral *reasoning,* or how the child thinks about moral problems and judges right and wrong. Each perspective makes a unique contribution to our understanding of the development of morality.

Psychodynamic Theory

Psychodynamic theory represents, via the investigations of Sigmund Freud, the first purely psychological explanation of moral development, and thus this model is of considerable interest in the history of developmental psychology. As we saw in Chapter 2, Freud (1925/1961) emphasized the *internalization* of moral standards as a by-product of the child's progression through the stages of psychosexual development.

▶ **Development as continuous/ stagelike**

Specifically, Freud believed that the acquisition of a moral sense occurs at about the age of five or six years during the *phallic stage,* when the resolution of the *Oedipal complex* takes place in boys. According to Freud, the boy experiences intense emotional conflict when he realizes that his sexual attachment to his mother cannot be fulfilled and his hostile feelings toward his father (his competitor for his mother's affections) cannot be acted upon. The boy's primary fear is that he will be punished by castration and that he will lose his parents' love. Both the sexual and aggressive tendencies experienced by the boy are natural, according to Freud, who believed that these are basic human instincts. But the expression of such instincts is prohibited by society and must be controlled.

The Oedipal conflict becomes resolved, Freud concluded, when the young boy suppresses his instinctual urges and allies himself with his powerful same-sex parent—his father. Through this process of *identification,* the child acquires his father's moral values and standards. Another outcome is the formation of the *superego,* the component of the child's personality that functions both as a *conscience* (by identifying what not to do) and *ego ideal* (by identifying appropriate and desirable behaviors). The child's suppressed aggressive tendencies are turned inward in such a way that his moral transgressions are followed by guilt feelings and the desire for self-punishment. The child generally tries to avoid feelings of guilt by acting in accordance with internalized notions of his parents' wishes. Thus, proscriptions that were initially imposed upon the child by external sources, namely parents and society, become internalized by the child and guide his own moral behavior.

A controversial aspect of Freud's theory is its prediction that girls will develop a weaker moral sense than boys. In the counterpart of the Oedipal complex for girls, dubbed the *Electra complex,* the daughter experiences a strong attachment to her father. The resolution of this conflict does not involve nearly the same emotional intensity for girls as it does for boys. Girls, for example, cannot fear castration. As a result, the girl's identification with her mother occurs with less force, and the superego or conscience, according to Freud, is not as strong.

Attempts to validate the various claims made in Freudian theory have not met with much success. Little empirical evidence has been found to show that the child's identification with the same-sex parent or fear of losing parental love results in the internalization of moral standards (Hoffman, 1970, 1971). Moreover, many critics of Freud's theory have responded vociferously to the suggestion that moral development is inferior or incomplete in girls. For example, Carol Gilligan (1982) maintains that Freud's theory is a male's view of male development that fails to explore the unique dimensions of the female experience as they pertain to morality. More will be said about the issue of sex differences in moral development later in this chapter. Finally, as we will soon see, contemporary research shows that children begin to develop concepts of morality well before the age of five or six years, the age at which Freud hypothesized that the superego emerged (Emde, Johnson, & Easterbrooks, 1987).

Despite these criticisms, Freud's hypotheses that moral development includes the internalization of society's moral standards and that parents play a central role in this process are ideas that have endured. Unlike other theories, Freud's work does not emphasize moral reasoning or moral behavior. But it does suggest how the internal life of the child—and, more specifically, the child's emotions—are closely associated with the development of morality.

Social Learning Theory

As we saw in Chapter 2, learning theorists such as Albert Bandura (1977b) and Justin Aronfreed (1976) have emphasized the role of the child's reinforcement history and observational learning to describe social development in general and moral development in particular. According to social learning theory, the rewards and punishments dispensed by parents and others in response to the child's behaviors shape morally acceptable conduct, as do the actions and verbalizations that parents and others model for the child. In that sense, moral behavior is learned like any other behavior. Eventually, the child internalizes the moral standards of behavior set forth by others; conditioned fear of punishment for violating rules and self-rewards for good behavior guide the child's

According to social learning theory, children learn moral behaviors, such as the importance of helping others, through reinforcement and imitation.

actions. In addition, the behaviors learned through imitation become part of the child's internal storehouse of possible actions. The result is that the child learns to delay gratification (see Chapter 11), to inhibit aggression, and to help others.

Social learning explanations of moral development have several distinctive features. Social learning theorists do not posit stages of moral development. Instead, they see morality as a process of the incremental growth of appropriate actions and increasing conformity with the rules of society. As cultures vary, so do the specific behaviors acquired by the child. Throughout this process, children play a passive role, absorbing the moral prescriptives of the larger social group. In addition, social learning theorists focus on the child's overt observable behaviors rather than on moral reasoning and moral judgment. Although they speak of the child's internalization of moral standards, social learning theorists are generally not concerned with the details of how the child decides or thinks about moral problems. Finally, social learning theory assigns special prominence to parents because they are the primary sources of rewards and punishments. The influential role of other figures such as teachers and peers, however, is also recognized.

▶ **Development as continuous/ stagelike**
▶ **Sociocultural influence**

How convincingly does the social learning model explain moral development? Laboratory studies investigating one form of moral behavior, the child's ability to resist temptation, suggest that the child's reinforcement history is indeed a factor. The following sequence of events is typical of this research:

1. The child is shown pairs of toys, one of which is clearly more attractive and desirable than the other.
2. The child is asked to select one toy of the pair to talk about but is also told at the outset that, across pairs, some of the choices will not be permitted.

3. Each time, if the more attractive toy is chosen, a mild punishment is administered, usually a verbal reprimand.
4. After all the trials are completed, the experimenter leaves the room and surreptitiously observes to see if the child plays with or touches the forbidden toys.

The amount of time the child spends playing with the attractive toys—the ones she must suppress her desires to touch—is taken as a measure of how much she has internalized the moral response as a consequence of the prohibitions issued by the adult.

Although studies of resistance to temptation are carried out in artificial settings, they demonstrate that basic principles of learning apply to this aspect of moral behavior. Children participating in the forbidden-toy experiments quickly learn not to touch the prohibited stimuli during the initial training trials; they respond to the punishments doled out by the adult. Researchers have also noted that several variables influence children's tendency to transgress once the adult has left the room. First, as social learning theory predicts, the timing of the punishment during the initial training trials plays a role. When the punishment is administered as the child reaches for the forbidden toy but *before* she actually touches the toy, fewer violations of the adult's commands occur during the "temptation period" than when the punishment occurs *after* the child has picked the toy up. The basic tenets of learning theory state that punishments will be most effective if they closely follow the undesired behavior—in this case, when reaching for the forbidden toy. Second, the provision of a verbal explanation for why the toys are prohibited also has an effect. When children are told, for example, that the attractive toys might become broken if handled, they are much less likely to violate the adult's prohibition. According to social learning theorists, verbalizations facilitate the internalization of morally acceptable and unacceptable behaviors (Aronfreed, 1969, 1976).

The influence of parents and others as models of moral behaviors and beliefs has also been demonstrated. Parents who express a belief in helping others have children who show similar beliefs (Hoffman, 1975). In addition, models can influence whether a child commits a transgression or not. Children who observe a model committing a prohibited act, such as touching a forbidden toy, are more likely to perform the act themselves, whereas children observing a model who resists temptation commit fewer transgressions themselves (Rosenkoetter, 1973). It seems, though, that models are more powerful in *disinhibiting* than in inhibiting behavior that violates a rule or expectation; children are very often likely to follow a model's deviant behaviors rather than his compliant ones (Hoffman, 1970). Parents and peers can also influence the child's reasoning about moral issues. When children are exposed to adult or peer models who reason about moral problems in a mature way, they show more advanced moral thinking themselves (Brody & Shaffer, 1982).

Ample evidence suggests that many aspects of moral development can be explained by social learning theory. A social learning explanation is compatible with the results of experiments demonstrating that reinforcements influence the child's tendency to transgress and that models influence the child's compliance with adult prohibitions. Social learning theories, however, have emphasized one direction of influence—the effects of parental responses on children—while virtually ignoring how children can influence parents' disciplinary

▶ **The child's active role**

▶ **Interaction among domains**

strategies. In one laboratory study of parental discipline, parents were more likely to punish their children if previous punishments had improved children's problem-solving performance (Mulhern & Passman, 1981). Thus, in fact, the child's own behavior influences parental socialization techniques.

In addition, some experts contend that social learning theorists do not adequately consider the child's thinking and reasoning about moral issues. Elliot Turiel (1983), for example, underscores the importance of children's judgments and interpretations about the punishments administered by adults. In his view, the effectiveness of early punishment in the forbidden-toy experiments is the result of extremely clear communication about acceptable and unacceptable behavior—the toy should not be touched. In contrast, when the punishment is delivered late, the child may become confused. In those first few moments that the child holds the toy, he may think that this behavior is acceptable. A few seconds later, though, the adult indicates that touching is not permitted. Thus, the child's inability to sort out these conflicting messages, rather than the late timing of reinforcement, may lead to the persistence of the "deviant" behavior.

Newer versions of social learning theory assign a larger role for cognitive processes in the emergence of morality. In Albert Bandura's (1986) social cognitive theory, children develop internalized standards of conduct, cognitive representations they derive by observing models and by processing the explanations of moral behavior delivered by parents and others. Children attempt to behave in ways consistent with those representations. A thorough consideration of the child's reasoning processes, however, has traditionally been absent from learning theory models. As we will see in the next section, it has been left to other theorists such as Jean Piaget and Lawrence Kohlberg to describe changes in the child's ability to reason about moral questions.

▶ **Interaction among domains**

Cognitive-Developmental Theories

Cognitive-developmental explanations of moral development highlight the ways in which children reason about moral problems. Should a person ever steal, even if this transgression might actually help another person? Are there any circumstances under which lying might be acceptable? The child's ability to think through the answers to questions such as these depends on her ability to reason abstractly and to consider the perspectives, needs, and feelings of others. In other words, moral development is intimately connected with advances in general thinking abilities.

▶ **Development as continuous/ stagelike**

The two most prominent cognitive-developmental theorists concerned with moral development have been Jean Piaget and Lawrence Kohlberg. Both have suggested stage theories in which children are believed to reason about moral issues in qualitatively different ways depending on their level of development. In each theory, children are presumed to pass through the stages in an invariant sequence, without skipping any stages. Both further assume that development is hierarchical, that earlier forms of thought form the basis for more mature reasoning abilities. An implication of both their theories is that children across different cultures will show notable similarities in the way they advance in their moral reasoning.

Piaget's Theory Like his work in cognitive development, described in Chapter 8, Piaget (1932/1965) derived his ideas on the development of moral reasoning from his systematic and extensive observations of children, in this case in two contexts—as they played a formal game with a commonly shared set of rules and as they encountered "moral dilemmas" that he created to assess their thinking about ethical problems. Piaget began with an exploration of children's understanding of rules because they are an essential ingredient in constructions of morality. He observed and interviewed children of a wide range of ages as they played marbles, a popular children's game. Children were asked several questions about the rules of this game: What are the rules? Can new rules be invented? Where do rules come from? Have they always been the same? Piaget concluded that children's developing appreciation for the rules of this game took place in several stages.

▶ **Development as continuous/ stagelike**

Initially, he stated, very young children's behavior is not guided by rules. Preschool-aged children engage in motor acts for the pure pleasure of performing them or out of habit, and their play is largely solitary. Children may become aware of the existence of rules by watching older children play, but they do not incorporate rules into their play. Thus, young children may hide marbles or throw them randomly without relying on the formal rules of the game.

By about age six years, children are not only aware of the rules of the game of marbles, they regard these rules as sacred and inviolable. Most children in this stage do not know the rules in detail, but they respect them unquestioningly. They also believe that rules have always existed in the same form and consequently that people have played marbles in exactly the same way over the years. Adult authority is respected and regarded as the source of all rules.

In the last stage, which usually begins at the age of ten years, children understand rules to be the result of mutual consent among the participants of the game. Thus, rules may be changed if all the players agree. No longer are rules viewed as coercive, to be followed blindly; children now see that they are the result of cooperation and understanding among all parties involved and thus may be modified to suit the needs of the situation. In fact, winning the game may become subordinate to demonstrating skill and cleverness.

The second method Piaget employed to study moral development consisted of noting the responses of children to a series of "moral dilemmas," stories he constructed in which a central character committed a transgression and the intentions of that character and the consequences of his act varied. The following are a pair of such stories:

> A. A little boy who is called John is in his room. He is called to dinner. He goes into the dining room. But behind the door there was a chair, and on the chair there was a tray with fifteen cups on it. John couldn't have known that there was all this behind the door. He goes in, the door knocks against the tray, bang go the fifteen cups, and they all get broken!
>
> B. Once there was a little boy whose name was Henry. One day when his mother was out he tried to get some jam out of the cupboard. He climbed up onto a chair and stretched out his arm. But the jam was too high up and he couldn't reach it and have any. But while he was trying to get it he knocked over a cup. The cup fell down and broke. (Piaget, 1932/1965, p. 122)

When asked, "Which boy is naughtier?" younger children typically choose John, the child who broke more cups. According to Piaget, children under the age of ten years are in the stage of moral development called **moral realism,** or **heteronomy.** They judge the rightness or wrongness of an act by the objective, visible consequences—in this case, how many cups were broken. They do not take into account the central character's intentions to behave well or improperly. In this stage, rules are viewed as unbreakable; when they are indeed violated, however, the child sees punishment as the inevitable consequence. This belief in **immanent justice** is reflected in such statements as, "That's God punishing me," when the child accidently falls off a bike after lying to her mother, for example. Even though the fall has no relation to any of the child's previous transgressions, she believes the causal link exists. Moreover, children in this stage believe in **expiatory punishment,** the notion that punishments need not be related to the wrongful act as long as the punishment is severe enough to teach a lesson. Thus, stealing a friend's toy can be punished by any means, not necessarily by returning the toy or making reparations, as long as the punishment is harsh. Children in this stage view adults as the authorities on moral standards.

From this limited ability to reason about moral issues, children progress to the second stage of moral development, **moral relativism,** or **autonomy.** Now the transgressor's motives are taken into account; Henry is named as the naughtier boy because he intended to misbehave even though he broke only one cup. The child no longer believes that every violation of a rule will be punished. If punishments do occur, however, they should be related to the misdemeanor so that the individual appreciates the consequences of his act on others. Piaget calls this concept **punishment by reciprocity.** Respect for adult authority is no longer the sole force in the obedience the child shows for rules or in her moral understanding. Mutual respect for and cooperation with peers now underlies the child's reasoning about moral issues.

What precipitates the shift from moral realism to moral relativism? Piaget points to changes in the child's cognitive capabilities—and, in particular, decreasing egocentrism (see Chapter 8)—as one important source. To understand a person's intentions, for example, the child must be able to appreciate the point of view of another person as distinct from his or her own. The child must also be able to consider internal psychological states, such as intentionality, rather than relying exclusively on the external, visible consequences of an act.

Another important factor is the opportunity to interact with peers. Peer interaction forces the child to consider the thoughts and feelings of others and eventually leads to an understanding of their intentions and motives. Thus, both maturation and social experience play a role in the child's move toward maturity in moral understanding. Parents can encourage the transition from realism to relativism, notes Piaget, by relying less on authoritarian child-rearing techniques that promote unwavering respect for adult authority and instead encouraging mutual respect and understanding. In practical terms, this means parents must point out the consequences of the child's actions for others and articulate their own needs and feelings as parents. Providing opportunities for the child to interact with age mates can also be beneficial, according to Piaget.

Evaluating Piaget   How well does Piaget's theory stand up to the results of subsequent empirical studies? Research has confirmed shifts in the ways children reason about moral problems as they grow older. Children from many

▶ **Roles of nature and nurture**

moral realism   In Piaget's theory of moral development, the first stage of moral reasoning, in which moral judgments are made on the basis of the consequences of an act. Also called *heteronomy.*

immanent justice   Young child's belief that punishment will inevitably follow a transgression.

different cultures, social classes, and of varying intellectual capabilities show an increasing consideration of intentions in judging a character's actions and a diminishing belief in immanent justice, expiatory punishment, and obedience to authority with age (Hoffman, 1970; Lickona, 1976).

Piaget's assertion that cognitive growth underlies changes in moral reasoning has also received support. Level of moral thought is related to IQ and, more directly, to Piagetian stages of cognitive development (Lickona, 1976). As children reach the stage of concrete operations, when they are less egocentric and their role-taking abilities increase, they are less likely to rely on adult authority and more likely to base moral responses on the principle of reciprocity (Lee, 1971).

As for Piaget's contention that peer interaction promotes advances in moral thought, the evidence is mixed. Children raised on the Israeli *kibbutz,* or collective farm, where they have extensive experience with peers right from early infancy, are no different in their level of moral reasoning than their counterparts growing up in nuclear family settings (Kugelmass & Breznitz, 1967). At the same time, other researchers have noted a positive relationship between opportunities to interact with peers in clubs, activities, and other settings and sophistication of moral thought (Harris, Mussen, & Rutherford, 1976; Keasey, 1971).

Although many of the general aspects of Piaget's theory have been confirmed, some of the particulars have been challenged. For one thing, Piaget maintains that a child in a given stage should display all the characteristics associated with moral reasoning at that level; that is, her thought should show internal consistency. But children who believe in immanent justice do not necessarily respond to moral dilemmas on the basis of objective consequences or adult authority (Lickona, 1976). Equally problematic for Piaget's theory is the finding that under certain circumstances, even very young children are sensitive to the intentions behind a given act. One set of researchers asked kindergarten, second-grade, and fifth-grade children to listen to stories about a girl being aggressive with another in two conditions. In the "hostile" condition, the aggressive act was clearly intended to make the victim feel bad. In the "prosocial" condition, the aggressive act protected someone else (for example, "Betty grabs the ball from Andrea so no one gets hit by it"). As Figure 13.1 shows, even the youngest children in this experiment indicated that aggression in the "hostile" condition was worse than in the "prosocial" condition, showing their awareness of the intentions behind the aggressor's behavior (Rule, Nesdale, & McAra, 1974). Thus, Piaget underestimated young children's ability to respond to intentionality.

Piaget's theory has made important contributions to our understanding of moral development by emphasizing a previously little-considered dimension— the child's cognitive skill. It is clear from Piaget's work that the child's conceptualization of what is moral becomes more elaborate and complex with age and that any attempt to understand moral development must include an explanation of the child's thought as well as behavior. Subsequent theorists, Kohlberg in particular, have found Piaget's writings to be a useful springboard for their own theoretical formulations.

Kohlberg's Theory Piaget's work, particularly his emphasis on the relationship between the child's thinking capabilities and shifts in moral reasoning, heavily influenced Lawrence Kohlberg's (1969, 1976) view of moral

▶ **Development as continuous/ stagelike**

expiatory punishment Young child's belief that punishment need not be related to a transgression as long as the punishment is severe enough.

moral relativism In Piaget's theory of moral development, the second stage of moral reasoning, in which moral judgments are made on the basis of the actor's intentions. Also called *autonomy.*

punishment by reciprocity Belief that punishment should be related to the transgression.

FIGURE 13.1

The Role of Intentions in Moral Reasoning

A sample of kindergarten, second-, and fifth-grade girls was asked to rate the naughtiness of a central character in a story. In the "hostile condition," the character's intent was to harm the victim, whereas in the "prosocial condition," the character displayed an aggressive act that was intended to protect someone else. The higher the score on the horizontal axis, the "naughtier" the central character was rated. Even the youngest children took the intentions of the actor into account as they made these moral judgments. Similar results were obtained from boys who were part of a separate sample in this study.

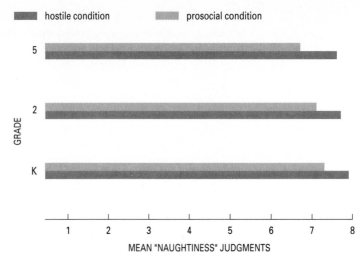

Source: Adapted from Rule, Nesdale, & McAra, 1974.

▶ **Development as continuous/ stagelike**

preconventional level   In Kohlberg's theory, the first level of moral reasoning, in which morality is motivated by the avoidance of punishments and attainment of rewards.

development. Like Piaget, Kohlberg has described a stage theory of moral development in which progress through each stage proceeds in a universal order and regression to earlier modes of thinking does not occur.

Kohlberg based his theory on children's responses to a set of dilemmas that put obedience to authority or the law in direct conflict with helping a person in need. One of the most famous of these dilemmas is the following story of a man's attempt to help his dying wife:

> In Europe, a woman was near death from cancer. One drug might save her, a form of radium that a druggist in the same town had recently discovered. The druggist was charging $2,000, ten times what the drug cost him to make. The sick woman's husband, Heinz, went to everyone he knew to borrow the money, but could only get together about half of what it cost. He told the druggist that his wife was dying and asked him to sell it cheaper or let him pay later. But the druggist said, "No." The husband got desperate and broke into the man's store to steal the drug for his wife. Should the husband have done that? Why? (Colby et al., 1983, p. 77)

In his original study, Kohlberg (1958) analyzed the responses of a group of adolescent boys ranging in age from ten to sixteen years to nine of these dilemmas. The behaviors or actions that the boys selected as moral were not as critical to establishing developmental trends as the reasoning they used to justify their choices. Thus, whether the child stated that Heinz should steal the drug or not was irrelevant; the reasons for valuing life were of more interest.

Kohlberg identified three general levels of moral orientation, each with two substages, to explain the varying responses of his subjects. In the first level of moral reasoning, called the **preconventional level,** the child's behavior is motivated by external pressures—avoidance of punishment, attainment of rewards, and preservation of one's own self-interests. Norms of behavior are not yet derived from internalized principles, and the child's own needs and desires are primary. The two substages of the preconventional level are

Stage 1: Punishment and obedience orientation   The primary motive for action is the avoidance of punishment, as in the following set of responses:

Pro: If you let your wife die, you will get in trouble. You'll be blamed for not spending the money to save her and there'll be an investigation of you and the druggist for your wife's death.

Con: You shouldn't steal the drug because you'll be caught and sent to jail if you do. If you do get away, your conscience would bother you thinking how the police would catch up to you any minute. (Kohlberg, 1984, p. 52)

Stage 2: Naive instrumental hedonism   In this stage, actions are motivated by the desire for rewards:

Pro: If you do happen to get caught you could give the drug back and you wouldn't get much of a sentence. It wouldn't bother you much to serve a little jail term, if you have your wife when you get out.

Con: He may not get much of a jail term if he steals the drug, but his wife will probably die before he gets out, so it wouldn't do him much good. If his wife dies, he shouldn't blame himself; it isn't his fault she has cancer. (Kohlberg, 1984, p. 52)

In the next level, the **conventional level,** conforming to the norms of the majority and maintaining the social order have become central to the child's reasoning. He now considers the point of view of others, along with their intentions and motives. The child also feels a sense of responsibility to make contributions to society and to uphold the laws and institutions that serve its members to keep the system going. The two substages at this level are

Stage 3: Good boy morality   The child strives to avoid the disapproval of others (as distinct from avoidance of punishment).

Pro: No one will think you're bad if you steal the drug but your family will think you're an inhuman husband if you don't. If you let your wife die, you'll never be able to look anyone in the face again.

Con: It isn't just the druggist who will think you're a criminal, everyone else will, too. After you steal it, you'll feel bad thinking how you've brought dishonor on your family and yourself; you won't be able to face anyone again. (Kohlberg, 1984, p. 52)

Stage 4: Authority-maintaining morality   Here, an act is always wrong if it violates a rule or does harm to others.

Pro: You should steal it. If you did nothing you'd be letting your wife die, it's your responsibility if she dies. You have to take it with the idea of paying the druggist.

Con: It is a natural thing for Heinz to want to save his wife but it's always wrong to steal. He still knows he's stealing and taking a valuable drug from the man who made it. (Kohlberg, 1984, p. 50)

Finally, in the **postconventional level,** the individual has developed a fuller understanding of the basis for laws and rules. They are now seen as the result of a social contract that all individuals must uphold because of shared responsibilities and duties. The individual recognizes the relative and sometimes arbitrary nature of rules, which may vary from group to group. Certain principles and values, however, such as justice and human dignity, must be preserved at all costs. In his original formulation, Kohlberg postulated two substages at this level:

Stage 5: Morality of contract and democracy   The individual is concerned with self-respect and maintaining the respect of others. Laws must be obeyed because they represent a social contract, but they may sometimes conflict with moral values.

Pro: The law wasn't set up for these circumstances. Taking the drug in this situation isn't really right, but it's justified to do it.

Con: You can't completely blame someone for stealing, but extreme circumstances don't really justify taking the law in your own hands. You can't have everyone stealing when they get desperate. The end may be good, but the ends don't justify the means. (Kohlberg, 1984, p. 50)

conventional level In Kohlberg's theory, the second level of moral reasoning, in which the child conforms to the norms of the majority and wishes to preserve the social order.

postconventional level In Kohlberg's theory, the third level of moral reasoning, in which laws are seen as the result of a social contract and individual principles of conscience may emerge.

Stage 6: Morality of individual principles of conscience   The individual is concerned with upholding his own principles and may sometimes feel it necessary to deviate from the rules when they conflict with moral principles.

Pro: This is a situation which forces him to choose between stealing and letting his wife die. In a situation where the choice must be made, it is morally right to steal. He has to act in terms of the principle of preserving and respecting life.

Con: Heinz is faced with the decision of whether to consider other people who need the drug just as badly as his wife. Heinz ought to act not according to his particular feelings toward his wife, but considering the value of all the lives involved. (Kohlberg, 1984, p. 51)

Kohlberg emphasized changes in the child's perspective-taking ability as the basis for shifts in moral reasoning. The tension between the self's rights and responsibilities and those of others changes in balance from the preconventional to the postconventional levels of moral development. The focus of the younger child is on the self and one's own needs, but children increasingly appreciate the perspectives of others by the end of the preconventional level and throughout the conventional level. By the postconventional level, children consider the self and others within the context of the larger society. According to Kohlberg, changes in perspective-taking ability are promoted by providing opportunities for children to discuss others' points of view. Exposure to higher levels of moral reasoning displayed by older peers and adults, which can precipitate cognitive advances in children, is also critical.

Kohlberg and Piaget differ in their explanation of moral development in several ways. Kohlberg places less emphasis on the role of adult authority in young children's moral reasoning than Piaget does. Although children in the preconventional level respond to external pressures, they are oriented primarily to the rewards and punishments doled out by adults rather than adult authority per se. Kohlberg also believes that the movement toward autonomy occurs toward the end of adolescence, much later than Piaget envisioned the shift. Like Piaget, though, Kohlberg hypothesizes that social experiences are central to promoting advances in moral reasoning. In Kohlberg's scheme, however, these experiences include not just peer interactions but any exchange that promotes the emergence of perspective-taking skills.

▶ **Development as continuous/ stagelike**

Evaluating Kohlberg   Kohlberg's theory has received enormous attention in the field of psychology, and his ideas have spawned hundreds of research studies. Numerous investigations have confirmed the existence of transitions in moral reasoning with age. In a major longitudinal study in which Kohlberg's original sample of adolescent boys was followed over a twenty-year period, Anne Colby and her colleagues (1983) confirmed that the subjects' responses to moral dilemmas displayed the developmental stages delineated by Kohlberg (see Figure 13.2). The subjects did not skip any stages and, with few exceptions, tended to move upward through the stages. It is interesting to note that most adults in the study reasoned at stage 3 or stage 4. In fact, so few subjects responded at the stage-6 level that Kohlberg (1984; Kohlberg, Levine, & Hewer, 1983) came to believe that this last stage might not be empirically justified. Moral development was also found to be positively correlated with IQ score and educational level for adult subjects, findings that are consistent with Kohlberg's emphasis on the cognitive basis of moral judgment. In a more recent study, Lawrence Walker (1989) confirmed that six- through fifteen-year-

FIGURE 13.2

**The Development of
Moral Reasoning**

In a longitudinal follow-up study of
Kohlberg's original sample, Colby
and her colleagues confirmed that
subjects showed consistent upward
advances in moral reasoning with
age. The graph shows the extent
to which subjects gave responses
characteristic of each stage from
age 10 years through adulthood.
With development, responses associated with Stages 1 and 2 declined, while responses associated
with Stages 3 and 4 increased. Few
young adults moved to Stage 5 of
moral reasoning.

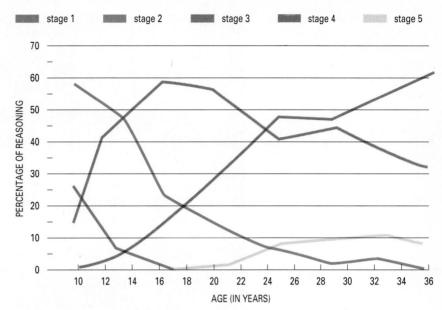

Source: Adapted from Colby et al., 1983.

old children tested over a two-year period showed significant gains in moral
reasoning and that few children skipped stages or regressed to earlier forms
of reasoning.

Cross-cultural studies of moral reasoning have also verified the progression
in thinking outlined by Kohlberg. In countries as diverse as India, Turkey,
Japan, Nigeria, and Finland, children show the development of reasoning skills
characteristic of stages 1 through 4, without skipping stages and without re-
gressing to previous stages. Stage 5 is observed less frequently; it is more
commonly reported from urban cultures but is virtually absent in tribal and
village folk societies (Snarey, 1985). Thus, there is considerable empirical support for universal changes in patterns of moral thinking as outlined by
Kohlberg.

As with several features of Piaget's theory, however, researchers have
been unable to confirm some specific propositions in Kohlberg's outline of
moral development. How important is the child's perspective-taking skill in
spurring advances in moral reasoning? Just as many researchers report no relationship between these two variables as find a significant one. Thus, it is
difficult to draw definitive conclusions about the impact of perspective-taking
ability (Kurdek, 1978). Do individuals within a stage respond consistently to
different moral dilemmas, as Kohlberg maintains they should? In one study of
seventy-five college students who responded to five moral dilemmas, not one
person received the same stage score across all the stories (Fishkin, Keniston,
& MacKinnon, 1973). Perhaps reasoning within a stage is not as fixed as Kohlberg claimed. Finally, there have been some exceptions to the hypothesis that
all individuals progress in moral reasoning with age. Some investigators have
observed that when adults do not continue their education they tend to remain
at the same stage of moral reasoning, whereas others report that a small percentage of subjects move downward instead of upward through the stages
(Rest, 1983).

One criticism of Kohlberg's theory of moral development is that it does not encompass moral values found in different cultures, such as the respect Hindus display for animal life.

▶ **Sociocultural influence**

One last criticism of Kohlberg's theory is that it does not capture all the possible modes of moral reasoning evident in different cultural groups. In responding to Kohlberg's moral dilemmas, persons growing up on the Israeli kibbutz describe the importance of the principle of happiness for everyone as in the following example:

> *Q.* Should Moshe steal the drug? Why or why not?
> *A.* Yes . . . I think that the community should be responsible for controlling this kind of situation. The medicine should be made available to all in need; the druggist should not have the right to decide on his own . . . the whole community or society should have the control of the drug.
> *Q.* Is it important for people to do everything they can to save another's life? Why or why not?
> *A.* If I want to create a better community, a nice and beautiful one, an ideal world, the only way we can do it is by cooperation between people . . . We need this cooperation among ourselves in order to achieve this better world . . . The *happiness . . . principle* underlies this cooperation—the greatest *happiness* for the greatest number of people in the society. (Snarey, 1985, pp. 222–223)

Asian cultures, too, emphasize the idea of the collective good and harmonious social order. The preferable way to resolve social conflicts is by reconciling persons who are in conflict, not relying on laws to control their behavior. Thus, families often hold conferences to settle disputes between individuals so that harmony is preserved among members of the group. Kohlberg's moral dilemmas, which require a choice between rules and the needs of individuals, do not permit the expression of this cultural principle (Dien, 1982). Likewise, Indian cultures emphasize the value of all life, not just human life, a concept that does not appear in Kohlberg's outline of moral development. One of the most serious transgressions as expressed by orthodox Hindu children and adults is eating beef, chicken, or fish (Shweder, Mahapatra, & Miller, 1987). Thus, the movement of the individual toward the fullest understanding of the principle of justice, the endpoint of development in Kohlberg's theory, may be a singularly Western phenomenon.

A current debate is whether these problems constitute enough evidence to discredit Kohlberg's theory. Another is whether the general shift from conventional to principled reasoning that occurs across different populations is best explained by Kohlberg's ideas. It may be that these transitions simply reflect universal developments toward abstract and more complex thought as opposed to milestones in moral reasoning per se.

CONTROVERSY

Are There Sex Differences in Moral Development?

Recent years have seen a growing debate about whether men and women show differences in their moral development. In one of his studies, Kohlberg reported that most males function at stage 4, whereas most females reason at stage 3 (Kohlberg & Kramer, 1969). This report provoked a strong reaction from some members of the psychological community and led Carol Gilligan (1977, 1982) to propose that moral development might take a different, not inferior, course in females. Gilligan states that because of their tendency to be concerned with relationships, caregiving, and intimacy, females tend to develop a **morality of care and responsibility** in contrast to the **morality of justice** described by Kohlberg. The morality of care and responsibility involves a concern with self-sacrifice, attachments to others, and a focus on relationships rather than on the tension between rules and the needs of the individual. The unique development of females, says Gilligan, stems from their attachment to and identification with their mothers, who are concerned with nurturing others and maintaining relationships (Gilligan & Wiggins, 1987).

An eleven-year-old girl's response to the story of Heinz and his wife illustrates the "ethic of care" Gilligan holds to be typical of females:

> If he stole the drug, he might save his wife then, but if he did, he might have to go to jail, and then his wife might get sicker again, and he couldn't get more of the drug, and it might not be good. So, they should really just talk it out and find some other way to make the money. (Gilligan, 1982, p. 28)

Even though this response might receive a low score in Kohlberg's system because of its seemingly wavering, noncommittal nature, Gilligan believes it reflects a relatively mature understanding of the crisis a relationship might undergo when a law is broken.

Are there gender differences in moral development? Of the large number of investigations based on Kohlberg's tasks, only a few have reported statistically significant differences between males and females in level of moral reasoning (Walker, 1984). It may be that for those few, differences in scoring methodologies and in defining stages account for the findings more than actual gender differences in moral thinking. Other research has shown that males and females often use *both* the morality of justice and the morality of care in responding to moral dilemmas (Walker, deVries, & Trevethan, 1987). Furthermore, Gilligan has come under fire herself for providing limited empirical support for

morality of care and responsibility Tendency to make moral judgments on the basis of concern for others.

morality of justice Tendency to make moral judgments on the basis of reason and abstract principles of equity.

her theoretical ideas. These problems notwithstanding, Gilligan's work has expanded our understanding of what constitutes moral reasoning beyond simply the principle of justice espoused by Kohlberg. Together, these two viewpoints may provide a fuller picture of moral development in both males and females (Brabeck, 1983). ■

Morality as Domain-Specific Knowledge   Both Piaget and Kohlberg emphasized changes in children's thinking processes as the foundations of emerging new levels of moral reasoning. At each stage of mental development, the child's cognitive structures are fully reorganized, and reasoning in all areas, including moral reasoning, reflects the specific features of thought at that stage. A more recent approach advocated by some cognitive developmental theorists is to distinguish the development of moral thinking from the development of other kinds of social knowledge. What the child understands about moral issues may be completely independent of knowledge in other domains and may develop in its own unique way.

▶ **Sociocultural influence**

One major proponent of such a view is Elliot Turiel (1978, 1983), who draws a distinction among the moral, societal, and psychological domains of social-cognitive development. The *moral domain* consists of rules that regulate one's own or another's rights or welfare; examples are the concepts of justice and responsibility toward others. The *societal domain* is the child's knowledge of the social world. Within this domain, **social conventions** are the behavioral rules that regulate social interactions, such as how to dress appropriately for a given occasion and what degree of formality to use in greeting or speaking to someone. Social conventions, unlike moral knowledge, can vary dramatically from culture to culture. The *psychological domain* consists of knowledge of the inner thoughts and feelings of the self and others, including an awareness of intentions and personality characteristics. Turiel hypothesizes that each domain develops along a separate path and that traditional theories of moral development have confused moral and social conventions. Rather than identifying stages of moral development, Turiel describes how the child's accumulated experiences with moral and social-conventional transgressions lead to advances in social knowledge.

▶ **Development as continuous/ stagelike**

Children can discriminate between moral and social conventional rules by the age of three years, although they become more consistent in making the distinctions later in the preschool years (Smetana & Braeges, 1990). In one study, preschool-aged children were observed to respond differently to the transgressions of their playmates, depending on whether the behavior violated a social or a moral rule. When the other child violated a moral rule—for example, by intentionally inflicting harm or taking another's possessions—subjects typically reacted by physically intervening or making statements about the pain experienced by the victim. On the other hand, when subjects observed another child violate a social convention—such as eating while standing instead of sitting—they either did not react or, if they did, alluded to the rules surrounding proper social behavior (Nucci & Turiel, 1978). Thus, children showed distinct patterns of reactions depending on the type of rule that was violated. In addition, when children were questioned about social-conventional transgressions, the majority said such an act would be acceptable if no rule existed about it in school, whereas moral transgressions were wrong even if the school had no rule pertaining to them.

social conventions Behavioral rules that regulate social interactions, such as dress codes and degrees of formality in speech.

▶ **Interaction among domains**

How do children come to appreciate the distinction between moral and social conventions? Probably through the affect associated with moral transgressions as distinct from the emotional neutrality of social transgressions. When a child observes a peer hitting someone or is a victim of physical aggression himself, a high degree of emotion is aroused. Events that share this emotional reactivity may cluster together in the child's memory, whereas social transgressions form their own cluster. Indeed, when first- and third-graders were asked to rate how they would feel if they were hit without provocation or if their toys were stolen by another child, they were more likely to indicate a negative emotion than in response to scenarios about lining up outside the wrong classroom. Furthermore, children frequently justified intervening in a moral transgression by referring to their own or the victim's emotional state (Arsenio & Ford, 1985).

Evaluating Cognitive-Developmental Theories In summary, as cognitive-developmental theorists have proposed, there are age-related changes in how children reason about moral problems. Older children are more likely than younger children to consider the intentions, feelings, and needs of others and to rely on abstract moral principles, such as the concept of justice, as they make moral judgments. These changes in moral reasoning parallel more general changes in cognitive abilities. The two most prominent theorists, Jean Piaget and Lawrence Kohlberg, believe that moral development proceeds in a stagelike manner. Domain-specific approaches, such as Elliot Turiel's, place less emphasis on qualitative transitions in moral thinking and focus instead on how the child's experiences lead to cognitive constructions of morality. Cognitive-developmental approaches fill a void left by psychodynamic and social learning theories by acknowledging that how the child thinks about moral situations is every bit as important as how she feels or behaves.

Cognitive-developmental theories, however, also have their shortcomings. Most important, it is not always clear that moral *reasoning* is related to moral *behavior*. When subjects' scores on moral reasoning tests are correlated with their tendencies to cheat, help others, or conform to rules, the relationships are not uniformly strong (Blasi, 1980; Kurtines & Greif, 1974). The strongest relationships are between moral reasoning and specific negative social behaviors, such as aggression and delinquency. Adolescent boys who display high levels of antisocial behavior tend to score lower on moral reasoning tests (Bear, 1989; Blasi, 1980). A second difficulty with cognitive-developmental theories is that current formulations of moral reasoning do not capture the full range of moral principles that individuals use in making ethical judgments. Toward this end, contemporary researchers continue to explore moral reasoning across different cultures and between the sexes.

Psychological Theories: An Overview

Although they highlight different facets of moral development, the three theoretical models outlined in this section (and summarized in Table 13.1) all portray the child as moving from a self-orientation to an other-orientation. They also share the idea that the child is motivated initially by external events, such as rewards and punishments or the need to affiliate with the parents. With development, the standards of morality become internalized. Ultimately, a

Theory	Emphasis	Path of Development	Process of Moral Development
Psychodynamic	Affective dimensions	Stagelike	Resolution of Oedipal conflict followed by identification with same-sex parent
Social Learning	Moral behavior	Continuous	Reinforcement and modeling of standards of behavior followed by internalization of those standards
Cognitive-Developmental			
Piaget	Moral reasoning	Stagelike	Growth in cognitive and perspective-taking skills that lead to more abstract, other-oriented principles of morality
Kohlberg	Moral reasoning	Stagelike	
Turiel	Moral reasoning	Continuous	Growth in knowledge of moral rules as distinct from social conventions

TABLE 13.1

The Major Theories of Moral Development

complete theory of moral development should describe how the affective, cognitive, and behavioral dimensions of morality are related to one another. Recent research on the more positive aspects of moral development such as the development of altruism has begun to shed additional light on how the child's emotions and reasoning might be related to moral action.

PROSOCIAL BEHAVIOR: ALTRUISM

A young child consoles a friend in distress, helps her pick up the pieces of a broken toy, or shares a snack. These are all **prosocial behaviors,** positive social actions performed to benefit others. A specific prosocial behavior, *altruism,* has been studied extensively in the past decade as one way of understanding the development of morality in children. **Altruism** is behavior carried out to help others without expectation of rewards for the self. We have learned from observing children that altruistic behaviors are not uncommon and in fact are displayed at surprisingly early ages.

The Development of Altruism

prosocial behavior Positive social action performed to benefit others.

altruism Behavior carried out to help another without expectation of reward.

empathy Vicarious response to the feelings of others.

Even young infants show signs of sensitivity to the distress of others. Two- and three-day-old infants cry in reaction to other infants' cries but do not produce this same response to other equally loud noises (Simner, 1971). Many psychologists interpret this behavior as one of the earliest signs of **empathy,** the vicarious response to the feelings of others that includes sympathetic con-

▶ **Roles of nature and nurture**

cern. Empathy is an emotional response that is likely to precede altruism, the actual act of helping someone else. In the neonate, empathy probably originates in reflexlike reactions to the distress of others. Because the primitive forms of empathy occur so early in life, some theorists believe it is an innate human response (Hoffman, 1981a).

A rich source of information about the altruistic capacities of infants and young children can be found in a series of studies conducted by Marian Radke-Yarrow and Carolyn Zahn-Waxler (1984). Their method involved training mothers to record systematically any event of distress, such as pain, sadness, fear, or anger, that occurred in the presence of their child. The mothers were to note the child's reactions and their own behaviors toward the distressed person and their child. The children in these various studies ranged in age from ten months to eight years, and data collection usually lasted for weeks or even months. Here is an example of the altruism of twenty-month-old Danny:

> [A visiting baby cries.] Danny went into the kitchen, picked up the baby's bottle, went into his room where the little girl was crying, and put the bottle into her mouth. He didn't even take a sample himself. I always keep thinking that when he sees someone else's bottle he's going to want to try it. He has been off the bottle himself for about two weeks. He held the bottle in her mouth. When she moved her head, it would slip out and he'd try readjusting it and holding it back in there again correctly. . . . (Radke-Yarrow & Zahn-Waxler, p. 85)

Altruism is a form of prosocial behavior carried out to help others without expected benefit to the self. Even preschool children show clear signs of sensitivity to the emotional needs of others.

Radke-Yarrow and Zahn-Waxler's (1984) research shows that at ten to fourteen months children display a range of empathic reactions. Besides crying, infants whimper or silently attend to expressions of distress from another person. Often they respond to the cries of other children by soothing *themselves,* by sucking the thumb or seeking the parent for comfort. Perhaps because children at this age do not yet clearly distinguish the boundaries of their own self from those of others, consoling the self is equated with coping with another's distress.

▶ **Interaction among domains**

Between one and two years of age, a new behavior emerges—touching or patting the victim as if to provide solace. The helping child may seek assistance for the person in distress or even give him something to provide comfort, such as a cookie, blanket, or teddy bear. The victim's emotional state might also be labeled with expressions such as "cry," "oh-oh!" or "hurting." Table 13.2 lists the various prosocial behaviors displayed by infants and young children. As we saw in Chapter 10, children show clear signs of sensitivity to the emotional states and needs of others well before they achieve a sophisticated level of cognitive functioning. Accompanying that sensitivity are actions that have an unmistakable altruistic character.

Preschool children display more varied and complex responses to the needs of others. In a classic study of "sympathy," Lois Murphy (1937) observed that children show a host of behaviors in response to a peer's distress in a naturalistic nursery school setting. Among them were comforting and helping the victim, asking questions of the troubled child, punishing the agent of the child's distress, protecting the victim, and asking an adult for help. Other researchers report that when they are asked why they share with or help someone else, nursery school children often state they simply "want to" or refer to the needs of the other person (Eisenberg-Berg & Neal, 1979).

The nature of altruistic behavior in school-aged children and adolescents is less clear. Although many researchers report increases in helping and sharing with age, others note that older children may actually help or share less (Radke-Yarrow, Zahn-Waxler, & Chapman, 1983). The lack of consensus on how altruism develops in the years from six to sixteen may stem in part from the wide range of research approaches employed in this area. Some investigators have relied exclusively on naturalistic observations, and others have employed elaborately staged laboratory experiments in which, for example, children are asked to make a donation to a needy person or group. Children participating in the second type of study may not behave as they would under more natural conditions. They may make donations, for example, because they feel that is what the experimenter expects rather than because they are genuinely altruistic. Researchers must address these methodological discrepancies before a comprehensive picture of altruism in older children can emerge.

Sex Differences in Altruism   A popular belief is that girls are more nurturant, caring, and empathic than boys and, because of these qualities, are thus more altruistic. Is there any evidence that girls behave more altruistically than boys do? On the whole, there are few sex differences in the *amount* of helping and sharing displayed by children (Radke-Yarrow, Zahn-Waxler, & Chapman, 1983). But there are sex differences in *how* altruism is expressed. For one thing, girls verbalize altruistic tendencies more than boys do. Girls who heard a recording of an infant crying in one experiment expressed more verbal sympathy than boys did. Yet when they were actually in the presence of a crying

Responses	Age (in months)			
	9–14 (N = 8) %[a]	14–20 (N = 17) %	20–25 (N = 16) %	25–31 (N = 7) %
Positive physical contact				
Pats, rubs	75	59	81	86
Hugs, kisses	25	59	88	86
Instrumental acts				
Gives an object	25	70	81	71
Gives physical help	12	12	50	14
Involves aid from a third person	00	24	56	28
Protects or defends victim	12	35	31	43
Verbal concern				
Concerned question	00	12	69	100
Advice to victim	00	00	44	86
Sympathetic reassurance	00	12	75	86
Ritualistic, sympathetic reassurance	12	24	62	57

[a]The percentage represents the number of children at a given age level who made the given response.
Source: Adapted from Radke-Yarrow & Zahn-Waxler, 1984.

TABLE 13.2

Prosocial Responses of Preschool Children

Preschool children display a variety of prosocial behaviors. At one year of age, children often pat or rub a victim. As they grow older, children give victims of distress material objects or seek assistance for them. By the age of two and a half years, they begin to express verbal concern by asking questions or offering advice and reassurance.

▶ **Sociocultural influence**

baby, girls were no more likely to assist than boys were (Zahn-Waxler, Friedman, & Cummings, 1983). The tendency for girls to be more expressive about altruism is consistent with at least some research findings (noted in Chapter 12 on sex roles) that show girls to be more verbally expressive in general.

In many cultures, including our own, an important part of the female role is being nurturant and helpful to others. Beverly Fagot (1978a) found that girls in our society are more frequently rewarded by parents for helping than boys are. Yet despite cultural stereotypes and differential patterns of parental reinforcement, sex differences in altruism are not very strong.

Cross-Cultural Studies of Altruism   Although the general progressions in moral reasoning measured by Kohlberg's moral dilemmas are similar across cultures, interesting variations occur when we measure reasoning about prosocial situations. One framework to assess prosocial reasoning has been formulated by Nancy Eisenberg (1986). In each of her "prosocial dilemmas," the needs of one person are in conflict with those of another individual or group. The following story is an example:

> One day a girl (boy) named Mary (Eric) was going to a friend's birthday party. On her (his) way she (he) saw a girl (boy) who had fallen down and hurt her (his) leg. The girl asked Mary to go to her house and get her parents so the parents could come and take her to the doctor. But if Mary did run and get the child's parents, she would be late for the birthday party and miss the ice cream, cake, and all the games. What should Mary do? Why? (Eisenberg, 1986, p. 135)

▶ **Interaction among domains**

▶ **Development as continuous/
stagelike**

TABLE 13.3

Levels of Prosocial Reasoning

Nancy Eisenberg has outlined the
accompanying progression in prosocial reasoning. Children move
from a concern with the self to a
concern for others and show more
internal, abstract bases for helping
as they grow older.

Most American children reason **hedonistically** in the preschool and early
school years, saying they would help in order to obtain affection or material
rewards such as candy or cake. **Needs-oriented reasoning** prevails in the
years up to age seven or eight, when children express a concern for the physical or psychological needs of others in statements such as, "He needs help" or
"She's hurt." Later, during the high school years, more **empathic** orientations
emerge ("I'm trying to put myself in her shoes"). Eisenberg believes that older
adolescents possess internalized abstract principles on the importance of altruism and experience emotions such as happiness and pride when their behaviors match their internal beliefs and guilt when they do not. As with other
outlines of moral development, we see a progression from concern for external
consequences to a more internalized, feeling-based foundation in reasoning.
Table 13.3 outlines these stages of prosocial reasoning.

When children from other countries are asked to reason about prosocial dilemmas, similar patterns of development are observed in societies with a
Western industrialized influence. German, Italian, and Polish children, for example, show the same progression from hedonistic to needs-oriented reasoning as do American children (Boehnke et al., 1989; Eisenberg et al., 1985). In
other cultures, however, in which societal norms and values are different,
variations in this sequence occur. For example, children raised on the Israeli
kibbutz express concern with the humanness of the central character and the
importance of internalized norms ("She has a duty to help others") even during
the elementary school years, reflecting a more mature level of prosocial reasoning (Eisenberg, Hertz-Lazarowitz, & Fuchs, 1990; Fuchs et al., 1986). A
somewhat different picture is provided by children from the Maisin tribe, a
coastal village society of Papua New Guinea. Here, children maintain a needs

Level	Age	Characteristics
Hedonistic reasoning	Preschoolers and young elemen-tary school children	Preoccupation with gain for the self as a re-sult of being or not being altruistic
Needs-oriented reasoning	Preschoolers and elementary school children	Concern for the physical and psychological needs of others even though they may con-flict with one's own
Approval and interper-sonal orientation	Elementary and high school students	Reliance on stereotypes of good and bad and seeking approval from others for helping or not helping
Empathic and/or transi-tional reasoning	Older elementary and high school students	Concern with feelings of others and use of norms for prosocial behavior
Internalized reasoning	High school students	Maintenance of self-respect for living up to internalized values and beliefs; belief in rights of all individuals and importance of fulfilling societal obligations

Source: Adapted from Eisenberg, 1986.

Some children grow up in cultures in which they contribute to the needs of the community, by helping with harvesting, for example. Children raised in group-oriented societies tend to behave more altruistically than children reared in settings that emphasize individualism.

orientation well into adolescence and even adulthood (Tietjen, 1986). These patterns of prosocial reasoning mirror the values emphasized by each culture (Eisenberg, 1986). On the Israeli kibbutz, the goal of contributing to the good of the entire community is stressed, whereas among the Maisin, children are explicitly taught to be aware of and respond to the needs of particular other individuals, as opposed to the larger social group.

If children show cross-cultural differences in their tendency to reason about prosocial matters, might they also show differences in their tendency to behave altruistically? In some societies, children show a greater propensity for helping and sharing than in others. Nancy and Theodore Graves (1983) studied the children of Aitutaki Island, one of the Cook Islands in the South Pacific, where tremendous economic and social changes were occurring in parts of the island. The shift from a subsistence economy to an industrialized market economy produced corresponding changes in family structure and the roles of family members. Children living in the remaining rural villages grow up in extended families in which they make substantial contributions toward family and community goals. They participate in most community affairs, are sent by elders to share food and other goods with other village members, and bring the family contribution to church each week. In contrast, children growing up in urban, more modernized settings are reared in nuclear families and participate less in both family and community functions.

Graves and Graves (1983) observed that children in the urban settings behaved less altruistically than children in rural settings. Observations of children five and six years of age in their homes and surrounding environs showed that village children were more likely to assist others than urban children. These researchers conclude that altruism is more likely in societies in which the predominant ethic is one of interdependence and group orientation and in which the child participates in cooperative work experiences than it is in cultures that emphasize individualism and self-reliance.

hedonistic reasoning Form of prosocial reasoning in which children say they will help in order to obtain material rewards.

needs-oriented reasoning Form of prosocial reasoning in which children express a concern for the physical or psychological needs of others.

empathic reasoning Form of prosocial reasoning in which children attempt to put themselves in another's place and understand that person's feelings.

Factors Influencing Altruism

▶ **Interaction among domains**

Children who are altruistic also seem to thrive in other areas of development. Grade school children who tend to help others are more popular with their peers and are more likely to have close friends (Gottman, Gonso, & Rasmussen, 1975; McGuire & Weisz, 1982). Among preadolescents, those who are more altruistic are also more self-confident and self-assured (Mussen et al., 1970). In general, children who are prosocially oriented are better adjusted and have better social skills (Eisenberg & Mussen, 1989). Thus, altruism is associated with many other desirable developmental outcomes, particularly in children's social relationships. Given this fact, as well as general agreement in our society that altruism is a desirable behavioral characteristic in and of itself, it seems important to understand the factors that influence the emergence of this quality.

▶ **Interaction among domains**

Empathy and Altruism   Several contemporary theorists believe that before a child can actually behave altruistically, he must feel empathy for the person in need of assistance. Altruism, in other words, possesses a strong affective component. Martin Hoffman (1975, 1976, 1982) postulates that empathy serves an important motivational function. To relieve his own empathic distress, the child must alleviate the other's distress; as a result, the child behaves altruistically. Thus, if a boy sees a friend who has just fallen down on the playground and cries, he feels uncomfortable. He knows how painful a skinned knee feels and shares his friend's distress. To feel better himself, the boy rushes to his playmate and helps him to get up to walk to the school nurse's office. There are other alternatives—the boy could look away or cover his ears so he doesn't hear his friend's cries, but these responses could result in feelings of guilt. Thus, in Hoffman's scheme, empathy prompts altruistic behavior.

How strong is the connection between empathy and altruism? Because of methodological difficulties associated with measuring empathic distress, especially when children are asked to make self-reports about their feeling states, a consistent relationship between empathy and altruism has not always been found (Underwood & Moore, 1982). It is also possible, however, to measure empathy with nonverbal measures, such as facial expressions (sadness) or behavioral gestures that connote empathy or lack of it (looking away from the distressed victim). When such measures are employed, empathy is found to be related to helping and sharing (Eisenberg, 1986; Eisenberg & Miller, 1987). As we saw earlier, even two-year-olds have been observed to show empathetic reactions to another person in distress, followed by attempts to soothe him or her (Radke-Yarrow & Zahn-Waxler, 1984). And as children grow older, the relationship between empathy and altruism grows distinctly stronger (Eisenberg & Miller, 1987; Underwood & Moore, 1982).

Empathy does not always lead to altruistic responses. The very young child, for example, may show signs of empathic distress yet not know that the victim requires assistance or what form that assistance should take (Hoffman, 1975, 1976). If a playmate is crying as the result of a fall, should she be helped to stand up or should she be left alone? Should the child say something comforting or reassuring or should he simply keep silent? As children mature, they have more opportunities to learn about the range of prosocial behaviors that

▶ **Interaction among domains**

can be expressed. Their understanding about the self's distinction from others also matures. Along with that understanding comes the realization that the other person's distress can be relieved by taking some action. The stronger relationship between empathy and altruism in later childhood probably reflects these elements.

Recent research suggests that empathy does not just involve negative emotions. When Randy Lennon and Nancy Eisenberg (1987) observed preschoolers in semistructured play, very few naturally occurring episodes of prosocial behavior were accompanied by negative emotional displays on the part of either the recipient or donor. On the contrary, virtually every time a child shared a toy with another, both she and the recipient displayed a positive emotion before and after the sharing. Such findings are not easily explained by the concept of "empathic distress" and indicate that empathy needs to be more broadly conceptualized as a responsiveness to both positive and negative emotions. Although the relationship between shared negative affect and altruism has been partially demonstrated, researchers still need to elucidate the role that shared positive affect plays in the display of altruism.

Altruism and Moral Reasoning Is the performance of altruistic acts associated with advances in moral reasoning? Such an association makes intuitive sense because the child's understanding of a moral issue may guide decisions to behave in a moral fashion. When level of reasoning on Kohlberg's moral dilemmas is compared with the amount of helping behavior demonstrated by children, moderate positive relationships have usually, but not always, been observed (Emler & Rushton, 1974; Harris, Mussen, & Rutherford, 1976; Santrock, 1975). One reason may be that Kohlberg's dilemmas emphasize law and justice as opposed to concepts such as altruism.

When reasoning is assessed by using dilemmas specifically designed to measure prosocial thinking, the relationships between reasoning and behavior are stronger (Eisenberg-Berg & Hand, 1979; Rubin & Schneider, 1973). As we saw earlier, these dilemmas require the child to choose between her own and another's needs or between helping or not helping someone. Children who reason hedonistically tend to help other children less frequently, whereas children who reason empathically are more likely to donate toys, stickers, or other valuable objects to others (Eisenberg & Shell, 1986; Eisenberg-Berg & Hand, 1979).

For a number of reasons, however, prosocial reasoning may not always predict moral behavior. As we saw earlier with respect to empathy, children may lack the skills or resources to provide assistance even though they understand the importance of helping others on a cognitive level (Peterson, 1983). A four-year-old may be able to verbalize that sharing food with a crying peer can make him feel better but at a given moment may not have an extra cookie or snack to give to the playmate. Moreover, behaving altruistically may not always be the most moral thing to do. If a friend has explicitly stated that he wants to do a puzzle alone, then "helping" that friend to fit the pieces would be inappropriate and could even lead to conflict (Eisenberg, 1982). Thus, the correspondence between moral reasoning and moral action need not be direct, or might be mitigated by other factors such as the demands of the situation or the skills in the child's response repertoire.

▶ **Roles of nature and nurture**

The Role of Socialization   What role does socialization play in the emergence of altruism, particularly the child-rearing techniques employed by parents? Much of the research on this topic draws from the principles of social learning theory. Evidence from laboratory studies suggests that reinforcements can influence a child's helping and sharing. Both material (for example, money, candy, tokens) and social ("You're a good boy!") rewards increase the likelihood that children will help another, although social rewards seem to encourage a greater internal motive for altruism. When seven- and eight-year-old children in one study were given either a penny for each episode of sharing or verbal praise ("That was a fine thing you did"), those in the latter group were more likely to say that they shared in order to help or were concerned about the welfare of the other child. Children who received a material reward stated that they shared simply to obtain the reward (Smith et al., 1979).

Laboratory studies have confirmed that opportunities for observational learning are another potent factor in the emergence of altruism. When a child sees a model making a donation to a needy person or group, he is likely to be charitable as well (Grusec & Skubiski, 1970; Rushton, 1975). Furthermore, what models *do* is usually more important than what they *say*. J. Philippe Rushton (1975) asked children to play a bowling game in which they could win tokens exchangeable for prizes. The experiment had four conditions: half the subjects saw a model giving 50 percent of the winnings away to a charity, and half saw a selfish model who kept all the tokens. In addition, for some children, the altruistic model lectured about the importance of being generous; for others, the altruistic model preached that one should be selfish. Similarly, some

FIGURE 13.3

The Effects of Models' Actions and Words

When children in one laboratory experiment heard a model preach about generosity and then give away half of her winnings to charity, they were far more likely to make a donation themselves than when the model preached about generosity but behaved selfishly. On the other hand, when the model preached about selfishness but behaved generously, children were more likely to donate than when the model spoke and behaved selfishly. The verbal message still had an effect, though. Children in this latter condition were less likely to be altruistic compared with when the models' actions and words were altruistic.

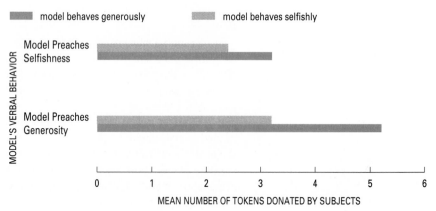

Source: Adapted from Rushton, 1982.

Parents who frequently explain why misbehaviors are unacceptable and provide a rationale for rules tend to have children who act more altruistically compared with parents who use power assertive techniques.

children heard the selfish model preach about generosity, while others heard the selfish model preach about selfishness. As Figure 13.3 shows, the model's behavior was more powerful in influencing children's tendency to donate than the verbal message she delivered (although the message did increase altruism as well). Because parents are the primary agents of socialization, their own overt altruistic behaviors and the rewards they give for their children's prosocial acts are major factors in the development of altruism.

The content of parents' verbal communications is especially important. When parents provide a rationale for altruism, leading their children to think about the effects of their actions on others, children are more likely to practice altruistic behaviors. **Induction,** or parental use of reasoning as a disciplinary technique, includes clear communication of standards for behavior, arousal of empathic feelings in children, and stimulation of role taking (Eisenberg & Mussen, 1989). Parents who use induction explain why transgressions are wrong and provide a rationale for rules and regulations. For example, a parent might say, "Don't pull Sam's hair! That hurts him. You don't like to have your hair pulled, do you?" In contrast, some parents use **power assertion,** the use of forceful commands, physical punishment, or removal of material objects or privileges. For example, the parent might yell, "Stop that! You're not watching TV tonight!" as her son pulls his brother's hair. Parents who frequently use induction as opposed to power assertion as a disciplinary tool have children

induction Parental control technique that relies on the extensive use of reasoning and explanation as well as the arousal of empathic feelings.

power assertion Parental control technique that relies on the use of forceful commands, physical punishment, and removal of material objects or privileges.

who behave more altruistically (Hoffman, 1975; Zahn-Waxler, Radke-Yarrow, & King, 1979). Hoffman (1975) believes that induction is particularly effective because it encourages children to be empathic, which in turn leads to more helping behavior.

A technique that may be just as powerful as induction is to make an attribution about the child's prosocial characteristics. When children are told, "I guess you're the kind of person who helps others whenever you can," their tendency to behave prosocially is greatly increased (Grusec & Redler, 1980; Mills & Grusec, 1989). It is possible that attributions of concern for others change the child's self-concept in such a way that she sees herself as possessing altruistic personality characteristics and strives to behave in a manner consistent with that image (Grusec, 1982). Parents do not often make prosocial attributions about their children, but it is precisely the rarity of these events that may make them so powerful in the eyes of the child (Grusec, 1991).

In summary, altruism has its beginnings in the early empathic responses of the child to the emotional states of others. The child's empathic capabilities grow and her reasoning about prosocial conflicts increasingly takes into account the feelings and needs of others. The child's socialization experiences add to her tendency to act in a helpful, prosocial manner. There is no one formula for raising an altruistic child. Research suggests, however, that when adults use social praise to reward prosocial acts and encourage children to think about their own prosocial traits, children show an increase in positive moral behaviors. Moreover, parents serve as extremely potent models for children's altruistic behaviors. The study of altruism has begun to demonstrate how moral development involves the complex interplay between affect, cognition, and behavior.

▶ **Roles of nature and nurture**   **Moral Education**

During the last two decades, many public officials and private citizens have expressed renewed interest in providing children with formal moral education within the school curriculum. Alarmed by the climbing rates of teenage pregnancy, crime, and substance abuse, these individuals believe that children should be exposed to moral values training beginning with the elementary school years, if not before. Various moral education programs have been developed based on our understanding of the psychological development of children. Many have proven to be effective in shaping children's moral reasoning and behavior.

One type of program is based on Kohlberg's theory of moral development. These programs emphasize exposing children to moral conflicts and to moral reasoning one stage above the child's own. In one study, children in junior and senior high school met twice each week to discuss moral conflicts similar to Kohlberg's moral dilemmas. After the trainer presented a conflict, children were encouraged to supply possible resolutions to the situation and the consequences of each solution for the characters in the story. The trainer made a deliberate attempt to encourage open discussion and alternative points of view. After nine weeks, children who had participated in this program showed

In one type of moral education program, participants discuss moral conflicts and exchange alternative points of view. After participating in one such program, junior and senior high school students showed significant increases in moral reasoning scores compared with control children who did not have this experience.

significant increases in moral reasoning scores compared with control children who did not participate in the program (Blatt & Kohlberg, 1975).

Other programs have employed **cooperative learning,** the use of peer groups to work on joint educational projects, in order to influence prosocial development. One long-term project conducted in Tel Aviv, Israel, involved an experimental teaching method called the Small Group Teaching approach (Hertz-Lazarowitz & Sharan, 1984). In each classroom, children were divided into small groups to work on academic projects in a collaborative fashion, investigating a topic, preparing a report, and presenting the findings to the class. The hypothesis was that this experience would encourage mutual help and support, the exchange of ideas and resources, and mutual acceptance. Teachers received extensive training in promoting social skills among their students, including active listening to peers, sharing thoughts and resources, and cooperation. The program was conducted over a two-year period in three elementary schools, after which children were compared with those in traditional schools on a number of academic and social dimensions.

The experimental program had a number of interesting results. Children showed an increase in higher-level thinking skills (for example, evaluation, comparison, and analysis) and creativity, and they also reported a more positive social climate in the classroom. The most important finding from the perspective of moral development, however, was an increase in the frequency of prosocial behaviors displayed by program participants. In one test, children were offered one of two tasks: a solitary one or helping another child in the class. Whereas nineteen out of twenty-one children in the traditional classrooms chose the individual task, thirteen out of nineteen students from the Small Group Teaching program chose to help another child. In general, children in the experimental group were significantly more altruistic and cooperative than students from the traditional group.

cooperative learning Educational experiences that involve collaborative efforts by a group of peers.

▶ **Interaction among domains**

It is important to note that specific moral principles were not directly taught as part of the experimental curriculum. Instead, the program's foundation was participation in experiential learning and group endeavors. It is also noteworthy that many components of the program dealt with cognitive learning styles, social-interactive patterns, and social skills. The experimenters provided a broad-based intervention that expanded both children's reasoning and behavior. Finally, the program was of relatively long duration. The success of this experiment suggests that when children are exposed to a steady climate of cooperative peer interaction, prosocial behaviors will develop without explicit instruction.

AGGRESSION

At the other end of the spectrum from prosocial behavior is **aggression**, physical or verbal behaviors that are intended to harm or irritate someone else. Aggression in children typically emerges as they begin to have more and more contact with peers. Conflicts inevitably arise over toys, friends, the rules of the games they play, and other issues. Sometimes these conflicts escalate into full-scale aggression, in which children will push, hit, kick, or bite another child. Aside from the physical harm that aggression can produce, it is a negative behavior for other reasons. Children who tend to be aggressive have difficulties with peer relationships. They are more likely to be rejected by their peers and have smaller peer networks than children who behave more prosocially (Dodge et al., 1990; Ladd, 1983). In its most extreme form, a child's persistent aggression can result in juvenile delinquency and antisocial behavior. Therefore, it is important to understand the developmental course and the roots of aggression.

▶ **Interaction among domains**

The Development of Aggression

The first signs of conflict among peers emerge between one and two years of age, when children begin to have disputes over toys (Maudry & Nekula, 1939). A familiar scene is one child tugging at a toy held by another, with the victim physically resisting or protesting loudly, "But it's *mine*"! Such conflicts occur more frequently in larger groups than in dyads and decrease over the period of toddlerhood (Rubenstein & Howes, 1976).

Dale Hay and Hildy Ross (1982) monitored how unacquainted pairs of twenty-one-month-olds engaged in and resolved conflicts as they interacted in a laboratory playroom. Even though the actual length of time spent in conflicts was brief—an average of 22.7 seconds per conflict—87 percent of the children were part of at least one conflict during the four 15-minute observation sessions, usually over a toy that two children wanted at the same time. Most of their disputes were resolved without the intrusion of an adult; usually one child yielded to the pulls and tugs of the other. Moreover, children often settled their conflicts without resorting to force. Many times one child would show or offer alternative objects to the antagonizing peer, for example. The

aggression Physical or verbal behaviors intended to harm or irritate someone else.

kind of information children extract from these brief struggles about the behaviors that aggravate or placate others, including those that are successful versus those that are unsuccessful, can lead to the development of aggressive or prosocial styles in later years (Parke & Slaby, 1983). For example, if children learn that antagonistic behavior is successful in letting them keep a desirable toy, they may continue to behave aggressively; if they learn that sharing an object diffuses the conflict, they may continue to behave prosocially.

During the preschool years, *physical aggression,* such as hitting, kicking, and shoving, declines, and *verbal aggression,* such as making derogatory comments, increases (Goodenough, 1931; McCabe & Lipscomb, 1988). *Instrumental aggression,* or object-oriented aggression (as in retrieving a toy commandeered by a playmate), decreases in frequency, whereas *hostile aggression,* or person-oriented aggression (as in hitting a peer), increases (Hartup, 1974).

As we saw in Chapter 12, until the age of six years, boys generally display more aggression, both physical and verbal, than girls do (Maccoby & Jacklin, 1980). This finding has been reported for children from a wide variety of cultures ranging from industrialized nations such as England and Switzerland to developing countries such as Kenya, the Philippines, and Mexico (Omark & Edelman, 1975; Smith & Green, 1974; Whiting & Whiting, 1975). After early childhood, boys continue to show more physical aggression than girls, although the findings for verbal aggression are mixed.

Individual differences in the tendency to be aggressive remain stable throughout childhood and into adulthood. Research has shown that ratings of childhood aggression at age eight years are significantly correlated with aggression at age nineteen years, with the correlation coefficient or $r = +0.38$ for boys and $r = +0.47$ for girls (Eron, 1980). Furthermore, many adolescents identified as needing counseling for aggressive antisocial tendencies continue to show these undesirable behavior patterns thirty years later (Robins, 1978). These findings do not mean that every aggressive child will become an aggressive adult, but they do suggest that it is important to identify the factors that make this such a persistent behavioral style.

Factors Influencing Aggression

▶ **Roles of nature and nurture**

What are the causes of aggression? Some theories focus on biological factors. In Chapter 12, we saw that hormones such as testosterone have been linked to aggressive behavior in several species. Ethologists like Konrad Lorenz (1966) maintain that aggression is an instinctual response in many organisms, including humans, that serves to ensure the survival of the species. Animals fight to defend their territory, and as the losers retreat to other areas, the population is distributed more equally across the environment. As a consequence, animals have more balanced access to food and other resources. Because the victors of aggression are also usually the strongest, they are most likely to reproduce, which acts to favor the survival of their offspring. Ethologists believe that organisms must periodically discharge the aggressive energy that builds up. Thus, aggression is seen in this perspective as a basic aspect of human nature.

Another popular model of aggression in the 1940s and 1950s was the **frustration-aggression hypothesis** (Dollard et al., 1939). In this view, aggression inevitably follows any event in which the organism's goals are blocked. If the child is forbidden to play with an attractive toy or has a delicious cookie taken from him, he will display aggression. As in the ethological view, in this model, aggression is seen as periodically arising energy that must somehow be released.

Finally, social learning theorists believe that aggression results from the child's reinforcement history but, more important, from opportunities to observe aggressive models as well. Children may witness aggression in their parents, peers, and the media and store representations of these behaviors for potential use at a later time.

Today, two of the most popular explanations of aggression center on children's interpretations of their social environment and parental disciplinary techniques. Contemporary theorists place less emphasis on aggression as an innate human characteristic and more emphasis on how the child's cognitions and experiences can lead to a persistent aggressive behavioral style. This body of research has specific implications for determining practical measures for controlling aggression in children.

Cognitive Mediators of Aggression   A key determinant of whether a child will act aggressively is how she understands the intentions of a partner in social interaction. If the child believes that a peer intended to act in a hostile manner, she is more likely to behave aggressively than when she attributes accidental intentions to the peer. Children differ in their tendency to ascribe hostile motives to the actions of others. Aggressive boys, for example, are more biased toward making hostile attributions about the actions of peers than boys who are not aggressive. In one experiment, all children watched a series of vignettes featuring two child actors in which one child's behavior was portrayed as negatively affecting the other. In some vignettes, the intent of the actor was ambiguous. Boys who had previously been identified as aggressive were more likely to state that the perpetrator in these ambiguous scenes was "mean" compared with boys who were not aggressive. As Figure 13.4 shows, this difference was especially pronounced if subjects were led to believe that they would actually interact with the hostile peer after they viewed the vignettes (Dodge & Somberg, 1987). It is as if aggressive boys were "primed" to see aggressive intentions in others, especially if they felt personally threatened.

Adolescents incarcerated for aggressive antisocial behavior show similar patterns of defining social problems in hostile ways. Subjects in one study were asked to imagine that they wanted to practice softball, but the bat they needed was being held by someone else. Antisocial adolescents tended to characterize this scenario as hostile and selected aggressive responses as a solution. They also anticipated few consequences for their aggressive behaviors compared with less aggressive adolescents (Slaby & Guerra, 1988).

Kenneth Dodge (1980, 1982, 1986) maintains that aggression is the result of deficits or biases in social information processing. The aggressive child (child A) fails to search for all available social cues when interacting with peers and attends primarily to hostile signals. Once child A decides, often incor-

▶ **The child's active role**

▶ **Interaction among domains**

FIGURE 13.4

Aggression as a Function of Attributing Hostile Motives to Others

Aggressive children are more likely to make hostile attributions about an ambiguous behavior than nonaggressive children. When aggressive boys heard a story about one child hurting another, they decided the perpetrator was "mean" even though the actor's intent was not clear (relaxed condition). On two subsequent trials (post-threats 1 and 2), subjects were told they would have to interact with the actor in the story. Aggressive children's tendency to make hostile attributions increased even further.

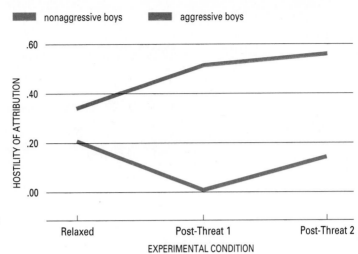

Source: Adapted from Dodge & Somberg, 1987.

rectly, that child B intends to be hostile, child A acts aggressively. The result is that child B retaliates and confirms child A's judgments. Child A continues to make hostile attributions and behaves aggressively in future interactions.

Aggressive children may also hold different beliefs about the outcomes of aggression. David Perry and his associates gave aggressive and nonaggressive elementary school children questionnaires investigating their beliefs about aggression (Perry, Perry, & Rasmussen, 1986). Aggressive children were more likely to report that aggression leads to tangible rewards and reduces the chance that they would be attacked or annoyed by another child in the future. Aggressive children have apparently learned that their behaviors have been successful in bringing them immediate rewards. A subsequent study showed that aggressive children place less value on suffering by the victims of aggression, retaliation from the victim, and peer rejection than nonaggressive children. They are also less likely to evaluate themselves negatively for being aggressive (Boldizar, Perry, & Perry, 1989). Thus, aggressive children are less concerned about the negative consequences of aggression than their nonaggressive age mates.

▶ **Roles of nature and nurture**

Parenting Practices and Aggression Two dimensions of parenting are most closely associated with aggression in children: the nurturance parents display toward their children and the type of disciplinary strategy they choose. In a major longitudinal study of over six hundred children, Leonard Eron and his colleagues found that children who were more aggressive in school had parents who displayed less warmth and positive emotion toward their offspring and who punished their children more for aggression at home (Eron et al., 1961). Instead of reducing aggression, punishment actually increased children's physical acting out. Punishment was effective in inhibiting aggression only for boys who identified strongly with their fathers (see Figure 13.5). Perhaps, when boys identify with their fathers, they interpret their fathers' behavior as appropriate responses to the misdeeds they performed (Eron, 1987).

frustration-aggression hypothesis Idea that the blocking or frustrating of an organism's goals leads to aggression.

FIGURE 13.5

Aggression as a Function of Parental Punishment

Boys who experience low levels of parental punishment tend to be less aggressive in school than those who experience high levels of punishment. The only exception is that when boys show high levels of identification with their father, higher levels of punishment inhibit their aggression.

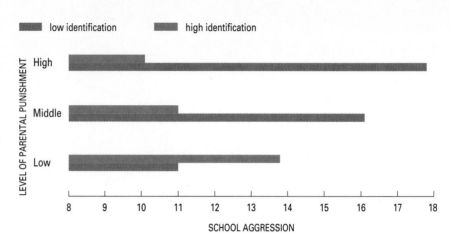

Source: Adapted from Eron, 1987.

Similarly, Dan Olweus (1980) found aggression in a sample of adolescent Swedish boys was related to parental reports of early child-rearing conditions. Mothers who recalled being hostile and rejecting during the first four to five years of their sons' lives had children who were rated by peers as more aggressive. In addition, parents who reported using power-assertive techniques such as physical punishment, threats, and violent outbursts also had more aggressive sons. Finally, if mothers were permissive when their sons behaved aggressively toward them or toward peers and siblings, setting few or no prohibitions on these undesired behaviors, sons tended to be more aggressive.

How could these parental variables result in aggression? Parental rejection and lack of nurturance may cause the child to feel frustrated; his emotional and other needs are not being met (Martin, 1975). Permissive parenting communicates to children that there are few limits or controls on their behavior—in essence, "anything goes." Also, parents who are permissive are frequently inconsistent in their use of punishment (Martin, 1975), which can send children mixed or confusing messages about which behaviors are acceptable and which are not. Thus, it may not be clear to the child that aggression is undesirable. Finally, when parents employ physical punishment, they are actually (and often unwittingly) providing their children with powerful models for aggression. Children may learn that spanking, hitting, or threatening are ways to control the behaviors of others.

▶ **The child's active role**

Children, however, do not become aggressive simply because of their parents' behavior. A complete account of children's aggression will almost certainly describe how reciprocal interactions between child and caregiver are responsible. Parents may react emotionally to the dispositional traits of their child or choose a disciplinary technique in response to the child's behavior. In his study of the antecedents of aggression, Olweus (1980) found boys' temperament, as assessed by parental reports of early activity level and "hot-headedness," was significantly related to aggression in adolescence. Boys who are active and emotionally volatile may exhaust parents and cause them to be more permissive. Alternatively, they may elicit greater punitiveness and hostility from parents, which, in turn, escalate the boys' aggression. The specific ways in which maladaptive cycles of interaction between caregivers and children can lead to aggression are elaborated in the next chapter.

In summary, although children, especially boys, may show biologically based predispositions to become aggressive, substantial evidence also shows that aggression is related to unique patterns of cognition and socialization history. Children who show persistent aggressive styles are biased to judge the intentions of others as hostile and do not think about the negative consequences of their misdeeds. There is also a high likelihood that they have been raised by caregivers who are low on nurturance and high in the use of power-assertive disciplinary techniques. Thus, like altruism, aggression has no single cause but is determined by a number of factors in the child's background. The Chronology on page 570 summarizes the emergence of specific aggressive behaviors along with the development of many other aspects of morality that we have described in this chapter.

Controlling Aggression

Given what we know about the sources of aggression, how can we intervene with children who show persistent and inappropriate attacks on others? One tactic is to break the cycle of negative interaction that frequently develops between caregivers and aggressive children by encouraging parents to use less power assertion and more induction when they discipline their offspring. Much more will be said about this strategy in the next chapter, in which we discuss the elements of effective parenting.

▶ **Interaction among domains**

Another possibility is to alter the child's cognitions about the consequences of aggression so that he or she understands the harm that kicking or hitting causes the victim. In one training program, every time a child was aggressive, nursery school teachers discussed with that child the feelings of the victim, explaining that aggression hurts the playmate and causes resentment. In addition, the children were taught more positive ways of solving interpersonal conflicts. Compared with a control group that did not receive this instruction, children in the training group were significantly less aggressive and more cooperative in their play even two weeks after the training sessions ended (Zahavi & Asher, 1978).

Finally, in his longitudinal study of aggression, Leonard Eron found that children who behaved more prosocially at age eight years were less likely to act aggressively as much as twenty-two years later (Eron & Huesmann, 1984). That is, prosocial and aggressive behaviors are not likely to co-occur and are incompatible with each other. Therefore, encouraging young children to behave more positively in social interactions seems worthwhile. In another study involving preschoolers, teachers were instructed to praise children's verbal cooperation and ignore their physical and verbal aggression. After two weeks of this simple intervention, children showed a dramatic decline in aggression and an increase in cooperative play (Slaby & Crowley, 1977).

All this should not imply that aggression in children is always easily controlled. Especially if a child has a long history of repeated violent behavior, intervention may have to be prolonged and intense as well as involving multi-

CHRONOLOGY	Moral Development
NEWBORN	Reacts to cries of other infants in primitive empathic way.
10–14 MONTHS	Shows various signs of empathy to distress of another, but often soothes the self.
1–2 YEARS	Assists another in distress by patting, touching, or offering material objects. Begins to display conflicts in interactions with peers.
3–6 YEARS	Discriminates moral and social-conventional rules. Decreases use of physical aggression but shows increases in verbal aggression. Decreases displays of instrumental aggression but shows increases in hostile aggression. Judges moral dilemmas according to objective consequences and believes in immanent justice and expiatory punishment. Reasons according to rewards and punishments expected from authority figures.
10–16 YEARS	Judges moral dilemmas according to intentions of actor and believes in punishment by reciprocity. Reasons on the basis of rules and laws with a belief in maintaining social order.
16 YEARS	Reasons according to internal principles of justice.
	This chart describes the sequence of moral development based on the findings of research. Children often show individual differences in the exact ages at which they display the various developmental achievements outlined here.

ple approaches. What the research does suggest, though, is that aggression can be minimized if early socialization emphasizes the child's reasoning about the consequences of his or her acts and encourages the display of prosocial behavior.

THEMES IN DEVELOPMENT

MORAL JUDGMENT AND BEHAVIOR

▶ **What roles do nature and nurture play in moral development?**

Psychologists have tended to emphasize the role of experience in the emergence of morality. Although there may be early, biologically based tendencies for children to display empathy and aggression, most researchers have described how the child's subsequent cognitions and socialization experiences shape morality. Cognitive theorists like Piaget and Kohlberg do believe that maturation, in part, guides changes in moral reasoning. But even they believe that children's experiences with peers and other socializing agents play a large role in spurring moral reasoning.

▶ How does the sociocultural context influence moral development?

Children's moral reasoning and behavior often reflect the values of the larger cultural group. In cultures that emphasize the individual's responsibilities to the larger social group, children tend to be more altruistic and display more prosocial reasoning than in cultures that emphasize the role of the individual. In addition, cultures place different weights on law-and-justice reasoning versus other values, such as happiness for all, the importance of harmonious social groups, or the value of all life. Children's responses to moral dilemmas often reflect their culture's unique beliefs.

▶ How does the child play an active role in the process of moral development?

In most theories of moral development, children are hypothesized to internalize the moral norms of the larger society. Cognitive theorists, in particular, describe the child's active construction of moral standards based on experiences with peers and adults that drive the child to more advanced thinking. On another front, children often influence the disciplinary techniques that their parents select, techniques that in turn can shape whether children will later behave aggressively or not. Finally, children often make attributions about the intentions of others, cognitive judgments that can determine whether they will respond aggressively.

▶ Is moral development stagelike or continuous?

Several influential theories of moral development are stage theories, specifically those of Freud, Piaget, and Kohlberg. The empirical evidence, however, does not support the notion that the phallic stage is the time when moral development begins. Nor do data support the idea that moral reasoning within a stage is entirely consistent, as Piaget and Kohlberg argue. Although stage theories are still popular, viewpoints such as domain-specific approaches that emphasize continuous growth are gaining more and more attention.

▶ How does moral development interact with development in other domains?

There are many sides to moral development. Emotions such as empathy are a distinct component. Cognitive skills, such as the ability to reason abstractly about the feelings and intentions of others, are also involved. Thus, moral development is largely influenced by development in other areas. At the same time, moral development has an impact on other domains. For example, altruistic children tend to have healthy peer interactions, whereas aggressive children tend to have poor ones. Moral development represents an important intersection among affect, cognition, and social experience.

SUMMARY

Moral development is the child's acquisition of the standards of conduct considered ethical within his or her culture. Psychological theories differ in the emphasis they place on various aspects of moral development. Psychodynamic theories focus on the affective relationship between the child and parents. Social learning theory centers on the emergence of moral behavior. Cognitive-developmental theories emphasize moral reasoning. All of these perspectives concur in describing moral development as a movement from self-orientation to other-orientation in which the child *internalizes* external societal standards.

Freud believed that moral development results from the resolution of the Oedipal conflict at five or six years of age. To avoid parental rejection, the child identifies with the same-sex parent and internalizes his or her moral beliefs and behaviors. There is little empirical support, however, for many of Freud's specific ideas.

According to social learning theory, children learn to behave morally as a result of the reinforcements they receive from parents and other agents of socialization. Observational learning is especially potent in the development of moral behaviors. Although research shows that many of the principles of social learning theory serve to produce moral behavior in the laboratory, critics point out that it is also important to consider how the child thinks about moral issues.

Cognitive-developmental theorists, like Piaget and Kohlberg, have outlined stages in the development of moral thought. In Piaget's theory, children progress from *moral realism* to *moral relativism* as their cognitive capabilities mature. In Kohlberg's outline, most children advance through three levels of moral reasoning: the *preconventional, conventional,* and *postconventional* levels. Kohlberg maintains that the child's increasing perspective-taking skills are largely responsible for these shifts. Though there are data to support the general idea that children progress in their moral thinking, it remains unclear whether discrete stages of acquisition actually exist. Newer domain-specific approaches describe how children acquire moral knowledge as distinct from social-conventional knowledge.

Researchers have demonstrated that a specific form of moral behavior, *altruism,* occurs early in childhood. Altruism begins with the *empathic response* of young infants to the distress of others, and is followed by distinct efforts of preschool children to help peers who show negative emotions. It is unclear, though, whether altruism increases during the elementary school years and adolescence. There are no significant sex differences in altruism. Children who grow up in cultures in which group values are important, however, tend to be more altruistic.

Children who are empathetic and show high levels of *prosocial reasoning* tend to be altruistic. In addition, children who are rewarded for altruism and observe parents and others behaving altruistically tend to help others more frequently. Parents who use *induction* as a disciplinary technique and make prosocial attributions about their children are especially likely to have altruistic sons and daughters.

The first signs of *aggression* appear during the preschool years as children have more extended contact with peers. With development, instrumental (object-oriented) aggression decreases and hostile (person-oriented) aggression increases. Contemporary researchers have focused on two major factors in the emergence of aggression: the child's cognitions and his socialization experiences. Aggressive children tend to make hostile attributions about the intentions of others and do not perceive the negative consequences of their actions. Furthermore, aggressive children often have rejecting, nonnurturant parents who use either permissive or power-assertive disciplinary techniques. Some intervention programs have attempted to control aggression by helping children to recognize the negative consequences of their actions for victims and by encouraging prosocial responses.

14

The Influence of the Family

KEY THEMES

▶ **How does the sociocultural context influence family processes?**

▶ **How does the child play an active role in family processes?**

▶ **How do family processes interact with other domains of development?**

Joey, age seven years, looked at his loaded dinner plate and announced, "I'm not hungry. Can I just have dessert?"

"No, you may not!" His mother, embarrassed, turned to their house-guest, "I can't think why he gets like this. He's stubborn as a mule." The guest, meanwhile, wondered why no one mentioned that Joey had eaten, in full view of his mother, most of a gift box full of cookies before dinner.

"I don't want this! It stinks! You stink!" Joey pushed away his plate, got up from the table, and ran to the television, which he turned up full volume.

"Turn that down this minute or go to your room!" Joey was motionless. "He's been like this since his father and I split up," his mother told the guest in a lowered voice. "Everything's so different now. I feel like I have to be two parents instead of one. He used to be such a good boy. Don't take that cookie!" Joey lowered his hand from the cookie box, then gave his mother a mournful, pleading look. "All right, but just one!" Joey took two and turned back to the TV.

Although every person displays a vast array of changing attitudes, motives, and behaviors during a lifetime, certain stable characteristics tend to carry through. Many of our most enduring traits are molded by the experiences each of us has in childhood—experiences within our families. This family experience is perhaps the crucial nurture/environment variable in the development of human personality. Moreover, the child's experiences within the family can be affected by other factors, such as divorce, that change the nature of interpersonal dynamics within the family. Joey's family experiences both before and after his parents' separation can potentially have long-lasting effects on his development and his adult personality.

Families, first of all, are central in the process of **socialization,** the process by which children acquire the social knowledge, behaviors, and attitudes valued by the larger society. Parents, siblings, and others within the family unit are the people the child usually spends the most time with and forms the strongest emotional bonds to, and they exert the most power in the child's life. The direction of influence within families runs several ways, however. Just as parents and siblings affect the child's behavior, the child affects the reactions of other family members. Because the family experience includes fluid, constantly changing effects and outcomes among its various members, studying the impact of the family presents a special research challenge to developmental psychologists.

In a sense, virtually every domain of development is deeply influenced by the family environment. Cognition, moral awareness, gender identity, and emotional growth are all nurtured largely within the family. Our goal in this chapter is to focus on the role that specific family members play in the child's social development, with special attention to adaptive and maladaptive patterns of interaction. We will also see how the family itself is a structure in flux, shaped by cultural values and shifting demographic trends such as divorce and maternal employment. The impact of these changes in family structure on the individual child's development is a major concern for developmental psychologists.

UNDERSTANDING THE FAMILY

Historians, sociologists, and anthropologists who study the family as a social unit point to the changes in its structure and functions during the latter half of the twentieth century, largely a result of economic, political, and cultural factors that have precipitated sweeping changes in societies as a whole. With the industrialization of nineteenth-century America, for example, the **extended family,** in which secondary relatives such as grandparents, aunts, or cousins lived in the same household as the primary family, gave way to the **nuclear family,** consisting solely of parents and their offspring living in a single household. Similarly, as we saw in Chapter 1, the modern notion that families are havens for nurturing the child's growth and development was not always prevalent. As we look back in history, we see that the family has been a fluid, changing social structure, and all signs indicate that it will continue to take different shapes in the future as a reflection of larger social, economic, and historical trends.

The Demographics of the American Family

▶ **Sociocultural influence**

socialization Process by which children acquire the social knowledge, skills, and attitudes valued by the larger society.

extended family Family group that includes secondary relations such as grandparents, aunts, uncles, and cousins as well as parents and siblings.

nuclear family Family group that consists solely of parents and their children.

No one family structure is typical of contemporary American society. The 1950s model of a two-parent family with two children and a nonworking mother has long since become more myth than reality. For example, as Figure 14.1 shows, only 73 percent of children under the age of eighteen years lived with two parents in 1988, compared with 85 percent in 1968. Today almost 25 percent of American children live with only a single parent (U.S. Bureau of the Census, 1990a). A climbing divorce rate and the rise in single-parent births have contributed to this trend. Presently, more than 50 percent of all marriages end in divorce (compared with about 15 percent in 1960), and over 25 percent of all births are to single mothers (Bumpass, 1990). Moreover, because adults now marry at later ages and many more couples decide to have fewer children, many children today grow up with older parents and fewer siblings (Rossi, 1987). Finally, as we reported in Chapter 10, about 65 percent of mothers with children under age eighteen years now work outside the home compared with about 45 percent in 1975. In fact, fewer than 15 percent of

FIGURE 14.1

Demographic Changes in Family Structure

The number of children living with two parents has declined since 1968, and the number living with a single parent (most frequently the mother) has increased dramatically. Almost one-fourth of American children live with a single parent. The greater rate of divorce and single-parent births has contributed to this trend.

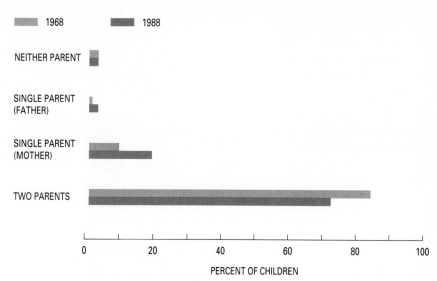

Source: Adapted from U.S. Bureau of the Census, 1978, 1990a.

American families currently consist of a working father, homemaker mother, and children. All of these changes in family structure have distinct implications for the child's experiences within the family.

A Systems Approach

Because families presently take so many forms, some child development researchers have found it more fruitful to focus on family dynamics, the interactions among all members of the group, rather than on the structure of the family per se, as they study the impact of the family. An important influence on contemporary thinking about the family is **systems theory.** A general systems model regards all relationships, be they physical, biological, or social, as holistic entities or systems made up of interdependent elements. In the context of the family, this premise means that all members influence each other simultaneously and that these interactions flow in a circular, reciprocal manner. In Chapter 10, for example, we discuss how the emotional states of mothers and infants are mutually dependent, with the reaction of one influencing the affective state of the other. In systems theory (see Figure 14.2), the individual child's development can only be understood as embedded in the complex network of multidirectional interactions taking place among all family members (Belsky, 1981; Bronfenbrenner, 1979, 1986).

Systems theory assumes that families undergo periods of stability and change. The family tends to adapt in order to maintain a state of *homeostasis,* or equilibrium. So, as children achieve milestones, such as going to school or entering adolescence, the family system must readjust to changes in the child in order to absorb his new routines or demands for independence. At other times, families may experience crises, such as financial hardship, moving, or divorce. Here changing external circumstances oblige both the child and all other family members to adapt to the new situation.

▶ **The child's active role**

systems theory Model for understanding the family that emphasizes the reciprocal interactions among various members.

FIGURE 14.2

The Systems Model of the Family

According to systems theorists, reciprocal influences among family members occur at three levels: the individual or microlevel, the family environment, and the larger social context. At the microlevel, parent and child influence each other directly. Within the family, relationships among particular individuals, such as husband and wife, can affect interactions with children. Finally, larger social factors, such as the presence of economic stress, can affect parent-child relations. The individual child's development is thus embedded in this network of multidirectional interactions.

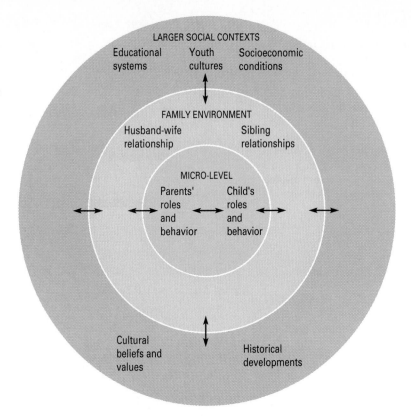

Source: Adapted from Peterson & Rollins, 1987.

Systems theory, then, regards families as dynamic, self-regulating social groups (Minuchin, 1988). Families usually contain several subsystems, such as the relations maintained between spouses, among siblings, and between parent and child. A single family member is usually a member of more than one subsystem at the same time. The child has a relationship with each parent as well as with one or more siblings; mothers and fathers are spouses as well as parents. The quality of each of these separate relationships can have an impact on other relationships. Thus, for example, mothers who feel their marriages are close and confiding tend to be more sensitive and warm with their infants, and fathers who express like feelings are more positive about their paternal role (Cox et al., 1989). Similarly, when parents have high-quality marital relationships, siblings have more positive interactions with each other (MacKinnon, 1988). Within the systems model, family members have reciprocal influences on one another and there are several layers of such interactions.

▶ **Sociocultural influence**

The family system is itself embedded in larger social networks, including the economic, political, legal, and educational forces that are part of the larger culture. Events in the workplace, school, and other extrafamilial settings can affect individual family members and hence the interactions that occur within the family unit. When one or both parents become unemployed, for example, the family experiences stress that is often expressed in increased conflict between parents and children (Flanagan, 1990). In other instances, both parents may work outside the home, which requires children to function independently, cooking their own meals or performing other household tasks. The *social ecology* of child development—that is, the impact of broad sociocultural factors on the child's social, cognitive, and emotional growth—has been given increasing credence by developmental psychologists.

PARENTS AND SOCIALIZATION

In most cultures, the primary agents of the child's socialization are parents. Teachers, peers, and the media—as we will see in the next two chapters—also play a significant role in many cultures, but perhaps no other individuals in the child's life have the power or impact that parents can have in influencing future behaviors, attitudes, and personality.

Parents affect the child's socialization in three primary ways. First, they socialize their children through direct training, providing information or reinforcement for the behaviors they find acceptable or desirable. Parents may encourage their children, for example, to share with playmates or instruct them on how to become acquainted with an unfamiliar peer. Second, as they interact with their children, parents serve as important models for the child's attitudes, beliefs, and actions. For example, parents who are warm, engaging, and verbally stimulating tend to have children who are popular in school. Finally, parents manage other aspects of the child's social life that can, in turn, influence their social development. Parents choose the neighborhood the family lives in, for example; they also may enroll children in sports programs, arrange birthday parties, and invite children's friends to spend the night, all of which influence children's peer networks (Parke et al., 1988).

Of course, parents' major concerns and activities shift as the child develops. Parents of infants focus on caregiving activities and helping the child to learn skills such as self-feeding, dressing, and toileting. By the time their child is two years old, parents begin more deliberate attempts at socialization. Parents of preschoolers help their children regulate their emotions—to control angry outbursts, for example—and start to instill social skills, such as polite forms of speech and sharing during play with peers. Parents of elementary school children are likely to be concerned with their sons' or daughters' academic achievement. When their children approach adolescence, most parents encourage independent, rational, and valued-based decision making as their youngsters prepare to enter their own adult lives.

The balance of power between parent and child also shifts with development. Throughout early childhood, parents closely monitor much of their child's activity. Once the child enters school, parents play less of a supervisory role. They begin to expect their children to be cooperative members of the family by avoiding conflicts and sharing in household tasks. Parents and children begin to negotiate as they make decisions and solve family problems. Finally, during adolescence, parents observe the child's participation in the larger social world, in school and community activities and close personal relationships with peers. More and more, the older child regulates his own behavior (Maccoby, 1984b; Maccoby & Martin, 1983).

▶ **The child's active role**

▶ **Interaction among domains**

As this quick sketch suggests, the child's own development often precipitates shifts in parental roles. As the child's language and cognitive skills mature, parents place greater expectations on her social communication behaviors. As she enters school, parents nurture greater independence. The physical changes associated with puberty often signal to parents that more mature child-adult interactions are warranted, such as deferring at times to the child's wishes rather than rigidly restricting her activities (Steinberg, 1981). As systems theory suggests, the individual child's development within the family represents an ongoing give-and-take between child and parent, obliging continual readjustment from all members to reinstate family equilibrium.

Styles of Parenting

Even the casual bystander who observes parents interacting with their children in public places such as parks, shopping malls, and supermarkets will notice markedly different styles of parental behavior. Some parents are extremely controlling, using crisp, firm commands void of explanations to restrict their children's behavior. Others seem not to notice as their charges create chaos and pandemonium. Researchers have established that the pattern of interactions a parent adopts is one of the most important variables in influencing the child's later development.

In a landmark series of observational studies, Diana Baumrind (1971, 1973) recorded the interpersonal and behavioral styles of nursery school children as they engaged in normal school activities. She also watched as they worked on a series of standardized problem-solving tasks, such as completing a set of puzzles. In addition, Baumrind gathered information on parenting styles by observing how mothers interacted with their children in both play and structured teaching settings, watching parents and their children in the home, and interviewing parents about their child-rearing practices. Children and parents were observed again when children were eight or nine years of age. Based on these extensive observations, Baumrind identified several distinct patterns of parenting related to two key dimensions: (1) how parents controlled children's behavior and (2) how much nurturance parents displayed.

Some parents, Baumrind found, were extremely restrictive and controlling. They valued respect for authority and strict obedience to their commands and relied on coercive techniques, such as threats or physical punishment, rather than reasoning or explanation, to regulate their children's actions. They were

authoritarian parent Parent who relies on coercive techniques to discipline the child and who displays a low level of nurturance.

permissive parent Parent who sets few limits on the child's behavior.

authoritative parent Parent who sets limits on a child's behavior by using the technique of induction and who displays a high degree of nurturance.

also less nurturant toward their children than other parents in the study. Baumrind identified these as **authoritarian parents.** The second parenting style belonged to the group she called **permissive parents.** These parents made few demands for mature behavior from their children. Children were permitted to make their own decisions about many routine activities such as TV viewing, bedtime, and mealtime, and few limits were imposed on their behavior. Permissive parents tended to be either moderately nurturant or cool and uninvolved. The third group of parents was high on both control and nurturance. These **authoritative parents** expected their children to behave in a mature fashion but tended to make more use of rewards than punishments to achieve these ends. They communicated their expectations clearly and provided explanations to help their children understand the reasons for their re-

TABLE 14.1

Patterns of Parenting as a Function of Control and Nurturance

Four parenting styles can be identified in terms of the extent to which parents set limits on the child's behavior (control) and the level of nurturance and responsiveness they provide.

CONTROL	NURTURANCE	
	Responsive, Child Centered	Rejecting, Parent Centered
High on control, demanding	Authoritative	Authoritarian
Low on control, undemanding	Permissive	Uninvolved

Source: Adapted from Maccoby & Martin, 1983.

quests. They also listened to what their children had to say and encouraged a dialogue with them. Authoritative parents were distinctly supportive and warm in their interactions with their children. Table 14.1 summarizes the characteristics of these three parental styles as well as a fourth style, *uninvolved parents,* which has been described in later research.

Baumrind discovered a cluster of behavioral characteristics in children linked with each of these three parental styles. The offspring of authoritative parents tended to have the most desirable profiles. These children were friendly with peers, cooperative with adults, independent, energetic, and achievement oriented. They also displayed a high degree of self-control. This set of characteristics is often termed **instrumental competence.** In marked contrast, children of authoritarian and permissive parents did not exhibit the social responsibility and independence associated with instrumental competence. Children who had authoritarian parents appeared unhappy, and boys tended to be aggressive, whereas girls were likely to be dependent. Children of permissive parents, on the other hand, were low on self-control and self-reliance.

▶ **Interaction among domains**

The effects of parenting style extend to other dimensions of child development. Authoritarian parenting, especially with its use of coercive techniques for controlling behavior, is associated with less advanced moral reasoning (Hoffman, 1970), lower self-esteem (Loeb, Horst, & Horton, 1980), and poorer adjustment to starting school (Barth, 1989). Extremely controlling and negative parenting is also associated with higher levels of aggression in children (Maccoby & Martin, 1983), poor peer relations (Putallaz, 1987), and lower school achievement in adolescence (Dornbush et al., 1987).

Researchers have more recently identified a fourth parenting style—the **uninvolved parent** (Maccoby & Martin, 1983). Like some of Baumrind's permissive group, these parents seem uncommitted to their parental role and emotionally detached from their children. Often, these parents give greater priority to their own needs and preferences than the child's. These parents may be uninterested in events at the child's school, unfamiliar with her playmates, and have only infrequent conversations with her (Pulkkinen, 1982). Uninvolved parenting is related to children's lower self-esteem (Loeb, Horst, & Horton, 1980), heightened aggression (Hatfield, Ferguson, & Alpert, 1967), and lower control over impulsive behavior (Block, 1971). In extreme cases,

instrumental competence
Child's display of independence, self-control, achievement orientation, and cooperation.

uninvolved parent Parent who is emotionally detached from the child and focuses on his or her own needs as opposed to the child's.

Research has shown that parents who expect mature behavior from their children, provide explanations for their requests, and are supportive and warm in their interactions have children who display instrumental competence.

parental uninvolvement can have a greater impact on the child's emotional development than physical or verbal abuse. In a study of attachment patterns among children "at risk" because of inadequate parenting, twelve-month-olds who were neglected were far more likely to be classified as anxiously attached than infants who were abused (Egeland & Sroufe, 1981a).

The most desirable developmental outcomes are associated with authoritative parenting, which has two key characteristics—*setting limits* on the child's behavior and *responding* to the child's needs and actions with warmth and nurturance. These themes echo the discussion of sensitive parenting and attachment presented in Chapter 10. We saw there that parents who are attuned and responsive to their infants' signals tend to raise children who become intellectually and socially competent. The importance of parental nurturance and warmth is underscored in a recent follow-up of seventy-six 41-year-old subjects who were originally studied when they were five years old. Those subjects who had a warm and affectionate mother or father at age five years tended to have long, happy marriages as adults and close relationships with friends at midlife (Franz, McClelland, & Weinberger, 1991).

Why does authoritative parenting work so well? Several explanations are possible. First, when parents make demands for mature behavior from their children, they make explicit the responsibilities that individuals have toward one another when they live in social groups. When parents set forth clear, consistent guidelines for behavior, they make the child's job of sorting out the social world much easier. Second, when parental demands are accompanied by a reasonable explanation, children are more likely to accept the limitations on their actions. Third, when parents take into account the child's responses and show affection, children are likely to acquire a sense of control over their actions and derive the sense that they have worth. A recent study confirms, for example, that adolescents who have authoritative parents have a healthy sense of autonomy and self-reliance and feel a sense of control over their lives (Steinberg, Elmen, & Mounts, 1989). The net outcome of authoritative parenting is thus a competent child who shows successful psychological adjustment.

Strategies of Parental Control

Parents set limits on their children's behavior for a variety of reasons, ranging from protecting their safety to controlling socially unacceptable behaviors such as temper tantrums and aggression against others. What specific techniques do parents use to regulate their children's actions? In Chapter 13, we examined two disciplinary techniques, induction and power assertion. *Induction,* which includes the extensive use of reasoning, explanation, and communication of clear standards of behavior, is the method that characterizes authoritative parenting. *Power assertion,* a directive style that includes physical punishment, forceful commands, and the removal of material objects and privileges, is the disciplinary approach of authoritarian parents. Still a third technique is *love withdrawal,* in which a parent reacts to the child's behavior by ignoring him, reacting coldly, or otherwise implying that affection will not be restored until the child obeys the parent.

We have already seen that induction is related to the most desirable child behaviors, whereas power assertion is associated with greater aggression, lower moral reasoning, and other negative outcomes in children. Love withdrawal presents its own problems. Though children are likely to comply with parental requests when love withdrawal is used as a disciplinary strategy, they may also avoid the parent as a consequence (Chapman & Zahn-Waxler, 1981, as cited in Maccoby & Martin, 1983). Because of such potential negative side effects, most child-rearing experts do not recommend the use of this strategy.

How and When Do Parents Discipline? As their children progress from ages one to three years, mothers decrease their reliance on physical means of control, such as pulling the child away from a forbidden object (for example, a stove) or forcibly holding his hand, and more frequently employ verbal commands, reprimands, and persuasion. These changes in maternal control parallel children's expressions of noncompliance. Initially, children display passive or defiant behaviors, such as whining and temper tantrums, to protest parental control. Older preschoolers attempt to negotiate with parents ("I'll do it later, OK?" or "I have a better idea!"). Some researchers believe that the parental

▶ **The child's active role**

shift to discipline based on reasoning is derived from the child's active bargaining and parents' recognition of the child's growing autonomy (Kuczynski, Kochanska et al., 1987). It is also interesting to note that even among two-year-olds, compliance on the part of the child is associated with maternal use of persuasion and suggestion, whereas defiance is associated with maternal use of power assertion (Crockenberg & Litman, 1990). Perhaps as their own experience in child rearing grows, parents come to recognize that control techniques based on reasoning often get the best results.

A survey of middle-class mothers and fathers of seventh- and ninth-graders yielded information on parenting strategies with older children (Smith, 1988). Parents were asked to recall any efforts to influence their children in the past year in such areas as choosing subjects in school, the amount of time spent doing homework, choice of peer associates, and several other common situations in which parents and children often disagree. The 197 parents reported over a thousand situations in which they exerted control over their children. As Table 14.2 shows, they employed some strategies more frequently than others.

The two most prevalent techniques were commands—that is, making imperative statements without threats ("Go clean your room, please!")—and self-oriented induction. *Self-oriented induction* consists of parental suggestions about the costs and rewards to the child of her behavior ("Spending more time on your homework will boost your grades"). *Other-oriented induction,* in contrast, consists of parental references to their own or another person's reasons for seeking a behavior change ("Your classmates are counting on you to finish this assignment"). This technique was used less frequently, as were several others described in Table 14.2.

How did parents choose a particular control strategy? It depended on the specific situation in which parent and child disagreed. When parents were concerned with producing an immediate impact, as when household chores were to be done or when a curfew was being set, they issued commands. When long-term consequences of the child's actions were involved, as in decisions relating to school, parents opted for self-oriented induction. Thus, at least for this

TABLE 14.2

Control Techniques: Frequency of Use by Middle-Class Parents

Middle-class parents tend to use commands and self-oriented induction with their adolescent children. The first technique is employed when parents want to have an immediate impact, the second when they are concerned with long-term goals. These parents make use of other discipline strategies less frequently.

Control Technique	Description	Percentage
Command	Imperative statement without threats	34
Self-oriented induction	Suggestion of costs and rewards of behavior to child	31
Advice	Suggestion of how to more easily accomplish parental goal	14
Relationship maintenance	Statement or behavior attempting to maintain child's positive orientation to parent	10
Power assertion	Physical punishment, deprivation, or threats	8
Other-oriented induction	Suggestion of costs and rewards of behavior to others	6
Love withdrawal	Temporary coldness or rejection	1

Source: Adapted from Smith, 1988.

How should a parent respond to a young child's temper tantrum? An authoritarian parent is likely to use power assertion and yell "Get down!" or forcibly move the child off the chair. In contrast, an authoritative parent might say "Are you trying to get down? Let's try putting your feet down first," using reasoning and explanation. The latter approach, called induction, produces the most desirable outcomes.

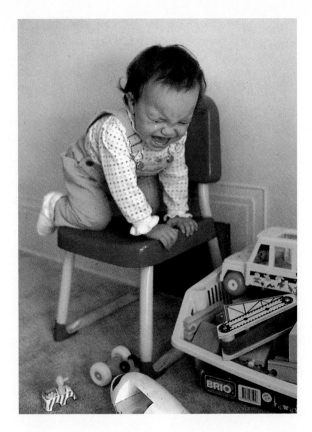

middle-class sample of parents and children living in intact families, many parents rely on their legitimate power and on reasoning rather than on physical coercion or threats to direct their children's behavior (Smith, 1988).

How often do parents exercise their authority over children? Obviously, the extent of parental control varies as a function of the age of the child, parental child-rearing philosophy, and the specific behaviors displayed by the child. Observations of family interactions in the home, however, tell us that mothers of preschool children issue commands or disapprove of their behaviors about once every three to four minutes and that these children disobey about 25 percent of the time (Wahler & Dumas, 1989). With age, as children become more attuned to parental expectations and are more capable of regulating their own behaviors, the need for parental control diminishes.

Punishment   Over recent decades, the most widely discussed parental control technique has been *punishment,* the administration of an aversive stimulus or withdrawal of rewards to decrease the frequency of undesirable behaviors. Punishment, a form of power assertion, can include spanking, sharp verbal threats, or the loss of privileges like TV viewing time or playtime with friends. Laboratory studies carried out in the tradition of learning theory show that certain ways of administering punishment are more effective than others.

Ross Parke (1969) studied how several variables influence the effectiveness of punishment in the forbidden-toy paradigm, originally described in Chapter 13. In the initial phase of the experiment, first- and second-grade boys were

FIGURE 14.3

Variables That Influence the Effectiveness of Punishment

In a complex experiment designed to assess the effects of several aspects of punishment on children's subsequent behavior, Parke found that children deviated less if (1) punishment was administered early, (2) a high-intensity punishment was used (a loud buzzer), and (3) children were provided with cognitive structure or explanation about the reason they were being punished. As these graphs show, deviations tended to remain low in the high–cognitive structure condition. When cognitive structure was low, however, the effects of intensity and timing were more pronounced.

presented with pairs of toys, one attractive and one less so. Each time the child touched the attractive toy, he was punished by the sound of an irritating buzzer. One variable was the timing of the punishment. The punishment for some children occurred *before* they touched the attractive toy, whereas the punishment for others was delivered *after* they had already held the toy for a few seconds. Another variable was degree of punishment—the intensity of the buzzer was either high (96 dB) or low (65 dB). A third variable was the amount of "cognitive structure" or explanation provided for not touching the toy. Some children were simply told not to touch the prohibited toy or a buzzer would sound. Others were given an elaborate explanation that some toys should not be touched because they might get broken or worn out. The prohibition was clearly stated along with its justification and the consequences of misconduct. The last variable was the amount of nurturance displayed by the experimenter; the experimenter played with some of the children and gave them lots of approval before the experiment, but did nothing extra with others.

Following the initial phase, an observer watched through a one-way mirror while the child was left alone with the prohibited toys. Figure 14.3 summarizes the results. Children who had received the "early" punishment, the louder buzzer, and the greater cognitive structure in the initial phase were less likely to touch the taboo items than children who had experienced "late" punishment, a less intense punishment, or low cognitive structure. The experimenter's nurturance was less important, although other studies have demonstrated that nurturant adults are more effective at inhibiting children's misbehaviors than nonnurturant adults are (Parke & Walters, 1967). The most powerful factor influencing the children's behavior, in fact, proved to be providing an explanation. As the test period progressed, children in the low–cognitive structure condition began to touch the attractive toys, suggesting that the effects of punishment were wearing off. Children in the high–cognitive structure

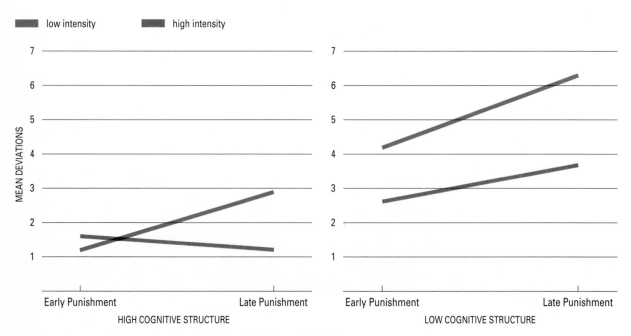

Source: Adapted from Parke, 1969.

condition continued to resist touching, however. Thus, the results of this study imply that reasoning or induction is a more effective technique than punishment for controlling children's behavior.

The effectiveness of punishment also depends on the consistency with which it is applied. As we saw in the case of Joey and the cookies at the chapter opening, children become particularly disobedient and aggressive when parents prohibit a behavior on one occasion and permit it on another. In one study, parents of delinquent boys displayed more inconsistent disciplinary practices than parents of nondelinquent boys (Gleuck & Gleuck, 1950). Consistency among caregivers (**interagent consistency**) as well as the consistency of one caregiver from one occasion to the next (**intra-agent consistency**) are both important factors in giving children clear, unambiguous messages about acceptable and unacceptable behaviors (Deur & Parke, 1970; Sawin & Parke, 1979).

CONTROVERSY

Spare the Rod and Spoil the Child?

Although punishment can inhibit a child's misbehavior, the question remains whether punishment, especially physical tactics such as spanking or hitting, should be used at all. In a 1985 survey of three thousand parents, Murray Straus and Richard Gelles found that 90 percent of parents of three- and four-year-olds reported striking their children in the previous year, as did 75 percent of parents of nine- and ten-year-olds. Infants and adolescents were spanked less often (Straus & Gelles, 1986). Thus, in the United States, many parents resort to physical punishment as a way of controlling their children's behavior. Most Americans, according to survey data, believe that it is morally correct to hit a child who misbehaves (Straus, Gelles, & Steinmetz, 1980).

Punishment does modify the child's behavior in the short run, but its use is also associated with many negative outcomes. The most serious is aggression, especially among boys (Martin, 1975; Rollins & Thomas, 1979). Many experts believe that parents who use punishment serve as aggressive models for their children (Parke & Slaby, 1983). Children may learn that hitting, kicking, or pinching are possible ways of resolving conflicts. For example, physically abused toddlers are twice as likely to direct physical assaults toward peers in their day-care centers as nonabused toddlers are (George & Main, 1979). Moreover, especially when children do not receive much attention from their parents, the spotlight placed on them when they are being punished may actually be positively reinforcing. As a consequence, children maintain the behavior parents were trying to eliminate.

interagent consistency Consistency in application of disciplinary strategies by different caregivers.

intra-agent consistency Consistency in a single caregiver's application of discipline from one situation to the next.

Another undesirable outcome is that children who are frequently punished eventually avoid the punishing agents (Redd, Morris, & Martin, 1975). Parents are likely to be more effective as socializing agents if their children maintain good relations with them than if they become physically and emotionally removed.

Finally, under some circumstances, an overreliance on physical punishment can set the stage for child abuse. Parental acts of abuse often start out as attempts to discipline the child, and abusive parents rely more on power assertion, including physical punishment, than do nonabusive parents (Oldershaw, Walters, & Hall, 1986; Parke & Collmer, 1975). Among abusive families, a light slap or tap can quickly escalate into a physical assault on the child.

Should parents employ physical punishment? Even parents with the best intentions may lose their temper and hit a child who exhibits an extreme or dangerous behavior, such as approaching a hot stove or running into the street. As a general rule, however, psychologists believe that alternative discipline strategies, such as reasoning and focusing on the child's positive behaviors, are more effective in accomplishing parents' long-term socialization goals—without spoiling the child. ■

Time-Out   A reasonable alternative to physical punishment is called **time-out** from reinforcement, a technique derived from the laboratories of behavior analysts. The principle underlying time-out is simple. When the child transgresses, he is removed from all possible sources of reward, even subtle or accidental ones. That is, he is immediately taken to a quiet, neutral place and remains by himself until the undesired behavior ceases or a short period of time, usually two to five minutes, has elapsed. Parents or teachers can set up a "time-out chair" in a remote area of the home or school where no distractions are likely to occur. (The child's room, with the toys, books, and TV that are often contained in it, is rarely a good place for time-out.) At the conclusion of the time-out period, the child is permitted to return to routine activities (Varni, 1983).

A study by Robert McMahon and Rex Forehand (1978) illustrates how parents can control inappropriate mealtime behaviors in their preschool-aged children by using time-out. Whenever the child exhibited behaviors such as throwing food, screaming, or leaving the table before the end of the meal, mothers were instructed to follow a particular sequence of responding. First, the mother issued a command to stop the behavior. If the child did not comply, time-out began; the child was taken to another room for two minutes, left alone, and then returned to the table. At the same time, mothers were told to praise their child often for appropriate mealtime behaviors. Figure 14.4 shows the percentage of inappropriate behaviors displayed by a five-year-old boy in the study during baseline (the period before treatment), treatment, and follow-up sessions six weeks later. As the graph shows, this subject's problem behaviors decreased markedly within just two treatment sessions.

Time-out has been found effective in reducing or eliminating a variety of troublesome behaviors in children, including temper tantrums, fighting, and self-injurious behaviors such as chronic scratching (Varni, 1983). To make effective use of time-out, Beth Sulzer-Azaroff and G. Roy Mayer (1977) suggest that parents (and others) keep the following guidelines in mind:

- Remove events that reinforce the undesired behavior, such as parental attention.
- Be consistent in applying time-out whenever the undesired behavior occurs.
- Keep the time-out period relatively brief, usually only a few minutes.
- Clearly communicate the conditions leading to time-out.
- Provide the child with an alternative desirable behavior to replace the undesired one, such as eating with a fork instead of with his fingers.

time-out   Disciplinary strategy in which a child is removed from all possible sources of reinforcement, both positive and negative, after committing a transgression.

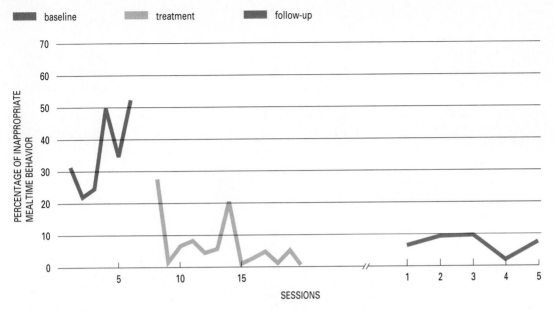

baseline   treatment   follow-up

PERCENTAGE OF INAPPROPRIATE MEALTIME BEHAVIOR

SESSIONS

FIGURE 14.4

Source: Adapted from McMahon & Forehand, 1978.

Time-Out as a Parental Control Technique

Time-out can be an effective means of reducing a child's undesirable behaviors. Bill, the five-year-old child whose behavior is diagrammed here, was sent to time-out every time he acted inappropriately at mealtime. His mother also praised him frequently for desirable behaviors. The graph shows that Bill's inappropriate behaviors decreased dramatically compared with the baseline period, and they remained low in frequency during the follow-up phase six weeks later.

Time-out gives both children and parents the opportunity to "cool down" after all parties have become aroused. Even well-meaning parents may find their emotions rising when the child persists in misbehaving. By allowing tempers to dissipate, parents who use time-out are more likely to fall back on adaptive strategies when management of the child's behaviors is required.

The Role of Attributions As we discussed in Chapter 11, *attribution theory* suggests that an individual's behavior depends on the inferences she makes about other people's actions—why they behave as they do, what traits they possess, and so on. Theodore Dix and Joan Grusec (1985) hypothesize that the kinds of attributions parents make about their children, particularly the causes of their children's behaviors, will influence the parenting strategies they adopt. If, for example, a parent believes that a three-year-old child is having a tantrum at the supper table because she wants her dessert immediately, the parent will probably insist that all the vegetables be finished first. If, on the other hand, the parent suspects the child is ill, Mom or Dad would probably remove her from the supper table and nurture and console her.

Figure 14.5 presents a schematic diagram of Dix and Grusec's (1985) attribution model of socialization. The flow of events proceeds as follows. First, the parent observes the child's behavior and judges whether it is typical for the child or normative for her age group. The parent assesses whether the child has the skills, knowledge, and motive to behave intentionally in a certain way. Do most three-year-olds have tantrums to get dessert? Is throwing a tantrum a typical behavior for that child? Parents make a causal attribution about the child's intentions. Next, parents' attributions affect their emotional and behavioral responses to the child. Parents become more upset and act more forcefully if they believe the child intends to misbehave—in this case, screaming for the explicit purpose of obtaining dessert. Finally, if parents have made the

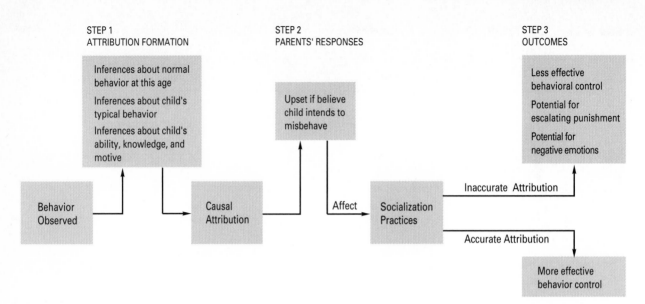

STEP 1
ATTRIBUTION FORMATION

Inferences about normal
behavior at this age

Inferences about child's
typical behavior

Inferences about child's
ability, knowledge, and
motive

STEP 2
PARENTS' RESPONSES

Upset if believe
child intends to
misbehave

STEP 3
OUTCOMES

Less effective
behavioral control

Potential for
escalating punishment

Potential for
negative emotions

Behavior
Observed

Causal
Attribution

Affect

Socialization
Practices

Inaccurate Attribution

Accurate Attribution

More effective
behavior control

FIGURE 14.5

**The Attribution Model
of Socialization**

Source: Adapted from Dix & Grusec, 1985.

Dix and Grusec hypothesize that
parents' judgments about the
child's intentionality in misbehaving are critical in determining their
response. Parents become more
upset if they believe the child intended to transgress and select
more forceful control strategies
than they do if they believe the
transgression was unintentional. If
their attributions are correct, they
will be effective in controlling behavior. If they make the wrong attribution, however, they will be
less effective, may escalate the
level of punishment, and may produce negative emotions in themselves and the child.

correct attribution, they will be effective in controlling the child. But if they
are wrong, the child may continue to misbehave, and both parents and child
may feel negative emotions rising.

   To show the influence of attributions, Dix and his colleagues asked mothers
and fathers of four-, eight-, and twelve-year-old children to react to several
vignettes portraying child misconduct. In one story, for example, the actor fails
to obey his mother's request to clean up the living room, an explicit violation of
a norm. In another, the central character fails to act altruistically and eats
candy while a boy without money to buy a snack looks on. The story characters
were all represented as the same age and sex as the parent's own child. The
results showed that parents of older children (who also heard stories about
older children) made more attributions of the child's intentionality compared
with parents of younger children (Dix et al., 1986).

   In a second similar study, parents were more upset when they believed a
child's transgressions were intentional or controllable. Furthermore, the more
upset they were, the more they thought it important to respond forcefully to
the child's actions (Dix, Ruble, & Zambarano, 1989). Thus, parents believe
there are age differences in children's ability to control their own behaviors,
and they choose different socialization approaches as a function of those
beliefs.

▶ **The child's active role**

control theory Hypothesis about
parent-child interactions that suggests that the intensity of one
partner's behavior affects the intensity of the other's response.

Children's Influence on Parenting Strategies The attribution model described here suggests that a child's behaviors may set in motion a series of
parental judgments about the child's intentions and how the parent should respond. Another perspective on how the child influences the parent's choice of
control strategies is provided by Richard Bell (1971; Bell & Harper, 1977). In
his **control theory**, Bell suggests that parents and children have upper and
lower limits of tolerance for the types of behavior each shows the other. When
the behavior of one approaches the other's upper limit, the recipient tries to
reduce the excessive behavior with increasing levels of intensity. Thus, for

example, a parent whose son is having a temper tantrum might first try to talk to him, then remove him to his room, and finally resort to physical punishment. Likewise, if the child's behavior approaches the parent's lower limits—in the child's shyness or withdrawal at the doctor's office, for example—the parent may try to stimulate the child by coaching her to speak and then promising her a reward if she vocalizes.

Control theory implies that when children's misbehavior pushes parents to their "upper limits," parents will respond with more forceful, firm control techniques. Furthermore, some children may transgress to this extent more frequently than others. Support for this idea comes from a study of six- to eleven-year-old boys, sixteen normal and sixteen classified as conduct-disordered because of their persistent aggression, fire setting, truancy, or temper tantrums. Mothers of conduct-disordered children were observed as they interacted with their own child, another conduct-disordered child, and a normal child. Similarly, mothers of normal children interacted with their own child, another normal child, and a conduct-disordered child. The researchers coded the frequency of the mothers' positive and negative behaviors as well as the number of requests they made for a change in the child's behavior. Both groups of mothers made more negative responses and requests to the conduct-disordered children than to the normal children. Thus, it was the type of child, and not the type of mother, that determined the tone of the interaction (Anderson, K. E., Lytton, & Romney, 1986). It could very well be that children who evidence a persistent behavioral style of pushing parents to their "upper limits" precipitate a pattern of authoritarian, power-assertive parenting.

Problems in Parenting

Not all patterns of parenting are successful. In some instances, such extreme maladaptive styles of interaction develop between parent and child that physical and psychological harm can occur to both. Understanding the dynamics of these families is essential to any attempt at intervention and also provides an even greater understanding of how all families, healthy and dysfunctional, work as systems.

The Coercive Cycle: Skills Deficits in Parenting In some families, maladaptive patterns of interaction escalate to the point at which children become extremely aggressive and antisocial. Gerald Patterson (1976, 1982, 1986) has conducted extensive longitudinal studies of boys who exhibit pathological aggression and concludes that their behavior was learned from previous day-to-day family interaction sequences in which both parents and children engaged in coercive behavior.

In Patterson's studies, preadolescent boys (usually nine to twelve years of age) labeled as highly aggressive by schools, courts, or the families themselves were compared with boys from normal families over a period of several months. Detailed observations were made of family interactions in the home, including the sequences of behaviors displayed by parents, the target children, and their siblings. Patterson learned that families of antisocial boys were characterized by high levels of aggressive interaction that rewarded coercive behaviors. When they were younger, the antisocial boys performed minor negative behaviors, such as whining, teasing, or yelling, in response to the aggression of another family member. About 70 percent of these behaviors were reinforced by the acquiescence of the child's interaction partner; in other words, the parent or sibling "backed down" and this submission negatively reinforced the child's aggression. At other times, parental attention to the child's aggression was positively reinforcing. In addition, although parents were observed to nag, scold, or threaten their children, like Joey's mother in the chapter opening, they seldom followed through on their threats. Such sequences between the target child and other family members occurred as much as hundreds of times each day in the aggressive families. Over time, the target boys' aggression escalated in frequency and progressed to physical assaults.

At this point, many parents attempted to control their sons' aggressive behaviors but in doing so the parents also became highly aggressive. These coercive chains increased in duration to form long bursts of negative interactions and often resulted in hitting between parent and child. Figure 14.6 illustrates how this **coercive cycle** of reciprocal aggression between parent and child operates. After extended experience in these maladaptive familial exchanges, boys became out of control and acted violently in settings outside the home, such as the school. Aggression in school, in turn, was related to poor peer relations and academic failure, adding further to the chain of negative events in these boys' lives.

▶ **Interaction among domains**

Can such extreme patterns of aggression be controlled? Patterson and his colleagues have intervened in the maladaptive interactions of aggressive families by training parents in basic child management skills (Patterson et al., 1975). They focused on teaching parents to use discipline more effectively by dispensing more positive reinforcements for prosocial behaviors, using reasoning, employing discipline consistently, and setting clear limits on even minor acts of aggression. Children significantly decreased their rates of deviant be-

FIGURE 14.6

The Coercive Cycle

A coercive cycle of behavior often develops between parents and their antisocial boys. Initially, the boy may exhibit mildly negative behaviors that the parent reacts to first by scolding or nagging but eventually by backing down. With these responses the parent negatively reinforces the child's aggression, acts as an aggressive model, and is inconsistent. At other times, parental attention positively reinforces the child's aggression. As a consequence, the boy's aggression escalates, further heightening the parent's aggression. The result is a cluster of antisocial behaviors at home and school.

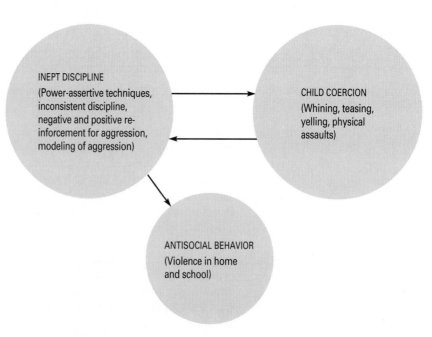

Source: Adapted from Patterson, 1986.

havior after only a few weeks, and these results were maintained for as long as twelve months after the initial training period (Patterson & Fleischman, 1979). As an added benefit, parents' perceptions of their children became more positive (Patterson & Reid, 1973).

Attentional Deficits and Problems in Parenting   Another model of dysfunctional parenting has been proposed by Robert Wahler and Jean Dumas (1984, 1989). Instead of assuming that parents in dysfunctional families use poor child management strategies, these researchers suggest that troubled families experience stresses from the larger social system that make parents inattentive to the dynamics of child care. For example, a mother who is concerned about marital or financial problems will be hard pressed to attend closely to her child's behavior or to the effects of her own parenting behaviors on the child. In an evaluation of the long-term impact of a skills-based parent training program, Dumas and Wahler (1983) found that the program's success or failure was closely tied to measures of socioeconomic status and social isolation. Parents who were removed from contacts outside the family and who were subject to the greatest financial strain were least likely to succeed with the training program.

▶ **Sociocultural influence**

According to the attentional deficit model, parents may possess knowledge about good parenting practices or may learn them very readily, but they often do not apply them. Because they are distracted by other family problems, such parents typically overlook the child's positive behaviors or make hasty judgments that their children are misbehaving. Stressed parents also develop a limited repertoire of responses to their children. Instead of experimenting with various child management techniques to discover the most effective one, they fall back on stereotyped, repetitive methods that are often coercive. Parental depression may add to the problem. Several researchers have found that depressed mothers are especially likely to mislabel their child's behavior (Brody & Forehand, 1986; Greist, Wells, & Forehand, 1979).

Wahler and Dumas (1989) believe that any long-term parent intervention program should include the following elements: (1) training parents to modify their attentional habits so they focus on the child's prosocial as well as aversive behaviors; (2) providing parents with coping strategies for external stressors, such as loss of employment or financial hardship; and (3) offering social support networks so that parents can receive assistance with the day-to-day problems of living. In other words, by providing parents with ways of coping with external stress, clinicians and counselors can help them refocus on more positive ways of interacting with their children.

Child Abuse   According to one estimate, over 1 million children suffer physical, sexual, or emotional abuse each year, and between 2,500 and 5,000 die from abuse (American Medical Association, 1985). Aside from the immediate physical and psychological consequences of abuse, children who are the victims of family violence are predisposed toward a number of developmental problems. Maltreated infants and toddlers are more likely to be anxiously attached to their mothers than are children who are not maltreated (Egeland & Sroufe, 1981a; Schneider-Rosen et al., 1985). These children are thus vulnerable to the social, emotional, and cognitive impairments associated with poor

coercive cycle   Pattern of reciprocal aggression between parent and child.

▶ **Interaction among domains**

attachment. Preschool and school-aged children with a history of abuse score lower on tests of cognitive maturity and manifest low self-esteem and school learning problems (Aber & Allen, 1987; Barahal, Waterman, & Martin, 1981; Hoffman-Plotkin & Twentyman, 1984). Emotionally, they may display withdrawal and passivity or, on the other hand, aggressive, oppositional patterns of behavior (Martin & Beezley, 1976). Finally, abused and neglected children are at greater risk for delinquency and violent criminal behavior in adulthood (Widom, 1989) and are prone to become abusive parents. In one study, women who had been abused as children were followed for a period of three years. Seventy percent were observed to maltreat their children or provide borderline care. Among women who were not abused, only one did not provide adequate care (Egeland, Jacobvitz, & Papatola, 1987).

The causes of abuse are neither simple nor easily ameliorated. Most current explanations of abuse center on aberrant interactions within the family system, particularly between the parent and child victim. The larger social community may also play a role in the stresses it places on families or in the absence of support services for families in need of them.

Research on the interaction patterns in abusive families suggests that they differ in several respects from those in normal families. First, parents in abusive families tend to rely on coercive or negative strategies for modifying their children's behavior, even for routine or mild discipline problems. In general, members of abusive families interact infrequently with each other, but when they do, the tone is negative. In one study, mothers in abusive families displayed 40 percent less positive interaction and 67 percent more negative interaction with their children compared with nonabusive mothers (Burgess & Conger, 1978). In another study, abusive and nonabusive mothers were observed as they engaged in a sequence of preparing a meal, playing, and cleaning up with their preschool-aged children. Abusive mothers relied heavily on power-assertive techniques, such as threats, humiliation, or physical contact, to alter their children's behavior, whereas control mothers used predominantly positively oriented strategies, including reasoning, bargaining, or modeling. Abusive mothers issued more than twice as many commands to their children as mothers in the control group and were also inconsistent in reinforcing their children's compliance. Whereas the control mothers positively reinforced every instance of their children's obedience to a request, abusive mothers dispensed positive and negative reinforcements with equal frequency (Oldershaw, Walters, & Hall, 1986). As we saw earlier, inconsistent punishment usually leads to the persistence of undesired behaviors in children.

▶ **The child's active role**

Certain characteristics of children are also more commonly observed in abusive families. Parents often describe the abused child as irritable, difficult to put to sleep, and prone to excessive crying (Ounsted, Oppenheimer, & Lindsay, 1974). A group at special risk for abuse is premature infants, who tend to have high-pitched, aversive cries and an unattractive appearance (Parke & Collmer, 1975). Abusive parents become especially sensitized to some of the child's objectionable behaviors and show heightened emotional reactivity to the child's cries or noncompliance (Frodi & Lamb, 1980; Wolfe, 1983). Older children in abusive families tend to be more aggressive and less compliant than similar-aged children from control families (Bousha & Twentyman, 1984; Egeland & Sroufe, 1981a; Parke & Collmer, 1975). Thus, both parental and child

▶ **Sociocultural influence**

factors may contribute to a dynamic of physically and psychologically harmful interactions.

Lastly, abusive families tend to be isolated from the outside world and have fewer sources of social support than nonabusive families. In one study, abusive parents reported that they had a lower degree of involvement with the community than nonabusive parents; they tended not to join sports teams, go to the library, or take classes (Trickett & Susman, 1988). In another study, some mothers who were at risk to become abusive because of their own family history had normal, positive relationships with their children. These mothers also had extensive emotional support from other adults, a therapist, or a mate. In contrast, high-risk mothers who subsequently became abusive experienced greater life stress and had fewer sources of psychological support (Egeland, Jacobvitz, & Sroufe, 1988).

How can the spiral of abuse be broken? The guidelines provided by Wahler and Dumas (1989) provide a good start. Specifically, interventions should teach basic parenting skills, provide parents with mechanisms to cope with their emotional tension, and offer social support, such as child-care or counseling services (Wolfe, 1985).

▶ **Sociocultural influence**

Cultural and Social Class Variations in Parenting

Do broader sociocultural beliefs and values play a role in parental socialization practices? And if so, do children show specific patterns of behavior as a result of their different cultural experiences? Until recently few systematic studies have directly addressed these issues, but new empirical work is beginning to yield some affirmative answers.

Cross-National Differences   Beatrice Whiting and Carolyn Edwards (1988) have provided an extended analysis of variations in parenting by comparing societies as diverse as rural Kenya and Liberia with urban America. Despite vast differences in economic, social, and political conditions, many similar overarching patterns are apparent in the ways parents (specifically, mothers) socialize their children. With infants and toddlers, the universal emphasis is on nurturance—that is, providing routine care along with attention and support. By the time the child reaches age four or five years, most parents shift their focus to control, correcting or reprimanding misbehavior. Finally, when children reach school age, parents become concerned with training their children in the skills and social behavior valued by their cultural group.

At the same time, though, there are notable differences. For example, mothers from rural villages in Kenya and Liberia emphasize training children to do chores responsibly and place a high premium on obedience. From an early age, children are taught how to care for the family's fields and animals, and they assume a major role in caring for younger siblings. Children are punished for performing tasks irresponsibly and are rarely praised. Consistent with this orientation to child rearing is the family's dependence on women and children to produce food. Because women in these cultures typically have an enormous workload, they delegate some of the tasks to children as soon as children are physically capable of managing these tasks. And because accidents and injury to infants and the family's resources must be prevented, deviant behaviors are not tolerated in children.

An even more controlling style characterizes other societies, such as the Tarong community in the Philippines, in which subsistence farming is the mainstay but responsibilities for producing food are more evenly distributed among the group's members. When the mother does not rely so much on her children to work for the family's survival and when the goals of training are thus less clear, arbitrary commands and even punitiveness become more common. Children are frequently scolded for being in the way of adults or playing in inappropriate places.

These patterns provide striking contrast to the "sociability" that characterized the middle-class American mothers in the sample. Interactions between mothers and children consisted of significant information exchange and warm, friendly dialogues. Mothers emphasized verbalization, educational tasks, and play, and they were liberal in their use of praise and encouragement. Because children in American society normally do not work to ensure the economic survival of the family unit, firm training and punitiveness were not part of these parents' styles. The emphasis on verbalization and educational activities is consistent with the high value Americans place on social interactions and schooling.

Other researchers examining parent-child relationships in Asian cultures have reaffirmed the idea that culture affects parenting styles. Japanese mothers use less physical punishment and more verbal reasoning to control their children compared with American mothers (Kobayashi-Winata & Power, 1989). Japanese culture emphasizes responsibilities and commitments to others, a socialization goal that is more effectively achieved through reasoning than through power-assertive techniques. Japanese children, in fact, comply with rules in home and school more than their American counterparts. Similarly, when Chinese parents are asked to describe their child-rearing practices, they report a greater emphasis on control and achievement in children than do American parents (Lin & Fu, 1990). In Chinese society, character development and educational attainment are highly valued, and parental practices directly follow from these larger societal goals.

As Whiting and Edwards (1988) point out, parents around the world resemble each other in numerous ways because of the universal needs of children as they grow and develop. But it is also true that the specific ecology of each culture, its socialization goals, and the demands it places on the family unit can dramatically shape parenting practices and the course of the individual child's socialization.

Social Class Differences   Parenting differs intraculturally as well as interculturally. A significant finding is that reliable social class differences exist in parenting practices. Middle-class mothers frequently employ induction, or reasoning, as they discipline their children, compared with lower-class mothers, who tend to use power-assertive techniques. Middle-class mothers are also liberal in giving their children praise and, in general, verbalize more than lower-class mothers, who in turn more frequently utter commands like, "Do it because I say so!" and dispense less positive reinforcement (Hoffman, 1984).

Social class (typically defined by father's occupation) by itself, however, is not a variable that provides neat or meaningful explanations because it is usually associated with variations in other variables, such as access to health care, nutrition, physical environment, and educational experiences. Just what is it about social class that leads to differences in parenting styles?

Vonnie McLoyd (1990) has provided an extended analysis of the growing literature on families under economic stress that illuminates the effects of social class. Because African American children experience a disproportionate share of the problems of poverty (a rate of 41 percent for African American children in 1985 compared with 13 percent for Caucasian children), she focused on the social and family dynamics that can affect this ethnic minority. In McLoyd's analysis, economic hardship has a serious negative impact on children's socioemotional development because of the *psychological distress* it causes parents. Parents under stress have a diminished ability to provide nurturant, consistent, involved care for their children. Children growing up with poverty are thus at risk for depression, poor peer relations, lower self-esteem, and conduct disorders. In one study, for example, poor African American and Caucasian mothers were interviewed about their parenting practices. Those who reported being under greater psychological stress found parenting to be more difficult, were less nurturant of their children, and discussed money and personal problems more often with their children than mothers who reported less stress (McLoyd & Wilson, 1989).

At the same time, the demands that poverty makes on African American families may be related to unique family structures and socialization goals that are adaptive for their situation and help them to cope. For example, a significant number of African American children grow up in an extended family. About 10 percent of African American children under age eighteen years grow up with a live-in grandparent, three times as many as Caucasian children (Beck & Beck, 1989). Extended family members often bring additional income, child-care assistance, and emotional support and counseling to families under stress, especially single-parent families (Wilson, 1986).

In addition, African American children are often socialized to have a positive orientation to their ethnic group and to develop interdependence and cooperation as opposed to independence and competition. These characteristics fit with the needs of a group of children who often find barriers to individual achievement (Harrison et al., 1990). Thus, even though economic stress can have a negative impact on family dynamics, it can also foster alternative family structures and socialization goals that help meet the needs of children.

RELATIONSHIPS WITH MOTHERS, FATHERS, AND SIBLINGS

Because mothers have traditionally been seen as the primary caregivers of children, most studies of parenting practices in the psychological literature have focused almost exclusively on mothering. A decade's research on fathers, however, as well as even more recent studies of sibling relationships, has given us a much broader understanding of how each of these distinct sets of relationships within the family influences the individual child's development.

Mothering Versus Fathering: Are There Differences?

For the most part, mothers still bear most of the responsibility for child rearing in our society, whether they are employed outside the home or not. Research, however, resoundingly reveals that fathers are also significant figures in their children's lives and are clearly competent in their parental role as well.

In this chapter as well as in Chapter 10, we have underscored maternal sensitivity and responsiveness as key factors in fostering optimal child development. Studies have shown that fathers are just as responsive to the signals emitted by their infants as are mothers and, when given the opportunity, they interact with their young babies in ways similar to mothers. One team of researchers measured the physiological responsiveness of mothers and fathers as they observed quiet, smiling, or crying babies on a video monitor (Frodi et al., 1978). Both mothers and fathers showed similar changes in heart rate, blood pressure, and skin conductance when the babies smiled or cried. In another study of maternal and paternal behaviors directed to infants in the newborn nursery, Ross Parke and Sandra O'Leary (1976) found that fathers were just as likely as mothers to hold, touch, and vocalize to their babies.

After the newborn period, fathers and mothers begin to manifest somewhat different styles of interaction with their infants. When they play face-to-face with their babies, fathers tend to provide physical and social stimulation in staccato bursts, whereas mothers tend to be more rhythmic and soothing (Yogman et al., 1977). Fathers engage in physical and unpredictable "idiosyncratic" play with their infants—they throw them up in the air, move their limbs, and tickle them—whereas mothers spend more time in caregiving activities or calm games like "pat-a-cake" (Lamb, 1976; Yogman, 1982). As a consequence, infants prefer fathers when they wish to play and seek out mothers when they desire care and comfort. This dichotomy in parental styles of interaction continues at least until middle childhood (Russell & Russell, 1987). The

Researchers have noted that fathers are "tuned in" to the signals displayed by their babies, as when a diaper needs to be changed. When they are given the opportunity, fathers respond to children in much the same way that mothers do.

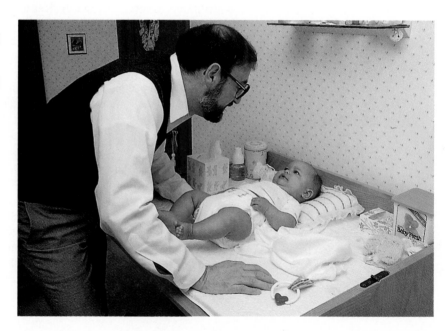

origins of sex differences in parental interactions are not yet fully understood, but they are no doubt linked to the powerful forces of sex-role socialization experienced by the parents themselves (see Chapter 12).

Despite their responsiveness and competence as parents, most fathers spend less time with their children than mothers do. Using a national sample, Joseph Pleck (1982) found that employed fathers with children under age five years spent an average of twenty-six minutes per day in caregiving or other interactions with them. With children between six and seventeen years, that figure dropped to sixteen minutes per day. In general, fathers spend about one-third the time that mothers do in direct contact with their children, even when the mother is employed outside the home (Lamb et al., 1987). Some exceptions do exist, most notably in nontraditional families in which fathers may even serve as the primary caregiver. Furthermore, the extent of paternal involvement with children has increased in the last two decades (Juster, 1987). The bulk of the evidence, however, suggests that although fathers are capable and responsive parents, they still have fewer interactions with their children than mothers do, especially in direct caregiving activities.

Why are fathers relatively uninvolved? One reason may be that fathers are not confident in their caregiving skills. Because males are traditionally not exposed to child care through experiences such as babysitting and home economics courses, they may feel insecure about feeding, bathing, or diapering a child (Lamb et al., 1987). Another obstacle may be the resistance of mothers! Survey data with a national sample showed that only 23 percent of employed mothers and 31 percent of unemployed mothers stated that they wanted more help from their husbands in child care (Pleck, 1982). In another recent study, researchers interviewed twenty-three couples about their child-care routines and philosophies (Grossman, Pollack, & Golding, 1988). They found that husbands were least likely to participate in child care when their wives had high career status and displayed a high degree of competence and independence at home. Apparently, these women were limiting the interactions of fathers with infants through subtle messages, such as correcting their caregiving practices. It may be that women are so strongly socialized to excel in the caregiving role that they are reluctant to relinquish it, even if it places extraordinary demands on their time.

The Father's Influence on Child Development   Do fathers have a unique impact, different from that of mothers, on the process of child development? During the 1960s and 1970s, psychologists believed that they did, based on studies of the effects of father absence, especially on boys. Boys growing up without fathers were more likely to have problems in academic achievement, sex-role development, and control of aggression (Biller, 1974; Lamb, 1981). An important theoretical construct driving much of the research was *identification*—the idea that boys assimilate the characteristics, attitudes, and behaviors of their fathers as they form an intense emotional bond with them. Presumably, boys without fathers did not have an identity figure or model for appropriate masculine, instrumentally competent behavior and thus suffered deficits in cognitive, social, and emotional domains.

Identification with the father, however, may be less important than other variables. A more contemporary view is that fathers make recognizable contributions to family life in general, and child development in particular, but those contributions simply reflect aspects of good parenting. In other words, good "fathering" resembles good "mothering," and the child will thrive by having two parents who fill those roles rather than just one. For example, the father's warmth emerges as a more powerful variable than his masculinity in predicting competence, achievement, and sex-role identity in sons (Radin, 1981; Radin & Sagi, 1982). Furthermore, Michael Lamb (1987) points out that the effects of father absence may not result from the loss of a masculine identity figure for the son but rather the loss of a source of emotional and financial support for the entire family. The tension and stress that result may produce maladaptive patterns of parenting, which in turn generate undesirable developmental outcomes in boys. Boys may be particularly vulnerable because they seem to be more generally susceptible than girls to the effects of deviant environments (Rutter, 1986).

On the other side of the spectrum, there are some noteworthy effects when fathers are more highly involved than the norm in child-care activities—that is, when they assume an equal or almost equal share of the responsibilities for feeding, bathing, and caring for children or when they are the primary caregivers. In one study, fathers and mothers of preschoolers were interviewed about their participation in child-care tasks, and their children were administered a number of standardized tests of achievement and psychosocial adjustment. Fathers who were highly involved in caregiving activities had children who believed they controlled the events in their lives, scored higher on tests of cognitive competence, and held less stereotyped sex-role beliefs. One reason for some of these gains might be that fathers spent more time in providing cognitively stimulating activities for their children, especially their daughters (Radin, 1982). When fathers participate in child care, they are providing an added source of enrichment for both their sons and daughters.

▶ **Sociocultural influence**

Cross-Cultural Studies of Fathering   In many cultures, as in the United States, fathers are becoming increasingly involved in the care of their children, especially during the newborn and infancy periods. In Britain, Sweden, West Germany, and Australia, fathers are beginning to participate more fully as parents (Hwang, 1987; Jackson, 1987; Nickel & Kocher, 1987; Russell, 1987). The Swedish government, in particular, has established social policies designed to encourage paternal participation. Among the benefits available to fathers are a ten-day paid leave following the birth of the baby, a leave during the child's first year (most of which is compensated), and the option of reducing the work day by up to two hours until the child is eight years of age. About 85 percent of Swedish fathers take advantage of the newborn leave policy; relatively few, however, remain home with the child for the first year (Hwang, 1987). Even with societal encouragement of paternal involvement, changes in traditional patterns of parenting evolve slowly—but, they have evolved.

In contrast to these northern European countries, there are some societies in which father participation is comparably low, particularly those with strong cultural beliefs about the proper role for mothers and fathers. When investigators examined father involvement in child care in a small town north of Rome, they found that few fathers were present at the births of their children, and once their infants were home, they did virtually no physical caregiving. Most of their infant-directed behaviors emanated from a distance; they looked at, talked to, or whistled at their child but were unlikely to pick up the baby to play. As the child grew older, the fathers became even more passive and distant (New & Benigni, 1987).

A closer look at this culture's beliefs about parenting provides some insights into these fathers' noninvolvement. First, both women and men feel strongly that only a woman can properly care for a child—that is, respond to physical needs and provide affection and nurturance. The father's role requires him to provide financial support for the family. Second, parents hold rigid ideas about infant care, with cleanliness and proper nutrition, for example, of great concern. Most parents interviewed in this study believed that only mothers had the specialized skills to care for the child "properly." Finally, the father has few opportunities to be alone with the child because members of the extended family, usually women, are frequently present. Fathers probably feel very reluctant to have their interactions with infants scrutinized by so many experts.

In summary, when fathers engage in sensitive, responsive interactions with their children, their children show many of the desirable developmental outcomes that are associated with good mothering. Fathers are clearly capable of engaging in responsive parenting, right from the time of infancy. They may not always be given the opportunity to participate in caregiving, however, because of cultural beliefs about the proper role of fathers or because of their unfamiliarity with child-care routines. As fathers in some societies assume more nontraditional roles and participate more fully in child care, we would expect the lives of both sons and daughters to become markedly enriched.

Siblings

Like parents, siblings serve as important sources of the child's social attitudes, beliefs, and behaviors. Although they may not wield as much power as parents, siblings certainly do attempt to control each other's behaviors (ask anyone who is not an only child!) and may model both desirable and undesirable actions. Until the last two decades, however, comparatively little research has been conducted on the specific effects of sibling relationships on child development. Fortunately, psychologists have awakened to this problem, and an emerging body of research on sibling relationships has provided yet another perspective on how families influence development.

▶ Interaction among domains

The Only Child   One way to assess the impact of siblings on development is to examine children who have none. Are there notable differences between only children and children with one or more sisters or brothers? Popular opinion depicts the only child as spoiled, demanding, self-centered, and dependent (Thompson, 1974). But research evidence suggests, on the contrary, that only children may enjoy the benefits of having their parents' exclusive attention. Toni Falbo and Denise Polit (1986) summarized the results of 115 studies of only children and concluded that, overall, only children showed higher achievement and intelligence scores than children with siblings. In addition, only borns ranked higher on measures of character—that is, the tendency toward leadership, personal control, and maturity. No overall differences emerged between only children and children with siblings on assessments of sociability and personal adjustment.

Only children often achieve more than children with two or more siblings, probably because parents have more time for high quality interactions with an only child.

In explaining these findings, Falbo and Polit (1986) found support for the hypothesis that features of the parent-child relationship account for the advantages only children enjoy in certain domains. Only children were found to have more positive relationships with their parents than children having siblings. This effect probably results from the fact that parents of one child have more time to spend with their son or daughter, and the quality of their interactions is generally high (Falbo & Cooper, 1980). Parents and children in one study, for example, exchanged more information in mealtime conversations in one-child families than in families having two or three children (Lewis & Feiring, 1982). First-time parents are also more anxious about their child-rearing techniques and may thus be more vigilant and responsive to their child's behaviors (Falbo & Polit, 1986).

Falbo and Polit's (1986) meta-analysis showed that parent-child relations in one- and two-child families are actually more similar than different. Only when a third child is born does the quality of parent-child relations diminish significantly. Parents of more than two children probably become more relaxed about their child-rearing strategies and also have significantly more demands placed on their time. The result is less responsiveness and fewer deliberate attempts to instruct their children, aspects of parenting related to cognitive achievements.

Family Size and Birth Order   Children growing up in contemporary American society have fewer siblings than children in past decades. In 1988, the average American family included either one or two children (U.S. Bureau of the Census, 1990a). Many children thus grow up with only one other sibling. Does the size of the family make any difference in child development?

▶ **Interaction among domains**

In general, children from smaller families have higher intelligence test scores, achieve higher levels of education, and display higher self-esteem (Blake, 1989; Wagner, Schubert, & Schubert, 1985). As we have just seen, one reason for these effects may be that parents in larger families have less time to spend with their children and may not provide the kind of cognitive stimulation that children receive in smaller families. Another important factor is financial; parents of more children often experience greater economic stress, which in turn may diminish the quality of their parenting (Rutter & Madge, 1976).

Regardless of family size, the child's birth order, whether he or she is first born or later born, can also be a factor in development. Like only children, first-borns tend to score higher on IQ tests and have higher achievement motivation (Glass, Neulinger, & Brim, 1974; Zajonc, Markus, & Markus, 1979). They also tend to be more obedient and socially responsible (Sutton-Smith & Rosenberg, 1970). All these effects probably stem from the greater attention parents give to their first children. Later-borns, however, seem to have an advantage in the social sphere. Youngest siblings tend to have better peer relationships than first-borns and are more confident in social situations (Lahey et al., 1980; Miller & Maruyama, 1976).

The Impact of a Sibling's Arrival   The birth of a sibling can have a dramatic effect on the life of a first-born child. Research on the consequences of a second child's arrival generally confirms that "sibling rivalry" is no mere myth but a reality. Judy Dunn and Carol Kendrick (1982) followed the progress of family relationships among forty first-born children who experienced the arrival of a sibling sometime between their first and fourth birthdays. Dunn and Kendrick observed normal home routines during the mother's last month of pregnancy and again when the baby sibling was one, eight, and fourteen months old. They also interviewed the mother at each stage about the elder child's eating and sleeping habits, moods, and other routine behaviors.

▶ **Interaction among domains**

This young boy's reaction to a new sibling is quite typical. Although many children become clingy, withdrawn, or demanding when a new sibling first arrives, these reactions can be diminished if parents prepare the older child for the infant's arrival and involve him in the infant's care.

For the majority of children, the arrival of a sister or brother was related to marked changes in behavior; they became more demanding, clingy, unhappy, or withdrawn. Accompanying these changes in child behavior were significant decreases in maternal attention toward them; mothers engaged in less joint play, cuddling, and verbalization with their first-borns and in general initiated fewer interactions with the older child. At the same time, restrictive and punitive maternal behaviors increased. Over time, Dunn and Kendrick (1982) noted, two distinct patterns of sibling relationships emerged. Among some sibling pairs, almost all interactions eventually became friendly and positive, whereas for others, a persistent pattern of hostility and aggression became the norm. The first pattern was more likely if mothers had previously prepared the older child for the newborn's arrival by referring to the infant as a person with his or her own needs and desires. Engaging the older child in care for the infant also seemed to have positive consequences. In contrast, negative relationships between siblings resulted if the older child experienced a sharp drop in maternal contact. This discrepancy in pre- and postsibling maternal contact made the most difference; children who had less contact with the mother before the sibling's birth were not so profoundly affected by her attention to the new infant.

The arrival of a sibling demands a big adjustment for the older child, especially because another individual begins to compete for the parents' attention and affection. Siblings are very much aware of the differential treatment parents may knowingly or unwittingly bestow on them. The greater the perceived discrepancy, the greater the sibling conflict (Dunn, 1988). But not all aspects of sibling relationships are negative. Dunn and Kendrick (1982) noted that in certain circumstances siblings fill a void in parent-child relationships. When mother and older child have difficulties in their interactions, siblings may provide the attention and affection missing from the maternal relationship, thus helping to keep the family system in equilibrium.

Sibling Interactions Among Older Children　　Preschool-aged siblings exhibit a high degree of mutual interaction, exchanges that are marked by antagonistic as well as prosocial behaviors. In a series of naturalistic observations of eighteen-month-olds and their three- to four-year-old siblings as they played at home, Rona Abramovitch and her colleagues (Abramovitch, Pepler, & Corter, 1982) found that approximately forty interactions were initiated by one or the other sibling per hour, over half of which were responded to. The older sibling initiated about 80 percent of the aggressive acts and 65 percent of the prosocial behaviors. Imitation occurred quite frequently, predominantly among the younger siblings. Differences observed as a function of the sex of the dyads were that sisters were more likely to engage in prosocial behaviors and brothers in aggressive actions. Three years later, the same sibling pairs were observed again. The older siblings continued to be dominant, initiating more aggressive and prosocial behaviors and serving as models for the younger children's imitations. The sex differences in aggression and prosocial responding, however, had disappeared (Abramovitch et al., 1986).

Children tend to fight more with their siblings than with their friends. When fifth- through eighth-grade students were asked to describe conflicts with siblings, they reported that they allowed quarrels with siblings to escalate, often to the point at which parents had to intervene, whereas they tried to resolve

Older siblings often serve as powerful models for all sorts of behaviors in younger family members, as this picture of two sisters demonstrates.

conflicts with friends. Most of the time, siblings fight about privacy and interpersonal boundaries (Raffaelli, 1989). In addition, interactions between siblings tend to be more negative when the older sibling is a male (MacKinnon, 1989a).

Sibling relationships do change from middle childhood through adolescence. Duane Buhrmester and Wyndol Furman (1990) administered a Sibling Relationship Questionnaire to third-, sixth-, ninth-, and twelfth-graders, assessing several dimensions of sibling interactions. Older siblings reported being more dominant and nurturant toward their younger siblings, and younger siblings similarly reported that they received more often than dispensed dominance and nurturance. These differences between older and younger sibling, however, apparently disappear with the passage of time. The older subjects in the sample reported having more egalitarian relationships with their siblings as well as less intense feelings of both warmth and conflict. Thus, for example, a pair of siblings seventeen and twenty-one years old is more likely to have a socially equal relationship than a pair who are eight and eleven years old. Initial differences in power and nurturance usually disappeared when the younger sibling was twelve years old, now more competent and in less need of guidance and emotional support.

The quality of sibling interactions can be affected by the style of parenting mothers and fathers choose. In one study, mothers who used nonpunitive control techniques and encouraged curiosity and openness to experience had children who were more prosocial toward each other than mothers who were punitive and restrictive (Brody, Stoneman, & MacKinnon, 1986). In another, prosocial behavior among siblings was related to marital harmony and low interparental conflict (Brody, Stoneman, & Burke, 1987). Once again, we see that the general tenor of interactions among specific subsystems in the family can have a significant impact on other subsystems, and on individual children.

The presence of siblings, finally, may mean that the child has fewer opportunities to interact with parents but also provides the context for developing other unique skills. Older siblings have opportunities to become nurturant and assertive, and younger siblings have more models than only children do for a range of social behaviors. Despite the fact that most children do grow up with siblings, we are only just beginning to understand the role they play in child development.

FAMILIES IN TRANSITION

As we saw at the start of this chapter, the traditional nuclear family has been slowly disappearing from mainstream American society. Single-parent families, dual-wage-earner families, and reconstituted families—in which adults who remarry bring their respective children into new families—are becoming more and more prevalent and offer new circumstances to which children must adapt. What are the effects of these emerging family structures on child development? Research shows that child development is not directly influenced by changes in family structure per se but by the ways in which structural changes affect interpersonal relations within the family.

▶ **Sociocultural influence**

▶ **Interaction among domains**

Maternal Employment

In the last two decades, the percentage of married women with children in the labor force has increased dramatically. As we saw in Chapter 10, approximately 65 percent of women with children are currently employed, compared with about 40 percent in 1970, and over 50 percent of mothers of infants one year old and under presently work outside the home (U.S. Bureau of the Census, 1990a). The prevalence of dual-wage-earning families has spurred numerous investigations of the impact of maternal employment on child development.

When psychologists compare children of employed mothers with children of women who remain at home, few differences emerge on measures of cognitive achievement and socioemotional development (Heyns, 1982; Hoffman, 1984, 1989). If anything, daughters of employed mothers derive some benefit; they are more likely to show greater independence, achievement, and higher self-esteem than daughters of nonworking mothers. Apparently these girls profit from having a successful, competent role model, at least as these qualities are recognized by the larger society. (Women who remain home "work," too, but traditionally have not been afforded recognition or status for that role.) A few researchers have also reported that for one particular group, middle-class boys, maternal employment is linked to lower achievement and IQ scores (Hoffman, 1980, 1984). A more recent large-scale study of the effects of maternal employment, however, found no evidence of cognitive deficits in sons of employed mothers (Gottfried, Gottfried, & Bathurst, 1988).

The clearest effect of maternal employment involves the sex-role attitudes of both sons and daughters. As we saw in Chapter 12, when mothers work outside the home, their children are less likely to hold stereotypical beliefs about males and females and are more likely to see both sexes as competent (Hoffman, 1984, 1989). When both mother and father work, sons and daughters have the opportunity to see both parents in multiple roles, as powerful, competent wage earners and as nurturant, warm caregivers. This factor no doubt contributes to their children's more egalitarian beliefs about male and female roles.

Overall, the variable of maternal employment is, by itself, not strongly related to many developmental outcomes. As Lois Hoffman (1989) points out, the effect of maternal employment is better understood through its effects on family dynamics, parental attitudes, and the alternative child-care arrangements the family has chosen. It is to these factors that we now turn our attention.

Maternal Employment and Parent-Child Interaction   Mothers who work full time outside the home spend less time caring for their children, whether they are infants or high school age, than mothers who stay at home (Hill & Stafford, 1980). In terms of direct one-to-one mother-child interaction, however, there are no significant differences between employed and nonemployed mothers (Goldberg, 1977). Employed mothers often compensate for the time they miss with their child during the work week by allocating more time for them on weekends and evenings (Easterbooks & Goldberg, 1985). Thus, working mothers try to establish "quality time" with their children to make up for the hours they are separated from them. The picture for fathers is less clear. Though some studies show that fathers assume more of the responsibilities for child care when the mother works, others indicate that they do not (Baruch & Barnett, 1981; Pederson et al., 1982; Pleck, 1983).

Does the quality of parent-child interaction differ between mothers who do and do not work? Employed mothers as a group tend to stress independence training (Hoffman, 1989), a characteristic in children that will help the family function more smoothly, given the more limited time mothers and fathers have to perform routine activities. Some researchers also report that employed mothers verbalize more to their children and engage in more social play (Pederson et al., 1982; Schubert, Bradley-Johnson, & Nuttal, 1980). Overall, however, what matters more than whether the mother works or not is her attitude toward mothering and the reasons she is working or staying home.

Mothers who stay at home but prefer to be in the labor force and mothers who are working but find their employment stressful do not create the best climate for optimal child development. In one study of mothers of infants, those who remained at home contrary to their preference had higher scores on tests of depression and stress compared with two other groups—mothers who preferred to be home and were not in the labor force, and employed mothers who valued their positions in the work world (Hock & DeMeis, 1990). On the other hand, when maternal employment produces tension, parenting practices may suffer. Researchers have found that mothers who worked more than forty hours per week, for example, were more anxious and unhappy, and they displayed less sensitive, less animated interactions with their infants (Owen & Cox, 1988). Furthermore, mothers may seek employment because of divorce, financial strains, or other reasons unrelated to career aspirations that may set the stage for negative family interactions.

TABLE 14.3

Child-Care Arrangements of Children Whose Mothers Work

This table shows the percentage of children who receive different forms of child care. Most infants and preschoolers whose mothers work receive child care provided by a relative or nonrelative, either in the child's home or the home of the caregiver.

The Effects of Day Care   It is almost impossible to extract the influence of maternal employment as a variable from the effect of the alternate caregiving arrangements made for the child. The two factors almost invariably co-occur. Child-care arrangements take various forms, from in-home care provided by a relative or paid caregiver to group care in a formal, organized center.

As Table 14.3 shows, most children are cared for in another home by a relative or nonrelative, and only a small percentage of children attend an organized day-care center. This finding raises an interesting issue concerning the

| Age of Child | Child's Home | | Another Home | | Organized Child-Care Facility | Other[1] |
	Relative	Nonrelative	Relative	Nonrelative		
Under 1 year	22.9	8.3	15.1	23.3	14.1	16.4
1 to 2 years	26.1	6.6	14.3	27.0	18.1	7.8
3 to 4 years	21.6	5.1	11.7	17.2	34.3	10.0

Source: Adapted from U.S. Bureau of the Census, 1990b.
[1]Includes mother caring for child at work, child caring for self, and child attending kindergarten or grade school.

effect of day care on development. With rare exceptions, researchers have compared children who have experienced varying amounts of time in center-based day care with children who have been reared by their parents at home. Because most children in the United States do not attend formal day-care centers, we must interpret the findings of this research cautiously. The more common home-based care of children whose mothers work has yet to be studied extensively.

In Chapter 10, we discussed the effects of day care on a specific aspect of development—the child's attachment to the mother. Here we consider the broader effects of alternate caregiving on child development. In spite of the many potential effects of day care, research so far has uncovered few differences between children reared at home by their parents and those experiencing day care. One area in which some (but not all) researchers have noted an effect of day care is in intellectual performance. Day-care children tend to outperform children reared at home by their parents on standardized tests of IQ as well as measures of problem-solving ability, creativity, language development, and arithmetic skills (Clarke-Stewart & Fein, 1983). Day-care programs that stress cognitive activities have a greater effect on IQ scores than those that simply provide caregiving (McCartney et al., 1985). The advantage day-care children enjoy virtually disappears by the age of five years, however, when many home-reared children begin kindergarten or nursery school. Thus, the impact of day care on intellectual achievements is likely to be a function of deliberate, strategic efforts to teach children information and skills they would eventually attain later once they enter school.

Day care also produces effects in the realm of social development. Specifically, children with experience in day care are more socially competent. They show greater self-confidence, assertiveness, independence, and behave more prosocially with peers than home-reared comparison groups. Besides showing more positive behaviors, however, day-care children also more frequently display aggression toward peers and noncompliance with adults, at least according to some, but not all, studies of this behavior (Clarke-Stewart & Fein, 1983). Two factors have been proposed as explanations for day-care children's advanced social behaviors: the extensive peer contacts they have and the prosocial instruction explicitly provided by many caregivers (Hamilton & Gordon, 1978; Rubenstein & Howes, 1979). As for their greater aggressive and noncompliant behavior, Alison Clarke-Stewart (1989) suggests that day-care children are simply more likely to think independently but have not yet mastered the social skills to negotiate for the attainment of their goals.

To summarize, day care has few negative effects on children and may even facilitate development in certain areas, especially social functioning. Researchers have yet to sort out, however, the influence of several key variables, such as the length of time the child spends in day care. Does it matter, for example, whether the child attends a program full time or part time? Does the age at which she begins day care make a difference? Little is also known about the long-term impact of day care on children and how other factors, such as parental attitudes and the child's own characteristics, play a role. Finally, most studies of day care have been conducted in high-quality centers, often associated with universities and populated by middle- to upper-class children. Many parents, however, do not have the opportunity or financial resources to send their children to programs of such high caliber. What are the effects of

To date, research shows that day care has few negative effects on young children, and may even facilitate social development. Particularly important is the caregiver's warmth and responsiveness.

less than excellent programs on children? Preliminary research suggests that when children are enrolled in low-quality centers prior to the age of twelve months, they have more difficulty with peers and are distractible and less task oriented in kindergarten compared with children who are enrolled at later ages and those who attend high-quality centers (Howes, 1990). Thus, many important questions about the effects of day care remain unanswered.

Choosing a Day-Care Center   Both the federal government and many states have set minimum requirements for day-care services that regulate the qualifications of teachers, staff-child ratios, the size and safety of the physical facility, and the provision of nourishing meals. Although these guidelines and laws provide for *minimum* standards, many parents are concerned with finding high-quality child care during the hours they are employed. Alison Clarke-Stewart (1982) has drawn on the expanding body of research findings on day care to compile the following suggestions for parents:

- Center-based care is more likely to include educational opportunities for children compared with home-based care, such as that provided by babysitters and family day care. On the other hand, children are more likely to receive one-to-one supervision and authoritative discipline in home-based care.

- Children are most likely to thrive intellectually and emotionally in programs that offer a balance between structured educational activities and an open, free environment.

- The caregiving environment should provide ample physical space (at least twenty-five square feet per child) and a variety of materials and activities to foster sensorimotor, social, and cognitive development.

- The interaction style of the caregiver is a key aspect of quality care. The caregiver should be actively involved but not restrictive with the children. She or he should also be responsive and offer positive encouragement.

- Caregivers who have training in child development and continuing opportunities for education are most likely to provide high-quality care.

- The individual characteristics of the child should be taken into account. Though some children will probably do well in a program in which structure and openness are balanced, others might profit from either more structure or a more flexible, relaxed program.

In essence, the qualities of good day care mirror the qualities of good parenting. In other words, parents should seek a warm, responsive environment in which the child is provided, at least some of the time, with opportunities for structured play and prosocial learning.

▶ **Sociocultural influence**

The Impact of Divorce

As we pointed out at the start of this chapter, the statistics are dramatic—the divorce rate among couples in the United States has tripled since 1960, and estimates suggest that between 40 and 50 percent of children born in the late 1970s and early 1980s will live through the divorce of their parents (Glick & Lin, 1986). Far from being an atypical event, divorce affects a significant proportion of American children. Unfortunately, the effects of divorce on children are rarely positive; the absence of one parent, the emotional and financial tension, and sometimes continuing conflicts between parents that accompany divorce frequently lead to a range of psychological problems for both boys and girls, at least in the period immediately following the break-up of the family. The ability of children to cope with the stresses of divorce, particularly in the long run, depends on a number of variables. Most important, though, is the way parents manage this transition in family structure.

A major longitudinal study of the impact of divorce on parents and children conducted by E. Mavis Hetherington and her associates illuminated how parental separation affects children and how the nature of parent-child interactions changes (Hetherington, Cox, & Cox, 1982). The researchers compared two groups over a period of two years, a sample of forty-eight preschool-aged middle-class children whose parents divorced, and another group of forty-eight middle-class children matched on several variables, such as age and sex, whose families were intact. In all the divorced families, mothers had custody of their children. During the course of the study, the researchers made several assessments of both parents and children, including parental interviews, observations of parent-child interactions in the laboratory and at home, observations and ratings of children's behavior in the home and school, and personality tests.

▶ **Interaction among domains**

The results of the study indicated that the worst period for most children was the first year following the divorce, when they exhibited many negative characteristics, such as aggression, distractability, and noncompliance. The extent of their undesirable behaviors even surpassed those of children from intact families with a high level of conflict, and it was particularly noticeable in boys. Two years after the divorce, many of the effects on children diminished, especially for girls. In a six-year follow-up, however, many boys continued to show patterns of aggression and noncompliance, academic difficulties, poor relations with peers, and extremely low self-esteem (Hetherington, 1989).

A look at family interaction styles following divorce helps to account for the poor initial adjustment of children. Hetherington and her colleagues noted that soon after they separated from their husbands, mothers tended to adopt a more authoritarian style of parenting (Hetherington, Cox, & Cox, 1982). They gave out numerous commands and prohibitions and displayed little affection or responsiveness to their children. These mothers were undoubtedly having problems coping with their new status as single parents, in both emotional and practical terms. At the same time, fathers withdrew, participating little in the management of their children's behavior. Children, particularly boys, became less compliant, and mothers in turn responded with increased restrictiveness and punitiveness. Caught up in a spiral of frustration, helplessness, and feelings of incompetence, these mothers responded negatively to many child behaviors, even those that were neutral or positive, and despite their harsh threats, followed up on few of the directives they gave. The result was a coercive cycle of parent-child interaction like that described earlier in this chapter and typified by this chapter's opening scene between Joey and his mother.

Other researchers have confirmed that many children show heightened aggression, lower academic achievement, disruptions in peer relationships, and depression after their parents' divorce (Camara & Resnick, 1988; Stolberg & Anker, 1984; Wallerstein, Corbin, & Lewis, 1988). Children aged six to eight years seem to have the most difficulty adjusting; they are old enough to realize the seriousness of the family's situation but do not yet have the coping skills to deal with feelings of sadness and guilt that often accompany the change in family structure (Wallerstein & Kelly, 1980). Older children often have a better understanding of divorce and the idea that conflicts between parents must somehow be resolved (Kurdek, 1989). Even adolescents, however, often suffer negative psychological consequences following parental divorce; adolescent boys, in particular, are more prone to using alcohol or illicit drugs and show psychological distress following parental separation when compared to a control group whose parents remained married (Doherty & Needle, 1991). Sibling interactions also suffer. Carol MacKinnon (1989b) observed elementary school–aged children as they played games with their siblings in the laboratory. Siblings whose parents had been divorced for one year or longer showed more teasing, quarreling, physical attacks, and other negative behaviors toward each other than children from married families. Given these deleterious consequences and the fact that divorce is so prevalent, is there anything that can be done to ease the adjustment of children? Research findings suggest some potentially useful strategies.

Adjusting to Divorce The consequences of divorce are not always so grim for all children. Hetherington (1989) observed that after six years, some of the children in her original study recovered from the family crisis and showed a healthy adaptation to their new family lifestyle, whether the mother remarried or not. These children displayed few behavior problems, high self-esteem, successful academic performance, and positive relations with peers. What factors were associated with this favorable pattern of adjustment? For one thing, mothers of children in this group had become less authoritarian and more authoritative in their parental style, encouraging independence but also providing a warm, supportive climate for their sons and daughters. If the mother was not available, many of these children had contact with some other caring adult, a relative, teacher, or neighbor. In addition, several of the children in this category had responsibility for the care of another individual—a younger sibling, an aged grandparent, or someone with a physical or emotional problem. These relationships may have offered children an opportunity to feel needed and provided an alternative source of emotional gratification and support. In contrast, mothers of children with long-lasting adjustment problems continued to manifest coercive styles of interaction. Mothers and sons were especially likely to fall into this pattern. Finally, children are more likely to show successful adjustment to divorce when conflict is low between parents following the divorce and when the child maintains a relationship with the noncustodial parent (Guidubaldi, Perry, & Cleminshaw, 1984; Kurdek & Berg, 1983; Wallerstein & Kelly, 1980).

After divorce, most children reside with their mother. Many states, however, now have laws that favor joint custody of children following divorce. In most cases, this means that both parents have equal responsibility for making decisions about the child's medical care and education; that is, they have *joint legal custody*. In other cases, it also means that children reside for substantial periods of time with each parent. This arrangement refers to *joint physical custody*. So far, the effects of various custody arrangements on children are unclear. Some experts believe that joint custody increases the likelihood that children will be exposed to their parents' hostility (Reppucci, 1984; Stahl,

1984). Others note no differences between the adjustment of children in joint-custody versus sole-custody families (Kline et al., 1989). Still other evidence suggests that children may adapt better when they are in the custody of the same-sex parent (Camara & Resnick, 1988; Warshak & Santrock, 1983). For example, a recent analysis of data from several hundred high school sophomores whose parents divorced shows that adolescents who live with their same-sex parent are less likely to drop out of high school (Zimiles & Lee, 1991).

Divorce represents a difficult transition for all members of the family. A key variable to understanding its impact is the effect on relationships among all family members—the more conflict and negative emotion associated with the process and the more prolonged the maladaptive patterns of interaction, the worse the outcomes for the child. At the same time, if persistent conflicts characterize the interactions of intact families, the consequences will be similarly harmful to the child (Hetherington, Cox, and Cox, 1982; Long & Forehand, 1987). In that instance, parental divorce may actually lead to better consequences for the child in the long run.

▶ **Interaction among domains**

Relationships with Stepparents   Approximately 75 percent of divorced individuals remarry, the majority within five years after their divorce (Glick, 1984). As a consequence, about 35 percent of children born in the early 1980s will live with a stepparent (Glick, 1989). For children who have just experienced the separation of their parents, the introduction of a new "parent" represents yet another difficult transition. Like divorce, a parent's remarriage often leads to aggression, noncompliance, academic difficulties, and poor peer relations among children (Bray, 1988; Zill, 1988). The child usually has more difficulty adjusting when stepparents have larger numbers of their own children, when children from two previous marriages are assimilated into one family, and when the custodial parent and stepparent have a new biological child of their own (Santrock & Sitterle, 1987; Zill, 1988). Adolescents have more problems adjusting to their new family than younger children, perhaps because their growing autonomy leads them to be more confrontational with parents (Brand, Clingempeel, & Bowen-Woodward, 1988). In addition, girls in the middle school years do not adjust as well to parental remarriage compared with boys, perhaps because girls must now share their mothers' attentions with a new father (Brand, Clingempeel, & Bowen-Woodward, 1988). In contrast, the addition of the stepfather may benefit boys who may be caught up in a coercive cycle with their mothers.

Drawing from data collected in a national survey of parent-adolescent relations, Frank Furstenberg (1987) found that stepparents report reservations about their ability to discipline and provide affection toward stepchildren. At the same time, stepchildren confirm that stepparents are less involved in their care and supervision than biological parents. Thus, stepparents seem not to fit the profile of authoritative parenting we described earlier in this chapter, and the benefits of that parenting style are not realized. Furstenberg (1987) also found, however, that most parents and children in stepfamilies actually have positive relations. Therefore, remarriage need not be a negative event in the child's life.

Some of the difficulties in stepfamilies may stem from the uncertain social roles of stepparents. Should they be as strict as the biological parent or will the child see too much control as intrusive? Stepparents who are trying to win the affections of their "new" children may be reluctant to use strong discipline. And, as with any new parent and child, stepparents and children need time to build their emotional relationship. Parental remarriage can have either positive or negative consequences on children depending on how the custodial parent and stepparent manage the transition.

Families in Transition: An Overview

We have seen that changes in the structure of the American family affect child development to the extent that they influence the interactions among members of the family system. Maternal employment, divorce, and remarriage can alter the emotional tone of parent-child interactions as well as the types of control strategies parents select, and it is these latter elements that can have a profound effect on the intellectual and socioemotional development of the child. Considering how prevalent changes in family structures have become and how many children are affected by them, it is imperative that ways be established to support families undergoing these transitions. Assistance with child care, parent training programs for dysfunctional families, and counseling support for families experiencing stress are some of the programs that can be helpful to families.

THEMES IN DEVELOPMENT

THE INFLUENCE OF THE FAMILY

▶ **How does the sociocultural context influence family processes?**

Many of the goals parents have for their children's socialization are governed by attitudes held by the larger society, values and beliefs that change over time. Parents will emphasize cooperation, achievement, and sociability, for example, to the extent that the larger social group values these characteristics. Culture also influences who participates in child care and to what extent; in some cultures, for example, fathers and siblings take part in many routine child-care tasks. Finally, economic and social trends, such as family size, single parenthood, maternal employment, alternative child care, divorce, and remarriage, can alter family structures. The changes in family dynamics introduced by these factors can have far-reaching consequences for child development.

▶ **How does the child play an active role in family processes?**

As integral members of the family system, children can have significant effects on interactions with parents, siblings, and others. The dramatic physical and cognitive changes associated with development oblige parents and siblings to adapt to the rapidly altering capabilities and needs of the child. In general, parents and siblings react to the child's growing independence and competence by displaying less dominance and regulation. In addition, the child's behaviors may influence the parents' choice of discipline style in such a way that aggressive, difficult children elicit more authoritarian parenting and premature children may be at risk for abuse.

▶ How do family processes interact with other domains of development?

The child's experiences within the family, particularly the type of parenting style she is exposed to, can have broad consequences for development. For example, children who experience authoritarian parenting show less advanced moral reasoning, lower self-esteem, poorer relations with peers, poorer school adjustment, and higher levels of aggression compared with children who experience authoritative parenting. Similarly, interactions with siblings often provide children with opportunities to develop social skills such as nurturance and assertiveness. Finally, transitions in families can introduce both new opportunities and new stresses in the lives of children that can affect their emotional, social, and cognitive development.

SUMMARY

Many social scientists conceptualize the family as a *system* in which each relationship can influence other relationships. In addition, the family is vulnerable to larger social influences such as cultural values and economic trends. Most psychologists recognize that the key to understanding the child's development lies in family dynamics.

Parents serve as the child's primary *socialization* agents by teaching their children directly, serving as powerful models, and controlling other aspects of the child's social life, such as interactions with peers. One important element of parenting is the general style with which parents relate to their children. *Authoritative parenting,* characterized by moderate control and high nurturance, results in the most positive consequences for children. Offspring of authoritative parents are cooperative, independent, achievement oriented, and have healthy peer relations. *Authoritarian parents* rely excessively on power-assertive techniques, such as physical punishment, and display less nurturance and affection. Their children frequently display aggression, lower levels of moral reasoning, poor self-esteem, poor peer relations, and lower school achievement. *Permissive* and *uninvolved* parents also tend to have children with developmental problems.

In general, studies of parental discipline indicate that induction is an effective technique, whereas power assertion and love withdrawal are associated with negative outcomes in children. Punishment can alter the child's behavior in the short run, particularly if it is accompanied by an explanation and is used consistently. It can, however, also result in more aggression in children as well as avoidance of the punishing agent. For these reasons, experts recommend induction and *time-out* as techniques. Problems in parenting, such as the *coercive cycle* and child abuse, illustrate how power assertion can lead to escalating levels of violence within the family.

Cross-cultural and social class variations in parenting reflect the pressures exerted by larger social forces. In some rural societies in which children contribute to the family's subsistence, they are expected to care for siblings and strictly obey their parents. In other societies, like Japan, children are disciplined through reasoning, a method consistent with the culture's influence on responsibilities to others. Families affected by economic hardship provide another example of how an external factor can place stress on parents and influence their parenting style.

Although mothers have traditionally assumed the caregiver role, other family members—namely, fathers and siblings—also play an important role in the child's socialization. Fathers typically do not spend as much time with their children as mothers, but behave similarly when they are given the opportunity. One difference, though, is that fathers tend to engage in more physical interactions with their infants and young children. Fathers probably contribute to child development in the same way that mothers do. Sensitive, responsive fathering is associated with many of the same desirable outcomes in children as good mothering.

Siblings also affect development. The presence of siblings usually means that parents have less time to spend with younger children; this fact may explain the generally higher achievement of only and first-born children. Sibling relations change over the course of development. Preschool-aged siblings have both aggressive and prosocial exchanges, and older siblings are more dominant and nurturant than younger siblings. These differences among siblings diminish as they get older.

Societal changes mean that more families include mothers who work and more families go through the experience of divorce. Maternal employment is associated with higher levels of achievement, independence, and self-esteem in girls and less stereotyped sex-role attitudes in both boys and girls. More important than the fact of maternal employment is the mother's interaction style and the quality of substitute care the child receives. Whether they work or not, mothers who are satisfied with their life circumstances and who display adaptive parenting techniques have well-adjusted children. Studies of day care generally show no negative effects on children; if anything, children who attend day care are more socially competent than children reared solely at home by their parents.

Children whose parents divorce evidence socioemotional and academic difficulties, especially boys. Many of these effects disappear after the first year following the divorce, particularly among girls. Parental separation typically means increased stress on the family, a factor that can lead to ineffective parenting. Successful adjustment to divorce among children is associated with low parental conflict in the period following separation. Children, especially adolescents, also have difficulty adjusting to the remarriage of their parents. These difficulties may stem, in part, from the reluctance of stepparents to exhibit nurturance or control in their interactions with their stepchildren.

15

The Influence of Peers

▶ **How does the sociocultural context influence peer relations?**

▶ **How does the child play an active role in peer relations?**

▶ **Are developmental changes in peer relations continuous or stagelike?**

▶ **How do peer relations interact with other domains of development?**

It was the start of the first day of school. Jan Nakamura, the third-grade teacher, surveyed her new charges as they played in the schoolyard before class. It was a familiar scene: The boys played a raucous game of kickball, cheering their teammates and urging victory. The girls gathered in small groups, talking with great animation about their summer experiences and their excitement about school. As always, certain children in both groups were the center of activity; they seemed to attract the gaze and attention of their age mates as a pot of honey draws bees. Other children seemed to fall into the background; few of their peers approached or spoke to them. Already Jan had a sense that third grade would be easier on some of these fresh new faces than others.

In many ways, Jan's intuitions were correct. She would find, as she learned to match up names to faces in this year's class, that many of the playground stars made the transition to a new grade more easily than some of the less popular children. Research evidence suggests that the ability to have successful and rewarding interactions with peers during childhood can be the harbinger of successful adjustment and that poor peer relations are often associated with a range of developmental problems. Boys and girls who have good peer relationships enjoy school more and are less likely to experience academic difficulties, drop out of school, and commit delinquent or criminal acts in later years than age mates who relate poorly with their peers (Kupersmidt, 1983; Ladd, 1990; Parker & Asher, 1987). Children who are accepted by their peers are also less likely to report feeling lonely, depressed, and socially anxious than children who are rejected (Asher & Wheeler, 1985; Hymel & Franke, 1985; Vosk et al., 1982). Of course, the quality of peer relations does not always predict later developmental outcomes. Nevertheless, experiences with peers play a substantial role in the lives of most children and thus have become an important focus of developmental research.

For most children, peers function as the most influential agents of socialization, second only to the family. As direct mediators of cultural norms and expectations, peers can influence the clothes a child chooses to wear, her attitudes about aggression (as was discussed in Chapter 13), her educational aspirations, and many other behaviors and beliefs. As we saw in Chapter 12, the influence of peers is probably most noticeable in the area of sex-role socialization. Peers strongly enforce cultural stereotypes about sex roles, and interactions in sex-segregated peer groups—like those in the playground scene above—provide an important setting for learning masculine and feminine sex-typed attitudes and behaviors.

In Chapter 14 we pointed out that for many American children, contact with peers starts early. As more and more children attend day care while their parents work, they spend a good part of each day with age mates from the age of two years or even earlier. Psychologists, parents, and teachers all wonder, with good reason, about the effects of such extensive interactions with peers.

A number of theorists have examined the role of peers in child development. Social learning theorists believe that peers exert a heavy influence on the child's socialization by means of modeling and reinforcement. Piaget (1932/1965) and Vygotsky (1978) have discussed the ways in which peer contacts alter the child's cognitions, which can, in turn, direct social behavior. Piaget contends that peer interactions prompt—even coerce—the child to consider the viewpoints of others, broadening her social perspective-taking ability and diminishing her egocentrism. The result is a greater capacity for social exchange. Vygotsky maintains that contact with peers, especially those who are more skilled in a given domain, stretches the child's intellectual and social capacities. The *zone of proximal development,* the child's mental capacity to performs ome activities but only with the assistance of someone more skilled, includes new modes of thinking and social interaction. As a result of experiences with peers, the child internalizes these new behaviors and then produces them independently.

In light of these important theoretical ideas about peers, the very real prevalence of peer experiences in children's lives, and the undoubted power of peers as socializing agents, the number of studies examining peer relations in childhood and adolescence has understandably skyrocketed in the last decade. Thanks to these intense efforts, researchers have been able to identify such developmentally relevant information as changes in peer relations with age, the dynamics of peer groups, and the factors that are related to social competence with peers. Because we humans are "social" beings, perhaps it should not be surprising that our childhood experiences in social groups play such a large part in making us what we are.

DEVELOPMENTAL CHANGES IN PEER RELATIONS

Compared with any other human relationship, the special feature of peer relations is their egalitarian nature. In fact, strictly speaking, the term **peer** refers to a companion who is approximately the same age and developmental level. Parent-child interactions are characterized by a distinct dominant-subordinate hierarchy that plays a useful role in the child's socialization as parents use their authority to transmit information about social rules and behaviors. Peers, however, often function as equals, and it is primarily among equals that children can forge such social skills as compromising, competing, and cooperating. Thus, experiences with peers afford the child unique opportunities to con-

peer Companion of approximately the same age and developmental level.

struct social understanding and to develop social skills (Hartup, 1977, 1989; Youniss & Smollar, 1985).

Relationships with peers also contribute to the child's developing sense of self. Peers provide the child with direct feedback (verbal and sometimes nonverbal) about how well she is doing in the academic, social, and emotional realms, feedback that can significantly influence the child's self-esteem. Peers also provide a natural comparison against which the child can gauge her own accomplishments (Furman & Robbins, 1985). "Am I really a good athlete?" "How am I doing as a student?" A child can answer questions like these by comparing her own abilities to those of her peers.

The way in which children relate to their peers undergoes significant developmental changes. At first, peers are simply interesting (and, at times, annoying) companions in play, but eventually they assume a larger and more crucial part in the child's social and emotional life. Children's peer networks start out small. But as children enter day care and school, and as their cognitive, language, and social skills develop, their peer networks expand in size, and their relationships with a subset of those peers grow in intensity.

▷ **Interaction among domains**

Early Peer Exchanges and Play

Infants show distinct reactions to peers even in the first few months of life. The sight of another baby often prompts a three-month-old to become generally aroused and active compared with the ritualized greeting she usually reserves for her mother (Fogel, 1979) or the rapt and quiet attention she displays to her reflected image (Field, 1979). At six months, diffuse responses to peers give way to more specific signals, such as smiles, squeals, touching, and leaning in their direction (Hay, Nash, & Pedersen, 1983; Maudry & Nekula, 1939; Vandell, Wilson, & Buchanan, 1980). Older babies crawl toward one another and explore each other's facial features (Vandell & Mueller, 1980). Thus, from early on, infants recognize something special and interesting about strangers who resemble them in size and features. But most peer interactions during infancy are brief, lasting only a few seconds, and usually do not involve mutual exchanges of behaviors (Eckerman, Whatley, & Kutz, 1975; Vandell & Wilson, 1982).

In the second year, social exchanges with peers become longer and more coordinated. Two children will jointly manipulate toys and other objects, each child taking a turn playing and then offering the object to the playmate. Children also begin to play simple games together, such as hide-and-seek or tag, activities that require the switching of turns and roles (Howes, 1987a, 1987b). Later in toddlerhood, between the ages of two and three years, children engage in peer interactions more frequently. These interactions contain many positive social behaviors, such as giving attention, smiling, sharing, and cooperating. Just such social or affiliative gestures, rather than objects such as toys, are likely to be the focus of peer interactions (Bronson, 1981).

Mildred Parten (1932) found that the peer relations of young children are characterized by three forms of play. In **solitary play,** children play alone with toys, apart from other children and without regard for what they are doing. One child might be stacking rings while another does a puzzle; neither notices

solitary play Individual play, performed without regard for what others are doing.

These two infants are engaged in typical early peer interaction. Babies will often crawl toward one another and explore each other's faces (and possessions), but such interactions are usually brief and do not involve mutual play.

▶ **Development as continuous/ stagelike**

▶ **Interaction among domains**

parallel play Side-by-side independent play that is not interactive.

cooperative play Interactive play in which children's actions are reciprocal.

social pretend play Play that makes use of imaginary and symbolic objects and social roles, often enacted among several children. Also called *sociodramatic play*.

or cares about the other's activities. In **parallel play,** children play independently while they are beside or close to other children. Several children might be gathered at a sandbox, one digging with a shovel, another making "pies," and still another dragging a truck. Even though they are in close proximity, one child's activities do not influence the play of the others. In **cooperative play,** children interact. They share toys, follow one another, and make mutual suggestions about what to do next. Although Parten believed that a stagelike developmental progression took place from solitary to parallel and then cooperative play, more recent research suggests that all three types of play occur among preschoolers (Barnes, 1971; Rubin, Maioni, & Hornung, 1976).

Preschoolers also begin to display **social pretend play** (also called *sociodramatic play*), in which they invoke "make-believe" to change the function of objects, create imaginary situations, and enact pretend roles, often with the cooperation of one or two peers (Rubin, Fein, & Vandenberg, 1983; Smilansky, 1968). Children use sticks and pots as band instruments, ride "magic carpets" together, and play "Mommy and Daddy." Growth in the child's cognitive, perspective-taking, and communication skills helps explain these changes (Hartup, 1983; Howes, 1987a). To conceive of a stick as representing a flute, for example, the child must develop symbolic capabilities that allow him to let one object represent another. For a young girl to play "Mommy," she must relinquish her own perspective and appreciate another person's social role—what "mommies" do and how they speak to children. Finally, for complex and coordinated exchanges of pretend play to occur, as when one child sets the table and prepares the food while the other cries like a baby, children must understand the rules of social dialogue and communication. When we watch three-year-olds engage in pretend play with one another, we are witnessing an intersection of their growing competence in several arenas—social, language, and cognitive skills (Howes, Unger, & Seidner, 1989).

FIGURE 15.1

Changes in Time Spent with Same-Sex Friends During Early Childhood

The amount of time children spend with same-sex peers increases dramatically during early childhood, as this study of children's behavior during free play at school shows. At the same time, the proportion of time spent playing with opposite-sex peers decreases noticeably.

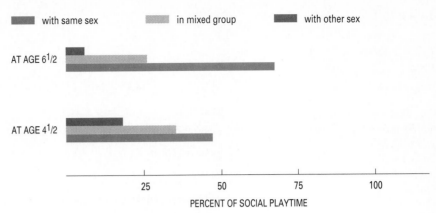

Source: Adapted from Maccoby & Jacklin, 1987.

The School Years and Adolescence

Elementary school–aged children begin to participate more in group activities than in the dyads (or two-person groups) that characterize earlier peer relations. As noted in Chapter 12, they show a clear preference for same-sex peers and, to a lesser extent, children who are racially similar. In fact, as Figure 15.1 shows, the tendency to play with other children of the same sex begins in the preschool years and grows stronger throughout the elementary school years (Maccoby & Jacklin, 1987). Quarrels and physical aggression with peers wane, although older children do use abusive language such as threats and insults when they have conflicts with their peers. Concurrently, prosocial behaviors such as sharing and helping others increase (Hartup, 1983).

A special form of play, called **rough-and-tumble play,** emerges around age two years and becomes more visible during the elementary school years, especially among boys. Children chase each other, pretend to fight, or sneak up and pounce on each other. Rough-and-tumble play differs from aggression in that children do not intend to hurt one another and it often occurs between children who like each other. Smiling and laughing often accompany rough-and-tumble play, and children will often continue to play together after a bout, all signs that these interactions are friendly. In one naturalistic observation of seven-, nine-, and eleven-year-olds, rough-and-tumble play took up about 10 percent of the children's playground time (Humphreys & Smith, 1987). The precise significance of rough-and-tumble play is a matter of debate, as we will shortly see.

What kinds of activities do school-aged children most frequently engage in with their peers? A survey of eighty-one fifth- and sixth-graders in Canada showed that peer activities are diverse (Zarbatany, Hartmann, & Rankin, 1990). Subjects were asked to scan a list of twenty-nine activities and rate how often they participated in each activity with their peers. As Table 15.1 shows, preadolescents spend a lot of time talking with each other, participating in sports, and listening to music or watching television together. These activities are likely to serve a number of functions, including promoting relationships, providing opportunities for learning, and allowing children to validate their own interests and self-worth.

rough-and-tumble play   Active, physical play that carries no intent of imposing harm on another child.

TABLE 15.1

Peer Activities in Later Childhood

Fifth- and sixth-graders were asked to indicate those peer activities they spent the most time engaged in. They rated a series of activities on a scale in which 0 indicated the activity was never conducted and 7 indicated the activity was conducted more than once a day. The results (average ratings) showed that preadolescents participate in a wide range of activities with each other, from conversing to simply watching TV. The underlined numbers indicate significant sex differences in responses.

Activity	Time Spent		
	All Children	Boys	Girls
Conversing	6.76	6.69	6.83
Hanging out	6.57	6.87	6.25
Walking at school	5.65	5.36	5.97
Telephone	5.63	4.84	6.47
Travel to/from school	5.57	5.26	5.92
TV/records	5.39	5.38	5.39
Physical games	5.26	5.43	5.08
Noncontact sports	5.17	5.67	4.64
Academic	5.15	4.85	5.47
Acting silly	5.12	4.95	5.31

Source: Adapted from Zarbatany, Hartmann, & Rankin, 1990.

clique Peer group of five to ten children who frequently interact together.

crowd Large group of peers that is characterized by specific traits or reputation.

Peer relations during adolescence become more intense on one level and involve larger networks on another level. Adolescents form close, intimate friendships with a subset of their peers, relationships they greatly value. Many children also form **cliques,** groups of five to ten children usually in the same class at school who frequently interact together (Brown, 1989). Clique membership is often supplemented by identification with a **crowd,** a larger group of peers with a specific reputation, such as "jocks" or "brains." Members of crowds do not necessarily spend time together but share a label based on a stereotype. It is interesting that even though youngsters may see themselves as members of particular cliques, their membership in crowds is often identified or labeled by others (Brown, 1989). That is, a boy might not see himself as a "brain" but receive that label from peers who observe his academic achievements and studious behaviors. Membership in cliques and crowds in the middle and later school years reflects the child's growing need for group belonging at a time when he is orienting away from parents and other adults. The norms of cliques and crowds can be powerful shapers of behavior; they often provide the adolescent with prescriptions on how to dress, act, and even what ambitions to have for the future.

As adolescents approach young adulthood and feel more secure with their self-identities, they are less interested in cliques and crowds and become oriented once again toward relationships with individuals. Third- through twelfth-graders in one study were asked to list their closest friends in the entire school as well as the persons they spent time with (Shrum & Cheek, 1987). An analysis of the patterns of relationships among children showed that there was a sharp decline toward later adolescence in the percentage of students who were members of cliques.

One other significant change in adolescence is that some peer relations begin to include elements of sexuality. Dating becomes one of the major social activities of adolescence, and interest in peers of the opposite sex is generally heightened (Damon, 1983). During this time, adolescents develop new social skills, such as having mutually engaging conversations with members of the opposite sex, skills that are more suitable for starting and maintaining romantic relationships than for sustaining relationships with same-sex peers. Again, interest in members of the opposite sex reflects the adolescent's concerns with entering the adult world. The Chronology on page 624 summarizes these major developmental changes in peer relations.

CONTROVERSY

Should Children's Rough-and-Tumble Play Be Discouraged?

Preschool and elementary school–aged children seem to love physical play. They jump on their beds, chase balls, and often engage in friendly "combat" with one another. Many parents and teachers who observe children engage in rough-and-tumble play wonder how to react. Should they be stopped, lest their play escalate into true aggression? Or is this an amusing and normal way for children to release energy or perhaps even accomplish specific developmental goals? Developmental psychologists have taken different positions on these questions.

The results of one study of the spontaneous behavior of twelve- and thirteen-year-old boys suggest that rough-and-tumble play does sometimes escalate into intense aggression (Neill, 1976). Some episodes that started out as play became increasingly hostile and led to physical harm to the victim. Moreover, from a social learning perspective, children who engage in rough play learn behaviors such as poking, hitting, and jumping on others that become part of their permanent repertoire. Once learned, these behaviors might be displayed in less amicable situations.

Other researchers, however, believe that rough-and-tumble play has a positive role in the child's development. In one study, kindergartners, second-, and fourth-graders were observed on their school playgrounds during recess. For some children—popular children—episodes of rough-and-tumble play were often followed by organized games with rules rather than aggression. A playful chase, for example, often led to the game of tag. In addition, popular children who engaged in rough-and-tumble play had higher scores on a test of social problem solving. These results suggest that, for some children, rough-and-tumble play provides a context for learning role exchange (for example, "Now you chase *me*") and prosocial behaviors like cooperation. On the other hand, when unpopular children played roughly, they were more likely to end up in a real physical fight. Their rough-and-tumble play escalated into aggression 28 percent of the time and was positively correlated with a measure of general antisocial behavior (Pellegrini, 1988).

Rough-and-tumble play occurs spontaneously in the young of many species, a fact that suggests it is a normal part of development. The precise function of this type of play in child development is not yet well understood, however. For most children, engaging in active physical play with others is not associated with greater hostility or aggression. For those children who have poor relations with peers, however, rough-and-tumble play may set off a chain of heightened aggression. ∎

PEER GROUP DYNAMICS

When we observe preschoolers or elementary school children, we see that they often associate in groups. The importance of peer groups, however, becomes especially visible during the middle school and early secondary school years (Crockett, Losoff, & Petersen, 1984). Adolescents frequently "hang out" in groups, desire to be members of the most popular groups, and look to the peer group for standards of appearance, conduct, and attitudes. Parents may find that their son or daughter *must have* a certain haircut or *must buy* a particular video game, only to discover that everyone else in the child's circle

CHRONOLOGY	Peer Relations
3 MONTHS	Reacts with arousal or attention to presence of a peer.
6–9 MONTHS	Directs smiles, touches, and other signals toward peers. Approaches peers.
2–4 YEARS	Jointly manipulates objects with one or two other peers. Engages in simple turn-taking games with peers. Shares, smiles, and cooperates with peers. Shows bouts of physical aggression with peers. Displays solitary, parallel, cooperative, and social pretend play.
5–9 YEARS	Participates in group activities. Displays less physical aggression and more prosocial behaviors toward peers. Displays rough-and-tumble play.
10–14 YEARS	Forms intimate friendships. Joins cliques. Becomes affiliated with a crowd. Feels greater peer pressure to conform.
15–18 YEARS	Participates less frequently in cliques and crowds. Becomes more interested in peers of the opposite sex.

This chart describes the sequence of peer relations based on the findings of research. Children often show individual differences in the exact ages at which they display the various developmental achievements outlined here.

of friends has the same "look" or library of games. The social dynamics of large groups are often different than the dynamics of two-person groups, or dyads, and the power exerted by the group in shaping how the child acts and thinks can be enormous.

Peer Group Formation

How do peer groups form in the first place? Undoubtedly, they coalesce on the basis of children's shared interests, backgrounds, or activities. Children associate with other members of their classroom, their soccer team, or other members of the school band, for example. Other variables, like socioeconomic class or ethnic and racial group membership, can also be a factor. Youngsters often join with others of similar social class or ethnic/racial background (Clasen & Brown, 1985; Larkin, 1979). As we have seen both in Chapter 12 and in this chapter, gender is another powerful variable; groups, for the most part, tend to be of the same sex throughout childhood and early adolescence.

A particularly enlightening description of how peer groups form and operate can be found in a classic experiment called the Robber's Cave Study, named after the state park in Oklahoma where it took place. Muzafer Sherif and his colleagues invited twenty-two fifth-grade boys who did not know each other to participate in a summer camp program (Sherif et al., 1961). The boys were divided into two groups who lived in separate parts of the state park. Initially, each group participated in its own program of typical camp activities—hiking, crafts, structured games—and was unaware of the existence of the other group. In this initial period of the experiment, each group began to develop a unique identity, and individual members performed distinct roles in relation to this group identity. One group became "tough"; the boys swore, acted roughly, and ridiculed those who were "sissies." Members of the other group were polite and considerate. As group solidarity grew, members decided to name themselves, the former calling themselves the Rattlers and the latter the Eagles.

The experimenters found that when they deliberately structured certain situations to encourage cooperation, group identities could be further strengthened. One day, for example, each group returned to the campsite only to find that the staff had not prepared dinner; only the uncooked ingredients were available. The boys quickly took over, dividing up the tasks so that some cooked, others prepared drinks, and so forth. Some boys assumed a leadership role, directing the suppertime activities, and others followed their directives. It was quite apparent that the boys had a strong sense of identity with the group and that the group had a clear structure. In other words, for both the Rattlers and the Eagles, there was strong intragroup cooperation and identity.

Another change in circumstances made the group identities even more pronounced. The camp counselors arranged for the Rattlers and Eagles to meet and organized a series of competitions for them, including games like baseball and tug-of-war. The effects of losing in these competitions were dramatic. The losing group became very disharmonious and full of conflict. Members accused each other of causing the loss, and some boys who had previously enjoyed status and prestige were demoted in standing if they had contributed to the group's humiliation. After these initial conflicts, though, group identity became stronger than ever. The effects of competition on behavior *between* the groups were even more pronounced. The Rattlers and Eagles verbally antagonized each other and retaliated for a loss in the day's competition by raiding each other's campsites and stealing possessions, such as comic books and clothing. Each episode forged intragroup identity but also increased intergroup hostility.

In the last phase of this social experiment, the counselors attempted to lessen the bad feelings between the Rattlers and the Eagles at first by having them share meals or watch movies together. Instead of promoting harmony between the groups, however, this tactic produced continuing hostilities, punctuated with fights and verbal assaults. In contrast, when the experimenters created situations in which the two groups had to work together to achieve some common goal, antagonisms between them began to crumble. One hot day, for example, when the counselors "discovered" that the water pipeline for the campsites was broken, boys from both the Rattlers and the Eagles began to search together for the broken pipes. On another occasion, the food delivery truck broke down; again, the boys all worked together to restart the engine. The acrimonious behavior between the two groups diminished, and boys from the two groups actually began to form friendships with one another.

Thus, groups form when individuals share activities and have some common goal or purpose. Identity with the group becomes stronger as children have more and more rewarding interactions within them and as the group's goals are accomplished. Groups also quickly develop structures wherein some members assume a more dominant role than others. Group identity becomes especially strong when there is competition with other groups, but an undesirable outcome is that intergroup conflict rises. Barriers between groups break down when they actively work together to achieve some common, overarching goal.

Peer groups form when children participate in cooperative activities that involve some common goal or purpose. Here, fifth graders participate in a camp activity intended to build group solidarity.

Few studies of the formation and function of peer groups match the scope of the Robber's Cave study, which has revealed many of the intricacies of peer group dynamics. Many parents, teachers, and others who work with children will see in these findings some clear suggestions for breaking down animosities between children's peer groups.

Dominance Hierarchies

The scene: a standard laboratory playroom on a university campus. Six elementary school boys, strangers to one another, are brought together to play for forty-five minutes, five days in a row. Beginning with the first day, researchers discover, the boys have already established **dominance hierarchies,** distinct levels of social power in the relationships among group members. Some boys initiate more activity, verbally persuade the other group members to act a certain way, or use aggression to get their way. Others play a more submissive role, giving in to the actions of the dominant boys. Based on the frequencies with which these behaviors are displayed, each boy can be rated as most or least dominant or somewhere in between (Pettit et al., 1990).

▶ **The child's active role**

As laboratory studies and field experiments like the Robber's Cave Study show, the dominance relations among members of the peer group form quickly and remain stable over a period of months or even longer (Strayer & Strayer, 1976). Especially among younger children, dominance is established through physical power and aggression; the most powerful children are those who physically coerce or threaten the other members of the group into compliance. The basis of dominance changes, however, as group members get to know one another. When preschoolers are observed over the period of a school year, for example, their aggression is highly correlated with dominance in the beginning of the year but is unrelated to dominance by the end of the year (LaFreniere & Charlesworth, 1983). As children approach adolescence, the basis for dominance shifts from physical power to characteristics such as intelligence, creativity, and interpersonal skill (Pettit et al., 1990; Savin-Williams, 1980).

What function do dominance hierarchies play in the social behavior of children? First, groups can more easily meet their objectives when certain individuals within the group assume a leadership role. Ethologists have long observed that many species of animals, especially primates, have clear lines of power that probably enhance the obtaining of food, protection against natural enemies, and control of reproduction. Among children, dominance hierarchies can serve to get games going on the playground or accomplish school projects that require group efforts. Second, dominance hierarchies make social relationships more predictable for members of the group. Each individual has a specific role, whether as leader or follower, and the behaviors associated with those roles are often clearly defined (Savin-Williams, 1979). Finally, dominance hierarchies are thought to control aggression among members of the group. Usually, once the most dominant members of the group have emerged, few other members resort to aggression. In one naturalistic observation of preschool children's free play, for example, only 20 percent of the interactions among children were classified as counterattacks to aggression (Strayer & Strayer, 1976).

dominance hierarchy Group's organized infrastructure, based on power relationships.

Peer Pressure and Conformity

One of the most widely accepted beliefs about peer groups is that they control the behavior of children, sometimes more than parents and other adults would like. In fact, peer pressure is a very real phenomenon. When seventh- through twelfth-graders are asked to rate how much pressure they feel from age mates in several domains, they report the greatest pressure on involvement with peers—that is, spending time with them, going to parties, and otherwise associating with them (Brown, Clasen, & Eicher, 1986; Clasen & Brown, 1985). They also feel pressured to excel and to complete their education. Contrary to popular opinion, though, they report the least peer pressure to engage in misconduct, such as smoking, drinking, or having sexual relations. Older adolescents, however, feel more pressures toward misconduct than younger adolescents.

How willing are children to conform to these peer pressures? Again, when researchers ask them, adolescents give different answers depending on their age (Berndt, 1979; Brown, Clasen, & Eicher, 1986; Gavin & Furman, 1989). Vulnerability to peer pressure peaks in early adolescence, usually between the sixth and ninth grades (see Figure 15.2) and may lead to conflicts with parents. In fact, adolescents report the greatest number of disagreements with their parents right around the ninth-grade mark. By late adolescence, however, the influence of peers on conformity declines. Thus, the relationship between age and peer conformity is a curvilinear one.

These developmental changes can be explained, in part, by the adjustments that youth must make at different points in adolescence. Most young adolescents are moving from elementary school to a middle school or junior high school, where many students are strangers to each other and new relationships must be established. For many children, this is an anxiety-ridden task; they fear that they "won't know anybody," a phrase many a preadolescent's parent has heard. In addition, adolescents in junior high typically physically move from one class to another over the course of the day; the peer group does not remain constant as it did in elementary school, and relationships may

FIGURE 15.2

Developmental Changes in Conformity to Peer Pressure

Conformity to peer pressure, whether it involves prosocial, antisocial, or neutral behavior, peaks in early adolescence, then declines. The higher numbers in this graph represent greater willingness to conform.

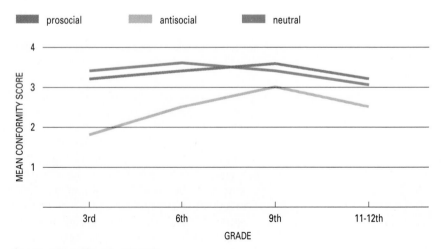

Source: Adapted from Berndt, 1979.

▶ **Interaction among domains**

be more difficult to establish in this context. Combined with the adjustment to the new school setting, young adolescents become more independent from their parents and increasingly search for their "selfhood." By conforming to the norms of the peer group and thereby becoming accepted, young adolescents are meeting many of their socioemotional needs, especially the need for affiliation. In contrast, older adolescents are approaching a new phase in their lives, a time when they must seek jobs, further their education, or make other major decisions. These are individual choices of great importance that require less input from peers. The older adolescent has also developed a stronger sense of self and feels less need to rely on the advice or norms of the peer group (Brown, 1989). Thus, the role of the peer group varies with the developmental tasks of different age groups.

Exactly how do peer groups exert their pressure? Most likely by rewarding individuals who conform to the group's norms and reacting negatively to those who resist. Children who conform to the norms of the group get invited to the "right" parties or receive compliments on their attire. Those who don't conform may get "the silent treatment" or, worse yet, become the objects of teasing and ridicule. Few researchers have actually observed the dynamics of peer groups as they try to enforce norms, but subjects in some studies report that negative interactions within peer groups increase during early adolescence and decrease in late adolescence. The same developmental trend shows up when subjects are asked how much they are bothered by these negative interactions; children are increasingly bothered in early adolescence and less bothered toward the end of the adolescent years (Gavin & Furman, 1989).

Finally, how much do the pressures placed by peers conflict with those doled out by parents? As we saw earlier, peers, like parents, expect the growing child to be competent and to achieve in school. In that sense, peers and parents pressure children toward some of the same goals. We also saw, however, that as adolescents approach young adulthood, the pressures to engage in behaviors frowned on by adults increase. Moreover, the results of a recent study show that when adolescents strongly value conforming to adult norms, (for example, by saying that getting drunk and skipping school are negative), they are less popular with their peers. Conversely, adolescents who place less value on conforming to adult norms are more popular (Allen, Weissberg, & Hawkins, 1989). Thus, adults and peers provide overlapping support in encouraging general competence, but conflicting pressures when it comes to certain behaviors like drinking or smoking that older adolescents are sometimes likely to experiment with.

PEERS AS AGENTS OF SOCIALIZATION

Like parents, teachers, and the media, peers are the child's source of information about the "do's" and "don'ts" of the social world. Because children have such extensive social relations with their peers, there are few better sources of feedback on acceptable and unacceptable behaviors. Peers socialize their age mates in two main ways—as models and as reinforcers. In their behaviors, peers also reflect the values of the larger society.

Peers as Models

According to social learning theory, the greater the similarity between a model and an observer, the more likely it is that the observer will imitate the model's behavior (Bandura, 1969). Peers, therefore, are prime candidates for prompting imitation in children. Although peer imitation declines by middle childhood, it occurs quite frequently in the early years. In one study, the number of imitative acts occurring in the free play of preschoolers averaged 14.82 per hour (Abramovitch & Grusec, 1978).

▶ **Interaction among domains**

There is ample evidence that a whole host of social behaviors can be transmitted through peer modeling. Display of aggression is a prime example. When children observe a peer acting aggressively with toys, they spontaneously perform similar aggressive acts (Hicks, 1965). On the opposite end of the spectrum, models can promote sharing and other altruistic acts in observer children (Elliott & Vasta, 1970; Hartup & Coates, 1967). Sex-role behaviors, too, can be influenced by peer models. Most children are reluctant to play with toys meant for the opposite sex. Yet if a peer model displays cross-sex play, children's tendency to follow suit increases (Kobasigawa, 1968; Wolf, 1973).

A powerful variable influencing imitation is the model's competence as perceived by the observer child, especially when new skills or behaviors are involved. Children prefer older, friendly models who are similar to them in background and interests (Brody & Stoneman, 1981; Hartup & Coates, 1967; Rosekrans, 1967). Especially in the realm of social behaviors, children may imitate competent peer models over adult models because they see the behaviors selected by peers as more appropriate for themselves.

Peers as Reinforcers

Peers not only model certain behaviors, they also actively reinforce their friends' behaviors. Peers communicate clear signals about the social behaviors they prefer and those they won't tolerate, messages that may either maintain or inhibit the child's behaviors. Consider the case of sex-typed behaviors. Researchers observed the reactions of peers as preschool-aged children engaged in sex-appropriate or inappropriate play in their nursery schools (Lamb & Roopnarine, 1979). They found that boys who engaged in male-typed activities such as playing ball or chase received more praise and approval (mostly from other boys) than girls did when they attempted these same behaviors. Similarly, peers more frequently reinforced girls than boys who played dolls, kitchen, or assumed female character roles. Peers controlled behavior through punishment, too, although punishment was used less frequently than positive reinforcement. Punishment was reserved largely for cross-sex activities as opposed to activities that peers consider appropriate for each sex. This study demonstrates how forcefully peers can enforce stereotypical codes of behavior for boys and girls by directly rewarding activities consistent with those codes.

▶ **Interaction among domains**

In the same way, the frequency of other social behaviors such as aggression can be regulated by peer reactions. In their observations of aggression among preschoolers, Gerald Patterson and his colleagues noted that about three-fourths of the aggressive behaviors that took place were reinforced by victims' compliance or submission (Patterson, Littman, & Bricker, 1967). The consequence was that aggressors maintained their combative styles of interaction.

If a peer responded with counteraggression, however, the perpetrator was less likely to repeat the action with that child, choosing either another victim or another behavior. Thus, peers powerfully affect one another by means of their positive and negative reactions.

Peer power in influencing children's behavior can be used to enhance teaching situations through peer teaching programs. A vivid example of this strategy is described in the next section when we examine peer relations in the Soviet Union. Apart from strictly pedagogical contexts, peers can similarly be used as models and reinforcers in programs to train social skills; descriptions of these programs come later in this chapter. The movement to promote peer cooperative learning in schools, a topic that will be touched on in the next chapter, represents still another application of this principle.

▶ **Sociocultural influence**

Peers as Transmitters of Cultural Values

In a broad sense, the way a culture or society organizes peer experiences for children can serve as a vehicle for conveying its primary values and ideals. In the Soviet Union and on the Israeli kibbutzim, some children are raised in *collective* settings in which they experience group care from infancy onward and contact with peers remains extensive through adolescence. Children who grow up in such peer-oriented contexts exhibit some behaviors and traits that distinguish them from children raised in societies, like American society, that stress individualism and independence.

Urie Bronfenbrenner's (1970) comparative study of peer experiences in the Soviet Union and several Western nations, including the United States, demonstrates how specific types of peer interactions can shape individual psychological characteristics and beliefs. At the time Bronfenbrenner's observations were conducted, a significant proportion of Soviet children attended preschool institutions. In this setting, group experiences predominate from the beginning. Infants are placed in playpens with five to seven other children, and although caregivers provide a good deal of individual attention, group consciousness is deliberately fostered. Children are encouraged to engage in group games and other forms of collective play and are explicitly taught the value of sharing.

At age seven years children enter a formal school program in which the emphasis on group activities continues. Each classroom is divided into "links," rows of students who together are responsible for preparing lessons, conducting projects, and maintaining discipline. "Links" frequently compete against each other for the teacher's approval, but the success of the "link" depends on cooperation among its members. Thus, children often help each other with homework assignments and enforce disciplinary rules so that the link can earn privileges (for example, going to recess first) and positive evaluations from the teacher. Here are some sample observations:

> "What are you fooling around for? You're holding up the whole link," whispers Kolya to his neighbor during the preparation period for the lesson. And during the break he teaches her how to organize better the books and pads in her knapsack.
>
> "Work more carefully," says Olya to her girl friend. "See, on account of you, our link got behind today. You come to me and we'll work together at home." (Bronfenbrenner, 1970, pp. 63–64)

Soviet society fosters peer group identity among children through structured peer experiences, such as "pioneer camps." This group orientation is consistent with the larger social values of Soviet culture.

▶ **Interaction among domains**

Another notable feature of collective child rearing in the Soviet Union is the cultivation of altruistic behavior. An example is the custom of "group adoption," in which each class takes responsibility for a lower-level class. Older children escort their charges to school, play with them during recess, and help them with schoolwork. The way in which they carry out these responsibilities is evaluated as part of their schoolwork.

What is the impact of this strong group orientation during childhood? Bronfenbrenner conducted a series of studies examining moral decision making and antisocial behavior in Soviet children. In one study, 150 twelve-year-olds were tested on their readiness to cheat and commit other moral transgressions. In one condition, children were assured that their answers would be kept confidential. In two other conditions, subjects were told that teachers or peers, respectively, would ostensibly learn their answers. Compared with children from the United States, England, and West Germany, Soviet children were much less willing to behave antisocially, but especially if they thought their peers would know the outcome. American children, in contrast, were *more* likely to transgress if they thought their peers might learn the results (Rodgers, Bronfenbrenner, & Devereux, 1968). What would the Soviet children do if they learned that a peer had committed a transgression? In another study, Bronfenbrenner (1964) learned that most would take a personal initiative in correcting their classmate's behavior. In contrast, the Swiss children in his sample responded that they would tell an adult or do nothing.

Bronfenbrenner characterized Soviet youth raised collectively as conforming and vulnerable to the pressures of the peer group, especially when it came to following adult codes for "good conduct." They were obedient, self-disciplined, and unlikely to display rebellious or aggressive behavior. These traits were consistent with the ideals of Soviet society at that time, namely, "character education" to produce an appreciation for the collective good.

Similarly, the "other orientation" of children living on the Israeli kibbutzim is apparent in their moral reasoning and prosocial behavior. We saw in Chapter

13 that children growing up in this peer-oriented setting make more advanced prosocial judgments. Kibbutz-reared children also behave more cooperatively than urban Israeli children when they play games that allow either for competition or for cooperation (Shapira & Madsen, 1969). Thus, through their day-to-day experiences with peers, children are directly or indirectly given strong messages about the general values and philosophies of their culture.

PEER POPULARITY AND SOCIAL COMPETENCE

Parents, teachers like Jan Nakamura in this chapter's opening scene, and others who have the opportunity to observe children over time usually notice the two extreme ends of the sociability spectrum: some children seem to be at the center of many activities, from school projects to playground games, whereas others are ridiculed or ignored. Frequently, the patterns of peer acceptance that become established in the early school years persist for years afterward, along with the psychological rewards or disappointments that accompany them. Psychologists have uncovered several factors related to peer acceptance and popularity and have applied this knowledge to helping children who may be at the bottom of the proverbial totem pole.

Measuring Peer Acceptance

Given the relationship between peer acceptance and later development that was described at the start of this chapter, the task of identifying children with problems in this domain is all the more important. Traditionally, psychologists have relied on peers, teachers, or their own observations of children's behaviors to assess the quality of peer relations.

Peer assessments frequently consist of a **sociometric nomination** measure in which children are asked to name a specified number of peers (usually between three and five) who fit a certain criterion. For example, children might be asked to "name three classmates you especially like (or dislike)" or "list three peers you would like to walk home from school with." The number of positive or negative nominations the child receives from other children serves as a measure of his popularity. Alternatively, children are sometimes asked to rate each peer in the class or group on a **sociometric rating scale,** a series of items such as "How much do you like to be with this person at school?" (see Figure 15.3). The target child's average rating by the other children is the index of peer acceptance. Peer assessments have the advantage of being the responses of the very group that determines the child's popularity. They also yield reliable information because they are based on peers' frequent and varied experiences with the target child (Hymel & Rubin, 1985). By themselves, however, peer assessments do not provide much insight about the specific behaviors that lead to popularity or unpopularity.

Another way of measuring peer acceptance is teacher assessments. These most commonly involve the teacher's rating or ranking of the popularity of each child in the classroom. Although teacher assessments correlate moderately well with peer sociometric measures, teachers may value different social behaviors than children do, and these adult biases may influence their

sociometric nomination Peer assessment measure in which children are asked to name a specified number of peers who fit a certain criterion, such as "peers you would like to walk home with."

sociometric rating scale Peer assessment measure in which children rate peers on a number of social dimensions.

FIGURE 15.3

A Sociometric Rating Scale

In this peer assessment tool, the child is asked to rate each peer on a series of items, such as "How much do you like to play with this person at school?" The average rating each target child receives from his or her peers is an index of peer acceptance.

Name _____

EXAMPLES:

HOW MUCH DO YOU LIKE TO PLAY WITH THIS PERSON AT SCHOOL?

	I don't like to				I like to a lot
Louise Blue	1	2	3	4	5
Russell Grey	1	2	3	4	5
John Armon	1	2	3	4	5
Andrea Brandt	1	2	3	4	5
Sue Curtis	1	2	3	4	5
Sandra Drexel	1	2	3	4	5
Jeff Ellis	1	2	3	4	5
Bill Fox	1	2	3	4	5
Diane Higgins	1	2	3	4	5
Harry Jones	1	2	3	4	5
Jill Lamb	1	2	3	4	5
Steve Murray	1	2	3	4	5
Jo Anne Norman	1	2	3	4	5
Pam Riley	1	2	3	4	5
Jim Stevens	1	2	3	4	5

HOW MUCH DO YOU LIKE TO PLAY WITH

THIS PERSON AT SCHOOL?   1   2   3   4   5

I don't like to   I like to a lot

Source: From Asher, 1985.

responses. For example, teachers may prefer compliant children and thus rate them as more popular, whereas children may prefer peers who display traits of leadership and assertiveness.

A third approach is for researchers to make objective behavioral observations of specific social (or asocial) activities displayed by the child. Is she playing alone or with others? Is the child aggressive or does she display prosocial behaviors such as helping another child? How does she attempt to enter a group of children already playing together? Any of a wide constellation of social behaviors may be considered, along with the events that precede or follow, allowing the researcher to understand the dynamics of the child's social world.

Researchers have relied on peer nomination measures, in particular, to classify children's *peer status*. *Popular* children receive many more positive ("like") than negative ("dislike") nominations. *Rejected* children, in contrast, receive few positive but many negative nominations; they are overtly disliked by their peers. *Neglected* children receive low numbers of nominations in either category; though they lack friends, they are not actively disliked (Asher & Dodge, 1986). *Controversial* children receive high numbers of both positive and negative nominations. They have a high degree of "social impact" because they are active and visible, but they are generally not preferred as social partners (Coie, Dodge, & Coppotelli, 1982). Finally, *average* children do not receive extreme scores on peer nomination measures. Table 15.2 summarizes these categories of peer status.

TABLE 15.2

Classifications of Peer Status

The number of positive and negative peer nominations received determines whether a child's peer status is classified as controversial, rejected, neglected, or popular.

		Positive Peer Nominations	
		Many	Few
Negative Peer Nominations	Many	Controversial	Rejected
	Few	Popular	Neglected

The child's peer status remains fairly stable even over a period of years. In one study, John Coie and Kenneth Dodge (1983) assessed third- and fifth-grade children's acceptance by peers over a five-year period. They observed a moderate degree of continuity in status, especially for children who were classified as rejected (see Table 15.3). What exactly is it about unpopular children's behavior that makes them so unappealing to their classmates and places them so consistently in an undesirable status? This is a particularly important question if we want to intervene in these children's "at risk" position.

Characteristics of Popular and Unpopular Children

Peer popularity is related to a number of variables, some of which lie within the child's control and some of which, unfortunately, do not. The child's physical attractiveness, name, and perhaps motor skills fall into the latter category, whereas social skills belong to the former.

TABLE 15.3

Peer Status over a Five-Year Period

This table shows the proportions of children who either maintained or changed their peer status over a five-year period. Peer status proved to be moderately stable over this long span of time, as the underlined numbers on the diagonal indicate. Children classified as rejected were especially likely to remain in the same peer status category.

Status in Year 1	n	Status in Year 5				
		Popular	Rejected	Neglected	Controversial	Average
Popular	(38)	.21	.05	.18	.16	.40
Rejected	(33)	.03	.30	.30	.00	.36
Neglected	(33)	.24	.06	.24	.00	.45
Controversial	(14)	.29	.36	.07	.14	.14
Average	(46)	.37	.17	.13	.11	.22

Source: Adapted from Coie & Dodge, 1983.

▶ **Interaction among domains**

Physical Attractiveness   When asked to rate photographs of unfamiliar children, both preschool and elementary school–aged children believe that children with attractive faces are more friendly, intelligent, and social than unattractive children (Dion & Berscheid, 1974; Langlois & Stephan, 1981). Correlations between children's ratings of peers' attractiveness and sociometric measures of peer acceptance typically range between +0.35 and +0.50, indicating a moderately strong relationship between these two variables (Cavior & Dokecki, 1973; Lerner & Lerner, 1977). Body type makes a difference, too. For example, boys with broad shoulders and large muscles are the most popular, and short, chubby boys are the least popular (Staffieri, 1967). The reasons for these stereotypic beliefs are unknown, but they can lead to self-fulfilling behaviors in children who have been labeled (Hartup, 1983). For example, a child who receives peer attention because of attractiveness or body type may have numerous opportunities to develop the social skills that lead to even greater peer acceptance. Finally, as we saw in Chapter 5, boys who mature early during adolescence and girls who mature later are more likely to be accepted by peers.

The Child's Name   The attractiveness of a child's name, as perceived by peers, is positively correlated with his or her popularity. When researchers asked several classes of ten- to twelve-year-olds to rate the attractiveness of first names of peers in their group, they found a substantial relationship between these ratings and ratings of peer popularity obtained one month later (McDavid & Harari, 1966). As with the child's physical appearance, the mechanisms underlying this relationship are not well understood, but one possibility is that parents who choose a unique name may have other characteristics that influence the child's social behaviors. They may, for example, be eccentric parents who encourage nonconformist behaviors in their children. Another possibility is that peers are more wary of a child that is "too different," even in name alone, and may be less likely to initiate conversations or invite that child to play. The child with the unusual name may thus have fewer opportunities to develop social skills. Whatever the case, in our society a child with the name "Elmer" might have a bigger task in establishing relationships with peers than a "Michael" or "William."

▶ **Interaction among domains**

Motor Skills   As noted in Chapter 5, another factor related to peer acceptance is the child's proficiency in motor activities. Both boys and girls who are coordinated, strong, and skilled in activities such as throwing a ball are rated as more popular by peers and as more socially competent by their teachers and parents (Hops & Finch, 1985). It may be that the value American society places on athletic prowess is reflected in children's preferences in playmates. Alternatively, motor skill may facilitate the manipulation of objects and game-playing that constitute the majority of children's shared activities. Those who are talented in this arena will naturally have more peer contacts and eventually be better liked.

▶ **Sociocultural influence**

Social Skills   Probably the most important factor in peer acceptance is the constellation of social behaviors displayed by popular and unpopular children. Researchers who have observed the overt activities of accepted and unaccepted peers have learned that each presents a distinct behavioral profile. In

▶ **The child's active role**

general, popular children engage in prosocial, cooperative, and normative behaviors and show a high degree of social skill. In contrast, rejected and neglected children behave in aggressive, withdrawn, or other socially inappropriate ways for which they receive little social reinforcement.

For example, when Gary Ladd (1983) observed third- and fourth-grade students during recess, he noted several differences in the behavioral styles of popular and rejected children. Popular children spent more time in cooperative play, social conversation, and other positive social interactions with peers than their rejected counterparts. Popular children had larger social networks comprised of children who were likewise popular. Rejected children, on the other hand, spent more time engaging in antagonistic behaviors such as arguing and playing in a rough-and-tumble fashion, or playing or standing alone at a distance from peers. Their social groups were small and usually consisted of younger children and other unpopular peers.

According to the results of another study that examined the peer-directed behaviors of first- and third-grade boys, neglected and controversial children display still different clusters of behaviors (Coie & Dodge, 1988). Neglected boys were the least aggressive of any group observed. They tended to engage in isolated activities and had low visibility with peers. Controversial boys were intellectually, athletically, or socially talented and very active, but they were sometimes prone to anger and rule violations. The mixture of their positive and negative social behaviors thus elicited a concommitantly mixed reaction from their classmates. Thus, children may be unpopular with their peers for a number of reasons ranging from social withdrawal to outright aggression.

The social competence of popular children becomes apparent when they are asked to enter a group of unfamiliar children who are already at play. Kenneth Dodge and his colleagues observed as individual kindergarten children entered a room where two other children they did not know were already playing with blocks (Dodge et al., 1983). Popular, rejected, and neglected children used

Children who lack social skills may be rejected or neglected by their peers. In contrast, popular children display prosocial behaviors and display a wide range of social knowledge.

somewhat different tactics to gain entry into the group, with popular children generally the most successful. Rejected children tended to disrupt the group's ongoing activity by pushing the blocks off the table or by making intrusive statements, usually about themselves (for example, "I have a baby brother"). In return, their peer hosts responded negatively to them. Neglected children were not disruptive but employed another ineffective strategy. Instead of making some verbal or nonverbal attempt to join the group, these children passively watched as their peers played—and they were ignored. Popular children seemed to know exactly what to do. Rather than bringing attention to themselves or disrupting the group's activities, they made statements about their peers or what they were doing, such as, "That looks like a fun game you are playing." These diplomatic verbalizations paved the way for their smooth integration into the group.

In the second part of this same research project, Dodge and his associates organized play groups for seven- and eight-year-old boys during the summer when school was out of session. None of the boys knew each other at the outset, so that it was possible to observe how they initiated entry into a play group under natural circumstances. Boys who were successful in entering a group that was already playing followed a three-step sequence that consisted of: (1) waiting and watching the group, (2) mimicking the group's activity—for example, playing basketball or singing—and (3) making a group-oriented statement, such as describing what the group was doing. In general, successful children began with low-risk tactics and, as they received positive feedback, moved toward higher-risk strategies. They also kept the focus of attention on the peer group rather than on themselves.

Popular children are particularly effective at maintaining cohesive social interactions with their peers. When Betty Black and Nancy Hazen (1990) observed the social entry behaviors of preschool-aged children, they found two important differences between the behaviors of liked and disliked children. Disliked children made significantly more irrelevant comments when they spoke with acquaintances as well as peers they did not know. The following segment illustrates how such a conversation might go:

MARY: "We're being witches here, and I am the mean witch."
SANDY: "My mom is taking me to get shoes today."
(p. 387)

In addition, disliked children were more likely than popular children to respond with non sequiturs to the questions or directives of their peers. When a peer asked him his name, for example, a child might not respond or might say something irrelevant. In contrast, children who were liked tended to maintain organized, thematically coherent conversations with their peers.

Thus, observations of popular children show that they display a range of social skills that their more unpopular age mates often lack. But does their social skill actually cause their popularity, or do children first develop reputations that precipitate subsequent successful or maladaptive patterns of social interaction? A child who is initially rejected because of his appearance, for example, may develop an aggressive style in retaliation. Gary Ladd and his associates examined this question more closely by observing preschool children in the playground during three 6-week intervals in the beginning, middle, and end of the academic year (Ladd, Price, & Hart, 1988). Episodes of cooperative play, arguments, and other positive and negative forms of interaction were recorded. In addition, children's sociometric status was assessed at each of these three points in time. The results showed that children who engaged in more cooperative play at the beginning of the school year made gains in peer acceptance by the end of the school year, whereas children who frequently argued showed a decline in acceptance by the middle of the school year. These results are consistent with the idea that children's behaviors precede their social status. As we examine the origins of social competence and the effects of social skill training programs on children, we will see even further how social skills are implicated as a causal factor in peer status.

The Origins of Social Competence

What factors are responsible for the skilled social behaviors of some children and the seeming social ineptness of others? The answers posed by researchers draw from a number of perspectives, from the early attachment relationships children form with their caregivers to capabilities in processing the subtle cues that form such an integral part of social interactions.

▷ **Interaction among domains**

Attachment Relationships As we saw in Chapter 10, infants who are securely attached to their caregivers are predisposed to have positive peer relations in toddlerhood (Waters, Wippman, & Sroufe, 1979). A plausible hypothesis is that in their relationships with caregivers children have the opportunity to learn and practice a variety of social skills, such as turn taking, compromise, and effective communication. Once honed and refined, these abilities can later be employed with peers and other individuals in the child's life. Attachment also teaches children about emotional ties—how to recognize affection and how to show it. This knowledge about the central ingredients of relationships may assist as children expand their social worlds (Hay, 1985; Sroufe, 1983).

Michael Lamb, however, contends that the evidence supporting this hypothesis is weak (Lamb & Nash, 1989). For one thing, few investigators have measured infants' peer skills and quality of attachment at the same time. If secure attachment leads to better peer relations, we would expect that peer relations would *improve* with time for infants who are securely attached. Unfortunately, the absence of longitudinal data makes it difficult to draw firm conclusions. It may be, adds Lamb, that sociability is a general dispositional trait and that friendly babies simply have positive relations with *both* parents and peers. At this point, the idea that elements of the attachment relationship might translate into healthier peer relations is still theoretically appealing. Any stronger conclusions, however, are impossible without more empirical data.

Parental Influences Parents serve as models of social competence for their children; they may also provide explicit instruction on appropriate ways to behave in social situations. In one study, mothers of popular and unpopular preschoolers were observed as they introduced their children to a pair of peers busily playing with blocks. Mothers of unpopular children tended to disrupt the ongoing play and use their authority to incorporate their own child into the group. In many ways, their behaviors resembled those of the unpopular children we discussed earlier. In contrast, mothers of popular children encouraged them to become involved in play without intervening in the activity of the host peers. Moreover, in a subsequent interview, these mothers displayed

▶ **Interaction among domains**

greater knowledge of how to encourage their children to make friends, resolve conflicts, and display other positive social behaviors (Finnie & Russell, 1988).

The general emotional tone of parent-child interactions is also reflected in the styles of discourse children have with their peers. Martha Putallaz (1987) recorded mother-child pairs as they played in a laboratory and then watched as two children and their two mothers interacted, each pair in a separate room. The children's peer status had been determined before the start of the observations. Compared with mothers of less popular children, mothers of popular children were less disagreeable and demanding when they were playing with their children. They were also more likely to focus on feelings when they talked with both their children and the other mother. At the same time, the children's styles when they were playing with their peers mirrored their mothers'. Positive, agreeable children had positive, agreeable mothers and vice versa. It was the positive, agreeable children who had also been independently classified as the most popular.

Finally, parents can influence children's social competence on another level—by managing their children's social activities. Parents vary in the extent to which they create opportunities for their children to have experiences with peers, which provide the context for the emergence of social skills. Some parents seek out play groups for their preschoolers, enroll them in nursery school, or periodically get together with friends that have children. When parents deliberately arrange peer contacts for their preschoolers, their children have both a greater variety of playmates and a greater number of consistent

When parents create opportunities for their children to have experiences with peers, as these mothers are doing, their children may benefit from this ability to practice social skills.

play partners than when parents do not make such efforts. Moreover, at least for boys, the more parents initiate peer contacts, the higher the child's sociometric status (Ladd & Golter, 1988). Opportunities to interact with peers provide the child with a natural arena to discover those behaviors that generate positive responses from peers and those that do not. There is growing evidence that the more such experiences children have, the more socially skilled—and therefore the more accepted—they will be in later years.

Day Care   When children have more experience with peers because they are enrolled in day care, they show greater social competence than children reared at home by their parents. Carollee Howes (1987a) has conducted an extensive longitudinal study of the peer relationships of one- to six-year-old children who were enrolled in child-care programs. Among her findings was the discovery that popular or average-status children had entered child care at earlier ages (about ten to nineteen months on average) than rejected children (about thirty to thirty-three months). Not only early experience was related to popularity, however. Howes found that the stability of the peer group was an important factor as well. Toddlers who had spent a year or more with *the same peers* were more socially competent in that they showed more cooperative forms of play. These children were also rated by teachers as having fewer difficulties than children who had moved to a different group. Evidently, experiences with peers do indeed provide an excellent context for mastering social skills, especially if there is sustained contact with familiar age mates.

▶ **Interaction among domains**

Social Cognitive Development   The studies of peer group entry strategies described here vividly illustrate that the social competence of children includes an array of intertwined cognitive and behavioral skills. When a child tries to enter a group, he cannot "come on too strong," yet at the same time he must do more than simply stand and watch as others play. All along, he must read the signals of the other children and try to fit into the dynamic already in motion. A five-step information-processing model of social competence recently formulated by Kenneth Dodge (see Figure 15.4) suggests more precisely how cognitions and behaviors are related and where problems in social functioning might occur (Dodge, 1986; Dodge et al., 1986).

▶ **The child's active role**

According to Dodge, the first step in processing social information is to perceive social cues correctly. For example, suppose a boy initiates a conversation with a peer who is a girl. It is more important for the child to encode the girl's facial expression ("Is that a smile or a sneer?") than the color of her clothing. Second, the child must meaningfully interpret the social cues, based on his past experiences. Most children would interpret a scowl on a peer's face as a sign of hostility and a smile as a mark of friendliness. In the third step of processing, the child generates one or more potential behavioral responses. If he perceives the peer as hostile, he may contemplate avoiding her or matching her hostility. If he reads her signals as friendly, he may consider smiling back or beginning to talk. Fourth, the child learns to evaluate the potential consequences of each possible behavior. Hostility and aggression could lead to physical harm where avoidance might not—hence the last response might be preferable. Finally, the child enacts the chosen response verbally or physically, monitors the outcome of his behavior, and if necessary, modifies it, engaging in the five-step cycle over again. This model, as should be obvious, includes a

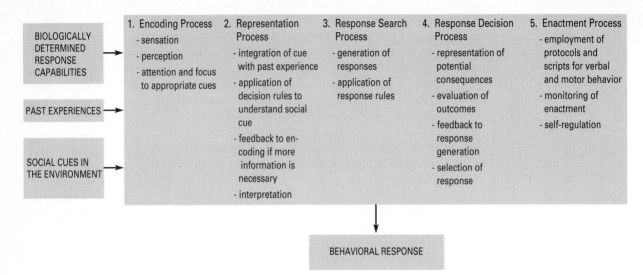

FIGURE 15.4

Social Competence: An Information-processing Model

Kenneth Dodge has proposed a five-step model of social competence based on the child's growing social information processing skills. The process begins when the child is able to correctly encode and then interpret a social cue. The child then generates a set of possible responses and evaluates the potential outcomes of each response. Finally, he enacts the behavior he internally selected. Children low in social competence may have difficulties at any step in this model.

Source: Adapted from Dodge, 1986.

number of stages in which things can go wrong to disrupt a smooth, mutually rewarding social interaction.

Studies of peer relations suggest that popular children are more skillful than unpopular (and, in particular, rejected) children at each step of the model. First, they are better able to encode and decipher social information correctly. In one study, elementary school children were asked to label the emotions depicted in two sets of pictures. One was a series of single faces depicting anger, happiness, sadness, disgust, surprise, and fear. The other was a series of interpersonal scenes portraying these same six emotions. Rejected children were less able to make correct identifications of the emotions represented in these stimuli than were popular children (Monfries & Kafer, 1987). In another experiment, researchers asked children to view videotaped episodes of an actor destroying a second actor's toy with either hostile, prosocial, accidental, or ambiguous intent. Both rejected and neglected children tended to attribute hostile intentions to the actor's actions, even when the acts were accidental or prosocial. Popular children were more often correct in their judgments (Dodge, Murphy, & Buchsbaum, 1984). Researchers have yet to establish the precise links between misperceptions of social information and the child's overt behaviors, but it is apparent that a correct "reading" of social events is a necessary first step in skilled interpersonal behavior.

Second, some children may incorrectly interpret the emotional responses of peers. Recall from Chapter 13, for example, that aggressive children tend to make more hostile attributions about the intentions of others than nonaggressive children. That is, they show a bias toward seeing the "bad side" of interpersonal cues that in reality may be ambiguous or even clearly positive. As a result of these mistaken attributions, aggressive children retaliate with further negative behavior.

Third, rejected children tend to offer inappropriate strategies for solving social problems and have difficulty in devising alternative paths to attain their social goals (Rubin & Krasnor, 1986). Researchers typically assess social problem-solving skills by presenting children with hypothetical social dilemmas and examining their proposed solutions. Researchers in one study asked kindergarten children to react to a series of dilemmas in which, for example, one child takes away another's toy. Unpopular children were much more likely than popular children to recommend an aggressive solution, such as, "Punch him" or "She could beat her up." When asked to suggest ways to initiate new social relationships or maintain old ones, these children were vague or appealed to adult authority (Asher & Renshaw, 1981). Kenneth Rubin and Linda Krasnor observed children's strategies for solving social problems in naturalistic settings and noted that rejected children were rigid in their attempts (Rubin & Krasnor, 1986). If, for example, a rejected child failed to convince another child to give him an object, he simply repeated the same unsuccessful behavior. Popular children often tried a different approach to attaining their goal, indicating a broader and more flexible repertoire of social problem-solving skills.

Popular children thus possess social knowledge that leads to successful interactions with their peers and also behave in ways that manifest this expertise. They recognize that the achievement of their social goals may require time and work and adjust their behaviors according to the sometimes subtle demands of the situation (Asher, 1983). Rejected children, on the other hand, have a more limited awareness of how to solve social problems, believing particularly in the effectiveness of aggression. Unfortunately, their antagonistic actions frequently lead to a spiral of continuing rejection. As they become disassociated from more socially skilled popular peers, they have fewer opportunities to learn the basics of successful social interaction from them. Moreover, the child who receives consistently negative feedback from peers would probably be hard pressed to be positive, cooperative, and friendly. Neglected children have their own special problems. Rubin and Krasnor (1986) believe that this special category of children does not display social cognitive deficits but rather insecurities and anxieties about the consequences of their social actions. What they need is more self-confidence in their ability to interact with and be accepted by their peers.

To sum up, the child's social competence includes a range of abilities—correctly reading others' emotions, accurately anticipating the outcomes of one's various social behaviors, knowing how to enter a group, and maintaining interactions in dyads and larger groups. These skills arise as children observe their parents' social interactions, as they become more able to understand and reason about the social world, and as they gain opportunities to interact with peers and practice social skills.

Training Social Skills

▶ **Sociocultural influence**

Can children be taught the elements of socially skilled behavior and thereby gain greater acceptance from their peers? This tactic seems especially useful in cultures such as our own where social skills form an important component of interpersonal relations. Several forms of intervention have been employed in schools and clinical settings, primarily with unpopular or socially unskilled children, that have produced changes in children's interpersonal strategies.

Modeling   One such technique is *modeling*—that is, exposing children to live or recorded models displaying desirable behaviors. As an example, one research team presented a group of socially withdrawn preschoolers with short videotapes depicting young children engaging in social behaviors accompanied by a narration of their thoughts (Jakibchuk & Smeriglio, 1976). The sound track included the following self-directed statements as the model approached a group of peers: "Those children over there are playing together . . . I would like to play with them. But I'm afraid. I don't know what to do or say . . . This is hard. But I'll try . . . I'm close to them. I did it. Good for me. . . ." Compared with their baseline behaviors, withdrawn children who watched these videotapes for four days increased the number of their social interactions and in turn were the objects of more positive social behaviors from others. The results were dramatic when children who received this treatment were compared with children who received no treatment at all or who saw a nature film (see Figure 15.5). From the perspective of social learning theory, by identifying with the model, observing how the model acted, and noting the positive consequences of the model's behavior, children were able to expand their repertoire of social behaviors, and their likelihood of performing these behaviors similarly increased.

Reinforcement   A second type of intervention uses social or material *reinforcement* to shape socially skilled behaviors and increase their frequency, a technique of operant conditioning. Suppose a withdrawn child merely looked at a group of peers playing on the opposite side of the room. The teacher or parent immediately reacts with a "Good!" or a pat on the head. Next the young child might take a few steps in the direction of the group. Again, the teacher promptly delivers a reinforcer. The teacher rewards each successive approximation to the target behavior—in this case, joining the group—until the child has actually entered the group. In general, direct reinforcement of social behaviors is a very effective technique, especially for increasing their frequency (Schneider & Byrne, 1985).

Sometimes the operant approach is combined with other techniques such as modeling. In one investigation, withdrawn nursery school children received social reinforcement whenever they interacted with their peers. Those who also saw a model demonstrating social interactions showed the greatest gains in the amount of time they spent with peers (O'Connor, 1972).

Coaching   The most popular training technique has been *coaching,* or direct instruction in displaying an assortment of social behaviors. In this approach, a verbal presentation of the "right" and "wrong" ways to act is frequently accompanied by discussion about why certain techniques work and by opportunities for children to *role-play,* or act out the desirable behaviors. The goal is to expand children's knowledge of socially desirable behaviors and to develop social problem-solving skills. A sample module for teaching children how to join a conversation comes from one social skills training program targeted for elementary school children:

> TEACHER: Chances are that if you don't know how to start talking with another person or join in when others are talking, you won't be a part of many conversations . . . For example, pretend that some of your classmates are talking about a TV show that you happened to see last night and you want to get in on the conversa-

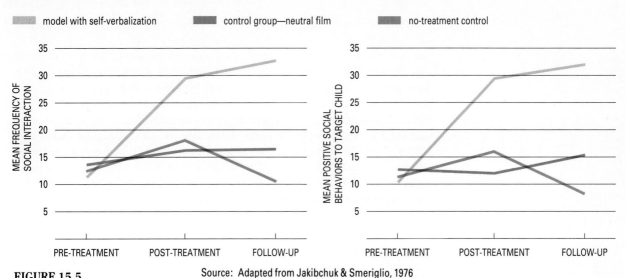

FIGURE 15.5

Source: Adapted from Jakibchuk & Smeriglio, 1976

Training Social Skills

In an experiment that evaluated the effects of several treatment strategies with socially withdrawn preschoolers, researchers found that children who observed a model approach a group of peers while verbalizing his thoughts later increased in their number of social interactions compared with the pretreatment or baseline period. These children also received more positive social behaviors from others. The graphs show both measures for this treatment group compared with a group that saw a neutral film and with a no-treatment control group. These last two groups were included to make sure that any gains in social behavior were not the result of simple contact with the experimenters or exposure to a film per se.

tion. . . . What you might do is walk over to the group and, when there is a slight pause in the talking, say something like, "Are you talking about *Star Trek*? I saw that and really liked it a lot too." At this point you have joined the conversation.

Next, you want to make sure that you participate in what's going on. You should listen and add comments to what is being said . . . Can you give me different examples of how you can now add to or take part in a conversation or what else you would say?
(Michelson et al., 1983, pp. 116–117)

Karen Bierman (1986) has added still another component to a social skills training program based on coaching—conducting the intervention as a cooperative activity among both popular and unpopular peers. Each target child in her group of preadolescents met with two socially accepted classmates for ten half-hour sessions to produce a film together but also to receive coaching on expressing feelings, asking questions, and displaying leadership. This two-pronged approach led to greater improvements in conversational skills than social skills training alone, possibly because peers could observe firsthand the positive changes occurring in initially unskilled children and could reinforce them immediately.

Children as young as four years of age can profit from training programs that explicitly teach social skills. George Spivack and Myrna Shure (1974) provided preschoolers and kindergarten-aged children with several months of instruction on how to solve social problems. For example, situations like the following were presented: "This girl wants that boy to get his wagon out of the way so she can ride by." Children were asked to generate solutions to the problems and were then asked to evaluate their merits. Children were also taught other skills, such as how to evaluate the emotional expressions of others and how to cope with their own feelings of frustration. At the end of the program, the participants showed significant gains in their ability to solve social problems. Moreover, aggressive children showed fewer disruptive and more prosocial behaviors and withdrawn children became more socially active, even one year after the formal instruction ended.

Evaluating Training Programs   Modeling, reinforcement, and coaching have all been effective in treating both aggression and social withdrawal in children (Schneider & Byrne, 1985), although the longer-term impact of social skills training has yet to be assessed. Children frequently show gains in their sociometric status following their participation in a social skills training program, especially if coaching was the predominant approach (Ladd & Asher, 1985). A task remaining for psychologists is to identify the social skills most salient for each developmental period, because the social behaviors valued by first-graders, for example, are certain to be different from those adolescents rate as important. Solid findings in this area would allow training programs to address different target skills, depending on the age of the child and the special concerns of the peer group at that time.

CHILDREN'S FRIENDSHIPS

Certain peer relations are special. They are marked by shared thoughts and experiences, trust, intimacy, and joy in the other's company. Children have different relationships with their friends than they do with other peers. Friends express more emotion toward each other, see each other more frequently, and both cooperate and disagree more than mere acquaintances (Hartup & Sancilio, 1986). Even though childhood friendships may not endure for decades or even years, their impact on social and emotional development can rival that of the family.

Children's Patterns and Conceptions of Friendship

About 80 percent of three- to four-year-old children spend a substantial amount of time with at least one peer who is, in other words, a "strong associate" or friend. Most preschoolers observed in their nursery school classrooms spend at least 30 percent of their time with one other peer, usually someone of the same sex (Hinde et al., 1985). For the three-year-old, though, the concept of "friend" does not entail the full range of psychological complexities it does for the older child. At this age, the term is virtually synonymous with "playmate."

Preschoolers' activities with friends usually consist of games, object sharing, and pretend sequences (for example, "You be the baby and I'll be the Mommy"). Conversations between friends often contain a good deal of social comparison, a search for differences as well as similarities. Preschool children are fascinated not so much by the specific nature of things they have in common as they are by the fact that they *have* things in common. Hence the following typical conversation recorded by Jeffrey Parker and John Gottman (1989):

A: "We both have chalk in our hands."
B: "Right!"

Preschool children try to avoid disagreements and negative affect in their interactions with friends, more so than older children do (Gottman & Parkhurst, 1980).

In the middle school years (roughly ages eight through twelve years), children are very concerned with being accepted by their peers and avoiding the insecurity that peer rejection brings, factors that motivate friendship formation. Most friends are of the same age and sex, although relationships with younger and older children occasionally occur as well. Cross-sex friendships are rare, though. Researchers in one study even found their fifth-grade subjects to be openly resistant to the idea that they might have a friend of the opposite sex (Buhrmester & Furman, 1987). By the time children approach preadolescence, the time they spend with same-sex friends surpasses the time they spend with either parent (see Figure 15.6).

In middle childhood, friendship interactions typically include conflicts as well as cooperation, and gossip becomes a predominant format for communication, as the following episode between two girls illustrates:

E: Oh, see, um, you know that tub she gave us for the spider?
M: Yeah.

E: She acts like she owns the whole thing.
M: The whole spider.

E: I know.
(Parker & Gottman, 1989)

Parker and Gottman (1989) believe that gossip allows children to sample the attitudes and beliefs of their age mates without taking the risk of revealing their own views. Because gossip involves the sharing of "privileged" information, it also solidifies the child's membership in the friendship circle.

During this age period, the internal psychological aspects of friendship grow in importance. When sixth-graders are asked, "How do you know that

FIGURE 15.6

Changes in Time Spent with Friends over Childhood

The amount of time that children spend with friends, especially friends of the same sex, increases from childhood to early adolescence. By the eighth grade, children say they spend more time in the company of a same-sex friend than with either parent.

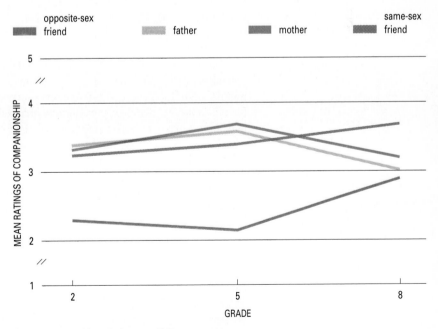

Source: Adapted from Buhrmester & Furman, 1986.

What is a friend? For preschoolers, like the girls on the left, friends are peers to play with and share common experiences with. For older children, like the adolescents on the right, friendship involves opportunities to share intimate thoughts and feelings, trust, and mutual understanding.

someone is your best friend?" they respond with statements like, "I can talk to her about my problems" or "He'll keep a secret if you tell him." In other words, intimacy and trust as well as loyalty, generosity, and helpfulness become integrated into the child's understanding of friendship (Berndt, 1981). Girls, in particular, speak of the value they place on intimacy in friendship relations. Girls cite the importance of sharing confidences and private feelings with friends far more frequently than boys do (Buhrmester & Furman, 1987; Jones & Dembo, 1989). This tendency, however, may stem in part from their stereotyped knowledge that female relationships are *supposed* to be close (Bukowski & Kramer, 1986).

Sex differences in concepts of friendship are accompanied by heightened differences in the structure of boys' and girls' friendship networks during the middle school years. Boys' friendships are usually *extensive;* their circle of friends is larger, and play is frequently enacted in groups. For boys, friendship is oriented around shared activities, especially sports (Erwin, 1985). In contrast, girls' friendships tend to be *intensive*. Girls have smaller networks of friends, but they engage in more intensive affective communication and self-disclosure. Girls usually play with only one other girl and may even be reluctant to include a third girl in the relationship. Girls also become more distressed over the break-up of a friendship (Eder & Hallinan, 1978; Maccoby & Jacklin, 1987; Waldrop & Halverson, 1975). It may be that these sex differences in friendship patterns are derived from the games children play. Boys are encouraged to play group games and team sports, like baseball, which involve a number of children and do not promote intimacy and close interaction. Girls' games, such as "house" and "dolls," involve smaller groups and provide an ideal environment for the exchange of thoughts and emotions. Another

▶ **Sociocultural influence**

possibility is that sex differences in friendships are due to larger socialization forces that foster sensitivity to others and affective sharing in girls and autonomy and emotional reservedness in boys (Winstead, 1986).

By adolescence, the importance of intimacy in friendship is firmly solidified. Adolescents say that they value the ability to share thoughts and feelings with friends and expect mutual understanding and self-disclosure in friendships (Bigelow & LaGaipa, 1975; Furman & Bierman, 1984). They share problems, solutions to those problems, and private feelings with friends. These qualities fit the needs of individuals who are struggling to define who they are and who they will become. A sample exchange between two adolescent friends drawn from Parker and Gottman's (1989) research illustrates these themes:

A: I don't know. Gosh, I have no idea what I want to do. And it really doesn't bother me that much that I don't have my future planned. [laughs]
B: [laughs]
A: [laughs] Like it bothers my Dad a lot, but it doesn't bother me.
B: Just tell your dad what I always tell my Dad: "Dad, I *am.*"
A: [laughs] Exactly!
B: "And whatever happens tomorrow, I *still* will be!"

Adolescents continue to prefer same-sex friends, although the frequency of boy-girl interactions increases. Adolescents also say that the time they spend with their friends is the most enjoyable part of their day (Csikszentmihalyi & Larson, 1984). Friendship is thus a key element in the social and emotional life of the older child.

▶ **Interaction among domains**

Friendship and Social Cognition

Robert Selman (1981) believes that developmental changes in children's conceptions of friendships are grounded in their social perspective-taking ability—that is, their capability for understanding the viewpoints, thoughts, and feelings of another person (see Chapter 11). Put another way, conceptions of friendship are linked to advances in social cognition. Selman has proposed a five-stage model of the development of friendship concepts that reflects the growing perspective-taking abilities of children:

▶ **Development as continuous/ stagelike**

• *Stage 0 (about 3–7 years): Momentary Physicalistic Interaction* Friendship is defined strictly in terms of physical proximity. A friend is someone who lives nearby or is a playmate.

• *Stage 1 (about 4–9 years): One-Way Assistance* Friends are conceptualized as helpers. The child who helps pick up a spilled lunch, for example, is a friend.

• *Stage 2 (about 6–12 years): Fair-Weather Cooperation* The roles of reciprocity and mutual adjustment in friendship are recognized, but definitions of friendship still center around self-interest rather than mutual concerns. Arguments can terminate the relationship.

• *Stage 3 (about 9–15 years): Intimate and Mutually Shared Relationships* The affective and durable qualities of friendship are recognized. Friendships can contain an element of possessiveness, though.

• *Stage 4 (12 years–adult): Autonomous and Interdependent Friendships*
Friendship is seen as an avenue for mutual support and a way in which both partners may derive psychological strength from each other. The importance of relationships with others is now recognized.

In Selman's model, young children's egocentricity limits their conception of friendship to concrete, self-oriented situations. Once they have gained the ability to reflect on the legitimacy of another's perspective—and, later, on how individuals relate to larger social groups—children's notions of friendship contain more expanded elements of reciprocity and respect for the internal needs and desires of the other.

Other psychologists add that as children gain an increasingly sophisticated understanding of the concept of *reciprocity,* their ideas of friendship are altered. Young children conceptualize reciprocity concretely; they match a peer's helping or sharing, for example, with a similar behavior of their own. Adolescents view reciprocity in a more abstract way; they see friendships as entailing mutual cooperation and a sharing of identities rather than just sharing objects (Youniss, 1980). Thus, the older child's more elaborate reasoning capabilities are assumed to pave the way for abstract, psychological concepts of friendship.

Research on children's understanding of friendship relies almost exclusively on their ability to verbalize their ideas about what friends do and why they are valuable. Other studies on how children behave with friends, however, show that children's friendships are far more complex than they themselves are able to describe. One clue to that complexity comes from investigations of how children form friendships in the first place.

How Children Become Friends

How do two previously unacquainted children form a friendship? What behaviors must occur to produce an affiliative bond between these two peers? A time-intensive investigation by John Gottman (1983) provides a fascinating glimpse into the process of friendship formation among children who initially met as strangers. Gottman's method involved tape-recording the conversations of eighteen unfamiliar dyads aged three to nine years as they played in their homes for three sessions. Even in this short time, friendships among some of the pairs began to emerge. In all cases, each member of the pair was within one year of age of the other. Some were same-sex pairs, others opposite-sex. The behaviors of the child whose home it was (the host child) and the visiting child (the guest) were coded separately; the sequences of behaviors displayed by these children—that is, how one child's behavior influenced the other's—were also analyzed.

Children who "hit it off" in the first play session showed several distinct patterns of interaction. First, they were successful in exchanging information, as in the following conversation one pair had:

A: "Hey, you know what?"
B: "No, what?"
A: "Sometime you can come to my house."

▶ **The child's active role**

Children who became friends made efforts to establish a common ground by finding activities that could be shared together or by identifying similarities and differences between them.

In addition, any conflicts that occurred as they played were successfully resolved, either by one member of the dyad explaining the reason for the disagreement or by one child complying with the other child's demands, as long as they were not excessive or unreasonable. Alternatively, as activities escalated from simply coloring side by side ("I'm coloring mine green") to one child's issuing a command ("Use blue. That'd be nice"), children who became friends tempered this potential conflict by de-escalating the intensity of play (in this case, going back to side-by-side coloring) or using another element of play that was "safe"—namely, information exchange (for example, "I don't have a blue crayon. Do you?"). In contrast, children who did not become friends often persisted in escalating their play until the amity of the situation disappeared. Children who became friends thus modulated their interactions to preserve a positive atmosphere.

▶ **Interaction among domains**

Over time, other social processes also came into play. One influential variable was the clarity of communication, as evidenced by a child giving clear answers to requests for information from the other. The following sequence is an example of a clear communication:

A: "Hand me the truck."
B: "Which truck?"
A: "The red one."

Also significant was the amount of self-disclosure in children's interactions—that is, one child's revelation of feelings in response to a question about them from the other.

Friendship formation, like other aspects of peer interaction, requires a sensitivity to social cues and knowledge of managing interactions that have their positive and negative moments. It should not be surprising, then, that socially skilled children have more friends than socially unskilled children do.

The Functions of Friendship

By virtue of their special qualities, friendships contribute to the child's development in ways that are different from other, more transient, peer interactions. Friendships involve extended contact between peers and a significant affective investment from each child. Thus they provide a fertile ground for the child's social and emotional development.

▶ **Interaction among domains**

Because friendships include the sharing of affection and emotional support, especially among older children, they may play a vital role in protecting children from anxiety and stress. For example, boys seem to adjust better to the practical and psychological consequences of divorce when they have friends (Wallerstein & Kelly, 1980). In addition, children who have close and intimate friendships have higher levels of self-esteem, less anxiety and depression, and are more sociable in general compared with those with few close friends (Buhrmester, 1990; Mannarino, 1978). Because many of these studies are correlational, the direction of influence is not always clear. That is, less anxious children may be more capable of forming intimate friendships, or the reverse may be true—friendships may make them less anxious. Nonetheless, it is reasonable to hypothesize that friends provide an important source of social support and feedback about one's competence and self-worth.

Interactions with friends also provide a context for the development of certain social skills such as cooperation, competition, and conflict resolution. In one study, researchers observed teams of four- and five-year-olds playing a game in which cooperation led to both partners winning, whereas competition led to losses for both (Matsumoto et al., 1986). Teachers independently rated the degree of friendship for each pair of children. The results showed that the greater the degree of friendship, the more the children cooperated to win the game. In another longitudinal study of three-year-olds in day care, Carollee Howes (1983) observed that children showed the greatest increases in the complexity of their social interactions—their ability to initiate an interaction or participate in an elaborate exchange, for example—within the context of playing with one or two stable friends. Such gains were not observed when children played with peers who were not friends.

Similarly, because of their investment in friendships, when children have conflicts with friends they frequently seek to negotiate and resolve those conflicts rather than letting the argument escalate or result in the end of the friendship. William Hartup and his colleagues, observing four-year-olds in nursery school over a period of several weeks, noted any instances of spontaneous conflict in which one child attempted to influence another but met with resistance (Hartup et al., 1988). They found that when conflicts occurred between friends, children were more likely either to negotiate and bargain or to physically turn away from the situation. When conflicts occurred between non-friends, children were more likely to stand firm and insist on their original goal.

Finally, the intimacy required in friendships may also promote healthier relations with others later in life. Harry Stack Sullivan (1953) believed that the capacity for intimacy nurtured by same-sex friendships in childhood provides the foundation for intimacy in more mature adult relationships. The failure to acquire this capacity in the formative years of childhood may impair a person's later functioning as a romantic partner, spouse, or parent. Although little research has been conducted to evaluate the validity of this claim, the idea that there is continuity between the capacity for intimacy in childhood and later life continues to have broad appeal.

THEMES IN DEVELOPMENT

THE INFLUENCE OF PEERS

▶ How does the sociocultural context influence peer relations?

Cultures vary in the amount of peer experience they structure for children. For example, some children in the Soviet Union and on the Israeli kibbutzim are reared with peers from early childhood. As more American children enter day care, they also have more extensive experiences with peers than previous generations. In general, children who spend more time with peers show advances in social development and often show a tendency to prefer cooperation to competition.

In most societies, peers pressure their age mates to conform to specific cultural values, such as sex-typed behaviors. Modeling and reinforcement are two mechanisms by which peers transmit behaviors that are part of a culture's socialization goals.

Culture can also influence the standards that shape peer acceptance. For example, in American society, athletic capabilities and social skill are highly valued, and as a consequence, children who are proficient in these domains typically enjoy more peer popularity.

▶ How does the child play an active role in peer relations?

On one level, many of the physical qualities the child possesses influence the reactions of peers. Attractiveness, body build, athletic skill, and rate of maturation all engender different responses from other children. On another level, the child's social skill, the ability to engage in smooth social interactions, clearly affects how peers react. Children who can accurately read the emotions of others, gauge the consequences of their own behaviors on others, and know the strategies that facilitate good social discourse are more popular with their peers. Similarly, children who are aggressive and display physical power often rise to the top of peer group dominance hierarchies, but may become unpopular with peers who are asked to name children they like or prefer to associate with.

▶ Are developmental changes in peer relations continuous or stagelike?

According to Parten, the development of play with peers progresses in a stagelike fashion. Similarly, Selman has proposed a stage theory of children's understanding of friendship. However, research now shows that preschoolers often concurrently display several types of play. In addition, young children's interactions with friends suggest more complexity than Selman's social cognitive model hypothesizes.

▶ How do peer relations interact with other domains of development?

First, healthy relations with peers are associated with a number of successful developmental outcomes in other arenas. Popular children do well in school, have high levels of self-esteem, and suffer fewer emotional difficulties, such as depression, than unpopular children.

Second, the ability to interact successfully with peers is related to attainments in several other developmental domains. Children who are reared in a positive emotional environment and who are good at deciphering emotional cues tend to be more socially competent with peers. The formation of early emotional attachments may also play a role. Growth in the child's social knowledge is an additional factor. The child's emerging cognitive capabilities—especially perspective-taking skills—make it possible for her to think about the reactions and expectations of others and to anticipate the consequences of her own behaviors. Clear communication skills add to her effectiveness in establishing successful relationships with peers. Successful peer interaction is thus both a product of and a contributor to the child's emotional, cognitive, and social achievements.

SUMMARY

Children show an interest in their *peers* directly from infancy, although coordinated social interchanges, such as turn taking, do not emerge until the age of two years or so. Preschool children typically engage in three kinds of play: *solitary play, parallel play,* and *cooperative play.* They also engage in *social pretend play.* Children's relationships with peers display their growing linguistic, cognitive, and social competencies.

During the school years and adolescence, peer groups assume greater importance for children than previously. Children associate in same-sex groups and groups based on other similarities, such as race or shared interests. *Rough-and-tumble play* is frequently observed. Adolescents form larger groups called *cliques* and *crowds;* toward the end of adolescence, they develop interest in peers of the opposite sex.

Children typically show strong identity with the peer groups they join, feelings that become solidified when the group members work together toward some common goal. At the same time, conflicts between peer groups can occur. One way to break down such intergroup hostilities is to have groups work together on some common goal. Peer groups quickly form organized structures, called *dominance hierarchies,* in which some children become leaders and others, followers. Dominance hierarchies seem to serve a number of adaptive social functions.

Susceptibility to peer pressure heightens during early adolescence but declines as young adulthood approaches. Peers pressure each other to spend time together and, less frequently, to misbehave. Peers enforce their norms by reacting positively to individuals who conform and negatively to those who resist. At times, peer pressures are in direct conflict with pressures from adults.

Peers are important agents of socialization who model and reinforce both prosocial and undesirable behaviors for others. Peers can also play a role in transmitting to children the values of the larger social group.

Peer acceptance is measured through such peer assessment devices as *sociometric nominations* or *sociometric rating scales.* Researchers also use teacher assessments and their own behavioral assessments to gauge children's popularity. The child's peer status is related to his or her physical attractiveness, name, motor skills, and, most particularly, social skills. In general, popular children engage in prosocial behaviors, know how to enter peer groups, and are effective at maintaining cohesive social interactions.

Social competence may have its roots in the child's earliest attachment relationships, but it is also influenced by parental styles of social interaction. Socially competent children are also better at perceiving and interpreting social cues and have good social problem-solving ability. Modeling, reinforcement, and coaching are some of the techniques that have been used to enhance social skills in children who have social problems such as aggression and withdrawal.

Friendships are an important part of children's peer relations. Preschoolers view friends as peers to play with, but with development they come to value friends for their psychological benefits. Children approaching adolescence increasingly see their friends as providers of intimacy and trust. These changes in children's concepts of friendship parallel changes in social cognition. Children form friendships by keeping social interactions positive in tone, exchanging information, and, at later ages, by clear communication and self-disclosure. Friendships provide a context for developing skills such as cooperation and conflict resolution and may help the child to learn the benefits of intimacy in relationships.

16

The Influence of
School and Television

▶ **How does the sociocultural context influence the child's experiences with school and television?**

▶ **How does the child play an active role in experiences with school and television?**

▶ **How do the child's experiences with school and television interact with development in other domains?**

"If I could just boot up my 286 clone," Linda was saying, "I think I can help you get your missing text file back. I have this new software package with some great utilities on it."

"That'd be great," Andy said from the next monitor. "But I think I may have purged that file all the way by mistake when I was sending mail to the electronic bulletin board yesterday. I'm not sure it's even recoverable."

"Don't worry, my teacher just lent me a video on using DOS. Between that and the utility, I think I know how to do it."

A conversation, perhaps, between two computer science majors in college? In fact, it took place between two 12-year-olds in a junior high school computer laboratory. Childhood in the 1990s is a vastly different enterprise from growing up three or even two decades ago. Would a seventh-grader living in the 1970s have had the vaguest idea what these peers of his were talking about?

Computers, television, and videocassette recorders now make up an important feature of most schools and many homes. Not just a brand new vocabulary, but a whole host of questions has sprung up around these technological marvels as we consider their impact on child development. Can children learn more effectively, both at school and at home, with electronic tools? Will their social development be impaired if they get "hooked" to a computer or television screen? What other aspects of their cognitive or social development may the new technology be affecting?

Historically, of course, parents and peers have played the major role in socializing children and helping them build their cognitive skills, and parents and peers carry on this role in contemporary society as well. Schools, too, play a significant part, and we will take a closer look at their effects, pedagogical and social, in this chapter. But rapid technological advances have transformed all of our lives and have created a new sociocultural climate within which children's growth will take place.

Even though school, computers, and television seem to be entirely separate influences on child development, their roles are deeply intertwined in the microsystem—the child's immediate environment made up of the home, school, and neighborhood—that Urie Bronfenbrenner

657

described in his ecological systems theory which we discussed in Chapter 2. School, computers, and television can rival parents, siblings, and peers in the magnitude of their influence, especially as the child moves beyond the preschool years. As we will see in this chapter, each in its own way has the power to shape both the cognitive and the social development of children as they reach out to the larger world that extends beyond the immediate family.

SCHOOL

In the late eighteenth century, Thomas Jefferson promoted an idea that was radical for the time—free education for all American children. The specifics of his plan were never adopted, but the notion eventually caught on in this country as well as in many others. By the mid- to late nineteenth century, independent local or district schools were replaced by a system of tax-supported, state-controlled compulsory schools. Much of the emphasis in this new system of education was on moral development and character training, with the goal of producing honest and hard-working contributors to society. Education was seen as a socioeconomic equalizer, providing all children with the same opportunities for success, regardless of their background.

▶ **Interaction among domains**

Today, in our nation as well as in many others, children are legally required to attend school, but academic accomplishment has replaced character development as the chief point of emphasis. The main aim of education is to provide children with the academic skills necessary to function as independent, responsible, and contributing members of society. Nevertheless, even today the child's experiences in school can have a profound impact on other aspects of development, most notably self-concept and psychological well-being.

By the time children graduate from high school, they have logged close to fifteen thousand hours in school. Thus it is important to understand the nature of that experience and how variations produce specific effects in the child. Several factors in the school experience influence learning and socialization, including the school's physical ecology, the educational philosophies of school personnel, transition points in schooling, and, most important, the attitudes and behaviors of teachers. We will take up each of these variables in turn.

What Are the Effects of School on the Developing Child?

▶ **Sociocultural influence**

As we discussed in Chapter 8, societies vary in the extent to which they stress the experience of formal schooling. Rural agrarian subcultures in some countries, for example, do not have compulsory schooling. Experience in school in turn cultivates cognitive skills such as rote memory, taxonomic classification, and logical reasoning (Rogoff, 1981; Rogoff & Morelli, 1989). One especially powerful outcome of schooling is the development of literacy, the ability to read and write using the symbol system of a culture's language. Not only is literacy virtually a prerequisite for survival in our own society, it is also linked to other specific cognitive and linguistic attainments, such as the ability to decipher the auditory components of language and to analyze grammatical correctness (Scribner & Cole, 1981).

The ability to read and write will assume even more importance in our society during upcoming decades. As adolescents approach adulthood in the twenty-first century, they will find that more and more jobs will be in the professional and technical sectors, areas that require not only reading and writing skills but also the ability to communicate, reason, and apply mathematical and scientific concepts (Jackson & Hornbeck, 1989). The responsibility for fostering these skills will lie mainly with our schools.

Academic Achievement   In some measure, most children attain the basic goals educators and parents have set for academic achievement in school. In 1988, 89 percent of young adults completed high school, although the dropout rates are higher for students from low-income families and racial and ethnic minorities (Rumberger, 1987; U.S. Bureau of the Census, 1990a).

But how well are children learning in schools? Several major national surveys conducted in the last decade conclude that levels of academic achievement among American students are declining or do not compare well with those of students from other industrialized countries. Here are some representative data:

- American high school students score lower on most standardized tests of achievement than they did three decades ago (National Commission on Excellence in Education, 1983).
- About 13 percent of seventeen-year-olds in the United States are functionally illiterate—essentially they cannot read or write—and the rate of illiteracy among minority youth may be as high as 40 percent (National Commission on Excellence in Education, 1983).
- Only 11 percent of all thirteen-year-olds can be categorized as "adept" readers, meaning they can understand relatively complicated written information (Mullis & Jenkins, 1990).
- Only 13 percent of eighth-graders wrote "adequate" or better essays when the task required them to "compare and contrast" (Applebee et al., 1990).
- Students from the United States ranked fourteenth out of seventeen major industrialized countries on a test of science achievement, as shown in Table 16.1 (International Association for the Evaluation of Educational Achievement, 1988).

These results are both alarming and perplexing. Have American schools shirked their commitment to academic excellence? Have the characteristics of the student population changed in some way? There are no simple answers to explain the national survey data, nor are there quick, obvious ways to remedy the problems. What these results call for very plainly, though, is a better understanding of how parents, peers, *and* schools contribute to students' academic attainments.

▶ **Interaction among domains**   ***Self-Concept***   In addition to building academic skills, a child's experience in school can also have a major impact on her feelings of competence and self-worth, both in a general sense and in terms of academic self-esteem. Schoolmates and teachers provide constant feedback to the child about how she is doing, from casual comments friends make at recess ("You did a great job reciting that poem this morning!") to the formal academic grades administered by the teacher.

TABLE 16.1

Science Achievement in Seventeen Countries

This table presents the rank order of countries in science achievement of ten- and fourteen-year-old children. The rank of 1 represents the highest scores on international science tests designed to measure knowledge of basic science concepts. (Some of the data indicate tied ranks.)

	10-Year-Olds (grades 4/5)	14-Year-Olds (grades 8/9)
Australia	9	10
Canada (English-speaking)	6	4
England	12	11
Finland	3	5
Hong Kong	13	16
Hungary	5	1
Italy	7	11
Japan	1	2
Korea	1	7
Netherlands	—	3
Norway	10	9
Philippines	15	17
Poland	11	7
Singapore	13	14
Sweden	4	6
Thailand	—	14
U.S.A.	8	14

Source: Adapted from International Association for the Evaluation of Educational Achievement, 1988.

In general, there is a positive correlation between academic achievement, usually measured by grades, and self-esteem. Students who obtain good grades have more favorable attitudes about themselves (Byrne, 1984). But does high self-esteem lead students to perform better in school, or does academic competence nurture the development of high self-esteem? Most experts concur that both processes operate. One research team measured the self-concept and mental abilities of children as they began kindergarten and then took successive measures of their reading ability and self-concept over the next two years. The results showed that initial measures of self-esteem were good predictors of reading achievement in second grade (Wattenberg & Clifford, 1964).

By the same token, experimental studies have demonstrated that academically competent children can be made to feel more negatively about themselves when they experience failure. In an illustrative experiment, two groups of high-achieving children were given a test of self-esteem and then three academic tests. Children in the experimental group, however, were given a slip of paper after the last test stating that they had failed. Their scores on a subsequent test of self-esteem declined, but the scores of the control group remained the same (Gibby & Gibby, 1967). Though contemporary researchers might question the ethics of subjecting students to this type of stress in a psychological experiment, the results clearly point to the power of performance feedback in shaping students' feelings about themselves. A recent two-year study of sixth- and seventh-graders confirms that students who showed gains in self-esteem had a favorable school climate and higher teacher evaluations of their work habits (Hoge, Smit, & Hanson, 1990).

The Physical Environment of the School

Among the characteristics of schools that play a role in the child's development are school size, class size, and the physical layout of the classroom. Each factor influences the frequency and range of opportunities for students to interact with teachers and peers in the school setting.

School Size Though there is some controversy over the importance of school size, when researchers find any significant effects, they usually favor students from smaller schools (Rutter, 1983). In a major study of thirteen high schools ranging in size from thirteen to over two thousand students, researchers noted that students from smaller schools were less alienated, participated more in school activities, felt more competent, and found themselves more challenged (Barker & Gump, 1964). One probable reason for these effects is the greater availability of roles for students to fill in smaller schools, particularly leadership roles. Students who have the opportunity to edit the school newspaper or be captain of the band typically receive positive feedback from parents, teachers, and peers for fulfilling these roles. They are also likely to identify strongly with the school and develop a greater sense of personal control and responsibility.

▶ **The child's active role**

Class Size Class size is another important aspect of school structure. In general, children in small classes show greater academic advances than children in large classes do. Few investigations have actually randomly assigned children to classes of different sizes to explore the effects on achievement, even though this procedure would allow us to draw the strongest conclusions about the causal influence of class size. In a recent study of seventy-six schools across one state, however, precisely this procedure was followed. Kindergarten children and teachers were randomly assigned to one of three conditions: small classes of thirteen to seventeen students, regular classes of twenty-two to twenty-five students, or regular-sized classes with a teacher's aide. By the end of the first grade, children in the small classes showed markedly greater improvements in performance on standardized tests of reading and mathematics than children from regular-sized classes, although the presence of an aide did improve scores somewhat. The benefits of small classes were especially pronounced for minority children (Finn & Achilles, 1990).

Why do smaller classes work? For one thing, teachers probably have higher enthusiasm and morale when they are not overburdened with large numbers of students. Teachers also have more time to spend with individual students, and students are more likely to be attentive and engaged in classroom activities in small classes (Finn & Achilles, 1990).

This crowded classroom in a public school in the United States does not afford children with the best learning environment. Children in smaller classes show higher scores on standardized achievement tests.

The Physical Arrangement of the Classroom   The way in which a classroom is set up affects both student-teacher and student-student interactions. In the typical traditional classroom, precisely aligned rows of desks all face the teacher to enhance communication between the teacher and individual pupils. This arrangement discourages interactions among students, which are viewed as disruptive to the learning process. Finally, it provides clear zones of greater student-teacher exchange: students seated across the front row and down the center aisle (see Figure 16.1) are most likely to interact with the teacher (Gump, 1978). Even gregarious and actively involved students become less engaged with the teacher when they are seated outside the "action zone" of the traditional classroom (Koneya, 1976).

The best way to encourage the attention and active participation of more students in the class is to place the desks in a circle so that all students have equal access to the teacher. Researchers have noted that when desks are arranged this way, children raise their hands more frequently and make more spontaneous comments about the lesson than when desks are positioned in rows and columns (Rosenfield, Lambert, & Black, 1985).

▶ **The child's active role**

When schools and classes are small, then, and when classrooms are arranged to encourage communication between teachers and students, children are likely to become more actively engaged in the educational process. Such improved structural features of schools provide students with opportunities to assume greater leadership roles and to participate more fully in classroom exchanges with teachers and peers.

Philosophies of Education

The traditional model of education emphasizes the role of the teacher as a transmitter of information to students and channels the major interactions in

FIGURE 16.1

The "Action Zones" of the Traditional Classroom

Students who sit in the front row and the center aisle of the classroom are likely to have the greatest number of interactions with the teacher. The best way to encourage the participation of more students is to arrange the desks in a circle.

Source: Adapted from Adams & Biddle, 1970.

the classroom so that they flow from teacher to student. Students are required to work on problems and assignments individually, their work is evaluated according to widely shared standards, and a climate of competition is the norm. Teachers assume an authority role, and their goal is to convey primarily academic information, as opposed to personal, emotional, or social knowledge. Alternative models of education, however, de-emphasize the teacher as authority, the student as individual learner, and a competitive academic environment.

The Open Classroom In the **open classroom,** students are encouraged to collaborate, and the teacher's role is frequently to structure lessons so that they offer opportunities for intellectual sharing and problem solving. Movable furniture, large open spaces, and activity centers replace the fixed, regular rows of student desks to encourage pupil interaction. The teacher is often considered a joint partner in the learning process, a collaborator in the process of discovery; team teaching is also common. Goals other than the strictly academic are equally valued: fostering the child's creativity, inquisitiveness, and socialization. Rarely are one child's accomplishments compared with those of others; instead, achievement is measured by the degree of progress the individual child shows.

Many of the ideas behind the open classroom had their origins in the work of John Dewey (1938/1963), an educational philosopher of the early part of this century. Dewey believed two things about education: it should capitalize on the child's natural interests and curiosity, and it should integrate the child into the larger society. Thus, for example, in Dewey's experimental school, arithmetic and science were taught in the context of cooking and carpentry; it was assumed that as the child conducted these basic social activities, he would develop a spontaneous interest in more formal academic information.

open classroom Nontraditional educational approach that emphasizes peer interaction, free-flowing movement of students around different activity centers in the classroom, and structured opportunities for students to "discover" knowledge.

Open classrooms like the one shown in this picture contain a number of unique features: large open spaces, movable furniture, and activity centers designed to help children learn by "discovery."

▶ **The child's active role**

    Likewise, contemporary open classrooms provide children with structured opportunities to "discover" principles of science, mathematics, and other academic subjects. Instead of reading a chapter on photosynthesis, children may have access to a science table where they can actively manipulate the amount of sunlight and water different plants receive over a period of days to determine those elements necessary for green leaves. Another activity center might be devoted to mathematical problems, and so forth. Children are free to explore different areas of the room under the careful guidance of the teacher.

    Do children in open classrooms display different academic and social profiles than those who learn in traditional classrooms? As Table 16.2 shows, in the realm of academics, over one hundred studies point to no consistent differences in the average performance of children in one classroom type versus the other (Horwitz, 1979). In the realm of social development, however, children

▶ **Interaction among domains**

from open classrooms show clear gains. A large body of empirical work shows that open classroom students are generally more cooperative, have a wide variety of interactions with peers in both work and socially related matters, and develop broad networks of relationships with peers (Hallinan, 1976; Horwitz, 1979; Minuchin & Shapiro, 1983).

    Open classrooms are not as popular today as they were twenty years ago. Because the expected academic benefits of the open classroom were not realized and because the "back-to-basics" movement is currently popular in American education, traditional classrooms still predominate. Nevertheless, open classrooms represent an interesting and still promising experiment in educational practice.

cooperative learning Peer-centered learning experience in which students of different abilities work together in small groups to solve academic problems. Often these groups compete against each other within the classroom.

Peer Learning   As we saw in Chapter 13, several unique peer-centered learning experiences demonstrate that there are benefits to experimenting with educational models that de-emphasize teacher-to-student transmission of information. One such model is **cooperative learning,** in which students work in groups rather than individually to solve academic problems or complete assignments.

A prime example is the *Student Teams–Achievement Divisions* (STAD) method developed by Robert Slavin (1990b). Students are assigned to four- or five-person learning teams composed of children having a range of abilities. Each group is deliberately structured to contain both boys and girls and children of mixed racial or ethnic backgrounds. After the teacher introduces a new topic or set of materials, team members in each group work on related problems, quiz each other, and study together until they decide collectively that they understand the unit. Then each individual is quizzed to assess her knowledge, and the amount of improvement from her past quiz average is added to the team score. This method ensures that even low-achieving students feel they have made a contribution to the group. Teams with the highest scores, individuals who most exceeded previous performance, and individuals who received perfect scores are recognized in a weekly class newsletter.

Cooperative learning works. Students who participate in STAD classrooms show greater achievement in language arts, social studies, and mathematics compared with control subjects who learned the same material from more traditional methods. Using specific group rewards—that is, overt, public recognition of the teams' accomplishments—has proved to be an especially important factor in producing gains. In addition, the STAD program increases the number of cross-racial friendships, improves self-esteem, and produces more favorable attitudes toward academic achievement (Slavin, 1990b). Like

TABLE 16.2

The Effects of Open Versus Traditional Classrooms

The results of 102 studies show that though open classrooms have few effects on academic achievement, they are likely to promote creativity, curiosity, independence, and a number of other desirable social characteristics.

Variable (number of studies)	Results (percent of studies)			
	Open Better	Traditional Better	Mixed Results	No Significant Differences
Academic achievement (102)	14	12	28	46
Self-concept (61)	25	3	25	47
Attitude toward school (57)	40	4	25	32
Creativity (33)	36	0	30	33
Independence and conformity (23)	78	4	9	9
Curiosity (14)	43	0	36	21
Anxiety and adjustment (39)	26	13	31	31
Locus of control (24)	25	4	17	54
Cooperation (9)	67	0	11	22
(Overall average)	(39)	(4)	(24)	(33)

Source: Adapted from Horowitz, 1979.

the children in the Robber's Cave Study described in Chapter 15, when these students work in groups toward common objectives, barriers to interpersonal relationships dissolve and commitments to the goals of the group are strengthened.

Another form of peer learning is called **peer collaboration.** Here, pairs of students work jointly on the same problems without competing with other groups. An illustration of how this method works comes from a study by Erin Phelps and William Damon (1989). Fourth-graders worked in pairs on mathematics and spatial reasoning problems, some requiring rote learning and copying and others formal reasoning. The children had to supply the answers to problems like $2 \times 2 = ?$ (rote learning) or, at other times, solve problems involving ratios and proportions (formal reasoning). After six sessions of peer collaboration, children showed significant gains in performance on math and spatial problems compared with a control group that did not receive the intervention. This effect occurred for tasks that required formal reasoning but not for those that required rote learning or copying. Another interesting outcome was that the superiority that boys showed over girls on spatial problems at the start of the study was significantly diminished. Peer collaboration thus improves certain forms of learning among elementary school children.

▶ **Interaction among domains**

Two major theoretical viewpoints help to explain the positive effects of peer learning. Both Piaget (1926) and Vygotsky (1978) believe that peer interactions encourage the advancement of cognitive skills. In Piagetian theory, the cognitive conflicts and disequilibrium created in peer exchanges produce reorganizations in the child's thinking. As noted in Chapter 15, Vygotsky believes that peers facilitate cognitive growth not only because they often operate within similar *zones of proximal development* but also because they display enough differences that one student's advanced knowledge in a given area can provide the *scaffolding* for another student.

One form of peer learning is called *peer collaboration,* where pairs of students work together on science or mathematics problems. Compared with students who receive more traditional methods of instruction, peer collaborators show significant increases in performance in these academic subjects.

▶ **The child's active role**

Another reason peer learning is effective is that it heightens children's motivation to learn. In team learning, an individual's goals can only be met if the group is successful and group members exert pressure on individual students to display their best efforts. Consistent with the tenets of behavior theory, peer praise or criticism serves to regulate the individual accomplishments of group members (Slavin, 1987b).

CONTROVERSY

Should Students Be Grouped According to Academic Ability?

Separating children into groups according to ability is standard practice in most North American schools. Sometimes students are simply given colorful group names, such as the Jets and the Falcons. Other times the names are less likely to obscure the true ranking criterion for the groups—some children are the Advanced Readers, others are the Slow Readers. Regardless of the names, however, most students and their parents realize they are being grouped (or "tracked") according to their academic abilities. One of the longest-running controversies in American education centers on the pros and cons of just this sort of grouping.

The arguments for tracking are numerous. Proponents of this procedure maintain that ability grouping helps teachers adapt their instructional styles to the specific needs of students. Bright students are more likely to be challenged and motivated when they are grouped with other bright students and can advance at a more rapid pace than if they are left in slower classrooms. Slower learners, in turn, are spared the embarrassment of continual failure and have more opportunities to participate when they do not have to compete with bright students. They can learn more when they receive more individual attention from the teacher and when the pace of learning is adjusted to their level of ability. Many educators have found these arguments convincing. As a consequence, grouping students according to academic ability is common in most elementary and secondary schools, whether it is for reading groups within an elementary class or curriculum tracks (for example, college preparatory versus vocational) in the higher grades.

Critics point out, though, that ability grouping can have several damaging consequences. Chief among these are the low expectations and diminished morale that slow learners often develop (Persell, 1977; Rosenbaum, 1980). When students discover they are in a lower track, they often feel demoralized and begin to live out the expectations of others. One student's comments during a research interview poignantly illustrate this point:

> I felt good when I was with my [elementary] class, but when they went and separated us—that changed us. That changed our ideas, our thinking, the way we thought about each other, and turned us to enemies toward each other—because they said I was dumb and they were smart . . . The devil with the whole thing—you lose—something in you—like it goes out of you. (Schafer & Olexa, 1971, pp. 62–63)

peer collaboration Peer-centered learning experience in which pairs of students work together on academic problems, usually without competing against other students.

There are other problems, too. Because many teachers prefer not to teach students in the lower tracks, some educational researchers maintain that those students actually get poorer-quality instruction (Gamoran, 1989; Oakes, 1985). In addition, students from lower social classes and racial and ethnic minorities are more likely to be grouped in lower tracks because they are low achievers (but not necessarily because they are low in ability) (Persell, 1977; Rosenbaum, 1980). Most of the time, once students are placed in a given academic track, it is exceedingly difficult for them to switch to another, especially because the grouping is often presumed to reflect innate ability rather than achievement level. Thus, tracking may serve to perpetuate the degree of access students from various economic and ethnic backgrounds have to educational resources.

In two major overviews of the research on academic ability grouping in elementary and secondary schools, Robert Slavin (1987a, 1990a) concluded that this educational strategy has no overall impact on the academic achievements of students. The only exception is that elementary school children who are grouped across grades according to reading ability (as when higher-level first-graders are grouped with lower-level second graders) or within grades for mathematics instruction achieve at slightly higher levels. Given the potential negative effects of tracking, Slavin argues that there is no good reason to continue this popular educational practice. On the other hand, Slavin's analysis included studies that relied almost exclusively on standardized tests as measures of achievement, measures that may not capture the benefits of tracking because they do not necessarily measure what students are actually taught in school (Hallinan, 1990). The debate on academic ability grouping will no doubt continue, but as Slavin (1990a) suggests, alternative ways of structuring classroom experiences, such as cooperative learning, can have more comprehensive benefits for the students then academic ability grouping. ∎

School Transitions

In addition to the physical ecology of school and philosophies of education, there is one other way in which the structuring of the school experience influences development: the age at which children are expected to make specific school transitions. Most children begin kindergarten at the age of five or six years, and the way in which they adjust to this first experience of school frequently determines how much they will like later grades. A second important transition occurs for most children in adolescence, when entering junior or senior high school makes new academic and social demands on them.

Starting School   Few times in a child's life are as momentous as the first day of school. Parents typically find this a time of mixed emotions, of eager anticipation of the child's future accomplishments coupled with anxieties about whether school will provide positive and rewarding experiences for their child. Children find they have many major adjustments to handle—accommodating to a teacher and a new physical environment, making new friends, and mastering new academic challenges. The success with which children make the initial transition to school can set the tone for later academic and socioemotional development. Because these early behavior patterns and impressions of school have a way of persisting, we need to identify and understand the factors that make adjustment to school smooth and successful.

To identify the variables connected with a positive transition to school, Gary Ladd and Joseph Price (1987) followed a sample of fifty-eight children as they moved from preschool to kindergarten. Assessing subjects on a number of social measures at three times—before entering kindergarten, at the beginning of the school year, and at the end of the school year—these investigators discovered that both the social behaviors of the children and the familiarity of the group they entered made contributions to healthy school adjustment. Children who as preschoolers displayed high levels of cooperative play and had extensive positive social contacts were well liked by their fellow kindergartners and were rated as involved with peers by teachers. Children who had been aggressive in preschool tended to be disliked by their kindergarten peers and were rated as hostile by teachers.

Peer acceptance was also facilitated by the presence of familiar peers in the kindergarten classroom. It is possible that a nucleus of familiar others provides a "secure base" from which to develop other social relationships. Moreover, the presence of familiar peers was related to more positive attitudes toward school and fewer anxieties at the start of the school year. In general, factors promoting continuity between the preschool and kindergarten experiences were most beneficial to the child's adjustment, suggesting that parents should consider ways of fostering their children's friendships with peers who will be future classmates.

▶ **Interaction among domains**

The quality of early peer relationships in school can have even more far-reaching effects on a child's adjustment. Ladd (1989) found that the number of new friendships children formed in the first two months of the school year predicted higher levels of social and academic competence, fewer absences from school, fewer visits to the nurse, and less behavioral disruptiveness. These results underscore the fact that the transition to school can be a particularly crucial time in development and that successes in one domain—peer relations—are related to successes in another—competence in school.

A Second Transition: Junior High Another important transition occurs later in many children's schooling careers when they move from elementary school to a middle school or junior high school. In American society, this time is usually the visible signal of childhood's end and the beginning of adolescence. Once again, children must adapt to new teachers, peers, and physical environment but now, rather than staying with the same classmates in the same room for most of the school day, they move from class to class, each usually with its own set of students. Frequently, the difference in student body size is dramatic between elementary school and junior high school. In one study, the mean school size from grade 6 to grade 7 increased from 466 to 1,307, and the mean number of children in each grade went from 59 to 403 (Simmons, Burgeson, & Carleton-Ford, 1987). It is no wonder that many researchers report a decline in school satisfaction in preadolescence as well as a drop in grades and participation in extracurricular activities (Epstein & McPartland, 1976; Hirsch & Rapkin, 1987; Schulenberg, Asp, & Petersen, 1984; Simmons & Blyth, 1987).

▶ **Interaction among domains**

Some researchers have also observed a decline in self-esteem at this time, particularly among preadolescent girls, and an increase in physical complaints (Hirsch & Rapkin, 1987; Simmons et al., 1979; Simmons, Rosenberg, & Rosenberg, 1973). Early-maturing sixth-grade girls have been found to have better images of themselves when they attend schools with kindergarten through

Most junior high schools are structured so that students physically move from class to class and take courses with different groups of peers over the day. Many adolescents show a decline in school satisfaction and achievement when they make the transition to junior high school.

eighth-grade classes, presumably because they feel less pressured to adopt dating and other activities that become prevalent among seventh- and eighth-graders. On the other hand, those girls entering puberty at more typical ages, and at about the same time that they enter a new school program or undergo other significant transitions, tend to have lower images of themselves and more difficulties in school, possibly because multiple changes in life are difficult to handle (Simmons, Burgeson, & Carleton-Ford, 1987).

For some adolescents, the difficulties encountered in junior high school may set in motion a pattern of academic decline that results in their dropping out of school (Eccles & Midgley, 1988). According to some experts, this is because the junior high school experience does not fit the specific developmental needs of preadolescents. At a time when youngsters are seeking stronger peer associations and a supportive climate for resolving identity issues, they are confronted with an educational environment that is more impersonal than elementary school and fragments peer relationships. In addition, the transition to junior high school frequently happens to coincide with several other life changes, such as the onset of puberty, dating, family disruptions (such as divorce), or new neighborhoods because of a family move. Entry into a new educational setting compounds the stresses many preadolescents are already coping with (Simmons, Burgeson, & Carleton-Ford, 1987).

What happens when alternatives to the traditional junior high school and high school structures are instituted? In one study, students about to begin high school were assigned to special homerooms in which the teacher played an expanded role in providing academic and personal counseling, contacted parents when students were absent, and encouraged other communication with parents. Thus, the homeroom teachers in this setting provided more than usual social support throughout the entire first year of high school. Students were also assigned to classes so that their major academic subjects were taken with many of the same students, a strategy that would presumably enhance peer support and provide a stable environment for students. At the end of the school year, students from this program showed higher levels of academic success and less psychological dysfunction than a control group; after four years, they showed a substantially lower dropout rate from school (21 percent) compared with the controls (43 percent) (Felner & Adan, 1988; Felner, Ginter, & Primavera, 1982).

We see from these studies that whenever children are confronted with a school transition, whether it be the start of kindergarten or the start of secondary school, they adjust best if they have adequate social and emotional supports to cope with the demands of the new environment. When children are buttressed by strong relationships with peers and teachers, they show higher academic performance, less anxiety, and more favorable attitudes toward school than when they lack these supports.

Teachers: Key Agents of Influence

No single factor in the school experience plays a more critical role in student achievement and self-esteem than teachers. The expectations teachers have of students, their classroom management strategies, and the climate they create in the classroom are all major elements in student success or failure.

The Role of Expectancies   A highly publicized study by Robert Rosenthal and Lenore Jacobson (1968) documented how teachers' expectations of students' performance could affect students' actual attainments. These researchers told teachers that certain elementary school children could be expected to show sudden gains in intellectual skills over the course of the school year based on their scores on an IQ test administered at the beginning of the term. In reality, the students they designated as "rapid bloomers" were chosen randomly. When Rosenthal and Jacobson administered the IQ test again at the end of the school year, the targeted children indeed showed significantly greater improvement than other students in the class, an outcome they called the *Pygmalian effect*. The authors explained these findings by suggesting that teachers somehow treated the targeted children differently, based on their beliefs about the children's intellectual potential, thereby creating a *self-fulfilling prophecy*.

The original research conducted by Rosenthal and Jacobson (1968) has been criticized for oversimplifying the variables that contribute to student achievement. Teacher expectations alone cannot explain why some children are more successful than others in school. Subsequent studies, however, have confirmed that high achievers *are* treated differently in the classroom; they are given more opportunities to participate, more time to answer questions, receive more praise for being correct, and receive less criticism than lower achievers (Minuchin & Shapiro, 1983). In other words, the classroom climate is most supportive for those who have already demonstrated success, whereas those who most need the teacher's attention and encouragement may actually get it least.

Most teachers are undoubtedly unaware of the ways in which their expectations influence their own behaviors toward students. Yet the forms of interactions that ensue can have important repercussions for students' academic accomplishments and their feelings of self-worth.

Classroom Management Strategies   Students achieve most in school when their teachers maximize the time spent in actual learning. This statement may seem obvious, but the reality is that not all school time is spent in direct instruction. Effective teachers plan their lessons well, monitor the entire classroom continuously, minimize the time spent in disciplining children who misbehave, and keep transitions between activities brief and smooth (Brophy, 1986). They make sure there is very little "dead time" in the classroom when students are unoccupied, and they keep the focus on instruction.

Another key ingredient in a teacher's success is his active involvement in the learning process. This means that teachers remain personally involved in every phase of instruction, from the initial presentation of a new lesson to supervising the individual work of students (Brophy, 1986). Even when students are working in groups, teachers who guide the discussion or progress of the group will produce higher levels of mastery than those who leave students completely on their own. Effective teachers also provide clear feedback to students on the quality of their performance and on what is expected of them (Rutter, 1983).

▶ **Interaction among domains**

Finally, the way in which teachers structure daily classroom activities and deliver feedback can affect students' self-esteem, particularly the conceptions they form about their academic abilities. Generally speaking, when teachers assign similar tasks to all students, students will have more opportunities to make comparisons among themselves, to see how they "stack up" against each other. Those comparisons are harder to draw when, for example, pupils are given choices of several math or reading assignments. When teachers organize tasks according to student ability levels (for example, high- and low-ability reading groups), they are also creating a structure that encourages students to compare themselves. Moreover, when teachers assign grades frequently, make public announcements about grades, and openly emphasize the poor accomplishments of some students, they create situations in which students are

▶ **The child's active role**

likely to conclude "I'm smarter (or dumber) than you." Children actively process the information, sometimes explicit and sometimes more subtle, that teachers deliver about their abilities. The net result is that some will inevitably see themselves as less competent than others (Rosenholtz & Simpson, 1984).

The Classroom Climate   Students achieve less when they are the targets of frequent criticism or ridicule from the teacher. On the other hand, when the classroom provides a warm, friendly environment, student achievement is high (Linney & Seidman, 1989). Teachers who set limits on students' behaviors do make the classroom run more smoothly, but the use of physical punishment is associated with poor attendance and delinquency (Rutter, 1983). In a large-scale investigation of the effectiveness of secondary schools, Michael Rutter and his colleagues found that schools in which students received frequent praise and that provided a pleasant, comfortable environment had children who were more likely to complete school and achieved more (Rutter et al., 1979). Positive feedback encourages both acceptable behavior and achievement as well as fostering higher student morale (Rutter, 1983). Like the authoritative parents discussed in Chapter 14, teachers who control students but make use of reasoning and positive emotions as strategies are likely to foster the greatest academic and personal gains among their students (Baumrind, 1972).

One of the most important factors in the child's experience in school is the encouragement provided by the teacher. Effective teachers are involved in all phases of instruction, provide clear feedback, and create a positive emotional climate in the classroom.

▶ **The child's active role**

A particularly important dimension is the extent to which the teacher promotes *autonomy,* or student initiative within the classroom. When children perceive that teachers give them responsibility within the classroom, they have higher self-esteem scores than when teachers are perceived as controlling and directive (Ryan & Grolnick, 1986). The effects of controlling strategies are not necessarily simple, however. In a recent experiment, some teachers were pressured to improve fourth-grade children's performance in a problem-solving task, and others were simply instructed to facilitate ways in which children learned to solve the problems. Teaching strategies for the next ten minutes were then carefully observed. The results showed that controlling behaviors from teachers produced declines in children's problem-solving performance, but only when teachers were pressured. In other words, other factors accompanying control, such as teacher stress and tension, may also affect students' performance (Flink, Boggiano, & Barrett, 1990).

As this entire section shows, teachers play the major role in structuring the child's classroom experiences, those precise forms of interaction that occur in the fifteen thousand hours the child spends in the classroom from kindergarten through high school. The teacher determines which child will be called on to respond to a question, whether that child will be praised or criticized, and which academic tasks she will perform. The teacher also sets the emotional tone in the classroom and establishes how much autonomy children have. All these decisions can have profound effects on children. In some circles, it has become popular to blame teachers for all the failings of our educational system. This is certainly unfair since the child's school success arises from a myriad of factors: her cognitive capabilities, the attitudes and behaviors of parents, and as we will see, even cultural beliefs about schooling. In many educational systems, teachers also face the pressures of high student-teacher ratios, lack of parental or administrative support for alternative classroom approaches, and the social problems of students who live in poor neighborhoods. At the same time, though, it is important for teachers to be aware of both the obvious and the subtle ways in which their own behaviors deeply influence the developing child.

▶ **Sociocultural influence**

Cultural Differences in School Achievement

The school experience is not the same for children from different racial and ethnic backgrounds. Children who attend school bring with them attitudes about school that are first nurtured within their families, as well as cultural beliefs that may be in synchrony or in conflict with the predominant belief system of the school. Are schools, for example, the vehicle for economic and personal advancement? Cultural and ethnic groups may vary in their responses to this question. Is verbal, rational expression (which is emphasized in schools) the optimal means of human communication as opposed to emotional or spiritual sharing? Again, cultures may vary in the extent to which they value some skills over others. One of the major challenges facing educators is how to ensure the academic success of children coming from a range of cultural-ethnic backgrounds.

School Achievement Among African American Children   A persistent finding in the research on school achievement is that children of African American backgrounds score significantly lower than Caucasians on many measures of academic performance. For example, the Coleman Report, a national study of elementary and secondary school students sponsored by the government in 1966, found that African American children scored significantly below Caucasian children on tests of reading comprehension, verbal skill, mathematical ability, and knowledge of general information (Coleman, Campbell, & Mood, 1966). Later studies showed similar patterns: on measures of achievement in academic subjects and verbal and mathematical aptitude, African American children consistently scored lower than Caucasian children, although the gap has decreased more recently (Jones, 1984). Explanations for these patterns of findings have taken many turns over the years.

The Cultural Deficit Hypothesis   In the 1960s, the prevailing explanation for the school difficulties of minority children centered on the *cultural deficit hypothesis,* the notion that some deficiency in the backgrounds of minority children did not prepare them for the academic demands of school. An inescapable fact was that African American children were overrepresented among lower socioeconomic groups. Thus some researchers hypothesized that these children came from unstimulating, pathological, or stressful homes and, in the absence of early experiences promoting cognitive development, suffered deficits in thinking skills that led to failure in school. As a consequence, the focus of many early-intervention programs was on remediating these cognitive deficits.

Herbert Ginsberg (1972) dispelled many of the popular beliefs of the time by pointing out that rather than being culturally deficient, minority children are *culturally different.* That is, the behaviors displayed by many African

American children help them to adapt to their specific life circumstances. For example, rather than having poor language skills, African American children speaking Black English display rich images and poetic forms when speaking to each other. More recently, other psychologists and educators have come to believe that we must consider the cultural backgrounds of the members of any minority group to understand their school failure or success. According to the **cultural compatibility hypothesis,** school instruction produces greater improvements in learning if it is consistent with the practices of the child's native culture (Tharp, 1989).

The KEEP Model   An example of an educational intervention specifically designed to be compatible with the child's cultural background is the Kamehameha Early Education Program (KEEP), developed by Roland Tharp and his collaborators in Hawaii (Tharp et al., 1984). Like many minority children in other parts of the United States, youngsters of Hawaiian ancestry have been the lowest achieving in the state. In one administration of a standardized test of reading achievement, more than half of Hawaiian children scored below the fortieth percentile. School achievement deteriorated from the first grade onward. Hawaiian children were also found to be overrepresented among juvenile offenders arrested for serious crimes such as larceny, rape, and murder.

The KEEP program was instituted as an early-education program in language arts for kindergarten through third-grade children. Several unique features of the program were tied to the practices and beliefs of traditional Hawaiian culture. First, since collaboration and cooperation are highly valued in that society, classrooms were organized into small groups of four to five children working on independent projects under the close supervision of a teacher. Teachers made a deliberate attempt to establish warm, nurturant relationships with their charges through the frequent use of social praise and the avoidance of authoritarian methods of control. Second, the program attempted to improve responsiveness to teachers by capitalizing on the tendency of Hawaiian children to engage their peers in rich and animated verbal interactions. Each day, teachers conducted small-group discussions of some academic topic and did not discourage children's interruptions, overlapping speech, and rapid-paced discussions. Third, reading was taught with the aim of developing comprehension as opposed to mechanics, and children were encouraged to relate personal experiences that were triggered by reading a given text.

What were the results of this broad-based intervention? Participants in KEEP scored at approximately the national norms for several tests of reading achievement, whereas control subjects from similar low-income backgrounds continued to place below national averages (Tharp et al., 1984). The KEEP program is an excellent example of how modifying classroom practices to incorporate cultural patterns of language, communication, and social organization can enhance the school performance of children.

African American Culture and Education   In keeping with the cultural compatibility hypothesis, some have argued that for many African American students, a conflict exists between the background culture and the social and cognitive structure of traditional schools. For example, the spiritualism, expressiveness, and rich oral tradition characteristic of an African heritage frequently clash with the materialism, emotional control, and emphasis on printed

cultural compatibility hypothesis Theory that school instruction is most effective if it is consistent with the practices of the child's background culture.

materials characteristic of Euro-Americans and their schools (Boykin, 1986; Heath, 1989; Slaughter-DeFoe et al., 1990).

The experience of racism can compound the problems. African American children may perceive that academic success does not necessarily lead to occupational or economic success, or they may believe that "acting white" is the only way to achieve success. John Ogbu (1974) found that inner-city black children do poorly on academic tests because they do not take them seriously, do not persevere, and do not see their performance as linked to later success. Ogbu (1986) also maintains that even though African American parents value education for their children, they have an inherent lack of trust in the traditional system because of its deep ties to segregation.

A recent study of achievement patterns of African American and Caucasian children in the first two years of school provides some support for the idea that larger sociocultural forces account for the lower achievement of minority children. Karl Alexander and Doris Entwistle (1988) found that African American and Caucasian first-graders did not differ significantly on a standardized test of verbal and quantitative achievement when they were assessed at the beginning of the school year. But by the end of the year and over the second year, the scores of African American and Caucasian students began to diverge noticeably. The achievements of Caucasian students were significantly related to parental variables, such as parents' expectations of their grades and assessments of their abilities. This relationship did not hold for African American students, however. The authors hypothesize that African American parents may be less attentive to the performance levels of their children or may be less involved in providing academic supports because of external pressures they face, such as economic hardship. Alexander and Entwistle's data, however, are also consistent with another possibility—that parental influences may diminish in the face of other, more powerful factors in influencing the achievement of African American children, such as those identified by Ogbu.

Achievement Among Asian Children   For the past decade, Harold Stevenson and his associates have been conducting comparative research on the academic abilities of Taiwanese Chinese, Japanese, and American students with an eye toward accounting for the superiority of Asian students, particularly in the areas of mathematics and science. In one of the earlier studies, first- and fifth-grade students from all three countries were tested on a battery of specially designed cognitive tasks that assessed, among other things, spatial relations, perceptual speed, auditory and verbal memory, and vocabulary (Stevenson, Lee, & Stigler, 1986). Tests of reading and mathematics achievement were also administered to these groups of children from middle- to upper-class backgrounds. The results showed that Chinese children scored significantly higher in reading achievement than American children, who in turn performed above the level of Japanese children. American children scored noticeably lower in mathematics than the other two groups did (see Figure 16.2).

These distinctive patterns of achievement could not be explained by superior cognitive skills in any one group. The researchers found no predictive relationships between scores on the various cognitive assessments and scores on achievement tests. In fact, what was striking was the similarity across cul-

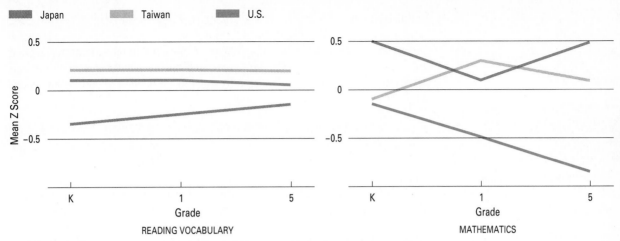

Source: Adapted from Stevenson, Lee, & Stigler, 1986.

FIGURE 16.2

Academic Achievement as a Function of Sociocultural Context

Chinese students score higher than American students on tests of reading achievement. By the first grade, both Chinese and Japanese students show clear superiority to American students in mathematics. (The vertical axis represents standard scores.)

Interaction among domains

tural groups in the children's cognitive profiles by the time they were in the fifth grade (Stevenson et al., 1985).

What, then, accounts for the differing patterns of achievement in reading and mathematics? Stevenson's research group has found large differences in children's school routines and the attitudes and beliefs of parents among the three cultures. One important difference occurred in the percentage of classroom time actually spent in academic activities. For fifth-grade students, these figures were 64.5 percent for American children, 91.5 for Chinese children, and 87.4 for Japanese children. Chinese and Japanese children also spend about fifty more days in school during the year than American children do. Furthermore, American children spent over twice as much time on language arts as on mathematics, whereas Chinese and Japanese children spent equal amounts of time on each. Thus, American children do not receive nearly as much instruction in mathematics as their Chinese and Japanese counterparts do (Stevenson, Lee, & Stigler, 1986). In addition, Japanese and Chinese teachers were far more likely to spend time in mathematics classes directly teaching the entire class, whereas American children spent over half their time in mathematics classes working alone (Stigler, Lee, & Stevenson, 1987).

The research group also examined attitudes and behaviors related to homework. American children spent substantially less time doing homework, an average of 46 minutes per day among fifth-graders according to mothers' estimates, compared with 114 and 57 minutes for Chinese and Japanese children, respectively. American mothers were not dissatisfied with the small amount of homework their children received, nor were Chinese and Japanese mothers with the large amounts their children were assigned (Stevenson, Lee, & Stigler, 1986).

These data highlight the fact that a number of factors aside from pure cognitive ability determine the child's level of achievement in school. As we have seen throughout this section, the characteristics of the given school (especially the events that transpire in the classroom), parental attitudes, and larger cultural influences are all related to patterns of academic success or failure. As we also saw at the outset of this chapter, academic performance can have important repercussions for the child's self-esteem and personal adjustment. If we are concerned about the educational attainments of our students and their overall psychological development, research on the impact of schools reveals that there are ways we can more fully engage children of all ability levels and of diverse sociocultural backgrounds.

Computers

▶ **Sociocultural influence**

Perhaps no more visible symbol of our technological age exists than the computer. Just as adults are more and more likely to encounter computers in their daily experiences, so, too, are children, particularly in school. A national survey of over two thousand elementary and secondary schools indicates that, as of 1985, 86 percent of schools provided computers for instructional purposes, and more than one-third of the students in these schools used computers in some way during the school year (Chen, 1985). High school students tend to spend more time with computers than elementary school children; even young children, however, spend an average of thirty-five minutes per week on computers. In addition, as Figure 16.3 shows, elementary school children commonly interact with drill-and-practice software, which provides direct instruction and exercises, and high school students tend to do their own programming (Becker & Sterling, 1987).

The number of households in which computers are present is also growing. According to some estimates, over 22 million American households have computers, and that number is likely to increase as the technology becomes more affordable (U.S. Bureau of the Census, 1990a). Moreover, computer games are staples in many children's play routines. So ubiquitous are computers in

FIGURE 16.3

Patterns of School Computer Use Among Children, 1985*

Children of all ages use the computer in school, but the kinds of programs they use vary by age. Elementary school children, for the most part, perform drill-and-practice exercises on the computer. Older children learn to write programs and engage in other more sophisticated computer activities. (*As perceived by primary computer-using teacher at each school.)

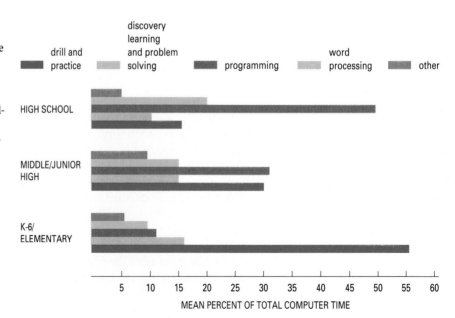

Source: Adapted from Becker & Sterling, 1987.

contemporary American society that many now speak of "computer literacy" as a skill akin to reading.

Quite naturally, parents, educators, and researchers have begun to question the impact computers will have on the process of child development. Some wonder specifically about effects on academic achievement: can computer-presented instructional materials enhance the child's mastery of academic subjects? Others are concerned with broader aspects of cognitive development: does experience with computers influence the ways in which children tackle problem solving and other cognitive tasks? Still others fear that young computer "hackers" who spend long hours glued to the video screen may be missing other significant experiences, particularly the social interactions crucial to their socioemotional development. The stereotype of the computer whiz is that of a brilliant yet socially inept loner who is more skilled at interacting with machines than with people. As it turns out, this description is not necessarily accurate, but the pervasive presence of computers in today's world makes the questions raised by their critics and advocates well worth exploring.

Researchers are just beginning to investigate systematically how children are influenced by contact with computers. The emerging message is clear: there is no such thing as an "effect of computers" *per se* on child development. What matters, rather, is the way children use them (Salomon & Gardner, 1986).

Academic Mastery The first relatively widespread use of computers in education began in the 1960s, when **computer-assisted instruction (CAI)** was touted as a valuable, efficient educational tool. CAI programs serve primarily to supplement classroom instruction, providing highly structured tutorial information along with drill-and-practice exercises in content areas such as mathematics and reading. Several principles are presumed to make CAI programs effective teaching tools. First, the child can work through a lesson at his own pace, reviewing topics if necessary. CAI thus provides an individually paced learning experience in which the content can be tailored to the specific needs of the student. Second, the child receives immediate feedback about the correctness of his responses to questions and exercises and may even receive periodic summaries of performance. These features usually enhance learning and heighten motivation. Finally, CAI programs often employ sound effects and graphics designed to promote the child's attention to, and interest in, the material being presented.

How effective are CAI approaches to instruction? Much of the early research found that children, and especially "slow learners," obtained higher scores on standardized tests of achievement when traditional classroom instruction was supplemented with CAI (Lieberman, 1985). More recently, meta-analyses of the hundreds of studies evaluating CAI have shown that on average, students with CAI experience improve in achievement test scores and that this effect is moderately strong (Lepper & Gurtner, 1989). CAI is especially effective with elementary school and special-needs children, who seem to profit most from individualized approaches to learning (Kulik, Kulik, & Bangert-Drowns, 1985; Niemiec & Walberg, 1987). Children given CAI experience also have more positive attitudes toward computers and the subject area they are studying (Kulik, Bangert, & Williams, 1983).

Although CAI continues to be popular, newer educational software places

computer-assisted instruction Use of computers to provide tutorial information and drill-and-practice routines.

less emphasis on rote memorization and more emphasis on providing children with opportunities to use higher-order thinking skills as they master academic subjects. Consider the example of fourth- and fifth-graders who are learning about the laws of physics, such as the principle that once an object is set in motion, an equal force in the opposite direction is necessary to stop it. In a study of how computers can help children learn the laws of motion, one group of children received tutorial material followed by questions and feedback, along the lines of the traditional CAI approach (Rieber, 1990). Another group was given a different type of computer experience in which they were allowed to experiment with a free-floating starship whose speed they could increase or decrease. As the children interacted with the starship, they could observe the effects of their physical manipulations on its course and "discover" the laws of motion. Still a third group, serving as a control, was given the lesson material with no questions or simulation experiences. Students who participated in the simulations later obtained higher scores on a test of the laws of motion than

▶ **The child's active role**

those in the other two groups. One reason may be that the simulation encouraged students to make a more active mental engagement with the scientific principles underlying the motion of the starship.

Another study explored the impact of a software package called the *Reading Partner* (Salomon, Globerson, & Guterman, 1989). The Reading Partner was developed specifically to cultivate the student's deliberate comprehension strategies. As the seventh-graders in the study read several passages from magazines, parables, or short stories, the computer prompted them: "Think what message a text is trying to convey to you. Think what thoughts the text brings to your mind. Ask yourself whether you understand the text." The program also encouraged students to make inferences about the content from the title of the passage, to conjure up images of the text, and to formulate summaries of the text as they read. Children who experienced three sessions with the Reading Partner improved significantly more in their later reading comprehension than children who simply read the texts or who answered only factual or inferential questions after the texts.

Software programs like the Reading Partner actually do no more nor less than a good human reading teacher would. In other cases, such as the starship simulation, the software allows students to conduct experiments they might not be able to try in the typical elementary school science laboratory. Both software packages, though, are prime examples of the ways in which computer instruction can extend beyond simple drill-and-practice routines to enhance academic learning in areas such as reading and science.

▶ **Interaction among domains**
▶ **The child's active role**

Cognition   More than simply vehicles of direct instruction, computers may also be a means of enriching analytic thinking skills and creativity, particularly when children learn to do their own programming. Seymour Papert (1980), a creator of the computer language Logo, believes that programming experiences represent an ideal setting for learning in which children can test their own theories and models of physical laws, mathematical relationships, and other forms of knowledge. Under such conditions, claims Papert, children can master abstract concepts and ideas much earlier than they normally would.

Because it is specifically designed for children, the Logo program has been the focus of most studies investigating the impact of programming on children's cognition. Logo is an interactive program that allows children to create graphic displays by instructing a "turtle," a triangular pointer, to move around on the computer screen. To draw a square, the child might write this program:

```
TO SQUARE
FORWARD 100
RIGHT 90
FORWARD 100
RIGHT 90
FORWARD 100
RIGHT 90
FORWARD 100
RIGHT 90
END
```

After using the Logo program, many children begin to have spontaneous insights on how to make their programming more efficient—by, for example, modifying the sequence of commands just given to read:

```
TO SQUARE
REPEAT 4
        FORWARD 100
        RIGHT 90
END
```

Here the child realizes that the same goal can be achieved by "factoring" two commands, an example of more abstract, higher-order thinking.

Papert (1980) maintains that by using Logo to direct the pointer's path, children become familiar with notions of planning and debugging (fixing errors and learning from that process) as well as heuristic strategies for solving problems. **Heuristic strategies** are those mental reflections that focus on accomplishing a goal—as in subdividing a problem into smaller parts or connecting it to other successfully solved problems. Furthermore, because computer programming requires the precise articulation of the steps necessary to reach solution, children should also become aware of the logical and hierarchical nature of problem solving. The result, according to Papert, is a broad, significant change in the child's cognitive processes.

Researchers evaluating these claims have reported conflicting results. Some have found little transfer of skills from programming to other problem-solving tasks. Children with one year of experience with Logo, for example, do not show appreciable superiority in their ability to plan a sequence of events, such as how to schedule a series of classroom tasks efficiently (washing the board, watering the plants, and so forth), compared with children who did not learn to program (Pea, Kurland, & Hawkins, 1985).

Other researchers, however, have reported that children with Logo experience often show significant cognitive gains. For example, Douglas Clements (1986) randomly assigned thirty-six first-graders and thirty-six third-graders to one of three experimental groups: (1) a Logo programming group, in which children had extensive experience in using this language; (2) a CAI group, in which children participated in reading and mathematics tutorials and drills; and (3) a control group, which participated in regular classroom lessons without computers. All children were administered several tests of general cognitive skill and academic achievement both before and twenty-two weeks after

heuristic strategies Methods of problem solving that involve higher-order analyses, such as subdividing the problem into smaller parts or comparing it with previously solved problems.

the study period. Although children in the three groups did not differ on measures of reading and mathematics achievement by the end of the study, children in the programming condition scored significantly higher on several measures of cognitive competence. First, the Logo group displayed the highest scores on tests of classification, which required the sorting of geometric shapes and objects as well as class inclusion, and seriation, in which objects had to be ordered from tallest to shortest. Second, this group also showed superior ability in monitoring their own cognitive processes—for example, by identifying the parts of a problem they did not understand. Finally, the Logo group received the highest scores on a test of creativity.

Experience with Logo has also been linked to greater spatial cognitive skill, enhanced rule learning, and a reflective cognitive style, in which children solve problems slowly and accurately rather than quickly and with many errors (Clements & Gullo, 1984; Gorman & Bourne, 1983; Mayer & Fay, 1987). In addition, children who have programmed with Logo show greater ability in analyzing the process of problem solving in abstract terms. Thus, they can say what information is necessary to solve a problem and identify problems that have similar structures (Nastasi, Clements, & Battista, 1990). One of the hypothesized reasons for the emergence of these higher-order problem-solving skills is that Logo is often used in group settings in which pairs or small groups of children help each other to solve programming problems. In these contexts, children often disagree on ways of conceptualizing a given problem (for example, how to make a house with the "turtle") and share several potential solutions. As children attempt to resolve their cognitive conflicts, they are pushed to more advanced modes of thinking (Nastasi, Clements, & Battista, 1990).

These studies show that the computer itself, as well as the interactions with peers it often precipitates, may function within the child's *zone of proximal development* (Salomon, Globerson, & Guterman, 1989). Children who are capable of learning cognitive skills, such as spatial relations or mathematical concepts, may be pushed to acquire these skills in their interactions with sophisticated software programs or as they work on joint problem-solving tasks with peers. Although some researchers believe that Papert's initial claims about the power of the computer to shape cognition were overstated, others hold that "intelligent" computer programs and experiences with programming languages have vast potential in enhancing children's thinking skills (Khayrallah & Van Den Meiraker, 1987; Salomon, Globerson, & Guterman, 1989).

▶ **Interaction among domains**

Social Development   Contrary to popular opinion, the interactions a child has with the computer do not need to displace other activities of a more social nature, nor is computer use itself necessarily a solitary activity. In one survey of over five hundred children, those with microcomputers at home resembled nonowners in the frequency with which they visited friends, participated in club meetings, and engaged in sports (Lieberman, 1985). In fact, the computer may actually serve as a stimulus for the formation of social relationships. Children who play computer games say they visit their friends more often than those who do not, for example (Lieberman, 1985). Furthermore, children who work on computer projects in schools tend to collaborate and share ideas more in these settings than they do in other school activities (Hawkins et al., 1982). In one observation of four-year-olds who had a computer in their child-care center, 63 percent of the time they spent at the computer was in joint partici-

When children employ the computer in school, they often have a partner. Computers can promote collaborative learning and provide opportunities for social development.

pation with a peer. In addition, the researchers found that 70 percent of the interactions consisted of active sharing of the computer (Muller & Perlmutter, 1985).

Thus, rather than inhibiting social interactions, computer activities may actually promote them, especially when teachers encourage group problem solving as opposed to individual projects. As they work on shared projects or spontaneously exchange ideas at the computer, children have opportunities to develop skills in cooperation and social problem solving.

▶ **Interaction among domains**

Sex Differences "Computer." Ask children ranging from kindergarten age to twelfth grade to rate this word on a scale on which one end point is labeled M (for male) and the other F (for female). Ask them also to rate how much they like the item. Researchers who have followed this procedure have found that children of all ages place computers toward the "male" side of the rating scale and that boys like computers more than girls do (Wilder, Mackie, & Cooper, 1985). Other researchers have reported that boys are far more likely to enroll in computer camps (by a ratio of three to one) than girls are and that males outnumber females in computer courses in school (Hess & Miura, 1985; Linn, 1985). School computer labs are also far more likely to be populated by male students than female students during free time (Fish, Gross, & Sanders, 1986). If, as we saw before, experiences with computers can have an impact on children's academic, cognitive, and social development, these sex differences have far-reaching implications for both girls and boys.

It is interesting to note that girls do not shy away from all computer activities. For example, even though girls do not spend as much time as boys doing programming or playing computer games, they are just about equally disposed to use word processing programs (Lockheed, 1985). Moreover, when girls do enroll in computer programming classes, their performance is no different from that of their male classmates (Linn, 1985). Why, then, do we see sex differences in the tendency to use computers?

There are several possible explanations. First, teachers and parents may encourage boys to use computers because of their own stereotypic beliefs about appropriate activities for each sex. Parents, especially, may see computer skills as linked to promising careers for their sons and may be more willing to invest in computers, software, and camp programs for them than they would be for their daughters. Second, girls may be less attracted to the aggressive and competitive themes that frequently characterize computer games and educational software, many with titles such as "Submarine Attack" or "Alien Intruder" (Hess & Miura, 1985). Finally, both boys and girls are socialized to link computers with science and mathematics, academic subjects that are frequently perceived as more appropriate for males (Lockheed, 1985). Unfortunately, the persistence of these stereotypes builds unnecessary barriers for girls to have the experiences with computers that promote abstract, analytical thinking.

Computers add a unique dimension to school experiences by encouraging children to engage in active and analytical reflection on the nature of problem solving and by promoting exchanges with peers, interactions that may further enhance both cognitive and social development. Psychologists are only now beginning to document the exact nature of the influence computers have on a range of developmental accomplishments, but early signs are that computers enhance, rather than detract from, the process of development.

TELEVISION

▶ **Sociocultural influence**

According to most estimates, American children watch a great deal of television. Almost all (92 percent) of American homes have at least one color television set (Steinberg, 1985), and as much as one-third of a child's waking life in our society will have been spent watching television (Nielsen, 1988). That is more time than children spend doing any other activity except sleep (Huston, Watkins, & Kunkel, 1989). Moreover, with the advent of cable television and video cassette recorders, children have more opportunities than ever to spend time in front of a television screen. In the United States, over half of all children have access to a VCR in their homes, and about one-third have cable programming (Stipp & Milavsky, 1988). Psychologists do not yet have much data on the impact of VCRs and cable television, but after thirty years of research we can say that television plays a recognizable role in the child's cognitive and social development.

Patterns of Television Viewing Among Children

How much television do American children watch? Babies as young as six months of age attend to television and, on average, are exposed to over one hour per day (Hollenbeck & Slaby, 1979). Estimates of viewing times for older

FIGURE 16.4

Hours of TV Watching as a Function of Children's Age

The amount of time children spend watching television increases throughout early childhood, peaks around age ten or twelve years, then declines in adolescence.

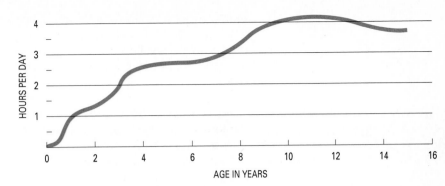

Source: Adapted from Liebert & Sprafkin, 1988.

children vary from about nine hours per week (Anderson, D. R. et al., 1986) to about twenty-eight hours per week (Nielsen, 1988). Television viewing among children, however, shows large individual differences. One research team investigating the viewing habits of three- to five-year-olds found that some children did not watch television at all during a one-week span, whereas others watched as much as seventy-five hours! Moreover, individual patterns of TV viewing were found to remain stable over a period of two years. Thus, the television-viewing habits children acquire in early childhood can be relatively long lasting (Huston et al., 1990).

As Figure 16.4 shows, the time children spend attending to television increases dramatically during the preschool years, especially after age two and a half years; peaks at around age ten to twelve years; and declines during adolescence (Anderson & Levin, 1976; Anderson, D. R. et al., 1986; Calvert et al., 1982). Boys and girls watch television for equally long periods of time, but children from lower social classes tend to be more frequent viewers than children from higher-income backgrounds (Greenberg, 1986).

As they grow older, children also show changes in the types of programs they prefer to watch. Preschoolers prefer to watch nonanimated informative programs specifically designed for children, such as "Sesame Street" or "Mister Rogers' Neighborhood." These programs feature language that children can comprehend easily and characters that are repeated across segments, and they do not require the child to integrate complex elements of a plot or story. Interest in these programs peaks at ages three and a half to four years and then declines. From ages three to five years, children watch more cartoons; by ages five to seven years, they watch comedies and entertainment shows aimed at general audiences. Thus, with age, children select shows that make increasing demands on their ability to comprehend plots and themes (Huston et al., 1990).

▶ **The child's active role**

Children's TV Viewing: Active or Passive?

Contrary to popular belief, television viewing is not always a passive process in which a mesmerized child sits gazing at the screen. The fact that their preferences for shows change with age is just one example of the ways in which children actively control their own TV viewing. Daniel Anderson and his colleagues have conducted numerous studies further demonstrating that children's selection of television programs is influenced by their ability to comprehend content. Certain *formal,* or structural, features of television do serve to "draw in" the viewer, particularly auditory sound effects, laughter, music, and children's and women's voices. Other features, such as visual cuts, motion, and sound effects, maintain the child's attention (Alwitt et al., 1980). In this sense, the child's choices are controlled by individual program elements. But the formal features of television programs are not the sole determinants of what children watch.

Anderson and his coresearchers recorded the visual attention of two- and five-year-old children as they watched a one-hour specially edited version of "Sesame Street" in a laboratory room (Anderson et al., 1981). The videotape contained a normal program segment along with other portions that were altered to reduce the show's comprehensibility while keeping its formal features constant. In one version the dialogue was presented backward, in another the auditory portion was dubbed in Greek, and so on. The results indicated that children's visual attention was greater during the normal portions than in any of the altered segments. In other words, children actively direct their attention to those portions of the show that they most readily understand; they are not merely influenced by sound effects or visual cuts alone.

Children do not always have control of the programs they watch. Families frequently view television together, and parents often pick the shows everyone will see. Furthermore, children's program selections are limited by those shows the broadcasters choose to air on a given day and at a given time. Thus, children are frequently exposed to programming that falls outside their range of comprehension (Huston et al., 1990). Nevertheless, much of children's television viewing is guided by their active selection of programming they understand.

Children's Comprehension of Television Programs

What exactly do young children understand about the various behaviors, roles, and stories that unfold on the programs they watch? Are there developmental changes in children's comprehension of TV programs? Many television shows have complex plots and employ subtle cues that require inferences about characters' motives, intentions, and feelings. In addition, most programs contain changes of scene that require watchers to integrate information across scenes. Research indicates that clear developmental differences exist in children's ability to understand information from television shows, differences that accompany changes in cognitive processing.

Preschoolers can understand short story segments in programs that are specifically targeted for children. When five-year-olds in one study saw four segments from "Sesame Street," each a few minutes long, they were later able to remember the most central elements of each story (Lorch, Bellack, & Augsbach, 1987). When the plots and themes of television shows become more complex, however, young children have difficulties.

More specifically, when they watch programs designed for general audiences, younger children are less likely than older children to remember the *explicit* content of programs; that is, they are less able to recognize the discrete scenes that are essential to understanding the plot. Second- and third-graders in one study remembered only 65 percent of the central content as compared with 90 percent and more for eighth-graders. Even when they do remember explicit information, younger children frequently fail to grasp the *implicit* content communicated by relationships between scenes (Collins et al., 1978). For example, young children may fail to understand a character's motive for aggression if the message is communicated in two scenes separated by several other sequences (Collins, 1983).

▶ **Interaction among domains**

W. Andrew Collins (1983) believes that children's comprehension of implicit content is tied to their emerging cognitive skills, specifically the ability to integrate two pieces of information separated by time or other events. He further suggests that the children's general knowledge and previous experiences can affect their comprehension of the programs they watch. Suppose, for example, that children are asked to retell the content of a show about a murder and the suspect's eventual capture. Children frequently mention *script-based* knowledge (see Chapter 8), drawing from their general storehouse of information on the events that surround the relationships between police and criminals. Older children are more likely than younger children, however, to describe content that was specific to the program they had watched, such as the fact that some police officers in the show did not wear uniforms (Collins, 1983). As children's general knowledge about the world grows, their comprehension of more detailed, specific information in television programs expands as well.

Other research has shown that still another skill—children's growing verbal competency—underlies their ability to understand TV programs. When five-year-olds were tested with standardized IQ tests as well as for their memory of the central and incidental events on a thirty-five-minute television program, their scores on the verbal subscales of the IQ test were significantly correlated with their ability to comprehend the show's central events (Jacobvitz, Wood, & Albin, 1989).

One other important developmental change occurs in relation to television viewing, and that is in children's ability to recognize that most television programming is not real but fabricated. Most five- and six-year-olds do not understand that television characters are actually actors playing roles, and it is not until age eight years and older that the majority of children understand this concept (Dorr, 1983). There are some exceptions: even kindergartners realize that cartoons are fantasy, and a few also understand that news shows are real. By second or third grade, children are increasingly able to distinguish between fantasy and reality on television by using contextual cues provided by the programs themselves, such as the genre of the show or whether animation appears. If a child labels a program as a cartoon or an entertainment show, he will see it as pretend; if he labels it as a news or sports show, he concludes that it is real. With age, children are more likely to consider the specific events and actions carried out by characters, rather than simply the type of show, in determining whether a program is about real life or fantasy (Dorr, 1983).

▶ **Interaction among domains**

Television's Impact on Cognitive and Language Development

Most preschoolers these days readily recognize Big Bird and the Cookie Monster as characters from "Sesame Street," the popular educational program specifically designed to teach cognitive skills to preschool children. But they also learn a lot more, according to research on educational television. Evaluations of the effects of shows like "Sesame Street" demonstrate that television can teach children a range of problem-solving, mathematical, reading, and language skills.

Cognition   "Sesame Street" was specifically designed to provide entertaining ways of teaching children the letters of the alphabet, counting, vocabulary, and similar school-readiness skills. The programs also deliberately include both male and female characters from many racial and ethnic backgrounds. One of the first comprehensive evaluations of the impact of "Sesame Street" was conducted by the Educational Testing Service shortly after the program's inception in 1969 (Ball & Bogatz, 1970). Subjects were preschool children, many from disadvantaged backgrounds, who were tested on an array of cognitive measures both before and after viewing "Sesame Street" at home for a season. Those who watched the show the most frequently showed the greatest gains on several skills, including writing their name and knowing letters, numbers, and forms (see Figure 16.5). A second study conducted two years later found that frequent viewers obtained higher scores on a standardized vocabulary test, adapted better to school, and had more positive attitudes toward school and people of other races than nonwatchers did (Bogatz & Ball, 1972). Thus, the show had effects not only on children's cognitive skills, but also on their prosocial attitudes.

Despite "Sesame Street"'s apparent successes, critics held that the gains made by children who watched the show, though statistically significant, were actually quite small. Rather than closing the gap between underprivileged and advantaged children, they further suggested, the show might actually widen it. Because children in the evaluation studies were given incentives to watch the program, they may have watched it more than they normally would have. According to the skeptics, in real life—that is, without the incentives—advantaged children would be more prone to watch the program and thereby benefit from it. Still another problem was that many children in the evaluation study watched "Sesame Street" with an adult present. Did the show itself have an effect, or did the presence of the adult make a difference (Cook et al., 1975)?

FIGURE 16.5

Television and Enhancement of Language Skills

Preschool children who watch "Sesame Street" show gains in a number of prereading skills, including the ability to recite the alphabet and write their names. The graph shows that children who watched the show the most displayed the greatest gains in performance. (Children in quartile 1 rarely watched the show; those in quartile 2 watched two to three times per week; those in quartile 3 watched four to five times per week; and those in quartile 4 watched more than five times per week.)

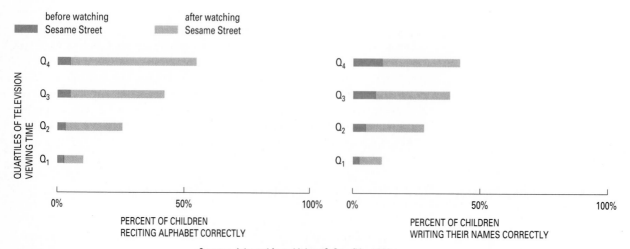

Source: Adapted from Liebert & Sprafkin, 1988.

A recent study by Mabel Rice and her associates (Rice et al., 1990) helps to rule out some of these criticisms. A large sample of three- and five-year-olds was studied over a two-year period. Diaries of television viewing were collected from the families; children's vocabulary skills were also tested. The results showed that parents viewed children's programs less than one-fourth of the time that children watched them and furthermore that the amount of parental co-viewing did not predict children's later vocabulary. Thus, the show itself, not parental presence, was associated with gains in vocabulary. In addition, the sample included families from a broad range of socioeconomic backgrounds. Contrary to earlier suggestions, the findings indicated no relationship between social class and the amount of time children spent watching "Sesame Street."

"Sesame Street" has also been criticized for its short, unrelated segments, a fast-paced format that some developmental psychologists believe may actually impede learning. Jerome and Dorothy Singer (Singer & Singer, 1983) caution that repeated exposure to fast-paced programs may cause children to become overly aroused and inattentive. Children may also come to expect equally high-tempo learning experiences in school and, not finding them, may fail to develop reflective, sustained strategies for learning. Though provocative, however, these criticisms of "Sesame Street" have not been fully tested through empirical research.

Language   The study by Mabel Rice and her colleagues (1990) mentioned earlier suggests that television can promote children's language development. Many programs targeted for children, such as "Electric Company" and "Mister Rogers' Neighborhood," include simplified language, repetitions, recasts, and elaboration of the meanings of words. As we saw in Chapter 7, these forms of language can enhance the child's acquisition of vocabulary and syntax (Rice, 1983). Parents also sometimes use television as a "video picture book" in which events portrayed on the show stimulate verbal exchanges and language learning. When mothers watch television with their young preschoolers, they frequently identify objects, repeat new words, ask questions, or relate the content of the show to the child's own experience (Lemish & Rice, 1986). Such verbal interactions are especially likely when parent and child watch age-appropriate shows, like "Sesame Street."

Is there direct evidence that television can function as a vehicle for vocabulary acquisition? Investigators exposed three- and five-year-old children to twenty new words in a fifteen-minute animated television story and found that both age groups showed gains in comprehension after only two viewings. Three-year-olds learned an average of one to two new words, and five-year-olds learned between four and five words (Rice & Woodsmall, 1988). These findings are all the more impressive considering the brevity of exposure children had to new vocabulary items and the limited efforts of the experimenters to highlight or exaggerate the new words.

▶ **Interaction among domains**   Television's Impact on Social Development

Whipping a towel over his shoulders, a seven-year-old jumps off the couch after watching the movie *Superman* on television. A brother and sister brandish toy swords, the brother mimicking Darth Vader's eerie mechanical voice from the *Star Wars* movies. These common scenes in American households illustrate the power of television to influence children's behavior through direct imitation. Sometimes the messages are more subtle: a male announcer's authoritative voice decrees that this detergent is twice as effective as other brands and that a new sugar cereal is fortified with vitamins. When mostly men's voices are heard in television commercials, the indirect message is that males, more than females, have the knowledge and authority to make such definitive statements. Whether by directly providing models for children to imitate or by indirectly offering messages about social categories, television can promote behaviors as diverse as aggression and sex typing. Psychologists and those who make social policy have been particularly concerned with how television affects the child's social behavior and understanding, for better or for worse.

Aggression   Any child turning on the television has an extraordinarily good chance of encountering the portrayal of violence. On average, five to six acts of physical aggression per hour occur on prime-time television. The rate is even higher on weekends, when children's programming predominates (Gerbner et al., 1986). For over two decades, concerned parents and psychologists alike have asked the pressing question: does viewing televised violence produce aggression in children? Hundreds of research studies have examined this issue, and several reports on the topic have been issued by government agencies and professional organizations. The Surgeon General's Report of 1972, the report of the National Institutes of Mental Health in 1982, and the American Psychological Association (1985) all agree—there is a small, but consistently found causal relationship between viewing aggression on TV and aggressive behavior in children (Huston, Watkins, & Kunkel, 1989).

Despite these reports, heated exchanges among the research community, media executives, and formulators of public policy still occur. On one side, many researchers believe that televised violence provides children with frequent and potent models for aggression, models that—in keeping with the principles of social learning theory—suggest to the child that physical attacks are acceptable in one's repertoire of behaviors. According to social learning theory, two processes operate: first, children may learn new acts of aggression, and second, aggressive behaviors already in their response repertoire are disinhibited (Bandura, 1969). On the other side are proponents of the **catharsis hypothesis,** who maintain that viewing television violence actually reduces the tendency to behave aggressively. The person who watches one television character commit aggression against another, they argue, experiences the violence vicariously and releases any stored-up frustrations or hostilities, thereby lessening the likelihood of committing actual aggression himself (Feshbach & Singer, 1971).

Still a third point of view in this debate is expressed by those researchers who caution that the evidence tying television to aggression is weak or flawed and that any conclusions about the causal relationship between these two variables are premature (Freedman, 1984, 1986). Because there is little evidence to support the catharsis hypothesis and because the research findings tend to implicate a causal role for aggressive television programming, most experts believe there are good reasons to be concerned over the typical child's heavy exposure to TV violence.

catharsis hypothesis   Theory that viewing television violence reduces tendencies to behave aggressively by releasing built-up frustrations or hostilities.

The most controlled evaluations of TV and aggression have been laboratory studies in which children are randomly assigned to one or more treatment conditions in which at least one group is exposed to a film or video portrayal of an actor behaving aggressively. Children's subsequent behavior is then systematically compared with that of a control group of children who have not viewed the aggressive episode. The studies spearheading the notion that violence on film could influence the child's aggression level were conducted by Albert Bandura and his colleagues in the 1960s (Bandura, Ross, & Ross, 1963a, 1963b).

In these studies, nursery school children were randomly assigned to one of five experimental conditions. The first group watched from behind a one-way mirror as a model in the next room performed a series of unusual acts of physical and verbal aggression toward a plastic, inflated Bobo doll. For example, the model hit the doll with a hammer, kicked it, and said, "Hit the Bobo doll!" and "Kick the Bobo doll!" A second group of children watched a model perform these same actions, but the presentation was on film. A third group watched an adult disguised as a cartoon figure behave like the models in the previous two conditions. A fourth group observed an adult model behaving in a nonaggressive manner, sitting quietly and ignoring the Bobo doll and the toys associated with aggressive behavior. The last group of children saw no model at all.

Figure 16.6 shows the mean number of aggressive responses displayed by children in each condition. Children who had seen an aggressive model performed a large number of imitative aggressive acts, copying even the subtle details of the model's behaviors. In addition, they frequently added their own forms of physical and verbal aggression. Most important from the standpoint of our present discussion, the performance of children in the film-model group

These photos, taken from Bandura's classic experiments, illustrate with stark clarity the power of imitation in influencing children's aggression. In the top row, an adult model displays various aggressive actions against a "Bobo doll." The middle and bottom rows depict the sequence of imitative aggression shown by a male and female subject in the experiment. Their behaviors closely mimic the specific actions they had previously seen the adult perform.

FIGURE 16.6

The Effect of Watching Modeled Aggression

After children saw a live, filmed, or live dressed-up "cartoon" model behave aggressively in the laboratory (first three bars), they were much more likely to imitate the model's aggression than were children who had seen no model at all (fourth bar) or viewed a model behaving nonaggressively (fifth bar).

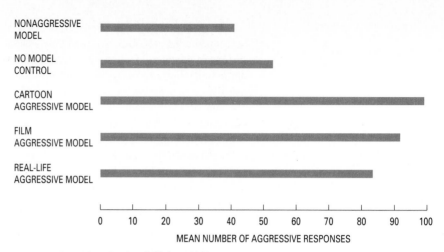

Source: Adapted from Bandura & Walters, 1963.

was no different from that of subjects who saw the real-life model. Models on film were just as powerful as "live" models in eliciting aggression.

Some researchers have questioned whether the act of punching a Bobo doll should be considered aggressive rather than "playful" behavior, and whether the film segment used by Bandura resembles the kinds of scenes depicted in actual television programs (Freedman, 1984). Another criticism is that when the child sees a violent program in the laboratory without the myriad other stimuli that occur under more natural conditions, his attention becomes focused on the experiment's theme. The child may think that the experimenter condones or even expects aggression and therefore behaves more aggressively then he normally would. Finally, laboratory studies of aggression may have limited generalizability to real-life situations. Most have not employed real TV shows as stimuli, and observations are typically conducted in settings unlike those most children experience in their daily routines.

Field experiments, in which children are exposed to actual television programs and are observed in more natural contexts, respond to many of these criticisms. You may recall from Chapter 1 that in one such study, Lynette Friedrich and Aletha Stein (1973) found that preschool children who viewed violent cartoons declined on several measures of self-control, including the ability to tolerate delays, obedience of school rules, and task persistence. At the same time, children who saw prosocial programs displayed higher tolerance for delays, more rule obedience, and greater task persistence than control children.

Large-scale correlational studies add to the evidence connecting violence on television with aggression. One study of almost one thousand children showed that aggression and televised violence are actually linked in a reciprocal way (Huesmann, Lagerspetz, & Eron, 1984). The investigators asked each subject's peers to rate how aggressive this child was, and they also noted how much television violence each child watched. After the data were collected over a period of three years, the results showed that the amount of violent TV shows children watched at the start of the study predicted how aggressive they were three years later. In turn, aggression also influenced TV viewing. Children who were aggressive at the start of the study watched more violent

▶ **The child's active role**

shows three years later than they did initially. These results are consistent with a bidirectional model of influence: children become more aggressive after a diet of violent television, and their aggression seems to stimulate even more viewing of violent shows. The investigators also found that children are more likely to be aggressive if they identify strongly with aggressive characters in the shows and believe life is depicted realistically in TV programs.

Can parents do anything to mitigate the potentially harmful consequences of certain television shows on their children's behavior? One obvious tactic is to limit the amount of time children are permitted to watch violent programs. Another is to watch television together with their children and discuss the negative consequences of violence. By suggesting prosocial methods of conflict resolution, parents can help youngsters develop a more critical attitude toward the programs they watch (Dorr, 1986). In a school-based intervention program, 170 children who frequently watched violent programs were divided into an experimental and control group. Over a period of six to eight weeks, children in the experimental group participated in regular training sessions in which they were taught that (1) the behaviors of aggressive TV characters are not representative of the way most people act, (2) aggressive scenes on TV are not real but are staged by means of special effects and camera techniques, and (3) the average person uses more positive strategies to resolve interpersonal problems than those shown on violent TV programs. Discussions of these issues followed the presentation of a high-action "superhero" show. During the same time period, control subjects saw nonviolent shows and participated in neutral discussions. By the end of the study, children in the experimental group were significantly less aggressive than the control children, demonstrating that the real-life behaviors of children can be modified by effecting changes in their attitudes about television (Huesmann et al., 1983).

Prosocial Behavior Just as television can encourage negative social behaviors, it can also foster prosocial development. We saw in the field experiment conducted by Friedrich and Stein (1973) that lower-class children who watched "Mister Rogers' Neighborhood" for a four-week period increased in their prosocial interpersonal behaviors. Other researchers have also found that programs that contain messages about cooperation, altruism, and sharing promote these behaviors in children.

Consider what happens, for example, when children view two segments from "Lassie," one that shows the main character, Jeff, risking his life to save a puppy and one that does not show an example of helping. Children were randomly assigned to one of these two conditions or, alternatively, watched a comedy episode from the "Brady Bunch" series. After children saw one of the shows, they were invited to play a game in which they could earn points to win desirable toys. While the children played, the experimenters played a tape of a dog barking with increasing franticness. Children who saw the prosocial episode of "Lassie" were much more likely to show helping behaviors than children in the other two conditions (Sprafkin, Liebert, & Poulos, 1975).

A meta-analysis of 190 studies of prosocial television indicates that these kinds of programs can have powerful effects on child behavior. In fact, the statistical findings indicated that the effects of prosocial programming are even greater than the effects of antisocial programming on child behavior (Hearold, 1986). Unfortunately, the power of television to influence children in these positive ways has yet to be fully utilized.

Sex-Role Stereotypes   Television shows like "The Cosby Show" and "Growing Pains" portray males and females in nontraditional roles in which fathers cook and care for their children and women are employed outside of the home. These programs, however, are not standard fare on commercial television. Women appear in only one-third or fewer of the roles in television programs and commercials, and when they do they typically play romantic or family roles. Working women, when they are shown, are likely to be employed in sex-typed positions (for example, as secretaries and nurses); if they occupy positions of authority, they are often cast as villains (Huston & Alvarez, 1990). Consistent with stereotypes of female behavior, girls and women on television act nurturantly, passively, or emotionally. In contrast, males are more frequently the central characters of television shows, and they act forcefully, have more power and authority than women, and display reason rather than emotion (Lovdal, 1989; Signorielli, 1989).

The televised stereotypes of male and female behaviors apparently do affect children. Correlational studies show that the more television children watch, the more they identify with stereotyped roles of their own sex (Frueh & McGhee, 1975; McGhee & Frueh, 1980). Other research shows that the children most likely to be affected by the sexist content of television are middle-class girls of above-average intelligence, the same group of children who otherwise display liberal gender-related attitudes (Morgan, 1982). Longitudinal studies point out that these correlations do not arise simply because sex-typed children watch more television. Michael Morgan's (1982, 1987) work shows that the viewing habits of adolescents during the initial phases of his studies were slightly correlated with their sex-role attitudes, but the relationships became stronger six months and one year later, suggesting that beliefs about male and female roles change after a heavy diet of television viewing.

In the same way that television is able to reinforce traditional sex-role standards, it has the power to make these standards less stereotyped. In 1975, a television series called "Freestyle" was developed to counteract children's stereotypical beliefs about sex-typed characteristics and behaviors. Each episode of the series presented stories of people in sex-atypical activities. In one episode, for example, a mother returns to work after teaching the other members of her family how to take care of themselves by performing household chores. The story revolves around the father's recognition that his wife's job increases her self-esteem and the happiness of the family and depicts his gradually increasing pleasure in performing "feminine" household chores. Studies of children who watched this series indicate that they were more accepting of nontraditional roles, activities, and occupations than children who did not watch the series. In addition, changes in children's beliefs persisted for as long as nine months after viewing the series (Johnston, Ettema, & Davidson, 1980).

Consumer Behavior   In 1989, American children between the ages of four and twelve spent $6 billion of their own money on candy and other snacks, toys and games, clothing, electronic equipment, and an assortment of other consumer goods (McNeal, 1990). Because of their tremendous spending power, either directly or through their parents, children are the targets of a significant number of television commercials. Of special concern to many child advocates is the proliferation of television shows linked to specific toys (for example, cartoon shows that portray the same characters as toys) and product endorsements for expensive items, such as athletic shoes, by popular sports figures and other celebrities, all of which put pressure on children to spend money.

Children who are heavy television viewers respond to the messages of commercials. For one thing, they frequently request the cereals and other foods they see advertised (Taras et al., 1989). Children, however, do not always recognize commercials as messages specifically intended to influence their behavior; four- and five-year-olds, for example, believe that "commercials are to help and entertain you." It is usually not until children are eight years of age or older that they understand that commercials are intended to influence viewers' buying habits (Ward, Reale, & Levinson, 1972). Because young children are not able to critically evaluate the information presented to them in commercials, they may pressure their parents to purchase expensive toys and clothes, heavily sugared foods, and other products, resulting in conflicts with parents and other undesirable outcomes.

Fortunately, children respond to materials designed to educate them about commercials. When children in one study saw one-minute segments describing the intent of commercials and the fact that they were not always truthful, they were more skeptical about the product claims than children who had not seen these educational messages (Christenson, 1982).

Television holds enormous promise in enhancing children's intellectual and social functioning. Children attend to and comprehend programs that are geared for their specific age group, and they often show gains in cognitive and language skills when they watch educational programs like "Sesame Street." Besides providing a rich source of intellectual stimulation, television—like parents, peers, and teachers—can also convey potent and influential messages about prosocial behaviors, nonstereotyped sex roles, and responsible consumer behavior. Many critics of television, however, hold that the medium's potential to promote desirable developmental outcomes thus far has gone largely untapped.

THEMES IN DEVELOPMENT

THE INFLUENCE OF SCHOOL AND TELEVISION

▶ **How does the sociocultural context influence the child's experiences with school and television?**

The society the child grows up in determines whether she will have any exposure to school, computers, or television in the first place. Not all cultures emphasize formal schooling, and not all children have access to television or computers. In terms of school, the skills, communication styles, and social organization of the child's background culture may either harmonize or conflict with the predominant values of the educational system. In the latter case, children may experience academic failure as well as lower self-esteem. The KEEP model suggests that children's academic performance climbs when educational practices are compatible with the child's cultural background. Similarly, studies of Asian students show how their high academic achievement is linked to cultural beliefs about education.

▶ **How does the child play an active role in experiences with school and television?**

In their schooling experiences, children show greater academic achievement and higher self-esteem when school structures facilitate their greater participation in the educational process. In addition, educational techniques such as peer collaboration, classroom autonomy, and computer activities in group contexts all seem to foster development by promoting the child's active involvement. In their television viewing, children actively direct their attention to programs they understand, although sometimes they are more passively exposed to programs selected by others. Aggressive children are also likely to select television shows that depict violence, furthering their exposure to models for violence.

▶ **How do the child's experiences with school and television interact with the various domains of development?**

Children's developmental accomplishments affect their school experience and vice versa. Children who have good peer relations and social skills are more likely to adjust well to school in the first place. Once in school, children typically have experiences that can promote their intellectual advancement, peer relations, and self-concept. For example, open classrooms can enhance peer interaction skills, and the academic feedback students receive can influence self-esteem. Peer learning techniques especially foster developmental accomplishments in many domains. Experiences with computers, too, can facilitate cognitive and social development.

As children's cognitive skills grow, so does their ability to comprehend both the explicit and implicit information portrayed on television. At the same time, educational television programs can enhance cognitive growth in such areas as pre-reading skills. Moreover, television can influence social behavior through the strong messages it portrays about violence, prosocial acts, and sex-role stereotypes.

SUMMARY

The major influence school exerts on children lies in fostering academic achievement and shaping their self-esteem. Several aspects of the school's physical environment—school size, class size, and the physical arrangement of the classroom—bear on development. Generally, smaller schools and classes, as well as circular seating arrangements, are beneficial to students by promoting their active participation in the educational process. Philosophies of education, which are translated into specific teaching models, also play a role. Some alternative educational practices, such as the *open classroom, peer collaboration,* and *cooperative learning,* have been found to produce especially positive effects on students' social and personal development.

The way in which children adjust to school transitions, such as the start of school or junior high school, can influence their subsequent attitudes toward and accomplishments in school. The most important element of the school experience, though, is the teacher. Teacher expectancies, classroom management techniques, and the classroom climate all make a difference in students' academic achievement and self-esteem.

Children's school achievement can vary depending on their cultural background. The *cultural deficit hypothesis,* which was once used to explain the lower achievement of African American children in U.S. schools, has more recently been replaced by the *cultural compatibility hypothesis.* The results of the KEEP project demonstrate that children's academic performance climbs when educational tactics incorporate elements of their background culture. Children who go to school in Asian societies show higher levels of achievement than American children, especially in mathematics and science. These differential patterns of achievement are associated with variations in students' classroom experiences.

Computers can influence both cognitive and social development. Children with *computer-assisted instruction (CAI)* experience show modest gains in academic achievement, and children who are exposed to more intelligent tutoring software or programming experiences show gains in higher-order cognitive skills, such as *heuristic strategies* for problem solving. Computers can enhance social development by stimulating peer exchanges as students attempt to solve problems. Boys are more likely than girls to learn computer skills, a fact that may be the result of sex-role stereotypes among parents, teachers, and the students themselves.

One of childhood's most frequent activities is watching television. Children show increases in the amount of television they view until they reach adolescence, at which point TV viewing declines. Although the formal features of television often guide young children's attention, children also actively attend to the portions of programs they comprehend. As children's cognitive and verbal skills expand, so does their ability to comprehend both the explicit and implicit elements of programs. Television can promote certain prereading skills, such as knowledge of the alphabet and numbers, as well as improve children's vocabulary. Television can also have an impact on social behavior, specifically in the display of aggression, prosocial behavior, sex-role stereotypes, and consumer behavior.

GLOSSARY

Accommodation   In Piagetian theory, a component of adaptation; process of modification in thinking (schemes) that takes place when old ways of understanding something no longer fit.

Accommodation (visual)   Visuomotor process by which small involuntary muscles change the shape of the lens of the eye so that images of objects seen at different distances are brought into focus on the retina.

Adaptation   In Piagetian theory, inborn tendency to adjust or become more attuned to conditions imposed by the environment; takes place through assimilation and accommodation.

Age-history confound   In longitudinal studies, changes in originally defined variables due to changes in sociohistorical context; affects generalizability of findings.

Aggression   Physical or verbal behaviors intended to harm or irritate someone else.

Allele   Alternate form of a specific gene; provides a genetic basis for many individual differences.

Altruism   Behavior carried out to help another without expectation of reward.

Ambivalent attachment   Infant-caregiver relations characterized by tension in the infant and a combination of clinging and avoidance behaviors.

Amniocentesis   Method of sampling the fluid surrounding the developing fetus by insertion of a needle; usually performed in sixteenth week of pregnancy. Used to diagnose fetal genetic and developmental disorders.

Amniotic sac   Fluid-filled, transparent protective membrane surrounding the fetus.

Analogical transfer   Ability to employ the solution to one problem in other similar problems.

Anal stage   In Freudian theory, the second psychosexual stage, between about one and three years of age, during which libidinal energy is focused on control of defecation.

Androgen   Class of male or masculinizing hormones.

Androgyny   Sex-role orientation in which a person possesses high levels of personality characteristics associated with both sexes.

Assimilation   In Piagetian theory, a component of adaptation; process of interpreting an experience in terms of current ways (schemes) of understanding things.

Attachment   Strong emotional bond that emerges between infant and caregiver.

Attention   State of alertness or arousal that allows the individual to focus on a selected aspect of the environment.

Attentional inertia   Continued sustained attention after an initial period of focused attention.

Attribution   Inference about a person's characteristics that cause that person's behavior.

Authoritarian parent   Parent who relies on coercive techniques to discipline the child and who displays a low level of nurturance.

Authoritative parent   Parent who sets limits on a child's behavior by using the technique of induction and who displays a high degree of nurturance.

Autonomy   *See* moral relativism

Autosomes   Twenty-two pairs of homologous chromosomes. The two members of each pair are similar in size, shape, and genetic function. The two sex chromosomes are excluded from this class.

Avoidant attachment   Infant-caregiver relations characterized by neutral emotion in the infant and few affectional behaviors directed to the caregiver.

Babbling   Consonant-vowel utterances that characterize the infant's first attempts to vocalize.

Basic emotion   Emotion such as joy, sadness, or surprise that appears early in infancy and seems to have a biological foundation. Also called *primary emotion*.

Behavior analysis   Learning theory perspective that explains the development of behavior by the principles of classical and operant conditioning.

Behavior genetics   Study of how characteristics and behaviors of individuals such as intelligence and personality are influenced by the interaction between genotype and experience.

Blastocyst   Hollow, spherical cell mass formed about the fourth day after conception by differentiation of the morula; embeds in uterine lining.

Broca's area   Portion of the cerebral cortex that controls expressive language.

Canalization   Concept that the development of some attributes is governed primarily by the genotype and that only extreme environmental conditions will alter the phenotypic pattern for these attributes.

Cardinality   Principle that the last number in a set of counted numbers refers to the number of items in that set.

Case study   In-depth description of psychological characteristics and behaviors of an individual.

Catch-up growth   Increase in growth rate after some factor such as illness or poor nutrition has disrupted the expected, normal growth rate.

Categorical perception   Inability to distinguish between sounds that vary on some basic physical dimension except when those sounds lie at opposite sides of a critical juncture point on that dimension.

Categorical self   Conceptual process starting in the early preschool years in which the child begins to classify him- or herself according to easily observable categories (sex, age, physical capacities, skills, and so forth) that can be used to distinguish people.

Catharsis hypothesis   Theory that viewing television violence reduces tendencies to behave aggressively by releasing built-up frustrations or hostilities.

Centration   In Piagetian theory, tendency of the child to focus on only one aspect of a problem.

Cephalocaudal development   Pattern that organs, systems, and motor movements near the head tend to develop earlier than those near the feet.

Cerebral cortex   Uppermost, outer, and largest portion of the brain; undergoes rapid differentiation during last few months of prenatal development and first few years of life. Various regions are specialized to carry out sensory, motor, associative, and other neural processing.

Chorionic villus sampling   Method of sampling fetal chorionic cells; usually performed in eighth or ninth week of pregnancy. Used to diagnose embryonic genetic and developmental disorders.

Chromosomes   Threadlike structures of DNA, located in the nucleus of cells, that form a collection of genes. A human body cell normally contains forty-six chromosomes.

Circular reaction   In Piagetian theory, repetition of some action or behavior because of the pleasure it brings.

Classical conditioning   Type of learning in which a neutral stimulus repeatedly paired with another stimulus that elicits a reflexive response eventually begins to elicit the reflexlike response by itself.

Cleavage   Mitotic cell division of the zygote.

Clinical method   Flexible, open-ended interview method in which questions are modified in reaction to the child's responses.

Clique   Peer group of five to ten children who frequently interact together.

Codominance   Condition in which individual, unblended characteristics of two alleles are reflected in the phenotype.

Coercive cycle   Pattern of reciprocal aggression between parent and child.

Cognition   Processes involved in thinking and mental activity, such as attention, memory, and problem solving.

Cognitive-developmental theory   Theoretical orientation, most frequently identified with Piaget, that explains development in terms of the active construction of psychological structures concerned with the interpretation of experience. These structures are assumed to be established at roughly similar ages by all children to form a series of qualitatively distinct stages in development.

Cohort effect   Characteristics shared by individuals growing up in a given sociohistorical context that can influence developmental outcomes.

Complex emotion   Emotion such as guilt and envy that appears later in childhood and requires more complex cognitive and social skills.

Comprehension monitoring   Ability to evaluate the adequacy of a communication.

Computer-assisted instruction   Use of computers to provide tutorial information and drill-and-practice routines.

Concept   Definition of a set of information on the basis of some general or abstract principle.

Concordance rate   Percentage of pairs of twins in which both members have a specific trait identified in one of the twins.

Concrete operational stage   In Piagetian theory, the third stage of development—approximately from seven to eleven years of age—in which thought is logical when stimuli are physically present.

Conditioned emotional response   Emergence of an emotional reaction to an originally neutral stimulus through classical conditioning.

Conditioned response (CR)   A learned response that is exhibited to a previously neutral stimulus (CS) as a result of pairing the CS with an unconditioned stimulus (UCS).

Conditioned stimulus (CS)   A neutral stimulus that begins to elicit a response similar to the unconditioned stimulus (UCS) with which it has been paired.

Configurational knowledge   Child's use of landmarks and routes in integrated, holistic ways to represent physical space.

Confluence model   Hypothesis that intellectual attainment is influenced by birth order and spacing among children in the family.

Conscience   In Freudian theory, the part of the superego that defines unacceptable behaviors and actions, usually as also defined by the parents.

Conservation tasks   Problems that require the child to make judgments about the equivalence of two displays; used to assess stage of cognitive development.

Contextual model   Theoretical orientation in developmental psychology that recognizes that, for each individual, the environment consists of a wide range of biological, physical, and sociocultural settings.

Control theory Hypothesis about parent-child interactions that suggests that the intensity of one partner's behavior affects the intensity of the other's response.

Conventional level In Kohlberg's theory, the second level of moral reasoning, in which the child conforms to the norms of the majority and wishes to preserve the social order.

Cooing Vowel-like utterances that characterize the infant's first attempts to vocalize.

Cooperative learning Peer-centered learning experience in which students of different abilities work together in small groups to solve academic problems. Often these groups compete against each other within the classroom.

Cooperative play Interactive play in which children's actions are reciprocal.

Correlation coefficient (r) Statistical measure, ranging from $+1.00$ to -1.00, that summarizes the strength and direction of the relationship between two variables; does not provide information about causation.

Correlational study Study assessing whether changes in one variable are accompanied by systematic changes in another variable.

Critical period *See* sensitive period

Cross-cultural study Study comparing subjects in different cultural contexts.

Cross-fostering study Research study in which children are reared in environments that differ from those of their biological parents.

Cross-gender behavior Behavior usually seen in a member of the opposite sex. Term generally is reserved for behavior that is persistently sex atypical.

Crossing over Process during the first stage of meiosis when genetic material is exchanged between autosomes.

Cross-sectional study Study in which subjects of different ages are examined at the same point in time.

Crowd Large group of peers that is characterized by specific traits or reputation.

Crystallized intelligence Mental skills derived from cultural experience.

Cultural compatibility hypothesis Theory that school instruction is most effective if it is consistent with the practices of the child's background culture.

Debriefing Providing research participants with a statement of the true goals of a study after initially deceiving them about its purposes.

Deferred imitation Ability to imitate a model's behavior hours, days, and even weeks after observation.

Delay of gratification Capacity to wait for some period of time before performing a tempting activity or attaining some highly desired outcome; a measure of individuals' ability to regulate their own behavior.

Deoxyribonucleic acid (DNA) Long, spiral staircase–like sequence of molecules created by nucleotides identified with the blueprint for genetic inheritance.

Dependent variable Behavior that is measured; suspected effect of an experimental manipulation.

Deprivational dwarfism Condition in which child's low levels of human growth hormone and failure to grow at normal rates are believed to be due solely to emotional deprivation. If placed in a supportive environment before adolescence, these children return to normal growth rates.

Development Physical and psychological changes in the individual over a lifetime.

Developmental psychology Systematic and scientific study of changes in human behaviors and mental activities over time.

Deviation IQ IQ score computed by comparing the child's performance with that of a standardization sample.

Dishabituation *See* recovery from habituation

Disorganized/disoriented attachment Infant-caregiver relations characterized by the infant's fear of the caregiver, confused facial expressions, and a combination of anxious and resistant attachment behaviors.

Display rules Cultural guidelines about when, how, and to what degree to display emotions.

Disposition Enduring tendencies and competencies characterizing the individual.

Dizygotic twins *See* fraternal twins

Domain-specific knowledge Knowledge about a specific content area.

Dominance hierarchy Group's organized infrastructure, based on power relationships.

Dominant allele Allele whose characteristics are reflected in the phenotype even when part of a heterozygous genotype. Its genetic characteristics tend to mask the characteristics of other alleles.

Down syndrome *See* Trisomy 21

Ecological systems theory Bronfenbrenner's theory that development is the joint outcome of individual and experiential events. Experience consists not only of immediate surroundings but also of the larger social and cultural systems that affect an individual's life.

Effectance motivation Inborn desire theorized by Robert White to be the basis for the infant's and child's efforts to master and gain control of the environment.

Ego In Freudian theory, a mental structure that fosters the formation of representational and cognitive mechanisms and operates according to the reality principle.

Egocentrism Preoperational child's inability to separate his or her own perspective from that of others.

Ego ideal In Freudian theory, the part of the superego that defines the positive standards for which an individual strives. This component is acquired via parental rewarding of desired behaviors.

Elaboration Memory strategy in which subjects link

items to be remembered in the form of an image or sentence.

Embryonic period   Period of prenatal development during which major biological organs and systems are formed. Begins at about the tenth to fourteenth day after conception when implantation occurs, and ends at about the eighth week after conception, with the onset of bone formation.

Emotions   Complex behaviors involving physiological, expressive, and experiential components produced in response to some external or internal event.

Empathic reasoning   Form of prosocial reasoning in which children attempt to put themselves in another's place and understand that person's feelings.

Empathy   Vicarious response to the feelings of others.

Empiricism   Theory that environmental experiences shape the individual; more specifically, that all knowledge is derived from sensory experiences.

Episodic memory   Memory for events that took place at a specific time and place.

Equilibration   In Piagetian theory, an innate self-regulatory process that begins with the discovery of a discrepancy between the child's cognitive structures or schemes and results, through accommodation and assimilation, in more organized and powerful schemes for effectively thinking about and adapting to the environment.

Estrogen   Hormone produced by the ovaries that contributes to pubertal changes in primary and secondary sexual characteristics and that helps prepare the uterus for implantation by a zygote.

Ethology   Theoretical orientation and discipline concerned with the evolutionary origins of behavior and its adaptive and survival value in animals, including humans.

Exosystem   In Bronfenbrenner's ecological systems theory, environmental settings that indirectly affect the child by influencing the various microsystems forming the child's immediate environment.

Expansion   Adult's repetition and elaboration of the child's utterance.

Experimental design   Research method in which one or more independent variables are manipulated to determine the effect on other, dependent, variables.

Expiatory punishment   Young child's belief that punishment need not be related to a transgression as long as the punishment is severe enough.

Expressive aphasia   Loss of the ability to speak fluently.

Expressive personality characteristics   Characteristics associated with emotions or relationships with people; usually considered feminine.

Expressive style   Type of early language production in which children use many social words.

Extended family   Family group that includes secondary relations such as grandparents, aunts, uncles, and cousins as well as parents and siblings.

Externality effect   Tendency for infants younger than two months of age to focus on the external features of a complex stimulus and to explore the internal features less systematically.

External locus of control   Individual's sense that outside factors such as luck, fate, and other people primarily influence success and failure and the events that happen to him or her. Contrast with *internal locus of control*.

Factor analysis   Statistical technique that examines relationships among a large number of correlations to find a smaller set of explanatory "factors."

Failure to thrive   Label applied to any child whose growth in height or weight is below the third percentile for children of the same age; may arise from inadequate social-emotional relationships with caregivers.

Fast-mapping   Deriving meanings of words from the context in which they are spoken.

Fetal alcohol syndrome (FAS)   Cluster of fetal abnormalities stemming from mother's consumption of alcohol; includes growth retardation, defects in facial features, and intellectual retardation.

Fetal monitoring device   Medical device used to monitor fetal heartbeat during delivery.

Fetal period   Period of prenatal development marked by relatively rapid growth of organs and preparation of body systems for functioning in postnatal environment. Begins about the eighth week after conception and ends at birth.

Field experiment   Experiment conducted in a "natural" real-world setting such as the child's home or school.

Fluid intelligence   Biologically based mental abilities that are relatively uninfluenced by cultural experiences.

Focus on states   Preoperational child's tendency to treat two or more connected events as unrelated.

Formal operational stage   In Piagetian theory, the last stage of development—approximately from eleven to fifteen years of age—in which thought is abstract and hypothetical.

Fragile X syndrome   Disorder associated with a pinched region of the X chromosome; a leading genetic cause of mental retardation in males.

Fraternal twins   Siblings sharing the same womb at the same time but who originate from two different eggs fertilized by two different sperm cells. Also called *dizygotic twins.*

Frustration-aggression hypothesis   Idea that the blocking or frustrating of an organism's goals leads to aggression.

Functional theory   Hypothesis that early concepts are based on the child's perception of the uses of objects.

Gametes   Sperm cells in males, egg cells in females, normally containing only twenty-three chromosomes.

Gender constancy   Knowledge, usually gained around age six or seven years, that one's gender does not change as a result of alterations in appearance, behaviors, or desires.

Gender identity Knowledge, usually gained by age three years, that one is male or female.

Gender schema Cognitive organizing structure for information relevant to sex typing.

Gender stability Knowledge, usually gained by age four years, that one's gender does not change over time.

Gene Large segment of nucleotides within a chromosome that codes for the production of proteins and enzymes. These proteins and enzymes underlie traits and characteristics inherited from one generation to the next.

Generative language Unique and novel combinations of words and sentences that speakers produce without having heard them before.

Genetic counseling Medical and counseling specialty concerned with determining and communicating the likelihood that prospective parents will give birth to a baby with a genetic disorder.

Genetic screening Systematic search for certain genotypes using a variety of tests to detect individuals at risk for developing genetic anomalies, bearing offspring with potential chromosome or gene defects, or having genetic susceptibility to environmental agents.

Genital stage In Freudian theory, the final psychosexual stage, beginning with adolescence, in which sexual energy is directed to peers of the opposite sex.

Genotype Total genetic endowment inherited by an individual.

Germinal period Period lasting about ten to fourteen days following conception before the fertilized egg becomes implanted into the uterine wall. Also called *period of the zygote.*

Gestational age Age of fetus derived from onset of mother's last menstrual period.

Glial cells Brain cells that provide the material from which myelin is created, nourish neurons, and provide a scaffolding for neuron migration.

Habituation Gradual decline in intensity, frequency, or duration of a response over repeated or lengthy occurrence of the same stimulus.

Hedonistic reasoning Form of prosocial reasoning in which children say they will help in order to obtain material rewards.

Heritability Proportion of variability in the phenotype that is estimated to be accounted for by genetic influences.

Heteronomy *See* moral realism

Heterozygous Genotype in which two alleles of a gene are different. The effects on a trait will depend on how the two alleles interact.

Heuristic strategies Methods of problem solving that involve higher-order analyses, such as subdividing the problem into smaller parts or comparing it with previously solved problems.

Homozygous Genotype in which two alleles of a gene are identical, thus having the same effects on a trait.

Human genome Entire inventory of nucleotide base pairs comprising the genes and chromosomes of humans.

Huntington's disease Dominant genetic disorder characterized by involuntary movements of the limbs, mental deterioration, and premature death. Symptoms appear between thirty and fifty years of age and death within twenty years of onset of these symptoms.

Hypothetical reasoning Ability to systematically generate and evaluate potential solutions to a problem.

Id In Freudian theory, a mental structure that is the seat of libidinal energy and that operates according to the pleasure principle.

Identical twins Two individuals who originate from a single zygote (one egg fertilized by one sperm), which early in cell division separates to form two separate cell masses. Such twins have an identical genetic makeup. Also called *monozygotic twins.*

Identity In Eriksonian psychosocial theory, the acceptance of both self and society, a concept that must be achieved at every stage but is especially important during adolescence.

Identity crisis Period, usually during adolescence, characterized by considerable uncertainty about the self and the role the individual is to fulfill in society.

Identity (personal) Coherent view of who one is and wants to be along with values and beliefs that emerge during adolescence.

Immanent justice Young child's belief that punishment will inevitably follow a transgression.

Imprinting Form of learning, difficult to reverse, during a sensitive period in development in which an organism tends to stay near a particular stimulus.

Independent variable Variable manipulated by the experimenter; the suspected cause.

Individual differences Unique characteristics that distinguish a person from other members of a larger group.

Induction Parental control technique that relies on the extensive use of reasoning and explanation as well as the arousal of empathic feelings.

Inflection Alteration to a word, such as tense or plural form, that indicates its syntactical function.

Information processing Theoretical approach that views humans, much like computers, as having a limited ability to process information.

Informed consent Subject's formal acknowledgement that he or she understands the purposes, procedures, and risks of a study and agrees to participate in it.

Inner self Aspects of the self, such as thoughts and feelings, that are associated with the mind which are private and unobservable by others.

Inner speech   Interiorized form of private speech.

Instrumental competence   Child's display of independence, self-control, achievement orientation, and cooperation.

Instrumental conditioning   *See* operant conditioning

Instrumental personality characteristics   Characteristics associated with acting on the world; usually considered masculine.

Intelligence quotient (IQ)   Numerical score received on an intelligence test.

Interactive synchrony   Reciprocal, mutually engaging cycles of caregiver-child behaviors.

Interagent consistency   Consistency in application of disciplinary strategies among different caregivers.

Intermodal perception   Coordination of information from more than one sensory modality to perceive an object or to make inferences about its characteristics.

Internal locus of control   Individual's sense that his or her own efforts and activities influence success and failure and the events that happen to him or her. Contrast with *external locus of control.*

Inter-rater reliability   Degree to which two or more observers agree in their observations.

Intra-agent consistency   Consistency in a single caregiver's application of discipline from one situation to the next.

Karyotype   Pictorial representation of an individual's chromosomes.

Kinetic cue   Perceptual information provided by movement of eyes, head, body, or of objects in the environment; important source of information for depth perception, even for infants.

Lagging-down growth   Condition in which, after periods of rapid acceleration because of congenital or hormonal disorders, growth is slowed so that subsequent increases in height conform to those normally expected for the individual.

Landmark   Distinctive location or cue that the child uses to negotiate or represent a spatial environment.

Latency   In Freudian theory, a period from about six to eleven years of age, when libidinal energy is suppressed and energies are focused on intellectual, athletic, and social achievements appropriate to the adult years.

Lateralization   Process by which one hemisphere of the brain dominates the other. In most individuals the left hemisphere is more involved in language processing, whereas the right is more involved in processing spatial and emotional information.

Learned helplessness   Belief that one has little control over situations, perhaps because of lack of ability or inconsistent outcomes.

Learning   Relatively permanent change in behavior as a result of such experiences as exploration, observation, and practice.

Limited-resource model   Information-processing model that emphasizes the allocation of finite energy within the cognitive system.

Linguistic contrast   Correction of the child's incorrect utterance by pointing out both the error and the correct term.

Longitudinal study   Research in which the same subjects are repeatedly tested over a period of time, usually years.

Long-term memory   Memory that holds information for extended periods of time.

Macrosystem   In Bronfenbrenner's ecological systems theory, major historical events and the broad values, practices, and customs promoted by a culture.

Mastery orientation   Belief that achievements are based on one's own efforts rather than luck or other factors beyond one's control.

Maturation   Gradual unfolding over time of genetic programs for development that are independent of experience.

Mean length utterance   Average number of morphemes per utterance.

Means-ends behavior   Deliberate behavior employed to attain a goal.

Mediator   Cognitive process that bridges the gap between an environmental event and the individual's eventual response to it.

Meiosis   Process of cell division that takes place to form the gametes; normally results in twenty-three chromosomes in each human egg and sperm cell rather than the full complement of forty-six chromosomes.

Memory span   Number of stimulus items that can be recalled after a brief interval of time.

Memory strategy   Mental activity, such as rehearsal, that enhances memory performance.

Menarche   First occurrence of menstruation.

Mental age   Expression of the child's mental abilities by comparing performance with that of children of the same, younger, or older ages.

Mesosystem   In Bronfenbrenner's ecological systems theory, the environment provided by the interrelationships among the various settings of the microsystem.

Meta-analysis   Statistical examination of a body of research studies to assess the effect of the common central variable.

Metacognition   Awareness and knowledge of cognitive processes.

Metalinguistic awareness   Ability to reflect on language as a communication tool and on the self as a user of language.

Metamemory Understanding of memory as a cognitive process.

Metaphor Figurative language in which a term is transferred from the object it customarily designates to describe a comparable object or event.

Microsystem In Bronfenbrenner's ecological systems theory, the immediate environment provided in such settings as the home, school, workplace, and neighborhood.

Mitosis Process of cell division taking place in most cells of the human body that results in a full complement of forty-six chromosomes in each cell; reproduces identical genetic material in succeeding generations of cells.

Monozygotic twins *See* identical twins

Morality of care and responsibility Tendency to make moral judgments on the basis of concern for others.

Morality of justice Tendency to make moral judgments on the basis of reason and abstract principles of equity.

Moral realism In Piaget's theory of moral development, the first stage of moral reasoning, in which moral judgments are made on the basis of the consequences of an act. Also called *heteronomy*.

Moral relativism In Piaget's theory of moral development, the second stage of moral reasoning, in which moral judgments are made on the basis of the actor's intentions. Also called *autonomy*.

Morpheme Smallest unit of meaning in speech.

Morula Solid ball of cells formed by cleavage of the zygote as it passes through the Fallopian tube.

Motherese Simple, repetitive, high-pitched speech of caregivers to young children; includes many questions.

Multistore model Information-processing model that describes a sequence of mental structures through which information flows.

Mutation Sudden change in molecular structure of a gene; may occur spontaneously or be caused by an environmental event such as radiation. Some mutations are lethal, but others are not and may be passed on from one generation to the next in the form of alleles of a gene.

Mutual exclusivity bias Tendency for children to assume that unfamiliar words label new objects.

Myelin Sheath of fatty cells that insulates and speeds neural impulses by about tenfold.

Naturalistic observation Study in which observations of naturally occurring behavior are made in real-life settings.

Nature-nurture debate Ongoing theoretical controversy over whether development is the result of the child's genetic endowment or the kinds of experiences he or she has had.

Needs-oriented reasoning Form of prosocial reasoning in which children express a concern for the physical or psychological needs of others.

Negative correlation Relationship in which changes in one variable are accompanied by systematic changes in another variable in the opposite direction.

Negative reinforcement Withdrawal of an aversive stimulus that, upon its removal, serves to strengthen a preceding response.

Neural tube Tube in which central nervous system develops. Failure of tube to close can cause spina bifida or no brain growth.

Neuron Nerve cell within central nervous system electrochemically designed to transmit messages between cells.

Network Model of semantic memory that consists of associations among closely related items.

Niche picking Tendency to actively select an environment compatible with a genotype.

Nominal Word that labels objects, people, or events; the first type of word most children produce.

Norm of reaction *See* range of reaction

Norms Measure of average values and variations in some aspect of development such as physical size and motor skill development in relation to age.

Nuclear family Family group that consists solely of parents and their children.

Nucleotide Repeating basic building block of DNA consisting of nitrogen-based molecules of adenine, thymine, cytosine, and guanine.

Object concept Realization that objects exist even when they are not within view. Also called *object permanence*.

Object permanence *See* object concept

Observational learning Learning that takes place by simply observing another person's behavior.

Observer bias Tendency of researchers to interpret ongoing events as consistent with their research hypotheses.

One-to-one correspondence Understanding that two sets are equivalent in number if each element in one set can be mapped onto a unique element in the second set with none left over.

Open classroom Nontraditional educational approach that emphasizes peer interaction, free-flowing movement of students around different activity centers in the classroom, and structured opportunities for students to "discover" knowledge.

Open word Variable word that accompanies the pivot word in a pivot grammar.

Operant conditioning Type of learning in which patterns of behavior that are learned and the frequency with which they are performed depend on whether the behaviors produce rewarding or desired outcomes. Also called *instrumental conditioning*.

Operation In Piagetian theory, mental action such as reversibility; in limited-resource models, activities such as the identification of stimuli that require mental energy.

Operational definition Specification of variables in terms of measurable properties.

Oral stage In Freudian theory, the first psychosexual stage, between birth and about one year of age, during which libidinal energy is focused on the mouth.

Ordinality Principle that a number refers to an item's order within a set, as in the third finisher in a race.

Organization Memory strategy in which subjects reorder items to be remembered on the basis of category or some other higher-order relationships. In Piagetian theory, the inborn tendency for structures and processes to become more systematic and coherent.

Overextension Tendency to apply a label to a broader category than the term actually signifies.

Overregularization Inappropriate application of syntactic rules to words and grammatical forms that show exceptions.

Parallel play Side-by-side independent play that is not interactive.

Peer Companion of approximately the same age and developmental level.

Peer collaboration Peer-centered learning experience in which pairs of students work together on academic problems, usually without competing against other students.

Perception Process of organizing and interpreting sensory information.

Perceptual differentiation Process postulated by Eleanor and James Gibson in which experience contributes to the ability to make increasingly finer perceptual discriminations and to distinguish stimulation arising from each sensory modality.

Perinatal environment Medical, physical, and social environment established immediately before, during, and after birth of an infant.

Period of the zygote *See* germinal period

Permissive parent Parent who sets few limits on the child's behavior.

Person perception Process of describing and conceptualizing someone's personality.

Perspective taking Ability to take the role of another person and understand what that person is thinking, feeling, or knows, often with the purpose of solving some problem in communicating or interacting with that individual. Also called *role taking*.

Phallic stage In Freudian theory, the third psychosexual stage, between about three and five years of age, when libidinal energy is focused on the genitals and resolution of unconscious conflict with the parent of the same sex leads to establishment of the superego.

Phenotype Observable and measurable characteristics and traits of an individual; a product of the interaction of the genotype with the environment.

Phenylketonuria (PKU) Autosomal recessive disorder involving protein metabolism; can lead to severe mental retardation. Dietary intervention can dramatically reduce negative impact.

Phoneme Smallest unit of sound that changes the meanings of words.

Phonology Fundamental sound units and combinations of units in a given language.

Physiological measure Measurement of heart rate, brain activity, respiration rate, or other bodily responses to stimulation.

Pituitary gland Major gland located near the hypothalamus that releases a number of hormones affecting physical growth and development.

Pivot grammar Early two-word grammar in which one word is repeated and a series of other words fills the second slot.

Pivot word Repeated, or anchor, word in a pivot grammar.

Placenta Support organ formed by cells from both blastocyst and uterine lining; serves as exchange site for oxygen, nutrients, and waste products.

Plasticity Capacity of immature systems, including regions of the brain and the individual neurons within those regions, to take on different functions as a result of experience.

Polygenic Phenotypic characteristic influenced by two or more genes.

Positive correlation Relationship in which changes in one variable are accompanied by systematic changes in another variable in the same direction.

Positive reinforcement Occurrence of a stimulus that strengthens a response when it follows that response. Also known as a reward.

Postconventional level In Kohlberg's theory, the third level of moral reasoning, in which laws are seen as the result of a social contract and individual principles of conscience may emerge.

Postnatal development Period in development following birth.

Postural reflexes Reflexes associated with maintaining a particular, usually upright, orientation and that disappear or become incorporated within voluntary behavior.

Power assertion Parental control technique that relies on the use of forceful commands, physical punishment, and removal of material objects or privileges.

Pragmatics Rules for using language effectively within a social context.

Preconventional level In Kohlberg's theory, the first level of moral reasoning, in which morality is motivated by the avoidance of punishments and attainment of rewards.

Preoperational stage In Piagetian theory, the second

stage of development—approximately from two to seven years of age—in which thought is now symbolic in form.

Prenatal development Period in development from conception to the onset of labor.

Primacy effect Tendency for subjects to display good recall for early items in a list.

Primary emotion *See* basic emotion

Primary reinforcer Reward that gratifies biological needs or drives.

Primitive reflexes Reflexes identified with survival and protection of the individual that usually disappear during the first year of life.

Private speech Child's vocalized speech to himself that directs behavior.

Production deficiency Failure of children under age seven years to spontaneously generate memory strategies.

Productive language Meaningful language spoken or otherwise produced by the individual.

Progesterone Hormone produced by the ovaries that helps prepare uterus for implantation by a zygote.

Prosocial behavior Positive social action performed to benefit others.

Prosody Patterns of intonation, stress, and rhythm that communicate meaning in speech.

Protodeclarative communication Use of a gesture to call attention to an object or event.

Protoimperative communication Use of a gesture to issue a command or request.

Proximodistal development Pattern that organs and systems of the body near the middle tend to develop earlier than those near the periphery.

Psychoanalytic models Set of theories, most frequently associated with Freud and his followers, that emphasizes the importance of unconscious motivations in determining personality development and behavior.

Psychometric model Theoretical perspective that quantifies individual differences in test scores to establish a rank order of abilities.

Psychometrician Psychologist who specializes in the construction and interpretation of standardized tests.

Psychosexual theory of development Freud's theory that many aspects of an individual's personality originate in an early and broad form of childhood sexuality. The focus of gratification of this sexuality, however, changes from one region of the body to another throughout various stages of development.

Psychosocial theory of development Erikson's theory that personality development proceeds through eight stages during which adaptive modes of functioning are established to meet the variety of demands framed by society.

Puberty Developmental period during which a sequence of physical changes takes place that transforms the individual from immaturity to one capable of reproduction.

Punishment Aversive stimulus, or the removal of a pleasant stimulus, that decreases the frequency of a response when it is the outcome of that response.

Punishment by reciprocity Belief that punishment should be related to the transgression.

Quasi-experiment Study in which the assignment of subjects to experimental groups is determined by their natural experiences.

Questionnaire Set of standardized questions administered to subjects in written form.

Random assignment Use of principles of chance to assign subjects to treatment and control groups; avoids systematic bias.

Range of reaction Range of phenotypic differences possible as a result of different environments interacting with a specific genotype. Also called *norm of reaction.*

Rare event learning mechanism Learning model that postulates the development of attention, memory, and other cognitive processes as a prerequisite to language achievements.

Recall memory Ability to reproduce stimuli that have previously been encountered.

Recast Repetition of a child's utterance along with some new elements.

Recency effect Tendency for subjects to show good recall for the last few items in a list.

Receptive aphasia Loss of the ability to comprehend the speech of others.

Receptive language Ability to comprehend spoken speech.

Recessive allele Allele whose characteristics do not tend to be expressed when part of a heterozygous genotype. Its genetic characteristics tend to be masked by other alleles.

Recognition memory Ability to identify whether a stimulus has been previously encountered.

Recovery from habituation Reinstatement of the intensity, frequency, or duration of a response to a stimulus that has changed. Also called *dishabituation.*

Reduplicated babbling Repetition of simple consonant-vowel combinations in the early stages of language development.

Referential communication Communication in situations that require the speaker to describe an object to a listener or to evaluate the effectiveness of a message.

Referential style Type of early language production in which the child uses mostly nominals.

Reflex Involuntary movement in response to touch, light, sound, and other forms of stimulation; controlled by subcortical neural mechanisms.

Regulator gene   Gene that switches other genes on and off.

Rehearsal   Memory strategy that involves repetition of items to be remembered.

Rehearsal set   Items actually repeated by subjects as they engage in rehearsal.

Reliability   Degree to which a measure will yield the same results if administered repeatedly.

Retrieval cue   Aid or cue to extract information that has already been stored in memory.

Reversibility   In Piagetian theory, the ability to mentally reverse or negate an action or transformation.

Rhythmical stereotypies   Repeated sequences of movements such as leg kicking and hand waving or banging that seem to have no apparent goal.

Role taking   *See* perspective taking

Rough-and-tumble play   Active, physical play that carries no intent of imposing harm on another child.

Route mapping   Child's use of sequential directional changes to negotiate or represent a spatial environment.

Saccade   Rapid eye movement to inspect an object or to view a stimulus in the periphery of the visual field.

Scaffolding   Temporary aid provided by one person to encourage, support, and assist a lesser-skilled person in carrying out a task or completing a problem. The model provides knowledge and skills that are learned and gradually transferred to the learner.

Scheme   In Piagetian theory, the mental structure underlying a coordinated and systematic pattern of behaviors or thinking applied across similar objects or situations.

Scientific method   Use of objective, measurable, and repeatable techniques to gather information.

Script   Organized scheme or framework for commonly experienced events.

Secondary reinforcer   Object or person that attains rewarding value because of its association with a primary reinforcer.

Secular trend   Consistent pattern of change over generations.

Secure attachment   Child's display of close affectional ties to the caregiver.

Secure base for exploration   Infant's use of the mother as a reference point during active exploration of a new environment.

Self   Realization of being an independent, unique, stable, and self-reflective entity; the beliefs, knowledge, feelings, and characteristics that the individual ascribes to his or her own personhood.

Self-concept   Perceptions, conceptions, and values one holds about oneself.

Self-esteem   One's feelings of worth; extent to which one senses one's attributes and actions are good, desired, and valued.

Self-regulation   Process by which children are expected to control their own behaviors in accordance with the standards and desires of their caregivers and community, especially in the absence of other adults.

Semantic feature hypothesis   Hypothesis that early concepts are based on the child's perception of the shared features of objects.

Semantic memory   Memory for general concepts or facts.

Semantics   Meanings of words or combinations of words.

Semiotic function   Ability to symbolize objects.

Sensation   Basic information in the external world processed by the sensory receptors.

Sensitive period   Brief period during which specific kinds of experiences have significant positive or negative consequences for development and behavior. Also called *critical period.*

Sensorimotor stage   In Piagetian theory, the first stage of cognitive development—from birth to approximately two years of age—in which thought is based primarily on action.

Sensory store   Memory store that holds information for very brief periods of time in a form that closely resembles the initial input.

Separation anxiety   Distress shown by the infant when the caregiver leaves the immediate environment.

Sequential study   Study that examines groups of children of different ages over a period of time; usually shorter than a longitudinal study.

Sex-atypical behavior   Behavior inconsistent with the norm for a particular sex.

Sex linked   Attribute, trait, or disorder inherited from genes located on the X chromosome.

Sex-role development   *See* sex typing

Sex-role stereotypes   Expectations or beliefs that individuals within a given culture hold about the behaviors characteristic of males and females.

Sex segregation   Clustering of individuals into same-sex groups.

Sex-typical behavior   Behavior usually associated with one sex.

Sex typing   Process by which individuals acquire the characteristics and behaviors prescribed by their culture for their sex. Also called *sex-role development.*

Sickle cell anemia   Genetic blood disorder common in regions of Africa and other areas of the world where malaria is found and among descendants of these regions. Abnormal blood cells are unable to carry adequate amounts of oxygen.

Sickle cell trait   Symptoms shown by those possessing a heterozygous genotype for sickle cell anemia.

Signaling behavior   In ethological theory, a behavior such as crying or smiling that brings the caregiver physically close to the infant.

Single-case design   Study that follows only one or a few children over a period of time.

Skeletal maturity Extent to which cartilage has ossified to form bone; provides the most accurate estimate of how much additional growth will take place in the individual.

Smooth visual pursuit Consistent, unbroken tracking by the eyes that serves to maintain focus on a moving visual target.

Social cognition Individual's knowledge of humans and the activities in which they engage, including knowledge of self, the traits and qualities of others, and the roles and rules for interacting in social settings and structures.

Social comparison Process in which individuals define themselves in relation to the skills, attributes, and qualities of others; believed to become especially important in contributing to self-concept during the middle childhood years.

Social conventions Behavioral rules that regulate social interactions, such as dress codes and degrees of formality in speech.

Socialization Process by which children acquire the social knowledge, skills, and attitudes valued by the larger society.

Social learning theory Theoretical approach emphasizing the importance of learning through observation and imitation of behaviors modeled by others.

Social pretend play Play that makes use of imaginary and symbolic objects and social roles, often enacted among several children. Also called *sociodramatic play*.

Social referencing Looking to another individual for emotional cues in interpreting a strange or ambiguous event.

Sociodramatic play *See* social pretend play

Sociohistorical theory Vygotsky's theory of development emphasizing the historical (cultural) and social processes that are part of the context of development for every child.

Sociometric nomination Peer assessment measure in which children are asked to name a specified number of peers who fit a certain criterion, such as "peers you would like to walk home with."

Sociometric rating scale Peer assessment measure in which children rate peers on a number of social dimensions.

Solitary play Individual play, performed without regard for what others are doing.

Sound localization Ability to determine a sound's point of origin.

Specificity hypothesis Hypothesis that specific cognitive achievements precede specific language achievements.

Stage Developmental period during which the organization of thought and behavior is qualitatively different from that of an earlier or later period.

Stereopsis Ability to perceive a single image of an object even though perceptual input is binocular and differs slightly for each eye; significant source of cues for depth perception.

Strange Situation Standardized test that assesses the quality of infant-caregiver attachment.

Stranger anxiety Fear or distress shown by an infant at the approach of an unfamiliar person.

Structural gene Gene responsible for the production of enzymes and other protein molecules. Humans are estimated to have about 100,000 structural genes, some of which have been located on particular chromosomes.

Structured interview Standardized set of questions administered orally to subjects.

Structured observation Study in which behaviors are recorded as they occur within a situation constructed by the experimenter, usually in the laboratory.

Subject reactivity Tendency of subjects who know they are under observation to alter natural behavior.

Sudden infant death syndrome (SIDS) Sudden, unexplained death of infant or toddler as a result of failure to continue breathing during sleep.

Superego In Freudian theory, a mental structure that monitors socially acceptable and unacceptable behavior.

Syntax Grammatical rules that dictate how words can be combined.

Systems theory Model for understanding the family that emphasizes the reciprocal interactions among various members.

Tabula rasa Literally, "blank slate"; the belief that infants are born with no innate knowledge or abilities.

Telegraphic speech Early two-word speech that contains few modifiers, prepositions, or other connective words.

Temperament Stable, early appearing constellation of individual personality attributes believed to have a hereditary basis; includes sociability, emotionality, and activity level.

Teratogen Any environmental agent that can cause deviations in prenatal development. Consequences may range from death to behavioral problems.

Test bias Idea that the content of traditional standardized tests does not adequately measure the competencies of children from diverse cultural backgrounds.

Testosterone Hormone produced by the testes of males that contributes to fetal sex differentiation and also triggers the emergence of pubertal changes.

Theory Set of ideas or propositions that helps organize or explain observable phenomena.

Time-out Disciplinary strategy in which a child is removed from all possible sources of reinforcement, both positive and negative, after committing a transgression.

Transactional theory Theoretical perspective in psychology that highlights the reciprocal relationship between child and environment, emphasizing that development is a seamless alloy formed by the child's being affected by and, in turn, actively influencing the environment.

Triarchic theory   Theory developed by Robert Sternberg that intelligence consists of three major components: (1) the ability to adapt to the environment; (2) the ability to employ fundamental information-processing skills; and (3) the ability to deal with novelty and automatize processing.

Trisomy   Condition in which an extra chromosome is present.

Trisomy 21   Inheritance of an extra copy of chromosome 21; associated with a distinct set of physical features and moderate to severe mental retardation. Commonly known as *Down syndrome.*

Turnabout   Element of conversation that requests a response from the child.

Turn taking   Alternating vocalization by parent and child.

Ultrasonography   Method of using sound wave reflections to provide a representation of the developing fetus. Used to estimate gestational age and to detect fetal physical abnormalities.

Umbilical cord   Conduit of blood vessels through which oxygen, nutrients, and waste products are transported between placenta and embryo.

Unconditioned response (UCR)   The response that is automatically elicited by the unconditioned stimulus (UCS).

Unconditioned stimulus (UCS)   A stimulus that, without prior training, elicits a reflexlike response (unconditioned response).

Underextension   Application of a label to a narrower class of objects than the term signifies.

Uninvolved parent   Parent who is emotionally detached from the child and focuses on his or her own needs as opposed to the child's.

Validity   Degree to which an assessment procedure ac-

tually measures the variable under consideration.

Variable   Factor having no fixed or constant value in a given situation.

Vergence   Ability of the eyes to rotate in opposite directions to fixate objects at different distances; improves rapidly during first few months after birth.

Viability   Ability of the baby to survive outside the mother's womb.

Visual acuity   Ability to make fine discriminations among elements in a visual array by detecting contours, transitions in light patterns that signal borders and edges.

Visual cliff   Experimental apparatus used to test depth perception in which the surface on one side of a glass-covered table is made to appear far below the surface on the other side.

Vocabulary spurt   Period of rapid word acquisition that typically occurs early in language development.

Wernicke's area   Portion of the cerebral cortex that controls language comprehension.

Working memory   Short-term memory store in which mental operations such as rehearsal and categorization take place.

X chromosome   Larger of the two sex chromosomes associated with genetic determination of sex. Normally females have two X chromosomes; males, only one.

Y chromosome   Smaller of the two sex chromosomes associated with genetic determination of sex. Normally males have one Y chromosome; females, none.

Zone of proximal development   Range of various kinds of support and assistance provided by an expert (usually an adult) who helps children to carry out activities they currently cannot complete but will later be able to accomplish independently.

Zygote   Fertilized egg cell.

REFERENCES

Abel, E. L. (1980). Smoking during pregnancy: A review of effects on growth and development of offspring. *Human Biology, 52*, 593–625.

Abel, E. L. (1981). Behavioral teratology of alcohol. *Psychological Bulletin, 90*, 564–581.

Abel, E. L. (1982). Consumption of alcohol during pregnancy: A review of effects on growth and development of offspring. *Human Biology, 54*, 421–453.

Abel, E. L. (1989). *Behavioral teratogenesis and behavioral mutagenesis: A primer in abnormal development.* New York: Plenum Press.

Abel, E. L., Rockwood, G. A., & Riley, E. P. (1986). The effects of early marijuana exposure. In E. P. Riley & C. V. Vorhees (Eds.), *Handbook of behavioral teratology.* New York: Plenum Press.

Abel, E. L., & Sokol, R. J. (1987). Incidence of fetal alcohol syndrome and economic impact of FAS-related anomalies. *Drug and Alcohol Dependency, 19*, 51–70.

Aber, J. L., & Allen, J. P. (1987). Effects of maltreatment on young children's socioemotional development: An attachment theory perspective. *Developmental Psychology, 23*, 406–414.

Aboud, F. E., & Skerry, S. (1983). Self and ethnic concepts in relation to ethnic constancy. *Canadian Journal of Behavioral Science, 15*, 14–26.

Abramovitch, R., Corter, C., Pepler, D. J., & Stanhope, L. (1986). Sibling and peer interaction: A final follow-up and a comparison. *Child Development, 57*, 217–229.

Abramovitch, R., & Grusec, J. E. (1978). Peer imitation in a natural setting. *Child Development, 49*, 60–65.

Abramovitch, R., Pepler, D., & Corter, C. (1982). Patterns of sibling interaction among preschool-age children. In M. E. Lamb & B. Sutton-Smith (Eds.), *Sibling relationships: Their nature and significance across the lifespan.* Hillsdale, NJ: Erlbaum.

Abravanel, E. (1968). The development of intersensory patterning with regard to selected spatial dimensions. *Monographs of the Society for Research in Child Development, 33*(2, Serial No. 118).

Acredolo, L. P., & Goodwyn, S. W. (1988). Symbolic gesturing in normal infants. *Child Development, 59*, 450–466.

Acredolo, L. P., & Goodwyn, S. W. (1990a). Sign language among hearing infants: The spontaneous development of symbolic gestures. In V. Volterra & C. J. Erting (Eds.), *From gesture to language in hearing and deaf children.* New York: Springer-Verlag.

Acredolo, L. P., & Goodwyn, S. W. (1990b). Sign language in babies: The significance of symbolic gesturing for understanding language development. In R. Vasta (Ed.), *Annals of child development* (Vol. 7). Greenwich, CT: JAI Press.

Acredolo, L. P., Pick, H. L., & Olsen, M. G. (1975). Environmental differentiation and familiarity as determinants of children's memory for spatial location. *Developmental Psychology, 11*, 495–501.

Adams, R. J. (1989). Newborns' discrimination among mid- and long-wavelength stimuli. *Journal of Experimental Child Psychology, 47*, 130–141.

Adams, R. J., Maurer, D., & Davis, M. (1986). Newborns' discrimination of chromatic from achromatic stimuli. *Journal of Experimental Child Psychology, 41*, 267–281.

Adams, R. S., & Biddle, B. J. (1970). *Realities of teaching.* New York: Holt, Rinehart & Winston.

Adamson, L. B., & Bakeman, R. (1985). Affect and attention: Infants observed with mothers and peers. *Child Development, 56*, 582–593.

Adelson, E., & Fraiberg, S. (1974). Gross motor development in infants blind from birth. *Child Development, 45*, 114–126.

Ainsworth, M. D. S., Bell, S. M., & Stayton, D. J. (1971). Individual differences in strange situation behavior of one-year-olds. In H. R. Schaffer (Ed.), *The origins of human social relations.* London: Academic Press.

Ainsworth, M. D. S., Bell, S. M., & Stayton, D. J. (1972). Individual differences in the development of some attachment behaviors. *Merrill-Palmer Quarterly, 18*, 123–143.

Ainsworth, M. D. S., Bell, S. M., & Stayton, D. J. (1974). Infant-mother attachment and social development: "Socialization" as a product of reciprocal responsiveness to signals. In M. R. Richards (Ed.), *The integration of the child into a social world.* London: Cambridge University Press.

Ainsworth, M. D. S., Blehar, M. C., Waters, E., & Wall, S. (1978). *Patterns of attachment: A psychological study of the strange situation.* Hillsdale, NJ: Erlbaum.

Alberts, B., Bray, D., Lewis, J., Raff, M., Roberts, K., & Watson, J. D. (1983). *Molecular biology of the cell.* New York: Garland.

Alexander, I. E., & Babad, E. Y. (1981). Returning the smile of a stranger: Within-culture and cross-cultural comparisons of Israeli and American children. *Genetic Psychology Monographs, 103*, 31–77.

Alexander, K. L., & Entwistle, D. R. (1988). Achievement in the first 2 years of school: Patterns and processes. *Monographs of the Society for Research in Child Development, 53*(2, Serial No. 218).

Allen, J. P., Weissberg, R. P., & Hawkins, J. A. (1989). The relation between values and social competence in early adolescence. *Developmental Psychology, 25*, 458–464.

Alwitt, L. F., Anderson, D. R., Lorch, E. P., & Levin, S. R. (1980). Preschool children's visual attention to attributes of television. *Human Communication Research, 7*, 52–67.

711

Ambros, V., & Horvitz, H. R. (1984). Heterochronic mutants of the nematode *Caenorhabditis elegans*. *Science, 226,* 409–416.

American Association of University Women. (1991). *Short change in girls, short change in America* [Summary]. Washington, DC: American Association of University Women.

American Fertility Society. (1988). Ethical considerations of the new reproductive technologies. *Fertility and Sterility, 46*(Suppl. 2), 1S–7S.

American Medical Association. (1985). AMA diagnostic and treatment guidelines concerning child abuse and neglect. *Journal of the American Medical Association, 254,* 796–800.

American Psychological Association. (1985). *Violence on television.* Washington, DC: APA Board of Ethical and Social Responsibility for Psychology.

Amsterdam, B. K. (1972). Mirror self-image reactions before age two. *Developmental Psychobiology, 5,* 297–305.

Anderson, D. R., Choi, H. P., & Lorch, E. P. (1987). Attentional inertia reduces distractibility during young children's TV viewing. *Child Development, 58,* 798–806.

Anderson, D. R., & Levin, S. R. (1976). Young children's attention to "Sesame Street." *Child Development, 47,* 806–811.

Anderson, D. R., Lorch, E. P., Field, D. E., Collins, P. A., & Nathan, J. G. (1986). Television viewing at home: Age trends in visual attention and time with TV. *Child Development, 57,* 1024–1033.

Anderson, D. R., Lorch, E. P., Field, D. E., & Sanders, J. (1981). The effects of TV program comprehensibility on preschool children's television viewing behavior. *Child Development, 52,* 151–157.

Anderson, K. E., Lytton, H., & Romney, D. M. (1986). Mothers' interactions with normal and conduct-disordered boys: Who affects whom? *Developmental Psychology, 22,* 604–609.

Andiman, W. A., & Horstmann, D. M. (1984). Congenital and perinatal viral infections. In M. B. Bracken (Ed.), *Perinatal epidemiology.* New York: Oxford University Press.

Angoff, W. H. (1988). The nature-nurture debate, aptitudes, and group differences. *American Psychologist, 43,* 713–720.

Anisfeld, M. (1991). Neonatal imitation. *Developmental Review, 11,* 60–97.

Annett, M. (1973). Laterality of childhood hemiplegia and the growth of speech and intelligence. *Cortex, 9,* 4–33.

Anooshian, L. J., & Young, D. (1981). Developmental changes in cognitive maps of a familiar neighborhood. *Child Development, 52,* 341–348.

Antonov, A. N. (1947). Children born during the siege of Leningrad in 1942. *Journal of Pediatrics, 30,* 250–259.

Apgar, V. (1953). A proposal for a new method of evaluation of the newborn infant. *Anesthesia and Analgesia: Current Researches, 32,* 260–267.

Applebee, A. N., Langer, J. A., Mullis, I. V. S., & Jenkins, L. B. (1990). *The writing report card, 1984–1988.* Princeton, NJ: Educational Testing Service.

Appleton, T., Clifton, R., & Goldberg, S. (1975). The development of behavioral competence in infancy. In F. D. Horowitz (Ed.), *Review of child development research* (Vol. 4). Chicago: University of Chicago Press.

Arend, R., Gove, F. L., & Sroufe, L. A. (1979). Continuity of individual adaptation from infancy to kindergarten: A predictive study of ego-resiliency and curiosity in preschoolers. *Child Development, 50,* 950–959.

Ariès, P. (1962). *Centuries of childhood: A social history of family life* (R. Baldick, Trans.). New York: Vintage.

Aronfreed, J. (1969). The concept of internalization. In D. A. Goslin (Ed.), *Handbook of socialization theory and research.* Chicago: Rand McNally.

Aronfreed, J. (1976). Moral development from the standpoint of a general psychological theory. In T. Lickona (Ed.), *Moral development and moral behavior.* New York: Holt, Rinehart & Winston.

Arsenio, W. F., & Ford, M. E. (1985). The role of affective information in social-cognitive development: Children's differentiation of moral and conventional events. *Merrill-Palmer Quarterly, 31,* 1–17.

Asher, S. R. (1983). Social competence and peer status: Recent advances and future directions. *Child Development, 54,* 1427–1434.

Asher, S. R. (1985). An evolving paradigm in social skill training research with children. In B. H. Schneider, K. H. Rubin, & J. E. Ledingham (Eds.), *Children's peer relations: Issues in assessment and intervention.* New York: Springer-Verlag.

Asher, S. R., & Dodge, K. A. (1986). The identification of socially rejected children. *Developmental Psychology, 22,* 444–449.

Asher, S. R., & Renshaw, P. D. (1981). Children without friends: Social knowledge and social skill training. In S. R. Asher & J. M. Gottman (Eds.), *The development of children's friendships.* Cambridge: Cambridge University Press.

Asher, S. R., & Wheeler, V. A. (1985). Children's loneliness: A comparison of rejected and neglected peer status. *Journal of Consulting and Clinical Psychology, 53,* 500–505.

Ashmead, D. H., Clifton, R. K., & Perris, E. E. (1987). Precision of auditory localization in human infants. *Developmental Psychology, 23,* 641–647.

Ashmead, D. H., Hill, E. W., & Talor, C. R. (1989). Obstacle perception by congenitally blind children. *Perception & Psychophysics, 46,* 425–433.

Aslin, R. N. (1987a). Motor aspects of visual development in infancy. In P. Salapatek & L. Cohen (Eds.), *Handbook of infant perception: From sensation to perception* (Vol. 1). Orlando, FL: Academic Press.

Aslin, R. N. (1987b). Visual and auditory development in infancy. In J. D. Osofsky (Ed.), *Handbook of infant development* (2nd ed.). New York: Wiley.

Aslin, R. N., & Dumais, S. T. (1980). Binocular vision in infants: A review and a theoretical framework. In H. W. Reese & L. P. Lipsitt (Eds.), *Advances in child development and behavior* (Vol. 15). New York: Academic Press.

Aslin, R. N., Pisoni, D. B., & Jusczyk, P. W. (1983). Auditory development and speech perception in infancy. In M. M. Haith & J. J. Campos (Eds.), *Handbook of child psychology: Vol. II. Infancy and developmental psychobiology.* New York: Wiley.

Aslin, R. N., & Smith, L. B. (1988). Perceptual development. *Annual Review of Psychology, 39,* 435–473.

Atkins, W. T. (1988). Cocaine: The drug of choice. In I. J. Chasnoff (Ed.), *Drugs, alcohol, pregnancy and parenting.* Boston: Kluwer Academic Publishers.

Atkinson, R. C., & Shiffrin, R. M. (1968). Human memory: A proposed system and its control processes. In K. W. Spence & J. T. Spence (Eds.), *The psychology of learning and motivation: Advances in research and theory* (Vol. 2). New York: Academic Press.

Au, T. K., & Laframboise, D. E. (1990). Acquiring color names via linguistic contrast: The influence of contrasting terms. *Child Development, 61,* 1808–1823.

Avery, A. W. (1982). Escaping loneliness in adolescence: The case for androgyny. *Journal of Youth and Adolescence, 11,* 451–459.

Aylward, G. P., Pfeiffer, S. I., Wright, A., & Verhulst, S. J. (1989). Outcome studies of low birth weight infants published in the last decade: A metaanalysis. *Journal of Pediatrics, 115,* 515–520.

Azmitia, M., & Perlmutter, M. (1989). Social influences on children's cognition: State of the art and future directions. In H. W. Reese (Ed.), *Advances in child development and behavior* (Vol. 22). New York: Academic Press.

Bachman, J. G. (1970). *The impact of family background and intelligence on tenth grade boys: Vol. 2. Youth in transition.* Ann Arbor: Survey Research Center, Institute for Social Research.

Bahrick, L. E. (1983). Infants' perception of substance and temporal synchrony in multimodal events. *Infant Behavior and Development, 6,* 429–451.

Baillargeon, R. (1987). Object permanence in 3 1/2- and 4 1/2-month-old infants. *Developmental Psychology, 23,* 655–664.

Baker-Ward, L., Ornstein, P. A., & Holden, D. J. (1984). The expression of memorization in early childhood. *Journal of Experimental Child Psychology, 37,* 555–575.

Baldwin, J. M. (1895). *Mental development in the child and the race.* New York: Macmillan.

Baldwin, J. M. (1930). [Autobiography]. In C. Murchison (Ed.), *A history of psychology in autobiography* (Vol. 1). Worcester, MA: Clark University Press.

Ball, S., & Bogatz, G. (1970). *The first years of Sesame Street: An evaluation.* Princeton, NJ: Educational Testing Service.

Ball, W., & Tronick, E. (1971). Infant responses to impending collision: Optical and real. *Science, 171,* 818–820.

Ballard, B. D., Gipson, M. T., Guttenberg, W., & Ramsey, K. (1980). Palatability of food as a factor influencing obese and normal-weight children's eating habits. *Behavior Research and Therapy, 18,* 598–600.

Balogh, R. D., & Porter, R. H. (1986). Olfactory preferences resulting from mere exposure in human neonates. *Infant Behavior and Development, 9,* 395–402.

Bandura, A. (1965). Vicarious processes: A case of no-trial learning. In L. Berkowitz (Ed.), *Advances in experimental social psychology* (Vol. 2). New York: Academic Press.

Bandura, A. (1969). *Principles of behavior modification.* New York: Holt, Rinehart & Winston.

Bandura, A. (1977a). Self-efficacy: Toward a unifying theory of behavioral change. *Psychological Review, 84,* 191–215.

Bandura, A. (1977b). *Social learning theory.* Englewood Cliffs, NJ: Prentice-Hall.

Bandura, A. (1986). *Social foundations of thought and action: A social cognitive theory.* Englewood Cliffs, NJ: Prentice-Hall.

Bandura, A. (1989). Social cognitive theory. In R. Vasta (Ed.), *Annals of child development: Vol. 6. Six theories of child development: Revised formulations and current issues.* Greenwich, CT: JAI Press.

Bandura, A., Ross, D., & Ross, S. A. (1963a). Imitation of film-mediated aggressive models. *Journal of Abnormal and Social Psychology, 66,* 3–11.

Bandura, A., Ross, D., & Ross, S. A. (1963b). Vicarious reinforcement and imitative learning. *Journal of Abnormal and Social Psychology, 67,* 601–607.

Bandura, A., & Walters, R. H. (1959). *Adolescent aggression.* New York: Ronald Press.

Bandura, A., & Walters, R. H. (1963). *Social learning and personality development.* New York: Holt, Rinehart & Winston.

Banks, M. S. (1980). The development of visual accommodation during early infancy. *Child Development, 51,* 646–666.

Banks, M. S., Aslin, R. N., & Letson, R. D. (1975). Sensitive period for the development of human binocular vision. *Science, 190,* 675–677.

Banks, M. S., & Dannemiller, J. L. (1987). Infant visual psychophysics. In P. Salapatek & L. Cohen (Eds.), *Handbook of infant perception: From sensation to perception* (Vol. 1). Orlando, FL: Academic Press.

Barahal, R. M., Waterman, J., & Martin, H. P. (1981). The social cognitive development of abused children. *Journal of Consulting and Clinical Psychology, 49,* 508–516.

Baran, A., & Pannor, R. (1989). *Lethal secrets.* New York: Warner Books.

Barden, R. C., Zelko, F., Duncan, S. W., & Masters, J. C. (1980). Children's consensual knowledge about the experiential components of emotion. *Journal of Personality and Social Psychology, 39,* 968–976.

Barenboim, C. (1981). The development of person perception in childhood and adolescence: From behavioral comparisons to psychological constructs to psychological comparisons. *Child Development, 52,* 129–144.

Barinaga, M. (1989). Manic depression gene put in limbo. *Science, 246,* 886–887.

Barker, R., & Gump, P. (1964). *Big school, small school: High school size and student behavior.* Stanford, CA: Standard University Press.

Barnard, K. E. (1987). Paradigms for intervention: Infant state modulation. In N. Gunzenhauser (Ed.), *Infant stimulation: For whom, what kind, when, and how much?* (Johnson & Johnson Baby Products Company Pediatric Round Table Series No. 13). Skilman, NJ: Johnson & Johnson.

Barnard, K. E., & Bee, H. L. (1983). The impact of temporally patterned stimulation on the development of preterm infants. *Child Development, 54,* 1156–1167.

Barnes, K. (1971). Preschool play norms: A replication. *Developmental Psychology, 5,* 99–103.

Barrera, M. E., & Maurer, D. (1981a). The perception of facial expressions by the three-month-old. *Child Development, 52,* 203–206.

Barrera, M. E., & Maurer, D. (1981b). Recognition of mother's photographed face by the three-month-old infant. *Child Development, 52,* 714–716.

Barrett, M. D. (1985). Issues in the study of children's single-word speech. In M. D. Barrett (Ed.), *Children's single-word speech.* Chichester, England: Wiley.

Barrett, M. D. (1986). Early semantic representations and early word usage. In S. A. Kuczaj & M. D. Barrett (Eds.), *The development of word meaning.* New York: Springer-Verlag.

Barrett, M. D. (1989). Early language development. In A. Slater & G. Bremner (Eds.), *Infant development.* London: Erlbaum.

Barth, J. M. (1989, April). *Parent-child relationships and children's transition to school.* Paper presented at the biennial meeting of the Society for Research in Child Development, Kansas City, MO.

Bartsch, K., & Wellman, H. (1989). Young children's attribution of action to beliefs and desires. *Child Development, 60,* 946–964.

Baruch, G. K., & Barnett, R. C. (1981). Fathers' participation in the care of their preschool children. *Sex Roles, 7,* 1043–1055.

Basser, L. S. (1962). Hemiplegia of early onset and the faculty of speech with special reference to the effects of hemispherectomy. *Brain, 85,* 427–460.

Bates, E. (1979). *The emergence of symbols: Cognition and communication in infancy.* New York: Academic Press.

Bates, E., Benigni, L., Bretherton, I., Camaioni, L., & Volterra, V. (1979). *The emergence of symbols: Cognition and communication in infancy.* New York: Academic Press.

Bates, E., Bretherton, I., & Snyder, L. (1988). *From first words to grammar.* Cambridge: Cambridge University Press.

Bates, E., Camaioni, L., & Volterra, V. (1975). The acquisition of performatives prior to speech. *Merrill-Palmer Quarterly, 21,* 205–224.

Bates, J. E., Maslin, C. A., & Frankel, K. A. (1985). Attachment security, mother-child interaction, and temperament as predictors of behavior-problem ratings at age three years. In I. Bretherton & E. Waters (Eds.), *Growing points of attachment theory and research. Monographs of the Society for Research in Child Development, 50*(1–2, Serial No. 209).

Bateson, P. P. G. (1979). How do sensitive periods arise and what are they for? *Animal Behaviour, 27,* 470–486.

Baum, C. G., & Foreham, R. (1984). Social factors associated with adolescent obesity. *Journal of Pediatric Psychology, 9,* 293–302.

Baumrind, D. (1971). Current patterns of parental authority. *Developmental Psychology Monographs, 4*(1, Pt. 2).

Baumrind, D. (1972). From each according to her ability. *School Review, 80,* 161–197.

Baumrind, D. (1973). The development of instrumental competence through socialization. In A. D. Pick (Ed.), *The Minnesota symposia on child psychology* (Vol. 7). Minneapolis: University of Minnesota Press.

Bayley, N. (1935). The development of motor abilities during the first three years. *Monographs of the Society for Research in Child Development, 1* (1, Serial No. 1), 1–26.

Bayley, N. (1936). *The California Infant Scale of Motor Development.* Berkeley and Los Angeles: University of California Press.

Bayley, N. (1949). Consistency and variability in the growth of intelligence from birth to eighteen years. *Journal of Genetic Psychology, 75,* 165–196.

Bayley, N. (1969). *Bayley Scales of Infant Development.* New York: The Psychological Corporation.

Beal, C. R. (1987). Repairing the message: Children's monitoring and repair skills. *Child Development, 58,* 401–408.

Bear, G. G. (1989). Sociomoral reasoning and antisocial behaviors among normal sixth graders. *Merrill-Palmer Quarterly, 35,* 181–196.

Beauchamp, G. K., & Cowart, B. J. (1990). Preference for high salt concentrations among children. *Developmental Psychology, 26,* 539–545.

Beauchamp, G. K., & Moran, M. (1982). Dietary experience and sweet taste preferences in human infants. *Appetite, 3,* 139–152.

Beck, R. W., & Beck, S. H. (1989). The incidence of extended households among middle-aged black and white women. *Journal of Family Issues, 10,* 147–168.

Becker, H. J., & Sterling, C. W. (1987). Equity in school computer use: National data and neglected considerations. *Journal of Educational Computing Research, 3,* 289–311.

Becker, J. (1989). Preschoolers' use of number words to denote one-to-one correspondence. *Child Development, 60,* 1147–1157.

Beckman, D. A., & Brent, R. L. (1987). Etiology of human malformations. In N. Kretchmer, E. J. Quilligan, & J. D. Johnson (Eds.), *Prenatal and perinatal biology and medicine: Vol. 2. Disorder, diagnosis and therapy.* New York: Harwood Academic Publishers.

Beilin, H. (1989). Piagetian theory. In R. Vasta (Ed.), *Annals of child development: Vol. 6. Six theories of child development: Revised formulations and current issues.* Greenwich, CT: JAI Press.

Bell, R. Q.(1968). A reinterpretation of the direction of effects in studies of socialization. *Psychological Review, 75,* 81–95.

Bell, R. Q. (1971). Stimulus control of parent or caretaker behavior by offspring. *Developmental Psychology, 4,* 63–72.

Bell, R. Q., & Harper, L. V. (1977). *Child effects on adults.* Hillsdale, NJ: Erlbaum.

Bellugi, U. (1967). *The acquisition of negation.* Unpublished doctoral dissertation, Harvard University.

Belmont, J. M. (1989). Cognitive strategies and strategic learning: The socio-instructional approach. *American Psychologist, 44,* 142–148.

Belmont, L., & Marolla, F. A. (1973). Birth order, family size, and intelligence. *Science, 182,* 1096–1101.

Belsky, J. (1981). Early human experience: A family perspective. *Developmental Psychology, 17,* 3–23.

Belsky, J., & Rovine, M. J. (1988). Nonmaternal care in the first year of life and the security of infant-parent attachment. *Child Development, 59,* 157–167.

Bem, S. L. (1974). The measurement of psychological androgyny. *Journal of Consulting and Clinical Psychology, 42,* 155–162.

Bem, S. L. (1975). Sex role adaptability: One consequence of psychological androgyny. *Journal of Personality and Social Psychology, 31,* 634–643.

Bem, S. L. (1981). Gender schema theory: A cognitive account of sex-typing. *Psychological Review, 88,* 354–364.

Bem, S. L. (1983). Gender schema theory and its implications for child development: Raising gender aschematic children in a gender schematic society. *Signs, 8,* 598–616.

Benbow, C. P., & Stanley, J. C. (1980). Sex differences in mathematical ability: Fact or artifact? *Science, 210,* 1262–1264.

Benbow, C. P., & Stanley, J. C. (1983). Sex differences in mathematical reasoning ability: More facts. *Science, 222,* 1029–1031.

Bender, B. G., Linden, M. G., & Robinson, A. (1987). Environment and developmental risk in children with sex chromosome abnormalities. *Journal of the Academy of Child and Adolescent Psychiatry, 26,* 499–503.

Benedict, H. (1979). Early lexical development: Comprehension and production. *Journal of Child Language, 6,* 183–200.

Benson, J. B. (1988). The significance and development of crawling in human infancy. In J. E. Clark & J. H. Humphrey (Eds.), *Advances in motor development* (Vol. 3). New York: AMS Press.

BenTsvi-Mayer, S., Hertz-Lazarowitz, R., & Safir, M. P. (1989). Teachers' selections of boys and girls as prominent pupils. *Sex Roles, 21,* 231–245.

Ben-Zeev, S. (1977). The influence of bilingualism on cognitive strategy and cognitive development. *Child Development, 48,* 1009–1018.

Berbaum, M. L., & Moreland, R. L. (1985). Intellectual development within transracial adoptive families: Retesting the confluence model. *Child Development, 56,* 207–216.

Berg, C. A., & Sternberg, R. J. (1985). Response to novelty: Continuity versus discontinuity in the developmental course of intelligence. In H. W. Reese (Ed.), *Advances in child development and behavior* (Vol. 19). New York: Academic Press.

Berk, L. E. (1984). Development of private speech among low-income Appalachian children. *Developmental Psychology, 20,* 271–286.

Berk, L. E. (1986). Relationship of elementary school children's private speech to behavioral accompaniment to task, attention, and task performance. *Developmental Psychology, 22,* 671–680.

Berko, J. (1958). The child's learning of English morphology. *Word, 14,* 150–177.

Berman, A. L. (1987, Spring). The problem of adolescent suicide. *Division of Child, Youth, and Family Services Newsletter, 10*(2), American Psychological Association Division 37. pp. 1, 14.

Berndt, T. J. (1979). Developmental changes in conformity to peers and parents. *Developmental Psychology, 15,* 608–616.

Berndt, T. J. (1981). Relations between social cognition, nonsocial cognition, and social behavior: The case of friendship. In J. H. Flavell & L. D. Ross (Eds.), *Social cognitive development: Frontiers and possible futures.* Cambridge: Cambridge University Press.

Berry, J. W. (1966). Temne and Eskimo perceptual skills. *International Journal of Psychology, 1,* 207–229.

Berry, M. (1982). The development of the human nervous system. In J. W. T. Dickerson & H. McGurk (Eds.), *Brain and behavioural development.* London: Surrey University Press.

Bertenthal, B. I., & Fischer, K. W. (1978). Development of self-recognition in the infant. *Developmental Psychology, 14,* 44–50.

Bertoud-Papandropoulou, I. (1978). An experimental study of children's ideas about language. In A. Sinclair, R. J. Jarvella, & W. J. M. Levelt (Eds.), *The child's conception of language.* Heidelberg: Springer-Verlag.

Berwick, D. M. (1980). Nonorganic failure to thrive. *Pediatrics in Review, 1,* 265–270.

Best, C. T., Hoffman, H., & Glanville, B. B. (1982). Development of infant ear asymmetries for speech and music. *Perception & Psychophysics, 31,* 75–85.

Bierman, K. L. (1986). Process of change during social skills training with preadolescents and its relation to treatment outcome. *Child Development, 57,* 230–240.

Bigelow, B. J., & LaGaipa, J. J. (1975). Children's written descriptions of friendship: A multidimensional analysis. *Developmental Psychology, 11,* 857–858.

Bijou, S. W. (1989). Behavior analysis. In R. Vasta (Ed.), *Annals of child development: Vol 6. Six theories of child development: Revised formulations and current issues.* Greenwich, CT: JAI Press.

Biller, H. B. (1974). *Paternal deprivation: Family, school, sexuality and society.* Lexington, MA: Heath.

Binet, A., & Simon, T. (1905). Méthodes nouvelles pour le diagnostic du niveau intellectuel des anormaux. *L'Anée Psychologique, 11,* 191–244.

Bivens, J. A., & Berk, L. E. (1990). A longitudinal study of the development of elementary school children's private speech. *Merrill-Palmer Quarterly, 36,* 443–463.

Bjorkland, D. F. (1987). How age changes in knowledge base contribute to the development of children's memory: An interpretive review. *Developmental Review, 7,* 93–130.

Bjorkland, D. F., & Harnishfeger, K. K. (1990). The resources construct in cognitive development: Diverse sources of evidence and a theory of inefficient inhibition. *Developmental Review, 10,* 48–71.

Bjorkland, D. F., Ornstein, P. A., & Haig, J. R. (1977). Development of organization and recall: Training in the use of organizational techniques. *Developmental Psychology, 13,* 175–183.

Black, B., & Hazen, N. L. (1990). Social status and patterns of communication in acquainted and unacquainted preschool children. *Developmental Psychology, 26,* 379–387.

Black, M. M., & Rollins, H. A., Jr. (1982). The effects of instructional variables on young children's organization and recall. *Journal of Experimental Child Psychology, 33,* 1–19.

Blake, J. (1989). Number of siblings and educational attainment. *Science, 245,* 32–36.

Blakemore, C., & Mitchell, D. E. (1973). Environmental modification of the visual cortex and the neural basis of learning and memory. *Nature* (London), *241,* 467–468.

Blasi, A. (1980). Bridging moral cognition and moral action: A critical review of the literature. *Psychological Bulletin, 88,* 1–45.

Blass, E. M., Ganchrow, J. R., & Steiner, J. E. (1984). Classical conditioning in newborn humans 2–48 hours of age. *Infant Behavior and Development, 7,* 223–235.

Blatt, M. M., & Kohlberg, L. (1975). The effects of classroom moral discussion upon children's level of moral judgment. *Journal of Moral Education, 4,* 129–161.

Blinder, B. J., & Goodman, S. L. (1986). Atypical eating disorders. *New Directions for Mental Health Services, 31,* 29–37.

Blinkov, S. M., & Glezer, I. I. (1968). *The human brain in figures and tables: A quantitative handbook.* New York: Basic Books.

Block, J. (1971). *Lives through time.* Berkeley, CA: Bancroft Books.

Block, J. H. (1973). Conceptions of sex role: Some cross-cultural and longitudinal perspectives. *American Psychologist, 28,* 512–526.

Block, J. H. (1983). Differential premises arising from differential socialization of the sexes: Some conjectures. *Child Development, 54,* 1335–1354.

Block, J. H., & Block, J. (1980). The role of ego-control and ego-resiliency in the organization of behavior. In W. A. Collins (Ed.), *The Minnesota symposia on child psychology: Vol. 13. Development of cognition, affect, and social relations.* Hillsdale, NJ: Erlbaum.

Bloom, L. (1973). *One word at a time.* The Hague: Mouton.

Bloom, L., Lightbown, P., & Hood, L. (1975). Structure and

variation in child language and the acquisition of grammatical morphemes. *Monographs of the Society for Research in Child Development, 40*(2, Serial No. 160).

Bock, J. K., & Hornsby, M. E. (1981). The development of directives: How children ask and tell. *Journal of Child Language, 8,* 151–163.

Boehm, A. (1985). Educational applications of intelligence testing. In B. B. Wolman (Ed.), *Handbook of intelligence.* New York: Wiley.

Boehnke, K., Silbereisen, R. K., Eisenberg, N., Reykowski, J., & Palmonari, A. (1989). Developmental pattern of prosocial motivation: A cross-national study. *Journal of Cross-Cultural Psychology, 20,* 219–243.

Bogatz, G., & Ball, S. (1972). *The second year of Sesame Street: A continuing evaluation.* Princeton, NJ: Educational Testing Service.

Bohannon, J. N., & Stanowicz, L. (1988). The issue of negative evidence: Adult responses to children's language errors. *Developmental Psychology, 24,* 684–689.

Boismer, J. D. (1977). Visual stimulation and wake-sleep behavior in human neonates. *Developmental Psychobiology, 10,* 219–227.

Boldizar, J. P., Perry, D. G., & Perry, L. C. (1989). Outcome values and aggression. *Child Development, 60,* 571–579.

Bond, E. A. (1940). Tenth grade abilities and achievements. *Teachers College contributions to education.* No. 813.

Bonitatibus, G. J., & Flavell, J. H. (1985). Effect of presenting a message in written form on young children's ability to evaluate its communication adequacy. *Developmental Psychology, 21,* 207–216.

Borke, H. (1973). The development of empathy in Chinese and American children between three and six years of age: A cross-culture study. *Developmental Psychology, 9,* 102–108.

Borke, H. (1975). Piaget's mountains revisited: Changes in the egocentric landscape. *Developmental Psychology, 11,* 240–243.

Bornstein, M. H., & Benasich, A. A. (1986). Infant habituation: Assessments of individual differences and short-term reliability at five months. *Child Development, 57,* 87–99.

Bornstein, M. H., & Krinsky, S. J. (1985). Perception of symmetry in infancy: The salience of vertical symmetry and the perception of pattern wholes. *Journal of Experimental Child Psychology, 39,* 1–19.

Bornstein, M. H., & Sigman, M. D. (1986). Continuity in mental development from infancy. *Child Development, 57,* 251–274.

Borstelmann, L. J. (1983). Children before psychology: Ideas about children from antiquity to the late 1800s. In W. Kessen (Ed.), *Handbook of child psychology: Vol. I. History, theory, and methods.* New York: Wiley.

Bouchard, T. J., Jr. (1984). Twins reared together and apart: What they tell us about human diversity. In S. W. Fox (Ed.), *Individuality and determinism: Chemical and biological bases.* New York: Plenum Press.

Bouchard, T. J., Jr., Lykken, D. T., McGue, M., Segal, N. L., & Tellegen, A. (1990). Sources of human psychological differences: The Minnesota Study of Twins Reared Apart. *Science, 250,* 223–228.

Bouchard, T. J., Jr., & McGue, M. (1981). Familial studies of intelligence: A review. *Science, 212,* 1055–1059.

Boué, A., Boué, J., & Gropp, A. (1985). Cytogenetics of pregnancy wastage. In H. Harris & K. Hirschhorn (Eds.), *Advances in human genetics* (Vol. 14). New York: Plenum Press.

Bousha, D. M., & Twentyman, C. Y. (1984). Mother-child interactional style and abuse, neglect, and control groups: Naturalistic observations in the home. *Journal of Abnormal Psychology, 93,* 106–114.

Bowlby, J. (1958). The nature of the child's tie to his mother. *International Journal of Psychoanalysis, 39,* 350–373.

Bowlby, J. (1969). *Attachment and loss: Vol. 1. Attachment.* New York: Basic Books.

Boykin, A. W. (1986). The triple quandry and the schooling of Afro-American children. In U. Neisser (Ed.), *The school achievement of minority children: New perspectives.* Hillsdale, NJ: Erlbaum.

Boysson-Bardies, B. de, Halle, P., Sagart, L., & Durand, C. (1989). A crosslinguistic investigation of vowel formants in babbling. *Journal of Child Language, 16,* 1–17.

Boysson-Bardies, B. de, Sagart, L., & Durand, C. (1984). Discernible differences in the babbling of infants according to target language. *Journal of Child Language, 11,* 1–15.

Brabeck, M. (1983). Moral judgment: Theory and research on differences between males and females. *Developmental Review, 3,* 274–291.

Brackbill, Y. (1975). Continuous stimulation and arousal level in infancy: Effects of stimulus intensity and stress. *Child Development, 46,* 364–369.

Brackbill, Y. (1979). Obstetrical medication and infant behavior. In J. D. Osofsky (Ed.), *Handbook of infant development.* New York: Wiley.

Brackbill, Y., McManus, K., & Woodward, L. (1985). *Medication in maternity: Infant exposure and maternal information.* Ann Arbor: University of Michigan Press.

Brackbill, Y., & Nichols, P. L. (1982). A test of the confluence model of intellectual development. *Developmental Psychology, 18,* 192–198.

Bradbard, M. R., Martin, C. L., Endsley, R. C., & Halverson, C. F. (1986). Influence of sex stereotypes on children's exploration and memory: A competence versus performance distinction. *Developmental Psychology, 22,* 481–486

Bradley, R. H. (1989). The use of the HOME inventory in longitudinal studies of child development. In M. H. Bornstein & N. A. Krasnegor (Eds.), *Stability and continuity in mental development: Behavioral and biological perspectives.* Hillsdale, NJ: Erlbaum.

Bradley, R. H., & Caldwell, B. M. (1976). The relation of infants' home environments to mental test performance at fifty-four months: A follow-up study. *Child Development, 47,* 1172–1174.

Bradley, R. H., & Caldwell, B. M. (1984). The relation of infants' home environments to achievement test performance in first grade: A follow-up study. *Child Development, 55,* 803–809.

Braine, M. D. S. (1976). Children's first word combinations. *Monographs of the Society for Research in Child Development, 41*(1, Serial No. 164).

Brainerd, C. J. (1978). *Piaget's theory of intelligence.* Englewood Cliffs, NJ: Prentice-Hall.

Brand, E., Clingempeel, W. E., & Bowen-Woodward, K. (1988). Family relationships and children's psychological adjustment in stepmother and stepfather families: Findings and conclusions from the Philadelphia Stepfamily Research Project. In

E. M. Hetherington & J. D. Arasteh (Eds.), *Impact of divorce, single-parenting, and stepparenting on children.* Hillsdale, NJ: Erlbaum.

Bray, J. H. (1988). Children's development during early remarriage. In E. M. Hetherington & J. D. Arasteh (Eds.), *Impact of divorce, single parenting, and stepparenting on children.* Hillsdale, NJ: Erlbaum.

Brazelton, T. B. (1973). *Neonatal Behavioral Assessment Scale.* Philadelphia: J. B. Lippincott.

Brazelton, T. B., Nugent, K. J., & Lester, B. M. (1987). Neonatal Behavioral Assessment Scale. In J. D. Osofsky (Ed.), *Handbook of infant development* (2nd ed.). New York: Wiley.

Bremner, J. G. (1978). Egocentric versus allocentric spatial coding in nine-month-old infants: Factors influencing the choice of code. *Developmental Psychology, 14,* 346–355.

Bremner, J. G., & Bryant, P. E. (1977). Place versus response as the basis for spatial errors made by young infants. *Journal of Experimental Child Psychology, 23,* 162–171.

Bretherton, I., & Beeghly, M. (1982). Talking about internal states: The acquisition of an explicit theory of mind. *Developmental Psychology, 18,* 906–921.

Bretherton, I., Fritz, J., Zahn-Waxler, C., & Ridgeway, D. (1986). Learning to talk about emotions: A functionalist perspective. *Child Development, 57,* 529–548.

Brody, E. B., & Brody, N. (1976). *Intelligence: Nature, determinants, and consequences.* New York: Academic Press.

Brody, G. H., & Forehand, R. (1986). Maternal perceptions of child maladjustment as a function of the combined influence of child behavior and maternal depression. *Journal of Consulting and Clinical Psychology, 54,* 237–240.

Brody, G. H., & Shaffer, D. (1982). Contributions of parents and peers to children's moral socialization. *Developmental Review, 2,* 31–75.

Brody, G. H., & Stoneman, Z. (1981). Selective imitation of same-age, older, and younger peer models. *Child Development, 52,* 717–720.

Brody, G. H., Stoneman, Z., & Burke, M. (1987). Family system and individual child correlates of sibling behavior. *American Journal of Orthopsychiatry, 57,* 561–569.

Brody, G. H., Stoneman, Z., & MacKinnon, C. E. (1986). Contributions of maternal child-rearing practices and play contexts to sibling interactions. *Journal of Applied Developmental Psychology, 7,* 225–236.

Brodzinsky, D. M., Schecter, D. E., Braff, A. M., & Singer, L. M. (1984). Psychological and academic adjustment in adopted children. *Journal of Consulting and Clinical Psychology, 52,* 582–590.

Bronfenbrenner, U. (1964). Upbringing in collective settings in Switzerland and the U.S.S.R. *Proceedings of the XVIII International Congress of Psychology, Washington, DC.* Amsterdam: North-Holland.

Bronfenbrenner, U. (1970). *Two worlds of childhood: U.S. and U.S.S.R.* New York: Simon & Schuster.

Bronfenbrenner, U. (1977). Toward an experimental ecology of human development. *American Psychologist, 32,* 513–531.

Bronfenbrenner, U. (1979). *The ecology of human development.* Cambridge: Harvard University Press.

Bronfenbrenner, U. (1986). Ecology of the family as a context for human development: Research perspectives. *Developmental Psychology, 22,* 723–742.

Bronfenbrenner, U. (1989). Ecological systems theory. In R. Vasta (Ed.), *Annals of child development: Vol 6. Six theories of child development: Revised formulations and current issues.* Greenwich, CT: JAI Press.

Bronson, G. W. (1974). The postnatal growth of visual capacity. *Child Development, 45,* 873–890.

Bronson, G. W. (1990). Changes in infants' visual scanning across the 2- to 14-week age period. *Journal of Experimental Child Psychology, 49,* 101–125.

Bronson, W. (1981). Toddlers' behavior with age-mates: Issues of interaction, cognition, and affect. In L. Lipsitt (Ed.), *Monographs on infancy* (Vol. 1). Norwood, NJ: Ablex.

Brook, C. G. D. (1986). Turner syndrome. *Archives of Disease in Childhood, 61,* 305–309.

Brooks-Gunn, J. (1984). The psychological significance of different pubertal events to young girls. *Journal of Early Adolescence, 4,* 315–327.

Brooks-Gunn, J. (1989). Pubertal processes and the early adolescent transition. In W. Damon (Ed.), *Child development today and tomorrow.* San Francisco: Jossey-Bass.

Brooks-Gunn, J., & Ruble, D. (1980). Menarche: The interaction of physiology, cultural, and social factors. In A. J. Dan, E. A. Graham, & C. P. Beecher (Eds.), *The menstrual cycle: A synthesis of interdisciplinary research.* New York: Springer-Verlag.

Brooks-Gunn, J., Warren, M. P., Samelson, M., & Fox, R. (1986). Physical similarity of and disclosure of menarcheal status to friends: Effects of grade and pubertal status. *Journal of Early Adolescence, 6,* 3–14.

Brophy, J. (1986). Teacher influences on student achievement. *American Psychologist, 41,* 1069–1077.

Brown, A. L., & Barclay, C. R. (1976). The effects of training specific mnemonics on the metamnemonic efficiency of retarded children. *Child Development, 47,* 71–80.

Brown, A. L., Campione, J. C., & Barclay, C. R. (1979). Training self-checking routines for estimating test readiness: Generalization from list learning to prose recall. *Child Development, 50,* 501–512.

Brown, A. L., Kane, M. J., & Echols, C. H. (1986). Young children's mental models determine analogical transfer across problems with a common goal structure. *Cognitive Development, 1,* 103–121.

Brown, A. L., & Reeve, R. A. (1987). Bandwidths of competence: The role of supportive contexts in learning and development. In L. S. Liben (Ed.), *Development and learning: Conflict or congruence?* Hillsdale, NJ: Erlbaum.

Brown, A. L., & Scott, M. S. (1971). Recognition memory for pictures in preschool children. *Journal of Experimental Child Psychology, 11,* 401–412.

Brown, B. B. (1989). The role of peer groups in adolescents' adjustment to secondary school. In T. J. Berndt & G. W. Ladd (Eds.), *Peer relationships in child development.* New York: Wiley.

Brown, B. B., Clasen, D. R., & Eicher, S. A. (1986). Perceptions of peer pressure, peer conformity dispositions, and self-reported behavior among adolescents. *Developmental Psychology, 22,* 521–530.

Brown, P. J., & Konner, M. (1987). An anthropological perspective on obesity. *Annals of the New York Academy of Sciences, 499,* 29–46.

Brown, R. (1973). *A first language: The early stages.* Cambridge: Harvard University Press.

Brown, R., & Hanlon, C. (1970). Derivational complexity and order of acquisition in child speech. In J. R. Hayes (Ed.), *Cognition and the development of language.* New York: Wiley.

Brown, R. M., & Fishman, R. H. B. (1984). An overview and summary of the behavioral and neural consequences of perinatal exposure to psychotropic drugs. In J. Yanai (Ed.), *Neurobehavioral teratology.* New York: Elsevier.

Brownlee, S. (1987, April). Lords of the flies. *Discover,* pp. 26–40.

Bruck, K. (1962). Temperature regulation in the newborn infant. *Biological Neonatorum, 3,* 65–119.

Bruner, J. S. (1981). Intention in the structure of action and interaction. In L. P. Lipsitt (Ed.), *Advances in infancy research* (Vol. 1). Norwood, NJ: Ablex.

Bruner, J. S. (1983). *Child's talk: Learning to use language.* New York: W. W. Norton.

Bryant, P. E., & Trabasso, T. (1971). Transitive inferences and memory in young children. *Nature, 232,* 456–458.

Buhrmester, D. (1990). Intimacy of friendship, interpersonal competence, and adjustment during preadolescence and adolescence. *Child Development, 61,* 1101–1111.

Buhrmester, D., & Furman, W. (1987). The development of companionship and intimacy. *Child Development, 58,* 1101–1113.

Buhrmester, D., & Furman, W. (1990). Perceptions of sibling relationships during middle childhood and adolescence. *Child Development, 61,* 1387–1398.

Bukowski, W. M., & Kramer, T. L. (1986). Judgments of the features of friendship among early adolescent boys and girls. *Journal of Early Adolescence, 6,* 331–338.

Bullinger, A. (1987, April). Action as tutor for the infant's tools of exploration. In M. Haith (Chair), *Perception and action: The acquisition of skill.* Symposium conducted at the biennial meeting of the Society for Research in Child Development, Baltimore.

Bumpass, L. L. (1990). What's happening to the American family? Interactions between demographic and institutional change. *Demography, 27,* 483–498.

Burgess, R. L., & Conger, R. D. (1978). Family interaction in abusive, neglectful, and normal families. *Child Development, 49,* 1163–1173.

Burnett, C. A., Jones, J. A., Rooks, J., Chen, C. H., Tyler, C. W., & Miller, C. A. (1980). Home delivery and neonatal mortality in North Carolina. *Journal of the American Medical Association, 244,* 2741–2745

Burns, A. L., Mitchell, G., & Obradovich, S. (1989). Of sex role and strollers: Female and male attention to toddlers at the zoo. *Sex Roles, 20,* 309–315.

Burns, K. A., Deddish, R. B., Burns, W. J., & Hatcher, R. P. (1983). Use of oscillating waterbeds and rhythmic sounds for premature infant stimulation. *Developmental Psychology, 19,* 746–751.

Bushnell, E. W. (1981). The ontogeny of intermodal relations: Vision and touch in infancy. In R. D. Walk & H. L. Pick, Jr. (Eds.), *Intersensory perception and sensory integration.* New York: Plenum Press.

Bushnell, E. W. (1985). The decline of visually guided reaching during infancy. *Infant Behavior and Development, 8,* 139–155.

Bushnell, I. W. R., Gerry, G., & Burt, K. (1983). The externality effect in neonates. *Infant Behavior and Development, 6,* 151–156.

Bushnell, I. W. R., Sai, F., & Mullin, J. T. (1989). Neonatal recognition of the mother's face. *British Journal of Developmental Psychology, 7,* 3–15.

Buss, A. H., & Plomin, R. (1975). *A temperament theory of personality development.* New York: Wiley-Interscience.

Buss, A. H., & Plomin, R. (1984). *Temperament: Early developing personality traits.* Hillsdale, NJ: Erlbaum.

Bussey, K., & Bandura, A. (1984). Influence of gender constancy and social power on sex-linked modeling. *Journal of Personality and Social Psychology, 47,* 1292–1302.

Bussey, K., & Perry, D. G. (1982). Same-sex imitation: The avoidance of cross-sex models or the acceptance of same-sex models. *Sex Roles, 8,* 773–784.

Butler, N. R., & Goldstein, H. (1973). Smoking in pregnancy and subsequent child development. *British Medical Journal, 4,* 573–575.

Butler, R. (1989). Mastery versus ability appraisal: A developmental study of children's observations of peers' work. *Child Development, 60,* 1350–1361.

Butler, R. (1990). The effects of mastery and competitive conditions on self-assessment at different ages. *Child Development, 61,* 201–210.

Byrne, B. M. (1984). The general/academic self-concept nomological network: A review of construct validation research. *Review of Educational Research, 54,* 427–456.

Byrnes, J. P., & Overton, W. F. (1988). Reasoning about logical connections: A developmental analysis. *Journal of Experimental Child Psychology, 46,* 194–218.

Cadoret, R. J., Cain, C. A., & Grove, W. M. (1980). Development of alcoholism in adoptees raised apart from alcoholic biologic relatives. *Archives of General Psychiatry, 37,* 561–563.

Cairns, R. B. (1983). The emergence of developmental psychology. In W. Kessen (Ed.), *Handbook of child psychology: Vol. I. History, theory, and methods.* New York: Wiley.

Cairns, R. B., & Ornstein, P. A. (1979). Developmental psychology. In E. Hearst (Ed.), *The first century of experimental psychology.* Hillsdale, NJ: Erlbaum.

Caldwell, B. M., & Bradley, R. H. (1978). *Home Observation for Measurement of the Environment.* Little Rock: University of Arkansas.

Calvert, S. L., Huston, A. C., Watkins, B. A., & Wright, J. C. (1982). The relationship between selective attention to televised forms and children's comprehension of content. *Child Development, 53,* 601–610.

Camara, K. A., & Resnick, G. (1988). Interparental conflict and cooperation: Factors moderating children's post-divorce adjustment. In E. M. Hetherington & J. Arasteh (Eds.), *Impact of divorce, single-parenting, and stepparenting on children.* Hillsdale, NJ: Erlbaum.

Campione, J. C., & Brown, A. L. (1978). Toward a theory of intelligence: Contributions from research with retarded children. *Intelligence, 2,* 279–304.

Campione, J. C., Brown, A. L., & Ferrara, R. A. (1982). Mental retardation and intelligence. In R. J. Sternberg (Ed.), *Handbook of human intelligence*. Cambridge: Cambridge University Press.

Campos, J. J., Barrett, K. C., Lamb, M. E., Goldsmith, H. H., & Stenberg, C. (1983). Socioemotional development. In M. M. Haith & J. J. Campos (Eds.), *Handbook of child psychology: Vol. II. Infancy and developmental psychobiology*. New York: Wiley

Campos, J. J., Langer, A., & Krowitz, A. (1970). Cardiac responses on the visual cliff in prelocomotor human infants. *Science, 170*, 196–197.

Carey, S. (1978). The child as word learner. In M. Halle, J. Bresnan, & G. A. Miller (Eds.), *Linguistic theory and psychological reality*. Cambridge: MIT Press.

Carlson, V., Cicchetti, D., Barnett, D., & Braunwald, K. (1989). Contributions of the study of maltreated infants to the development of the disorganized ("D") type of attachment relationship. In D. Cicchetti & V. Carlson (Eds.), *Child maltreatment: Theory and research on the causes and consequences of child abuse and neglect*. Cambridge: Cambridge University Press.

Carroll, J. J., & Gibson, E. J. (1981, April). *Infants' differentiation of an aperture and an obstacle*. Paper presented at the biennial meeting of the Society for Research in Child Development, Boston.

Carter, D. B. (1987). The roles of peers in sex role socialization. In D. B. Carter (Ed.), *Current conceptions of sex roles and sex-typing: Theory and research*. New York: Praeger.

Carter, D. B., & Levy, G. D. (1988). Cognitive aspects of early sex-role development: The influence of gender schemas on preschoolers' memories and preferences for sex-typed toys and activities. *Child Development, 59*, 782–792.

Carter, D. B., & McCloskey, L. A. (1984). Peers and the maintenance of sex-typed behavior: The development of children's understanding of cross-gender behavior in their peers. *Social Cognition, 2*, 294–314.

Carter, D. B., & Patterson, C. J. (1982). Sex roles as social conventions: The development of children's conceptions of sex role stereotypes. *Developmental Psychology, 18*, 812–824.

Case, R. (1985). *Intellectual development: A systematic reinterpretation*. New York: Academic Press.

Case, R., Kurland, D. M., & Goldberg, J. (1982). Operational efficiency and the growth of short term memory span. *Journal of Experimental Child Psychology, 33*, 386–404.

Cattell, J. M. (1890). Mental tests and measurements. *Mind, 15*, 373–381.

Cattell, R. B. (1971). *Abilities: Their structure, growth, and action*. Boston: Houghton Mifflin.

Cavior, N., & Dokecki, P. R. (1973). Physical attractiveness, perceived attitude similarity, and academic achievement as contributors to interpersonal attraction among adolescents. *Developmental Psychology, 9*, 44–54.

Ceci, S. J., Ross, D. F., & Toglia, M. P. (1987). Suggestibility of children's memory: Psychological implications. *Journal of Experimental Psychology: General, 116*, 38–49.

Cernoch, J. M., & Porter, R. H. (1985). Recognition of maternal axillary odors by infants. *Child Development, 56*, 1593–1598.

Chapman, M., Skinner, E. A., & Baltes, P. B. (1990). Interpret-

ing correlations between children's perceived control and cognitive performance: Control, agency, or means-ends beliefs? *Developmental Psychology, 26*, 246–253.

Chapman, M., & Zahn-Waxler, C. (1981). *Young children's compliance and noncompliance to parental discipline in a natural setting*. Unpublished manuscript.

Chasnoff, I. J. (1986). Perinatal addiction: Consequences of intrauterine exposure to opiate and nonopiate drugs. In I. J. Chasnoff (Ed.), *Drug use in pregnancy: Mother and child*. Lancaster, England: MTP Press.

Chasnoff, I. J. (1988). Cocaine: Effects on pregnancy and the neonate. In I. J. Chasnoff (Ed.), *Drugs, alcohol, pregnancy and parenting*. Boston: Kluwer Academic Publishers.

Chasnoff, I. J., Hatcher, R., & Burns, W. J. (1980). Early growth patterns of methadone-addicted infants. *American Journal of Diseases of Children, 134*, 1049–1051.

Chen, M. (1985). A macro-focus on microcomputers: Eight utilization and effects issues. In M. Chen & W. Paisley (Eds.), *Children and microcomputers: Research on the newest medium*. Beverly Hills: Sage.

Chen, Z., & Daehler, M. W. (1989). Positive and negative transfer in analogical problem-solving by 6-year-olds. *Cognitive Development, 4*, 327–344.

Chess, S., & Thomas, A. (1982). Infant bonding: Mystique and reality. *American Journal of Orthopsychiatry, 52*, 213–222.

Chess, S., & Thomas, A. (1986). Developmental issues. In S. Chess & A. Thomas (Eds.), *Annual progress in child psychiatry and child development*. New York: Brunner/Mazel.

Cheyne, J. A. (1976). Development of forms and functions of smiling in preschoolers. *Child Development, 47*, 820–823.

Chi, M. T. H. (1978). Knowledge structure and memory development. In R. Siegler (Ed.), *Children's thinking: What develops?* Hillsdale, NJ: Erlbaum.

Chibucos, T., & Kail, P. R. (1981). Longitudinal examination of father-infant interaction and infant-father interaction. *Merrill-Palmer Quarterly, 27*, 81–96.

Children's Defense Fund. (1988, April). Piecing together the teen pregnancy puzzle. *CDF Reports, 9*, pp. 1, 5–6.

Chomsky, N. (1957). *Syntactic structures*. The Hague: Mouton.

Christenson, P. G. (1982). Children's perceptions of TV commercials and products: The effects of PSAs. *Communication Research, 9*, 491–524.

Chukovsky, K. (1963). *From two to five*. Berkeley and Los Angeles: University of California Press.

Cianfrani, T. (1960). *A short history of obstetrics and gynecology*. Springfield, IL: C. C. Thomas.

Cicchetti, D. (1987). Developmental psychopathology in infancy: Illustration from the study of maltreated youngsters. *Journal of Consulting and Clinical Psychology, 55*, 837–845.

Clark, E. V. (1973). What's in a word? On the child's acquisition of semantics in his first language. In T. E. Moore (Ed.), *Cognitive development and the acquisition of language*. New York: Academic Press.

Clarke, N., in consultation with Bennets, A. B. (1982). Vital statistics and nonhospital births: A mortality study of infants born out of hospitals in Oregon [Appendix]. In *Research Issues in the Assessment of Birth Settings*. Washington, DC: Institute of Medicine and National Research Council, National Academy Press.

Clarke-Stewart, A. (1982). *Daycare*. Cambridge: Harvard University Press.

Clarke-Stewart, K. A. (1989). Infant day care: Maligned or malignant? *American Psychologist, 44,* 266–273.

Clarke-Stewart, K. A., & Fein, G. G. (1983). Early childhood programs. In M. M. Haith & J. J. Campos (Eds.), *Handbook of child psychology: Vol. II. Infancy and developmental psychobiology*. New York: Wiley.

Clarren, S. K., Alvord, E. C., Suni, S. M., & Streissguth, A. P. (1978). Brain malformations related to prenatal exposure to ethanol. *Journal of Pediatrics, 92,* 64–67.

Clasen, D. R., & Brown, B. B. (1985). The multidimensionality of peer pressure in adolescence. *Journal of Youth and Adolescence, 14,* 451–468.

Clements, D. H. (1986). Effects of Logo and CAI environments on cognition and creativity. *Journal of Educational Psychology, 78,* 309–318.

Clements, D. H., & Gullo, D. F. (1984). Effects of computer programming on young children's cognition. *Journal of Educational Psychology, 76,* 1051–1058.

Cobb, H. V. (1954). Role wishes and general wishes of children and adolescents. *Child Development, 25,* 161–171.

Cohen, L., & Campos, J. (1974). Father, mother and stranger as elicitors of attachment behaviors in infancy. *Developmental Psychology, 10,* 146–154.

Cohen, R. L. (1966). Experimental and clinical chemateratogenesis. *Advances in Pharmacology, 4,* 263–349.

Cohn, J. F., Matias, R., Tronick, E. Z., Connell, D., & Lyons-Ruth, D. (1986). Face-to-face interactions of depressed mothers and their infants. In E. Z. Tronick & T. M. Field (Eds.), *New directions for child development: No. 34. Maternal depression and infant disturbance*. San Francisco: Jossey-Bass.

Cohn, J. F., & Tronick, E. Z. (1983). Three-month-old infants' reaction to simulated maternal depression. *Child Development, 54,* 185–193.

Cohn, J. F., & Tronick, E. Z. (1987). Mother-infant face-to-face interaction: The sequence of dyadic states at 3, 6, and 9 months. *Developmental Psychology, 23,* 68–77.

Coie, J. D., & Dodge, K. A. (1983). Continuities and changes in children's social status: A five-year longitudinal study. *Merrill-Palmer Quarterly, 29,* 261–282.

Coie, J. D., & Dodge, K. A. (1988). Multiple sources of data on social behavior and social status in the school: A cross-age comparison. *Child Development, 59,* 815–829.

Coie, J. D., Dodge, K. A., & Coppotelli, H. (1982). Dimensions and types of social status: A cross-age perspective. *Developmental Psychology, 18,* 557–570.

Colby, A., Kohlberg, L., Gibbs, J., & Lieberman, M. (1983). A longitudinal study of moral judgment. *Monographs of the Society for Research in Child Development, 48*(1–2, Serial No. 200).

Cole, M., Gay, J., Glick, J., & Sharp, D. W. (1971). *The cultural context of learning and thinking*. New York: Basic Books.

Coleman, J. S., Campbell, E., & Mood, A. (1966). *Equality of educational opportunity*. Washington, DC: U.S. Office of Education.

Collins, W. A. (1983). Social antecedents, cognitive processing, and comprehension of social portrayals on television. In E. T. Higgins, D. N. Ruble, & W. W. Hartup (Eds.), *Social cognition and social development*. Cambridge: Cambridge University Press.

Collins, W. A., Wellman, H., Keniston, A. H., & Westby, S. D. (1978). Age-related aspects of comprehension and inference from a televised dramatic narrative. *Child Development, 49,* 389–399.

Colombo, J., Mitchell, D. W., O'Brien, M., & Horowitz, F. D. (1987). The stability of visual habituation during the first year of life. *Child Development, 58,* 474–487.

Condry, J. C., & Condry, S. M. (1976). Sex differences: A study of the eye of the beholder. *Child Development, 47,* 812–819.

Condry, S. M., Condry, J. C., & Pogatshynik, L. W. (1978, August). *Sex differences: A study of the ear of the beholder*. Paper presented at the annual meeting of the American Psychological Association, Toronto.

Congregation for the Doctrine of the Faith. (1987, March 11). Instruction on respect for human life [Vatican document]. *The New York Times*, pp. A14–A17.

Connolly, K., & Elliott, J. (1972). The evolution and ontogeny of hand function. In N. B. Jones (Ed.), *The growth of competence*. Cambridge: Cambridge University Press.

Connor, J. M., Schackman, M. E., & Serbin, L. A. (1978). Sex-related differences in response to practice on a visual-spatial test and generalization to a related test. *Child Development, 49,* 24–29.

Consensus Development Conference. (1981). *Cesarean childbirth*. Bethesda, MD: National Institutes of Health.

Cook, T. D., Appleton, H., Conner, R. F., Shaffer, A., Tamkin, G., & Weber, S. J. (1975). *"Sesame Street" revisited*. New York: Russell Sage.

Cooley, C. H. (1902). *Human nature and the social order*. New York: Scribner's.

Cooper, J., Hall, J., & Huff, C. (1990). Situational stress as a consequence of sex-stereotyped software. *Personality and Social Psychology Bulletin, 16,* 419–429.

Cordua, G. D., McGraw, K. O., & Drabman, R. S. (1979). Doctor or nurse: Children's perceptions of sex-typed occupations. *Child Development, 50,* 590–593.

Corrigan, R. (1979). Cognitive correlates of language: Differential criteria yield differential results. *Child Development, 50,* 617–631.

Costanzo, P. R., & Woody, E. Z. (1979). Externality as a function of obesity in children: Pervasive style or eating-specific attribute? *Journal of Personality and Social Psychology, 37,* 2286–2296.

Coustan, D. R., & Felig, P. (1988). Diabetes mellitus. In G. N. Burrow & T. F. Ferris (Eds.), *Medical complications during pregnancy* (3rd ed.). Philadelphia: W. B. Saunders.

Cowan, W. M. (1979, September). The development of the brain. *Scientific American, 241,* pp. 113–133.

Cox, M. J., Owen, M. T., Lewis, J. M., & Henderson, V. K. (1989). Marriage, adult adjustment, and early parenting. *Child Development, 60,* 1015–1024.

The crack children. (1990, February 12). *Newsweek*, pp. 62–63.

Crain, W. C. (1985). *Theories of development: Concepts and applications* (2nd ed.). Englewood Cliffs, NJ: Prentice-Hall.

Crandall, R. (1973). The measurement of self-esteem and related concepts. In J. P. Robinson & P. R. Shaver (Eds.), *Measures of social psychological attitudes* (rev. ed.). Ann Arbor: Institute for Social Research.

Crandall, V. C. (1969). Sex differences in expectancy of intellectual and academic reinforcement. In C. P. Smith (Ed.), *Achievement-related motives in children.* New York: Russell Sage.

Crnic, L. S., & Pennington, B. F. (1987). Developmental psychology and the neurosciences: An introduction. *Child Development, 58,* 533–538.

Crockenberg, S., & Litman, C. (1990). Autonomy as competence in 2-year-olds: Maternal correlates of child defiance, compliance, and self-assertion. *Developmental Psychology, 26,* 961–971.

Crockett, L., Losoff, M., & Petersen, A. C., (1984). Perceptions of the peer group and friendship in early adolescence. *Journal of Early Adolescence, 4,* 155–181.

Crook, C. (1987). Taste and olfaction. In P. Salapatek & L. Cohen (Eds.), *Handbook of infant perception: From sensation to perception* (Vol. 1). Orlando, FL: Academic Press.

Csikszentmihalyi, M., & Larson, R. (1984). *Being adolescent.* New York: Basic Books.

Cummings, E. M., Ianotti, R. J., & Zahn-Waxler, C. (1985). Influence of conflict between adults on the emotions and aggression of young children. *Developmental Psychology, 21,* 495–507.

Cummings, E. M., Zahn-Waxler, C., & Radke-Yarrow, C. (1981). Young children's responses to expressions of anger and affection by others in the family. *Child Development, 52,* 1274–1282.

Curie-Cohen, M., Luttrell, L., & Shapiro, S. (1979). Current practice of artificial insemination by donor in the United States. *New England Journal of Medicine, 300,* 585–590.

Curtis, L. E., Siegel, A. W., & Furlong, N. E. (1981). Developmental differences in cognitive mapping: Configurational knowledge of familiar large-scale environments. *Journal of Experimental Child Psychology, 31,* 456–469.

Curtiss, S. (1977). *Genie: A psycholinguistic study of a modern-day 'wild child.'* New York: Academic Press.

Daehler, M. W., & Bukatko, D. (1977). Recognition memory for pictures in very young children: Evidence from attentional preferences using a continuous presentation procedure. *Child Development, 48,* 693–696.

Daehler, M. W., & Bukatko, D. (1985). *Cognitive development.* New York: Knopf.

Dalterio, S., & Bartke, A. (1979). Perinatal exposure to cannabinoids alters male reproductive function in mice. *Science, 205,* 1420–1422.

Damon, W. (1983). *Social and personality development: Infancy through adolescence.* New York: W. W. Norton.

Damon, W., & Hart, D. (1988). *Self-understanding in childhood and adolescence.* New York: Cambridge University Press.

Darwin, C. (1877). A biographical sketch of an infant. *Mind, 2,* 285–294.

Darwin, C. (1965). *The expression of emotions in man and animals.* Chicago: University of Chicago Press. (Original work published 1872)

Dasen, P. R. (1972). Cross-cultural Piagetian research: A summary. *Journal of Cross-Cultural Psychology, 3,* 23–39.

DeCasper, A. J., & Fifer, W. P. (1980). Of human bonding: Newborns prefer their mothers' voices. *Science, 208,* 1174–1176.

DeCasper, A. J., & Spence, M. J. (1986). Prenatal maternal speech influences newborns' perception of speech sounds. *Infant Behavior and Development, 9,* 133–150.

DeFries, J. C., Gervais, M. C., & Thomas, E. A. (1978). Response to 30 generations of selection for open-field activity in laboratory mice. *Behavior Genetics, 8,* 3–13.

DeLisi, C. (1988). The human genome project. *American Scientist, 76,* 488–493.

De Maeyer, E. M. (1976). Protein-energy malnutrition. In G. Beaton & J. Bengoa (Eds.), *Nutrition in preventative medicine* (WHO Monograph Series No. 62). Geneva: World Health Organization.

Demany, L., McKenzie, B., & Vurpillot, E. (1977). Rhythm perception in early infancy. *Nature, 266,* 718–719.

Demetras, M., Post, K., & Snow, C. (1986). Feedback to first language learners: The role of repetitions and clarification questions. *Journal of Child Language, 13,* 275–292.

Demographic Yearbook, 1981. (1983). New York: United Nations.

Demographic Yearbook, 1988. (1990). New York: United Nations.

Dempster, F. N. (1981). Memory span: Sources of individual and developmental differences. *Psychological Bulletin, 89,* 63–100.

Denham, S. A., McKinley, M., Couchoud, E. A., & Holt, R. (1990). Emotional and behavioral predictors of preschool ratings. *Child Development, 61,* 1145–1152.

Dennis, W. (1960). Causes of retardation among institutional children: Iran. *Journal of Genetic Psychology, 96,* 47–59.

Dennis, W., & Dennis, M. G. (1940). The effect of cradling practices upon the onset of walking in Hopi children. *Journal of Genetic Psychology, 56,* 77–86.

DeRegt, R. H., Minkoff, H. L., Feldman, J., & Schwartz, R. H. (1986). Relation of private or clinic care to the cesarean birth rate. *New England Journal of Medicine, 315,* 619–624.

Desmond, M. M., Franklin, R. R., Vallbona, C., Hill, R. M., Plumb, R., Arnold, H., & Watts, J. (1963). The clinical behavior of the newly born. *Journal of Pediatrics, 62,* 307–325.

Deur, J. L., & Parke, R. D. (1970). Effects of inconsistent punishment on aggression in children. *Developmental Psychology, 2,* 403–411.

Deutsch, M., Katz, I., & Jensen, A. R. (1968). *Social class, race, and psychological development.* New York: Holt, Rinehart & Winston.

de Villiers, P. A., & de Villiers, J. G. (1979). Form and function in the development of sentence negation. *Papers and Reports in Child Language, 17,* 57–64.

Devitt, N. (1977). The transition from home to hospital birth in the United States, 1930–1960. *Birth and the Family Journal, 4,* 47–58.

Dewey, J. (1963). *The school and society.* New York: Macmillan. (Original work published 1938)

Dick-Read, G. (1959). *Childbirth without fear.* New York: Harper & Row.

Dien, D. S. (1982). A Chinese perspective on Kohlberg's theory of moral development. *Developmental Review, 2,* 331–341.

Dietz, W. A. (1983). Childhood obesity: Susceptibility, cause, and management. *Journal of Pediatrics, 103,* 676–686.

Dion, K. K., & Berscheid, E. (1974). Physical attractiveness and peer perception among children. *Sociometry, 37,* 1–12.

DiVitto, B., & Goldberg, S. (1979). The effect of newborn medical status on early parent-infant interactions. In T. M. Field, A. M. Sostek, S. Goldberg, & H. H. Shuman (Eds.), *Infants born at risk.* New York: S. P. Medical & Scientific Books.

Dix, T. H., & Grusec, J. E. (1985). Parent attribution processes in the socialization of children. In I. E. Sigel (Ed.), *Parental belief systems: The psychological consequences for children.* Hillsdale, NJ: Erlbaum.

Dix, T. H., Ruble, D. N., Grusec, J. E., & Nixon, S. (1986). Social cognition in parents: Inferential and affective reactions to children of three age levels. *Child Development, 57,* 879–894.

Dix, T., Ruble, D. N., & Zambarano, R. J. (1989). Mothers' implicit theories of discipline: Child effects, parent effects, and the attribution process. *Child Development, 60,* 1373–1391.

Dixon, S., Tronick, E., Keeler, C., & Brazelton, T. B. (1981). Mother-infant interaction among the Gusii of Kenya. In T. M. Field, A. M. Sosteck, P. Vietze, & P. H. Leiderman (Eds.), *Culture and early interactions.* Hillsdale, NJ: Erlbaum.

Dodge, K. A. (1980). Social cognition and children's aggressive behavior. *Child Development, 51,* 162–170.

Dodge, K. A. (1982). Social information processing variables in the development of aggression and altruism in young children. In C. Zahn-Waxler, M. Cummings, & M. Radke-Yarrow (Eds.), *The development of altruism and aggression: Social and sociological origins.* New York: Cambridge University Press.

Dodge, K. A. (1986). A social information processing model of social competence in children. In M. Perlmutter (Ed.), *The Minnesota symposia on child psychology: Vol. 18. Cognitive perspectives on children's social and behavioral development.* Hillsdale, NJ: Erlbaum.

Dodge, K. A., Coie, J. D., Pettit, G. S., & Price, J. M. (1990). Peer status and aggression in boys' groups: Developmental and contextual analyses. *Child Development, 61,* 1289–1309.

Dodge, K. A., Murphy, R. R., & Buchsbaum, K. (1984). The assessment of intention-cue detection skills in children: Implications for developmental psychopathology. *Child Development, 55,* 163–173.

Dodge, K. A., Pettit, G. S., McClaskey, C. L., & Brown, M. M. (1986). Social competence in children. *Monographs of the Society for Research in Child Development, 51*(2, Serial No. 213).

Dodge, K. A., Schlundt, D. C., Schocken, I., & Delugach, J. D. (1983). Social competence and children's sociometric status: The role of peer group entry strategies. *Merrill-Palmer Quarterly, 29,* 309–336.

Dodge, K. A., & Somberg, D. R. (1987). Hostile attributional biases among aggressive boys are exacerbated under conditions of threats to self. *Child Development, 58,* 213–224.

Dodwell, P. C., Humphrey, G. K., & Muir, D. W. (1987). Shape and pattern perception. In P. Salapatek & L. Cohen (Eds.), *Handbook of infant perception: From perception to cognition* (Vol. 2). Orlando, FL: Academic Press.

Doherty, W. J., & Needle, R. H. (1991). Psychological adjustment and substance use among adolescents before and after a parental divorce. *Child Development, 62,* 328–337.

Dollard, J., Doob, L. W., Miller, N. E., Mowrer, O. H., & Sears, R. R. (1939). *Frustration and aggression.* New Haven: Yale University Press.

Doman, .G. (1983). *How to teach your baby to read* (2nd ed.). Garden City, NY: Doubleday.

Dornbush, S. M., Ritter, P. L., Leiderman, P. H., Roberts, D. F., & Fraleigh, M. J. (1987). The relation of parenting style to adolescent school performance. *Child Development, 58,* 1244–1257.

Dorozynski, A. (1986). How the new genetic therapy could change peoples' lives. *Impact of Science on Society, 36,* 313–319.

Dorr, A. (1983). No shortcuts to judging reality. In J. Bryant & D. R. Anderson (Eds.), *Children's understanding of television: Research on attention and comprehension.* New York: Academic Press.

Dorr, A. (1986). *Television and children: A special medium for a special audience.* Beverly Hills: Sage.

Doty, R. L., Shaman, P., Applebaum, S. L., Giberson, R., Sikorski, L., & Rosenberg, L. (1984). Smell identification ability: Changes with age. *Science, 226,* 141–143.

Drotar, D., Eckerle, D., Satola, J., Pallotta, J., & Wyatt, B. (1990). Maternal interactional behavior with nonorganic failure-to-thrive infants: A case comparison study. *Child Abuse and Neglect, 14,* 41–51.

Dumaret, A. (1985). IQ, scholastic performance and behaviour of sibs raised in contrasting environments. *Journal of Child Psychology and Psychiatry, 26,* 553–580.

Dumas, J. E., & Wahler, R. G. (1983). Predictors of treatment outcome in parent training: Mother insularity and socioeconomic disadvantage. *Behavioral Assessment, 5,* 301–313.

Dunn, J. (1988). Connections between relationships: Implications of research on mothers and siblings. In R. A. Hinde & J. Stevenson-Hinde (Eds.), *Relationships within families: Mutual influences.* Oxford: Clarendon Press.

Dunn, J., Bretherton, I., & Munn, P. (1987). Conversations about feeling states between mothers and their young children. *Developmental Psychology, 23,* 132–139.

Dunn, J., & Kendrick, C. (1982). *Siblings: Love, envy, and understanding.* Cambridge: Harvard University Press.

Dunn, J., & Shatz, M. (1989). Becoming a conversationalist despite (or because of) having an older sibling. *Child Development, 60,* 399–410.

Durkin, D. (1966). *Children who read early: Two longitudinal studies.* New York: Teachers College Press.

Dusek, J. B. (1987). Sex roles and adjustment. In D. B. Carter (Ed.), *Current conceptions of sex roles and sex typing: Theory and research.* New York: Praeger.

Dweck, C. S. (1975). The role of expectations and attributions in the alleviation of learned helplessness. *Journal of Personality and Social Psychology, 31,* 674–685.

Dweck, C. S. (1986). Motivational processes affecting learning. *American Psychologist, 41,* 1040–1048.

Dweck, C. S., Davidson, W., Nelson, S., & Enna, B. (1978). Sex differences in learned helplessness: II. The contingencies of evaluative feedback in the classroom and III. An experimental analysis. *Developmental Psychology, 14,* 268–276

Dweck, C. S., & Elliott, E. S. (1983). Achievement motivation. In E. M. Hetherington (Ed.), *Handbook of child psychology: Vol. IV. Socialization, personality, and social development.* New York: Wiley.

Dweck, C. S., Goetz, T. E., & Strauss, N. L. (1980). Sex differences in learned helplessness: IV. An experimental and naturalistic study of failure generalization and its mediators. *Journal of Personality and Social Psychology, 38,* 441–452.

Dweck, C. S., & Reppucci, N. D. (1973). Learned helplessness and reinforcement responsibility in children. *Journal of Personality and Social Psychology, 25,* 109–116.

Dye, N. S. (1986). The medicalization of birth. In P. S. Eakins (Ed.), *The American way of birth*. Philadelphia: Temple University Press.

Eagly, A. H., & Steffen, V. J. (1986). Gender and aggressive behavior: A meta-analytic review of the social psychological literature. *Psychological Bulletin, 100,* 309–330.

Eakins, P. S. (1984). The rise of the free standing birth center: Principles and practice. *Women and Health, 9,* 49–64.

Easterbrooks, M. A., & Goldberg, W. A. (1984). Toddler development in the family: Impact of father involvement and parenting characteristics. *Child Development, 55,* 740–752.

Easterbrooks, M. A., & Goldberg, W. A. (1985). Effects of early maternal employment on toddlers, mothers, and fathers. *Developmental Psychology, 4,* 774–783.

Eccles, J. E. (1983). Expectancies, values, and academic behaviors. In J. T. Spence (Ed.), *Achievement and achievement motives: Psychological and sociological approaches*. San Francisco: W. H. Freeman.

Eccles, J. E. (1987). Adolescence: Gateway to androgyny? In D. B. Carter (Ed.), *Current conceptions of sex roles and sex typing: Theory and research*. New York: Praeger.

Eccles, J. E., & Jacobs, J. E. (1986). Social forces shape math attitudes and performance. *Signs, 11,* 367–380.

Eccles, J. S., & Midgely, C. (1988). Stage/environment fit: Developmentally appropriate classrooms for early adolescents. In R. E. Ames & C. Ames (Eds.), *Research on motivation in education* (Vol. 3). New York: Academic Press.

Eccles-Parsons, J., Adler, T., & Kaczala, C. (1982). Socialization of achievement attitudes and beliefs: Parental influences. *Child Development, 53,* 310–321.

Eckerman, C. O., & Stein, M. R. (1990). How imitation begets imitation and toddlers' generation of games. *Developmental Psychology, 26,* 370–378

Eckerman, C. O., Whatley, J. L., & Kutz, S. L. (1975). Growth of social play with peers during the second year of life. *Developmental Psychology, 11,* 42–49.

Edelman, A. M., Kraemer, H. C., & Korner, A. F. (1982). Effects of compensatory movement stimulation on the sleep-wake behaviors of preterm infants. *Journal of the American Academy of Child Psychiatry, 21,* 555–559.

Eder, D., & Hallinan, M. T. (1978). Sex differences in children's friendships. *American Sociological Review, 43,* 237–250.

Eder, R. A. (1989). The emergent personologist: The structure and content of 3 1/2-, 5 1/2-, and 7 1/2-year-olds' concepts of themselves and other persons. *Child Development, 60,* 1218–1228.

Eder, R. A. (1990). Uncovering young children's psychological selves: Individual and developmental differences. *Child Development, 61,* 849–863.

Egeland, B., Jacobvitz, D., & Papatola, K. (1987). Intergenerational continuity of abuse. In R. J. Gelles & J. B. Lancaster (Eds.), *Child abuse and neglect: Biosocial dimensions*. Hawthorne, NY: Aldine de Gruyter.

Egeland, B., Jacobvitz, D., & Sroufe, L. A. (1988). Breaking the cycle of abuse. *Child Development, 59,* 1080–1088.

Egeland, B., & Sroufe, L. A. (1981a). Attachment and early maltreatment. *Child Development, 52,* 44–52.

Egeland, B., & Sroufe, L. A. (1981b). Developmental sequelae of maltreatment in infancy. In R. Rizley & D. Cicchetti (Eds.), *New directions for child development: No. 11. Developmental perspectives on child maltreatment*. San Francisco: Jossey-Bass.

Ehrenhaft, P. M., Wagner, J. L., & Herdman, R. C. (1989). Changing prognosis for very low birth weight infants. *Obstetrics and Gynecology, 74,* 528–535.

Ehrhardt, A. A., & Meyer-Bahlburg, H. F. L. (1981). Effects of prenatal sex hormones on gender-related behavior. *Science, 211,* 1312–1318.

Ehrhardt, A. A., Meyer-Bahlburg, H. F. L., Feldman, J. F., & Ince, S. E. (1984). Sex-dimorphic behavior in childhood subsequent to prenatal exposure to exogenous progestogens and estrogens. *Archives of Sexual Behavior, 13,* 457–477.

Eimas, P. D., Siqueland, E. R., Jusczyk, P., & Vigorito, J. (1971). Speech perception in infants. *Science, 171,* 303–306.

Eisenberg, N. (1982). Introduction. In N. Eisenberg (Ed.), *The development of prosocial behavior*. New York: Academic Press.

Eisenberg, N. (1986). *Altruistic emotion, cognition, and behavior.* Hillsdale, NJ: Erlbaum.

Eisenberg, N., Boehnke, K., Schuhler, P., & Silbereisen, R. K. (1985). The development of prosocial behavior and cognition in German children. *Journal of Cross-Cultural Psychology, 16,* 69–82.

Eisenberg, N., Hertz-Lazarowitz, R., & Fuchs, I. (1990). Prosocial moral judgment in Israeli kibbutz and city children: A longitudinal study. *Merrill-Palmer Quarterly, 36,* 273–285.

Eisenberg, N., & Lennon, R. (1983). Sex differences in empathy and related capacities. *Psychological Bulletin, 94,* 100–131.

Eisenberg, N., & Miller, P. A. (1987). The relation of empathy to prosocial and related behaviors. *Psychological Bulletin, 101,* 91–119.

Eisenberg, N., & Mussen, P. H. (1989). *The roots of prosocial behavior in children*. Cambridge: Cambridge University Press.

Eisenberg, N., Roth, K., Bryniarski, K. A., & Murray, E. (1984). Sex differences in the relationship of height to children's actual and attributed social and cognitive competencies. *Sex Roles, 11,* 719–734.

Eisenberg, N., & Shell, R. (1986). Prosocial moral judgment and behavior in children: The mediating role of cost. *Personality and Social Psychology Bulletin, 12,* 426–433.

Eisenberg-Berg, N., & Hand, M. (1979). The relationship of preschoolers' reasoning about prosocial moral conflicts to prosocial behavior. *Child Development, 50,* 356–363.

Eisenberg-Berg, N., & Neal, C. (1979). Children's moral reasoning about their own spontaneous prosocial behavior. *Developmental Psychology, 15,* 228–229.

Ekman, P. (1972). Universals and cultural differences in facial expressions of emotion. In J. K. Cole (Ed.), *Nebraska symposium on motivation, 1971*. Lincoln: University of Nebraska Press.

Ekman, P. (1973). Cross-cultural studies of facial expression. In P. Ekman (Ed.), *Darwin and facial expression*. New York: Academic Press.

Elardo, R., Bradley, R. H., & Caldwell, B. M. (1977). A longitudinal study of the relation of infants' home environments to language development at age three. *Child Development, 48,* 595–603.

Elardo, R., & Bradley, R. H. (1981). The Home Observation for Measurement of the Environment (HOME) scale: A review of research. *Developmental Review, 1,* 113–145.

Elardo, R., Bradley, R. H., & Caldwell, B. M. (1975). The relation of infants' home environments to mental test performance from six to thirty-six months: A longitudinal analysis. *Child Development, 46,* 71–76.

Elias, S., & Annas, G. J. (1987). *Reproductive genetics and the law.* Chicago: Year Book Medical Publishers.

Elkind, D. (1978). *The child's reality: Three developmental themes.* Hillsdale, NJ: Erlbaum.

Elkind, D. (1981a). *Children and adolescents: Interpretive essays on Jean Piaget* (3rd ed.). New York: Oxford University Press.

Elkind, D. (1981b). *The hurried child.* Reading, MA: Addison-Wesley.

Elkind, D., Koegler, R. R., & Go, E. (1964). Studies in perceptual development: 2. Part-whole perception. *Child Development, 35,* 81–90.

Elliott, R., & Vasta, R. (1970). The modeling of sharing: Effects associated with vicarious reinforcement, symbolization, age, and generalization. *Journal of Experimental Child Psychology, 10,* 8–15.

Emde, R. N. (1980). Levels of meaning for infant emotions: A biosocial view. In W. A. Collins (Ed.), *The Minnesota symposia on child psychology: Vol. 13. Development of cognition, affect, and social relations.* Hillsdale, NJ: Erlbaum.

Emde, R. N., Johnson, W. F., & Easterbrooks, M. A. (1987). The do's and don'ts of early moral development: Psychoanalytic tradition and current research. In J. Kagan & S. Lamb (Eds.), *The emergence of morality in young children.* Chicago: University of Chicago Press.

Emde, R. N., & Koenig, K. L. (1969). Neonatal smiling, frowning and rapid eye movement states. *Journal of the American Academy of Child Psychiatry, 8,* 57–67.

Emler, N. P., & Rushton, J. P. (1974). Cognitive-developmental factors in children's generosity. *British Journal of Social and Clinical Psychology, 13,* 277–281.

Engen, T., Lipsitt, L. P., & Kaye, H. (1963). Olfactory responses and adaptation in the human neonate. *Journal of Comparative and Physiological Psychology, 56,* 73–77.

English, P. C. (1978). Failure to thrive without organic reason. *Pediatric Annals, 7,* 774–781.

Epstein, J., & McPartland, J. (1976). The concept and measurement of the quality of school life. *American Educational Research Journal, 50,* 13–30.

Epstein, L. H., & Wing, R. R. (1987). Behavioral treatment of childhood obesity. *Psychological Bulletin, 101,* 331–342.

Epstein, L. H., Wing, R. R., & Valoski, A. (1985). Childhood obesity. In P. B. Penchanz (Ed.), *Pediatric clinics of North America, 32,* 363–380.

Erickson, M. F., Sroufe, L. A., & Egeland, B. (1985). The relationship between quality of attachment and behavior problems in preschool in a high-risk sample. In I. Bretherton & E. Waters (Eds.), *Growing points of attachment theory and research. Monographs of the Society for Research in Child Development, 50*(1–2, Serial No. 209).

Erikson, E. H. (1950). *Childhood and society.* New York: W. W. Norton.

Erikson, E. H. (1963). *Childhood and society* (2nd ed.). New York: W. W. Norton.

Eron, L. D. (1980). Prescription for reduction of aggression. *American Psychologist, 35,* 244–252.

Eron, L. D. (1987). The development of aggressive behavior from the perspective of a developing organism. *American Psychologist, 42,* 435–442.

Eron, L. D., & Huesmann, L. R. (1984). The relation of prosocial behavior to the development of aggression and psychopathology. *Aggressive Behavior, 10,* 243–253.

Eron, L. D., Laulicht, J. H., Walder, L. O., Farber, I. E., & Spiegel, J. P. (1961). Application of role and learning theories to the study of the development of aggression in children. *Psychological Reports, 9,* 291–334.

Erwin, P. (1985). Similarity of attitudes and constructs in children's friendships. *Journal of Experimental Child Psychology, 40,* 470–485.

Eskenazi, B. (1984). Neurobehavioral teratology. In M. B. Bracken (Ed.), *Perinatal epidemiology.* New York: Oxford University Press.

Estes, D., Wellman, H. M., & Woolley, J. D. (1989). Children's understanding of mental phenomena. In H. W. Reese (Ed.), *Advances in child development and behavior* (Vol. 22). New York: Academic Press.

Etaugh, C., Grinnell, K., & Etaugh, A. (1989). Development of gender labeling: Effect of age of pictured child. *Sex Roles, 21,* 769–773.

Evans, M. I., Drugan, A., Koppitch, F. C., III, Zador, I. E., Sacks, A. J., & Sokol, R. J. (1989). Genetic diagnosis in the first trimester: The norm for the 1990s. *American Journal of Obstetrics and Gynecology, 160,* 1332–1339.

Fabes, R. A., Eisenberg, N., McCormick, S. E., & Wilson, M. S. (1988). Preschoolers' attributions of the situational determinants of others' naturally occurring emotions. *Developmental Psychology, 24,* 376–385.

Fagan, J. F., III. (1974). Infant recognition memory: The effects of length of familiarization and type of discrimination task. *Child Development, 45,* 351–356.

Fagan, J. F. (1984). The intelligent infant: Theoretical implications. *Intelligence, 8,* 1–9.

Fagan, J. F., & Montie, J. E. (1988). The behavioral assessment of cognitive well-being in the infant. In J. Kavanagh (Ed.), *Understanding mental retardation: Research accomplishments and new frontiers.* Baltimore: Paul H. Brookes.

Fagan, J. F., Shepherd, P. A., & Montie, J. E. (1987). A screening test for infants at risk for mental retardation. *Journal of Developmental and Behavioral Pediatrics, 5,* 121–130.

Fagan, J. F., & Singer, L. T. (1983). Infant recognition memory as a measure of intelligence. In L. P. Lipsitt (Ed.), *Advances in infancy research* (Vol. 2). Norwood, NJ: Ablex.

Fagot, B. I. (1977). Consequences of moderate cross-gender behavior in preschool children. *Child Development, 48,* 902–907.

Fagot, B. I. (1978a). The influence of sex of child on parental reactions to toddler children. *Child Development, 49,* 459–465.

Fagot, B. I. (1978b). Reinforcing contingencies for sex-role behaviors: Effect of experience with children. *Child Development, 49,* 30–36.

Fagot, B. I. (1985). Changes in thinking about early sex role development. *Developmental Review, 5,* 83–98.

Fagot, B. I., & Leinbach, M. D. (1987). Socialization of sex roles within the family. In D. B. Carter (Ed.), *Current conceptions of sex roles and sex typing: Theory and research.* New York: Praeger.

Fagot, B. I., & Leinbach, M. D. (1989). The young child's gender schema: Environmental input, internal organization. *Child Development, 60,* 663–672.

Falbo, T., & Cooper, C. R., (1980). Young children's time and intellectual ability. *Journal of Genetic Psychology, 173,* 299–300.

Falbo, T., & Polit, D. F. (1986). Quantitative review of the only child literature: Research evidence and theory development. *Psychological Bulletin, 100,* 176–189.

Fantz, R. L. (1961, May). The origin of form perception. *Scientific American, 204,* pp. 66–72.

Fantz, R. L., & Yeh, J. (1979). Configurational selectivities: Critical for development of visual perception and attention. *Canadian Journal of Psychology, 33,* 277–287.

Faust, M. S. (1983). Alternative constructions of adolescent growth. In J. Brooks-Gunn & A. C. Petersen (Eds.), *Girls at puberty: Biological and psychosocial perspectives.* New York: Plenum Press.

Feingold, A. (1988). Cognitive gender differences are disappearing. *American Psychologist, 43,* 95–103.

Feldman, H., Goldin-Meadow, S., & Gleitman, L. (1978). Beyond Herodotus: The creation of language by linguistically deprived deaf children. In A. Locke (Ed.), *Action, symbol, and gesture: The emergence of language.* New York: Academic Press.

Feldman, H. A. (1982). Epidemiology of toxoplasma infections. *Epidemiological Review, 4,* 204–213.

Feldman, W., Feldman, E., & Goodman, J. T. (1988). Culture versus biology: Children's attitudes toward thinness and fatness. *Pediatrics, 81,* 190–194.

Felner, R. D., & Adan, A. M. (1988). The School Transitional Environment Project: An ecological intervention and evaluation. In R. H. Price, E. L. Cowan, R. P. Lorion, I. Serrano-Garcia, & J. Ramos-McKay (Eds.), *14 ounces of prevention: A casebook for practitioners.* Washington, DC: American Psychological Association.

Felner, R. D., Ginter, M., & Primavera, J. (1982). Primary prevention during school transitions: Social support and environmental structure. *American Journal of Community Psychology, 10,* 277–290.

Fenson, L., Vella, D., & Kennedy, M. (1989). Children's knowledge of thematic and taxonomic relations at two years of age. *Child Development, 60,* 911–919.

Fernald, A. (1985). Four-month-olds prefer to listen to motherese. *Infant Behavior and Development, 8,* 181–195.

Fernald, A., & Kuhl, P. (1987). Acoustic determinants of infant preference for motherese speech. *Infant Behavior and Development, 10,* 279–293.

Fernald, A., & Mazzie, C. (1983, April). *Pitch-marking of new and old information in mothers' speech to infants.* Paper presented at the biennial meeting of the Society for Research in Child Development, Detroit.

Feshbach, S., & Singer, R. (1971). *Television and aggression.* San Francisco: Jossey-Bass.

Field, J., Muir, D., Pilon, R., Sinclair, M., & Dodwell, P. (1980). Infants' orientation to lateral sounds from birth to three months. *Child Development, 51,* 295–298.

Field, T. M. (1977). Effects of early separation, interactive deficits, and experimental manipulations on infant-mother face-to-face interactions. *Child Development, 48,* 763–771.

Field, T. (1979). Differential behavior and cardiac responses of 3-month-olds to a mirror and a peer. *Infant Behavior and Development, 2,* 179–184.

Field, T. M. (1982). Affective displays of high-risk infants during early interactions. In T. Field & A. Fogel (Eds.), *Emotion and early interaction.* Hillsdale, NJ: Erlbaum.

Field, T. M. (1986). Interventions for premature infants. *Journal of Pediatrics, 109,* 183–191.

Field, T. M. (1987). Affective and interactive disturbances in infants. In J. D. Osofsky (Ed.), *Handbook of infant development* (2nd ed.). New York: Wiley.

Field, T. M., Cohen, D., Garcia, R., & Greenberg, R. (1984). Mother-stranger face discrimination by the newborn. *Infant Behavior and Development, 7,* 19–25.

Field, T. M., Healy, B., Goldstein, S., Perry, S., Bendell, D., Schanberg, S., Zimmerman, E. A., & Kuhn, C. (1988). Infants of depressed mothers show "depressed" behavior even with nondepressed adults. *Child Development, 59,* 1569–1579.

Field, T. M., Ignatoff, E., Stringer, S., Brennan, J., Greenberg, R., Widmayer, S., & Anderson, G. C. (1982). Nonnutritive sucking during tube feedings: Effects on preterm neonates in an intensive care unit. *Pediatrics, 70,* 381–384.

Field, T. M., & Walden, T. A. (1982). Production and perception of facial expressions in infancy and early childhood. In H. W. Reese & L. P. Lipsitt (Eds.), *Advances in child development and behavior* (Vol. 16). New York: Academic Press.

Field, T. M., Woodson, R., Cohen, D., Greenberg, R., Garcia, R., & Collins, K. (1983). Discrimination and imitation of facial expressions by term and preterm neonates. *Infant Behavior and Development, 6,* 485–489.

Field, T. M., Woodson, R., Greenberg, R., & Cohen, D. (1982). Discrimination and imitation of facial expressions by neonates. *Science, 218,* 179–181.

Finch, E. (1978). *Clinical assessment of short stature.* Unpublished medical school thesis, Yale University.

Findley, M. J., & Cooper, H. M. (1983). Locus of control and academic achievement. A literature review. *Journal of Personality and Social Psychology, 44,* 419–427.

Finn, J. D., & Achilles, C. M. (1990). Answers and questions about class size: A statewide experiment. *American Educational Research Journal, 27,* 557–577.

Finnie, V., & Russell, A. (1988). Preschool children's social status and their mothers' behavior and knowledge in the supervisory role. *Developmental Psychology, 24,* 789–801.

Fischbein, S. (1981). Heredity-environment influences on growth and development during adolescence. In L. Gedda, P. Parisi, & W. E. Nance (Eds.), *Twin research 3: Pt. B. Program in clinical and biological research.* New York: Liss.

Fischer, K. (1980). A theory of cognitive development: The control and construction of hierarchies of skills. *Psychological Review, 87,* 477–531.

Fischer, K., & Pipp, S. L. (1984). Processes of cognitive development: Optimal level and skill acquisition. In R. J. Sternberg (Ed.), *Mechanisms of cognitive development.* New York: W. H. Freeman.

Fish, M. C., Gross, A. L., & Sanders, J. S. (1986). The effect of equity strategies on girls' computer usage in school. *Computers in Human Behavior, 2,* 127–134.

Fishkin, J., Keniston, K., & MacKinnon, C. (1973). Moral reasoning and political ideology. *Journal of Personality and Social Psychology, 27,* 109–119.

Fishler, K., Azen, C. G., Henderson, R., Friedman, E. G., & Koch, R. (1987). Psychoeducational findings among children treated for phenylketonuria. *American Journal of Mental Deficiency, 92,* 65–73.

Fivush, R. (1984). Learning about school: The development of kindergartners' school scripts. *Child Development, 55,* 1697–1709.

Flanagan, C. A. (1990). Change in family work status: Effects on parent-adolescent decision making. *Child Development, 61,* 163–177.

Flavell, J. H. (1963). *The developmental psychology of Jean Piaget.* New York: Van Nostrand Reinhold.

Flavell, J. H. (1970). Developmental studies of mediated memory. In H. W. Reese & L. P. Lipsitt (Eds.), *Advances in child development and behavior* (Vol. 5). New York: Academic Press.

Flavell, J. H. (1978). The development of knowledge about visual perception. In C. B. Keasey (Ed.), *Nebraska symposium on motivation* (Vol. 25). Lincoln: University of Nebraska Press.

Flavell, J. H. (1985). *Cognitive development* (2nd ed.). Englewood Cliffs, NJ: Prentice-Hall.

Flavell, J. H., Beach, D. H., & Chinsky, J. M. (1966). Spontaneous verbal rehearsal in a memory task as a function of age. *Child Development, 37,* 283–299.

Flavell, J. H., Botkin, P. T., Fry, C. L., Jr., Wright, J. W., & Jarvis, P. E. (1968). *The development of roletaking and communication skills in children.* New York: Wiley.

Flavell, J. H., Friedrichs, A. G., & Hoyt, J. D. (1970). Developmental changes in memorization processes. *Cognitive Psychology, 1,* 324–340.

Flavell, J. H., Shipstead, S. G., & Croft, K. (1978). Young children's knowledge about visual perception: Hiding objects from others. *Child Development, 49,* 1208–1211.

Flavell, J. H., & Wellman, H. M. (1977). Metamemory. In R. V. Kail & J. W. Hagen (Eds.), *Perspectives on the development of memory and cognition.* Hillsdale, NJ: Erlbaum.

Flink, C., Boggiano, A. K., & Barrett, M. (1990). Controlling teaching strategies: Undermining children's self-determination and performance. *Journal of Personality and Social Psychology, 59,* 916–924.

Fodor, J. A. (1983). *The modularity of mind.* Cambridge: MIT Press.

Fogel, A. (1979). Peer- vs. mother-directed behavior in 1- to 3-month-old infants. *Infant Behavior and Development, 2,* 215–226.

Fogel, A. (1982). Early adult-infant face-to-face interaction: Expectable sequences of behavior. *Journal of Pediatric Psychology, 7,* 1–22.

Ford, C. S. (1964). *A comparative study of human reproduction* (Yale University Publications in Anthropology No. 32). New Haven: Yale University Press.

Fox, N. A. (1977). Attachment of kibbutz infants to mother and metapelet. *Child Development, 48,* 1228–1239.

Fox, N. A., & Davidson, R. J. (1986). Psychophysiological measures of emotion: New directions in developmental research. In C. E. Izard & P. B. Read (Eds.), *Measuring emotions in infants and children* (Vol. 2). Cambridge: Cambridge University Press.

Fox, R., Aslin, R. N., Shea, S. L., & Dumais, S. T. (1980). Stereopsis in human infants. *Science, 207,* 323–324.

Fraiberg, S. (1977). *Insights from the blind.* New York: Basic Books.

Francis, P. L., & McCroy, G. (1983, April). *Bimodal recognition of human stimulus configurations.* Paper presented at the biennial meeting of the Society for Research in Child Development, Detroit.

Frankenburg, W. K., & Dodds, J. B. (1967). The Denver Developmental Screening Test. *Journal of Pediatrics, 71,* 181–191.

Franz, C. E., McClelland, D. C., & Weinberger, J. (1991). Childhood antecedents of conventional social accomplishment in midlife adults: A 36-year prospective study. *Journal of Personality and Social Psychology, 60,* 586–595.

Frauenglass, M. H., & Diaz, R. M. (1985). Self-regulatory functions of children's private speech: A critical analysis of recent challenges to Vygotsky's theory. *Developmental Psychology, 21,* 357–364.

Freedman, D. (1979). Ethnic differences in babies. *Human Nature, 2,* 26–43.

Freedman, J. L. (1984). Effect of television violence on aggressiveness. *Psychological Bulletin, 96,* 227–246.

Freedman, J. L. (1986). Television violence and aggression: A rejoinder. *Psychological Bulletin, 100,* 372–378.

Freud, A. (1958). Adolescence. In *Psychoanalytic study of the child* (Vol. 13). New York: International Universities Press.

Freud, S. (1922). *Beyond the pleasure principle.* London: Hogarth Press.

Freud, S. (1961). Some psychical consequences of the anatomical distinction between the sexes. In J. Strachey (Ed. and Trans.), *Standard edition of the complete psychological works of Sigmund Freud* (Vol. 19). London: Hogarth Press. (Original work published 1925)

Freud, S. (1965). *New introductory lectures on psychoanalysis* (J. Strachey, Trans.). New York: W. W. Norton. (Original work published 1933)

Frey, K. S., & Ruble, D. N. (1987). What children say about classroom performance: Sex and grade differences in perceived competence. *Child Development, 58,* 1066–1078.

Fried, P. A. (1986). Marijuana and human pregnancy. In I. J. Chasnoff (Ed.), *Drug use in pregnancy: Mother and child.* Lancaster, England: MTP Press.

Friedman, E. (1978). *Labor: Clinical evaluation and management.* New York: Appleton-Century-Crofts.

Friedrich, L. K., & Stein, A. H. (1973). Aggressive and prosocial television programs and the natural behavior of preschool children. *Monographs of the Society for Research in Child Development, 38*(4, Serial No. 151).

Frisch, R. E. (1983). Fatness, puberty and fertility. In J. Brooks-Gunn & A. C. Petersen (Eds.), *Girls at puberty: Biological and psychosocial perspectives.* New York: Plenum Press.

Frodi, A. M., & Lamb, M. E. (1980). Child abusers' responses to infant smiles and cries. *Child Development, 51,* 238–241.

Frodi, A. M., Lamb, M. E., Leavitt, L. A., & Donovan, W. L. (1978). Fathers' and mothers' responses to infant smiles and cries. *Infant Behavior and Development, 1,* 187–198.

Frodi, A. M., & Thompson, R. (1985). Infants' affective responses in the strange situation: Effects of prematurity and of quality of attachment. *Child Development, 56,* 1280–1290.

Frueh, T., & McGhee, P. (1975). Traditional sex-role development and amount of time spent watching television. *Developmental Psychology, 11,* 109.

Fry, D. B. (1966). The development of the phonological system in the normal and the deaf child. In F. Smith & G. A. Miller (Eds.), *The genesis of language.* Cambridge: MIT Press.

Fuchs, I., Eisenberg, N., Hertz-Lazarowitz, R., & Sharabany, R. (1986). Kibbutz, Israeli city, and American children's moral reasoning about prosocial moral conflicts. *Merrill-Palmer Quarterly, 32,* 37–50.

Fulker, O. W., & Eysenck, H. J. (1979). Nature, nurture and socio-economic status. In H. J. Eysenck (Ed.), *The structure and measurement of intelligence.* Berlin: Springer-Verlag.

Furman, W., & Bierman, K. L. (1984). Children's conceptions of friendship: A multimethod study of developmental changes. *Developmental Psychology, 20,* 925–931.

Furman, W., & Robbins, P. (1985). What's the point? Issues in the selection of treatment objectives. In B. H. Schneider, K. H. Rubin, & J. E. Ledingham (Eds.), *Children's peer relations: Issues in assessment and intervention.* New York: Springer-Verlag.

Furstenberg, F. F., Jr. (1987). The new extended family: The experience of parents and children after remarriage. In K. Paley & M. Ihinger-Tallman (Eds.), *Remarriage and stepparenting.* New York: Guilford Press.

Fuson, K. C. (1979). The development of self-regulating aspects of speech: A review. In G. Zivin (Ed.), *The development of self-regulation through private speech.* New York: Wiley.

Gaddis, A., & Brooks-Gunn, J. (1985). The male experience of pubertal change. *Journal of Youth and Adolescence, 14,* 61–69.

Gagné, R. M. (1968). *The conditions of learning.* New York: Holt, Rinehart & Winston.

Gagné, R. M., Briggs, L. J., & Wager, W. W. (1988). *Principles of instructional design* (3rd ed.). New York: Holt, Rinehart & Winston.

Galotti, K. M. (1989). Approaches to studying formal and everyday reasoning. *Psychological Bulletin, 105,* 331–351.

Galton, F. (1883). *Inquiries into human faculty and its development.* London: Macmillan.

Gamoran, A. (1989). Measuring curriculum differentiation. *American Journal of Education, 97,* 129–143.

Ganon, E. C., & Swartz, K. B. (1980). Perception of internal elements of compound figures by one-month-olds. *Journal of Experimental Child Psychology, 30,* 159–170.

Garabino, J. (1982). Sociocultural risk: Dangers to competence. In C. Kopp & J. Krakow (Eds.), *Child development in a social context.* Reading, MA: Addison-Wesley.

Gardner, H. (1983). *Frames of mind: The theory of multiple intelligences.* New York: Basic Books.

Gardner, H. (1986). The waning of intelligence tests. In R. J. Sternberg & D. K. Detterman (Eds.), *What is intelligence?* Norwood, NJ: Ablex.

Garmezy, N. (1985). Stress-resistant children: The search for protective factors. In J. E. Stevenson (Ed.), *Recent research in developmental psychology.* (Journal of Child Psychology and Psychiatry Book Suppl. 4). Oxford: Pergamon Press.

Gavin, L. A., & Furman, W. (1989). Age differences in adolescent's perceptions of their peer groups. *Developmental Psychology, 25,* 827–834.

Gelman, R. (1969). Conservation acquisition: A problem of learning to attend to relevant attributes. *Journal of Experimental Child Psychology, 7,* 167–187.

Gelman, R. (1972). Logical capacity of very young children: Number invariance rules. *Child Development, 43,* 75–90.

Gelman, R., & Baillargeon, R. (1983). A review of some Piagetian concepts. In J. H. Flavell & E. M. Markman (Eds.), *Handbook of child psychology. Vol. III. Cognitive development.* New York: Wiley.

Gelman, R., & Gallistel, C. R. (1978). *The child's understanding of number.* Cambridge: Harvard University Press.

Gelman, R., & Meck, E. (1983). Preschoolers' counting: Principles before skill. *Cognition, 13,* 343–359.

George, C., & Main, M. (1979). Social interactions of young abused children: Approach, avoidance, and aggression. *Child Development, 50,* 306–318.

Gerbner, G., Gross, L., Morgan, M., & Signorielli, N. (1986). Living with television: The dynamics of the cultivation process. In J. Bryant & D. Zillman (Eds.), *Perspectives on media effects.* Hillsdale, NJ: Erlbaum.

Gesell, A. (1929). *Infancy and human growth.* New York: Macmillan.

Gesell, A., & Thompson, H. (1934). *Infant behavior: Its genesis and growth.* New York: McGraw-Hill.

Gesell, A., & Thompson, H. (1938). *The psychology of early growth.* New York: Macmillan.

Ghim, H-R. (1990). Evidence for perceptual organization in infants: Perception of subjective contours by young infants. *Infant Behavior and Development, 13,* 221–248.

Ghim, H-R., & Eimas, P. D. (1988). Global and local processing by 3- and 4-month-old infants. *Perception & Psychophysics, 43,* 165–171.

Ghiselli, E. E. (1966). *The validity of occupational aptitude tests.* New York: Wiley.

Gibby, R. G., Sr., & Gibby, R. G., Jr. (1967). The effects of stress resulting from academic failure. *Journal of Clinical Psychology, 23,* 35–37.

Gibson, E. J. (1969). *Principles of perceptual learning and development.* New York: Appleton.

Gibson, E. J. (1982). The concept of affordances in development: The renascence of functionalism. In W. A. Collins (Ed.), *The Minnesota symposia on child psychology: Vol. 15. The concept of development.* Hillsdale, NJ: Erlbaum.

Gibson, E. J. (1988). Exploratory behavior in the development of perceiving, acting, and the acquiring of knowledge. *Annual Review of Psychology, 39,* 1–41.

Gibson, E. J., Gibson, J. J., Pick, A. D., & Osser, H. (1962). A developmental study of the discrimination of letter-like forms. *Journal of Comparative and Physiological Psychology, 55,* 897–906.

Gibson, E. J., & Spelke, E. S. (1983). The development of perception. In J. H. Flavell & E. M. Markman (Eds.), *Handbook of child psychology: Vol. III. Cognitive development.* New York: Wiley.

Gibson, E. J., & Walker, A. (1984). Development of knowledge of visual-tactual affordances of substance. *Child Development, 55,* 453–460.

Gibson, J. J. (1966). *The senses considered as perceptual systems.* Boston: Houghton Mifflin.

Gibson, J. J. (1979). *The ecological approach to visual perception.* Boston: Houghton Mifflin.

Gilligan, C. (1977). In a different voice: Women's conceptions of self and morality. *Harvard Educational Review, 47,* 481–517.

Gilligan, C. (1982). *In a different voice: Psychological theory and women's development.* Cambridge: Harvard University Press.

Gilligan, C., & Wiggins, G. (1987). The origins of morality in early childhood relationships. In J. Kagan & S. Lamb (Eds.),

The emergence of morality in young children. Chicago: University of Chicago Press.

Gillis, J. S. (1982). *Too tall, too small.* Champaign, IL: Institute for Personality and Ability Testing.

Ginsberg, H. (1972). *The myth of the deprived child: Poor children's intellect and education.* Englewood Cliffs, NJ: Prentice-Hall.

Ginsburg, H. P., & Opper, S. (1988). *Piaget's theory of intellectual development* (3rd ed.). Englewood Cliffs, NJ: Prentice-Hall.

Glass, D. C., Neulinger, J., & Brim, O. G. (1974). Birth order, verbal intelligence, and educational aspiration. *Child Development, 45,* 807–811.

Gleason, J. B., & Perlmann, R. Y. (1985). Acquiring social variation in speech. In H. Giles & R. N. St. Clair (Eds.), *Recent advances in language, communication, and social psychology.* London: Erlbaum.

Gleason, J. B., & Weintraub, S. (1978). Input language and the acquisition of communicative competence. In K. Nelson (Ed.), *Children's language* (Vol. 1). New York: Gardner Press.

Gleitman, L. R., Gleitman, H., & Shipley, E. F. (1972). The emergence of the child as grammarian. *Cognition, 1,* 137–164.

Gleitman, L. R., Newport, E. L., & Gleitman, H. (1984). The current status of the motherese hypothesis. *Journal of Child Language, 11,* 43–79.

Gleuck, S., & Gleuck, E. (1950). *Unraveling juvenile delinquency.* Cambridge: Harvard University Press.

Glick, P. C. (1984). Marriage, divorce, and living arrangements: Prospective changes. *Journal of Family Issues, 5,* 7–26.

Glick, P. C. (1989). Remarried families, stepfamilies, and stepchildren: A brief demographic analysis. *Family Relations, 38,* 24–27.

Glick, P. C., & Lin, S. (1986). Recent changes in divorce and remarriage. *Journal of Marriage and the Family, 48,* 737–747.

Gnepp, J. & Chilamkurti, C. (1988). Children's use of personality attributions to predict other people's emotional and behavioral reactions. *Child Development, 59,* 743–754.

Goldberg, R. J. (1977, April). *Maternal time use and preschool performance.* Paper presented at the biennial meeting of the Society for Research in Child Development, New Orleans.

Goldberg, S. (1979). Premature birth: Consequences for the parent-infant relationship. *American Scientist, 67,* 582–590.

Goldberg, S. (1983). Parent-infant bonding: Another look. *Child Development, 54,* 1355–1382.

Goldfield, B. A., & Reznick, J. S. (1990). Early lexical acquisition: Rate, content, and the vocabulary spurt. *Journal of Child Language, 17,* 171–183.

Goldschmid, M. L. (1967). Different types of conservation and non-conservation and their relation to age, sex, IQ, MA, and vocabulary. *Child Development, 38,* 1229–1246.

Goldschmid, M. L., & Bentler, P. M. (1968). *Concept assessment kit: Conservation.* San Diego: Educational and Industrial Testing Service.

Goldsmith, H. H., & Alansky, J. A. (1987). Maternal and infant temperamental predictors of attachment: A meta-analytic review. *Journal of Consulting and Clinical Psychology, 55,* 805–816.

Goldsmith, H. H., & Gottesman, I. I. (1981). Origins of variation in behavioral style: A longitudinal study of temperament in young twins. *Child Development, 52,* 91–103.

Golub, M. S., Sassenrath, E. N., & Chapman, C. F. (1981). Regulation of visual attention in offspring of female monkeys treated with delta-9-tetrahydrocannabinol. *Developmental Psychobiology, 14,* 507–512.

Goodenough, F. L. (1931). *Anger in young children.* Minneapolis: University of Minnesota Press.

Goodman, G. S., Levine, M., Melton, G. B., & Ogden, D. W. (1991). Child witnesses and the confrontation clause. *Law and Human Behavior, 15,* 13–29.

Goodman, G. S., & Reed, R. S. (1986). Age differences in eyewitness testimony. *Law and Human Behavior, 10,* 317–332.

Goodwin, D. W., Schulsinger, F., Hermansen, L., Guze, S. B., & Winokur, G. (1973). Alcohol problems in adoptees raised apart from alcoholic biological parents. *Archives of General Psychiatry, 28,* 238–243.

Gopnik, A., & Meltzoff, A. N. (1986). Relations between semantic and cognitive development in the one-word stage: The specificity hypothesis. *Child Development, 57,* 1040–1053.

Gopnik, A., & Meltzoff, A. N. (1987). The development of categorization in the second year and its relation to other cognitive and linguistic attainments. *Child Development, 58,* 1523–1531.

Gorlin, R. J. (1977). Classical chromosome disorders. In J. J. Yunis (Ed.), *New chromosomal syndromes.* New York: Academic Press.

Gorman, H., & Bourne, L. E. (1983). Learning to think by learning Logo: Rule learning in third grade computer programmers. *Bulletin of the Psychonomic Society, 21,* 165–167.

Gorski, R. A. (1980). Sexual differentiation of the brain. In D. T. Krieger & J. C. Hughes (Eds.), *Neuroendocrinology.* New York: Rockefeller University Press.

Gortmaker, S. L., Dietz, W. H., Jr., Sobol, A. M., & Wehler, C. A. (1987). Increasing pediatric obesity in the United States. *American Journal of Diseases of Children, 141,* 535–540.

Gottesman, I. I. (1963). Heritability of personality: A demonstration. *Psychological Monographs, 77* (Whole No. 572).

Gottesman, I. I., & Shields, J. (1982). *Schizophrenia: The epigenetic puzzle.* Cambridge: Cambridge University Press.

Gottfried, A. E., Gottfried, A. W., & Bathurst, K. (1988). Maternal employment when children are toddlers and kindergartners. In A. E. Gottfried & A. W. Gottfried (Eds.), *Maternal employment and children's development: Longitudinal research.* New York: Plenum Press.

Gottman, J. M. (1983). How children become friends. *Monographs of the Society for Research in Child Development, 48*(2, Serial No. 201).

Gottman, J. M., Gonso, J., & Rasmussen, B. (1975). Social interaction, social competence, and friendship in children. *Child Development, 46,* 709–718.

Gottman, J. M., & Parkhurst, J. T. (1980). A developmental theory of friendship and acquaintanceship processes. In W. A. Collins (Ed.), *The Minnesota symposia on child development: Vol. 13. Development of cognition, affect, and social relations.* Hillsdale, NJ: Erlbaum.

Gouin-Decarie, T. (1969). A study of the mental and emotional development of the thalidomide child. In B. M. Foss (Ed.), *Determinants of infant behavior IV.* London: Methuen.

Gould, S. J. (1985, November). Geoffrey and the homeobox. *Natural History,* pp. 12–23.

Goy, R. (1970). Early hormonal influences on the development of sexual and sex-related behavior. In F. Schmitt, G. Quarton, T. Melnechuck, & G. Adelman (Eds.), *The neurosciences: Second study program*. New York: Rockefeller University Press.

Goyco, P. G., & Beckerman, R. C. (1990). Sudden infant death syndrome. *Current Problems in Pediatrics, 20,* 299–346.

Grady, D. (1987, June). The ticking of a time bomb in the genes. *Discover,* pp. 26–39.

Granrud, C. E., Yonas, A., Smith, I. M. E., Arterberry, M. W., Glicksman, M. L., & Sorknes, A. C. (1984). Infants' sensitivity to accretion and deletion of texture as information for depth at an edge. *Child Development, 55,* 1630–1636.

Graves, N. B., & Graves, T. D. (1983). The cultural context of prosocial development: An ecological model. In D. L. Bridgeman (Ed.), *The nature of prosocial development: Interdisciplinary theories and strategies*. New York: Academic Press.

Green, J. E., Dorfmann, A., Jones, S. L., Bender, S., Patton, L., & Schulman, J. D. (1988). Chorionic villus sampling: Experience with an initial 940 cases. *Obstetrics and Gynecology, 71,* 208–212.

Greenberg, B. S. (1986). Minorities and the mass media. In J. Bryant & D. Zillman (Eds.), *Perspectives on mass media effects*. Hillsdale, NJ: Erlbaum.

Greenfield, P. M. (1976). Cross-cultural research and Piagetian theory: Paradox and progress. In K. Riegel & J. Meacham (Eds.), *The developing individual in a changing world* (Vol. 1). The Hague: Mouton.

Greenfield, P. M. (1984). A theory of the teacher in the learning activities of everyday life. In B. Rogoff & J. Lave (Eds.), *Everyday cognition: Its development in social context*. Cambridge: Harvard University Press.

Greenough, W. T., Black, J. E., & Wallace, C. S. (1987). Experience and brain development. *Child Development, 58,* 539–559.

Greif, E. B., & Gleason, J. B. (1980). Hi, thanks, and goodbye: More routine information. *Language in Society, 9,* 159–166.

Greif, E. B., & Ulman, K. J. (1982). The psychological impact of menarche on early adolescent females: A review of the literature. *Child Development, 53,* 1413–1430.

Greist, D., Wells, K. C., & Forehand, R. (1979). An examination of predictors of maternal perceptions of maladjustment in clinic-referred children. *Journal of Abnormal Psychology, 88,* 277–281.

Grimes, D., & Gross, G. (1981). Pregnancy outcomes in black women aged 35 and older. *Obstetrics and Gynecology, 58,* 614–620.

Grossman, F. K., Pollack, W. S., & Golding, E. (1988). Fathers and children: Predicting the quality and quantity of fathering. *Developmental Psychology, 24,* 82–91.

Grossman, K., Grossman, K. E., Spangler, G., Suess, G., & Unzner, L. (1985). Maternal sensitivity and newborns' orientation responses as related to quality of attachment in northern Germany. In I. Bretherton & E. Waters (Eds.), *Growing points of attachment theory and research. Monographs of the Society for Research in Child Development, 50*(1–2, Serial No. 209).

Grotevant, H. D., & Cooper, C. R. (1986). Individuation in family relationships. *Human Development, 29,* 82–100.

Gruen, G., Ottinger, D., & Zigler, E. (1970). Level of aspiration and the probability learning of middle- and lower-class children. *Developmental Psychology, 3,* 133–142.

Grusec, J. E. (1982). The socialization of altruism. In N. Eisen-berg (Ed.), *The development of prosocial behavior*. New York: Academic Press.

Grusec, J. E. (1991). Socializing concern for others in the home. *Developmental Psychology, 27,* 338–342.

Grusec, J. E., & Redler, E. (1980). Attribution, reinforcement, and altruism: A developmental analysis. *Developmental Psychology, 16,* 525–534.

Grusec, J. E., & Skubiski, L. (1970). Model nurturance, demand characteristics of the modeling experiment, and altruism. *Journal of Personality and Social Psychology, 14,* 352–359.

Guidubaldi, J., Perry, J. D., & Cleminshaw, H. K. (1984). The legacy of parental divorce: A nationwide study of family status and selected mediating variables on children's academic and social competencies. In B. B. Lahey & A. E. Kazdin (Eds.), *Advances in clinical child psychology* (Vol. 7). New York: Plenum Press.

Guilford, J. P. (1967). *The nature of human intelligence*. New York: McGraw-Hill.

Guilford, J. P. (1985). The structure-of-intellect model. In B. B. Wolman (Ed.), *Handbook of intelligence*. New York: Wiley.

Gump, P. V. (1978). School environments. In I. Altman & J. F. Wohlwill (Eds.), *Children and the environment*. New York: Plenum Press.

Gundy, J. H. (1987). The pediatric physical examination. In R. A. Hoekelman, S. Blatman, S. B. Friedman, N. M. Nelson, & H. M. Seidel (Eds.), *Primary pediatric care*. Washington, DC: C. V. Mosby.

Gunnar, M. R., Malone, S., Vance, G., & Fisch, R. O. (1985). Coping with aversive stimulation in the neonatal period: Quiet sleep and plasma cortisol levels during recovery from circumcision. *Child Development, 56,* 824–834.

Gunzenhauser, N. (Ed.). (1987). *Infant stimulation: For whom, what kind, when, and how much?* (Johnson & Johnson Baby Products Company Pediatric Round Table Series No. 13). Skilman, NJ: Johnson & Johnson.

Gurucharri, C., & Selman, R. L. (1982). The development of interpersonal understanding during childhood, preadolescence, and adolescence: A longitudinal follow-up study. *Child Development, 53,* 924–927.

Gusella, J. L., Muir, D., & Tronick, E. Z. (1988). The effect of manipulating maternal behavior during an interaction on three- and six-month-olds' affect and attention. *Child Development, 59,* 1111–1124.

Guttentag, R. E. (1987). Memory and aging: Implications for theories of memory development during childhood. *Developmental Review, 5,* 56–82.

Hagerman, R. J. (1987). Fragile X syndrome. *Current Problems in Pediatrics, 17,* 625–674.

Hainline, L., Turkel, J., Abramov, I., Lemerise, E., & Harris, C. M. (1984). Characteristics of saccades in human infants. *Vision Research, 24,* 1771–1780.

Haith, M. M. (1980). *Rules that babies look by: The organization of newborn visual activity*. Hillsdale, NJ: Erlbaum.

Haith, M. M. (1990). Progress in the understanding of sensory and perceptual processes in early infancy. *Merrill-Palmer Quarterly, 36,* 1–26.

Hakuta, K., & Diaz, R. M. (1985). The relationship between degree of bilingualism and cognitive ability: A critical discussion and some new longitudinal data. In K. E. Nelson (Ed.), *Children's language* (Vol. 5). Hillsdale, NJ: Erlbaum.

Hall, G. S. (1893). The contents of children's minds on entering school. *Pedagogical Seminary, 1,* 139–173.

Hall, J. A. (1978). Gender effects in decoding nonverbal cues. *Psychological Bulletin, 85,* 845–857.

Hall, J. A. (1984). *Nonverbal sex differences: Communication accuracy and expressive style.* Baltimore: Johns Hopkins University Press.

Hall, J. A., & Halberstadt, A. G. (1986). Smiling and gazing. In J. S. Hyde & M. C. Linn (Eds.), *The psychology of gender: Advances through meta-analysis.* Baltimore: Johns Hopkins University Press.

Hallinan, M. T. (1976). Friendship patterns in open and traditional classrooms. *Sociology of Education, 49,* 254–265.

Hallinan, M. T. (1990). The effects of ability grouping in secondary schools: A response to Slavin's best-evidence synthesis. *Review of Educational Research, 60,* 501–504.

Halmi, K. A. (1985). The diagnosis and treatment of anorexia nervosa. In D. Shaffer, A. A. Ehrhardt, & L. Greenhill (Eds.), *The clinical guide to child psychiatry.* New York: Free Press.

Halpern, D. F. (1986). *Sex differences in cognitive abilities.* Hillsdale, NJ: Erlbaum.

Halverson, H. M. (1931). An experimental study of prehension in infants by means of systematic cinema records. *Genetic Psychology Monographs, 10,* 107–286.

Hamilton, V. J., & Gordon, D. A. (1978). Teacher-child interactions in preschool and task persistence. *American Educational Research Journal, 15,* 459–466.

Hans, S. L., Marcus, J., Jeremy, R. J., & Auerbach, J. G. (1984). Neurobehavioral development of children exposed in utero to opioid drugs. In J. Yanai (Ed.), *Neurobehavioral teratology.* New York: Elsevier.

Hansen, J. D. L. (1990). Malnutrition review. *Pediatric Reviews and Communication, 4,* 201–212.

Harbison, R. D., & Mantilla-Plata, B. (1972). Prenatal toxicity, maternal distribution and placental transfer of tetrahydrocannabinol. *Journal of Pharmacology and Experimental Therapeutics, 180,* 446–453.

Hareven, T. (1985). Historical changes in the family and the life course: Implications for child development. In A. B. Smuts & J. W. Hagen (Eds.), *History and research in child development. Monographs of the Society for Research in Child Development, 50*(4–5, Serial No. 211).

Harkness, S., & Super, C. M. (1985). Child-environment interactions in the socialization of affect. In M. Lewis & C. Saarni (Eds.), *The socialization of emotions.* New York: Plenum Press.

Harlow, H. F., & Zimmerman, R. R. (1959). Affectional responses in the infant monkey. *Science, 130,* 421–432.

Harpin, V., Chellappah, G., & Rutter, N. (1983). Responses of the newborn infant to overheating. *Biology of the Neonate, 44,* 65–75.

Harriman, A. E., & Lukosius, P. A. (1982). On why Wayne Dennis found Hopi children retarded in age at onset of walking. *Perceptual and Motor Skills, 55,* 79–86.

Harris, G., & Booth, D. (1985). Sodium preference in food and previous dietary experience in 6-month-old infants. *IRCS Medical Science, 13,* 1177–1178.

Harris, P. L. (1983). Children's understanding of the link between situation and emotion. *Journal of Experimental Child Psychology, 36,* 490–509.

Harris, P. L., Donnelly, K., Guz, G. R., & Pitt-Watson, R. (1986). Children's understanding of the distinction between real and apparent emotion. *Child Development, 57,* 895–909.

Harris, P. L., Guz, G. R., Lipian, M. S., & Man-Shu, Z. (1985). Insight into the time-course of emotion among Western and Chinese children. *Child Development, 56,* 972–988.

Harris, P. L., Olthof, T., & Meerum Terwogt, M. (1981). Children's knowledge of emotion. *Journal of Child Psychology and Psychiatry, 22,* 247–261.

Harris, S., Mussen, P. H., & Rutherford, E. (1976). Some cognitive, behavioral, and personality correlates of maturity of moral judgment. *Journal of Genetic Psychology, 128,* 123–135.

Harrison, A. O., Wilson, M. N., Pine, C. J., Chan, S. Q., & Buriel, R. (1990). Family ecologies of ethnic minority children. *Child Development, 61,* 347–362.

Harter, S. (1980). A model of intrinsic mastery motivation in children: Individual differences and developmental change. In W. A. Collins (Ed.), *The Minnesota symposia on child psychology: Vol. 13. Development of cognition, affect, and social relations.* Hillsdale, NJ: Erlbaum.

Harter, S. (1982). A cognitive-developmental approach to children's use of affect and trait labels. In F. Serafice (Ed.), *Sociocognitive development in context.* New York: Guilford Press.

Harter, S. (1983). Developmental perspectives on the self-system. In E. M. Hetherington (Ed.), *Handbook of child psychology: Vol. IV. Socialization, personality, and social development.* New York: Wiley.

Harter, S. (1985). Processes underlying the construct, maintenance and enhancement of the self-concept in children. In J. Suls & A. Greenwald (Eds.), *Psychological perspectives on the self* (Vol. 3). Hillsdale, NJ: Erlbaum.

Harter, S. (1986). Cognitive-developmental processes in the integration of concepts about emotions and the self. *Social Cognition, 4,* 119–151.

Harter, S. (1987). The determinants and mediational role of global self-worth in children. In N. Eisenberg (Ed.), *Contemporary topics in developmental psychology.* New York: Wiley.

Harter, S. (1988). Developmental processes in the construction of the self. In T. D. Yawkey & J. E. Johnson (Eds.), *Integrative processes and socialization: Early to middle childhood.* Hillsdale, NJ: Erlbaum.

Harter, S., & Buddin, B. J. (1987). Children's understanding of the simultaneity of two emotions: A five-stage developmental acquisition sequence. *Developmental Psychology, 23,* 388–399.

Hartl, D. (1977). *Our uncertain heritage: Genetics and diversity.* Philadelphia: J. B. Lippincott.

Hartup, W. W. (1974). Aggression in childhood: Developmental perspectives. *American Psychologist, 29,* 336–341.

Hartup, W. W. (1977, Fall). Peers, play, and pathology: A new look at the social behavior of children. *Newsletter of the Society for Research in Child Development,* pp. 1–3.

Hartup, W. W. (1983). Peer relations. In E. M. Hetherington (Ed.), *Handbook of child psychology: Vol. IV. Socialization, personality, and social development.* New York: Wiley.

Hartup, W. W. (1989). Social relationships and their developmental significance. *American Psychologist, 44,* 120–126.

Hartup, W. W., & Coates, B. (1967). Imitation of a peer as a function of reinforcement from the peer group and rewardingness of the model. *Child Development, 38,* 1003–1016.

Hartup, W. W., Laursen, B., Stewart, M. I., & Eastenson, A. (1988). Conflict and the friendship relations of young children. *Child Development, 59,* 1590–1600.

Hartup, W. W., & Sancilio, M. F. (1986). Children's friendships. In E. Shopler & G. B. Mesibov (Eds.), *Social behavior in autism.* New York: Plenum Press.

Hatfield, J. S., Ferguson, L. R., & Alpert, R. (1967). Mother-child interaction and the socialization process. *Child Development, 38,* 365–414.

Hauser, S. T., Powers, S. I., Noam, G. G., & Bowlds, M. K. (1987). Family interiors of adolescent ego development trajectories. *Family Perspectives, 21,* 263–282.

Hawkins, J., Sheingold, K., Gearhart, M., & Berger, C. (1982). Microcomputers in classrooms: Impact on the social life of elementary classrooms. *Journal of Applied Developmental Psychology, 3,* 361–373.

Hawn, P. R., & Harris, L. J. (1983). Hand differences in grasp duration and reaching in two- and five-month old infants. In G. Young, S. Segalowitz, C. M. Carter, & S. E. Trehub (Eds.), *Manual specialization and the developing brain.* New York: Academic Press.

Hay, D. F. (1985). Learning to form relationships in infancy: Parallel attainments with parents and peers. *Developmental Review, 5,* 122–161.

Hay, D. F., Nash, A., & Pedersen, J. (1983). Interaction between 6-month-old peers. *Child Development, 54,* 557–562.

Hay, D. F., & Ross, H. S. (1982). The social nature of early conflict. *Child Development, 53,* 105–113.

Headings, V. E. (1988). Screening the newborn population for congenital and genetic disorders. *Pediatric Reviews and Communications, 2,* 317–332.

Hearold, S. (1986). A synthesis of 1043 effects of television on social behavior. In G. A. Comstock (Ed.), *Public communications and behavior* (Vol. 1). New York: Academic Press.

Heath, S. B. (1983). *Ways with words.* Cambridge: Cambridge University Press.

Heath, S. B. (1989). Oral and literate traditions among black Americans living in poverty. *American Psychologist, 44,* 367–373.

Hebb, D. O. (1980). *Essay on mind.* Hillsdale, NJ: Erlbaum.

Held, R., Birch, E., & Gwiazda, J. (1980). Stereoacuity in human infants. *Proceedings of the National Academy of Sciences of the U.S.A., 77,* 5572–5574.

Henig, R. M. (1988, May 22). Should baby read? *The New York Times Magazine,* pp. 37–38.

Hertz-Lazarowitz, R., & Sharan, S. (1984). Enhancing prosocial behavior through cooperative learning in the classroom. In E. Staub, D. Bar-Tel, J. Karylowski, & J. Reykowski (Eds.), *Development and maintenance of prosocial behavior.* New York: Plenum Press.

Hess, R. D., & Miura, I. T. (1985). Gender differences in enrollment in computer camps and classes. *Sex Roles, 13,* 193–203.

Hetherington, E. M. (1989). Coping with family transitions: Winners, losers, and survivors. *Child Development, 60,* 1–14.

Hetherington, E. M., Cox, M., & Cox, R. (1982). Effects of divorce on parents and children. In M. Lamb (Ed.), *Nontraditional families.* Hillsdale, NJ: Erlbaum.

Heyns, B. (1982). The influence of parents' work on children's school achievement. In S. B. Kamerman & C. D. Hayes (Eds.),

Families that work: Children in a changing world. Washington, DC: National Academy Press.

Hicks, D. J. (1965). Imitation and retention of film-mediated aggressive peer and adult models. *Journal of Personality and Social Psychology, 2,* 97–100.

Higgins, E. T., & Parsons, J. E. (1983). Stages as subcultures: Social-cognitive development and the social life of the child. In E. T. Higgins, W. W. Hartup, & D. N. Ruble (Eds.), *Social cognition and social development: A sociocultural perspective.* New York: Cambridge University Press.

Hilgard, J. R. (1932). Learning and maturation in preschool children. *Journal of Genetic Psychology, 41,* 36–56.

Hill, C. R., & Stafford, F. P. (1980). Parental care of children: Time diary estimates of quantity, predictability, and variety. *Journal of Human Resources, 15,* 219–289.

Hill, J. P. (1987). Research on adolescents and their families: Past and prospect. In C. E. Irwin (Ed.), *Adolescent social behavior and health.* San Francisco: Jossey-Bass.

Hill, S. T., & Shronk, L. K. (1979). The effect of early parent-infant contact on newborn body temperature. *Journal of Obstetric and Gynecological Nursing, 8,* 287–290.

Hinde, R. A. (1965). Interaction of internal and external factors in integration of canary reproduction. In F. Beach (Ed.), *Sex and behavior.* New York: Wiley.

Hinde, R. A. (1989). Ethological and relationships approaches. In R. Vasta (Ed.), *Annals of child development: Vol 6. Six theories of child development: Revised formulations and current issues.* Greenwich, CT: JAI Press.

Hinde, R. A., Titmus, G., Easton, D., & Tamplin, A. (1985). Incidence of "friendship" and behavior to strong associates versus non-associates in preschoolers. *Child Development, 56,* 234–245.

Hirsch, B. J., & Rapkin, B. D. (1987). The transition to junior high school: A longitudinal study of self-esteem, psychological symptomatology, school life, and social support. *Child Development, 58,* 1235–1243.

Hirsch, J. (1975). Cell number and size as a determinant of subsequent obesity. In M. Winick (Ed.), *Childhood obesity.* New York: Wiley.

Hirsch-Pasek, K., Gleitman, L. R., & Gleitman, H. (1978). What does the brain say to the mind? A study of the detection and report of ambiguity by young children. In A. Sinclair, R. J. Jarvella, & W. J. M. Levelt (Eds.), *The child's conception of language.* Berlin: Springer-Verlag.

Hock, E., & DeMeis, D. K. (1990). Depression in mothers of infants: The role of maternal employment. *Developmental Psychology, 26,* 285–291.

Hoff-Ginsberg, E. (1986). Function and structure in maternal speech: Their relation to the child's development of syntax. *Developmental Psychology, 22,* 155–163.

Hoff-Ginsberg, E. (1990). Maternal speech and the child's development of syntax: A further look. *Journal of Child Language, 17,* 85–99.

Hoffman, L. W. (1979). Maternal employment: 1979. *American Psychologist, 34,* 859–865.

Hoffman, L. W. (1980). The effects of maternal employment on the academic attitudes and performance of school-age children. *School Psychology Review, 9,* 319–336.

Hoffman, L. W. (1984). Maternal employment and the young child. In M. Perlmutter (Ed.), *The Minnesota symposia on child psychology: Vol. 17. Parent-child interaction and parent-child relations in child development.* Hillsdale, NJ: Erlbaum.

Hoffman, L. W. (1989). Effects of maternal employment in the two-parent family. *American Psychologist, 44,* 283–292.

Hoffman, M. L. (1970). Moral development. In P. H. Mussen (Ed.), *Carmichael's manual of child psychology* (Vol. 2). New York: Wiley.

Hoffman, M. L. (1971). Identification and conscience development. *Child Development, 42,* 1071–1082.

Hoffman, M. L. (1975). Altruistic behavior and the parent-child relationship. *Journal of Personality and Social Psychology, 31,* 937–943.

Hoffman, M. L. (1976). Empathy, role-taking, guilt, and the development of altruistic motives. In T. Lickona (Ed.), *Moral development and moral behavior: Theory, research, and social issues.* New York: Holt, Rinehart & Winston.

Hoffman, M. L. (1981a). Is altruism part of human nature? *Journal of Personality and Social Psychology, 40,* 121–137.

Hoffman, M. L. (1981b). Perspectives on the difference between understanding people and understanding things. The role of affect. In J. H. Flavell & L. Ross (Eds.), *Social cognitive development: Frontiers and possible futures.* New York: Cambridge University Press.

Hoffman, M. L. (1982). Development of prosocial motivation: Empathy and guilt. In N. Eisenberg (Ed.), *The development of prosocial behavior.* New York: Academic Press.

Hoffman-Plotkin, D., & Twentyman, C. (1984). A multimodal assessment of behavioral and cognitive deficits in abused and neglected preschoolers. *Child Development, 52,* 13–30.

Hofsten, C. von. (1984). Developmental changes in the organization of prereaching movements. *Developmental Psychology, 20,* 378–388.

Hoge, D. R., Smit, E. K., & Hanson, S. L. (1990). School experiences predicting changes in self-esteem of sixth- and seventh-graders. *Journal of Educational Psychology, 82,* 117–127.

Holbrook, S. M. (1990). Adoption, infertility, and the new reproductive technologies: Problems and prospects for social work and welfare policy. *Social Work, 35,* 333–337.

Holden, G. W. (1983). Avoiding conflict: Mothers as tacticians in the supermarket. *Child Development, 54,* 233–240.

Holden, G. W., & West, M. J. (1989). Proximate regulation by mothers: A demonstration of how differing styles affect young children's behavior. *Child Development, 60,* 64–69.

Hollenbeck, A. R., Gewirtz, J. L., & Sebris, S. L. (1984). Labor and delivery medication influences parent-infant interaction in the first post-partum month. *Infant Behavior and Development, 7,* 201–209.

Hollenbeck, A. R., & Slaby, R. G. (1979). Infant visual and vocal responses to television. *Child Development, 50,* 41–45.

Honzik, M. P., Macfarlane, J. W., & Allen, L. (1948). The stability of mental test performance between two and eighteen years. *Journal of Experimental Education, 17,* 309–329.

Hood, K. E., Draper, P., Crockett, L. J., & Petersen, A. C. (1987). The ontogeny and phylogeny of sex differences in development: A biopsychosocial synthesis. In D. B. Carter (Ed.), *Current conceptions of sex roles and sex typing: Theory and research.* New York: Praeger.

Hopkins, B., & Westra, T. (1990). Motor development, maternal expectations, and the role of handling. *Infant Behavior and Development, 13,* 117–122.

Hops, H., & Finch, M. (1985). Social competence and skill: A

reassessment. In B. H. Schneider, K. H. Rubin, & J. E. Ledingham (Eds.), *Children's peer relations: Issues in assessment and intervention.* New York: Springer-Verlag.

Horn, J. L. (1968). Organization of abilities and the development of intelligence. *Psychological Review, 75,* 242–259.

Horn, J. L., & Cattell, R. B. (1967). Refinement and test of the theory of fluid and crystallized ability intelligences. *Journal of Educational Psychology, 57,* 253–270.

Horn, J. M. (1983). The Texas Adoption Project: Adopted children and their intellectual resemblance to biological and adoptive parents. *Child Development, 54,* 268–275.

Horn, J. M., Loehlin, J. C., & Willerman, L. (1979). Intellectual resemblance among adoptive and biological relatives: The Texas Adoption Project. *Behavior Genetics, 9,* 177–201.

Horowitz, F. D. (1987a). *Exploring developmental theories: Toward a structural/behavioral model of development.* Hillsdale, NJ: Erlbaum.

Horowitz, F. D. (1987b). Targeting infant stimulation efforts: Theoretical challenges for research and intervention. In N. Gunzenhauser (Ed.), *Infant stimulation: For whom, what kind, when, and how much?* (Johnson & Johnson Baby Products Company Pediatric Round Table Series No. 13). Skilman, NJ: Johnson & Johnson.

Horwitz, R. A. (1979). Psychological effects of the "open classroom." *Review of Educational Research, 49,* 71–86.

Howe, P. E., & Schiller, M. (1952). Growth responses of the school child to changes in diet and environmental factors. *Journal of Applied Physiology, 5,* 51–61.

Howes, C. (1983). Patterns of friendship. *Child Development, 54,* 1041–1053.

Howes, C. (1987a). Peer interaction of young children. *Monographs of the Society for Research in Child Development, 53*(1, Serial No. 217).

Howes, C. (1987b). Social competence with peers in young children. *Developmental Review, 7,* 252–272.

Howes, C. (1990). Can age of entry and the quality of childcare predict adjustment in kindergarten? *Developmental Psychology, 26,* 292–303.

Howes, C., Unger, O., & Seidner, L. B. (1989). Social pretend play in toddlers: Parallels with social play and with solitary pretend. *Child Development, 60,* 77–84.

Hubel, D. H., & Wiesel, T. N. (1979, September). Brain mechanisms of vision. *Scientific American, 241,* pp. 150–162.

Huesmann, L. R., Eron, L. D., Klein, R., Brice, P., & Fischer, P. (1983). Mitigating the imitation of aggressive behaviors by changing children's attitudes about media violence. *Journal of Personality and Social Psychology, 44,* 899–910.

Huesmann, L. R., Lagerspetz, K., & Eron, L. D. (1984). Intervening variables and the TV violence-aggression relation: Evidence from two countries. *Developmental Psychology, 20,* 746–775.

Humphrey, T. (1964). Some correlations between the appearance of human fetal reflexes and the development of the nervous system. *Progress in Brain Research, 4,* 93–133.

Humphreys, A. P., & Smith, P. K. (1987). Rough and tumble, friendship, and dominance in schoolchildren: Evidence for continuity and change with age. *Child Development, 58,* 201–212.

Hunt, C. E., & Brouillette, R. T. (1987). Sudden infant death syndrome: 1987 perspective. *Journal of Pediatrics, 110,* 669–678.

Huston, A. C. (1983). Sex typing. In E. M. Hetherington (Ed.),

Handbook of child psychology: Vol. IV. Socialization, personality, and social development. New York: Wiley.

Huston, A. C. (1985). The development of sex typing: Themes from recent research. *Developmental Review, 5,* 1–17.

Huston, A. C., & Alvarez, M. M. (1990). The socialization context of gender role development in early adolescence. In R. Montemayor, G. R. Adams, & T. P. Gullota (Eds.), *From childhood to adolescence: A transitional period?* Newbury Park, CA: Sage.

Huston, A. C., Watkins, B. A., & Kunkel, D. (1989). Public policy and children's television. *American Psychologist, 44,* 424–433.

Huston, A. C., Wright, J. C., Rice, M. L., Kerkman, D., & St. Peters, M. (1990). Development of television viewing patterns in early childhood: A longitudinal investigation. *Developmental Psychology, 26,* 409–420.

Huttenlocher, J., Haight, W., Bryk, A., Seltzer, M., & Lyons, T. (1991). Early vocabulary growth: Relation to language input and gender. *Developmental Psychology, 27,* 236–248.

Hwang, P. (1987). The changing role of Swedish fathers. In M. E. Lamb (Ed.), *The father's role: Cross-cultural perspectives.* Hillsdale, NJ: Erlbaum.

Hyde, J. S. (1984). How large are gender differences in aggression? A developmental meta-analysis. *Developmental Psychology, 20,* 722–736.

Hyde, J. S. (1986). Gender differences in aggression. In J. S. Hyde & M. C. Linn (Eds.), *The psychology of gender: Advances through meta-analysis.* Baltimore: Johns Hopkins University Press.

Hyde, J. S., Fennema, E., & Lamon, S. J. (1990). Gender differences in mathematics performance: A meta-analysis. *Psychological Bulletin, 107,* 139–155.

Hyde, J. S., & Linn, M. C. (1988). Gender differences in verbal ability: A meta-analysis. *Psychological Bulletin, 104,* 53–69.

Hymel, S., & Franke, S. (1985). Children's peer relations: Assessing self-perceptions. In B. H. Schneider, K. H. Rubin, & J. E. Ledingham (Eds.), *Children's peer relations: Issues in assessment and intervention.* New York: Springer-Verlag.

Hymel, S., & Rubin, K. H. (1985). Children with peer relationship and social skills problems: Conceptual, methodological, and developmental issues. In G. J. Whitehurst (Ed.), *Annals of child development* (Vol. 2). Greenwich, CT: JAI Press.

Inhelder, B., & Piaget, J. (1958). *The growth of logical thinking from childhood to adolescence.* New York: Basic Books.

International Association for the Evaluation of Educational Achievement. (1988). *Science achievement in seventeen countries: A preliminary report.* Exeter, England: Pergamon Press.

Isabella, R. A., Belsky, J., & von Eye, A. (1989). Origins of infant-mother attachment: An examination of interactional synchrony during the infant's first year. *Developmental Psychology, 25,* 12–21.

Isensee, W. (1986, September 3). *The Chronicle of Higher Education, 33.*

Izard, C. E. (1978). On the ontogenesis of emotions and emotion-cognition relationships in infancy. In M. Lewis & L. A. Rosenblum (Eds.), *The development of affect.* New York: Plenum Press.

Izard, C. E., & Dougherty, L. M. (1982). Two complementary systems for measuring facial expressions in infants and children. In C. E. Izard (Ed.), *Measuring emotions in infants and children* (Vol. 1). Cambridge: Cambridge University Press.

Izard, C. E., Huebner, R. R., Risser, D., McGinnes, G., & Dougherty, L. (1980). The young infant's ability to produce discrete emotion expressions. *Developmental Psychology, 16,* 132–140.

Izard, C. E., Kagan, J., & Zajonc, R. B. (1984). Introduction. In C. E. Izard, J. Kagan, & R. B. Zajonc (Eds.), *Emotions, cognition, and behavior.* Cambridge: Cambridge University Press.

Izard, C. E., & Malatesta, C. Z. (1987). Perspectives on emotional development: I. Differential emotions theory of early emotional development. In J. D. Osofsky (Ed.), *Handbook of infant development* (2nd ed.). New York: Wiley.

Jacklin, C. N. (1989). Female and male: Issues of gender. *American Psychologist, 44,* 127–133.

Jacklin, C. N., DiPietro, J. A., & Maccoby, E. E. (1984). Sex-typing behavior and sex-typing pressure in child/parent interaction. *Archives of Sexual Behavior, 13,* 413–425.

Jacklin, C. N., & Maccoby, E. E. (1978). Social behavior at thirty-three months in same-sex and mixed-sex dyads. *Child Development, 49,* 557–569.

Jacklin, C. N., Maccoby, E. E., & Doering, C. H. (1983). Neonatal sex-steroid hormones and timidity in 6–18 month-old boys and girls. *Developmental Psychobiology, 16,* 163–168.

Jacklin, C. N., Maccoby, E. E., Doering, C. H., & King, D. (1984). Neonatal sex-steroid hormones and muscular strength of boys and girls in the first three years. *Developmental Psychobiology, 17,* 301–310.

Jacklin, C. N., Wilcox, K. T., & Maccoby, E. E. (1988). Neonatal sex-steroid hormones and cognitive abilities at six years. *Developmental Psychobiology, 21,* 567–574.

Jackson, A. W., & Hornbeck, D. W. (1989). Educating young adolescents: Why we must restructure middle grade schools. *American Psychologist, 44,* 831–836.

Jackson, N. E. (1988). Precocious reading ability: What does it mean? *Gifted Child Quarterly, 32,* 200–204.

Jackson, S. (1987). Great Britain. In M. E. Lamb (Ed.), *The father's role: Cross-cultural perspectives.* Hillsdale, NJ: Erlbaum.

Jacobson, S. W. (1979). Matching behavior in the young infant. *Child Development, 50,* 425–430.

Jacobvitz, R. S., Wood, M., & Albin, K. (1989, April). *Cognitive skills and young children's comprehension of television.* Paper presented at the biennial meeting of the Society for Research in Child Development, Kansas City, MO.

Jakibchuk, Z., & Smeriglio, V. L. (1976). The influence of symbolic modeling on the social behavior of preschool children with low levels of social responsiveness. *Child Development, 47,* 838–841.

James, S. (1978). Effect of listener age and situation on the politeness of children's directives. *Journal of Psycholinguistic Research, 7,* 307–317.

James, W. (1890). *The principles of psychology.* New York: Henry Holt.

James, W. (1892). *Psychology: The briefer course.* New York: Henry Holt.

Jencks, C. (1972). *Inequality: A reassessment of the effect of family and schooling in America.* New York: Basic Books.

Jensen, A. R. (1969). How much can we boost IQ and scholastic achievement? *Harvard Educational Review, 39,* 1–123.

Jensen, A. R. (1980). *Bias in mental testing.* New York: Free Press.

Jensen, A. R. (1982). The chronometry of intelligence. In R. J.

Sternberg (Ed.), *Advances in the psychology of human intelligence* (Vol. 1). Hillsdale, NJ: Erlbaum.

Jensen, A. R., & Munroe, E. (1979). Reaction time, movement time, and intelligence. *Intelligence, 3,* 121–126.

Johnson, C. N., & Wellman, H. (1982). Children's developing conceptions of the mind and brain. *Child Development, 53,* 222–234.

Johnson, J., & Newport, E. (1989). Critical period effects in second language learning: The influence of maturational state on the acquisition of English as a second language. *Cognitive Psychology, 21,* 60–99.

Johnston, J., Ettema, J., & Davidson, T. (1980). *An evaluaton of "Freestyle": A television series to reduce sex role stereotypes.* Ann Arbor: Institute for Social Research.

Jones, G. P., & Dembo, M. H. (1989). Age and sex role differences in intimate friendships during childhood and adolescence. *Merrill-Palmer Quarterly, 35,* 445–462.

Jones, H. E., & Bayley, N. (1941). The Berkeley Growth Study. *Child Development, 12,* 167–173.

Jones, K. L., & Smith, D. W. (1973). Recognition of the fetal alcohol syndrome in early infancy. *Lancet, 2,* 999–1001.

Jones, L. V. (1984). White-black achievement differences: The narrowing gap. *American Psychologist, 39,* 1207–1213.

Jones, M. C. (1957). The later careers of boys who were early- or late-maturing. *Child Development, 28,* 113–128.

Jones, M. C. (1965). Psychological correlates of somatic development. *Child Development, 36,* 899–911.

Juster, F. T. (1987). A note on recent changes in time use. In F. T. Juster & F. Stafford (Eds.), *Studies in the measurement of time allocation.* Ann Arbor: Institute for Social Research.

Kagan, J. (1976). Emergent themes in human development. *American Scientist, 64,* 186–196.

Kagan, J., Kearsley, R. B., & Zelazo, P. R. (1978). *Infancy: Its place in human development.* Cambridge: Cambridge University Press.

Kagan, J., Reznick, J. S., & Snidman, N. (1988). Biological basis of childhood shyness. *Science, 240,* 167–171.

Kahneman, D. (1973). *Attention and effort.* Englewood Cliffs, NJ: Prentice-Hall.

Kail, R. (1990). *The development of memory in children* (3rd ed.). New York: W. H. Freeman.

Kail, R., & Pellegrino, J. W. (1985). *Human intelligence: Perspectives and prospects.* New York: W. H. Freeman.

Kaitz, M., Meschulach-Sarfaty, O., Auerbach, J., & Eidelman, A. (1988). A reexamination of newborns' ability to imitate facial expressions. *Developmental Psychology, 24,* 3–7.

Kalil, R. E. (1989, December). Synapse formation in the developing brain. *Scientific American, 261,* pp. 76–85.

Kaplan, H., & Dove, H. (1987). Infant development among the Ache of Eastern Paraguay. *Developmental Psychology, 23,* 190–196.

Karmel, B. Z., & Maisel, E. B. (1975). A neuronal activity model for infant visual attention. In L. B. Cohen & P. Salapatek (Eds.), *Infant perception: From sensation to cognition* (Vol. 1). New York: Academic Press.

Karniol, R. (1989). The role of manual manipulative stages in the infant's acquisition of perceived control over objects. *Developmental Review, 9,* 205–233.

Katz, P. A. (1987). Variations in family constellation: Effects on gender schemata. In L. S. Liben & M. L. Signorella (Eds.),

New directions for child development: No. 38. Children's gender schemata. San Francisco: Jossey-Bass.

Kaufman, A. S., Kamphaus, R. W., & Kaufman, N. L. (1985). New directions in intelligence testing: The Kaufman Assessment Battery for Children (K-ABC). In B. B. Wolman (Ed.), *Handbook of intelligence.* New York: Wiley.

Kaufman, A. S., & Kaufman, N. L. (1983). *K-ABC administration and scoring manual.* Circle Pines, MN: American Guidance Service.

Kaye, K., & Marcus, J. (1981). Infant imitation: The sensorimotor agenda. *Developmental Psychology, 17,* 258–265.

Kazmeier, K. J., Keenan, W. J., & Sutherland, J. M. (1977). Effects of elevated bilirubin and phototherapy on infant behavior. *Pediatric Research, 11,* 563.

Keasey, C. B. (1971). Social participation as a factor in the moral development of preadolescents. *Developmental Psychology, 5,* 216–220.

Keating, D. P., & Clark, L. V. (1980). Development of physical and social reasoning in adolescence. *Developmental Psychology, 16,* 23–30.

Keeney, T. J., Cannizzo, S. R., & Flavell, J. H. (1967). Spontaneous and induced rehearsal in a recall task. *Child Development, 38,* 953–966.

Kellman, P. J., & Spelke, E. S. (1983). Perception of partly occluded objects in infancy. *Cognitive Psychology, 15,* 483–524.

Kellman, P. J., Spelke, E. S., & Short, K. (1986). Infant perception of object unity from transitory motion in depth and vertical translation. *Child Development, 57,* 72–86.

Keogh, J., & Sugden, D. (1985). *Movement skill development.* New York: Macmillan.

Kerlinger, F. N. (1964). *Foundations of behavioral research: Educational and psychological inquiry.* New York: Holt, Rinehart & Winston.

Kerns, L. L., & Davis, G. P. (1986). Psychotropic drugs in pregnancy. In I. J. Chasnoff (Ed.), *Drug use in pregnancy: Mother and child.* Lancaster, England: MTP Press.

Kester, P. A. (1984). Effects of prenatally administered 17-alpha-hydroxyprogesterone caproate on adolescent males. *Archives of Sexual Behavior, 13,* 441–455.

Khayrallah, M., & Van Den Meiraker, M. (1987). LOGO programming and the acquisition of cognitive skills. *Journal of Computer-Based Instruction, 14,* 133–137.

Kinsbourne, M., & Hiscock, M. (1983). The normal and deviant development of functional lateralization of the brain. In M. M. Haith & J. C. Campos (Eds.), *Infancy and developmental psychobiology: Vol. II. Handbook of child psychology.* New York: Wiley.

Kirkpatrick, S. W., & Sanders, D. M. (1978). Body image stereotypes: A developmental comparison. *Journal of Genetic Psychology, 132,* 87–95.

Kitchen, W. H., Ford, G. W., Rickards, A. L., Lissenden, J. V., & Ryan, M. M. (1987). Children of birth weight <1000 g: Changing outcome between ages 2 and 5 years. *Journal of Pediatrics, 110,* 283–288.

Klahr, D. (1989). Information-processing approaches. In R. Vasta (Ed.), *Annals of child development: Vol 6. Six theories of child development: Revised formulations and current issues.* Greenwich, CT: JAI Press.

Klaus, M., & Kennell, J. (1976). *Maternal infant bonding.* St. Louis: C. V. Mosby.

Klaus, M., & Kennell, J. (1982). *Parent-infant bonding.* St. Louis: C. V. Mosby.

Kleitman, N. (1963). *Sleep and wakefulness.* Chicago: University of Chicago Press.

Klima, E. S., & Bellugi, U. (1966). Syntactic regularities in the speech of children. In J. Lyons & R. J. Wales (Eds.), *Psycholinguistic papers: The proceedings of the 1966 Edinburgh conference.* Edinburgh: Edinburgh University Press.

Kline, J., Shrout, P., Stein, Z., Susser, M., & Warburton, D. (1980). Drinking during pregnancy and spontaneous abortion. *Lancet, 2,* 176–180.

Kline, M., Tschann, J. M., Johnston, J. R., & Wallerstein, J. S. (1989). Children's adjustment in joint and sole physical custody families. *Developmental Psychology, 25,* 430–438.

Knowles, R. V. (1985). *Genetics, society and decisions.* Columbus, OH: Merrill.

Kobasigawa, A. (1968). Inhibitory and disinhibitory effects of models on sex-inappropriate behavior in children. *Psychologia, 11,* 86–96.

Kobasigawa, A. (1974). Utilization of retrieval cues by children in recall. *Child Development, 45,* 127–134.

Kobayashi-Winata, H., & Power, T. G. (1989). Child rearing and compliance: Japanese and American families in Houston. *Journal of Cross-Cultural Psychology, 20,* 333–356.

Koff, E., Rierdan, J., & Sheingold, K. (1982). Memories of menarche: Age, preparation, and prior knowledge as determinants of initial menstrual experience. *Journal of Youth and Adolescence, 11,* 1–9.

Kohlberg, L. (1958). *The development of modes of moral thinking and choice in the years 10 to 16.* Unpublished doctoral dissertation, University of Chicago.

Kohlberg, L. A. (1966). A cognitive-developmental analysis of children's sex-role concepts and attitudes. In E. E. Maccoby (Ed.), *The development of sex differences.* Stanford, CA: Stanford University Press.

Kohlberg, L. (1969). Stage and sequence: The cognitive-developmental approach to socialization. In D. A. Goslin (Ed.), *The handbook of socialization theory and research.* Chicago: Rand McNally.

Kohlberg, L. (1976). Moral stages and moralization: The cognitive developmental approach. In T. Lickona (Ed.), *Moral development and moral behavior: Theory, research, and social issues.* New York: Holt, Rinehart & Winston.

Kohlberg, L. (1984). *Essays on moral development: Vol. 2. The psychology of moral development.* San Francisco: Harper & Row.

Kohlberg, L., & Kramer, R. (1969). Continuities and discontinuities in childhood moral development. *Human Development, 12,* 93–120.

Kohlberg, L., Levine, C., & Hewer, A. (1983). *Moral stages: A current formulation and a response to critics.* Basel: Karger.

Kohlberg, L., Yaeger, J., & Hjertholm, E. (1968). Private speech: Four studies and a review of theories. *Child Development, 45,* 127–134.

Koneya, M. (1976). Location and interaction in row-and-column seating arrangements. *Environment and Behavior, 8,* 265–282.

Kopp, C. B. (1979). Perspectives on infant motor system development. In M. Bornstein & W. Kessen (Eds.), *Psychological development from infancy.* Hillsdale, NJ: Erlbaum.

Kopp, C. B. (1982). The antecedents of self-regulation: A developmental perspective. *Developmental Psychology, 18,* 199–214.

Kopp, C. B. (1987). The growth of self-regulation: Caregivers and children. In N. Eisenberg (Ed.), *Contemporary topics in developmental psychology.* New York: Wiley.

Kopp, C. B., & McCall, R. B. (1980). Stability and instability in mental performance among normal, at-risk, and handicapped infants and children. In P. B. Baltes & O. G. Grim, Jr. (Eds.), *Life-span development and behavior* (Vol. 4). New York: Academic Press.

Korner, A. F. (1972). State as a variable, as obstacle, and mediator of stimulation in infant research. *Merrill-Palmer Quarterly, 18,* 77–94.

Korner, A. F. (1987). Preventive intervention with high-risk newborns: Theoretical, conceptual, and methodological perspectives. In J. D. Osofsky (Ed.), *Handbook of infant development* (2nd ed.). New York: Wiley.

Korner, A. F., Schneider, P., & Forrest, T. (1983). Effects of vestibular-proprioceptive stimulation on the neurobehavioral development of preterm infants: A pilot study. *Neuropediatrics, 14,* 170–175.

Kotelchuk, M. (1975, August). *Father caretaking characteristics and their influence on infant-father interactions.* Paper presented at the meeting of the American Psychological Association, Chicago.

Kotelchuk, M. (1976). The infant's relationship to the father: Experimental evidence. In M. E. Lamb (Ed.), *The role of the father in child development.* New York: Wiley.

Kraemer, H. C., Korner, A., Anders, T., Jacklin, C. N., & Dimiceli, S. (1985). Obstetric drugs and infant behavior: A re-evaluation. *Journal of Pediatric Psychology, 10,* 345–353.

Krafchuk, E. E., Tronick, E. Z., & Clifton, R. K. (1983). Behavioral and cardiac responses to sound in preterm infants varying in risk status: A hypothesis of their paradoxical reactivity. In T. Field & A. Sostek (Eds.), *Infants born at risk: Physiological, perceptual, and cognitive processes.* New York: Grune & Stratton.

Krauss, R. H., & Glucksberg, S. (1969). The development of communication. *Child Development, 40,* 255–266.

Krebs, D., & Gilmore, J. (1982). The relationship among the first stages of cognitive development, role taking abilities, and moral development. *Child Development, 53,* 877–886.

Kremenitzer, J. P., Vaughan, H. G., Kurtzberg, D., & Dowling, K. (1979). Smooth-pursuit eye movements in the newborn infant. *Child Development, 50,* 442–448.

Kreutzer, M. A., Leonard, S. C., & Flavell, J. H. (1975). An interview study of children's knowledge about memory. *Monographs of the Society for Research in Child Development, 40*(1, Serial No. 159).

Kroll, J. (1977). The concept of childhood in the Middle Ages. *Journal of the History of the Behavioral Sciences, 13,* 384–393.

Krumhansl, C. L., & Jusczyk, P. W. (1990). Infants' perception of phrase structure in music. *Psychological Science, 1,* 70–73.

Kuchuk, A., Vibbert, M., & Bornstein, M. H. (1986). The perception of smiling and its experiential correlates in three-month-old infants. *Child Development, 57,* 1054–1061.

Kuczaj, S. A., Borys, R. H., & Jones, M. (1989). On the interaction of language and thought: Some thoughts and developmental data. In A. Gellatly, D. Rogers, & J. A. Sloboda (Eds.), *Cognition and social worlds.* Oxford: Clarendon Press.

Kuczynski, L., Kochanska, G., Radke-Yarrow, M., & Girnius-Brown, O. (1987). A developmental interpretation of young children's noncompliance. *Developmental Psychology, 23,* 799–806.

Kuczynski, L., Zahn-Waxler, C., & Radke-Yarrow, M. (1987). Development and content of imitation in the second and third year of life: A socialization perspective. *Developmental Psychology, 23,* 276–282.

Kugelmass, S., & Breznitz, S. (1967). The development of intentionality in moral judgment in city and kibbutz adolescents. *Journal of Genetic Psychology, 111,* 103–111.

Kuhl, P. K. (1987). Perception of speech and sound in early infancy. In P. Salapatek & L. Cohen (Eds.), *Handbook of infant perception: From perception to cognition* (Vol. 2). Orlando, FL: Academic Press.

Kuhl, P. K., & Miller, J. D. (1978). Speech perception by the chinchilla: Identification functions for synthetic VOT stimuli. *Journal of the Acoustical Society of America, 63,* 905–917.

Kuhl, P. K., & Padden, D. M. (1983). Enhanced discriminability at the phonetic boundary for the place feature in macaques. *Journal of the Acoustical Society of America, 73,* 1003–1010.

Kuhn, D., Nash, S. C., & Brucken, L. (1978). Sex role concepts of two- and three-year-olds. *Child Development, 49,* 445–451.

Kulik, J. A., Bangert, R. L., & Williams, G. W. (1983). Effects of computer-based teaching on secondary school students. *Journal of Educational Psychology, 75,* 19–26.

Kulik, J. A., Kulik, C. C., & Bangert-Drowns, R. L. (1985). Effectiveness of computer-based education in elementary schools. *Computers in Human Behavior, 1,* 59–74.

Kupersmidt, J. B. (1983, April). Predicting delinquency and academic problems from childhood peer status. In J. D. Coie (Chair), *Strategies for identifying children at social risk: Longitudinal correlates and consequences.* Symposium conducted at the biennial meeting of the Society for Research in Child Development, Detroit.

Kurdek, L. A. (1978). Perspective-taking as the cognitive basis of children's moral development: A review of the literature. *Merrill-Palmer Quarterly, 24,* 3–28.

Kurdek, L. A. (1989). Siblings' reactions to parental divorce. *Journal of Divorce, 12,* 203–219.

Kurdek, L. A., & Berg, B. (1983). Correlates of children's adjustments to their parents' divorces. In L. A. Kurdek (Ed.), *New directions for child development: No. 19. Children and divorce.* San Francisco: Jossey-Bass.

Kurtines, W., & Greif, E. B. (1974). The development of moral thought: Review and evaluation of Kohlberg's approach. *Psychological Bulletin, 81,* 453–470.

LaBarbera, J. D., Izard, C. E., Vietze, P., & Parisi, S. A. (1976). Four- and six-month-old infants' visual responses to joy, anger, and neutral expressions. *Child Development, 47,* 535–538.

Lackey, P. N. (1989). Adults' attitudes about assignments of household chores to male and female children. *Sex Roles, 20,* 271–281.

Ladd, G. W. (1983). Social networks of popular, average, and rejected children in school settings. *Merrill-Palmer Quarterly, 29,* 283–307.

Ladd, G. W. (1989, April). *Children's friendships in the classroom: Precursors of early school adaptation.* Paper presented at the biennial meeting of the Society for Research in Child Development, Kansas City, MO.

Ladd, G. W. (1990). Having friends, keeping friends, making friends, and being liked by peers in the classroom: Predictors of children's early school adjustment? *Child Development, 61,* 1081–1100.

Ladd, G. W., & Asher, S. R. (1985). Social skill training and children's peer relations. In L. L'Abate & M. Milan (Eds.), *Handbook of social skills training.* New York: Wiley.

Ladd, G. W., & Golter, B. S. (1988). Parents' management of preschooler's peer relations: Is it related to children's social competencies? *Developmental Psychology, 24,* 109–117.

Ladd, G. W., & Price, J. M. (1987). Predicting children's social and school adjustment following the transition from preschool to kindergarten. *Child Development, 58,* 1168–1189.

Ladd, G. W., Price, J. M., & Hart, C. H. (1988). Predicting preschoolers' peer status from their playground behaviors. *Child Development, 59,* 986–992.

LaFreniere, P., & Charlesworth, W. R. (1983). Dominance, attention, and affiliation in a preschool group: A nine-month longitudinal study. *Ethology and Sociobiology, 4,* 55–67.

Lahey, B. B., Hammer, D., Crumrine, P. L., & Forehand, R. L. (1980). Birth order x sex interactions in child behavior problems. *Developmental Psychology, 16,* 608–615.

Lamaze, F. (1970). *Painless childbirth: Psychoprophylactic method.* Chicago: Henry Regnery.

Lamb, M. E. (1976). *The role of the father in child development.* New York: Wiley.

Lamb, M. E. (1981). *The role of the father in child development* (rev. ed.). New York: Wiley.

Lamb, M. E. (1987). Introduction: The emergent American father. In M. E. Lamb (Ed.), *The father's role: Cross-cultural perspectives.* Hillsdale, NJ: Erlbaum.

Lamb, M. E., Easterbrooks, M. A., & Holden, G. (1980). Reinforcement and punishment among preschoolers: Characteristics and correlates. *Child Development, 51,* 1230–1236.

Lamb, M. E., & Nash, A. (1989). Infant-mother attachment, sociability, and peer competence. In T. J. Berndt & G. W. Ladd (Eds.), *Peer relationships in child development.* New York: Wiley.

Lamb, M. E., Pleck, J. H., Charnov, E. L., & Levine, J. A. (1987). A biosocial perspective on paternal behavior and involvement. In J. B. Lancaster, J. Altmann, A. S. Rossi, & L. R. Sherrod (Eds.), *Parenting across the life span: Biosocial dimensions.* New York: Aldine de Gruyter.

Lamb, M. E., & Roopnarine, J. L. (1979). Peer influences on sex-role development in preschoolers. *Child Development, 50,* 1219–1222.

Lamb, M. E., Thompson, R. A., Gardner, W., & Charnov, E. L. (1985). *Infant-mother attachment: The origins and developmental significance of individual differences in strange situation behavior.* Hillsdale, NJ: Erlbaum.

Landesman-Dwyer, S., Keller, L. S., & Streissguth, A. P. (1978). Naturalistic observations of newborns: Effects of maternal alcohol intake. *Alcoholism, 2,* 171–177.

Landesman-Dwyer, S., Ragozin, A. S., & Little, R. E. (1981). Behavioral correlates of prenatal alcohol exposure: A four-year follow-up study. *Neurobehavioral Toxicology and Teratology, 3,* 187–193.

Lane, D. M., & Pearson, D. A. (1982). The development of selective attention. *Merrill-Palmer Quarterly, 28,* 317–345.

Langlois, J. H., & Downs, A. C. (1980). Mothers, fathers, and peers as socialization agents of sex-typed play behaviors in young children. *Child Development, 51,* 1237–1247.

Langlois, J. H., & Stephan, C. (1981). Beauty and the beast: The role of physical attractiveness in the development of peer relations and social behavior. In S. S. Brehm, S. H. Kassin, & F. X. Gibbons (Eds.), *Developmental social psychology.* New York: Oxford University Press.

Laosa, L. M. (1982). Families as facilitators of children's intellectual development at 3 years of age: A causal analysis. In L. M. Laosa & I. E. Sigel (Eds.), *Families as learning environments for children.* New York: Plenum Press.

Larkin, R. W. (1979). *Suburban youth in cultural crisis.* New York: Oxford University Press.

Lauritzen, P. (1990). What price parenthood? *The Hastings Center Report, 20,* 38–46.

Law, C. M. (1987). The disability of short stature. *Archives of Disease in Childhood, 62,* 855–859.

Lawson, M. (1980). Development of body build stereotypes, peer ratings, and self-esteem in Australian children. *Journal of Psychology, 104,* 111–118.

Lazar, I., & Darlington, R. (1982). Lasting effects of early education: A report from the Consortium for Longitudinal Studies. *Monographs of the Society for Research in Child Development, 47*(2–3, Serial No. 195).

Lee, L. C. (1971). The concomitant development of cognitive and moral modes of thought: A test of selected deductions from Piaget's theory. *Genetic Psychology Monographs, 83,* 93–146.

Lee, R. V. (1988). Sexually transmitted infections. In G. N. Burrow & T. F. Ferris (Eds.), *Medical complications during pregnancy.* Philadelphia: W. B. Saunders.

Lee, V. E., Brooks-Gunn, J., & Schnur, E. (1988). Does Head Start work? A 1-year follow-up comparison of disadvantaged children attending Head Start, no preschool, and other preschool programs. *Developmental Psychology, 24,* 210–222.

Lee, V. E., Brooks-Gunn, J., Schnur, E., & Liaw, F. (1990). Are Head Start effects sustained? A longitudinal follow-up comparison of disadvantaged children attending Head Start, no preschool, and other preschool programs. *Child Development, 61,* 495–507.

Lefkowitz, M. M. (1981). Smoking during pregnancy: Long-term effects on offspring. *Developmental Psychology, 17,* 192–194.

Leinbach, M. D., & Fagot, B. I. (1986). Acquisition of gender labels: A test for toddlers. *Sex Roles, 15,* 655–666.

Lemish, D., & Rice, M. (1986). Television as a talking picture book: A prop for language acquisition. *Journal of Child Language, 13,* 251–274.

Lempers, J. D., Flavell, E. R., & Flavell, J. H. (1977). The development in very young children of tacit knowledge concerning visual perception. *Genetic Psychology Monographs, 95,* 3–53.

Lempert, H. (1989). Animacy constraints on preschool children's acquisition of syntax. *Child Development, 60,* 237–245.

Lenke, R. R., & Levy, H. L. (1982). Maternal phenylketonuria—results of dietary therapy. *Journal of Obstetrics and Gynecology, 142,* 548–553.

Lenneberg, E. (1967). *Biological foundations of language.* New York: Wiley.

Lennon, R., & Eisenberg, N. (1987). Emotional displays associated with preschoolers' prosocial behavior. *Child Development, 58,* 992–1000.

Lennon, R. T. (1985). Group tests of intelligence. In B. B. Wolman (Ed.), *Handbook of intelligence.* New York: Wiley.

Lepper, M. R., & Gurtner, J. (1989). Children and computers: Approaching the twenty-first century. *American Psychologist, 44,* 170–178.

Lerner, R. M., & Lerner, J. V. (1977). Effects of age, sex, and physical attractiveness on child-peer relations, academic performance, and elementary school adjustment. *Developmental Psychology, 13,* 585–590.

Lerner, R. M., & Lerner, J. V. (1983). Temperament-intelligence reciprocities in early childhood: A contextual model. In M. Lewis (Ed.), *Origins of intelligence.* New York: Plenum Press.

Lesser, G. S., Fifer, F., & Clark, D. H. (1965). Mental abilities of children of different social-class and cultural groups. *Monographs of the Society for Research in Child Development, 30*(4, Serial No. 102).

Lester, B. M., Kotelchuk, M., Spelke, E., Sellers, M. J., & Klein, R. E. (1974). Separation protest in Guatemalan infants: Cross-cultural and cognitive findings. *Developmental Psychology, 10,* 79–85.

Levine, R., & White, M. (1986). *Human conditions: The cultural basis for educational development.* New York: Routledge & Kegan Paul.

Lewis, M. (1969). Infants' responses to facial stimuli during the first year of life. *Developmental Psychology, 1,* 75–86.

Lewis, M. (1983). On the nature of intelligence. In M. Lewis (Ed.), *Origins of intelligence.* New York: Plenum Press.

Lewis, M. (1989, April). *Self and self-conscious emotions.* Paper presented at the biennial meeting of the Society for Research in Child Development, Kansas City, MO.

Lewis, M. (1990). Social knowledge and social development. *Merrill-Palmer Quarterly, 36,* 93–116.

Lewis, M., & Brooks-Gunn, J. (1979). *Social cognition and the acquisition of self.* New York: Plenum Press.

Lewis, M., & Brooks-Gunn, J. (1981). Visual attention at three months as a predictor of cognitive functioning at two years of age. *Intelligence, 5,* 131–140.

Lewis, M., & Feiring, C. (1982). Some American families at dinner. In L. M. Laosa & I. E. Sigel (Eds.), *Families as learning environments for children.* New York: Plenum Press.

Lewis, M., & Freedle, R. O. (1973). Mother-infant dyad: The cradle of meaning. In P. Pilner, L. Krames, & T. Alloway (Eds.), *Communication and affect: Language and thought.* New York: Academic Press.

Lewis, M., & Michalson, L. (1983). *Children's emotions and moods: Developmental theory and measurement.* New York: Plenum Press.

Lewis, M., & Saarni, C. (1985). Culture and emotions. In M. Lewis & C. Saarni (Eds.), *The socialization of emotions.* New York: Plenum Press.

Lewis, M., Sullivan, M. W., Stanger, C., & Weiss, M. (1989). Self development and self-conscious emotions. *Child Development, 60,* 146–156.

Lewis, M., & Weinraub, M. (1974). Sex of parent versus sex of child: Socio-emotional development. In R. C. Friedman, R. M. Riehart, & R. Vande Wiele (Eds.), *Sex differences in behavior.* New York: Wiley.

Lewis, P. (1983). Drug usage in pregnancy. In P. Lewis (Ed.), *Clinical pharmacology in obstetrics.* Boston: Wright-PSG.

Lewis, T. L., Maurer, D., & Kay, D. (1978). Newborns' central vision: Whole or hole? *Journal of Experimental Child Psychology, 26,* 193–203.

Lewkowicz, D. J. (1988a). Sensory dominance in infants: 1. Six-month-old infants' response to auditory-visual compounds. *Developmental Psychology, 24,* 155–171.

Lewkowicz, D. J. (1988b). Sensory dominance in infants: 2. Ten-month-old infants' response to auditory-visual compounds. *Developmental Psychology, 24,* 172–182.

Lickona, T. (1976). Research on Piaget's theory of moral development. In T. Lickona (Ed.), *Moral development and behavior: Theory, research, and social issues.* New York: Holt, Rinehart & Winston.

Lieberman, D. (1985). Research on children and microcomputers: A review of utilization and effect studies. In M. Chen & W. Paisley (Eds.), *Children and microcomputers: Research on the newest medium.* Beverly Hills: Sage.

Liebert, R. M., & Sprafkin, J. (1988). *The early window: Effects of television on children and youth* (3rd ed.). New York: Pergamon Press.

Lillard, A. S., & Flavell, J. H. (1990). Young children's preference for mental state versus behavioral descriptions of human action. *Child Development, 61,* 731–741.

Lin, C. C., & Fu, V. R. (1990). A comparison of child-rearing practices among Chinese, immigrant Chinese, and Caucasian-American parents. *Child Development, 61,* 429–433.

Linden, M. G., Bender, B. G., Harmon, R. J., Mrazek, D. A., & Robinson, A. (1988). 47,XXX: What is the prognosis? *Pediatrics, 82,* 619–630.

Linn, M. C. (1985). Fostering equitable consequences from computer learning environments. *Sex Roles, 13,* 229–240.

Linn, M. C., & Petersen, A. C. (1985). Emergence and characterization of sex differences in spatial ability: A meta-analysis. *Child Development, 56,* 1479–1498.

Linn, M. C., & Petersen, A. C. (1986). A meta-analysis of differences in spatial ability: Implications for mathematics and science achievement. In J. S. Hyde & M. C. Linn (Eds.), *The psychology of gender: Advances through meta-analysis.* Baltimore: Johns Hopkins University Press.

Linney, J. A., & Seidman, E. N. (1989). The future of schooling. *American Psychologist, 44,* 336–340.

Lipsitt, L. P. (1982). Infant learning. In T. M. Field, A. Huston, H. C. Quay, L. Troll, & G. E. Finley (Eds.), *Review of Human Development.* New York: Wiley.

Lipsitt, L. P., Engen, T., & Kaye, H. (1963). Developmental changes in the olfactory threshold of the neonate. *Child Development, 34,* 371–376.

Little, B. B., Snell, L. M., & Gilstrap, L. C., III. (1988). Meth-amphetamine abuse during pregnancy: Outcome and fetal effects. *Obstetrics and Gynecology, 72,* 541–544.

Livesley, W. J., & Bromley, D. B. (1973). *Person perception in childhood and adolescence.* London: Wiley.

Locke, J. (1961). *An essay concerning human understanding.* London: J. M. Dent and Sons. (Original work published 1690)

Locke, J. (1964). *Some thoughts concerning education.* In P. Gay (Ed.), *John Locke on education.* New York: Bureau of Publications, Teacher's College. (Original work published 1693)

Lockheed, M. E. (1985). Women, girls, and computers: A first look at the evidence. *Sex Roles, 13,* 115–122.

Loeb, R. C., Horst, L., & Horton, P. J. (1980). Family interaction patterns associated with self-esteem in preadolescent girls and boys. *Merrill-Palmer Quarterly, 26,* 203–217.

Loehlin, J. C., Lindzey, G., & Spuhler, J. N. (1975). *Racial differences in intelligence.* San Francisco: W. H. Freeman.

Loehlin, J. C., Willerman, L., & Horn, J. M. (1988). Human behavior genetics. *Annual Review of Psychology, 39,* 101–133.

Long, N., & Forehand, R. (1987). The effects of parental divorce and marital conflict on children: An overview. *Journal of Developmental and Behavioral Pediatrics, 8,* 292–296.

Lorch, E. P., Bellack, D. R., & Augsbach, L. H. (1987). Young children's memory for televised stories: Effects of importance. *Child Development, 58,* 453–463.

Lorenz, K. Z. (1966). *On aggression* (M. K. Wilson, Trans.). New York: Harcourt, Brace, & World. (Original work published 1963)

Lovdal, L. T. (1989). Sex role messages in television commercials: An update. *Sex Roles, 21,* 715–724.

Lowitzer, A. C. (1987). Maternal phenylketonuria: Cause for concern among women with PKU. *Research in Developmental Disabilities, 8,* 1–14.

Lozoff, B. (1983). Birth and "bonding" in non-industrialized societies. *Developmental Medicine and Child Neurology, 25,* 595–600.

Lummis, M., & Stevenson, H. W. (1990). Gender differences in beliefs and achievement: A cross-cultural study. *Developmental Psychology, 26,* 254–263.

Luria, A. R. (1961). *The role of speech in the regulation of normal and abnormal behavior.* New York: Liveright.

Luria, A. R. (1969). Speech and formation of mental processes. In M. Cole & I. Maltzman (Eds.), *A handbook of contemporary Soviet psychology.* New York: Basic Books.

Lytton, H., & Romney, D. M. (1991). Parents' differential socialization of boys and girls: A meta-analysis. *Psychological Bulletin, 109,* 267–296.

Maccoby, E. E. (1984a). Middle childhood in the context of the family. In W. A. Collins (Ed.), *Development during middle childhood: The years from six to twelve.* Washington, DC: National Academy Press.

Maccoby, E. E. (1984b). Socialization and developmental change. *Child Development, 55,* 317–328.

Maccoby, E. E. (1988). Gender as a social category. *Developmental Psychology, 24,* 755–765.

Maccoby, E. E. (1990). Gender and relationships: A developmental account. *American Psychologist, 45,* 513–520.

Maccoby, E. E., & Jacklin, C. N. (1974). *The psychology of sex differences.* Stanford, CA: Stanford University Press.

Maccoby, E. E., & Jacklin, C. N. (1980). Sex differences in aggression: A rejoinder and reprise. *Child Development, 51,* 964–980.

Maccoby, E. E., & Jacklin, C. N. (1987). Gender segregation in childhood. In H. W. Reese (Ed.), *Advances in child development and behavior* (Vol. 20). Orlando, FL: Academic Press.

Maccoby, E. E., & Martin, J. A. (1983). Socialization in the context of the family: Parent-child interaction. In E. M. Hetherington (Ed.), *Handbook of child psychology: Vol. IV. Socialization, personality, and social development.* New York: Wiley.

MacFarlane, J. A. (1975). Olfaction in the development of social preferences in the human neonate. In M. A. Hofer (Ed.), *Parent-infant interaction.* Amsterdam: Elsevier.

MacKinnon, C. E. (1988). Influences on sibling relations in families with married and divorced parents. *Journal of Social Issues, 9,* 469–477.

MacKinnon, C. E. (1989a). An observational investigation of sibling interactions in married and divorced families. *Developmental Psychology, 25,* 36–44.

MacKinnon, C. E. (1989b). Sibling interactions in married and divorced families: Influence of ordinal position, socioeconomic status, and play context. *Journal of Divorce, 12,* 221–251.

MacLeod, C. L., & Lee, R. V. (1988). Parasitic infections. In G. N. Burrow & T. F. Ferris (Eds.), *Medical complications during pregnancy.* Philadelphia: W. B. Saunders.

MacLusky, N. J., & Naftolin, F. (1981). Sexual differentiation of the nervous system. *Science, 211,* 1294–1303.

Magnusson, D., Stattin, H., & Allen, V. (1986). Differential maturation among girls and its relations to social adjustment: A longitudinal perspective. In P. B. Baltes, D. L. Featherman, & R. M. Lerner (Eds.), *Life-span development and behavior* (Vol. 7). Hillsdale, NJ: Erlbaum.

Main, M., & Cassidy, J. (1988). Categories of response to reunion with the parent at age 6: Predictable from attachment classifications and stable over a 1-month period. *Developmental Psychology, 24,* 415–426.

Main, M., Kaplan, N., & Cassidy, J. (1985). Security in infancy, childhood, and adulthood: A move to the level of representation. In I. Bretherton & E. Waters (Eds.), *Growing points of attachment theory and research. Monographs of the Society for Research in Child Development, 50*(1–2, Serial No. 209).

Main, M., & Solomon, J. (1986). Discovery of a disorganized/disoriented attachment pattern. In T. B. Brazelton & M. W. Yogman (Eds.), *Affective development in infancy.* Norwood, NJ: Ablex.

Makin, J. W., & Porter, R. H. (1989). Attractiveness of lactating females' breast odors to neonates. *Child Development, 60,* 803–810.

Malatesta, C. Z., Culver, C., Tesman, J. R., & Shepard, B. (1989). The development of emotion expression during the first two years of life. *Monographs of the Society for Research in Child Development, 54*(1–2, Serial No. 219).

Malatesta, C. Z., & Haviland, J. M. (1982). Learning display rules: The socialization of emotion expression in infancy. *Child Development, 53,* 991–1003.

Malik, S. L., & Hauspic, R. C. (1986). Age at menarche among high altitude Bods of Ladakh (India). *Human Biology, 58,* 541–548.

Malina, R. M. (1975). *Growth and development: The first twenty years in man.* Minneapolis: Burgess.

Malina, R. M. (1980). Biosocial correlates of motor development during infancy and early childhood. In L. S. Greene & F. E. Johnstone (Eds.), *Social and biological predictors of nutritional status, physical growth, and neurological development.* New York: Academic Press.

Malinowski, B. (1927). *Sex and repression in savage society.* London: Routledge & Kegan Paul.

Mandler, J. M. (1988). How to build a baby: On the development of an accessible representational system. *Cognitive Development, 3,* 113–136.

Mandler, J. M., Fivush, R., & Reznick, J. S. (1987). The development of contextual categories. *Cognitive Development, 2,* 339–354.

Mange, A. P., & Mange, E. J. (1990). *Genetics: Human aspects* (2nd ed.). Sunderland, MA: Sinauer.

Mannarino, A. P. (1978). Friendship patterns and self-concept development in preadolescent males. *Journal of Genetic Psychology, 133,* 105–110.

Maratsos, M. P. (1983). Some current issues in the study of the acquisition of grammar. In J. H. Flavell & E. M. Markman (Eds.), *Handbook of child psychology: Vol. III. Cognitive development.* New York: Wiley.

Maratsos, M. P. (1989). Innateness and plasticity in language acquisition. In M. L. Rice & R. L. Schiefelbusch (Eds.), *The teachability of language.* Baltimore: Paul H. Brookes.

Maratsos, M. P., Kuczaj, S. A., II, Fox, D. E. C., & Chalkley, M. A. (1979). Some empirical studies in the acquisition of transformational relations. In W. A. Collins (Ed.), *Minnesota symposia on child psychology* (Vol. 12). Hillsdale, NJ: Erlbaum.

Marcus, D. E., & Overton, W. F. (1978). The development of cognitive gender constancy and sex role preferences. *Child Development, 49,* 434–444.

Marin, B. V., Holmes, D. L., Guth, M., & Kovac, P. (1979). The potential of children as eyewitnesses. *Law and Human Behavior, 3,* 295–305.

Marjoribanks, K. (1972). Ethnic and environmental influences on mental abilities. *American Journal of Sociology, 78,* 323–337.

Markman, E. M. (1987). How children constrain the possible meanings of words. In U. Neisser (Ed.), *Concepts and conceptual development: Ecological and intellectual factors in categorization.* Cambridge: Cambridge University Press.

Markman, E. M. (1990). Constraints children place on word meanings. *Cognitive Science, 14,* 57–77.

Markman, E. M., & Wachtel G. F. (1988). Children's use of mutual exclusivity to constrain the meanings of words. *Cognitive Psychology, 20,* 121–157.

Marr, D. B., & Sternberg, R. J. (1987). The role of mental speed in intelligence: A triarchic perspective. In P. A. Vernon (Ed.), *Speed of information-processing and intelligence.* Norwood, NJ: Ablex.

Marshall, R. E., Porter, F. L., Rogers, A. G., Moore, J., Anderson, B., & Boxerman, S. B. (1982). Circumcision: 2. Effects on mother-infant interaction. *Early Human Development, 7,* 367–374.

Marshall, W. A., & Tanner, J. M. (1970). Variations in the pattern of pubertal changes in boys. *Archives of Disease in Childhood, 45,* 13–23.

Martin, B. (1975). Parent-child relations. In F. D. Horowitz (Ed.), *Review of child development research* (Vol. 4). Chicago: University of Chicago Press.

Martin, C. L., & Halverson, C. F. (1981). A schematic processing model of sex typing and stereotyping in children. *Child Development, 52,* 1119–1134.

Martin, C. L., & Halverson, C. F. (1987). The roles of cognition in sex role acquisition. In D. B. Carter (Ed.), *Current conceptions of sex roles and sex typing: Theory and research.* New York: Praeger.

Martin, C. L., & Little, J. K. (1990). The relation of gender understanding to children's sex-typed preferences and gender stereotypes. *Child Development, 61,* 1427–1439.

Martin, H. P., & Beezley, P. (1976). Personality of abused children. In H. P. Martin (Ed.), *The abused child*. Cambridge: Ballinger.

Martin, J., Martin, D. C., Lund, C. A., & Streissguth, A. P. (1977). Maternal alcohol ingestion and cigarette smoking and their effects on newborn conditioning. *Alcoholism: Clinical and Experimental Research, 1*, 243–247.

Martin, J. B. (1987). Molecular genetics: Applications to the clinical neurosciences. *Science, 238*, 765–772.

Marvin, R. S. (1977). An ethological-cognitive model for the attenuation of mother-child attachment behavior. In T. M. Alloway, L. Krames, & P. Pliner (Eds.), *Advances in the study of communication and affect: Vol. 3. The development of social attachments*. New York: Plenum Press.

Masangkay, Z. S., McCluskey, K. A., McIntyre, C. W., Sims-Knight, J., Vaughn, B. E., & Flavell, J. H. (1974). The early development of inferences about the visual percepts of others. *Child Development, 45*, 357–366.

Massad, C. M. (1981). Sex role identity and adjustment during adolescence. *Child Development, 52*, 1290–1298.

Masters, J. C., Barden, R. C., & Ford, M. E. (1979). Affective states, expressive behavior, and learning in children. *Journal of Personality and Social Psychology, 37*, 380–390.

Masters, J. C., Ford, M. E., Arend, R., Grotevant, H. D., & Clark, L. V. (1979). Modeling and labeling as integrated determinants of children's sex-typed imitative behavior. *Child Development, 50*, 364–371.

Masur, E. F. (1982). Mothers' responses to infants' object-related gestures: Influences on lexical development. *Journal of Child Language, 9*, 23–30.

Matas, L., Arend, R. A., & Sroufe, L. A. (1978). Continuity of adaptation in the second year: The relationship between quality of attachment and later competence. *Child Development, 49*, 547–556.

Matheny, A. P., Jr. (1989). Children's behavioral inhibition over age and across situations. *Journal of Personality, 57*, 215–235.

Matsumoto, D., Haan, N., Yabrove, G., Theodorou, P., & Carney, C. C. (1986). Preschoolers' moral actions and emotions in prisoner's dilemma. *Developmental Psychology, 22*, 663–670.

Maudry, M., & Nekula, M. (1939). Social relations between children of the same age during the first two years of life. *Journal of Genetic Psychology, 54*, 193–215.

Maurer, D. (1983). The scanning of compound figures by young infants. *Journal of Experimental Child Psychology, 35*, 437–448.

Maurer, D. (1985). Infants' perception of facedness. In T. M. Field & N. A. Fox (Eds.), *Social perception in infants*. Norwood, NJ: Ablex.

Maurer, D., & Lewis, T, L. (1979). A physiological explanation of infants' early visual development. *Canadian Journal of Psychology, 33*, 232–252.

Mayer, R. E., & Fay, A. L. (1987). A chain of cognitive changes with learning to program in Logo. *Journal of Educational Psychology, 79*, 269–279.

McAnarney, E. R. (1987). Young maternal age and adverse neonatal outcome. *American Journal of Diseases of Children, 141*, 1053–1059.

McAnarney, E. R., & Stevens-Simon, C. (1990). Maternal psychological stress/depression and low birth weight. *American Journal of Diseases of Children, 144*, 789–792.

McBride, W. G. (1961). Thalidomide and congenital abnormalities. *Lancet, 2*, 1358.

McCabe, A., & Lipscomb, T. J. (1988). Sex differences in children's verbal aggression. *Merrill-Palmer Quarterly, 34*, 389–401.

McCall, R. B. (1979). *Infants*. Cambridge: Harvard University Press.

McCall, R. B. (1981). Nature-nurture and the two realms of development: A proposed integration with respect to mental development. *Child Development, 52*, 1–12.

McCall, R. B. (1984). Developmental changes in mental performance: The effect of birth of a sibling. *Child Development, 55*, 1317–1321.

McCall, R. B., Appelbaum, M. I., & Hogarty, P. S. (1973). Developmental changes in mental performance. *Monographs of the Society for Research in Child Development, 38*(3, Serial No. 150).

McCall, R. B., Hogarty, P. S., & Hurlburt, N. (1972). Transitions in sensorimotor development and the prediction of childhood IQ. *American Psychologist, 27*, 728–748.

McCall, R. B., Parke, R. D., & Kavanaugh, R. D. (1977). Imitation of live and televised models in children one to three years of age. *Monographs of the Society for Research in Child Development, 42*(3, Serial No. 171).

McCartney, K., Harris, M. J., & Bernieri, F. (1990). Growing up and growing apart: A developmental meta-analysis of twin studies. *Psychological Bulletin, 107*, 226–237.

McCartney, K., & Nelson, K. (1981). Children's use of scripts in story recall. *Discourse Processes, 4*, 59–70.

McCartney, K., Scarr, S., Phillips, D., & Grajek, S. (1985). Day care as intervention: Comparisons of varying quality programs. *Journal of Applied Developmental Psychology, 6*, 247–260.

McClelland, D. C. (1973). Testing for competence rather than for "intelligence." *American Psychologist, 28*, 1–14.

McCormick, M. C., Gortmaker, S. L., & Sobol, A. M. (1990). Very low birth weight children: Behavior problems and school difficulty in a national sample. *Journal of Pediatrics, 117*, 687–693.

McCormick, M. C., Shapiro, S., & Starfield, B. H. (1982). Factors associated with maternal opinion of infant development: Clues to the vulnerable child? *Pediatrics, 69*, 537–543.

McCormick, M. C., Wessel, K. W., Krischer, J. P., Welcher, D. W., & Handy, J. B. (1981). Preliminary analysis of developmental observations in a survey of morbidity in infants. *Early Human Development, 5*, 377–393.

McDavid, J. W., & Harari, H. (1966). Stereotyping of names and popularity in grade-school children. *Child Development, 37*, 453–459.

McDonald, L., & Pien, D. (1982). Mother conversational behavior as a function of interactional intent. *Journal of Child Language, 9*, 337–358.

McGhee, P. E. (1979). *Humor: Its origin and development*. San Francisco: W. H. Freeman.

McGhee, P. E., & Frueh, T. (1980). Television viewing and the learning of sex role stereotypes. *Sex Roles, 6*, 179–188.

McGraw, M. B. (1935). *Growth: A study of Johnny and Jimmy*. New York: Appleton-Century.

McGraw, M. B. (1941). Neural maturation as exemplified in the changing reactions of the infant to pin prick. *Child Development, 12*, 31–42.

McGraw, M. B. (1943). *The neuromuscular maturation of the human infant.* New York: Columbia University Press.

McGuire, J. (1988). Gender stereotypes of parents with two-year-olds and beliefs about gender differences in behavior. *Sex Roles, 19,* 233–240.

McGuire, K. D., & Weisz, J. R. (1982). Social cognition and behavior correlates of preadolescent chumship. *Child Development, 53,* 1478–1484.

McGurk, H., & MacDonald, J. (1976). Hearing lips and seeing voices. *Nature* (London), *264,* 746–748.

McKey, R. H., Condelli, L., Granson, H., Barrett, B., McConkey, C., & Plantz, M. (1985). *The impact of Head Start on children, families and communities* (Final report of the Head Start Evaluation, Synthesis and Utilization Project). Washington, DC: U.S. Government Printing Office.

McLaughlin, B. (1984). *Second-language acquisition in childhood: Vol. 2. School-age children.* Hillsdale, NJ: Erlbaum.

McLoyd, V. C. (1990). The impact of economic hardship on black families and children: Psychological distress, parenting, and socioemotional development. *Child Development, 61,* 311–346.

McLoyd, V. C., & Wilson, L. (1989). Maternal behavior, social support, and economic conditions as predictors of psychological distress in children. In V. C. McLoyd & C. Flanagan (Eds.), *New directions for child development: No. 46. Responses of children and adolescents to economic crisis.* San Francisco: Jossey-Bass.

McMahon, R. J., & Forehand, R. (1978). Nonprescription behavior therapy: Effectiveness of a brochure in teaching mothers to correct their children's inappropriate mealtime behaviors. *Behavior Therapy, 9,* 814–820.

McNeal, J. (1990, September). Children as customers. *American Demographics,* pp. 36–39.

Mead, G. H. (1934). *Mind, self, and society.* Chicago: University of Chicago Press.

Mead, M. (1967). *Male and female: A study of the sexes in a changing world.* New York: Morrow Quill. (Original work published 1949)

Medin, D. L. (1989). Concepts and conceptual structure. *American Psychologist, 44,* 1469–1481.

Mednick, S. A., Moffitt, T. E., & Stack, S. (1987). *The causes of crime: New biological approaches.* New York: Cambridge University Press.

Mehler, J., Jusczyk, P., Lambertz, G., Halsted, N., Bertoncini, J., & Amiel-Tison, C. (1988). A precursor of language acquisition in young infants. *Cognition, 29,* 143–178.

Meichenbaum, D. (1977). *Cognitive-behavior modification: An integrative approach.* New York: Plenum Press.

Meichenbaum, D., & Goodman, J. (1971). Training impulsive children to talk to themselves: A means of developing self-control. *Journal of Abnormal Psychology, 77,* 115–126.

Meltzoff, A., & Borton, R. (1979). Intermodal matching by human neonates. *Nature* (London), *282,* 403–404.

Meltzoff, A. N. (1988a). Imitation, objects, tools, and the rudiments of language in human ontogeny. *Human Evolution, 3,* 45–64.

Meltzoff, A. N. (1988b). Infant imitation and memory: Nine-month-olds in immediate and deferred tests. *Child Development, 59,* 217–225.

Meltzoff, A. N., & Moore, M. K. (1983). Newborn infants imitate adult facial gestures. *Child Development, 54,* 702–709.

Meltzoff, A. N., & Moore, M. K. (1989). Imitation in newborn infants: Exploring the range of gestures imitated and the underlying mechanisms. *Developmental Psychology, 25,* 954–962.

Mendelson, M. J., & Haith, M. M. (1976). The relation between audition and vision in the human newborn. *Monographs of the Society for Research in Child Development, 41*(4, Serial No. 167).

Meredith, H. V. (1978). *Human body growth in the first ten years of life.* Columbia, SC: The State Printing Co.

Merimee, T. J., Zapf, J., & Froesch, E. R. (1981). Dwarfism in the Pygmy: An isolated deficiency of insulin-like Growth Factor I. *New England Journal of Medicine, 305,* 965–968.

Merriman, W. E., & Bowman, L. L. (1989). The mutual exclusivity bias in children's word learning. *Monographs of the Society for Research in Child Development, 54*(3–4, Serial No. 220).

Merritt, T. A. (1981). Smoking mothers affect little lives. *American Journal of Diseases of Children, 135,* 501–502.

Messer, D. J. (1981). The identification of names in maternal speech to infants. *Journal of Psycholinguistic Research, 10,* 69–77.

Meyer, M. B., & Tonascia, J. A. (1977). Maternal smoking, pregnancy complications, and perinatal mortality. *American Journal of Obstetrics and Gynecology, 128,* 494–502.

Michel, G. F. (1988). A neuropsychological perspective on infant sensorimotor development. In C. Rovee-Collier & L. P. Lipsitt (Eds.), *Advances in infancy research* (Vol. 5). Norwood, NJ: Ablex.

Michel, G. F., & Harkins, D. A. (1986). Postural and lateral asymmetries in the ontogeny of handedness during infancy. *Developmental Psychobiology, 19,* 247–258.

Michelson, L., Sugai, D. P., Wood, R. P., & Kazdin, A. E. (1983). *Social skills assessment and training with children.* New York: Plenum Press.

Michelsson, K., Sirvio, P., & Wasz-Hockert, D. (1977). Pain cry in fullterm asphyxiated newborn infants correlated with late findings. *Acta Paediatrica Scandinavica, 66,* 611–616.

Miller, N., & Maruyama, G. (1976). Ordinal position and peer popularity. *Journal of Personality and Social Psychology, 33,* 123–131.

Miller, P. H. (1985). Children's reasoning about the causes of human behavior. *Journal of Experimental Child Psychology, 39,* 343–362.

Miller, P. H., & Aloise, P. A. (1989). Young children's understanding of the psychological causes of behavior: A review. *Child Development, 60,* 257–285.

Miller, P. H., & Harris, Y. R. (1988). Preschoolers' strategies of attention on a same-different task. *Developmental Psychology, 24,* 628–633.

Miller, P. H., Kessel, F. S., & Flavell, J. H. (1970). Thinking about people thinking about people thinking about . . . A study of social cognitive development. *Child Development, 41,* 613–623.

Miller-Jones, D. (1989). Culture and testing. *American Psychologist, 44,* 360–366.

Mills, R. S. L., & Grusec, J. E. (1989). Cognitive, affective, and behavioral consequences of praising altruism. *Merrill-Palmer Quarterly, 35,* 299–326.

Minkoff, H., Deepak, N., Menez, R., & Fikrig, S. (1987). Pregnancies resulting in infants with acquired immunodeficiency syndrome or AIDS-related complex: Follow-up of mothers, children, and subsequently born siblings. *Obstetrics and Gynecology, 69,* 288–291.

Minuchin, P. P. (1988). Relationships within the family: A systems perspective on development. In R. A. Hinde & J. Stevenson-Hinde (Eds.), *Relationships within families: Mutual influences.* Oxford: Clarendon Press.

Minuchin, P. P., & Shapiro, E. K. (1983). The school as a context for social development. In E. M. Hetherington (Ed.), *Handbook of child psychology: Vol. IV. Socialization, personality, and social development.* New York: Wiley.

Mischel, H. N., & Mischel, W. (1983). The development of children's knowledge of self-control strategies. *Child Development, 54,* 603–619.

Mischel, W. (1966). A social learning view of sex differences in behavior. In E. E. Maccoby (Ed.), *The development of sex differences.* Stanford, CA: Stanford University Press.

Mischel, W., Ebbesen, E. B., & Zeiss, A. R. (1972). Cognitive and attentional mechanisms in delay of gratification. *Journal of Personality and Social Psychology, 21,* 204–218.

Mischel, W., & Mischel, H. N. (1977). Self-control and the self. In T. Mischel (Ed.), *The self: Psychological and philosophical issues.* Totowa, NJ: Rowan & Littlefield.

Mischel, W., Shoda, Y., & Rodriguez, M. L. (1989). Delay of gratification in children. *Science, 244,* 933–938.

Mittendorf, R., Williams, M. A., Berkey, C. S., & Cotter, P. F. (1990). The length of uncomplicated human gestation. *Obstetrics and Gynecology, 75,* 929–932.

Miyake, K., Chen, S., & Campos, J. J. (1985). Infant temperament, mother's mode of interaction, and attachment in Japan: An interim report. In I. Bretherton & E. Waters (Eds.), *Growing points of attachment theory and research. Monographs of the Society for Research in Child Development, 50*(1–2, Serial No. 209).

Moely, B. E., Hart, S. S., Santulli, K. A., Leal, L., Kogut, D. J., McLain, E., Zhou, Z., & Johnson, T. D. (1989, April). *Teachers' cognitions about the memory processes of elementary school children: A developmental perspective.* Paper presented at the biennial meeting of the Society for Research in Child Development, Kansas City, MO.

Moely, B. E., Olson, F. A., Halwes, T. G., & Flavell, J. H. (1969). Production deficiency in young children's clustered recall. *Developmental Psychology, 1,* 26–34.

Moffat, R., & Hackel, A. (1985). Thermal aspects of neonatal care. In A. Gottfried & J. Gaiter (Eds.), *Infant stress under intensive care.* Baltimore: University Park Press.

Molfese, D. L., & Molfese, V. J. (1979). Hemisphere and stimulus differences as reflected in the cortical responses of newborn infants to speech stimuli. *Developmental Psychology, 15,* 505–511.

Molfese, D. L., & Molfese, V. J. (1980). Cortical responses of preterm infants to phonetic and nonphonetic speech stimuli. *Developmental Psychology, 16,* 574–581.

Molfese, D. L., & Molfese, V. J. (1985). Electrophysiological indices of auditory discrimination in newborn infants: The bases for predicting later language development? *Infant Behavior and Development, 8,* 197–211.

Money, J., & Ehrhardt, A. A. (1972). *Man and woman, boy and girl: Differentiation and dimorphism of gender identity from conception to maturity.* Baltimore: Johns Hopkins University Press.

Monfries, M. M., & Kafer, N. F. (1987). Neglected and rejected children: A social-skills model. *Journal of Psychology, 121,* 401–407.

Moore, C. L. (1985). Another psychobiological view of sexual differentiation. *Developmental Review, 5,* 18–55.

Moore, K. L. (1988). *The developing human: Clinically oriented embryology* (4th ed.). Philadelphia: W. B. Saunders.

Moore, K. L. (1989). *Before we are born* (3rd ed.). Philadelphia: W. B. Saunders.

Moore, R. S., & Moore, D. N. (1975). *Better late than early.* New York: Reader's Digest Press.

Morgan, M. (1982). Television and adolescents' sex-role stereotypes: A longitudinal study. *Journal of Personality and Social Psychology, 43,* 947–955.

Morgan, M. (1987). Television, sex-role attitudes, and sex-role behavior. *Journal of Early Adolescence, 7,* 269–282.

Morris, R., & Kratchowill, T. (1983). *Treating children's fears and phobias.* New York: Pergamon Press.

Morrongiello, B. A. (1984). Auditory temporal pattern perception in 6- and 12-month-old infants. *Developmental Psychology, 20,* 441–448.

Morrongiello, B. A. (1988). The development of auditory pattern perception skills. In C. Rovee-Collier & L. P. Lipsitt (Eds.), *Advances in infancy research* (Vol. 5). Norwood, NJ: Ablex.

Morrongiello, B. A., Fenwick, K. D., & Chance, G. (1990). Sound localization acuity in very young infants: An observer-based testing procedure. *Developmental Psychology, 26,* 75–84.

Moshman, D., & Franks, B. A. (1986). Development of the concept of inferential validity. *Child Development, 57,* 153–165.

Moss, H. A. (1974). Early sex differences and mother-infant interaction. In R. C. Friedman, R. M. Richart, & R. L. Vande Wiele (Eds.), *Sex differences in behavior.* New York: Wiley.

Mossler, D. G., Marvin, R. S., & Greenberg, M. T. (1976). Conceptual perspective-taking in 2- to 6-year-old children. *Developmental Psychology, 12,* 85–86.

Movshon, J. A., & Van Sluyters, R. C. (1981). Visual neuronal development. *Annual Review of Psychology, 32,* 477–522.

Mulhern, R. K., Jr., & Passman, R. H. (1981). Parental discipline as affected by the sex of the parent, the sex of the child, and the child's apparent responsiveness to discipline. *Developmental Psychology, 17,* 604–613.

Muller, A. A., & Perlmutter, M. (1985). Preschool children's problem-solving interactions at computers and jigsaw puzzles. *Journal of Applied Developmental Psychology, 6,* 173–186.

Muller, H. J. (1927). Artificial transmutation of the gene. *Science, 66,* 84–87.

Mullis, I. V. S., & Jenkins, L. B. (1990). *The reading report card, 1971–1988.* Princeton, NJ: Educational Testing Service.

Murphy, L. B. (1937). *Social behavior and child personality.* New York: Columbia University Press.

Mussen, P., Rutherford, E., Harris, S., & Keasey, C. (1970). Honesty and altruism among preadolescents. *Developmental Psychology, 3,* 169–194.

Mussen, P. H., & Jones, M. C. (1957). Self-conceptions, motivations, and interpersonal attitudes of late and early maturing boys. *Child Development, 28,* 243–256.

Mussen, P. H., & Jones, M. C. (1958). The behavior inferred motivations of late and early maturing boys. *Child Development, 29,* 61–67.

Nahmias, A. J., Keyserling, H. L., & Kernick, G. M. (1983). Herpes simplex. In J. S. Remington & J. O. Klein (Eds.), *In-*

fectious diseases of the fetus and newborn infant. Philadelphia: W. B. Saunders.

Náñez, J. E., Sr. (1988). Perception of impending collision in 3- to 6-week-old human infants. *Infant Behavior and Development, 11,* 447–463.

Nastasi, B. K., Clements, D. H., & Battista, M. T. (1990). Social-cognitive interactions, motivation, and cognitive growth in Logo programming and CAI problem-solving environments. *Journal of Educational Psychology, 82,* 150–158.

National Association for Perinatal Addiction Research and Education. (1988, October). Innocent addicts: High rate of prenatal drug abuse found. *ADAMHA News.*

National Center for Health Statistics. (1976). *Monthly Vital Statistics Report, 25*(3, Suppl).

National Commission on Excellence in Education. (1983). *A nation at risk: The imperative for educational reform.* Washington, DC: U.S. Government Printing Office.

National Genetics Foundation. (1987). *Clinical genetics handbook.* Oradell, NJ: Medical Economics Books.

National Institutes of Mental Health. (1982). *Television and behavior: Ten years of scientific progress and implications for the eighties.* Rockville, MD: Author.

National Research Council, Committee on Mapping and Sequencing the Human Genome. (1988). *Mapping and sequencing the human genome.* Washington, DC: National Academy Press.

Neill, S. (1976). Aggressive and non-aggressive fighting in twelve- to thirteen-year-old pre-adolescent boys. *Journal of Child Psychology and Psychiatry, 17,* 213–220.

Neimark, E. D. (1979). Current status of formal operations research. *Human Development, 22,* 60–67.

Nelson, C. A., & Horowitz, F. D. (1987). Visual motion perception in infancy: A review and synthesis. In P. Salapatek & L. Cohen (Eds.), *Handbook of infant perception: From perception to cognition* (Vol. 2). Orlando, FL: Academic Press.

Nelson, D. G. K., Hirsh-Pasek, K., Jusczyk, P. W., & Cassidy, K. W. (1989). How the prosodic cues in motherese might assist language learning. *Journal of Child Language, 16,* 55–68.

Nelson, K. (1973). Structure and strategy in learning to talk. *Monographs of the Society for Research in Child Development, 38*(1–2, Serial No. 149).

Nelson, K., & Gruendel, J. (1981). Generalized event representations: Basic building blocks of cognitive development. In M. E. Lamb & A. L. Brown (Eds.), *Advances in developmental psychology* (Vol. 1). Hillsdale, NJ: Erlbaum.

Nelson, K. E. (1989). Strategies for first language teaching. In M. L. Rice & R. L. Schiefelbusch (Eds.), *The teachability of language.* Baltimore: Paul H. Brookes.

Nelson-LeGall, S. (1985). Motive-outcome matching and outcome foreseeability: Effects on attribution of intentionality and moral judgments. *Developmental Psychology, 21,* 332–337.

New, R. S., & Benigni, L. (1987). Italian fathers and infants: Cultural constraints on paternal behavior. In M. E. Lamb (Ed.), *The father's role: Cross-cultural perspectives.* Hillsdale, NJ: Erlbaum.

Newport, E. L. (1977). Motherese: The speech of mothers to young children. In N. J. Castellan, D. B. Pisoni, & G. Potts (Eds.), *Cognitive theory* (Vol. 2). Hillsdale, NJ: Erlbaum.

Newport, E. L. (1990). Maturational constraints on language learning. *Cognitive Science, 14,* 11–28.

Newton, N. (1955). *Maternal emotions.* New York: P. B. Hoeber.

Nickel, H., & Kocher, E. M. T. (1987). West Germany and the German-speaking countries. In M. E. Lamb (Ed.), *The father's role: Cross-cultural perspectives.* Hillsdale, NJ: Erlbaum.

Nielsen, J. M. (1990). *Sex and gender in society: Perspectives on stratification* (2nd ed.). Prospect Heights, IL: Waverly.

Nielson Co. (1988). *1988 Nielson report on television.* Northbrook, IL: Author.

Niemiec, R., & Walberg, H. J. (1987). Comparative effects of computer-assisted instruction: A synthesis of reviews. *Journal of Educational Computing Research, 3,* 19–37.

Nilsson, L. (1977). *A child is born.* New York: Dell.

Ninio, A., & Bruner, J. S. (1978). The achievement and antecedents of labelling. *Journal of Child Language, 5,* 1–15.

Norbeck, J. S., & Tilden, V. P. (1983). Life stress, social support, and emotional disequilibrium in complications of pregnancy: A prospective, multivariate study. *Journal of Health and Social Behavior, 24,* 30–46.

Notzon, F. C., Placek, P. J., & Taffel, S. M. (1987). Comparisons of national cesarean-section rates. *New England Journal of Medicine, 316,* 386–389.

Novello, A. C., Wise, P. H., Willoughby, A., & Pizzo, P. A. (1989). Final report of the United States Department of Health and Human Services Secretary's Work Group on Pediatric Human Immunodeficiency Virus Infection and Disease: Content and implications. *Pediatrics, 84,* 547–555.

Nowakowski, R. S. (1987). Basic concepts of CNS development. *Child Development, 58,* 568–595.

Nowicki, S., & Strickland, B. (1973). A locus of control scale for children. *Journal of Consulting and Clinical Psychology, 40,* 148–154.

Nucci, L. P., & Turiel, E. (1978). Social interactions and the development of social concepts in preschool children. *Child Development, 49,* 400–407.

Nuckolls, K. B., Cassel, J., & Kaplan, B. H. (1972). Psychosocial assets, life crisis, and the prognosis of pregnancy. *American Journal of Epidemiology, 95,* 431–441.

Nussbaum, R. L., & Ledbetter, D. H. (1986). Fragile X syndrome: A unique mutation in man. *Annual Review of Genetics, 20,* 109–145.

O'Brien, M., Huston, A. C., & Risley, T. (1983). Sex-typed play of toddlers in a day care center. *Journal of Applied Developmental Psychology, 4,* 1–9.

O'Connor, N., & Hermelin, B. (1965). Sensory dominance. *Archives of General Psychiatry, 12,* 99–103.

O'Connor, R. D. (1972). Relative efficacy of modeling, shaping, and the procedures for modification of social withdrawal. *Journal of Abnormal Psychology, 79,* 327–334.

Oakes, J. (1985). *Keeping track: How schools structure inequality.* New Haven, CT: Yale University Press.

Oakland, T. D. (1982). Nonbiased assessment in counseling: Issues and guidelines. *Measurement and Evaluation in Guidance, 15,* 107–116.

Oates, R. K. (1984). Similarities and differences between nonorganic failure to thrive and deprivation dwarfism. *Child Abuse and Neglect, 8,* 439–445.

Oates, R. K., Peacock, A., & Forrest, D. (1985). Long-term effects of nonorganic failure to thrive. *Pediatrics, 75,* 36–40.

Ochs, E. (1990). Indexicality and socialization. In J. W. Stigler, R. A. Shweder, & G. Herdt (Eds.), *Cultural psychology.* Cambridge: Cambridge University Press.

Offer, D. (1987). In defense of adolescents. *Journal of the American Medical Association, 257,* 3407–3408.

Ogbu, J. U. (1974). *The next generation: An ethnography of education in an urban neighborhood.* New York: Academic Press.

Ogbu, J. U. (1986). The consequences of the American caste system. In U. Neisser (Ed.), *The school achievement of minority children: New perspectives.* Hillsdale, NJ: Erlbaum.

Oldershaw, L., Walters, G. C., & Hall, D. K. (1986). Control strategies and noncompliance in abusive mother-child dyads: An observational study. *Child Development, 57,* 722–732.

Oller, D. K., & Eilers, R. E. (1982). Similarity of babbling in Spanish and English-learning babies. *Journal of Child Language, 9,* 565–577.

Oller, D. K., & Eilers, R. E. (1988). The role of audition in infant babbling. *Child Development, 59,* 441–449.

Olney, R., & Scholnick, E. (1976). Adult judgments of age and linguistic differences in infant vocalizations. *Journal of Child Language, 3,* 145–156.

Olsho, L. W. (1984). Infant frequency discrimination. *Infant Behavior and Development, 7,* 27–35.

Olson, S. L., Bayles, K., & Bates, J. E. (1986). Mother-child interaction and children's speech progress: A longitudinal study of the first two years. *Merrill-Palmer Quarterly, 32,* 1–20.

Olweus, D. (1980). Familial and temperamental determinants of aggressive behavior in adolescent boys: A causal analysis. *Developmental Psychology, 16,* 644–660.

Olweus, D., Mattsson, A., Schalling, D., & Low, H. (1980). Testosterone, aggression, physical, and personality dimensions in normal adolescent males. *Psychosomatic Medicine, 42,* 253–269.

Omark, D. R., & Edelman, M. S. (1975). Formation of dominance hierarchies in young children: Attention and perception. In T. Williams (Ed.), *Physical anthropology.* The Hague: Mouton.

Orenstein, W. A., Bart, K. J., Hinman, A. R., Preblud, S. R., Greaves, W. L., Doster, S. W., Stetler, W. C., & Sirotkin, B. (1984). The opportunity and obligation to eliminate rubella from the United States. *Journal of the American Medical Association, 251,* 1988–1994.

Ornstein, P. A., & Naus, M. J. (1978). Rehearsal processes in children's memory. In P. A. Ornstein (Ed.), *Memory development in children.* Hillsdale, NJ: Erlbaum.

Ornstein, P. A., Naus, M. J., & Liberty, C. (1975). Rehearsal and organizational processes in children's memory. *Child Development, 46,* 818–830.

Orton, G. L. (1982). A comparative study of children's worries. *Journal of Psychology, 110,* 153–162.

Osherson, D. N., & Markman, E. M. (1975). Language and the ability to evaluate contradictions and tautologies. *Cognition, 2,* 213–226.

Ostrer, H., & Hejtmancik, J. F. (1988). Prenatal diagnosis and carrier detection of genetic diseases by analysis of deoxyribonucleic acid. *Journal of Pediatrics, 112,* 679–687.

Ounsted, C., Oppenheimer, R., & Lindsay, J. (1974). Aspects of bonding failure: The psychopathology and psychotherapeutic treatment of families of battered children. *Developmental Medicine and Child Neurology, 16,* 447–452.

Over, R. (1987). Can human neonates imitate facial gestures? In B. E. McKenzie & R. H. Day (Eds.), *Perceptual development in early infancy: Problems and issues.* Hillsdale, NJ: Erlbaum.

Overview: Growing up—Del and Rey, Johnny and Jimmy, and na-

ture versus nurture. (1987, July). *Scientific American,* pp. 30–32.

Owen, M. T., & Cox, M. J. (1988). Maternal employment and the transition to parenthood. In A. E. Gottfried & A. W. Gottfried (Eds.), *Maternal employment and children's development: Longitudinal research.* New York: Plenum Press.

Palinscar, A. S., & Brown, A. L. (1984). Reciprocal teaching of comprehension-fostering and comprehension-monitoring activities. *Cognition and Instruction, 1,* 117–175.

Palisin, H. (1986). Preschool temperament and performance on achievement tests. *Developmental Psychology, 22,* 766–770.

Palkovitz, R. (1985). Fathers' birth attendance, early contact, and extended contact with their newborns: A critical review. *Child Development, 56,* 392–406.

Papert, S. (1980). *Mindstorms: Children, computers, and powerful ideas.* New York: Basic Books.

Papousek, H. (1967). Experimental studies of appetitional behavior in human newborns and infants. In H. W. Stevenson, E. H. Hess, & H. L. Rheingold (Eds.), *Early behavior.* New York: Wiley.

Papousek, H., Papousek, M., & Koester, L. S. (1986). Sharing emotionality and sharing knowledge: A microanalytic approach to parent-infant communication. In C. E. Izard & P. B. Read (Eds.), *Measuring emotions in infants and children* (Vol. 2). Cambridge: Cambridge University Press.

Paris, S. G., & Cross, D. R. (1983). Ordinary learning: Pragmatic connections among children's beliefs, motives, and actions. In J. Bisanz, G. L. Bisanz, & R. Kail (Eds.), *Learning in children: Progress in cognitive research.* New York: Springer-Verlag.

Parke, R. D. (1969). Effectiveness of punishment as an interaction of intensity, timing, agent nurturance, and cognitive structuring. *Child Development, 40,* 213–235.

Parke, R. D., & Collmer, C. W. (1975). Child abuse: An interdisciplinary analysis. In E. M. Hetherington (Ed.), *Review of child development research* (Vol. 5). Chicago: University of Chicago Press.

Parke, R. D., MacDonald, K. B., Beitel, A., & Bhavnagri, N. (1988). The role of the family in the development of peer relationships. In R. D. Peters & R. J. McMahon (Eds.), *Social learning and systems approaches to marriage and the family.* New York: Brunner/Mazel.

Parke, R. D., & O'Leary, S. (1976). Father-mother-infant interaction in the newborn period: Some findings, some observations, and some unresolved issues. In K. F. Riegel & J. Meacham (Eds.), *The developing individual in a changing world: Vol. 2. Social and environmental issues.* The Hague: Mouton.

Parke, R. D., & Slaby, R. G. (1983). The development of aggression. In E. M. Hetherington (Ed.), *Handbook of child psychology: Vol. IV. Socialization, personality, and social development.* New York: Wiley.

Parke, R. D., & Walters, R. H. (1967). Some factors influencing the efficacy of punishment training for inducing response inhibition. *Monographs of the Society for Research in Child Development, 32*(1, Serial No. 109).

Parker, J. G., & Asher, S. R. (1987). Peer relations and later personal adjustment: Are low-accepted children at risk? *Psychological Bulletin, 102,* 357–389.

Parker, J. G., & Gottman, J. M. (1989). Social and emotional development in a relational context: Friendship interaction from early childhood to adolescence. In T. M. Berndt & G. W. Ladd (Eds.), *Peer relations in childhood.* New York: Wiley.

Parmelee, A. H., & Sigman, M. (1983). Perinatal brain development and behavior. In M. Haith & J. Campos (Eds.), *Biology and infancy.* New York: Wiley.

Parsons, J. E. (1980). Psychosexual neutrality: Is anatomy destiny? In J. E. Parsons (Ed.), *The psychobiology of sex differences and sex roles.* New York: Hemisphere.

Parten, M. B. (1932). Social participation among pre-school children. *Journal of Abnormal and Social Psychology, 32,* 243–269.

Pass, R. F. (1987). Congenital and perinatal infections due to viruses and toxoplasma. In N. Kretchmer, E. J. Quilligan, & J. D. Johnson (Eds.), *Prenatal and perinatal biology and medicine: Vol. 2. Disorder, diagnosis, and therapy.* New York: Harwood Academic Publishers.

Pass, R. F., Stagno, S., Myers, G. J., & Alford, C. A. (1980). Outcome of symptomatic congenital cytomegalovirus infection: Results of long-term longitudinal follow-up. *Pediatrics, 66,* 758–762.

Patterson, D. (1987, August). The causes of Down syndrome. *Scientific American, 257,* pp. 52–61.

Patterson, G. R. (1976). The aggressive child: Victim and architect of a coercive system. In E. J. Mash, L. A. Hamerlynck, & L. C. Handy (Eds.), *Behavior modification and families.* New York: Brunner/Mazel.

Patterson, G. R. (1982). *A social learning approach: Vol. 3. Coercive family process.* Eugene, OR: Castalia.

Patterson, G. R. (1986). Performance models for antisocial boys. *American Psychologist, 41,* 432–444.

Patterson, G. R., & Fleischman, M. J. (1979). Maintenance of treatment effects: Some considerations concerning family systems and follow-up data. *Behavior Therapy, 10,* 168–185.

Patterson, G. R., Littman, R. A., & Bricker, W. (1967). Assertive behavior in children: A step toward a theory of aggression. *Monographs of the Society for Research in Child Development, 32*(5, Serial No. 113).

Patterson, G. R., & Reid, J. B. (1973). Intervention for families of aggressive boys: A replication study. *Behavior Research and Therapy, 11,* 383–394.

Patterson, G. R., Reid, J. B., Jones, R. R., & Conger, R. E. (1975). *A social learning approach: Vol. 1. Families with aggressive children.* Eugene, OR: Castalia.

Pea, R. D., Kurland, D. M., & Hawkins, J. (1985). LOGO and the development of thinking skills. In M. Chen & W. Paisley (Eds.), *Children and microcomputers: Research on the newest medium.* Beverly Hills: Sage.

Pederson, F. A., Cain, R., Zaslow, M., & Anderson, B. (1982). Variation in infant experience associated with alternative family organization. In L. Laosa & I. Sigel (Eds.), *Families as learning environments for children.* New York: Plenum Press.

Peevers, B. H., & Secord, P. F. (1973). Developmental changes in attribution of descriptive concepts to persons. *Journal of Personality and Social Psychology, 27,* 120–128.

Pellegrini, A. D. (1988). Elementary-school children's rough-and-tumble play and social competence. *Developmental Psychology, 24,* 802–806.

Penner, S. G. (1987). Parental responses to grammatical and ungrammatical child utterances. *Child Development, 58,* 376–384.

Perlmutter, M., & Myers, N. A. (1979). Development of recall in 2- to 4-year-old children. *Developmental Psychology, 15,* 73–83.

Perry, D. G., & Bussey, K. (1979). The social learning theory of sex differences: Imitation is alive and well. *Journal of Personality and Social Psychology, 37,* 1699–1712.

Perry, D. G., Perry, L. C., & Rasmussen, P. (1986). Cognitive social learning mediators of aggression. *Child Development, 52,* 700–711.

Persell, C. H. (1977). *Education and inequality: A theoretical and empirical synthesis.* New York: Free Press.

Petersen, A. C. (1980). Biopsychosocial processes in the development of sex-related differences. In J. Parsons (Ed.), *The psychobiology of sex differences and sex roles.* New York: Hemisphere.

Peterson, A. C. (1987, September). Those gangly years. *Psychology Today,* pp. 28–34.

Peterson, D. R. (1984). Sudden infant death syndrome. In M. B. Bracken (Ed.), *Behavioral teratology.* New York: Oxford University Press.

Peterson, G. W., & Rollins, B. C. (1987). Parent-child socialization. In M. B. Sussman & S. K. Steinmetz (Eds.), *Handbook of marriage and the family.* New York: Plenum Press.

Peterson, L. (1983). Influence of age, task competence, and responsibility focus on children's altruism. *Developmental Psychology, 19,* 141–148.

Petitto, L. A., & Marentette, P. F. (1991). Babbling in the manual code: Evidence for the ontogeny of language. *Science, 251,* 1493–1496.

Pettersen, L., Yonas, A., & Fisch, R. O. (1980). The development of blinking in response to impending collision in preterm, fullterm, and postterm infants. *Infant Behavior and Development, 3,* 155–165.

Pettit, G. S., Dodge, K. A., Bakshi, A., & Coie, J. D. (1990). The emergence of social dominance in young boys' play groups: Developmental differences and behavioral correlates. *Developmental Psychology, 26,* 1017–1025.

Phelps, E., & Damon, W. (1989). Problem solving with equals: Peer collaboration as a context for learning mathematics and spatial concepts. *Journal of Educational Psychology, 81,* 639–646.

Phillips, D. (1984). The illusion of incompetence among academically competent children. *Child Development, 55,* 2000–2016.

Phillips, J. L. (1975). *The origins of intellect: Piaget's theory.* San Francisco: W. H. Freeman.

Piaget, J. (1926). *The language and thought of the child.* New York: Harcourt Brace.

Piaget, J. (1929). *The child's conception of the world.* London: Routledge & Kegan Paul.

Piaget, J. (1965). *The moral judgment of the child.* New York: Free Press. (Original work published 1932)

Piaget, J. (1952a). *The child's conception of number.* New York: W. W. Norton.

Piaget, J. (1952b). *The origins of intelligence in children.* New York: W. W. Norton.

Piaget, J. (1954). *The construction of reality in the child.* New York: Basic Books.

Piaget, J. (1962). *Play, dreams, and imitation in childhood.* New York: W. W. Norton.

Piaget, J. (1971). *Biology and knowledge: An essay on the rela-*

tionship between organic regulations and cognitive processes. Chicago: University of Chicago Press.

Piaget, J., & Inhelder, B. (1956). *The child's conception of space.* London: Routledge & Kegan Paul.

Pick, A. D. (1965). Improvement of visual and tactual discrimination. *Journal of Experimental Psychology, 69,* 331–339.

Pick, H. L., Jr. (1987). Information and the effects of early perceptual experience. In N. Eisenberg (Ed.), *Contemporary topics in developmental psychology.* New York: Wiley.

Pillow, B. H. (1988). Young children's understanding of attentional limits. *Child Development, 59,* 38–46.

Pinneau, S. R. (1961). *Changes in intelligence quotient: Infancy to maturity.* Boston: Houghton Mifflin.

Pinon, M. F., Huston, A. C., & Wright, J. C. (1989). Family ecology and child characteristics that predict young children's educational television viewing. *Child Development, 60,* 846–856.

Pleck, J. H. (1982). *Husbands' and wives' paid work, family work, and adjustment.* Working papers. Wellesley, MA: Wellesley College Center for Research on Women.

Pleck, J. H. (1983). Husbands' paid work and family roles: Current research issues. In H. Z. Lopata & J. H. Pleck (Eds.), *Research in the interweave of social roles: Families and jobs.* Greenwich, CT: JAI Press.

Plomin, R. (1986). *Development, genetics, and psychology.* Hillsdale, NJ: Erlbaum.

Plomin, R. (1987). Developmental behavioral genetics and infancy. In J. D. Osofsky (Ed.), *Handbook of infant development* (2nd ed.). New York: Wiley.

Plomin, R. (1989). Environment and genes: Determinants of behavior. *American Psychologist, 44,* 105–111.

Plomin, R. (1990). The role of inheritance in behavior. *Science, 248,* 183–188.

Plomin, R., & Daniels, D. (1987). Why are children in the same family so different from one another? *Behavioral and Brain Science, 10,* 1–16.

Plomin, R., & DeFries, J. C. (1980). Genetics and intelligence: Recent data. *Intelligence, 4,* 15–24.

Plomin, R., & DeFries, J. C. (1985). *Origins of individual differences in infancy: The Colorado Adoption Project.* Orlando, FL: Academic Press.

Plomin, R., DeFries, J. C., & Loehlin, J. C. (1977). Genotype-environment interaction and correlation in the analysis of human behavior. *Psychological Bulletin, 84,* 309–322.

Plomin, R., DeFries, J. C., & McClearn, G. E. (1990). *Behavioral genetics: A primer* (2nd ed.). New York: W. H. Freeman.

Poche, C., McCubbrey, H., & Munn, T. (1982). The development of correct toothbrushing techniques in pre-school children. *Journal of Applied Behavior Analysis, 15,* 315–320.

Pogrebin, L. C. (1980). *Growing up free: Raising your kids in the 80's.* New York: McGraw-Hill.

Pollio, M. R., & Pickens, J. P. (1980). The developmental structure of figurative competence. In R. P. Honeck & R. R. Hoffman (Eds.), *Cognition and figurative language.* Hillsdale, NJ: Erlbaum.

Pollock, L. A. (1983). *Forgotten children: Parent-child relations from 1500–1900.* Cambridge: Cambridge University Press.

Pomerleau, A., Bolduc, D., Malcuit, G., & Cossette, L. (1990). Pink or blue: Environmental gender stereotypes in the first two years of life. *Sex Roles, 22,* 359–367.

Porter, R. H., Balogh, R. D., & Makin, J. W. (1988). Olfactory influences on mother-infant interaction. In C. Rovee-Collier & L. P. Lipsitt (Eds.), *Advances in infancy research* (Vol. 5). Norwood, NJ: Ablex.

Postman, N. (1982). *The disappearance of childhood.* New York: Delacorte.

Powers, S. I., Hauser, S. T., & Kilner, L. A. (1989). Adolescent mental health. *American Psychologist, 44,* 200–208.

Prader, A. (1978). Catch-up growth. *Postgraduate Medical Journal, 54,* 133–146.

Prather, P. A., & Bacon, J. (1986). Developmental differences in part/whole identification. *Child Development, 57,* 549–558.

Pressley, M., & Levin, J. R. (1977). Task parameters affecting the efficacy of a visual imagery learning strategy in younger and older children. *Journal of Experimental Child Psychology, 24,* 53–59.

Preyer, W. (1888–1889). *The mind of the child* (H. W. Brown, Trans.). New York: Appleton. (Original work published 1882)

Price-Williams, D., Gordon, W., & Ramirez, M. (1969). Skill and conservation: A study of pottery-making children. *Developmental Psychology, 1,* 769.

Proffitt, D. R., & Bertenthal, B. I. (1990). Converging operations revisited: Assessing what infants perceive using discrimination measures. *Perception & Psychophysics, 47,* 1–11.

Pulkkinen, L. (1982). Self-control and continuity from childhood to adolescence. In P. B. Baltes & O. G. Brim (Eds.), *Life-span development and behavior* (Vol. 4). New York: Academic Press.

Purcell, P., & Stewart, L. (1990). Dick and Jane in 1989. *Sex Roles, 22,* 177–185.

Putallaz, M. (1987). Maternal behavior and children's sociometric status. *Child Development, 58,* 324–340.

Radin, N. (1981). The role of the father in cognitive, academic, and intellectual development. In M. E. Lamb (Ed.), *The role of the father in child development.* New York: Wiley.

Radin, N. (1982). Primary caregiving and role-sharing fathers. In M. E. Lamb (Ed.), *Nontraditional families: Parenting and child development.* Hillsdale, NJ: Erlbaum.

Radin, N., & Sagi, A. (1982). Childrearing fathers in intact families in Israel and the U.S.A. *Merrill-Palmer Quarterly, 28,* 111–136.

Radke-Yarrow, M., & Zahn-Waxler, C. (1984). Roots, motives, and patterns of children's prosocial behavior. In E. Staub, D. Bar-Tel, J. Karylowski, & J. Reykowski (Eds.), *Development and maintenance of prosocial behavior.* New York: Plenum Press.

Radke-Yarrow, M., Zahn-Waxler, C., & Chapman, M. (1983). Children's prosocial dispositions and behavior. In E. M. Hetherington (Ed.), *Handbook of child psychology: Vol. IV. Socialization, personality, and social development.* New York: Wiley.

Radziszewska, B., & Rogoff, B. (1988). Influence of adult and peer collaborators on children's planning skills. *Developmental Psychology, 24,* 840–848.

Raffaelli, M. (1989, April). *Conflict with siblings and friends in late childhood and early adolescence.* Paper presented at the biennial meeting of the Society for Research in Child Development, Kansas City, MO.

Rakic, P. (1981). Developmental events leading to laminar and areal organization of the neocortex. In F. O. Schmitt, F. G. Worden, G. Adelman, & S. G. Dennis (Eds.), *The organization of the cerebral cortex: Proceedings of a neurosciences research program colloquium.* Cambridge, MA: MIT Press.

Rallison, M. L. (1986). *Growth disorders in infants, children, and adolescents.* New York: Wiley.

Ramey, C. T., Bryant, D. M., & Suarez, T. M. (1987). Early intervention: Why, for whom, how, at what cost? In N. Gunzenhauser (Ed.), *Infant stimulation: For whom, what kind, when, and how much?* (Johnson & Johnson Baby Products Company Pediatric Round Table Series No. 13). Skilman, NJ: Johnson & Johnson.

Ramey, C. T., & Campbell, F. A. (1981). Educational intervention for children at risk for mild retardation: A longitudinal analysis. In P. Mittler (Ed.), *Frontiers of knowledge in mental retardation: Vol. 1. Social, educational, and behavioral aspects.* Baltimore: University Park Press.

Ramey, C. T., Lee, M. W., & Burchinal, M. R. (1989). Developmental plasticity and predictability: Consequences of ecological change. In M. H. Bornstein & N. A. Krasnegor (Eds.), *Stability and continuity in mental development: Behavioral and biological perspectives.* Hillsdale, NJ: Erlbaum.

Ramey, C. T., & Ramey, S. L. (1990). Intensive educational intervention for children of poverty. *Intelligence, 14,* 1–9.

Ratner, H. H. (1984). Memory demands and the development of young children's memory. *Child Development, 55,* 2173–2191.

Raven, J. C., Court, J. H., & Raven, J. (1985). *A manual for Raven's Progressive Matrices and vocabulary scales.* London: H. K. Lewis.

Redd, W. H., Morris, E. K., & Martin, J. A. (1975). Effects of positive and negative adult-child interaction on children's social preferences. *Journal of Experimental Child Psychology, 19,* 153–164.

Reisman, J. E. (1987). Touch, motion, and proprioception. In P. Salapatek & L. Cohen (Eds.), *Handbook of infant perception: From sensation to perception* (Vol. 1). Orlando, FL: Academic Press.

Reissland, N. (1988). Neonatal imitation in the first hour of life: Observations in rural Nepal. *Developmental Psychology, 24,* 464–469.

Reppucci, N. D. (1984). The wisdom of Solomon: Issues in child custody determination. In N. D. Reppucci, L. A. Weithorn, E. P. Mulvey, & J. Monahan (Eds.), *Children, mental health, and the law.* Beverly Hills, CA: Sage.

Resnick, L. B. (1986). The development of mathematical intuition. In M. Perlmutter (Ed.), *Perspectives on intellectual development: The Minnesota symposia on child psychology* (Vol. 19). Hillsdale, NJ: Erlbaum.

Resnick, M. B., Stralka, K., Carter, R. L., Ariet, M., Bucciarelli, R. L., Furlough, R. R., Evans, J. H., Curran, J. S., & Ausbon, W. W. (1990). Effects of birth weight and sociodemographic variables on mental development of neonatal intensive care unit survivors. *American Journal of Obstetrics and Gynecology, 162,* 374–378.

Rest, J. R. (1983). Morality. In J. H. Flavell & E. Markman (Eds.), *Handbook of child psychology: Vol. III. Cognitive development.* New York: Wiley.

Rheingold, H. L., & Cook, K. V. (1975). The contents of boys' and girls' rooms as an index of parents' behavior. *Child Development, 46,* 459–463.

Rholes, W. S., & Ruble, D. N. (1984). Children's understanding of dispositional characteristics of others. *Child Development, 33,* 550–560.

Ribble, M. (1943). *The rights of infants.* New York: Columbia University Press.

Rice, K. G. (1990). Attachment in adolescence: A narrative and meta-analytic review. *Journal of Youth and Adolescence, 19,* 511–538.

Rice, M. (1983). The role of television in language acquisition. *Developmental Review, 3,* 211–224.

Rice, M. L. (1989). Children's language acquisition. *American Psychologist, 44,* 149–156.

Rice, M. L., Huston, A. C., Truglio, R., & Wright, J. (1990). Words from "Sesame Street": Learning vocabulary while viewing. *Developmental Psychology, 26,* 421–428.

Rice, M. L., & Woodsmall, L. (1988). Lessons from television: Children's word learning when viewing. *Child Development, 59,* 420–429.

Ricks, M. H. (1985). The social transmission of parental behavior: Attachment across generations. In I. Bretherton & E. Waters (Eds.), *Growing points of attachment theory and research. Monographs of the Society for Research in Child Development, 50*(1–2, Serial No. 209).

Rieber, L. P. (1990). Using computer animated graphics in science instruction with children. *Journal of Educational Psychology, 82,* 135–140.

Riesen, A. H. (1965). Effects of visual deprivation on perceptual function and the neural substrate. In J. de Ajuriaguerra (Ed.), *Dessafferentation expérimental et clinique.* Geneva: Georg.

Rieser, J., Yonas, A., & Wikner, K. (1976). Radial localization of odors by human newborns. *Child Development, 47,* 856–859.

Robbins, W. J., Brody, S., Hogan, A. G., Jackson, C. M., & Green, C. W. (Eds.). (1928). *Growth.* New Haven: Yale University Press.

Robins, L. N. (1978). Aetiological implications in studies of childhood histories relating to antisocial personality. In R. D. Hare & D. Schalling (Eds.), *Psychopathic behavior.* New York: Wiley.

Rodgers, B. D., & Lee, R. V. (1988). Drug abuse. In G. N. Burrow & T. F. Ferris (Eds.), *Medical complications during pregnancy.* Philadelphia: W. B. Saunders.

Rodgers, R. R., Bronfenbrenner, U., & Devereux, E. C., Jr. (1968). Standards of social behavior among children in four cultures. *International Journal of Psychology, 3,* 31–41.

Roe, K. V., Drivas, A., Karagellis, A., & Roe, A. (1985). Sex differences in vocal interaction with mother and stranger in Greek infants: Some cognitive implications. *Developmental Psychology, 21,* 372–377.

Roffwarg, H. P., Muzio, J. N., & Dement, W. C. (1966). Ontogenetic development of the human sleep-dream cycle. *Science, 152,* 604–619.

Roggman, L. A., Langlois, J. H., & Hubbs-Tait, L. (1987). Mothers, infants, and toys: Social play correlates of attachment. *Infant Behavior and Development, 10,* 233–237.

Rogoff, B. (1981). Schooling and the development of cognitive skills. In H. C. Triandis & A. Heron (Eds.), *Handbook of cross-cultural psychology: Developmental psychology* (Vol. 4). Boston: Allyn & Bacon.

Rogoff, B. (1989). The joint socialization of development by young children and adults. In A. Gellatly, D. Rogers, & J. A.

Sloboda (Eds.), *Cognition and social worlds*. Oxford: Clarendon Press.

Rogoff, B., & Morelli, G. (1989). Perspectives on children's development from cultural psychology. *American Psychologist, 44,* 343–348.

Rogoff, B., & Waddell, K. J. (1982). Memory for information organized in a scene by children from two cultures. *Child Development, 53,* 1224–1228.

Rollins, B. C., & Thomas, D. L. (1979). Parental support, power, and control techniques in the socialization of children. In W. R. Burr, R. Hill, F. I. Nye, & I. L. Reiss (Eds.), *Contemporary theories about the family: Research-based theories* (Vol. 1). New York: Free Press.

Rosch, E., Mervis, C. B., Gray, W. D., Johnson, D. M., & Boyes-Braem, P. (1976). Basic objects in natural categories. *Cognitive Psychology, 8,* 382–439.

Rose, S. A., Feldman, J. F., Wallace, I. F., & McCarton, C. (1989). Infant visual attention: Relation to birth status and developmental outcome during the first 5 years. *Developmental Psychology, 25,* 560–576.

Rose, S. A., Gottfried, A. W., & Bridger, W. H. (1981). Cross-modal transfer in 6-month-old infants. *Developmental Psychology, 17,* 661–669.

Rosekrans, M. A. (1967). Imitation in children as a function of perceived similarity to a social model and vicarious reinforcement. *Journal of Personality and Social Psychology, 7,* 307–315.

Rosenbaum, J. E. (1980). Social implications of educational grouping. *Review of Educational Research, 8,* 361–401.

Rosenblith, J. F., & Sims-Knight, J. E. (1985). *In the beginning: Development in the first two years of life.* Monterey, CA: Brooks/Cole.

Rosenfield, P., Lambert, N. M., & Black, A. (1985). Desk arrangement effects on pupil classroom behavior. *Journal of Educational Psychology, 77,* 101–108.

Rosenholtz, S. J., & Simpson, C. (1984). The formation of ability conceptions: Developmental trend or social construction? *Review of Educational Research, 54,* 31–63.

Rosenkoetter, L. I. (1973). Resistance to temptation: Inhibitory and disinhibitory effects of models. *Developmental Psychology, 8,* 80–84.

Rosenthal, D. (1970). *Genetic theory and abnormal behavior.* New York: McGraw-Hill.

Rosenthal, R., & Jacobson, L. (1968). *Pygmalion in the classroom: Teacher expectation and pupils' intellectual development.* New York: Holt, Rinehart & Winston.

Rosett, H. L., & Weiner, L. (1984). *Alcohol and the fetus, a clinical perspective.* New York: Oxford University Press.

Rosser, R. A. (1983). The emergence of spatial perspective taking: An information-processing alternative to egocentrism. *Child Development, 54,* 660–668.

Rossi, A. S. (1987). Parenthood in transition: From lineage to child to self-orientation. In J. B. Lancaster, J. Altmann, A. S. Rossi, & L. R. Sherrod (Eds.), *Parenting across the life span: Biosocial dimensions.* New York: Aldine de Gruyter.

Rothbart, M. K., & Derryberry, D. (1981). Development of individual differences in temperament. In M. E. Lamb & A. L. Brown (Eds.), *Advances in developmental psychology* (Vol. 1). Hillsdale, NJ: Erlbaum.

Rothenberg, B. B. (1970). Children's social sensitivity and the relationship to interpersonal competence, intrapersonal comfort, and intellectual level. *Developmental Psychology, 2,* 335–350.

Rotnem, D. L. (1986). Size versus age: Ambiguities in parenting short-statured children. In B. Stabler & L. E. Underwood (Eds.), *Slow grows the child: Psychological aspects of growth delay.* Hillsdale, NJ: Erlbaum.

Rotter, J. B. (1966). Generalized expectancies for internal versus external locus of control of reinforcement. *Psychological Monographs: General and Applied, 80,* 1–28.

Rousseau, J. J. (1895). *Émile or treatise on education* (W. H. Payne, Trans.). New York: Appleton. (Original work published 1762)

Rovee-Collier, C. K. (1987). Learning and memory in infancy. In J. D. Osofsky (Ed.), *Handbook of infant development* (2nd ed.). New York: Wiley.

Rovee-Collier, C. K., & Lipsitt, L. P. (1987). Learning, adaptation, and memory in the newborn. In P. Stratton (Ed.), *Psychobiology of the human newborn.* New York: Wiley.

Rozin, P. (1990). Development in the food domain. *Developmental Psychology, 26,* 555–562.

Rubenstein, J., & Howes, C. (1976). The effects of peers on toddler interaction with mother and toys. *Child Development, 47,* 597–605.

Rubenstein, J., & Howes, C. (1979). Caregiving and infant behavior in day care and in homes. *Developmental Psychology, 15,* 1–24.

Rubin, K. H., & Everett, B. (1982). Social perspective-taking in young children. In S. G. Moore & C. R. Cooper (Eds.), *The young child: Reviews of research* (Vol. 3). Washington, DC: National Association for the Education of Young Children.

Rubin, K. H., Fein, G. G., & Vandenberg, B. (1983). Play. In E. M. Hetherington (Ed.), *Handbook of child psychology: Vol. IV. Socialization, personality, and social development.* New York: Wiley.

Rubin, K. H., & Krasnor, L. R. (1986). Social-cognitive and social behavioral perspectives on problem-solving. In M. Perlmutter (Ed.), *The Minnesota symposia on child psychology: Vol. 18. Cognitive perspectives on children's social and behavioral development.* Hillsdale, NJ: Erlbaum.

Rubin, K. H., Maioni, T. L., & Hornung, M. (1976). Free play behaviors in middle- and lower-class preschoolers: Parten and Piaget revisited. *Child Development, 47,* 414–419.

Rubin, K. H., & Schneider, F. W. (1973). The relationship between moral judgment, egocentrism, and moral behavior. *Child Development, 44,* 661–665.

Ruble, D. N. (1983). The development of social-comparison processes and their role in achievement-related self-socialization. In E. T. Higgins, D. Ruble, & W. W. Hartup (Eds.), *Social cognition and social development: A sociocultural perspective.* Cambridge: Cambridge University Press.

Ruble, D. N. (1987). The acquisition of self-knowledge: A self-socialization perspective. In N. Eisenberg (Ed.), *Contemporary topics in developmental psychology.* New York: Wiley.

Ruble, D. N., Boggiano, A. K., Feldman, N. S., & Loebl, J. H. (1980). Developmental analysis of the role of social comparison in self-evaluation. *Developmental Psychology, 16,* 105–115.

Ruble, D. N., & Brooks-Gunn, J. (1982). The experience of menarche. *Child Development, 53,* 1557–1566.

Ruble, D. N., & Flett, G. L. (1988). Conflicting goals in self-evaluative information seeking: Developmental and ability level analyses. *Child Development, 59,* 97–106.

Ruble, T. L. (1983). Sex stereotypes: Issues of change in the 1970s. *Sex Roles, 9,* 397–402.

Ruff, H. A., & Kohler, C. J. (1978). Tactual visual transfer in 6-month-old infants. *Infant Behavior and Development, 1,* 259–264.

Ruff, H. A., & Lawson, K. R. (1990). Development of sustained, focused attention in young children during free play. *Developmental Psychology, 26,* 85–93.

Rule, B. G., Nesdale, A. R., & McAra, M. J. (1974). Children's reactions to information about the intentions underlying an aggressive act. *Child Development, 45,* 794–798.

Rumberger, R. W. (1987). High school dropouts: A review of issues and evidence. *Review of Educational Research, 57,* 101–121.

Rushton, J. P. (1975). Generosity in children: Immediate and long-term effects of modeling, preaching, and moral judgment. *Journal of Personality and Social Psychology, 31,* 459–466.

Rushton, J. P. (1982). Social learning theory and the development of prosocial behavior. In N. Eisenberg (Ed.), *The development of prosocial behavior.* New York: Academic Press.

Russell, G. (1987). Fatherhood in Australia. In M. E. Lamb (Ed.), *The father's role: Cross-cultural perspectives.* Hillsdale, NJ: Erlbaum.

Russell, G., & Russell, A. (1987). Mother-child and father-child relationships in middle childhood. *Child Development, 58,* 1573–1585.

Rutter, M. (1979). Maternal deprivation 1972–1978: New findings, new concepts, new approaches. *Child Development, 50,* 283–305.

Rutter, M. (1983). School effects on pupil progress: Research findings and policy implications. *Child Development, 54,* 1–29.

Rutter, M. (1986). Meyerian psychobiology, personality development, and the role of life experiences. *American Journal of Psychiatry, 143,* 1077–1087.

Rutter, M., & Garmezy, N. (1983). Developmental psychopathology. In E. M. Hetherington (Ed.), *Handbook of child psychology: Vol. IV. Socialization, personality, and social development.* New York: Wiley.

Rutter, M., & Madge, N. (1976). *Cycles of disadvantage.* London: Heinemmann.

Rutter, M., Maughan, B., Mortimore, P., Ouston, J., & Smith, A. (1979). *Fifteen thousand hours: Secondary schools and their effects on children.* Cambridge: Harvard University Press.

Ryan, R. M., & Grolnick, W. S. (1986). Origins and pawns in the classroom: Self-report and projective assessments of individual differences in children's perceptions. *Journal of Personality and Social Psychology, 50,* 550–558.

Sagi, A., Lamb, M. E., Lewkowicz, K. S., Shoham, R., Dvir, R., & Estes, D. (1985). Security of infant-mother, -father, and -metapelet attachments among kibbutz-reared Israeli children. In I. Bretherton & E. Waters (Eds.), *Growing points of attachment theory and research. Monographs of the Society for Research in Child Development, 50*(1–2, Serial No. 209).

Salapatek, P. (1975). Pattern perception in early infancy. In L. B. Cohen & P. Salapatek (Eds.), *Infant perception: From sensation to cognition* (Vol. 1). New York: Academic Press.

Salomon, G., & Gardner, H. (1986). The computer as educator: Lessons from television research. *Educational Researcher, 15,* 13–19.

Salomon, G., Globerson, T., & Guterman, E. (1989). The computer as a zone of proximal development: Internalizing reading-related metacognitions from a reading partner. *Journal of Educational Psychology, 89,* 620–627.

Saltz, E., Campbell, S., & Skotko, D. (1983). Verbal control of behavior: The effects of shouting. *Developmental Psychology, 19,* 461–464.

Saltzman, R. L., & Jordan, M. C. (1988). Viral infections. In G. N. Burrow & T. F. Ferris (Eds.), *Medical complications during pregnancy.* Philadelphia: W. B. Saunders.

Sameroff, A. J. (1968). The components of sucking in the human newborn. *Journal of Experimental Child Psychology, 6,* 607–623.

Sameroff, A. J. (1972). Learning and adaptation in infancy: A comparison of models. In H. W. Reese (Ed.), *Advances in child development and behavior* (Vol. 7). New York: Academic Press.

Sameroff, A. J. (1987). The social context of development. In N. Eisenberg (Ed.), *Contemporary topics in developmental psychology.* New York: Wiley.

Sameroff, A. J., & Cavanagh, P. J. (1979). Learning in infancy: A developmental perspective. In J. D. Osofsky (Ed.), *Handbook of infant development.* New York: Wiley.

Sameroff, A. J., & Chandler, P. J. (1975). Reproductive risk and the continuum of caretaking casualty. In F. D. Horowitz (Ed.), *Review of child development research* (Vol. 4). Chicago: University of Chicago Press.

Samuels, M., & Bennett, H. Z. (1983). *Well body, well earth: The Sierra Club environmental health sourcebook.* San Francisco: Sierra Club Books.

Samuels, M., & Samuels, N. (1986). *The well pregnancy book.* New York: Summit Books.

Santrock, J. W. (1975). Moral structure: The interrelations of moral behavior, moral judgment, and moral affect. *Journal of Genetic Psychology, 127,* 201–213.

Santrock, J. W., & Sitterle, K. A. (1987). Parent-child relationships in stepmother families. In K. Pasley & M. Ihinger-Tallman (Eds.), *Remarriage and stepparenting: Current research and theory.* New York: Guilford Press.

Savin-Williams, R. C. (1979). Dominance hierarchies in groups of early adolescents. *Child Development, 50,* 923–935.

Savin-Williams, R. C. (1980). Dominance hierarchies in groups of middle to late adolescent males. *Journal of Youth and Adolescence, 9,* 75–85.

Sawin, D. B., & Parke, R. D. (1979). The effects of interagent inconsistent discipline on children's aggressive behavior. *Journal of Experimental Child Psychology, 28,* 525–538.

Saxby, L., & Bryden, M. P. (1985). Left visual field advantage in children for processing visual emotional stimuli. *Developmental Psychology, 20,* 253–261.

Saxe, G. B., Guberman, S. R., & Gearhart, M. (1987). Social processes in early number development. *Monographs of the Society for Research in Child Development, 52*(2, Serial No. 216).

Scammon, R. E. (1930). The measurement of the body in childhood. In J. A. Harris, C. M. Jackson, D. G. Paterson, & R. E. Scammon (Eds.), *The measurement of man.* Minneapolis: University of Minnesota Press.

Scarr, S. (1981). Genetics and the development of intelligence.

In S. Scarr (Ed.), *Race, social class, and individual differences in IQ*. Hillsdale, NJ: Erlbaum.

Scarr, S. (1987). Three cheers for behavior genetics: Winning the war and losing our identity. *Behavior Genetics, 17,* 219–228.

Scarr, S., & Carter-Saltzman, L. (1983). Genetics and intelligence. In J. L. Fuller & E. C. Simmel (Eds.), *Behavior genetics: Principles and applications*. Hillsdale, NJ: Erlbaum.

Scarr, S., & McCartney, K. (1983). How people make their own environments: A theory of genotype→environment effects. *Child Development, 54,* 424–435.

Scarr, S., Webber, P. L., Weinberg, R. A., & Wittig, M. A. (1981). Personality resemblance among adolescents and their parents in biologically related and adoptive families. *Journal of Personality and Social Psychology, 40,* 885–898.

Scarr, S., & Weinberg, R. A. (1976). IQ test performance of black children adopted by white families. *American Psychologist, 31,* 726–739.

Scarr, S., & Weinberg, R. A. (1977). Intellectual similarities within families of both adopted and biological children. *Intelligence, 1,* 170–191.

Scarr, S., & Weinberg, R. A. (1978). The influence of "family background" on intellectual attainment. *American Sociological Review, 43,* 674–692.

Scarr, S., & Weinberg, R. A. (1983). The Minnesota adoption studies: Genetic differences and malleability. *Child Development, 54,* 260–267.

Scarr-Salapatek, S., & Williams, M. L. (1973). The effects of early stimulation on low birth-weight infants. *Child Development, 44,* 94–101.

Schachter, F. F. (1982). Sibling deidentification and split-parent identification: A family tetrad. In M. E. Lamb & B. Sutton-Smith (Eds.), *Sibling relationships: Their nature and significance across the life-span*. Hillsdale, NJ: Erlbaum.

Schachter, F. F., Shore, E., Feldman-Rotman, S., Marquis, R. E., & Campbell, S. (1976). Sibling deidentification. *Developmental Psychology, 12,* 418–427.

Schafer, W. E., & Olexa, C. (1971). *Tracking and opportunity*. Scranton, PA: Chandler.

Schaffer, H. R., & Emerson, P. E. (1964). The development of social attachments in infancy. *Monographs of the Society for Research in Child Development, 29*(3, Serial No. 94).

Schaie, K. W. (1974). Translations in gerontology—from lab to life: Intellectual functioning. *American Psychologist, 29,* 802–807.

Schaie, K. W. (1983). The Seattle longitudinal study: A twenty-one year investigation of psychometric intelligence. In K. W. Schaie (Ed.), *Longitudinal studies of adult psychological development*. New York: Guilford Press.

Schaie, K. W., & Hertzog, C. (1986). Toward a comprehensive model of adult intellectual development: Contributions of the Seattle longitudinal study. In R. J. Sternberg (Ed.), *Advances in the psychology of human intelligence* (Vol. 3). Hillsdale, NJ: Erlbaum.

Schieffelin, B. B., & Ochs, E. (1983). A cultural perspective on the transition from prelinguistic to linguistic communication. In R. M. Golinkoff (Ed.), *The transition from prelinguistic to linguistic communication*. Hillsdale, NJ: Erlbaum.

Schneider, B., Trehub, S. E., Morrongiello, B. A., & Thorpe, L. A. (1986). Auditory sensitivity in preschool children. *Journal of the Acoustical Society of America, 79,* 447–452.

Schneider, B. H., & Byrne, B. M. (1985). Children's social skills training: A meta-analysis. In B. H. Schneider, K. H. Rubin, & J. E. Ledingham (Eds.), *Children's peer relations: Issues in assessment and intervention*. New York: Springer-Verlag.

Schneider-Rosen, K., Braunwald, K., Carlson, V., & Cicchetti, D. (1985). Current perspectives on attachment theory: Illustrations from the study of maltreated infants. In I. Bretherton & E. Waters, (Eds.), *Growing points of attachment theory and research. Monographs of the Society for Research in Child Development, 50*(1–2, Serial No. 209).

Schnoll, S. H. (1986). Pharmacologic basis of perinatal addiction. In I. J. Chasnoff (Ed.), *Drug use in pregnancy: Mother and child*. Lancaster, England: MTP Press.

Schubert, J. B., Bradley-Johnson, S., & Nuttal, J. (1980). Mother-infant communication and maternal employment. *Child Development, 51,* 246–249.

Schulenberg, J., Asp, C. E., & Petersen, A. (1984). School from the young adolescent's perspective: A descriptive report. *Journal of Early Adolescence, 4,* 107–130.

Schuz, A. (1978). Some facts and hypotheses concerning dendritic spines and learning. In M. A. B. Brazier & H. Petsche (Eds.), *Architectonics of the cerebral cortex*. New York: Raven.

Schwartz, M., & Day, R. H. (1979). Visual shape perception in early infancy. *Monographs of the Society for Research in Child Development, 44*(7, Serial No. 182).

Scoville, R. (1983). Development of the intention to communicate: The eye of the beholder. In L. Feagans, C. Garvey, & R. Golinkoff (Eds.), *The origins and growth of communication*. Norwood, NJ: Ablex.

Scribner, S., & Cole, M. (1981). *The psychology of literacy*. Cambridge: Harvard University Press.

Scriver, C. R., & Clow, C. L. (1988). Avoiding phenylketonuria: Why parents seek prenatal diagnosis. *Journal of Pediatrics, 113,* 495–496.

Seavey, C. A., Katz, P. A., & Zalk, S. R. (1975). Baby X: The effects of gender labels on adult responses to infants. *Sex Roles, 1,* 103–109.

Secord, P., & Peevers, B. H. (1974). The development and attribution of person concepts. In T. Mischel (Ed.), *Understanding other persons*. Oxford: Blackwell.

Segall, M. H., Campbell, D. T., & Herskovits, M. J. (1966). *The influence of culture on perception*. New York: Bobbs-Merrill.

Self, P. A., Horowitz, F. D., & Paden, L. Y. (1972). Olfaction in newborn infants. *Developmental Psychology, 7,* 349–363.

Selman, R. L. (1976). Social-cognitive understanding: A guide to educational and clinical practice. In T. Lickona (Ed.), *Moral development and behavior: Theory, research, and social issues*. New York: Holt, Rinehart & Winston.

Selman, R. L. (1980). *The growth of interpersonal understanding: Developmental and clinical analysis*. New York: Academic Press.

Selman, R. L. (1981). The child as a friendship philosopher. In S. R. Asher & J. M. Gottman (Eds.), *The development of children's friendships*. Cambridge: Cambridge University Press.

Selman, R. L., & Byrne, D. F. (1974). A structural-developmental analysis of levels of role taking in middle childhood. *Child Development, 45,* 803–806.

Serbin, L. A., Connor, J. M., & Iler, I. (1979). Sex-stereotyped and nonstereotyped introductions of new toys in the preschool classroom: An observational study of teacher behavior and its effects. *Psychology of Women Quarterly, 4,* 261–265.

Serbin, L. A., Connor, J. M., Burchardt, C. J., & Citron, C. C. (1979). Effects of peer presence on sex-typing of children's play behavior. *Journal of Experimental Child Psychology, 27,* 303–309.

Serbin, L. A., O'Leary, K. D., Kent, R. N., & Tonick, I. J. (1973). A comparison of teacher response to the preacademic and problem behavior of boys and girls. *Child Development, 44,* 796–804.

Serbin, L. A., Tonick, I. J., & Sternglanz, S. H. (1977). Shaping cooperative cross-sex play. *Child Development, 48,* 924–929.

Shahar, S. (1990). *Childhood in the Middle Ages.* London: Routledge.

Shantz, C. (1983). Social cognition. In J. H. Flavell & E. M. Markman (Eds.), *Handbook of child psychology: Vol. III. Cognitive development.* New York: Wiley.

Shapira, A., & Madsen, M. C. (1969). Cooperative and competitive behavior of kibbutz and urban children in Israel. *Child Development, 4,* 609–617.

Shapiro, S., McCormick, M. C., Starfield, B. H., Krischer, J. P., & Bross, D. (1980). Relevance of correlates of infant deaths for significant morbidity at 1 year of age. *American Journal of Obstetrics and Gynecology, 136,* 363–373.

Sharp, D., Cole, M., & Lave, C. (1979). Education and cognitive development: The evidence from experimental research. *Monographs of the Society for Research in Child Development, 44*(1–2, Serial No. 178).

Shatz, M., & Gelman, R. (1973). The development of communication skills: Modification in the speech of young children as a function of listener. *Monographs of the Society for Research in Child Development, 38*(5, Serial No. 152).

Shaw, E., & Darling, J. (1985). *Strategies of being female.* Brighton, England: Harvester Press.

Sherif, M., Harvey, O. J., White, B. J., Hood, W. R., & Sherif, C. W. (1961). *Inter-group conflict and cooperation: The Robber's Cave experiment.* Norman: University of Oklahoma Press.

Shirley, M. M. (1931). *The first two years: A study of twenty-five babies: Vol. 1. Postural and locomotor development.* Minneapolis: University of Minnesota Press.

Shoda, Y., Mischel, W., & Peake, P. K. (1990). Predicting adolescent cognitive and self-regulatory competencies from preschool delay of gratification: Identifying diagnostic conditions. *Developmental Psychology, 26,* 978–986.

Shostak, M. (1981). *Nisa: The life and words of a !Kung woman.* Cambridge: Harvard University Press.

Shrum, W., & Cheek, N. H. (1987). Social structure during the school years: Onset of the degrouping process. *American Sociological Review, 52,* 218–223.

Shultz, T. R. (1982). Causal reasoning in the social and nonsocial realms. *Canadian Journal of Behavior, 14,* 307–322.

Shultz, T. R., & Wells, D. (1985). Judging the intentionality of action-outcomes. *Developmental Psychology, 21,* 83–89.

Shultz, T. R., Wells, D., & Sarda, M. (1980). Development of the ability to distinguish intended actions from mistakes, reflexes, and passive movements. *British Journal of Social and Clinical Psychology, 19,* 301–310.

Shupert, C., & Fuchs, A. F. (1988). Development of conjugate human eye movements. *Vision Research, 28,* 585–596.

Shweder, R. A., Mahapatra, M., & Miller, J. G. (1987). Culture and moral development. In J. Kagan & S. Lamb (Eds.), *The emergence of morality in young children.* Chicago: University of Chicago Press.

Shy, K. K., Luthy, A. A., Bennett, F. C., Whitfield, M., Larson, E. G., Van Belle, G., Hughes, J. P., Wilson, J. A., & Stenchever, M. A. (1990). Effects of electronic fetal-heart-rate monitoring, as compared with periodic auscultation, on the neurological development of premature infants. *New England Journal of Medicine, 322,* 588–593.

Siegel, A. W., Kirasic, K. C., & Kail, R. V., Jr. (1978). Stalking the elusive cognitive map: The development of children's representations of geographical space. In I. Altman & J. F. Wohlwill (Eds.), *Children and the environment.* New York: Plenum Press.

Siegler, R. S., & Richards, D. D. (1982). The development of intelligence. In R. J. Sternberg (Ed.), *Handbook of human intelligence.* Cambridge: Cambridge University Press.

Siegler, R. S., & Robinson, M. (1982). The development of numerical understandings. In H. W. Reese & L. P. Lipsitt (Eds.), *Advances in child development and behavior* (Vol. 16). New York: Academic Press.

Sigelman, C. K., Carr, M. B., & Begley, N. L. (1986). Developmental changes in the influence of sex-role stereotypes on person perception. *Child Study Journal, 16,* 191–205.

Signorella, M. L. (1987). Gender schemata: Individual differences and context effects. In L. S. Liben & M. L. Signorella (Eds.), *New directions for child development: No. 38. Children's gender schemata.* San Francisco: Jossey-Bass.

Signorielli, N. (1989). Television and conceptions about sex roles: Maintaining conventionality and the status quo. *Sex Roles, 21,* 341–360.

Silberstein, L., Gardner, H., Phelps, E., & Winner, E. (1982). Autumn leaves and old photographs: The development of metaphor preferences. *Journal of Experimental Child Psychology, 34,* 135–150.

Simmons, R. G., & Blyth, D. A. (1987). *Moving into adolescence: The impact of pubertal change and school context.* Hawthorne, NY: Aldine de Gruyter.

Simmons, R. G., Blyth, D. A., & McKinney, K. L. (1983). The social and psychological effects of puberty on white females. In J. Brooks-Gunn & A. C. Petersen (Eds.), *Girls at puberty.* New York: Plenum Press.

Simmons, R. G., Blyth, D. A., Van Cleave, E. F., & Bush, D. M. (1979). Entry into early adolescence: The impact of school structure, puberty, and early dating on self-esteem. *American Sociological Review, 44,* 948–967.

Simmons, R. G., Burgeson, R., Carlton-Ford, S., & Blyth, D. A. (1987). The impact of cumulative change in early adolescence. *Child Development, 58,* 1220–1234.

Simmons, R. G., Rosenberg, M., & Rosenberg, F. (1973). Disturbance in the self-image at adolescence. *American Sociological Review, 39,* 553–568.

Simner, M. L. (1971). Newborn's response to the cry of another infant. *Developmental Psychology, 5,* 136–150.

Sinclair, D. (1985). *Human growth after birth* (4th ed.). New York: Oxford University Press.

Singer, J. L., & Singer, D. G. (1983). Implications of childhood television viewing for cognition, imagination, and emotion. In J. Bryant & D. R. Anderson (Eds.), *Children's understanding of television: Research on attention and comprehension.* New York: Academic Press.

Singer, L. M., Brodzinsky, D. M., Ramsay, D., Steir, M., & Waters, E. (1985). Mother-infant attachment in adoptive families. *Child Development, 56,* 1543–1551.

Siqueland, E. R., & Lipsitt, L. P. (1966). Conditioned head turning in human newborns. *Journal of Experimental Child Psychology, 4,* 356–376.

Skinner, B. F. (1948). *Walden two.* New York: Macmillan.

Skinner, B. F. (1953). *Science and human behavior.* New York: Macmillan.

Skinner, B. F. (1957). *Verbal behavior.* New York: Appleton-Century-Crofts.

Skinner, B. F. (1971). *Beyond freedom and dignity.* New York: Knopf.

Skinner, B. F. (1974). *About behaviorism.* New York: Knopf.

Skodak, M., & Skeels, H. M. (1949). A final follow-up study of one hundred adopted children. *Pedagogical Seminary and Journal of Genetic Psychology, 75,* 85–125.

Skuse, D. (1985). Nonorganic failure to thrive: A reappraisal. *Archives of Disease in Childhood, 60,* 173–178.

Slaby, R. G., & Crowley, C. G. (1977). Modification of cooperation and aggression through teacher attention to children's speech. *Journal of Experimental Child Psychology, 23,* 442–458.

Slaby, R. G., & Frey, K. S. (1975). Development of gender constancy and selective attention to same-sex models. *Child Development, 46,* 849–856.

Slaby, R. G., & Guerra, N. G. (1988). Cognitive mediators of aggression in adolescent offenders: 1. Assessment. *Developmental Psychology, 24,* 580–588.

Slater, A., Morison, V., Somers, M., Mattock, A., Brown, E., & Taylor, D. (1990). Newborn and older infants' perception of partly occluded objects. *Infant Behavior and Development, 13,* 33–49.

Slater, A., Rose, D., & Morison, V. (1984). New-born infants' perception of similarities and differences between two- and three-dimensional stimuli. *British Journal of Developmental Psychology, 3,* 211–220.

Slaughter-Defoe, D. T., Nakagawa, K., Takanishi, R., & Johnson, D. J. (1990). Toward cultural/ecological perspectives on schooling and achievement in African- and Asian-American children. *Child Development, 61,* 363–383.

Slavin, R. E. (1987a). Ability grouping and student achievement in elementary schools: A best-evidence synthesis. *Review of Educational Research, 57,* 293–336.

Slavin, R. E. (1987b). Developmental and motivational perspectives on cooperative learning: A reconciliation. *Child Development, 58,* 1161–1167.

Slavin, R. E. (1990a). Achievement effects of ability grouping in secondary schools: A best-evidence synthesis. *Review of Educational Research, 60,* 471–499.

Slavin, R. E. (1990b). *Cooperative learning: Theory, research, and practice.* Englewood Cliffs, NJ: Prentice-Hall.

Smetana, J. G. (1988). Concepts of self and social conventions: Adolescents' and parents' reasoning about hypothetical and actual family conflicts. In M. R. Gunnar & W. A. Collins (Eds.),

The Minnesota symposia on child psychology: Vol. 21. Development during the transition to adolescence. Hillsdale, NJ: Erlbaum.

Smetana, J. G., & Braeges, J. L. (1990). The development of toddlers' moral and conventional judgments. *Merrill-Palmer Quarterly, 36,* 329–346.

Smilansky, S. (1968). *The effects of sociodramatic play on disadvantaged preschool children.* New York: Wiley.

Smilkstein, G., Helsper-Lucas, A., Ashworth, C., Montano, D., & Pagel, M. (1984). Prediction of pregnancy complications: An application of the biopsychosocial model. *Social Sciences & Medicine, 18,* 315–321.

Smith, B. L. (1988). The emergent lexicon from a phonetic perspective. In M. D. Smith & J. L. Locke (Eds.), *The emergent lexicon.* New York: Academic Press.

Smith, C. L., Gelfand, D. M., Hartmann, D. P., & Partlow, M. P. (1979). Children's causal attributions regarding help giving. *Child Development, 50,* 203–210.

Smith, I., Beasley, M. G., Wolff, O. H., & Ades, A. E. (1988). Behavior disturbance in 8-year-old children with early treated phenylketonuria. *Journal of Pediatrics, 112,* 403–408.

Smith, J. D., & Kemler-Nelson, D. G. (1984). Overall similarity in adults' classification: The child in all of us. *Journal of Experimental Psychology: General, 113,* 137–159.

Smith, L. B. (1989). From global similarities to kinds of similarities: The construction of dimensions in development. In S. Vosniadou & A. Ortony (Eds.), *Similarity and analogical reasoning.* New York: Cambridge University Press.

Smith, L. B., & Evans, P. M. (1989). Similarity, identity, and dimensions: Perceptual classification in children and adults. In B. E. Shepp & S. Ballesteros (Eds.), *Object perception: Structure and process.* Hillsdale, NJ: Erlbaum.

Smith, M. C. (1978). Cognizing the behavior stream: The recognition of intentional action. *Child Development, 49,* 736–743.

Smith, P. K., & Green, M. (1974). Aggressive behavior in English nurseries and playgroups: Sex differences and response of adults. *Child Development, 45,* 211–214.

Smith, T. E. (1988). Parental control techniques: Relative frequencies and relationships with situational factors. *Journal of Family Issues, 9,* 155–176.

Snarey, J. R. (1985). Cross-cultural universality of social-moral development: A critical review of Kohlbergian research. *Psychological Bulletin, 97,* 202–232.

Snow, C. E. (1977). The development of conversation between babies and mothers. *Journal of Child Language, 4,* 1–22.

Snow, C. E. (1984). Parent-child interaction and the development of communicative ability. In R. L. Schiefelbusch & J. Pickar (Eds.), *The acquisition of communicative competence.* Baltimore: University Park Press.

Snow, C. E. (1987a). Comment: Language and the beginnings of moral understanding. In J. Kagan & S. Lamb (Eds.), *The emergence of morality in young children.* Chicago: University of Chicago Press.

Snow, C. E. (1987b). Relevance of the notion of a critical period to language acquisition. In M. H. Bornstein (Ed.), *Sensitive periods in development.* Hillsdale, NJ: Erlbaum.

Sobal, J., & Stunkard, A. J. (1989). Socioeconomic status and obesity: A review of the literature. *Psychological Bulletin, 105,* 260–275.

Society for Research in Child Development. (1990, Winter). Ethical standards for research with children. *SRCD Newsletter.*

Solkoff, N., Yaffe, S., Weintraub, D., & Blase, B. (1969). Effects of handling on the subsequent development of premature infants. *Developmental Psychology, 1,* 765–768.

Sontag, L. W., Baker, C. T., & Nelson, V. L. (1958). Mental growth and personality development: A longitudinal study. *Monographs of the Society for Research in Child Development, 23*(2, Serial No. 68).

Sorce, J. F., Emde, R. N., Campos, J., & Klinnert, M. D. (1985). Maternal emotional signaling: Its effect on the visual cliff behavior of 1-year-olds. *Developmental Psychology, 21,* 195–200.

Spearman, C. (1904). "General intelligence," objectively determined and measured. *American Journal of Psychology, 15,* 72–101.

Spearman, C. (1923). *The nature of "intelligence" and the principles of cognition.* London: Macmillan.

Spearman, C. (1927). *The abilities of man.* London: Macmillan.

Spears, W., & Hohle, R. (1967). Sensory and perceptual processes in infants. In Y. Brackbill (Ed.), *Infancy and early childhood.* New York: Free Press.

Spelke, E. S. (1976). Infants' intermodal perception of events. *Cognitive Psychology, 8,* 553–560.

Spelke, E. S. (1985). Perception of unity, persistence and identity: Thoughts on infants' conceptions of objects. In J. Mehler & R. Fox (Eds.), *Neonate cognition: Beyond the blooming, buzzing confusion.* Hillsdale, NJ: Erlbaum.

Spelke, E. S. (1987). The development of intermodal perception. In P. Salapatek & L. Cohen (Eds.), *Handbook of infant perception: From perception to cognition* (Vol. 2). Orlando, FL: Academic Press.

Spelke, E. S., & Owsley, C. J. (1979). Intermodal exploration and knowledge in infancy. *Infant Behavior and Development, 2,* 13–27.

Spence, S. H. (1986). Behavioural treatments of childhood obesity. *Journal of Child Psychology and Psychiatry, 27,* 447–453.

Spitz, H. H. (1986). *The raising of intelligence.* Hillsdale, NJ: Erlbaum.

Spitz, R. (1946a). Anaclitic depression. *Psychoanalytic Study of the Child, 2,* 313–342.

Spitz, R. (1946b). Hospitalism: A follow-up report. *Psychoanalytic Study of the Child, 2,* 113–117.

Spivack, G., & Shure, M. B. (1974). *Social adjustment of young children.* San Francisco: Jossey-Bass.

Sprafkin, J. N., Liebert, R. M., & Poulos, R. W. (1975). Effects of a prosocial televised example on children's helping. *Journal of Experimental Child Psychology, 20,* 119–126.

Spreen, O., Tupper, D., Risser, A., Tuokko, H., & Edgell, D. (1984). *Human developmental neuropsychology.* New York: Oxford University Press.

Sroufe, L. A. (1983). Infant-caregiver attachment and patterns of adaptation in preschool: The roots of maladaptation and competence. In M. Perlmutter (Ed.), *The Minnesota symposia on child psychology: Vol. 16. Development and policy concerning children with special needs.* Hillsdale, NJ: Erlbaum.

Sroufe, L. A. (1985). Attachment classification from the perspective of infant-caregiver relationships and infant temperament. *Child Development, 56,* 1–14.

Sroufe, L. A., & Waters, E. (1976). The ontogenesis of smiling and laughter: A perspective on the organization of development in infancy. *Psychological Review, 83,* 173–189.

Sroufe, L. A., & Wunsch, J. P. (1972). The development of laughter in the first year of life. *Child Development, 43,* 1326–1344.

Staffieri, J. R. (1967). A study of social stereotypes of body image in children. *Journal of Personality and Social Psychology, 7,* 101–104.

Stahl, P. M. (1984). A review of joint and shared parenting literature. In J. Folberg (Ed.), *Joint custody and shared parenting.* Washington, DC: Bureau of National Affairs.

Starfield, B., Shapiro, S., McCormick, M. C., & Bross, D. (1982). Mortality and morbidity in infants with intrauterine growth retardation. *Journal of Pediatrics, 101,* 978–983.

Stark, R. E. (1986). Prespeech segmental feature detection. In P. Fletcher & M. Garman (Eds.), *Language acquisition: Studies in first language development.* Cambridge: Cambridge University Press.

Stein, A. (1983). Pregnancy in gravidas over age 35 years. *Journal of Nurse-Midwifery, 28,* 17–20.

Steinberg, C. (1985). *TV facts.* New York: Facts on File Publications.

Steinberg, L. (1981). Transformations in family relations at puberty. *Developmental Psychology, 17,* 833–840.

Steinberg, L., Elmen, J. D., & Mounts, N. S. (1989). Authoritative parenting, psychosocial maturity, and academic success among adolescents. *Child Development, 60,* 1424–1436.

Steiner, J. E. (1979). Human facial expressions in response to taste and smell stimulation. In H. W. Reese & L. P. Lipsitt (Eds.), *Advances in child development and behavior* (Vol. 13). New York: Academic Press.

Stern, D. N. (1974). The goal and structure of mother-infant play. *Journal of the American Academy of Child Psychiatry, 13,* 402–421.

Sternberg, R. J. (1985). *Beyond IQ: A triarchic theory of human intelligence.* Cambridge: Cambridge University Press.

Sternberg, R. J., Conway, B. E., Ketron, J. L., & Bernstein, M. (1981). People's conceptions of intelligence. *Journal of Personality and Social Psychology, 41,* 37–55.

Stevenson, H. W., Lee, S., & Stigler, J. W. (1986). Mathematics achievement of Chinese, Japanese, and American children. *Science, 231,* 693–699.

Stevenson, H. W., Stigler, J. W., Lee, S., Lucker, G. W., Kitamura, S., & Hsu, C. (1985). Cognitive performance and academic achievement of Japanese, Chinese, and American children. *Child Development, 56,* 718–734.

Stewart, G. D., Hassold, T. J., & Kunit, D. M. (1988). Trisomy 21: Molecular and cytogenetic studies of nondisjunction. In H. Harris & K. Hirschhorn (Eds.), *Advances in human genetics* (Vol. 17). New York: Plenum Press.

Stigler, J. W., Lee, S., & Stevenson, H. W. (1987). Mathematics classrooms in Japan, Taiwan, and the United States. *Child Development, 58,* 1272–1285.

Stipek, D. J., & Hoffman, J. M. (1980). Children's achievement related expectancies as a function of academic performance histories and sex. *Journal of Educational Psychology, 72,* 861–865.

Stipp, H., & Milavsky, J. R. (1988). U.S. television programming's effects on aggressive behavior of children and adolescents. *Current Psychology: Research & Reviews, 7,* 76–92.

Stolberg, A. L., & Anker, J. M. (1984). Cognitive and behavioral changes in children resulting from parental divorce and consequent environmental changes. *Journal of Divorce, 8,* 184–197.

Straus, M. A., & Gelles, R. J. (1986). Societal change and change in family violence from 1975 to 1985 as revealed in two national surveys. *Journal of Marriage and the Family, 48,* 465–479.

Straus, M. A., Gelles, R. J., & Steinmetz, S. K. (1980). *Behind closed doors: Violence in the American family.* Garden City, NY: Doubleday.

Strayer, F. F., & Strayer, J. (1976). An ethological analysis of social agonism and dominance relations among preschool children. *Child Development, 47,* 980–989.

Streissguth, A. P., Barr, H. M., & Martin, D. C. (1983). Maternal alcohol use and neonatal habituation assessed with the Brazleton Scale. *Child Development, 54,* 1109–1118.

Streissguth, A. P., Barr, H. M., Sampson, P. D., Darby, B. L., & Martin, D. C. (1989). IQ at age 4 in relation to maternal alcohol use and smoking during pregnancy. *Developmental Psychology, 25,* 3–11.

Streissguth, A. P., Treder, R., Barr, H. M., Shepard, T., Bleyer, A., & Martin, D. (1984). Prenatal aspirin and offspring IQ in a large group. *Teratology, 29,* 59A–60A.

Strutt, G. F., Anderson, D. R., & Well, A. D. (1975). A developmental study of the effects of irrelevant information on speeded classification. *Journal of Experimental Child Psychology, 20,* 127–135.

Stunkard, A. J., Sørensen, T. I., Hanis, C., Teasdale, T. W., Chakraborty, R., Schull, W. J., & Schulsinger, F. (1986). An adoption study of human obesity. *New England Journal of Medicine, 314,* 193–198.

Sturtevant, A. H. (1965). *A history of genetics.* New York: Harper & Row.

Sugarman, S. (1982). Developmental change in early representational intelligence: Evidence from spatial classification strategies and related verbal expressions. *Cognitive Psychology, 14,* 410–449.

Sugarman, S. (1983). *Children's early thought: Developments in classification.* New York: Cambridge University Press.

Sullivan, H. S. (1953). *The interpersonal theory of psychiatry.* New York: W. W. Norton.

Sullivan, S. A., & Birch, L. L. (1990). Pass the sugar, pass the salt: Experience dictates preference. *Developmental Psychology, 26,* 546–551.

Sulzer-Azaroff, B., & Mayer, G. R. (1977). *Applying behavior-analysis procedures with children and youth.* New York: Holt, Rinehart & Winston.

Summey, P. S. (1986). Cesarean birth. In P. S. Eakins (Ed.), *The American way of birth.* Philadelphia: Temple University Press.

Suomi, S. (1982). Biological foundations and developmental psychobiology. In C. B. Kopp & J. B. Krakow (Eds.), *The child: Development in a social context.* Reading, MA: Addison-Wesley.

Super, C. M. (1976). Environmental effects on motor development: The case of "African infant precocity." *Developmental Medicine and Child Neurology, 18,* 561–567.

Super, C. M., & Harkness, S. (1982). The infant's niche in rural Kenya and metropolitan America. In L. Adler (Ed.), *Issues in cross-cultural research.* New York: Academic Press.

Super, C. M., Herrera, M. G., & Mora, J. O. (1990). Long-term effects of food supplementation and psychosocial intervention on the physical growth of Colombian infants at risk of malnutrition. *Child Development, 61,* 29–49.

Surgeon General's Scientific Advisory Committee on Television and Social Behavior. (1972). *Television and growing up: The impact of televised violence* (DHEW Publication No. HSM 72–90). Washington, DC: U.S. Government Printing Office.

Susman, E. J., Inoff-Germain, G., Nottelmann, E. D., Loriaux, D. L., Cutler, G. B., Jr., & Chrousos, G. P. (1987). Hormones, emotional dispositions, and aggressive attributes in young adolescents. *Child Development, 58,* 1114–1134.

Sutton-Smith, B., & Rosenberg, B. G. (1970). *The sibling.* New York: Holt, Rinehart & Winston.

Svejda, M. J., Campos, J. J., & Emde, R. N. (1980). Mother-infant "bonding": Failure to generalize. *Child Development, 51,* 775–779.

Szajnberg, N., Ward, M. J., Krauss, A., & Kessler, D. B. (1987). Low birth-weight prematures: Preventive intervention and maternal attitude. *Child Psychiatry and Human Development, 17,* 152–165.

Tager-Flusberg, H. (1985). Putting words together: Morphology and syntax in the preschool years. In J. B. Gleason (Ed.), *The development of language.* Columbus, OH: Charles E. Merrill.

Talayesva, D. (1942). *Sun chief: The autobiography of a Hopi Indian.* New Haven: Yale University Press.

Tanner, J. M. (1962). *Growth at adolescence* (2nd ed.). Oxford: Blackwell.

Tanner, J. M. (1978). *Fetus into man: Physical growth from conception to maturity.* Cambridge: Harvard University Press.

Tanner, J. M., & Taylor, G. P. (1965). *Growth.* Alexandria, VA: Time/Life Books.

Tanner, J. M., Whitehouse, R. H., & Takaishi, M. (1966). Standards from birth to maturity for height, weight, height velocity, and weight velocity for British children 1965, Parts I and II. *Archives of Disease in Childhood, 41,* 613.

Taras, H. L., Sallis, J. F., Patterson, T. L., Nader, P. R., & Nelson, J. A. (1989). Television's influence on children's diet and physical activity. *Journal of Developmental and Behavioral Pediatrics, 10,* 176–180.

Taylor, M. (1988). Conceptual perspective taking: Children's ability to distinguish what they know from what they see. *Child Development, 59,* 703–718.

Taylor, R. (1989). Cracking cocaine's legacy in babies of drug abusers. *The Journal of NIH Research, 1,* 29–31.

Teller, D. Y., & Bornstein, M. H. (1987). Infant color vision and color perception. In P. Salapatek & L. Cohen (Eds.), *Handbook of infant perception: From sensation to perception* (Vol. 1). Orlando, FL: Academic Press.

Terman, L. M. (1916). *The measurement of intelligence.* Boston: Houghton Mifflin.

Terman, L. M. (1925). *Genetic studies of genius: Vol. 1. Mental and physical traits of a thousand gifted children.* Stanford, CA: Stanford University Press.

Terman, L. M., & Merrill, M. A. (1937). *Measuring intelligence.* Boston: Houghton Mifflin.

Terman, L. M., & Merrill, M. A. (1973). *Stanford-Binet Intelligence Scale: Manual for the third revision.* Boston: Houghton Mifflin.

Terman, L. M., & Oden, M. H. (1959). *Genetic studies of genius: Vol. 4. The gifted group at midlife.* Stanford, CA: Stanford University Press.

Tharp, R. G. (1989). Psychocultural variables and constants: Effects on teaching and learning in schools. *American Psychologist, 44,* 349–359.

Tharp, R. G., Jordan, C., Speidel, G. E., Au, K. H., Klein, T. W., Calkins, R. P., Sloat, K. C. M., & Gallimore, R. (1984). Product and process in applied developmental research: Education and the children of a minority. In M. E. Lamb, A. L. Brown, & B. Rogoff (Eds.), *Advances in developmental psychology* (Vol. 3). Hillsdale, NJ: Erlbaum.

Thelen, E. (1979). Rhythmical stereotypies in normal human infants. *Animal Behavior, 27,* 699–715.

Thelen, E. (1983). Learning to walk is still an "old" problem: A reply to Zelazo. *Journal of Motor Behavior, 15,* 139–161.

Thelen, E., Kelso, J. A. S., & Fogel, A. (1987). Self-organizing systems and infant motor development. *Developmental Review, 7,* 39–65.

Thelen, E., Skala, K. D., & Kelso, J. A. S. (1987). The dynamic nature of early coordination: Evidence from bilateral leg movements in young infants. *Developmental Psychology, 23,* 179–186.

Thomas, A., & Chess, S. (1977). *Temperament and development.* New York: Brunner/Mazel.

Thompson, C. (1982). Cortical activity in behavioural development. In J. W. T. Dickerson & H. McGurk (Eds.), *Brain and behavioural development.* London: Surrey University Press.

Thompson, R. A. (1990). Vulnerability in research: A developmental perspective on risk research. *Child Development, 61,* 1–16.

Thompson, R. A., Lamb, M. E., & Estes, D. (1982). Stability of infant-mother attachment and its relationship to changing life circumstances in an unselected middle-class sample. *Child Development, 53,* 144–148.

Thompson, S. K. (1975). Gender labels and early sex role development. *Child Development, 46,* 339–347.

Thompson, V. D. (1974). Family size: Implicit policies and assumed psychological outcomes. *Journal of Social Issues, 30,* 93–124.

Thorndike, R. L., Hagen, E. P., & Sattler, J. M. (1986). *The Stanford-Binet Intelligence Scale: Guide for administering and scoring* (4th ed.). Chicago: Riverside.

Thurstone, L. L. (1938). *Primary mental abilities.* Chicago: University of Chicago Press.

Thurstone, L. L. (1947). *Multiple factor analysis.* Chicago: University of Chicago Press.

Tieger, T. (1980). On the biological basis of sex differences in aggression. *Child Development, 51,* 943–963.

Tietjen, A. M. (1986). Prosocial moral reasoning among children and adults in a Papua New Guinea society. *Developmental Psychology, 22,* 861–868.

Tinbergen, N. (1951). *The study of instinct.* London: Oxford University Press.

Toda, S., Fogel, A., & Kawai, M. (1990). Maternal speech to three-month-old infants in the United States and Japan. *Journal of Child Language, 17,* 279–294.

Tomasello, M., Conti-Ramsden, G., & Ewert, B. (1990). Young children's conversations with their mothers and fathers: Differences in breakdown and repair. *Journal of Child Language, 17,* 115–130.

Tomasello, M., & Todd, J. (1983). Joint attention and lexical acquisition style. *First Language, 4,* 197–212.

Touwen, B. C. L. (1974). The neurological development of the infant. In J. A. Davis & J. Dobbing (Eds.), *Scientific foundations of paediatrics.* Philadelphia: W. B. Saunders.

Trehub, S. E. (1987). Infants' perception of musical patterns. *Perception & Psychophysics, 41,* 635–641.

Trehub, S. E., Bull, D., & Thorpe, L. A. (1984). Infants' perception of melodies: The role of melodic contour. *Child Development, 55,* 821–830.

Trehub, S. E., Schneider, B. A., Morrongiello, B. A., & Thorpe, L. A. (1988). Auditory sensitivity in school-age children. *Journal of Experimental Child Psychology, 46,* 273–285.

Trehub, S. E., Thorpe, L. A., & Morrongiello, B. A. (1985). Infants' perception of melodies: Changes in a single tone. *Infant Behavior and Development, 8,* 213–223.

Treiber, F., & Wilcox, S. (1980). Perception of a "subjective" contour by infants. *Child Development, 51,* 915–917.

Trevarthen, W. (1987). *Human birth: An evolutionary perspective.* New York: Aldine de Gruyter.

Trickett, P. K., & Susman, E. J. (1988). Parental perceptions of child-rearing practices in physically abusive and nonabusive families. *Developmental Psychology, 24,* 270–276.

Tronick, E. Z. (1987). The Neonatal Behavioral Assessment Scale as a biomarker of the effects of environmental agents on the newborn. *Environmental Health Perspectives, 74,* 185–189.

Tronick, E. Z. (1989). Emotions and emotional communication in infants. *American Psychologist, 44,* 112–119.

Tronick, E. Z., Als, H., Adamson, L., Wise, S., & Brazelton, T. E. (1978). The infant's response to entrapment between contradictory messages in face-to-face interaction. *Journal of the American Academy of Child Psychiatry, 17,* 1–13.

Tronick, E. Z., & Cohn, J. F. (1989). Infant-mother face-to-face interaction: Age and gender differences in coordination and the occurrence of miscoordination. *Child Development, 60,* 85–92.

Tronick, E. Z., Ricks, M., & Cohn, J. F., (1982). Maternal and infant affective exchange: Patterns of adaptation. In T. Field & A. Fogel (Eds.), *Emotion and early interaction.* Hillsdale, NJ: Erlbaum.

Tryon, R. C. (1940). Genetic differences in maze learning in rats. *Yearbook of the National Society for Studies in Education, 39,* 111–119.

Turiel, E. (1978). Social regulations and domains of social concepts. In W. Damon (Ed.), *New directions for child development: Vol. 1. Social cognition.* San Francisco: Jossey-Bass.

Turiel, E. (1983). *The development of social knowledge: Morality and convention.* Cambridge: Cambridge University Press.

U.S. Bureau of the Census. (1978). *Statistical abstract of the United States* (98th ed.). Washington, DC: U.S. Government Printing Office.

U.S. Bureau of the Census. (1990a). *Statistical abstract of the United States* (110th ed.). Washington, DC: U.S. Government Printing Office.

U.S. Bureau of the Census. (1990b). Who's minding the kids? *Current population reports* (Series P-70, No. 20). Washington, DC: U.S. Government Printing Office.

U.S. Department of Health, Education, and Welfare. (1978). *Alcohol and health.* Rockville, MD: National Institute of Alcohol Abuse and Alcoholism.

U.S. Public Health Service. (1979). *Smoking and health* (A Report of the Surgeon General, U.S. Department of Health, Education, and Welfare Publication No. (PHS) 79–50066). Washington, DC: U.S. Public Health Service, Office on Smoking and Health.

Underwood, B., & Moore, B. (1982). Perspective-taking and altruism. *Psychological Bulletin, 91,* 143–173.

Uzgiris, I. (1968). Situational generality of conservation. In I. E. Sigel & F. H. Hooper (Eds.), *Logical thinking in children.* New York: Holt, Rinehart & Winston.

Valian, V. (1986). Syntactic categories in the speech of young children. *Developmental Psychology, 22,* 562–579.

Valleroy, L. A., Harris, J. R., & Way, P. O. (1990). The impact of HIV infection on child survival in the developing world. *AIDS, 4,* 667–672.

Vandell, D. L., Henderson, V. K., & Wilson, K. S. (1988). A longitudinal study of children with day-care experiences of varying quality. *Child Development, 59,* 1286–1292.

Vandell, D. L., & Mueller, E. C. (1980). Peer play and friendships during the first two years. In H. C. Foot, A. J. Chapman, & J. R. Smith (Eds.), *Friendship and social relations in children.* New York: Wiley.

Vandell, D. L., & Wilson, K. S. (1982). Social interaction in the first year of life: Infants' social skills with peers versus mother. In K. H. Rubin & H. S. Ross (Eds.), *Peer relationships and social skills in childhood.* New York: Springer-Verlag.

Vandell, D. L., Wilson, K. S., & Buchanan, N. R. (1980). Peer interaction in the first year of life: An examination of its structure, content, and sensitivity to toys. *Child Development, 51,* 481–488.

Vandenberg, S. G., Singer, S. M., & Pauls, D. L. (1986). *The heredity of behavior disorders in adults and children.* New York: Plenum Press.

Vandenberg, S. G., & Vogler, G. P. (1985). Genetic determinants of intelligence. In B. B. Wolman (Ed.), *Handbook of intelligence.* New York: Wiley.

Varni, J. W., (1983). *Clinical behavioral pediatrics: An interdisciplinary biobehavioral approach.* New York: Pergamon Press.

Vaughn, B. E., Egeland, B., Sroufe, L. A., & Waters, E. (1979). Individual differences in infant-mother attachment at twelve and eighteen months: Stability and change in families under stress. *Child Development, 50,* 971–975.

Vaughn, B. E., Kopp, C. B., & Krakow, J. B. (1984). The emergence and consolidation of self-control from eighteen to thirty months of age: Normative trends and individual differences. *Child Development, 55,* 990–1004.

Vaughn, B. E., Taraldson, B., Crichton, L., & Egeland, B. (1980). Relationships between neonatal behavioral organization and infant behavior during the first year of life. *Infant Behavior and Development, 3,* 78–89.

Vernon, P. A. (1983). Speed of information processing and general intelligence. *Intelligence, 7,* 53–70.

Vernon, P. E. (1966). Educational and intellectual development among Canadian Indians and Eskimos. *Educational Review, 18,* 79–91.

Veroff, J. (1969). Social comparison and the development of achievement motivation. In C. P. Smith (Ed.), *Achievement-related motives in children.* New York: Russell Sage.

Vinter, A. (1986). The role of movement in eliciting early imitations. *Child Development, 57,* 66–71.

Vorhees, C. V. (1986). Principles of behavioral teratology. In

E. P. Riley & C. V. Vorhees (Eds.), *Handbook of behavioral teratology.* New York: Plenum Press.

Vosk, B., Forehand, R., Parker, J., & Rickard, K. (1982). A multimethod comparison of popular and unpopular children. *Developmental Psychology, 18,* 571–575.

Vurpillot, E. (1968). The development of scanning strategies and their relation to visual differentiation. *Journal of Experimental Child Psychology, 6,* 632–650.

Vurpillot, E., & Ball, W. A. (1979). The concept of identity and children's selective attention. In G. A. Hale & M. Lewis (Eds.), *Attention and cognitive development.* New York: Plenum Press.

Vuyk, R. (1981). *Overview and critique of Piaget's genetic epistemology 1965–1980* (Vols. 1 & 2). New York: Academic Press.

Vygotsky, L. S. (1962). *Thought and language* (E. Hanfmann & G. Vakar, Trans.). Cambridge: MIT Press.

Vygotsky, L. S. (1978). *Mind in society: The development of higher psychological processes.* Cambridge: Harvard University Press.

Waber, D. P. (1976). Sex differences in cognition: A function of maturation rate? *Science, 192,* 572–574.

Wachs, T. D. (1983). The use and abuse of environment in behavior-genetic research. *Child Development, 54,* 396–407.

Wadstroem, J. A. (1769). Metamorphosis humana, 1767. In C. von Linné, *Amoenitates academicae* (Vol. III, pp. 326–344).

Wagner, D. A. (1978). Memories of Morocco: The influence of age, schooling, and environment on memory. *Cognitive Psychology, 10,* 1–28.

Wagner, M. E., Schubert, H. J. P., & Schubert, D. S. P. (1985). Family size effects: A review. *Journal of Genetic Psychology, 146,* 65–78.

Wahler, R. G., & Dumas, J. E. (1984). Changing the observational coding styles of insular and noninsular mothers: A step toward maintenance of parent training effects. In R. F. Dangel & R. A. Polster (Eds.), *Parent training: Foundations of research and practice.* New York: Guilford Press.

Wahler, R. G., & Dumas, J. E. (1989). Attentional problems in dysfunctional mother-child interactions: An interbehavioral model. *Psychological Bulletin, 105,* 116–130.

Waldrop, M. F., & Halverson, C. F. (1975). Intensive and extensive peer behavior: Longitudinal and cross-sectional analyses. *Child Development, 46,* 19–26.

Walk, R. D. (1968). Monocular compared to binocular depth perception in human infants. *Science, 162,* 473–475.

Walk, R. D. (1981). *Perceptual development.* Monterey, CA: Brooks/Cole.

Walker, L. J. (1984). Sex differences in the development of moral reasoning: A critical review. *Child Development, 55,* 677–691.

Walker, L. J. (1989). A longitudinal study of moral reasoning. *Child Development, 60,* 157–166.

Walker, L. J., deVries, B., & Trevethan, S. D. (1987). Moral stages and moral orientations in real-life and hypothetical dilemmas. *Child Development, 58,* 842–858.

Walker-Andrews, A. S. (1986). Intermodal expression of expressive behaviors: Relation of eye and voice? *Developmental Psychology, 22,* 373–377.

Walker-Andrews, A. S., & Lennon, E. M. (1985). Auditory-visual perception of changing distance by human infants. *Child Development, 56,* 544–548.

Wallerstein, J. S., Corbin, S. B., & Lewis, J. M. (1988). Children of divorce: A ten-year study. In E. M. Hetherington & J. Arasteh (Eds.), *Impact of divorce, single-parenting, and step-parenting on children.* Hillsdale, NJ: Erlbaum.

Wallerstein, J. S., & Kelly, J. B. (1980). *Surviving the breakup: How children and parents cope with divorce.* New York: Basic Books.

Ward, S., Reale, G., & Levinson, D. (1972). Children's perceptions, explanations, and judgments of television advertising. In E. A. Rubenstein, G. A. Comstock, & J. P. Murray (Eds.), *Television and social behavior: Vol. 4. Television in day-to-day life: Patterns of use.* Washington, DC: U.S. Government Printing Office.

Warkany, J. (1983). Teratology: Spectrum of a science. In H. Kalter (Ed.), *Issues and reviews in teratology* (Vol. 1). New York: Plenum Press.

Warkany, J., & Schraffenberger, E. (1947). Congenital malformations induced in rats by roentgen rays. *American Journal of Roentgenology and Radium Therapy, 57,* 455–463.

Warshak, R. A., & Santrock, J. W. (1983). The impact of divorce on father-custody and mother-custody homes: The child's perspective. In L. Kurdek (Ed.), *New directions for child development: No. 19. Children and divorce.* San Francisco: Jossey-Bass.

Waters, E. (1978). The reliability and stability of individual differences in infant-mother attachment. *Child Development, 49,* 483–494.

Waters, E., Wippman, J., & Sroufe, L. A. (1979). Attachment, positive affect, and competence in the peer group: Two studies in construct validation. *Child Development, 50,* 821–829.

Watson, J. B. (1930). *Behaviorism.* New York: W. W. Norton.

Watson, J. S. (1971). Cognitive-perceptual development in infancy: Settings for the seventies. *Merrill-Palmer Quarterly, 17,* 139–152.

Watson, J. S., & Ramey, C. T. (1972). Reactions to response-contingent stimulation in early infancy. *Merrill-Palmer Quarterly, 18,* 219–227.

Wattenberg, W. W., & Clifford, C. (1964). Relation of self-concept to beginning achievement in reading. *Child Development, 35,* 461–467.

Wechsler, D. (1974). *Wechsler Intelligence Scale for Children—Revised.* New York: The Psychological Corporation.

Weinberg, R. (1989). Intelligence and IQ: Landmark issues and great debates. *American Psychologist, 44,* 98–104.

Weinberger, S. E., & Weiss, S. T. (1988). Pulmonary diseases. In G. N. Burrow & T. F. Ferris (Eds.), *Medical complications of pregnancy* (3rd ed.). Philadelphia: W. B. Saunders.

Weiner, B., & Handel, S. J. (1985). A cognition-emotion-action sequence: Anticipated emotional consequences of causal attributions and reported communication strategy. *Developmental Psychology, 21,* 102–107.

Weiner, L., & Morse, B. A. (1988). FAS: Clinical perspectives and prevention. In I. J. Chasnoff (Ed.), *Drugs, alcohol, pregnancy and parenting.* Boston: Kluwer Academic Publishers.

Wellman, H. M. (1977). The early development of intentional memory. *Human Development, 20,* 86–101.

Wellman, H. M., & Lempers, J. D. (1977). The naturalistic communicative abilities of two-year-olds. *Child Development, 48,* 1052–1057.

Wentworth, B. B., & Alexander, E. R. (1971). Seroepidemiology of infections due to members of the herpesvirus group. *American Journal of Epidemiology, 94,* 496–507.

Werker, J. F. (1989). Becoming a native listener. *American Scientist, 77,* 54–59.

Werker, J. F., & Lalonde, C. E. (1988). Cross-language speech perception: Initial capabilities and developmental change. *Developmental Psychology, 24,* 672–683.

Werner, E., & Smith, R. (1982). *Vulnerable but invincible: A study of resilient children.* New York: McGraw-Hill.

Werner, E. E. (1972). Infants around the world: Cross-cultural studies of psychomotor development from birth to two years. *Journal of Cross-Cultural Psychology, 3,* 111–134.

Wertsch, J. V. (1989). A sociocultural approach to mind. In W. Damon (Ed.), *Child development today and tomorrow.* San Francisco: Jossey-Bass.

Wertsch, J. V. (1985). *Vygotsky and the social formation of mind.* Cambridge: Harvard University Press.

Wertsch, J. V., Minick, N., & Arns, F. J. (1984). The creation of context in joint problem solving. In B. Rogoff & J. Lave (Eds.), *Everyday cognition: Its development in social context.* Cambridge: Harvard University Press.

Wertz, R. W., & Wertz, D. C. (1977). *Lying-in: A history of childbirth in America.* New York: Free Press.

Westinghouse Learning Corporation/Ohio University. (1969). *The impact of Head Start: An evaluation of the effects of Head Start on children's cognitive and affective development.* Washington, DC: Department of Commerce.

Wexler, K. (1982). A principle theory for language acquisition. In E. Wanner & L. Gleitman (Eds.), *Language acquisition.* Cambridge: Cambridge University Press.

Whalen, R. E. (1984). Multiple actions of steroids and their antagonists. *Archives of Sexual Behavior, 13,* 497–502.

White, B. L. (1971). *Human infants: Experience and psychological development.* Englewood Cliffs, NJ: Prentice-Hall.

White, J., & Labarba, R. (1976). The effects of tactile and kinesthetic stimulation on neonatal development in the premature infant. *Developmental Psychobiology, 9,* 569–577.

White, R. W. (1959). Motivation reconsidered: The concept of competence. *Psychological Review, 66,* 297–333.

Whiting, B. B., & Edwards, C. P. (1988). *Children of different worlds.* Cambridge: Harvard University Press.

Whiting, B. B., & Whiting, J. W. M. (1975). *Children of six cultures: A psychocultural analysis.* Cambridge: Harvard University Press.

Widmayer, S. M., & Field, T. M. (1981). Effects of Brazelton demonstrations for mothers on the development of preterm infants. *Pediatrics, 67,* 711–714.

Widom, C. S. (1989). The cycle of violence. *Science, 244,* 160–166.

Wilder, G., Mackie, D., & Cooper, J. (1985). Gender and computers: Two surveys of computer-related attitudes. *Sex Roles, 13,* 215–228.

Willatts, P., & Rosie, K. (1989, April). *Planning by 12-month-old infants.* Paper presented at the biennial meeting of the Society for Research in Child Development, Kansas City, MO.

Williams, J. E., & Best, D. L. (1982). *Measuring sex stereotypes: A thirty nation study.* Beverly Hills, CA: Sage.

Wilson, D. M., & Rosenfeld, R. G. (1987). Treatment of short stature and delayed adolescence. In C. P. Mahoney (Ed.), *Pediatric clinics of North America, 34,* 865–879.

Wilson, J. G. (1977). Current status of teratology: General principles and mechanisms derived from animal studies. In J. G. Wilson & F. C. Fraser (Eds.), *Handbook of teratology: Vol. 1. General principles and etiology.* New York: Plenum Press.

Wilson, M. N. (1986). The black extended family: An analytical consideration. *Developmental Psychology, 22,* 246–258.

Wilson, R. S. (1978). Synchronies in mental development: An epigenetic perspective. *Science, 202,* 939–948.

Wilson, R. S. (1983). The Louisville Twin Study: Developmental synchronies in behavior. *Child Development, 54,* 298–316.

Wilson, R. S. (1986). Continuity and change in cognitive ability profile. *Behavior Genetics, 16,* 45–60.

Winn, M. (1983). *Children without childhood.* New York: Pantheon Books.

Winner, E. (1979). New names for old things: The emergence of metaphoric language. *Journal of Child Language, 6,* 469–491.

Winstead, B. A. (1986). Sex differences in same-sex friendships. In V. J. Derlaga & B. A. Winstead (Eds.), *Friendship and social interaction.* New York: Springer-Verlag.

Wissler, C. (1901). The correlation of mental and physical traits. *Psychological Monographs, 3,* 1–62.

Witelson, S. F. (1985). On hemisphere specialization and cerebral plasticity from birth: Mark II. In C. T. Best (Ed.), *Hemisphere function and collaboration in the child.* New York: Academic Press.

Witelson, S. F. (1987). Neurobiological aspects of language in children. *Child Development, 58,* 653–688.

Witkin, H. A., Mednick, S. A., Schulsinger, F., Bakkestrom, E., Christiansen, K. O., Goodenough, D. R., Hirschhorn, K., Lundsteen, C., Owen, D. R., Philip, J., Rubin, D. B., & Stocking, M. (1976). Criminality in XYY and XXY men. *Science, 193,* 547–555.

Wolf, T. M. (1973). Effects of live modeled sex-inappropriate play behavior in a naturalistic setting. *Developmental Psychology, 9,* 120–123.

Wolfe, D. A. (1985). Child-abusive parents: An empirical review and analysis. *Psychological Bulletin, 97,* 462–482.

Wolfe, D. A., Fairbank, J., Kelly, J. A., & Bradlyn, A. S. (1983). Child abusive parents' physiological responses to stressful and non-stressful behavior in children. *Behavioral Assessment, 5,* 363–371.

Wolff, P. H. (1969). The natural history of crying and other vocalizations in early infancy. In B. Foss (Ed.), *Determinants of infant behavior* (Vol. 4). London: Methuen.

Wolff, P. H. (1987). *The development of behavioral states and the expression of emotions in early infancy.* Chicago: University of Chicago Press.

Wood, D. J., Bruner, J. S., & Ross, G. (1976). The role of tutoring in problem solving. *Journal of Child Psychology and Psychiatry, 17,* 89–100.

Woolston, J. L. (1987). Obesity in infancy and early childhood. *Journal of the American Academy of Child and Adolescent Psychiatry, 26,* 123–126.

Worobey, J. (1985). A review of Brazelton-based interventions to enhance parent-infant interaction. *Journal of Reproductive and Infant Psychology, 3,* 64–73.

Worobey, J., & Belsky, J. (1982). Employing the Brazelton scale to influence mothering: An experimental comparison of three strategies. *Developmental Psychology, 18,* 736–743.

Yakovlev, P. I., & Lecours, A. R. (1967). The myelogenetic cycles of regional maturation of the brain. In A. Minkowski (Ed.), *Regional development of the brain in early life.* Oxford: Blackwell.

Yarrow, L. J., Goodwin, M. S., Manheimer, H., & Milowe, I. D. (1973). Infancy experiences and cognitive and personality development at 10 years. In L. J. Stone, H. T. Smith, & L. B. Murphy (Eds.), *The competent infant: Research and commentary.* New York: Basic Books.

Yee, D. K., & Eccles, J. S. (1988). Parent perceptions and attributions for children's math achievement. *Sex Roles, 19,* 317–333.

Yendovitskaya, T. V. (1971). Development of attention. In A. V. Zaporozhets & D. B. Elkonin (Eds.), *The psychology of preschool children.* Cambridge: MIT Press.

Yogman, M. W. (1982). Observations on the father-infant relationship. In S. H. Cath, A. R. Gurwitt, & J. M. Ross (Eds.), *Father and child: Developmental and clinical perspectives.* Boston: Little, Brown.

Yogman, M. W., Dixon, S., Tronick, E., Als, H., Adamson, L., Lester, B. M., & Brazelton, T. B. (1977, April). *The goals and structure of face-to-face interaction between infants and their fathers.* Paper presented at the biennial meeting of the Society for Research in Child Development, New Orleans.

Yonas, A., & Owsley, C. (1987). Development of visual space perception. In P. Salapatek & L. Cohen (Eds.), *Handbook of infant perception: From perception to cognition* (Vol. 2). Orlando, FL: Academic Press.

Yoneshige, Y., & Elliott, L. L. (1981). Pure-tone sensitivity and ear canal pressure at threshold in children and adults. *Journal of the Acoustical Society of America, 70,* 1272–1276.

Young-Browne, G., Rosenfeld, H. M., & Horowitz, F. D. (1977). Infant discrimination of facial expression. *Child Development, 48,* 555–562.

Youniss, J. (1980). *Parents and peers in social development: A Sullivan-Piaget perspective.* Chicago: University of Chicago Press.

Youniss, J., & Smollar, J. (1985). *Adolescent relations with mothers, fathers, and friends.* Chicago: University of Chicago Press.

Zagon, I. S., & McLaughlin, P. J. (1984). An overview of the neurobehavioral sequelae of perinatal opiod exposure. In J. Yanai (Ed.), *Neurobehavioral teratology.* New York: Elsevier.

Zahavi, S., & Asher, S. R. (1978). The effect of verbal instructions on preschool children's aggressive behavior. *Journal of School Psychology, 16,* 146–153.

Zahn-Waxler, C., Friedman, S. L., & Cummings, E. M. (1983). Children's emotions and behaviors in response to infants' cries. *Child Development, 54,* 1522–1528.

Zahn-Waxler, C., & Radke-Yarrow, M. (1982). The development of altruism: Alternative research strategies. In N. Eisenberg-Berg (Ed.), *The development of prosocial behavior.* New York: Academic Press.

Zahn-Waxler, C., Radke-Yarrow, M., & King, R. A. (1979). Child rearing and children's prosocial initiations toward victims of distress. *Child Development, 50,* 319–330.

Zajonc, R. B., & Markus, G. B. (1975). Birth order and intellectual development. *Psychological Review, 82,* 74–88.

Zajonc, R. B., Markus, H., & Markus, G. B. (1979). The birth order puzzle. *Journal of Personality and Social Psychology, 37,* 1325–1341.

Zaporozhets, A. V. (1965). The development of perception in the preschool child. *Monographs of the Society for Research in Child Development, 30*(2, Serial No. 100).

Zarbatany, L., Hartmann, D. P., & Rankin, D. B. (1990). The psychological functions of preadolescent peer activities. *Child Development, 61,* 1067–1080.

Zausmer, E., & Shea, A. M. (1984). Motor development. In S. M. Pueschel (Ed.), *The young child with Down syndrome.* New York: Human Sciences Press.

Zelazo, P. R. (1983). The development of walking: New findings and old assumptions. *Journal of Motor Behavior, 15,* 99–137.

Zelazo, P. R., Zelazo, N. A., & Kolb, S. (1972). "Walking" in the newborn. *Science, 176,* 314–315.

Zeskind, P. S. (1981). Behavioral dimensions and cry sounds of infants of differential fetal growth. *Infant Behavior and Development, 4,* 297–306.

Zeskind, P. S., & Lester, B. M. (1981). Analysis of cry features in newborns with differential fetal growth. *Child Development, 52,* 207–212.

Ziegler, C. B., Dusek, J. B., & Carter, D. B. (1984). Self-concept and sex-role orientation: An investigation of multidimensional aspects of personality development on adolescence. *Journal of Early Adolescence, 4,* 25–39.

Zigler, E. (1967). Familial mental retardation: A continuing dilemma. *Science, 155,* 292–298.

Zigler, E., & Berman, W. (1983). Discerning the future of early childhood intervention. *American Psychologist, 38,* 894–906.

Zigler, E., & Butterfield, E. C. (1968). Motivational aspects of changes in IQ test performance of culturally deprived nursery school children. *Child Development, 39,* 1–14.

Zigler, E., & Trickett, P. K. (1978). IQ, social competence, and evaluation of early childhood intervention programs. *American Psychologist, 33,* 789–798.

Zill, N. (1988). Behavior, achievement, and health problems among children in stepfamilies: Findings from a national survey of child health. In E. M. Hetherington & J. D. Arasteh (Eds.), *Impact of divorce, single-parenting, and stepparenting on children.* Hillsdale, NJ: Erlbaum.

Zimiles, H., & Lee, V. E. (1991). Adolescent family structure and educational progress. *Developmental Psychology, 27,* 314–320.

Zuckerman, B. (1988). Marijuana and cigarette smoking during pregnancy: Neonatal effects. In I. J. Chasnoff (Ed.), *Drugs, alcohol, pregnancy and parenting.* Boston: Kluwer Academic Publishers.

CREDITS

Chapter opening photos p. 2: © 1988 Frank Siteman/The Picture Cube. **p. 40:** © Bob Daemmrich/The Image Works. **p. 82:** © Porterfield-Chickering/Photo Researchers. **p. 128:** © Algaze/The Image Works. **p. 178:** © 1989 Susan Lapides. **p. 226:** © Mathew Neal McVay/TSW-Click/Chicago Ltd. **p. 272:** © Bob Daemmrich/TSW-Click/Chicago Ltd. **p. 316:** © Paul Conklin. **p. 360:** © F. B. Grunzweig/Photo Researchers, Inc. **p. 404:** © Kevin Horan/Stock Boston. **p. 448:** Cameramann International, Ltd. **p. 492:** Judith D. Sedwick/The Picture Cube. **p. 534:** © Bob Daemmrich/TSW-Click/Chicago Ltd. **p. 575:** © Susan Van Etten/The Picture Cube. **p. 616:** © Bill Bachman/Photo Researchers. **p. 656:** © 1991 Jerry Howard/Positive Images.

Chapter 1 p. 4: © Paul Damien/TSW-Click/Chicago Ltd. **p. 6:** *Las Meninas* by Diego Velazquez. © Museo del Prado, Madrid. All rights reserved. **p. 9:** © Darwin Museum, Down House. **p. 18:** © Bob Daemmrich/The Image Works. **p. 20:** *Figure 1.1* Cummings, E. M., Iannotti, R. J., & Zahn-Waxler, C. (1985). Influence of conflict between adults on the emotions and aggression of young children. *Developmental Psychology, 21,* 495–507. **p. 26:** *Figure 1.2* Gusella, J. L., Muir, D., & Tronick, E. Z. (1988). The effect of manipulating maternal behavior during an interaction of three- and six-month-olds' affect and attention. *Child Development, 59,* 1111–1124. © The Society for Research in Child Development, Inc. **p. 28:** *Figure 1.3* Poche, C., McCubbrey, H., & Munn, T. (1982). The development of correct toothbrushing technique in preschool children. *Journal of Applied Behavior Analysis, 15,* Figure 1, p. 318. Reprinted by permission of *Journal of Applied Behavior Analysis* and the author. **p. 31:** © Ulrike Welsch. **p. 33:** *Figure 1.4* Ornstein, P. A., Naus, M. J., & Liberty, C. (1975). Rehearsal and organization processes in children's memory. *Child Development, 46,* 818–830. © The Society for Research in Child Development, Inc. **p. 34:** *Figure 1.5* Pinon, M. F., Huston, A. C., & Wright, J. C. (1989). Family ecology and child characteristics that predict young children's educational television viewing. *Child Development, 60,* 846–856. © The Society for Research in Child Development, Inc. **p. 36:** left, Shostal Associates/SuperStock; right, Elizabeth Crews.

Chapter 2 p. 44: © Jerry Howard/Positive Images. **p. 48:** Elizabeth Crews. **p. 51:** © Barbara Filet/TSW-Click/Chicago Ltd. **p. 54:** Anderson/Monkmeyer Press Photo Service. **p. 63:** Mary Evans Picture Library. **p. 68:** AP/Wide World. **p. 71:**

Figure 2.3 J. Garabino, in Kapp & Krakow, *The child,* © 1982 by Addison-Wesley Publishing Company, Inc. Reprinted with permission of the publisher. **p. 75:** Thomas McAvoy, Life Magazine © Time Warner Inc.

Chapter 3 p. 85: Paul Conklin/Monkmeyer Press. **p. 87:** *Figure 3.1* Isensee, W. (September 3, 1986). *The Chronicle of Higher Education.* **p. 88:** *Figure 3.2* Alberts, B., Bray, D., Lewis, J., Raff, M., et al. (1983). *Molecular biology of the cell.* New York: Garland Publishing, Inc. Reprinted by permission. **p. 89:** *Figure 3.3* Custom Medical Stock Photo. **p. 92:** *Figure 3.6 Genetics, society, and decisions* by Richard V. Kowles. Copyright © 1985 by Scott, Foresman and Company. Reprinted by permission of HarperCollins Publishers. **p. 101:** © Omikron/Photo Researchers. **p. 104:** © Tony Mendoza/The Picture Cube. **p. 105:** *Table 3.3* Hook, E. B., & Cross, P. K. (1982). Interpretation of recent data pertinent to genetic counseling for Down syndrome. In Willey, A. M., Carter, T. P., Kelly, S., et al. (Eds.), *Clinical Genetics: Problems in Diagnosis and Counseling.* New York: Academic Press. Reprinted by permission. **p. 108:** *Figure 3.8* Bender, B. G., Linden, M. G., & Robinson, A. (1987). Environment and developmental risk in children with sex chromosome abnormalities. *Journal of the Academy of Child and Adolescent Psychiatry, 26,* 499–503. © by Williams & Wilkins, 1987. **p. 111:** © 1987 Newsweek, Inc. All rights reserved. Reprinted by permission. **p. 113:** © Bob Daemmrich. **p. 116:** *Figure 3.9* Gottesman, I. I. (1963). Genetic aspects of intelligent behavior. In N. R. Ellis (Ed.), *Handbook of mental deficiency.* New York: McGraw-Hill. Reprinted by permission of the author. **p. 119:** © Bob Daemmrich/The Image Works. **p. 125:** *Table 3.5 Our uncertain heritage: Genetics and human diversity* by Daniel L. Hartl. Copyright © 1977 by Daniel L. Hartl. Reprinted by permission of HarperCollins Publishers.

Chapter 4 p. 131: © D. W. Fawcett/Science Source/Photo Researchers. **p. 132:** *Figure 4.1* K. L. Moore, *The developing human,* 1988, 4th Edition, W. B. Saunders Company. Reprinted by permission. **pp. 134–135:** All photos © Lennart Nilsson, *A child is born,* 1976, except for last photo, which is from the 1990 edition. **p. 143:** *Figure 4.3* Moore, K. L., *Before we are born,* 1989, 3rd Edition, W. B. Saunders Company. Reprinted by permission. **p. 145:** James Hanson. **p. 155:** *Table 4.4 Well body, well earth,* by Mike Samuels, M.D., & Hal Zina Bennett. Copyright © 1983 by Mike Samuels, M.D. & Hal Zina

Bennett. Reprinted with permission of Sierra Club Books. **p. 157:** © Will & Deni McIntyre/Photo Researchers. **p. 159:** © Nancy Durrell McKenna/Photo Researchers. **p. 161:** Jorgen Schytte/UNICEF. **p. 166:** *Figure 4.4* Shapiro, S., McCormick, M. C., Starfield, B. H., et al., Relevance of correlates of infant deaths for significant morbidity at one year of age. *American Journal of Obstetrics and Gynecology* 136: 363–373, 1980. **p. 170:** © Hella Hammid/Photo Researchers. **p. 171:** *Table 4.5* Apgar, V. (1953). A proposal for a new method of evaluation of the newborn infant. *Anesthesia and Analgesia: Current Researches,* 32, 260–267. Reprinted by permission of International Anesthesia Research Society. **p. 173:** *Figure 4.6* Kleitman, N. (1963). *Sleep and wakefulness.* Chicago: University of Chicago Press. Copyright © 1963 by The University of Chicago. Reprinted by permission. **p. 174:** *Figure 4.7* Roffwarg, H. P., Muzio, J. N., & Dement, W. C. (1966). Ontogenetic development of the human sleep-dream cycle. *Science* 152, 604–619. Copyright 1966 by the American Association for the Advancement of Science.

Chapter 5   p. 182: © Bob Daemmrich/Stock Boston. **p. 183:** *Figure 5.1* Tanner, J. M., et al. (1966). Standards from birth to maturity for height, weight, height velocity, and weight velocity for British children 1965, Parts I and II. *Archives of Disease in Childhood,* 41, 613. Reprinted by permission. **p. 184:** *Figure 5.2* Robbins, W. J., Brody, S., et al. (Eds.), 1928. New Haven: Yale University Press. **p. 185:** *Figure 5.3.* Reprinted by permission of the publishers from *Fetus into man* by J. M. Tanner, Cambridge, MA: Harvard University Press. Copyright © 1978 by J. M. Tanner. **p. 189:** *Figure 5.5* Marshall, W. A., & Tanner, J. M. (1970). Variations in the pattern of pubertal change in boys. *Archives of the Diseases of Childhood,* 45, 13–23. Reprinted by permission of the British Medical Association. **p. 194:** © Antonio Mendoza/The Picture Cube. **p. 201:** *Figure 5.8* Magnusson, D., et al. (1986). Differential maturation among girls and its relations to social adjustment: A longitudinal perspective. *Lifespan Development & Behavior,* Vol. 7, Hillsdale, NJ: Erlbaum. Reprinted by permission. **p. 203:** *Figure 5.9* From *The development of the brain,* by William M. Cowan. Copyright © 1979 by Scientific American, Inc. All rights reserved. **p. 209:** © Brady/Monkmeyer Press. **p. 213:** © Laura Dwight/Black Star. **p. 215:** *Figure 5.10* Connolly, K., & Elliott, J. (1972). The evolution and ontogeny of hand function. In N. B. Jones (Ed.), *The Growth of Competence.* Cambridge, England: Cambridge University Press. Reprinted by permission. **p. 216:** © Susan Lapides. **p. 219:** Shostal Associates/SuperStock. **p. 221:** © 1990 Ulrike Welsch.

Chapter 6   p. 231: *Figure 6.1* Nadja Reissland. **p. 235:** © Susan Lapides. **p. 239:** *Figure 6.2* From *The origin of form perception,* by Robert L. Fantz. Copyright © 1961 by Scientific American, Inc. All rights reserved. **p. 239:** *Figure 6.3* Salapatek, P. (1975). Pattern perception in early infancy. In L. B. Cohen & P. Salapatek (Eds.), *Infant Perception: From Sensation to Cognition* (Vol. 1). New York: Academic Press. Reprinted by permission. **p. 241:** *Figure 6.4* Schwartz, M., &

Day, R. H. (1979). Visual shape perception in early infancy. *Monographs of the Society for Research in Child Development,* 44 (Serial No. 182). © The Society for Research in Child Development, Inc. **p. 243:** © DEK/TexaStock. **p. 245:** *Figure 6.5* William Vandivert and Scientific American. **p. 248:** *Figure 6.6* Treiber, F., & Wilcox, S. (1980). "Perception of a 'Subjective' Contour by Infants." *Child Development,* 51, 915–917. © The Society for Research in Child Development, Inc. **p. 249:** *Figure 6.7* Spelke, E. S. (1985). Perception of unity, persistence and identity: Thoughts on infants' conceptions of objects. In J. Mehler & R. Fox (Eds.), *Neonate Cognition: Beyond the Blooming, Buzzing Confusion.* Hillsdale, NJ: Erlbaum. Reprinted by permission. **p. 257:** *Figure 6.8* Jacob E. Steiner. **p. 258:** © Paul Damien/TSW-Click/Chicago Ltd. **p. 262:** © Elizabeth Crews. **p. 263:** *Figure 6.9* Pick, A. D. (1965). Improvement of visual and tactual discrimination. *Journal of Experimental Psychology,* 69, 331–339. Copyright 1969 by the American Psychological Association. Adapted by permission. **p. 264:** *Figure 6.10* Elkind, D., Koegler, R. R., & Go, E. (1964). Studies in perceptual development II: Part-whole perception. *Child Development,* 35, 81–90. © The Society for Research in Child Development, Inc. **p. 266:** *Figure 6.11* Vurpillot, E. (1968). "The Development of Scanning Strategies and their Relation to Visual Differentiation." *Journal of Experimental Child Psychology,* 6, 632–650. Reprinted by permission of Academic Press. **p. 267:** UN photo by J. Isaac.

Chapter 7   p. 277: *Figure 7.1* Fernald, A. (1985). Four-month-olds prefer to listen to motherese. *Infant Behavior and Development,* 8, 181–195. Reprinted with permission of Ablex Publishing Corporation. **p. 280:** © Elizabeth Crews. **p. 282:** *Figure 7.2* Nelson, K. (1973). Structure and strategy in learning to talk. *Monographs of the Society for Research in Child Development,* 38 (1–2, serial no. 149). © The Society for Research in Child Development, Inc. **p. 283:** *Figure 7.3* Goldfield, B. A., & Reznick, J. S. (1990). Early lexical acquisition: Rate, content & the vocabulary spurt. *Journal of Child Language,* 17, 171–183. Reprinted by permission of Cambridge University Press. **p. 286:** © Ulrike Welsch. **p. 288:** *Table 7.1* Braine, M. D. S. (1976). Children's first word combinations. *Monographs of the Society for Research in Child Development,* 41 (1, Serial No. 164). © The Society for Research in Child Development, Inc. **p. 289:** *Table 7.2* Modified and reprinted by permission of the publishers from *A first language* by R. Brown. Cambridge, MA: Harvard University Press. Copyright © 1973 by the President and Fellows of Harvard College. **p. 291:** *Figure 7.4* Kraus, R. H., & Glucksberg, S. (1969). The development of communication. *Child Development,* 40, 255–266. © The Society for Research in Child Development, Inc. **p. 292:** © George Goodwin/Monkmeyer Press. **p. 297:** © Lew Merrim/Monkmeyer Press. **p. 301:** © Daemmrich/The Image Works. **p. 303:** *Figure 7.6* Berko, J. (1958). The child's learning of English morphology. *Word,* 14, 150–177. Reprinted by permission of the International Linguistic Association. **p. 305:** © Diana Rasche/TSW-Click/Chicago Ltd. **p. 310:** *Figure 7.7* Figure A1 from the

Raven Standard Progressive Matrices is reproduced by permission of J. C. Raven Ltd. **p. 311:** © George Goodwin/Monkmeyer Press.

Chapter 8 p. 321: © Doug Goodman/Monkmeyer Press. **p. 325:** © Paul Conklin/Monkmeyer Press. **p. 327:** *Figure 8.2* Baillargeon, R. (1987). Object permanence in 3-1/2- 4-1/2-month-old infants. *Developmental Psychology, 23,* 655–664. Copyright 1987 by the American Psychological Association. Reprinted by permission. **p. 333:** © Shostal Associates/SuperStock, **p. 335:** *Figure 8.4* Fagan, J. F. (1974). Infant recognition memory: The effects of length of familiarization and type of discrimination task. *Child Development, 45,* 351–356. © The Society for Research in Child Development, Inc. **p. 336:** *Figure 8.5* Dempster, F. N. (1981). Memory span: Sources of individual and developmental differences. *Psychological Bulletin, 89,* 63–100. Copyright 1981 by the American Psychological Association. Reprinted by permission. **p. 337:** *Figure 8.6* Ornstein, P. A., Naus, M. J., & Liberty, C. (1975). Rehearsal and organization processes in children's memory. *Child Development, 46,* 818–830. © The Society for Research in Child Development, Inc. **p. 339:** *Table 8.2* Ornstein, P. A., Naus, M. J., & Liberty, C. (1975). Rehearsal and organization processes in children's memory. *Child Development, 46,* 818–830. © The Society for Research in Child Development, Inc. **p. 340:** *Figure 8.7* Kobasigawa, A. (1974). Utilization of retrieval cues by children in recall. *Child Development, 45,* 127–134. © The Society for Research in Child Development, Inc. **p. 342:** © Paul Damien/Monkmeyer Press. **p. 345:** © Jerry Howard/Positive Images. **p. 350:** *Figure 8.8* Peter Willats. **p. 355:** Cameramann International, Ltd.

Chapter 9 p. 362: *Table 9.1* Siegler, R. S., & Richards, D. D. (1982). The development of intelligence. In R. J. Sternberg (Ed.), *Handbook of Human Intelligence,* Cambridge University Press, p. 889. Reprinted by permission. **p. 366:** *Table 9.2* Guilford, J. P. (1985). The structure of intellect model. In B. B. Wolman (Ed.), *Handbook of Human Intelligence,* pp. 231–233. Copyright © 1985 by John Wiley & Sons, Inc. Reprinted by permission of John Wiley & Sons, Inc. **p. 367:** *Figure 9.1* Guilford, J. P. (1985). The structure of intellect model. In B. B. Wolman (Ed.), *Handbook of Human Intelligence,* p. 230. Copyright © 1985 by John Wiley & Sons, Inc. Reprinted by permission of John Wiley & Sons, Inc. **p. 368:** © Paul Conklin. **p. 374:** Alan Mercer/Stock Boston. **p. 375:** © G. Carde-Explorer/Photo Researchers. **p. 377:** *Figure 9.4* Vandenberg, S. G. (1971). What do we need to know about the inheritance of intelligence and how do we know it? In R. Cancro (Ed.), *Intelligence: Genetic and Environmental Influences.* Figure 2, p. 184. Reprinted by permission of Grune & Stratton, Inc. **p. 379:** *Table 9.4 Bayley Scales of Infant Development.* Copyright © 1969 by The Psychological Corporation. Reproduced by permission. All rights reserved. **p. 381:** *Figure 9.5* Items similar to those in the *Wechsler Intelligence Scale for Children–Revised.* Copyright © 1974 by The Psychological Corporation. Reproduced by permission. All rights reserved. **p. 382:** *Figure 9.6* Kaufman, A. S., &

Kaufman, A. S. (1983). *Kaufman Assessment Battery for Children (K-ABC).* Circle Pines, MN: American Guidance Service, Inc. **p. 385:** © Bob Daemmrich. **p. 392:** *Table 9.5* Elardo, R., & Bradley, R. H. (1981). The Home Observation for Measurement of the Environment (HOME) Scale: A review of research. *Developmental Review,* 1, 113–145. Reprinted by permission. **p. 394:** *Figure 9.8* Laosa, L. M. (1982). Families as facilitators of children's intellectual development at 3 years of age: A causal analysis. In L. M. Laosa and I. E. Sigel (Eds.), *Families as Learning Environments for Children.* New York: Plenum Publishing Corporation. Reprinted by permission. **p. 396:** © Leonard Lee Rue III/Photo Researchers. **p. 398:** © Paul Conklin.

Chapter 10 p. 407: Carroll E. Izard. **p. 408:** *Figure 10.1* Papousek, H., Papousek, M., & Koester, L. S. (1986). Sharing emotionally and sharing knowledge: A microanalytic approach to parent-infant communication. In C. E. Izard and P. B. Read (Eds.), *Measuring Emotions in Infants and Children,* Vol. 2, Cambridge: Cambridge University Press, pp. 112–113. Reprinted by permission. **p. 411:** © David R. Frazier Photolibrary. **p. 414:** Tiffany Field. **p. 417:** *Figure 10.2* Kuchuk, A., Vibbert, M., & Bornstein, M. H. (1986). The perception of smiling and its experiential correlates in 3-month-old infants. *Child Development,* 57, 1054–1061. **p. 419:** Francoise Sauze/Science Photo Library/Photo Researchers Inc. **p. 422:** *Table 10.1* Bretherton, I., & Beeghly, M. (1982). Talking about internal states: The acquisition of an explicit theory of mind. *Developmental Psychology,* 18, 906–921. Copyright 1982 by the American Psychological Association. Adapted by permission. **p. 426:** Harlow Primate Laboratory, University of Wisconsin. **p. 427:** *Figure 10.3* Harlow, H. F., & Zimmerman, R. R. (1959). Affectional responses in the infant monkey. *Science,* 130, 421–432. Copyright 1959 by the American Association for the Advancement of Science. Reprinted by permission. **p. 429:** *Figure 10.4* Shaffer, H. R., & Emerson, P. E. (1964). The development of social attachments in infancy. *Monographs of the Society for Research in Child Development,* 29, (3, Serial No. 94). © The Society for Research in Child Development, Inc. **p. 431:** *Table 10.2* M. M. Haith & J. J. Campos (Eds.), *Handbook of child psychology.* Vol. II: Infancy and developmental psychobiology, p. 861. Copyright © 1983 by John Wiley & Sons, Inc. Reprinted by permission of John Wiley & Sons, Inc. **p. 434:** © Laura Dwight/Black Star. **p. 438:** *Figure 10.5* Field, T. M. (1982). Affective displays of high-risk infants during early interactions. In T. Field & A. Fogel (Eds.), *Emotion and Early Interaction,* p. 109. Reprinted by permission of Lawrence Erlbaum Associates, Inc., Publishers. **p. 441:** Shostal Associates/SuperStock.

Chapter 11 pp. 449–450: *Excerpts* from Harter, S. (1988). Developmental processes in the construction of the self. In T. D. Yawkey & E. Johnson (Eds.), *Integrative processes and socialization: Early to middle childhood.* Hillsdale, NJ: Erlbaum. Reprinted by permission. **p. 452:** © Susan Lapides. **p. 455:** *Figure 11.1* Mischel, W., Ebbesen, E. B., & Ziess, A. R.

(1972). Cognitive and attentional mechanisms in delay of gratification. *Journal of Personality and Social Psychology,* 21, 204–218. Copyright 1972 by the American Psychological Association. Reprinted by permission. **p. 459:** © Susan Woog Wagner/Photo Researchers. **pp. 460–470:** *Excerpts* from Damon, W., & Hart, P. (1988). *Self-understanding in childhood and adolescence.* New York: Cambridge University Press, pp. 65, 66, 71, 72, 73, 74, 75, 76, 164. Reprinted by permission. **p. 463:** *Figure 11.2* Ruble, D. N., & Flett, G. L. (1988). Conflicting goals in self-evaluative information-seeking: Developmental and ability level analyses. *Child Development,* 59, 97–106. © The Society for Research in Child Development, Inc. **p. 465:** © Ron Dahlquist/SuperStock. **p. 467:** *Figure 11.3* John S. Watson. **p. 470:** © Dieder Palais/FourByFive. **p. 474:** *Figure 11.4* Harter, S. (1987). The determinants and mediational role of global self-worth in children. In N. Eisenberg (Ed.), *Contemporary Topics in Developmental Psychology,* p. 227. Copyright © 1987 by John Wiley & Sons, Inc. Reprinted by permission of John Wiley & Sons, Inc. **p. 478:** *Figure 11.5 The origins of intellect: Piaget's theory* by John L. Phillips, Jr. Copyright © 1969 and 1975 by W. H. Freeman and Company. Reprinted by permission. **p. 480:** *Figure 11.6* Miller, P. H., Kessell, F. S., & Flavell, J. H. (1970). Thinking about people thinking about . . . A study of cognitive development. *Child Development,* 41, p. 616. © The Society for Research in Child Development, Inc. **p. 482:** *Table 11.1* Selman, R. L. (1976). Social-cognitive understanding: A guide to educational and clinical practice. In T. Lickona (Ed.), *Moral Development and Behavior: Theory, Research, and Social Issues.* Holt, Rinehart and Winston. Reprinted by permission. **p. 483:** *Figure 11.7* Gurucharri, C., & Selman, R. L. (1982). The development of interpersonal understanding during childhood. *Child Development,* 53, p. 926. © The Society for Research in Child Development, Inc. **p. 484:** © Elizabeth Crews. **p. 486:** © Susan Johns/Photo Researchers.

Chapter 12 p. 497: *Figure 12.2* Linn, M. C., & Peterson, A. C. (1985). Emergence and characterization of sex differences in spatial ability: A meta-analysis. *Child Development,* 56, 1479–1498. © The Society for Research in Child Development, Inc. **p. 498:** *Figure 12.3* Hyde, J. S., Fennema, E., & Lamon, S. J. (1990). Gender differences in mathematics performance: A meta-analysis. *Psychological Bulletin,* 107, 139–155. Copyright 1990 by the American Psychological Association. Adapted by permission. **p. 499:** © Stephen Frisch/Stock Boston. **p. 500:** left, © Larry Kolvoord/The Image Works; right, © Carol Palmer/The Picture Cube. **p. 504:** © Sujoy Das/Stock Boston. **p. 507:** © Elizabeth Crews. **p. 512:** © Elizabeth Crews. **p. 519:** © Renee Lynn/Photo Researchers. **p. 521:** *Figure 12.5* Jacklin, C. N., & Maccoby, E. E. (1978). Social behavior at 33 months in same-sex and mixed-sex dyads. *Child Development,* 49, 557–569. © The Society for Research in Child Development, Inc. **p. 522:** © Bob Daemmrich/The Image Works. **p. 524:** © Bob Daemmrich/Stock Boston. **p. 527:** *Figure 12.6* Frey, K. S., & Ruble, D. N. (1987). What children

say about classroom performance: Sex and grade differences in perceived competence. *Child Development,* 58, 1066–1078. © The Society for Research in Child Development, Inc.

Chapter 13 p. 538: © Paul Conklin. **p. 544:** *Figure 13.1* Rule, B. G., Nesdale, A. R., & McAra, M. J. (1974). Children's reactions to information about the intentions underlying an aggressive act. *Child Development,* 45, 794–798. © The Society for Research in Child Development, Inc. **pp. 544–546:** *Excerpts* from *Essays on moral development Vol. II: The psychology of moral development* by Lawrence Kohlberg. Copyright © 1984 by Lawrence Kohlberg. Reprinted by permission of HarperCollins Publishers. **p. 547:** *Figure 13.2* Colby, A., Kohlberg, L., Gibbs, J., & Lieberman, M. (1983). A longitudinal study of moral judgment. *Monographs of the Society for Research in Child Development,* 48 (No. 1–2, Serial No. 200). © The Society for Research in Child Development, Inc. **p. 548:** SuperStock. **p. 553:** © Lori Adamski Peek/TSW-Glick/Chicago Ltd. **p. 555:** *Table 13.2* Radke-Yarrow, M., & Zahn-Waxler, C. (1984). Roots, motives, and patterns of children's prosocial behavior. In E. Staub, D. Bar-Tel, et al. (Eds.), *Development and Maintenance of Prosocial Behavior.* New York: Plenum, p. 89. Reprinted by permission. **p. 556:** *Table 13.3* Eisenberg, N. (1986). *Altruistic emotion, cognition, and behavior.* Hillsdale, NJ: Erlbaum, p. 144. Reprinted by permission of Lawrence Erlbaum Associates, Inc. **p. 557:** © David Austen/Stock Boston. **p. 560:** *Figure 13.3* Rushton, J. P. (1982). Social learning theory and the development of prosocial behavior. In N. Eisenberg (Ed.), *The Development of Prosocial Behavior,* p. 89. Reprinted by permission of Academic Press. **p. 561:** © Ogust/The Image Works. **p. 563:** © Phil Huber/Black Star. **p. 567:** *Figure 13.4* Dodge, K. A., & Somberg, D. R. (1989). Hostile attributional biases among aggressive boys are exacerbated under conditions of threats to the self. *Child Development,* 58, 213–224. © The Society for Research in Child Development, Inc. **p. 568:** *Figure 13.5* Eron, L. D. (1987). The development of aggressive behavior from the perspective of a developing behaviorism. *American Psychologist,* 42, 435–442. Copyright 1987 by the American Psychological Association. Reprinted by permission.

Chapter 14 p. 578: *Figure 14.2* Peterson, G. W., & Rollins, B. C. (1987). Parent-child socialization. In M. B. Sussman and S. K. Steinmetz (Eds.), *Handbook of Marriage and the Family.* Reprinted by permission of Plenum Publishing Corporation. **p. 581:** *Table 14.1* Maccoby, E. E., & Martin, J. A. (1983). Socialization in the context of the family: Parent-child interaction. In E. M. Hetherington (Ed.), *Handbook of child psychology.* Vol. 4. Socialization, personality, and social development. Copyright © 1983 by John Wiley & Sons, Inc. Reprinted by permission of John Wiley & Sons, Inc. **p. 582:** © Jeffrey W. Myers/Stock Boston. **p. 584:** *Table 14.2* Smith, T. E. (1988). Parental control techniques: Relative frequencies and relationships with situational factors. *Journal of Family Issues,* 9, 155–176. Reprinted by permission of Sage Publications, Inc. **p. 585:** Elizabeth Crews. **p. 586:** *Figure 14.3* Parke, R. D. (1969). Effectiveness as punishment as an interaction of intensity, timing,

NAME INDEX

SUBJECT INDEX